# McDougal Littell
# CLASSZONE

D0931194

## Visit classzone.com and get connected.

*ClassZone* resources provide instruction, practice and learning support for students and parents.

### Literature and Reading Center

- Selection-specific content includes vocabulary practice, research links, and extension activities for writing and critical thinking
- Author Online provides information about each author, as well as in-depth author studies on selected writers
- English Learner support for a variety of languages includes audio summaries of selections and a Multi-Language Academic Glossary

### Vocabulary and Spelling Center

- Vocabulary practice and games
- Spelling lessons

### Writing and Grammar Center

- Quick-Fix Editing Machine provides grammar help in a student-friendly format
- Writing Templates and graphic organizers promote clear, orderly communication

### Media Center

- Media Analysis Guides encourage critical thinking skills
- Project Ideas, Storyboards, and Production Templates inspire creative media projects

**Access the online version of your textbook at classzone.com**

Your complete text is available for immediate use!

## McDougal Littell
### Where Great Lessons Begin

McDougal Littell

# LITERATURE

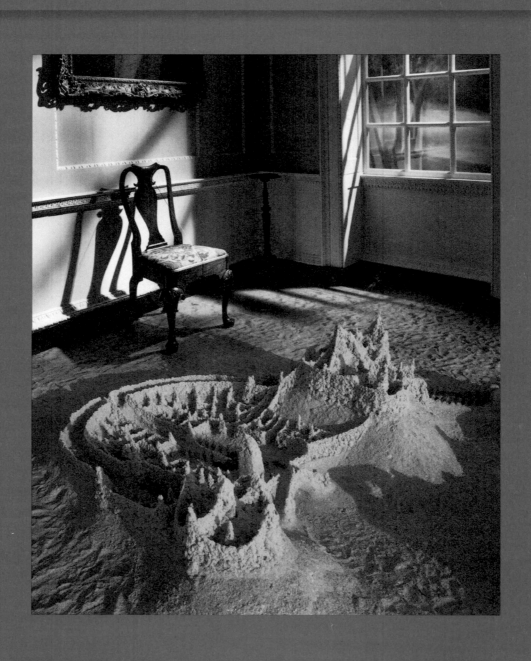

## ACKNOWLEDGMENTS

### INTRODUCTORY UNIT

**Scholastic:** Excerpt from *Slam!* by Walter Dean Myers. Copyright © 1996 by Walter Dean Myers. Used by permission of Scholastic Inc./Scholastic Press.

**Arte Público Press:** "Teenagers," from *Communion* by Pat Mora. Copyright © 1991 by Pat Mora. Reprinted with permission from the publisher Arte Público Press.

**Gary DaSilva:** Excerpt from *Brighton Beach Memoirs* by Neil Simon. Copyright © 1984 by Neil Simon. Reprinted by permission of Gary DaSilva, agent for Neil Simon.

**Lerner Books:** Excerpt from *Steve Jobs: Thinks Different* by Ann Brashares. Copyright © 2001 by The Millbrook Press. Used by permission of Lerner Books.

**McIntosh & Otis:** Excerpt from "The Winter Hibiscus" by Minfong Ho, from *Join In: Multiethnic Short Stories by Outstanding Writers for Young Adults* edited by Donald R. Gallo. Copyright © 1993 by Minfong Ho. Reprinted by permission of McIntosh & Otis.

*Continued on page R147*

## ART CREDITS

### COVER, TITLE PAGE

Untitled (1990), Jerry N. Uelsmann. © Jerry N. Uelsmann.

*Continued on page R151*

ISBN 13: 978-0-618-90184-5        ISBN 10: 0-618-90184-1

3 4 5 6 7 8 9—DWO—12  11  10  09  08

# INDIANA

## McDougal Littell
# LITERATURE

Janet Allen

Arthur N. Applebee

Jim Burke

Douglas Carnine

Yvette Jackson

Robert T. Jiménez

Judith A. Langer

Robert J. Marzano

Mary Lou McCloskey

Donna M. Ogle

Carol Booth Olson

Lydia Stack

Carol Ann Tomlinson

*Covered bridge near Kokomo, Indiana © Corbis*

## McDougal Littell
EVANSTON, ILLINOIS • BOSTON • DALLAS

## SENIOR PROGRAM CONSULTANTS

**JANET ALLEN** Reading and Literacy Specialist; creator of the popular "It's Never Too Late"/"Reading for Life" Institutes. Dr. Allen is an internationally known consultant who specializes in literacy work with at-risk students. Her publications include *Tools for Content Literacy; It's Never Too Late: Leading Adolescents to Lifelong Learning; Yellow Brick Roads: Shared and Guided Paths to Independent Reading; Words, Words, Words: Teaching Vocabulary in Grades 4–12;* and *Testing 1, 2, 3 ... Bridging Best Practice and High-Stakes Assessments.* Dr. Allen was a high school reading and English teacher for more than 20 years and has taught courses in both subjects at the University of Central Florida. She directed the Central Florida Writing Project and received the Milken Foundation National Educator Award.

**ARTHUR N. APPLEBEE** Leading Professor, School of Education at the University at Albany, State University of New York; Director of the Center on English Learning and Achievement. During his varied career, Dr. Applebee has been both a researcher and a teacher, working in institutional settings with children with severe learning problems, in public schools, as a staff member of the National Council of Teachers of English, and in professional education. Among his many books are *Curriculum as Conversation: Transforming Traditions of Teaching and Learning; Literature in the Secondary School: Studies of Curriculum and Instruction in the United States;* and *Tradition and Reform in the Teaching of English: A History.* He was elected to the International Reading Hall of Fame and has received, among other honors, the David H. Russell Award for Distinguished Research in the Teaching of English.

**JIM BURKE** Lecturer and Author; Teacher of English at Burlingame High School, Burlingame, California. Mr. Burke is a popular presenter at educational conferences across the country and is the author of numerous books for teachers, including *School Smarts: The Four Cs of Academic Success; The English Teacher's Companion; Reading Reminders; Writing Reminders;* and *ACCESSing School: Teaching Struggling Readers to Achieve Academic and Personal Success.* He is the recipient of NCTE's Exemplary English Leadership Award and was inducted into the California Reading Association's Hall of Fame.

**DOUGLAS CARNINE** Professor of Education at the University of Oregon; Director of the Western Region Reading First Technical Assistance Center. Dr. Carnine is nationally known for his focus on research-based practices in education, especially curriculum designs that prepare instructors of K–12 students. He has received the Lifetime Achievement Award from the Council for Exceptional Children and the Ersted Award for outstanding teaching at the University of Oregon. Dr. Carnine frequently consults on educational policy with government groups, businesses, communities, and teacher unions.

**YVETTE JACKSON** Executive Director of the National Urban Alliance for Effective Education. Nationally recognized for her work in assessing the learning potential of underachieving urban students, Dr. Jackson is also a presenter for the Harvard Principal Center and is a member of the Differentiation Faculty of the Association for Supervision and Curriculum Development. Dr. Jackson's research focuses on literacy, gifted education, and cognitive mediation theory. She designed the Comprehensive Education Plan for the New York City Public Schools and has served as their Director of Gifted Programs and Executive Director of Instruction and Professional Development.

**ROBERT T. JIMÉNEZ** Professor of Language, Literacy, and Culture at Vanderbilt University. Dr. Jiménez's research focuses on the language and literacy practices of Latino students. A former bilingual education teacher, he is now conducting research on how written language is thought about and used in contemporary Mexico. Dr. Jiménez has received several research and teaching honors, including two Fulbright awards from the Council for the International Exchange of Scholars and the Albert J. Harris Award from the International Reading Association. His published work has appeared in the *American Educational Research Journal, Reading Research Quarterly, The Reading Teacher, Journal of Adolescent and Adult Literacy,* and *Lectura y Vida.*

**JUDITH A. LANGER** Distinguished Professor at the University at Albany, State University of New York; Director of the Center on English Learning and Achievement; Director of the Albany Institute for Research in Education. An internationally known scholar in English language arts education, Dr. Langer specializes in developing teaching approaches that can enrich and improve what gets done on a daily basis in classrooms. Her publications include *Getting to Excellent: How to Create Better Schools* and *Effective Literacy Instruction: Building Successful Reading and Writing Programs.* She was inducted into the International Reading Hall of Fame and has received many other notable awards, including an honorary doctorate from the University of Uppsala, Sweden, for her research on literacy education.

**ROBERT J. MARZANO** Senior Scholar at Mid-Continent Research for Education and Learning (McREL); Associate Professor at Cardinal Stritch University in Milwaukee, Wisconsin; President of Marzano & Associates. An internationally known researcher, trainer, and speaker, Dr. Marzano has developed programs that translate research and theory into practical tools for K–12 teachers and administrators. He has written extensively on such topics as reading and writing instruction, thinking skills, school effectiveness, assessment, and standards implementation. His books include *Building Background Knowledge for Academic Achievement; Classroom Management That Works: Research-Based Strategies for Every Teacher;* and *What Works in Schools: Translating Research Into Action.*

**DONNA M. OGLE** Professor of Reading and Language at National-Louis University in Chicago, Illinois; Past President of the International Reading Association. Creator of the well-known KWL strategy, Dr. Ogle has directed many staff development projects translating theory and research into school practice in middle and secondary schools throughout the United States and has served as a consultant on literacy projects worldwide. Her extensive international experience includes coordinating the Reading and Writing for Critical Thinking Project in Eastern Europe, developing integrated curriculum for a USAID Afghan Education Project, and speaking and consulting on projects in several Latin American countries and in Asia. Her books include *Coming Together as Readers; Reading Comprehension: Strategies for Independent Learners; All Children Read;* and *Literacy for a Democratic Society.*

**CAROL BOOTH OLSON** Senior Lecturer in the Department of Education at the University of California, Irvine; Director of the UCI site of the National Writing Project. Dr. Olson writes and lectures extensively on the reading/writing connection, critical thinking through writing, interactive strategies for teaching writing, and the use of multicultural literature with students of culturally diverse backgrounds. She has received many awards, including the California Association of Teachers of English Award of Merit, the Outstanding California Education Research Award, and the UC Irvine Excellence in Teaching Award. Dr. Olson's books include *Reading, Thinking, and Writing About Multicultural Literature* and *The Reading/Writing Connection: Strategies for Teaching and Learning in the Secondary Classroom.*

**CAROL ANN TOMLINSON** Professor of Educational Research, Foundations, and Policy at the University of Virginia; Co-Director of the University's Institutes on Academic Diversity. An internationally known expert on differentiated instruction, Dr. Tomlinson helps teachers and administrators develop effective methods of teaching academically diverse learners. She was a teacher of middle and high school English for 22 years prior to teaching at the University of Virginia. Her books on differentiated instruction have been translated into eight languages. Among her many publications are *How to Differentiate Instruction in Mixed-Ability Classrooms* and *The Differentiated Classroom: Responding to the Needs of All Learners.*

## ENGLISH LEARNER SPECIALISTS

**MARY LOU McCLOSKEY** Past President of Teachers of English to Speakers of Other Languages (TESOL); Director of Teacher Development and Curriculum Design for Educo in Atlanta, Georgia. Dr. McCloskey is a former teacher in multilingual and multicultural classrooms. She has worked with teachers, teacher educators, and departments of education around the world on teaching English as a second and foreign language. She is author of *On Our Way to English, Voices in Literature, Integrating English,* and *Visions: Language, Literature, Content.* Her awards include the Le Moyne College Ignatian Award for Professional Achievement and the TESOL D. Scott Enright Service Award.

**LYDIA STACK** International ESL consultant. Her areas of expertise are English language teaching strategies, ESL standards for students and teachers, and curriculum writing. Her teaching experience includes 25 years as an elementary and high school ESL teacher. She is a past president of TESOL. Her awards include the James E. Alatis Award for Service to TESOL (2003) and the San Francisco STAR Teacher Award (1989). Her publications include *On Our Way to English; Wordways: Games for Language Learning;* and *Visions: Language, Literature, Content.*

## CURRICULUM SPECIALIST

**WILLIAM L. McBRIDE** Curriculum Specialist. Dr. McBride is a nationally known speaker, educator, and author who now trains teachers in instructional methodologies. A former reading specialist, English teacher, and social studies teacher, he holds a Masters in Reading and a Ph.D. in Curriculum and Instruction from the University of North Carolina at Chapel Hill. Dr. McBride has contributed to the development of textbook series in language arts, social studies, science, and vocabulary. He is also known for his novel *Entertaining an Elephant,* which tells the story of a burned-out teacher who becomes re-inspired with both his profession and his life.

## MEDIA SPECIALISTS

**DAVID M. CONSIDINE** Professor of Instructional Technology and Media Studies at Appalachian State University in North Carolina. Dr. Considine has served as a media literacy consultant to the U.S. government and to the media industry, including Discovery Communications and Cable in the Classroom. He has also conducted media literacy workshops and training for county and state health departments across the United States. Among his many publications are *Visual Messages: Integrating Imagery into Instruction,* and *Imagine That: Developing Critical Viewing and Thinking Through Children's Literature.*

**LARKIN PAULUZZI** Teacher and Media Specialist; trainer for the New Jersey Writing Project. Ms. Pauluzzi puts her extensive classroom experience to use in developing teacher-friendly curriculum materials and workshops in many different areas, including media literacy. She has led media literacy training workshops in several districts throughout Texas, guiding teachers in the meaningful and practical uses of media in the classroom. Ms. Pauluzzi has taught students at all levels, from Title I Reading to AP English IV. She also spearheads a technology club at her school, working with students to produce media and technology to serve both the school and the community.

**LISA K. SCHEFFLER** Teacher and Media Specialist. Ms. Scheffler has designed and taught media literacy and video production curriculum, in addition to teaching language arts and speech. Using her knowledge of mass communication theory, coupled with real classroom experience, she has developed ready-to-use materials that help teachers incorporate media literacy into their curricula. She has taught film and television studies at the University of North Texas and has served as a contributing writer for the Texas Education Agency's statewide viewing and representing curriculum.

## INDIANA TEACHER ADVISORS

**JoAnn Amato**
LaSalle Intermediate School
South Bend, IN

**Mrs. Desiree Brooks**
Belzer Middle School
Indianapolis, IN

**Rebecca Carr**
Wilson Middle School
Muncie, IN

**April Isaacs**
Tri High School
Straughn, IN

**Sherri Miller**
New Haven Middle School
New Haven, IN

**Theresa Mueller**
Northwood Middle School
Fort Wayne, IN

**Susan Pape**
Portage Middle School
Fort Wayne, IN

**Karen Snipes**
South Side Middle School
Anderson, IN

## TEACHER ADVISORS

These are some of the many educators from across the country who played a crucial role in the development of the tables of contents, the lesson design, and other key components of this program:

**Virginia L. Alford,** MacArthur High School, San Antonio, Texas

**Yvonne L. Allen,** Shaker Heights High School, Shaker Heights, Ohio

**Dave T. Anderson,** Hinsdale South High School, Darien, Illinois

**Kacy Colleen Anglim,** Portland Public Schools District, Portland, Oregon

**Beverly Scott Bass,** Arlington Heights High School, Fort Worth, Texas

**Jordana Benone,** North High School, Torrance, California

**Patricia Blood,** Howell High School, Farmingdale, New Jersey

**Marjorie Bloom,** Eau Gallie High School, Melbourne, Florida

**Edward J. Blotzer,** Wilkinsburg Junior/Senior High School, Wilkinsburg, Pennsylvania

**Stephen D. Bournes,** Evanston Township High School, Evanston, Illinois

**Barbara M. Bowling,** Mt. Tabor High School, Winston-Salem, North Carolina

**Kiala Boykin-Givehand,** Duval County Public Schools, Jacksonville, Florida

**Laura L. Brown,** Adlai Stevenson High School, Lincolnshire, Illinois

**Cynthia Burke,** Yavneh Academy, Dallas, Texas

**Hoppy Chandler,** San Diego City Schools, San Diego, California

**Gary Chmielewski,** St. Benedict High School, Chicago, Illinois

**Delorse Cole-Stewart,** Milwaukee Public Schools, Milwaukee, Wisconsin

**Kathy Dahlgren,** Skokie, Illinois

**Diana Dilger,** Rosa Parks Middle School, Dixmoor, Illinois

**L. Calvin Dillon,** Gaither High School, Tampa, Florida

**Dori Dolata,** Rufus King High School, Milwaukee, Wisconsin

**Jon Epstein,** Marietta High School, Marietta, Georgia

**Helen Ervin,** Fort Bend Independent School District, Sugarland, Texas

**Sue Friedman,** Buffalo Grove High School, Buffalo Grove, Illinois

**Chris Gee,** Bel Air High School, El Paso, Texas

**Paula Grasel,** The Horizon Center, Gainesville, Georgia

**Christopher Guarraia,** Centreville High School, Clifton, Virginia

**Rochelle L. Greene-Brady,** Kenwood Academy, Chicago, Illinois

**Michele M. Hettinger,** Niles West High School, Skokie, Illinois

**Elizabeth Holcomb,** Forest Hill High School, Jackson, Mississippi

**Jim Horan,** Hinsdale Central High School, Hinsdale, Illinois

**James Paul Hunter,** Oak Park-River Forest High School, Oak Park, Illinois

**Susan P. Kelly,** Director of Curriculum, Island Trees School District, Levittown, New York

**Beverley A. Lanier,** Varina High School, Richmond, Virginia

**Pat Laws,** Charlotte-Mecklenburg Schools, Charlotte, North Carolina

**Diana R. Martinez,** Treviño School of Communications & Fine Arts, Laredo, Texas

**Natalie Martinez,** Stephen F. Austin High School, Houston, Texas

**Elizabeth Matarazzo,** Ysleta High School, El Paso, Texas

**Carol M. McDonald,** J. Frank Dobie High School, Houston, Texas

**Amy Millikan,** Consultant, Chicago, Illinois

# INDIANA

## OVERVIEW
### Indiana Student's Edition

 Look for the Indiana symbol throughout the book. It highlights targeted performance indicators to help you succeed on your test.

**INDIANA CONTENTS**

*Covered bridge near Kokomo, Indiana © Corbis*

## Online LITERATURE CLASSZONE.COM

**LITERATURE AND READING CENTER**
- Author Biographies
- Additional Selection Background
- Literary Analysis Frames
- Power Thinking Activities

**WRITING AND GRAMMAR CENTER**
- Writing Templates and Graphic Organizers
- Publishing Options
- Quick-Fix Editing Machine

**VOCABULARY AND SPELLING CENTER**
- Vocabulary Strategies and Practice
- Multi-Language Glossary of Academic Vocabulary
- Vocabulary Flash Cards
- Spelling Lessons

**MEDIA CENTER**
- Production Templates
- Analysis Guides

**RESEARCH CENTER**
- Web Research Guide
- Citation Guide

 **ASSESSMENT CENTER**
- ISTEP+ PRACTICE AND TEST-TAKING TIPS
- SAT/ACT PRACTICE AND TIPS

### MORE TECHNOLOGY

*eEdition*
- Interactive Selections
- Audio Summaries

*WriteSmart*
- Writing Prompts and Templates
- Interactive Student Models
- Interactive Graphic Organizers
- Interactive Revision Lessons
- Rubric Generator

*MediaSmart* DVD
- Media Lessons
- Interactive Media Studies

# *The Main Events*
# PLOT AND CONFLICT

• IN FICTION • IN DRAMA • IN MEDIA • IN NONFICTION • IN POETRY

**VOCABULARY STRATEGIES**

Compound words, *p. 44*

Prefixes: *com-, p. 60*

Suffixes that form nouns, *p. 74*

Reference aids, *p. 85*

Latin roots: *dict, p. 117*

Onomatopoeia, *p. 130*

# Through Different Eyes
# CHARACTER AND POINT OF VIEW
• IN FICTION • IN MEDIA • IN NONFICTION • IN POETRY

> ### VOCABULARY STRATEGIES
>
> Similes, *p. 180*               Analogies, *p. 252*
>
> Specialized vocabulary, *p. 220*    Synonyms as context clues, *p. 272*
>
> Prefixes: *fore-* and *mal-, p. 236*   Multiple-meaning words, *p. 281*

# UNIT 3
## INDIANA

# The Place to Be
# SETTING AND MOOD

• IN FICTION • IN NONFICTION • IN POETRY

### VOCABULARY STRATEGIES

Idioms, *p. 325*

Homographs, *p. 356*

Latin roots: *cred, p. 372*

Recognizing base words, *p. 394*

Prefixes: *inter-, p. 414*

# UNIT 4
## INDIANA

# A World of Meaning
# THEME AND SYMBOL

• IN FICTION • IN POETRY • IN DRAMA • IN MEDIA

**INDIANA STANDARDS**

> **VOCABULARY STRATEGIES**
>
> Reference aids, *p. 461*          Suffixes: *-ly, p. 474*

# Painting with Words
# POETRY

**INDIANA STANDARDS**

*Forms, Speaker, Sound Devices, Rhythm and Rhyme*

*Stanza, Metaphor, Simile*

*Couplet, Analyze Figurative Language*

*Free Verse, Speaker, Clarify Meaning*

*Recurring Theme, Set a Purpose for Reading*

**VOCABULARY STRATEGIES**

Word origins, *p. 595*          Latin roots: *carn, p. 631*

## *A Unique Imprint*
# STYLE, VOICE, AND TONE

• IN FICTION • IN NONFICTION • IN POETRY

> ### VOCABULARY STRATEGIES
> Multiple-meaning words, *p. 680*        Latin roots: *leg, p. 713*
> Connotation and denotation, *p. 693*    Idioms, *p. 726*

# UNIT 7
## INDIANA

*Our Place in the World*
# HISTORY, CULTURE, AND THE AUTHOR
• IN FICTION • IN NONFICTION • IN MEDIA • IN POETRY

**VOCABULARY STRATEGIES**

Analogies, *p. 780*                    Similes, *p. 828*
Homographs, *p. 798*                   Denotation and connotation, *p. 845*

## UNIT 8 INDIANA

## Believe It or Not
# FACTS AND INFORMATION

• IN NONFICTION • IN MEDIA

**INDIANA STANDARDS**

## HEALTH AND MEDICINE

### VOCABULARY STRATEGIES

Recognizing base words, *p. 892*          Suffixes that form adjectives, *p. 926*

Word origins, *p. 903*                    Latin roots: *pend, p. 937*

Denotation and connotation, *p. 917*

# UNIT 9
## INDIANA

# *State Your Case*
# ARGUMENT AND PERSUASION

- IN NONFICTION • IN MEDIA • IN LITERATURE

### INDIANA STANDARDS

*Elements of an Argument, Persuasive Techniques*

*Argument, Distinguish Fact and Opinion*

*Persuasion in Advertising*

*Persuasion, Set a Purpose for Reading*

**VOCABULARY STRATEGIES**

Greek roots: *exo, p. 978*

Latin words: *gressus, p. 992*

Related words, *p. 1001*

Antonyms and context clues, *p. 1009*

*Investigation and Discovery*
# THE POWER OF RESEARCH

**INDIANA STANDARDS**

*Use Reference Materials and Technology, Evaluate Sources*

**WRITING PRACTICE**

*Research, Synthesis*

# Student Resource Bank

# Selections by Genre

## FICTION

## NONFICTION

### POETRY

### DRAMA

# Selections by Genre

 **LITERATURE CENTER** at ClassZone.com

 **MEDIA CENTER** at ClassZone.com

 WriteSmart

 **MediaSmart** DVD

## VOCABULARY STRATEGIES

## GRAMMAR AND WRITING

# INDIANA

# STUDENT GUIDE TO ISTEP+ SUCCESS

*Covered bridge near Kokomo, Indiana © Corbis*

**ISTEP+ SUCCESS**

# *Understanding the* Indiana Academic Standards

## What are the Indiana Academic Standards?

The Indiana Academic Standards outline what you should know and be able to do at each grade level, not only for success in taking tests like the ISTEP+, but also so that you will be well equipped for everyday life and the workplace. Your teacher uses the standards to create a course of instruction that will help you develop the skills and knowledge you are expected to have by the end of grade 8.

## How will I learn the Indiana Academic Standards?

Your textbook is closely aligned to the Indiana Academic Standards for English/language arts, so that every time you learn or practice a skill, you are mastering one of the standards. Each unit, each selection, and each workshop connects to one or more of the standards which are listed on the opening page of the section.

*For a complete listing of Indiana Academic Standards for English/ language arts see page S1*

There are seven Indiana Academic Standards for English/ language arts.

**1. READING:** Word Recognition, Fluency, and Vocabulary Development

**2. READING:** Comprehension and Analysis of Nonfiction and Informational Text

**3. READING:** Comprehension and Analysis of Literary Text

**4. WRITING:** Processes and Features

**5. WRITING:** Applications (Different Types of Writing and Their Characteristics)

**6. WRITING:** English Language Conventions

**7. LISTENING AND SPEAKING:** Skills, Strategies, and Applications

These seven standards are further broken down into performance indicators. Performance indicators describe what you must learn to master the standard. Indiana uses a special numbering system to identify the grade level, the standard, and the performance indicator.

---

**INDIANA ACADEMIC STANDARD DECODER**

# 8 . 3 . 4

*Indicates a grade 8 standard*

*Indicates Standard 3:*

**READING: Comprehension and Analysis of Literary Text**

*Students read and respond to grade-level-appropriate historically or culturally significant works of literature, such as the selections in the* **Indiana Reading List** *(www.doe.state.in.us/standards/readinglist.html), which illustrate the quality and complexity of the materials to be read by students. At Grade 8, students read a wide variety of fiction, such as classic and contemporary literature, historical fiction, fantasy, science fiction, mysteries, adventures, folklore, mythology, poetry, short stories, dramas, and other genres.*

*Identifies the performance indicator:*

**4.** Analyze the importance of setting to the mood, tone, or meaning of the text.

# Embedded Assessment Practice

Each unit has a formatted practice test that covers specific standards-based skills.

# Preparing for the ISTEP+

## What is the ISTEP+ ?

ISTEP+ stands for the Indiana Statewide Testing for Educational Progress–Plus. Indiana students in Grades 3 through 10 must take the ISTEP+ to measure understanding of the Indiana Academic Standards in every grade that you have completed. The English/language arts portion of the ISTEP+ consists of multiple-choice and short-answer items as well as writing prompts for essay questions.

## How can I be successful on the ISTEP+ ?

You can use the passages and questions on the following pages to prepare for the English/language arts portion of the ISTEP+. This section will familiarize you with the format of test items. The tips and strategies in blue will guide you through reading the passages and answering the questions.

- Read the passages carefully, as well as the tips in the margins. The tips help you to focus on important points in the reading so that you will be better prepared to answer the questions that follow.

Here we learn events that have already happened in the story. Huck also finds out what is happening now—that the search for him and Jim is underway.

It's a long way to the upper end of town. You better stay here all night. Take off your bonnet."

"No," I says. "I'll rest awhile and go on."

She said she wouldn't let me go by myself. Her husband would be in soon, and she'd send him along with me. Then she got to talking about her family and her moving here and all that she'd heard. She told me about me and Tom Sawyer finding the six thousand dollars. She also knew all about Pap. At last she got down to where I was killed.

"Who done it?" I asked.

"Well, I reckon people here would like to know who killed him. Some thinks old Finn [Huckleberry's father] done it himself."

"Is that so?"

"Most everybody thought it at first. He'll never know how close he come to getting lynched. But before night, they decided it was done by a runaway slave named Jim."

"Why he—" I stopped. I thought I'd better keep still. She went on.

"He run off the very night Huck Finn was killed. So there's a reward out for him—three hundred dollars. The next day back comes old Finn. He went

- Each question tests a particular performance indicator. There are also strategies for answering the types of questions you will encounter on the English/language arts portion of the ISTEP+.

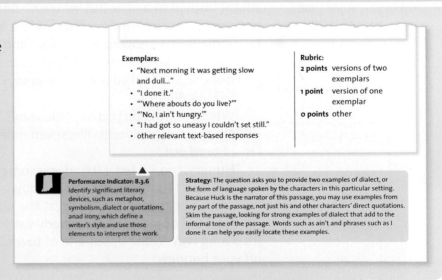

**Exemplars:**
- "Next morning it was getting slow and dull…"
- "I done it."
- "'Where abouts do you live?'"
- "'No, I ain't hungry.'"
- "I had got so uneasy I couldn't set still."
- other relevant text-based responses

**Rubric:**
2 points versions of two exemplars
1 point version of one exemplar
0 points other

**Performance Indicator: 8.3.6** Identify significant literary devices, such as metaphor, symbolism, dialect or quotations, anad irony, which define a writer's style and use those elements to interpret the work.

**Strategy:** The question asks you to provide two examples of dialect, or the form of language spoken by the characters in this particular setting. Because Huck is the narrator of this passage, you may use examples from any part of the passage, not just his and other characters' direct quotations. Skim the passage, looking for strong examples of dialect that add to the informal tone of the passage. Words such as ain't and phrases such as I done it can help you easily locate these examples.

# ISTEP+ Strategies and Preparation

The following section introduces you to how the English/language arts portion of the ISTEP+ will look and what kinds of questions you may encounter. Look for tips and strategies in blue boxes throughout this section.

# Excerpted and adapted from *The Adventures of Huckleberry Finn*

## *by Mark Twain*

This passage is an excerpt from a much longer story. This background information lets you know what has happened before this part of the story begins.

At the time this story was written, girls and boys were supposed to act certain ways. Although Huck was dressed up as a girl, he also had to walk and act the way girls at the time were expected to walk and act.

*After faking his own death, Huckleberry Finn is on the run with his good friend, the escaped slave Jim.*

Next morning it was getting slow and dull, and I wanted to stir things up. I thought I would cross the river and find out what was going on. Jim liked that idea. Then he said, couldn't I dress up like a girl? That was a good idea. So we shortened up one of the dresses, and I turned up my pant legs. I put on the sun bonnet and tied it under my chin. Jim said nobody would know me, even in the daytime, hardly. I practiced all day to get used to the things. Jim said I didn't walk like a girl, and he said I must quit pulling up my gown to get at my pants pocket. I tried to do better.

I took the boat across the river just after dark. At the bottom end of town, a light burned in a little hut where no one had lived for a long time. I went up and peeped in the window. There was a woman about forty years old, knitting by candlelight. I knocked at the door and tried to act like a girl.

"Come in," says the woman, and I did. "Take a chair."

I done it. She looked me over and says, "What might your name be?"

"Sarah Williams."

"Where abouts do you live? Close by?"

"No, ma'am. In Hookerville, seven miles below. I've walked all the way, and I'm all tired out."

"Hungry, too, I'll bet. I'll find you something."

"No, I ain't hungry. My mother's down sick, and out of money. I come to tell my uncle, Abner Moore. He lives at the upper end of town. Do you know him?"

"No, but I don't know everybody yet. I haven't lived here quite two weeks. It's a long way to the upper end of town. You better stay here all night. Take off your bonnet."

"No," I says. "I'll rest awhile and go on."

She said she wouldn't let me go by myself. Her husband would be in soon, and she'd send him along with me. Then she got to talking about her family and her moving here and all that she'd heard. She told me about me and Tom Sawyer finding the six thousand dollars. She also knew all about Pap. At last she got down to where I was killed.

"Who done it?" I asked.

"Well, I reckon people here would like to know who killed him. Some thinks old Finn [Huckleberry's father] done it himself."

"Is that so?"

"Most everybody thought it at first. He'll never know how close he come to getting lynched. But before night, they decided it was done by a runaway slave named Jim."

"Why he—" I stopped. I thought I'd better keep still. She went on.

"He run off the very night Huck Finn was killed. So there's a reward out for him—three hundred dollars. The next day back comes old Finn. He went crying to Judge Thatcher to get some money to hunt Jim. The judge gave him some, and he got drunk. He went off with a couple of mean-looking strangers. Well, he ain't come back since. People think now that he killed his boy and fixed things so folks would think robbers done it. Then he'd get Huck's money without a lawsuit."

"Has everybody quit thinking the runaway slave done it?"

"Oh, not everybody. But they'll get him pretty soon, now, and maybe they can scare the truth out of him."

"They're still after him?"

"Of course they are. Do people get the chance for a three-hundred-dollar reward every day?"

I had got so uneasy I couldn't set still. I had to do something with my hands, so I took up a needle and tried to put the thread through the hole. My hands shook, and I was doing a bad job. The woman looked at me and smiled a little. I put down the needle.

The woman kept looking at me funny. Pretty soon she says, "What did you say your name was, honey?"

"M-Mary Williams."

"Honey, I thought you said it was Sarah when you first come in?"

"Oh yes, I did. Sarah Mary Williams. Sarah's my first name. Some calls me Sarah, some calls me Mary."

The woman fell to talking about how hard times were, and how the rats owned the place. She said she had to have things handy to throw at them. She said she was a good shot but she'd hurt her arm a day or two ago. She watched for a rat and banged away at him but missed him. Then she told me to try for the next one. The first rat that showed his nose, I let him have it. She said that was first rate. She said, "Keep your eyes on the rats. You better have something handy to throw."

Here we learn events that have already happened in the story. Huck also finds out what is happening now—that the search for him and Jim is underway.

Huck pretends to know nothing about any of these events. He asks questions to get more information from the woman.

While girls at the time would know how to thread a needle, boys would probably not. Huck's nervousness makes the task even more difficult.

What do you think is the real reason she drops the lead into Huck's lap?

► So she dropped a lump of lead into my lap, and I clapped my legs on it. Then she looked me in the eyes and says, "Come now, what's your real name?"

"Wh-what, mum?"

"What's your real name? Is it Bill, or Tom, or Bob?"

I shook like a leaf. She said, "I ain't going to hurt you, and I ain't going to tell on you. You keep your secret, and trust me. There ain't no harm in running away. You've been treated bad, I suppose. Bless you, child, I wouldn't tell on you. And don't go around in that old dress. You do a girl pretty poor. The way you hold the thread, the way you throw things at a rat, and the way you catch a lump of lead, why, I spotted you as a boy all along. Now go along to your uncle."

I went up to the bank and then back to where my boat was. I ran through the woods and up the ridge, into the cavern. There Jim laid, sound asleep. I says, "Get up, Jim! There ain't no time to lose! They're after us!"

**1** **The author's use of a narrator who tells the story in first person helps the reader to**

  **A** know what the woman knows

  **B** learn the history of the town

  **C** understand what Jim is thinking

  **D** see the events as Huck sees them

▲

**Performance Indicator: 8.3.8**
Contrast points of view—such as first person, third person, third person limited and third person omniscient, and subjective and objective—in narrative text and explain how they affect the overall theme of the work.

**Strategy:** When a story is told in first person, the narrator tells the story using *I*. The observations are affected by the viewpoint, or perspective, of the narrator. In other words, you are "seeing the world" through the narrator's eyes. *A* is not correct. We do not know what the woman knows until she tells Huck what is happening. *B* is not correct; we do not get all the facts about the town. *C* would not result from first-person narration. Huck, as the narrator, does not help you understand what Jim is thinking. You see the events as Huck sees them, so *D* is correct.

**2** **How does Huck's trip into town advance the plot of the story?**

  **A** It reveals that Huck's mother is sick.

  **B** It explains why everyone thought Huck had been killed.

  **C** It makes Huck want the three-hundred-dollar reward for himself.

  **D** It shows that Jim is in danger.

▲

**Performance Indicator: 8.3.2**
Evaluate the structural elements of the plot, such as subplots, parallel episodes, and climax; the plot's development; and the way in which conflicts are (or are not) addressed and resolved.

**Strategy:** Think about why Huck goes into town. Huck says that he wants to "stir things up" and to "find out what was going on." Ironically, when Huck finds out that there is a reward for Jim's capture, he realizes that they have already "stirred things up." Huck tells the woman in the hut that his mother is sick, but he is just making it up. You already know why everyone thinks Huck had been killed—the introduction says that he faked his own death. His trip into town does nothing to clarify that. At the end of the passage, Huck runs back to get Jim, so he is not interested in turning Jim in to claim the reward for himself. *D* is correct.

**3** This passage has an informal, or conversational, tone. Give TWO examples of dialect in the passage that help create this tone.

1) _____

_____

2) _____

_____

**Exemplars:**

- "Next morning it was getting slow and dull..."
- "I done it."
- "'Where abouts do you live?'"
- "'No, I ain't hungry.'"
- "I had got so uneasy I couldn't set still."
- other relevant text-based responses

**Rubric:**

**2 points** versions of two exemplars

**1 point** version of one exemplar

**0 points** other

**Performance Indicator: 8.3.6**
Identify significant literary devices, such as metaphor, symbolism, dialect or quotations, anad irony, which define a writer's style and use those elements to interpret the work.

**Strategy:** The question asks you to provide two examples of dialect, or the form of language spoken by the characters in this particular setting. Because Huck is the narrator of this passage, you may use examples from any part of the passage, not just his and other characters' direct quotations. Skim the passage, looking for strong examples of dialect that add to the informal tone of the passage. Words such as *ain't* and phrases such as *I done it* can help you easily locate these examples.

# In the Zone

From the title and the introduction, you can infer that this article deals with an issue related to time zones. The first sentence in the second paragraph confirms this.

Communication technology is so advanced that with the push of a button a person can speak to someone on the other side of the planet, as long as that someone is not sound asleep. Even with such advanced technology, human beings have not yet developed a way to control the spinning of the earth. A person in Tampa, Florida, who calls a relative in Sydney, Australia, at 12:00 P.M. Tampa time had better be prepared for a groggy answer. It would be 2:00 A.M. in Australia, and that relative would most likely be sleeping.

Pay close attention to definitions given in the text. They will often be the subject of test questions.

The person in Florida lives in one time zone, while the relative in Australia lives in another. A time zone is a specific area of the earth's surface, stretching east and west, that shares the same time. It is defined by a line of longitude, which is an imaginary line stretching north and south across the earth between the North and South Poles. These time zones were invented in order to standardize time for everyone in the world, so that you know what time it is no matter where you are.

In 1884, members of the governments of several different countries, including the United States, met in Washington, D.C., to talk about ways to standardize time. The officials at this conference agreed to divide the world into 24 different time zones. Since they needed a place to start, they drew a line of longitude through Greenwich, England, and called it the Prime Meridian, or zero degrees. Then, every 15 degrees, they drew another line of longitude (meridian) and called the area from 7.5 degrees west of each line to 7.5 degrees east of each line a time zone.

This method seemed flawless until someone pointed out that the 24th meridian was the same as the Prime Meridian. For this reason, times zones east of the Prime Meridian are each an hour later than the previous zone, while those west of the Prime Meridian are each one hour earlier than the previous zone. This means that the time zone 12 hours east of the Prime Meridian is the same as the time zone 12 hours west of the Prime Meridian.

The author does not explain why the officials chose to divide the world into 24 zones. You can use prior knowledge to infer that the reason has something to do with the 24 hours in a day.

The meridian that defines this time zone is called the International Date Line. A person crossing the International Date Line from east to west moves one day forward. A person crossing the line from west to east moves one day backward. For example, a person leaving Western Samoa on Saturday would arrive in Fiji on Sunday. The flight may only be a couple of hours, but crossing the International Date Line means the person loses a day.

The time zone plan appeared to be a good one, but some countries, upon hearing about the plan at a later date, rejected it. Governments in Saudi Arabia, Mongolia, and Afghanistan decide for themselves what time it is. Whenever the sun goes down in Saudi Arabia, it is 12:00.

This means people in Saudi Arabia have to set their watches differently every night. People in countries that adopted the plan would have to change their watches more often as well if it weren't for some alterations. Sometimes, time zone lines are moved around cities to make timekeeping a little simpler.

In spite of certain political changes and exceptions, the time zones adopted in 1884 are fairly easy to understand. They make it possible to figure out what time it is anywhere in the world at any given moment. They assist in the conduct of business and travel around the world. However, if you prefer to leave your watch as it is when you travel, simply head due north or due south.

> From the explanation of how the International Date Line works, you can infer that Samoa is east of Fiji

> This paragraph explains some of the benefits of time zones.

**4** **What conclusion can you draw based on information in the article?**

**A** People in Saudi Arabia, Mongolia, and Afghanistan don't understand time.

**B** People in Saudi Arabia, Mongolia, and Afghanistan don't use watches.

**C** Saudi Arabia, Mongolia, and Afghanistan are in the same time zone.

**D** Representatives from Saudi Arabia, Mongolia, and Afghanistan did not attend the conference.

**Performance Indicator: 8.2.9**
Make reasonable statements and draw conclusions about a text, supporting them with accurate examples.

**Strategy:** To answer this question, first locate the part of the passage where Saudi Arabia, Mongolia, and Afghanistan are mentioned, and reread it. Then, examine each of the answer choices and decide which one could best be supported with information from that part of the passage. There is no support for the claim made in *A*. The claim made in *B* is directly refuted by the passage, which specifically mentions people in Saudi Arabia setting their watches. *C* is incorrect. Even if you do not know the geographic location of these countries, there is no support for this claim anywhere in the passage. This leaves you with *D*, which is the correct answer. The passage specifically mentions that these countries heard about the plan "at a later date." So, you can infer that representatives from these countries did not attend the conference. If they had, they would have known about the plan during the conference.

**5** **Read this sentence from the passage.**

*Then, every 15 degrees, they drew another line of longitude (meridian) and called the area from 7.5 degrees west of each line to 7.5 degrees east of each line a time zone.*

**Why did the author put the word *meridian* in parentheses?**

**A** to contrast a line of longitude with a meridian

**B** to compare a meridian with a time zone

**C** to clarify that a meridian is a line of longitude

**D** to identify the location of the Prime Meridian

**Performance Indicator: 8.1.3**
Verify the meaning of a word in its context, even when its meaning is not directly stated, through the use of definition, restatement, example, comparison, or contrast.

**Strategy:** The correct answer is *C*. Putting the word *meridian* in parentheses clarifies that a meridian is a line of longitude. Often, an author will include a word or explanation in parentheses to clarify word meanings. *A* is the opposite of *C* and is incorrect. *B* is incorrect; the words *time zone* do not appear anywhere in the sentence. *D* is incorrect; the Prime Meridian is not mentioned in this sentence.

**6** Give TWO examples of how this passage would be different if it were an instructional manual on how to understand time zones.

1) _____

_____

2) _____

_____

**Exemplars:**

- An instructional manual would have a list of steps.
- An instructional manual would not include the history of how time zones were developed.
- An instructional manual would not explain the benefits of using time zones.
- An instructional manual might have a diagram for the example.
- other relevant text-based response

**Rubric:**

**2 points** versions of two exemplars

**1 point** version of one exemplar

**0 points** other

**Performance Indicator: 8.2.7**
Analyze the structure, format, and purpose of informational materials (such as textbooks, newspapers, instructional or technical manuals, and public documents).

**Strategy:** "In the Zone" is an informational passage that explains some of the history behind the creation of time zones. You are asked to think about how it would be different if it were written as an instructional manual. Think about how an instructional manual differs from an informational passage, such as "In the Zone." An instructional manual would be written from a different perspective. A manual would include instructions and stick to technical details. It might be helpful to jot down some ideas and pick the strongest two for your answer.

**7** Suppose you are writing an article about time zones using "In the Zone" as a reference. Write a paragraph or two that assesses how the evidence in the passage supports the claim that time zones are a good thing.
**Be sure to use at least two examples from the passage for support.**

**SCORED FOR READING**

**Exemplars:**

- The author does not offer many opinions in the factual parts of the passage.
- The evidence in the passage can be easily proven using other sources.
- The author admits that not everyone thought the time-zone plan was a good one.
- The author uses the story of how time zones were created to show that they were created to help people.
- other relevant text-based response

**Rubric:**

**2 points** position is taken and response includes versions of two exemplars

**1 point** position is taken and response includes version of one exemplar

**0 points** other

**ALSO SCORED FOR WRITING**

**Apply 4-point Extended-Response Writing Applications Rubric, Grades 6–12, pages S8–S11 (overview on page IN49)**

**Apply 4-point Language Conventions Rubric, Grades 6–12, page IN50**

**Performance Indicator: 8.2.9** Make reasonable statements and draw conclusions about a text, supporting them with accurate examples.

**Strategy:** Here, you must assess the evidence that supports the claim that time zones are a good thing. You may use any evidence from the passage that you want, but be sure it adequately supports the claim. Think about why time zones might be a good thing. What are the effects of time zones? Why is it useful to have so many countries participate? Look carefully through the passage again and notice any details that indicate that time zones are a good thing. You are asked to use two examples from the original passage. Make sure that you do so. You do not want to lose points because you did not follow directions and included only one example. Use the rubrics on the following pages to see what a teacher scoring your response might look for.

# Extended Response Writing Applications Overview
## Grades 6–12

| Score | Does the writing sample |
|-------|-------------------------|
| **4** | • fully accomplish the task?<br>• include many relevant ideas?<br>• organize ideas logically?<br>• exhibit very good word usage?<br>• demonstrate very good writing technique?<br>• demonstrate effective adjustment of language and tone to task and reader? |
| **Score** | **Does the writing sample** |
| **3** | • accomplish the task?<br>• include relevant ideas?<br>• organize ideas logically?<br>• exhibit good word usage?<br>• demonstrate good writing technique?<br>• demonstrate an attempt to adjust language and tone to task and reader? |
| **Score** | **Does the writing sample** |
| **2** | • minimally accomplish the task?<br>• include some relevant ideas?<br>• exhibit an attempt to organize ideas logically?<br>• exhibit ordinary word usage?<br>• demonstrate adequate writing technique?<br>• demonstrate an attempt to adjust language and tone to task and reader? |
| **Score** | **Does the writing sample** |
| **1** | • only partially accomplish or fail to accomplish the task?<br>• include few relevant ideas?<br>• exhibit a minimal attempt to organize ideas logically?<br>• exhibit minimal word usage?<br>• demonstrate minimal or less than minimal writing technique?<br>• demonstrate language and tone that may be inappropriate to task and reader? |

**NOTE:** This chart is only a brief summary of the score points. It is not appropriate to use this summary as the sole tool in scoring student papers. The more in-depth Extended Response Writing Applications Rubric on pages S8-S11 is used for the actual scoring of ISTEP+ student papers. These scoring rubrics are used for students tested on the fall ISTEP+ assessment in Grades 6–12.

# Language Conventions Rubric
## Grades 6–12

| Score | Does the writing sample exhibit a good command of language skills? |
|---|---|
| **4** | In a Score Point 4 paper, there are no errors that impair the flow of communication. Errors are infrequent and will generally be of the first-draft variety; they have a minor impact on the overall communication.<br>• Do words have very few or no capitalization errors?<br>• Do sentences have very few or no punctuation errors?<br>• Do words have very few or no spelling errors?<br>• Do sentences have very few or no grammar or word usage errors?<br>• Writing has very few or no paragraphing errors.<br>• Writing has very few or no run-on sentences or sentence fragments. |

| Score | Does the writing sample exhibit an adequate command of language skills? |
|---|---|
| **3** | In a Score Point 3 paper, errors are occasional but do not impede the flow of communication; the writer's meaning is not seriously obscured by errors in language conventions.<br>• Do words have occasional capitalization errors?<br>• Do sentences have occasional punctuation errors?<br>• Do words have occasional spelling errors?<br>• Do sentences have occasional grammar or word usage errors?<br>• Writing may have occasional paragraphing errors.<br>• Writing may have run-on sentences or sentence fragments. |

| Score | Does the writing sample exhibit a minimal command of language skills? |
|---|---|
| **2** | In a Score Point 2 paper, errors are typically frequent and may cause the reader to stop and reread part of the writing. While some aspects of the writing may be more consistently correct than others, the existing errors do impair communication. With a little extra effort on the reader's part, it is still possible to discern most, if not all, of what the writer is trying to communicate.<br>• Do words have frequent capitalization errors?<br>• Do sentences have frequent punctuation errors?<br>• Do words have frequent spelling errors?<br>• Do sentences have frequent grammar or word usage errors?<br>• Writing may have errors in paragraphing, or paragraphing may be missing.<br>• Writing is likely to have run-on sentences or sentence fragments. |

| Score | Does the writing sample exhibit a less than minimal command of language skills? |
|---|---|
| **1** | In a Score Point 1 paper, errors are serious and numerous; they often cause the reader to struggle to discern the writer's meaning. Errors are frequently of a wide variety. There may be sections where it is impossible to ascertain what the writer is attempting to communicate.<br>• Do words have many capitalization errors?<br>• Do sentences have many punctuation errors?<br>• Do words have many spelling errors?<br>• Do sentences have many grammar and word usage errors?<br>• Writing may have errors in paragraphing, or paragraphing may be missing.<br>• Writing is likely to have run-on sentences or sentence fragments. |

**NOTE:** These rubrics are applied holistically, with no element of the rubric intended to supersede any other element. The variety and proportion of errors in relation to the length of the writing sample are considered. A very brief paper, consisting of two or three sentences, may receive no more than 2 score points.

# Excerpted from
## *The Importance of Being Earnest*

### by Oscar Wilde

This is an example of irony—Jack is using humor by suggesting the opposite of what is true. How can Jack amuse neighbors whom he has never met?

ALGERNON: How are you, my dear Ernest? What brings you up to town?

JACK: Oh, pleasure, pleasure! What else should bring one anywhere? Eating as usual, I see, Algy!

ALGERNON: [*stiffly*] I believe it is customary in good society to take some slight refreshment at five o'clock. Where have you been since last Thursday?

JACK: [*sitting down on the sofa*] In the country.

ALGERNON: What on earth do you do there?

JACK: [*pulling off his gloves*] When one is in town one amuses oneself. When one is in the country one amuses other people. It is excessively boring.

ALGERNON: And who are the people you amuse?

JACK: [*airily*] Oh, neighbors, neighbors.

ALGERNON: Got nice neighbors in your part of Shropshire?

JACK: Perfectly horrid! Never speak to one of them.

Irony occurs when a character says one thing but means another. A marriage proposal is generally understood to be a pleasurable experience. Algernon's reaction to the news is the opposite of what readers or viewers might expect.

ALGERNON: How immensely you must amuse them! [*Goes over and takes a sandwich*] By the way, Shropshire is your county, is it not?

JACK: Eh? Shropshire? Yes, of course. Hallo! Why all these cups? Why cucumber sandwiches? Why such reckless extravagance in one so young? Who is coming to tea?

ALGERNON: Oh! merely Aunt Augusta and Gwendolen.

JACK: How perfectly delightful!

ALGERNON: Yes, that is all very well; but I am afraid Aunt Augusta won't quite approve of your being here.

JACK: May I ask why?

ALGERNON: My dear fellow, the way you flirt with Gwendolen is perfectly disgraceful. It is almost as bad as the way Gwendolen flirts with you.

JACK: I am in love with Gwendolen. I have come up to town expressly to propose to her.

Authors write for different reasons: to persuade, inform, describe, explain, or amuse. As you read Algernon's final dialogue, note your reaction. Do you find yourself laughing? Think about the author's purpose in writing such dialogue.

ALGERNON: I thought you had come up for pleasure?... I call that business.

JACK: How utterly unromantic you are!

ALGERNON: I really don't see anything romantic in proposing. It is very romantic to be in love. But there is nothing romantic about a definite proposal. Why, one may be accepted. One usually is, I believe. Then the excitement is all over. The very essence of romance is uncertainty. If ever I get married, I'll certainly try to forget the fact.

**8** **Read this quotation from the passage.**

*Why all these cups? Why cucumber sandwiches? Why such reckless extravagance in one so young?*

**The use of the phrase *reckless extravagance* is an example of**

A hyperbole.

B imagery.

C metaphor.

D simile.

▲

**Performance Indicator: 8.3.6**
Identify significant literary devices, such as metaphor, symbolism, dialect or quotations, and irony, which define a writer's style and use those elements to interpret the work.

**Strategy:** Recall what you know about figurative language. Hyperbole is a statement of exaggeration. Imagery is the creation of a mental picture through sensory descriptions. A metaphor is a comparison of two seemingly unrelated things. A simile compares two things using the words *like* or *as*. The "reckless extravagance" that the author refers to is simply cups and cucumber sandwiches, which is perhaps special, but not extravagant, or beyond what is appropriate. Therefore, *A* is correct.

**9** **Read this quotation from the passage.**

*I believe it is customary in good society to take some slight refreshment at five o'clock.*

**What does the word *refreshment* mean in this context?**

A rest

B entertainment

C food

D wine

▲

**Performance Indicator: 8.1.3**
Verify the meaning of a word in its context, even when its meaning is not directly stated, through the use of definition, restatement, example, comparison, or contrast.

**Strategy:** Reread the lines surrounding Algernon's comment about refreshment. In the line immediately before Algernon's comment, Jack notes that Algernon is eating. From the stage direction directly preceding Algernon's response (*[stiffly]*), you can tell that Algernon has been offended by Jack's comment about his eating. Therefore, to "take some slight refreshment" must mean "to eat." *C* is correct.

**10** Name TWO things you can conclude about the setting of the passage, based on the characters' dialogue and/or the stage directions.

1. _____

_____

2. _____

_____

**Exemplars:**

- It is "in town," or in an urban area.
- It is home to cultured people.
- It is home to educated people.
- other relevant text-based responses.

**Rubric:**

**2 points** versions of two exemplars

**1 point** version of one exemplar

**0 points** other

**Performance Indicator: 8.3.9**
Analyze the relevance of setting (places, times, customs) to mood, tone, and meaning of text.

**Strategy:** Think about what you know of the characters. What kind of setting does their conversation most likely take place in? We know they are indoors, and the stage direction [*sitting down on the sofa*] tells us that they are in some kind of sitting or living room. We know that the setting is somewhere "in town," because the characters compare it to "the country," and Algernon asks Jack, "What brings you up to town?" From the dialogue, you can also tell that the setting is one familiar to educated and cultured, or refined, people.

# Invictus

## by William Ernest Henley

In a poem, the end of a line does not necessarily signify the end of a sentence. Here, the entire stanza forms one sentence. It is often helpful to read stanzas in poems as sentences to help you understand them.

▶

Out of the night that covers me,
Black as the Pit from pole to pole,
I thank whatever gods may be
For my unconquerable soul.

In the fell clutch of circumstance
I have not winced nor cried aloud.
Under the bludgeonings of chance
My head is bloody, but unbowed.

Beyond this place of wrath and tears
Looms but the Horror of the shade,
And yet the menace of the years
Finds, and shall find, me unafraid.

Rhyming is a common literary feature of poems. In this poem, every other line within a stanza rhymes. This is called an *abab* rhyme scheme.

▶

It matters not how strait the gate,
How charged with punishments the scroll,
I am the master of my fate;
I am the captain of my soul.

**11** **Which of the following is true about the imagery in the poem?**

   **A**  It conveys how afraid the character is.

   **B**  It paints a picture of a defiant fighter.

   **C**  It shows the cruelty of the character's soul.

   **D**  It gives a literal picture of the character's body.

**Performance Indicator: 8.3.6** Identify significant literary devices, such as metaphor, symbolism, dialect or quotations, and irony, which define a writer's style and use those elements to interpret the work.

**Strategy:** Imagery is when an author uses language to create vivid pictures in the reader's mind. In this poem, the narrator can best be described as a defiant fighter, based on the use of imagery. For example, the narrator says, "I have not winced nor cried aloud. / Under the bludgeonings of chance / My head is bloody, but unbowed." Therefore, *B* is correct. Since the narrator is defiant, he is not afraid, so *A* is incorrect. The narrator's soul is not cruel, so eliminate *C*. *D* is incorrect. Nothing in this poem presents a literal picture.

**12** **Read the following lines from the poem.**

*Beyond this place of wrath and tears*

*Looms but the Horror of the shade,*

**What does the speaker MOST LIKELY mean by "the Horror of the shade"?**

   **A**  rain

   **B**  night

   **C**  death

   **D**  hardship

**Performance Indicator: 8.1.1** Analyze idioms and comparisons—such as analogies, metaphors, and similes—to infer the literal and figurative meanings of phrases.

**Strategy:** Review the third stanza of the poem. The speaker is using figurative language when he says that the "horror of the shade" is "beyond this place of wrath and tears." "The horror of the shade" is a metaphor for something the speaker has yet to experience. *A* and *B* are incorrect because the shade is figurative, not literal. *D* is also incorrect because "hardship" does not make sense in the context of the stanza. Though the speaker has obviously experienced hardship, he does not necessarily know what to expect "beyond this place of wrath and tears." "This place of wrath and tears" refers to life, and therefore, "the horror of the shade" is death. *C* is correct.

**13** **Give TWO themes that appear in this poem.**

1. _____

   _____

2. _____

   _____

**Exemplars:**

- Good *vs.* evil
- Bravery
- Faith
- Perseverance
- other relevant text-based response

**Rubric:**

**2 points**  versions of two exemplars

**1 point**  version of one exemplar

**0 points**  other

**Performance Indicator: 8.3.5**
Identify and analyze recurring themes (such as good versus evil) that appear frequently across traditional and contemporary works.

**Strategy:** A theme is an idea central to a work of literature. Some themes are universal, such as good *vs.* evil. A theme is communicated by the author through a work, but it is important to remember that different people interpret literature and, in this case, poetry, in different ways. In addition, there can be more than one theme in a work. In this question, you are asked to find two themes. Make sure the contents of the poem support the themes that you choose.

# Writing Prompt

**Read the writing prompt below and complete the writing activity.**

**Your school is holding an essay contest. You need to write a story about a time that you met up with someone that you did not expect to see.**

**Before you begin to write, think about unexpected meetings or reunions you have had and pick one to write about. What happened? Why was it unexpected? Where were you? Who was the person you did not expect to meet?**

**Write a narrative essay describing what happened when you met up with a person you did not expect to see. Be sure to include sensory details in your essay. Use the following tips for help with your essay.**

Be sure to include
- specific details about the place
- information about why the meeting was unexpected
- a description of what happened when you met
- an introduction, a body, and a conclusion to your essay

**Strategy:** For this writing activity, you are asked to write a narrative essay. When you write a narrative essay, you are trying to tell your readers about a series of events or a situation in which something happened. For this essay, you are trying to describe an unexpected meeting. You may want to make the meeting unexpected for your readers as well, so that the readers are surprised by the meeting, too. Be sure to describe the scene as clearly as possible so that your readers can visualize the sensory details. Where were you? Who did you meet? Why was it unexpected? How did it end? Be sure that your essay does not spend so much time describing the place that the action stops. Before you write, you may want to jot down as much as you remember about the situation. Keep your essay focused on the topic. Remember to proofread your essay for errors in grammar, spelling, and mechanics.

The Writing Applications Overview below and Language Conventions Rubric on page IN50 provide a way to evaluate your writing. The rubrics outline the level to which your writing demonstrates your ability to develop ideas; organize information logically; make appropriate word choices; and show mastery of grammar, usage, and mechanics. Your writing will be compared to the rubrics and scored appropriately. Read the rubrics to see what a teacher reading your essay might look for.

# Writing Applications Overview
## Grades 6–12

| Score Level | Ideas and Content | Organization | Style | Voice |
|---|---|---|---|---|
| | Does the writing sample: | Does the writing sample: | Does the writing sample: | Does the writing sample: |
| 6 | • fully accomplish the task?<br>• include thorough, relevant, and complete ideas? | • organize ideas logically? | • exhibit exceptional word usage?<br>• demonstrate exceptional writing technique? | • demonstrate effective adjustment of language and tone to task and reader? |
| 5 | • fully accomplish the task?<br>• include many relevant ideas? | • organize ideas logically? | • exhibit very good word usage?<br>• demonstrate very good writing technique? | • demonstrate effective adjustment of language and tone to task and reader? |
| 4 | • accomplish the task?<br>• include relevant ideas? | • organize ideas logically? | • exhibit good word usage?<br>• demonstrate good writing technique? | • demonstrate an attempt to adjust language and tone to task and reader? |
| 3 | • minimally accomplish the task?<br>• include some relevant ideas? | • exhibit an attempt to organize ideas logically? | • exhibit ordinary word usage?<br>• demonstrate average writing technique? | • demonstrate an attempt to adjust language and tone to task and reader? |
| 2 | • only partially accomplish the task?<br>• include few relevant ideas? | • exhibit a minimal attempt to organize ideas logically? | • exhibit minimal word usage?<br>• demonstrate minimal writing technique? | • demonstrate language and tone that may be inappropriate to task and reader? |
| 1 | • fail to accomplish the task?<br>• include very few relevant ideas? | • organize ideas illogically? | • exhibit less than minimal word usage?<br>• demonstrate less than minimal writing technique? | • demonstrate language and tone that may be inappropriate to task and reader? |

**NOTE:** This chart is only a brief summary of the score points. It is not appropriate to use this summary as the sole tool in scoring student papers. The complete Writing Applications Rubric on pages S14–S19 is used for actual scoring.

Copyright © 2006 by State of Indiana Department of Education

**For Number 14, read the following sentences. Choose which sentence should come FIRST if all sentences were written in a single paragraph.**

**14** **A** He always takes the time to explain concepts we have trouble understanding.

**B** Our class is nominating him for Teacher of the Year.

**C** Mr. Grimes is the best teacher in our grade.

**D** Because of this, most students do really well in his class.

**Performance Indicator: 8.4.9**
Revise writing for word choice; appropriate organization; consistent point of view; and transitions among paragraphs, passages, and ideas.

**Strategy:** When you encounter a question like this, think hard about the organization of the sentences. How would they best be organized into a paragraph? If it helps, number the sentences and read them in the order that you have numbered them. If the paragraph does not make sense, renumber and try again. Another way to approach a question like this is to read all of the sentences and determine the main idea. Most often, the main idea you come up with will match one of the answer choices—the correct answer choice. In this case, each of the sentences supports the main idea that Mr. Grimes is a great teacher. This is close to *C*, the correct answer choice. The other answer choices are all supporting details and could not represent the main idea of this paragraph.

**15** **Which of the following sentences is MOST CLEARLY written?**

**A** Around the block she played with her friends.

**B** She played with her friends from around the block.

**C** Her friends played with her from around the block.

**D** Her friends, from around the block, and the girl played.

**Performance Indicator: 8.4.7**
Review, evaluate, and revise writing for meaning and clarity.

**Strategy:** When you evaluate and revise writing, it is important to be as clear as possible. For this question, *B* is the most clear and simply written sentence and is the correct answer. *A* is incorrect; it is awkwardly worded. *C* is incorrect because "around the block" is misplaced—did her friends come only as close as around the block when they played with her? *D* is also incorrect; it does not make grammatical sense as written.

**For Numbers 16 and 17, read the paragraph and answer the questions that follow.**

▼¹Soccer is the most important sport in our school. ▼²Our school's soccer teams are ranked number one in the county each year. ³My friends (Marci and June) and I do not play soccer, but we like to go to games and cheer on the team. ▼⁴Marci likes to eat pizza, too. ⁵When we are done watching the game, we eat dinner and hang out with friends. ▼⁶The next day, we read about the game in the school paper.

**16** **Which sentence does not belong in the paragraph?**

   **A** Sentence 2

   **B** Sentence 3

   **C** Sentence 4

   **D** Sentence 5

**Performance Indicator: 8.4.9**
Revise writing for word choice; appropriate organization; consistent point of view; and transitions among paragraphs, passages, and ideas.

**Strategy:** When you are asked to read a paragraph for questions like this, make sure to read it carefully. As you read, evaluate the paragraph for clarity and logical organization. Look for awkward transitions or sentences that do not belong. Any errors you find might very well be the subject of test questions, like the question above. Sentence 4 does not belong in the paragraph. It does not add anything to the paragraph, and it strays off topic. Therefore, *C* is the correct answer. The other answer choices (sentences) make sense and are logical parts of the paragraph.

**17** The author wants to add this sentence to her paragraph on soccer.

*In fact, almost everyone in our school either plays soccer*
*or watches school soccer games.*

**Where would this sentence BEST fit in the paragraph?**

**A** before Sentence 1

**B** between Sentence 1 and Sentence 2

**C** after Sentence 5

**D** after Sentence 6

**Performance Indicator: 8.4.7**
Review, evaluate, and revise
writing for meaning and clarity.

**Strategy:** The best place to insert this sentence is between Sentence 1 and Sentence 2 of this paragraph. "In fact" provides a nice transition between the idea that soccer is an important sport and the fact that almost everyone plays or watches soccer. Therefore, *B* is the correct answer. It would not make sense to place the sentence before Sentence 1; Sentence 1 is a topic sentence, and the sentence being inserted is a supporting detail. Eliminate *A*. It simply would not make sense to insert the sentence after Sentence 5 or Sentence 6, so you can eliminate *C* and *D*.

**18** **Choose the sentence that is punctuated correctly.**

**A** The king cobra's large size makes it seem frightening
but it is actually less aggressive than many smaller snakes.

**B** The king cobra's large size makes it seem frightening,
but it is actually less aggressive than many smaller snakes.

**C** The king cobra's large size makes it seem frightening;
but it is actually less aggressive than many smaller snakes.

**D** The king cobra's large size makes it seem frightening,
but, it is actually less aggressive than many smaller snakes.

**Performance Indicator: 8.6.5** Use
correct punctuation.

**Strategy:** Notice that the sentence has two independent clauses joined by the conjunction *but*. Remember that a comma must be used before the conjunction that joins the two independent clauses of a compound sentence. Therefore, *B* is correct.

**19** **Choose the sentence that uses correct parallelism.**

    **A**  A good employee is a person who is prompt, sharp, and likes responsibility.

    **B**  A good employee is a person who is prompt, sharp, and acts responsibly.

    **C**  A good employee is a person who is prompt, sharp, and responsible.

    **D**  A good employee is a person who likes to be prompt, sharp, and behave in a responsible way.

**Performance Standard: 8.6.2**
Identify and use parallelism (use consistent elements of grammar when compiling a list) in all writing to present items in a series and items juxtaposed for emphasis.

**Strategy:** In order to maintain parallelism in a sentence, corresponding words, phrases, or clauses should be constructed in the same way. Note that *prompt* and *sharp* are adjectives. The phrase *likes responsibility* in *A* departs from this structure. Only *C* has parallel structure by using the adjectives *prompt, sharp*, and *responsible*.

**20** **Which is written with the infinitive form of a verb?**

    **A**  He goes to the early movie on Sundays.

    **B**  She wants to go to the movies on Saturday.

    **C**  This weekend, the group of friends sees one movie too many.

    **D**  She admitted to her friends that she hated the movie.

**Performance Indicator: 8.6.8**
Identify and use infinitives (the word *to* followed by the base form of a verb, such as *to understand* or *to learn*) and participles (made by adding *-ing, -d, -ed, -n, -en,* or *-t* to the base form of the verb, such as *dreaming, chosen, built,* and *grown*).

**Strategy:** The infinitive form of a verb is the base form of the verb preceded by the word *to*. Examples of infinitives are *to run, to go, to eat, to drink*, and *to learn. A* is incorrect; the verb is "goes," which is not in the infinitive form. *B* is correct. "To go" is an infinitive. *C* is incorrect; "sees" is the verb, and is not an infinitive. *D* is incorrect; "admitted" is the verb, and it is not an infinitive.

**21** **Read this sentence.**

*The coach tried to <u>console</u> her defeated team.*

**In which sentence does the underlined word have the same meaning?**

**A**  A console supported the shelf of old books.

**B**  Our sound engineer sat down at the console.

**C**  The beautiful day did not console the lonely child.

**D**  An antique organ console filled the tiny annex.

**Performance Indicator: 8.1.3** Verify the meaning of a word in its context, even when its meaning is not directly stated, through the use of definition, restatement, example, comparison, or contrast.

**Strategy:** Consider the multiple meanings and pronunciations of the word *console*. It can be a verb that means "to comfort" or a noun that means "a cabinet or supporting bracket." The context of the sentence tells you which meaning is intended—the coach tried *to comfort* her defeated team. *A*, *B*, and *D* all use the word as a noun and place the emphasis on the first syllable. Only *C* has the same meaning and pronunciation of the word as in the original sentence.

**22** **Choose the sentence that uses the correct capitalization.**

**A**  We had to read *the Red badge of Courage* last year in English class.

**B**  We had to read *the red badge of courage* last year in English class.

**C**  We had to read *the Red Badge Of Courage* last year in English class.

**D**  We had to read *The Red Badge of Courage* last year in English class.

**Performance Indicator: 8.6.6** Use correct capitalization.

**Strategy:** Here, you are being tested on the proper capitalization of a book title: *The Red Badge of Courage*. *D* is the correct answer. In a title, the first and last words are always capitalized. In general, the only words that are not capitalized in a title (unless they are the first or last words) are prepositions, conjunctions, and articles. Therefore, the only word in this title that is not capitalized is *of*, which is a preposition and appears in the middle of the title. *A* is incorrect because *badge* is not capitalized. *B* is incorrect because none of the words in the title are capitalized. *C* is incorrect because *of* is capitalized.

**23** **Read this sentence.**

*The business venture did not end very <u>profitabley</u> for the partners.*

**Which of these is spelled correctly and BEST replaces the underlined word in the sentence?**

**A** profitebly

**B** profitibely

**C** profitably

**D** profitobley

**Performance Indicator: 8.6.7**
Use correct spelling conventions.

**Strategy:** This question tests spelling. More specifically, it tests your knowledge of proper suffixes and their spelling. The correct answer is *C*. It is the only version of the word *profitable* with the correctly spelled suffix among the answer choices. If you encounter this type of question and do not know the correct spelling, read each answer choice slowly and sound it out. This will usually lead you to the correct answer choice.

**24** **Choose the sentence that is punctuated correctly.**

**A** She will be busy tomorrow; so she wants to finish the book tonight.

**B** She will be busy tomorrow and she wants to finish the book tonight.

**C** She wants to finish the book tonight; she will be busy tomorrow.

**D** She wants to finish; the book and she will be busy tomorrow.

**Performance Indicator: 8.6.5**
Use correct punctuation.

**Strategy:** *A* is not correct. The two independent clauses are joined by the conjunction *so*, which should be preceded by a comma, not a semicolon. *B* is also a compound sentence that should have a comma before the coordinating conjunction *and*, so *B* is not correct. *C* is correct. A semicolon joins the two independent clauses when there is no coordinating conjunction. *D* does not make sense as written.

# The Power of Ideas

## INTRODUCING THE ESSENTIALS

- Literary Genres Workshop
- Reading Strategies Workshop
- Writing Process Workshop

## What Are Life's Big Questions?

We never stop searching for answers to life's big questions. Asking questions such as the ones shown here is our way of making sense of who we are, where we're going, and how we fit into the world. While our own experiences can guide us toward answers, good literature can also help. Through reading, writing, and talking about literature, we can explore the big questions in life and gain meaningful insights into our own lives and the world.

## *What does it mean to* BELONG?

Humans are naturally social beings. We create groups—families, friends, communities—that bind us together. But what happens when you're on the outside of a group and can't find a way in? Explore the meaning of belonging through the writing of Naomi Shihab Nye, Daniel Keyes, David Sedaris, and others. Then ask yourself: Is it always good to belong?

## *Why does the* PAST *matter?*

There's an old saying: "History repeats itself"—in other words, everything that happens in the world is bound to happen again. If that's the case, then we can look to the past to help us understand conflicts and issues that challenge us in the present. In this book, you'll read about the Civil War, Paul Revere, and Harriet Tubman. Find out what we can still learn from them all these years later.

# *Are people basically* GOOD?

In her diary, Anne Frank wrote: ". . . I still believe, in spite of everything, that people are truly good at heart." This sentiment is surprising, given that Anne was one of the millions of Jews who lost their lives in Nazi concentration camps during World War II. Today, we might find ourselves asking this same question. After all, war and crime are still facts of life. What do you think? Are people really good?

# *What's really* IMPORTANT?

Some objects, such as flashy cars and diamonds, are worth a lot of money. But then there are other things—a photograph or a beautiful sunset, for instance—that are priceless. Authors such as Sandra Cisneros, Walter Dean Myers, and Joseph Bruchac all write about the things people treasure most. Reading about what others value can help you decide for yourself what's really important to *you*.

# Exploring Ideas in Literature

How do you answer important questions in life? For most people, the answers don't come easily. Throughout history, people have turned to everything from ancient cave walls, fragile paper manuscripts, and up-to-the-minute blogs in search of answers to life's big questions. Exploring literature of all types can help you think about these questions—and answers—in new and exciting ways.

## The Genres

What draws you to the books you read or the movies you see? Most likely, their ideas appeal to you. Family relationships, competition between friends, impossible decisions—powerful ideas such as these are at the heart of all good literature, not just the novels and movies you encounter today. Believe it or not, centuries-old poetry, classic dramas, and inspiring biographies can also help you grapple with ideas that are thought-provoking and relevant in today's world.

In this book, you'll explore ideas in a variety of **genres,** or forms, of literature. You'll even consider the ideas in popular media forms, such as ads and movies. First, though, familiarize yourself with the characteristics of each genre.

**INDIANA STANDARDS**

**READING & WRITING STANDARDS**
**8.3.5** Identify and analyze recurring themes (such as good versus evil) that appear frequently across traditional and contemporary works.

**8.5.7** Write for different purposes and to a specific audience or person, adjusting tone and style as necessary.

### GENRES AT A GLANCE

**FICTION**
Fiction refers to stories about made-up events and characters.
- short stories
- novels
- novellas

**POETRY**
Poetry is a type of literature in which words are chosen and arranged in a precise way to create certain sounds and meanings.
- odes
- sonnets
- narrative poems
- lyric poems

**DRAMA**
Drama is meant to be performed. Characters and conflicts are developed through dialogue and action.
- comedies
- radio plays
- historical dramas

**NONFICTION**
Nonfiction is writing that tells about real people, events, and places.
- autobiographies
- essays
- news articles
- biographies
- speeches
- feature articles

### TYPES OF MEDIA

*Media* refers to forms of communication that reach large numbers of people.
- TV shows
- advertising
- Web sites

## FICTION

Does fiction mean "fake"? Some authors dream up every element of a story, from the setting to the plot and the characters. Others may be inspired by real events and people, and build a story around them. Whether it's an original product of an author's imagination or an idea "ripped straight from the headlines," all good fiction guarantees a stirring **plot,** a vivid **setting,** and compelling **characters.** Most works of fiction also have **themes,** or larger messages about life. Fiction usually takes one of three forms.

- A **short story** often focuses on a single event or incident. Most stories are short enough to be read without taking a break.
- A **novel** is a longer work of fiction that weaves together many different events, storylines, and characters.
- A **novella** is generally longer than a short story but shorter than a novel. Novellas usually feature a limited number of characters.

**Read the Model** In the novel *Slam!,* Greg Harris has just transferred from a high school in Harlem to a more academically challenging school for the arts. At his old school, Greg was the star of his basketball team. Will he still shine on the court now that he's on unfamiliar ground? As you read this excerpt, notice how Greg describes his athletic abilities. In what ways does his attitude help you to understand the **key idea** of self-confidence?

*from*

# SLAM!

### Novel by **Walter Dean Myers**

Basketball is my thing. I can hoop. Case closed. I'm six four and I got the moves, the eye, and the heart. You can take my game to the bank and wait around for the interest. With me it's not like playing a game, it's like the only time I'm being for real. Bringing the ball down the court makes me feel like
5  a bird that just learned to fly. I see my guys moving down in front of me and everything feels and looks right. Patterns come up and a small buzz comes into my head that starts to build up and I know it won't end until the ball swishes through the net. If somebody starts messing with my game it's like they're getting into my head. But if I've got the ball it's okay, because I can take care of
10  the situation. That's the word and I know it the same way I know my tag, Slam. Yeah, that's it. Slam. But without the ball, without the floorboards under my feet, without the mid-court line that takes me halfway home, you can get to me.

So when Mr. Tate, the principal at my new school, started talking about me laying low for the season until I got my grades together I was like seriously
15  turned out. The night after he talked to my moms I couldn't sleep. It wasn't the hissing of the radiator or my little brother talking in his sleep in the other bed, it was the idea of not playing ball that was bouncing crazylike through my head.

**Close Read**

1. Characters and conflicts are two key elements of good fiction. Which characters are introduced in this excerpt? What is Greg's conflict?

2. **Key Idea: Self-Confidence** Greg's confidence springs from his "game." Other than athletic ability, what else can be a source of **self-confidence?**

snow softly swirls

## POETRY

"Poetry: the best words in the best order." This is how British poet Samuel Taylor Coleridge summed up the goal and the struggle of writing poetry. Poets search for the perfect words and then arrange them in precise ways to achieve specific effects. The result can be both ear-catching and unforgettable.

As you know, poetry looks different on the page than fiction or nonfiction. Poems are made up of **lines,** which are often arranged into groups called **stanzas.** In some poems, the lines and stanzas reflect the rules of a particular form, such as a haiku or a sonnet. In others, there is no recognizable form; instead, the poet lets the ideas drive what the poem looks like on the page.

In poetry, sounds and language are just as important as form. Does the poem have a brisk **rhythm** or singsong **rhymes?** What sensory details help readers clearly picture what's being described? Every choice a poet makes can affect the overall meaning and sound of the poem.

**Read the Model** You already know what it's like to be a teenager—but how about the parent of one? As you read this poem, think about the **key idea** of relationships, especially between parents and teenagers.

# Teenagers

Poem by **Pat Mora**

One day they disappear
into their rooms.
Doors and lips shut
and we become strangers
5   in our own home.

I pace the hall, hear whispers,
a code I knew but can't remember,
mouthed by mouths I taught to speak.

Years later the door opens.
10   I see faces I once held,
open as sunflowers in my hands. I see
familiar skin now stretched on long bodies
that move past me
glowing almost like pearls.

---

### ACADEMIC VOCABULARY FOR POETRY

- form
- line
- stanza
- speaker
- rhyme
- rhythm
- sound devices
- imagery

---

### Close Read

1. What specific characteristics tell you that "Teenagers" is a poem, rather than a work of fiction?

2. **Key Idea: Relationships** According to this poem, how do parents view their **relationships** with their teenaged children? How might teenagers' views differ?

## DRAMA

You may use the term *drama* in everyday speech to mean something or somebody acting in a dramatic way (as in, "What a drama queen!"). In literature, though, a **drama** is any work that is written to be performed on a stage. A drama has all the elements of good fiction—plot, characters, setting, and theme. Unlike a work of fiction, however, a drama is usually divided into **scenes,** with several scenes grouped into **acts.**

A drama is primarily written as **dialogue** between characters. The playwright, or author, describes the setting, characters' movements, and props as **stage directions,** written in *italics* throughout the play. These notes represent the playwright's vision of the performance. However, a great deal is left to the imagination of the director, the actors, and readers.

**Read the Model** This drama takes place in Brooklyn in 1937. Fourteen-year-old Eugene has just discovered that his oldest brother, Stanley, is leaving home. Stanley is ashamed because he gambled away his paycheck, which the family relies on to make ends meet. In this excerpt, Eugene offers Stanley "his life savings" for train fare. As you read, consider the **key idea** of admiration.

**ACADEMIC VOCABULARY FOR DRAMA**
- plot
- character
- act
- scene
- stage directions
- dialogue

*from* Brighton Beach Memoirs

Drama by **Neil Simon**

**Eugene.** You're leaving home?

**Stanley.** When I'm gone, you tell Aunt Blanche what happened to my salary. Then she'll know why Mom was so angry. Tell her please not to leave, because it was all my fault, not Mom's. Will you do that?

5     (*He takes the coins out of the cigar box*)

**Eugene.** I have eight cents' worth of stamps, if you want that too.

**Stanley.** Thanks. (*He picks up a small medal*) What's this?

**Eugene.** The medal you won for the hundred-yard dash two years ago.

**Stanley.** From the Police Athletic League. I didn't know you still had this.

10 **Eugene.** You gave it to me. You can have it back if you want it.

**Stanley.** It's not worth anything.

**Eugene.** It is to me.

**Close Read**

1. How does Eugene feel about Stanley? Cite details from the dialogue and the stage directions to support your answer.

2. **Key Idea: Admiration** Think of a person you look up to or **admire.** If that person made a mistake, would your opinion of him or her change? Why or why not?

## NONFICTION AND INFORMATIONAL TEXT

Some works of nonfiction, such as biographies and true-life adventures, read like gripping novels. There's a key difference, though. In nonfiction, the events actually happened, and the characters are real people. Informational nonfiction, however, is nothing like fiction. It includes texts such as news articles, manuals, and directions to a friend's house—sources you consult for information. Since you read all kinds of nonfiction texts daily, you should know what to expect from them.

| TYPE OF NONFICTION | CHARACTERISTICS |
|---|---|
| **AUTOBIOGRAPHY/ BIOGRAPHY** The true story of a person's life, told by that person (autobiography) or by another person (biography) | • Provides details about a person's life <br>• Written from the first-person point of view (autobiography) or from the third-person point of view (biography) <br>• Presents the writer's own version of his or her life (autobiography) or an outside writer's research (biography) |
| **ESSAY** A short work of nonfiction that focuses on a single subject. Common types include reflective, persuasive, and descriptive essays. | • Is intended to share a personal experience, to express feelings, to inform, to entertain, or to persuade <br>• May be written in a **formal** style, with an academic tone <br>• May be written in an **informal** style, with a conversational tone |
| **SPEECH** An oral presentation of the ideas, beliefs, or proposals of a speaker | • May be intended to share a personal experience, to express feelings, to inform, to entertain, or to persuade <br>• Relies on powerful language, as well as the speaker's voice and gestures |
| **NEWS/FEATURE ARTICLES** Informative writing in newspapers and magazines. **News articles** report on recent events. **Feature articles** offer in-depth coverage of human-interest topics. | • Are primarily intended to inform or entertain <br>• Use headlines, subheadings, photographs, and graphic aids to present information <br>• Strive to be objective and fair |
| **FUNCTIONAL DOCUMENTS** Writing that serves a practical purpose. Types include consumer documents, such as user manuals, and workplace documents, such as résumés. | • Are written to inform a specific audience (for example, employees or consumers) <br>• Often include charts, diagrams, or other helpful graphic aids |

**Zoos: Myth and Reality** Rob Laidlaw

In recent years, zoos have become the target of intense public scrutiny and criticism. In response, many have tried to repackage themselves as institutions devoted to wildlife conservation, public education, and animal welfare. But most zoos fail to live up to their own **propaganda** and vast numbers of zoo animals continue to endure lives of misery and **deprivation.**

Nearly every zoo, from the smallest amateur operation to the largest professional facilities, claims to be making important contributions to conservation, usually through participation in endangered species...

**Over the Top** The True Adventures of a Volcano Chaser Renee Skelton

**Chicago to Kenosha**

| STATIONS | 303 AM | 305 AM | 307 AM |
|---|---|---|---|
| OGILVIE TRANSPORTATION CENTER LV: | 6:24 | 6:35 | 6:5 |
| Clybourn | | 6:43 | 6:5 |
| Ravenswood | | 6:48 | 7:0 |
| Rogers Park | | 6:53 | 7:0 |
| Main St., Evanston | ↓ | 6:56 | 7:1 |
| Davis St., Evanston | 6:43 | 6:59 | 7:1 |
| Central St., Evanston | | 7:03 | |
| Wilmette | | 7:05 | |
| Kenilworth | | 7:07 | |
| Indian Hill | ↓ | 7:09 | |
| Winnetka | 6:57 | 7:11 | 7:2 |
| Hubbard Woods | — | 7:14 | |

## MODEL 1: BIOGRAPHY

As the cofounder and CEO of a major technology corporation, Steve Jobs helped develop some of the first user-friendly personal computers. As you read this excerpt from a biography of Jobs, keep in mind the **key idea** of initiative—the ability to take action.

*from*

# Steve Jobs: [Thinks Different]

### Biography by **Ann Brashares**

At thirteen, Jobs's interest in electronics was blossoming. One day he was building an electronic counting machine, and he needed some parts. He knew he could get them from Hewlett-Packard, a giant electronics company not far from his house. Jobs looked up the phone number of Bill Hewlett, the

5 cofounder of Hewlett-Packard. Some kids would have been afraid to dial up one of the richest and most important men in California. Not Steve Jobs.

He boldly chatted with Bill Hewlett for twenty minutes, and Hewlett was so impressed and surprised by the young man that he not only gave him the parts he needed but offered him a summer job, too. That phone call taught an early

10 lesson: If you ask for what you want, you often get it.

**Close Read**

1. How can you tell that this excerpt is from a biography rather than an autobiography?

2. **Key Idea: Initiative** Jobs was a "go-getter" even at the age of 13. What qualities do you think people must have in order to take **initiative?**

## MODEL 2: FEATURE ARTICLE

Did you know that the first computer weighed *30 tons?* As you read this excerpt from a feature article on computer history, look for other mind-boggling facts. Also, consider the **key idea** of progress.

# WIRELESS EVOLUTION: THANK YOU ENIAC

WAY BACK WHEN, ONE COMPUTER COULD FILL AN ENTIRE MIDDLE SCHOOL CAFETERIA. TODAY, YOU CAN WEAR ONE ON YOUR BELT LOOP.

**by David Santos**

**Far from a Handheld** The first computerized "counting machine" was called ENIAC—Electronic Numerical Integrator and Computer. Completed

5 in 1946, covering three walls, standing eight feet high, and weighing 30 tons, ENIAC required 7,468 vacuum tubes and 6,000 manual switches just to get warmed up!

10 ENIAC could execute thousands of calculations in seconds. However, reprogramming it took a team of people, three days, and lots of patience.

15 ENIAC's advanced technology, even with its massive shortcomings, was critical in spurring on the decades of computer evolution that followed.

**Close Read**

1. What characteristics make this article different from the biography you just read?

2. **Key Idea: Progress** Think about the role technology plays in our society. What are the dangers of technological **progress,** or is it all positive?

## MEDIA

The World Wide Web alerts you to breaking news. A blockbuster movie keeps you on the edge of your seat for two action-packed hours. A clever ad campaign convinces you to buy a product you probably don't need. Media messages are all around you, and they influence your beliefs and actions more than you might realize. That's why it's important to become **media literate**—to learn how to "read" all types of media messages, including the ones shown here.

| TYPE OF MEDIA | CHARACTERISTICS | |
|---|---|---|
| **FEATURE FILMS** Motion pictures that use narrative elements to tell stories | • Created for entertainment and to make money<br>• Rely on music, cinematography, sets, and actors to tell interesting stories<br>• Are at least one hour in length |  |
| **NEWS MEDIA** Accounts of current events in newspapers and magazines, as well as on television, the radio, and the Web | • Designed to inform and entertain viewers<br>• Present information differently in each medium (TV, Web, print)<br>• Can include bias and inaccuracies, so must be closely examined |  |
| **TV SHOWS** Programs broadcast on television, including dramas, sitcoms, talk shows, documentaries, and reality shows | • Are usually created to entertain or inform<br>• Are sponsored by advertisers who pay to market their products during commercial breaks<br>• Use camera techniques and dramatic music to make stories more compelling<br>• Typically last for a half hour or an hour |  |
| **ADVERTISING** Paid promotion of products, services, candidates, or public service messages using print, electronic, and broadcast media | • Is designed to persuade a target audience to buy a product, use a service, or agree with an idea<br>• Uses visuals, sound effects, and actors to persuade viewers<br>• Is presented when and where the target audience is likely to see it |  |
| **WEB SITES** Collections of "pages" on the World Wide Web. Users navigate to pages by clicking menus or hyperlinks. | • Present information through text, graphics, audio, video, animation, and interactive features<br>• Require careful evaluation, as most Web sites are not checked for credibility |  |

# Strategies That Work: Literature

## ❶ Ask the Right Questions

It's one thing to "get through" a work of literature but another to really enjoy and participate in the story. To get the most from what you read, make sure you ask the right questions.

| Stage of Reading | Kinds of Questions |
|---|---|
| **Before Reading** Preview the selection and get your bearings. ▶ | • Based on the title, the subheadings, and the first paragraph, what do I think this text is about? <br> • What is my purpose for reading? |
| **During Reading** Pause occasionally to monitor understanding. ▶ | • What just happened? <br> • What details help me to visualize the characters or events? <br> • What do I predict might happen next? |
| **After Reading** Analyze the selection and explore its key ideas. ▶ | • How would I summarize the main idea or the basic plot? <br> • What are the key ideas in the story? Did I gain any new insights? |

## ❷ Make Connections

The conflicts and themes in literature can help you make sense of your own life. Use these tips to make connections.

- **Key Ideas** Take time to think about how the key ideas and big questions in this book are relevant to your life. For example, where do you think confidence comes from? Has someone you admire ever disappointed you?

- **Discussion/Journaling** Jot down your thoughts and opinions as you read, or share them with others. You might want to record
  - conflicts or events that you can relate to
  - characters who remind you of people you know
  - ideas you strongly agree or disagree with

## ❸ Record Your Reactions

Keeping a **Reader's Notebook** can help you organize your questions, thoughts, and analysis. Experiment with different formats to find out which works best for you.

**JOURNAL**

Pause as you read to record your impressions, predictions, or questions.

> *Brighton Beach Memoirs*
>
> *I wonder how Stanley's family will react when he leaves home.*
>
> *I predict that Eugene will have a hard time dealing with his brother's absence.*

**GRAPHIC ORGANIZER**

After reading, create a graphic organizer to help you analyze characters and events.

*Eugene's Character Traits*

*Eager to Please* Wants to help out his brother

*Selfless* Offers life savings

*Honest* Lets Stanley know the medal is important to him

# Becoming an Active Reader

Are you sometimes tempted to race through your reading just to get it done? Have you ever skipped ahead a few scenes or chapters to find out what happens? While you might save time, you probably won't enjoy the experience as much. Reading actively means taking the time to ask questions, clarify, and connect to what you're reading, whether it's a message-board posting, a novel, or even a TV drama. Use these skills and strategies to stay engaged in the process.

## SKILLS AND STRATEGIES FOR ACTIVE READING

### Preview
**Become familiar with the text before you start to read.**
- Look at the title, the graphics, and subheadings.
- Skim the first paragraph to get a feel for what the text is about.

### Set a Purpose
**Know why you are reading.**
- Ask: Am I reading for pure entertainment, information, or another reason?
- Think about how your purpose affects your approach. Should you take notes or sit back and enjoy?

### Connect
**Find something you can personally relate to.**
- Consider whether any characters remind you of people in your life.
- Ask: If I were in this situation, would I react differently?

### Use Prior Knowledge
**Recall what you already know about a topic.**
- Before reading, jot down what you already know.
- As you read, connect what you know to what you are learning.

### Predict
**Guess what's going to happen next.**
- Pay attention to certain clues, such as important statements made by characters or repeated details.
- Resist the urge to read ahead.
- Ask: Was my prediction on target, or did I miss the mark?

### Visualize
**Get a clear mental picture of what is being described.**
- Notice the author's description of characters, settings, and events.
- Use these descriptions to help you "see" what's happening like a movie in your mind.

### Monitor
**Check your own understanding.**
- Ask **questions** like, What just happened? Why did the character do that?
- **Clarify** your understanding by rereading confusing parts.
- **Evaluate** yourself as a reader. Ask: How well am I understanding this?

### Make Inferences
**Make logical guesses by considering the text and your own experiences.**
- Record specific details in the text about characters and events.
- Use common sense and your own experiences to help you "read between the lines."

| Details in "The Winter Hibiscus" | What I Know | My Inference |
|---|---|---|
| Saeng is nervous about passing the driver's test. | It's easy to make mistakes when you're nervous. | Saeng's nerves probably interfered with her judgment during the test. |

## MODEL: SHORT STORY

This story is about a 16-year-old girl named Saeng, who has moved with her family from Laos to the United States. The time has come for Saeng to take her driver's test. The stakes are high because Saeng's family is counting on her to be their sole driver. In this excerpt, David, a fellow classmate, is letting Saeng borrow his car to take the exam. As you read, use the **Close Read** questions to practice the skills and strategies you just learned.

from *The*
*Winter*
*Hibiscus*

Short story by **Minfong Ho**

"Ready?" David asked, eyebrow arched quizzically as he handed her his car keys.

Saeng nodded. Her mouth suddenly felt dry, and she licked her lips.

"Don't forget: Step on the gas real gently. You don't want to jerk the car 5 forward the way you did last time," David said with a grin.

"I won't," Saeng said, and managed a smile.

Another car drove up, and the test instructor stepped out of it and onto the curb in front of them. He was a pale, overweight man whose thick lips jutted out from behind a bushy moustache. On his paunch[1] was balanced a 10 clipboard, which he was busy marking.

Finally he looked up and saw Saeng. "Miss Saeng Panouvong?" he asked, slurring the name so much that Saeng did not recognize it as her own until she felt David nudge her slightly.

"Y—yes, sir," Saeng answered.

15 "Your turn. Get in."

Then Saeng was behind the wheel, the paunchy man seated next to her, clipboard on his lap.

"Drive to the end of the street and take a right," the test instructor said. He spoke in a low, bored staccato[2] that Saeng had to strain to understand.

20 Obediently, she started up the car, careful to step on the accelerator very slowly, and eased the car out into the middle of the street. *Check the rearview mirror, make the hand gestures, take a deep breath,* Saeng told herself.

---

1. **paunch:** a protruding belly.
2. **staccato:** short, crisp sounds, or way of speaking.

**Close Read**

1. **Make Inferences** Given David's comments in lines 4–5, what can you infer about Saeng and David's relationship?

2. **Monitor** How can you tell that Saeng is nervous? Cite details from lines 1–22 to support your answer.

So far, so good. At the intersection at the end of the street, she slowed down. Two cars were coming down the cross street toward her at quite a high speed. Instinctively, she stopped and waited for them both to drive past. Instead, they both stopped, as if waiting for her to proceed.

Saeng hesitated. Should she go ahead and take the turn before them or wait until they went past?

Better to be cautious, she decided, and waited, switching gears over to neutral.

For what seemed an interminable[3] moment, nobody moved. Then the other cars went through the intersection, one after the other. Carefully, Saeng then took her turn (*turn signal, hand signal, look both ways*).

As she continued to drive down the street, out of the corner of her eye she saw the instructor mark down something on his clipboard.

*A mistake,* she thought. *He's writing down a mistake I just made. But what did I do wrong?* She stole a quick look at his face. It was stern but impassive. *Maybe I should ask him right now, what I did wrong,* Saeng wondered.

"Watch out!" he suddenly exclaimed. "That's a stop sign!"

Startled, Saeng jerked the car to a stop—but not soon enough. They were right in the middle of the crossroads.

The instructor shook his head. An almost imperceptible[4] gesture, but Saeng noted it with a sinking feeling in her stomach.

"Back up," he snapped.

Her heart beating hard, Saeng managed to reverse the car and back up to the stop sign that she had just gone through.

"You might as well go back to where we started out," the instructor said. "Take a right here, and another right at the next intersection."

*It's over,* Saeng thought. *He doesn't even want to see me go up the hill or parallel park or anything. I've failed.*

Swallowing hard, she managed to drive the rest of the way back. In the distance she could see the big M archway outside the McDonald's restaurant, and as she approached, she noticed David standing on the opposite curb, hands on his hips, watching their approach.

With gratitude she noticed that he had somehow managed to stake out two parking spaces in a row so that she could have plenty of space to swerve into place.

She breathed a deep sigh of relief when the car was safely parked. Only after she had turned off the ignition did she dare look the instructor in the face.

"How—how did I do, sir?" she asked him, hating the quaver in her own voice.

"You'll get your results in the mail next week," he said in that bored monotone again, as if he had parroted the same sentence countless times. Then he must have seen the anxious, pleading look on Saeng's face, for he seemed to soften somewhat. "You stopped when you didn't need to—you had right of way[5] at that first intersection," he said. "Then at the second intersection, when you should have stopped at the stop sign, you went right through it."

He shrugged. "Too bad," he mumbled. . . .

---

3. **interminable:** seeming to be without end.

4. **imperceptible:** extremely subtle; hard to notice.

5. **right of way:** customary or legal right of one car to pass in front of another.

## Close Read

3. **Visualize** Reread the boxed text, picturing where each car stops. Then give a short summary of what happened at the intersection. (Hint: Sketch the scene in your notebook.)

4. **Predict** Given what's happened so far, do you think Saeng will pass the test? Give a reason for your prediction.

5. **Connect** Do most people perform well under pressure, or are they more likely to make mistakes? Support your opinion.

6. **Make Inferences** What do you think Saeng might be thinking or feeling as the instructor is evaluating her performance on the test?

# Strategies That Work: Reading

## ❶ Know Your Purpose

Determining ahead of time *why* you are reading will help focus your effort. Make sure you're using the best strategy for your purpose.

| Purpose | Strategy |
|---------|----------|
| For Enjoyment ▶ | Don't feel you have to hurry. Read at a comfortable pace for you. |
| To Learn ▶ | Take notes on the main ideas and supporting details as you read. |
| For Research ▶ | Remember that you don't have to read every word. Use subheadings, captions, and graphic aids to help you quickly locate information. |
| To Follow Directions ▶ | Closely follow each step. Use illustrations or photographs as guides. |

## ❷ Use Graphic Organizers

Recording your ideas in a graphic organizer can help you analyze and make sense of characters, relationships, and events. Depending on your purpose, you might use a cluster diagram, a Y-chart, or a time line.

## ❸ Create a Personal Word List

Tracking down the meanings of words can enrich your understanding of any story—and expand your vocabulary. Start a personal word list and keep adding to it.

- **Choose new words.** The words you include are up to you. As a starting point, you might list the vocabulary words for the selections in this book.
- **Meaning goes beyond the definition.** You have to be able to do more than remember dictionary definitions. Make sure you know synonyms and antonyms for the word and can use it in a sentence.
- **Get some practice.** Visit the **Vocabulary Center** at **ClassZone.com** for interactive practice.
- **Add a word a day.** Find new words in magazines and on Web sites, or be listening for them in conversation. Find their meanings, and make them yours!

| Word | Meaning |
|------|---------|
| *quiz-z-ically* adv. "The Winter Hibiscus," line 1 | **Definition:** expressing doubt, curiosity, or confusion. **Synonyms:** curiously, questioningly **Antonyms:** knowingly, seriously **Sentence:** "So, you finished all your homework?" my mother asked *quiz-z-ically* when she saw me watching TV. |

# Expressing Ideas in Writing

Writing is a way to let others know who you are and how your mind works. Through the right words, you can express laugh-out-loud humor, inspiring thoughts, or strong opinions and then share those ideas with the world. You might be writing to your favorite musician, a teacher, an e-mail buddy, or the entire blogosphere. In each case, your words can carry an important message.

## Consider Your Options

Any work of writing starts with careful planning. Long before your polished ideas hit the page or screen, take the time to ask some basic questions about the **purpose** and **format** of your writing, and your intended **audience**. Are you crafting a research paper for class or posting a short movie review to an online database? Questions like these can help you get off to a good start—and stay on track later on.

### PURPOSE

**Why am I writing?**
- to entertain
- to inform or explain
- to persuade
- to describe
- to express thoughts and feelings
- to inspire

### AUDIENCE

**Who are my readers?**
- classmates
- teachers
- friends
- community members
- customer service at a company
- Web users

### FORMAT

**Which format will best suit my purpose and audience?**
- essay
- letter
- poem
- review
- script
- power presentation
- speech
- research paper
- short story
- journal entry
- Web site

# Continue with the Process

The more you write, the more you'll understand your own process of writing. It takes practice, but eventually you will find what works best for you. As you tackle the **Writing Workshops** in this book, begin by following this basic process.

## THE WRITING PROCESS

### What Should I Do?

### What Does It Look Like?

---

**PREWRITING**

Explore your ideas and decide what you want to write about. To get your ideas flowing, try **freewriting, listing,** or using one of the other prewriting strategies described on page 19.

**LISTING**

Ideas from <u>Slam!</u>
- passion for an activity
- what activities am I good at?
- what if I had to give up doing something I love? (possible short story idea?)

---

**DRAFTING**

Transform your prewriting efforts into a rough draft. For a formal essay, it might be helpful to **draft from an outline.** For an informal essay, **draft to discover**—in other words, let your ideas take shape as you write. If you're writing a short story, create a **story map.**

**STORY MAP**

**Setting:** High school; Midwestern town.
**Characters:** Judy Brack (student); Mr. Brack (Judy's dad); Mr. Valdez (basketball coach)
**Conflict:** Judy joins boys' basketball team without parents' approval. They want her to quit the team. Should she?

---

**REVISING AND EDITING**

Review your draft. Look for ways to clarify the ideas, style, and structure of your writing.
- Review the **rubric** (page 18).
- Ask a classmate to review your work.
- **Proofread** for errors in spelling and grammar.

**PEER SUGGESTIONS**

Judy scored a basket as the buzzer sounded. Her teammates cheered, but she didn't feel like celebrating.

**Suggestion:** Add details to convey the excitement of the game. Try: "Swoosh. From the three-point line, Judy heard the familiar sound of the ball gliding through the net."

---

**PUBLISHING**

Share your finished piece with others. Your purpose, audience, and format will determine your publishing choices. Visit the **Writing Center** at **ClassZone.com** for options.

**PUBLISHING OPTIONS**

# Do a Self-Check

Professional writers know they can never check their work too often or too thoroughly. Use this **key traits rubric** to evaluate any rough draft.

## KEY TRAITS RUBRIC

| | Strong | Average | Weak |
|---|---|---|---|
| **Ideas** 1 | • centers around a clear, focused topic<br>• is supported by vivid, well-chosen details | • has a topic, but it could use more development<br>• contains general statements with some details | • has no clear topic<br>• lacks details or has unclear details |
| **Organization** 2 | • opens in an engaging way and wraps up with a satisfying conclusion<br>• flows in a logical manner | • has both an introduction and a conclusion, but they are uninteresting<br>• lacks some transitions | • has no real introduction or conclusion<br>• contains a confusing jumble of ideas |
| **Voice** 3 | • conveys a strong sense of individual style<br>• uses a tone that is well suited to the purpose and audience | • sounds "flat" in some places<br>• lapses into an inappropriate tone at times | • has little or no "life"<br>• employs a completely inappropriate tone for the intended purpose and audience |
| **Word Choice** 4 | • uses words that are precise and colorful<br>• conveys meaning in a powerful yet natural-sounding manner | • uses words that are correct, but ordinary<br>• gets meaning across, but is not memorable | • uses words that are vague or incorrect<br>• fails to convey meaning clearly |
| **Sentence Fluency** 5 | • includes sentences of varied lengths and structures<br>• creates a pleasing flow from one idea to the next | • has some sentence variety but not enough<br>• lacks flow in some places | • includes mostly short or rambling sentences<br>• is awkward or repetitious |
| **Conventions** 6 | • shows a strong grasp of grammar and usage<br>• has few problems with mechanics (spelling, capitalization, and punctuation) | • has minor grammar and usage problems<br>• contains some mechanical errors | • has such poor grammar and usage that meaning is unclear<br>• contains so many mechanical errors that the writing is hard to read |

# Strategies That Work: Writing

## ❶ Use Prewriting Strategies

Anyone who has ever faced a blank page or screen knows how difficult the first steps can be. Try these strategies.

- **Freewrite.** Write for ten minutes, letting whatever comes to you flow without interruption.

- **Get visual.** Use a graphic organizer, such as a cluster diagram or a chart, to flesh out your ideas.

- **Brainstorm with others.** Bounce ideas off other writers for their feedback.

- **Ask big questions.** "Who was the most courageous person in history?" Ask fun or serious questions in search of a topic.

## ❷ Get Feedback from Peers

Often, it is easier to see trouble spots when the writing is not your own. When you exchange feedback with classmates, keep these guidelines in mind.

| When You're the Writer | When You're the Reader |
|---|---|
| • Ask for specific feedback. Should readers comment on your ideas, look for errors, or both? <br><br> • Invite your readers to offer honest feedback. Respect their opinions, even if you don't agree. <br><br> • Clarify their suggestions. Review them on your own, and use the suggestions most helpful to your piece. | • Be respectful of the writer; offer positive feedback first. <br><br> • Give reasons for your opinions, as well as specific suggestions for improvement. <br><br> • Offer your feedback, and then let the writer decide on his or her own which changes to make. |

## ❸ Read, Read, Read

Reading will help your writing. Take advantage of reading both peer and professional work. Consider these sources.

**LITERATURE**
See what worked for the classic and contemporary authors featured in this book. Seek other sources as well, including novels, magazines, and newspapers.

**WRITING COMMUNITY**
Form a writing group with other students to share your process, works in progress, and finished products.

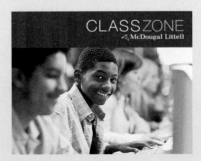

**ONLINE RESOURCES**
Check out online sources, including the **Writing Center** at ClassZone.com for links to blogs and student publications.

# The Main Events

## PLOT AND CONFLICT

- In Fiction
- In Drama
- In Media
- In Nonfiction
- In Poetry

# What makes a STORY worth telling?

A great **story** can make you laugh, cry, or gasp in surprise, but one thing is for sure: you'll give it your full attention. You might even forget your own troubles as the story unfolds or gain an insight that will change the way you view your life. Something about the fabulous setting, the compelling characters, or the unusual situations presented will stay with you long after you close the book or turn away from the screen.

**ACTIVITY** Think about the last time you thought to yourself, "That's a great story!" With a group of classmates, discuss the following:

- What story did you think was special?

- Why did you like that story so much?

- How do your reasons for liking it compare with others' reasons for liking what they did?

Based on your discussion, come up with a list of qualities that make a story worth telling.

**INDIANA STANDARDS**

# Preview Unit Goals

| | |
|---|---|
| **LITERARY ANALYSIS** | • Identify and analyze stages of plot, including exposition, rising action, climax, falling action, and resolution |
| | • Identify and analyze types of conflicts |
| | • Analyze suspense |
| | • Identify and analyze foreshadowing and flashback |
| **READING** | • Identify and analyze sequence and cause-effect relationships |
| | • Use study skills, including taking notes and skimming |
| **WRITING AND GRAMMAR** | • Write a personal narrative |
| | • Use apostrophes to punctuate possessive nouns correctly |
| | • Maintain pronoun-antecedent agreement |
| | • Use subject and object pronouns correctly |
| **SPEAKING, LISTENING, AND VIEWING** | • Identify and analyze film elements; analyze plot in a film |
| | • Stage a scene |
| **VOCABULARY** | • Use knowledge of word roots, base words, and affixes to understand word meaning |
| | • Use reference aids, including a dictionary and a thesaurus |
| **ACADEMIC VOCABULARY** | • stages of plot   • flashback   • personal narrative |
| | • conflict   • foreshadowing |

# Plot and Conflict

Will the hero save the world *and* win the girl? Can the young soldier survive the war? How will the family stay alive on the deserted island? Good stories are all around you—in novels and short stories, on television, and in movies. How do they capture your imagination and keep you riveted? Read on to find out.

**INDIANA STANDARDS**

**READING STANDARD**
**8.3.2** Evaluate the structural elements of the plot, such as subplots, parallel episodes, and climax; the plot's development; and the way in which conflicts are (or are not) addressed and resolved.

## Part 1: Conflict—The Fuel of a Story

A knight must slay a fierce dragon. A girl faces the consequences of betraying her friend. No matter what they're about, all good stories are fueled by conflict. A **conflict,** or a struggle between opposing forces, can be external or internal.

- An **external conflict** involves a struggle between a character and an outside force, such as another character, a force of nature, or society.

- An **internal conflict** is a struggle that takes place within a character's own mind, as he or she wrestles with difficult thoughts, feelings, or choices.

Whether it is external or internal, a conflict is what drives a story forward, from its beginning to its end. How will the characters handle the conflict? What obstacles will they face? Such questions prompt you to keep turning the pages.

Examine the different types of conflicts described in this graphic.

**TYPES OF CONFLICTS**

### External

**Character vs. Character**
Ling overhears Julian bragging about his malicious plan to ridicule her best friend. Angered, she confronts Julian and becomes even more incensed when he denies every word. (*Ling vs. Julian*)

### External

**Character vs. Force of Nature**
A blinding snowstorm hits while Yoni is hiking in unfamiliar territory. Suddenly, he loses his bearings and has no idea how to find his way home. (*Yoni vs. snowstorm*)

### External

**Character vs. Society**
The year is 1961. Sarah works in a factory at a time when workers must put in long hours and deal with dismal, even dangerous, conditions on the job. (*Sarah vs. poor working conditions*)

### Internal

**Character vs. Self**
Hannah accepted Raj's marriage proposal against the strong wishes of her family. If she marries him, they will never speak to her again. It's one day before the wedding, and Hannah is doubting her decision. (*marry Raj and alienate her family vs. call off the wedding and lose her true love*)

## MODEL 1: EXTERNAL CONFLICT

Johnny Tremain, a poor orphaned silversmith, believes he is related to the wealthy merchant Mr. Lyte. Johnny has proof—a cup engraved with the Lyte family name. How does Mr. Lyte react to the news?

### from Johnny Tremain

Novel by **Esther Forbes**

"I think," said Mr. Lyte quietly, "all of you ladies and gentlemen will agree that this cup our—ah, cousin, is it?—has brought back tonight is one of this set?"

There was a murmur of assent. Johnny could hear the tiny tinkle, seemingly far away, of Miss Lavinia's spinet.[1]

5 "It is perfectly obvious that this cup now stands where it belongs. The question is how was it ever separated from its fellows?"

Johnny felt that everyone there except himself knew the answer to this question.

"In fact," the merchant's voice was as smooth as oil, "I declare this to be the very cup which was stolen from me by thieves. They broke through yonder window on the twenty-third of last August. Sheriff, I order you to arrest this boy for burglary."

---

1. **spinet:** a small, compact upright piano.

**Close Read**

1. In your own words, describe the conflict that Johnny is facing.

2. Johnny's conflict isn't fully revealed until lines 11–12. What details earlier in the excerpt suggest that a problem is brewing?

## MODEL 2: INTERNAL CONFLICT

Eva is thrilled when her friend Kenisha moves back to town. Most of the time, Kenisha is too involved with the popular crowd to acknowledge her old friend. In fact, Kenisha is only nice when she wants to copy Eva's homework. How does Eva feel after she lets Kenisha copy her work?

### from Eva and the Mayor

Short story by **Jean Davies Okimoto**

Eva knew it wasn't right to copy other people's work, but it wasn't as bad as cheating on a test, and a lot of people did it. She knew that didn't make it right, but still it didn't seem like such a big sin, and besides, she wasn't the copier. The whole thing made her feel pretty mixed up.

5 She didn't know for sure if she had let Kenisha copy her work because of all that stuff Gramma Evelyn said about being nice to Kenisha or because she wanted to get in with Kenisha and be one of the cool people.

**Close Read**

1. What details suggest that Eva is conflicted about her decision to let Kenisha copy her homework? One detail is boxed.

2. In your opinion, is Eva overcome with guilt? Support your answer.

# Part 2: Stages of Plot

To draw readers into a story and maintain their interest, a writer must do more than simply introduce an intriguing conflict. He or she has to show how that conflict develops at every twist and turn, at every stage in the story's plot. A **plot,** or the series of events in a story, typically includes five stages. It's important to remember, though, that not every story follows this exact pattern.

Take a look at the following graphic, which shows a traditional plot structure. Notice what happens to the conflict at the different stages.

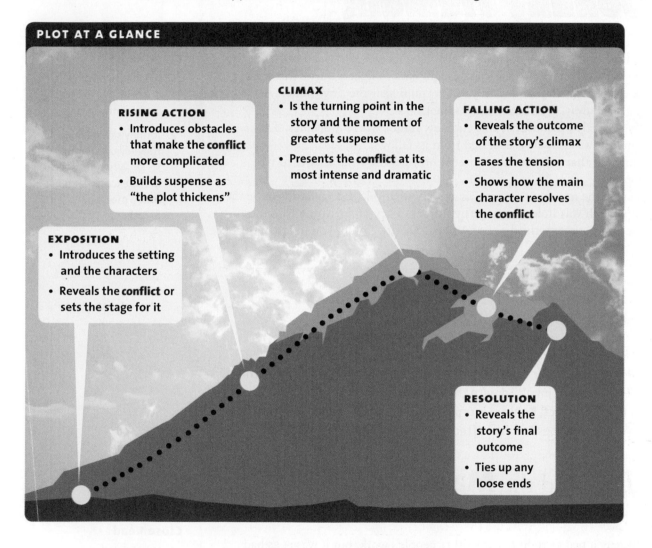

**PLOT AT A GLANCE**

**RISING ACTION**
- Introduces obstacles that make the **conflict** more complicated
- Builds suspense as "the plot thickens"

**CLIMAX**
- Is the turning point in the story and the moment of greatest suspense
- Presents the **conflict** at its most intense and dramatic

**FALLING ACTION**
- Reveals the outcome of the story's climax
- Eases the tension
- Shows how the main character resolves the **conflict**

**EXPOSITION**
- Introduces the setting and the characters
- Reveals the **conflict** or sets the stage for it

**RESOLUTION**
- Reveals the story's final outcome
- Ties up any loose ends

# Part 3: Analyze the Literature

"The Elevator" is about a boy named Martin who recently moved with his father to a new apartment. Living on the seventeenth floor, Martin has no choice but to take the elevator. The idea of the elevator terrifies him. What exactly is Martin so afraid of? Use what you've learned about plot and conflict to analyze this unsettling story.

Short story by **William Sleator**

It was an old building with an old elevator—a very small elevator, with a maximum capacity of three people. Martin, a thin twelve-year-old, felt nervous in it from the first day he and his father moved into the apartment. Of course he was always uncomfortable in elevators, afraid that they would
5  fall, but there was something especially unpleasant about this one. Perhaps its baleful[1] atmosphere was due to the light from the single fluorescent ceiling strip, bleak and dim on the dirty brown walls. Perhaps the problem was the door, which never stayed open quite long enough, and slammed shut with such ominous, clanging finality. Perhaps it was the way the mechanism
10  shuddered in a kind of exhaustion each time it left a floor, as though it might never reach the next one. Maybe it was simply the dimensions of the contraption that bothered him, so small that it felt uncomfortably crowded even when there was only one other person in it.
　　Coming home from school the day after they moved in, Martin tried the
15  stairs. But they were almost as bad, windowless, shadowy, with several dark landings where the light bulbs had burned out. His footsteps echoed behind him like slaps on the cement, as though there was another person climbing, getting closer. By the time he reached the seventeenth floor, which seemed to take forever, he was winded and gasping.
20  　　His father, who worked at home, wanted to know why he was so out of breath. "But why didn't you take the elevator?" he asked, frowning at Martin when he explained about the stairs. Not only are you skinny and weak and bad at sports, his expression seemed to say, but you're also a coward. After that, Martin forced himself to take the elevator. He would have to get used to it, he
25  told himself, just the way he got used to being bullied at school, and always picked last when they chose teams. The elevator was an undeniable fact of life.

---

1. **baleful:** sinister; ominous.

**Close Read**
**Exposition** (lines 1–40)

1. Reread the boxed details. What do you learn about the main character Martin in the exposition?

He didn't get used to it. He remained tense in the trembling little box, his eyes fixed on the numbers over the door that blinked on and off so haltingly, as if at any moment they might simply give up. Sometimes he forced himself to look away from them, to the Emergency Stop button, or the red Alarm button. What would happen if he pushed one of them? Would a bell ring? Would the elevator stop between floors? And if it did, how would they get him out?

That was what he hated about being alone on the thing—the fear of being trapped there for hours by himself. But it wasn't much better when there were other passengers. He felt too close to any other rider, too intimate. And he was always very conscious of the effort people made *not* to look at one another, staring fixedly at nothing. Being short, in this one situation, was an advantage, since his face was below the eye level of adults, and after a brief glance they ignored him.

Until the morning the elevator stopped at the fourteenth floor, and the fat lady got on. She wore a threadbare green coat that ballooned around her; her ankles bulged above dirty sneakers. As she waddled into the elevator, Martin was sure he felt it sink under her weight. She was so big that she filled the cubicle; her coat brushed against him, and he had to squeeze into the corner to make room for her—there certainly wouldn't have been room for another passenger. The door slammed quickly behind her. And then, unlike everyone else, she did not stand facing the door. She stood with her back to the door, wheezing, staring directly at Martin.

For a moment he met her gaze. Her features seemed very small, squashed together by the loose fleshy mounds of her cheeks. She had no chin, only a great swollen mass of neck, barely contained by the collar of her coat. Her sparse red hair was pinned back by a plastic barrette. And her blue eyes, though tiny, were sharp and penetrating, boring into Martin's face.

Abruptly he looked away from her to the numbers over the door. She didn't turn around. Was she still looking at him? His eyes slipped back to hers, then quickly away. She *was* still watching him. He wanted to close his eyes; he wanted to turn around and stare into the corner, but how could he? The elevator creaked down to twelve, down to eleven. Martin looked at his watch; he looked at the numbers again. They weren't even down to nine yet. And then, against his will, his eyes slipped back to her face. She was still watching him. Her nose tilted up; there was a large space between her nostrils and her upper lip, giving her a piggish look. He looked away again, clenching his teeth, fighting the impulse to squeeze his eyes shut against her.

She had to be crazy. Why else would she stare at him this way? What was she going to do next?

She did nothing. She only watched him, breathing audibly, until the elevator reached the first floor at last. Martin would have rushed past her to get

2. Consider what you've read so far about the setting and Martin's feelings about his surroundings. What do you think the main conflict will be about?

**Close Read**
**Rising Action**
**begins** (lines 41–80)

3. What event sets the rising action in motion?

4. Martin seems to perceive the strange lady as a threat. In your opinion, is this conflict real or in his head? Support your answer.

out, but there was no room. He could only wait as she turned—reluctantly, it
70 seemed to him—and moved so slowly out into the lobby. And then he ran. He
didn't care what she thought. He ran past her, outside into the fresh air, and he
ran almost all the way to school. He had never felt such relief in his life.

He thought about her all day. Did she live in the building? He had never
seen her before, and the building wasn't very big—only four apartments
75 on each floor. It seemed likely that she didn't live there, and had only been
visiting somebody.

But if she were only visiting somebody, why was she leaving the building at
seven thirty in the morning? People didn't make visits at that time of day. Did
that mean she *did* live in the building? If so, it was likely—it was a certainty—
80 that sometime he would be riding with her on the elevator again.

He was apprehensive as he approached the building after school. In the
lobby, he considered the stairs. But that was ridiculous. Why should
he be afraid of an old lady? If he *was* afraid of her, if he let it control him, then
he was worse than all the names they called him at school. He pressed the
85 button; he stepped into the empty elevator. He stared at the lights, urging the
elevator on. It stopped on three.

At least it's not fourteen, he told himself; the person she was visiting lives
on fourteen. He watched the door slide open—revealing a green coat, a
piggish face, blue eyes already fixed on him as though she knew he'd be there.
90 It wasn't possible. It was like a nightmare. But there she was, massively real.
"Going up!" he said, his voice a humiliating squeak.

She nodded, her flesh quivering, and stepped on. The door slammed. He
watched her pudgy hand move toward the buttons. She pressed, not fourteen,
but eighteen, the top floor, one floor above his own. The elevator trembled
95 and began its ascent.[2] The fat lady watched him.

He knew she had gotten on at fourteen this morning. So why was she
on three, going up to eighteen now? The only floors *he* ever went to were
seventeen and one. What was she doing? Had she been waiting for him? Was
she riding with him on purpose?
100 But that was crazy. Maybe she had a lot of friends in the building. Or else
she was a cleaning lady who worked in different apartments. That had to be
it. He felt her eyes on him as he stared at the numbers slowly blinking on
and off—slower than usual, it seemed to him. Maybe the elevator was having
trouble because of how heavy she was. It was supposed to carry three adults,
105 but it was old. What if it got stuck between floors? What if it fell?

They were on five now. It occurred to him to press seven, get off there, and
walk the rest of the way. And he would have done it, if he could have reached
the buttons. But there was no room to get past her without squeezing against
her, and he could not bear the thought of any physical contact with her. He
110 concentrated on being in his room. He would be home soon, only another

---

2. **ascent:** the act of climbing or rising upward.

**Close Read
Rising Action
continues** (lines 81–174)

5. What internal conflict is
plaguing Martin in lines
81–84?

6. Tension builds as Martin
and the lady meet again.
What details in lines
88–105 help to create
suspense about what
might happen? One
detail is boxed.

minute or so. He could stand anything for a minute, even this crazy lady watching him.

Unless the elevator got stuck between floors. Then what would he do? He tried to push the thought away, but it kept coming back. He looked at her. She was still staring at him, no expression at all on her squashed little features.

When the elevator stopped on his floor, she barely moved out of the way. He had to inch past her, rubbing against her horrible scratchy coat, terrified the door would close before he made it through. She quickly turned and watched him as the door slammed shut. And he thought, *Now she knows I live on seventeen.*

"Did you ever notice a strange fat lady on the elevator?" he asked his father that evening.

"Can't say as I have," he said, not looking away from the television.

He knew he was probably making a mistake, but he had to tell somebody. "Well, she was on the elevator with me twice today. And the funny thing was, she just kept staring at me, she never stopped looking at me for a minute. You think . . . you know of anybody who has a weird cleaning lady or anything?"

"What are you so worked up about now?" his father said, turning impatiently away from the television.

"I'm not worked up. It was just funny the way she kept staring at me. You know how people never look at each other in the elevator. Well, she just kept looking at me."

"What am I going to do with you, Martin?" his father said. He sighed and shook his head. "Honestly, now you're afraid of some poor old lady."

"I'm not afraid."

"You're afraid," said his father, with total assurance. "When are you going to grow up and act like a man? Are you going to be timid all your life?"

He managed not to cry until he got to his room—but his father probably knew he was crying anyway. He slept very little.

And in the morning, when the elevator door opened, the fat lady was waiting for him.

She was expecting him. She knew he lived on seventeen. He stood there, unable to move, and then backed away. And as he did so, her expression changed. She smiled as the door slammed.

He ran for the stairs. Luckily, the unlit flight on which he fell was between sixteen and fifteen. He only had to drag himself up one and a half flights with the terrible pain in his leg. His father was silent on the way to the hospital, disappointed and annoyed at him for being such a coward and a fool.

It was a simple fracture. He didn't need a wheelchair, only a cast and crutches. But he was condemned to the elevator now. Was that why the fat lady had smiled? Had she known it would happen this way?

At least his father was with him on the elevator on the way back from the hospital. There was no room for the fat lady to get on. And even if she did, his

7. What details in lines 121–139 suggest a conflict between father and son?

8. Review your answer to question 4. Then consider the lady's behavior each time Martin sees her on the elevator. Has your answer changed? Explain.

father would see her, he would realize how peculiar she was, and then maybe
155   he would understand. And once they got home, he could stay in the apartment
for a few days—the doctor had said he should use the leg as little as possible.
A week, maybe—a whole week without going on the elevator. Riding up with
his father, leaning on his crutches, he looked around the little cubicle and felt
a kind of triumph. He had beaten the elevator, and the fat lady, for the time
160   being. And the end of the week was very far away.

    "Oh, I almost forgot," his father reached out his hand and pressed nine.

    "What are you doing? You're not getting off, are you?" he asked him, trying
not to sound panicky.

    "I promised Terry Ullman I'd drop in on her," his father said, looking at his
165   watch as he stepped off.

    "Let me go with you. I want to visit her, too," Martin pleaded, struggling
forward on his crutches.

    But the door was already closing. "Afraid to be on the elevator alone?" his
father said, with a look of total scorn. "Grow up, Martin." The door slammed
170   shut.

    Martin hobbled to the buttons and pressed nine, but it didn't do any good.
The elevator stopped at ten, where the fat lady was waiting for him. She
moved in quickly; he was too slow, too unsteady on his crutches to work his
way past her in time. The door sealed them in; the elevator started up.
175   "Hello, Martin," she said, and laughed, and pushed the Stop button.

9. In lines 145–160, the story takes an unexpected turn. How might this development affect Martin's conflict?

**Close Read**
**Climax** (line 175)

10. Line 175 is the climax, or turning point, of the story. Do you think Martin is in danger? Explain your opinion.

**Close Read**
**Falling Action and Resolution**

11. The author ends this story at the climax and doesn't indicate how the conflict between Martin and the lady is resolved. Why do you think the author made this choice?

## Raymond's Run
### Short Story by Toni Cade Bambara

# *What's worth* the EFFORT?

**INDIANA STANDARDS**

**READING STANDARDS**

**8.2.9** Make reasonable statements and draw conclusions about a text, supporting them with accurate examples.

**8.3.2** Evaluate the structural elements of the plot, such as subplots, parallel episodes, and climax; the plot's development; and the way in which conflicts are (or are not) addressed and resolved.

*KEY IDEA* Have you ever wanted something so badly you'd do anything to achieve it? If so, you've felt **motivation**, the drive that causes people to strive toward a goal. In the story you are about to read, a spunky young girl does what it takes to be the fastest runner in her neighborhood.

*QUICKWRITE* Jot down a list of things you've been willing to work for. Choose a favorite and write a short paragraph telling what motivates you.

1. Hold record for most chin-ups
2. Learn new dance

## ● LITERARY ANALYSIS: PLOT

A story wouldn't be a story if nothing happened. The series of events that happen in a story make up its **plot.** Most plots include the following parts, or stages:

- **Exposition**—introduces the main characters, the setting, and sometimes the conflict
- **Rising action**—increases tension and builds the conflict
- **Climax**—the point of greatest interest, or the turning point in the story
- **Falling action**—shows the result of the climax and brings the story to a close
- **Resolution**—reveals the final outcome of events and ties up loose ends

As you read "Raymond's Run," notice how each stage of the plot helps build a powerful story.

## ● READING SKILL: MAKE INFERENCES

When you make an **inference** while reading, you use clues from the story and your own knowledge to guess about things the author doesn't say directly. As you read "Raymond's Run," make inferences to better understand the main character's feelings, thoughts, and ideas. Record your inferences in equations.

| Squeaky says her dad is the only one faster than she is. | + | Kids like when their parents are talented. | = | Squeaky is proud of her father. |
|---|---|---|---|---|

## ▲ VOCABULARY IN CONTEXT

The boldfaced words help Toni Cade Bambara tell a story about a race that's important in more ways than one. Use context clues to figure out what each word means.

1. Teams of three or four usually compete in **relay** races.
2. The talented young sprinter was considered a track **prodigy.**
3. Mai's teammate is also her good friend, or **sidekick.**
4. Ben is **liable** to get injured if he doesn't warm up before the race.
5. At the start of a race, runners **crouch** close to the ground.
6. The winner might **clutch** the blue ribbon to her chest.

# Author Online

**Creativity and Concern**
Raised in urban neighborhoods of New York and New Jersey in the 1940s and 1950s, Toni Cade spent much time daydreaming and exploring her world. Her mother encouraged her to do so. In the dedication of her award-winning novel *The Salt Eaters,*

**Toni Cade Bambara**
**1939–1995**

Bambara thanks her "mama . . . who in 1948, having come upon me daydreaming in the middle of the kitchen floor, mopped around me." One day, while looking through an old trunk, Toni found her great-grandmother's sketchbook. The name inscribed there was "Bambara." Impressed with her ancestor's creative drive, she decided to add that name to her own.

**"A Tremendous Responsibility"** Toni Cade Bambara went on to careers as a teacher, community activist, and documentary filmmaker. She continued to write, sharing her personal concern for and understanding of the lives of African-American families and communities. She was always aware of the influence that writers, artists, and cultural workers have on others. "It's a tremendous responsibility," she said. "One's got to see what the factory worker sees, what the prisoner sees, what the welfare children see . . . in order to tell the truth and not get trapped."

**MORE ABOUT THE AUTHOR**
For more on Toni Cade Bambara, visit the **Literature Center** at ClassZone.com.

# RRRAARAYMOND'S RRRUN

## TONI CADE BAMBARA

I don't have much work to do around the house like some girls. My mother does that. And I don't have to earn my pocket money by hustling; George runs errands for the big boys and sells Christmas cards. And anything else that's got to get done, my father does. All I have to do in life is mind my brother Raymond, which is enough.

Sometimes I slip and say my little brother Raymond. But as any fool can see he's much bigger and he's older too. But a lot of people call him my little brother cause he needs looking after cause he's not quite right. And a lot of smart mouths got lots to say about that too, especially when George was
10 minding him. But now, if anybody has anything to say to Raymond, anything to say about his big head,[1] they have to come by me. And I don't play the dozens[2] or believe in standing around with somebody in my face doing a lot of talking. I much rather just knock you down and take my chances even if I am a little girl with skinny arms and a squeaky voice, which is how I got the name Squeaky. And if things get too rough, I run. And as anybody can tell you, I'm the fastest thing on two feet. **A**

There is no track meet that I don't win the first place medal. I used to win the twenty-yard dash when I was a little kid in kindergarten. Nowadays, it's the fifty-yard dash. And tomorrow I'm subject to run the quarter-meter
20 **relay** all by myself and come in first, second, and third. The big kids call me Mercury[3] cause I'm the swiftest thing in the neighborhood. Everybody knows that—except two people who know better, my father and me. He can beat me to Amsterdam Avenue with me having a two fire hydrant headstart and him running with his hands in his pockets and whistling. But that's private information. Cause can you imagine some thirty-five-year-old man stuffing himself into PAL shorts to race little kids? So as far as everyone's concerned, I'm

**ANALYZE VISUALS**
From her posture and her expression, what can you **infer** about the girl in this photograph?

**A PLOT: EXPOSITION**
What have you learned about Squeaky so far?

**relay** (rē'lā) *n.* a race in which several team members take turns running to complete the race

---

1. **big head:** a result of hydrocephalus, or fluid in parts of the brain, that causes enlargement of the skull.
2. **play the dozens:** exchange rhyming insults.
3. **Mercury:** in Roman mythology, the swift messenger of the gods.

the fastest and that goes for Gretchen, too, who has put out the tale that she is going to win the first-place medal this year. Ridiculous. In the second place, she's got short legs. In the third place, she's got freckles. In the first place, no one can
30  beat me and that's all there is to it.

I'm standing on the corner admiring the weather and about to take a stroll down Broadway so I can practice my breathing exercises, and I've got Raymond walking on the inside close to the buildings, cause he's subject to fits of fantasy and starts thinking he's a circus performer and that the curb is a tightrope strung high in the air. And sometimes after a rain he likes to step down off his tightrope right into the gutter and slosh around getting his shoes and cuffs wet. Then I get hit when I get home. Or sometimes if you don't watch him he'll dash across traffic to the island in the middle of Broadway and give the pigeons a fit. Then I have to go behind him apologizing to all
40  the old people sitting around trying to get some sun and getting all upset with the pigeons fluttering around them, scattering their newspapers and upsetting the waxpaper lunches[4] in their laps. So I keep Raymond on the inside of me, and he plays like he's driving a stage coach which is O.K. by me so long as he doesn't run me over or interrupt my breathing exercises, which I have to do on account of I'm serious about my running, and I don't care who knows it. **B**

Now some people like to act like things come easy to them, won't let on that they practice. Not me. I'll high-prance down 34th Street like a rodeo pony to keep my knees strong even if it does get my mother uptight so that she walks ahead like she's not with me, don't know me, is all by herself on a
50  shopping trip, and I am somebody else's crazy child. Now you take Cynthia Procter for instance. She's just the opposite. If there's a test tomorrow, she'll say something like, "Oh, I guess I'll play handball this afternoon and watch television tonight," just to let you know she ain't thinking about the test. Or like last week when she won the spelling bee for the millionth time, "A good thing you got 'receive,' Squeaky, cause I would have got it wrong. I completely forgot about the spelling bee." And she'll **clutch** the lace on her blouse like it was a narrow escape. Oh, brother. But of course when I pass her house on my early morning trots around the block, she is practicing the scales on the piano over and over and over and over. Then in music class she always lets herself get
60  bumped around so she falls accidentally on purpose onto the piano stool and is so surprised to find herself sitting there that she decides just for fun to try out the ole keys. And what do you know—Chopin's waltzes[5] just spring out of her fingertips and she's the most surprised thing in the world. A regular **prodigy.** I could kill people like that. I stay up all night studying the words for the spelling bee. And you can see me any time of day practicing running. I never walk if I can trot, and shame on Raymond if he can't keep up. But of course he does, cause if he hangs back someone's **liable** to walk up to him and get

**B MAKE INFERENCES**
Reread lines 31–45. How do you think Squeaky feels about taking care of her brother? Use an equation to note your inference.

**clutch** (klŭch) *v.* to grasp and hold tightly

**prodigy** (prŏd'ə-jē) *n.* a person with an exceptional talent

**liable** (lī'ə-bəl) *adj.* likely to

---

4. **waxpaper lunches:** sandwiches wrapped in wax paper.

5. **Chopin's** (shō'pănz') **waltzes:** music by composer Frédéric Chopin.

smart, or take his allowance from him, or ask him where he got that great big pumpkin head. People are so stupid sometimes.

70 So I'm strolling down Broadway breathing out and breathing in on counts of seven, which is my lucky number, and here comes Gretchen and her <u>**sidekicks:**</u> Mary Louise, who used to be a friend of mine when she first moved to Harlem from Baltimore and got beat up by everybody till I took up for her on account of her mother and my mother used to sing in the same choir when they were young girls, but people ain't grateful, so now she hangs out with the new girl Gretchen and talks about me like a dog; and Rosie, who is as fat as I am skinny and has a big mouth where Raymond is concerned and is too stupid to know that there is not a big deal of difference between herself and Raymond and that she can't afford to throw stones. So they are steady coming up

80 Broadway and I see right away that it's going to be one of those Dodge City[6] scenes cause the street ain't that big and they're close to the buildings just as we are. First I think I'll step into the candy store and look over the new comics and let them pass. But that's chicken and I've got a reputation to consider. So then I think I'll just walk straight on through them or even over them if necessary. But as they get to me, they slow down. I'm ready to fight, cause like I said I don't feature a whole lot of chit-chat, I much prefer to just knock you down right from the jump and save everybody a lotta precious time. **C**

"You signing up for the May Day races?" smiles Mary Louise, only it's not a smile at all. A dumb question like that doesn't deserve an answer. Besides,

90 there's just me and Gretchen standing there really, so no use wasting my breath talking to shadows.

"I don't think you're going to win this time," says Rosie, trying to signify with her hands on her hips all salty, completely forgetting that I have whupped her behind many times for less salt than that.

"I always win cause I'm the best," I say straight at Gretchen who is, as far as I'm concerned, the only one talking in this ventriloquist-dummy routine. Gretchen smiles, but it's not a smile, and I'm thinking that girls never really smile at each other because they don't know how and don't want to know how and there's probably no one to teach us how, cause grown-up girls don't know

100 either. Then they all look at Raymond who has just brought his mule team to a standstill. And they're about to see what trouble they can get into through him.

"What grade you in now, Raymond?"

"You got anything to say to my brother, you say it to me, Mary Louise Williams of Raggedy Town, Baltimore."

"What are you, his mother?" sasses Rosie.

"That's right, Fatso. And the next word out of anybody and I'll be *their* mother too." So they just stand there and Gretchen shifts from one leg to the other and so do they. Then Gretchen puts her hands on her hips and is about to say something with her freckle-face self but doesn't. Then she walks

---

6. **Dodge City:** an Old West town, famous for showdowns between outlaws and lawmen.

**sidekick** (sīd′kǐk′) *n.* a close friend

**C** **PLOT: RISING ACTION**
Why does Gretchen's approach cause tension for Squeaky?

**VISUAL VOCABULARY**

**ventriloquist-dummy** *n.* A ventriloquist controls his or her voice and moves the mouth of a puppet, or dummy, to make it appear to be talking.

110 around me looking me up and down but keeps walking up Broadway, and her sidekicks follow her. So me and Raymond smile at each other and he says, "Gidyap" to his team and I continue with my breathing exercises, strolling down Broadway toward the ice man on 145th with not a care in the world cause I am Miss Quicksilver[7] herself.

I take my time getting to the park on May Day because the track meet is the last thing on the program. The biggest thing on the program is the May Pole dancing, which I can do without, thank you, even if my mother thinks it's a shame I don't take part and act like a girl for a change. You'd think my mother'd be grateful not to have to make me a white organdy dress with a big satin sash and buy me new white baby-doll shoes that can't be taken out of 120 the box till the big day. You'd think she'd be glad her daughter ain't out there prancing around a May Pole getting the new clothes all dirty and sweaty and trying to act like a fairy or a flower or whatever you're supposed to be when you should be trying to be yourself, whatever that is, which is, as far as I am concerned, a poor Black girl who really can't afford to buy shoes and a new dress you only wear once a lifetime cause it won't fit next year. **D**

I was once a strawberry in a Hansel and Gretel pageant when I was in nursery school and didn't have no better sense than to dance on tiptoe with my arms in a circle over my head doing umbrella steps and being a perfect fool just 130 so my mother and father could come dressed up and clap. You'd think they'd know better than to encourage that kind of nonsense. I am not a strawberry. I do not dance on my toes. I run. That is what I am all about. So I always come late to the May Day program, just in time to get my number pinned on and lay in the grass till they announce the fifty-yard dash.

I put Raymond in the little swings, which is a tight squeeze this year and will be impossible next year. Then I look around for Mr. Pearson, who pins the numbers on. I'm really looking for Gretchen, if you want to know the truth, but she's not around. The park is jam-packed. Parents in hats and corsages and breast-pocket handkerchiefs peeking up. Kids in white dresses 140 and light-blue suits. The parkees[8] unfolding chairs and chasing the rowdy kids from Lenox[9] as if they had no right to be there. The big guys with their caps on backwards, leaning against the fence swirling the basketballs on the tips of their fingers, waiting for all these crazy people to clear out the park so they can play. Most of the kids in my class are carrying bass drums and glockenspiels[10] and flutes. You'd think they'd put in a few bongos or something for real like that. **E**

Then here comes Mr. Pearson with his clipboard and his cards and pencils and whistles and safety pins and 50 million other things he's always dropping all over the place with his clumsy self. He sticks out in a crowd because he's

**D MAKE INFERENCES**
Reread lines 115–126. What do you think Squeaky's relationship with her mother is like?

**E MAKE INFERENCES**
Reread lines 135–136. How is Squeaky's life affected by having to take care of Raymond? Think about how she might deal with Raymond next year.

---

7. **Miss Quicksilver:** a reference to how fast quicksilver (mercury) flows.

8. **parkees:** people who regularly gather in the park.

9. **Lenox:** street in Harlem in New York City.

10. **glockenspiels** (glŏk′ən-spēlz′): musical instruments with tuned metal bars played with light hammers.

150 on stilts. We used to call him Jack and the Beanstalk to get him mad. But I'm
the only one that can outrun him and get away, and I'm too grown for that
silliness now.

"Well, Squeaky," he says, checking my name off the list and handing me
number seven and two pins. And I'm thinking he's got no right to call me
Squeaky, if I can't call him Beanstalk.

"Hazel Elizabeth Deborah Parker," I correct him and tell him to write it
down on his board.

"Well, Hazel Elizabeth Deborah Parker, going to give someone else a break
this year?" I squint at him real hard to see if he is seriously thinking I should
160 lose the race on purpose just to give someone else a break. "Only six girls
running this time," he continues, shaking his head sadly like it's my fault all

**ANALYZE VISUALS**
How does the boy in this picture **compare** with the way you imagine Raymond?

of New York didn't turn out in sneakers. "That new girl should give you a run for your money." He looks around the park for Gretchen like a periscope[11] in a submarine movie. "Wouldn't it be a nice gesture if you were . . . to ahhh . . ."

I give him such a look he couldn't finish putting that idea into words. Grownups got a lot of nerve sometimes. I pin number seven to myself and stomp away, I'm so burnt. And I go straight for the track and stretch out on the grass while the band winds up with "Oh, the Monkey Wrapped His Tail Around the Flag Pole," which my teacher calls by some other name. The man
170 on the loudspeaker is calling everyone over to the track and I'm on my back looking at the sky, trying to pretend I'm in the country, but I can't, because even grass in the city feels hard as sidewalk, and there's just no pretending you are anywhere but in a "concrete jungle" as my grandfather says.

The twenty-yard dash takes all of two minutes cause most of the little kids don't know no better than to run off the track or run the wrong way or run smack into the fence and fall down and cry. One little kid, though, has got the good sense to run straight for the white ribbon up ahead so he wins. Then the second-graders line up for the thirty-yard dash and I don't even bother to turn my head to watch cause Raphael Perez always wins. He wins before he
180 even begins by psyching the runners, telling them they're going to trip on their shoelaces and fall on their faces or lose their shorts or something, which he doesn't really have to do since he is very fast, almost as fast as I am. After that is the forty-yard dash which I used to run when I was in first grade. Raymond is hollering from the swings cause he knows I'm about to do my thing cause the man on the loudspeaker has just announced the fifty-yard dash, although he might just as well be giving a recipe for angel food cake cause you can hardly make out what he's sayin for the static. I get up and slip off my sweat pants and then I see Gretchen standing at the starting line, kicking her legs out like a pro. Then as I get into place I see that ole Raymond is on line on
190 the other side of the fence, bending down with his fingers on the ground just like he knew what he was doing. I was going to yell at him but then I didn't. It burns up your energy to holler. **F**

Every time, just before I take off in a race, I always feel like I'm in a dream, the kind of dream you have when you're sick with fever and feel all hot and weightless. I dream I'm flying over a sandy beach in the early morning sun, kissing the leaves of the trees as I fly by. And there's always the smell of apples, just like in the country when I was little and used to think I was a choo-choo train, running through the fields of corn and chugging up the hill to the orchard. And all the time I'm dreaming this, I get lighter and lighter until I'm
200 flying over the beach again, getting blown through the sky like a feather that weighs nothing at all. But once I spread my fingers in the dirt and **crouch** over the Get on Your Mark, the dream goes and I am solid again and am telling

**F** PLOT: RISING ACTION
What details in this paragraph increase the excitement and tension?

**crouch** v. to stoop with bent knees

---

11. **periscope:** a tube with mirrors or prisms inside through which a person can see the reflection of an object at the other end.

myself, Squeaky you must win, you must win, you are the fastest thing in the world, you can even beat your father up Amsterdam if you really try. **G** And then I feel my weight coming back just behind my knees then down to my feet then into the earth and the pistol shot explodes in my blood and I am off and weightless again, flying past the other runners, my arms pumping up and down and the whole world is quiet except for the crunch as I zoom over the gravel in the track. I glance to my left and there is no one. To the right, a
210 blurred Gretchen, who's got her chin jutting out as if it would win the race all by itself. And on the other side of the fence is Raymond with his arms down to his side and the palms tucked up behind him, running in his very own style, and it's the first time I ever saw that and I almost stop to watch my brother Raymond on his first run. But the white ribbon is bouncing toward me and I tear past it, racing into the distance till my feet with a mind of their own start digging up footfuls of dirt and brake me short. Then all the kids standing on the side pile on me, banging me on the back and slapping my head with their May Day programs, for I have won again and everybody on 151st Street can walk tall for another year.

220     "In first place . . ." the man on the loudspeaker is clear as a bell now. But then he pauses and the loudspeaker starts to whine. Then static. And I lean down to catch my breath and here comes Gretchen walking back, for she's overshot the finish line too, huffing and puffing with her hands on her hips taking it slow, breathing in steady time like a real pro and I sort of like her a little for the first time. "In first place . . ." and then three or four voices get all mixed up on the loudspeaker and I dig my sneaker into the grass and stare at Gretchen who's staring back, we both wondering just who did win. I can hear old Beanstalk arguing with the man on the loudspeaker and then a few others running their mouths about what the stopwatches say. Then I hear Raymond
230 yanking at the fence to call me and I wave to shush him, but he keeps rattling the fence like a gorilla in a cage like in them gorilla movies, but then like a dancer or something he starts climbing up nice and easy but very fast. And it occurs to me, watching how smoothly he climbs hand over hand and remembering how he looked running with his arms down to his side and with the wind pulling his mouth back and his teeth showing and all, it occurred to me that Raymond would make a very fine runner. Doesn't he always keep up with me on my trots? And he surely knows how to breathe in counts of seven cause he's always doing it at the dinner table, which drives my brother George up the wall. And I'm smiling to beat the band cause if I've lost this race, or if
240 me and Gretchen tied, or even if I've won, I can always retire as a runner and begin a whole new career as a coach with Raymond as my champion. After all, with a little more study I can beat Cynthia and her phony self at the spelling bee. And if I bugged my mother, I could get piano lessons and become a star. And I have a big rep as the baddest thing around. And I've got a roomful of ribbons and medals and awards. But what has Raymond got to call his own? **H**

**G** MAKE INFERENCES
Why do you think Squeaky always feels this way before a race?

**H** PLOT: CLIMAX
Why is this a **turning point** in the story?

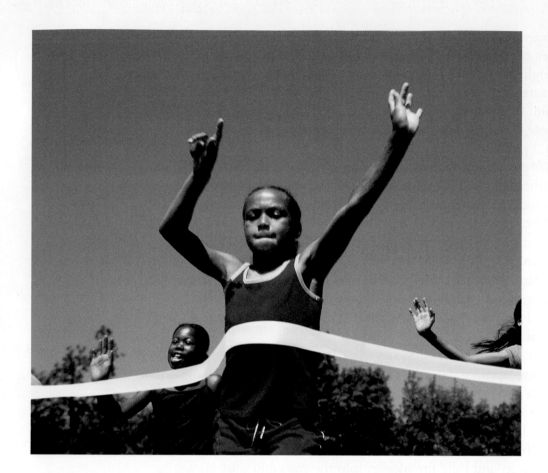

**ANALYZE VISUALS**
What can you **infer** about how the girl in red feels about herself? Tell what clues you used to make your inference.

So I stand there with my new plans, laughing out loud by this time as Raymond jumps down from the fence and runs over with his teeth showing and his arms down to the side, which no one before him has quite mastered as a running style. And by the time he comes over I'm jumping up and down so
250 glad to see him—my brother Raymond, a great runner in the family tradition. But of course everyone thinks I'm jumping up and down because the men on the loudspeaker have finally gotten themselves together and compared notes and are announcing, "In first place—Miss Hazel Elizabeth Deborah Parker." (Dig that.) "In second place—Miss Gretchen P. Lewis." And I look over at Gretchen wondering what the "P" stands for. And I smile. Cause she's good, no doubt about it. Maybe she'd like to help me coach Raymond; she obviously is serious about running, as any fool can see. And she nods to congratulate me and then she smiles. And I smile. We stand there with this big smile of respect between us. It's about as real a smile as girls can do for each other, considering
260 we don't practice real smiling every day, you know, cause maybe we too busy being flowers or fairies or strawberries instead of something honest and worthy of respect . . . you know . . . like being people. ◗ ❶

❶ **PLOT: FALLING ACTION AND RESOLUTION**
How does Squeaky react to the announcement that she won the race?

# Comprehension

**INDIANA STANDARDS**

**READING STANDARD**
**8.3.2** Evaluate the structural elements of the plot ....

1. **Recall** Tell what nickname the big kids have given Squeaky. Why do they call her that?

2. **Clarify** Why does Squeaky feel the May Pole dance is a waste of time?

3. **Clarify** Describe Squeaky's reaction when she sees Raymond running parallel to her in the race.

# Literary Analysis

4. **Make Inferences** Review the inference equations you created as you read the story. Use these **inferences** to answer this question: Why might Squeaky react to other people the way she does? Give details from the story to support your answer.

5. **Compare and Contrast** What are some differences between Squeaky and Gretchen? What are some similarities?

6. **Analyze Plot** The plot of "Raymond's Run" revolves around Squeaky's desire to win the May Day race. Using a diagram like the one shown, note the events that happen at each stage of the **plot.**

7. **Draw Conclusions** How do the events in the story change the way Squeaky views competition?

8. **Evaluate a Character** Does the character Squeaky seem like a real person? Why or why not?

# Extension and Challenge

9. **Big Question Activity** Review the Quickwrite activity on page 32. If Squeaky were in your class, what do you think her response to this activity would be? Complete the activity again, writing about her **motivation** as if you were she.

10. **Inquiry and Research** According to Squeaky, Raymond has a "big head." Find out more about hydrocephalus, the condition he has. With the medical advances of today, is there a treatment or cure for hydrocephalus? What is known about the causes of it? Present your findings to the class.

 **RESEARCH LINKS**
For more on hydrocephalus, visit the **Research Center** at **ClassZone.com.**

# Vocabulary in Context

## VOCABULARY PRACTICE

Answer each question to show your understanding of the vocabulary words.

1. Is a **sidekick** likely to be a friend or someone you just met?
2. If you were to **clutch** something, would you be tossing it away or holding it close?
3. Which would you expect a sports **prodigy** to be—clumsy or talented?
4. When are you more likely to **crouch**—picking a flower from the garden or reaching for a glass in the cabinet?
5. If a person is **liable** to do something, does that mean it's likely or unlikely to happen?
6. What's more important in a **relay** race—one good runner or a team effort?

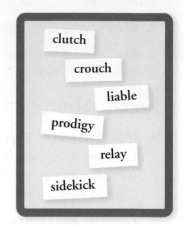

clutch

crouch

liable

prodigy

relay

sidekick

## VOCABULARY IN WRITING

Pretend you are going to run in a race with Squeaky. Using at least two vocabulary words, write a paragraph about your thoughts and feelings at the starting line. You could begin like this.

> **EXAMPLE SENTENCE**
>
> *I'm going to run in this race, even if I'm not __liable__ to win.*

## VOCABULARY STRATEGY: COMPOUND WORDS

Compound words are made up of two or more smaller words. Sometimes the meaning of a compound word can be figured out from the meaning of the two words. Other times, as with the word *sidekick,* you would have to look at context clues or the dictionary to find out the meaning.

**INDIANA STANDARDS**

**READING STANDARD**
**8.1.3** Verify the meaning of a word in its context . . . .

*PRACTICE* Use context clues to figure out the meaning of each boldfaced compound word. Then write the definition. You can consult a dictionary if you need to.

1. Traffic was at a **standstill** after the semitrailer blocked the highway.
2. When the children get to the **crosswalk,** have them look both ways before crossing the street.
3. If the audience is having trouble hearing you, make the announcement over the **loudspeaker.**
4. Since you heard it directly from the source, it's **firsthand** knowledge.
5. We couldn't find the tools, so we used a metal pole as a **makeshift** hammer.

**VOCABULARY PRACTICE**
For more practice, go to the **Vocabulary Center** at ClassZone.com.

# Reading-Writing Connection

Increase your understanding of "Raymond's Run" by responding to these prompts. Then complete the **Grammar and Writing** exercise.

| WRITING PROMPTS | SELF-CHECK |
|---|---|
| **A. Short Response: Describe a Character's World**<br>Squeaky's personality and experiences are influenced by her environment. Write **one paragraph** describing Squeaky's neighborhood and how it affected her. | *A strong description will . . .*<br>• provide details about the streets and traffic<br>• show Squeaky's relationship to neighborhood people and places |
| **B. Extended Response: Write an Article**<br>Imagine you are a newspaper writer covering the May Day events at the park. You are assigned to interview runners and ask them about their **motivation** for participating. Write a **two- or three-paragraph** article that will appear in the next day's paper. | *A thorough article will . . .*<br>• answer *who, what, when, where,* and *why* questions<br>• include quotes from characters in the story |

## GRAMMAR AND WRITING

**AVOID SENTENCE FRAGMENTS**  A **sentence fragment** is an incomplete sentence. It is missing a subject (whom or what the sentence is about), a predicate (what the subject is or does), or both. The missing part(s) must be added in order to fix, or complete, the sentence.

**INDIANA STANDARDS**

**WRITING STANDARD**
**8.4.8** Edit and proofread one's own writing, as well as that of others . . . .

Original:   My brother. (*This is a sentence fragment because it is missing a predicate.*)  He likes movies with a lot of action.

Revised:   My brother likes movies with a lot of action. (*This is now a complete sentence because it contains the subject "My brother" and the predicate "likes movies with a lot of action."*)

**PRACTICE**  Decide whether the following sentence fragments in bold are missing a subject, a predicate, or both. Then combine each fragment with the sentence before it, inserting any additional words as needed.

1. The crowd gathered in the park. **For the May Day festivities.**
2. They gathered, as usual. **The regulars, or parkees.**
3. For many, the May Pole dance is the highlight. **For others, the races.**
4. I'm sure I'll win again. **Always do.**
5. He was the surprise of the day. **Squeaky's brother Raymond.**

*For more help with fragments, see page R64 in the **Grammar Handbook**.*

## The Ransom of Red Chief
Short Story by O. Henry

# *Is any plan* FOOLPROOF?

**INDIANA STANDARDS**

**READING STANDARDS**

**8.2.9** Make reasonable statements and draw conclusions about a text, supporting them with accurate examples.

**8.3.2** Evaluate the structural elements of the plot, such as subplots, parallel episodes, and climax; the plot's development; and the way in which conflicts are (or are not) addressed and resolved.

*KEY IDEA* You can make a list. You can check it twice. You can go over every last detail of a plan in your mind. But even when you think you've thought of everything, **the unexpected** can change the outcome in surprising, terrible, or sometimes hysterically funny ways. In the story you are about to read, the main characters have a plan for making some quick money, but things don't work out the way they had hoped.

*LIST IT* With a partner, plan a surprise party for a friend by making a list of what you need to do. Then, next to each item, write down something unexpected that could possibly happen to spoil that part of the plan.

Lu's Party!

| E-mail our group to invite them. | Forget to take Lu off the list. |
| --- | --- |
| | |

46

## ● LITERARY ANALYSIS: CONFLICT AND RESOLUTION

A story's plot centers on **conflicts,** or struggles between opposing forces. By the end of the story, the conflicts are usually **resolved,** or settled. For example, a fight between two characters might be resolved when one character wins and one character loses. As you read "The Ransom of Red Chief," pay attention to the conflicts and note how they are resolved.

## ● READING STRATEGY: PREDICT

When you watch TV shows or read books, do you ever try to guess what will happen next? If you do, you're making **predictions.** As you read this story, use clues from the text and your own common sense to make predictions. Keep track of whether your predictions were right, or whether you were surprised by the way events unfolded.

| My Prediction | Actual Event | Correct or Surprised? |
|---|---|---|
| The boy will fight back when kidnapped. | Boy fights back. | correct |

*Review:* **Make Inferences**

## ▲ VOCABULARY IN CONTEXT

O. Henry's characters use the words listed, but they aren't as smart as their big vocabulary suggests. See how many words you can match with their numbered definitions.

| WORD LIST | | |
|---|---|---|
| collaborate | diatribe | provisions |
| commend | impudent | ransom |
| comply | proposition | |

1. payment demanded for the release of a person or property
2. to act according to a command or request
3. verbal attack; harsh criticism
4. bold and disrespectful
5. to work together on a project
6. to praise
7. necessary supplies, especially food
8. a suggested plan

# Author On|ine

**Unexpected Twists**
The early life of O. Henry, whose real name was William Sydney Porter, was filled with ups, downs, and unexpected turns. As a young man, he held many different jobs. He clerked in his uncle's drugstore, worked as a ranch hand, and became a bank teller. Several

O. Henry
1862–1910

years after leaving his position at the bank, he was convicted of having embezzled, or stolen, money from his employer. It certainly wasn't his plan to be put in jail, but that's where he found his next occupation.

**A Trailblazing Storyteller** While behind bars, Porter began penning stories to help support his young daughter. Upon his release, he changed his name to O. Henry, became a fiction writer, and contributed weekly stories to newspapers. He grew into one of the country's best-loved authors. O. Henry wrote adventure stories, humorous stories, and slice-of-life tales of ordinary people. The stories often had surprise endings. Today, stories that end with an unexpected twist are said to be written in the "O. Henry style."

 **MORE ABOUT THE AUTHOR**
For more on O. Henry, visit the **Literature Center** at **ClassZone.com.**

# THE RANSOM OF RED CHIEF

## O. HENRY

**ANALYZE VISUALS**
What personality **traits** might the boy in the painting possess?

It looked like a good thing; but wait till I tell you. We were down South, in Alabama—Bill Driscoll and myself—when this kidnapping idea struck us. It was, as Bill afterward expressed it, "during a moment of temporary mental apparition";[1] but we didn't find that out till later.

There was a town down there, as flat as a flannel-cake, and called Summit, of course. It contained inhabitants of as undeleterious[2] and self-satisfied a class of peasantry as ever clustered around a Maypole.

Bill and me had a joint capital of about six hundred dollars, and we needed just two thousand dollars more to pull off a fraudulent town-lot scheme
10 in Western Illinois with. We talked it over on the front steps of the hotel. Philoprogenitiveness,[3] says we, is strong in semi-rural communities; therefore, and for other reasons, a kidnapping project ought to do better there than in the radius of newspapers that send reporters out in plain clothes to stir up talk about such things. We knew that Summit couldn't get after us with anything stronger than constables, and, maybe, some lackadaisical bloodhounds and a **diatribe** or two in the *Weekly Farmers' Budget*. So, it looked good.

We selected for our victim the only child of a prominent citizen named Ebenezer Dorset. The father was respectable and tight, a mortgage fancier and a stern, upright collection-plate passer and forecloser. The kid was a boy of ten,
20 with bas-relief[4] freckles, and hair the color of the cover of the magazine you buy at the news-stand when you want to catch a train. Bill and me figured that Ebenezer would melt down for a **ransom** of two thousand dollars to a cent. But wait till I tell you. **A**

**diatribe** (dī′ə-trīb′) *n.* bitter, abusive criticism

**ransom** (răn′səm) *n.* payment demanded for the release of a person or property

**A** **PREDICT**
Reread lines 17–23. Based on Sam's final comment, do you think the men's plan will be successful? Add this prediction to your chart.

---

1. **apparition** (ăp′ə-rĭsh′ən): a sudden or unusual sight.
2. **undeleterious** (ŭn-dĕl′ĭ-tîr′ē-əs): harmless.
3. **philoprogenitiveness** (fĭl′ō-prō-jĕn′ĭ-tĭv-nĕs): love for one's own children.
4. **bas-relief** (bä′rĭ-lēf′): slightly raised.

About two miles from Summit was a little mountain, covered with a dense cedar brake.[5] On the rear elevation of this mountain was a cave. There we stored **provisions.**

One evening after sundown, we drove in a buggy past old Dorset's house. The kid was in the street, throwing rocks at a kitten on the opposite fence.

"Hey, little boy!" says Bill, "would you like to have a bag of candy and a
30 nice ride?"

The boy catches Bill neatly in the eye with a piece of brick.

"That will cost the old man an extra five hundred dollars," says Bill, climbing over the wheel.

That boy put up a fight like a welter-weight cinnamon bear; but, at last, we got him down in the bottom of the buggy and drove away. We took him up to the cave, and I hitched the horse in the cedar brake. After dark I drove the buggy to the little village, three miles away, where we had hired it, and walked back to the mountain. **B**

Bill was pasting court plaster[6] over the scratches and bruises on his features.
40 There was a fire burning behind the big rock at the entrance of the cave, and the boy was watching a pot of boiling coffee, with two buzzard tail feathers stuck in his red hair. He points a stick at me when I come up, and says:

"Ha! cursed paleface, do you dare to enter the camp of Red Chief, the terror of the plains?" **C**

"He's all right now," says Bill, rolling up his trousers and examining some bruises on his shins. "We're playing Indian. We're making Buffalo Bill's show look like magic-lantern views[7] of Palestine in the town hall. I'm Old Hank, the Trapper, Red Chief's captive, and I'm to be scalped at daybreak. By Geronimo! that kid can kick hard."

50     Yes, sir, that boy seemed to be having the time of his life. The fun of camping out in a cave had made him forget that he was a captive himself. He immediately christened me Snake-eye, the Spy, and announced that, when his braves returned from the warpath, I was to be broiled at the stake at the rising of the sun.

Then we had supper; and he filled his mouth full of bacon and bread and gravy, and began to talk. He made a during-dinner speech something like this:

"I like this fine. I never camped out before; but I had a pet 'possum once, and I was nine last birthday. I hate to go to school. Rats ate up sixteen of Jimmy Talbot's aunt's speckled hen's eggs. Are there any real Indians in these
60 woods? I want some more gravy. Does the trees moving make the wind blow? We had five puppies. What makes your nose so red, Hank? My father has lots of money. Are the stars hot? I whipped Ed Walker twice, Saturday. I don't like girls. You dassent[8] catch toads unless with a string. Do oxen make any noise?

---

5. **brake:** a thick grouping of trees.

6. **court plaster:** adhesive cloth for covering cuts and scratches.

7. **magic-lantern views:** slides.

8. **dassant:** dare not.

provisions (prə-vĭzh'ənz)
*n.* necessary supplies; food

**B** CONFLICT
Who is in conflict and why?

**C** PREDICT
How do you think the boy will respond to being held in captivity?

SOCIAL STUDIES CONNECTION

In 1883, William F. Cody began producing Buffalo Bill's Wild West Show, a traveling extravaganza celebrating and glorifying the American West.

Why are oranges round? Have you got beds to sleep on in this cave? Amos Murray has got six toes. A parrot can talk, but a monkey or a fish can't. How many does it take to make twelve?" **D**

Every few minutes he would remember that he was an Indian, and pick up his stick rifle and tiptoe to the mouth of the cave to search for the scouts of the hated paleface. Now and then he would let out a war whoop that made Old
70 Hank the Trapper shiver. That boy had Bill terrorized from the start.

"Red Chief," says I to the kid, "would you like to go home?"

"Aw, what for?" says he. "I don't have any fun at home. I hate to go to school. I like to camp out. You won't take me back home again, Snake-eye, will you?"

"Not right away," says I. "We'll stay here in the cave awhile."

"All right!" says he. "That'll be fine. I never had such fun in all my life."

We went to bed about eleven o'clock. We spread down some wide blankets and quilts and put Red Chief between us. We weren't afraid he'd run away. He kept us awake for three hours, jumping up and reaching for his rifle and screeching: "Hist! pard," in mine and Bill's ears, as the fancied crackle of
80 a twig or the rustle of a leaf revealed to his young imagination the stealthy approach of the outlaw band. At last, I fell into a troubled sleep, and dreamed that I had been kidnapped and chained to a tree by a ferocious pirate with red hair.

Just at daybreak, I was awakened by a series of awful screams from Bill. They weren't yells, or howls, or shouts, or whoops, or yawps, such as you'd expect from a manly set of vocal organs—they were simply indecent, terrifying, humiliating screams, such as women emit when they see ghosts or caterpillars. It's an awful thing to hear a strong, desperate, fat man scream incontinently in a cave at daybreak.
90 I jumped up to see what the matter was. Red Chief was sitting on Bill's chest, with one hand twined in Bill's hair. In the other he had the sharp case-knife we used for slicing bacon; and he was industriously and realistically trying to take Bill's scalp, according to the sentence that had been pronounced upon him the evening before.

I got the knife away from the kid and made him lie down again. But, from that moment, Bill's spirit was broken. He laid down on his side of the bed, but he never closed an eye again in sleep as long as that boy was with us. I dozed off for a while, but along toward sun-up I remembered that Red Chief had said I was to be burned at the stake at the rising of the sun. I wasn't nervous or
100 afraid; but I sat up and leaned against a rock. **E**

"What you getting up so soon for, Sam?" asked Bill.

"Me?" says I. "Oh, I got a kind of a pain in my shoulder. I thought sitting up would rest it."

"You're a liar!" says Bill. "You're afraid. You was to be burned at sunrise, and you was afraid he'd do it. And he would, too, if he could find a match. Ain't it awful, Sam? Do you think anybody will pay out money to get a little imp like that back home?"

**D PREDICT**
On your chart, note whether the boy's response to captivity matches your prediction. Do you think the boy's current attitude about his captivity will make the men's plan go more smoothly?

**E CONFLICT**
In what way has his interaction with the boy affected Bill?

"Sure," said I. "A rowdy kid like that is just the kind that parents dote on. Now, you and the Chief get up and cook breakfast, while I go up on the top of this mountain and reconnoiter."[9]

I went up on the peak of the little mountain and ran my eye over the contiguous vicinity. Over toward Summit I expected to see the sturdy yeomanry of the village armed with scythes and pitchforks beating the countryside for the dastardly kidnappers. But what I saw was a peaceful landscape dotted with one man plowing with a dun mule. Nobody was dragging the creek; no couriers dashed hither and yon, bringing tidings of no news to the distracted parents. There was a sylvan[10] attitude of somnolent sleepiness pervading that section of the external outward surface of Alabama that lay exposed to my view. "Perhaps," says I to myself, "it has not yet been discovered that the wolves have borne away the tender lambkin from the fold. Heaven help the wolves!" says I, and I went down the mountain to breakfast.

When I got to the cave I found Bill backed up against the side of it, breathing hard, and the boy threatening to smash him with a rock half as big as a coconut.

"He put a red-hot boiled potato down my back," explained Bill, "and then mashed it with his foot; and I boxed his ears. Have you got a gun about you, Sam?"

I took the rock away from the boy and kind of patched up the argument. "I'll fix you," says the kid to Bill. "No man ever yet struck the Red Chief but what he got paid for it. You better beware!"

---

9. **reconnoiter** (rē′kə-noi′tər): to seek information about an enemy's whereabouts.

10. **sylvan** (sĭl′vən): like woods or forests.

**ANALYZE VISUALS**
Who seems to be winning the **conflict** in the painting? Tell how you know.

After breakfast the kid takes a piece of leather with strings wrapped around it out of his pocket and goes outside the cave unwinding it.

"What's he up to now?" says Bill anxiously. "You don't think he'll run away, do you, Sam?" **F**

"No fear of it," says I. "He don't seem to be much of a homebody. But we've got to fix up some plan about the ransom. There don't seem to be much excitement around Summit on account of his disappearance; but maybe they haven't realized yet that he's gone. His folks may think he's spending the night with Aunt Jane or one of the neighbors. Anyhow, he'll be missed today.

140 Tonight we must get a message to his father demanding the two thousand dollars for his return."

Just then we heard a kind of war whoop, such as David might have emitted when he knocked out the champion Goliath. It was a sling that Red Chief had pulled out of his pocket, and he was whirling it around his head.

I dodged, and heard a heavy thud and a kind of a sigh from Bill, like a horse gives out when you take his saddle off. A rock the size of an egg had caught Bill just behind his left ear. He loosened himself all over and fell in the fire across the frying pan of hot water for washing the dishes. I dragged him out and poured cold water on his head for half an hour.

150 By and by, Bill sits up and feels behind his ear and says: "Sam, do you know who my favorite Biblical character is?"

"Take it easy," says I. "You'll come to your senses presently."

"King Herod,"[11] says he. "You won't go away and leave me here alone, will you, Sam?"

I went out and caught that boy and shook him until his freckles rattled.

"If you don't behave," says I, "I'll take you straight home. Now, are you going to be good, or not?"

"I was only funning," says he, sullenly. "I didn't mean to hurt Old Hank. But what did he hit me for? I'll behave, Snake-eye, if you won't send me home, 160 and if you'll let me play the Scout today." **G**

"I don't know the game," says I. "That's for you and Mr. Bill to decide. He's your playmate for the day. I'm going away for a while, on business. Now, you come in and make friends with him and say you are sorry for hurting him, or home you go, at once." **H**

I made him and Bill shake hands, and then I took Bill aside and told him I was going to Poplar Cove, a little village three miles from the cave, and find out what I could about how the kidnapping had been regarded in Summit. Also, I thought it best to send a peremptory letter to old man Dorset that day, demanding the ransom and dictating how it should be paid.

170 "You know, Sam," says Bill, "I've stood by you without batting an eye in earthquakes, fire, and flood—in poker games, dynamite outrages, police raids, train robberies, and cyclones. I never lost my nerve yet till we kidnapped that

**F** MAKE INFERENCES
How do you think Bill is starting to feel about the plan to get two thousand dollars?

**G** PREDICT
Do you expect that the boy will behave better going forward? Add the prediction to your chart.

**H** CONFLICT
In what ways has the conflict changed since the beginning of the story?

---

11. **King Herod:** an ancient king of Judea who once ordered the execution of all Bethlehem boys under the age of two.

two-legged skyrocket of a kid. He's got me going. You won't leave me long with him, will you, Sam?"

"I'll be back sometime this afternoon," says I. "You must keep the boy amused and quiet till I return. And now we'll write the letter to old Dorset."

Bill and I got paper and pencil and worked on the letter while Red Chief, with a blanket wrapped around him, strutted up and down, guarding the mouth of the cave. Bill begged me tearfully to make the ransom fifteen
180  hundred dollars instead of two thousand. "I ain't attempting," says he, "to decry[12] the celebrated moral aspect of parental affection, but we're dealing with humans, and it ain't human for anybody to give up two thousand dollars for that forty-pound chunk of freckled wildcat. I'm willing to take a chance at fifteen hundred dollars. You can charge the difference up to me."

So, to relieve Bill, I acceded, and we **collaborated** a letter that ran this way:

EBENEZER DORSET, ESQ.:
We have your boy concealed in a place far from Summit. It is useless for you or the most skillful detectives to attempt to find him. Absolutely, the only terms on which you can have him restored to you are these: We demand
190  fifteen hundred dollars in large bills for his return: the money to be left at midnight at the same spot and in the same box as your reply—as hereinafter described. If you agree to these terms, send your answer in writing by a solitary messenger tonight at half-past eight o'clock. After crossing Owl Creek on the road to Poplar Cove, there are three large trees about a hundred yards apart, close to the fence of the wheat field on the right-hand side. At the bottom of the fence post, opposite the third tree, will be found a small pasteboard box.

The messenger will place the answer in this box and return immediately to Summit.
200  If you attempt any treachery or fail to **comply** with our demand as stated, you will never see your boy again.

If you pay the money as demanded, he will be returned to you safe and well within three hours. These terms are final, and if you do not accede to them no further communication will be attempted.

TWO DESPERATE MEN. ⓘ

I addressed this letter to Dorset and put it in my pocket. As I was about to start, the kid comes up to me and says:

"Aw, Snake-eye, you said I could play the Scout while you was gone."

"Play it, of course," says I. "Mr. Bill will play with you. What kind of a
210  game is it?"

"I'm the Scout," says Red Chief, "and I have to ride to the stockade to warn the settlers that the Indians are coming. I'm tired of playing Indian myself. I want to be the Scout."

---

12. **decry:** to criticize.

> **collaborate**
> (kə-lăb′ə-rāt′) *v.* to work together on a project

> **comply** (kəm-plī′) *v.* to act according to a command or request

> ⓘ **PREDICT**
> How do you think the boy's father will respond to the men's demands? Add the prediction to your chart.

"All right," says I. "It sounds harmless to me. I guess Mr. Bill will help you foil the enemy."

"What am I to do?" asks Bill, looking at the kid suspiciously.

"You are the hoss," says Scout. "Get down on your hands and knees. How can I ride to the stockade without a hoss?"

"You'd better keep him interested," said I, "till we get the scheme going.
220 Loosen up."

Bill gets down on his all fours, and a look comes in his eye like a rabbit's when you catch it in a trap.

"How far is it to the stockade, kid?" he asks, in a husky manner of voice.

"Ninety miles," says the Scout. "And you have to hurry to get there on time. Whoa, now!"

The Scout jumps on Bill's back and digs his heels in his side.

"For Heaven's sake," says Bill, "hurry back, Sam, as soon as you can. I wish we hadn't made the ransom more than a thousand. Say, you quit kicking me or I'll get up and warm you good." **J**

230     I walked over to Poplar Cove and sat around the post office and store, talking with the chawbacons that came in to trade. One whiskerando says that he hears Summit is all upset on account of Elder Ebenezer Dorset's boy having been lost or stolen. That was all I wanted to know. I referred casually to the price of black-eyed peas, posted my letter surreptitiously and came away. The postmaster said the mail carrier would come by in an hour to take the mail on to Summit. **K**

When I got back to the cave Bill and the boy were not to be found. I explored the vicinity of the cave, and risked a yodel or two, but there was no response.

240     So I sat down on a mossy bank to await developments.

In about half an hour I heard the bushes rustle, and Bill wabbled out into the little glade in front of the cave. Behind him was the kid, stepping softly like a scout, with a broad grin on his face. Bill stopped, took off his hat and wiped his face with a red handkerchief. The kid stopped about eight feet behind him.

"Sam," says Bill, "I suppose you think I'm a renegade, but I couldn't help it. I'm a grown person with masculine proclivities and habits of self-defense, but there is a time when all systems of egotism and predominance fail. The boy is gone. I have sent him home. All is off. There was martyrs in old times,"
250 goes on Bill, "that suffered death rather than give up the particular graft they enjoyed. None of 'em ever was subjugated to such supernatural tortures as I have been. I tried to be faithful to our articles of depredation;[13] but there came a limit." **L**

"What's the trouble, Bill?" I asks him.

"I was rode," says Bill, "the ninety miles to the stockade, not barring an inch. Then, when the settlers was rescued, I was given oats. Sand ain't a

**J** CONFLICT
Who seems to be winning the struggle?

**K** PREDICT
What do you think will happen now that the letter has been posted?

**L** CONFLICT
Reread lines 241–253. Bill thinks the conflict has been resolved. What details let the reader know that he is wrong?

---

13. **depredation** (dĕp′rĭ-dā′shən): robbery.

palatable substitute. And then, for an hour I had
to try to explain to him why there was nothin' in
holes, how a road can run both ways and what
makes the grass green. I tell you, Sam, a human
can only stand so much. I takes him by the neck
of his clothes and drags him down the mountain.
On the way he kicks my legs black and blue from
the knees down; and I've got to have two or three
bites on my thumb and hand cauterized.[14]

"But he's gone"—continues Bill—"gone home.
I showed him the road to Summit and kicked him
about eight feet nearer there at one kick. I'm sorry
we lose the ransom; but it was either that or Bill
Driscoll to the madhouse."

Bill is puffing and blowing, but there is a look
of ineffable peace and growing content on his
rose-pink features.

"Bill," says I, "there isn't any heart disease in
your family, is there?"

"No," says Bill, "nothing chronic except malaria
and accidents. Why?"

"Then you might turn around," says I, "and have a look behind you."

Bill turns and sees the boy, and loses his complexion and sits down plump
on the ground and begins to pluck aimlessly at grass and little sticks. For an
hour I was afraid of his mind. And then I told him that my scheme was to put
the whole job through immediately and that we would get the ransom and
be off with it by midnight if old Dorset fell in with our **proposition.** So Bill
braced up enough to give the kid a weak sort of a smile and a promise to play
the Russian in a Japanese war with him as soon as he felt a little better.

I had a scheme for collecting that ransom without danger of being caught
by counterplots that ought to **commend** itself to professional kidnappers. The
tree under which the answer was to be left—and the money later on—was
close to the road fence with big, bare fields on all sides. If a gang of constables
should be watching for anyone to come for the note they could see him a long
way off crossing the fields or in the road. But no, sirree! At half-past eight I
was up in that tree as well hidden as a tree toad, waiting for the messenger to
arrive.

Exactly on time, a half-grown boy rides up the road on a bicycle, locates the
pasteboard box at the foot of the fence post, slips a folded piece of paper into it
and pedals away again back toward Summit.

I waited an hour and then concluded the thing was square. I slid down the
tree, got the note, slipped along the fence till I struck the woods, and was back
at the cave in another half an hour. I opened the note, got near the lantern,

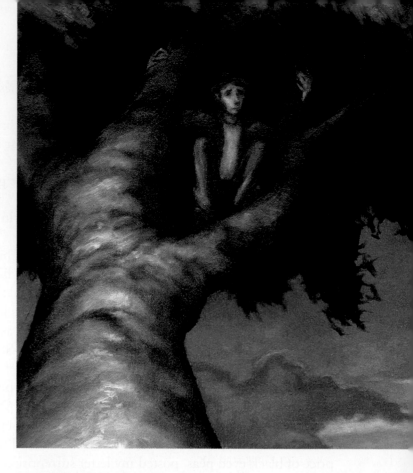

**proposition**
(prŏp′ə-zĭsh′ən) *n.*
a suggested plan

**commend** (kə-mĕnd′)
*v.* to speak highly of; to
praise; to recommend

---

14. **cauterized** (kô′tə-rīzd′): burned a wound to stop bleeding.

300 and read it to Bill. It was written with a pen in a crabbed hand, and the sum and substance of it was this:

TWO DESPERATE MEN.

GENTLEMEN: I received your letter today by post, in regard to the ransom you ask for the return of my son. I think you are a little high in your demands, and I hereby make you a counter-proposition, which I am inclined to believe you will accept. You bring Johnny home and pay me two hundred and fifty dollars in cash, and I agree to take him off your hands. You had better come at night, for the neighbors believe he is lost, and I couldn't be responsible for what they would do to anybody they saw bringing him back.

310
Very respectfully,

EBENEZER DORSET. **M**

**M** MAKE INFERENCES
Reread the note from Ebenezer Dorset. From this passage, what can you infer about how well he knows his son?

"Great Pirates of Penzance!" says I; "of all the **impudent**—"

But I glanced at Bill, and hesitated. He had the most appealing look in his eyes I ever saw on the face of a dumb or a talking brute.

**impudent**
(ĭm′pyə-dənt) *adj.* bold and disrespectful

"Sam," says he, "what's two hundred and fifty dollars, after all? We've got the money. One more night of this kid will send me to bed in Bedlam.[15] Besides being a thorough gentleman, I think Mr. Dorset is a spendthrift for making us such a liberal offer. You ain't going to let the chance go, are you?"

"Tell you the truth, Bill," says I, "this little he ewe lamb has somewhat
320 got on my nerves, too. We'll take him home, pay the ransom, and make our getaway." **N**

We took him home that night. We got him to go by telling him that his father had bought a silver-mounted rifle and a pair of moccasins for him, and we were going to hunt bears the next day.

It was just twelve o'clock when we knocked at Ebenezer's front door. Just at the moment when I should have been abstracting the fifteen hundred dollars from the box under the tree, according to the original proposition, Bill was counting out two hundred and fifty dollars into Dorset's hand.

When the kid found out we were going to leave him at home he started up
330 a howl like a calliope[16] and fastened himself as tight as a leech to Bill's leg. His father peeled him away gradually, like a porous plaster.

"How long can you hold him?" asks Bill.

"I'm not as strong as I used to be," says old Dorset, "but I think I can promise you ten minutes."

"Enough," says Bill. "In ten minutes I shall cross the Central, Southern, and Middle Western States, and be legging it trippingly for the Canadian border."

And, as dark as it was, and as fat as Bill was, and as good a runner as I am, he was a good mile and a half out of Summit before I could catch up with him. **O**

**N** CONFLICT AND RESOLUTION
Who wins out in the conflict between the kidnappers and the boy's father?

**O** CONFLICT AND RESOLUTION
How is the conflict between the men and the boy finally resolved?

---

15. **Bedlam:** an insane asylum.

16. **calliope** (kə-lī′ə-pē′): an instrument with steam whistles.

**ANECDOTE** O. Henry was a master of unexpected plot twists. In the following anecdote, which was originally read on the radio, you will learn about a happy coincidence that involves an undiscovered O. Henry story.

# Manuscript Found in an Attic

## MARCUS ROSENBAUM

O. Henry

When I told my father that I was moving to Des Moines, he told me about the only time he'd been there. It was in the 1930s, he said, when he was the business manager of the literary magazine of Southern Methodist University in Dallas. His friend Lon Tinkle was the magazine's editor. Lon also taught English at SMU, and there was a student in his class who had a severely deformed back. It was the Depression, and the young woman came from a family that was so poor she couldn't afford the operation that would correct the problem.

Her mother, who ran a boardinghouse in Galveston, was cleaning out the attic one day when she came across an old dusty manuscript. Scribbled across the top were the words, "By O. Henry." It was a nice story, and she sent it along to her daughter at SMU, who showed it to Lon. Lon had never seen the story before, but it *sounded* like O. Henry, it had an O. Henry story line, and he knew that William Sydney Porter, aka O. Henry, had lived in Houston at one time. So it was entirely possible that the famous author had gone to the beach and stayed in the Galveston boardinghouse, had written the story while he was there, and had inadvertently left the manuscript behind. Lon showed the manuscript to my father, who contacted an O. Henry expert at Columbia University in New York. The expert said he'd like to see it, so my father got on a train and took it to him.

The expert authenticated the story as O. Henry's, and my father set out to sell it. Eventually, he found himself in Des Moines, meeting with Gardner Cowles, a top editor at the Des Moines *Register.* Cowles loved the story and bought it on the spot. My father took the proceeds to the young woman in Lon Tinkle's class. It was just enough for her to have the operation she so desperately needed—and, as far as we know, to live happily ever after.

My father never told me what the O. Henry story was about. But I doubt that it could have been better than his own story: a story about O. Henry that was an O. Henry story itself.

## Comprehension

INDIANA
STANDARDS

READING STANDARD
8.3.2 Evaluate the structural
elements of the plot . . . .

1. **Recall**  Why do Sam and Bill need two thousand dollars?

2. **Clarify**  Why does the boy prefer to stay with Sam and Bill rather than go home?

3. **Represent**  Reread lines 24–26 on page 50.  Use the details in this paragraph to draw a simple map showing Summit, the mountain, and the cave.

## Literary Analysis

4. **Predict**  Look back at the chart you created as you read.  Which outcomes surprised you and which did not?  Tell what **unexpected** circumstances affected Bill and Sam's plan to get money.

5. **Analyze Conflict and Resolution**  When an outcome is the opposite of what might be expected, it is said to be **ironic.**  Which of the resolutions to this story's conflicts are ironic?  Show your thinking in two graphics like the ones shown.

6. **Draw Conclusions**  Look back at lines 8–16.  From the vocabulary Sam uses, as well as the way he presents himself and Bill to the reader at the beginning of the story, do you think the partners are typically successful in their schemes? Cite evidence to support your conclusion.

## Extension and Challenge

7. **Creative Project: Music**  Choose a familiar tune and rewrite the words to retell the story of "The Ransom of Red Chief."  Include details that bring out the **irony** in the story.

8. **Literary Criticism**  O. Henry's short stories remain popular with readers in part because they often have **surprise endings.**  Read the article "Manuscript Found in an Attic" on page 58.  What do you think the author means when he describes it as "a story about O. Henry that was an O. Henry story itself"?

# Vocabulary in Context

## VOCABULARY PRACTICE

Choose the vocabulary word that best completes each the sentence.

collaborate    impudent

commend    proposition

comply    provisions

diatribe    ransom

1. The kidnappers demanded a _____ before they returned the boy.
2. They had enough _____ stashed in a cave to last a week.
3. Since neither of them could complete the scheme alone, the kidnappers had to _____.
4. The worst they expected was a _____ in the local paper.
5. Red Chief was so _____, adults didn't like being around him.
6. The father did not _____ with the terms of the letter.
7. Red Chief's father had a different _____ for the kidnappers.
8. You can't _____ the parent's actions, but you can certainly understand them.

## VOCABULARY IN WRITING

What is your reaction to the end of this story? Use two or more vocabulary words to write a one-paragraph answer. You could start like this.

> **EXAMPLE SENTENCE**
>
> I was surprised at how the kidnappers' **_proposition_** got turned around.

## VOCABULARY STRATEGY: THE PREFIX *com-*

The vocabulary word *commend* contains the prefix *com-*, which means "together" or "with." The prefix can be spelled *com-*, *col-*, *cor-*, or *con-*, depending on the letter that follows it. Learning to recognize this prefix with its various spellings can help you remember the meanings of many words.

*PRACTICE* Choose the word from the list that matches each numbered definition. If necessary, consult a dictionary.

collect    combine    concur    confirm

1. to join together
2. to establish that something is true
3. to bring together in a group, gather
4. to be in agreement, or harmony

**VOCABULARY PRACTICE**
For more practice, go to the **Vocabulary Center** at **ClassZone.com.**

# Reading-Writing Connection

Demonstrate your understanding of "The Ransom of Red Chief" by responding to these prompts. Then complete the **Grammar and Writing** exercise.

| WRITING PROMPTS | SELF-CHECK |
|---|---|
| **A. Short Response: Write a Postcard**<br>For the boy, being with Sam and Bill was like being at camp. Write a **one-paragraph postcard** that he might have sent to his father while he was gone. | ***A good postcard will . . .***<br>• include words and phrases similar to those used by the boy in the story<br>• cite events from the story from the boy's perspective |
| **B. Extended Response: Analyze What Went Wrong**<br>Bill and Sam thought they had a brilliant scheme to make money, but they didn't plan for the **unexpected.** In **two or three paragraphs,** tell why they thought their plan would work and what they were mistaken about. | ***A successful analysis will . . .***<br>• include a topic sentence<br>• identify mistakes the men made in their thinking |

## GRAMMAR AND WRITING

***AVOID RUN-ON SENTENCES*** A **run-on sentence,** sometimes called a run-on, is two or more sentences written as though they were a single sentence. To correct a run-on, you can

**INDIANA STANDARDS**

WRITING STANDARD
**8.4.8** Edit and proofread one's own writing, as well as that of others . . . .

- insert an end mark and start a new sentence
- insert a **coordinating conjunction,** such as *and, but,* or *so,* after a comma
- change a comma to a **semicolon**

> *Original:* I thought Randy would win the class elections, Mary believed Ling would be the winner.
>
> *Revised:* I thought Randy would win the class elections, but Mary believed Ling would be the winner.

***PRACTICE*** Rewrite the following sentences so that they are no longer run-ons.

1. I thought I wouldn't like being away from home, it's actually really fun.
2. I promised to behave, they threatened to send me home.
3. There weren't daily newspapers, nosy reporters wouldn't be coming around.
4. They didn't count on the boy's adventurous spirit they were surprised by it.
5. Parents worry about keeping their children safe, they don't worry about keeping people safe from their children.

*For more help with run-on sentences, see page R64 in the **Grammar Handbook.***

## Clean Sweep
Short Story by Joan Bauer

# When does trash become
# TREASURE?

**INDIANA STANDARDS**

**READING STANDARD**
**8.3.2** Evaluate the structural elements of the plot, such as subplots, parallel episodes, and climax; the plot's development; and the way in which conflicts are (or are not) addressed and resolved.

**KEY IDEA** There is an old saying, "One man's trash is another man's **treasure.**" A scrap of cloth, a wrinkled photo, or a worn, torn book can have great value to a person if there are special memories attached. In "Clean Sweep," a girl finds out not only that a simple object can hold good memories, but also that those memories can help heal.

**WEB IT** What do you value that someone else might be tempted to throw away? Create a web to show some memories that are connected to that item. Expand your web by adding details that explain what makes the object special to you.

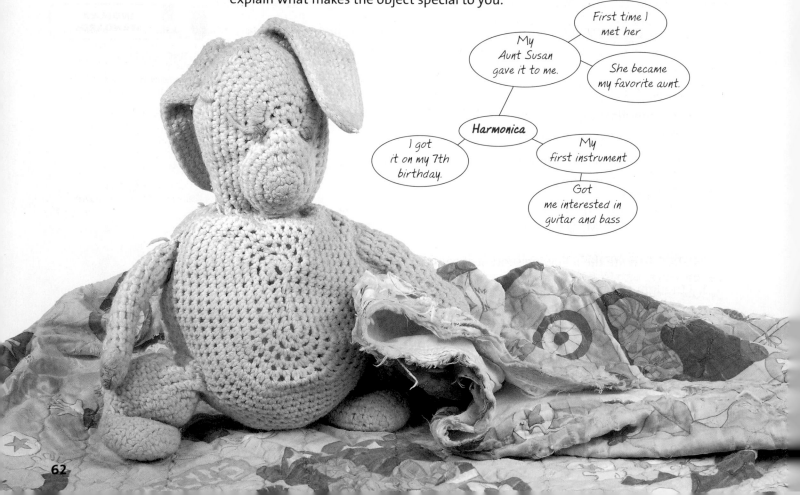

First time I met her

My Aunt Susan gave it to me.

She became my favorite aunt.

Harmonica

I got it on my 7th birthday.

My first instrument

Got me interested in guitar and bass

## ● LITERARY ANALYSIS: INTERNAL AND EXTERNAL CONFLICT

You already know that a **conflict** is a struggle between opposing forces. It creates the tension or suspense in a story or play. Recognizing the types of conflict can help you better understand the actions of the characters.

- **External conflict** is a struggle between a character and an outside force. The outside force could be another character, society, or a force of nature.
- **Internal conflict** is a struggle within a character's mind. This type of conflict may occur when the character has to make a difficult decision or deal with contradictory feelings.

As you read "Clean Sweep," notice how a past event causes internal and external conflict.

## ● READING SKILL: SEQUENCE

To fully understand a story, you must recognize the **sequence,** or order, of the events described. While events are often presented in the order in which they occur, sometimes the action is interrupted to present a scene from an earlier time. This scene, called a **flashback,** can help explain a character's actions. To help you figure out when events occurred, look for signal words and phrases such as these:

*four years ago        moments later        while*

As you read "Clean Sweep," keep track of the sequence by recording important events on a sequence chart.

*Review:* **Predict**

## ▲ VOCABULARY IN CONTEXT

The boldfaced words help Joan Bauer tell about one teenager's experience with loss and familial responsibility. To see how many you know, substitute a different word or words for each.

1. The room was dark and **dingy.**
2. A **minuscule** amount of light came through the window.
3. Her sense of **propriety** kept her from interrupting him.
4. She acted calm in front of her class, but she was in **turmoil.**
5. I can't stand the **vileness** of rotten eggs.
6. It was an **aberration,** not what she usually sees.

# Author Online

**Laughter and Life**
As a child, Joan Bauer dreamed of becoming a comedian or a comedy writer when she grew up. The funny adults in her life inspired her. Her mother loved to make people laugh, and her grandmother, Nana, was a storyteller whose tales always included humor. But

**Joan Bauer
born 1951**

real life wasn't always amusing. When Joan was eight years old, her parents divorced. This and other family troubles proved devastating. However, she continued writing, finding that it helped ease her pain. Now an award-winning author, Joan Bauer admits to often drawing from these difficult life experiences while creating her touching, amusing stories.

**Hope and Humor** "I want to create stories that link life's struggles with laughter," Bauer has said. "Laughter is a gift we've been given . . . not just to make us feel good, but to empower us to overcome dark times." Her novels and stories are about how we can help each other by sharing both the struggle and the laughter.

 **MORE ABOUT THE AUTHOR**
For more on Joan Bauer, visit the **Literature Center** at ClassZone.com.

# Clean Sweep

## Joan Bauer

"Have you ever seen a dust mite?"

My mother always lowers her voice when she asks this; it adds to the emotional impact. Never in the four years since she's had the cleaning business has anyone ever said they've seen one. That's because the only people who have seen dust mites are scientists who put dust balls on slides and look at them under microscopes. Personally I have better things to do than look at **minuscule** animals who cause great torture among the allergic, but my mother has a photo of a dust mite blown up to ten gazillion times its size—she is holding it up now, as she always does in this part of her
10 presentation—and the two women who sit on the floral couch before her gasp appropriately and shut their eyes, because dust mites, trust me, are ugly. Think *Invasion of the Body Snatchers* meets *The Hunchback of Notre Dame*, and you're just beginning to enter into the **vileness** of this creature.

"They're everywhere," Mom says to the women. "Under the bed, on the sheets, clinging to the blinds; hiding, waiting. And at Clean Sweep," she offers quietly, but dramatically, "we *kill* them for you. We hate them even more than you do. *This* is why we're in business."

The two women look at each other and say *yes,* they want the cleaning service to start immediately.

20 Mom tells them our price. One woman, as expected, says, "That sounds a little high." People are so cheap. Everyone wants quality, no one wants to pay for it. Here's the suburban dream—to hire great workers who are such meek morons that they don't have the guts to ask for a living wage. Ⓐ

This is not my mother's problem. She holds up the dust mite enlargement to make the point. "We cost more because we know where he and his army are hiding."

ANALYZE VISUALS
What can you **conclude** about this girl's feelings toward housework?

**minuscule** (mĭn′ə-skyōōl′) *adj.* very small; tiny

**vileness** (vīl′nəs) *n.* unpleasantness; disgusting quality

Ⓐ **CONFLICT**
What conflicts do the main character and her family face with each job?

She used to say "we know where he and his friends are hiding," but "army" sounds more fierce, and when you are serious about eliminating dust, you'd better let everyone know it's war.

30    "Well . . . ," the other woman says, unsure.

Mom presses in. "We suggest two cleanings per week for one month to achieve total elimination. Then weekly cleanings should do, unless you have special needs."

Special needs in the cleaning world range from cleaning out attics to detoxification[1] of teenage bedrooms. I am a specialist in cleaning rooms of kids who have just gone off to college. It takes nerves of steel. And I have them.

My brother Benjamin doesn't. To begin with, he's allergic to dust—bad news when the family business is dedicated to eliminating it. To end with, he's a devoted underachiever, in stark contrast to myself. And Benjamin knows
40 how to get out of work—he could give seminars on this. He gets the perfect look of abject[2] pain over his face, says he's not feeling too well, he's sorry, he doesn't want to be a *burden*. He talks about the pain moving across his back, down his leg, and into his ankle. Then he gets dizzy and has to sit down; lying down comes moments later after his face gets a little pale (I don't know how he does this) and his hand touches his forehead which, I swear, has small drops of sweat on it. Then he'll try to get up and help, but by this time, you feel like such a snake that a sick person is going to get sicker because of your insensitive demands that you say, no, you rest, I'll do it.  **B**

This is what he's done to me today, and I'm not in the mood for the game.
50 He tells me, groaning, he'll *try* to make it to Mrs. Leonardo's today to help her pack up her attic, but he's not sure he can even sit. He's lying on the couch in misery saying if he can sit, he will try to stand, and if he attempts standing, he will attempt actual walking—Mrs. Leonardo's house being four houses down the street. I throw my book bag at him. Suggest he *crawl* to Mrs. Leonardo's house and he says, "Thanks, Katie. Just thanks." To which I reply, "Look, Benny Boy, I'm getting sick of carrying your weight around here. If you think I'm going to do your job and mine until I die, think again." Benjamin groans deep, turns off the light, closes his eyes and says his headache is cosmic and could I please go get him some aspirin. **C**

60    I don't get the aspirin. It's a big bad world out there and he needs to find it out now, at fourteen. This is what big sisters are for.

So I'm basically crabby and bitter all day; taking it out on random people. After school I have mounds of homework. You wonder what teachers are thinking—I have three hundred pages of reading in three textbooks plus a paper due on Friday. Have you ever noticed that it takes a textbook dozens of pages to say what normal people can cover fast?

Example:

What was the full impact of World War II?

---

1. **detoxification** (dē-tŏk′sə-fĭ-kā′shən): the process of removing toxic substances.

2. **abject** (ăb′jĕkt): of the most miserable kind; wretched.

**SCIENCE
CONNECTION**

Dust mites are microscopic organisms found in house dust the world over. Some people are allergic to the feces and skin shed by the mites.

**B CONFLICT**
How does the narrator feel about her brother's behavior? Tell how she handles it.

**C SEQUENCE**
Reread lines 49–51. What words or phrases show that the specific events of this story are starting now? Record the event on your chart.

Clear-cut teenage answer: We won.

70  So I'm close to dying young from excessive homework, and I have to help Mrs. Leonardo clean out her attic. She is paying big bucks for this, and, believe me, my family needs the money.

Mrs. Leonardo wants people there on time and working like ants. Ants carry their weight on their backs and are thrilled as anything to be abused. But that is the insect world; I am not one of them. I'm not in the mood to sit with her in her **dingy** attic and lug tons of garbage down the stairs and listen to her stories of how her family deserted her. I know that sounds mean, but Mrs. Leonardo is a mean person. It's easy to see why she's alone. The big joke is that when her husband died, he had a big smile on his face in the casket that he'd

80  never had in real life. The funeral director said they tried to wipe that grin off his face, but they couldn't do it.

So I'm on my knees in the dust, putting things in bags, while Mrs. Leonardo tells me about her selfish brother Horace who deserted her, and her uncaring, money-grubbing cousin Cynthia who backed out of the driveway eight years ago and never came back. She tells me how she helped them and loaned them money which they never paid back. She's going on and on about how the world is a dark, dark place. I clear my throat: "Boy, Mrs. Leonardo, you've got a lot of stuff up here. Are you sure you want to keep it all?" **D**

**T**his is the wrong thing to say. Mrs. Leonardo's gray eyes get spitting mad and

90  she says, *well,* she's seventy-six years old and she's had a *very* interesting life and she doesn't want to throw out anything of value. I look in a box with IRS tax forms dating back to 1955.

"Mrs. Leonardo, the IRS says you only need to keep tax records from the last three years. We could dump this whole box . . ." My mother told me this.

She lunges as much as a seventy-six-year-old person can and says she isn't giving her tax records to anyone so they can steal her secrets. Like tons of thieves are out there ready to pounce on this.

But at twenty-five dollars per hour, you learn to be patient. "Think of the money," my mother always says, "and the graciousness will come." So I'm

100  taping the box and writing IMPORTANT PAPERS 1955–1963. Maybe she could turn this attic into a museum and people could walk through and learn all the things you should never hold on to.

Benjamin would have cracked under this pressure. Mrs. Leonardo is kneeling by a huge trunk, saying how the younger generation (mine) doesn't understand about manners, **propriety,** or simple human decency. Her grandniece, Veronica, walks around with her belly button showing. She pulls old clothes out of the trunk and yanks this old lace tablecloth out and just looks at it. Finally, she says she got it when she was married and she's only used it once. She waited for a special occasion and only one came—her twentieth anniversary. No

110  other occasion was special enough, and then her husband died right before

**dingy** (dĭn′jē) *adj.* dirty or discolored

**D  SEQUENCE**
Reread lines 82–88. What words help signal that the narrator is returning to the main story she is telling?

**propriety** (prə-prī′ĭ-tē) *n.* the quality of being proper; appropriateness their twenty-fifth anniversary and the tablecloth has been in this trunk ever since—only used once, she keeps saying—beautiful Egyptian linen. She looks kind of sad, though stiff. I say, "You could start using it now, Mrs. Leonardo," which is the wrong thing to say. She shuts that trunk and asks me just who do I think she's going to invite to dinner since everyone she's ever done anything for has either deserted her or died. **E**

I don't know how to answer a question like this. My mother didn't cover it during Clean Sweep boot camp training where I learned how to scour a bathtub that a toddler spilled ink in, how to clean pet stains from any carpet known to man, how to wash windows and not leave streaks, how to open a refrigerator with year-old meat and not gag in front of the client. I pledged that the customer was always right and I, the lowly dust eliminator, was always, always wrong.

But I'm not sure what to do. If I agree with her, I'm not helping, and if I listen, I won't get the job done. The truth is, I don't like Mrs. Leonardo—so there's a big part of me that doesn't care—even though I know this is probably inhumane because she's a sad person, really. Kneeling there in the dust, surrounded by the boxes of her so-called interesting life, going on and on

**E CONFLICT**
What causes Mrs. Leonardo to be upset with Katie?

**ANALYZE VISUALS**
What do the **details** in the picture tell you about the person or people who live here?

about people who are gone. I'm thinking about the next stage of the job—the
130 actual cleaning of the attic which is going to take two people, and I know
Benjamin will be hurled into monumental physical **aberrations** up here.

    I'm tired, too, and my paper is late on King Lear who, in my opinion,
thought too much and couldn't deliver. I'm thinking about my personal life—
yes, dust eliminators have them. We have feelings; we have needs, dreams.
I'm feeling that I work too much and I wish my mom had another business
because what I do all day at school is exhausting enough without having to do
heavy lifting after school and on the weekends. I think about when my dad
died four years ago, and because of disorganization—that is, getting behind
on paying his life insurance premiums—his insurance policy was cancelled
140 and we got no insurance money when he died. He never meant to hurt us,
but it was so scary not knowing if we could keep the house mixed with all the
pain of losing him. We never got a regular time of mourning because we were
fighting to stay afloat. Mom was trying to sort through Dad's huge piles of
papers. We loved him so much, but he could never get rid of what Mom called
his "clutter demons." **F**

    It took several months, but we got his papers sorted. We learned firsthand
how you get organized, clean up, and obliterate dust. We became total aces at
it; learned how widespread the problem truly is. We knew then we needed to
share what we'd learned with others who were suffering, and felt that twenty-
150 five dollars an hour was reasonable. **G**

    I'm not sure if Mrs. Leonardo wants someone to help or someone to
complain to. Between you and me, I feel that listening to complaining *and*
busting dust should earn thirty-five dollars per hour. But, I'm remembering
being in our attic after my dad died; trying to go through his things. He had
a trunk that his grandfather had given him—inside were all his photos and
papers from school. I remember reading some of his essays from high school
and just crying. I couldn't throw those out. Mom said going through all that
was therapeutic[3] for me because it was like being with him, kind of. He was
forty-one years old when he died. Had a heart attack at work and was dead by
160 the time the ambulance came. **H**

    Just thinking about the day makes me shaky. Over the years I've dissected
every last thing I remember about the last morning I saw him. I should have
made him breakfast—I knew how much he liked it when I did. I should have
hugged him when he went out the door, but I was on the phone with Roger
Rugsby who was my biology partner who needed me to go over my lab notes
or he would fail. I missed the bus and Dad missed his train and he took me to
school. I was late, so I hurled myself out of the car and he said, "Go get 'em,
kiddo." That's the last thing he ever said to me. But I did better than Benjamin
who overslept and didn't even see Dad that morning. **I**

170     Mrs. Leonardo leans over a trunk like the one my father had. I want to say
something encouraging to her, like, "Gee, Mrs. Leonardo, I know how hard it

**aberration** (ăb'ə-rā'shən)
*n.* an abnormal alteration

**F** **CONFLICT**
What internal and
external conflicts does
Katie face as a result of
her dad's death?

**G** **SEQUENCE**
When did Katie's mother
form Clean Sweep?

**H** **CONFLICT**
Reread lines 153–158.
How does Katie react
while looking through her
father's things?

**I** **SEQUENCE**
Reread lines 161–163.
Note the phrase that
lets you know a **flashback**
is coming. When do the
events in this paragraph
take place?

---

3. **therapeutic** (thĕr'ə-pyōō'tĭk): having healing powers.

must be going through all these memories," or, "I hope sorting through all this is helping you the way it helped me." Memories are the only things we have left sometimes. You can hold a photo of a person you loved who's gone, but it isn't alive. Memories—the best ones—are filled with sights, smells, love, and happiness. I try to hold some of those in my heart for my dad each day.

She goes through the trunk, stony-faced. I can't tell what she's found, can't tell if she's going to torch the contents or hold them to her heart. I lug a big bag over and throw old newspapers inside. Mrs. Leonardo stops going through 180 the trunk. She's holding something in her hands, not moving. I look at her stiff face and for a moment in the weird light of the attic, she looks like she's going to cry. But that's impossible. Then I hear a sniff and she says softly, "My mother read this book to my sister and me every night before bed."

I look at the book—a well-worn brown leather cover. Doesn't look like much.

"I thought she had it," Mrs. Leonardo says sadly.

"Who had it?"

"My sister, Helen. I thought she had the book. She always wanted it."

In these situations it's best to say, "Oh."

"I thought . . . I thought I'd sent it to her after Mother died." She looks down.

190 I say, "It's hard to remember what you've done after someone important dies."

"But, she'd asked me for it. It was the one thing she'd wanted."

"Well . . ."

"I haven't talked to her since Mother died. I thought she . . ."

I'm not sure how to ask this. Is Helen still alive?

I dance around it. "What do you think you should do with the book, Mrs. Leonardo?" She doesn't answer.

I try again. "Why did Helen want it so bad?"

She hands me the book. "She said these stories were her best memories of childhood." I look through it. "The Naughty Little Frog," "The Little 200 Lost Tulip," "Spanky, the Black Sheep." It's amazing what we put up with as children. But then I remember my favorite bedtime story—"Rupert, the Church Mouse"—about this little mouse who lives in a church and polishes all the stained glass windows every night before he goes to sleep so the light can come forth every morning.

"I know she lives in Vermont," Mrs. Leonardo offers. "I heard from a cousin a while ago . . ." Her voice trails off. **J**

"I think you should call her, Mrs. Leonardo."

She shakes her old head. No—she couldn't possibly.

"I think you should call her and tell her you've got the book."

210 She glares at me. "I believe we're done for today." She grabs the book from my hands, puts it back in the trunk.

"Sorry, ma'am. I didn't mean . . ."

She heads down the attic stairs.

**J** **PREDICT**
Now that she's found the book, what do you think Mrs. Leonardo might do in regard to her sister?

I tell Benjamin that I don't want to hear about his problems, that his back looks strong to me, the shooting pain in his leg will go away eventually, and his headache is just a reflection of his deep, inner **turmoil.** I say this as we're walking to Mrs. Leonardo's house.

"I think my whole left side is going numb," he whispers pitifully as we walk up her steps.

220 *"Deal with it."*

Mrs. Leonardo is waiting for us. We're late. I don't mention that having to drag a hypochondriac[4] four doors down the street takes time. Great food smells swirl from her kitchen. **Ⓚ**

Mrs. Leonardo looks Benjamin up and down, not impressed. "You've not been here before," she says. Benjamin half smiles and rubs his tennis elbow,[5] which makes me nuts because he doesn't play tennis.

I introduce them. Tell her Benjamin is here to help with dust elimination and heavy lifting, at which point Benjamin leans painfully against the wall and closes his eyes.

230 "He's a very dedicated worker once he gets started, Mrs. Leonardo."

I jam my elbow into his side.

Okay, so we're cleaning this cavernous[6] attic like there's no tomorrow. We've got all the trunks and boxes wiped down and pushed to the far side. We're running the turbo-charged Clean Sweep Frankenstein portable vacuum that is so powerful it can suck up pets and small children if they get too close. Benjamin is wearing a dust mask over his nose and mouth—he wrote *The Terminator* over it. This boy is appropriately miserable, pulling down spiders' webs, sucking up dust mites. I can almost hear their little screams of terror. Almost, but not quite. My mother claims she can hear dust mites shrieking for mercy and uses this in her 240 presentation if she thinks potential clients can handle it.

"Get the lace tablecloth from the trunk!" Mrs. Leonardo shouts from downstairs.

What's she want with that?

"And bring the book, too," she hollers impatiently.

I don't mention that we've shoved everything in the corner like she said to, that I'll have to move it all to get to the trunk, and, by the way, I'm going as fast as I can. I get the book and the lace tablecloth that's been folded in very old plastic. I look at the book—reddish brown leather—*Aunt Goody's Good Night Stories,* it's called. Benjamin comes over looking like some kind of cosmic 250 alien with his mask, takes the book, starts laughing.

"The Naughty Little Frog," he says reading. "Once upon a time there was a naughty little frog named Edmond. Edmond was so naughty that

**Ⓚ CONFLICT**
In what ways is Katie responsible for her brother?

---

4. **hypochondriac** (hī'pə-kŏn'drē-ăk'): a person who continually thinks he or she is ill or about to become ill.

5. **tennis elbow:** pain around the elbow, often caused from playing tennis or similar activities.

6. **cavernous** (kăv'ər-nəs): filled with caverns; like a cave.

he never, ever cleaned his lily pad. It got so dirty that his mother had to make him stay on that lily pad several times each day to—"

"You're going to have to wait for the end." I yank the book from his hands and head down the creaky attic stairs with the tablecloth. Mrs. Leonardo is in the kitchen wearing a frilly apron, stirring a pot of something that smells beyond great.

260 She turns to look at me, puts her wooden spoon down.

"Help me put it on the table," she orders.

I'm smiling a little now because I know this tablecloth's history. I'm wondering who's coming to dinner.

"Looks like you're having a party," I offer as we get the tablecloth squared perfectly on the table.

Mrs. Leonardo says nothing, sets the table for two with what looks like the good silverware, the good napkins. Then she puts the storybook in front of one of the place settings.

"My sister, you see . . ." She pauses emotionally. "Well, she's . . . 270 coming to dinner."

"You mean the one you haven't seen for a long time?"

"I only have *one* sister."

I'm just grinning now and I tell her I hope they have the best dinner in the world.

"Well, I do too." She looks nervously out the window and says whatever work we haven't finished can be done tomorrow. "You were right about . . . calling her, Katie."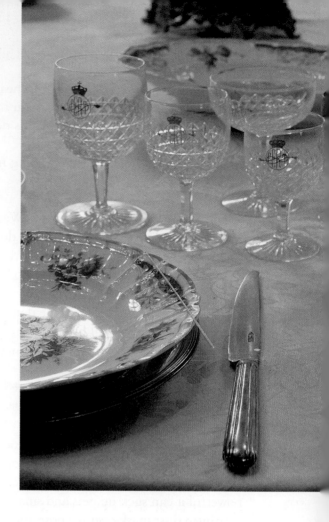

I smile brightly, wondering if she's going to offer me some of her great-smelling food to show her gratitude. She doesn't. I head up the attic stairs 280 and drag Benjamin to safety. He's sneezing like he's going to die. I take off his Terminator dust mask and lean him against a wall. Half of me wants to give Mrs. Leonardo a little hug of encouragement, but the other half warns, *Don't touch clients because they can turn on you.*

"Whatever you're cooking, Mrs. Leonardo, it sure smells good," I shout. "Your sister's going to love it." I'm not sure she hears all of that. Benjamin is into his fifth sneezing attack.

She nods from the kitchen; I push Benjamin out on the street.

"I could have died up there," he shouts, blowing his nose.

"But you didn't."

290 And I remember the book my dad would read to us when we were little about the baby animals and their parents and how each mother and father animal kissed their babies good night. That book was chewed to death, ripped, stained, and missing the last two pages, but I wouldn't give it up for anything.

We walk back home almost silently, except for Benjamin's sniffs, sneezes, and groans. People just don't understand what important things can be hiding in the dust.

Mom says that all the time in her presentation. ∾

**L SEQUENCE**
What steps has Mrs. Leonardo taken to prepare for her sister's visit? Add these to your chart.

# Comprehension

**INDIANA STANDARDS**

READING STANDARD
**8.3.2** Evaluate the structural elements of the plot....

1. **Recall** What job does the Clean Sweep company do?

2. **Clarify** Why does Katie resent her brother?

3. **Summarize** For Katie, what makes working for Mrs. Leonardo so difficult?

# Literary Analysis

4. **Identify Sequence** Review the chart you created as you read. Which event or events in the sequence occur as **flashbacks?** What information do you learn about Katie from the flashbacks?

5. **Examine Conflict** Note the internal and external conflicts Katie faces after her dad's death. By the end of the story, which of these conflicts are resolved? Explain.

6. **Identify Subplot** A subplot is a minor plot that involves an additional **conflict** in the story. Use the following graphic to record details of the subplot involving Mrs. Leonardo and her sister. How does this subplot help shed light on Katie's story?

| Characters Involved: |
| Mrs. Leonardo and her sister |
| Conflict: |
| Resolution: |

7. **Analyze Character Motivations** Why do you think Mrs. Leonardo decided to reconnect with her sister?

8. **Make Judgments** Reread lines 221–229 and footnote 4. Would you say that Katie's brother is a hypochondriac? Use examples from the text to support your answer.

# Extension and Challenge

9. **Big Question Activity** Look again at the Web It activity on page 62. Imagine you are Katie, and her **treasure** is the book she mentions on page 72, lines 290–293. Complete a new web and include the good memories Katie might connect to the book.

10.  **SCIENCE CONNECTION** Katie's family earns a living fighting dust mites. Look back at the information about dust mites on page 66. Research more about them to find out whether they are seriously harmful to people and whether it is possible to get rid of all dust mites in a home. Is Katie's mother being honest in her presentation? Present your findings to the class.

> **RESEARCH LINKS**
> For more on dust mites, visit the **Research Center** at **ClassZone.com.**

# Vocabulary in Context

## VOCABULARY PRACTICE

Decide whether the words in each pair are synonyms (words that mean the same) or antonyms (words that mean the opposite).

1. propriety/rudeness
2. vileness/niceness
3. dingy/shabby
4. minuscule/huge
5. aberration/sameness
6. turmoil/chaos

**INDIANA STANDARDS**

READING STANDARD
**8.1.3** Verify the meaning of a word in its context . . . .

## VOCABULARY IN WRITING

What was the state of Mrs. Leonardo's attic when Katie first saw it? Use at least two vocabulary words to write a one-paragraph description. You could start this way.

> **EXAMPLE SENTENCE**
>
> *The attic was **dingy** and dusty, and it was filled with old clothes and papers.*

## VOCABULARY STRATEGY: SUFFIXES THAT FORM NOUNS

A suffix is a word part that appears at the end of a root or base word to form a new word. Some suffixes, such as those in *vileness* and *aberration*, can be added to words to form nouns. The web shown includes other suffixes that have a similar meaning.

If a word seems unfamiliar, see if you can break it into a familiar root and suffix. For example, the word *embellishment* can be broken into *embellish* and *–ment,* which might help you understand that an embellishment is something that is decorated.

happi**ness**   wreck**age**

**state or process; quality or state of**

argu**ment**   toler**ance**   rebell**ion**

*PRACTICE* Identify the base word and suffix in each boldfaced word. Then define the nouns that have been made by adding the suffixes.

1. Winning the state championship was quite an **achievement.**
2. To make the **connection,** your flight will have to arrive on time.
3. His **performance** in the concert was superb.
4. One could see the **sadness** in their faces.
5. We have a **shortage** of paper towels in the kitchen.

**VOCABULARY PRACTICE**
For more practice, go to the **Vocabulary Center** at **ClassZone.com.**

# Reading-Writing Connection

Increase your understanding of "Clean Sweep" by responding to these prompts. Then complete the **Grammar and Writing** exercise.

| WRITING PROMPTS | SELF-CHECK |
|---|---|

**A. Short Response: Write a Dialogue**
Reread lines 151–160. Write a **half-page of dialogue** between Katie and her mother that might have occurred while they sorted through her dad's things after his death.

*An effective dialogue will . . .*
- include details about what they found
- use words and phrases that show how they feel

**B. Extended Response: Compare and Contrast**
Write **two or three paragraphs** comparing and contrasting Mrs. Leonardo's loss and Katie's loss. How did the losses occur? How did each person react? Explain how forgotten **treasures** helped both characters come to terms with their losses.

*A detailed response will . . .*
- describe each character's loss
- show the connection between the treasure and the characters' feelings

## GRAMMAR AND WRITING

**PUNCTUATE POSSESSIVES CORRECTLY** When you're writing about people's possessions, be sure to put the apostrophe in the correct place. To help keep your writing clear, follow these guidelines for punctuating possessive nouns:

**INDIANA STANDARDS**

**WRITING STANDARD**
**8.6.5** Use correct punctuation.

- **Singular nouns:** Add an apostrophe and *s*, even if the word ends in *s* (*dog's leash, princess's crown*)
- **Plural nouns ending in *s*:** Add an apostrophe (*hosts' party, employees' benefits*)
- **Plural nouns not ending in *s*:** Add an apostrophe and *s* (*children's toys, mice's footprints*)

> *Original:* When I lifted the trunks' lid, it wobbled and creaked.
>
> *Revised:* When I lifted the trunk's lid, it wobbled and creaked.

**PRACTICE** In the following sentences, decide which possessives are used correctly. If incorrect, revise them.

1. We have to categorize the family's papers.
2. I had no idea he could write until I read through Dads' essays.
3. Some of the essays' titles reminded me of how he talked when he helped me with homework.
4. The death of Katies father was out of her control.
5. Childrens' books can hold powerful memories.

*For more help with possessives, see page R46 in the* **Grammar Handbook**.

## The Tell-Tale Heart
Short Story by Edgar Allan Poe

# *What makes you* SUSPICIOUS?

**INDIANA STANDARDS**

**READING STANDARDS**

**8.2.9** Make reasonable statements and draw conclusions about a text, supporting them with accurate examples.

**8.3.2** Evaluate the structural elements of the plot, such as subplots, parallel episodes, and climax; the plot's development; and the way in which conflicts are (or are not) addressed and resolved.

***KEY IDEA*** Has something or someone ever seemed dangerous or untrustworthy to you? The feeling you had was **suspicion.** While suspicion might come from a misunderstanding, it can also be a warning that something is very wrong. In this story, you'll meet a man whose own suspicions are his downfall.

***DISCUSS*** With a small group, discuss suspicious characters you've read about or seen on television shows. In what ways did these characters look or act differently from other characters? Continue your discussion by creating a list of warning signs that should make a person suspicious.

Suspicious Actions
1. Avoiding eye contact
2.

## ● LITERARY ANALYSIS: SUSPENSE

Writers often "hook" readers by creating a sense of excitement, tension, dread, or fear about what will happen next. This feeling is called **suspense.** Techniques used by Edgar Allan Poe to develop suspense include

- describing a character's anxiety or fear
- relating vivid descriptions of dramatic sights and sounds
- repeating words, phrases, or characters' actions

As you read "The Tell-Tale Heart," notice what causes you to feel suspense.

## ● READING SKILL: EVALUATE NARRATOR

Have you ever suspected someone was not telling you the truth? Just as you can't trust every person you meet, you can't believe all **narrators,** or characters who tell a story. To evaluate a narrator's **reliability,** or trustworthiness, pay attention to his or her actions, attitudes, and statements. Do any raise your suspicions? As you read "The Tell-Tale Heart," record any clues that reveal whether the narrator is reliable or not.

| Narrator's Reliability | |
|---|---|
| Makes Me Suspicious: | Makes Me Trust Him: |
| • | • |
| • | • |
| • | • |

## ▲ VOCABULARY IN CONTEXT

Poe uses the following words to reveal how the main character is acting, feeling, and thinking. For each word, choose the numbered word or phrase closest in meaning.

| WORD LIST | acute | crevice | stealthily | vehemently |
|---|---|---|---|---|
| | audacity | derision | stifled | vex |
| | conceive | hypocritical | | |

1. annoy
2. cautiously
3. intense
4. crack
5. deceptive
6. smothered
7. ridicule
8. think of
9. strongly
10. shameless daring

# The Tell-Tale Heart

*Edgar Allan Poe*

True!—nervous—very, very dreadfully nervous I had been and am! but why *will* you say that I am mad? The disease had sharpened my senses—not destroyed—not dulled them. Above all was the sense of hearing **acute.** I heard all things in the heaven and in the earth. I heard many things in hell. How, then, am I mad? Hearken! and observe how healthily—how calmly I can tell you the whole story.

It is impossible to say how first the idea entered my brain; but once **conceived,** it haunted me day and night. Object there was none. Passion there was none. I loved the old man. He had never wronged me. He had never given 10 me insult. For his gold I had no desire. I think it was his eye! yes, it was this! He had the eye of a vulture—a pale blue eye, with a film over it. Whenever it fell upon me, my blood ran cold; and so by degrees—very gradually—I made up my mind to take the life of the old man, and thus rid myself of the eye forever.

Now this is the point. You fancy me mad. Madmen know nothing. But you should have seen *me.* You should have seen how wisely I proceeded—with what caution—with what foresight—with what dissimulation[1] I went to work! **A**

I was never kinder to the old man than during the whole week before I killed him. And every night, about midnight, I turned the latch of his door and opened it—oh, so gently! And then, when I had made an opening sufficient for my head, 20 I put in a dark lantern, all closed, closed, so that no light shone out, and then I thrust in my head. Oh, you would have laughed to see how cunningly I thrust it in! I moved it slowly—very, very slowly, so that I might not disturb the old

---

1. **dissimulation** (dĭ-sĭm′yə-lā′shən): a hiding of one's true feelings.

Illustrations by Howard Simpson.

man's sleep. It took me an hour to place my whole head within the opening so far that I could see him as he lay upon his bed. Ha!—would a madman have been so wise as this? And then, when my head was well in the room, I undid the lantern cautiously—oh, so cautiously—cautiously (for the hinges creaked)—I undid it just so much that a single thin ray fell upon the vulture eye. And this I did for seven long nights—every night just at midnight—but I found the eye always closed; and so it was impossible to do the work; for it was not the old man who **vexed** me, but his Evil Eye. And every morning, when the day broke, I went boldly into the chamber, and spoke courageously to him, calling him by name in a hearty tone, and inquiring how he had passed the night. So you see he would have been a very profound old man, indeed, to suspect that every night, just at twelve, I looked in upon him while he slept. **B**

Upon the eighth night I was more than usually cautious in opening the door. A watch's minute hand moves more quickly than did mine. Never before that night had I *felt* the extent of my own powers—of my sagacity.[2] I could scarcely contain my feelings of triumph. To think that there I was, opening the door, little by little, and he not even to dream of my secret deeds or thoughts. I fairly chuckled at the idea; and perhaps he heard me; for he moved on the bed suddenly, as if startled. Now you may think that I drew back—but no. His room was as black as pitch with the thick darkness (for the shutters were close fastened, through fear of robbers), and so I knew that he could not see the opening of the door, and I kept pushing it on steadily, steadily.

I had my head in, and was about to open the lantern, when my thumb slipped upon the tin fastening, and the old man sprang up in the bed, crying out—"Who's there?"

I kept quite still and said nothing. For a whole hour I did not move a muscle, and in the meantime I did not hear him lie down. He was still sitting up in the bed listening,—just as I have done, night after night, hearkening to the death watches[3] in the wall. **C**

Presently I heard a slight groan, and I knew it was the groan of mortal terror. It was not a groan of pain or grief—oh, no!—it was the low, **stifled** sound that arises from the bottom of the soul when overcharged with awe. I knew the sound well. Many a night, just at midnight, when all the world slept, it has welled up from my own bosom, deepening, with its dreadful echo, the terrors that distracted me. I say I knew it well. I knew what the old man felt, and pitied him, although I chuckled at heart. I knew that he had been lying awake ever since the first slight noise, when he had turned in the bed. His fears had been ever since growing upon him. He had been trying to fancy them causeless, but could not. He had been saying to himself—"It is nothing but the wind in the chimney—it is only a mouse crossing the floor," or "it is merely a cricket which has made a single chirp." Yes, he has been trying to comfort himself with these suppositions; but he had found all in vain. *All in vain;* because Death,

vex (vĕks) v. to disturb; to annoy

**B SUSPENSE**
Note the actions the narrator repeats. Why does this repetition create a sense of dread?

**C SUSPENSE**
In what way does the characters' inaction create tension?

stifled (stī'fəld) adj. smothered **stifle** v.

---

2. **sagacity** (sə-găs'ĭ-tē): sound judgment.

3. **death watches**: deathwatch beetles—insects that make a tapping sound with their heads.

in approaching him, had stalked with his black shadow before him, and enveloped the victim. And it was the mournful influence of the unperceived shadow that caused him to feel—although he neither saw nor heard—to *feel* the presence of my head within the room.

When I had waited a long time, very patiently, without hearing him lie down, I resolved to open a little—a very, very little **crevice** in the lantern. So I opened it—you cannot imagine how **stealthily**, stealthily—until, at length, a single dim ray, like the thread of the spider, shot from out the crevice and fell full upon the vulture eye.

It was open—wide, wide open—and I grew furious as I gazed upon it. I saw it with perfect distinctness—all a dull blue, with a hideous veil over it that chilled the very marrow in my bones; but I could see nothing else of the old man's face or person: for I had directed the ray as if by instinct, precisely upon the damned spot.

And now have I not told you that what you mistake for madness is but over-acuteness of the senses?—now, I say, there came to my ears a low, dull, quick sound, such as a watch makes when enveloped in cotton. I knew *that* sound well too. It was the beating of the old man's heart. It increased my fury, as the beating of a drum stimulates the soldier into courage. **D**

But even yet I refrained and kept still. I scarcely breathed. I held the lantern motionless. I tried how steadily I could maintain the ray upon the eye. Meantime the hellish tattoo[4] of the heart increased. It grew quicker and quicker, and louder and louder every instant. The old man's terror *must* have been extreme! It grew louder, I say, louder every moment!—do you mark me well? I have told you that I am nervous: so I am. And now at the dead hour of the night, amid the dreadful silence of that old house, so strange a noise as this excited me to uncontrollable terror. Yet, for some minutes longer I refrained and stood still. But the beating grew louder, louder! I thought the heart must burst. And now a new anxiety seized me—the sound would be heard by a neighbor! The old man's hour had come! With a loud yell, I threw open the lantern and leaped into the room. He shrieked once—once only. In an instant I dragged him to the floor, and pulled the heavy bed over him. I then smiled gaily, to find the deed so far done. But, for many minutes, the heart beat on with a muffled sound. This, however, did not vex me; it would not be heard through the wall. At length it ceased. The old man was dead. I removed the bed and examined the corpse. Yes, he was stone, stone dead. I placed my hand upon the heart and held it there many minutes. There was no pulsation. He was stone dead. His eye would trouble me no more. **E**

If still you think me mad, you will think so no longer when I describe the wise precautions I took for the concealment of the body. The night waned,[5] and I worked hastily, but in silence. First of all I dismembered the corpse. I cut off the head and the arms and the legs.

---

4. **hellish tattoo:** awful drumming.

5. **waned:** approached its end.

**crevice** (krĕv′ĭs) *n.* crack

**stealthily** (stĕl′thə-lē) *adv.* cautiously; secretly

**D EVALUATE NARRATOR**
What does the narrator claim to be hearing? Decide whether you think he is correct.

**E SUSPENSE**
Reread lines 84–102. What is the scariest or most exciting part of this paragraph? Tell what details contribute to this feeling.

I then took up three planks from the flooring of the chamber, and deposited all between the scantlings.[6] I then replaced the boards so cleverly, so cunningly, that no human eye—not even *his*—could have detected anything wrong. There was nothing to wash out—no stain of any kind—no blood-spot whatever. I had been too wary for that. A tub had caught all—ha! ha!

When I made an end of these labors, it was four o'clock—still dark as midnight. As the bell sounded the hour, there came a knocking at the street door. I went down to open it with a light heart,—for what had I *now* to fear?

---

6. **scantlings:** small wooden beams supporting the floor.

There entered three men, who introduced themselves, with perfect suavity,[7] as officers of the police. A shriek had been heard by a neighbor during the night: suspicion of foul play had been aroused; information had been lodged at the police office, and they (the officers) had been deputed[8] to search the premises.

I smiled,—for *what* had I to fear? I bade the gentlemen welcome. The shriek, I said, was my own in a dream. The old man, I mentioned, was absent in the country. I took my visitors all over the house. I bade them search— search *well*. I led them, at length, to *his* chamber. I showed them his treasures, secure, undisturbed. In the enthusiasm of my confidence, I brought chairs into the room, and desired them *here* to rest from their fatigues, while I myself, in the wild **audacity** of my perfect triumph, placed my own seat upon the very spot beneath which reposed[9] the corpse of the victim.

The officers were satisfied. My *manner* had convinced them. I was singularly at ease. They sat, and while I answered cheerily, they chatted of familiar things. But, ere long, I felt myself getting pale and wished them gone. My head ached, and I fancied a ringing in my ears: but still they sat and still chatted. The ringing became more distinct:—it continued and became more distinct: I talked more freely to get rid of the feeling: but it continued and gained definitiveness—until at length, I found that the noise was *not* within my ears.

No doubt I now grew *very* pale;—but I talked more fluently, and with a heightened voice. Yet the sound increased—and what could I do? It was *a low, dull, quick sound—much such a sound as a watch makes when enveloped in cotton.* I gasped for breath—and yet the officers heard it not. I talked more quickly—more **vehemently;** but the noise steadily increased. I arose and argued about trifles, in a high key and with violent gesticulations,[10] but the noise steadily increased. Why *would* they not be gone? I paced the floor to and fro with heavy strides, as if excited to fury by the observation of the men—but the noise steadily increased. What *could* I do? I foamed—I raved— I swore. I swung the chair upon which I had been sitting, and grated it upon the boards, but the noise arose over all and continually increased. It grew louder—louder—*louder!* And still the men chatted pleasantly, and smiled. Was it possible they heard not?—no, no! They heard!—they suspected!—they *knew!*—they were making a *mockery* of my horror!—this I thought, and this I think. But anything was better than this agony! Anything was more tolerable than this **derision!** I could bear those **hypocritical** smiles no longer! I felt that I must scream or die!—and now—again!—hark! louder! louder! *louder!*— 🅕

"Villains!" I shrieked, "dissemble[11] no more! I admit the deed!—tear up the planks!—here, here!—it is the beating of his hideous heart!" ❧

---

7. **suavity** (swä′vĭ-tē): graceful politeness.

8. **deputed:** appointed as a representative.

9. **reposed:** rested.

10. **gesticulations** (jĕ-stĭk′yə-lā′shəns): energetic gestures of the hands or arms.

11. **dissemble:** pretend.

**audacity** (ô-dăs′ĭ-tē) *n.* shameless daring or boldness

**vehemently** (vē′ə-mənt-lē) *adv.* with intense emotion

**derision** (dĭ-rĭzh′ən) *n.* ridicule

**hypocritical** (hĭp′ə-krĭt′ĭ-kəl) *adj.* false or deceptive

🅕 **SUSPENSE**
Think about the emotions that the narrator is feeling. How does Poe help the reader feel the same way?

# Comprehension

1. **Recall**  Why does the narrator want to kill the old man?

2. **Clarify**  Why does the narrator believe he will not be caught after murdering the old man?

3. **Summarize**  What actions does the narrator take to prepare for the crime and cover up?

**INDIANA STANDARDS**

READING STANDARD
**8.3.2** Evaluate the structural elements of the plot....

# Literary Analysis

4. **Make Inferences**  Reread lines 7–13. From this passage, what do you think was the relationship between the narrator and the old man?

5. **Analyze Suspense**  Which of Poe's techniques for creating suspense is most effective for you? To find out, review the following story sections. List the techniques used in each section, and then rank the sections from 1–4, with 1 being the most suspenseful.

| Rank | | | | |
|---|---|---|---|---|
| Lines | 1–78 | 79–111 | 112–133 | 134–152 |
| Techniques | 1. | 1. | 1. | 1. |
| | 2. | 2. | 2. | 2. |

6. **Evaluate Narrator**  How reliable is the narrator of the story? Should you believe what he tells you about himself? Support your answer with details from the chart you created as you read.

7. **Draw Conclusions**  Do you think the police knew the narrator was guilty at any point before he confessed? If so, when do you think the police became **suspicious?** Give reasons for your answer.

# Extension and Challenge

8. **Readers' Circle**  With a group, brainstorm a list of horror stories and movies that most of you are familiar with. Choose at least two of these titles and discuss the techniques the authors or directors used to create suspense. Which of the techniques are similar to the ones Poe uses?

9. **Inquiry and Research**  Do research on lie detection to find out what are the most reliable ways of finding out if someone is telling the truth. Present your findings to the class. Does what you learn change your opinion about whether the narrator is reliable?

**RESEARCH LINKS**
For more on lie detection, visit the **Research Center** at ClassZone.com.

# Vocabulary in Context

## VOCABULARY PRACTICE

Choose *true* or *false* for each statement.

1. It is difficult to hide a **stifled** yawn.
2. If you have the **audacity** to do something, you are bold and daring.
3. **Derision** is something you feel toward someone you respect.
4. A lion would approach its prey **stealthily.**
5. You could not hear much if you had an **acute** sense of hearing.
6. If someone **conceived** of a plan, he or she heard it from someone else.
7. A person could trip over a **crevice** in the sidewalk.
8. When a person is **hypocritical,** he is honest and true.
9. To **vex** is to delight in something.
10. If you react **vehemently** to something, you don't care much about it.

acute
audacity
conceived
crevice
derision
hypocritical
stealthily
stifled
vehemently
vex

## VOCABULARY IN WRITING

Using three or more vocabulary words, write a paragraph about how the narrator felt before the murder. Here is a sample beginning.

> **EXAMPLE SENTENCE**
>
> The man **conceived** an idea that haunted him.

## VOCABULARY STRATEGY: USING REFERENCE AIDS

Choosing the perfect word can make a difference between good and great writing. One reason Poe's writing is still so popular is because of his masterful use of language. When you want to find the most accurate words to express yourself, the following reference aids can help you.

- A **thesaurus** is a reference book of **synonyms,** words with similar meanings. Most word processing software provides an electronic thesaurus tool.

  **vex** *verb* aggravate, annoy, bother, bug, disturb, provoke

- A **dictionary** lists synonyms after the definitions of some words.

  **vex** (věks) *v.* 1. To annoy. 2. To cause perplexity in. 3. To bring distress or suffering to. **syn** BOTHER, PUZZLE, PLAGUE, AFFLICT

**PRACTICE** Use a dictionary or thesaurus to find a synonym for each word. Use each synonym in a sentence that matches its distinct meaning.

1. commend    2. dupe    3. impish    4. menace

**VOCABULARY PRACTICE**
For more practice, go to the **Vocabulary Center** at **ClassZone.com.**

## The Hitchhiker
Radio Play by Lucille Fletcher

# *Is seeing* BELIEVING?

**KEY IDEA** Occasionally, something happens so quickly or unexpectedly, you can't be sure what you've seen. Was that a rabbit racing through the field, or was it just wind in the grass? Did you see a man hiding in the alley, or did you see only a shadow? To be convinced that something is real, you need **proof,** or solid evidence. In *The Hitchhiker*, a man is desperate for proof that what he's seeing can be explained.

**DISCUSS** Think of something you've seen that you can't explain. Maybe it was oddly shaped footprints in an empty lot, or a bright shape flying through the sky. Share your experience with a small group, and together brainstorm possible explanations. Then tell what proof you'd need to determine which explanation is the right one.

## ● LITERARY ANALYSIS: FORESHADOWING

While reading a story or watching a movie, have you ever gotten a hint about what might happen later on? A device that prepares readers for an event or action occurring later in the plot is called **foreshadowing.** For example, if a character says, "Whatever you do, don't open that door," you might suspect that the door will eventually be opened to create a dramatic effect. Anticipating that event can make you more excited to find out what happens next.

As you read *The Hitchhiker*, make a chart to note events or dialogue that might foreshadow what happens later. You'll complete the chart at the end of the selection.

| Foreshadowing | Events That Were Foreshadowed |
|---|---|
|  |  |

## ■ READING STRATEGY: READING A RADIO PLAY

A **radio play** is a play written for radio broadcast, which means that it was originally meant to be heard, not seen. When you're reading a radio play, you'll understand it best if you try to imagine what it would sound like being performed. As you read, look for the following elements, written in italics. Use the information these elements provide to "hear" the radio play in your mind.

- **Stage directions,** or instructions, for the actor will help you know how a line is spoken.
- **Sound effects** are often used to suggest what is happening in the play. They help a listener "see" the action.
- The term *music in* will indicate when and sometimes what kind of music is used to mark a change of scene or show the passing of time.

## ▲ VOCABULARY IN CONTEXT

The words in Column A help Lucille Fletcher tell about one man's encounter with a mysterious hitchhiker. Match each word with the word or phrase in Column B that is closest in meaning.

| Column A | Column B |
|---|---|
| 1. lark | a. guarantee |
| 2. junction | b. carefree adventure |
| 3. sinister | c. evil |
| 4. assurance | d. sameness |
| 5. monotony | e. place of joining |

## Author On[line]

**Suspenseful Stories**
As a young adult, Lucille Fletcher wanted to become a novelist. After she took her first job as a script typist and began reading scripts by other writers, she decided she wanted to write plays as well. She was successful at both. Fletcher penned more than

**Lucille Fletcher**
**1912–2000**

20 radio plays, including the well-known *Sorry, Wrong Number* and *The Hitchhiker*. In addition, she wrote several novels. Her works were suspenseful, full of mystery, and often terrifying.

> **MORE ABOUT THE AUTHOR**
> For more on Lucille Fletcher, visit the **Literature Center** at **ClassZone.com.**

## *Background*

**Radio Plays** Though the television was invented in the 1920s, most American households did not have television sets until the late 1950s. Before then, families gathered around the radio to listen to their favorite radio plays. These plays took the form of dramas, mysteries, or comedies. Actors at the radio station read their lines into the microphone with dramatic flair. Background music helped set the mood.

**Hearing Is Believing** Sound effects were an important part of a radio play. They were often produced in the radio studio. Sheet metal, shaken up and down, replicated rolling thunder. A wooden match, broken close to the microphone, sounded like a baseball bat striking a ball. Coconut halves clapped against wood imitated the sound of horses' hooves.

# The Hitchhiker

## Lucille Fletcher

**CAST OF CHARACTERS**

| | |
|---|---|
| **Orson Welles** | **Girl** |
| **Ronald Adams** | **Operator** |
| **Adams's Mother** | **Long-Distance Operator** |
| **Voice of Hitchhiker** | **Albuquerque Operator** |
| **Mechanic** | **New York Operator** |
| **Henry,** a sleepy man | **Mrs. Whitney** |
| **Woman's Voice,** Henry's wife | |

**Welles.** Good evening, this is Orson Welles . . . (*music in*) Personally I've never met anybody who didn't like a good ghost story, but I know a lot of people who think there are a lot of people who don't like a good ghost story. For the benefit of these, at least, I go on record at the outset of this evening's entertainment with the sober **assurance** that although blood may be curdled on this program none will be spilt. There's no
10 shooting, knifing, throttling, axing or poisoning here. No clanking chains, no cobwebs, no bony and/or hairy hands appearing from secret panels or, better yet, bedroom curtains. If it's any part of that dear old *phosphorescent*[1] foolishness that people who don't like ghost stories don't like, then again I promise you we haven't got it. What we do have is a thriller. If it's half as good as we think it is you can call it a shocker, and we present it proudly and without apologies. After
20 all a story doesn't have to appeal to the heart— it can also appeal to the spine. Sometimes you want your heart to be warmed—sometimes you want your spine to tingle. The tingling, it's to be hoped, will be quite audible as you listen tonight to *The Hitchhiker*—That's the name of our story, *The Hitchhiker*—

---

1. **phosphorescent** (fŏs′fə-rĕs′ənt): glowing with a cold light.

*(sound: automobile wheels humming over concrete road)*

*(music: something weird and shuddery)*

30 **Adams.** I am in an auto camp on Route Sixty-six just west of Gallup, New Mexico. If I tell it perhaps it will help me. It will keep me from going mad. But I must tell this quickly. I am not mad now. I feel perfectly well, except that I am running a slight temperature. My name is Ronald Adams. I am thirty-six years of age, unmarried, tall, dark, with a black mustache. I drive a 1940 Ford V-8, license number 6V-7989. I was born in Brooklyn. All this I know. I know that I am at 40 this moment perfectly sane. That it is not I, who has gone mad—but something else—something utterly beyond my control. But I must speak quickly. At any moment the link with life may break. This may be the last thing I ever tell on earth . . . the last night I ever see the stars. . . .

*(music in)*

**Adams.** Six days ago I left Brooklyn, to drive to California . . .

**Mother.** Goodbye, son. Good luck to you, my 50 boy . . .

**Adams.** Goodbye, mother. Here—give me a kiss, and then I'll go . . .

**Mother.** I'll come out with you to the car.

**Adams.** No. It's raining. Stay here at the door. Hey—what is this? Tears? I thought you promised me you wouldn't cry.

**Mother.** I know dear. I'm sorry. But I—do hate to see you go.

**Adams.** I'll be back. I'll only be on the coast three 60 months.

**Mother.** Oh—it isn't that. It's just—the trip. Ronald—I wish you weren't driving.

**Adams.** Oh—mother. There you go again. People do it every day.

**Mother.** I know. But you'll be careful, won't you. Promise me you'll be extra careful. Don't fall asleep—or drive fast—or pick up any strangers on the road . . .

**Adams.** Of course not! You'd think I was still 70 seventeen to hear you talk—

**Mother.** And wire me as soon as you get to Hollywood, won't you, son?

**Adams.** Of course I will. Now don't you worry. There isn't anything going to happen. It's just eight days of perfectly simple driving on smooth, decent, civilized roads, with a hotdog or a hamburger stand every ten miles . . . *(fade)*

*(sound: auto hum)*

*(music in)*

80 **Adams.** I was in excellent spirits. The drive ahead of me, even the loneliness, seemed like a **lark.** But I reckoned without *him.*

*(Music changes to something weird and empty.)*

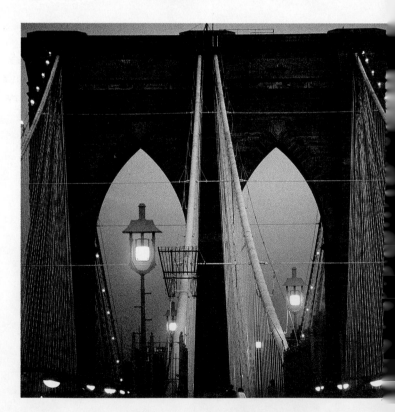

**Adams.** Crossing Brooklyn Bridge that morning in the rain, I saw a man leaning against the cables. He seemed to be waiting for a lift. There were spots of fresh rain on his shoulders. He was carrying a cheap overnight bag in one hand. He was thin, nondescript, with a cap pulled down 90 over his eyes. He stepped off the walk, and if I hadn't swerved, I'd have hit him.

(*sound: terrific skidding*)

(*music in*)

**Adams.** I would have forgotten him completely, except that just an hour later, while crossing the Pulaski Skyway over the Jersey flats, I saw him again. At least, he looked like the same person. He was standing now, with one thumb pointing west. I couldn't figure out how he'd got there, but 100 I thought probably one of those fast trucks had picked him up, beaten me to the Skyway, and let him off. I didn't stop for him. Then—late that night, I saw him again.

(*music changing*)

**Adams.** It was on the new Pennsylvania Turnpike between Harrisburg and Pittsburgh. It's 265 miles long, with a very high speed limit. I was just slowing down for one of the tunnels—when I saw him—standing under an arc light by the side of 110 the road. I could see him quite distinctly. The bag, the cap, even the spots of fresh rain spattered over his shoulders. He hailed me this time . . .

**Voice** (*very spooky and faint*). Hall-ooo . . . (*echo as through tunnel*) Hall-ooo . . . !

**Adams.** I stepped on the gas like a shot. That's lonely country through the Alleghenies,[2] and I had no intention of stopping. Besides, the coincidence, or whatever it was, gave me the willies.[3] I stopped at the next gas station.

120 (*sound: auto tires screeching to stop . . . horn honk*)

**Mechanic.** Yes, sir.

**Adams.** Fill her up.

**Mechanic.** Certainly, sir. Check your oil, sir?

**Adams.** No, thanks.

(*sound: gas being put into car . . . bell tinkle, et cetera*)

**Mechanic.** Nice night, isn't it?

**Adams.** Yes. It—hasn't been raining here recently, has it?

130 **Mechanic.** Not a drop of rain all week.

**Adams.** Hm. I suppose that hasn't done your business any harm.

**Mechanic.** Oh—people drive through here all kinds of weather. Mostly business, you know. There aren't many pleasure cars out on the turnpike this season of the year.

**Adams.** I suppose not. (*casually*) What about hitchhikers?

**Mechanic** (*half laughing*). Hitchhikers *here*?

140 **Adams.** What's the matter? Don't you ever see any?

**Mechanic.** Not much. If we did, it'd be a sight for sore eyes.

**Adams.** Why?

**Mechanic.** A guy'd be a fool who started out to hitch rides on this road. Look at it. It's 265 miles long, there's practically no speed limit, and it's a straightaway. Now what car is going to stop to pick up a guy under those conditions? Would you stop?

150 **Adams.** No. (*slowly, with puzzled emphasis*) Then you've never seen anybody?

**Mechanic.** Nope. Mebbe they get the lift before the turnpike starts—I mean, you know—just before the toll house—but then it'd be a mighty long ride. Most cars wouldn't want to pick up a guy for that long a ride. And you know—this is pretty lonesome country here—mountains, and woods . . . You ain't seen anybody like that, have you?

**Adams.** No. (*quickly*) Oh no, not at all. It was—160 just a—technical question.

---

2. **Alleghenies** (ăl'ĭ-gā'nēz): The Allegheny Mountains, a range extending from northern Pennsylvania to western Virginia.

3. **gave me the willies:** made me nervous.

**Mechanic.** I see. Well—that'll be just a dollar forty-nine—with the tax . . . (*fade*)

(*sound: auto hum up*)

(*music changing*)

**Adams.** The thing gradually passed from my mind, as sheer coincidence. I had a good night's sleep in Pittsburgh. I did not think about the man all next day—until just outside of Zanesville, Ohio, I saw him again.

170 (*music: dark, ominous note*)

**Adams.** It was a bright sunshiny afternoon. The peaceful Ohio fields, brown with the autumn stubble, lay dreaming in the golden light. I was driving slowly, drinking it in, when the road suddenly ended in a detour. In front of the barrier, *he* was standing.

(*music in*)

**Adams.** Let me explain about his appearance before I go on. I repeat. There was nothing **sinister** about
180 him. He was as drab as a mud fence. Nor was his attitude menacing. He merely stood there, waiting, almost drooping a little, the cheap overnight bag in his hand. He looked as though he had been waiting there for hours. Then he looked up. He hailed me. He started to walk forward.

**Voice** (*far off*). Hall-ooo . . . Hall-ooo . . .

**Adams.** I had stopped the car, of course, for the detour. And for a few moments, I couldn't seem to find the new road. I knew he must be thinking
190 that I had stopped for him.

**Voice** (*closer*). Hall-ooo . . . Hallll . . . ooo . . .

(*sound: gears jamming . . . sound of motor turning over hard . . . nervous accelerator*)

**Voice** (*closer*). Halll . . . oooo . . .

**Adams** (*panicky*). No. Not just now. Sorry . . .

**Voice** (*closer*). Going to California?

(*sound: starter starting . . . gears jamming*)

**Adams** (*as though sweating blood*). No. Not today. The other way. Going to New York. Sorry . . .
200 sorry . . .

(*sound: car starts with squeal of wheels on dirt . . . into auto hum*)

(*music in*)

**Adams.** After I got the car back onto the road again, I felt like a fool. Yet the thought of picking him up, of having him sit beside me was somehow unbearable. Yet, at the same time, I felt, more than ever, unspeakably alone.

(*sound: auto hum up*)

210 **Adams.** Hour after hour went by. The fields, the towns ticked off, one by one. The lights changed. I knew now that I was going to see him again. And though I dreaded the sight, I caught myself searching the side of the road, waiting for him to appear.

(*sound: auto hum up . . . car screeches to a halt . . . impatient honk two or three times . . . door being unbolted*)

**Sleepy Man's Voice.** Yep? What is it? What do you
220 want?

**Adams** (*breathless*). You sell sandwiches and pop here, don't you?

**Voice** (*cranky*). Yep. We do. In the daytime. But we're closed up now for the night.

**Adams.** I know. But—I was wondering if you could possibly let me have a cup of coffee—black coffee.

**Voice.** Not at this time of night, mister. My wife's the cook and she's in bed. Mebbe further down
230 the road—at the Honeysuckle Rest . . .

(*sound: door squeaking on hinges as though being closed*)

**Adams.** No—no. Don't shut the door. (*shakily*) Listen—just a minute ago, there was a man standing here—right beside this stand—a suspicious looking man . . .

**Woman's Voice** (*from distance*). Hen-ry? Who is it, Hen-ry?

**Henry.** It's nobuddy, mother. Just a feller thinks he
240 wants a cup of coffee. Go back into bed.

**Adams.** I don't mean to disturb you. But you see, I was driving along—when I just happened to look—and there he was . . .

**Henry.** What was he doing?

**Adams.** Nothing. He ran off—when I stopped the car.

**Henry.** Then what of it? That's nothing to wake a man in the middle of his sleep about. (*sternly*) Young man, I've got a good mind to turn you over to the sheriff.

**Adams.** But—I—

**Henry.** You've been taking a nip, that's what you've been doing. And you haven't got anything better to do than to wake decent folk out of their hard-earned sleep. Get going. Go on.

**Adams.** But—he looked as though he were going to rob you.

**Henry.** I ain't got nothin' in this stand to lose. Now—on your way before I call out Sheriff Oakes. (*fades*)

(*sound: auto hum up*)

**Adams.** I got into the car again and drove on slowly. I was beginning to hate the car. If I could have found a place to stop . . . to rest a little. But I was in the Ozark Mountains of Missouri now. The few resort places there were closed. Only an occasional log cabin, seemingly deserted, broke the **monotony** of the wild wooded landscape. I *had* seen him at that roadside stand; I knew I would see him again—perhaps at the next turn of the road. I knew that when I saw him next, I would run him down . . .

(*sound: auto hum up*)

**Adams.** But I did not see him again until late next afternoon . . .

(*sound: of railroad warning signal at crossroads*)

**Adams.** I had stopped the car at a sleepy little **junction** just across the border into Oklahoma—to let a train pass by—when he appeared, across the tracks, leaning against a telephone pole.

(*sound: distant sound of train chugging . . . bell ringing steadily*)

**Adams** (*very tense*). It was a perfectly airless, dry day. The red clay of Oklahoma was baking under the south-western sun. Yet there were spots of fresh rain on his shoulders. I couldn't stand that. Without thinking, blindly, I started the car across the tracks.

(*sound: train chugging closer*)

**Adams.** He didn't even look up at me. He was staring at the ground. I stepped on the gas hard, veering the wheel sharply toward him. I could hear the train in the distance now, but I didn't care. Then something went wrong with the car. It stalled right on the tracks.

(*sound: Train chugging closer. Above this sound of car stalling.*)

**Adams.** The train was coming closer. I could hear its bell ringing, and the cry of its whistle. Still
300 he stood there. And now—I knew that he was beckoning—beckoning me to my death.

(*sound: Train chugging close. Whistle blows wildly. Then train rushes up and by with pistons going, et cetera.*)

**Adams.** Well—I frustrated him that time. The starter had worked at last. I managed to back up. But when the train passed, he was gone. I was all alone in the hot dry afternoon.

(*sound: Train retreating. Crickets begin to sing.*)
310 (*music in*)

**Adams.** After that, I knew I had to do something. I didn't know who this man was or what he wanted of me. I only knew that from now on, I must not let myself be alone on the road for one moment.

(*sound: Auto hum up. Slow down. Stop. Door opening.*)

**Adams.** Hello, there. Like a ride?

**Girl.** What do you think? How far you going?

320 **Adams.** Amarillo . . . I'll take you to Amarillo.

**Girl.** Amarillo, Texas.

**Adams.** I'll drive you there.

**Girl.** Gee!

(*sound: Door closes—car starts.*)

(*music in*)

**Girl.** Mind if I take off my shoes? My dogs[4] are killing me.

**Adams.** Go right ahead.

**Girl.** Gee, what a break this is. A swell car, a decent
330 guy, and driving all the way to Amarillo. All I been getting so far is trucks.

**Adams.** Hitchhike much?

**Girl.** Sure. Only it's tough sometimes, in these great open spaces, to get the breaks.

**Adams.** I should think it would be. Though I'll bet if you get a good pick-up in a fast car, you can get to places faster than—say, another person, in another car?

**Girl.** I don't get you.

340 **Adams.** Well, take me, for instance. Suppose I'm driving across the country, say, at a nice steady clip of about 45 miles an hour. Couldn't a girl like you, just standing beside the road, waiting for lifts, beat me to town after town—provided she got picked up every time in a car doing from 65 to 70 miles an hour?

**Girl.** I dunno. Maybe she could and maybe she couldn't. What difference does it make?

**Adams.** Oh—no difference. It's just a—crazy idea
350 I had sitting here in the car.

**Girl** (*laughing*). Imagine spending your time in a swell car thinking of things like that!

**Adams.** What would you do instead?

**Girl** (*admiringly*). What would I do? If I was a good-looking fellow like yourself? Why—I'd just *enjoy* myself—every minute of the time. I'd sit back, and relax, and if I saw a good-looking girl along the side of the road . . . (*sharply*) Hey! Look out!

**Adams** (*breathlessly*). Did you see him too?

360 **Girl.** See who?

**Adams.** That man. Standing beside the barbed wire fence.

**Girl.** I didn't see—anybody. There wasn't nothing, but a bunch of steers—and the barbed wire fence. What did you think you was doing? Trying to run into the barbed wire fence?

**Adams.** There was a man there, I tell you . . . a thin gray man, with an overnight bag in his hand. And I was trying to—run him down.

370 **Girl.** Run him down? You mean—kill him?

---

4. **dogs:** a slang term for feet.

**Adams.** He's a sort of—phantom. I'm trying to get rid of him—or else prove that he's real. But (*desperately*) you say you didn't see him back there? You're sure?

**Girl.** I didn't see a soul. And as far as that's concerned, mister . . .

**Adams.** Watch for him the next time, then. Keep watching. Keep your eyes peeled on the road. He'll turn up again—maybe any minute now.

380 (*excitedly*) There. Look there—

(*sound: Auto sharply veering and skidding. Girl screams.*)

(*sound: Crash of car going into barbed wire fence. Frightened lowing[5] of steer.*)

**Girl.** How does this door work? I—I'm gettin' outta here.

**Adams.** Did you see him that time?

**Girl** (*sharply*). No. I didn't see him that time. And personally, mister, I don't expect never to see him.

390 All I want to do is to go on living—and I don't see how I will very long driving with you—

**Adams.** I'm sorry. I—I don't know what came over me. (*frightened*) Please—don't go . . .

**Girl.** So if you'll excuse me, mister—

**Adams.** You can't go. Listen, how would you like to go to California? I'll drive you to California.

**Girl.** Seeing pink elephants all the way? No thanks.

**Adams** (*desperately*). I could get you a job there. You wouldn't have to be a waitress. I have friends

400 there—my name is Ronald Adams—You can check up.

(*sound: door opening*)

**Girl.** Uhn-hunh. Thanks just the same.

**Adams.** Listen. Please. For just one minute. Maybe you think I am half cracked. But this man. You see, I've been seeing this man all the way across the country. He's been following me. And if you could only help me—stay with me—until I reach the coast—

410 **Girl.** You know what I think you need, big boy? Not a girl friend. Just a good dose of sleep. . . . There, I got it now.

(*sound: door opens . . . slams*)

**Adams.** No. You can't go.

**Girl** (*screams*). Leave your hands offa me, do you hear! Leave your—

**Adams.** Come back here, please, come back.

(*sound: struggle . . . slap . . . footsteps running away on gravel . . . lowing of steer*)

420 **Adams.** She ran from me, as though I were a monster. A few minutes later, I saw a passing truck pick her up. I knew then that I was utterly alone.

(*sound: lowing of steer up*)

**Adams.** I was in the heart of the great Texas prairies. There wasn't a car on the road after the truck went by. I tried to figure out what to do, how to get hold of myself. If I could find a place to rest. Or even, if I could sleep right here in the car for a few hours, along the side of the road . . .

430 I was getting my winter overcoat out of the back seat to use as a blanket, (Hall-ooo) when I saw him coming toward me, (Hall-ooo), emerging from the herd of moving steer . . .

**Voice.** Hall-ooo . . . Hall-oooo . . .

(*sound: auto starting violently . . . up to steady hum*)

(*music in*)

**Adams.** I didn't wait for him to come any closer. Perhaps I should have spoken to him then, fought it out then and there. For now he began

440 to be everywhere. Whenever I stopped, even for a moment—for gas, for oil, for a drink of pop, a cup of coffee, a sandwich—he was there.

(*music faster*)

**Adams.** I saw him standing outside the auto camp in Amarillo that night, when I dared to slow down. He was sitting near the drinking fountain in a little camping spot just inside the border of New Mexico.

---

5. **lowing:** mooing.

(*music faster*)

450 **Adams.** He was waiting for me outside the Navajo Reservation, where I stopped to check my tires. I saw him in Albuquerque[6] where I bought 12 gallons of gas . . . I was afraid now, afraid to stop. I began to drive faster and faster. I was in lunar landscape now—the great arid mesa country of New Mexico. I drove through it with the indifference of a fly crawling over the face of the moon.

(*music faster*)

460 **Adams.** But now he didn't even wait for me to stop. Unless I drove at 85 miles an hour over those endless roads—he waited for me at every other mile. I would see his figure, shadowless, flitting before me, still in its same attitude, over the cold and lifeless ground, flitting over dried-up rivers, over broken stones cast up by old glacial upheavals, flitting in the pure and cloudless air . . .

(*music strikes sinister note of finality.*)

470 **Adams.** I was beside myself when I finally reached Gallup, New Mexico, this morning. There is an auto camp here—cold, almost deserted at this time of year. I went inside, and asked if there was a telephone. I had the feeling that if only I could speak to someone familiar, someone that I loved, I could pull myself together.

(*sound: nickel put in slot*)

**Operator.** Number, please?

**Adams.** Long distance.

480 **Operator.** Thank you.

(*sound: return of nickel; buzz*)

**Long-Distance Opr.** This is long distance.

**Adams.** I'd like to put in a call to my home in Brooklyn, New York. I'm Ronald Adams. The number is Beechwood 2-0828.

**Long-Distance Opr.** Thank you. What is your number?

---

6. **Albuquerque** (ăl'bə-kûr'kē): a city in central New Mexico.

**Adams.** 312.

**Albuquerque Opr.** Albuquerque.

490 **Long-Distance Opr.** New York for Gallup. (*pause*)

**New York Opr.** New York.

**Long-Distance Opr.** Gallup, New Mexico calling Beechwood 2-0828. (*fade*)

**Adams.** I had read somewhere that love could banish demons. It was the middle of the morning. I knew Mother would be home. I pictured her, tall, white-haired, in her crisp house-dress, going about her tasks. It would be enough, I thought, merely to hear the even calmness of her voice . . .

500 **Long-Distance Opr.** Will you please deposit three dollars and 85 cents for the first three minutes? When you have deposited a dollar and a half, will you wait until I have collected the money?

(*sound: clunk of six coins*)

**Long-Distance Opr.** All right, deposit another dollar and a half.

(*sound: clunk of six coins*)

**Long-Distance Opr.** Will you please deposit the remaining 85 cents.

510 (*sound: clunk of four coins*)

**Long-Distance Opr.** Ready with Brooklyn—go ahead please.

**Adams.** Hello.

**Mrs. Whitney.** Mrs. Adams' residence.

**Adams.** Hello. Hello—Mother?

**Mrs. Whitney** (*very flat and rather proper . . . dumb, too, in a frizzy sort of way*). This is Mrs. Adams' residence. Who is it you wished to speak to, please?

**Adams.** Why—who's this?

520 **Mrs. Whitney.** This is Mrs. Whitney.

**Adams.** Mrs. Whitney? I don't know any Mrs. Whitney. Is this Beechwood 2-0828?

**Mrs. Whitney.** Yes.

**Adams.** Where's my mother? Where's Mrs. Adams?

**Mrs. Whitney.** Mrs. Adams is not at home. She is still in the hospital.

**Adams.** The hospital!

**Mrs. Whitney.** Yes. Who is this calling, please? Is it 530 a member of the family?

**Adams.** What's she in the hospital for?

**Mrs. Whitney.** She's been prostrated[7] for five days. Nervous breakdown. But who is this calling?

**Adams.** Nervous breakdown? But—my mother was never nervous . . .

**Mrs. Whitney.** It's all taken place since the death of her oldest son, Ronald.

**Adams.** Death of her oldest son, Ronald . . . ? Hey—what is this? What number is this?

540 **Mrs. Whitney.** This is Beechwood 2-0828. It's all been very sudden. He was killed just six days ago in an automobile accident on the Brooklyn Bridge.

**Long-Distance Opr.** (*breaking in*). Your three minutes are up, sir. (*silence*) Your three minutes are up, sir. (*pause*) Your three minutes are up, sir. (*fade*) Sir, your three minutes are up. Your three minutes are up, sir.

**Adams** (*in a strange voice*). And so, I am sitting here in this deserted auto camp in Gallup, New 550 Mexico. I am trying to think. I am trying to get hold of myself. Otherwise, I shall go mad . . . Outside it is night—the vast, soulless night of New Mexico. A million stars are in the sky. Ahead of me stretch a thousand miles of empty mesa, mountains, prairies—desert. Somewhere among them, he is waiting for me. Somewhere I shall know who he is, and who . . . I . . . am . . .

(*music up*)

---

7. **prostrated:** in a state of mental collapse.

# Comprehension

**INDIANA STANDARDS**

**READING STANDARD**
**8.3.6** Identify significant literary devices . . . .

1. **Recall**  What is Ronald Adams's original destination?

2. **Clarify**  Why does the repeated sight of the hitchhiker give Adams "the willies"?

3. **Clarify**  What does Adams learn about his mother at the end of the play?

# Literary Analysis

4. **Make Inferences**  What kind of relationship did Ronald Adams have with his mother? Cite evidence to support your answer.

5. **Examine Foreshadowing**  Now that you've read the play, is there anything you'd like to change or add to the first column of your foreshadowing chart? Make the adjustments and then fill in the second column of the chart. Note which use of foreshadowing was most effective in increasing the suspense you felt as you read.

6. **Analyze the Radio Play**  Reread lines 377–384. Tell what actions and emotions are communicated through stage directions and sound effects. Could listeners fully understand what was taking place in this scene if these elements weren't included? Explain.

7. **Draw Conclusions**  Who do you think the hitchhiker is? Give **proof** from the play to support your conclusion.

8. **Compare Across Texts**  What are some similarities and differences between "The Tell-Tale Heart" and *The Hitchhiker*? Think about the main characters, the settings, and the endings. Present your answers in a Venn diagram like the one shown.

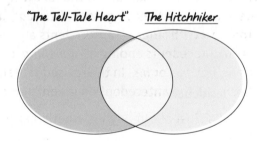

"The Tell-Tale Heart"    The Hitchhiker

# Extension and Challenge

9. **Readers' Circle**  Ask one member of your group to reread Adams's last speech aloud. Then discuss what might happen as he continues his journey. Make sure your guesses are based on details from the selection.

10. **Creative Project: Drama**  With a small group, choose a scene from *The Hitchhiker* that you think is especially suspenseful. Practice performing the scene, remembering to include sound effects and to follow stage directions. Then perform for the class. Afterward, explain why your group chose the scene you did.

# Reading-Writing Connection

Show your understanding of *The Hitchhiker* by responding to these prompts.
Then complete the **Grammar and Writing** exercise.

**A. Short Response: Evaluate Ronald Adams**
The play opens with Adams telling the listeners, "I am not mad." On the basis of what you learn in the rest of the play, do you agree with his assessment? Write a **one-paragraph evaluation** of Adams's sanity.

**B. Extended Response: Write a Scene**
What if the hitchhiker Adams picked up went to the police to report him? Write a **one- or two-page scene** in which she explains to an officer what happened and what **proof** she has for thinking Adams might be mad or even dangerous.

**A *good evaluation* will . . .**
• present an opinion about Adams's mental state
• support that opinion with details from the play

**An *interesting scene* will . . .**
• include dialogue about what the girl saw or didn't see while in the car
• show whether or not the officers believe her

## GRAMMAR AND WRITING

*MAINTAIN PRONOUN-ANTECEDENT AGREEMENT* An antecedent is the noun or pronoun to which a pronoun refers. For example, in the following sentence, the pronoun *their* refers to the antecedent *they: They took their seats at the café.* Be sure to use singular pronouns with singular antecedents and plural pronouns with plural antecedents. Pair antecedents ending in *one, thing,* or *body* with singular pronouns, such as *he, her, she,* or *his.* In the revised sentence, notice how the pronouns (in yellow) and the antecedent (in green) **agree in number.**

**INDIANA STANDARDS**

WRITING STANDARD
**8.4.8** Edit and proofread one's own writing, as well as that of others . . . .

> *Original:*  Adams would ask just about anyone whether they had seen the hitchhiker.
>
> *Revised:*  Adams would ask just about anyone whether he or she had seen the hitchhiker.

*PRACTICE* Correct the pronoun antecedent error in each sentence.

1. Adams first saw someone holding their bag on the bridge.
2. Everyone thought Adams was crazy because they could never see the hitchhiker.
3. Adams's scary story would make anybody fear for their life.
4. Nobody could have suspected that they got a ride from a dead man!

*For more help with pronoun-antecedent agreement, see page R52 in the* ***Grammar Handbook.***

# Hoot

Novel by Carl Hiaasen

## Meet Carl Hiaasen

Carl Hiaasen (hīˈə-sən) is a Florida native to the core. He began writing about his home state at age six, when his father gave him his first typewriter. Over the years, Hiassen developed the humorous writing style that has made him famous. He is an award-winning reporter and longtime columnist for the *Miami Herald*, as well as being the author of numerous best-selling mystery novels for adults. *Hoot* is his first young adult novel.

Much of Hiaasen's writing reflects his deep love of the outdoors. The heroes in his novels are often fierce protectors of the natural habitats and native species in Florida. The villains represent corporate greed and abuse of the environment. A reviewer once noted that Hiaasen "displays no mercy for anyone perceived as being responsible for defiling his home environment."

**Carl Hiaasen**
**born 1954**

**Other Book by Carl Hiaasen**
- *Flush*

## Try a Mystery Novel

What makes a book a **mystery novel?** First, you need a crime or unexplained event. There will be various clues left behind and possible motives for what happened. Suspense will build as further clues are revealed. Characters in the story will try to solve the mystery, but you, as the reader, might figure it out before they do. You can never be too sure of the answer, though—there might be a plot twist that changes everything.

## Read a Great Book

Roy Eberhardt didn't know what he was in for when his family moved from Bozeman, Montana, to Coconut Cove, Florida. He's getting bullied on the bus, but he's used to that. In fact, since his family moves around a lot, he's encountered enough bullies to consider himself "an expert on the breed." It's the stuff that he isn't used to that makes his new home seem strange. For starters, he spies a barefoot boy sprinting alongside the school bus at a speed that would put track stars in state-of-the-art running shoes to shame. Then there's the big, threatening girl who knows too much about him and won't tell him how. Roy needs to find some answers to his questions, but it won't be easy.

*from*

# HOOT

"Are there any other schools around here?" Roy asked Garrett.

"Why? You sick of this one already?" Garrett cackled and plunged a spoon into a lump of clammy apple crisp.

"No way. The reason I asked, I saw this weird kid today at one of the bus stops. Except he didn't get on the bus, and he's not here at school," Roy said, "so I figured he must not go to Trace."

"I don't know *anyone* who doesn't go to Trace," Garrett said. "There's a Catholic school up in Fort Myers, but that's a long ways off. Was he wearing a uniform, this kid? Because the nuns make everybody wear uniforms."

"No, he definitely wasn't in a uniform."

"You're sure he was in middle school? Maybe he goes to Graham," Garrett suggested. Graham was the public high school nearest to Coconut Cove.

Roy said, "He didn't look big enough for high school."

"Maybe he was a midget." Garrett grinned and made a funny noise with one of his cheeks.

"I don't think so," said Roy.

"You said he was weird."

20 "He wasn't wearing any shoes," Roy said, "and he was running like crazy."

"Maybe somebody was after him. Did he look scared?"

"Not really."

Garrett nodded. "High school kid. Betcha five bucks."

To Roy, that still didn't make sense. Classes at Graham High started fifty-five minutes earlier than the classes at Trace; the high school kids were off the streets long before the middle school buses finished their routes.

"So he was skippin' class. Kids skip all the time," Garrett said.

30 "You want your dessert?"

Roy pushed his tray across the table. "You ever skip school?"

"Uh, yeah," Garrett said sarcastically. "Buncha times."

"You ever skip alone?"

Garrett thought for a moment. "No. It's always me and my friends."

"See. That's what I mean."

"So maybe the kid's just a psycho. Who cares?"

"Or an outlaw," said Roy.

Garrett looked skeptical. "An outlaw? You mean like Jesse James?"

"No, not exactly," Roy said, though there *had* been something wild 40 in that kid's eyes.

Garrett laughed again. "An outlaw—that's rich, Eberhardt. You got a seriously whacked imagination."

"Yeah," said Roy, but already he was thinking about a plan. He was determined to find the running boy.

❧

The next morning, Roy traded seats on the school bus to be closer to the front door. When the bus turned onto the street where he had seen the running boy, Roy slipped his backpack over his shoulders and scouted out the window, waiting. Seven rows back, Dana Matherson was tormenting a sixth grader named Louis. Louis was from Haiti and 50 Dana was merciless.

As the bus came to a stop at the intersection, Roy poked his head out the window and checked up and down the street. Nobody was running. Seven kids boarded the bus, but the strange shoeless boy was not among them.

∾

It was the same story the next day, and the day after that. By Friday, Roy had pretty much given up. He was sitting ten rows from the door, reading an X-Man comic, as the bus turned the familiar corner and began to slow down. A movement at the corner of his eye made Roy glance up from his comic book—and there he was on the 60 sidewalk, running again! Same basketball jersey, same grimy shorts, same black-soled feet.

As the brakes of the school bus wheezed, Roy grabbed his backpack off the floor and stood up. At that instant, two big sweaty hands closed around his neck.

"Where ya goin', cowgirl?"

"Lemme go," Roy rasped, squirming to break free.

The grip on his throat tightened. He felt Dana's ashtray breath on his right ear: "How come you don't got your boots on today? Who ever heard of a cowgirl wearing Air Jordans?"

70 "They're Reeboks," Roy squeaked.

The bus had stopped, and the students were starting to board. Roy was furious. He had to get to the door fast, before the driver closed it and the bus began to roll.

But Dana wouldn't let go, digging his fingers into Roy's windpipe. Roy was having trouble getting air, and struggling only made it worse.

"Look at you," Dana chortled from behind, "red as a tomato!"

Roy knew the rules against fighting on the bus, but he couldn't think of anything else to do. He clenched his right fist and brought it up

80 blindly over his shoulder, as hard as he could. The punch landed on something moist and rubbery.

There was a gargled cry; then Dana's hands fell away from Roy's neck. Panting, Roy bolted for the door of the bus just as the last student, a tall girl with curly blond hair and red-framed eyeglasses, came up the steps. Roy clumsily edged past her and jumped to the ground.

"Where do you think you're going?" the girl demanded.

"Hey, wait!" the bus driver shouted, but Roy was already a blur.

The running boy was way ahead of him, but Roy figured he could
90 stay close enough to keep him in sight. He knew the kid couldn't go at full speed forever.

He followed him for several blocks—over fences, through shrubbery, weaving through yapping dogs and lawn sprinklers and hot tubs. Eventually Roy felt himself tiring. This kid is amazing, he thought. Maybe he's practicing for the track team.

Once Roy thought he saw the boy glance over his shoulder, as if he knew he was being pursued, but Roy couldn't be certain. The boy was still far ahead of him, and Roy was gulping like a beached trout. His shirt was soaked and perspiration poured off his forehead, stinging
100 his eyes.

The last house in the subdivision was still under construction, but the shoeless boy dashed heedlessly through the lumber and loose nails. Three men hanging drywall stopped to holler at him, but the boy never broke stride. One of the same workers made a one-armed lunge at Roy but missed.

Suddenly there was grass under his feet again—the greenest, softest grass that Roy had ever seen. He realized that he was on a golf course, and that the blond kid was tearing down the middle of a long, lush fairway.
110 On one side was a row of tall Australian pines, and on the other side was a milky man-made lake. Roy could see four brightly dressed figures ahead, gesturing at the barefoot boy as he ran by.

Roy gritted his teeth and kept going. His legs felt like wet cement, and his lungs were on fire. A hundred yards ahead, the boy cut sharply to the right and disappeared into the pine trees. Roy doggedly aimed himself for the woods.

An angry shout echoed, and Roy noticed that the people in the fairway were waving their arms at him, too. He kept right on running. Moments later there was a distant glint of sunlight on 120 metal, followed by a muted *thwack*. Roy didn't actually see the golf ball until it came down six feet in front of him. He had no time to duck or dive out of the way. All he could do was turn his head and brace for the blow.

The bounce caught him squarely above the left ear, and at first it didn't even hurt. Then Roy felt himself swaying and spinning as a brilliant gout of fireworks erupted inside his skull. He felt himself falling for what seemed like a long time, falling as softly as a drop of rain on velvet.

When the golfers ran up and saw Roy facedown in the sand trap, 130 they thought he was dead. Roy heard their frantic cries but he didn't move. The sugar-white sand felt cool against his burning cheeks, and he was very sleepy. ◡

## Keep Reading

Roy has gone from reading mysteries to being right in the middle of one. But the barefoot boy is just one of the mysteries in Roy's new hometown, where reptile wranglers are listed in the phone book because you just might find an alligator in your toilet. While Roy is trying to find out who the strange boy is, the Coconut Cove Public Safety Department has another mystery on its hands. Someone is sabotaging the construction of a pancake house, and no one knows why. Keep reading to see how the mystery unfolds.

### *from* **The Sisterhood of the Traveling Pants**
Film Clip on **MediaSmart** DVD

# *How do* GREAT *stories begin?*

**INDIANA STANDARDS**

**LISTENING/SPEAKING STANDARD 8.7.9** Interpret and evaluate the various ways in which visual image makers (such as graphic artists, illustrators, and news photographers) communicate information and affect impressions and opinions.

*KEY IDEA* Quite often, a popular book is made into a major motion picture. Fans of the book form long lines at theaters, eager to experience big-screen portrayals of gripping moments they know so well. What **movie versions** of books have you enjoyed? What made those movies worthwhile? Prepare to watch a clip from a movie that's based on a well-loved novel. You'll explore what filmmakers do to draw you into the plot of a movie.

## Background

**A Perfect Fit** The novel *The Sisterhood of the Traveling Pants* is about four lifelong best friends who are about to spend their first summer apart. Before their vacations begin, these girls make an amazing discovery. A pair of jeans purchased in a thrift shop fits each one of them perfectly. To stay connected that summer, they agree to mail the jeans to each other. This book's popularity led to sequels to the novel as well as a movie. The scene you'll watch occurs fairly early in the movie and focuses on Carmen, who is about to visit her dad.

# Media Literacy: Plot in Movies

The **exposition** stage of a story is the part that introduces the characters, setting, and conflict. Movies unfold in a similar way, introducing the characters and their struggles. For a movie director, the first steps in developing a plot are to show characters' relationships and predicaments, and to make viewers like you care about these characters. Filmmakers position the characters and the camera in certain ways to help you to follow and react to what's happening.

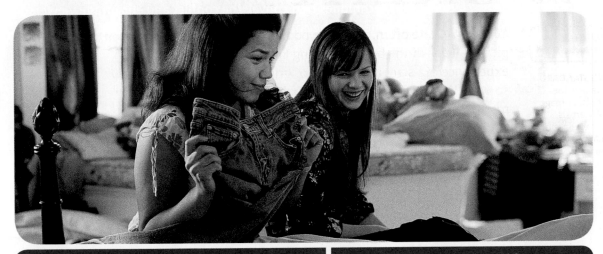

## HOW DIRECTORS TELL THEIR STORIES

**Directors position characters to portray relationships.**

To show how characters relate to each other in a scene, directors use **blocking,** the arrangement of the characters within a film frame.

**Directors position the camera to reveal how what's happening affects the characters.**

A **close-up shot** is a detailed view of a character or an object. Close-ups can reveal a character's personality and often hint at a character's emotions or thoughts. **Medium shots** show a character from the waist up. This type of shot can capture movements that reveal a character's behavior.

**Directors try to stir viewers' emotions.**

Directors not only want you to understand what's happening in a story but to get you emotionally involved. They want you to follow the plot complications closely and to make you wonder about the outcome.

## STRATEGIES FOR VIEWING

Notice how close or how far apart characters stand to one another. Their positions may offer clues about their relationships or their emotions.

To watch for what might be revealed in close-up or medium shots, ask yourself:

- What reactions or thoughts can I infer from a character's facial expressions?
- What does a character's body language tell me about how he or she feels about what's happening?

As you watch a conflict unfold in a scene, ask yourself:

- How am I reacting to what's happening?
- What does the director do to make me care about what will happen?
- What is the mood of the music? Is it upbeat? Sad? How is it affecting me?

- **Film:** *The Sisterhood of the Traveling Pants*
- **Director:** Ken Kwapis
- **Genre:** Drama
- **Running Time:** 2.5 minutes

# The Sisterhood of the Traveling Pants

The scene you'll watch focuses on Carmen, who has just arrived to spend the summer with her dad. First, watch the clip to follow what's happening in the scene. Then view the clip a few times to spot techniques that convey the conflict and encourage viewers to connect to the characters. Answer these questions to help you analyze the clip.

## NOW VIEW

### FIRST VIEWING:  Comprehension

1. **Recall**  Carmen surprises her dad with her grades. What is the surprise Carmen's dad reveals to her?

2. **Clarify**  What is shown from outside of the moving car that gets Carmen's attention?

### CLOSE VIEWING:  Media Literacy

3. **Analyze Character**  How do the filmmakers show Carmen's excitement at spending the summer with her father?

4. **Analyze Blocking**  This image of the three characters is an example of how a director can position characters in a film frame to signal character relationships. Through blocking, what is the director communicating to viewers about Carmen's relationship to the others?

5. **Analyze Techniques**  One song plays throughout the scene. What effect do you think the song is intended to have on you?

6. **Evaluate Techniques**  The scene focuses on two characters having a conversation that leads to a tense moment. How well do the filmmakers set the stage for a conflict that will develop as the movie progresses? Base your opinion on these elements:

   - the details about the characters that are delivered through dialogue
   - the shots the filmmakers use to make the characters' emotions visible
   - your own emotional reactions to what happens in the scene

# Write or Discuss

**Analyze Film** You've viewed a clip from *The Sisterhood of the Traveling Pants* to look at how directors portray characters and conflicts. Now put yourself in the shoes of the movie's director. How might the scene be different if it focused less on Carmen and more on her dad and his news? Write a short description of this new version. Think about

- which character would have more close-ups
- how viewers might sympathize more with him
- how the music might differ

# Produce Your Own Media

**MEDIA TOOLS**

For help with creating a storyboard, visit the **Media Center** at **ClassZone.com.**

**Create a Storyboard** A **storyboard** is a device filmmakers use to plan the shooting of a movie. A storyboard can serve as a visual map and is made up of a few images and brief descriptions. Choose an important scene from a novel you've recently read or any of the stories from this unit. With a partner, make a storyboard that portrays a conflict.

*HERE'S HOW* Use these as tips for creating your storyboard:

- Make your storyboard simple rather than beautiful. Draw or sketch the images, making sure they're easy to understand.
- Within the six separate frames, include close-ups or medium shots that reveal a character's reactions or emotions.
- Show shots that reveal a conflict. Show how at least one character reacts.
- Underneath each frame, write out a specific description or a line of dialogue.

**STUDENT MODEL**

"Runners, take your places at the starting line!"

Medium shot of Squeaky getting ready

Close-up shot of Raymond watching

Medium shot of Squeaky running

Medium shot of Raymond running

Medium shot of squeaky winning the race

**Tech Tip**

Use a word processing program to type the descriptions or dialogue for the storyboard.

## My First Free Summer

Memoir by Julia Alvarez

# When is it time to LEAVE?

**INDIANA STANDARDS**

**READING STANDARDS**
**8.3.2** Evaluate the structural elements of the plot, such as subplots, parallel episodes, and climax; the plot's development; and the way in which conflicts are (or are not) addressed and resolved.

**8.3.7** Analyze a work of literature, showing how it reflects the heritage, traditions, attitudes, and beliefs of its author.

**KEY IDEA** Even under the best of circumstances, **leaving** someone or something behind can be difficult. Familiar people and places often provide us with a sense of safety and security. In the memoir you are about to read, Julia Alvarez faces the pain of leaving her homeland, even as she realizes the dangers of staying.

**QUICKWRITE** Reflect on times when you have had to leave a special person or place. Choose one experience and write a journal entry that explores your feelings about leaving. Were you looking forward to moving on? What were you worried about?

## ● LITERARY ANALYSIS: MEMOIR

A **memoir** is a form of autobiographical writing in which a writer describes important events in his or her life. Most memoirs

- use the first-person point of view
- are true accounts of actual events
- describe conflicts faced by the writer
- include the writer's feelings about historical events or social issues

As you read "My First Free Summer," look for places where Julia Alvarez shares her feelings about the historical events taking place in the Dominican Republic.

## ● READING SKILL: CAUSE AND EFFECT

Events are often related by **cause and effect,** which means that one event brings about the other. The first event is the **cause,** and what follows is the **effect.** Sometimes, one cause can have many effects. Recognizing cause and effect relationships can help you understand important turning points, because you'll be aware of the consequences of events and actions.

As you read, look for the effects that the political struggle in Alvarez's homeland had on her life. Use a chart like the one shown to help you keep track of these effects.

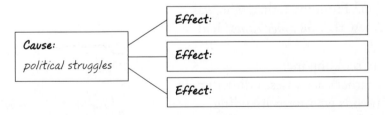

Cause:
political struggles

Effect:

Effect:

Effect:

## ▲ VOCABULARY IN CONTEXT

Alvarez uses the vocabulary words to help describe a traumatic childhood experience. See how many you know. Make a chart like the one shown. Put each word in the appropriate column.

| WORD LIST | contradiction | replete | unravel |
| --- | --- | --- | --- |
| | interrogation | summon | |

| Know Well | Think I Know | Don't Know at All |
| --- | --- | --- |
| | | |

# Author Online

**Julia Alvarez**
**born 1950**

**Where Is Home?** Julia Alvarez emigrated from the Dominican Republic to the United States when she was ten. Her father had taken part in an underground plot against dictator Rafael Trujillo (rä-fä′yəl′ trōō-hē′yō), so the family's safety was in jeopardy. Although Alvarez and her family escaped, she found it difficult being cut off from her homeland and adjusting to a new country. Books offered Alvarez a world where she did not feel alone. Through writing, she could begin to connect her two cultures. She likes to quote another poet in saying, "Language is the only homeland."

**A Poet First** Poetry first drew Alvarez to writing. After receiving degrees in literature and writing, she spent 13 years teaching poetry at several universities. *Homecoming,* a book of her poems, was published in 1984. Since then, Alvarez has gone on to write in a variety of genres, including fiction for both children and adults.

## Background

**A Brutal Dictator** The people of the Dominican Republic suffered under the brutal dictatorship of Rafael Trujillo and his supporters for 31 years (from 1930–1961). Under his rule, masses of people were slaughtered for "crimes" as minor as not hanging his portrait in their homes. Many brave Dominicans, including Alvarez's father, tried to overthrow this government. Those caught faced terrible consequences.

**MORE ABOUT THE AUTHOR AND BACKGROUND**
To learn more about Julia Alvarez and the Dominican Republic, visit the **Literature Center** at ClassZone.com.

# My First Free Summer

## JULIA ALVAREZ

**ANALYZE VISUALS**
Look at the girl's expression, posture, and clothing, as well as the window she leans near. What do these **details** suggest about her situation?

I never had summer—I had summer school. First grade, summer school. Second grade, summer school. Thirdgradesummerschoolfourthgradesummerschool. In fifth grade, I vowed I would get interested in fractions, the presidents of the United States, Mesopotamia; I would learn my English.

That was the problem. English. My mother had decided to send her children to the American school so we could learn the language of the nation that would soon be liberating us. For thirty years, the Dominican Republic had endured a bloody and repressive dictatorship.[1] From my father, who was involved in an underground plot, my mother knew that *los américanos*[2] had 10 promised to help bring democracy to the island.

"You have to learn your English!" Mami kept scolding me.

"But why?" I'd ask. I didn't know about my father's activities. I didn't know the dictator was bad. All I knew was that my friends who were attending Dominican schools were often on holiday to honor the dictator's birthday, the dictator's saint day, the day the dictator became the dictator, the day the dictator's oldest son was born, and so on. They marched in parades and visited the palace and had their picture in the paper.

Meanwhile, I had to learn about the pilgrims with their funny witch hats, about the 50 states and where they were on the map, about Dick and Jane[3] and 20 their tame little pets, Puff and Spot, about freedom and liberty and justice for all—while being imprisoned in a hot classroom with a picture of a man wearing a silly wig hanging above the blackboard. And all of this learning I had to do in that impossibly difficult, rocks-in-your-mouth language of English! **A**

**A CAUSE AND EFFECT**
What effect does Mr. Alvarez's political involvement have on Julia's life? Include this in your chart.

---

1. **dictatorship** (dĭk-tā′tər-shĭp′): a government under an absolute ruler, or dictator.
2. *los américanos* (lōs ə-měr′ĭ-kä′nōs) *Spanish:* the Americans.
3. **Dick and Jane:** characters in a children's reading textbook.

Detail of *The Stillness of an Afternoon* (2003), Bo Bartlett. Oil on panel, 18½″ × 21″. Courtesy of the artist and P.P.O.W. Gallery, New York.

Somehow, I managed to scrape by. Every June, when my prospects looked iffy, Mami and I met with the principal. I squirmed in my seat while they arranged for my special summer lessons.

"She is going to work extra hard. Aren't you, young lady?" the principal would quiz me at the end of our session.

My mother's eye on me, I'd murmur, "Yeah."

30  "Yes, what?" Mami coached.

"Yes." I sighed. "Sir."

It's a wonder that I just wasn't thrown out, which was what I secretly hoped for. But there were extenuating circumstances,[4] the grounds on which the American school stood had been donated by my grandfather. In fact, it had been my grandmother who had encouraged Carol Morgan to start her school. The bulk of the student body was made up of the sons and daughters of American diplomats and business people, but a few Dominicans—most of them friends or members of my family—were allowed to attend.

"You should be grateful!" Mami scolded on the way home from our

40  meeting. "Not every girl is lucky enough to go to the Carol Morgan School!"

In fifth grade, I straightened out. "Yes, ma'am!" I learned to say brightly. "Yes, sir!" To wave my hand in sword-wielding swoops so I could get called on with the right answer. What had changed me? Gratitude? A realization of my luckiness? No, sir! The thought of a fun summer? Yes, ma'am! I wanted to run with the pack of cousins and friends in the common yard that connected all our properties. To play on the trampoline and go off to *la playa*[5] and get brown as a berry. I wanted to be free. Maybe American principles had finally sunk in! **B**

The summer of 1960 began in bliss: I did not have to go to summer school! *Attitude much improved. Her English progressing nicely. Attentive and cooperative*

50  *in classroom.* I grinned as Mami read off the note that accompanied my report card of Bs.

But the yard **replete** with cousins and friends that I had dreamed about all year was deserted. Family members were leaving for the United States, using whatever connections they could drum up. The plot had **unraveled.** Every day there were massive arrests. The United States had closed its embassy and was advising Americans to return home.

My own parents were terrified. Every night black Volkswagens blocked our driveway and stayed there until morning. "Secret police," my older sister whispered.

60  "Why are they secret if they're the police?" I asked.

"Shut up!" my sister hissed. "Do you want to get us all killed?"

Day after day, I kicked a deflated beach ball around the empty yard, feeling as if I'd been tricked into good behavior by whomever God put in charge of the lives of 10-year-olds. I was bored. Even summer school would have been better than this! **C**

---

4   **extenuating circumstances** (ĭk-stĕn′yōō-ā′tĭng sûr′kəm-stăn′səs): a situation or condition that provides an excuse for an action.

5.  *la playa* (lä plä′yä) *Spanish:* the beach.

**SOCIAL STUDIES CONNECTION**

Dictator Trujillo established the SIM (Military Intelligence Service), a secret police force that spied on fellow Dominicans and engaged in torture and murder at Trujillo's request.

**B  MEMOIR**
What does freedom mean to Alvarez at this point in her life?

**replete** (rĭ-plēt′) *adj.* abundantly supplied

**unravel** (ŭn-răv′əl) *v.* to undo; come apart

**C  CAUSE AND EFFECT**
What's causing Alvarez to have a boring summer?

One day toward the end of the summer, my mother **summoned** my sisters and me. She wore that too-bright smile she sometimes pasted on her terrified face.

"Good news, girls! Our papers and tickets came! We're leaving for the United States!"

70 Our mouths dropped. We hadn't been told we were going on a trip anywhere, no less to some place so far away.

I was the first to speak up. "But why?"

My mother flashed me the same look she used to give me when I'd ask why I had to learn English.

I was about to tell her that I didn't want to go to the United States, where summer school had been invented and everyone spoke English. But my mother lifted a hand for silence. "We're leaving in a few hours. I want you all to go get ready! I'll be in to pack soon." The desperate look in her eyes did not allow for **contradiction**. We raced off, wondering how to fit the contents of our 80 Dominican lives into four small suitcases. **D**

Our flight was scheduled for that afternoon, but the airplane did not appear. The terminal filled with soldiers, wielding machine guns, checking papers, escorting passengers into a small **interrogation** room. Not everyone returned.

"It's a trap," I heard my mother whisper to my father.

This had happened before, a cat-and-mouse game[6] the dictator liked to play. Pretend that he was letting someone go, and then at the last minute, their family and friends conveniently gathered together—wham! The secret police would haul the whole clan away.

Of course, I didn't know that this was what my parents were dreading. 90 But as the hours ticked away, and afternoon turned into evening and evening into night and night into midnight with no plane in sight, a light came on in my head. If the light could be translated into words, instead, they would say: Freedom and liberty and justice for all . . . I knew that ours was not a trip, but an escape. We had to get to the United States. **E**

The rest of that night is a blur. It is one, then two the next morning. A plane lands, lights flashing. We are walking on the runway, climbing up the stairs into the cabin. An American lady wearing a cap welcomes us. We sit down, ready to depart. But suddenly, soldiers come on board. They go seat by seat, looking at our faces. Finally, they leave, the door closes, and with a powerful 100 roar, we lift off and I fall asleep.

Next morning, we are standing inside a large, echoing hall as a stern American official reviews our documents. What if he doesn't let us in? What if we have to go back? I am holding my breath. My parents' terror has become mine.

He checks our faces against the passport pictures. When he is done, he asks, "You girls ready for school?" I swear he is looking at me.

"Yes, sir!" I speak up.

The man laughs. He stamps our papers and hands them to my father. Then, wonderfully, a smile spreads across his face. "Welcome to the United States," he says, waving us in. ❧

---

6. **cat-and-mouse game:** cruel, playful game to torment another.

**contradiction**
(kŏn'trə-dĭk'shən) *n.*
a denial; an expression that is opposite to

**D** **CAUSE AND EFFECT**
Why is Alvarez's family leaving for the United States on such short notice? Mark this in your chart.

**interrogation**
(ĭn-tĕr'ə-gā'shən) *n.*
an official or formal questioning

**E** **MEMOIR**
Reread lines 89–94. What changes have occurred in Alvarez's thinking about the Dominican Republic and the United States?

# Comprehension

1. **Recall** Why was Alvarez allowed to attend the American school?

2. **Clarify** What happened at the airport as the Alvarez family waited for the plane?

INDIANA
STANDARDS

READING STANDARD
**8.3.7** Analyze a work of literature, showing how it reflects ... attitudes ... of its author.

# Literary Analysis

3. **Interpret Memoir** What do you think the title of the memoir means? Consider the possible meanings of the word "free." Cite evidence from the selection to support your interpretation.

4. **Analyze Personality Traits** Choose three words or phrases to describe Alvarez as a child. Include them in a web like the one shown. Expand the web by providing specific examples from the memoir that support each description.

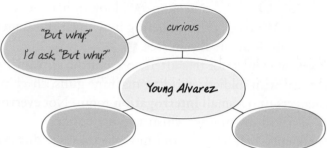

5. **Analyze Perspective** Although the events depicted in the memoir take place when Alvarez was a child, she writes about the experience many years later. Find at least two examples from the selection that show her adult perspective, or view on the topic. What does she know as an adult that she didn't know at the time?

6. **Generalize About Cause and Effect** Review the chart you created as you read. On the basis of the information you collected, make a general statement about how politics can affect one's personal life.

7. **Draw Conclusions** Why do Alvarez's feelings about **leaving** her homeland change by the end of the memoir?

# Extension and Challenge

8. **SOCIAL STUDIES CONNECTION** Research one of the following topics to find out more about the Dominican Republic during Trujillo's rule. Present your findings in a poster.

   • The 14th of June Movement
   • "The Butterflies"
   • Trujillo's assassination

   **RESEARCH LINKS**
   For more on Dominican Republic, visit the **Research Center** at ClassZone.com.

# Vocabulary in Context

## VOCABULARY PRACTICE

Choose the word from the list that is the best substitute for each boldfaced word or phrase.

1. Julia had hoped her summer would be **filled** with free time and fun.
2. Her plans for a carefree summer were soon to **come apart.**
3. When Julia's mother spoke, there was no room for **disagreement.**
4. Officials started to **call** the passengers for questioning.
5. The **questioning** took place in a small room.

contradiction

interrogation

replete

summon

unravel

## VOCABULARY IN WRITING

Write a paragraph explaining the challenges that Julia and her family faced in the summer of 1960. Use at least two vocabulary words. You might begin this way.

> **EXAMPLE SENTENCE**
>
> When events started to **unravel**, Julia's family had to leave the country.

**INDIANA STANDARDS**

READING STANDARD
**8.1.3** Verify the meaning of a word in its context . . . .

## VOCABULARY STRATEGY: THE LATIN ROOT *dict*

The vocabulary word *contradiction* contains the Latin root *dict* (also spelled *dic*), which means "say" or "speak." Your understanding of this root can help you to figure out the meaning of other words formed from *dict*.

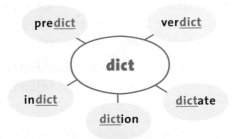

pre**dict**  ver**dict**  **dict**  in**dict**  **dict**ate  **dict**ion

*PRACTICE* Look up each word that appears in the web. Then decide which word best completes each sentence. Be ready to explain how the meaning of the root is reflected in each word.

1. The jury stated its findings by announcing the _____.
2. To say that someone has done something wrong is to _____ him.
3. The ruler with absolute power will ____ the laws of the land.
4. Were you able to _____, or tell in advance, what would happen?
5. Her precise way of speaking showed that she had wonderful _____.

**VOCABULARY PRACTICE**
For more practice, go to the **Vocabulary Center** at **ClassZone.com.**

## The Great Rat Hunt

Memoir by Laurence Yep

# When is it OK to be SCARED?

**INDIANA STANDARDS**

**READING STANDARD**
**8.3.2** Evaluate the structural elements of the plot, such as subplots, parallel episodes, and climax; the plot's development; and the way in which conflicts are (or are not) addressed and resolved.

**KEY IDEA** A spider. A roller coaster. A hurricane. We're all **scared** of something. Even so, it can be hard to admit to being afraid. If your friends think it's fun to jump off the high dive, you might not want them to know that heights frighten you. In the selection you are about to read, Laurence Yep tells about a time he tried to overcome his fear in order to impress his father.

**SURVEY** What scares you and your classmates? Find out by conducting an informal survey. On your own, jot down three or four of your fears. Then meet with a small group, combine your lists, and tally the results. Which fears are most common? Which surprised you?

| What Scares You? | |
| --- | --- |
| Fears | Number of People |
| 1. Heights | )))) |
| 2. Thunder | )) |
| 3. The dark | ))) |
| 4. | |

## LITERARY ANALYSIS: CONFLICT IN NONFICTION

In the memoir you're about to read, Laurence Yep relates an event from his childhood. To tell this real-life story, he uses some of the same literary elements that appear in his award-winning fiction. For example, the narrative centers around **conflicts,** or struggles between opposing forces. As you read "The Great Rat Hunt," identify the conflicts the young Laurence Yep faces.

## READING SKILL: CHRONOLOGICAL ORDER

Memoirs are often organized in **chronological order,** which means that events are presented in the order in which they happened. To make sure you know when each event occurs, follow these steps:

- Identify individual events taking place.
- Look for words and phrases that signal order, such as *before, after, first, next, then, while, the next day,* or *an hour and a half later.*

As you read "The Great Rat Hunt," keep track of the chronology. In a chart like the one shown, record key events in order, using parallel boxes when two actions occur at the same time.

Father sets out traps. →

## ▲ VOCABULARY IN CONTEXT

The boldfaced words help Laurence Yep relate a story from his childhood. To see how many you know, substitute a different word or phrase for each one.

1. **barricade** the doorway
2. **rationalize** a bad habit
3. **wince** in pain
4. **perpetual** motion
5. an **improvised** comedy skit
6. known for his quiet **reserve**
7. **vigilant** watchdog
8. the **ravage** caused by the flood
9. embarrassed by my **ineptitude**
10. spoken to me **brusquely**

# Author Online

**A Man of Accomplishment**
Laurence Yep has said that he approaches American culture as "somewhat of a stranger." Born in San Francisco, California, Yep was always surrounded by people of various backgrounds, none quite like his own. He was

**Laurence Yep
born 1948**

raised in an African-American community and commuted to a bilingual school in Chinatown. There, his classmates teased him for not knowing Chinese. Yep began submitting his work to magazines when a high school English teacher made publishing a story a requirement for getting an A in the class. He became a published author at 18 and went on to publish dozens of stories, as well as earning a college degree and a PhD. Many of the main conflicts in his works involve feeling like an outsider.

**A Father's Pride** Yep's writing has gained him numerous awards, including more than ten for his book *Dragonwings*—a book that, like many of his more recent works, explores Chinese mythology. Yep's success as a writer greatly pleased his father, who displayed his son's writing medals and plaques "in lieu of athletic accomplishments."

 **MORE ABOUT THE AUTHOR**
For more on Laurence Yep, visit the
**Literature Center** at ClassZone.com.

# THE GREAT RAT HUNT

**Laurence Yep**

I had asthma[1] when I was young, so I never got to play sports much with my father. While my brother and father practiced, I could only sit in bed, propped up by a stack of pillows. As I read my comic books, I heard them beneath our apartment window. In the summer, it was the thump of my brother's fastball into my father's mitt. In the fall, it was the smack of a football. In the winter, it was the airy bounce of a basketball.

Though my father had come from China when he was eight, he had taken quickly to American games. When he and Mother were young, they had had the same dances and sports leagues as their white schoolmates—but kept
10 separate in Chinatown. (He had met Mother when she tripped him during a co-ed basketball game at the Chinatown Y.)

Father was big as a teenager and good at sports. In fact, a social club in Chinatown had hired him to play football against social clubs in other Chinatowns. There he was, a boy playing against grown men.

During a game in Watsonville, a part-time butcher had broken Father's nose. It never properly healed, leaving a big bump at the bridge. There were other injuries too from baseball, basketball, and tennis. Each bump and scar on his body had its own story, and each story was matched by a trophy or medal.

20 Though he now ran a grocery store in San Francisco, he tried to pass on his athletic skills to my older brother Eddy and me. During the times I felt well, I tried to keep up with them, but my lungs always failed me. **Ⓐ**

---

1. **asthma** (ăz′mə): a lung disease that at times makes breathing difficult.

**ANALYZE VISUALS**
What can you **infer** about the relationship between the man and the boy in this painting?

**Ⓐ CONFLICT**
How does Yep's asthma affect his relationship with his father and brother?

Illustrations by Jan Peng Wang.

When I had to sit down on the curb, I felt as if I had let my father down. I'd glance up anxiously when I felt his shadow over me; but he looked neither angry nor disgusted—just puzzled, as if he could not understand why my lungs were not like his.

"S-s-sorry." I panted.

"That's okay." He squatted and waved his hat, trying to fan more air at me. In the background, Eddy played catch with himself, waiting impatiently for the lessons to begin again. Ashamed, I would gasp. "Go on . . . and play."

And Father and Eddy would start once more while I watched, doomed to be positively un-American, a weakling, a **perpetual** spectator, an outsider. Worse, I felt as if Eddy were Father's only true son. **B**

And then came the day when the rat invaded our store. It was Eddy who first noticed it while we were restocking the store shelves. I was stacking packages of pinto beans when Eddy called me. "Hey, do you know what this is?" He waved me over to the cans of soup. On his palm lay some dark drops. "Is it candy?"

Father came out of the storeroom in the rear of our store. Over his back, he carried a huge hundred pound sack of rice. He let it thump to the floor right away. "Throw that away."

"What is it, Father?" I asked.

"Rat droppings," he said. "Go wash your hands."

"Yuck." Eddy flung the droppings down.

While Eddy washed his hands, I helped Father get rid of the evidence. Then he got some wooden traps from a shelf and we set them out.

However, the traps were for mice and not for rats. The rat must have gotten a good laugh while it stole the bait and set off the springs. **C**

Then Father tried poison pellets, but the rat avoided them all. It even left a souvenir right near the front door.

Father looked grim as he cleaned it up. "I'm through fooling around." **D**

So he called up his exterminator[2] friend, Pete Wong, the Cockroach King of Chinatown. While Pete fumigated[3] the store, we stayed with my Aunt Nancy over on Mason, where the cable cars kept me up late. They always rang their bells when they rounded the corner. Even when they weren't there, I could hear the cable rattling in its channel beneath the street. It was OK, though, because my cousin Jackie could tell stories all night.

The next day, when we went back home, Father searched around the store, sniffing suspiciously for deadly chemicals. Mother went upstairs to our apartment over the store to get our electric fan. **E**

She came right back down empty-handed. "I think he's moved up there. I could hear him scratching behind the living room walls."

Father stared at the ceiling as if the rat had gone too far. "Leave it to me," he said. He fished his car keys from his pocket.

---

2. **exterminator** (ĭk-stûr′mə-nā′tər): a person whose job it is to get rid of insects or rodents.

3. **fumigated** (fyōō′mĭ-gāt′d): used smoke or fumes to kill rodents or insects.

**perpetual**
(pər-pĕch′ōō-əl) *adj.* continuing without interruption

**B CONFLICT**
Reread lines 28–33. Why does Yep feel "un-American" and "as if Eddy were Father's only true son"?

**C CONFLICT**
What **external conflict** is the Yep family facing?

**D CHRONOLOGICAL ORDER**
Describe Father's first two attempts to catch the rat. Add them to your chart.

**E CHRONOLOGICAL ORDER**
Reread lines 52–60. What words make clear the order in which events occurred? Add the events to your chart.

"Where are you going?" Mother asked.

Father, though, was a man of few words. He preferred to speak by his actions. "I'll be back soon."

An hour and a half later he returned with a rifle. He held it up for the three of us to examine. "Isn't it a beaut? Henry Loo loaned it to me." Henry Loo was
70 a pharmacist and one of Father's fishing buddies.

Mother frowned. "You can't shoot that cannon off in my house."

"It's just a twenty-two." Father tugged a box of cartridges out of his jacket pocket. "Let's go, boys."

Mother sucked in her breath sharply. "Thomas!"

Father was surprised by Mother's objection. "They've got to learn sometime."

Mother turned to us urgently. "It means killing. Like buying Grandpop's chickens. But you'll be the ones who have to make it dead."

"It's not the same," Father argued. "We won't have to twist its neck."

80 Buying the chicken was a chore that everyone tried to avoid at New Year's when Mother's father insisted on it. To make sure the chicken was fresh, we had to watch the poulterer[4] kill it. And then we had to collect the coppery-smelling blood in a jar for a special dish that only Mother's father would eat. For a moment, I felt queasy.

"You're scaring the boys," Father scolded her.

Mother glanced at him over her shoulder. "They ought to know what they're getting into."

I didn't believe in killing—unless it was a bug like a cockroach. However, I felt different when I saw a real rifle—the shiny barrel, the faint smell of oil,
90 the decorated wooden stock. I **rationalized** the hunt by telling myself I was not murdering rabbits or deer, just a mean old rat—like a furry kind of cockroach.

"What'll it be, boys?" Father asked.

Taking a deep breath, I nodded my head. "Yes, sir."

Father turned expectantly to Eddy and raised an eyebrow.

From next to me, though, Eddy murmured, "I think I'll help Mother." He wouldn't look at me.

Father seemed just as shocked as Mother and I. "Are you sure?"

Eddy drew back and mumbled miserably. "Yes, sir."

Mother gave me a quick peck on the cheek. "I expect you to still have ten
100 toes and ten fingers when you finish."

As we left the store, I felt funny. Part of me felt triumphant. For once, it was Eddy who had failed and not me. And yet another part of me wished I were staying with him and Mother. **F**

Father said nothing as we left the store and climbed the back stairs. As I trailed him, I thought he was silent because he was disappointed: He would rather have Eddy's help than mine.

**rationalize**
(răsh′ə-nə-liz′) *v.* to make explanations for one's behavior

**F** **CONFLICT**
Reread lines 88–103. Why is Yep torn between staying with his mother and going to help his father?

---

4. **poulterer** (pōl′tər-ər): a person who sells domestic fowls, such as chickens, turkeys, ducks, or geese.

At the back door of our apartment, he paused and said **brusquely,** "Now for some rules. First, never, never aim the rifle at anyone."

110 I listened as attentively as I had the disastrous times he'd tried to teach me how to dribble, or catch a football, or handle a pop foul. "I won't." I nodded earnestly.

Father pulled a lever near the middle of the gun. "Next, make sure the rifle is empty." He let me inspect the breech.[5] There was nothing inside.

"Yes, sir," I said and glanced up at him to read his mood. Because Father used so few words, he always sounded a little impatient whenever he taught me a lesson. However, it was hard to tell this time if it was genuine irritation or his normal **reserve.** **G**

He merely grunted. "Here. Open this." And he handed me the box of cartridges.

120 I was so nervous that the cartridges clinked inside the box when I took it. As I fumbled at the lid, I almost felt like apologizing for not being Eddy.

Now, when I got edgy, I was the opposite of Father: I got talkier. "How did you learn how to hunt?" I asked. "From your father?"

My father rarely spoke of his father, who had died before I was born. He **winced** now as if the rat had just nipped him. "My old man? Nah. He never had the time. I learned from some of my buddies in Chinatown."[6] He held out his hand.

I passed him a cartridge. "What did you hunt? Bear?"

"We shot quail." Father carefully loaded the rifle.

130 I was uncomfortable with the idea of shooting the cute little birds I saw in cartoons. "You did?"

He clicked the cartridge into the rifle. "You have to be tough in this world, boy. There are going to be some times when nobody's around to help—like when I first came to America."

That was a long speech for Father. "You had your father." His mother had stayed back in China, because in those days, America would not let her accompany her husband.

"He was too busy working." Father stared back down the stairs as if each step were a year. "When I first came here, I got beaten up by the white kids.
140 And when the white kids weren't around, there were the other Chinese kids."

I furrowed my forehead in puzzlement. I handed him another cartridge. "But they were your own kind."

He loaded the rifle steadily as I gave him the ammunition. "No, they weren't. The boys born here, they like to give a China-born a hard time. They thought I'd be easy pickings. But it was always a clean fight. No knives. No guns. Just our feet and fists. Not like the punks nowadays." He snapped the last cartridge into the rifle. "Then I learned how to play their games, and I made them my friends." He said the last part with pride. **H**

---

5. **breech:** the part of a gun behind the barrel.

6. **Chinatown:** the name given to some neighborhoods in which there is a large Chinese population with prominent Chinese cultural influence.

**brusquely** (brŭsk'lē) *adv.* in an abrupt, sudden manner

**reserve** (rĭ-zûrv') *n.* self-restraint in the way one looks or acts

**G** **CONFLICT**
How does Yep think his father sees him?

**wince** (wĭns) *v.* to flinch or shrink in pain or distress

**H** **CHRONOLOGICAL ORDER**
What action is taking place at the same time the father is talking about his past?

And suddenly I began to understand all the trophies and medals in our
150 living room. They were more than awards for sports. Each prize was a sign
that my father belonged to America—and at the same time, to Chinatown.
And that was why he tried so hard now to teach sports to Eddy and me.

When I finally understood what sports really meant to my father, it only
magnified the scale of my **ineptitude.** "I'm not good at fighting." As I closed
the lid on the box of ammunition, I thought I ought to prepare him for future
disappointments. "I'm not much good at anything."

Careful to keep the rifle pointed away from me, Father unlocked the door.
"I said you have to be tough, not stupid. No reason to get a beat-up old mug[7]
like mine."

160 I shook my head, bewildered. "What's wrong with your face?"

Father seemed amused. He stepped away from the door and jerked his head
for me to open it. "It's nothing that a steamroller couldn't fix."

"But you have an interesting face," I protested as I grabbed the doorknob.

"Are you blind, boy? This mug isn't ever going to win a beauty contest." He
chuckled. "I've been called a lot of names in my time, but never 'interesting.'
You've got a way with words."

ANALYZE VISUALS
How would you describe
the **mood** of this painting?
Tell what elements of the
image contribute to the
mood.

**ineptitude**
(ĭn-ĕp′tĭ-tōōd′) *n.*
clumsiness; lack of
competence

---

7. **mug:** face.

The doorknob was cold in my hand. "I do?"

Father adjusted his grip on the rifle. "I wouldn't buy any real estate from you." And he gave me an encouraging grin. "Now let's kill that rat."

170 When I opened the door, our home suddenly seemed as foreign to me as Africa. At first, I felt lonely—and a little scared. Then I heard Father reassure me, "I'm with you, boy."

Feeling more confident, I crept through the kitchen and into the living room. Father was right behind me and motioned me to search one half of the room while he explored the other. When I found a hole in the corner away from the fireplace, I caught Father's eye and pointed.

He peered under a chair with me and gave me an approving wink. "Give me a hand," he whispered.

In silent cooperation, we moved the chair aside and then shifted the 180 sofa over until it was between us and the rat hole. Bit by bit, Father and I constructed an upholstered **barricade.** I couldn't have been prouder if we'd built a whole fort together.

Father considerately left the lighter things for me to lift, and I was grateful for his thoughtfulness. The last thing I wanted was to get asthma now from overexertion. When we were done, Father got his rifle from the corner where he had left it temporarily.

As we crouched down behind our **improvised** wall, Father rested the rifle on it. "We'll take turns watching."

"Yes, sir," I said, peering over the barrier. There wasn't so much as a whisker 190 in the hole.

While I scanned the hole with intense radar eyes, Father tried to make himself comfortable by leaning against the sofa. It made me feel important to know Father trusted me; and I was determined to do well. In the center of the living room wall was the fireplace, and on its mantel stood Father's trophies like ranks of soldiers reminding me to be **vigilant.**

We remained in companionable silence for maybe three quarters of an hour. Suddenly, I saw something flicker near the mouth of the hole. "Father," I whispered. ❶

Father popped up alertly and took his rifle. Squeezing one eye shut, he 200 sighted on the rat hole. His crouching body grew tense. "Right." He adjusted his aim minutely. "Right. Take a breath," he recited to himself. "Take up the slack. Squeeze the trigger." Suddenly, he looked up, startled. "Where'd it go?"

As the gray shape darted forward, I could not control my panic. "It's coming straight at us."

The rifle barrel swung back and forth wildly as Father tried to aim. "Where?"

I thought I could see huge teeth and beady, violent eyes. The teeth were the size of daggers and the eyes were the size of baseballs, and they were getting bigger by the moment. It was the rat of all rats. "Shoot it!" I yelled.

**barricade** (băr′ĭ-kād′) *n.* a structure that blocks passage

**improvised** (ĭm′prə-vīzd′) *adj.* to put together with little preparation or planning **improvise** *v.*

**vigilant** (vĭj′ə-lənt) *adj.* watchful; alert

❶ **CONFLICT**
Reread line 196. Compare the "companionable silence" Yep describes here with an earlier statement, "I thought he was silent because he was disappointed." Why does Yep view the silence differently the second time?

210 "Where?" Father shouted desperately.

My courage evaporated. All I could think of was escape. "It's charging." Springing to my feet, I darted from the room.

"Oh, man," Father said, and his footsteps pounded after me.

In a blind panic, I bolted out of the apartment and down the back stairs and into the store. **J**

"Get the SPCA[8]. I think the rat's mad," Father yelled as he slammed the door behind him.

Mother took the rifle from him. "I'd be annoyed too if someone were trying to shoot me."

220 "No." Father panted. "I mean it's rabid."[9] We could hear the rat scurrying above us in the living room. It sounded as if it were doing a victory dance.

Mother made Father empty the rifle. "You return that to Henry Loo tomorrow," she said. "We'll learn to live with the rat."

As she stowed the rifle in the storeroom, Father tried to regather his dignity. "It may have fleas," he called after her.

Now that my panic was over, I suddenly became aware of the enormity of what I had done. Father had counted on me to help him, and yet I had run, leaving him to the **ravages** of that monster. I was worse than a failure. I was a coward. I had deserted Father right at the time he needed me most. I wouldn't

230 blame him if he kicked me out of his family.

It took what little nerve I had left to look up at my father. At that moment, he seemed to tower over me, as grand and remote as a monument. "I'm sorry," I said miserably.

He drew his eyebrows together as he clinked the shells in his fist. "For what?"

It made me feel even worse to have to explain in front of Eddy. "For running," I said wretchedly.

He chuckled as he dumped the cartridges into his shirt pocket. "Well, I ran too. Sometimes it's smart to be scared."

240 "When were you ever scared?" I challenged him.

He buttoned his pocket. "Plenty of times. Like when I came to America. They had to pry my fingers from the boat railing."

It was the first time I'd ever heard my father confess to that failing. "But you're the best at everything."

"Nobody's good at everything." He gave his head a little shake as if the very notion puzzled him. "Each of us is good at some things and lousy at others. The trick is to find something that you're good at."

I thought again of the mantel where all of Father's sports trophies stood. Eddy gave every promise of collecting just as many, but I knew I would be

250 lucky to win even one.

"I'm lousy at sports," I confessed.

**J** CHRONOLOGICAL ORDER
How much time do you think passes from when Yep and his father begin their rat hunt until they give up? Explain your reasoning.

**ravage** (răv'ĭj) *n.* serious damage or destruction

---

8. **SPCA:** Society for the Prevention of Cruelty to Animals.

9. **rabid:** affected by the viral disease rabies.

His eyes flicked back and forth, as if my face were a book open for his inspection. He seemed surprised by what he read there.

Slowly his knees bent until we were looking eye to eye. "Then you'll find something else," he said and put his arm around me. My father never let people touch him. In fact, I hardly ever saw him hug Mother. As his arm tightened, I felt a real love and assurance in that embrace.

Shortly after that, the rat left as mysteriously as it had come. "I must've scared it off," Father announced.

260 Mother shook her head. "That rat laughed itself to death."

Father disappeared into the storeroom: and for a moment we all thought Mother had gone too far. Then we heard the electric saw that he kept back there. "What are you doing?" Mother called.

He came back out with a block of wood about two inches square. He was carefully sandpapering the splinters from the edges. "Maybe some day we'll find the corpse. Its head ought to look real good over the fireplace."

Mother was trying hard to keep a straight face. "You can't have a trophy head unless you shoot it."

"If it died of laughter like you said, then I killed it," he insisted proudly. 270 "Sure as if I pulled the trigger." He winked at me. "Get the varnish out for our trophy will you?"

I was walking away when I realized he had said "our." I turned and said, "That rat was doomed from the start." I heard my parents both laughing as I hurried away. ❧

**K** CONFLICT
How has Yep's relationship with his father changed since the beginning of the story?

## Comprehension

**INDIANA STANDARDS**

**READING STANDARD**
**8.3.2** Evaluate the structural elements of the plot ....

1. **Recall** How do Laurence and his brother differ?

2. **Recall** What compliment does Laurence's father give him?

3. **Clarify** What happens to the rat at the end of the selection?

## Literary Analysis

4. **Identify Chronological Order** Review the chart you made as you read. Does it contain all the important events of the selection? If not, add them now. Then use your chart to tell what happened right before Father ran out of the apartment. What happened right after?

5. **Examine Conflict** In a conflict map like the one shown, note one of the selection's most important conflicts and the events that lead to its **resolution,** or outcome.

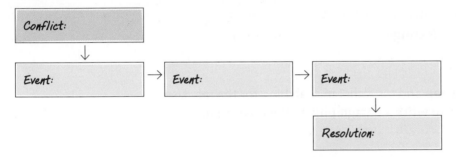

6. **Analyze Characters** Even though Yep was **scared,** he still agreed to help his father capture the rat. What do you learn about Yep from his actions?

7. **Compare and Contrast** Compare Yep's feelings about his role in the family in the beginning of the selection with his feelings at the end. How are they different?

8. **Interpret Meaning** Reread lines 270–271. What do you think it means that Yep's father uses the word "our" to refer to the trophy?

## Extension and Challenge

9. **Creative Project: Drama** With two other classmates, rehearse a dramatic reading of the rat-hunt scene. Have one student play the role of Father, one student play the role of Yep, and one student act as the narrator. Perform your reading for the class.

10. **Readers' Circle** Yep's father says, "Sometimes it's smart to be scared." Do you think the encounter with the rat was one of those times, or is Yep's father just trying to make himself and his son feel better? Refer to the selection as you discuss the question.

# Vocabulary in Context

## VOCABULARY PRACTICE

For each item, choose the word that differs most in meaning from the other words.

1. (a) justify, (b) rationalize, (c) multiply, (d) explain
2. (a) improvised, (b) ad-libbed, (c) invented, (d) practiced
3. (a) openness, (b) modesty, (c) reserve, (d) coolness
4. (a) destruction, (b) ravage, (c) construction, (d) ruin
5. (a) keen, (b) inattentive, (c) observant, (d) vigilant
6. (a) ineptitude, (b) awkwardness, (c) incompetence, (d) gracefulness
7. (a) finite, (b) infinite, (c) constant, (d) perpetual
8. (a) abruptly, (b) gruffly, (c) brusquely, (d) kindly
9. (a) walkway, (b) barricade, (c) fence, (d) obstruction
10. (a) flinch, (b) wince, (c) strut, (d) cringe

barricade  rationalize
brusquely  ravage
improvised  reserve
ineptitude  vigilant
perpetual  wince

## VOCABULARY IN WRITING

Imagine you are trying to assist Yep and his father in searching for the rat. Use three or more vocabulary words to write a paragraph about your experience. You could start like this.

> **EXAMPLE SENTENCE**
>
> The appearance of the rat made me **wince**.

## VOCABULARY STRATEGY: ONOMATOPOEIA

Onomatopoeia is the use of words whose sounds suggest their meaning. Yep uses onomatopoeia in "The Great Rat Hunt" when he writes: "In the fall, it was the smack of a football." *Smack* is a word that sounds like what it means.

**PRACTICE** In the following sentences, identify the words that are examples of onomatopoeia.

1. You could hear the tick-tock of the clock.
2. The fire crackled as the logs burned.
3. I love to pop popcorn.
4. The crowd was buzzing with excitement.
5. He plopped down in the chair to watch the movie.

**VOCABULARY PRACTICE**
For more practice, go to the **Vocabulary Center** at **ClassZone.com**.

# Reading-Writing Connection

Broaden your understanding of "The Great Rat Hunt" by responding to these prompts. Then complete the **Grammar and Writing** exercise.

| WRITING PROMPTS | SELF-CHECK |
|---|---|
| **A. Short Response: Write a Description**<br>Write a **one-paragraph description** of the rat hunt from the rat's point of view. In the rat's own words (using the pronoun *I*), tell how you outsmarted Mr. Yep and whether you were ever **scared.** | *A strong description will . . .*<br>• relate the main events of the rat hunt<br>• give a believable account from the rat's point of view |
| **B. Extended Response: Compare and Contrast**<br>Both Laurence Yep and his father felt like outsiders. In **two or three paragraphs,** compare their experiences, including the conflicts each person faced and how he dealt with them. | *A detailed response will . . .*<br>• identify similarities and differences between the son's and father's experiences<br>• cite the conflicts each faced |

## GRAMMAR AND WRITING

 INDIANA STANDARDS

**WRITING STANDARD**
**8.4.8** Edit and proofread one's own writing, as well as that of others . . . .

***USE CORRECT PRONOUN CASE*** People often misuse the subject and object cases of personal pronouns, especially in sentences containing a compound subject. **Subject pronouns** function as just that—the subject of a sentence. They include the words *I, he, she, we,* and *they.* **Object pronouns** function as the object of a sentence and include the words *me, him, her, us,* and *them.* (*You* and *it* function as both subject and object pronouns.)

> *Original:* Him and his brother have different interests and abilities.
>
> *Revised:* He and his brother have different interests and abilities.
> (*The pronoun is functioning as a subject, so it should be* he.)

> *Original:* I outsmarted his father and he.
>
> *Revised:* I outsmarted his father and him. (*The pronoun is functioning as an object, so it should be* him, *not* he.)

***PRACTICE*** Choose the correct pronoun to complete each sentence.

1. Laurence thinks his father is disappointed in (him, he).
2. One day, (they, them) and the rat confront each other.
3. (Him, He) and his father both have something in common, Laurence discovers.
4. As readers, you and (me, I) learn that even his father isn't perfect.

*For more help with pronoun cases, see page R53 in the **Grammar Handbook.***

## Paul Revere's Ride
Poem by Henry Wadsworth Longfellow

# When does truth become
# LEGEND?

**INDIANA STANDARDS**

**READING STANDARDS**
**8.3.1** Determine and articulate the relationship between the purposes and characteristics of different forms of poetry . . . .

**8.3.2** Evaluate the structural elements of the plot, such as subplots, parallel episodes, and climax; the plot's development; and the way in which conflicts are (or are not) addressed and resolved.

**KEY IDEA** George Washington was an amazing leader, but did he really never, ever lie? When highly regarded people are famous for long enough, they sometimes become **legends,** and the stories about them are exaggerated. You're about to read a poem featuring one such person.

**DISCUSS** In a small group, come up with a list of people you consider legendary. Think about sports heroes, performers, and historical figures. What do these people have in common? Why do you think they became legends? Share your ideas with the class.

## ● LITERARY ANALYSIS: NARRATIVE POETRY

You've read fictional stories, true stories, and stories presented dramatically. Now you're about to read a **narrative poem,** which is a poem that tells a story. Like a short story, a narrative poem has the following elements:

- a **plot,** or series of events that center on a conflict faced by a main character

- a **setting,** the time and place(s) where the story occurs; setting is usually established in the exposition stage of the plot

- **character(s),** or the individual or individuals who take part in the action

As you read "Paul Revere's Ride," notice how Longfellow uses story elements to describe Paul Revere's adventures.

*Review:* **Suspense**

## ● READING SKILL: PARAPHRASE

Have you ever explained a complex idea using easier language, or retold a story in your own words? Restating complete information in simpler terms is called **paraphrasing.** A good paraphrase includes all of the main ideas and supporting details of the original source and is usually just as long, or longer. Paraphrasing challenging passages can help you better understand them. As you read "Paul Revere's Ride," use a chart like the one shown to paraphrase parts of the poem, such as the following lines, that may be difficult to understand:

Original: *Meanwhile, his friend through alley and street*
*Wanders and watches, with eager ears . . .*

Paraphrase: *At the same time, his friend walks through quiet streets and alleys, looking and listening carefully.*

| Line Numbers | Paraphrase |
|---|---|
|  |  |

# Author Online

**An Accomplished Teenager** When he was just 14, Henry Wadsworth Longfellow was accepted into Bowdoin College in Maine. He did well in his studies and had nearly 40 poems published before he graduated. He learned French, Italian, and Spanish and translated famous literary works into English.

Henry Wadsworth
Longfellow
1807–1882

**World Fame** After traveling in Europe, Longfellow returned to teach at Harvard University. He continued to write poetry that explored many important American themes. Works such as *The Song of Hiawatha* and *Tales of a Wayside Inn,* which includes "Paul Revere's Ride," brought American history to the attention of readers around the world. Though the death of his wife in 1861 made Longfellow deeply depressed, he remained extraordinarily kind, courteous, and generous. He never refused to give an autograph or welcome visitors who sometimes lingered around his house, hoping for a glimpse of the famous author.

## *Background*

By 1775, many American colonists had begun to rebel against the British government's interference in their affairs. On the night of April 18, British troops left Boston, heading to Concord to arrest the rebel leaders and seize their weapons stockpile. Hoping to warn the rebel leaders of the British advance, Paul Revere, along with William Dawes and Dr. Samuel Prescott, set off on a ride that would make Revere a legend.

**MORE ABOUT THE AUTHOR AND BACKGROUND**
To learn more about Longfellow and the Revolutionary War, visit the **Literature Center** at ClassZone.com.

# Paul Revere's Ride

## HENRY WADSWORTH LONGFELLOW

Listen, my children, and you shall hear
Of the midnight ride of Paul Revere,
On the eighteenth of April, in Seventy-five;
Hardly a man is now alive
5 Who remembers that famous day and year.

He said to his friend, "If the British march
By land or sea from the town to-night,
Hang a lantern aloft in the belfry arch
Of the North Church tower as a signal light,—
10 One if by land, and two if by sea;
And I on the opposite shore will be,
Ready to ride and spread the alarm
Through every Middlesex[1] village and farm,
For the country folk to be up and to arm." **A**

**ANALYZE VISUALS**
What **mood** does this
painting convey?

**A NARRATIVE POETRY**
According to the first two
stanzas, where does the
poem take place?

---

1. **Middlesex:** a county in eastern Massachusetts—the setting of the first
battle of the Revolutionary War on April 19, 1775.

Illustration by Christopher Bing.

15 Then he said "Good-night!" and with muffled oar
Silently rowed to the Charlestown shore,
Just as the moon rose over the bay,
Where swinging wide at her moorings[2] lay
The *Somerset,* British man-of-war;[3]
20 A phantom ship, with each mast and spar[4]
Across the moon like a prison bar,
And a huge black hulk, that was magnified
By its own reflection in the tide. **B**

Meanwhile, his friend through alley and street
25 Wanders and watches, with eager ears,
Till in the silence around him he hears
The muster of men at the barrack door,
The sound of arms, and the tramp of feet,
And the measured tread of the grenadiers,[5]
30 Marching down to their boats on the shore.

**B** **NARRATIVE POETRY**
What is the **conflict** being described?

---

2. **moorings:** the place where the ship is docked.

3. **man-of-war:** a warship, often a large sailing ship, bearing canons and other guns.

4. **spar:** a pole supporting a ship's sail.

5. **grenadiers** (grĕn´ə-dîrz´): British foot soldiers.

Then he climbed the tower of the Old North Church,
By the wooden stairs, with stealthy tread,[6]
To the belfry chamber overhead,
And startled the pigeons from their perch
35 On the somber[7] rafters, that round him made
Masses and moving shapes of shade,—
By the trembling ladder, steep and tall,
To the highest window in the wall,
Where he paused to listen and look down
40 A moment on the roofs of the town
And the moonlight flowing over all. **C**

Beneath, in the churchyard, lay the dead,
In their night encampment on the hill,
Wrapped in silence so deep and still
45 That he could hear, like a sentinel's[8] tread,
The watchful night-wind, as it went
Creeping along from tent to tent,
And seeming to whisper, "All is well!"
A moment only he feels the spell
50 Of the place and the hour, and the secret dread
Of the lonely belfry and the dead;
For suddenly all his thoughts are bent
On a shadowy something far away,
Where the river widens to meet the bay,—
55 A line of black that bends and floats
On the rising tide like a bridge of boats. **D**

Meanwhile, impatient to mount and ride,
Booted and spurred, with a heavy stride
On the opposite shore walked Paul Revere.
60 Now he patted his horse's side,
Now he gazed at the landscape far and near,
Then, impetuous,[9] stamped the earth,
And turned and tightened his saddle girth;[10]
But mostly he watched with eager search

---

6. **stealthy tread:** quiet footsteps.

7. **somber:** gloomy.

8. **sentinel:** a guard or sentry.

9. **impetuous** (ĭm-pĕch'o͞o-əs): acting suddenly, on impulse.

10. **saddle girth:** the strap attaching a saddle to a horse's body.

65 The belfry tower of the Old North Church,
As it rose above the graves on the hill,
Lonely and spectral[11] and somber and still.
And lo! as he looks, on the belfry's height
A glimmer, and then a gleam of light!
70 He springs to the saddle, the bridle he turns,
But lingers and gazes, till full on his sight
A second lamp in the belfry burns. **E**

A hurry of hoofs in a village street,
A shape in the moonlight, a bulk in the dark,
75 And beneath, from the pebbles, in passing, a spark
Struck out by a steed flying fearless and fleet;
That was all! And yet, through the gloom and the light,
The fate of a nation was riding that night;
And the spark struck out by that steed, in his flight,
80 Kindled the land into flame with its heat.
He has left the village and mounted the steep,
And beneath him, tranquil and broad and deep,
Is the Mystic,[12] meeting the ocean tides;
And under the alders[13] that skirt its edge,
85 Now soft on the sand, now loud on the ledge,
Is heard the tramp of his steed as he rides. **F**

It was twelve by the village clock,
When he crossed the bridge into Medford town.
He heard the crowing of the cock,
90 And the barking of the farmer's dog,
And felt the damp of the river fog,
That rises after the sun goes down.

It was one by the village clock,
When he galloped into Lexington.
95 He saw the gilded weathercock
Swim in the moonlight as he passed,
And the meeting-house windows, black and bare,
Gaze at him with a spectral glare,
As if they already stood aghast[14]
100 At the bloody work they would look upon.

**E NARRATIVE POETRY**
Who are the **characters** in
this narrative poem?

**F PARAPHRASE**
Reread the lines 73–80.
What's happening in this
passage? Paraphrase the
passage and add it to
your chart.

---

11. **spectral:** ghostly.
12. **Mystic:** a short river flowing into Boston Harbor.
13. **alder:** tree of the birch family.
14. **aghast:** (ə-găst'): terrified.

It was two by the village clock,
When he came to the bridge in Concord town.
He heard the bleating[15] of the flock,
And the twitter of birds among the trees,
105 And felt the breath of the morning breeze
Blowing over the meadow brown.
And one was safe and asleep in his bed
Who at the bridge would be first to fall,
Who that day would be lying dead,
110 Pierced by a British musket ball.

You know the rest. In the books you have read
How the British Regulars[16] fired and fled,—
How the farmers gave them ball for ball,
From behind each fence and farmyard wall,
115 Chasing the redcoats down the lane,
Then crossing the fields to emerge again
Under the trees at the turn of the road,
And only pausing to fire and load. **G**

So through the night rode Paul Revere;
120 And so through the night went his cry of alarm
To every Middlesex village and farm,—
A cry of defiance, and not of fear,
A voice in the darkness, a knock at the door,
And a word that shall echo for evermore!
125 For, borne on the night-wind of the Past,
Through all our history, to the last,
In the hour of darkness and peril[17] and need,
The people will waken and listen to hear
The hurrying hoof-beats of that steed,
130 And the midnight message of Paul Revere.

**G** **NARRATIVE POETRY**
What is the **climax** of the plot? Give reasons for your answer.

---

15. **bleating:** the cry of sheep.
16. **British Regulars:** members of Great Britain's standing army.
17. **peril:** danger.

## Comprehension

**INDIANA STANDARDS**

**READING STANDARD**
**8.3.1** Determine and articulate the …characteristics of different forms of poetry….

1. **Recall** How many lanterns were hung in the belfry of the Old North Church? What do they signify?

2. **Summarize** In your own words, describe what Paul Revere hoped to accomplish with his late-night ride.

3. **Represent** Reread lines 37–56. Draw what you think Revere's friend sees from the bell tower.

## Literary Analysis

4. **Analyze Narrative Poetry** In a chart like the one shown, note the story elements in "Paul Revere's Ride." Then tell the main conflict and how it is resolved.

| | "Paul Revere's Ride" |
|---|---|
| Setting | |
| Characters | |
| Main Plot Events | • <br> • |

5. **Understand Paraphrasing** Now that you've read the whole poem, review the paraphrases you wrote in your chart as you read. Did you capture the correct meaning in each case? If not, revise your paraphrases.

6. **Analyze Suspense** How did Longfellow create tension and excitement in the poem? Consider the way he used **language, rhythm, rhyme,** and **repetition.** Cite specific details to support your answer.

7. **Evaluate Sensory Details** "Paul Revere's Ride" is full of descriptive language that appeals to the senses. List two or three images that you find most striking. Why did you choose these?

8. **Draw Conclusions** Reread lines 119–130. On the basis of this stanza, why do you think Paul Revere became an American **legend?**

## Extension and Challenge

9.  **SOCIAL STUDIES CONNECTION** Paul Revere did more in his life than ride to warn the colonists that the British army was on its way. Find out where he lived, what he did for a living, and about his involvement in the "Sons of Liberty" before and during the American Revolution. Share your findings with the class.

> **RESEARCH LINKS**
> For more on Paul Revere, visit the **Research Center** at **ClassZone.com.**

# The Other Riders
History Article

## What's the Connection?

The poem you just read celebrates Paul Revere, but did you know he was not the only brave rider on the eve of the Revolutionary War? The following article tells about two equally important but lesser-known heroes: William Dawes and Samuel Prescott.

## Skill Focus: Take Notes

When you read an article for social studies or science class, how do you absorb all the facts? One good way to digest a lot of information is to **take notes.** Writing down important facts and ideas can help you remember them.

Here are some tips for note-taking:

- First, preview the article by looking at its title, subheadings, topic sentences, and graphic aids to determine its topic and main ideas.

- Next, decide how to organize your notes. Can you use the subheadings to create a simple outline or a graphic organizer like the one shown?

- As you take notes, record the main ideas and only the most important facts and details under the appropriate headings. Be sure to include the names, dates, and terms that are necessary for a full understanding of the material.

For help taking notes on the following selection, use a graphic organizer like the one started here.

Use with "Paul Revere's Ride," page 134.

INDIANA STANDARDS

**READING & WRITING STANDARDS**
**8.2.7** Analyze the structure, format, and purpose of informational materials (such as textbooks, newspapers, instructional or technical manuals, and public documents).

**8.5.7** Write for different purposes and to a specific audience or person, adjusting tone and style as necessary.

| Subheadings | Notes |
|---|---|
| Rumors of a March on Concord | Night of April 18, 1775, a rumor reaches William Dawes that the British are planning to take ammunition in Concord.<br><br>Dawes tells Paul Revere; both get orders from Dr. Joseph Warren to ride to inform the leaders of the Provincial Congress of what's going on. |
| Sneaking Past Guards | |

BACK   FORWARD   STOP   REFRESH   HOME   PRINT

# The Other Riders

 PBS

Late on the night of April 18, 1775, Boston patriot Joseph Warren learned of a British military operation planned for the next day. To warn John Hancock and Samuel Adams, who were across the Charles River in Lexington, Warren dispatched two riders, Paul Revere and William Dawes. Revere's ride has been celebrated in poems and textbooks, but
10 Dawes's role was at least as important.

*William Dawes* (unknown), attributed to John Johnston. Oil on canvas, 35″ × 29″. © Collection of the Evanston Historical Society, Evanston, Illinois.

## Rumors of a March on Concord

On the night of April 18, 1775, rumors of a planned British action to seize ammunition in the town of Concord raced through Boston. Word reached William Dawes, a tanner, who told Paul Revere—who had heard about it from two others already. The two men received orders from Dr. Joseph Warren to ride to inform the leaders of the Provincial Congress of the developments.

## Sneaking Past Guards

Dawes's route led him to the British guards at the gate of Boston Neck—the narrowest part of the isthmus—as he rode south out of the
20 city. A naturally witty and friendly man, Dawes had spent numerous afternoons sneaking in and out of the city without being stopped. He would disguise himself as a peddler, smuggling gold coins disguised as buttons that he wore sewn on his coat. Dawes also befriended any British guards who seemed amicable. On the historic night, one of his buddies was on duty. When the guard opened the gate for some British soldiers, Dawes slipped through with them. **A**

## Spreading the Word

On his ride west, Dawes alerted more riders, who in turn rallied companies from neighboring towns: Dedham, Needham, Framingham, Newton and Watertown. Avoiding trouble, Dawes made good time and
30 caught up to Revere in Lexington just after midnight. After notifying Hancock and Adams, Dawes and Revere set out for Concord together,

**F**OCUS ON FORM
You are about to read a **history article,** a nonfiction article about real events and people of historical importance.

**A** TAKE NOTES
What is the most important information in this section? Make sure to note it under the subheading.

joined by Dr. Samuel Prescott, a Concord resident who had been visiting a girlfriend.

### A Clever Escape

Revere, riding in front, ran into a British roadblock. Dawes and Prescott were captured before they could be warned. As the British tried to lead them into a 40 meadow, Prescott signaled that they should make their escape, and all three rode off. Back on the road towards Lexington, Dawes realized that his horse was too tired to outrun the Redcoats. As he pulled up in the yard of a house, he reared his horse and shouted, "I've got two of them—surround them!" His trick succeeded in scaring off his pursuers, although he fell from his horse and lost his watch.

This map of eastern Massachusetts shows the route of each rider. **B**

### Prescott Warns Concord

Prescott, the local, rode off toward Concord through fields and creek beds 50 that he knew, quickly outdistancing his would-be captors. It was Prescott who warned the town of Concord of the impending British march. **C**

### So Forgotten It's Funny

Over the years, Dawes's relative anonymity has become something of a joke. In 1896, Helen F. Moore published a parody of Longfellow's famous poem about the historic night, entitled "The Midnight Ride of William Dawes," one verse of which reads:

> 'Tis all very well for the children to hear
> Of the midnight ride of Paul Revere;
> But why should my name be quite forgot,
> Who rode as boldly and well, God wot?
> 60   Why should I ask? The reason is clear—
> My name was Dawes and his Revere.

A cartoon in the early 1960s turned on the same humor, namely that "Dawes" was a name less suited for rhyming than "Revere" (in that comic strip, Longfellow is stuck on "Listen my children while I pause, to tell the ride of William Dawes." when his wife suggests using the name of that other rider). **D**

---

**B  HISTORY ARTICLE**
History articles often contain maps, timelines, and other graphic aids to help you track the details presented in the text. As you read this article, follow Revere's, Dawes's, and Prescott's progress on this map.

**C  TAKE NOTES**
What surprising fact do you learn from this section? Be sure to add this to your notes.

**D  HISTORY ARTICLE**
This history article primarily tells about the true story of the people and events of April 18, 1775. What does the additional information in this last section help you understand?

# Comprehension

1. **Recall** Who was sent to warn John Hancock and Samuel Adams about a British military operation?

2. **Clarify** What kind of person was William Dawes?

3. **Clarify** What "near miss" did the riders encounter as they rode to Concord?

# Critical Analysis

4. **Use Your Notes** Use your notes to create a timeline of the historic events that occurred on the night of April 18, 1775.

5. **Understand a History Article** Now that you've read this history article, what do you think are the main points the author wants to make about the events of April 18, 1775?

**INDIANA STANDARDS**

**READING & WRITING STANDARDS**
**8.2.7** Analyze the structure, format, and purpose of informational materials (such as textbooks, newspapers, instructional or technical manuals, and public documents).

**8.5.7** Write for different purposes and to a specific audience or person, adjusting tone and style as necessary.

# Read for Information: Compare and Contrast

**WRITING PROMPT**

How does the information in "The Other Riders" match up with the story told in "Paul Revere's Ride"? In a paragraph, compare and contrast the legend in the poem with the true account of that night as it is presented in the historical article.

Remember that when you **compare and contrast,** you identify the ways in which two or more things are alike and different. Then follow these steps:

1. In a chart like the one shown, identify the main people and events in the poem. Then identify the main people and events in the article.

2. Note the differences between the two accounts in the last column of the chart.

3. In a sentence, make a general statement about the similarities and differences in the accounts. Support your statement with specific examples.

| | from "Paul Revere's Ride" | from "The Other Riders" | Differences |
|---|---|---|---|
| Main Participants | | | |
| Main Events | | | |

# Writing Workshop

# Personal Narrative

Like the characters in this unit, you have played a part in many memorable events. Check out the **Writer's Road Map** to get started writing your own personal narrative about something unforgettable that happened to you.

## WRITER'S ROAD MAP

### Personal Narrative

#### WRITING PROMPT 1

**Writing from Your Life** Write a personal narrative telling about a special experience in your life. Include details that will help your reader understand what the experience was like. Be sure to explain why it was important to you.

**Experiences to Consider**

- your first day in a new place
- a special accomplishment

#### WRITING PROMPT 2

**Writing from Literature** Sometimes an incident or a conflict in a literary work can remind you of a similar experience in your own life. Choose an incident or conflict from one of the stories in this unit. Describe the event and tell what similar thing happened to you.

**Experiences and Literary Works to Consider**

- a time when you learned something new about another person ("Raymond's Run")
- a time when you felt guilty ("The Tell-Tale Heart")

**WRITING TOOLS**
For prewriting, revision, and editing tools, visit the **Writing Center** at **ClassZone.com**.

### KEY TRAITS

**1. IDEAS**
- Focuses on a single **experience**
- Re-creates the experience with **descriptive details** and **dialogue**

**2. ORGANIZATION**
- "Hooks" readers with an attention-getting **introduction**
- Uses transitions to make the **order of events** clear
- Has a **conclusion** that summarizes the meaning of the experience

**3. VOICE**
- Has a **style** that reflects the writer's personality

**4. WORD CHOICE**
- Brings the experience alive for the reader with **sensory language**

**5. SENTENCE FLUENCY**
- Includes a variety of **sentence types** (statements, questions, and exclamations)

**6. CONVENTIONS**
- Uses **correct grammar, spelling, and punctuation**

# Part 1: Analyze a Student Model

**WRITING STANDARD**
**8.5.1** Write biographies, autobiographies, and short stories....

**Joe Sanders**
**Humphrey Middle School**

**Jalapeños, Anyone?**

**KEY TRAITS IN ACTION**

It was an ingenious idea. It was *my* idea. During lunch one day, we loaded up two trays with as many jalapeño peppers as they would hold. Then the fun began.

> Intriguing **introduction** makes the reader want to find out about the writer's **experience.**

Let me tell you how it all started. Tom and I were in the cafeteria,
5  eating. It was fourth period in May. I grunted with a mouth full of ham, "I got an idea." Tom was so busy eating his hot dog with everything on it that he didn't hear me.

"*Tom!*" I yelled, sending bits of ham onto his tray.

"What? Huh?" he replied, looking up from his hot dog momentarily.

> Includes **dialogue** that matches what people said at the time, even if it contains slang or mistakes in grammar.

10 Tom is my best friend, and he looks exactly like me. If we told you we were twins with different last names, you would probably believe us. We have brown hair and blue eyes. We also wear rimless glasses. We think alike, too.

"So let's hear this great idea of yours," Tom stated, brushing ham
15 from his fries.

> **Descriptive details** and **sensory language** bring the people and action to life.

"Well, seeing as you like your jalapeños. . . ." I paused for a moment and pointed at his hot dog, which was covered in them. "Maybe you would like to have an eating contest with someone." He didn't hesitate. We decided that Anahi, who is Mexican (and in our heads used to hot
20 stuff), should be the other contestant. She thought it was a good idea, too.

After they each had a tray full of jalapeños in front of them, I started the countdown. "On your mark, get set, go!" Anahi put two in her mouth, then spat them out and ran to the drinking fountain, forfeiting the contest. The rules stated that once you took a drink or ate anything
25 else, you were out of the running.

> Transition words make the **order of events** clear.

Meanwhile, Tom was stuffing peppers 37 and 38 in his mouth. He just kept eating, as though he didn't know that his rival had given up. We turned our attention to him and started counting off the jalapeños as he shoveled them in.

30     "Come on, Tom. You can do it!" I encouraged, pounding the table. "50, 51, 52, 53, 54 . . . Come on . . . 55, 56, 57."

"Yahoo!" Tom shouted. He threw up his hands in triumph even though he looked like he would actually throw up.

The crowd went wild. "All right, Tom!" I yelled. People around us

35 started clapping as he ran frantically to the drinking fountain. When he got back, I handed him his prize—a bag of candy, as promised.

"I am never eating another jalapeño pepper in my life," Tom proclaimed after stuffing his face with chocolate bars. I couldn't do anything but laugh.

40     It's a little harder to get Tom to partake in my other schemes since I sent him to the drinking fountain for hours! I still have hope that he can pack down 58 peppers if he just works at it, though. I'm sure you can imagine how much luck I'm having convincing him to try.

What about you? Bon appétit!

> Includes more **dialogue** to show, rather than tell about, Tom's victory.

> This writer's **style** is informal and humorous.

> Different **sentence types** (statements, questions, and exclamations) keep the narrative lively. **Conclusion** explains why the writer remembers the experience.

2

# Part 2: Apply the Writing Process

**WRITING STANDARD**
**8.4.1** Discuss ideas for writing . . . and use graphic organizers to plan writing.

## PREWRITING

| *What Should I Do?* | *What Does It Look Like?* |
|---|---|

**1. Choose an experience to share.**
Take a trip through your memory. List funny, sad, or exciting experiences you have had. Put a star by the one that would be most interesting for you to write about and for your audience to read.

**TIP** **If you are having trouble thinking of experiences, look back at the Writer's Road Map on page 144.**

▶

**Interesting Experiences**
jalapeño contest ✱
whale-watching trip
baby-sitting the Salgado twins
kitchen fire at Aunt Erica's
breaking my arm during spring vacation

**2. What happened? When?**
Use a spider map, a cluster diagram, or another graphic organizer to help you gather important facts about the incident. Thinking about the major elements of a story—characters, setting, and action—can help jog your memory.

**TIP** **If this experience is too personal to share with your teacher and classmates, go back to your list and choose a different event.**

▶

**3. Re-create the action for your reader.**
Think of lively words to describe what happened. Write down the actual words that others said. These descriptions and quotations will help your reader feel like he or she is experiencing the event right alongside you.

▶

**Descriptions:**
It was my ingenious idea...
Tom ran frantically to the water fountain.
**Quotations:**
"So let's hear this great idea of yours."
"Come on, Tom. You can do it!"

**4. Think about what the experience meant to you.**
Write a sentence or two explaining the meaning of your experience. You will probably want to include this statement in your narrative, but thinking about it as you draft can also keep your writing on track.

▶

Why do I remember the contest? It was a fantastic idea, and it made me laugh. Also, Tom is more cautious about going along with my schemes now.

| What Should I Do? | What Does It Look Like? |
|---|---|

**1. Plan how to tell your narrative.**
Use a flow chart to get organized. Make sure you haven't left out any important steps.

Describing the incident in **chronological order** (also called time order) is usually the clearest way to help readers understand what happened. If you want, you can include a **flashback**. That's an event that took place before the start of your narrative.

Tom and I are eating lunch.
↓
I get the idea of having a jalapeño-eating contest.
↓
Tom and Anahi agree to do it.
↓
We collect two trays of peppers.
↓
Anahi forfeits.
↓
Tom eats 57 peppers.
↓
I give him his prize.
↓
He vows not to eat jalapeños again.

**2. Capture your reader's interest.**
Write an introduction that makes your reader curious. Set the scene, describe a character, explain an action, or include a quotation. Some narratives begin by asking the reader a question.

It was an ingenious idea. It was <u>my</u> idea. During lunch one day, we loaded up two trays with as many jalapeño peppers as they would hold. Then the fun began.

Let me tell you how it all started. Tom and I were in the cafeteria, eating. It was fourth period in May. I grunted with a mouth full of ham, "I got an idea." Tom was so busy eating his hot dog with everything on it that he didn't hear me.

**3. Make the most of dialogue.**
Instead of writing "this happened, and then this happened," try including dialogue that shows your reader what happened.

**See page 150:** Check Your Grammar

**TIP** Before you revise, look back at the **key traits on page 144** and the **rubric and peer-reader questions on page 150.**

**From prewriting notes . . .**
I got the idea of having a jalapeño-eating contest. Then I told Tom about it.

**. . . to draft**
"Well, seeing as you like your jalapeños. . . ." I paused for a moment and pointed at his hot dog, which was covered in them. "Maybe you would like to have an eating contest with someone."

## REVISING AND EDITING

| **What Should I Do?** | **What Does It Look Like?** |

**1. Check the sequence of events.**
- Ask a peer reader to <u>underline</u> events that seem confusing or out of order.
- Add transitions or move information around to specify what happened when.

**See page 150:** Ask a Peer Reader

▶ People around us started clapping, ^as He ran frantically to the drinking fountain, I handed him his prize—a bag of candy, as promised.
When he got back,

**2. Add sensory language.**
- (Circle) words that describe how things looked, sounded, tasted, felt, or smelled.
- If your narrative doesn't have many circles, add precise sensory details.

▶ Tom is my best friend, and (he looks exactly like me.) If we told you we were twins with different last names, you would probably believe us. We have brown hair and blue eyes. We also wear rimless glasses.

**3. Make your narrative stylish.**
- Reread your narrative. Does it give your reader a sense of your attitude and personality? Do your descriptions of others help readers understand their likes, dislikes, strengths, and weaknesses?
- Revise your narrative as needed so that your style shines through. Your narrative might be formal or informal, fast-paced or leisurely, serious or lighthearted.

▶ ~~Tom ate all the candy and said he didn't like peppers anymore.~~
   "I am never eating another jalapeño pepper in my life," Tom proclaimed after stuffing his face with chocolate bars. I couldn't do anything but laugh.

**4. Conclude strongly.**
- [Bracket] the part of your conclusion that explains why you chose to describe this experience or what you learned from it.
- If you have nothing to bracket, add one or more sentences that explain the meaning of the incident.

▶ It's a little harder to get Tom to partake in my other schemes since I sent him to the drinking fountain for hours! I still have hope that he can pack down 58 peppers if he just works at it, though. I'm sure you can imagine how much luck I'm having convincing him to try.
What about you? Bon appétit!

## Personal Narrative

## Apply the Rubric

**A strong personal narrative . . .**

☑ describes a single incident

☑ has an intriguing introduction

☑ includes transitions that show the order of events

☑ presents dialogue and specific details to describe exactly what happened

☑ uses sensory language to make the experience come alive

☑ has a distinctive style that reveals the writer's personality

☑ varies sentence types (statements, questions, and exclamations)

☑ concludes by explaining what the experience meant to the writer

## Ask a Peer Reader

• Do any events seem out of order or confusing? If so, which ones?

• What else would you like to know about this experience?

• How can I make my introduction more interesting?

## Check Your Grammar

• To include dialogue in your narrative, enclose each person's exact words in quotation marks. Begin a new paragraph for each new speaker.

> "Come on, Tom. You can do it!" I encouraged, pounding the table. "50, 51, 52, 53, 54 . . . Come on . . . 55, 56, 57."
>
> "Yahoo!!" Tom shouted.

• If the speaker's words are a statement, use a comma to separate them from the rest of the text. If they are a question or an exclamation, use a question mark or an exclamation point instead of a comma.

> "So let's hear this great idea of yours," Tom stated, brushing ham from his fries.

> "What? Huh?" he replied, looking up from his hot dog.

> "All right, Tom!" I yelled.

**See page R49:** Quick Reference: Punctuation

## Writing Online

**PUBLISHING OPTIONS**
For publishing options, visit the **Writing Center** at ClassZone.com.

**ASSESSMENT PREPARATION**
For writing and grammar assessment practice, go to the **Assessment Center** at ClassZone.com.

**SPEAKING AND LISTENING**

## Staging a Scene

Remember how your own heart pounded while you were reading "The Tell-Tale Heart"? You can help give people that exciting "you are there" feeling by staging a scene from your own narrative.

### Preparing the Scene

1. **Choose a scene.** Read through your personal narrative. Look for a scene that has exciting action and funny or dramatic dialogue. You may need to rewrite it a little to give explanations or background information.

2. **Pick the actors, props, and scenery.** List the characters involved in the scene. Ask your classmates to volunteer to act the parts. Collect props and scenery. For example, you might look for rimless glasses for the main characters as well as a long table and a few cafeteria trays to suggest a lunchroom. Keep props and scenery simple so they won't distract your audience.

3. **Create a script.** Mark up your scene with directions telling the actors where they should stand or sit and how they should say their lines. Give a copy to each actor.

> Tom and Anahi sit at a long table in front of trays loaded with jalapeños. Joe and their other classmates gather around.
>
> **Joe** (sounding serious and official) "On your mark, get set, go!"
>
> The contestants begin stuffing peppers into their mouths.
>
> **Anahi** (with eyes bugging out, runs for the water fountain) "Aarrgghh! Yeecchh! Wwaaaterrr!"
>
> **Joe** (pounding the table) "Come on, Tom! You can do it! 50, 51, 52 . . ."

4. **Rehearse.** Set up the scenery and props. Have the actors practice the scene several times until they feel comfortable.

### Presenting the Scene

1. **Action!** Have the actors deliver their lines clearly enough to be heard at the back of the room.

2. **Show emotion.** The actors' facial expressions and body language should convey feelings clearly but without exaggeration.

3. **Pay attention to pacing.** Signal the actors to speed up if the audience seems bored or slow down if they seem confused.

**See page R82:** Evaluate an Oral Interpretation

# Reading Comprehension

**DIRECTIONS** *Read this selection and answer the questions that follow.*

# The Invaders

### Jack Ritchie

None of them left the ship on the first day of its arrival, but I knew that they would be watching carefully for signs of human life.

The skies were dark with scudding clouds, and the cold wind moved high in the trees. Thin snow drifted slowly to the ground.

From the cover of the forest, I now watched as a small, heavily armed group of them left the large craft. When they reached the edge of the woods, they hesitated for a few moments and then moved cautiously forward.

I had seen them before and I knew that in appearance, at least, they were not monsters. They looked very much like us. There were some differences, of

10 course, but all in all, we were really quite similar to them.

I met them first when I was almost a boy and I had been without caution. I approached them and they seemed friendly, but then suddenly they seized me and carried me off in their strange ship.

It was a long journey to their land and when our ship made a landing, I was shown about and exhibited as though I were some kind of animal.

I saw their cities, and I was shown plants and animals completely strange to me. I learned to wear their clothing and even to eat their food.

They taught me to communicate in their strange and difficult tongue until I could, at times, even think in their language.

20 I had almost given up the hope of ever seeing my home again, but they one day put me back on one of their ships and told me that they were returning me because they wished to establish friendly relations with my people. But by now, I knew enough of them to know that this was not true. However, I nodded and smiled and watched for my opportunity to escape.

When the ship landed, I went out with the first search party. It was near evening and as the darkness gathered, I edged away from them and finally I fled into the blackness and safety of the forest.

They came after me, of course, but I was hidden deep in the woods where they could not find me.

30 Finally they gave up and I watched their ship become smaller and finally disappear, and I hoped fervently that they would never return.

But now they were back again.

I felt a coldness inside of me as I watched them moving slowly through the trees. They seemed somehow different from the others who had been here before. It was not so much in their appearance as in the air about them— the way they walked, the way they looked about with speculating eyes.

Slowly and instinctively, I realized that this time they were not here on just another raid for a captive or two.

This time they had come to stay.

40 What could we do now? Could we lure them deeper into the forest and kill them? Could we take their weapons and learn how to use them?

No, I thought despairingly. There were so many more of the invaders on the ship. And more weapons. They would come out and hunt us down like animals. They would hunt us down and kill us all.

I sighed. We must find out what it was that they wanted this time and whatever it might be, we must learn to adjust and to hope for the best.

But I still retreated silently before them, afraid to approach. I watched them search the ground ahead of them and knew they were looking for footprints, for some signs of life. But there was not yet enough snow on the ground to 50 track us down.

Their strangely colored eyes glanced about warily. They were cautious, yes.

They could be a cruel race, I knew. I had seen with my own eyes how they treated their animals and even their own kind.

I sighed again. Yes, we could be cruel, too. In this respect we could not claim to be superior to the invaders.

They paused now in a clearing, their eyes gleaming beneath their helmets.

It was time for me to approach them.

I took a deep breath and stepped into the open.

Their weapons quickly pointed at me.

60 "Welcome," I said.

They stared at me, and then one of them turned to their bearded leader. "It appears that this savage can speak some English, Captain Standish."

"Welcome," I said again. But I wondered what they would do to my land and my people now

# Comprehension

**DIRECTIONS** *Answer these questions about "The Invaders."*

1. Which event happens first in the story?
   - O The invaders look at the ground for footprints.
   - O The invaders leave the ship and enter the woods.
   - O The narrator thinks about attacking the invaders.
   - O The narrator steps into view and greets the invaders.

2. In the exposition of the story, you learn that
   - O the narrator speaks English
   - O the invaders are cruel people
   - O Captain Standish is a leader
   - O the weather is cold and snowy

3. Which phrase helps to develop suspense in the story?
   - O "first day of its arrival" (line 1)
   - O "I knew that they would be watching" (lines 1–2)
   - O "thin snow drifted slowly" (line 4)
   - O "we were really quite similar to them" (line 10)

4. Which conflict does the narrator struggle with in this story?
   - O choosing whether to return with the invaders to their country
   - O deciding which response to the invaders will be best for his people
   - O sharing food with the invaders or hiding it from them
   - O betraying his people by helping the invaders find what they want

5. Which conflict is not resolved by the end of this story?
   - O what will happen between the invaders and the narrator's people
   - O how the narrator will decide to communicate with the invaders
   - O whether the invaders can make their way off the ship and into the forest
   - O if the narrator will choose to stay hidden from the invaders

6. Which line comes at the beginning of the rising action?
   - O "They looked very much like us." (line 9)
   - O "I learned to wear their clothing and even to eat their food." (line 17)
   - O "But now they were back again." (line 32)
   - O "Yes, we could be cruel, too." (line 54)

7. In line 42, why is the narrator losing hope?
   - O He fears that his people are outnumbered and will be killed.
   - O His hiding places in the snowy forest are too visible.
   - O He thinks that the invaders are looking for another captive.
   - O His footprints might lead the invaders to his people.

8. Which line introduces the flashback within the story?
   - O "I met them first when I was almost a boy and I had been without caution." (line 11)
   - O "But by now, I knew enough of them to know that this was not true." (lines 22–23)
   - O "There were so many more of the invaders on the ship." (lines 42–43)
   - O "But I still retreated silently before them, afraid to approach." (line 47)

9. The flashback reveals that the narrator

   ○ carefully watched the invaders when they left their ship
   ○ was captured as a child by invaders and taken to their land
   ○ grew to believe that the invaders had friendly intentions
   ○ had many habits in common with the invaders

10. The climax of the story occurs when the narrator

    ○ steps out and speaks to the invaders
    ○ hides from the invaders in the woods
    ○ returns home after being held captive
    ○ hears the invaders talk to their leader

11. Why does the narrator hide from the new invaders?

    ○ He distrusts the invaders and is trying to decide what to do.
    ○ Other people are coming to help him.
    ○ He wants to surprise the invaders from a well-protected location.
    ○ A search party is looking for him.

12. Which phrase from the story helps you figure out when an event occurs?

    ○ "There were some differences . . . "
    ○ "It was a long journey . . ."
    ○ "I could, at times, . . ."
    ○ "They paused now . . ."

13. The narrator rejects the idea of attacking the invaders because

    ○ the strangers have enough people and weapons to harm the local people
    ○ the strangers are peaceful and hope to do good deeds
    ○ neither the strangers nor the local people want to have a fight
    ○ the narrator can speak the strangers' language

14. During the falling action, you discover that the invaders

    ○ arrive on a large ship
    ○ have strangely colored eyes
    ○ are led by an English captain
    ○ mistreat their animals and each other

## Constructed Response

**SHORT ANSWER**  *Write two or three sentences to answer each question.*

15. Identify one technique the author uses to create suspense.  Give an example from the text to support your choice.

16. In the flashback, what steps does the narrator take to escape the invaders?

**ESSAY**  *Write a paragraph to answer the following question.*

17. Reread lines 37–46. What does the narrator realize about the invaders? Explain how this realization helps him to resolve his conflict.

**GO ON** ➡

# Vocabulary

**DIRECTIONS** *Use context clues and the Latin word and root definitions to answer the following questions.*

1. The Latin prefix *ex-* means "out," and the Latin word *habere* means "to hold" or "to see." What is the most likely meaning of the word *exhibited* as it is used in line 15?

   ○ made to work hard
   ○ presented in public
   ○ held captive in a prison
   ○ soothed with kind words

2. The word *establish* comes from the Latin word *stabilis*, which means "firm." What is the most likely meaning of the word *establish* as it is used in line 22?

   ○ to end quickly
   ○ to damage beyond repair
   ○ to bring about using trickery
   ○ to set up and make solid

3. The Latin word *fervere* means "to boil." What is the most likely meaning of the word *fervently* as it is used in line 31?

   ○ in a dreamy way
   ○ for a long time
   ○ with great emotion
   ○ while cooking

4. The Latin word *speculari* means "to observe." What is the most likely meaning of the word *speculating* as it is used in line 36?

   ○ creating a new object
   ○ thinking about or guessing
   ○ taking a risk in the hope of gain
   ○ accepting something as true

**DIRECTIONS** *Use the dictionary entry to answer the following questions.*

**craft** (krăft) *noun* **1.** A boat, ship, or aircraft. **2.** Skill in doing or making something **3.** An occupation or trade. *verb* **1.** To make by hand. **Synonyms:** *noun*: vehicle, talent, profession, trickery; *verb:* create.

5. Which definition best matches the meaning of the word *craft* as it is used in line 6?

   ○ noun definition 1
   ○ noun definition 2
   ○ noun definition 3
   ○ verb definition 1

6. In which sentence is the word *craft* used as a verb?

   ○ She learned her craft from her father, who was a carpenter.
   ○ The fine workmanship revealed the sculptor's craft.
   ○ He tried to craft a set of bookshelves for the library.
   ○ The small craft was tossed about by the rough waves.

7. Which synonym would best replace the word *craft* in the following sentence?

   The wily fox used <u>craft</u> to outsmart the hunters.

   ○ vehicle
   ○ talent
   ○ profession
   ○ trickery

# Writing & Grammar

**DIRECTIONS** *Read this passage and answer the questions that follow.*

---

(1) When the Pilgrims first landed at Plymouth in 1620, everyone had their dream of a better life. (2) They agreed that they should work together to build a common house for all of the <u>colonists</u> meetings and religious services. (3) <u>Peoples</u> lives were difficult though, especially because there was a shortage of food. (4) Nobody knew whether they would survive. (5) In fact, many settlers died during his first winter in the colony. (6) The Native American Squanto helped everyone who remained find where they could fish and trap animals for food. (7) The Native <u>Americans</u> willingness to share their knowledge of agriculture helped the Pilgrims survive in the new land. (8) Today, the national holiday of Thanksgiving recalls the <u>Pilgrims</u> celebration of their first harvest in Plymouth.

---

**1.** To maintain pronoun-antecedent agreement in sentence 1, change *their* to

- ○ theirs
- ○ its
- ○ his or her
- ○ they

**2.** Choose the correct way to punctuate the underlined word in sentence 2.

- ○ colonist's
- ○ colonists'
- ○ colonists's
- ○ colonist's's

**3.** Choose the correct way to punctuate the underlined word in sentence 3.

- ○ Peopleses'
- ○ Peoples'
- ○ Peoples's
- ○ People's

**4.** To maintain pronoun-antecedent agreement in sentence 4, change *they* to

- ○ he or she
- ○ them
- ○ his or her
- ○ its

**5.** To maintain pronoun-antecedent agreement in sentence 5, change *his* to

- ○ their
- ○ its
- ○ his or her
- ○ her

**6.** To maintain pronoun-antecedent agreement in sentence 6, change *they* to

- ○ it
- ○ its
- ○ their
- ○ he or she

**7.** Choose the correct way to punctuate the underlined word in sentence 7.

- ○ American's
- ○ Americans's
- ○ Americanses'
- ○ Americans'

**8.** Choose the correct way to punctuate the underlined word in sentence 8.

- ○ Pilgrims'es
- ○ Pilgrims'
- ○ Pilgrims's
- ○ Pilgrim's

STOP

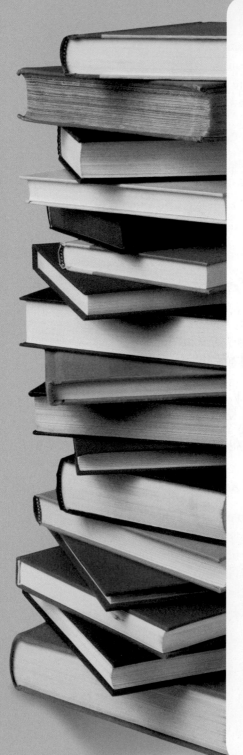

# More Great Reads

## Ideas for Independent Reading

Which questions from Unit 1 made an impression on you? Continue exploring them with these books.

## What's worth the effort?

### The Circuit: Stories from the Life of a Migrant Child
*by Francisco Jiménez*

In the 1940s, Francisco and his family crossed the Mexican border. Together they worked picking crops in California, struggling to make a life and a permanent home in a new country.

### Dancing at the Odinochka
*by Kirkpatrick Hill*

Erinia and her family live on a small trading post in Russian America. Life is hard, but Erinia is happy. When America buys the territory, life changes. Will the Pavaloffs be able to survive?

### Lord of the Deep
*by Graham Salisbury*

This summer, 13-year-old Mikey is the youngest deckhand in the marina. He soon realizes that working on his stepdad's boat is complicated. When two customers ask for "special" treatment, Mikey has to decide where his loyalty lies.

## Is seeing believing?

### The Kite Rider
*by Geraldine McCaughrean*

In thirteenth-century China, Hayou works as a kite rider. It's a terrifying job, but as he soars through the clouds he sometimes sees his father's spirit. Can these sightings give Hayou the wisdom and courage to save his mother and himself?

### Sorceress
*by Celia Rees*

Agnes grew up on a Mohawk reservation in upstate New York. When she starts dreaming of a 17th-century ancestor, she goes home to her Aunt M for help. Is Agnes going crazy, or is someone trying to tell her secrets of her family's past?

### The True Confessions of Charlotte Doyle
*by Avi*

At only 13, Charlotte is a perfect young lady. When she's on a ship traveling to America, she swears she will never leave her cabin, but by the end of the voyage she's been accused of murder, tried, and found guilty.

## When is it OK to be scared?

### Code Orange
*by Caroline B. Cooney*

Mitty panics when he remembers his biology paper. He grabs some old medical books from his mother's office and finds an envelope of smallpox scabs from 1912. Has Mitty just unleashed a deadly virus on New York City?

### A Girl Named Disaster
*by Nancy Farmer*

Nhamo isn't even 12 when she's forced to marry a cruel man with three wives. Her grandmother convinces her to run away, and Nhamo must find her way from Mozambique to Zimbabwe on her own.

### The Rag and Bone Shop
*by Robert Cormier*

A little girl has been murdered. Trent, an expert interrogator, is brought to Monument, Massachusetts to meet the 12-year-old suspect, Jason Dorrant. If Trent can get the boy's confession it'll make his career, but is Jason really guilty?

# Through Different Eyes

## CHARACTER AND POINT OF VIEW

- In Fiction
- In Media
- In Nonfiction
- In Poetry

159

# What brings a
# CHARACTER
## *to life?*

A great **character** might start out as a few words jotted on a page or as a lump of clay squeezed between an artist's fingers. How can these humble beginnings result in a person—or a dog, a rabbit, or a robot— who can seem as familiar as your best friend? A skilled creator knows how to add layers of details that make someone who doesn't even exist in real life seem like someone you've known forever.

***ACTIVITY*** Can you bring a character to life? Follow these steps to give it a try:

- Look through magazines and find a picture of someone or something that looks like he, she, or it could be an interesting character.

- Invent a life for that character. Think about things like where the character lives, what the character cares about most, and how he, she, or it responds to triumphs and challenges.

- Introduce your character to your group. Which of the details you provide most help your classmates feel like they know the person or creature you've invented?

**INDIANA STANDARDS**

# Preview Unit Goals

| | |
|---|---|
| **LITERARY ANALYSIS** | • Identify and analyze point of view, including first-person, third-person limited, and third-person omniscient<br>• Identify and analyze character traits and motives<br>• Identify and analyze methods of characterization<br>• Identify, analyze, and evaluate sound devices |
| **READING** | • Make inferences and draw conclusions<br>• Identify scope of ideas and information in different texts<br>• Evaluate usefulness of information from different sources |
| **WRITING AND GRAMMAR** | • Write a descriptive essay<br>• Identify and use comparative and superlative forms correctly<br>• Combine sentences by using coordinating conjunctions<br>• Identify and use verb tenses correctly. |
| **SPEAKING, LISTENING, AND VIEWING** | • Identify and analyze visual elements and editing in film<br>• Conduct an interview |
| **VOCABULARY** | • Use context to determine the meaning of multiple-meaning words<br>• Use knowledge of base words and affixes to determine the meaning of words |
| **ACADEMIC VOCABULARY** | • point of view    • inferences    • characterization<br>• traits    • scope of ideas    • motives |

## Reader's Workshop

# Character and Point of View

For a story to really resonate, it must have characters you can care about, relate to, understand, or even love to hate. How do writers create characters that trigger these kinds of reactions? How does *who* tells the story affect your feelings? In this workshop, you'll look closely at characterization and point of view, two techniques that help shape your reactions and opinions.

**INDIANA STANDARDS**

**READING STANDARD**
**8.3.8** Contrast points of view — such as first person, third person limited and third person omniscient, and subjects and objective — in narrative text and explain how they affect the overall theme of the work.

## Part 1: Point of View

**Point of view**—the vantage point from which a story is told—can affect your understanding of characters and events. Point of view is created by a writer's choice of **narrator,** the voice that tells the story. The narrator may be a character in the story or an outside observer.

This chart describes three points of view. You'll notice that all the examples focus on two students vying to win a school election. In each example, how does the choice of narrator influence your impressions of the characters?

| POINT OF VIEW | | EXAMPLE |
|---|---|---|
| **FIRST-PERSON**<br>*The narrator*<br><br>• is a main or minor character in the story<br>• uses the pronouns *I* and *me* to refer to himself or herself<br>• shares his or her thoughts, feelings, and opinions of other characters and events<br>• doesn't know the thoughts, feelings, and opinions of other characters |  | Nervously, I eyed Gwen, my competition in the election, and flashed her a gracious smile. Believe me—I wasn't feeling very gracious.<br><br>After Gwen began her speech, I relaxed. What kind of campaign speech is *that?* I thought. There's no way I'll lose now! |
| **THIRD-PERSON LIMITED**<br>*The narrator*<br><br>• is not a character in the story but an outside observer<br>• zooms in on the thoughts, feelings, and opinions of one character |  | Devin had trouble wiping the smile off his face as he listened to Gwen fumble through her speech. For a brief moment, he felt a wave of sympathy for Gwen. Then Devin forgot about his opponent and started planning his acceptance speech in his head. |
| **THIRD-PERSON OMNISCIENT**<br>*The narrator*<br><br>• is not a character in the story but an outside observer<br>• is "all knowing"—that is, he or she has access to the thoughts, feelings, and opinions of all the characters |  | Feeling confident and superior, Devin gave his opponent, Gwen, a genuine smile as she walked past him.<br><br>Though Gwen returned Devin's smile, she was suspicious of his kindness. He's probably gloating over my mistakes, Gwen thought angrily. |

## MODEL 1: FIRST-PERSON

Emily, the young narrator of this novel, is visiting her sick grandmother, Ola. Emily and Ola have spent the entire day together trying on Ola's old hats and scarves. In this excerpt, Emily describes their special relationship.

### *from* Toning the Sweep

Novel by **Angela Johnson**

Ola and I lie on our backs in the kitchen, scarves and hats everywhere. I look over at the night-light by the table. It's the only light in the room now. Ola's eyes are closed, but I don't think she's asleep.

I have always loved my grandmother, but I know that she is a strange
5  woman. I know that not too many of my friends would spend an evening trying on hats with their grandmothers. A few years ago they would have. Now most of them don't even admit that they like their grandparents, though they do.

I'm clueless about how to be cool. I've always told my friends that I like
10  my grandmother. Since most of them only get a glimpse of who she is by the books and strange things she sends through the mail, I think secretly they think she's cool. That makes up for me being clueless, I guess.

**Close Read**

1. One sentence that reflects the first-person point of view has been boxed. Identify another one.

2. Suppose Emily's grandmother was the narrator of this novel. How might that change what you learn about the woman and her granddaughter?

## MODEL 2: THIRD-PERSON OMNISCIENT

The narrator of this story shares the thoughts of more than one character. Alfonso is thrilled when Sandra agrees to go on a bike ride with him. Before his date, Alfonso breaks the chain on his bike. Will his brother help him out?

### *from* Broken Chain

Short story by **Gary Soto**

"Come on, man, let me use it," Alfonso pleaded. "Please, Ernie, I'll do anything."

Although Ernie could see Alfonso's desperation, he had plans with his friend Raymundo. They were going to catch frogs at the Mayfair canal. He felt sorry for
5  his brother, and gave him a stick of gum to make him feel better, but there was nothing he could do. The canal was three miles away, and the frogs were waiting.

Alfonso took the stick of gum, placed it in his shirt pocket, and left the bedroom with his head down. . . .

At four he decided to get it over with and started walking to Sandra's house,
10  trudging slowly, as if he were waist-deep in water. Shame colored his face. How could he disappoint his first date? She would probably laugh.

**Close Read**

1. How does Ernie feel about Alfonso's predicament? How does Alfonso himself feel? Cite details to support your answers.

2. Suppose the narrator had not revealed Ernie's thoughts in lines 3–6. How might this affect your impression of Ernie?

# Part 2: Character Traits and Motivation

As a reader, you can't help but have strong reactions to the people you meet on the page. Did you know that writers use different methods of characterization to create these responses in you? Read on to find out exactly how writers develop lifelike characters with distinct traits and motivations.

## CHARACTER TRAITS

Loyal, outgoing, lazy—you might use words like these to describe people in your life. You may not realize it, but you learn about people's qualities, or **traits,** by observing the way they look, talk, and act. For example, a new neighbor probably wouldn't introduce herself by saying, "Hi! I'm outgoing." Instead, you would infer this trait by noticing her big smile and confident voice.

Like people, characters in literature have unique personalities and traits. Sometimes, a narrator will directly tell you what a character is like. More often, you have to infer a character's traits the same way you would a person's—by considering his or her appearance and behavior, for instance.

Writers show you what their characters are like by using the following **indirect methods of characterization.** Look at this graphic, noting the descriptions of the girl Madeleine. What traits can you infer?

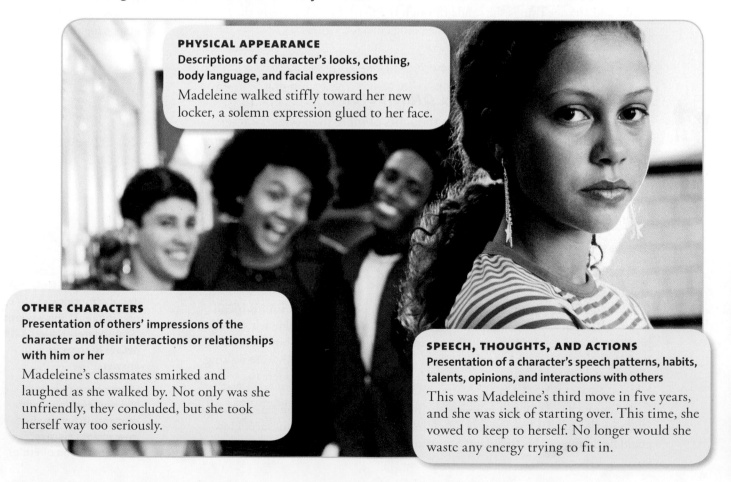

**PHYSICAL APPEARANCE**
**Descriptions of a character's looks, clothing, body language, and facial expressions**
Madeleine walked stiffly toward her new locker, a solemn expression glued to her face.

**OTHER CHARACTERS**
**Presentation of others' impressions of the character and their interactions or relationships with him or her**
Madeleine's classmates smirked and laughed as she walked by. Not only was she unfriendly, they concluded, but she took herself way too seriously.

**SPEECH, THOUGHTS, AND ACTIONS**
**Presentation of a character's speech patterns, habits, talents, opinions, and interactions with others**
This was Madeleine's third move in five years, and she was sick of starting over. This time, she vowed to keep to herself. No longer would she waste any energy trying to fit in.

## MODEL 1: CHARACTERIZATION

The narrator of this story takes the 8:12 train to work everyday; he sees the same commuters and sits in the same corner seat. Today, however, he notices a stranger on the platform. What do you learn about the stranger from this brief excerpt?

*from* # Galloping Foxley

Short story by **Roald Dahl**

The stranger was standing plumb in the middle of the platform, feet apart and arms folded, looking for all the world as though he owned the whole place. He was a biggish, thickset man, and even from behind he somehow managed to convey a powerful impression of arrogance and oil. Very
5   definitely, he was not one of us. He carried a cane instead of an umbrella, his shoes were brown instead of black, the grey hat was cocked at a ridiculous angle, and in one way and another there seemed to be an excess of silk and polish about his person. More than this I did not care to observe.

### Close Read

1. What methods of characterization has the author used to describe the stranger?

2. What kind of person do you think the stranger is? Cite specific details that affected your impression of him.

## MODEL 2: CHARACTER TRAITS

Sopeap is a Cambodian teenager whose family recently moved to the United States. One day, a classmate walks into her family's store, lugging a green armchair. How does Sopeap respond to the classmate's request for help?

*from* # The Green Armchair

Short story by **Minfong Ho**

*Thomas Ramsey.* For an awful moment she thought she had said his name out loud, but then realized it had only been in her mind.
Sopeap forced a smile. "Sure," she said, pleasantly surprised by how casual, how American, she sounded. "Be right with you."
5   "Hey, aren't you in my history class?" he asked.
"Algebra," she said quietly. At least he recognized her. She had long since noticed him, intrigued by the aloof, easy banter he carried on with his classmates, as if he were looking at them from the wrong end of a telescope. A bit of a loner, and liking it that way. *Sort of like me*, she had sometimes
10   thought, clutching onto her solitude as tightly as she held her textbooks. . . .

### Close Read

1. How would you describe Thomas? Identify at least two details in this excerpt that influenced your impression of him.

2. Reread the boxed descriptions of Sopeap's thoughts and feelings. What do these descriptions suggest about her traits?

## CHARACTER MOTIVATION

Why did the boy decide to volunteer at the animal shelter? What prompted the woman to risk her life for a stranger? A big part of understanding characters is analyzing their **motivations,** or the reasons behind their actions. For instance, did the boy volunteer at the shelter because of his passion for animals or because he has a crush on someone who works there? Think about what each motivation might suggest about the boy's traits.

To uncover a character's motivation, you often have to look for details in the story. As you read, consider the following:

- the narrator's direct comments about a character's motivation

- a character's actions, thoughts, and values

- your own understanding of the emotions—love, greed, ambition, jealousy— that drive human behavior

In this story, 17-year-old Mike finally decides to visit his grandmother in the nursing home. What factors are motivating his actions?

## from The Moustache

Short story by **Robert Cormier**

. . . I told my mother I'd go, anyway. I hadn't seen my grandmother since she'd been admitted to Lawnrest. Besides, the place is located on the Southwest Turnpike, which meant I could barrel along in my father's new Le Mans. My ambition was to see the speedometer hit 75. Ordinarily, I used the
5   old station wagon, which can barely stagger up to 50.

Frankly, I wasn't too crazy about visiting a nursing home. They reminded me of hospitals, and hospitals turn me off. I mean, the smell of ether makes me nauseous, and I feel faint at the sight of blood. And as I approached Lawnrest—which is a terrible cemetery kind of name, to begin with—I was
10   sorry I hadn't avoided the trip. Then I felt guilty about it. I'm loaded with guilt complexes. Like driving like a madman after promising my father to be careful. Like sitting in the parking lot, looking at the nursing home with dread and thinking how I'd rather be with Cindy. Then I thought of all the Christmas and birthday gifts my grandmother had given me, and I got out of
15   the car, guilty as usual.

### Close Read

1. Reread the boxed text. What is the narrator's initial motivation for visiting his grandmother?

2. The narrator has second thoughts about his visit once he's in the parking lot. What eventually motivates him to go inside?

3. Consider the two motivating factors that influence the narrator's actions. What do they tell you about him?

# Part 3: Analyze the Literature

Meet Gene, a high school student in Mrs. Tibbetts' second-period class. Gene and his fellow classmates have just found out that Mrs. Tibbetts is taking the advanced English class to a poetry reading. What happens when Mrs. Tibbetts unexpectedly extends the invitation to Gene's class? Read on to find out.

 *from*
# I GO ALONG
Short story by **Richard Peck**

Since it's only the second period of the day, we're all feeling pretty good. Also it's a Tuesday, a terrible TV night. Everybody in the class puts up their hands. I mean everybody. Even Marty Crawshaw. . . . And Pink Hohenfield, who's in class today for the first time this month. I put up mine. I go along.

5　Mrs. Tibbetts looks amazed. She's never seen this many hands up in our class. She's never seen anybody's hand except Darla's. . . .

But then she sees we have to be putting her on. So she just says, "Anyone who would like to go, be in the parking lot at five-thirty. And eat first. No eating on the bus."

10　Mrs. Tibbetts can drive the school bus. Whenever she's taking the advanced class anywhere, she can go to the principal for the keys. She can use the bus anytime she wants to, unless the coach needs it.

Then she opens her attendance book, and we tune out. And at five-thirty that night I'm in the parking lot. I have no idea why. Needless to say, I'm the only one here from second period. Marty Crawshaw and Pink Hohenfield will be out on the access highway about now, at 7-Eleven, sitting on their hoods. Darla couldn't make it either. Right offhand I can't think of anybody who wants to ride a school bus thirty miles to see a poet. Including me.

The advanced-English juniors are milling around behind school. I'm still
20　in my car, and it's almost dark, so nobody sees me.

Then Mrs. Tibbetts wheels the school bus in. She's got the amber fogs flashing, and you can see the black letters along the yellow side: CONSOLIDATED SCHOOL DIST. She swings in and hits the brakes, and the doors fly open. The advanced class starts to climb aboard. They're
25　more orderly than us, but they've got their groups too. . . . I'm settling behind my dashboard. The last kid climbs the bus.

And I seem to be sprinting across the asphalt. I'm on the bus, and the door's hissing shut behind me. When I swing past the driver's seat, I don't look at Mrs. Tibbetts, and she doesn't say anything. I wonder where I'm supposed to sit.

30　They're still milling around in the aisle, but there are plenty of seats. I find an empty double and settle by the window, pulling my ball cap down in front. It doesn't take us long to get out of town, not in this town. When we go past 7-Eleven, I'm way down in the seat with my hand shielding my face on the window side. Right about then, somebody sits down next to me. I flinch.

## Close Read

1. From what point of view is this story told? Explain how you can tell.

2. Reread the boxed sentences. What do they suggest about Gene's character traits?

3. How would this excerpt be different if Mrs. Tibbetts were the narrator?

4. Examine lines 32–34. Why do you think Gene hides when the bus passes the 7–Eleven?

5. Consider Gene's actions and body language in lines 27–34. Based on these details, what can you infer about his personality?

## The Treasure of Lemon Brown

Short Story by Walter Dean Myers

# *What do you* CHERISH?

**INDIANA STANDARDS**

**READING STANDARDS**

**8.2.9** Make reasonable statements and draw conclusions about a text, supporting them with accurate examples.

**8.3.8** Contrast points of view—such as first person, third person limited and third person omniscient, and subjects and objective—in narrative text and explain how they affect the overall theme of the work.

**KEY IDEA** Think of what you most **cherish,** or hold dear. Is it worth a lot of money, or is it valuable because of a memory that is important only to you? For example, a photograph of a favorite friend or relative wouldn't bring much money at an auction, but the memories it holds might make it one of the first things you'd save if your home were on fire. In "The Treasure of Lemon Brown," a boy's encounter with an old blues musician helps him discover what he treasures most.

**LIST IT** Make a list of three to five things that you cherish. They might be tangible (things you can touch, such as a pair of jeans or a pet) or intangible (things you cannot touch, such as a memory or an idea like freedom). Explain why these things are important to you.

## ● LITERARY ANALYSIS: THIRD-PERSON LIMITED POINT OF VIEW

In a story told from the **third-person limited point of view,** the narrator is outside the story and tells what one character sees, thinks, and feels. Look at the following example:

*Report cards were due in a week, and Greg had been hoping for the best.*

In this sentence, the narrator tells the reader how Greg feels about the report card he's about to receive.

As you read, pay attention to how much the narrator allows you to know about each character's thoughts and feelings and how this affects your understanding of the story.

## ● READING SKILL: MAKE INFERENCES

Writers rarely explain everything to their readers. They provide certain clues and expect readers to use the clues and their own experience to fill in the gaps. This is called **making inferences.**

Often you will need to make inferences to understand the characters in a story. As you read "The Treasure of Lemon Brown," watch for clues that tell you what a character is like and why the character acts a particular way. Use a chart like the one shown to note details about the characters.

| Details About Character | What I Infer |
|---|---|
| Greg's father lectures Greg about his poor effort in math. | Greg's father wants him to succeed in life. |

## ▲ VOCABULARY IN CONTEXT

Walter Dean Myers uses the boldfaced words to tell about an old man who has a hard and dangerous life, but also a precious treasure. To see how many of the words you know, substitute a different word or phrase for each one.

1. The door was **ajar** and let in a small amount of light.
2. There was a **tremor** in his voice as he told the sad tale.
3. The silence was **ominous** and scary.
4. He would **commence** his trip when the rain stopped.
5. Years of hard work left him with **gnarled** hands.
6. Get his attention and **beckon** him to come closer.
7. The hallway was dark, so he moved **tentatively.**
8. We had an **impromptu** meeting at the street corner.

# Author Online

**Walter Dean Myers**
**born 1937**

**Contest to Career**
Walter Dean Myers was born to a large family in West Virginia. After his mother died when he was two years old, his father could no longer care for all the children. Myers grew up with foster parents in New York City. A speech impediment made it difficult for him to speak, so he began writing poetry and stories with the encouragement of a teacher who thought writing would help him express himself. Still, he didn't think he could earn a living as an author. After unhappily working as a post-office clerk and a messenger, Myers saw an advertisement for a children's book-writing contest. He had never written for young people before, but he won the contest and began a highly successful writing career.

**Writing His Life** Myers frequently draws on his own experience in his writing. Many of his characters belong to low-income families and deal with urban problems. He has also written biographies of prominent African Americans, including Malcolm X and Muhammad Ali. Myers has said, "As a black writer, I want to talk about my people." But the characters he creates and the issues he addresses have universal appeal.

 **MORE ABOUT THE AUTHOR**
For more on Walter Dean Myers, visit the **Literature Center** at ClassZone.com.

## Background

**Harlem** "The Treasure of Lemon Brown" takes place in Harlem, the neighborhood in which Myers grew up in New York City. Since about 1910, it has been one of the largest African-American communities in the United States.

# The Treasure of Lemon Brown

*Walter Dean Myers*

**ANALYZE VISUALS**
This collage was created by Walter Dean Myers's son. What can you **infer** about Harlem from the details in this image?

The dark sky, filled with angry, swirling clouds, reflected Greg Ridley's mood as he sat on the stoop[1] of his building. His father's voice came to him again, first reading the letter the principal had sent to the house, then lecturing endlessly about his poor efforts in math.

"I had to leave school when I was 13," his father had said, "that's a year younger than you are now. If I'd had half the chances that you have, I'd . . ."

Greg had sat in the small, pale green kitchen listening, knowing the lecture would end with his father saying he couldn't play ball with the Scorpions. He had asked his father the week before, and his father had said it depended on his
10 next report card. It wasn't often the Scorpions took on new players, especially 14-year-olds, and this was a chance of a lifetime for Greg. He hadn't been allowed to play high school ball, which he had really wanted to do, but playing for the Community Center team was the next best thing. Report cards were due in a week, and Greg had been hoping for the best. But the principal had ended the suspense early when she sent that letter saying Greg would probably fail math if he didn't spend more time studying. **A**

"And you want to play *basketball?*" His father's brows knitted over deep brown eyes. "That must be some kind of a joke. Now you just get into your room and hit those books."

20 That had been two nights before. His father's words, like the distant thunder that now echoed through the streets of Harlem, still rumbled softly in his ears.

**A** **POINT OF VIEW**
Whose thoughts and feelings is the **narrator** describing?

---

1. **stoop:** a porch or staircase at the entrance of a building.

Illustrations by Christopher Myers.

It was beginning to cool. Gusts of wind made bits of paper dance between the parked cars. There was a flash of nearby lightning, and soon large drops of rain splashed onto his jeans. He stood to go upstairs, thought of the lecture that probably awaited him if he did anything except shut himself in his room with his math book, and started walking down the street instead. Down the block there was an old tenement that had been abandoned for some months. Some of the guys had held an **impromptu** checker tournament there the week before, and Greg had noticed that the door, once boarded over, had been slightly **ajar.**

Pulling his collar up as high as he could, he checked for traffic and made a dash across the street. He reached the house just as another flash of lightning changed the night to day for an instant, then returned the graffiti-scarred building to the grim shadows. He vaulted over the outer stairs and pushed **tentatively** on the door. It was open, and he let himself in.

The inside of the building was dark except for the dim light that filtered through the dirty windows from the streetlamps. There was a room a few feet from the door, and from where he stood at the entrance, Greg could see a squarish patch of light on the floor. He entered the room, frowning at the musty smell. It was a large room that might have been someone's parlor at one time. Squinting, Greg could see an old table on its side against one wall, what looked like a pile of rags or a torn mattress in the corner, and a couch, with one side broken, in front of the window.

He went to the couch. The side that wasn't broken was comfortable enough, though a little creaky. From this spot he could see the blinking neon sign over the bodega[2] on the corner. He sat a while, watching the sign blink first green then red, allowing his mind to drift to the Scorpions, then to his father. His father had been a postal worker for all Greg's life, and was proud of it, often telling Greg how hard he had worked to pass the test. Greg had heard the story too many times to be interested now. **B**

For a moment Greg thought he heard something that sounded like a scraping against the wall. He listened carefully, but it was gone.

Outside the wind had picked up, sending the rain against the window with a force that shook the glass in its frame. A car passed, its tires hissing over the wet street and its red tail lights glowing in the darkness.

Greg thought he heard the noise again. His stomach tightened as he held himself still and listened intently. There weren't any more scraping noises, but he was sure he had heard something in the darkness—something breathing!

He tried to figure out just where the breathing was coming from; he knew it was in the room with him. Slowly he stood, tensing. As he turned, a flash of lightning lit up the room, frightening him with its sudden brilliance. He saw nothing, just the overturned table, the pile of rags and an old newspaper on the floor. Could he have been imagining the sounds? He continued listening,

---

2. **bodega** (bō-dä′gə): a small grocery store.

---

**impromptu**
(ĭm-prŏmp′tōō) *adj.*
unplanned

**ajar** (ə-jär′) *adj.* partially open

**tentatively** (tĕn′tə-tĭv-lē) *adv.* uncertainly or hesitantly

**B  MAKE INFERENCES**
Reread lines 48–51. What can you infer about Greg's attitude toward his father?

but heard nothing and thought that it might have just been rats. Still, he thought, as soon as the rain let up he would leave. He went to the window and was about to look out when he heard a voice behind him.

"Don't try nothin' 'cause I got a razor here sharp enough to cut a week into nine days!"

70 Greg, except for an involuntary **tremor** in his knees, stood stock still. The voice was high and brittle, like dry twigs being broken, surely not one he had ever heard before. There was a shuffling sound as the person who had been speaking moved a step closer. Greg turned, holding his breath, his eyes straining to see in the dark room.

The upper part of the figure before him was still in darkness. The lower half was in the dim rectangle of light that fell unevenly from the window. There were two feet, in cracked, dirty shoes from which rose legs that were wrapped in rags.

"Who are you?" Greg hardly recognized his own voice.

"I'm Lemon Brown," came the answer. "Who're you?"

80 "Greg Ridley."

"What you doing here?" The figure shuffled forward again, and Greg took a small step backward.

"It's raining," Greg said.

"I can see that," the figure said.

The person who called himself Lemon Brown peered forward, and Greg could see him clearly. He was an old man. His black, heavily wrinkled face was surrounded by a halo of crinkly white hair and whiskers that seemed to separate his head from the layers of dirty coats piled on his smallish frame. His pants were bagged to the knee, where they were met with rags that went 90 down to the old shoes. The rags were held on with strings, and there was a rope around his middle. Greg relaxed. He had seen the man before, picking through the trash on the corner and pulling clothes out of a Salvation Army box. There was no sign of the razor that could "cut a week into nine days." **C**

"What are you doing here?" Greg asked.

"This is where I'm staying," Lemon Brown said. "What you here for?"

"Told you it was raining out," Greg said, leaning against the back of the couch until he felt it give slightly.

"Ain't you got no home?"

"I got a home," Greg answered.

100 "You ain't one of them bad boys looking for my treasure, is you?" Lemon Brown cocked his head to one side and squinted one eye. "Because I told you I got me a razor."

"I'm not looking for your treasure," Greg answered, smiling. *"If* you have one."

"What you mean, *if* I have one," Lemon Brown said. "Every man got a treasure. You don't know that, you must be a fool!"

"Sure," Greg said as he sat on the sofa and put one leg over the back. "What do you have, gold coins?"

"Don't worry none about what I got," Lemon Brown said. "You know who I am?"

**tremor** (trĕm′ər) *n.* nervous trembling

**C** **POINT OF VIEW**
How does knowing Greg's thoughts and actions affect your impression of Lemon Brown?

**ANALYZE VISUALS**
How does the man in the picture **compare** with the way you imagine Lemon Brown?

110     "You told me your name was orange or lemon or something like that."

    "Lemon Brown," the old man said, pulling back his shoulders as he did so, "they used to call me Sweet Lemon Brown." **D**

    "Sweet Lemon?" Greg asked.

    "Yessir. Sweet Lemon Brown. They used to say I sung the blues³ so sweet that if I sang at a funeral, the dead would **commence** to rocking with the beat. Used to travel all over Mississippi and as far as Monroe, Louisiana, and east on over to Macon, Georgia. You mean you ain't never heard of Sweet Lemon Brown?"

**D** **MAKE INFERENCES**
Why does the man pull back his shoulders as he tells Greg his name?

**commence** (kə-mĕns')
*v.* to begin

---

3. **blues:** a style of music developed from southern African-American songs.

"Afraid not," Greg said. "What . . . what happened to you?"

"Hard times, boy. Hard times always after a poor man. One day I got tired,
120 sat down to rest a spell and felt a tap on my shoulder. Hard times caught up
with me."

"Sorry about that."

"What you doing here? How come you didn't go on home when the rain
come? Rain don't bother you young folks none."

"Just didn't." Greg looked away.

"I used to have a knotty-headed boy just like you." Lemon Brown had half
walked, half shuffled back to the corner and sat down against the wall. "Had
them big eyes like you got. I used to call them moon eyes. Look into them
moon eyes and see anything you want."

130 "How come you gave up singing the blues?" Greg asked.

"Didn't give it up," Lemon Brown said. "You don't give up the blues; they
give you up. After a while you do good for yourself, and it ain't nothing but
foolishness singing about how hard you got it. Ain't that right?"

"I guess so."

"What's that noise?" Lemon Brown asked, suddenly sitting upright.

Greg listened, and he heard a noise outside. He looked at Lemon Brown
and saw the old man was pointing toward the window.

Greg went to the window and saw three men, neighborhood thugs, on the
stoop. One was carrying a length of pipe. Greg looked back toward Lemon
140 Brown, who moved quietly across the room to the window. The old man
looked out, then **beckoned** frantically for Greg to follow him. For a moment
Greg couldn't move. Then he found himself following Lemon Brown into the
hallway and up darkened stairs. Greg followed as closely as he could. They
reached the top of the stairs, and Greg felt Lemon Brown's hand first lying on
his shoulder, then probing down his arm until he finally took Greg's hand into
his own as they crouched in the darkness. **E**

"They's bad men," Lemon Brown whispered. His breath was warm against
Greg's skin.

"Hey! Rag man!" a voice called. "We know you in here. What you got up
150 under them rags? You got any money?"

Silence.

"We don't want to have to come in and hurt you, old man, but we don't
mind if we have to."

Lemon Brown squeezed Greg's hand in his own hard, **gnarled** fist.

There was a banging downstairs and a light as the men entered. They banged
around noisily, calling for the rag man.

"We heard you talking about your treasure." The voice was slurred. "We just
want to see it, that's all."

"You sure he's here?" One voice seemed to come from the room with the sofa.

160 "Yeah, he stays here every night."

"There's another room over there; I'm going to take a look. You got that
flashlight?"

**beckon** (běk'ən) v.
to signal to come

**E** MAKE INFERENCES
Why does Lemon Brown
hold Greg's hand?

**gnarled** (närld) adj.
roughened, as from age
or work

"Yeah, here, take the pipe too."

Greg opened his mouth to quiet the sound of his breath as he sucked it in uneasily. A beam of light hit the wall a few feet opposite him, then went out.

"Ain't nobody in that room," a voice said. "You think he gone or something?"

"I don't know," came the answer. "All I know is that I heard him talking about some kind of treasure. You know they found that shopping bag lady with that money in her bags."

170 "Yeah. You think he's upstairs?"

"HEY, OLD MAN, ARE YOU UP THERE?"

Silence.

"Watch my back. I'm going up."

There was a footstep on the stairs, and the beam from the flashlight danced crazily along the peeling wallpaper. Greg held his breath. There was another step and a loud crashing noise as the man banged the pipe against the wooden banister. Greg could feel his temples throb as the man slowly neared them. Greg thought about the pipe, wondering what he would do when the man reached them—what he *could* do. **F**

180 Then Lemon Brown released his hand and moved toward the top of the stairs. Greg looked around and saw stairs going up to the next floor. He tried waving to Lemon Brown, hoping the old man would see him in the dim light and follow him to the next floor. Maybe, Greg thought, the man wouldn't follow them up there. Suddenly, though, Lemon Brown stood at the top of the stairs, both arms raised high above his head.

"There he is!" a voice cried from below.

"Throw down your money, old man, so I won't have to bash your head in!"

Lemon Brown didn't move. Greg felt himself near panic. The steps came closer, and still Lemon Brown didn't move. He was an eerie sight, a bundle of
190 rags standing at the top of the stairs, his shadow on the wall looming over him. Maybe, the thought came to Greg, the scene could be even eerier.

Greg wet his lips, put his hands to his mouth and tried to make a sound. Nothing came out. He swallowed hard, wet his lips once more and howled as evenly as he could.

*"What's that?"*

As Greg howled, the light moved away from Lemon Brown, but not before Greg saw him hurl his body down the stairs at the men who had come to take his treasure. There was a crashing noise, and then footsteps. A rush of warm air came in as the downstairs door opened, then there was only an
200 **ominous** silence. **G**

Greg stood on the landing. He listened, and after a while there was another sound on the staircase.

"Mr. Brown?" he called.

"Yeah, it's me," came the answer. "I got their flashlight."

Greg exhaled in relief as Lemon Brown made his way slowly back up the stairs.

"You O.K.?"

"Few bumps and bruises," Lemon Brown said.

**F POINT OF VIEW**
Whose feelings about the intruders do you learn more about, Greg's or Lemon Brown's?

**ominous** (ŏm'ə-nəs) *adj.* threatening

**G POINT OF VIEW**
Reread lines 196–200. How would this passage be different if you knew what Lemon Brown was thinking?

"I think I'd better be going," Greg said, his breath returning to normal. "You'd better leave, too, before they come back." **H**

210 "They may hang around outside for a while," Lemon Brown said, "but they ain't getting their nerve up to come in here again. Not with crazy old rag men and howling spooks. Best you stay awhile till the coast is clear. I'm heading out West tomorrow, out to east St. Louis."

"They were talking about treasures," Greg said. "You *really* have a treasure?"

"What I tell you? Didn't I tell you every man got a treasure?" Lemon Brown said. "You want to see mine?"

"If you want to show it to me," Greg shrugged.

"Let's look out the window first, see what them scoundrels be doing," Lemon Brown said.

220 They followed the oval beam of the flashlight into one of the rooms and looked out the window. They saw the men who had tried to take the treasure sitting on the curb near the corner. One of them had his pants leg up, looking at his knee.

"You sure you're not hurt?" Greg asked Lemon Brown.

"Nothing that ain't been hurt before," Lemon Brown said. "When you get as old as me all you say when something hurts is 'Howdy, Mr. Pain, sees you back again.' Then when Mr. Pain see he can't worry you none, he go on mess with somebody else."

Greg smiled.

230 "Here, you hold this." Lemon Brown gave Greg the flashlight.

He sat on the floor near Greg and carefully untied the strings that held the rags on his right leg. When he took the rags away, Greg saw a piece of plastic. The old man carefully took off the plastic and unfolded it. He revealed some yellowed newspaper clippings and a battered harmonica.

"There it be," he said, nodding his head. "There it be."

Greg looked at the old man, saw the distant look in his eye, then turned to the clippings. They told of Sweet Lemon Brown, a blues singer and harmonica player who was appearing at different theaters in the South. One of the clippings said he had been the hit of the show, although not the headliner.

240 All of the clippings were reviews of shows Lemon Brown had been in more than 50 years ago. Greg looked at the harmonica. It was dented badly on one side, with the reed holes on one end nearly closed.

"I used to travel around and make money for to feed my wife and Jesse— that's my boy's name. Used to feed them good, too. Then his mama died, and he stayed with his mama's sister. He growed up to be a man, and when the war come he saw fit to go off and fight in it. I didn't have nothing to give him except these things that told him who I was, and what he come from. If you know your pappy did something, you know you can do something too. **I**

"Anyway, he went off to war, and I went off still playing and singing.

250 'Course by then I wasn't as much as I used to be, not without somebody to make it worth the while. You know what I mean?"

**H MAKE INFERENCES**
Why does Greg think he should leave?

**I MAKE INFERENCES**
Reread lines 247–248. How might Greg apply this idea to his own life?

"Yeah," Greg nodded, not quite really knowing.

"I traveled around, and one time I come home, and there was this letter saying Jesse got killed in the war. Broke my heart, it truly did.

"They sent back what he had with him over there, and what it was is this old mouth fiddle and these clippings. Him carrying it around with him like that told me it meant something to him. That was my treasure, and when I give it to him he treated it just like that, a treasure. Ain't that something?"

"Yeah, I guess so," Greg said. **J**

260    "You *guess* so?" Lemon Brown's voice rose an octave as he started to put his treasure back into the plastic. "Well, you got to guess 'cause you sure don't know nothing. Don't know enough to get home when it's raining."

"I guess . . . I mean, you're right."

"You O.K. for a youngster," the old man said as he tied the strings around his leg, "better than those scalawags[4] what come here looking for my treasure. That's for sure."

"You really think that treasure of yours was worth fighting for?" Greg asked. "Against a pipe?"

"What else a man got 'cepting what he can pass on to his son, or his 270 daughter, if she be his oldest?" Lemon Brown said. "For a big-headed boy you sure do ask the foolishest questions."

Lemon Brown got up after patting his rags in place and looked out the window again.

"Looks like they're gone. You get on out of here and get yourself home. I'll be watching from the window so you'll be all right."

Lemon Brown went down the stairs behind Greg. When they reached the front door the old man looked out first, saw the street was clear and told Greg to scoot on home.

"You sure you'll be O.K.?" Greg asked.

280    "Now didn't I tell you I was going to east St. Louis in the morning?" Lemon Brown asked. "Don't that sound O.K. to you?"

"Sure it does," Greg said. "Sure it does. And you take care of that treasure of yours."

"That I'll do," Lemon said, the wrinkles about his eyes suggesting a smile. "That I'll do."

The night had warmed and the rain had stopped, leaving puddles at the curbs. Greg didn't even want to think how late it was. He thought ahead of what his father would say and wondered if he should tell him about Lemon Brown. He thought about it until he reached his stoop, and decided against 290 it. Lemon Brown would be O.K., Greg thought, with his memories and his treasure.

Greg pushed the button over the bell marked Ridley, thought of the lecture he knew his father would give him, and smiled. ❧ **K**

**J** **POINT OF VIEW**
What does Greg think about Lemon Brown's treasure?

**K** **MAKE INFERENCES**
Why does the thought of his father's lecture make Greg smile?

---

4. **scalawags** (skăl′ə-wăgz′): rascals.

## Comprehension

1. **Recall** How does Greg meet Lemon Brown?

2. **Recall** How does Lemon Brown scare off the intruders?

3. **Clarify** Why does Lemon Brown **cherish** his treasure?

**INDIANA STANDARDS**

**READING STANDARD**
**8.3.8** Contrast points of view ... and explain how they affect the overall theme of the work.

## Literary Analysis

4. **Examine Third-Person Limited Point of View** Whose sights, thoughts, and feelings does the narrator present? Explain how the story might be different if readers knew more about the thoughts of the other characters.

5. **Understand Events** How do Greg's feelings toward Lemon Brown change over time? In a graphic like the one shown, note important events from the story. Under each event, tell how Greg feels about Lemon Brown at that point.

6. **Make Inferences** Review the inferences you noted in your chart. How do you think Lemon Brown's life story helps Greg see his relationship with his father in a new way?

7. **Analyze Dialect** One way writers create realistic characters is to include the characters' **dialect,** the language spoken by people in a particular place or group. Dialect can include unique uses for words and nonstandard grammar. Find three examples of Lemon Brown's dialect. Explain how his language contributes to your understanding of his character.

8. **Draw Conclusions About Characters** In fiction, a character may be either static or dynamic. **Static** characters experience little change over the course of a story. **Dynamic** characters change and grow during a story. Which characters in this story are static? Which are dynamic? Explain.

## Extension and Challenge

9. **Readers' Circle** Walter Dean Myers believes it is important for young people to have role models. Discuss with a small group of classmates what makes a good role model and in what ways Lemon Brown is a role model for Greg.

10. **Inquiry and Research** Lemon Brown describes singing the blues as "singing about how hard you got it." Research the blues and find some representative songs. Is Lemon Brown's description of the blues accurate? Play parts of the songs for the class and talk about the kind of life the songs suggest.

 **RESEARCH LINKS**
For more on the blues, visit the **Research Center** at **ClassZone.com.**

# Vocabulary Practice

## VOCABULARY PRACTICE

Synonyms are words that have the same meaning. **Antonyms** are words that have the opposite meaning. Explain the meaning of the words in each pair and then decide whether they are synonyms or antonyms.

1. beckon/call
2. tentatively/cautiously
3. ominous/haunting
4. gnarled/smooth
5. ajar/open
6. impromptu/planned
7. tremor/stillness
8. commence/stop

ajar

beckon

commence

gnarled

impromptu

ominous

tentatively

tremor

## VOCABULARY IN WRITING

Use at least three vocabulary words to write a paragraph describing Greg's experience hiding from the neighborhood thugs. You might start like this.

> **EXAMPLE SENTENCE**
>
> Greg and Lemon Brown climbed the darkened staircase **tentatively**.

## VOCABULARY STRATEGY: SIMILES

Similes compare two things that are not alike using the words *like* or *as*. In this selection, Lemon Brown's voice is said to be "high and brittle, **like** dry twigs being broken." This simile helps you hear and understand what the character's voice sounds like.

Similes can also provide a context clue to help you figure out the meaning of an unknown word. If you know the sound of dry twigs being broken, you understand what the word *brittle* means.

*PRACTICE* Pay attention to the comparison being made by each simile. Use it as a context clue to help you define the boldfaced word.

1. The windows were as **murky** as the muddy waters of the Mississippi.
2. Like a mule unwilling to move, the **obstinate** child held his ground.
3. As she danced across the stage, she looked as **nimble** as a graceful deer.
4. The **persistent** detective looked for clues like a dog sniffing out a bone.
5. Their friendship was becoming as **tenuous** as a fraying rope.

**INDIANA STANDARDS**

**READING STANDARD**
**8.1.1** Analyze idioms and comparisons … to infer the literal and figurative meanings of phrases.

**VOCABULARY PRACTICE**
For more practice, go to the **Vocabulary Center** at **ClassZone.com**.

# Reading-Writing Connection

Increase your appreciation of "The Treasure of Lemon Brown" by responding to these prompts. Then complete the **Grammar and Writing** exercise.

| WRITING PROMPTS | SELF-CHECK |
|---|---|

**A. Short Response: Describe a Character**

Imagine that a friend of yours had to find Lemon Brown in a crowd. What would you tell your friend to look for? Write a **one-paragraph description** of Lemon Brown that includes details about his appearance and the treasure he **cherishes.**

*A strong description will ...*

- include words and phrases that bring Lemon Brown to life
- provide details from the story

**B. Extended Response: Write a Dialogue**

What do you think Greg and his father might have said to one another when Greg returned home? Write a **one-page dialogue** between the two of them in which they address the subject of the report card and their feelings about each other.

*A creative dialogue will ...*

- refer to details from the story
- sound like a real teenager and adult are speaking

## GRAMMAR AND WRITING

*USE CORRECT VERB TENSE* **Verb tense** indicates the time that an action or condition takes place—whether in the **past, present,** or **future.** In your writing, use the same verb tense to describe actions that take place at the same time, and change the verb tense when an action or condition happens at a different time.

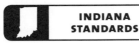 INDIANA STANDARDS

**WRITING STANDARD**
**8.4.8** Edit and proofread one's own writing, as well as that of others ....

*Original:* I always have a good time when I went to the beach. Last week, I swim and collect seashells. (Have *and* went *are in two different tenses.* Swim *and* collect *are present tense.*)

*Revised:* I always have a good time when I go to the beach. Last week, I swam and collected seashells. (*In the first sentence, both verbs need to be in the present tense. In the second sentence, the action is happening in the past, so the verbs should be in the past tense.*)

*PRACTICE* Choose the correct verb tenses in the following paragraph.

I (meet, met, will meet) an old blues musician earlier tonight. He (carries, carried, will carry) a harmonica around in his pocket every day because it reminds him of his son. He (helps, helped, will help) me realize that I should treasure people in my life more. I (work, worked, will work) harder in school to make you proud.

*For more help with verb tenses, see page R56 in the **Grammar Handbook.***

# Blues: A National Treasure

- Timeline
- History Article
- Feature Article

Use with "The Treasure of Lemon Brown," page 170.

**INDIANA STANDARDS**

**READING STANDARDS**
**8.2.3** Find similarities and differences between texts in the treatment, amount of coverage, or organization of ideas.

**8.2.7** Analyze the structure, format, and purpose of informational materials (such as textbooks, newspapers, instructional or technical manuals, and public documents).

## What's the Connection?

In "The Treasure of Lemon Brown," you met a blues musician, but do you know what blues music is? Where it came from? The other kinds of music it inspired? The selections that follow will tell you about all that and more.

## Skill Focus: Identify Scope

**Scope** refers to a work's range, or breadth, of coverage. In general, the fewer people, places, events, and ideas a work covers, the narrower its scope. For example, the "The Treasure of Lemon Brown" has a narrow scope because it covers just a few key interactions between a couple of characters on a single rainy evening. A story or article with a broad scope might introduce many people or events or cover a long period of time.

To identify how wide or narrow the scope of a selection is, consider how the writer covers the following:

- **People**—How many people are introduced? How well do you get to know them?
- **Places**—How many places, or settings, are described? How much do you get to know about them?
- **Events**—How many events are covered? How much time do these events span? How much do you learn about them?
- **Topic**—What is the topic? How many aspects of it are discussed?

As you read the selections that follow, keep track of your answers to these questions. Then, use your answers to estimate each selection's scope.

|  | Timeline | History Article | Feature Article |
|---|---|---|---|
| How many people does it introduce? How well do you get to know them? |  |  |  |
| How many places does it describe? |  |  |  |
| How many events does it cover? How much time do they span? |  |  |  |
| What is the topic? How many aspects of it are discussed? |  |  |  |

# Timeline: Evolution of the Blues  Ⓐ

The blues emerged as a new form of music in the 20th century, but its roots date back to the music created by enslaved African Americans.

| 🎼 | THE BLUES | AFRICAN-AMERICAN HISTORY |
|---|---|---|
| **1910s** | **1912** W. C. Handy writes the first blues song. He later becomes known as "the father of the blues." | **The Great Migration** Many African Americans leave the South in search of greater opportunity in Northern cities. |
| **1920s** | **1923** Ma Rainey, "the mother of the blues," releases her first album. | **The Harlem Renaissance** African-American music, art, and writing thrive in Harlem, New York. |
| **1930s** | **1933** Billie Holiday is discovered; she becomes one of the most famous jazz singers of all time. Her style is characteristic of the blues. | **The Great Depression** African Americans, along with the population as a whole, experience massive unemployment. |
| **1940s** | **1943** Blues musician Muddy Waters moves to Chicago, which becomes the center of a new style of blues. | **World War II** More than one million African Americans serve in the military despite widespread segregation and discrimination. |
| **1950s** | **1954** Elvis Presley records his first song. Influenced by blues and country music, he becomes known as "the king of rock and roll." | **A Landmark Court Case** In 1954, racial segregation in schools is declared unconstitutional in *Brown* v. *Board of Education.* |
| **1960s** | **1962** The Rolling Stones form. Influenced by the blues, the band creates a new hard-rock style that inspires countless bands to follow. | **The Civil Rights Movement** Congress passes the Civil Rights Act, which makes racial discrimination illegal in public places. |
| **1970s to present** | **1973** Kool Herc begins to DJ in the Bronx. He is seen as the father of hip-hop, a musical style that has blues roots and is Ⓑ known for rapping and instrumental "beats." | **Struggles and Accomplishments** Though racial tensions still exist, African Americans gain broader economic opportunity than they had in previous decades. |

**Ⓕ OCUS ON FORM**
A timeline is a graphic aid that identifies key events during a certain time period. Labels usually tell the specific time in which notable events occurred.

**Ⓐ TIMELINE**
**Preview** the timeline's title and headings. Based on these, what kinds of events will the timeline include?

**Ⓑ IDENTIFY SCOPE**
What period of time does the entire timeline cover?

BACK    FORWARD    STOP    REFRESH    HOME    PRINT

MUDDY WATERS     MA RAINEY     W. C. HANDY     BESSIE SMITH

# Basic Blues:
## An American Art Form

**W.C.** Handy knew about music. The composer, cornet player, and orchestra leader had traveled a lot, and he had encountered many different types of music along the way. But while waiting for a train late one night, Handy discovered a style of music unlike anything he had ever heard or played: the blues.

The legend goes like this: One night in 1903, Handy arrived at a train station in Tutwiler, Mississippi, to find that his train was about nine hours behind schedule. His companion on the platform was a raggedly dressed fellow with a guitar. The man had an odd style of playing. He slid the back of a knife
10 blade up and down the guitar's strings, creating a warbling sound. As he sang, he repeated an odd refrain—"goin' where the Southern cross the Dog"—which meant nothing to Handy. It turned out that the guitar-playing fellow was a traveling musician headed to a town called Moorhead, which was located at the intersection of two railroads, the Southern and the Yellow Dog. Handy was so intrigued by the musician's unique style and lyrics that he decided to put something similar down on paper. In the years to come, Handy would be known as the "Father of the Blues."

The American blues that Handy heard that night had its roots in the soulful songs of enslaved African Americans, which in turn were influenced by the call-
20 and-response style of singing found in Africa.  Field hollers, work songs, and

BACK   FORWARD   STOP   REFRESH   HOME   PRINT

spirituals were all sung by enslaved people as a way of expressing both their suffering and their dreams. After the Civil War, some solo musicians in the South adapted these sounds into songs they sang while accompanying themselves on guitar. The term "the blues" goes back to the 18th century, when being sad or depressed meant that you were experiencing the "blue devils." Since many of the songs were about emotional pain and loss, the name fit.

In 1912, Handy became one of the first composers to release sheet music for a blues song, "Memphis Blues." In 1920, Mamie Smith, a vaudeville performer, became the first African American to record a blues record. "Crazy Blues" sold 30  75,000 copies in its first month. Such "race records," as they were called, were originally marketed to African-American consumers, but by the end of the 1920s, both African-American and white listeners were snapping up copies of blues recordings from such artists as Ma Rainey and Bessie Smith. Blues artists went from doing informal performances in taverns to large-scale stage performances in theaters and nightclubs, and blues musicians were no longer a phenomenon of the South alone. **C**

Throughout the first half of the 20th century, many African Americans began relocating to the North, looking for a better life with more opportunity. When they moved to cities like Chicago and Detroit, they brought blues music with 40  them. Blues musicians at the time invented new ways to play the blues as a means of reflecting the changes they had experienced. One artist, Muddy Waters, traded in his acoustic guitar for an electric one and added new instruments such as an upright bass, drums, and a harmonica. The new blues was livelier, gave folks something to dance to, and paved the way for rhythm and blues and rock and roll.

Waters's style of "electrified blues" was popular until the early 1950s. But then rock and roll took over the American airwaves. This could have been the end of the blues, but starting in the 1960s, a new wave of white musicians from England and the United States revived interest with their own versions 50  of classic blues tunes. Groups like the Rolling Stones, Cream, and Led Zeppelin brought the blues back to the forefront of the American music scene. However, some blues musicians resented the success of these white musicians, who were gaining fortune and fame using the sounds of lesser-known African-American musicians. **D**

In recent years, new artists such as Jonny Lang, Shemekia Copeland, and Susan Tedeschi have contributed their own styles to the evolution of blues music. These new artists have managed to keep the genre fresh, while at the same time paying tribute to generations of past musicians who taught the United States— and the world—how to sing the blues.

**C  IDENTIFY SCOPE**
How many people has the writer mentioned so far? Note how much you learn about each one of them.

**D  IDENTIFY SCOPE**
Over what period of time do the events in this paragraph take place?

The New York Times

SUNDAY, MARCH 21, 2004                                    B16

# Musicians Know the Blues Firsthand

*Andrew Jacobs*

No one ever said the blues was any way to make a living. . . . Broke even in good times, Little Freddie King survived by playing juke joints in New Orleans until old age left his body broken. Deprived of a steady income, he went without dentures or glasses, and one night, a heavy rain brought down the ceiling of his
10 bedroom.

Without an audience for his quirky style of music, Haskel "Whistling Britches" Thompson ended up in a Winston-Salem homeless shelter. . . .

"These people are our culture, our folk musicians, and no one is looking after them," said the bluesman Taj Mahal. "We're always putting our hands over our heart and saying the
20 Pledge of Allegiance and honoring Davy Crockett, yet we're allowing these people and their music to fall through the cracks."

In the 1980s, Tim Duffy came to a similar realization. As a student studying folklore at the University of North Carolina, he grew obsessed with preserving the sounds of these unheralded musicians. But as he
30 traveled the rural South with recording equipment, he grew even more troubled by the poverty that left many artists without instruments and too strapped for heating oil or medicine.

"Their music ended up in archives but the problem is no one gets to hear it," said Mr. Duffy, who lives in Hillsborough, N.C. "And the recordings don't put food on their
40 table, it doesn't get them a gig."

Over the last two decades, Mr. Duffy, 41, has turned his passion into a nonprofit organization, the Music Maker Foundation, which is part recording company, part artist management service, and part social welfare agency. For those able to perform, the foundation promotes roots music and offers artists a touring career;
50 for those too old or sickly, he sends monthly checks that average $100.

When unexpected hardships strike, as in the case of Little Freddie King's collapsing ceiling, Mr. Duffy provides emergency cash. . . .

The foundation also puts CDs into the hands of men like Cootie Stark, a blind guitarist from Greenville, S.C., who had never had his music recorded
60 until he met Mr. Duffy at age 68. Mr. Stark, now 77, has since taken to the stages of Lincoln Center, the Rockport Rhythm and Blues Festival at Newport, and other concert venues. He earns about $8,000 a year selling his CDs.

"It should have happened 45 years ago, but I finally got a break," he said. **E**

**E** IDENTIFY SCOPE
What is this article about? What time period does it focus on? Jot this information in your chart.

# Comprehension

1. **Recall** Who became known as "the father of the blues" and why?

2. **Summarize** In a few sentences, summarize what gave rise to electrified blues.

3. **Clarify** Reread lines 15–23 in "Musicians Know the Blues Firsthand." What is Taj Mahal pointing out here?

# Critical Analysis

4. **Compare Scope** Which of the three selections has the narrowest scope? How do the scopes of the other two selections compare? Use the chart you made as you read to give reasons for your answers.

5. **Draw Conclusions About a Timeline** Why do you suppose a timeline called "Evolution of the Blues" includes key events in African-American history?

**INDIANA STANDARDS**

**READING STANDARDS**
**8.2.3** Find similarities and differences between texts in the treatment, amount of coverage, or organization of ideas.

**8.2.7** Analyze the structure, format, and purpose of informational materials (such as textbooks, newspapers, instructional or technical manuals, and public documents).

# Read for Information: Evaluate Sources for Usefulness

### WRITING PROMPT

Imagine you have chosen one of the following topics for a report:

- the birth of blues music and how blues has changed over the years
- important events in African-American history
- the life of blues musicians

Explain which selection you would use as a source of information for this topic and why. If more than one selection would be useful to you, be sure to explain what each would provide.

To answer this prompt, first identify the topic you would want to focus on. Then follow these steps:

1. Using the chart you filled in, consider the focus of each selection you just read. What kinds of information does each selection provide?

| Topic of Report: _____ | |
|---|---|
| Selection I Would Use | Why I Would Use It |
| | |

2. In a paragraph, identify the topic you picked, the selection(s) you would use for a report on that topic, and a brief explanation as to why the selection(s) would be useful to you.

## Flowers for Algernon
Short Story by Daniel Keyes

### *from* Charly
Screenplay by Stirling Silliphant

# When is it better not to
# KNOW?

**INDIANA STANDARDS**

**READING STANDARD**
**8.3.2** Evaluate the structural elements of the plot, such as subplots, parallel episodes, and climax; the plot's development; and the way in which conflicts are (or are not) addressed and resolved.

**KEY IDEA** As young children, we want to know everything: why the sky is blue, how computers work, why people can talk but dogs can't. Humans have a natural thirst for **knowledge.** But as we grow up, we sometimes find there are things it's not necessary, or even desirable, to know. In the short story you are about to read, a man learns that knowledge can bring with it some unpleasant truths.

**DISCUSS** If it were possible, would you want to see what the future holds for you in ten years, even if you couldn't change it? Discuss this question with a small group. Consider the benefits of knowing what your life will be like, as well as the potential negatives.

## ● LITERARY ANALYSIS: CHARACTER TRAITS

Literary characters are as unique as real people. They have distinct personalities, appearances, and likes and dislikes. These qualities are called **character traits,** and a reader must often infer them based on characters' words and actions.

In "Flowers for Algernon," the main character undergoes a dramatic transformation. As you read, use a Y-chart to note which of his character traits change and which stay the same.

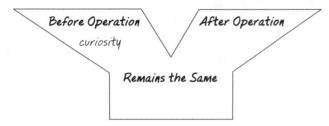

*Before Operation*
curiosity

*After Operation*

*Remains the Same*

*Review:* **Point of View**

## ● READING STRATEGY: READING A LONG STORY

Have you ever felt overwhelmed when reading a long story? The following strategies can help you stay on track:

- Look for ways to break up a long story into smaller parts.
- Pause at the end of these sections and ask yourself questions.
- Think about how later sections relate to earlier ones.

"Flowers for Algernon" is already divided into parts; it is made up of a series of journal entries. As you read, notice the dates, lengths, and language of the journal entries and consider how these things affect your understanding of the selection.

## ▲ VOCABULARY IN CONTEXT

The boldfaced words help Daniel Keyes tell about a man who is the subject of a medical experiment. Try to figure out what each word means in the context of its sentence.

1. Receiving the medal made his success more **tangible.**
2. He's an **opportunist** because he'll do anything to get ahead.
3. The doctor had a **specialization** in brain development.
4. The research findings created a **sensation** at the conference.
5. Will you **refute** the results, or do you believe them, too?
6. His understanding is **proportional** to his intelligence.
7. His long work hours could **impair** his social life.
8. They laughed at his **absurd** moves when dancing.

# Author On|ine

**Daniel Keyes: Wondering, What If?** Writing "Flowers for Algernon" brought together two of Daniel Keyes's interests: pyschology and literature. Keyes started his career as an English teacher. A struggling student once approached him and said, "I want to be smart." Keyes wondered what would happen if science discovered a way to increase a person's intelligence, and he explored the idea in "Flowers for Algernon." He later expanded the story into a novel, published in 1966.

**Daniel Keyes born 1927**

**Stirling Silliphant: Screenwriter** Stirling Silliphant's career included winning the Academy Award for best screenplay in 1968. Known for action-filled scripts, he showed the range of his abilities by writing the screenplay for *Charly* (1969), based on the novel *Flowers for Algernon.*

**Stirling Silliphant 1918–1996**

**MORE ABOUT THE AUTHOR**
For more on the authors, visit the **Literature Center** at **ClassZone.com.**

## *Background*

**IQ** In "Flowers for Algernon," the main character takes tests to measure his IQ, or intelligence quotient. IQ is a number that is thought to provide a measurement of a person's intelligence. IQ tests involve memory, reasoning, and numerical ability. Intelligence tests were once considered to be a reliable measure, but today, questions remain about the accuracy of such tests.

# Flowers *for* Algernon

## Daniel Keyes

**progris riport 1—martch 5 1965**

Dr. Strauss says I shud rite down what I think and evrey thing that happins to me from now on. I dont know why but he says its importint so they will see if they will use me. I hope they use me. Miss Kinnian says maybe they can make me smart. I want to be smart. My name is Charlie Gordon. I am 37 years old and 2 weeks ago was my brithday. I have nuthing more to rite now so I will close for today.

**progris riport 2—martch 6**

I had a test today. I think I faled it. and I think that maybe now they wont use me. What happind is a nice young man was in the room and he had some white cards with ink spillled all over them. He sed Charlie what do you see on
10  this card. I was very skared even tho I had my rabits foot in my pockit because when I was a kid I always faled tests in school and I spillled ink to. Ⓐ
    I told him I saw a inkblot. He said yes and it made me feel good. I thot that was all but when I got up to go he stopped me. He said now sit down Charlie we are not thru yet. Then I dont remember so good but he wantid me to say what was in the ink. I dint see nuthing in the ink but he said there was picturs there other pepul saw some picturs. I coudnt see any picturs. I reely tryed to see. I held the card close up and then far away. Then I said if I had my glases I coud see better I usally only ware my glases in the movies or TV but I said they are in the closit in the hall. I got them. Then I said let me see that card
20  agen I bet Ill find it now.

Illustration by Sylvia Chesley Smith.
All other illustrations by Todd Davidson.

---

**ANALYZE VISUALS**
What is the **mood** of this illustration? Tell how the colors and brush strokes help create that mood.

Ⓐ **CHARACTER TRAITS**
What can you **infer** about Charlie's abilities and personality?

I tryed hard but I still coudnt find the picturs I only saw the ink. I told him maybe I need new glases. He rote somthing down on a paper and I got skared of faling the test. I told him it was a very nice inkblot with littel points all around the eges. He looked very sad so that wasnt it. I said please let me try agen. Ill get it in a few minits becaus Im not so fast somtimes. Im a slow reeder too in Miss Kinnians class for slow adults but I'm trying very hard.

He gave me a chance with another card that had 2 kinds of ink spillled on it red and blue.

30 He was very nice and talked slow like Miss Kinnian does and he explaned it to me that it was a *raw shok.* He said pepul see things in the ink. I said show me where. He said think. I told him I think a inkblot but that wasnt rite eather. He said what does it remind you—pretend somthing. I closd my eyes for a long time to pretend. I told him I pretned a fowntan pen with ink leeking all over a table cloth. Then he got up and went out.

I dont think I passd the *raw shok* test. **B**

**progris report 3—martch 7**

Dr Strauss and Dr Nemur say it dont matter about the inkblots. I told them I dint spill the ink on the cards and I coudnt see anything in the ink. They said that maybe they will still use me. I said Miss Kinnian never gave me tests like that one only spelling and reading. They said Miss Kinnian told that I was her
40 bestist pupil in the adult nite scool becaus I tryed the hardist and I reely wantid to lern. They said how come you went to the adult nite scool all by yourself Charlie. How did you find it. I said I askd pepul and sumbody told me where I shud go to lern to read and spell good. They said why did you want to. I told them becaus all my life I wantid to be smart and not dumb. But its very hard to be smart. They said you know it will probly be tempirery. I said yes. Miss Kinnian told me. I dont care if it herts. **C**

Later I had more crazy tests today. The nice lady who gave it me told me the name and I asked her how do you spellit so I can rite it in my progris riport. THEMATIC APPERCEPTION TEST.[1] I dont know the frist 2 words but I
50 know what *test* means. You got to pass it or you get bad marks. This test lookd easy becaus I coud see the picturs. Only this time she dint want me to tell her the picturs. That mixd me up. I said the man yesterday said I shoud tell him what I saw in the ink she said that dont make no difrence. She said make up storys about the pepul in the picturs.

I told her how can you tell storys about pepul you never met. I said why shud I make up lies. I never tell lies any more becaus I always get caut.

She told me this test and the other one the raw-shok was for getting personalty. I laffed so hard. I said how can you get that thing from inkblots and fotos. She got sore and put her picturs away. I dont care. It was sily. I gess
60 I faled that test too.

---

1. **Thematic Apperception** (thĭ-mǎt′ĭk ăp′ər-sĕp′shən) **Test:** test for analyzing personality on the basis of stories people make up about a series of pictures.

**VISUAL VOCABULARY**

**Rorschach** (rôr′shäk′) **test** *n.* the name of a personality test that uses inkblot designs

**B READING A LONG STORY**
In what ways are Charlie's journal entries unique?

**C CHARACTER TRAITS**
What do lines 41–46 tell you about Charlie's desire to change?

Later some men in white coats took me to a difernt part of the hospitil and gave me a game to play. It was like a race with a white mouse. They called the mouse Algernon. Algernon was in a box with a lot of twists and turns like all kinds of walls and they gave me a pencil and a paper with lines and lots of boxes. On one side it said START and on the other end it said FINISH. They said it was *amazed*[2] and that Algernon and me had the same *amazed* to do. I dint see how we could have the same *amazed* if Algernon had a box and I had a paper but I dint say nothing. Anyway there wasnt time because the race started.

One of the men had a watch he was trying to hide so I woudnt see it so
70 I tryed not to look and that made me nervus.

Anyway that test made me feel worser than all the others because they did it over 10 times with difernt *amazeds* and Algernon won every time. I dint know that mice were so smart. Maybe thats because Algernon is a white mouse. Maybe white mice are smarter then other mice. **D**

### progris riport 4—Mar 8

Their going to use me! Im so exited I can hardly write. Dr Nemur and Dr Strauss had a argument about it first. Dr Nemur was in the office when Dr Strauss brot me in. Dr Nemur was worryed about using me but Dr Strauss told him Miss Kinnian rekemmended me the best from all the people who she was teaching. I like Miss Kinnian becaus shes a very smart teacher. And she said
80 Charlie your going to have a second chance. If you volenteer for this experament you mite get smart. They dont know if it will be perminint but theirs a chance. Thats why I said ok even when I was scared because she said it was an operashun. She said dont be scared Charlie you done so much with so little I think you deserv it most of all.

So I got scaird when Dr Nemur and Dr Strauss argud about it. Dr Strauss said I had something that was very good. He said I had a good *motor-vation*.[3] I never even knew I had that. I felt proud when he said that not every body with an eye-q[4] of 68 had that thing. I dont know what it is or where I got it but he said Algernon had it too. Algernons *motor-vation* is the cheese they put
90 in his box. But it cant be that because I didnt eat any cheese this week.

Then he told Dr Nemur something I dint understand so while they were talking I wrote down some of the words.

He said Dr Nemur I know Charlie is not what you had in mind as the first of your new brede of intelek** (coudnt get the word) superman. But most people of his low ment** are host** and uncoop** they are usualy dull apath** and hard to reach. He has a good natcher hes intristed and eager to please. **E**

Dr Nemur said remember he will be the first human beeng ever to have his intelijence trippled by surgicle meens.

2. **amazed:** Charlie's way of writing *a maze*.

3. **motor-vation:** Charlie's way of writing *motivation*.

4. **eye-q:** Charlie's way of writing *IQ* (abbreviation for *intelligence quotient*).

**D POINT OF VIEW**
Because this story is told in the **first-person point of view,** you learn about Charlie's thought process directly from him. What do you learn about his mental capacity?

**E CHARACTER TRAITS**
What have you learned about Charlie through the comments of Miss Kinnian and the doctors?

Dr Strauss said exakly. Look at how well hes lerned to read and write for his
100 low mentel age its as grate an acheve** as you and I lerning einstines therey of
**vity[5] without help. That shows the intenss motor-vation. Its comparat** a
tremen** achev** I say we use Charlie. **F**

I dint get all the words and they were talking to fast but it sounded like
Dr Strauss was on my side and like the other one wasnt.

Then Dr Nemur nodded he said all right maybe your right. We will use
Charlie. When he said that I got so exited I jumped up and shook his hand for
being so good to me. I told him thank you doc you wont be sorry for giving
me a second chance. And I mean it like I told him. After the operashun Im
gonna try to be smart. Im gonna try awful hard.

**progris ript 5—Mar 10**

110 Im skared. Lots of people who work here and the nurses and the people who
gave me the tests came to bring me candy and wish me luck. I hope I have
luck. I got my rabits foot and my lucky penny and my horse shoe. Only a black
cat crossed me when I was comming to the hospitil. Dr Strauss says dont be
supersitis Charlie this is sience. Anyway Im keeping my rabits foot with me.

I asked Dr Strauss if Ill beat Algernon in the race after the operashun and
he said maybe. If the operashun works Ill show that mouse I can be as smart as
he is. Maybe smarter. Then Ill be abel to read better and spell the words good
and know lots of things and be like other people. I want to be smart like other
people. If it works perminint they will make everybody smart all over the
120 wurld. **G**

They dint give me anything to eat this morning. I dont know what that
eating has to do with getting smart. Im very hungry and Dr Nemur took away
my box of candy. That Dr Nemur is a grouch. Dr Strauss says I can have it
back after the operashun. You cant eat befor a operashun . . .

**Progress Report 6—Mar 15**

The operashun dint hurt. He did it while I was sleeping. They took off the
bandijis from my eyes and my head today so I can make a PROGRESS
REPORT. Dr Nemur who looked at some of my other ones says I spell
PROGRESS wrong and he told me how to spell it and REPORT too. I got
to try and remember that.

130 I have a very bad memary for spelling. Dr Strauss says its ok to tell about
all the things that happin to me but he says I shoud tell more about what I feel
and what I think. When I told him I dont know how to think he said try.
All the time when the bandijis were on my eyes I tryed to think. Nothing
happened. I dont know what to think about. Maybe if I ask him he will tell
me how I can think now that Im suppose to get smart. What do smart people
think about. Fancy things I suppose. I wish I knew some fancy things alredy.

**F CHARACTER TRAITS**
Which of Charlie's traits
convince Dr. Strauss
to use him in the
experiment?

**G CHARACTER TRAITS**
What hopes does Charlie
have for the operation?

---

5. **einstines therey of **vity:** Charlie's way of writing *Einstein's theory of relativity*, the theory of space
and time developed by Albert Einstein.

### Progress Report 7—mar 19

Nothing is happining. I had lots of tests and different kinds of races with Algernon. I hate that mouse. He always beats me. Dr Strauss said I got to play those games. And he said some time I got to take those tests over again. Thse 140 inkblots are stupid. And those pictures are stupid too. I like to draw a picture of a man and a woman but I wont make up lies about people.

I got a headache from trying to think so much. I thot Dr Strauss was my frend but he dont help me. He dont tell me what to think or when Ill get smart. Miss Kinnian dint come to see me. I think writing these progress reports are stupid too. **H**

### Progress Report 8—Mar 23

Im going back to work at the factery. They said it was better I shud go back to work but I cant tell anyone what the operashun was for and I have to come to the hospitil for an hour evry night after work. They are gonna pay me mony every month for lerning to be smart.

**ANALYZE VISUALS**
What is the **connection** between this illustration and what happens to Charlie?

**H** **READING A LONG STORY**
In what ways is the March 19 progress report different from the other reports so far? Think about its length and language.

150      Im glad Im going back to work because I miss my job and all my frends and all the fun we have there.

     Dr Strauss says I shud keep writing things down but I dont have to do it every day just when I think of something or something speshul happins. He says dont get discoridged because it takes time and it happins slow. He says it took a long time with Algernon before he got 3 times smarter then he was before. Thats why Algernon beats me all the time because he had that operashun too. That makes me feel better. I coud probly do that *amazed* faster than a reglar mouse. Maybe some day Ill beat Algernon. Boy that would be something. So far Algernon looks like he mite be smart perminent.

160 *Mar 25* (I dont have to write PROGRESS REPORT on top any more just when I hand it in once a week for Dr Nemur to read. I just have to put the date on. That saves time)

     We had a lot of fun at the factery today. Joe Carp said hey look where Charlie had his operashun what did they do Charlie put some brains in. I was going to tell him but I remembered Dr Strauss said no. Then Frank Reilly said what did you do Charlie forget your key and open your door the hard way. That made me laff. Their really my friends and they like me.

     Sometimes somebody will say hey look at Joe or Frank or George he really pulled a Charlie Gordon. I dont know why they say that but they always laff. 170 This morning Amos Borg who is the 4 man at Donnegans used my name when he shouted at Ernie the office boy. Ernie lost a packige. He said Ernie for godsake what are you trying to be a Charlie Gordon. I dont understand why he said that. I never lost any packiges. ❶

*Mar 28* Dr Straus came to my room tonight to see why I dint come in like I was suppose to. I told him I dont like to race with Algernon any more. He said I dont have to for a while but I shud come in. He had a present for me only it wasnt a present but just for lend. I thot it was a little television but it wasnt. He said I got to turn it on when I go to sleep. I said your kidding why shud I turn it on when Im going to sleep. Who ever herd of a thing like that. But he said if I want to get 180 smart I got to do what he says. I told him I dint think I was going to get smart and he put his hand on my sholder and said Charlie you dont know it yet but your getting smarter all the time. You wont notice for a while. I think he was just being nice to make me feel good because I dont look any smarter.

     Oh yes I almost forgot. I asked him when I can go back to the class at Miss Kinnians school. He said I wont go their. He said that soon Miss Kinnian will come to the hospitil to start and teach me speshul. I was mad at her for not comming to see me when I got the operashun but I like her so maybe we will be frends again.

*Mar 29* That crazy TV kept me up all night. How can I sleep with something 190 yelling crazy things all night in my ears. And the nutty pictures. Wow. I dont know what it says when Im up so how am I going to know when Im sleeping.

❶ **CHARACTER TRAITS**
Why does Charlie think these men are his friends? Note whether he is a good judge of character at this point.

Dr Strauss says its ok. He says my brains are lerning when I sleep and that will help me when Miss Kinnian starts my lessons in the hospitl (only I found out it isnt a hospitil its a labatory. I think its all crazy. If you can get smart when your sleeping why do people go to school. That thing I dont think will work. I use to watch the late show and the late late show on TV all the time and it never made me smart. Maybe you have to sleep while you watch it.

## PROGRESS REPORT 9—April 3

Dr Strauss showed me how to keep the TV turned low so now I can sleep. I dont hear a thing. And I still dont understand what it says. A few times I play it over
200 in the morning to find out what I lerned when I was sleeping and I dont think so. Miss Kinnian says Maybe its another langwidge or something. But most times it sounds american. It talks so fast faster than even Miss Gold who was my teacher in 6 grade and I remember she talked so fast I coudnt understand her.

I told Dr Strauss what good is it to get smart in my sleep. I want to be smart when Im awake. He says its the same thing and I have two minds. Theres the *subconscious* and the *conscious*[6] (thats how you spell it). And one dont tell the other one what its doing. They dont even talk to each other. Thats why I dream. And boy have I been having crazy dreams. Wow. Ever since that night TV. The late late late late late show.

210 I forgot to ask him if it was only me or if everybody had those two minds.

(I just looked up the word in the dictionary Dr Strauss gave me. The word is *subconscious. adj. Of the nature of mental operations yet not present in consciousness; as, subconscious conflict of desires.*) There's more but I still dont know what it means. This isnt a very good dictionary for dumb people like me.

Anyway the headache is from the party. My frends from the factery Joe Carp and Frank Reilly invited me to go with them to Muggsys Saloon for some drinks. I dont like to drink but they said we will have lots of fun. I had a good time.

Joe Carp said I shoud show the girls how I mop out the toilet in the factory
220 and he got me a mop. I showed them and everyone laffed when I told that Mr Donnegan said I was the best janiter he ever had because I like my job and do it good and never come late or miss a day except for my operashun.

I said Miss Kinnian always said Charlie be proud of your job because you do it good.

Everybody laffed and we had a good time and they gave me lots of drinks and Joe said Charlie is a card when hes potted.[7] I dont know what that means but everybody likes me and we have fun. I cant wait to be smart like my best frends Joe Carp and Frank Reilly. **J**

I dont remember how the party was over but I think I went out to buy a
230 newspaper and coffe for Joe and Frank and when I came back there was no one

**J** **POINT OF VIEW**
How does hearing about the party from Charlie's **point of view** affect your reaction to his coworkers?

---

6. **the subconscious** (sŭb-kŏn′shəs) **and the conscious** (kŏn′shəs): psychological terms. *Subconscious* refers to mental activity a person is not aware of; *conscious* refers to mental activity of which a person is aware.

7. **Charlie is a card when he's potted:** Charlie is funny when he's drunk.

their. I looked for them all over till late. Then I dont remember so good but I think I got sleepy or sick. A nice cop brot me back home. Thats what my landlady Mrs Flynn says.

But I got a headache and a big lump on my head and black and blue all over. I think maybe I fell but Joe Carp says it was the cop they beat up drunks some times. I don't think so. Miss Kinnian says cops are to help people. 240 Anyway I got a bad headache and Im sick and hurt all over. I dont think Ill drink anymore.

*April 6* I beat Algernon! I dint even know I beat him until Burt the tester told me. Then the second time I lost because I got so exited I fell off the chair before I finished. But after that I beat him 8 more times. I must be getting smart to beat a smart mouse like Algernon. But I dont *feel* smarter.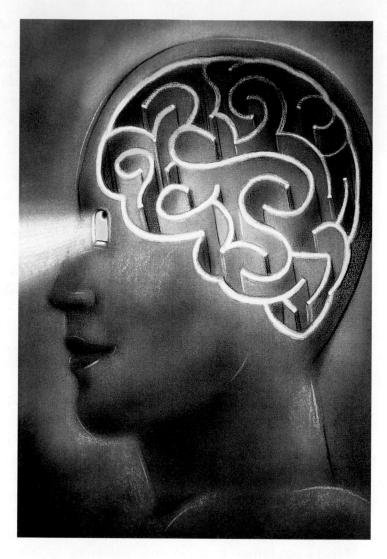

I wanted to race Algernon some more but 250 Burt said thats enough for one day. They let me hold him for a minit. Hes not so bad. Hes soft like a ball of cotton. He blinks and when he opens his eyes their black and pink on the eges.

I said can I feed him because I felt bad to beat him and I wanted to be nice and make frends. Burt said no Algernon is a very specshul mouse with an operashun like mine, and he was the first of all the animals to stay smart so long. He told me 260 Algernon is so smart that every day he has to solve a test to get his food. Its a thing like a lock on a door that changes every time Algernon goes in to eat so he has to lern something new to get his food. That made me sad because if he coudnt lern he woud be hungry.

I dont think its right to make you pass a test to eat. How woud Dr Nemur like it to have to pass a test every time he wants to eat. I think Ill be frends with Algernon. **L**

*April 9* Tonight after work Miss Kinnian was at the laboratory. She looked like she was glad to see me but scared. I told her dont worry Miss Kinnian Im not smart yet and she laffed. She said I have confidence in you Charlie the way 270 you struggled so hard to read and right better than all the others. At werst you will have it for a littel wile and your doing somthing for sience.

**K** **READING A LONG STORY**
Note the date on this journal entry. What significant changes have happened in the story since the first entries one month ago?

**L** **CHARACTER TRAITS**
In lines 249–266, what does Charlie's treatment of Algernon reveal about his character?

We are reading a very hard book. I never read such a hard book before. Its called *Robinson Crusoe* about a man who gets merooned on a dessert Iland. Hes smart and figers out all kinds of things so he can have a house and food and hes a good swimmer. Only I feel sorry because hes all alone and has no frends. But I think their must be somebody else on the iland because theres a picture with his funny umbrella looking at footprints. I hope he gets a frend and not be lonly.

*April 10* Miss Kinnian teaches me to spell better. She says look at a word and
280 close your eyes and say it over and over until you remember. I have lots of truble with *through* that you say *threw* and *enough* and *tough* that you dont say *enew* and *tew*. You got to say *enuff* and *tuff*. Thats how I use to write it before I started to get smart. Im confused but Miss Kinnian says theres no reason in spelling.

*Apr 14* Finished *Robinson Crusoe*. I want to find out more about what happens to him but Miss Kinnian says thats all there is. *Why*

*Apr 15* Miss Kinnian says Im lerning fast. She read some of the Progress Reports and she looked at me kind of funny. She says Im a fine person and Ill show them all. I asked her why. She said never mind but I shoudnt feel bad if
290 I find out that everybody isnt nice like I think. She said for a person who god gave so little to you done more then a lot of people with brains they never even used. I said all my frends are smart people but there good. They like me and they never did anything that wasnt nice. Then she got something in her eye and she had to run out to the ladys room. ⓜ

*Apr 16* Today, I lerned, the *comma*, this is a comma (,) a period, with a tail, Miss Kinnian, says its important, because, it makes writing, better, she said, sombeody, coud lose, a lot of money, if a comma, isnt, in the, right place, I dont have, any money, and I dont see, how a comma, keeps you, from losing it,
    But she says, everybody, uses commas, so Ill use, them too,

300 *Apr 17* I used the comma wrong. Its punctuation. Miss Kinnian told me to look up long words in the dictionary to lern to spell them. I said whats the difference if you can read it anyway. She said its part of your education so now on Ill look up all the words Im not sure how to spell. It takes a long time to write that way but I think Im remembering. I only have to look up once and after that I get it right. Anyway thats how come I got the word *punctuation* right. (Its that way in the dictionary). Miss Kinnian says a period is punctuation too, and there are lots of other marks to lern. I told her I thot all the periods had to have tails but she said no.
    You got to mix them up, she showed? me" how. to mix! them(up,. and
310 now; I can! mix up all kinds" of punctuation, in! my writing? There, are lots! of rules? to lern; but Im gettin'g them in my head.

ⓜ **CHARACTER TRAITS**
What can you **infer** about Miss Kinnian from her conversation with Charlie?

One thing I? like about, Dear Miss Kinnian: (thats the way it goes in a business letter if I ever go into business) is she, always gives me' a reason" when—I ask. She's a gen'ius! I wish! I cou'd be smart" like, her;

(Punctuation, is; fun!)

*April 18*  What a dope I am! I didn't even understand what she was talking about. I read the grammar book last night and it explanes the whole thing. Then I saw it was the same way as Miss Kinnian was trying to tell me, but I didn't get it. I got up in the middle of the night, and the whole thing straightened out in my mind.

Miss Kinnian said that the TV working in my sleep helped out. She said I reached a plateau. Thats like the flat top of a hill.

After I figgered out how punctuation worked, I read over all my old Progress Reports from the beginning. Boy, did I have crazy spelling and punctuation! I told Miss Kinnian I ought to go over the pages and fix all the mistakes but she said, "No, Charlie, Dr. Nemur wants them just as they are. That's why he let you keep them after they were photostated, to see your own progress. You're coming along fast, Charlie."

That made me feel good. After the lesson I went down and played with Algernon. We don't race any more.

*April 20*  I feel sick inside. Not sick like for a doctor, but inside my chest it feels empty like getting punched and a heartburn at the same time.

I wasn't going to write about it, but I guess I got to, because its important. Today was the first time I ever stayed home from work.

Last night Joe Carp and Frank Reilly invited me to a party. There were lots of girls and some men from the factory. I remembered how sick I got last time I drank too much, so I told Joe I didn't want anything to drink. He gave me a plain coke instead. It tasted funny, but I thought it was just a bad taste in my mouth.

We had a lot of fun for a while. Joe said I should dance with Ellen and she would teach me the steps. I fell a few times and I couldn't understand why because no one else was dancing besides Ellen and me. And all the time I was tripping because somebody's foot was always sticking out.

Then when I got up I saw the look on Joe's face and it gave me a funny feeling in my stomach. "He's a scream," one of the girls said. Everybody was laughing.

Frank said, "I ain't laughed so much since we sent him off for the newspaper that night at Muggsy's and ditched him."

"Look at him. His face is red."

"He's blushing. Charlie is blushing."

"Hey, Ellen, what'd you do to Charlie? I never saw him act like that before."

I didn't know what to do or where to turn. Everyone was looking at me and laughing and I felt naked. I wanted to hide myself. I ran out into the street and

I threw up. Then I walked home. It's a funny thing I never knew that Joe and Frank and the others liked to have me around all the time to make fun of me.

Now I know what it means when they say "to pull a Charlie Gordon."

I'm ashamed. **N**

## PROGRESS REPORT 10

*April 21* Still didn't go into the factory. I told Mrs. Flynn my landlady to call and tell Mr. Donnegan I was sick. Mrs. Flynn looks at me very funny lately
360 like she's scared of me.

I think it's a good thing about finding out how everybody laughs at me. I thought about it a lot. It's because I'm so dumb and I don't even know when I'm doing something dumb. People think it's funny when a dumb person can't do things the same way they can.

Anyway, now I know I'm getting smarter every day. I know punctuation and I can spell good. I like to look up all the hard words in the dictionary and I remember them. I'm reading a lot now, and Miss Kinnian says I read very fast. Sometimes I even understand what I'm reading about, and it stays in my mind. There are times when I can close my eyes and think of a page and it all
370 comes back like a picture.

Besides history, geography, and arithmetic, Miss Kinnian said I should start to learn a few foreign languages. Dr. Strauss gave me some more tapes to play while I sleep. I still don't understand how that conscious and unconscious mind works, but Dr. Strauss says not to worry yet. He asked me to promise that when I start learning college subjects next week I wouldn't read any books on psychology—that is, until he gives me permission. **O**

I feel a lot better today, but I guess I'm still a little angry that all the time people were laughing and making fun of me because I wasn't so smart. When I become intelligent like Dr. Strauss says, with three times my I.Q. of 68, then
380 maybe I'll be like everyone else and people will like me and be friendly.

I'm not sure what an *I.Q.* is. Dr. Nemur said it was something that measured how intelligent you were—like a scale in the drugstore weighs pounds. But Dr. Strauss had a big arguement with him and said an I.Q. didn't weigh intelligence at all. He said an I.Q. showed how much intelligence you could get, like the numbers on the outside of a measuring cup. You still had to fill the cup up with stuff.

Then when I asked Burt, who gives me my intelligence tests and works with Algernon, he said that both of them were wrong (only I had to promise not to tell them he said so). Burt says that the I.Q. measures a lot of different
390 things including some of the things you learned already, and it really isn't any good at all.

So I still don't know what I.Q. is except that mine is going to be over 200 soon. I didn't want to say anything, but I don't see how if they don't know *what* it is, or *where* it is—I don't see how they know *how much* of it you've got.

Dr. Nemur says I have to take a *Rorschach Test* tomorrow. I wonder what *that* is.

**N CHARACTER TRAITS**
Why is Charlie ashamed now? Why wasn't he ashamed a couple of weeks ago?

**O POINT OF VIEW**
How might your understanding of Charlie's progress be different if you knew what others were thinking?

*April 22* I found out what a *Rorshach* is. It's the test I took before the operation—the one with the inkblots on the pieces of cardboard. The man who gave me the test was the same one.

400   I was scared to death of those inkblots. I knew he was going to ask me to find the pictures and I knew I wouldn't be able to. I was thinking to myself, if only there was some way of knowing what kind of pictures were hidden there. Maybe there weren't any pictures at all. Maybe it was just a trick to see if I was dumb enough to look for something that wasn't there. Just thinking about that made me sore at him.

"All right, Charlie," he said, "you've seen these cards before, remember?"

"Of course I remember."

The way I said it, he knew I was angry, and he looked surprised. "Yes, of course. Now I want you to look at this one. What might this be? What do you
410   see on this card? People see all sorts of things in these inkblots. Tell me what it might be for you—what it makes you think of."

I was shocked. That wasn't what I had expected him to say at all. "You mean there are no pictures hidden in those inkblots?"

He frowned and took off his glasses. "What?"

"Pictures. Hidden in the inkblots. Last time you told me that everyone could see them and you wanted me to find them too."

He explained to me that the last time he had used almost the exact same words he was using now. I didn't believe it, and I still have the suspicion that he misled me at the time just for the fun of it. Unless—I don't know any
420   more—could I have been *that* feeble-minded?

We went through the cards slowly. One of them looked like a pair of bats tugging at something. Another one looked like two men fencing with swords. I imagined all sorts of things. I guess I got carried away. But I didn't trust him any more, and I kept turning them around and even looking on the back to see if there was anything there I was supposed to catch. While he was making his notes, I peeked out of the corner of my eye to read it. But it was all in code that looked like this:

WF+A  DdF-Ad orig.  WF-A  SF+obj

The test still doesn't make sense to me. It seems to me that anyone could
430   make up lies about things that they didn't really see. How could he know I wasn't making a fool of him by mentioning things that I didn't really imagine? Maybe I'll understand it when Dr. Strauss lets me read up on psychology. 🄿

*April 25* I figured out a new way to line up the machines in the factory, and Mr. Donnegan says it will save him ten thousand dollars a year in labor and increased production. He gave me a $25 bonus.

I wanted to take Joe Carp and Frank Reilly out to lunch to celebrate, but Joe said he had to buy some things for his wife, and Frank said he was meeting his cousin for lunch. I guess it'll take a little time for them to get

🄿 **CHARACTER TRAITS**
How is Charlie's second experience with the Rorschach test different from his first experience?

used to the changes in me. Everybody seems to
440 be frightened of me. When I went over to Amos
Borg and tapped him on the shoulder, he jumped
up in the air.

People don't talk to me much any more or kid
around the way they used to. It makes the job
kind of lonely.

*April 27* I got up the nerve today to ask Miss
Kinnian to have dinner with me tomorrow night
to celebrate my bonus.

At first she wasn't sure it was right, but I asked
450 Dr. Strauss and he said it was okay. Dr. Strauss
and Dr. Nemur don't seem to be getting along so
well. They're arguing all the time. This evening
when I came in to ask Dr. Strauss about having
dinner with Miss Kinnian, I heard them shouting.
Dr. Nemur was saying that it was *his* experiment
and *his* research, and Dr. Strauss was shouting
back that he contributed just as much, because he
found me through Miss Kinnian and he
performed the operation. Dr. Strauss said that
460 someday thousands of neurosurgeons[8] might be
using his technique all over the world.

Dr. Nemur wanted to publish the results of the
experiment at the end of this month. Dr. Strauss
wanted to wait a while longer to be sure. Dr.
Strauss said that Dr. Nemur was more interested in the Chair of Psychology at
Princeton[9] than he was in the experiment. Dr. Nemur said that Dr. Strauss was
nothing but an **opportunist** who was trying to ride to glory on *his* coattails.

When I left afterwards, I found myself trembling. I don't know why for
sure, but it was as if I'd seen both men clearly for the first time. I remember
470 hearing Burt say that Dr. Nemur had a shrew of a wife who was pushing him
all the time to get things published so that he could become famous. Burt said
that the dream of her life was to have a big shot husband.

Was Dr. Strauss really trying to ride on his coattails?

*April 28* I don't understand why I never noticed how beautiful Miss Kinnian
really is. She has brown eyes and feathery brown hair that comes to the top of
her neck. She's only thirty-four! I think from the beginning I had the feeling
that she was an unreachable genius—and very, very old. Now, every time I see
her she grows younger and more lovely.

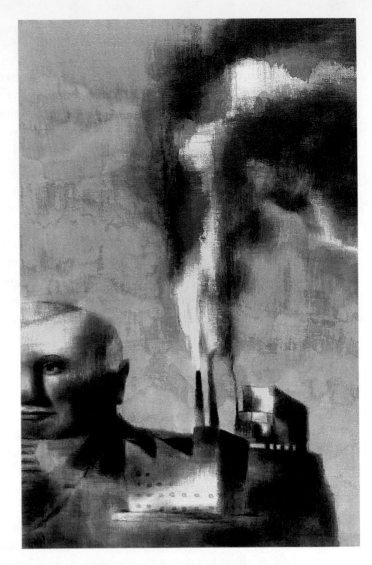

**opportunist**
(ŏp′ər-tōō′nĭst) *n.*
a person who takes
advantage of any
opportunity, without
moral regard, to achieve
a goal

---

8. **neurosurgeons** (nŏŏr′ō-sûr′jənz): doctors who perform surgery on the brain and nervous system.

9. **Chair of Psychology at Princeton:** head of the psychology department at Princeton University.

We had dinner and a long talk. When she said that I was coming along so
480 fast that soon I'd be leaving her behind, I laughed.

"It's true, Charlie. You're already a better reader than I am. You can read a whole page at a glance while I can take in only a few lines at a time. And you remember every single thing you read. I'm lucky if I can recall the main thoughts and the general meaning."

"I don't feel intelligent. There are so many things I don't understand."

She took out a cigarette and I lit it for her. "You've got to be a *little* patient. You're accomplishing in days and weeks what it takes normal people to do in half a lifetime. That's what makes it so amazing. You're like a giant sponge now, soaking things in. Facts, figures, general knowledge. And soon you'll
490 begin to connect them, too. You'll see how the different branches of learning are related. There are many levels, Charlie, like steps on a giant ladder that take you up higher and higher to see more and more of the world around you.

"I can see only a little bit of that, Charlie, and I won't go much higher than I am now, but you'll keep climbing up and up, and see more and more, and each step will open new worlds that you never even knew existed." She frowned. "I hope . . . I just hope to God—"

"What?"

"Never mind, Charles. I just hope I wasn't wrong to advise you to go into this in the first place."

500 I laughed. "How could that be? It worked, didn't it? Even Algernon is still smart."

We sat there silently for a while and I knew what she was thinking about as she watched me toying with the chain of my rabbit's foot and my keys. I didn't want to think of that possibility any more than elderly people want to think of death. I *knew* that this was only the beginning. I knew what she meant about levels because I'd seen some of them already. The thought of leaving her behind made me sad.

I'm in love with Miss Kinnian. ◉

## PROGRESS REPORT 11

*April 30* I've quit my job with Donnegan's Plastic Box Company. Mr.
510 Donnegan insisted that it would be better for all concerned if I left. What did I do to make them hate me so?

The first I knew of it was when Mr. Donnegan showed me the petition. Eight hundred and forty names, everyone connected with the factory, except Fanny Girden. Scanning the list quickly, I saw at once that hers was the only missing name. All the rest demanded that I be fired.

Joe Carp and Frank Reilly wouldn't talk to me about it. No one else would either, except Fanny. She was one of the few people I'd known who set her mind to something and believed it no matter what the rest of the world

◉ **CHARACTER TRAITS**
What new aspects of Charlie's personality are revealed in this scene with Miss Kinnian?

proved, said or did—and Fanny did not believe that I should have been fired.
520 She had been against the petition on principle and despite the pressure and
threats she'd held out.

"Which don't mean to say," she remarked, "that I don't think there's
something mighty strange about you, Charlie. Them changes. I don't know.
You used to be a good, dependable, ordinary man—not too bright maybe, but
honest. Who knows what you done to yourself to get so smart all of a sudden.
Like everybody around here's been saying, Charlie, it's not right."

"But how can you say that, Fanny? What's wrong with a man becoming
intelligent and wanting to acquire knowledge and understanding of the world
around him?"

530 She stared down at her work and I turned to leave. Without looking at me,
she said: "It was evil when Eve listened to the snake and ate from the tree of
knowledge. It was evil when she saw that she was naked. If not for that none
of us would ever have to grow old and sick, and die." [10]

Once again now I have the feeling of shame burning inside me. This
intelligence has driven a wedge between me and all the people I once knew
and loved. Before, they laughed at me and despised me for my ignorance and
dullness; now, they hate me for my knowledge and understanding. What in
God's name do they want of me?

They've driven me out of the factory. Now I'm
540 more alone than ever before . . .

ANALYZE VISUALS
What might the flask
in this illustration
**symbolize?**

*May 15* Dr. Strauss is very angry at me for not
having written any progress reports in two
weeks. He's justified because the lab is now
paying me a regular salary. I told him I was too
busy thinking and reading. When I pointed
out that writing was such a slow process that it
made me impatient with my poor handwriting,
he suggested that I learn to type. It's much
easier to write now because I can type nearly
550 seventy-five words a minute. Dr. Strauss
continually reminds me of the need to speak
and write simply so that people will be able to
understand me.

I'll try to review all the things that
happened to me during the last two weeks.
Algernon and I were presented to the *American
Psychological Association* sitting in convention

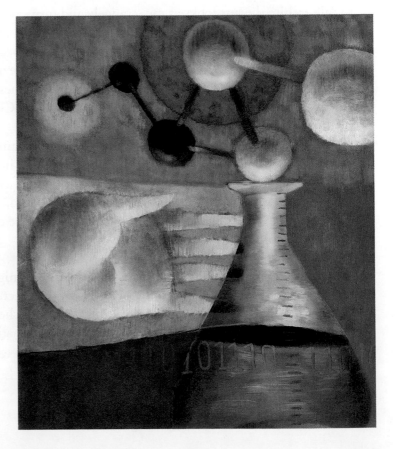

---

10. **It was evil . . . die:** a reference to the biblical story of Adam
and Eve (Genesis 2–3).

with the *World Psychological Association* last Tuesday. We created quite a
**sensation.** Dr. Nemur and Dr. Strauss were proud of us.

560    I suspect that Dr. Nemur, who is sixty—ten years older than Dr. Strauss—
finds it necessary to see **tangible** results of his work. Undoubtedly the result of
pressure by Mrs. Nemur.

Contrary to my earlier impressions of him, I realize that Dr. Nemur is not
at all a genius. He has a very good mind, but it struggles under the specter of
self-doubt. He wants people to take him for a genius. Therefore, it is important
for him to feel that his work is accepted by the world. I believe that Dr. Nemur
was afraid of further delay because he worried that someone else might make a
discovery along these lines and take the credit from him.

Dr. Strauss on the other hand might be called a genius, although I feel that
570  his areas of knowledge are too limited. He was educated in the tradition of
narrow **specialization;** the broader aspects of background were neglected far
more than necessary—even for a neuro-surgeon.

I was shocked to learn that the only ancient languages he could read were
Latin, Greek, and Hebrew, and that he knows almost nothing of mathematics
beyond the elementary levels of the calculus of variations.[11] When he admitted
this to me, I found myself almost annoyed. It was as if he'd hidden this part
of himself in order to deceive me, pretending—as do many people I've
discovered—to be what he is not. No one I've ever known is what he appears
to be on the surface.

580    Dr. Nemur appears to be uncomfortable around me. Sometimes when I try
to talk to him, he just looks at me strangely and turns away. I was angry at first
when Dr. Strauss told me I was giving Dr. Nemur an inferiority complex.[12]
I thought he was mocking me and I'm oversensitive at being made fun of.

How was I to know that a highly respected psycho-experimentalist like
Nemur was unacquainted with Hindustani[13] and Chinese? It's **absurd** when
you consider the work that is being done in India and China today in the very
field of his study.

I asked Dr. Strauss how Nemur could **refute** Rahajamati's attack on his
method and results if Nemur couldn't even read them in the first place. That
590  strange look on Dr. Strauss' face can mean only one of two things. Either he
doesn't want to tell Nemur what they're saying in India, or else—and this
worries me—Dr. Strauss doesn't know either. I must be careful to speak and
write clearly and simply so that people won't laugh. **R**

*May 18*   I am very disturbed. I saw Miss Kinnian last night for the first time
in over a week. I tried to avoid all discussions of intellectual concepts and to
keep the conversation on a simple, everyday level, but she just stared at me
blankly and asked me what I meant about the mathematical variance
equivalent in Dorbermann's *Fifth Concerto*.

---

11.  **calculus** (kăl′kyə-ləs) **of variations:** a branch of higher mathematics.

12.  **inferiority complex:** feelings of worthlessness.

13.  **Hindustani** (hĭn′dŏŏ-stä′nē): a group of languages used in India.

**sensation** (sĕn-sā′shən)
*n.* a state of great interest
and excitement

**tangible** (tăn′jə-bəl) *adj.*
able to be seen, touched,
or understood

**specialization**
(spĕsh′ə-lĭ-za′shən) *n.*
a focus on a particular
area of study

**absurd** (əb-sûrd′) *adj.*
ridiculously unreasonable

**refute** (rĭ-fyōōt′) *v.*
to prove as false

**R**  **READING A LONG
STORY**
What do the length
and language of the
May 15 progress report
reveal about Charlie's
intelligence?  Think about
how this report differs
from those in March
and April.

When I tried to explain she stopped me and laughed. I guess I got angry,
600  but I suspect I'm approaching her on the wrong level. No matter what I try
to discuss with her, I am unable to communicate. I must review Vrostadt's
equations on *Levels of Semantic Progression.* I find that I don't communicate
with people much any more. Thank God for books and music and things I
can think about. I am alone in my apartment at Mrs. Flynn's boarding house
most of the time and seldom speak to anyone. **S**

*May 20*  I would not have noticed the new dishwasher, a boy of about sixteen,
at the corner diner where I take my evening meals if not for the incident of the
broken dishes.

They crashed to the floor, shattering and sending bits of white china under
610  the tables. The boy stood there, dazed and frightened, holding the empty tray
in his hand. The whistles and catcalls from the customers (the cries of "hey,
there go the profits!" . . . "*Mazeltov!*" . . . and "well, *he* didn't work here very
long . . ." which invariably seems to follow the breaking of glass or dishware in
a public restaurant) all seemed to confuse him.

When the owner came to see what the excitement was about, the boy cowered
as if he expected to be struck and threw up his arms as if to ward off the blow.

"All right! All right, you dope," shouted the owner, "don't just stand there!
Get the broom and sweep that mess up. A broom . . . a broom, you idiot!
It's in the kitchen. Sweep up all the pieces."

620  The boy saw that he was not going to be punished. His frightened
expression disappeared and he smiled and hummed as he came back with
the broom to sweep the floor. A few of the rowdier customers kept up the
remarks, amusing themselves at his expense.

"Here, sonny, over here there's a nice piece behind you . . ."

"C'mon, do it again . . ."

"He's not so dumb. It's easier to break 'em than to wash 'em . . ."

As his vacant eyes moved across the crowd of amused onlookers, he slowly
mirrored their smiles and finally broke into an uncertain grin at the joke
which he obviously did not understand.

630  I felt sick inside as I looked at his dull, vacuous smile, the wide, bright eyes
of a child, uncertain but eager to please. They were laughing at him because
he was mentally retarded.

And I had been laughing at him too.

Suddenly, I was furious at myself and all those who were smirking at him.
I jumped up and shouted, "Shut up! Leave him alone! It's not his fault he can't
understand! He can't help what he is! But for God's sake . . . he's still a human
being!" **T**

The room grew silent. I cursed myself for losing control and creating a
scene. I tried not to look at the boy as I paid my check and walked out without
640  touching my food. I felt ashamed for both of us.

**S  CHARACTER TRAITS**
How has Charlie's
attitude toward
socializing changed?

**T  CHARACTER TRAITS**
Why does Charlie defend
the dishwasher? Tell
what you can **infer** about
his personality based on
his behavior.

How strange it is that people of honest feelings and sensibility, who would not take advantage of a man born without arms or legs or eyes—how such people think nothing of abusing a man born with low intelligence. It infuriated me to think that not too long ago I, like this boy, had foolishly played the clown.

And I had almost forgotten.

I'd hidden the picture of the old Charlie Gordon from myself because now that I was intelligent it was something that had to be pushed out of my mind. But today in looking at that boy, for the first time I saw what I had been. *I was* 650 *just like him!*

Only a short time ago, I learned that people laughed at me. Now I can see that unknowingly I joined with them in laughing at myself. That hurts most of all.

I have often reread my progress reports and seen the illiteracy, the childish naïveté, the mind of low intelligence peering from a dark room, through the keyhole, at the dazzling light outside. I see that even in my dullness I knew that I was inferior, and that other people had something I lacked—something denied me. In my mental blindness, I thought that it was somehow connected with the ability to read and write, and I was sure that if I could get those skills I would automatically have intelligence too.

660 Even a feeble-minded man wants to be like other men.

A child may not know how to feed itself, or what to eat, yet it knows of hunger.

This then is what I was like. I never knew. Even with my gift of intellectual awareness, I never really knew.

This day was good for me. Seeing the past more clearly, I have decided to use my knowledge and skills to work in the field of increasing human intelligence levels. Who is better equipped for this work? Who else has lived in both worlds? These are my people. Let me use my gift to do something for them. **U**

Tomorrow, I will discuss with Dr. Strauss the manner in which I can work in 670 this area. I may be able to help him work out the problems of widespread use of the technique which was used on me. I have several good ideas of my own.

There is so much that might be done with this technique. If I could be made into a genius, what about thousands of others like myself? What fantastic levels might be achieved by using this technique on normal people? On *geniuses?*

There are so many doors to open. I am impatient to begin.

## PROGRESS REPORT 12

*May 23* It happened today. Algernon bit me. I visited the lab to see him as I do occasionally, and when I took him out of his cage, he snapped at my hand. I put him back and watched him for a while. He was unusually disturbed and vicious.

*May 24* Burt, who is in charge of the experimental animals, tells me that 680 Algernon is changing. He is less cooperative; he refuses to run the maze any more; general motivation has decreased. And he hasn't been eating. Everyone is upset about what this may mean.

**U CHARACTER TRAITS**
How does Charlie's concern for others affect his goals?

*May 25*  They've been feeding Algernon, who now refuses to work the shifting-lock problem. Everyone identifies me with Algernon. In a way we're both the first of our kind. They're all pretending that Algernon's behavior is not necessarily significant for me. But it's hard to hide the fact that some of the other animals who were used in this experiment are showing strange behavior.

690 Dr. Strauss and Dr. Nemur have asked me not to come to the lab any more. I know what they're thinking but I can't accept it. I am going ahead with my plans to carry their research forward. With all due respect to both of these fine scientists, I am well aware of their limitations. If there is an answer, I'll have to find it out for myself. Suddenly, time has become very important to me.

*May 29*  I have been given a lab of my own and permission to go ahead with the research. I'm on to something. Working day and night. I've had a cot moved into the lab. Most of my writing time is spent on the notes which I keep in a separate folder, but from time to time I feel it necessary to put down my moods and my thoughts out of sheer habit.

I find the *calculus of intelligence* to be a fascinating study. Here is the place for the application of all the knowledge I have acquired. In a sense it's the 700 problem I've been concerned with all my life.

**ANALYZE VISUALS**
In what way does this illustration **represent** the actions Charlie describes in his May 29 entry?

*May 31* Dr. Strauss thinks I'm working too hard. Dr. Nemur says I'm trying to cram a lifetime of research and thought into a few weeks. I know I should rest, but I'm driven on by something inside that won't let me stop. I've got to find the reason for the sharp regression in Algernon. I've got to know *if* and *when* it will happen to me.

*June 4*

LETTER TO DR. STRAUSS (*copy*)

Dear Dr. Strauss:

Under separate cover I am sending you a copy of my report entitled, "The
710    Algernon-Gordon Effect: A Study of Structure and Function of Increased
Intelligence," which I would like to have you read and have published.

As you see, my experiments are completed. I have included in my report
all of my formulae, as well as mathematical analysis in the appendix.
Of course, these should be verified.

Because of its importance to both you and Dr. Nemur (and need I say to
myself, too?) I have checked and rechecked my results a dozen times in the
hope of finding an error. I am sorry to say the results must stand. Yet for the
sake of science, I am grateful for the little bit that I here add to the
knowledge of the function of the human mind and of the laws governing
720    the artificial increase of human intelligence.

I recall your once saying to me that an experimental *failure* or the
*disproving* of a theory was as important to the advancement of learning as a
success would be. I know now that this is true. I am sorry, however, that my
own contribution to the field must rest upon the ashes of the work of two
men I regard so highly.

Yours truly,
Charles Gordon **V**

encl.: rept.

*June 5* I must not become emotional. The facts and the results of my
730    experiments are clear, and the more sensational aspects of my own rapid climb
cannot obscure the fact that the tripling of intelligence by the surgical technique
developed by Dr.'s Strauss and Nemur must be viewed as having little or no
practical applicability (at the present time) to the increase of human intelligence.

As I review the records and data on Algernon, I see that although he is still
in his physical infancy, he has regressed mentally. Motor activity[14] is **impaired**;
there is a general reduction of glandular activity; there is an accelerated loss of
coordination.

There are also strong indications of progressive amnesia.[15]

As will be seen by my report, these and other physical and mental
740    deterioration syndromes can be predicted with statistically significant results
by the application of my formula.

---

**V** **READING A LONG STORY**
What is different about the June 4 entry? Tell what you learn about Charlie and his future from this section.

**impair** (ĭm-pâr´) *v.*
to weaken; damage

---

14. **motor activity:** movement produced by use of the muscles.

15. **progressive amnesia** (prə-grĕs´ĭv ăm-nē´zhə): a steadily worsening loss of memory.

The surgical stimulus to which we were both subjected has resulted in an intensification and acceleration of all mental processes. The unforeseen development, which I have taken the liberty of calling the *Algernon-Gordon Effect,* is the logical extension of the entire intelligence speed-up. The hypothesis here proven may be described simply in the following terms: Artificially increased intelligence deteriorates at a rate of time directly **proportional** to the quantity of the increase.

I feel that this, in itself, is an important discovery.

750  As long as I am able to write, I will continue to record my thoughts in these progress reports. It is one of my few pleasures. However, by all indications, my own mental deterioration will be very rapid.

I have already begun to notice signs of emotional instability and forgetfulness, the first symptoms of the burn-out.

*June 10* Deterioration progressing. I have become absent-minded. Algernon died two days ago. Dissection shows my predictions were right. His brain had decreased in weight and there was a general smoothing out of cerebral convolutions as well as a deepening and broadening of brain fissures.[16]

I guess the same thing is or will soon be happening to me. Now that it's
760 definite, I don't want it to happen.

I put Algernon's body in a cheese box and buried him in the back yard. I cried. **W**

*June 15* Dr. Strauss came to see me again. I wouldn't open the door and I told him to go away. I want to be left to myself. I have become touchy and irritable. I feel the darkness closing in. It's hard to throw off thoughts of suicide. I keep telling myself how important this introspective journal will be.

It's a strange sensation to pick up a book that you've read and enjoyed just a few months ago and discover that you don't remember it. I remembered how great I thought John Milton was, but when I picked up *Paradise Lost* I couldn't
770 understand it at all. I got so angry I threw the book across the room.

I've got to try to hold on to some of it. Some of the things I've learned. Oh, God, please don't take it all away.

*June 19* Sometimes, at night, I go out for a walk. Last night I couldn't remember where I lived. A policeman took me home. I have the strange feeling that this has all happened to me before—a long time ago. I keep telling myself I'm the only person in the world who can describe what's happening to me.

*June 21* Why can't I remember? I've got to fight. I lie in bed for days and I don't know who or where I am. Then it all comes back to me in a flash.

**proportional**
(prə-pôr'shə-nəl) *adj.*
having a constant relation in degree or number

**W** **READING A LONG STORY**
What does Charlie's language in the June 10 entry tell you about what is happening to his intelligence? Think about how this might affect Charlie's attitude toward Algernon's death.

---

16. **cerebral convolutions** (sĕr'ə-brəl kŏn'-və-lōō'shən) . . . **brain fissures** (fĭsh'ərz): cerebral convolutions are ridges or folds on the brain's surface; fissures are grooves that divide the brain into sections.

Fugues[17] of amnesia. Symptoms of senility—second childhood. I can watch
780 them coming on. It's so cruelly logical. I learned so much and so fast. Now
my mind is deteriorating rapidly. I won't let it happen. I'll fight it. I can't help
thinking of the boy in the restaurant, the blank expression, the silly smile,
the people laughing at him. No—please—not that again . . . ⊗

*June 22*  I'm forgetting things that I learned recently. It seems to be following
the classic pattern—the last things learned are the first things forgotten. Or is
that the pattern? I'd better look it up again. . . .

I reread my paper on the *Algernon-Gordon Effect* and I get the strange feeling
that it was written by someone else. There are parts I don't even understand.

Motor activity impaired. I keep tripping over things, and it becomes
790 increasingly difficult to type.

*June 23*  I've given up using the typewriter completely. My coordination is bad.
I feel that I'm moving slower and slower. Had a terrible shock today. I picked
up a copy of an article I used in my research, Krueger's *Uber psychische
Ganzheit,* to see if it would help me understand what I had done. First I
thought there was something wrong with my eyes. Then I realized I could
no longer read German. I tested myself in other languages. All gone.

*June 30*  A week since I dared to write again. It's slipping away like sand through
my fingers. Most of the books I have are too hard for me now. I get angry with
them because I know that I read and understood them just a few weeks ago.
800      I keep telling myself I must keep writing these reports so that somebody
will know what is happening to me. But it gets harder to form the words and
remember spellings. I have to look up even simple words in the dictionary now
and it makes me impatient with myself.

Dr. Strauss comes around almost every day, but I told him I wouldn't see or
speak to anybody. He feels guilty. They all do. But I don't blame anyone.
I knew what might happen. But how it hurts.

*July 7*  I don't know where the week went. Todays Sunday I know because I
can see through my window people going to church. I think I stayed in bed
all week but I remember Mrs. Flynn bringing food to me a few times. I keep
810 saying over and over Ive got to do something but then I forget or maybe its
just easier not to do what I say Im going to do.

I think of my mother and father a lot these days. I found a picture of
them with me taken at a beach. My father has a big ball under his arm and
my mother is holding me by the hand. I dont remember them the way they
are in the picture. All I remember is my father drunk most of the time and
arguing with mom about money.

⊗ **POINT OF VIEW**
What effect does learning
about Charlie's feelings
through his own words
have on you?

---

17. **fugues** (fyōōgz): psychological states where people seem to act consciously but later have no memory
of the action.

He never shaved much and he used to scratch my face when he hugged me. My mother said he died but Cousin Miltie said he heard his mom and dad say that my father ran away with another woman. When I asked my mother she slapped my face and said my father was dead. I dont think I ever found out which was true but I dont care much. (He said he was going to take me to see cows on a farm once but he never did. He never kept his promises . . .)

*July 10* My landlady Mrs Flynn is very worried about me. She says the way I lay around all day and dont do anything I remind her of her son before she threw him out of the house. She said she doesnt like loafers. If Im sick its one thing, but if Im a loafer thats another thing and she wont have it. I told her I think Im sick.

I try to read a little bit every day, mostly stories, but sometimes I have to read the same thing over and over again because I dont know what it means. And its hard to write. I know I should look up all the words in the dictionary but its so hard and Im so tired all the time.

Then I got the idea that I would only use the easy words instead of the long hard ones. That saves time. I put flowers on Algernons grave about once a week. Mrs Flynn thinks Im crazy to put flowers on a mouses grave but I told her that Algernon was special.

*July 14* Its sunday again. I dont have anything to do to keep me busy now because my television set is broke and I dont have any money to get it fixed. (I think I lost this months check from the lab. I dont remember)

I get awful headaches and asperin doesnt help me much. Mrs Flynn knows Im really sick and she feels very sorry for me. Shes a wonderful woman whenever someone is sick.

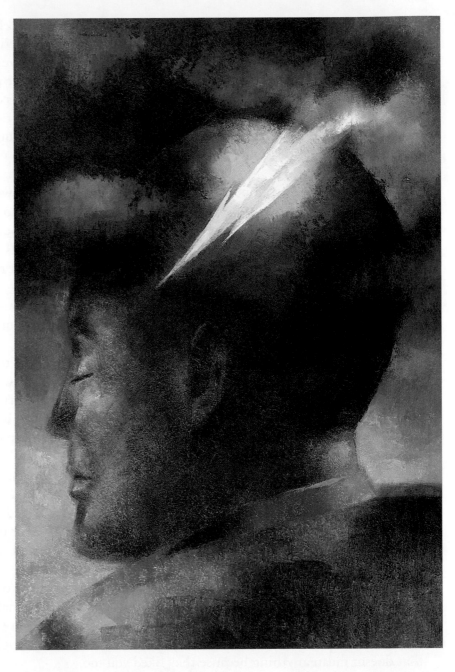

**ANALYZE VISUALS**
What can you **infer** about what is happening to the man in the picture?

860 *July 22* Mrs Flynn called a strange doctor to see me. She was afraid I was going to die. I told the doctor I wasnt too sick and that I only forget sometimes. He asked me did I have any friends or relatives and I said no I dont have any. I told him I had a friend called Algernon once but he was a mouse and we used to run races together. He looked at me kind of funny like he thought I was crazy.

He smiled when I told him I used to be a genius. He talked to me like I was a baby and he winked at Mrs Flynn. I got mad and chased him out because he was making fun of me the way they all used to.

*July 24* I have no more money and Mrs Flynn says I got to go to work somewhere and pay the rent because I havent paid for over two months. I dont 870 know any work but the job I used to have at Donnegans Plastic Box Company. I dont want to go back there because they all knew me when I was smart and maybe they'll laugh at me. But I dont know what else to do to get money.

*July 25* I was looking at some of my old progress reports and its very funny but I cant read what I wrote. I can make out some of the words but they dont make sense.

Miss Kinnian came to the door but I said go away I dont want to see you. She cried and I cried too but I wouldnt let her in because I didnt want her to laugh at me. I told her I didn't like her any more. I told her I didn't want to be smart any more. Thats not true. I still love her and I still want to be smart but 880 I had to say that so shed go away. She gave Mrs. Flynn money to pay the rent. I dont want that. I got to get a job.

Please . . . please let me not forget how to read and write . . . **Y**

*July 27* Mr. Donnegan was very nice when I came back and asked him for my old job of janitor. First he was very suspicious but I told him what happened to me then he looked very sad and put his hand on my shoulder and said Charlie Gordon you got guts.

Everybody looked at me when I came downstairs and started working in the toilet sweeping it out like I used to. I told myself Charlie if they make fun of you dont get sore because you remember their not so smart as you once thot 890 they were. And besides they were once your friends and if they laughed at you that doesnt mean anything because they liked you too.

One of the new men who came to work there after I went away made a nasty crack he said hey Charlie I hear your a very smart fella a real quiz kid. Say something intelligent. I felt bad but Joe Carp came over and grabbed him by the shirt and said leave him alone you lousy cracker or Ill break your neck. I didnt expect Joe to take my part so I guess hes really my friend.

Later Frank Reilly came over and said Charlie if anybody bothers you or trys to take advantage you call me or Joe and we will set em straight. I said thanks Frank and I got choked up so I had to turn around and go into the 900 supply room so he wouldnt see me cry. Its good to have friends.

**Y READING A LONG STORY**
Compare the July 25 progress report to those from previous months. How does it help you understand what has happened to Charlie?

*July 28* I did a dumb thing today I forgot I wasnt in Miss Kinnians class at the adult center any more like I use to be. I went in and sat down in my old seat in the back of the room and she looked at me funny and she said Charles. I dint remember she ever called me that before only Charlie so I said hello Miss Kinnian Im redy for my lesin today only I lost my reader that we was using. She startid to cry and run out of the room and everybody looked at me and I saw they wasnt the same pepul who use to be in my class.

Then all of a suddin I rememberd some things about the operashun and me getting smart and I said holy smoke I reely pulled a Charlie Gordon that time.
910 I went away before she come back to the room.

Thats why Im going away from New York for good. I dont want to do nothing like that agen. I dont want Miss Kinnian to feel sorry for me. Evry body feels sorry at the factery and I dont want that eather so Im going someplace where nobody knows that Charlie Gordon was once a genus and now he cant even reed a book or rite good.

Im taking a cuple of books along and even if I cant reed them Ill practise hard and maybe I wont forget every thing I lerned. If I try reel hard maybe Ill be a littel bit smarter then I was before the operashun. I got my rabits foot and my luky penny and maybe they will help me.

920 If you ever reed this Miss Kinnian dont be sorry for me Im glad I got a second chanse to be smart becaus I lerned a lot of things that I never even new were in this world and Im grateful that I saw it all for a littel bit. I dont know why Im dumb agen or what I did wrong maybe its becaus I dint try hard enuff. But if I try and practis very hard maybe Ill get a littl smarter and know what all the words are. I remember a littel bit how nice I had a feeling with the blue book that has the torn cover when I red it. Thats why Im gonna keep trying to get smart so I can have that feeling agen. Its a good feeling to know things and be smart. I wish I had it rite now if I did I woud sit down and reed all the time. Anyway I bet Im the first dumb person in the
930 world who ever found out somthing importent for sience. I remember I did somthing but I dont remember what. So I gess its like I did it for all the dumb pepul like me. **Z**

Goodbye Miss Kinnian and Dr. Strauss and evreybody. And P.S. please tell Dr Nemur not to be such a grouch when pepul laff at him and he woud have more frends. Its easy to make frends if you let pepul laff at you. Im going to have lots of frends where I go.

P.P.S. Please if you get a chanse put some flowrs on Algernons grave in the bak yard . . . ᔆ

**Z** **CHARACTER TRAITS**
What does Charlie's attitude toward his experience suggest about the kind of person he is?

# Charly[1]

## Stirling Silliphant

---

**CHARACTERS**

Charlie    Dr. Strauss    Dr. Nemur    Alice Kinnian

---

**Charlie.** Boy!

(*He straightens, looks at* Dr. Nemur *and* Dr. Strauss *who stand at one end of the cage.* Alice Kinnian *is just to one side of* Charlie *in a laboratory around which cages containing mice, rats, and monkeys are arranged. Here and there in the background lab assistants are at work.* Dr. Strauss *reaches in a piece of cheese, rewards the mouse.*)

10 **Dr. Strauss.** Well, Charlie, what do you think of Algernon?

**Charlie** (*grinning*). Pretty fancy name for a mouse!

**Dr. Strauss.** Algernon's a pretty special mouse.

(Charlie *turns back to the cage, rubs the tip of his fingers along the mesh and baby-talks to the mouse.* Algernon *twitches its nose and waggles its whiskers.*)

(*favoring* Dr. Nemur)

20 **Dr. Nemur** (*to* Alice). How much does Charlie understand about the operation?

**Alice Kinnian.** Charlie?

(Charlie *looks up.*)

**Charlie.** Yeh?

**Alice Kinnian.** What do you remember about the operation we discussed? The reason I brought you here?

---

1.  **Charly:** The screenwriter might have chosen to misspell Charlie's name as "Charly" to convey the main character's struggle with spelling.

Movie still from the 1969 film *Charly*

(Charlie *straightens, looks the two doctors straight in the eye—this is his big moment—and the* 30 *words come now, tumbling.*)

**Charlie.** All my life I wantid to be smart not dumb. It's very hard to be smart. It's—kind of—slow. I mean, I *try*—but it's—slow. Even when I learn something in Miss Kinnian's class at the Training Center where I try the hardest it's slow—and I ferget. I used to think maybe it's because I talk to myself a lot—you know, I say, hey, Charlie—and stuff like that—but that don't slow me down—because I don't 40 listen to myself.

(*He stops, out of breath, discovers that* Alice— *and the two doctors—still seem to expect more from him.*)

**Charlie.** Oh—the operashun! The operashun will make me smart. (*a beat—then to* Alice) Is that what you told me?

**Alice Kinnian** (*softly*). We *hope* it will, Charlie. But nobody knows for sure. Anyway . . . (*looking at the doctors*) . . . the doctors have to 50 talk to a lot of other people too—before they decide who'll be the first to have this operation. (*favoring* Dr. Strauss)

**Dr. Strauss.** Charlie . . . how would you like to race Algernon?

**Charlie** (*grinning*). Sure, but . . . (*He looks down at the cage.*)

**Charlie.** I can't fit in there.

(Dr. Strauss *hands* Charlie *a long metal rod.*)

**Dr. Strauss.** We call this an electric stylus.

60 (*She guides* Charlie's *hand holding the stylus into the open space between the walls of a maze which sits next to* Algernon's *cage on the long bench before which they stand.*)

**Dr. Strauss.** When I say START—move the pencil along this line until you come to . . . that place there—the FINISH. If you move the wrong way, you'll get a shock.

(*She causes* Charlie's *hand to touch the wall of a cul-de-sac.* Charlie *reacts.*)

70 **Dr. Strauss.** Did that hurt?

**Charlie.** Naw.

**Dr. Strauss.** That shock is a signal . . . it tells you to back up the stylus and go down another row.

**Alice Kinnian.** You understand, Charlie?

(Charlie *nods reassuringly, smiles broadly. This is FUN.* Dr. Nemur *moves* Algernon *from the finish box to the start box.*)

**Dr. Strauss.** Ready?

80 (Charlie, *eager to begin, nods. He holds up his left hand, exhibiting the rabbit's foot.* Alice *smiles at him reassuringly.*)

**Dr. Strauss.** Start.

(Dr. Strauss *waits until she sees that* Charlie *has already begun to guide the stylus, then she lifts the hatch and releases* Algernon. *Camera shots alternate between* Charlie *and* Algernon *as each "runs" his race.* Charlie's *race is hardly run—it is actually one shock after another, one* 90 *bafflement piled on top another, one dead end after another—then all too quickly* Algernon's *telltale victory squeak is heard.* Charlie *looks over at* Algernon *in the finish box.* Dr. Strauss *is feeding him a small piece of cheese. Close-up on* Charlie *as he considers what has just happened. He looks up at* Alice, *who is smiling reassuringly.* Dr. Nemur's *face is without expression.* Charlie *brings the stylus out of the maze. He shrugs.*)

100 **Charlie.** Anybody so stoopid even a little mouse can beat him you sure don't want to give *him* no operashun. I don't blame you!

(*He puts down the stylus, leans closer to the cage, and smiles in wonder at* Algernon.)

**Charlie.** I dint know mice was so smart.

## Comprehension

1. **Recall**  What type of operation does Charlie undergo?

2. **Clarify**  Why does Charlie decide to leave New York at the end of the story?

3. **Clarify**  In *Charly*, what is the purpose of the electric stylus?

## Literary Analysis

4. **Identify Character Traits**  If you haven't done this yet, fill in the bottom of your Y-chart with traits that Charlie showed throughout the story.  How much did the operation change Charlie's character?  Use notes on your chart to support your answer.

5. **Understand Plot Elements**  The technique of hinting about something that will occur later in a story is called **foreshadowing**.  Explain how Algernon's death is an example of this technique.

6. **Analyze a Long Story**  This story covers a period of five months.  Analyze the progress reports from each of these months to determine the change in Charlie's abilities.  Track your results on a graph like the one shown.  How quickly did Charlie Gordon's intelligence rise and fall?

7. **Analyze Parallel Episodes**  A **parallel episode** is a repeated element in a story's plot.  For example, Charlie races Algernon both before he has the operation and after.  Identify at least three other parallel episodes in this story.  What is the purpose of repeating these elements?

8. **Compare Texts**  Think about the ways that the short story and the screenplay present the scene in which Charlie meets Algernon.  What are the similarities and differences?  Consider the amount of detail each selection provides.

## Extension and Challenge

9. **Big Question Activity**  Discuss the following question with a small group: Would Charlie have been better off if he had never gained the **knowledge** he did?  Consider how he feels at different points in the story.

10. **Literary Criticism**  A literary critic wrote that "Flowers for Algernon" has "one of the most perfect and perfectly controlled narrative arcs in the entire history of the short story...."  A **narrative arc** is the shape a story's plot takes as it slowly rises, reaches a high point, and then falls to reach a resolution.  What do you think the critic meant by this comment?

# Vocabulary in Context

## VOCABULARY PRACTICE

Show that you understand the boldfaced words. Decide if each statement is true or false.

absurd refute

impair sensation

opportunist specialization

proportional tangible

1. Something that causes a **sensation** is not of much interest.
2. A **specialization** means a little knowledge about a lot of things.
3. If something is **absurd,** it's unusual or ridiculous.
4. You cannot touch something that is **tangible.**
5. To **refute** something is to agree with it wholeheartedly.
6. Lack of sleep can **impair** your ability to stay alert.
7. An **opportunist** might take advantage of someone to achieve a goal.
8. When two things are **proportional,** they are not at all related to each other.

## VOCABULARY IN WRITING

Were the doctors right to experiment on Charlie? Use at least three vocabulary words in a paragraph that states and supports your opinion. Here is a sample beginning.

> **EXAMPLE SENTENCE**
>
> *Just because research might cause a **sensation** doesn't mean doctors should conduct it.*

## VOCABULARY STRATEGY: SPECIALIZED VOCABULARY

Many of the words used in this selection are specialized terms that relate to the study of psychology. Knowing the meanings of these words can help you understand more about this field of study.

**PRACTICE** Match the word in the first column with its definition in the second column. Use a dictionary if you need help.

1. hypothesis    **a.** symptoms that characterize a disease or disorder
2. syndrome    **b.** a return to a less developed condition
3. regression    **c.** an assumption used as the basis for research
4. introspective    **d.** examining one's own thoughts, feelings, and sensations

**VOCABULARY PRACTICE**
For more practice, go to the **Vocabulary Center** at **ClassZone.com.**

# Reading-Writing Connection

Explore the issues raised in "Flowers for Algernon" by responding to these prompts. Then complete the **Grammar and Writing** exercise.

| WRITING PROMPTS | SELF-CHECK |
|---|---|

**A. Short Response: Write a Progress Report**
What do you think happens to Charlie after the story ends? Write a progress report that Charlie might have written after he left New York. Model the sentence structure, grammar, and spelling in your **one-paragraph report** on the reports in the story.

▶

*A successful report will . . .*
- accurately portray Charlie's character traits
- use language that reflects Charlie's intelligence level

**B. Extended Response: Evaluate Traits**
After reading this story, do you think having **knowledge** makes a person happier, kinder, or generally better? Write a **two- or three-paragraph response,** citing as evidence two or more characters.

▶

*A good evaluation will . . .*
- include a statement that answers the question
- support the statement with appropriate details

## GRAMMAR AND WRITING

**COMPARE CORRECTLY** The **comparative form** of a modifier is used to compare only two people or things. For most one-syllable modifiers, add *-er* (brighter, closer) to form the comparative. For most modifiers with two or more syllables, use the word *more* (more important, more easily).

The **superlative form** is used to compare three or more people or things. For most one-syllable modifiers, add *-est* (brightest, closest). For most modifiers with two or more syllables, use the word *most* (most important, most easily).

> *Example:*  Dr. Strauss is closer to being a genius than Dr. Nemur. (*Two things are being compared, and* close *has one syllable.*)

> *Example:*  Even the most intelligent person in the world must be unhappy sometimes. (*More than two things are being compared, and* intelligent *has more than one syllable.*)

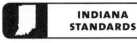

**INDIANA STANDARDS**

**WRITING STANDARD**
**8.4.8** Edit and proofread one's own writing, as well as that of others . . . .

**PRACTICE** Choose the correct form to complete each sentence.

1. Charlie Gordon becomes (smarter, more smart) than he was before.
2. Dr. Strauss and Dr. Nemur might be the (brightest, most bright) doctors in their field, but they do not always make good decisions.
3. At first, Charlie is (more content, contenter) at his job than at the lab.
4. Miss Kinnian is the person (more, most) worried about Charlie's well-being.

*For more help with comparative and superlative forms, see page R58 in the* ***Grammar Handbook.***

## Rules of the Game

Short Story by Amy Tan

# *Can allies be* OPPONENTS?

**INDIANA STANDARDS**

**READING STANDARDS**

**8.2.9** Make reasonable statements and draw conclusions about a text, supporting them with accurate examples.

**8.3.8** Contrast points of view—such as first person, third person limited and third person omniscient, and subjects and objective—in narrative text and explain how they affect the overall theme of the work.

*KEY IDEA* Family, friends, coaches—these are people who usually want the best for you. Then why can it feel like they're always giving you a hard time? Understanding people's good intentions can be challenging, and it may even feel like your supporters aren't on your side. In "Rules of the Game," find out why a young girl sees her mother—who is her biggest fan—as her main **opponent.**

*QUICKWRITE* Think of one or two people in your life who want you to be the best you can be. Then write a brief journal entry about your relationship with them. In what ways does their support help you? In what ways does their support make things harder for you?

## ● LITERARY ANALYSIS: FIRST-PERSON POINT OF VIEW

When a writer uses the **first-person point of view,** the narrator is a character in the story—usually the main character. A story is told in the first-person point of view when the narrator

- describes people and events as he or she experiences them
- uses the pronouns *I* and *me* to talk about himself or herself
- doesn't know what other characters are thinking and feeling

As you read, notice how seeing people and events through the narrator's eyes affects your understanding of the selection.

## ● READING SKILL: DRAW CONCLUSIONS

In reading and in life, you often have to **draw conclusions,** or make logical judgments, about things that are not directly stated. Follow these steps to draw a conclusion:

- Gather evidence from the literature.
- Consider your own experience and knowledge.
- Make a judgment that combines both.

As you read, use a chart like the one shown to help you form conclusions about Waverly's relationship with her mother.

| Evidence | My Thoughts | Conclusion |
|---|---|---|
| Mrs. Jong scolds Waverly for crying out for salted plums. | I know parents try to teach their kids how to behave. | Mrs. Jong wants Waverly to learn self control. |

**Review: Visualize**

## ▲ VOCABULARY IN CONTEXT

Amy Tan uses the words listed to help her describe one girl's conflicts with her mother. Place each word in the appropriate column of a chart like the one shown.

| WORD LIST | | |
|---|---|---|
| adversary | impart | pungent |
| benefactor | malodorous | retort |
| concession | ponder | tactic |
| foresight | | |

| Know Well | Think I Know | Don't Know at All |
|---|---|---|
| | | |

# Author On|ine

**Amy Tan**
**born 1952**

**Change of Heart**
The daughter of Chinese immigrants, Amy Tan grew up in California having little interest in her heritage. When she was a teenager, her father and older brother died. Their deaths devastated her, and her rocky relationship with her mother became worse. Tan's mother wanted her to become a doctor or a concert pianist, but Tan became a business writer instead. She later turned to fiction writing as a hobby, which helped her express her emotions about her family and embrace her Chinese heritage as an important part of her identity. Tan's hobby became her new career.

**Mother-Daughter Ties** Tan wrote "Rules of the Game" for a writing workshop in 1985. She later used it as part of her first novel, *The Joy Luck Club,* which is a series of interconnected stories about four Chinese mothers and their Chinese-American daughters. Tan's family stories have inspired her writing. She once said of her mother, "My books have amounted to taking her stories—a gift to me—and giving them back to her."

 **MORE ABOUT THE AUTHOR**
For more on Amy Tan, visit the **Literature Center** at **ClassZone.com.**

## *Background*

**An Old Game Lives On** Although the game of chess is hundreds of years old, competitive chess remains a popular pastime today. A special class of players strives for the title of grand master, which only the top 0.02% of tournament players worldwide earn. A player must accumulate at least 2,500 points in tournament play to be recognized as a grand master by the World Chess Federation.

# Rules of the Game

## Amy Tan

I was six when my mother taught me the art of invisible strength. It was a strategy for winning arguments, respect from others, and eventually, though neither of us knew it at the time, chess games.

"Bite back your tongue," scolded my mother when I cried loudly, yanking her hand toward the store that sold bags of salted plums. At home, she said, "Wise guy, he not go against wind. In Chinese we say, Come from South, blow with wind—poom!—North will follow. Strongest wind cannot be seen."

The next week I bit back my tongue as we entered the store with the forbidden candies. When my mother finished her shopping, she quietly
10 plucked a small bag of plums from the rack and put it on the counter with the rest of the items. **A**

My mother **imparted** her daily truths so she could help my older brothers and me rise above our circumstances. We lived in San Francisco's Chinatown. Like most of the other Chinese children who played in the back alleys of restaurants and curio shops,[1] I didn't think we were poor. My bowl was always full, three five-course meals every day, beginning with a soup full of mysterious things I didn't want to know the names of.

We lived on Waverly Place, in a warm, clean, two-bedroom flat that sat above a small Chinese bakery specializing in steamed pastries and dim sum.[2]

---

1. **curio shops:** shops that sell curious or unusual objects.

2. **dim sum:** small portions of a variety of Chinese foods and dumplings.

**ANALYZE VISUALS**
Note which **details** of this photograph are in focus and which are blurry. What effect does this have on you, the viewer?

**A POINT OF VIEW**
Identify who is telling this story. What has she suggested about her relationship with her mother so far?

**impart** (ĭm-pärt′) *v.* to make known; reveal

20　In the early morning, when the alley was still quiet, I could smell fragrant red beans as they were cooked down to a pasty sweetness. By daybreak, our flat was heavy with the odor of fried sesame balls and sweet curried chicken crescents. From my bed, I would listen as my father got ready for work, then locked the door behind him, one-two-three clicks.

At the end of our two-block alley was a small sandlot playground with swings and slides well-shined down the middle with use. The play area was bordered by wood-slat benches where old-country people sat cracking roasted watermelon seeds with their golden teeth and scattering the husks to an impatient gathering of gurgling pigeons. The best playground, however, was
30　the dark alley itself. It was crammed with daily mysteries and adventures. My brothers and I would peer into the medicinal herb shop, watching old Li[3] dole out onto a stiff sheet of white paper the right amount of insect shells, saffron-colored seeds, and **pungent** leaves for his ailing customers. It was said that he once cured a woman dying of an ancestral curse that had eluded the best of American doctors. Next to the pharmacy was a printer who specialized in gold-embossed wedding invitations and festive red banners. **B**

Farther down the street was Ping Yuen[4] Fish Market. The front window displayed a tank crowded with doomed fish and turtles struggling to gain footing on the slimy green-tiled sides. A hand-written sign informed tourists,
40　"Within this store, is all for food, not for pet." Inside, the butchers with their bloodstained white smocks deftly gutted the fish while customers cried out their orders and shouted, "Give me your freshest," to which the butchers always protested, "All are freshest." On less crowded market days, we would inspect the crates of live frogs and crabs which we were warned not to poke, boxes of dried cuttlefish, and row upon row of iced prawns, squid, and slippery fish. The sanddabs made me shiver each time; their eyes lay on one flattened side and reminded me of my mother's story of a careless girl who ran into a crowded street and was crushed by a cab. "Was smash flat," reported my mother.

At the corner of the alley was Hong Sing's, a four-table café with a recessed
50　stairwell in front that led to a door marked "Tradesmen." My brothers and I believed the bad people emerged from this door at night. Tourists never went to Hong Sing's, since the menu was printed only in Chinese. A Caucasian man with a big camera once posed me and my playmates in front of the restaurant. He had us move to the side of the picture window so the photo would capture the roasted duck with its head dangling from a juice-covered rope. After he took the picture, I told him he should go into Hong Sing's and eat dinner. When he smiled and asked me what they served, I shouted, "Guts and duck's feet and octopus gizzards!" Then I ran off with my friends, shrieking with laughter as we scampered across the alley and hid in the entryway grotto[5] of the China Gem
60　Company, my heart pounding with hope that he would chase us. **C**

**pungent** (pŭn'jənt) *adj.* sharp or intense

**B** VISUALIZE
Reread lines 25–36. What words help you picture the neighborhood?

**C** POINT OF VIEW
Reread lines 49–60. What do the narrator's words and actions tell you about her attitude toward taking risks?

---

3. **Li** (lē).

4. **Ping Yuen** (bĭng yü'ĕn).

5. **grotto** (grŏt'ō): an artificial structure made to resemble a cave or cavern.

**ANALYZE VISUALS**
This photograph shows a Chinese market in San Francisco. How would you describe the **setting?**

**M**y mother named me after the street that we lived on: Waverly Place Jong, my official name for important American documents. But my family called me Meimei,[6] "Little Sister." I was the youngest, the only daughter. Each morning before school, my mother would twist and yank on my thick black hair until she had formed two tightly wound pigtails. One day, as she struggled to weave a hard-toothed comb through my disobedient hair, I had a sly thought.

I asked her, "Ma, what is Chinese torture?" My mother shook her head. A bobby pin was wedged between her lips. She wetted her palm and smoothed
70 the hair above my ear, then pushed the pin in so that it nicked sharply against my scalp.

"Who say this word?" she asked without a trace of knowing how wicked I was being. I shrugged my shoulders and said, "Some boy in my class said Chinese people do Chinese torture."

"Chinese people do many things," she said simply. "Chinese people do business, do medicine, do painting. Not lazy like American people. We do torture. Best torture." **D**

My older brother Vincent was the one who actually got the chess set. We had gone to the annual Christmas party held at the First Chinese Baptist
80 Church at the end of the alley. The missionary ladies had put together a Santa bag of gifts donated by members of another church. None of the gifts had names on them. There were separate sacks for boys and girls of different ages.

**D** **DRAW CONCLUSIONS**
How does Waverly feel about her mother fixing her hair?

---

6. **Meimei** (mā´mā).

One of the Chinese parishioners had donned a Santa Claus costume and a stiff paper beard with cotton balls glued to it. I think the only children who thought he was the real thing were too young to know that Santa Claus was not Chinese. When my turn came up, the Santa man asked me how old I was. I thought it was a trick question; I was seven according to the American formula and eight by the Chinese calendar. I said I was born on March 17, 1951. That seemed to satisfy him. He then solemnly asked if I had been a very, very good
90 girl this year and did I believe in Jesus Christ and obey my parents. I knew the only answer to that. I nodded back with equal solemnity.

Having watched the other children opening their gifts, I already knew that the big gifts were not necessarily the nicest ones. One girl my age got a large coloring book of biblical characters, while a less greedy girl who selected a smaller box received a glass vial of lavender toilet water. The sound of the box was also important. A ten-year-old boy had chosen a box that jangled when he shook it. It was a tin globe of the world with a slit for inserting money. He must have thought it was full of dimes and nickels, because when he saw that it had just ten pennies, his face fell with such undisguised disappointment that
100 his mother slapped the side of his head and led him out of the church hall, apologizing to the crowd for her son who had such bad manners he couldn't appreciate such a fine gift.

As I peered into the sack, I quickly fingered the remaining presents, testing their weight, imagining what they contained. I chose a heavy, compact one that was wrapped in shiny silver foil and a red satin ribbon. It was a twelve-pack of Life Savers and I spent the rest of the party arranging and rearranging the candy tubes in the order of my favorites. My brother Winston chose wisely as well. His present turned out to be a box of intricate plastic parts; the instructions on the box proclaimed that when they were properly assembled he
110 would have an authentic miniature replica of a World War II submarine.

Vincent got the chess set, which would have been a very decent present to get at a church Christmas party, except it was obviously used and, as we discovered later, it was missing a black pawn and a white knight. My mother graciously thanked the unknown **benefactor,** saying, "Too good. Cost too much." At which point, an old lady with fine white, wispy hair nodded toward our family and said with a whistling whisper, "Merry, merry Christmas."

When we got home, my mother told Vincent to throw the chess set away. "She not want it. We not want it," she said, tossing her head stiffly to the side with a tight, proud smile. My brothers had deaf ears. They were already lining
120 up the chess pieces and reading from the dog-eared instruction book. **E**

I watched Vincent and Winston play during Christmas week. The chessboard seemed to hold elaborate secrets waiting to be untangled. The chessmen were more powerful than Old Li's magic herbs that cured ancestral curses. And my brothers wore such serious faces that I was sure something was at stake that was greater than avoiding the tradesmen's door to Hong Sing's.

"Let me! Let me!" I begged between games when one brother or the other would sit back with a deep sigh of relief and victory, the other annoyed, unable

**benefactor**
(bĕn′ə-făk′tər) *n.* a person who gives monetary or other aid

**E** DRAW CONCLUSIONS
Why does Mrs. Jong want Vincent to throw away his chess set?

to let go of the outcome. Vincent at first refused to let me play, but when I offered my Life Savers as replacements for the buttons that filled in for the missing pieces, he relented. He chose the flavors: wild cherry for the black pawn and peppermint for the white knight. Winner could eat both.

As our mother sprinkled flour and rolled out small doughy circles for the steamed dumplings that would be our dinner that night, Vincent explained the rules, pointing to each piece. "You have sixteen pieces and so do I. One king and queen, two bishops, two knights, two castles, and eight pawns. The pawns can only move forward one step, except on the first move. Then they can move two. But they can only take men by moving crossways like this, except in the beginning, when you can move ahead and take another pawn."

"Why?" I asked as I moved my pawn. "Why can't they move more steps?"

"Because they're pawns," he said.

"But why do they go crossways to take other men? Why aren't there any women and children?"

"Why is the sky blue? Why must you always ask stupid questions?" asked Vincent. "This is a game. These are the rules. I didn't make them up. See. Here. In the book." He jabbed a page with a pawn in his hand. "Pawn. P-A-W-N. Pawn. Read it yourself."

My mother patted the flour off her hands. "Let me see book," she said quietly. She scanned the pages quickly, not reading the foreign English symbols, seeming to search deliberately for nothing in particular.

"This American rules," she concluded at last. "Every time people come out from foreign country, must know rules. You not know, judge say, Too bad, go back. They not telling you why so you can use their way go forward. They say, Don't know why, you find out yourself. But they knowing all the time. Better you take it, find out why yourself." She tossed her head back with a satisfied smile.

I found out about all the whys later. I read the rules and looked up all the big words in a dictionary. I borrowed books from the Chinatown library. I studied each chess piece, trying to absorb the power each contained.

I learned about opening moves and why it's important to control the center early on; the shortest distance between two points is straight down the middle. I learned about the middle game and why **tactics** between two **adversaries** are like clashing ideas; the one who plays better has the clearest plans for both attacking and getting out of traps. I learned why it is essential in the endgame to have **foresight,** a mathematical understanding of all possible moves, and patience; all weaknesses and advantages become evident to a strong adversary and are obscured to a tiring opponent. I discovered that for the whole game one must gather invisible strengths and see the endgame before the game begins.

I also found out why I should never reveal "why" to others. A little knowledge withheld is a great advantage one should store for future use. That is the power of chess. It is a game of secrets in which one must show and never tell.

I loved the secrets I found within the sixty-four black and white squares. I carefully drew a handmade chessboard and pinned it to the wall next to my

● SOCIAL STUDIES
CONNECTION
Waverly's mother might be suggesting something larger about American rules. Between the years 1882 and 1965, Chinese immigration to the U.S. was restricted. Those who were let into the country were not granted the same rights as other Americans.

**tactic** (tăk′tĭk) *n.* a maneuver to achieve a goal

**adversary** (ăd′vər-sĕr′ē) *n.* an opponent

**foresight** (fôr′sīt) *n.* perception of the significance of events before they have occurred bed, where at night I would stare for hours at imaginary battles. Soon I no longer lost any games or Life Savers, but I lost my adversaries. Winston and Vincent decided they were more interested in roaming the streets after school in their Hopalong Cassidy cowboy hats. **F**

On a cold spring afternoon, while walking home from school, I detoured through the playground at the end of our alley. I saw a group of old men, two seated across a folding table playing a game of chess, others smoking pipes, eating peanuts, and watching. I ran home and grabbed Vincent's chess set, which was bound in a cardboard box with rubber bands. I also carefully selected two prized rolls of Life Savers. I came back to the park and approached a man who was observing the game.

"Want to play?" I asked him. His face widened with surprise and he grinned as he looked at the box under my arm.

"Little sister, been a long time since I play with dolls," he said, smiling benevolently. I quickly put the box down next to him on the bench and displayed my **retort.**

Lau Po,[7] as he allowed me to call him, turned out to be a much better player than my brothers. I lost many games and many Life Savers. But over the weeks, with each diminishing roll of candies, I added new secrets. Lau Po gave me the names. The Double Attack from the East and West Shores. Throwing Stones on the Drowning Man. The Sudden Meeting of the Clan. The Surprise from the Sleeping Guard. The Humble Servant Who Kills the King. Sand in the Eyes of Advancing Forces. A Double Killing Without Blood.

---

7. **Lau Po** (lou bō).

**F** POINT OF VIEW
What do Waverly's descriptions of her thoughts and actions reveal about her?

**retort** (rĭ-tôrt') *n.* a quick, sharp, witty reply

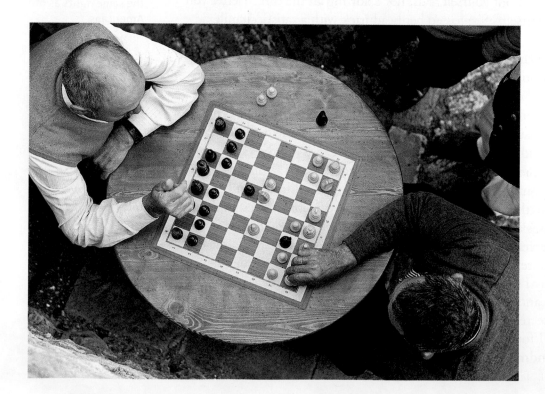

**ANALYZE VISUALS**
How does the angle at which this photograph was taken affect what you first notice in the picture?

There were also the fine points of chess etiquette. Keep captured men in neat rows, as well-tended prisoners. Never announce "Check"[8] with vanity, lest someone with an unseen sword slit your throat. Never hurl pieces into the sandbox after you have lost a game, because then you must find them again, by yourself, after apologizing to all around you. By the end of the summer, Lau Po had taught me all he knew, and I had become a better chess player.

A small weekend crowd of Chinese people and tourists would gather as I played and defeated my opponents one by one. My mother would join the crowds during these outdoor exhibition games.[9] She sat proudly on the bench, telling my admirers with proper Chinese humility, "Is luck." **G**

A man who watched me play in the park suggested that my mother allow me to play in local chess tournaments. My mother smiled graciously, an answer that meant nothing. I desperately wanted to go, but I bit back my tongue. I knew she would not let me play among strangers. So as we walked home I said in a small voice that I didn't want to play in the local tournament. They would have American rules. If I lost, I would bring shame on my family. **H**

"Is shame you fall down nobody push you," said my mother.

During my first tournament, my mother sat with me in the front row as I waited for my turn. I frequently bounced my legs to unstick them from the cold metal seat of the folding chair. When my name was called, I leapt up. My mother unwrapped something in her lap. It was her *chang,* a small tablet of red jade which held the sun's fire. "Is luck," she whispered, and tucked it into my dress pocket. I turned to my opponent, a fifteen-year-old boy from Oakland. He looked at me, wrinkling his nose.

As I began to play, the boy disappeared, the color ran out of the room, and I saw only my white pieces and his black ones waiting on the other side. A light wind began blowing past my ears. It whispered secrets only I could hear.

"Blow from the South," it murmured. "The wind leaves no trail." I saw a clear path, the traps to avoid. The crowd rustled. "Shhh! Shhh!" said the corners of the room. The wind blew stronger. "Throw sand from the East to distract him." The knight came forward ready for the sacrifice. The wind hissed, louder and louder. "Blow, blow, blow. He cannot see. He is blind now. Make him lean away from the wind so he is easier to knock down."

"Check," I said, as the wind roared with laughter. The wind died down to little puffs, my own breath.

My mother placed my first trophy next to a new plastic chess set that the neighborhood Tao society had given to me. As she wiped each piece with a soft cloth, she said, "Next time win more, lose less."

"Ma, it's not how many pieces you lose," I said. "Sometimes you need to lose pieces to get ahead."

**G** DRAW CONCLUSIONS
Why does Waverly start winning more chess games?

**H** POINT OF VIEW
Reread lines 208–211. How are Waverly's thoughts and words different from each other? What does this tell you about her?

---

8. **check:** a move in chess that places an opponent's king under direct attack.

9. **exhibition games:** public showings or demonstrations.

"Better to lose less, see if you really need."

At the next tournament, I won again, but it was my mother who wore the triumphant grin.

"Lost eight pieces this time. Last time was eleven. What I tell you? Better
240 off lose less!" I was annoyed, but I couldn't say anything. ▣

I attended more tournaments, each one farther away from home. I won all games, in all divisions. The Chinese bakery downstairs from our flat displayed my growing collection of trophies in its window, amidst the dust-covered cakes that were never picked up. The day after I won an important regional tournament, the window encased a fresh sheet cake with whipped-cream frosting and red script saying, "Congratulations, Waverly Jong, Chinatown Chess Champion." Soon after that, a flower shop, headstone engraver, and funeral parlor offered to sponsor me in national tournaments. That's when my mother decided I no longer had to do the dishes. Winston and Vincent had to do my chores.

250 "Why does she get to play and we do all the work?" complained Vincent.

"Is new American rules," said my mother. "Meimei play, squeeze all her brains out for win chess. You play, worth squeeze towel."

By my ninth birthday, I was a national chess champion. I was still some 429 points away from grand-master status, but I was touted as the Great American Hope, a child prodigy and a girl to boot. They ran a photo of me in *Life* magazine next to a quote in which Bobby Fischer[10] said, "There will never be a woman grand master." "Your move, Bobby," said the caption.

The day they took the magazine picture I wore neatly plaited braids clipped with plastic barrettes trimmed with rhinestones. I was playing in a large high
260 school auditorium that echoed with phlegmy coughs and the squeaky rubber knobs of chair legs sliding across freshly waxed wooden floors. Seated across from me was an American man, about the same age as Lau Po, maybe fifty. I remember that his sweaty brow seemed to weep at my every move. He wore a dark, **malodorous** suit. One of his pockets was stuffed with a great white kerchief on which he wiped his palm before sweeping his hand over the chosen chess piece with great flourish.

In my crisp pink-and-white dress with scratchy lace at the neck, one of two my mother had sewn for these special occasions, I would clasp my hands under my chin, the delicate points of my elbows poised lightly on the table in the
270 manner my mother had shown me for posing for the press. I would swing my patent leather shoes back and forth like an impatient child riding on a school bus. Then I would pause, suck in my lips, twirl my chosen piece in midair as if undecided, and then firmly plant it in its new threatening place, with a triumphant smile thrown back at my opponent for good measure.

▎I no longer played in the alley of Waverly Place. I never visited the playground
 where the pigeons and old men gathered. I went to school, then directly home
to learn new chess secrets, cleverly concealed advantages, more escape routes.

▣ **DRAW CONCLUSIONS**
Why does Waverly feel she can't correct her mother?

**malodorous**
(măl-ō′dər-əs) *adj.*
having a bad odor

---

10. **Bobby Fischer:** a well-known chess player who, at 15, was the world's youngest grand master.

But I found it difficult to concentrate at home. My mother had a habit of standing over me while I plotted out my games. I think she thought of herself as my protective ally. Her lips would be sealed tight, and after each move I made, a soft "Hmmmmph" would escape from her nose.

"Ma, I can't practice when you stand there like that," I said one day. She retreated to the kitchen and made loud noises with the pots and pans. When the crashing stopped, I could see out of the corner of my eye that she was standing in the doorway. "Hmmmph!" Only this one came out of her tight throat. **J**

My parents made many **concessions** to allow me to practice. One time I complained that the bedroom I shared was so noisy that I couldn't think. Thereafter, my brothers slept in a bed in the living room facing the street. I said I couldn't finish my rice; my head didn't work right when my stomach was too full. I left the table with half-finished bowls and nobody complained. But there was one duty I couldn't avoid. I had to accompany my mother on Saturday market days when I had no tournament to play. My mother would proudly walk with me, visiting many shops, buying very little. "This my daughter Wave-ly Jong," she said to whoever looked her way.

One day, after we left a shop I said under my breath, "I wish you wouldn't do that, telling everybody I'm your daughter." My mother stopped walking. Crowds of people with heavy bags pushed past us on the sidewalk, bumping into first one shoulder, then another.

"Aiii-ya. So shame be with mother?" She grasped my hand even tighter as she glared at me.

I looked down. "It's not that, it's just so obvious. It's just so embarrassing."

"Embarrass you be my daughter?" Her voice was cracking with anger.

"That's not what I meant. That's not what I said."

"What you say?"

I knew it was a mistake to say anything more, but I heard my voice speaking. "Why do you have to use me to show off? If you want to show off, then why don't you learn to play chess." **K**

My mother's eyes turned into dangerous black slits. She had no words for me, just sharp silence.

I felt the wind rushing around my hot ears. I jerked my hand out of my mother's tight grasp and spun around, knocking into an old woman. Her bag of groceries spilled to the ground.

"Aii-ya! Stupid girl!" my mother and the woman cried. Oranges and tin cans careened down the sidewalk. As my mother stooped to help the old woman pick up the escaping food, I took off.

I raced down the street, dashing between people, not looking back as my mother screamed shrilly, "Meimei! Meimei!" I fled down an alley, past dark curtained shops and merchants washing the grime off their windows. I sped into the sunlight, into a large street crowded with tourists examining trinkets and souvenirs. I ducked into another dark alley, down another street, up another alley. I ran until it hurt and I realized I had nowhere to go, that I was not running from anything. The alleys contained no escape routes.

**J** POINT OF VIEW
Reread lines 278–285. How does knowing only Waverly's point of view affect your impression of her mother?

**concession** (kən-sĕsh'ən) *n.* the act of yielding or conceding

**K** DRAW CONCLUSIONS
Why is Waverly embarrassed by her mother's behavior?

My breath came out like angry smoke. It was cold. I sat down on an upturned plastic pail next to a stack of empty boxes, cupping my chin with my hands, thinking hard. I imagined my mother, first walking briskly down one street or another looking for me, then giving up and returning home to await my arrival. After two hours, I stood
330 up on creaking legs and slowly walked home.

The alley was quiet and I could see the yellow lights shining from our flat like two tiger's eyes in the night. I climbed the sixteen steps to the door, advancing quietly up each so as not to make any warning sounds. I turned the knob; the door was locked. I heard a chair moving, quick steps, the locks turning—click! click! click!—and then the door opened.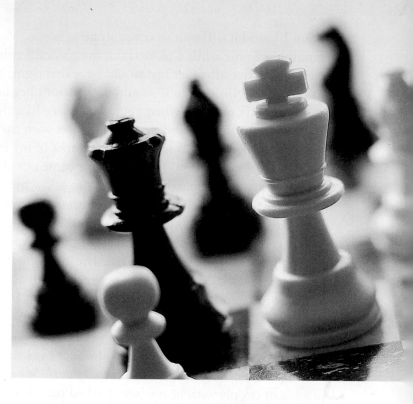

"About time you got home," said Vincent.
340 "Boy, are you in trouble."

He slid back to the dinner table. On a platter were the remains of a large fish, its fleshy head still connected to bones swimming upstream in vain escape. Standing there waiting for my punishment, I heard my mother speak in a dry voice.

"We not concerning this girl. This girl not have concerning for us."

Nobody looked at me. Bone chopsticks clinked against the insides of bowls being emptied into hungry mouths.

I walked into my room, closed the door, and lay down on my bed. The
350 room was dark, the ceiling filled with shadows from the dinnertime lights of neighboring flats.

In my head, I saw a chessboard with sixty-four black and white squares. Opposite me was my opponent, two angry black slits. She wore a triumphant smile. "Strongest wind cannot be seen," she said.

Her black men advanced across the plane, slowly marching to each successive level as a single unit. My white pieces screamed as they scurried and fell off the board one by one. As her men drew closer to my edge, I felt myself growing light. I rose up into the air and flew out the window. Higher and higher, above the alley, over the tops of tiled roofs, where I was gathered up
360 by the wind and pushed up toward the night sky until everything below me disappeared and I was alone.

I closed my eyes and **pondered** my next move. ❧

**ANALYZE VISUALS**
What is the **mood** of this photograph?

**L VISUALIZE**
Reread lines 331–338. What **images** help you picture Waverly's walk home?

**ponder** (pŏn′dər) *v.* to think or consider carefully

# Comprehension

1. **Recall** How does Waverly's family get a chess set?

2. **Clarify** What does Waverly learn from the old man in the park?

3. **Clarify** What events cause Waverly to run away from her mother at the market?

**INDIANA STANDARDS**

**READING STANDARD**
**8.3.8** Contrast points of view…and explain how they affect the overall theme of the work.

# Literary Analysis

4. **Visualize** What scene in this story can you picture most vividly? Reread that part of the selection, noting at least three words or phrases that help you visualize the people, places, or events.

5. **Compare and Contrast** Use a Venn diagram like the one shown to compare and contrast Waverly before she learns chess and after she learns chess. How does she change? How does she stay the same?

6. **Analyze First-Person Point of View** How would "Rules of the Game" be different if you knew what Waverly's mother was thinking?

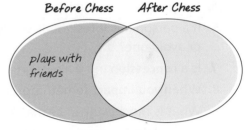

Before Chess    After Chess

plays with friends

7. **Draw Conclusions** Review the chart you made as you read. Why does Waverly view her mother as her **opponent?** Use evidence from the story and your own ideas to support your conclusion.

8. **Evaluate Conflict** Give one or two reasons why Waverly and her mother might be in conflict with each other. Do you think they treat each other fairly? Explain.

# Extension and Challenge

9. **Literary Criticism** Amy Tan once mentioned in an interview that even though "Rules of the Game" is fiction and she never played chess, it is the closest she has come to describing her own life with her mother. She spoke of the "invisible force" her mother taught her. Tan uses the image of the wind throughout the story to represent this invisible force. Look for specific passages in the story in which Tan writes about the wind. With a small group, discuss the wind's effect on Waverly and her chess game.

10. **SOCIAL STUDIES CONNECTION** What challenges did Chinese immigrants face when they moved to the United States in the 1940s and 1950s, as Waverly's mother probably did? Research what it was like for newly arrived people to find jobs and housing and how the government responded to immigration from China. Share your findings with the class.

> **RESEARCH LINKS**
> For more on Chinese immigration to the United States, visit the **Research Center** at **ClassZone.com.**

# Vocabulary in Context

## VOCABULARY PRACTICE

Answer each question to show your understanding of the vocabulary words.

1. Is a **retort** a high-pitched sound or a sharp reply?
2. When you **ponder,** do you think carefully or wander around a pond?
3. Which is an **adversary**—an opponent or an advisor?
4. Would a **tactic** help you more in playing sports or watching a movie?
5. Is a **pungent** smell faint or sharp?
6. If a person has **foresight,** is she likely to make a mistake or avoid one?
7. Is a **concession** more like giving in or letting loose?
8. When you **impart** something, do you hide it or reveal it?
9. What is more likely to be **malodorous**—flowers or garbage?
10. Is a **benefactor** someone who gives money or takes it away?

> adversary
> malodorous
> benefactor
> ponder
> concession
> pungent
> foresight
> retort
> impart
> tactic

## VOCABULARY IN WRITING

Write a paragraph summarizing what happened to Waverly in this story. Use at least three vocabulary words. You could start like this.

> **EXAMPLE SENTENCE**
>
> *At first, Waverly's brothers did not want to **impart** their knowledge of chess to her.*

## VOCABULARY STRATEGY: THE PREFIXES *fore-* AND *mal-*

The prefixes *fore-* and *mal-* are used in the vocabulary words *foresight* and *malodorous.* The prefix *fore-* means "in front" or "before," and the prefix *mal-* means "bad" or "badly."

**PRACTICE** Decide which prefix, *fore-* or *mal-,* should be added to each word to make it match the definition provided.

1. _____ **cast:** to predict the weather conditions in advance
2. _____ **content:** dissatisfied with existing conditions
3. _____ **function:** to function improperly
4. _____ **arm:** part of the arm between the wrist and elbow
5. _____ **word:** a preface or introductory note in a book
6. _____ **practice:** improper treatment of a patient

**VOCABULARY PRACTICE**
For more practice, go to the **Vocabulary Center** at **ClassZone.com.**

# Reading-Writing Connection

Show how well you know the characters in "Rules of the Game" by responding to these prompts. Then complete the **Grammar and Writing** exercise.

| WRITING PROMPTS | SELF-CHECK |
| --- | --- |
| **A. Short Response: Describe a Character**<br>What steps does Waverly take to learn the game of chess and improve her skills? Write **one paragraph** to describe how she prepares herself to defeat her **opponents.** | **An effective description will . . .**<br>• include a topic sentence that introduces the topic<br>• provide details about how Waverly improves her skills |
| **B. Extended Response: Explore Point of View**<br>If Waverly's mother were telling the story, what might she say? In **two or three paragraphs,** retell from Waverly's mother's point of view the scenes in which Waverly runs away from the market and then returns home. | **A creative response will . . .**<br>• use the pronouns *I, me, we,* and *us*<br>• show an understanding of the mother's character |

## GRAMMAR AND WRITING

*COMBINE SENTENCES* Using too many short sentences can make your writing sound choppy. One way to solve this problem is to use a **coordinating conjunction** to combine two shorter sentences. Coordinating conjunctions include the words *for, and, or, nor, but, so,* and *yet.* To combine two sentences, place a comma and a coordinating conjunction between them. Be sure to choose a coordinating conjunction that best shows the relationship between the two ideas.

**INDIANA STANDARDS**

**WRITING STANDARD**
**8.6.1** Use correct and varied sentence types . . . to present a lively and effective personal style.

> *Original:* Waverly wanted salted plums. Her mother wouldn't let her have any.
>
> *Revised:* Waverly wanted salted plums, but her mother wouldn't let her have any.

*PRACTICE* Combine the two sentences in each item below using an appropriate coordinating conjunction.

1. Waverly received candy at the Christmas party. Vincent received a chess set.
2. Mrs. Jong wanted Vincent to throw away the chess set. He decided to keep it.
3. Waverly wanted to learn about chess. She watched men play in the park.
4. Mrs. Jong is proud of Waverly's chess skills. Waverly feels like her mother is using her to show off.

*For more help with coordinating conjunctions, see page R63 in the **Grammar Handbook.***

## The Medicine Bag
Short Story by Virginia Driving Hawk Sneve

## Who Are You Today, María?
Vignette by Judith Ortiz Cofer

# *What shows others* WHO *we are?*

**INDIANA STANDARDS**

**READING STANDARDS**
**8.3.3** Compare and contrast the motivations and reactions of literary characters....

**8.3.7** Analyze a work of literature, showing how it reflects the heritage, traditions, attitudes, and beliefs of its author.

**KEY IDEA** The clothes we wear, the way we speak, and the traditions we follow are just a few of the ways we show others who we are. Our families and our heritage can also play important roles in shaping our **identity,** which is how we see ourselves and how we want others to see us. In the stories you are about to read, two young people must decide which parts of their identities they want to share with the world.

**PICTURE IT** Create a collage or drawing that reflects your identity. Think of ways to visually represent your background, the beliefs that are important you, and the meaningful activities and relationships in your life.

## ● LITERARY ANALYSIS: MAIN CHARACTER

Short stories usually focus on one **main character.** Since the plot of the story revolves around this person, understanding him or her is important to understanding the selection as a whole. As you read each of the following stories, get to know the main character just as you would get to know a real person. Ask questions like these:

- Where does the character live, and how does that place affect him or her?

- With whom does the character have important relationships? What are these relationships like?

- What is the character's social background or cultural heritage? How does the character feel about who he or she is?

## ● READING STRATEGY: SET A PURPOSE FOR READING

In this lesson, your **purpose** for reading is to compare two main characters. As you read, begin filling in a chart like the one shown. You will be asked to add to this chart later.

|  | Martin | María |
|---|---|---|
| How does his or her environment affect him or her? |  |  |
| What is his or her relationship with grandparent like? |  |  |
| What is his or her attitude toward cultural heritage? |  |  |

## ▲ VOCABULARY IN CONTEXT

The words in the box help tell two stories of family relationships. Match each numbered word or phrase with a vocabulary word.

| WORD LIST | authentic | conspiracy | sheepishly |
|---|---|---|---|
|  | commotion | descendant | unseemly |

1. excitement
2. improper
3. son or daughter
4. not fake
5. scheme
6. timidly

# Author Online

**Virginia Driving Hawk Sneve: Sioux Storyteller** Born at the height of the Great Depression, Virginia Driving Hawk Sneve grew up on the Rosebud Sioux reservation in South Dakota. Since her parents often had to leave the reservation to find work, Sneve spent a great deal of time with her grandmothers, whose tales inspired many of her books. Sneve has said that her goal in writing is to present accurate portrayals of Native American life. "The Medicine Bag" describes a tradition in which Native American boys create medicine bags, small pouches that hold items of religious significance and that symbolize the wearer's transition to adulthood.

**Virginia Driving Hawk Sneve
born 1933**

**Judith Ortiz Cofer: A Rich Identity**
Judith Ortiz Cofer was born in Puerto Rico, but she spent much of her childhood in New Jersey after her father joined the U.S. Navy. When her father was at sea, the family returned to Puerto Rico for extended visits with Cofer's grandmother. At times, Cofer felt that she did not fit in either culture—American or Puerto Rican. She uses her writing to explore the difficulties and rewards of her dual identity.

**Judith Ortiz Cofer
born 1952**

 **MORE ABOUT THE AUTHOR**
For more on Virginia Driving Hawk Sneve and Judith Ortiz Cofer, visit the **Literature Center** at ClassZone.com.

# The Medicine Bag

Virginia Driving Hawk Sneve

My kid sister Cheryl and I always bragged about our Sioux grandpa, Joe Iron Shell. Our friends, who had always lived in the city and only knew about Indians from movies and TV, were impressed by our stories. Maybe we exaggerated and made Grandpa and the reservation sound glamorous, but when we'd return home to Iowa after our yearly summer visit to Grandpa we always had some exciting tale to tell.

We always had some **authentic** Sioux article to show our listeners. One year Cheryl had new moccasins that Grandpa had made. On another visit he gave me a small, round, flat, rawhide drum which was decorated with a painting of
10 a warrior riding a horse. He taught me a real Sioux chant to sing while I beat the drum with a leather-covered stick that had a feather on the end. Man, that really made an impression. **A**

We never showed our friends Grandpa's picture. Not that we were ashamed of him, but because we knew that the glamorous tales we told didn't go with the real thing. Our friends would have laughed at the picture, because Grandpa wasn't tall and stately like TV Indians. His hair wasn't in braids, but hung in stringy, gray strands on his neck and he was old. He was our great-grandfather, and he didn't live in a tipi, but all by himself in a part log, part tar-paper shack on the Rosebud Reservation in South Dakota. So when Grandpa
20 came to visit us, I was so ashamed and embarrassed I could've died.

There are a lot of yippy poodles and other fancy little dogs in our neighborhood, but they usually barked singly at the mailman from the safety of their own yards. Now it sounded as if a whole pack of mutts were barking together in one place. **B**

ANALYZE VISUALS
What **details** of the man's face tell you the most about him?

**authentic** (ô-thĕn′tĭk) *adj.* having a verifiable origin; not counterfeit

**A** MAIN CHARACTER
Why did the narrator and his sister exaggerate when they talked about their grandfather?

**B** MAIN CHARACTER
What **conclusions** can you draw about the narrator's neighborhood?

Detail of *They Moved Them* (1991), David Behrens.
Oil glazing, 9¼″ × 14½″. © David Behrens.

I got up and walked to the curb to see what the **commotion** was. About a block away I saw a crowd of little kids yelling, with the dogs yipping and growling around someone who was walking down the middle of the street.

I watched the group as it slowly came closer and saw that in the center of the strange procession was a man wearing a tall black hat. He'd pause now and 30 then to peer at something in his hand and then at the houses on either side of the street. I felt cold and hot at the same time as I recognized the man. "Oh, no!" I whispered. "It's Grandpa!"

I stood on the curb, unable to move even though I wanted to run and hide. Then I got mad when I saw how the yippy dogs were growling and nipping at the old man's baggy pant legs and how wearily he poked them away with his cane. "Stupid mutts," I said as I ran to rescue Grandpa.

When I kicked and hollered at the dogs to get away, they put their tails between their legs and scattered. The kids ran to the curb where they watched me and the old man.

40 "Grandpa," I said and felt pretty dumb when my voice cracked. I reached for his beat-up old tin suitcase, which was tied shut with a rope. But he set it down right in the street and shook my hand.

"*Hau,*[1] *Takoza,* Grandchild," he greeted me formally in Sioux.

All I could do was stand there with the whole neighborhood watching and shake the hand of the leather-brown old man. I saw how his gray hair straggled from under his big black hat, which had a drooping feather in its crown. His rumpled black suit hung like a sack over his stooped frame. As he shook my hand, his coat fell open to expose a bright-red, satin shirt with a beaded bolo tie under the collar. His getup wasn't out of place on the reservation, but it sure 50 was here, and I wanted to sink right through the pavement. **C**

"Hi," I muttered with my head down. I tried to pull my hand away when I felt his bony hand trembling, and looked up to see fatigue in his face. I felt like crying. I couldn't think of anything to say so I picked up Grandpa's suitcase, took his arm, and guided him up the driveway to our house.

Mom was standing on the steps. I don't know how long she'd been watching, but her hand was over her mouth and she looked as if she couldn't believe what she saw. Then she ran to us.

"Grandpa," she gasped. "How in the world did you get here?"

She checked her move to embrace Grandpa and I remembered that such 60 a display of affection is **unseemly** to the Sioux and would embarrass him.

"*Hau,* Marie," he said as he shook Mom's hand. She smiled and took his other arm.

As we supported him up the steps the door banged open and Cheryl came bursting out of the house. She was all smiles and was so obviously glad to see Grandpa that I was ashamed of how I felt.

"Grandpa!" she yelled happily. "You came to see us!"

---

1. *Hau Sioux:* hello.

**commotion** (kə-mō′shən)
*n.* a disturbance

## 🌐 SOCIAL STUDIES CONNECTION

The Rosebud Reservation in South Dakota

**C** **MAIN CHARACTER**
How does Martin feel about his grandfather's outfit?

**unseemly** (ŭn-sēm′lē)
*adj.* inappropriate

Grandpa smiled and Mom and I let go of him as he stretched out his arms to my 10-year-old sister, who was still young enough to be hugged.

"*Wicincala,*[2] little girl," he greeted her and then collapsed.

70 He had fainted. Mom and I carried him into her sewing room, where we had a spare bed.

After we had Grandpa on the bed Mom stood there helplessly patting his shoulder.

"Shouldn't we call the doctor, Mom?" I suggested, since she didn't seem to know what to do.

"Yes," she agreed with a sigh. "You make Grandpa comfortable, Martin."

I reluctantly moved to the bed. I knew Grandpa wouldn't want to have Mom undress him, but I didn't want to, either. He was so skinny and frail that his coat slipped off easily. When I loosened his tie and opened his shirt collar, 80 I felt a small leather pouch that hung from a thong around his neck. I left it alone and moved to remove his boots. The scuffed old cowboy boots were tight and he moaned as I put pressure on his legs to jerk them off. **D**

I put the boots on the floor and saw why they fit so tight. Each one was stuffed with money. I looked at the bills that lined the boots and started to ask about them, but Grandpa's eyes were closed again.

Mom came back with a basin of water. "The doctor thinks Grandpa is suffering from heat exhaustion," she explained as she bathed Grandpa's face. Mom gave a big sigh, "*Oh hinh,* Martin. How do you suppose he got here?"

We found out after the doctor's visit. Grandpa was angrily sitting up in bed 90 while Mom tried to feed him some soup.

"Tonight you let Marie feed you, Grandpa," spoke my dad, who had gotten home from work just as the doctor was leaving. "You're not really sick," he said as he gently pushed Grandpa back against the pillows. "The doctor said you just got too tired and hot after your long trip."

Grandpa relaxed, and between sips of soup, he told us of his journey. Soon after our visit to him Grandpa decided that he would like to see where his only living **descendants** lived and what our home was like. Besides, he admitted **sheepishly,** he was lonesome after we left.

I knew everybody felt as guilty as I did—especially Mom. Mom was all 100 Grandpa had left. So even after she married my dad, who's a white man and teaches in the college in our city, and after Cheryl and I were born, Mom made sure that every summer we spent a week with Grandpa.

I never thought that Grandpa would be lonely after our visits, and none of us noticed how old and weak he had become. But Grandpa knew and so he came to us. He had ridden on buses for two and a half days. When he arrived in the city, tired and stiff from sitting for so long, he set out, walking, to find us. **E**

He had stopped to rest on the steps of some building downtown and a policeman found him. The cop, according to Grandpa, was a good man who

**D MAIN CHARACTER**
Reread lines 77–82. Which details in these lines indicate that Martin is uneasy around his grandfather?

**descendant** (dĭ-sĕn′dənt) *n.* a person whose descent can be traced to an individual or group

**sheepishly** (shē′pĭsh-lē) *adv.* meekly; with embarrassment

**E MAIN CHARACTER**
Reread lines 99–106. What do you learn about Martin's relationship with his grandfather?

2. **Wicincala** *Sioux:* girl.

took him to the bus stop and waited until the bus came and told the driver to
110 let Grandpa out at Bell View Drive. After Grandpa got off the bus, he started
walking again. But he couldn't see the house numbers on the other side when
he walked on the sidewalk so he walked in the middle of the street. That's
when all the little kids and dogs followed him.

I knew everybody felt as bad as I did. Yet I was proud of this 86-year-old
man, who had never been away from the reservation, having the courage to
travel so far alone. **F**

"You found the money in my boots?" he asked Mom.

"Martin did," she answered, and roused herself to scold. "Grandpa, you
shouldn't have carried so much money. What if someone had stolen it from you?"

120 Grandpa laughed. "I would've known if anyone tried to take the boots off
my feet. The money is what I've saved for a long time—a hundred dollars—for
my funeral. But you take it now to buy groceries so that I won't be a burden to
you while I am here."

"That won't be necessary, Grandpa," Dad said. "We are honored to
have you with us and you will never be a burden. I am only sorry that we
never thought to bring you home with us this summer and spare you the
discomfort of a long trip."

Grandpa was pleased. "Thank you," he answered. "But do not feel bad
that you didn't bring me with you for I would not have come then. It was
130 not time." He said this in such a way that no one could argue with him. To
Grandpa and the Sioux, he once told me, a thing would be done when it was
the right time to do it and that's the way it was.

"Also," Grandpa went on, looking at me, "I have come because it is soon
time for Martin to have the medicine bag."

We all knew what that meant. Grandpa thought he was going to die and he
had to follow the tradition of his family to pass the medicine bag, along with
its history, to the oldest male child.

"Even though the boy," he said still looking at me, "bears a white man's
name, the medicine bag will be his."

140 I didn't know what to say. I had the same hot and cold feeling that I had
when I first saw Grandpa in the street. The medicine bag was the dirty
leather pouch I had found around his neck. "I could never wear such a
thing," I almost said aloud. I thought of having my friends see it in gym
class, at the swimming pool, and could imagine the smart things they would
say. But I just swallowed hard and took a step toward the bed. I knew I
would have to take it. **G**

But Grandpa was tired. "Not now, Martin," he said, waving his hand in
dismissal, "it is not time. Now I will sleep."

So that's how Grandpa came to be with us for two months. My friends kept
150 asking to come see the old man, but I put them off. I told myself that I didn't
want them laughing at Grandpa. But even as I made excuses I knew it wasn't
Grandpa that I was afraid they'd laugh at.

**F MAIN CHARACTER**
What is Martin's attitude
toward his grandfather's
journey?

**G MAIN CHARACTER**
How does Martin feel
about receiving the
medicine bag?

Nothing bothered Cheryl about bringing her friends to see Grandpa. Every day after school started there'd be a crew of giggling little girls or round-eyed little boys crowded around the old man on the patio, where he'd gotten in the habit of sitting every afternoon.

Grandpa would smile in his gentle way and patiently answer their questions, or he'd tell them stories of brave warriors, ghosts, animals, and the kids listened in awed silence. Those little guys thought Grandpa was great.

160     Finally, one day after school, my friends came home with me because nothing I said stopped them. "We're going to see the great Indian of Bell View Drive," said Hank, who was supposed to be my best friend. "My brother has seen him three times so he oughta be well enough to see us." **Ⓗ**

When we got to my house Grandpa was sitting on the patio. He had on his red shirt, but today he also wore a fringed leather vest that was decorated with beads. Instead of his usual cowboy boots he had solidly beaded moccasins on his feet that stuck out of his black trousers. Of course, he had his old black hat on—he was seldom without it. But it had been brushed and the feather in the beaded headband was proudly erect, its tip a brighter white. His hair lay in 170 silver strands over the red shirt collar.

I stared just as my friends did and I heard one of them murmur, "Wow!"

Grandpa looked up and when his eyes met mine they twinkled as if he were laughing inside. He nodded to me and my face got all hot. I could tell that he had known all along I was afraid he'd embarrass me in front of my friends.

"*Hau, hoksilas,* boys," he greeted and held out his hand.

My buddies passed in a single file and shook his hand as I introduced them. They were so polite I almost laughed. "How, there, Grandpa," and even a "How-do-you-do, sir."

"You look fine, Grandpa," I said 180 as the guys sat on the lawn chairs or on the patio floor.

"*Hanh,* yes," he agreed. "When I woke up this morning it seemed the right time to dress in the good clothes. I knew that my grandson would be bringing his friends."

"You guys want some lemonade or something?" I offered. No one answered. They were listening to 190 Grandpa as he started telling how he'd killed the deer from which his vest was made.

Grandpa did most of the talking while my friends were there. I was so proud of him and amazed at how respectfully quiet my buddies

**Ⓗ MAIN CHARACTER**
What bothers Martin about bringing his friends home to meet his grandfather?

**ANALYZE VISUALS**
**Compare** this picture of a medicine bag to the way you imagine the medicine bag in the story. How is it similar?

were. Mom had to chase them home at supper time. As they left they shook Grandpa's hand again and said to me:

"Martin, he's really great!"

200 "Yeah, man! Don't blame you for keeping him to yourself."

"Can we come back?" ❶

But after they left, Mom said, "No more visitors for a while, Martin. Grandpa won't admit it, but his strength hasn't returned. He likes having company, but it tires him."

That evening Grandpa called me to his room before he went to sleep. "Tomorrow," he said, "when you come home, it will be time to give you the medicine bag."

I felt a hard squeeze from where my heart is supposed to be and was scared, but I answered, "OK, Grandpa."

210 All night I had weird dreams about thunder and lightning on a high hill. From a distance I heard the slow beat of a drum. When I woke up in the morning I felt as if I hadn't slept at all. At school it seemed as if the day would never end and, when it finally did, I ran home. ❷

Grandpa was in his room, sitting on the bed. The shades were down and the place was dim and cool. I sat on the floor in front of Grandpa, but he didn't even look at me. After what seemed a long time he spoke.

"I sent your mother and sister away. What you will hear today is only for a man's ears. What you will receive is only for a man's hands." He fell silent and I felt shivers down my back.

220 "My father in his early manhood," Grandpa began, "made a vision quest to find a spirit guide for his life. You cannot understand how it was in that time, when the great Teton Sioux were first made to stay on the reservation. There was a strong need for guidance from *Wakantanka,* the Great Spirit. But too many of the young men were filled with despair and hatred. They thought it was hopeless to search for a vision when the glorious life was gone and only the hated confines of a reservation lay ahead. But my father held to the old ways.

"He carefully prepared for his quest with a purifying sweat bath and then he went alone to a high butte[3] top to fast and pray. After three days he received 230 his sacred dream—in which he found, after long searching, the white man's iron. He did not understand his vision of finding something belonging to the white people, for in that time they were the enemy. When he came down from the butte to cleanse himself at the stream below, he found the remains of a campfire and the broken shell of an iron kettle. This was a sign which reinforced his dream. He took a piece of the iron for his medicine bag, which he had made of elk skin years before, to prepare for his quest.

"He returned to his village, where he told his dream to the wise old men of the tribe. They gave him the name *Iron Shell,* but neither did they understand the

---

3. **butte** (byo͞ot): an abruptly rising hill with sloping sides and a flat top.

❶ **MAIN CHARACTER**
Why is Martin proud of his grandfather?

❷ **MAIN CHARACTER**
How have Martin's feelings about receiving the medicine bag changed?

meaning of the dream. This first Iron Shell kept the piece of iron with him at all
240 times and believed it gave him protection from the evils of those unhappy days.

"Then a terrible thing happened to Iron Shell. He and several other young
men were taken from their homes by the soldiers and sent far away to a white
man's boarding school. He was angry and lonesome for his parents and the young
girl he had wed before he was taken away. At first Iron Shell resisted the teachers'
attempts to change him and he did not try to learn. One day it was his turn to
work in the school's blacksmith shop. As he walked into the place he knew that
his medicine had brought him there to learn and work with the white man's iron.

"Iron Shell became a blacksmith and worked at the trade when he returned to
the reservation. All of his life he treasured the medicine bag. When he was old,
250 and I was a man, he gave it to me, for no one made the vision quest any more."

Grandpa quit talking and I stared in disbelief as he covered his face with his
hands. His shoulders were shaking with quiet sobs and I looked away until he
began to speak again.

"I kept the bag until my son, your mother's father, was a man and had to
leave us to fight in the war across the ocean. I gave him the bag, for I believed
it would protect him in battle, but he did not take it with him. He was afraid
that he would lose it. He died in a faraway place." **K**

Again Grandpa was still and I felt his grief around me.

"My son," he went on after clearing his throat, "had only a daughter and it
260 is not proper for her to know of these things."

He unbuttoned his shirt, pulled out the leather pouch, and lifted it over his
head. He held it in his hand, turning it over and over as if memorizing how it
looked.

"In the bag," he said as he opened it and removed two objects, "is the
broken shell of the iron kettle, a pebble from the butte, and a piece of the
sacred sage." He held the pouch upside down and dust drifted down.

"After the bag is yours you must put a piece of prairie sage within and never
open it again until you pass it on to your son." He replaced the pebble and the
piece of iron and tied the bag.

270 I stood up, somehow knowing I should. Grandpa slowly rose from the bed
and stood upright in front of me holding the bag before my face. I closed my
eyes and waited for him to slip it over my head. But he spoke.

"No, you need not wear it." He placed the soft leather bag in my right hand
and closed my other hand over it. "It would not be right to wear it in this time
and place where no one will understand. Put it safely away until you are again
on the reservation. Wear it then, when you replace the sacred sage."

Grandpa turned and sat again on the bed. Wearily he leaned his head
against the pillow. "Go," he said. "I will sleep now."

"Thank you, Grandpa," I said softly and left with the bag in my hands.

280 That night Mom and Dad took Grandpa to the hospital. Two weeks later
I stood alone on the lonely prairie of the reservation and put the sacred sage
in my medicine bag. ∾ **L**

**K** **MAIN CHARACTER**
What is Martin learning
about his heritage?

**L** **MAIN CHARACTER**
What does Martin's
return to the reservation
suggest about his
attitude toward his
heritage?

# Who Are You Today, María?

*Judith Ortiz Cofer*

Abuela[1] knocks on my bedroom door. She has come to my room this morning to watch me choose my outfit for Who You Are Day at school. This is a day when we are allowed to dress in clothes that we think tell the world who we really are. (Within reason, our principal warned—no extremes will be tolerated. I hope that her definition of the word *extreme* is the same as my friend Whoopee's. Nothing that she will put on this morning has ever been seen on this planet, much less at school.)

Abuela makes herself comfortable on my bed as I put on my costume of myself made up of pieces of my life. I thought about my Who You Are Day
10 outfit a lot. Mr. Golden told us in English class to think about our choices: are you going to walk around as a joke or as a poem? I have a suspicion that our teachers have allowed us this chance to dress up as ourselves for a reason. Our school is already a united nations, a carnival, and a parade all at once. There are students from dozens of different countries, and we do not always get along. Most of us are too shy to talk to others outside our little circles, and so misunderstandings come up. The principal has tried almost everything. The Who You Are Day is another of her crazy ideas to get us to communicate. In each of my classes, the teacher said, let us know something about what has made you who you are by what you wear to school tomorrow. It all sounds like
20 a **conspiracy** to me. But I like dressing up so I do not complain like the boys have been doing. Most of them hate the idea! **Ⓜ**

Abuela looks at my choices hanging on the door and shakes her head, smiling, like she did when we went to see *Cats*. It is a smile that says, I do not understand, but if it is important to María, I will bear it the best I can. She is elegant even at 7:00 A.M. in her embroidered silk robe and red velvet slippers. She has wrapped a shawl over her shoulders because she is always cold in our *cueva,*[2] as she calls the apartment. The shawl was handmade by her mother and it is Abuela's most prized possession. As a little girl, I liked to put it over

---

1. **Abuela** (ä-bwā'lä) *Spanish:* grandmother.
2. *cueva* (kwâ'vä) *Spanish:* cave.

### ANALYZE VISUALS
Based on the **details** in this painting, what impression do you get of the girl?

**conspiracy**
(kən-spîr'ə-sē) *n.* an agreement to perform together an illegal or wrongful act

**Ⓜ MAIN CHARACTER**
What can you **infer** about the community in which María lives?

*Frida* (2004), María Sanchez. Acrylic on canvas. C. Perez Collection. © María Sanchez.

my head because the pattern of sequins made a night sky full of stars and
30 because it smelled like Abuela. **N**

Abuela sips from her cup of café con leche[3] as she watches me.

I feel a little strange about being in my underwear in front of her and go in my closet with my choices, which are:

My mother's red skirt that she wore when she had a part in a musical play on the Island. I have played dress-up with it since I was five years old, but it finally fits me perfectly. It is the kind of skirt that opens like an umbrella when you turn in circles.

A top I sewed together from an old sari[4] Uma's mother was going to throw away. It is turquoise blue with silver edges.

40 And finally, over my sari, I will wear my father's sharkskin[5] suit jacket—it's big on me but I can roll up the sleeves. It is what he likes to wear when he sings at rent parties. Under the light, it changes colors and seems to come alive as the design shifts and moves. Papi says it is great for dancing; you don't even need a partner.

And finally, tall platform shoes we found buried deep in Whoopee's closet, circa 1974, she told me. Whoopee collects antique shoes to go with her science fiction outfits. It is a fashion statement; she will tell anyone who asks. No one knows what the statement means, and that is just fine with Whoopee.

When I part the clothes in my closet and come out like an actor in a play,
50 Abuela's eyes open wide. Before she can say anything, I point to each piece of my outfit and say a name: Mami, Papi, Uma, and Whoopee.

Abuela's face changes as she begins to understand the meaning of my fashion statement.

*"Ahora sé quién eres, María, y quién puedes ser, si quieres. Ven acá, mi amor."*

Abuela says that she knows who I am and who I may be if I choose. I have heard those words before but I don't remember when or where. Abuela embraces me and kisses my face several times. This is a Puerto Rican thing. It goes on for a while. I close my eyes to wait it out and I suddenly inhale a familiar scent. When I open my eyes, I see a starry sky. Abuela has put her
60 shawl over my head.

*"Algo mío para tu día de ser quien eres, mi hija,"* she tells me. *Something of mine for your day of being who you are.* She is letting me borrow her mother's beautiful shawl! **O**

All day at school, I feel elegant. Whenever anyone tries to make fun of my costume, I think of the words my grandmother quoted to me: *I know who you are and who you may be if you choose.* And when I go into Mr. Golden's class and his eyes ask me, *Who are you today, María?* I will say by the way I walk in, head held high, that today I am a poem. ❧

---

3. **café con leche** (kă-fā kŏn lĕch'ā) *Spanish:* coffee with milk.

4. **sari** (sä'rē): a traditional Indian women's garment.

5. **sharkskin:** a synthetic fabric with a smooth, shiny surface.

**N MAIN CHARACTER**
What can you **infer** about María's relationship with her grandmother?

**O MAIN CHARACTER**
Reread lines 55–63. What is María's attitude toward her grandmother's Puerto Rican customs and clothing?

## Comprehension

1. **Recall** In "The Medicine Bag," why does Martin's grandfather come to visit?

2. **Recall** What does the medicine bag contain?

3. **Represent** Create a sketch of María in her Who You Are Day outfit. Make sure your sketch reflects the details in the selection.

## Literary Analysis

4. **Make Inferences** In "The Medicine Bag," how do Martin's mother, father, and sister each feel about Grandpa? Cite details from the story to support your answer.

5. **Draw Conclusions** How are Martin's feelings about his grandfather and his Sioux heritage affected by the kind of neighborhood he lives in?

6. **Interpret Ideas** In "Who Are You Today, María?" what do you think María's English teacher means in line 11 when he asks, "are you going to walk around as a joke or as a poem"?

7. **Compare and Contrast** Compare Martin's relationship with Grandpa to María's relationship with Abuela. How are the relationships similar and different?

8. **Analyze Theme** What message about **identity** does each story contain?

## Comparing Characters

Now that you've read both stories, finish filling in your chart. Then add the final question and answer it, too.

|  | Martin | María |
|---|---|---|
| How does his or her environment affect him or her? |  |  |
| What is his or her relationship with grandparent like? |  |  |
| What is his or her attitude toward cultural heritage? |  |  |
| Does the character change in any way? Explain. |  |  |

**INDIANA STANDARDS**

**READING STANDARD**
**8.3.3** Compare and contrast the motivations and reactions of literary characters . . . .

# Vocabulary in Context

## VOCABULARY PRACTICE

For each item, choose the word that differs most in meaning from the other words. Refer to a dictionary if you need help.

1. (a) uprising, (b) commotion, (c) calmness, (d) racket
2. (a) unseemly, (b) crude, (c) rude, (d) proper
3. (a) phony, (b) factual, (c) real, (d) authentic
4. (a) heir, (b) descendant, (c) parent, (d) child
5. (a) shyly, (b) self-consciously, (c) sheepishly, (d) boldly
6. (a) conspiracy, (b) loyalty, (c) plot, (d) trickery

## VOCABULARY IN WRITING

Imagine that Joe Iron Shell is your grandfather. Using two or more vocabulary words, write a paragraph explaining how you feel about receiving the medicine bag. You could start this way.

> **EXAMPLE SENTENCE**
>
> I **sheepishly** accept the medicine bag.

## VOCABULARY STRATEGY: ANALOGIES

An **analogy** is a relationship between pairs of words. To complete an analogy, identify the relationship between the words in the first pair. The second pair of words must relate to each other in the same way. For example, if the first pair are **antonyms** (words with opposite meanings), the second pair should also be antonyms. If the first pair of words show a **cause-effect relationship,** the second pair of words should show a cause-effect relationship, too.

Analogies are often written as follows—big : small :: soft : rough. If the analogy is read aloud, you would say, "big **is to** small **as** soft **is to** rough."

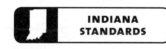

**INDIANA STANDARDS**

**READING STANDARD**
**8.1.1** Analyze idioms and comparisons . . . to infer the literal and figurative meanings of phrases.

*PRACTICE* Choose a word from the box to complete each analogy.

| flood | hinder | mature | murky |
|-------|--------|--------|-------|

1. old : immature :: young : _____
2. gather : scatter :: benefit : _____
3. match : fire :: storm : _____
4. bright : drab :: clear : _____

**VOCABULARY PRACTICE**
For more practice, go to the **Vocabulary Center** at ClassZone.com.

# Writing for Assessment

## 1. READ THE PROMPT

In writing assessments, you will often be asked to compare and contrast main characters from different selections.

**PROMPT**

In four or five paragraphs, compare and contrast the main characters in "The Medicine Bag" and "Who Are You Today, María?" Consider the environments they came from, their relationships with their grandparents, and their attitudes toward their cultural heritage. In your conclusion, explain whether the characters change in any important ways. Support your response with details from the two stories.

◀ **STRATEGIES IN ACTION**

1. *I need to discuss the* **similarities and differences** *between the two characters.*

2. *I need to* **give examples** *to show how the characters' environments, relationships, and heritage are* **alike** *or* **different.**

3. *In the conclusion, I need to* **describe** *whether the characters change, and if so, how.*

## 2. PLAN YOUR WRITING

Review the chart you filled out on page 251. Use the chart to help you identify the characters' similarities and differences. Then think about how you will set up the body of your essay.

- Do you want to compare the characters' environments in one paragraph, relationships with their grandparents in the next paragraph, and attitudes toward their cultural heritage in a third paragraph?

- Do you want to describe the characters in separate paragraphs and then discuss their similarities and differences in a third paragraph?

*I. Introduction*
*II. Environments they came from*
*III. Relationships with grandparents*
*IV. Attitudes toward cultural heritage*
*V. Conclusion*

Once you have decided on an organization, create an outline.
Then write a thesis statement that describes the main idea or purpose of your essay.

## 3. DRAFT YOUR RESPONSE

**Introduction** Provide the titles and authors of both selections as well as a sentence telling what each is about. Include your thesis statement.
**Body** Discuss characters' similarities and differences, using your outline as a guide. Support your ideas with story details.
**Conclusion** Remind readers of your thesis statement. End by noting whether either character changed in any important way.
**Revision** Make sure your essay answers the question in the writing prompt.

*from* **Whale Rider**

Film Clips on  **MediaSmart** DVD

# *What puts a* CHARACTER *in focus?*

**INDIANA STANDARDS**

**LISTENING/SPEAKING STANDARD 8.7.9** Interpret and evaluate the various ways in which visual image makers (such as graphic artists, illustrators, and news photographers) communicate information and affect impressions and opinions.

**KEY IDEA** Think about your favorite fictional **characters.** What is it that draws you to them? Is it the things they say, the way they behave, the lives they lead? As you read about or watch these characters, perhaps you imagine how you would act if you were in their shoes. In this lesson, you'll view two clips from *Whale Rider* to explore the tools filmmakers use to create believable characters.

## Background

**Out with the Old** In *Whale Rider,* a young native New Zealand girl named Paikea, or Pai, must challenge the old ways of her tribe to fulfill her destiny. For over 1,000 years, Paikea's tribe has been ruled by a male. The current chief is Koro, Paikea's grandfather. When Paikea's father refuses his rightful place as chief, Koro must decide who will take his place. Although Paikea is descended from the chief, Koro doesn't believe a girl can lead.

Koro starts a school to train the young men of the tribe in the old ways of their people. He will choose one among them to succeed him. You'll watch the conflict that arises between the determined Paikea and her stubborn grandfather when she tries to join the school.

# Media Literacy: Characters in Movies

The best books and movies develop characters that feel like real people. You laugh with them and cry with them. You're drawn into their stories and you truly care what happens to them. An author provides detail and background through descriptive passages to develop his or her characters. A filmmaker has to rely on his or her camera work, the performances of the actors, and the skills of the film editor to create true-to-life characters.

| FILMMAKING TECHNIQUES | STRATEGIES FOR VIEWING |
| --- | --- |
| **Camera Shots**<br>• A **close-up shot** provides a detailed view of a person or object.<br>• A **long shot** provides a wide view of a scene. It can show distance between characters and establish location.<br>• A **reaction shot** shows a person react to what occurred in the previous shot. | • Notice how close-ups focus on facial expressions. Ask yourself what the character might be feeling.<br>• Watch how long shots can reveal relationships. A shot of two people standing apart can show emotional distance. A long shot of one character can single him or her out from a group.<br>• Watch for reaction shots. What does the character's response to an event say about his or her feelings? |
| **Performance**<br>• **Physical appearance,** including height, weight, hairstyle, and clothing<br>• **Behavior,** including **facial expressions** and **body language**<br>• **Dialogue,** both what the character says and how he or she says it | • Pay attention to how a main character's appearance provides clues about his or her personality.<br>• Watch a character's posture and facial expressions. These can convey feelings, reactions, or self-image.<br>• Listen to the dialogue. Is the character's tone of voice happy, calm, or angry? What does speech reveal about a character's background and intelligence? |
| **Editing**<br>**Editing** is the process of choosing and arranging shots in a sequence. Filmmakers combine the shots they've filmed to create an overall effect on the audience. | • Notice the different types of shots the editor uses. How do they reflect the emotion of the scene?<br>• Watch for reaction shots that are edited into a scene. How do they reveal characters' thoughts and feelings?<br>• Notice how long each shot stays on the screen. How does shot length change as emotion rises in a scene? |

*Viewing Guide for*
# Whale Rider

In these scenes, Koro, the chief, starts to teach the tribe's traditions to the boys of the village. You'll see what happens when Paikea attempts to join the school. As you watch, notice how the director's choice of shots, the actors' performances, and the editing work together to create memorable characters. Pay special attention to the techniques that are used when the emotion rises. Use the questions to analyze the scenes. You may want to view the clips more than once.

## NOW VIEW

### FIRST VIEWING: Comprehension

1. **Recall** Why doesn't Koro get angry when the boy hits him in the back with his stick?

2. **Clarify** Paikea doesn't say a single word to her grandfather in these scenes. How does she defy his wishes without speaking?

### CLOSE VIEWING: Media Literacy

3. **Identify Film Technique** A **long shot** is used to show Paikea's loneliness when she walks away from the group in the beginning of these clips. Find another example from the clips of how the director separates Paikea from the group.

4. **Analyze Shots** Why do you think the director chose to show **reaction shots** of the grandmother when Paikea defies Koro?

5. **Analyze Editing** Even though these scenes are short, they cover several days in Paikea's life. Cite evidence from the clips that tell you the scenes took place over more than one day.

6. **Compare Characters** Even though Koro and Paikea are at odds throughout these scenes, they are similar in many ways. Compare the two characters by listing descriptive traits of each in a Venn diagram. As a starting point, think of the qualities of a chief that Koro mentions in the scenes: strength, courage, intelligence, and leadership.

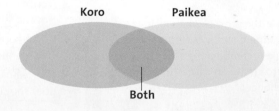

Koro          Paikea

Both

## Write or Discuss

**Evaluate Film** In this lesson, you learned some of the techniques filmmakers use to create believable characters. Think about Paikea's predicament. She believes she can be a leader, but she has to defy her grandfather to prove it. Write a paragraph describing how the filmmaking techniques you learned were used in the scene. In your opinion, were the filmmakers successful in making Paikea into a believable character? Think about

- the types of shots the filmmakers use
- the appearance and performance of the actor playing Paikea
- the editing of the scene

## Produce Your Own Media

**Plan a Scene** Imagine you're a movie director. You're planning a scene that is designed to show the relationship between two characters. Create a shot-by-shot description of a two-person scene. You can choose a scene from a story you've read or create your own. Your description should include a brief overall description of what happens in the scene, a list of shots describing what happens in each, and a sketch of each shot.

*HERE'S HOW* Use these tips to help you plan your scene:

- Remember that conflict drives a story. Consider creating a scene in which your two characters are in a disagreement.
- Include any dialogue that will be spoken in your description of each shot.
- Identify each type of shot you will use. **Close-up shots** are perfect for capturing facial expressions in **reaction shots. Long shots** work better for showing body language and distance between characters.

**MEDIA TOOLS**

For help with creating a shot-by-shot scene description, visit the **Media Center** at **ClassZone.com.**

**Tech Tip**

If a camera is available, shoot photographs of your classmates acting out your scene in place of the sketches.

**STUDENT MODEL**

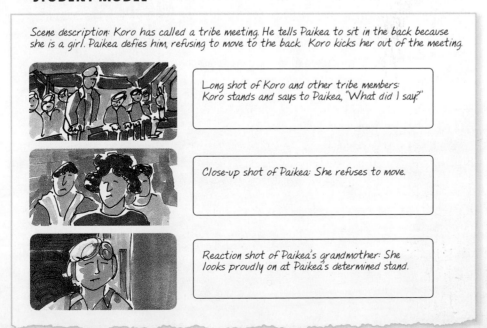

Scene description: Koro has called a tribe meeting. He tells Paikea to sit in the back because she is a girl. Paikea defies him, refusing to move to the back. Koro kicks her out of the meeting.

Long shot of Koro and other tribe members: Koro stands and says to Paikea, "What did I say?"

Close-up shot of Paikea: She refuses to move.

Reaction shot of Paikea's grandmother: She looks proudly on at Paikea's determined stand.

## from **Harriet Tubman: Conductor on the Underground Railroad**
Biography by Ann Petry

# When is a **RISK** worth taking?

**INDIANA STANDARDS**

**READING STANDARD**
**8.2.9** Make reasonable statements and draw conclusions about a text, supporting them with accurate examples.

**KEY IDEA** Some people **risk** their lives needlessly looking for a thrill. Others hold themselves back from accomplishment because they are afraid to take a chance. How can you be sure when it's right to put your safety or reputation on the line? In the biography you are about to read, you will meet a woman who took enormous risks to help others because she believed all people have the right to freedom.

**QUICKWRITE** Think about a time when you took a risk. In a brief paragraph, describe the risk and why you took it. What were the results? Looking back, was the risk worth taking?

## ● LITERARY ANALYSIS: CHARACTERIZATION

Whether they are describing fictional characters or real people, skillful writers can make you feel as if you've met the person you're reading about. To bring figures to life in this way, writers use the following methods of **characterization:**

- describing the person's physical appearance
- presenting the person's own thoughts, speech, and actions
- revealing other people's reactions to the person
- directly commenting on the person

As you read, pay attention to the methods Ann Petry uses to create a portrait of the biography's subject, Harriet Tubman.

## ● READING STRATEGY: MONITOR

Have you ever found yourself reading without fully understanding the words in front of you? If so, pause and ask yourself **questions** about confusing parts. When you read to find the answers, you will probably find that more information stays with you.

As you read this biography, take time to note places where you become confused or lose track of ideas. Use a chart like the one shown to record your questions and their answers.

| My Questions | Answers |
|---|---|
| How does Harriet Tubman avoid getting caught? | |

## ▲ VOCABULARY IN CONTEXT

The boldfaced words help Ann Petry tell about one of Harriet Tubman's journeys for freedom. Try to figure out what each word means in the context of its sentence.

1. After days of wear, his shirt was wrinkled and **disheveled.**
2. A good leader can **instill** a feeling of confidence in others.
3. Music can often **evoke** a pleasant memory.
4. Days on their feet made them long to **linger** at each stop.
5. She used clever stories to **cajole** them to take risks.
6. His **sullen** attitude discouraged others in the group.
7. Her positive attitude helped **dispel** their fears.
8. Her **eloquence** helped convince them to follow her.

# Author On[l]ine

**Ann Petry**
**1908–1997**

**Making History Speak**
The descendant of a runaway slave from Virginia, Ann Petry grew up in a comfortable middle-class household in Old Saybrook, Connecticut. Hers was the only African-American family in town. Despite her father's respected position as the town's pharmacist, Petry experienced racism growing up. Much of her writing describes the struggles of African Americans against prejudice in New England and in Harlem, where she moved in the 1930s. After Petry had a daughter of her own, she became interested in writing for young readers. In addition to her biography of Harriet Tubman, Petry wrote four other books for young people and four books for adults. She said that writing about the lives of real people helped her "make history speak across the centuries." She wanted to remind readers of the important contributions that African-American men and women have made to American history.

**MORE ABOUT THE AUTHOR**
For more on Ann Petry, visit the **Literature Center** at ClassZone.com.

## *Background*

**The Underground Railroad** In the period before and during the Civil War, many people enslaved in the South fled north to freedom using a secret network of escape routes known as the Underground Railroad. The "conductors" on the Underground Railroad were brave men and women who provided the escaping people with food, hiding places, and guidance to the next "station." Harriet Tubman was one of the most famous of these conductors.

# Harriet Tubman:
## Conductor on the Underground Railroad

### Ann Petry

### The Railroad Runs to Canada

Along the Eastern Shore of Maryland, in Dorchester County, in Caroline County, the masters kept hearing whispers about the man named Moses, who was running off slaves. At first they did not believe in his existence. The stories about him were fantastic, unbelievable. Yet they watched for him. They offered rewards for his capture. **A**

They never saw him. Now and then they heard whispered rumors to the effect that he was in the neighborhood. The woods were searched. The roads were watched. There was never anything to indicate his whereabouts. But a few days afterward, a goodly number of slaves would be gone from the
10 plantation. Neither the master nor the overseer had heard or seen anything unusual in the quarter.[1] Sometimes one or the other would vaguely remember having heard a whippoorwill call somewhere in the woods, close by, late at night. Though it was the wrong season for whippoorwills. **B**

Sometimes the masters thought they had heard the cry of a hoot owl, repeated, and would remember having thought that the intervals between the low moaning cry were wrong, that it had been repeated four times in succession instead of three. There was never anything more than that to suggest that all was not well in the quarter. Yet when morning came, they invariably discovered that a group of the finest slaves had taken to their heels.
20 Unfortunately, the discovery was almost always made on a Sunday. Thus a whole day was lost before the machinery of pursuit could be set in motion. The posters offering rewards for the fugitives could not be printed until Monday.

**ANALYZE VISUALS**
What **symbols** do you notice in this painting?

**A MONITOR**
What are you wondering about Moses?

**B CHARACTERIZATION**
Reread lines 6–13. What does the author tell you about Moses' actions?

---

1. **quarter:** the area in which enslaved people lived.

*Harriet Tubman* (1945), William H. Johnson. Oil on paperboard, sheet, 29⅜″ × 23⅜″. Smithsonian American Art Museum, Washington, D.C.

The men who made a living hunting for runaway slaves were out of reach, off in the woods with their dogs and their guns, in pursuit of four-footed game, or they were in camp meetings saying their prayers with their wives and families beside them. **C**

Harriet Tubman could have told them that there was far more involved in this matter of running off slaves than signaling the would-be runaways by imitating the call of a whippoorwill, or a hoot owl, far more involved than a 30 matter of waiting for a clear night when the North Star was visible.

In December, 1851, when she started out with the band of fugitives that she planned to take to Canada, she had been in the vicinity of the plantation for days, planning the trip, carefully selecting the slaves that she would take with her.

She had announced her arrival in the quarter by singing the forbidden spiritual—"Go down, Moses, 'way down to Egypt Land"[2]—singing it softly outside the door of a slave cabin, late at night. The husky voice was beautiful even when it was barely more than a murmur borne[3] on the wind. **D**

Once she had made her presence known, word of her coming spread from 40 cabin to cabin. The slaves whispered to each other, ear to mouth, mouth to ear,

---

2. **"Go down, Moses, 'way down to Egypt Land":** a line from an African-American folk song.

3. **borne:** carried.

**C MONITOR**
Why does Moses choose Saturday night to help enslaved people escape?

**D MONITOR**
What is Harriet Tubman's relationship to Moses?

**ANALYZE VISUALS**
Consider the colors, shapes, and figures in this painting. What **mood** do they convey?

*Through Forest, Through Rivers, Up Mountains* (1967), Jacob Lawrence. Tempera, gouache and pencil on paper, 15 11/16″ × 26 7/8″. Smithsonian Institution, Hirshhorn Museum and Sculpture Garden. © 2007 The Jacob and Gwendolyn Lawrence Foundation, Seattle/Artists Rights Society (ARS), New York.

"Moses is here." "Moses has come." "Get ready. Moses is back again." The ones who had agreed to go North with her put ashcake and salt herring in an old bandanna, hastily tied it into a bundle, and then waited patiently for the signal that meant it was time to start.

There were eleven in this party, including one of her brothers and his wife. It was the largest group that she had ever conducted, but she was determined that more and more slaves should know what freedom was like.

She had to take them all the way to Canada. The Fugitive Slave Law[4] was no longer a great many incomprehensible words written down on the country's

50 lawbooks. The new law had become a reality. It was Thomas Sims, a boy, picked up on the streets of Boston at night and shipped back to Georgia. It was Jerry and Shadrach, arrested and jailed with no warning.

She had never been in Canada. The route beyond Philadelphia was strange to her. But she could not let the runaways who accompanied her know this. As they walked along she told them stories of her own first flight, she kept painting vivid word pictures of what it would be like to be free. **E**

But there were so many of them this time. She knew moments of doubt when she was half-afraid, and kept looking back over her shoulder, imagining that she heard the sound of pursuit. They would certainly be pursued. Eleven

60 of them. Eleven thousand dollars' worth of flesh and bone and muscle that belonged to Maryland planters. If they were caught, the eleven runaways would be whipped and sold South, but she—she would probably be hanged.

They tried to sleep during the day but they never could wholly relax into sleep. She could tell by the positions they assumed, by their restless movements. And they walked at night. Their progress was slow. It took them three nights of walking to reach the first stop. She had told them about the place where they would stay, promising warmth and good food, holding these things out to them as an incentive to keep going. **F**

When she knocked on the door of a farmhouse, a place where she and her

70 parties of runaways had always been welcome, always been given shelter and plenty to eat, there was no answer. She knocked again, softly. A voice from within said, "Who is it?" There was fear in the voice.

She knew instantly from the sound of the voice that there was something wrong. She said, "A friend with friends," the password on the Underground Railroad.

The door opened, slowly. The man who stood in the doorway looked at her coldly, looked with unconcealed astonishment and fear at the eleven **disheveled** runaways who were standing near her. Then he shouted, "Too many, too many. It's not safe. My place was searched last week. It's not safe!"

80 and slammed the door in her face.

She turned away from the house, frowning. She had promised her passengers food and rest and warmth, and instead of that, there would be

**E** CHARACTERIZATION
What do Tubman's words to the runaways tell you about her?

**F** MONITOR
What questions do you have about the journey?

**disheveled** (dĭ-shĕv′əld) *adj.* messy; untidy

---

4. **Fugitive Slave Law:** a law by which enslaved people who escaped could be recovered by their owners.

hunger and cold and more walking over the frozen ground. Somehow she would have to **instill** courage into these eleven people, most of them strangers, would have to feed them on hope and bright dreams of freedom instead of the fried pork and corn bread and milk she had promised them.

They stumbled along behind her, half-dead for sleep, and she urged them on, though she was as tired and as discouraged as they were. She had never been in Canada but she kept painting wondrous word pictures of what it would be like. She managed to **dispel** their fear of pursuit, so that they would not become hysterical, panic-stricken. Then she had to bring some of the fear back, so that they would stay awake and keep walking though they drooped with sleep.

Yet during the day, when they lay down deep in a thicket, they never really slept, because if a twig snapped or the wind sighed in the branches of a pine tree, they jumped to their feet, afraid of their own shadows, shivering and shaking. It was very cold, but they dared not make fires because someone would see the smoke and wonder about it.

She kept thinking, eleven of them. Eleven thousand dollars' worth of slaves. And she had to take them all the way to Canada. Sometimes she told them about Thomas Garrett, in Wilmington. She said he was their friend even though he did not know them. He was the friend of all fugitives. He called them God's poor. He was a Quaker[5] and his speech was a little different from that of other people. His clothing was different, too. He wore the wide-brimmed hat that the Quakers wear.

She said that he had thick white hair, soft, almost like a baby's, and the kindest eyes she had ever seen. He was a big man and strong, but he had never used his strength to harm anyone, always to help people. He would give all of them a new pair of shoes. Everybody. He always did. Once they reached his house in Wilmington, they would be safe. He would see to it that they were.

She described the house where he lived, told them about the store where he sold shoes. She said he kept a pail of milk and a loaf of bread in the drawer of his desk so that he would have food ready at hand for any of God's poor who should suddenly appear before him, fainting with hunger. There was a hidden room in the store. A whole wall swung open, and behind it was a room where he could hide fugitives. On the wall there were shelves filled with small boxes—boxes of shoes—so that you would never guess that the wall actually opened.

While she talked, she kept watching them. They did not believe her. She could tell by their expressions. They were thinking, New shoes, Thomas Garrett, Quaker, Wilmington—what foolishness was this? Who knew if she told the truth? Where was she taking them anyway?

That night they reached the next stop—a farm that belonged to a German. She made the runaways take shelter behind trees at the edge of the fields before she knocked at the door. She hesitated before she approached the door, thinking, suppose that he, too, should refuse shelter, suppose— Then she

---

**instill** (ĭn-stĭl′) v. to supply gradually

**dispel** (dĭ-spĕl′) v. to drive away

🌐 SOCIAL STUDIES CONNECTION

In the years leading up to the Civil War, the United States was bitterly divided about slavery. Many enslaved people in the South escaped all the way to Canada to reach freedom.

---

5. **Quaker:** a member of a religious group called the Society of Friends.

thought, Lord, I'm going to hold steady on to You and You've got to see me through—and knocked softly. **G**

She heard the familiar guttural voice say, "Who's there?"

She answered quickly, "A friend with friends."

He opened the door and greeted her warmly. "How many this time?" he asked.

130 "Eleven," she said and waited, doubting, wondering.

He said, "Good. Bring them in."

He and his wife fed them in the lamplit kitchen, their faces glowing, as they offered food and more food, urging them to eat, saying there was plenty for everybody, have more milk, have more bread, have more meat.

They spent the night in the warm kitchen. They really slept, all that night and until dusk the next day. When they left, it was with reluctance. They had all been warm and safe and well-fed. It was hard to exchange the security offered by that clean warm kitchen for the darkness and the cold of a December night.

## "Go On or Die"

140 **H**arriet had found it hard to leave the warmth and friendliness, too. But she urged them on. For a while, as they walked, they seemed to carry in them a measure of contentment; some of the serenity and the cleanliness of that big warm kitchen **lingered** on inside them. But as they walked farther and farther away from the warmth and the light, the cold and the darkness entered into them. They fell silent, **sullen,** suspicious. She waited for the moment when some one of them would turn mutinous. It did not happen that night.

Two nights later she was aware that the feet behind her were moving slower and slower. She heard the irritability in their voices, knew that soon someone
150 would refuse to go on.

She started talking about William Still and the Philadelphia Vigilance Committee.[6] No one commented. No one asked any questions. She told them the story of William and Ellen Craft and how they escaped from Georgia. Ellen was so fair that she looked as though she were white, and so she dressed up in a man's clothing and she looked like a wealthy young planter. Her husband, William, who was dark, played the role of her slave. Thus they traveled from Macon, Georgia, to Philadelphia, riding on the trains, staying at the finest hotels. Ellen pretended to be very ill—her right arm was in a sling, and her right hand was bandaged, because she was supposed to have
160 rheumatism. Thus she avoided having to sign the register at the hotels for she could not read or write. They finally arrived safely in Philadelphia, and then went on to Boston. **H**

No one said anything. Not one of them seemed to have heard her.

**G CHARACTERIZATION**
What do Tubman's thoughts suggest about the way she deals with hardship?

**linger** (lĭng′gər) *v.*
to remain or stay longer

**sullen** (sŭl′ən) *adj.*
showing silent resentment; sulky

**H MONITOR**
Why does Tubman tell stories of how other enslaved people escaped?

---

6. **Philadelphia Vigilance Committee:** fundraising organization that helped people who escaped enslavement.

She told them about Frederick Douglass,[7] the most famous of the escaped slaves, of his **eloquence,** of his magnificent appearance. Then she told them of her own first vain effort at running away, **evoking** the memory of that miserable life she had led as a child, reliving it for a moment in the telling.

But they had been tired too long, hungry too long, afraid too long, footsore too long. One of them suddenly cried out in despair, "Let me go back. It is 170 better to be a slave than to suffer like this in order to be free."

She carried a gun with her on these trips. She had never used it—except as a threat. Now as she aimed it, she experienced a feeling of guilt, remembering that time, years ago, when she had prayed for the death of Edward Brodas, the Master, and then not too long afterward had heard that great wailing cry that came from the throats of the field hands, and knew from the sound that the Master was dead.

One of the runaways said, again, "Let me go back. Let me go back," and stood still, and then turned around and said, over his shoulder, "I am going back."

She lifted the gun, aimed it at the despairing slave. She said, "Go on with us 180 or die." The husky low-pitched voice was grim. **❶**

He hesitated for a moment and then he joined the others. They started walking again. She tried to explain to them why none of them could go back to the plantation. If a runaway returned, he would turn traitor, the master and the overseer would force him to turn traitor. The returned slave would disclose the stopping places, the hiding places, the cornstacks they had used with the full knowledge of the owner of the farm, the name of the German farmer who had fed them and sheltered them. These people who had risked their own security to help runaways would be ruined, fined, imprisoned.

She said, "We got to go free or die. And freedom's not bought with dust." **❶** 190 This time she told them about the long agony of the Middle Passage[8] on the old slave ships, about the black horror of the holds, about the chains and the whips. They too knew these stories. But she wanted to remind them of the long hard way they had come, about the long hard way they had yet to go. She told them about Thomas Sims, the boy picked up on the streets of Boston and sent back to Georgia. She said when they got him back to Savannah, got him in prison there, they whipped him until a doctor who was standing by watching said, "You will kill him if you strike him again!" His master said, "Let him die!"

Thus she forced them to go on. Sometimes she thought she had become nothing but a voice speaking in the darkness, **cajoling,** urging, threatening. 200 Sometimes she told them things to make them laugh, sometimes she sang to them, and heard the eleven voices behind her blending softly with hers, and then she knew that for the moment all was well with them.

She gave the impression of being a short, muscular, indomitable woman who could never be defeated. Yet at any moment she was liable to be seized by one of those curious fits of sleep, which might last for a few minutes or for hours.

---

**eloquence** (ĕl'ə-kwəns) *n.* an ability to speak powerfully and persuasively

**evoke** (ĭ-vōk') *v.* to call forth; to summon

**❶ CHARACTERIZATION**
Why does Tubman take such a drastic action? Consider what this tells you about her character.

**❶ CHARACTERIZATION**
How does Tubman's statement reflect her attitude about the journey?

**cajole** (kə-jōl') *v.* to urge gently; to coax

---

7. **Frederick Douglass:** African-American leader who worked to end slavery.

8. **Middle Passage:** sea route along which enslaved Africans were transported to the Americas.

Even on this trip, she suddenly fell asleep in the woods. The runaways, ragged, dirty, hungry, cold, did not steal the gun as they might have, and set off by themselves, or turn back. They sat on the ground near her and waited patiently until she awakened. They had come to trust her implicitly, totally. They, too, had come to believe her repeated statement, "We got to go free or die." She was leading them into freedom, and so they waited until she was ready to go on. **K**

Finally, they reached Thomas Garrett's house in Wilmington, Delaware. Just as Harriet had promised, Garrett gave them all new shoes, and provided carriages to take them on to the next stop.

By slow stages they reached Philadelphia, where William Still hastily recorded their names, and the plantations whence they had come, and something of the life they had led in slavery. Then he carefully hid what he had written, for fear it might be discovered. In 1872 he published this record

**K** CHARACTERIZATION
What do the runaways' actions tell you about Tubman?

*An Underground Railroad* (1967), Jacob Lawrence. Gouache and tempera on paper, 14¼″ × 13″. © 2007 The Jacob and Gwendolyn Lawrence Foundation, Seattle/Artists Rights Society (ARS), New York.

**ANALYZE VISUALS**
What can you **infer** about the people in the painting?

in book form and called it *The Underground Railroad*. In the foreword to his
220  book he said: "While I knew the danger of keeping strict records, and while
I did not then dream that in my day slavery would be blotted out, or that the
time would come when I could publish these records, it used to afford me
great satisfaction to take them down, fresh from the lips of fugitives on the
way to freedom, and to preserve them as they had given them." **L**

William Still, who was familiar with all the station stops on the
Underground Railroad, supplied Harriet with money and sent her and her
eleven fugitives on to Burlington, New Jersey.

Harriet felt safer now, though there were danger spots ahead. But the biggest
part of her job was over. As they went farther and farther north, it grew colder;
230  she was aware of the wind on the Jersey ferry and aware of the cold damp in
New York. From New York they went on to Syracuse, where the temperature
was even lower.

In Syracuse she met the Reverend J. W. Loguen, known as "Jarm" Loguen.
This was the beginning of a lifelong friendship. Both Harriet and Jarm Loguen
were to become friends and supporters of Old John Brown.[9]

From Syracuse they went north again, into a colder, snowier city—
Rochester. Here they almost certainly stayed with Frederick Douglass, for he
wrote in his autobiography:

On one occasion I had eleven fugitives at the same time under my roof,
240  and it was necessary for them to remain with me until I could collect
sufficient money to get them to Canada. It was the largest number I ever
had at any one time, and I had some difficulty in providing so many with
food and shelter, but, as may well be imagined, they were not very fastidious
in either direction, and were well content with very plain food, and a strip
of carpet on the floor for a bed, or a place on the straw in the barnloft.

Late in December, 1851, Harriet arrived in St. Catharines, Canada West (now
Ontario), with the eleven fugitives. It had taken almost a month to complete this
journey; most of the time had been spent getting out of Maryland.

That first winter in St. Catharines was a terrible one. Canada was a strange
250  frozen land, snow everywhere, ice everywhere, and a bone-biting cold the like of
which none of them had ever experienced before. Harriet rented a small frame
house in the town and set to work to make a home. The fugitives boarded with
her. They worked in the forests, felling trees, and so did she. Sometimes she took
other jobs, cooking or cleaning house for people in the town. She cheered on
these newly arrived fugitives, working herself, finding work for them, finding
food for them, praying for them, sometimes begging for them. **M**

Often she found herself thinking of the beauty of Maryland, the mellowness
of the soil, the richness of the plant life there. The climate itself made for an
ease of living that could never be duplicated in this bleak, barren countryside.

**L MONITOR**
What do you want to know about the people who help the escapees?

**M CHARACTERIZATION**
How does Tubman help the fugitives?

---

9. **Old John Brown:** anti-slavery leader who was executed.

*Harriet and the Promised Land No. 15: Canada Bound* (1967), Jacob Lawrence. Gouache and tempera on paper, 16½″ × 28¼″. The University of Michigan Museum of Art. © 2007 The Jacob and Gwendolyn Lawrence Foundation, Seattle/Artists Rights Society (ARS), New York.

260　In spite of the severe cold, the hard work, she came to love St. Catharines, and the other towns and cities in Canada where black men lived. She discovered that freedom meant more than the right to change jobs at will, more than the right to keep the money that one earned. It was the right to vote and to sit on juries. It was the right to be elected to office. In Canada there were black men who were county officials and members of school boards. St. Catharines had a large colony of ex-slaves, and they owned their own homes, kept them neat and clean and in good repair. They lived in whatever part of town they chose and sent their children to the schools.

When spring came she decided that she would make this small Canadian
270　city her home—as much as any place could be said to be home to a woman who traveled from Canada to the Eastern Shore of Maryland as often as she did.

In the spring of 1852, she went back to Cape May, New Jersey. She spent the summer there, cooking in a hotel. That fall she returned, as usual, to Dorchester County, and brought out nine more slaves, conducting them all the way to St. Catharines, in Canada West, to the bone-biting cold, the snow-covered forests—and freedom.

She continued to live in this fashion, spending the winter in Canada, and the spring and summer working in Cape May, New Jersey, or in Philadelphia. She made two trips a year into slave territory, one in the fall and another in
280　the spring. She now had a definite crystallized purpose, and in carrying it out, her life fell into a pattern which remained unchanged for the next six years. ॰ **N**

**ANALYZE VISUALS**
What **details** do you notice in this painting that portray the escapees' journey?

**N** **CHARACTERIZATION**
What does the way Tubman lives her life tell you about her?

**LETTER** Frederick Douglass, a vocal African-American statesman and journalist, had a very different style of leadership than Harriet Tubman did. Douglass wrote the following letter when the first biography of Tubman was about to be published.

**August 29, 1868**

Dear Harriet:

I am glad to know that the story of your eventful life has been written by a kind lady, and that the same is soon to be published. You ask for what you do not need when you call upon me for a word of commendation.[1] I need such words from you far more than you can need them from me, especially where your superior labors and devotion to the cause of the lately enslaved of our land are known as I know them. The difference between us is very marked. Most that I have done and suffered in the service of our cause has been in public, and I have received much encouragement at every step of the way. You, on the other hand, have labored in a private way. I have wrought in the day—you in the night. I have had the applause of the crowd and the satisfaction that comes of being approved by the multitude, while the most that you have done has been witnessed by a few trembling, scarred, and footsore bondmen and women, whom you have led out of the house of bondage, and whose heartfelt "God bless you" has been your only reward. The midnight sky and the silent stars have been the witnesses of your devotion to freedom and of your heroism. Excepting John Brown—of sacred memory—I know of no one who has willingly encountered more perils and hardships to serve our enslaved people than you have. Much that you have done would seem improbable to those who do not know you as I know you. It is to me a great pleasure and a great privilege to bear testimony to your character and your works, and to say to those to whom you may come, that I regard you in every way truthful and trustworthy.

Your friend,

*Fred.* Douglass

Frederick Douglass

---

1. **commendation** (kŏm'ən-dā'shən): an expression of praise or recommendation.

## Comprehension

1. **Recall** What is the purpose of Harriet Tubman's trips to Maryland?

2. **Clarify** Why does the man at the first stop on the Underground Railroad turn away the group of runaways?

3. **Summarize** How does life for the runaways change in Canada?

**INDIANA STANDARDS**

**READING STANDARD**
**8.2.9** Make reasonable statements and draw conclusions about a text . . . .

## Literary Analysis

4. **Monitor** Review the chart of questions and answers you made as you read. Which questions added the most to your understanding of the selection? Why?

5. **Identify Anecdote** An **anecdote** is a brief account of an interesting incident. Identify three anecdotes the author uses to describe Harriet Tubman. What do these anecdotes help readers understand about Tubman?

6. **Examine Characterization** Review the four methods of **characterization.** Which method of characterization does Petry use the most in her biography? Tell what you learn about Tubman through this method.

7. **Analyze a Character** Complete a character map for Harriet Tubman like the one shown. Then create a one-sentence description of her.

8. **Make Judgments** Read the "Letter to Harriet Tubman" by Frederick Douglass. Why does Douglass believe that Harriet Tubman is "superior" to him? Decide why Douglass might have felt this way, and support your opinion with details from the biography and the letter.

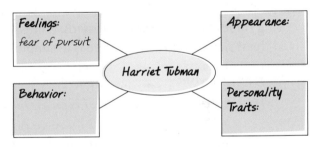

## Extension and Challenge

9. **Readers' Circle** Based on the information in the selection, would you have been willing to trust Harriet Tubman with your life? Discuss which of Tubman's qualities make her a good leader and why you might be hesitant to follow her.

10. **SOCIAL STUDIES CONNECTION** Because the Fugitive Slave Law allowed slave owners to recover enslaved people who escaped, Harriet Tubman led escapees on Underground Railroad routes to Canada, where they reached freedom. Research more about the approximately 18 other trips to Canada that Tubman led and present your findings to the class. Consider what continued to motivate her to **risk** her life to help others.

**RESEARCH LINKS**
For more on the Underground Railroad, visit the **Research Center** at **ClassZone.com.**

Harriet Tubman's route from Maryland to Canada

# Vocabulary in Context

## VOCABULARY PRACTICE

Choose the word from the list that makes the most sense in each sentence.

1. Harriet had to make sure that they didn't _____ too long in any one place.
2. She had to work hard to _____ a sense of hope.
3. At times, it was difficult for Harriet to _____ feelings of despair.
4. When she saw the _____ looks on people's faces, she knew it was time for another encouraging story.
5. When they arrived at a destination, they were hungry and their appearance was _____.
6. Harriet often had to _____ the fugitives into moving toward their next stop.
7. Harriet said that Frederick Douglass was a man of great _____.
8. Harriet tried to _____ in the fugitives a sense of responsibility.

> cajole
> evoke
> disheveled
> instill
> dispel
> linger
> eloquence
> sullen

## VOCABULARY IN WRITING

Using three or more vocabulary words, write a paragraph describing how Harriet led the 11 slaves to freedom. Here is a sample of how you might begin.

> **EXAMPLE SENTENCE**
>
> *Harriet had to **evoke** a feeling of hope as they walked along on their journey.*

## VOCABULARY STRATEGY: SYNONYMS AS CONTEXT CLUES

Context clues are often found in the words and sentences that surround an unfamiliar word. These clues can help you figure out the meaning of the word. A **synonym,** or a word that has a similar definition, can be a context clue. For example, a sentence from the selection refers to "a voice speaking in the darkness, cajoling, urging. . . ." If you know the word *urging,* you can figure out what *cajoling* means because they are synonyms.

*PRACTICE* Identify the synonyms of each boldfaced word. Then define the word.

1. They had come to trust her **implicitly,** just as they believed in her totally.
2. She was considered **indomitable** because of her undefeatable spirit.
3. Harriet longed for **contentment,** but would never be satisfied until the journey ended.
4. The group was not **fastidious** or fussy about what they ate or where they slept.
5. In the end, the lure of freedom was its own **incentive.**
6. The escape was unimaginable, and the journey almost **incomprehensible.**

**INDIANA STANDARDS**

**READING STANDARD**
**8.1.3** Verify the meaning of a word in its context . . . .

**VOCABULARY PRACTICE**
For more practice, go to the **Vocabulary Center** at **ClassZone.com.**

# Reading-Writing Connection

Demonstrate your understanding of "Harriet Tubman: Conductor on the Underground Railroad" by responding to these prompts. Then complete the **Grammar and Writing** exercise.

| WRITING PROMPTS | SELF-CHECK |
|---|---|
| **A. Short Response: Analyze Motivation**<br>Why do you think Harriet Tubman and others who broke the Fugitive Slave Law were willing to take that **risk?** Write a **one-paragraph response,** including details from the biography and the letter from Frederick Douglass. | **An effective analysis will . . .**<br>• describe the risks that Harriet Tubman took<br>• clearly explain her motivations based on evidence from the texts |
| **B. Extended Response: Write a Character Sketch**<br>You learned about Harriet Tubman from the way Ann Petry characterized her. Now it's your turn to describe this historic figure for an elementary school audience. Write a **two- or three-paragraph character sketch** that uses various methods of characterization to capture the personality of Harriet Tubman. | **An interesting character sketch will . . .**<br>• use at least two methods of characterization<br>• be written in words an elementary school student can understand |

## GRAMMAR AND WRITING

**INDIANA STANDARDS**

**WRITING STANDARD**
**8.6.1** Use correct and varied sentence types . . . .

***AVOID CLAUSES AS FRAGMENTS*** A clause is a group of words that contains a subject and a verb. An **independent clause** expresses a complete thought and can stand alone as a sentence. A **dependent,** or **subordinate, clause** cannot. Dependent clauses begin with words such as *although, before, because, so that, when, while,* and *that.* To avoid a sentence fragment, join a dependent clause (shown in yellow) to an independent clause.

*Original:* Harriet Tubman was willing to take risks. Because she wanted everyone to be free.

*Revised:* Harriet Tubman was willing to take risks because she wanted everyone to be free.

***PRACTICE*** Find four fragments in the following paragraph. Then fix the fragments by combining independent and dependent clauses.

Harriet Tubman would be hanged. If slaveholders caught her. Tubman was willing to kill. So that the Underground Railroad would remain a secret. It made Tubman happy. When former slaves had the right to vote. Although her work was dangerous. She did not ask for any reward.

*For more help with clauses, see page R62 in the **Grammar Handbook.***

## The Mysterious Mr. Lincoln
Biography by Russell Freedman

# *What are the signs of* GREATNESS?

**INDIANA STANDARDS**

**READING STANDARDS**
**8.2.7** Analyze the structure, format, and purpose of informational materials (such as textbooks, newspapers, instructional or technical manuals, and public documents).

**8.2.9** Make reasonable statements and draw conclusions about a text, supporting them with accurate examples.

**KEY IDEA** People can be noticed for a variety of reasons. A brilliant mind, confident personality, strong work ethic, or generous spirit can make someone shine. When people use these qualities to improve the world and inspire others, they are said to have **greatness.** The biography you are about to read describes the complicated personality—and extraordinary leadership—of one of the greatest U.S. presidents, Abraham Lincoln.

**WEB IT** Think of two or three people you consider to have qualities of greatness. You can include public figures, friends, or family members. For each person, create a web like the one shown to show the qualities that make him or her great. Then compare your web with your classmates' webs. What qualities come up more than once?

continued in the face of threats

bravery

Martin Luther King Jr.

## ● LITERARY ANALYSIS: BIOGRAPHY

Real people often inspire fascinating pieces of writing. A true account of a person's life that's written by someone else is called a **biography**. Writers of biographies

- use the third-person point of view
- present facts and opinions from a variety of sources
- provide an interpretation of a person's character

As you read this biography, watch for ways Russell Freedman highlights President Lincoln's strengths and weaknesses.

## ● READING SKILL: IDENTIFY MAIN IDEA AND DETAILS

Nonfiction writing is usually organized around **main ideas,** which are the most important ideas a writer wants to convey about a topic. The writer develops the main ideas through **supporting details,** which can include

- **facts:** statements that can be proven
- **anecdotes:** brief stories that reveal important points
- **quotations:** direct statements from relevant people

Sometimes writers state their main ideas clearly, often at the beginning or end of paragraphs. Other times, you must **infer** the main ideas from the details provided. As you read, note the main ideas and details on a rough outline like the one shown.

> I. Lincoln had a distinctive, changing appearance.
>    A. Tall with long legs
>    B.
> II.

## ▲ VOCABULARY IN CONTEXT

The following phrases could have been headlines at the time Abraham Lincoln lived. Replace each boldfaced term with a word or words that means something similar.

1. Southern States **Denounce** the War
2. A **Melancholy** Nation Faces Civil War
3. Soldiers **Defy** the Odds
4. Lincoln to **Patronize** Local Business
5. Exhausted Generals Grow **Listless** as War Rages On
6. Senators **Meddle** in Lincoln's War Plans

# Author Online

**The Art of Nonfiction**
Russell Freedman's father worked for a publishing company and often brought authors home to have dinner with the family. "I wanted to be like them," Freedman says. To improve his writing skills, he got a job as a news reporter. His interest in writing biographies started when he learned about a blind 16-year-old boy who had invented a Braille typewriter. Fascinated by the boy's story, Freedman wrote his first book, *Teenagers Who Made History* (1961). When asked why he specializes in writing nonfiction for young readers, Freedman says he enjoys the challenge of conveying "the spirit and essence of a life."

**Russell Freedman**
**born 1929**

## Background

**Abraham Lincoln** Despite being born into a poor family with few opportunities, Abraham Lincoln managed to educate himself. He became a successful lawyer and state politician, but he had even greater ambitions. In 1860, he achieved them; he won the presidency. He steered the country through the long and bloody Civil War (1861–1865), which resulted in an end to slavery in the United States. In April 1865, Lincoln was assassinated by John Wilkes Booth, a southerner who wanted slavery to continue. Lincoln has held an enduring fascination for historians who often find new facets of his personality to examine. As Russell Freedman has pointed out, "Every ten years Lincoln changes character dramatically."

 **MORE ABOUT THE AUTHOR AND BACKGROUND**
To learn more about Russell Freedman and President Lincoln, visit the **Literature Center** at ClassZone.com.

# The Mysterious
# MR. LINCOLN

## Russell Freedman

**ANALYZE VISUALS**
Look at this photograph of Lincoln. How would you **describe** the expression on his face?

*"If any personal description of me is thought desirable, it may be said, I am, in height, six feet, four inches, nearly; lean in flesh, weighing, on average, one hundred and eighty pounds dark complexion, with coarse black hair and grey eyes—no other marks or brands recollected."*

Abraham Lincoln wasn't the sort of man who could lose himself in a crowd. After all, he stood six feet four inches tall, and to top it off, he wore a high silk hat.

His height was mostly in his long bony legs. When he sat in a chair, he seemed no taller than anyone else. It was only when he stood up that he towered above other men.

At first glance, most people thought he was homely. Lincoln thought so too, referring once to his "poor, lean, lank face." As a young man he was sensitive about his gawky looks, but in time, he learned to laugh at himself. When a

10 rival called him "two-faced" during a political debate, Lincoln replied: "I leave it to my audience. If I had another face, do you think I'd wear this one?" **Ⓐ**

According to those who knew him, Lincoln was a man of many faces. In repose,[1] he often seemed sad and gloomy. But when he began to speak, his expression changed. "The dull, **listless** features dropped like a mask," said a Chicago newspaperman. "The eyes began to sparkle, the mouth to smile, the whole countenance[2] was wreathed in animation, so that a stranger would have said 'Why, this man, so angular and solemn a moment ago, is really handsome!'" **Ⓑ**

**Ⓐ MAIN IDEA AND DETAILS**
Reread lines 7–11. What type of detail does the author use to help convey Lincoln's appearance? Add this to your outline.

**listless** (lĭst'lĭs) *adj.* lacking energy

**Ⓑ BIOGRAPHY**
Who thinks Lincoln is "a man of many faces"? Tell how you know this.

---

1. **repose** (rĭ-pōz'): the act of resting.

2. **countenance** (koun'tə-nəns): the face; expression of the face.

Lincoln was the most photographed man of his time, but his friends insisted
20 that no photo ever did him justice. It's no wonder. Back then, cameras required
long exposures. The person being photographed had to "freeze" as the seconds
ticked by. If he blinked an eye, the picture would be blurred. That's why Lincoln
looks so stiff and formal in his photos. We never see him laughing or joking.

Artists and writers tried to capture the "real" Lincoln that the camera
missed, but something about the man always escaped them. His changeable
features, his tones, gestures, and expressions, seemed to **defy** description.

Today it's hard to imagine Lincoln as he really was. And he never cared to
reveal much about himself. In company he was witty and talkative, but he rarely
betrayed his inner feelings. According to William Herndon, his law partner, he
30 was "the most secretive—reticent—shut-mouthed man that ever lived."

In his own time, Lincoln was never fully understood even by his closest friends.
Since then, his life story has been told and retold so many times, he has become
as much a legend as a flesh-and-blood human being. While the legend is based on
truth, it is only partly true. And it hides the man behind it like a disguise. **C**

The legendary Lincoln is known as Honest Abe, a humble man of the
people who rose from a log cabin to the White House. There's no doubt that
Lincoln was a poor boy who made good. And it's true that he carried his
folksy manners and homespun speech to the White House with him. He said
"howdy" to visitors and invited them to "stay a spell." He greeted diplomats
40 while wearing carpet slippers, called his wife "mother" at receptions, and told
bawdy[3] jokes at cabinet meetings.

Lincoln may have seemed like a common man, but he wasn't. His friends
agreed that he was one of the most ambitious people they had ever known.
Lincoln struggled hard to rise above his log-cabin origins, and he was proud
of his achievements. By the time he ran for president he was a wealthy man,
earning a large income from his law practice and his many investments. As for
the nickname Abe, he hated it. No one who knew him well ever called him
Abe to his face. They addressed him as Lincoln or Mr. Lincoln.

Lincoln is often described as a sloppy dresser, careless about his appearance. In
50 fact, he **patronized** the best tailor in Springfield, Illinois, buying two suits a year.
That was at a time when many men lived, died, and were buried in the same suit.

It's true that Lincoln had little formal "eddication," as he would have
pronounced it. Almost everything he "larned" he taught himself. All his life he
said "thar" for *there*, "git" for *get*, "kin" for *can*. Even so, he became an eloquent
public speaker who could hold a vast audience spellbound, and a great writer
whose finest phrases still ring in our ears. He was known to sit up late into the
night, discussing Shakespeare's plays with White House visitors. **D**

He was certainly a humorous man, famous for his rollicking stories. But he
was also moody and **melancholy,** tormented by long and frequent bouts of
60 depression. Humor was his therapy. He relied on his yarns,[4] a friend observed,
to "whistle down sadness."

---

3. **bawdy** (bô′dē): vulgar.

4. **yarn**: an entertaining tale.

**defy** (dĭ-fī′) *v.* to boldly
oppose or resist

**C MAIN IDEA AND
DETAILS**
What is the main idea
in this paragraph? Add it
to your outline.

**patronize** (pā′trə-nīz′) *v.*
to go to as a customer

**D MAIN IDEA AND
DETAILS**
Note the details about
Lincoln's words and
actions. What main idea
do they support?

**melancholy**
(mĕl′ən-kŏl′ē) *adj.*
sad; depressed

He had a cool, logical mind, trained in the courtroom, and a practical, commonsense approach to problems. Yet he was deeply superstitious, a believer in dreams, omens, and visions. **E**

We admire Lincoln today as an American folk hero. During the Civil War, however, he was the most unpopular president the nation had ever known. His critics called him a tyrant, a hick, a stupid baboon who was unfit for his office. As commander in chief of the armed forces, he was **denounced** as a bungling amateur who **meddled** in military affairs he knew nothing about. But he also
70 had his supporters. They praised him as a farsighted statesman, a military mastermind who engineered the Union victory.

Lincoln is best known as the Great Emancipator, the man who freed the slaves. Yet he did not enter the war with that idea in mind. "My paramount object in this struggle *is* to save the Union," he said in 1862, "and is *not* either to save or destroy slavery." As the war continued, Lincoln's attitude changed. Eventually he came to regard the conflict as a moral crusade to wipe out the sin of slavery.

No black leader was more critical of Lincoln than the fiery abolitionist[5] writer and editor Frederick Douglass. Douglass had grown up as a slave.
80 He had won his freedom by escaping to the North. Early in the war, impatient with Lincoln's cautious leadership, Douglass called him "preeminently the white man's president, entirely devoted to the welfare of white men." Later, Douglass changed his mind and came to admire Lincoln. Several years after the war, he said
90 this about the sixteenth president:

"His greatest mission was to accomplish two things: first, to save his country from dismemberment and ruin; and, second, to free his country from the great crime of slavery. . . . taking him for all in all, measuring the tremendous magnitude of the work before him, considering the necessary means to
100 ends, and surveying the end from the beginning, infinite wisdom has seldom sent any man into the world better fitted for his mission than Abraham Lincoln." ❧

---

5. **abolitionist** (ăb′ə-lĭsh′ə-nĭst): one who advocated the end of slavery.

**E** **BIOGRAPHY**
Which of the qualities described would you expect a great leader to have, and which would you not?

**denounce** (dĭ-nouns′) *v.*
to condemn; to criticize

**meddle** (mĕd′l) *v.*
to intrude or interfere

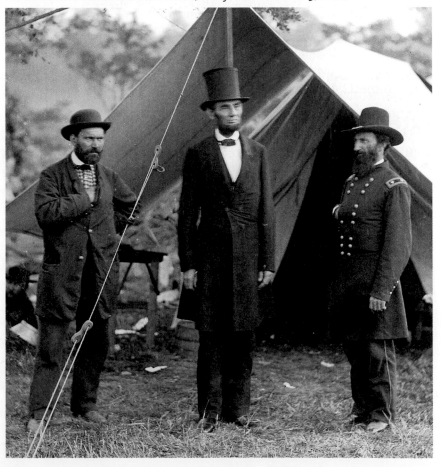

Allan Pinkerton, President Abraham Lincoln, and Major General John A. McClernand at Antietam Battle Site, Maryland. October 3, 1862.

# Comprehension

1. **Recall** According to the author, why does Abraham Lincoln look "so stiff and formal" in photographs?

2. **Recall** What was Lincoln's original reason for entering into the Civil War?

3. **Clarify** What caused Frederick Douglass to change his opinion of Lincoln?

INDIANA STANDARDS

READING STANDARD
**8.2.7** Analyze the structure, format, and purpose of informational materials....

# Literary Analysis

4. **Identify Main Idea and Details** Review the outline you filled in as you read. Based on the main ideas and details you noted, what do you think is the overall main idea of the selection?

5. **Analyze Characterization** One method of characterization is to present the way a person talks. Review the quotations from Lincoln that Freedman includes in this biography. In what way do Lincoln's words add to your understanding of his character? Cite one or two specific quotations to support your answer.

6. **Make Judgments** What signs of **greatness** did Lincoln exhibit in his life? Support your response with evidence from the text.

7. **Evaluate Biography** List the strengths and weaknesses of Lincoln in a chart like the one shown. In your opinion, does the author provide a balanced portrait of his subject? Explain.

| Strengths | Weaknesses |
|---|---|
| sense of humor | |

# Extension and Challenge

8. **Readers' Circle** People often say that Abraham Lincoln would have a difficult time winning an election today. Why do you think they say that? Discuss the question with your group. Then decide whether or not you agree. Support your opinion with examples from the biography.

9.  **SOCIAL STUDIES CONNECTION** In 1922, President Harding dedicated the Lincoln Memorial, a magnificent structure built in Washington D.C. to honor Abraham Lincoln. Research the memorial to find out what is included within it and what it stands for.

Lincoln Memorial

**RESEARCH LINKS**
For more about the Lincoln Memorial, visit the **Research Center** at **ClassZone.com.**

# Vocabulary in Context

## VOCABULARY PRACTICE

For each sentence, choose the vocabulary word that has a similar meaning to the boldfaced word or phrase.

1. It's easy now, after the fact, to say that you **condemn** the awful crime.
2. I **shop regularly at** the corner grocery.
3. Why must you always **interfere** in things that are not your business?
4. He thought it was wrong to **oppose** his parents.
5. That particular music made them feel **sad.**
6. Because he felt so **tired,** he began taking vitamins.

defy
denounce
listless
meddle
melancholy
patronize

## VOCABULARY IN WRITING

What negative things did people say about President Lincoln when he was in office? Use two or more vocabulary words to write your answer in a paragraph. Here is a sample opening sentence.

> **EXAMPLE SENTENCE**
>
> During the Civil War, plenty of people took the opportunity to **denounce** Lincoln's military decisions.

## VOCABULARY STRATEGY: MULTIPLE-MEANING WORDS

Many English words have more than one meaning. The vocabulary word *patronize* is one of these words. In the selection, *patronize* means "to visit as a customer," but another definition is "to treat in a condescending manner."

*PRACTICE* Each boldfaced word below has multiple meanings. Read the sentence and figure out the meaning of the boldfaced word based on context clues. Use a dictionary to check your answer. Then find another meaning for the word and use the word in a new sentence.

1. My grandmother knit a sweater using yellow **yarn.**
2. I can **sink** the basketball in the net even when I'm nervous.
3. The **pipe** below the sink was rusty from age.
4. When I am hungry, I **gorge** myself on pancakes and eggs.

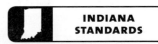

**INDIANA STANDARDS**

READING STANDARD
**8.1.3** Verify the meaning of a word in its context....

**VOCABULARY PRACTICE**
For more practice, go to the **Vocabulary Center** at **ClassZone.com.**

# Barbara Frietchie
Poem by John Greenleaf Whittier

# John Henry
Traditional Poem

## *Is it ever right to* GIVE UP?

**INDIANA STANDARDS**

**READING STANDARDS**
**8.3.1** Determine and articulate the relationship between the purposes and characterisitics of different forms of poetry (including ballads, lyrics, couplets, epics, elegies, odes, and sonnets).

**8.3.6** Identify significant literary devices ....

**KEY IDEA** Think of a time when you kept trying something without success. Did you get discouraged, or did the experience make you try harder? When some of us might give up, other people find the strength to **persevere**. In the poems you are about to read, you will meet two characters who refuse to take no for an answer.

**QUICKWRITE** Think of a situation in which you gave up doing something—perhaps playing an instrument or being on a team. Write a brief paragraph explaining the positive and negative consequences of your decision.

## ● LITERARY ANALYSIS: CHARACTERIZATION IN POETRY

The two works you are about to read are **narrative poems,** which means they tell a story. Like short stories, narrative poems always feature characters. Poets can bring their characters to life, or **characterize** them, in just a few words. A telling image, a carefully chosen scrap of dialogue, or a striking detail can suggest a great deal about a character's traits, behavior, and values.

As you read "Barbara Frietchie" and "John Henry," pay attention to what the poets' language suggests about the characters. Then note information about each main character in the appropriate part of a graphic like the one shown.

Details

Barbara Frietchie

Dialogue                                    Images

## ● READING SKILL: RECOGNIZE SOUND DEVICES

One way that narrative poems differ from short stories is the extent to which they use **sound devices** to add meaning and interest. The three Rs of sound devices are

- **Rhyme:** the repetition of sounds at the ends of words

  *Over the mountains winding <u>down</u>,*
  *Horse and foot, into Frederick <u>town</u>.*

- **Rhythm:** the pattern of stressed and unstressed syllables in the lines of a poem

  *She leaned far out on the window-sill*

- **Repetition:** repeated sounds, words, or phrases that are used for emphasis

  *You must be a steel driving man like me,*
  *You must be a steel driving man like me.*

Reading a poem aloud can help you appreciate the sound devices. As you read "Barbara Frietchie" and "John Henry," notice the effect the devices have on the sound and sense of the poem.

# Author Onine

**Fiery Abolitionist**
Although John Greenleaf Whittier had little formal schooling, he was naturally drawn to poetry. His career began in 1826 when a local newspaper published one of his poems, which his older sister had submitted without his knowledge. William Lloyd Garrison, a noted abolitionist, was the newspaper's editor, and his passion for ending slavery affected Whittier. Whittier's poems about the evils of slavery were published in 1846 under the title *Voices of Freedom.*

**John Greenleaf Whittier**
**1807–1892**

➤ **MORE ABOUT THE AUTHOR**
For more on John Greenleaf Whittier, visit the **Literature Center** at ClassZone.com.

## *Background*

**"Barbara Frietchie" and the Civil War**
As an abolitionist, John Greenleaf Whittier strongly supported the Union side in the Civil War. He wrote "Barbara Frietchie" to honor a legendary act of courage. Barbara Frietchie was a citizen of Frederick, Maryland, who was fiercely loyal to the Union. According to legend, as Confederate soldiers marched through the town, she defiantly waved a Union flag.

**John Henry** It is not known if John Henry actually existed, but the character may have been based on a real steel driver in the early 1870s. Steel drivers used hammers and steel drills to pound holes into mountains. Then explosives blasted deeper into the mountains to create tunnels for railroads. The speed and efficiency of machines like steam drills eventually threatened the livelihood of steel drivers. John Henry's story is often sung as a ballad.

# Barbara Frietchie

## John Greenleaf Whittier

Up from the meadows rich with corn,
Clear in the cool September morn,

The clustered spires of Frederick stand
Green-walled by the hills of Maryland.

5 Round about them orchards sweep,
Apple and peach tree fruited deep,

Fair as the garden of the Lord
To the eyes of the famished rebel horde,[1]

On that pleasant morn of the early fall
10 When Lee[2] marched over the mountain wall;

Over the mountains winding down,
Horse and foot, into Frederick town. **A**

**ANALYZE VISUALS**
This union flag flew during the Civil War. What **conclusions** can you draw about why the flag looks the way it does?

**A SOUND DEVICES**
Which sound devices do you notice in lines 1–12?

---

1. **horde:** a large group or crowd.
2. **Lee:** a general for the Confederate army during the Civil War.

Forty flags with their silver stars,
Forty flags with their crimson bars,

15 Flapped in the morning wind: the sun
Of noon looked down, and saw not one.

Up rose old Barbara Frietchie then,
Bowed with her fourscore years and ten;[3]

Bravest of all in Frederick town,
20 She took up the flag the men hauled down.

In her attic window the staff she set,
To show that one heart was loyal yet. **B**

Up the street came the rebel tread,
Stonewall Jackson[4] riding ahead.

25 Under his slouched hat left and right
He glanced; the old flag met his sight.

"Halt!"—the dust-brown ranks stood fast.
"Fire!"—out blazed the rifle-blast.

It shivered the window, pane and sash;
30 It rent[5] the banner with seam and gash.

Quick, as it fell, from the broken staff
Dame Barbara snatched the silken scarf. **C**

She leaned far out on the window-sill,
And shook it forth with a royal will.

35 "Shoot, if you must, this old gray head,
But spare your country's flag," she said.

**B CHARACTERIZATION**
Reread lines 17–22.
What do you learn about
Barbara Frietchie?

**C SOUND DEVICES**
In lines 31–32, what is
different about the use
of **rhyme?** Tell what
effect this has on your
reading of the poem.

---

3. **fourscore years and ten:** ninety years.

4. **Stonewall Jackson:** a general for the Confederate army
during the Civil War.

5. **rent:** tore apart.

A shade of sadness, a blush of shame,
Over the face of the leader came;

The nobler nature within him stirred
40 To life at that woman's deed and word;

"Who touches a hair of yon gray head
Dies like a dog! March on!" he said. **D**

All day long through Frederick street
Sounded the tread of marching feet:

45 All day long that free flag tost
Over the heads of the rebel host. **E**

Ever its torn folds rose and fell
On the loyal winds that loved it well;

And through the hill-gaps sunset light
50 Shone over it with a warm good-night.

Barbara Frietchie's work is o'er,
And the Rebel rides on his raids no more.

Honor to her! and let a tear
Fall, for her sake, on Stonewall's bier.[6]

55 Over Barbara Frietchie's grave,
Flag of Freedom and Union, wave!

Peace and order and beauty draw
Round thy symbol of light and law;

And ever the stars above look down
60 On thy stars below in Frederick town!

**D CHARACTERIZATION**
In lines 35–42, what traits and behavior does Barbara Frietchie display that make Stonewall Jackson feel shame?

**E SOUND DEVICES**
Reread lines 43–46? What does the **repetition** emphasize about the events in Frederick?

---

6. **bier** (bîr): a stand on which a coffin is placed before a burial.

# John Henry

Traditional

When John Henry was a little boy,
Sitting upon his father's knee,
His father said, "Look here, my boy,
You must be a steel driving man like me,
5 You must be a steel driving man like me." **F**

John Henry went up on the mountain,
Just to drive himself some steel.
The rocks was so tall and John Henry so small,
He said lay down hammer and squeal,
10 He said lay down hammer and squeal.

John Henry had a little wife,
And the dress she wore was red;
The last thing before he died,
He said, "Be true to me when I'm dead,
15 Oh, be true to me when I'm dead."

John Henry's wife ask him for fifteen cents,
And he said he didn't have but a dime,
Said, "If you wait till the rising sun goes down,
I'll borrow it from the man in the mine,
20 I'll borrow it from the man in the mine."

John Henry started on the right-hand side,
And the steam drill started on the left.
He said, "Before I'd let that steam drill beat me down,
I'd hammer my fool self to death,
25 Oh, I'd hammer my fool self to death." **G**

**F** SOUND DEVICES
What part of John Henry's
life does the **repetition** in
lines 4–5 emphasize?

**G** CHARACTERIZATION
How would you describe
John Henry's attitude?

The steam drill started at half-past six,
John Henry started the same time.
John Henry struck bottom at half-past eight,
And the steam drill didn't bottom till nine,
30 And the steam drill didn't bottom till nine.

John Henry said to his captain,
"A man, he ain't nothing but a man,
Before I'd let that steam drill beat me down,
I'd die with the hammer in my hand,
35 Oh, I'd die with the hammer in my hand."

John Henry said to his shaker, [1]
"Shaker, why don't you sing just a few more rounds?
And before the setting sun goes down,
You're gonna hear this hammer of mine sound,
40 You're gonna hear this hammer of mine sound."

John Henry hammered on the mountain,
He hammered till half-past three,
He said, "This big Bend Tunnel on the C. & O. road [2]
Is going to be the death of me,
45 Lord! is going to be the death of me."

John Henry had a little baby boy,
You could hold him in the palm of your hand.
The last words before he died,
"Son, you must be a steel driving man,
50 Son, you must be a steel driving man." **H**

John Henry had a little woman,
And the dress she wore was red,
She went down the railroad track and never come back,
Said she was going where John Henry fell dead,
55 Said she was going where John Henry fell dead.

John Henry hammering on the mountain,
As the whistle blew for half-past two,
The last word I heard him say,
"Captain, I've hammered my insides in two,
60 Lord, I've hammered my insides in two." **I**

**H** **CHARACTERIZATION**
Why do you think it is important to John Henry that his son follows in his footsteps?

**I** **SOUND DEVICES**
Read lines 56–57 aloud with a natural **rhythm.** Which syllables are stressed?

---

1. **shaker:** the person who holds the steel drill for the steel driving man and shakes the drill to remove it from the rock.

2. **big Bend . . . road:** Construction work on the Big Bend Tunnel on the Chesapeake & Ohio Railroad in West Virginia took place from 1870 to 1873.

**COMIC STRIP** John Henry has been the subject of ballads, children's books, feature films, and more. In this comic, cartoonist John Steventon shows one of the ways he's been inspired by this American folk hero.

# Cartoon Tribute to
# John Henry

John Henry was a childhood hero of mine, and he was probably one of the biggest influences on who I am and how I live my life. To me, the legend and the man are the same; I still see him as a regular guy who was confident in himself and who never, ever gave up. When he needed a job, he went and got one, convincing the boss that he was the right man for it. And when that job of Steel Driving Man was threatened by automation, he challenged that Steam Drill to a contest and won. Sure, he died in the process, but that just adds to his legend. The point is, he said he would win and did, against all odds. What a role model for young and old alike!

## Comprehension

1. **Recall** What causes Barbara Frietchie to hold a flag out her window?

2. **Clarify** Why does John Henry have a contest with the steam drill?

## Literary Analysis

3. **Make Inferences** Reread lines 23–42 of "Barbara Frietchie." Why do you think Stonewall Jackson decides to protect the woman who defied him?

4. **Interpret Symbol** What do you think John Henry's victory over the steam drill **symbolizes,** or stands for beyond its usual meaning?

5. **Analyze Ballad** "John Henry" is a **ballad,** a poem that tells a story and was originally meant to be sung. What elements of the poem make it songlike?

6. **Compare and Contrast** Using a Venn diagram like the one shown, compare and contrast the characters of Barbara Frietchie and John Henry. Are they more similar or different?

Frietchie    Henry

elderly

7. **Analyze Characterization** Review the character maps you created as you read. Based on the information you collected, describe each character in detail. What are they like? What do they believe in?

8. **Draw Conclusions** Why do you think Barbara Frietchie and John Henry captured the American imagination? Think about why Americans value the traits these characters display in the poems.

9. **Evaluate Sound Devices** Read several stanzas of each poem aloud. For each poem, tell whether you think the **rhythm, rhyme,** or **repetition** affects the meaning most. Explain your answer.

10. **Compare Texts** In the "Cartoon Tribute to John Henry," how does Bobby's encounter with Dr. Dampflok parallel John Henry's experience in the poem?

## Extension and Challenge

11. **Readers' Circle** Considering the outcome, do you think John Henry was right to **persevere** at his work on the railroad? Explain.

**INDIANA STANDARDS**

**READING STANDARD**
**8.3.1** Determine and articulate . . . characterisitics of different forms of poetry . . . .

## Writing Workshop

# Describing a Person

In Unit 2 you read about some incredible people, including Abraham Lincoln and Harriet Tubman. Now you will have a chance to write about someone who fascinates you—either a person you know or a literary character. Read the **Writer's Road Map** and get started describing someone unforgettable.

### WRITER'S ROAD MAP

#### Describing a Person

**WRITING PROMPT 1**

**Writing from Your Life** Write a focused description of a person who is important to you. Your description should include anecdotes and details to help your readers visualize the person.

**People to Consider**

- a friend you know very well
- a person who taught you something important
- a family member who helped you

**WRITING PROMPT 2**

**Writing from Literature** The literature in this unit is full of memorable characters. Choose one of the characters you read about and describe that person as clearly as you can.

**Characters to Consider**

- Greg in "The Treasure of Lemon Brown"
- Charlie in "Flowers for Algernon"
- Waverly in "Rules of the Game"

 **WRITING TOOLS**
For prewriting, revision, and editing tools, visit the **Writing Center** at ClassZone.com.

**KEY TRAITS**

**1. IDEAS**

- Provides a **focused description** of a clearly identified person or character
- Includes **anecdotes and details** to describe the person
- Uses **dialogue** to show the subject's personality

**2. ORGANIZATION**

- Has a clear **organization,** with an introduction, a body, and a conclusion
- Uses **transitions** to connect ideas
- Provides any **background information** the reader may need
- **Concludes** by showing why the person is important

**3. VOICE**

- Has an appropriate and respectful **tone**

**4. WORD CHOICE**

- Uses **sensory details** to show the reader what the person or character is like

**5. SENTENCE FLUENCY**

- Varies the **lengths of sentences** to make the description lively and interesting

**6. CONVENTIONS**

- Uses **correct grammar, spelling, and punctuation**

# Part 1: Analyze a Student Model

**WRITING STANDARD**
8.5.7 Write for different purposes and to a specific audience....

Madison Delgado
Flaherty Junior High School

### Coach Sand's Swimming Lesson

"Are you going to do it, or should we go home for lunch while you make up your mind?" Coach Sand's booming voice shook the diving board as I stood with my knees trembling and toes white and numb from gripping the edge. He was only 17, but planted below me at the
5   side of the pool, he looked even shorter than his 5 feet 6 inches or so and much broader and more muscular—almost like King Kong.

"I'm not afraid of you," I muttered. I *was* afraid of him, though, and so was everyone else.

A group of us had signed up for Coach Sand's Pool School during
10   winter break, thinking that it would be a fun way to improve our swimming and diving. He was the star diver on the high school team and had just gotten a scholarship to the state university. My friends and I had seen him in a few local competitions. We couldn't believe how anyone so short and stocky could turn himself into a graceful arrow that
15   hit the water like a bull's-eye every time.

Coach was the boss of the water and of his students, and he made sure we knew it. The first day, he made us wait for 15 minutes huddled and shivering in our baggy Pool School bathing suits. When he finally came marching into the pool area, he was fully dressed in jeans, cowboy
20   boots, and a black leather jacket. His boot heels cracked the tiles at every step and echoed off the pool walls. Right away, that made us feel scrawny and scared.

"I'm not going to dive into the pool to save any of you," he said, "so listen up and do as I say. You're going to find out that you can swim and
25   dive a lot better than you think you can."

## KEY TRAITS IN ACTION

Creates a **focused impression** of Coach Sand with a quotation and highlighted descriptive **details** that show his personality.

Provides important **background information** about the coach's qualifications. Putting this information early in the description is a sign of clear **organization**.

An **anecdote** and **sensory details** make Coach Sand leap off the page.

My friends and I looked at each other, wondering what we had gotten ourselves into. We were all on the middle school swim team, so we thought that we knew what we could do. Coach Sand disagreed. When my friend Angela raised her hand, Coach barked, "I'll ask the

30   questions around here. Your job is to come up with the answers—or try." Then he lined us all up and had us dive into the pool and swim laps for the next 45 minutes. If anyone stopped to rest or switched to an easy stroke like the sidestroke, he would yell from the deck, "What are you doing, taking a bath? Front crawl, breaststroke, or backstroke."

35   What kept us going was his challenge to do more than we thought we could do. Every day for a week, he made us do laps and more laps. Finally, he showed up in a bathing suit one day and climbed up to the high dive without saying a word. He did a perfect back somersault with a double twist and entered the water without a splash. We gasped.

40   "Okay, you saw that," he said. "Now show me what you can do."

"I'm not afraid of you," I muttered, standing on that diving board. I leaped off and did a simple, clean dive. As I came out of the water, Coach Sand reached down to give me a hand.

"Way to go," he said proudly. I had learned his lesson.

Highlighted **transitions** help the reader see how ideas are related. **Tone** is informal without being slangy.

Varying the **lengths of sentences** helps to maintain reader interest. **Dialogue** helps the reader understand Coach Sand and the writer's reaction to him.

Thoughtful **conclusion** shows why the coach is important to this writer.

2

# Part 2: Apply the Writing Process

**WRITING STANDARD**
**8.4.7** Review, evaluate, and revise writing for meaning and clarity.

## PREWRITING

| What Should I Do? | What Does It Look Like? |
|---|---|

**1. Choose a person or a character.**
Carefully read the prompts on page 292. Decide which one you will answer. Then list people who are important to you or characters from literature who stick in your mind. Note what is special about each one. (Circle) your first choice.

**TIP** For Prompt 1, think about people who make you laugh, who annoy you, or who have taught you something. For Prompt 2, think of characters you like or dislike.

▶

| People | Why They Are Important |
|---|---|
| Joe Dean | Is always doing something goofy |
| (Coach Sand) | Got me to do my best |
| Lily | Stood up for me with Mom and Dad |

**2. Identify the most important impression.**
Jot down a sentence or two that focuses on what makes this person or character so memorable.

▶

Coach Sand was really hard on us, but he helped us do more than we ever thought we could.

**3. Collect information.**
Use a cluster diagram to organize details about the person or character's physical appearance, speech, beliefs, thoughts, and actions. Don't forget **anecdotes**—brief stories about the person or character. These can clearly show his or her personality.

▶

Words: "I'll ask the questions around here."

Anecdote: the first time he showed us how to dive

Coach Sand

Belief: that we could do more than we thought we could

**4. Brainstorm sensory details.**
Try to think of specific sights, sounds, smells, tastes, textures, and other qualities associated with the person or character. These will make your writing vivid and distinctive.

▶

| Sights | Sounds | Smells |
|---|---|---|
| • short and stocky (like King Kong!) | • echo of boot heels off the pool walls<br>• booming voice | • chlorine<br>• Coach's leather jacket |

| What Should I Do? | What Does It Look Like? |
|---|---|

**1. Decide which points to include.**
How will you support your main impression of the person? Which details or anecdotes will you use to describe each point? Use a chart, list, or outline to get organized.

▶

| Main Points | Details |
|---|---|
| • scary at first | • tough and sarcastic (use examples of what he said) |
| • got us to do more than we thought we could | • after we saw him dive, wanted to show him what we could do |

**2. Craft an intriguing introduction.**
Try starting with a surprising statement, a quotation, or a description that makes your reader want to know more about the person or character.

▶

**Surprising statement**
Who's afraid of a swimming coach? I was.

**Quotation**
"Are you going to do it, or should we go home for lunch while you make up your mind?"

**Description**
He was 17. He looked like King Kong. His voice shook the diving board under my feet.

**3. Show, don't tell.**
Instead of just telling about your subject's personality, include details and anecdotes that show your subject in action. Try using some of the sensory words and phrases you came up with on page 295 .

▶

**Telling**
Coach Sand was always very strict.

**Showing**
"I'm not going to dive into the pool to save any of you," he said, "so listen up and do as I say."

**3. Explain the importance.**
Conclude by making it clear why this person or character matters to you. For example, the writer of the student model realized that her coach was proud of her.

**TIP** Before you revise, look back at the key traits on page 292 and the rubric and peer-reader questions on page 298.

▶

"I'm not afraid of you," I muttered again. I leaped off the board and did a simple, clean dive. As I came out of the water, Coach Sand reached down to give me a hand.

"Way to go," he said proudly. I had learned his lesson.

## REVISING AND EDITING

| *What Should I Do?* | *What Does It Look Like?* |
|---|---|

**1. Stay focused.**
- Your description should give a focused impression of the person or character. For example, Coach Sand is tough but fair.
- Reread your draft. Delete information that wanders from your main point.

▶ He was the star diver on the high school team and had just gotten a scholarship to the state university. ~~Now he is majoring in accounting, and he works part time at a sporting-goods store in Saugus.~~

**2. Provide helpful background information.**
- Have a peer reader draw a box around parts of your description that don't give enough information.
- Add explanations or details that keep your reader from becoming frustrated or confused.

▶ Then he lined us all up and had us dive into the pool and swim laps for the next 45 minutes. He'd yell from the deck, "What are you doing, taking a bath? Front crawl, breaststroke, or backstroke."
If anyone stopped to rest or switched to an easy stroke like the sidestroke,

**3. Vary the length of your sentences.**
- Pick a paragraph and count the number of words in each sentence. Do they all have about the same number of words? Do any sentences begin the same way?
- If your writing sounds choppy or droning, revise or combine some sentences to create a pleasing rhythm.

▶ ~~We looked at each other. We wondered what we had gotten ourselves into. All of us were on the middle school swim team. We thought that we knew what we could do. It turned out that Coach Sand disagreed with us.~~
My friends and I looked at each other, wondering what we had gotten ourselves into. We were all on the middle school swim team, so we thought that we knew what we could do. Coach Sand disagreed.

**4. Pay attention to tone.**
- Ask a peer reader to [bracket] any parts of your description that use slang or that seem too informal.
- Revise your description so that it is appropriate and respectful throughout.

**See page 298:** Ask a Peer Reader

▶ ~~[The dude] did a [wicked] dive. The rest of us were completely [bugging out!!! ]~~
He did a perfect back somersault with a double twist and entered the water without a splash. We gasped.

# Describing a Person

## Apply the Rubric

**A strong description of a person or character . . .**

- ☑ uses details to create a focused description
- ☑ uses dialogue, anecdotes, and sensory details to reveal the subject's personality
- ☑ includes helpful background information
- ☑ is sensibly organized
- ☑ uses transitions to show the order of events
- ☑ maintains an appropriate tone
- ☑ varies sentence lengths
- ☑ ends by summarizing why the person is important to the writer

## Ask a Peer Reader

- Why is this person or character important to me?
- What else would you like to know about him or her?
- Is my tone appropriate? If not, where are some problem areas?

## Stay Away from Clichés

**Cliché:** I was **scared to death.**

**Rewrite:** I stood with my knees trembling.

**Cliché:** The diver was **the best of the best.**

**Rewrite:** The diver was a graceful arrow who hit the water like a bull's-eye every time.

**Cliché:** We were **as cold as ice.**

**Rewrite:** We were huddled and shivering.

**Cliché:** He was **as strong as an ox.**

**Rewrite:** He looked like King Kong.

## Check Your Grammar

- Use *who* as a subject or a predicate pronoun.

  *Who suggested that you go to Pool School?*
  *He is the person who coached me.*

- Use *whom* for a direct object, indirect object, or object of a preposition.

  *Whom will you nominate for the award?*
  *They gave whom a diving trophy?*

**See page R54:** Interrogative Pronouns

## Writing On**l**ine

**PUBLISHING OPTIONS**
For publishing options, visit the **Writing Center** at ClassZone.com.

**ASSESSMENT PREPARATION**
For writing and grammar assessment practice, go to the **Assessment Center** at ClassZone.com.

**LISTENING/SPEAKING STANDARD**
**8.7.1** Paraphrase (restate) a speaker's purpose and point of view and ask questions . . . .

# Conducting an Interview

Interviewing someone gives you a chance to see the world from another person's perspective.

## Planning the Interview

1. **Pick your person.** You can decide to interview the person you wrote about or someone else who interests you. To learn more about your family history, you could interview a relative. You also could think of a subject—like a sport you enjoy—and find someone who knows a great deal about it.

   **TIP** **If you want to practice interviewing before you start your real interview, have a classmate role-play a favorite character from literature.**

2. **Set up the interview.** Get in touch with the person face-to-face or by telephone, e-mail, or letter. Ask for permission to conduct an interview. If you want to make a video or audio recording of the interview, mention that as well. Then decide on a time and place. You might agree to meet in a public place, talk by phone, or send instant messages.

3. **Do your research.** Learn all you can about the person beforehand. Make a list of specific questions. Think of questions that can't be answered "yes" or "no." Ask open-ended questions to encourage the person to talk at length about his or her experiences, feelings, and ideas.

## Conducting the Interview

1. **Listen carefully and take notes.** Taking notes is important, even if you are recording the interview. Don't be afraid to ask the person to repeat something or to wait while you finish writing.

2. **Ask follow-up questions.** Encourage the person to tell you more. "What happened then?" and "Why do you feel that way?" are good follow-up questions.

3. **Be respectful.** Be attentive and enthusiastic during the interview, and thank the person when you're through. Send a handwritten note or e-card the next day.

4. **Record what you have learned.** Your teacher will explain how to summarize the interview. You might write a summary, produce a partial transcript (a word-for-word re-creation of what was said), or create an audio or video presentation.

   **See page R84:** Evaluate an Interview

# Reading Comprehension

**DIRECTIONS** *Read these selections and answer the questions that follow.*

## *from* A Year Down Yonder

**Richard Peck**

As the train pulled out behind me, there came Grandma up the platform steps. My goodness, she was a big woman. I'd forgotten. And taller still with her spidery old umbrella held up to keep off the sun of high noon. A fan of white hair escaped the big bun on the back of her head. She drew nearer till she blotted out the day.

You couldn't call her a welcoming woman, and there wasn't a hug in her. She didn't put out her arms, so I had nothing to run into.

Nobody had told Grandma that skirts were shorter this year. Her skirttails brushed her shoes. I recognized the dress. It was the one she put on in hot 10 weather to walk uptown in. Though I was two years older, two years taller than last time, she wasn't one for personal comments. The picnic hamper quivered, and she noticed. "What's in there?"

"Bootsie," I said. "My cat."

"Hoo-boy," Grandma said. "Another mouth to feed." Her lips pleated. "And what's that thing?" She nodded to my other hand.

"My radio." But it was more than a radio to me. It was my last touch with the world.

"That's all we need." Grandma looked skyward. "More noise."

She aimed one of her chins down the platform. "That yours?" She meant 20 the trunk. It was the footlocker Dad had brought home from the Great War.

"Leave it," she said. "They'll bring it to the house." She turned and trudged away, and I was supposed to follow. I walked away from my trunk, wondering if I'd ever see it again. It wouldn't have lasted long on the platform in Chicago. Hot tongs wouldn't have separated me from Bootsie and my radio.

The recession of thirty-seven had hit Grandma's town harder than it had hit Chicago. Grass grew in the main street. Only a face or two showed in the window of The Coffee Pot Cafe. Moore's Store was hurting for trade. Weidenbach's bank looked to be just barely in business.

On the other side of the weedy road, Grandma turned the wrong way, away 30 from her house. Two old slab-sided dogs slept on the sidewalk. Bootsie knew because she was having a conniption in the hamper. And my radio was getting heavier. I caught up with Grandma.

"Where are we going?"

"Going?" she said, the picture of surprise. "Why, to school. You've already missed pretty nearly two weeks."

# *from* Luke Baldwin's Vow

## Morley Callaghan

That summer when twelve-year-old Luke Baldwin came to live with his
Uncle Henry in the house on the stream by the sawmill, he did not forget that
he had promised his dying father he would try to learn things from his uncle;
so he used to watch him very carefully.

Uncle Henry, who was the manager of the sawmill, was a big, burly man
weighing more than two hundred and thirty pounds, and he had a rough-
skinned, brick-colored face. He looked like a powerful man, but his health
was not good. He had aches and pains in his back and shoulders which
puzzled the doctor. The first thing Luke learned about Uncle Henry was
10  that everybody had great respect for him. The four men he employed in the
sawmill were always polite and attentive when he spoke to them. His wife,
Luke's Aunt Helen, a kindly, plump, straightforward woman, never argued
with him. "You should try and be like your Uncle Henry," she would say to
Luke. "He's so wonderfully practical. He takes care of everything in a sensible,
easy way."

Luke used to trail around the sawmill after Uncle Henry, not only because
he liked the fresh, clean smell of the newly cut wood and the big piles of
sawdust, but because he was impressed by his uncle's precise, firm tone when
he spoke to the men.

20  Sometimes Uncle Henry would stop and explain to Luke something about
a piece of timber. "Always try and learn the essential facts, son," he would say.
"If you've got the facts, you know what's useful and what isn't useful, and no
one can fool you."

He showed Luke that nothing of value was ever wasted around the mill. Luke
used to listen, and wonder if there was another man in the world who knew
so well what was needed and what ought to be thrown away. Uncle Henry
had known at once that Luke needed a bicycle to ride to his school, which was
two miles away in town, and he bought him a good one. He knew that Luke
needed good, serviceable clothes. He also knew exactly how much Aunt Helen
30  needed to run the house, the price of everything, and how much a woman
should be paid for doing the family washing. In the evenings Luke used to sit
in the living room watching his uncle making notations in a black notebook
which he always carried in his vest pocket, and he knew that he was assessing
the value of the smallest transaction that had taken place during the day.

# Comprehension

**DIRECTIONS** *Answer these questions about the excerpt from* A Year Down Yonder.

1. You can tell that this story is told from the first person point of view because the narrator
   - ○ is a minor character in the story who reveals some information
   - ○ is an outside observer rather than a character in the story
   - ○ reveals the grandmother's and the girl's thoughts
   - ○ uses the pronouns *I* and *me* to refer to herself

2. The author brings Grandma's character to life mainly by revealing
   - ○ the townspeople's opinions of Grandma
   - ○ Grandma's own thoughts about her granddaughter
   - ○ the granddaughter's reactions to Grandma
   - ○ a detailed description of Grandma's life

3. The narrator makes you aware that Grandma is not a sentimental person when she says
   - ○ "My goodness, she was a big woman."
   - ○ "She drew nearer till she blotted out the day."
   - ○ "You couldn't call her a welcoming woman, and there wasn't a hug in her."
   - ○ "She aimed one of her chins down the platform."

4. Which term best describes Grandma?
   - ○ easygoing
   - ○ no-nonsense
   - ○ generous
   - ○ self-important

5. Which character trait do the narrator and her grandmother seem to share?
   - ○ determination
   - ○ lightheartedness
   - ○ talkativeness
   - ○ idealism

6. Reread lines 21–23. Why does the narrator wonder if she'll ever see her trunk again?
   - ○ Grandma does not want the trunk at her house.
   - ○ People in the town could use many of the things in the trunk.
   - ○ She comes from a large city, where the trunk could be stolen if left on the platform.
   - ○ The trunk is too heavy to carry to Grandma's house.

7. From her comment in lines 16–17 that the radio is "my last touch with the world," you can infer that the narrator
   - ○ is afraid that her radio will be stolen
   - ○ thinks that people in Grandma's town don't have radios
   - ○ does not want to make friends in Grandma's town
   - ○ feels she has arrived in an isolated place

8. Why is Grandma surprised when the narrator asks, "Where are we going?"
   - ○ She expects her granddaughter to know that school is the only interesting place to go in town.
   - ○ The question sounds rude to Grandma.
   - ○ School has begun, and Grandma thinks that is where her granddaughter belongs.
   - ○ Her granddaughter doesn't usually ask questions.

**DIRECTIONS** *Answer these questions about the excerpt from* "Luke Baldwin's Vow."

9. The reader learns about Uncle Henry mainly through the eyes of
   - ○ Luke
   - ○ Uncle Henry
   - ○ Aunt Helen
   - ○ the sawmill employees

**10.** You can tell that this excerpt is told from a third-person limited point of view because the narrator

- ○ is a main character in the story
- ○ tells about the thoughts and feelings of all of the characters in the story
- ○ is outside the story and tells what one character sees, thinks, and feels
- ○ describes his or her own thoughts

**11.** You can infer that Luke views Uncle Henry with

- ○ pity
- ○ irony
- ○ suspicion
- ○ admiration

**12.** What first motivates Luke to watch his uncle carefully?

- ○ Aunt Helen suggests that it is a good idea to pay attention to his uncle.
- ○ Luke promised his father that he would try to learn things from his uncle.
- ○ Uncle Henry knows more about what is needed than anyone else Luke has met.
- ○ The family wants Luke to succeed as a worker at the sawmill.

**13.** Which method of characterization is used in lines 13–15 to describe Uncle Henry?

- ○ a description of his physical appearance
- ○ another character's opinion of him
- ○ Uncle Henry's own thoughts about life
- ○ the author's direct comment about him

**14.** Uncle Henry's words and actions in lines 20–23 show him to be a

- ○ strict boss
- ○ patient teacher
- ○ fun-loving relative
- ○ dishonest businessman

**15.** Luke learns about Uncle Henry mainly by

- ○ reading his uncle's black notebook
- ○ listening to Aunt Helen's stories
- ○ remembering his father's descriptions
- ○ watching and listening to his uncle

**16.** From the description of Uncle Henry in this excerpt, you can infer that he is

- ○ unconcerned about the feelings of other people
- ○ very shy and forgetful about business dealings
- ○ careful and smart in his work and personal business
- ○ confident that he has good health and will live a long time

**DIRECTIONS** *Answer this question about both selections.*

**17.** The granddaughter and Luke can both be described as

- ○ cheerful
- ○ observant
- ○ confused
- ○ spoiled

## Constructed Response

**SHORT ANSWER** *Write two or three sentences to answer this question.*

**18.** Reread lines 8–11 in the excerpt from *A Year Down Yonder.* What can you infer about the grandmother from this description?

**19.** Reread lines 16–19 in the excerpt from "Luke Baldwin's Vow." What motivates Luke to follow Uncle Henry around the sawmill?

**ESSAY** *Write a paragraph to answer this question.*

**20.** Describe two ways in which Peck brings Grandma's character to life and Callaghan brings Uncle Henry's character to life. Give examples from the excerpts to support your answer.

GO ON

# Vocabulary

DIRECTIONS *Use context clues and your knowledge of multiple-meaning words to answer the following questions.*

1. Which meaning of the word *trail* is used in line 16 of the excerpt from "Luke Baldwin's Vow"?

   "Luke used to <u>trail</u> around the sawmill after Uncle Henry. . . ."

   ○ stream along        ○ follow behind
   ○ drag heavily        ○ track closely

2. Which meaning of the word *platform* is used in line 1 of the excerpt from *A Year Down Yonder?*

   ". . . there came Grandma up the <u>platform</u> steps."

   ○ a statement of principles
   ○ a place for discussion
   ○ a device for drilling
   ○ a raised surface

3. Which meaning of the word *trunk* is used in line 22 of the excerpt from *A Year Down Yonder?*

   "I walked away from my <u>trunk</u>, wondering if I'd ever see it again."

   ○ a storage compartment
   ○ a piece of luggage
   ○ a tree stem
   ○ the center of the body

4. Which meaning of the word *trade* is used in line 27 of the excerpt from *A Year Down Yonder?*

   "Moore's Store was hurting for <u>trade</u>."

   ○ the customers of a business
   ○ an exchange of one thing for another
   ○ an occupation that requires skilled training
   ○ the people who work in a certain kind of business

DIRECTIONS *Use context clues and your knowledge of prefixes to answer the following questions.*

5. One meaning of the prefix *re-* is "again," and the Latin word *cognoscere* means "to get to know." What is the meaning of the word *recognize* as it is used in line 9 of the excerpt from *A Year Down Yonder?*

   "I <u>recognized</u> the dress."

   ○ learned from someone else
   ○ had forgotten once more
   ○ knew from before
   ○ could not remember

6. Another meaning of the prefix *re-* is "back," and the Latin word *cedere* means "to go." What is the meaning of the word *recession* as it is used in line 25 of the excerpt from *A Year Down Yonder?*

   "The <u>recession</u> of thirty-seven had hit Grandma's town harder than it had hit Chicago."

   ○ the act of performing again
   ○ a period when business activity falls away
   ○ a departing procession
   ○ a short time set aside for rest

7. One meaning of the prefix *trans-* is "transfer." What is the most likely meaning of the word *transaction* as it is used in line 34 of the excerpt from "Luke Baldwin's Vow"?

   ". . . he knew that he was assessing the value of the smallest <u>transaction</u> that had taken place during the day."

   ○ a sudden burst of activity
   ○ an immigration to a new land
   ○ the passage of goods by sale or barter
   ○ the distribution of the business profits

# Writing & Grammar

**DIRECTIONS** *Read the passage and answer the questions that follow.*

> (1) On October 29, 1929, the stock market <u>will crash</u>, sending the United States into an economic depression. (2) Because it was the <u>more devastating</u> depression ever to afflict the country, it was called the Great Depression. (3) Herbert Hoover, the president at the time, <u>will refuse</u> to provide direct federal relief to the poor. (4) Americans <u>are</u> furious about Hoover's lack of action, and in 1932, the country elected Franklin D. Roosevelt as the new president. (5) Roosevelt was <u>most willing</u> than Hoover was to provide aid. (6) He supplied immediate relief to the poor and aid to farms and businesses. (7) Although a lot of people remained unemployed, their circumstances were <u>more better</u> than they had been before.

1. Choose the correct verb tense to replace the underlined words in sentence 1.
   - ○ is crashing
   - ○ crashed
   - ○ will be crashing
   - ○ has crashed

2. Choose the correct superlative to replace the underlined word in sentence 2.
   - ○ more devastatinger
   - ○ most devastatingest
   - ○ devastatinger
   - ○ most devastating

3. Choose the correct verb tense to replace the underlined words in sentence 3.
   - ○ refused
   - ○ will be refusing
   - ○ is refusing
   - ○ has refused

4. Choose the correct verb tense to replace the underlined word in sentence 4.
   - ○ will be
   - ○ were
   - ○ are becoming
   - ○ have been

5. Choose the correct comparative to replace the underlined words in sentence 5.
   - ○ more willing
   - ○ willingest
   - ○ willinger
   - ○ more willinger

6. Choose the correct comparative to replace the underlined words in sentence 7.
   - ○ best
   - ○ most better
   - ○ betterer
   - ○ better

**STOP**

## Ideas for Independent Reading

Which questions from Unit 2 made an impression on you?
Continue exploring them with these books.

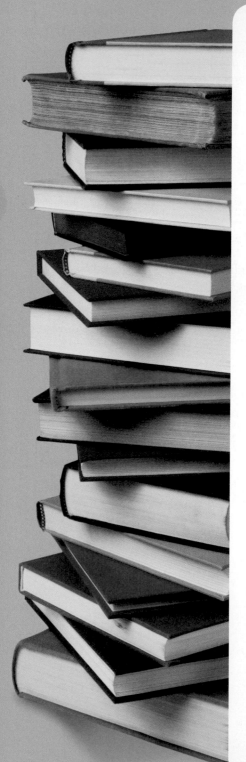

# What do you cherish?

### A Thief in the House of Memory
*by Tim Wynne-Jones*

Declan barely remembers his mother, but this year the memories have started coming back. Sometimes he thinks he can see and hear her in his old house. Can Declan recall his "real" mom and still trust his dad?

### Hope Was Here
*by Joan Bauer*

Hope and her aunt are starting over again—this time at a diner in small-town Wisconsin. When G.T., the owner, decides to run for mayor even though he has a terminal illness, Hope gets sucked into the campaign.

### Song of the Trees
*by Mildred D. Taylor*

Times are tough for Cassie Logan and her family. They don't even have enough to eat. But when someone offers to buy the trees that have whispered outside of her window for as long as she can remember, Cassie knows she must protect them.

# What shows others who we are?

### I, Juan de Pareja
*by Elizabeth Borton de Treviño*

A man named Juan de Pareja is enslaved in Spain during the 1600s. By watching his owner, a famous artist, Juan learns to paint—a skill forbidden to slaves. If he reveals his true talent, will he be celebrated, or punished?

### Stargirl
*by Jerry Spinelli*

Leo knows Stargirl is different from the rest of Mica High. She has a pet rat and a ukulele and at basketball games she cheers for the other team. When Leo falls in love with her, he likes her just the way she is—at first.

### An Innocent Soldier
*by Josef Holub*

Adam is only 16 when he's forced to serve in Napoleon's army in the place of his employer's son. He is trapped in freezing Russia with a sick lieutenant his own age. Slowly the two boys become friends, but will they survive?

# What are the signs of greatness?

### The Voice that Challenged a Nation: Marian Anderson and the Struggle for Equal Rights
*by Russell Freedman*

Marian Anderson was an acclaimed singer, but there were some segregated concert halls that wouldn't let her perform. She helped to erase these barriers.

### Sir Walter Raleigh and the Quest for El Dorado
*by Marc Aronson*

Walter Ralegh was a favorite courtier of Queen Elizabeth. After her death, he tried to regain his glory by returning to South America in search of El Dorado, the fabled city of gold.

### Summerland
*by Michael Chabon*

Ethan is the worst ballplayer in the league. He's called Dog Boy because "he's always hoping for a walk." Surprised when a mysterious talent scout chooses him to help save Summerland, the home of baseball, Ethan hopes he's up for the task.

# The Place to Be

## SETTING AND MOOD

- In Fiction
- In Nonfiction
- In Poetry

# Where can IMAGINATION take you?

Close your eyes and picture a place you've always wanted to visit. Maybe you're diving down to a sunken ship, swimming slowly through the murky waters. Maybe you're in the locker room of your favorite team on the night they won the world championship. Wherever you are, your **imagination** is what takes you there. Good writers know how to spark your imagination and transport you to faraway places or times.

*ACTIVITY*

- With a partner, make a list called "Stories That Have Taken Me Places." In it, include at least four books, stories, or movies with settings that made you feel you had visited another time or place.

- Make another list called "Places I'd Like to Visit." Include at least four settings you'd like to explore.

- Then question others to see if any of the places you'd like to visit are featured in their "Stories That Have Taken Me Places" list. What can your classmates tell you about the places you want to go?

PUFFIN CLASSICS

JULES VERNE

JOURNEY TO THE CENTRE of THE EARTH

**INDIANA STANDARDS**

# Preview Unit Goals

| | |
|---|---|
| **LITERARY ANALYSIS** | • Identify and analyze setting and how setting affects plot<br>• Identify and analyze mood<br>• Identify, analyze, and evaluate imagery |
| **READING** | • Develop strategies for reading, including visualizing, predicting, connecting, and setting a purpose for reading<br>• Make inferences<br>• Compare scope of events as presented in two accounts<br>• Read and analyze a primary source |
| **WRITING AND GRAMMAR** | • Write a comparison-contrast essay<br>• Maintain subject-verb agreement |
| **SPEAKING, LISTENING, AND VIEWING** | • Produce and deliver a power presentation |
| **VOCABULARY** | • Use context clues to determine the meaning of idioms and homographs<br>• Use structural analysis to identify base words and affixes<br>• Use knowledge of word roots, base words, and affixes to determine the meaning of words |
| **ACADEMIC VOCABULARY** | • setting • imagery • primary source<br>• mood • scope • subject-verb agreement |

**Reader's Workshop**

# Setting and Mood

Suppose you are immersed in a story about ten castaways stranded on an island. What makes the story such a page-turner? At first, you might credit the intriguing conflicts and characters. However, the setting and the atmosphere may also be responsible for drawing you in. The perilous terrain, the raging storms, the lurking wildlife—details like these can transport you to the world that a writer describes. Read on to find out how setting and mood can make you feel as if you are there.

**INDIANA STANDARDS**

**READING STANDARDS**
**8.3.4** Analyze the importance of the setting to the mood, tone, and meaning of the text.

**8.3.9** Analyze the relevance of setting (places, times, customs) to mood, tone, and meaning of text.

## Part 1: Setting

You know that the **setting** of a story is the time and place in which the action occurs. The time can be a particular season, year, time of day, or historical period. The place can be anywhere—from a Civil War battlefield to a spaceship hurtling toward Mars.

A writer reveals a setting by describing the details of a time and place. Often, he or she also includes descriptions of the characters' clothing and lifestyles. Such descriptions allow readers to visualize a setting in vivid detail.

In some stories, the setting takes center stage, serving as more than just a backdrop for the unfolding action. As this chart shows, a setting can affect the characters or create conflicts for them to endure.

| ROLE OF SETTING | EXAMPLE | |
|---|---|---|
| **Setting can affect characters by**<br>• determining the jobs and living conditions available to them<br>• influencing their values, attitudes, and emotions | Small-town rural life had taken its toll on Garrett. He was sick of being around people who had no intention of finishing school or exploring the world. Garrett was determined to do more with his life than settle for a job on his family's farm. |  |
| **Setting can create conflicts by**<br>• exposing the characters to dangerous weather or natural disasters<br>• making the characters live through difficult time periods, events, or situations, such as poverty or war | The flood had ravaged their home beyond repair and destroyed their personal belongings. For the Tilak family, the loss was devastating. It would take months, even years, for them to rebuild their lives. |  |

## MODEL 1: SETTING AND CHARACTERS

For Sun-hee's entire life, Korea has been under the rule of the Japanese emperor, who has, by law, forbidden the practicing of Korean customs. When World War II breaks out, life becomes even more difficult for the people of Korea. While no battles are fought on Korean soil, Japanese soldiers patrol the streets, and school classes are replaced by war drills.

*from* **When My Name Was *Keoko*** Novel by **Linda Sue Park**

It seemed as if the war would never end. Day after day of too much hard work, not enough food, constant exhaustion—and no chance to make or do anything beautiful. If a war lasts long enough, is it possible that people would completely forget the idea of beauty? That they'd only be able to do what they
5   needed to survive and would no longer remember how to make and enjoy beautiful things?

I was determined not to let this happen to me. At school every day, while I was working with my hands, I let my mind float away to think of something beautiful.

**Close Read**

1. How has the war affected people's daily lives?

2. Reread the boxed text. How does the narrator fear a long-lasting war could shape people's attitude toward their surroundings?

## MODEL 2: SETTING AND CONFLICT

In this science fiction novel, a chain of volcanic explosions has caused ash to seep into the atmosphere. Miles and his family live in Minneapolis, where the air has become increasingly murky.

*from* **Memory Boy** Novel by **Will Weaver**

"I'm not leaving," Sarah said, jerking away from me. "Everybody's going to die anyway, so why can't we die in our own house?" She plopped down onto the lawn. Pale pumice[1] puffed up around her and hung in the air like a ghostly double. That was the weird thing about the volcanic ash; it had been falling
5   softly, softly falling, for over two years now—and sometimes it was almost beautiful. Tonight the rock flour suspended in the air made a wide, furry-white halo around the moon. Its giant, raccoon-like eyeball stared down and made the whole neighborhood look X-rayed.

"Nobody's going to die," I said. "Though if we stay in the city, we might,"
10   I muttered to myself.

**Close Read**

1. Find two details that help you to understand the effects of the volcanic explosions on Minneapolis.

2. How do Sarah and Miles each view the conflict that the setting has created for their family?

---

1. pumice: a powdery substance that comes from volcanic glass.

## Part 2: Mood

The way a writer describes a setting can make you feel as if "you are there," whether "there" is a war-torn country or a city threatened by volcanic explosions. Like setting, mood is responsible for prompting this reaction in you.

**Mood** is the feeling or atmosphere that a writer creates for readers. A mood can be described as *exciting, somber, terrifying, cheerful, carefree,* or something else. To identify the mood in a work of literature, notice the following elements.

- **Descriptions of Setting** Does the story take place in an abandoned house on a stormy night or on a crowded beach during the summer? The writer's choice of setting and the words he or she uses to describe it can create a mood.

- **Imagery** Writers use **imagery**—language that appeals to your senses of sight, hearing, smell, taste, or touch—to affect your emotions and establish a mood. For instance, images such as *squeals of laughter* and *a rainbow of beach umbrellas* help to convey a cheerful mood.

- **Descriptions of Characters' Speech or Feelings** Pay attention to what the characters say, think, or feel about the setting and the conflict. Are they scared, joyful, or depressed? The characters' reactions often reflect the mood the writer is trying to create.

Examine this graphic. Notice how these three elements work together to create a terrifying mood.

**DESCRIPTIONS OF SETTING**
The forest at the edge of town was even more ominous at night. There wasn't a house or store within two miles. So far, no one in Jake's class had been brave enough to explore it.

**IMAGERY**
He walked hesitantly, leaves crunching under his feet. Bare trees hovered over him, casting armlike shadows across his path. His heart hammered in his chest as he inched forward.

**CHARACTERS' SPEECH OR FEELINGS**
Jake couldn't believe he accepted the dare. "What was I thinking?" he muttered to himself, stopping suddenly when he heard approaching footsteps. Fear paralyzed him.

**MODEL 1: COMPARING MOOD**

Set in New England during the Civil War years, *Little Women* follows the lives of the four March sisters. This excerpt describes the day on which Meg, the oldest sister, is to get married. As you read, pay attention to the descriptions of the setting and the roses.

*from* Little Women

Novel by **Louisa May Alcott**

The June roses over the porch were awake bright and early on that morning, rejoicing with all their hearts in the cloudless sunshine, like friendly little neighbors, as they were. Quite flushed with excitement were their ruddy faces, as they swung in the wind, whispering to one another what they had
5   seen; for some peeped in at the dining-room windows, where the feast was spread, some climbed up to nod and smile at the sisters, as they dressed the bride, others waved a welcome to those who came and went on various errands in garden, porch and hall, and all, from the rosiest full-blown flower to the palest baby-bud, offered their tribute of beauty and fragrance to the gentle
10   mistress who had loved and tended them so long.

**Close Read**

1. In the boxed text, the roses are described as if they were human. What details help you understand the roses' "feelings" about the wedding?

2. What imagery is used to describe the setting?

3. How would you describe the mood of this scene?

**MODEL 2: COMPARING MOOD**

The mood of this scene is dramatically different from the one you identified in the *Little Women* excerpt. As you read this passage, look closely at the descriptions that help to create this different mood.

*from* **MAX**

Short story by **Chaim Potok**

That night it stormed, and a school bus turned slowly into our small street from the main road, one block away. Our new house was only two blocks from my school, and yellow school buses went up and down the street mornings and afternoons. But never during the night! Now the bus moved
5   carefully along the rain-drenched asphalt, and about fifty feet from our house, it picked up speed. Lying in my bed, I heard the revving of the engine and stepped quickly to the window—in time to see the bus skid from the street and mount the curb, barely missing our sycamore tree. It advanced solemnly, ponderously, as if in slow motion. . . .

**Close Read**

1. In what ways is this setting different from the one described in *Little Women*?

2. Consider the boxed examples of imagery, as well as the descriptions of the setting. How would you describe the mood?

# Part 3: Analyze the Literature

Now, you'll use what you've learned about setting and mood to analyze the following two novel excerpts. In each, the main character is seeing his or her new home for the first time.

The first excerpt is from *Journey to Topaz*, which is about a Japanese-American family being moved to an internment camp, or holding facility, during World War II. How will life change for Yuki and her family?

# from Journey to TOPAZ

### Novel by Yoshiko Uchida

The eager hopeful voices on the bus died down and soon stopped altogether. Mother said nothing more and Yuki herself grew silent. At the western rim of the desert they could see a tall range of mountains, but long before they reached their sheltering shadows the buses made a sharp left
5 turn, and there in the midst of the desert, they came upon rows and rows of squat tar-papered barracks sitting in a pool of white dust that had once been the bottom of a lake. They had arrived at Topaz, the Central Utah War Relocation Center, which would be their new home.

Ken turned to look at Yuki. "Well, here we are," he said dryly. "This is
10 beautiful Topaz."

The minute Yuki stepped off the bus, she felt the white powdery dust of the desert engulf her like a smothering blanket. The Boy Scout Drum and Bugle Corp had come out to welcome the incoming buses, but now they looked like flour-dusted cookies that had escaped from a bakery.

15 Yuki coughed while one of the team of doctors inspected her throat and then she ran quickly to talk to Emi while Ken finished registering the family.

"We've been assigned to Block 7, Barrack 2, Apartment C," she informed her. "Try to get the room next door."

Emi nodded. "OK, I'll tell Grandma," she said, for they both knew that if
20 anybody could manage such an arrangement, Grandma could.

A boy about Ken's age offered to take them out to their new quarters. He had come in one of the earlier contingents and already knew his way around the big, sprawling barrack city.

"It's a mile square," he explained as they started toward Block 7, and like a
25 guide on a tour he told them all he knew about Topaz.

"There're forty-two blocks and each block has twelve barracks with a mess hall and a latrine-washroom in the center," he pointed out. "When the barracks are all finished and occupied, we'll be the fifth largest city in Utah."

"Imagine!" Mother said.

30 It sounded impressive, but Yuki thought she had never seen a more dreary place in all her life. There wasn't a single tree or a blade of grass to break the monotony of the sun-bleached desert.

## Close Read

1. Where does this scene take place? Find three details that reveal the setting.

2. What conflicts has the setting created for the characters?

3. Reread the boxed lines, which reveal Yuki's first impression of her new home. Which word best describes the mood of this scene?

   a. hopeful
   b. bleak
   c. threatening

Now read this excerpt from the novel *The House of Dies Drear*. Thomas Small and his family are driving across states toward their new house, which is rumored to have a long, interesting history. During the Civil War years, the house was owned by an abolitionist who hid fugitive slaves there. How will Thomas react when he sees his new home for the first time?

# *from* THE HOUSE *of* DIES DREAR

Novel by **Virginia Hamilton**

Thomas did not wake in time to see the Ohio River. Mr. Small was glad he didn't, for through the gloom of mist and heavy rain, most of its expanse was hidden. What was visible looked much like a thick mud path, as the sedan crossed over it at Huntington.

5  Thomas lurched awake a long time after. The car went slowly; there was hardly any rain now. His mother spoke excitedly, and Thomas had to shake his head rapidly in order to understand what she was saying.

"Oh dear! My heavens!" Mrs. Small said. "Why it's huge!"

Mr. Small broke in eagerly, turning around to face Thomas. You've waited
10  a long time," he said. "Take a good look, son. There's our new house!"

Thomas looked carefully out of his window. He opened the car door for a few seconds to see better, but found the moist air too warm and soft. The feel of it was not nice at all, and he quickly closed the door. He could see well enough out of the window, and what he saw made everything inside him grow
15  quiet for the first time in weeks. It was more than he could have dreamed.

The house of Dies Drear loomed out of mist and murky sky, not only gray and formless, but huge and unnatural. It seemed to crouch on the side of a hill high above the highway. And it had a dark, isolated look about it that set it at odds with all that was living.
20  A chill passed over Thomas. He sighed with satisfaction. The house of Dies Drear was a haunted place, of that he was certain.

"Well," Mr. Small said, "what do you think of it, Thomas?"

"It must be the biggest house anyone ever built," Thomas said at last. "And to think—it's our new house! Papa, let's get closer, let's go inside!"

## Close Read

1. What clues in the text could help you determine the location of the Small family's new house?

2. What images in lines 16–19 help you to visualize the Small's new house?

3. Pay attention to Thomas's thoughts and speech in lines 11–24. How does he feel about the setting? Support your answer.

4. Review your answers to the preceding two questions. How would you describe the mood of the scene when Thomas first sees the house?

## The Drummer Boy of Shiloh
Short Story by Ray Bradbury

# Does every CONTRIBUTION count?

**INDIANA STANDARDS**

**READING STANDARDS**
**8.2.9** Make reasonable statements and draw conclusions about a text, supporting them with accurate examples.

**8.3.4** Analyze the importance of the setting to the mood, tone, and meaning of the text.

**KEY IDEA** When there are 12 people on the team, and you're not even a starter, you might think that staying for extra practice doesn't matter. But one good assist can make the difference between victory and defeat. In sports, as in many areas of life, every **contribution** counts. You are about to read a short story in which a young drummer boy learns that even he can make a difference.

**CHART IT** Think of a situation in which one person's contribution affects the outcome. What would happen if that person didn't do his or her part? Create a cause-and-effect chain like the one shown.

| Cause | Effect/Cause | Effect |
|---|---|---|
| Alicia forgets to practice her solo for the concert. | | |

316

## ● LITERARY ANALYSIS: SETTING

The **setting** of a story is the time and place in which events occur. Setting is particularly important in **historical fiction,** which features real places and events from the past and might also include characters based on real people. To give readers a sense of the past, writers of historical fiction

- refer to historically significant events
- use descriptive details that help readers see, hear, and smell what life was like at a different time

As you read, note the ways Ray Bradbury captures what life was like during the Civil War.

## ● READING STRATEGY: MAKE INFERENCES

When you **make inferences** as you read, you make logical guesses based on information in the story and your own knowledge and experience. For example, if a character sighs and puts her face in her hands, you could infer that she is sad. By suggesting rather than stating things directly, a writer can better engage a reader and build suspense.

As you read the story, use a chart like the one shown to note inferences you make about what the drummer boy is feeling. To make these inferences, record details from the story and what you know from your own experience.

| Details from the Story | What I Know from Experience | Inference |
|---|---|---|
|  |  |  |

*Review:* **Monitor**

## ▲ VOCABULARY IN CONTEXT

These vocabulary words help Ray Bradbury convey what it was like to fight in the Civil War. To see how many you know, match each numbered word or phrase with the word closest in meaning.

| WORD LIST | askew | muted | solemn |
|---|---|---|---|
|  | legitimately | resolute | strew |

1. muffled
2. serious
3. to one side
4. lawfully
5. determined
6. scatter

# Author Online

**Ray Bradbury born 1920**

**An Idea Man**
Fans often ask Ray Bradbury, "Where do you get your ideas?" Bradbury says that he often wakes up with a great idea and immediately turns it into a story. He has written nearly 600 short stories—showing his fans that he's not short on ideas.

**More than a Science-Fiction Writer**
Because much of his work explores the effect of scientific development on human lives, Ray Bradbury is often called a science-fiction writer; however, he doesn't accept this label, and he actually avoids some of the most common technological conveniences. For example, Bradbury does not drive a car or own a computer. In addition to science fiction, he's written plays, mysteries, fantasies, realistic stories and novels, and various types of nonfiction—much of it on an old-fashioned typewriter.

## *Background*

**A "Deeply Felt" Story** One morning over 40 years ago, Bradbury read in the paper about an actor whose great-grandfather was known as the drummer boy of Shiloh. Struck by the phrase, Bradbury rushed to his typewriter and wrote the first draft of this story in one day. Later, he researched the Civil War and revised the story to make it historically accurate. He says it's one of the most "deeply felt" stories he's ever written. The Battle of Shiloh, upon which this story is based, took place in April, 1862, in southwestern Tennessee. This major battle was the bloodiest yet seen in the U.S.

**MORE ABOUT THE AUTHOR AND BACKGROUND**
To learn more about Ray Bradbury and the Battle of Shiloh, visit the **Literature Center** at ClassZone.com.

# THE
# Drummer Boy
## OF Shiloh

## RAY BRADBURY

In the April night, more than once, blossoms fell from the orchard trees and lit with rustling taps on the drumskin. At midnight a peach stone left miraculously on a branch through winter, flicked by a bird, fell swift and unseen, struck once, like panic, which jerked the boy upright. In silence he listened to his own heart ruffle away, away, at last gone from his ears and back in his chest again.

After that, he turned the drum on its side, where its great lunar[1] face peered at him whenever he opened his eyes. **A**

His face, alert or at rest, was **solemn.** It was indeed a solemn time and a
10 solemn night for a boy just turned fourteen in the peach field near the Owl Creek not far from the church at Shiloh.

". . . thirty-one, thirty-two, thirty-three . . ."

Unable to see, he stopped counting.

Beyond the thirty-three familiar shadows, forty thousand men, exhausted by nervous expectation, unable to sleep for romantic dreams of battles yet unfought, lay crazily **askew** in their uniforms. A mile yet farther on, another army was **strewn** helter-skelter, turning slow, basting themselves with the thought of what they would do when the time came: a leap, a yell, a blind plunge their strategy, raw youth their protection and benediction.[2]

20 Now and again the boy heard a vast wind come up, that gently stirred the air. But he knew what it was, the army here, the army there, whispering to itself in the dark. Some men talking to others, others murmuring to themselves, and all so quiet it was like a natural element arisen from south or north with the motion of the earth toward dawn.

**A** MAKE INFERENCES
Note the boy's reaction when the peach pit strikes the drum. Why do you think he reacted that way?

**solemn** (sŏl'əm) *adj.* deeply serious

**askew** (ə-skyōō') *adj.* to one side; awry

**strew** (strōō) *v.* to spread here and there; scatter

---

1. **lunar** (lōō'nər): of or relating to the moon.
2. **benediction** (bĕn'ĭ-dĭk'shən): a blessing.

*The Musician,* Dale Gallon. Courtesy of Gallon Historical Art, Gettysburg, Pennsylvania.

*Letter from Home*, Mort Künstler. © Mort Künstler, Inc. www.mkunstler.com.

**ANALYZE VISUALS**
Based on this image, what can you **conclude** about what life was like in a Civil War army camp?

What the men whispered the boy could only guess, and he guessed that it was: Me, I'm the one, I'm the one of all the rest won't die. I'll live through it. I'll go home. The band will play. And I'll be there to hear it.

Yes, thought the boy, that's all very well for them, they can give as good as they get!

30   For with the careless bones of the young men harvested by night and bindled[3] around campfires were the similarly strewn steel bones of their rifles, with bayonets[4] fixed like eternal lightning lost in the orchard grass. **B**

Me, thought the boy, I got only a drum, two sticks to beat it, and no shield.

There wasn't a man-boy on this ground tonight did not have a shield he cast, riveted or carved himself on his way to his first attack, compounded of remote but nonetheless firm and fiery family devotion, flag-blown patriotism and cocksure immortality strengthened by the touchstone[5] of very real gunpowder, ramrod, minnieball and flint.[6] But without these last the boy felt his family move yet farther off away in the dark, as if one of those great prairie-burning

**B SETTING**
Reread lines 30–32. What **details** help you to imagine this particular time and place?

---

3. **bindled:** fastened or wrapped by encircling, as with a belt.

4. **bayonets** (bā´ə-nĕts´): blades adapted to fit the muzzle end of a rifle; used in close combat.

5. **touchstone:** a reference point against which other things are compared or measured.

6. **ramrod, minnieball,** and **flint:** items used to fire a rifle.

40 trains had chanted them away never to return, leaving him with this drum
which was worse than a toy in the game to be played tomorrow or some day
much too soon. **C**

The boy turned on his side. A moth brushed his face, but it was peach
blossom. A peach blossom flicked him, but it was a moth. Nothing stayed put.
Nothing had a name. Nothing was as it once was.

If he lay very still, when the dawn came up and the soldiers put on their
bravery with their caps, perhaps they might go away, the war with them, and
not notice him lying small here, no more than a toy himself. **D**

"Well, by God, now," said a voice.

50 The boy shut up his eyes, to hide inside himself, but it was too
late. Someone, walking by in the night, stood over him.

"Well," said the voice quietly, "here's a soldier crying *before* the fight. Good.
Get it over. Won't be time once it all starts."

And the voice was about to move on when the boy, startled, touched the
drum at his elbow. The man above, hearing this, stopped. The boy could feel
his eyes, sense him slowly bending near. A hand must have come down out of
the night, for there was a little rat-tat as the fingernails brushed and the man's
breath fanned his face.

"Why, it's the drummer boy, isn't it?"

60 The boy nodded, not knowing if his nod was seen. "Sir, is that *you?*" he said.

"I assume it is." The man's knees cracked as he bent still closer.

He smelled as all fathers should smell, of salt sweat, ginger tobacco, horse
and boot leather, and the earth he walked upon. He had many eyes. No, not
eyes, brass buttons that watched the boy. **E**

He could only be, and was, the General.

"What's your name, boy?" he asked.

"Joby," whispered the boy, starting to sit up.

"All right, Joby, don't stir." A hand pressed his chest gently, and the boy
relaxed. "How long you been with us, Joby?"

70 "Three weeks, sir."

"Run off from home or joined **legitimately,** boy?"

Silence.

"Damn-fool question," said the General. "Do you shave yet, boy? Even more
of a damn-fool. There's your cheek, fell right off the tree overhead. And the
others here not much older. Raw, raw, damn raw, the lot of you. You ready for
tomorrow or the next day, Joby?"

"I think so, sir."

"You want to cry some more, go on ahead. I did the same last night."

"*You,* sir?"

80 "God's truth. Thinking of everything ahead. Both sides figuring the other
side will just give up, and soon, and the war done in weeks, and us all home.
Well, that's not how it's going to be. And maybe that's why I cried."

**C** MONITOR
Reread lines 34–42.
Do you understand what
the man-boys' shields
represent? If not, reread
this paragraph slowly and
refer to the footnotes.

**D** MAKE INFERENCES
What feelings is the boy
experiencing? Include
them in your chart, along
with the clues that help
you infer the feelings.

**E** SETTING
Reread lines 62–64.
What do the **descriptive
details** about the General
suggest about how men
lived in the 1800s?

**legitimately**
(lə-jĭt′ə-mĭt-lē) *adv.*
lawfully

"Yes, sir," said Joby.

The General must have taken out a cigar now, for the dark was suddenly filled with the Indian smell of tobacco unlit as yet, but chewed as the man thought what next to say.

"It's going to be a crazy time," said the General. "Counting both sides, there's a hundred thousand men, give or take a few thousand out there tonight, not one as can spit a sparrow off a tree, or knows a horse clod from a minnieball. Stand up, bare the breast, ask to be a target, thank them and sit down, that's us, that's them. We should turn tail and train four months, they should do the same. But here we are, taken with spring fever and thinking it blood lust, taking our sulphur with cannons instead of with molasses[7] as it should be, going to be a hero, going to live forever. And I can see all of them over there nodding agreement, save the other way around. It's wrong, boy, it's wrong as a head put on hind side front and a man marching backward through life. It will be a double massacre if one of their itchy generals decides to picnic his lads on our grass. More innocents will get shot out of pure Cherokee enthusiasm than ever got shot before. Owl Creek was full of boys splashing around in the noonday sun just a few hours ago. I fear it will be full of boys again, just floating, at sundown tomorrow, not caring where the tide takes them."

The General stopped and made a little pile of winter leaves and twigs in the darkness, as if he might at any moment strike fire to them to see his way through the coming days when the sun might not show its face because of what was happening here and just beyond.

The boy watched the hand stirring the leaves and opened his lips to say something, but did not say it. The General heard the boy's breath and spoke himself.

"Why am I telling you this? That's what you wanted to ask, eh? Well, when you got a bunch of wild horses on a loose rein somewhere, somehow you got to bring order, rein them in. These lads, fresh out of the milkshed, don't know what I know, and I can't tell them: men actually die, in war. So each is his own army. I got to make *one* army of them. And for that, boy, I need you."

"Me!" The boy's lips barely twitched.

"Now, boy," said the General quietly, "you are the heart of the army. Think of that. You're the heart of the army. Listen, now."

And, lying there, Joby listened.

And the General spoke on.

If he, Joby, beat slow tomorrow, the heart would beat slow in the men. They would lag by the wayside.[8] They would drowse in the fields on their muskets.[9] They would sleep forever, after that, in those same fields, their hearts slowed by a drummer boy and stopped by enemy lead.

---

7. **taking our sulphur with cannons instead of with molasses:** sulphur was an ingredient in gunpowder that was used to fire cannons; at that time sulphur was also used as a tonic or medical treatment. Molasses is a thick, brown syrup, used to mask the unpleasant taste of medicines.

8. **lag by the wayside:** fall behind.

9. **musket:** shoulder gun with a long barrel.

SOCIAL STUDIES CONNECTION

The Battle of Shiloh took place near Shiloh Church, on the banks of Owl Creek.

**F SETTING**
What do you learn about the Civil War from the General's **dialogue?**

But if he beat a sure, steady, ever faster rhythm, then, then their knees would come up in a long line down over that hill, one knee after the other, like a wave on the ocean shore! Had he seen the ocean ever? Seen the waves rolling in like a well-ordered cavalry charge to the sand? Well, that was it, that's what he wanted, that's what was needed! Joby was his right hand and his left. He gave the orders, but Joby set the pace!

So bring the right knee up and the right foot out and the left knee up and the left foot out. One following the other in good time, in brisk time. Move the blood up the body and make the head proud and the spine stiff and the jaw **resolute.** Focus the eye and set the teeth, flare the nostrils and tighten the hands, put steel armor all over the men, for blood moving fast in them does indeed make men feel as if they'd put on steel. He must keep at it, at it! Long and steady, steady and long! Then, even though shot or torn, those wounds got in hot blood—in blood he'd helped stir—would feel less pain. If their blood was cold, it would be more than slaughter, it would be murderous nightmare and pain best not told and no one to guess. **G**

The General spoke and stopped, letting his breath slack off. Then, after a moment, he said, "So there you are, that's it. Will you do that, boy? Do you know now you're general of the army when the General's left behind?"

The boy nodded mutely.

"You'll run them through for me then, boy?"

"Yes, sir."

"Good. And, God willing, many nights from tonight, many years from now, when you're as old or far much older than me, when they ask you what you did in this awful time, you will tell them—one part humble and one part proud—'I was the drummer boy at the battle of Owl Creek,' or the Tennessee River, or maybe they'll just name it after the church there. 'I was the drummer boy at Shiloh.' Good grief, that has a beat and sound to it fitting for Mr. Longfellow.[10] 'I was the drummer boy at Shiloh.' Who will ever hear those words and not know you, boy, or what you thought this night, or what you'll think tomorrow or the next day when we must get up on our legs and *move!*"

The general stood up. "Well, then. God bless you, boy. Good night."

"Good night, sir." **H**

And, tobacco, brass, boot polish, salt sweat and leather, the man moved away through the grass.

Joby lay for a moment, staring but unable to see where the man had gone. He swallowed. He wiped his eyes. He cleared his throat. He settled himself. Then, at last, very slowly and firmly, he turned the drum so that it faced up toward the sky.

He lay next to it, his arm around it, feeling the tremor, the touch, the **muted** thunder as, all the rest of the April night in the year 1862, near the Tennessee River, not far from the Owl Creek, very close to the church named Shiloh, the peach blossoms fell on the drum. ◑

**resolute** (rĕz′ə-lo͞ot′) *adj.* firm or determined

**G MONITOR**
Reread lines 119–138. To make sure you understand it, **summarize** the General's advice to Joby.

**H MAKE INFERENCES**
What can you tell about Joby's feelings toward the General from the way he speaks and listens to him throughout the story?

**muted** (myo͞o′tĭd) *adj.* muffled; softened

---

10. **Longfellow:** Henry Wadsworth Longfellow (1807–1882), popular American author of "Paul Revere's Ride" and *The Song of Hiawatha.*

# Comprehension

**INDIANA STANDARDS**

**READING STANDARD**
**8.3.4** Analyze the importance of the setting to the mood, tone, and meaning of the text.

1. **Recall** At the beginning of the story, what does Joby guess that the men were whispering about?

2. **Clarify** What causes the General to stop and talk with Joby rather than continue walking?

3. **Clarify** According to the General, why was he telling Joby his thoughts about the war?

# Literary Analysis

4. **Make Inferences About Characters** Review the chart in which you made inferences about Joby's feelings. Mark the entries that show how Joby felt after the General talked to him. How did the General affect Joby?

5. **Examine Setting** What details of setting help you understand what it was like the night before this Civil War battle? Take notes in a chart like the one shown.

| Descriptive Details | References to Events |
|---|---|
| blossoms falling | |

6. **Interpret an Event** Reread lines 1–8. Then reread lines 159–161. At the story's end, what does it mean that Joby turns the drum up toward the sky?

7. **Evaluate Historical Fiction** The information about the Civil War that is found in the story can also be found in numerous works of nonfiction. Tell whether you think Bradbury's use of **historical fiction** is an effective way to learn about the kinds of people who fought in the Civil War. Support your opinion with examples from the story.

# Extension and Challenge

8. **Big Question Activity** There was no clear winner in the Battle of Shiloh, and nearly 24,000 lives were lost. Given this outcome, do you think the General still would have told Joby that his **contribution** mattered? Discuss your answer in a small group.

9.  **SOCIAL STUDIES CONNECTION** Conduct some research about Johnny Clem, a real drummer boy at the Battle of Shiloh, or about another hero or battle of the American Civil War. Share your findings with your classmates.

> **RESEARCH LINKS**
> For more about Johnny Clem, visit the **Research Center** at **ClassZone.com**.

# Vocabulary in Context

## VOCABULARY PRACTICE

For each item, choose the word that differs most in meaning from the other words.

1. (a) legally, (b) legitimately, (c) lawfully, (d) illegally
2. (a) askew, (b) tidy, (c) crooked, (d) awry
3. (a) softened, (b) muted, (c) harsh, (d) indistinct
4. (a) scatter, (b) arrange, (c) jumble, (d) strew
5. (a) bright, (b) heavy, (c) solemn, (d) glum
6. (a) paralyzed, (b) strong, (c) persistent, (d) resolute

askew

legitimately

muted

resolute

solemn

strew

## VOCABULARY IN WRITING

If you were the drummer boy, how would you describe the soldiers' camp? Write a one-paragraph journal entry using two or more vocabulary words. Here is a sample beginning.

> **EXAMPLE SENTENCE**
>
> The General is **solemn** yet kind.

## VOCABULARY STRATEGY: IDIOMS

**INDIANA STANDARDS**

**READING STANDARD**
**8.1.1** Analyze idioms and comparisons ... to infer the literal and figurative meanings of phrases.

An idiom is an expression in which the meaning of the entire phrase is different from the meaning of the individual words in it. For example, in the story, the General says that the marching soldiers would "lag by the wayside" if Joby beat his drum too slowly. The General meant that the soldiers would fall behind. Today we use the phrase "fall by the wayside" to mean the same thing.

You won't be familiar with every idiom you encounter. To figure out the meaning of an idiom you don't understand, use context clues. Also, idioms appear in some dictionaries. Try looking up the first word of the phrase.

**PRACTICE** Using context clues from the sentences, decide what each idiom means.

1. My old computer finally **bit the dust;** it had been working poorly for weeks.
2. Amanda wanted to continue arguing with her sister, but she decided to **leave well enough alone.**
3. I've always been a good dancer, so learning the routine was **a piece of cake.**
4. After signing up for four after-school activities, Max realized that he had **bitten off more than he could chew.**
5. I'm bringing my umbrella, because it's **raining cats and dogs** out there.
6. Maria **let the cat out of the bag** and told Lamar about the surprise party.

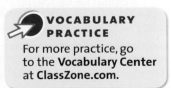

**VOCABULARY PRACTICE**
For more practice, go to the **Vocabulary Center** at **ClassZone.com.**

# Civil War Journal
Journal

Use with *The Drummer Boy of Shiloh*, page 318.

## What's the Connection?

Historical fiction such as "The Drummer Boy of Shiloh" can give you an idea about what it was like during the Civil War, but reading about the time period from someone who was actually there can be even more revealing. Louisa May Alcott, who wrote the famous novel *Little Women*, kept a journal during the war years.

## Skill Focus: Read a Primary Source

One of the best ways to learn about past events is through **primary sources,** materials that were written or made by people who took part in the events. Journals, photographs, and even personal letters are all examples of primary sources. When you study them, you get direct knowledge, rather than someone else's interpretation, of people, places, and events.

When gathering information from a primary source, it's important to consider what the source is and how its form might limit or affect what it conveys. For example, a business letter is not likely to contain colorful details or gossip. You should also think about other factors that would have shaped the source's contents, such as when and where it was created, for whom, and the creator's position in society.

As you read Alcott's journal entries, keep these considerations in mind. Also note what her journal entries tell you about life during the Civil War. Completing a chart such as the one started here can help.

| | |
|---|---|
| What is the form and purpose of this text? | The text is a journal. It was most likely written to reflect on experiences. |
| Who was its author? What do you know about her? | Louisa May Alcott; she was the author of <u>Little Women</u> and other novels. |
| When and where was it written? | |
| What do you already know about life at that time and place? | |
| Who was its intended audience? | |
| What does this document reveal about life at the time it was written? | |

# Civil War Journal

Portrait of the author

## Louisa May Alcott

**1861** **A**

*April.*—War declared with the South, and our Concord company went to Washington. A busy time getting them ready, and a sad day seeing them off; for in a little town like this we all seem like one family in times like these. At the station the scene was very dramatic, as the brave boys went away perhaps never to come back again.

I've often longed to see a war, and now I have my wish. I long to be a man; but as I can't fight, I will content myself with working for those who can. . . .

**1862** **B**

*September, October.*—War news bad. Anxious faces, beating hearts, and busy minds.

10     I like the stir in the air, and long for battle like a warhorse when he smells powder. The blood of the Mays is up!

*November.*—Thirty years old. Decided to go to Washington as a nurse if I could find a place. Help needed, and I love nursing, and *must* let out my pent-up energy in some new way. Winter is always a hard and a dull time, and if I am away there is one less to feed and warm and worry over.

**A** **JOURNAL**
**Preview** the journal entries' headings. In what years were they written?

**B** **READ A PRIMARY SOURCE**
What do you already know about the times in which these entries were written? Add this information to your chart.

I want new experiences, and am sure to get 'em if I go. So I've sent in my name, and bide my time writing tales, to leave all snug behind me, and mending up my old clothes,—for nurses don't need nice things, thank Heaven!

Patients in a military hospital, 1865

**C** VIEW A PRIMARY SOURCE

What do you learn about Civil War hospitals from this photograph?

*December.*—On the 11th I received a note from Miss H[annah] M. Stevenson
20 telling me to start for Georgetown next day to fill a place in the Union Hotel Hospital. Mrs. Ropes of Boston was matron, and Miss Kendall of Plymouth was a nurse there, and though a hard place, help was needed. I was ready, and when my commander said "March!" I marched. Packed my trunk, and reported in B[oston] that same evening.

We had all been full of courage till the last moment came; then we all broke down. I realized that I had taken my life in my hand, and might never see them all again. I said, "Shall I stay, Mother?" as I hugged her close. "No, go! and the Lord be with you!" answered the Spartan woman; and till I turned the corner she bravely smiled and waved her wet handkerchief on the doorstep. Shall I ever see
30 that dear old face again?

So I set forth in the December twilight, with May and Julian Hawthorne as escort, feeling as if I was the son of the house going to war.

Friday, the 12th, was a very memorable day, spent in running all over Boston to get my pass, etc., calling for parcels, getting a tooth filled, and buying a veil,— my only purchase. A. C. gave me some old clothes, the dear Sewalls money for myself and boys, lots of love and help; and at 5 P.M., saying "good-by" to a group of tearful faces at the station, I started on my long journey, full of hope and sorrow, courage and plans. **D**

**D** READ A PRIMARY SOURCE

Reread lines 33–38. How does Alcott spend her last day in Boston? What do her activities suggest about her needs and values?

A most interesting journey into a new world full of stirring sights and sounds,
40 new adventures, and an evergrowing sense of the great task I had undertaken.

I said my prayers as I went rushing through the country white with tents, all alive with patriotism, and already red with blood.

A solemn time, but I'm glad to live in it; and am sure it will do me good whether I come out alive or dead.

All went well, and I got to Georgetown one evening very tired. Was kindly welcomed, slept in my narrow bed with two other roommates, and on the morrow began my new life by seeing a poor man die at dawn, and sitting all day between a boy with pneumonia and a man shot through the lungs. A strange day, but I did my best; and when I put mother's little black shawl round the boy while he sat up
50 panting for breath, he smiled and said, "You are real motherly, ma'am." I felt as if I was getting on. The man only lay and stared with his big black eyes, and made me very nervous. But all were well behaved; and I sat looking at the twenty strong faces as they looked back at me,—hoping that I looked "motherly" to them; for my thirty years made me feel old, and the suffering round me made me long to comfort every one. . . . **E**

#### 1863

*January.*—I never began the year in a stranger place than this; five hundred miles from home, alone among strangers, doing painful duties all day long, & leading a life of constant excitement in this greathouse surrounded by 3 or 4 hundred men in all stages of suffering, disease & death. Though often home sick, heart sick &
60 worn out, I like it—find real pleasure in comforting tending & cheering these poor souls who seem to love me, to feel my sympathy though unspoken, & acknowledge my hearty good will in spite of the ignorance, awkwardness, & bashfulness which I cannot help showing in so new & trying a situation. The men are docile, respectful, & affectionate, with but few exceptions; truly lovable & manly many of them. John Suhre a Virginia blacksmith is the prince of patients, & though what we call a common man, in education & condition, to me is all that I could expect or ask from the first gentleman in the land. Under his plain speech & unpolished manner I seem to see a noble character, a heart as warm & tender as a woman's, a nature fresh & frank as any child's. He is about thirty, I think, tall & handsome, mortally
70 wounded & dying royally, without reproach, repining, or remorse. Mrs. Ropes & myself love him & feel indignant that such a man should be so early lost, for though he might never distinguish himself before the world, his influence & example cannot be without effect, for real goodness is never wasted.

Mon 4th—I shall record the events of a day as a sample of the days I spend—

Up at six, dress by gas light, run through my ward & fling up the windows though the men grumble & shiver; but the air is bad enough to breed a pestilence & as no notice is taken of our frequent appeals for better ventilation I must do what I can. Poke up the fire, add blankets, joke, coax, & command; but continue to
80 open doors & windows as if life depended on it; mine does, & doubtless many

**E** **JOURNAL**
Reread lines 45–55. How does Alcott spend her first day as a nurse? What does she hope and feel?

another, for a more perfect pestilence-box than this house I never saw—cold, damp, dirty, full of vile odors from wounds, kitchens, wash rooms, & stables. No competent head, male or female, to right matters, & a jumble of good, bad, & indifferent nurses, surgeons & attendants to complicate the Chaos still more.

After this unwelcome progress through my stifling ward I go to breakfast with what appetite I may; find the inevitable fried beef, salt butter, husky bread & washy coffee; listen to the clack of eight women & a dozen men; the first silly, stupid or possessed of but one idea, the last absorbed in their breakfast & themselves to a degree that is both ludicrous and provoking, for all the dishes are
90 ordered down the table *full* & returned *empty;* the conversation is entirely among themselves & each announces his opinion with an air of importance that frequently causes me to choke in my cup or bolt my meals with undignified speed lest a laugh betray to these pompous beings that a "child's among them takin notes." Till noon I trot, trot, giving out rations, cutting up food for helpless "boys," washing faces, teaching my attendants how beds are made or floors swept, dressing wounds, taking Dr. Fitz Patrick's orders, (privately wishing all the time that he would be more gentle with my big babies,) dusting tables, sewing bandages, keeping my tray tidy, rushing up & down after pillows, bed linen, sponges, books & directions, till it seems as if I would joyfully pay down all I
100 possess for fifteen minutes rest.

At twelve the big bell rings & up comes dinner for the boys who are always ready for it & never entirely satisfied. Soup, meat, potatoes & bread is the bill of fare. Charley Thayer the attendant travels up & down the room serving out the rations, saving little for himself yet always thoughtful of his mates & patient as a woman with their helplessness. When dinner is over some sleep, many read, & others want letters written. This I like to do for they put in such odd things & express their ideas so comically I have great fun interiorly while as grave as possible exteriorly. A few of the men word their paragraphs well & make excellent letters. John's was the best of all I wrote. The answering of letters from friends
110 after some one has died is the saddest & hardest duty a nurse has to do.

Supper at five sets every one to running that can run & when that flurry is over all settle down for the evening amusements which consist of newspapers, gossip, Drs last round, & for such as need them the final doses for the night. At nine the bell rings, gas is turned down & day nurses go to bed.

Night nurses go on duty, & sleep & death have the house to themselves. . . . **F**

My work is changed to night watching or half night & half day, from twelve to twelve. I like it as it leaves me time for a morning run which is what I need to keep well, for bad air, food, water, work & watching are getting to be too much for me. I trot up & down the streets in all directions, some times to the Heights,
120 then half way to Washington, again to the hill over which the long trains of army wagons are constantly vanishing & ambulances appearing. That way the fighting lies, & I long to follow.

**F READ A PRIMARY SOURCE**
What do you learn about hospital conditions and the nurses' routine activities?

# Comprehension

1. **Recall** When war is declared, how do the people of Concord respond?

2. **Summarize** Review Alcott's 1861 and 1862 journal entries. Then, in a few sentences, summarize why Alcott wants to serve as a nurse.

# Critical Analysis

3. **Gather Information from a Primary Source** Reread lines 64–73. Which of John Suhre's qualities does Alcott find most notable? Tell what you learn about her values from her opinions about this soldier.

4. **Identify Characteristics of a Journal** If you had stumbled across the original, handwritten version of this journal in a drawer, what characteristics of it would help you identify it as a journal?

**INDIANA STANDARDS**

**READING STANDARDS**
**8.2.7** Analyze the structure, format, and purpose of informational materials (such as textbooks, newspapers, instructional or technical manuals, and public documents).

**8.2.9** Make reasonable statements and draw conclusions about a text, supporting them with accurate examples.

# Read for Information: Draw a Conclusion

## WRITING PROMPT

A **conclusion** is a judgment or belief about something. To reach a solid conclusion, you need to use sound reasoning, evidence, and experience. In a paragraph, state and support a conclusion you have reached about one of the following topics:

- Louisa May Alcott
- Civil War soldiers
- being a nurse in a military hospital
- Civil War military hospitals

To answer this prompt, first identify the topic you would like to focus on. Then follow these steps:

1. Jot down ideas and information about it.

2. Based on this information, reach a conclusion about the topic.

3. Pick out strong support for your conclusion from Alcott's journal, Bradbury's historical fiction, and/or the lesson text.

4. State your conclusion in a topic sentence. Then present your reasons and evidence for arriving at that conclusion.

# Hallucination
Short Story by Isaac Asimov

## How do you find your
# PURPOSE?

**INDIANA STANDARDS**

**READING STANDARDS**
**8.3.4** Analyze the importance of the setting to the mood, tone, and meaning of the text.

**8.3.6** Identify significant literary devices ....

*KEY IDEA* Maybe you've heard about a pop star who began performing onstage at the age of three, or about a writer who published her first poem in grade school. Maybe you, too, have always known what your **purpose** is. But most of us have to search, question, and take a few wrong turns before we find out how to put our talents to their best use. In the story you are about to read, a 15-year-old boy discovers his purpose by traveling to a rather unusual place.

*QUICKWRITE* What might your purpose be? Explore the question by listing the five things you most enjoy doing. Make a separate list of personal qualities that you are proud of, such as kindness, sensitivity, or intelligence. Reflect upon how you can combine these interests and qualities to make a contribution of some sort. Record your reflections in your journal.

## ● LITERARY ANALYSIS: SETTING AND PLOT

As you probably recall, the time and place in which a story occurs is called the **setting.** When and where a story happens can create a conflict or influence a character's decisions. Therefore, setting can play an important role in a story's **plot,** or sequence of related events. For example, in "The Drummer Boy of Shiloh," a story set on the eve of a Civil War battle, the main character must gather his courage for the next day's fight. As you read "Hallucination," look for ways the story's setting affects its plot.

## ● READING STRATEGY: VISUALIZE

You're about to read a story that's set on an imaginary planet. How will you be able to understand what the environment is like? One way is to visualize as you read. When you **visualize,** you form mental pictures using details from the story plus your own knowledge and imagination. **Sensory details**—words telling how things look, sound, smell, taste, and feel—can help.

As you read, take note of details that help you form mental pictures. Use a chart like the one shown to sketch your visualizations.

| Details | Visualization |
|---|---|
| transparent dome 1,000 meters high stretched farther than he could see |  |

*Review:* **Make Inferences**

## ▲ VOCABULARY IN CONTEXT

The boldfaced words help Isaac Asimov tell the story of a boy who discovers his purpose despite opposition. Use context clues to figure out what each word means, and then write a synonym or phrase that means the same.

1. He held a strong **conviction** that something wasn't right.
2. The boy wasn't **insolent;** he tried hard to be respectful.
3. It's difficult to **refrain** from doing something that you enjoy.
4. Losing this game could **diminish** our chances for the finals.
5. Those in **opposition** to the plan were told to keep quiet.
6. She overcame her **inertia** and began seeking a cure.

# Author On|ine

**Candy as Inspiration** A candy store had an unlikely influence on Isaac Asimov's life and work. The store was a family operation owned by Asimov's father. The new science fiction magazines sold in the store sparked young Asimov's interest in science fiction.

**Isaac Asimov**
**1920–1992**

**Science Fact and Science Fiction** Asimov grew up to combine his interests in both science and science fiction. He earned a PhD in biochemistry and was a well-respected contributor to the field of robotics, the study of robot technology. He was also famous for his dedication to his writing. He often spent 12-hour days in front of his typewriter, and he was able to type more than 90 words per minute. In addition to fiction, Asimov wrote books on a wide variety of topics, including science, math, history, and poetry. In all, Asimov wrote over 450 books, totaling over seven million words.

**MORE ABOUT THE AUTHOR**
For more on Isaac Asimov, visit the **Literature Center** at **ClassZone.com.**

## *Background*

**Science Fiction** In science fiction, writers often explore what life might be like in the future. They do so by blending scientific facts and theories and familiar elements of real life with their own ideas to create imaginary worlds and unique situations. Writers of science fiction, including Isaac Asimov, also often use their stories to comment on current political and social conditions.

# HALLUCINATION

## ISAAC ASIMOV

## PART ONE

Sam Chase arrived on Energy Planet on his fifteenth birthday.

It was a great achievement, he had been told, to have been assigned there, but he wasn't at all sure he felt that at the moment.

It meant a three-year separation from Earth and from his family, while he continued a specialized education in the field, and that was a sobering thought. It was not the field of education in which he was interested, and he could not understand why Central Computer had assigned him to this project, and that was downright depressing.

He looked at the transparent dome overhead. It was quite high, perhaps a
10 thousand meters high, and it stretched in all directions farther than he could clearly see. He asked, "Is it true that this is the only Dome on the planet, sir?"

The information-films he had studied on the spaceship that had carried him here had described only one Dome, but they might have been out-of-date.

Donald Gentry, to whom the question had been addressed, smiled. He was a large man, a little chubby, with dark brown, good-natured eyes, not much hair, and a short, graying beard.

He said, "The only one, Sam. It's quite large, though, and most of the housing facilities are underground, where you'll find no lack of space. Besides, once your basic training is done, you'll be spending most of your time in space.
20 This is just our planetary base." **A**

**ANALYZE VISUALS**
What can you **infer** from this photograph about where the story will take place?

**A SETTING AND PLOT**
What have you learned so far about where and when the story takes place?

"I see, sir," said Sam, a little troubled.

Gentry said, "I am in charge of our basic trainees so I have to study their records carefully. It seems clear to me that this assignment was not your first choice. Am I right?"

Sam hesitated, and then decided he didn't have much choice but to be honest about it. He said, "I'm not sure that I'll do as well as I would like to in gravitational engineering."

"Why not? Surely the Central Computer, which evaluated your scholastic record and your social and personal background can be trusted in its 30 judgments. And if you do well, it will be a great achievement for you, for right here we are on the cutting edge of a new technology."

"I know that, sir," said Sam. "Back on Earth, everyone is very excited about it. No one before has ever tried to get close to a neutron star and make use of its energy."

"Yes?" said Gentry. "I haven't been on Earth for two years. What else do they say about it? I understand there's considerable **opposition?**"

His eyes probed the boy.

Sam shifted uneasily, aware he was being tested. He said, "There are people on Earth who say it's all too dangerous and might be a waste of money."

40 "Do you believe that?"

"It might be so, but most new technologies have their dangers and many are worth doing despite that. This one is, I think." **B**

"Very good. What else do they say on Earth?"

Sam said, "They say the Commander isn't well and that the project might fail without him." When Gentry didn't respond, Sam said, hastily, "That's what they say."

Gentry acted as though he did not hear. He put his hand on Sam's shoulder and said, "Come, I've got to show you to your Corridor, introduce you to your roommate, and explain what your initial duties will be." As they walked 50 toward the elevator that would take them downward, he said, "What was your first choice in assignment, Chase?"

"Neurophysiology,[1] sir."

"Not a bad choice. Even today, the human brain continues to be a mystery. We know more about neutron stars than we do about the brain, as we found out when this project first began."

"Oh?"

"Indeed! At the start, various people at the base—it was much smaller and more primitive then—reported having experienced hallucinations.[2] They never caused any bad effects, and after a while, there were no further reports. We 60 never found out the cause."

Sam stopped, and looked up and about again, "Was that why the Dome was built, Dr. Gentry?"

**opposition** (ŏp'ə-zĭsh'ən) *n.* the act of opposing or resisting

**B** **SETTING AND PLOT**
Reread lines 28–42. What do the humans hope to achieve on Energy Planet?

**VISUAL VOCABULARY**

**corridor** (kôr'ĭ-dôr') *n.* a narrow hallway, often with rooms opening onto it.

---

1. **neurophysiology** (nŏŏr'ō-fĭz'ē-ŏl'ə-jē): the study of the functions of the nervous system.

2. **hallucination** (hə-lōō'sə-nā'shən): a perception of objects that don't really exist.

"No, not at all. We needed a place with a completely Earth-like environment, for various reasons, but we haven't isolated ourselves. People can go outside freely. There are no hallucinations being reported now."

Sam said, "The information I was given about Energy Planet is that there is no life on it except for plants and insects, and that they're harmless."

"That's right, but they're also inedible, so we grow our own vegetables, and keep some small animals, right here under the Dome. Still, we've found nothing hallucinogenic about the planetary life."

"Anything unusual about the atmosphere, sir?"

Gentry looked down from his only slightly greater height and said, "Not at all. People have camped in the open overnight on occasion and nothing has happened. It is a pleasant world. There are streams but no fish, just algae and water-insects. There is nothing to sting you or poison you. There are yellow berries that look delicious and taste terrible but do no other harm. The weather's pretty nearly always good. There are frequent light rains and it is sometimes windy, but there are no extremes of heat and cold." **C**

"And no hallucinations anymore, Dr. Gentry?"

"You sound disappointed," said Gentry, smiling.

Sam took a chance. "Does the Commander's trouble have anything to do with the hallucinations, sir?"

The good nature vanished from Gentry's eyes for a moment, and he frowned. He said, "What trouble do you refer to?"

Sam flushed and they proceeded in silence.

Sam found few others in the Corridor he had been assigned to, but Gentry explained it was a busy time at the forward station, where the power system was being built in a ring around the neutron star—the tiny object less than ten miles across that had all the mass of a normal star, and a magnetic field of incredible power.

It was the magnetic field that would be tapped. Energy would be led away in enormous amounts and yet it would all be a pinprick, less than a pinprick, to the star's rotational energy, which was the ultimate source. It would take billions of years to bleed off all that energy, and in that time, dozens of populated planets, fed the energy through hyperspace, would have all they needed for an indefinite time.

Sharing his room was Robert Gillette, a dark-haired, unhappy-looking young man. After cautious greetings had been exchanged, Robert revealed the fact that he was sixteen and had been "grounded" with a broken arm, though the fact didn't show since it had been pinned internally.

Robert said, ruefully, "It takes a while before you learn to handle things in space. They may not have weight, but they have **inertia** and you have to allow for that."

**C** VISUALIZE
Reread lines 66–78. What words help you form a mental picture of Energy Planet? Add these words to your chart.

**inertia** (ĭ-nûr'shə) *n.* resistance to motion, action, or change

Sam said, "They always teach you that in—" He was going to say that it was taught in fourth-grade science, but realized that would be insulting, and stopped himself.

Robert caught the implication, however, and flushed. He said, "It's easy to know it in your head. It doesn't mean you get the proper reflexes, till you've practiced quite a bit. You'll find out."

110 Sam said, "Is it very complicated to get to go outside?"

"No, but why do you want to go? There's nothing there."

"Have you ever been outside?"

"Sure," but he shrugged, and volunteered nothing else.

Sam took a chance. He said, very casually, "Did you ever see one of these hallucinations they talk about?"

Robert said, "*Who* talks about?"

Sam didn't answer directly. He said, "A lot of people used to see them, but they don't anymore. Or so they say."

"So *who* say?"

120 Sam took another chance. "Or if they see them, they keep quiet about them."

Robert said gruffly, "Listen, let me give you some advice. Don't get interested in these—whatever they are. If you start telling yourself you see—uh—something, you might be sent back. You'll lose your chance at a good education and an important career." **D**

Robert's eyes shifted to a direct stare as he said that.

**D MAKE INFERENCES**
Why doesn't Robert want to talk about the hallucinations?

**ANALYZE VISUALS**
What words would you use to describe the **setting** pictured here?

Sam shrugged and sat down on the unused bunk. "All right for this to be my bed?"

"It's the only other bed here," said Robert, still staring. "The bathroom's to your right. There's your closet, your bureau. You get half the room. There's a gym here, a library, a dining area." He paused and then, as though to let bygones be bygones,[3] said, "I'll show you around later." **E**

"Thanks," said Sam. "What kind of a guy is the Commander?"

"He's aces. We wouldn't be here without him. He knows more about hyperspatial technology than anyone, and he's got pull with the Space Agency, so we get the money and equipment we need."

Sam opened his trunk and, with his back to Robert, said casually, "I understand he's not well."

"Things get him down. We're behind schedule, there are cost overruns, and things like that. Enough to get anyone down."

"Depression, huh? Any connection, you suppose, with—"

Robert stirred impatiently in his seat, "Say, why are you so interested in all this?"

"Energy physics isn't really my deal. Coming here—"

"Well, here's where you are, mister, and you better make up your mind to it, or you'll get sent home, and then you won't be anywhere. I'm going to the library."

Sam remained in the room alone, with his thoughts.

It was not at all difficult for Sam to get permission to leave the Dome. The Corridor-Master didn't even ask the reason until after he had checked him off.

"I want to get a feel for the planet, sir."

The Corridor-Master nodded. "Fair enough, but you only get three hours, you know. And don't wander out of sight of the Dome. If we have to look for you, we'll find you, because you'll be wearing this," and he held out a transmitter which Sam knew had been tuned to his own personal wavelength, one which had been assigned him at birth. "But if we have to go to that trouble, you won't be allowed out again for a pretty long time. And it won't look good on your record, either. You understand?"

*It won't look good on your record.* Any reasonable career these days had to include experience and education in space, so it was an effective warning. No wonder people might have stopped reporting hallucinations, even if they saw them. **F**

Even so, Sam was going to have to take his chances. After all, the Central Computer *couldn't* have sent him here just to do energy physics. There was nothing in his record that made sense out of that.

As far as looks were concerned, the planet might have been Earth, some part of Earth anyway, some place where there were a few trees and low bushes and lots of tall grass.

----

3. **let bygones be bygones:** decide to forget past disagreements.

**E VISUALIZE**
What clues do you get about the boys' living area? Add these details to your chart.

**F SETTING AND PLOT**
Why is Sam's assignment on Energy Planet so important to his future?

There were no paths and with every cautious step, the grass swayed, and tiny flying creatures whirred upward with a soft, hissing noise of wings.

170　One of them landed on his finger and Sam looked at it curiously. It was very small and, therefore, hard to see in detail, but it seemed hexagonal, bulging above and concave below. There were many short, small legs so that when it moved it almost seemed to do so on tiny wheels. There were no signs of wings till it suddenly took off, and then four tiny, feathery objects unfurled. **G**

What made the planet different from Earth, though, was the smell. It wasn't unpleasant, it was just different. The plants must have had an entirely different chemistry from those on Earth; that's why they tasted bad and were inedible. It was just luck they weren't poisonous.

The smell **diminished** with time, however, as it saturated Sam's nostrils.

180　He found an exposed bit of rocky ledge he could sit on and considered the prospect. The sky was filled with lines of clouds, and the Sun was periodically obscured, but the temperature was pleasant and there was only a light wind. The air felt a bit damp, as though it might rain in a few hours.

Sam had brought a small hamper with him and he placed it in his lap and opened it. He had brought along two sandwiches and a canned drink so that he could make rather a picnic of it.

He chewed away and thought: Why should there be hallucinations?

Surely those accepted for a job as important as that of taming a neutron star would have been selected for mental stability. It would be surprising to have

190　even one person hallucinating, let alone a number of them. Was it a matter of chemical influences on the brain?

They would surely have checked that out.

Sam plucked a leaf, tore it in two and squeezed. He then put the torn edge to his nose cautiously, and took it away again. A very acrid, unpleasant smell. He tried a blade of grass. Much the same.

Was the smell enough? It hadn't made him feel dizzy or in any way peculiar.

He used a bit of his water to rinse off the fingers that had held the plants and then rubbed them on his trouser leg. He finished his sandwiches slowly, and tried to see if anything else might be considered unnatural about the planet.

200　All that greenery. There ought to be animals eating it, rabbits, cows, whatever. Not just insects, innumerable insects, or whatever those little things might be, with the gentle sighing of their tiny feathery wings and the very soft crackle of their munch, munch, munchings of leaves and stalks. **H**

What if there were a cow—a big, fat cow—doing the munching? And with the last mouthful of his second sandwich between his teeth, his own munching stopped.

There was a kind of smoke in the air between himself and a line of hedges. It waved, billowed, and altered: a very thin smoke. He blinked his eyes, then shook his head, but it was still there.

**G VISUALIZE**
What details help you visualize the insects Sam discovers? Add a sketch of what you "see" on your chart.

**diminish** (dĭ-mĭn'ĭsh') *v.* to become smaller or less

**H SETTING AND PLOT**
What does Sam observe about the planet?

210     He swallowed hastily, closed his lunch box, and slung it over his shoulder by its strap. He stood up.

    He felt no fear. He was only excited—and curious.

    The smoke was growing thicker, and taking on a shape. Vaguely, it looked like a cow, a smoky, insubstantial shape that he could see through. Was it a hallucination? A creation of his mind? He had just been thinking of a cow.

    Hallucination or not, he was going to investigate.

    With determination, he stepped toward the shape.

## PART TWO

Sam Chase stepped toward the cow outlined in smoke on the strange, far planet on which his education and career were to be advanced.

220     He was convinced there was nothing wrong with his mind. It was the "hallucination" that Dr. Gentry had mentioned, but it was no hallucination. Even as he pushed his way through the tall rank[4] grasslike greenery, he noted the silence, and knew not only that it was no hallucination, but what it really *was*.

    The smoke seemed to condense and grow darker, outlining the cow more sharply. It was as though the cow were being painted in the air.

    Sam laughed, and shouted, "Stop! Stop! Don't use me. I don't know a cow well enough. I've only seen pictures. You're getting it all wrong."

    It looked more like a caricature[5] than a real animal and, as he cried out, the outline wavered and thinned. The smoke remained but it was as though an
230 unseen hand had passed across the air to erase what had been written. **I**

    Then a new shape began to take form. At first, Sam couldn't quite make out what it was intended to represent, but it changed and sharpened quickly. He stared in surprise, his mouth hanging open and his hamper bumping emptily against his shoulder blade.

    The smoke was forming a human being. There was no mistake about it. It was forming accurately, as though it had a model it could imitate, and of course it did have one, for Sam was standing there.

    It was becoming Sam, clothes and all, even the outline of the hamper and the strap over his shoulder. It was another Sam Chase.
240     It was still a little vague, wavering a bit, insubstantial, but it firmed as though it were correcting itself, and then, finally, it was steady.

    It never became entirely solid. Sam could see the vegetation dimly through it, and when a gust of wind caught it, it moved a bit as if it were a tethered balloon. **J**

    But it was real. It was no creation of his mind. Sam was sure of that.

    But he couldn't just stand there, simply facing it. Diffidently, he said, "Hello, there."

**I** VISUALIZE
Close your eyes and picture the cow described here. Add this "picture" to your chart.

**J** SETTING AND PLOT
Do you think that what Sam sees is a real part of the planet, or is it a hallucination?

---

4. **rank:** yielding an excessive crop.

5. **caricature** (kăr′ĭ-kə-chŏŏr′): a comic or exaggerated picture.

Somehow, he expected the Other Sam to speak, too, and, indeed, its mouth opened and closed, but no sound came out. It might just have been imitating 250 the motion of Sam's mouth.

Sam said, again, "Hello, can you speak?"

There was no sound but his own voice, and yet there was a tickling in his mind, a **conviction** that they could communicate.

Sam frowned. What made him so sure of that? The thought seemed to pop into his mind.

He said, "Is this what has appeared to other people, human people—my kind—on this world?"

No answering sound, but he was quite sure what the answer to his question was. This had appeared to other people, not necessarily in their own shape, but 260 *something*. And it hadn't worked.

What made him so sure of *that?* Where did these convictions come from in answer to his questions?

Yes, of course, they *were* the answers to his questions. The Other Sam was putting thoughts into his mind. It was adjusting the tiny electric currents in his brain cells so that the proper thoughts would arise.

He nodded thoughtfully at *that* thought, and the Other Sam must have caught the significance of the gesture, for it nodded, too.

It had to be so. First a cow had formed, when Sam had thought of a cow, and then it had shifted when Sam had said the cow was imperfect. The Other 270 Sam could grasp his thoughts somehow, and if it could grasp them, then it could modify them, too, perhaps.

Was this what telepathy[6] was like, then? It was not like talking. It was having thoughts, except that the thoughts originated elsewhere and were not created entirely of one's own mental operations. But how could you tell your own thoughts from thoughts imposed from outside?

Sam knew the answer to that at once. Right now, he was unused to the process. He had never had practice. With time, as he grew more skilled at it, he would be able to tell one kind of thought from another without trouble.

In fact, he could do it now, if he thought about it. Wasn't he carrying 280 on a conversation in a way? He was wondering, and then knowing. The wondering was his own question, the knowing was the Other Sam's answer. Of course it was.

There! The "of course it was," just now, was an answer.

"Not so fast, Other Sam," said Sam, aloud. "Don't go too quickly. Give me a chance to sort things out, or I'll just get confused."

He sat down suddenly on the grass, which bent away from him in all directions.

The Other Sam slowly tried to sit down as well.

conviction (kən-vĭk'shən)
*n.* a strong belief

---

6. **telepathy** (tə-lĕp'ə-thē): communication directly from one person's mind to another.

Sam laughed. "Your legs are bending in the wrong place."

290 That was corrected at once. The Other Sam sat down, but remained very stiff from the waist up.

"Relax," said Sam.

Slowly, the Other Sam slumped, flopping a bit to one side, then correcting that. **K**

Sam was relieved. With the Other Sam so willing to follow his lead, he was sure good will was involved. It was! Exactly!

"No," said Sam. "I said, not so fast. Don't go by my thoughts. Let me speak out loud, even if you can't hear me. *Then* adjust my thoughts, so I'll know it's an adjustment. Do you understand?"

300 He waited a moment and was then sure the Other Sam understood.

Ah, the answer had come, but not right away. Good!

"Why do you appear to people?" asked Sam.

He stared earnestly at the Other Sam, and knew that the Other Sam wanted to communicate with people, but had failed.

No answer to that question had really been required. The answer was obvious. But then, *why* had they failed?

He put it in words. "Why did you fail? You are successfully communicating with me."

**ANALYZE VISUALS**
What details in this picture help you **visualize** the Other Sam?

**K** **VISUALIZE**
What does the Other Sam do to copy Sam's movements? Sketch your mental picture.

Sam was beginning to learn how to understand the alien manifestation.[7] It was as if his mind were adapting itself to a new technique of communication, just as it would adapt itself to a new language. Or was Other Sam influencing Sam's mind and teaching him the method without Sam even knowing it was being done?

Sam found himself emptying his mind of immediate thoughts. After he asked his question, he just let his eyes focus at nothing and his eyelids droop, as though he were about to drop off to sleep, and then he knew the answer. There was a little clicking, or something, in his mind, a signal that showed him something had been put in from outside.

He now knew, for instance, that the Other Sam's previous attempts at communication had failed because the people to whom it had appeared had been frightened. They had doubted their own sanity. And because they feared, their minds . . . tightened. Their minds would not receive. The attempts at communication gradually diminished, though they had never entirely stopped.

"But you're communicating with me," said Sam.

Sam was different from all the rest. He had not been afraid.

"Couldn't you have made them not afraid first? Then talked to them?"

It wouldn't work. The fear-filled mind resisted all. An attempt to change might damage. It would be wrong to damage a thinking mind. There had been one such attempt, but it had not worked.

"'What is it you are trying to communicate, Other Sam?"

A wish to be left alone. *Despair!*

Despair was more than a thought; it was an emotion; it was a frightening sensation. Sam felt despair wash over him intensely, heavily—and yet it was not part of himself. He felt despair on the surface of his mind, keenly, but underneath it, where his own mind was, he was free of it.

Sam said, wonderingly, "It seems to me as though you're giving up. Why? We're not interfering with you?"

Human beings had built the Dome, cleared a large area of all planetary life and substituted their own. And once the neutron star had its power station— once floods of energy moved outward through hyperspace to power-thirsty worlds—more power stations would be built and still more. Then what would happen to *Home.* (There must be a name for the planet that the Other Sam used but the only thought Sam found in his mind was *Home* and, underneath that, the thought: *ours—ours—ours—*)

This planet was the nearest convenient base to the neutron star. It would be flooded with more and more people, more and more Domes, and their Home would be destroyed. ❶

"But you could change our minds if you had to, even if you damaged a few, couldn't you?"

**❶ SETTING AND PLOT**
What **conflict** is being introduced?

---

7. **manifestation** (măn'ə-fĕ-stā'shən): an indication of the presence of something.

350　If they tried, people would find them dangerous. People would work out what was happening. Ships would approach, and from a distance, use weapons to destroy the life on Home, and then bring in People-life instead. This could be seen in the people's minds. People had a violent history; they would stop at nothing.

"But what can I do?" said Sam. "I'm just an apprentice. I've just been here a few days. What can I do?"

*Fear. Despair.*

There were no thoughts that Sam could work out, just the numbing layer of fear and despair.

360　He felt moved. It was such a peaceful world. They threatened nobody. They didn't even hurt minds when they could. **Ⓜ**

It wasn't their fault they were conveniently near a neutron star. It wasn't their fault they were in the way of expanding humanity.

He said, "Let me think."

He thought, and there was the feeling of another mind watching. Sometimes his thoughts skipped forward and he recognized a suggestion from outside.

There came the beginning of hope. Sam felt it, but wasn't certain.

He said doubtfully, "I'll try."

370　He looked at the time-strip[8] on his wrist and jumped a little. Far more time had passed than he had realized. His three hours were nearly up. "I must go back now," he said.

He opened his lunch hamper and removed the small thermos of water, drank from it thirstily, and emptied it. He placed the empty thermos under one arm. He removed the wrappings of the sandwich and stuffed it in his pocket.

The Other Sam wavered and turned smoky. The smoke thinned, dispersed and was gone.

Sam closed the hamper, swung its strap over his shoulder again and turned 380　toward the Dome.

His heart was hammering. Would he have the courage to go through with his plan? And if he did, would it work?

When Sam entered the Dome, the Corridor-Master was waiting for him and said, as he looked ostentatiously at his own time-strip, "You shaved it rather fine, didn't you?"

Sam's lips tightened and he tried not to sound **insolent.** "I had three hours, sir."

"And you took two hours and fifty-eight minutes."

"That's less than three hours, sir."

390　"Hmm." The Corridor-Master was cold and unfriendly. "Dr. Gentry would like to see you."

**Ⓜ SETTING AND PLOT**
What have you learned about the beings who inhabit this planet?

**insolent** (ĭn′sə-lənt) *adj.*
insulting; arrogant

---

8. **time-strip:** watch.

"Yes, sir. What for?"

"He didn't tell me. But I don't like you cutting it that fine your first time out, Chase. And I don't like your attitude either, and I don't like an officer of the Dome wanting to see you. I'm just going to tell you once, Chase—if you're a troublemaker, I won't want you in this Corridor. Do you understand?"

"Yes, sir. But what trouble have I made?"

"We'll find that out soon enough." **N**

**N** **MAKE INFERENCES**
Why do you think the Corridor-Master believes that Sam is a troublemaker?

400   **S**am had not seen Donald Gentry since their one and only meeting the day the young apprentice had reached the Dome. Gentry still seemed good natured and kindly, and there was nothing in his voice to indicate anything else. He sat in a chair behind his desk, and Sam stood before it, his hamper still bumping his shoulder blade.

Gentry said, "How are you getting along, Sam? Having an interesting time?"

"Yes, sir," said Sam.

"Still feeling you'd rather be doing something else, working somewhere else?"

Sam said, earnestly, "No, sir. This is a good place for me."

"Because you're interested in hallucinations?"

"Yes, sir."

410   "You've been asking others about it, haven't you?"

"It's an interesting subject to me, sir."

"Because you want to study the human brain?"

"Any brain, sir."

"And you've been wandering about outside the Dome, haven't you?"

"I was told it was permitted, sir."

"It is. But few apprentices take advantage of that so soon. Did you see anything interesting?"

Sam hesitated, then said, "Yes, sir."

"A hallucination?"

420   "No, sir." He said it quite positively.

Gentry stared at him for a few moments, and there was a kind of speculative hardening of his eyes. "Would you care to tell me what you did see? Honestly."

Sam hesitated again. Then he said, "I saw and spoke to an inhabitant of this planet, sir."

"An intelligent inhabitant, young man?"

"Yes, sir."

Gentry said, "Sam, we had reason to wonder about you when you came. The Central Computer's report on you did not match our needs, though it was favorable in many ways, so I took the opportunity to study you that first

430   day. We kept our collective eye on you, and when you left to wander about the planet on your own, we kept you under observation."

"Sir," said Sam, indignantly. "That violates my right of privacy."

"Yes, it does, but this is a most vital project and we are sometimes driven to bend the rules a little. We saw you talking with considerable animation for a substantial period of time."

"I just told you I was, sir."

"Yes, but you were talking to *nothing*, to empty air. You were experiencing a hallucination, Sam!"

## PART THREE

S am Chase was speechless. A hallucination? It couldn't be a hallucination. Less than half an hour ago, he had been speaking to the Other Sam, had been experiencing the thoughts of the Other Sam. He knew exactly what had happened then, and he was still the same Sam Chase he had been during that conversation and before. He put his elbow over his lunch hamper as though it were a connection with the sandwiches he had been eating when the Other Sam had appeared.

He said, with what was almost a stammer, "Sir—Dr. Gentry—it wasn't a hallucination. It was real."

440

Gentry shook his head. "My boy, I saw you talking with animation to nothing at all. I didn't hear what you said, but you were talking. Nothing else was there except plants. Nor was I the only one. There were two other witnesses, and we have it all on record."

"On record?"

"On a television cassette. Why should we lie to you, young man? This has happened before. At the start it happened rather frequently. Now it happens only very rarely. For one thing, we tell the new apprentices of the hallucinations at the start, as I told you, and they generally avoid the planet until they are more acclimated, and then it doesn't happen to them."

"You mean you scare them," blurted out Sam, "so that it's not likely to happen. And they don't tell you if it does happen. But I wasn't scared."

Gentry shook his head. "I'm sorry you weren't, if that was what it would have taken you to keep from seeing things."

"I wasn't seeing things. At least, not things that weren't there."

"How do you intend to argue with a television cassette, which will show you staring at nothing?"

"Sir, what I saw was not opaque. It was smoky, actually; foggy, if you know what I mean."

"Yes, I do. It looked as a hallucination might look, not as reality. But the television set would have seen even smoke."

"Maybe not, sir. My mind must have been focused to see it more clearly. It was probably less clear to the camera than to me."

"It focused your mind, did it?" Gentry stood up, and he sounded rather sad. "That's an admission of hallucination. I'm really sorry, Sam, because you are clearly intelligent, and the Central Computer rated you highly, but we can't use you."

"Will you be sending me home, sir?"

"Yes, but why should that matter? You didn't particularly want to come here."

"I want to stay here *now*."

"But I'm afraid you cannot."

"You can't just send me home. Don't I get a hearing?"

"You certainly can, if you insist, but in that case, the proceedings will be official and will go on your record, so that you won't get another apprenticeship anywhere. As it is, if you are sent back unofficially, as better suited to an apprenticeship in neurophysiology, you might get that, and be better off, actually, than you are now."

"I don't want that. I want a hearing—before the Commander."

"Oh, no. Not the Commander. He can't be bothered with that."

"It *must* be the Commander," said Sam, with desperate force, "or this Project will fail." ◉

◉ **SETTING AND PLOT**
Why does Sam so badly want to stay on Energy Planet?

"Unless the Commander gives you a hearing? Why do you say that? Come,
490 you are forcing me to think that you are unstable in ways other than those involved with hallucinations."

"Sir." The words were tumbling out of Sam's mouth now. "The Commander is ill—they know that even on Earth—and if he gets too ill to work, this Project will fail. I did not see a hallucination and the proof is that I know why he is ill and how he can be cured."

"You're not helping yourself," said Gentry.

"If you send me away, I tell you the Project will fail. Can it hurt to let me see the Commander? All I ask is five minutes."

"Five minutes? What if he refuses?"

500 "*Ask* him, sir. Tell him that I say the same thing that caused his depression can remove it."

"No, I don't think I'll tell him that. But I'll ask him if he'll see you."

The Commander was a thin man, not very tall. His eyes were a deep blue and they looked tired.

His voice was very soft, a little low-pitched, definitely weary. **P**

"You're the one who saw the hallucination?"

"It was not a hallucination, Commander. It was real. So was the one *you* saw, Commander." If that did not get him thrown out, Sam thought, he might have a chance. He felt his elbow tightening on his hamper again. He still had
510 it with him.

The Commander seemed to wince. "The one *I* saw?"

"Yes, Commander. It said it had hurt one person. They had to try with you because you were the Commander, and they . . . did damage."

The Commander ignored that and said, "Did you ever have any mental problems before you came here?"

"No, Commander. You can consult my Central Computer record."

Sam thought: *He* must have had problems, but they let it go because he's a genius and they had to have him.

Then he thought: Was that my own idea? Or had it been put there?

520 The Commander was speaking. Sam had almost missed it. He said, "What you saw can't be real. There is no intelligent life-form on this planet."

"Yes, sir. There is."

"Oh? And no one ever discovered it till you came here, and in three days you did the job?" The Commander smiled very briefly. "I'm afraid I have no choice but to—"

"Wait, Commander," said Sam, in a strangled voice. "We know about the intelligent life-form. It's the insects, the little flying things."

"You say the insects are intelligent?"

**P** **VISUALIZE**
What does the Commander look like? Note the details that help you picture him, and then sketch him in your chart.

"Not an individual insect by itself, but they fit together when they want to, like little jigsaw pieces. They can do it in any way they want. And when they do, their nervous systems fit together, too, and build up. A lot of them *together* are intelligent." **Q**

The Commander's eyebrows lifted. "That's an interesting idea, anyway. Almost crazy enough to be true. How did you come to that conclusion, young man?"

"By observation, sir. Everywhere I walked, I disturbed the insects in the grass and they flew about in all directions. But once the cow started to form, and I walked toward it, there was nothing to see or hear. The insects were gone. They had gathered together in front of me and they weren't in the grass anymore. That's how I knew."

"You talked with a cow?"

"It was a cow at first, because that's what I thought of. But they had it wrong, so they switched and came together to form a human being—*me*."

"You?" And then, in a lower voice, "Well, that fits anyway."

"Did you see it that way, too, Commander?"

The Commander ignored that. "And when it shaped itself like you, it could talk as you did? Is that what you're telling me?"

"No, Commander. The talking was in my mind."

"Telepathy?"

**Q SETTING AND PLOT**
Reread lines 529–532. How do the insects communicate with humans?

550 "Sort of."

"And what did it say to you, or think to you?"

"It wanted us to **refrain** from disturbing this planet. It wanted us not to take it over." Sam was all but holding his breath. The interview had lasted more than five minutes already, and the Commander was making no move to put an end to it, to send him home.

"Quite impossible."

"Why, Commander?"

"Any other base will double and triple the expense. We're having enough trouble getting grants as it is. Fortunately, it is all a hallucination, young man,

560 and the problem does not arise." He closed his eyes, then opened them and looked at Sam without really focusing on him. "I'm sorry, young man. You will be sent back—officially."

Sam gambled again. "We can't afford to ignore the insects, Commander. They have a lot to give us."

The Commander had raised his hand halfway as though about to give a signal. He paused long enough to say, "Really? What do they have that they can give us?"

"The one thing more important than energy, Commander. An understanding of the brain."

570 "How do you know that?"

**ANALYZE VISUALS**
In what ways is the setting captured by this photo different from how you pictured Energy Planet? In what ways is it similar?

**refrain** (rĭ-frān') *v.* to hold oneself back; to stop

**R** **SETTING AND PLOT**
Why is it so important to the Commander to remain on the planet?

"I can demonstrate it. I have them here." Sam seized his hamper and swung it forward onto the desk.

"What's that?"

Sam did not answer in words. He opened the hamper, and a softly whirring, smoky cloud appeared.

The Commander rose suddenly and cried out. He lifted his hand high and an alarm bell sounded.

Through the door came Gentry, and others behind him. Sam felt himself seized by the arms, and then a kind of stunned and motionless silence prevailed 580 in the room.

The smoke was condensing, wavering, taking on the shape of a Head, a thin head, with high cheekbones, a smooth forehead and receding hairline. It had the appearance of the Commander.

"I'm seeing things," croaked the Commander.

Sam said, "We're all seeing the same thing, aren't we?" He wriggled and was released. **s**

Gentry said in a low voice, "Mass hysteria."

"No," said Sam, "it's real." He reached toward the Head in midair, and brought back his finger with a tiny insect on it. He flicked it and it could just 590 barely be seen making its way back to its companions.

No one moved.

Sam said, "Head, do you see the problem with the Commander's mind?"

Sam had the brief vision of a snarl in an otherwise smooth curve, but it vanished and left nothing behind. It was not something that could be easily put into human thought. He hoped the others experienced that quick snarl. Yes, they had. He knew it.

The Commander said, "There is no problem."

Sam said, "Can you adjust it, Head?"

Of course, they could not. It was not right to invade a mind.

600 Sam said, "Commander, give permission."

The Commander put his hands to his eyes and muttered something Sam did not make out. Then he said, clearly, "It's a nightmare, but I've been in one since—Whatever must be done, I give permission."

Nothing happened.

Or nothing seemed to happen.

And then slowly, little by little, the Commander's face lit in a smile.

He said, just above a whisper, "Astonishing. I'm watching a sun rise. It's been cold night for so long, and now I feel the warmth again." His voice rose high. "I feel wonderful."

610 The Head deformed at that point, turned into a vague, pulsing fog, then formed a curving, narrowing arrow that sped into the hamper. Sam snapped it shut.

**s VISUALIZE**
Imagine what the Commander sees when Sam opens his hamper. Sketch this scene in your chart.

He said, "Commander, have I your permission to restore these little insect-things to their own world?"

"Yes, yes," said the Commander, dismissing that with a wave of his hand. "Gentry, call a meeting. We've got to change all our plans." **T**

Sam had been escorted outside the Dome by a stolid guard and had then been confined to his quarters for the rest of the day.

It was late when Gentry entered, stared at him thoughtfully, and said,
620 "That was an amazing demonstration of yours. The entire incident has been fed into the Central Computer and we now have a double project— neutron-star energy and neurophysiology. I doubt that there will be any question about pouring money into this project now. And we'll have a group of neurophysiologists arriving eventually. Until then you're going to be working with those little things and you'll probably end up the most important person here."

Sam said, "But will we leave their world to them?"

Gentry said, "We'll have to if we expect to get anything out of them, won't we? The Commander thinks we're going to build elaborate settlements in orbit
630 about this world and shift all operations to them except for a skeleton crew in this Dome to maintain direct contact with the insects—or whatever we'll decide to call them. It will cost a great deal of money, and take time and labor, but it's going to be worth it. No one will question that." **U**

Sam said, "Good!"

Gentry stared at him again, longer and more thoughtfully than before.

"My boy," he said, "it seems that what happened came about because you did not fear the supposed hallucination. Your mind remained open, and that was the whole difference. Why was that? Why weren't you afraid?"

Sam flushed. "I'm not sure, sir. As I look back on it, though, it seemed to
640 me I was puzzled as to why I was sent here. I had been doing my best to study neurophysiology through my computerized courses, and I knew very little about astrophysics. The Central Computer had my record, all of it, the full details of everything I had ever studied and I couldn't imagine why I had been sent here.

"Then, when you first mentioned the hallucinations, I thought, 'That must be it. I was sent here to look into it.' I just made up my mind that was the thing I had to do. I had no *time* to be afraid, Dr. Gentry. I had a problem to solve and I—I had faith in the Central Computer. It wouldn't have sent me here, if I weren't up to it."

650 Gentry shook his head. "I'm afraid I wouldn't have had that much faith in that machine. But they say faith can move mountains, and I guess it did in this case." ❧

**T SETTING AND PLOT**
What did the insects do to make the Commander change his plans?

**U SETTING AND PLOT**
Reread lines 619–633. What **resolution** have the humans reached regarding their plans for Energy Planet, and for Sam?

**PERSONAL ESSAY** Much like Sam Chase in "Hallucination," Isaac Asimov found his purpose in a place far from where he was born. When Asimov was three, he and his parents emigrated from Russia to the U.S. His father never fully mastered English, and both father and son wanted the boy to succeed at reading and writing.

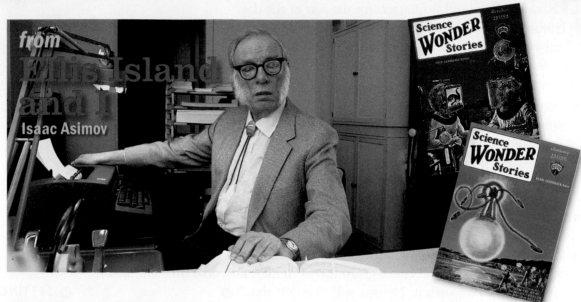

from **Ellis Island and I**

Isaac Asimov

Only in one point did we clash in this matter of reading, and that was over the newsstand in the candy store. I wanted to read the magazines and my father was unalterably opposed. He felt that I would be reading trash and contaminating what he obviously was beginning to think was going to be a first-class mind.

For a while all my arguments fell on deaf ears, and then I discovered science-fiction magazines, which I took surreptitious peeks at while my father was taking his afternoon nap. In particular, I found one called *Science Wonder Stories,* and I pointed out to my father that since the stories were about science, they were bound to be educational.

It was a good time to attack, for my mother was pregnant with what turned out to be my younger brother, and my father was feeling as though he had a lot more on his mind than questions over whether I could read a magazine or not. He gave in.

That started me, at the age of nine, on my career as a science-fiction reader. By the time I was eleven, I felt that I just could not get enough science fiction from the magazines (there were only three, and they came out only once a month), and it struck me that I might write my own.

I didn't quite write science fiction at first, but I managed to get to it when I was fifteen, and by the time I was eighteen I sold a story to one of the magazines and was off and running.

I cannot say how things would have been for me had I not come into the United States as an immigrant. I can't go back and live life over under changed circumstances. Still, as I think about it, it seems to me I needed something to rise above.

To be brief, I'm glad I came here—and I'm glad I had to come here. Life might have been too easy for me if my ancestors had beat me to the punch and had come here on the Mayflower.

# Comprehension

**INDIANA STANDARDS**

**READING STANDARD**
**8.3.4** Analyze the importance of the setting to the mood, tone, and meaning of the text.

1. **Recall**  Why does Sam succeed in communicating with the life forms on Energy Planet?

2. **Recall**  Why does the Other Sam feel despair?

3. **Clarify**  Why does Sam bring his lunch box to his meeting with the Commander?

# Literary Analysis

4. **Visualize**  Choose three sketches from the chart you completed as you read. For each sketch, tell which parts are based on the author's description and which parts, if any, came from your imagination.

5. **Analyze Setting and Plot**  How does the setting of "Hallucination" affect the plot of the story?  Use examples from the selection to support your answer.

6. **Interpret Science Fiction**  Writers of science fiction often comment on present society by writing about the future.  What message about contemporary culture might Asimov have been communicating with "Hallucination"?  Cite evidence from the story to support your interpretation.

7. **Compare Characters**  Think back to your reading of "The Drummer Boy of Shiloh" on page 318.  Although the setting is different from that of "Hallucination," both selections feature teenaged main characters who face big challenges.  In a chart like the one shown, compare and contrast these characters in terms of their motivations for taking on the challenge, their traits, and their reactions to events and characters.

| | Joby | Sam | Similarities and Differences |
|---|---|---|---|
| Motivations | | | |
| Traits | | | |
| Reactions | | | |

# Extension and Challenge

8. **Literary Criticism**  Isaac Asimov once wrote that, for science fiction writers, "each year sees possible plots destroyed" as real-life technology and information catches up with the imaginary.  With a group, discuss whether this means that science fiction written many years ago is no longer relevant. "Hallucination" was written in the last century.  Do its messages still hold up today?

9. **Readers' Circle**  Read the selection "Ellis Island and I" on page 354, taking note of the young Isaac Asimov's personality traits.  What characteristics do Asimov and Sam Chase share?  How did each young man realize his **purpose?** Share your ideas with a group.

# Vocabulary in Context

## VOCABULARY PRACTICE

Decide whether the words in each pair are synonyms (words that mean the same) or antonyms (words that mean the opposite).

1. refrain/persist
2. opposition/resistance
3. inertia/activity
4. diminish/decrease
5. insolent/insulting
6. conviction/doubt

conviction
diminish
inertia
insolent
opposition
refrain

## VOCABULARY IN WRITING

Imagine you are Dr. Gentry, writing a report on Sam, a new arrival. How is Sam different from the other humans on Energy Planet? Use two or more vocabulary words to write a one-paragraph report. You might start like this.

> **EXAMPLE SENTENCE**
>
> Sam's **conviction** that the hallucinations are real is disturbing to the others.

## VOCABULARY STRATEGY: HOMOGRAPHS

Homographs are words that are spelled the same but have different meanings, origins, and sometimes pronunciations. The vocabulary word *refrain* is a homograph. Notice the following two different definitions of *refrain*:

**refrain**[1] (rĭ-frān′) *v.* to hold oneself back; restrain

**refrain**[2] (rĭ-frān′) *n.* a phrase or verse repeated at intervals in a poem or song

If you see a word used in a way that is unfamiliar to you, check the dictionary. You'll know a word is a homograph if there are two separate entries for the word.

***PRACTICE*** Use a dictionary to find two or three homographs for each listed word. Note the origin of each word. Then write sentences that show the differences in meaning for each.

1. row
2. well
3. sound
4. fine
5. wind
6. found

**VOCABULARY PRACTICE**
For more practice, go to the **Vocabulary Center** at ClassZone.com.

# Reading-Writing Connection

Broaden your understanding of "Hallucination" by responding to these prompts. Then complete the **Grammar and Writing** exercise.

| WRITING PROMPTS | SELF-CHECK |
|---|---|
| **A. Short Response: Analyze Cause and Effect**<br>By the end of the story, Dr. Gentry tells Sam, "You'll probably end up the most important person here." How did Sam gain this position so quickly?  In **one paragraph,** describe how Sam's actions made this new opportunity possible. | *A strong analysis will . . .*<br>• describe the events that led up to Sam's promotion<br>• use specific details and examples from the story |
| **B. Extended Response: Write a Letter**<br>Suppose Sam wrote home to describe his experience on Energy Planet.  How would he explain how he found his **purpose** there?  Write a **one-page letter** from Sam to his parents.  Be sure your letter is based on facts from the story. | *A creative letter will . . .*<br>• identify Sam's **purpose** and summarize the events of the story<br>• tell Sam's experiences from his point of view |

## GRAMMAR AND WRITING

*AVOID MISPLACED MODIFIERS*  A **prepositional phrase** consists of a preposition, such as *above, at, for, from, with,* or *on;* its object (a noun or pronoun); and any modifiers of the object.

**INDIANA STANDARDS**

**WRITING STANDARD**
**8.4.8** Edit and proofread one's own writing, as well as that of others . . . .

> *Example:*   The massive dome stretched in all directions.
>                          preposition   modifier   object

When you use a prepositional phrase in your writing, place it close to the word it modifies.  Otherwise, you may end up confusing your readers.

> *Original:*   From the grass, I saw thousands of tiny insects flying.
>                  (*Who or what was in the grass?*)

> *Revised:*   I saw thousands of tiny insects flying from the grass.
>                  (*The insects were in the grass.*)

**PRACTICE**  Move each misplaced prepositional phrase to the correct place.

1. I wondered why I had been sent to this planet with my background.
2. The smells are different from Earth's smells on this planet.
3. The shape began to look like me in the smoke.
4. The Commander sat in his office behind a desk.

*For more help with misplaced modifiers, see page R59 in the **Grammar Handbook.***

## The Monkey's Paw
Short Story by W. W. Jacobs

# *Are you* SUPERSTITIOUS?

**INDIANA STANDARDS**

**READING STANDARDS**
**8.2.9** Make reasonable statements and draw conclusions about a text, supporting them with accurate examples.

**8.3.4** Analyze the importance of the setting to the mood, tone, and meaning of the text.

**KEY IDEA** Many people say they aren't **superstitious.** But those same people might own a lucky charm or get nervous on Friday the 13th. Usually these superstitions are harmless, but sometimes they can interfere with a person's life. In the selection you are about to read, curiosity about the power of an unusual object brings unexpected consequences.

**DISCUSS** What kinds of superstitious behaviors do you or people you know believe in? In a small group, brainstorm a list of common superstitions. Then discuss which you think are harmless, and which might cause problems or interfere with someone's life. Share your findings with the class.

## ● LITERARY ANALYSIS: MOOD

If you've ever felt nervous or peaceful while reading a book, you've been affected by the story's mood. **Mood** is the feeling or atmosphere the writer creates for the reader. There are as many moods as there are emotions: cheerful, gloomy, anxious, lighthearted—the list goes on. Writers create mood through

- the choice of setting, including time and place
- **imagery**—descriptions that appeal to the reader's senses
- conversations between characters

If you are sensitive to a story's mood, you'll become more involved in the story. As you read "The Monkey's Paw," notice how the story makes you feel and which words or passages make you feel that way.

## ● READING STRATEGY: PREDICT

When you make a **prediction,** you use clues from the selection plus your own knowledge and experience to make a reasonable guess about what will happen. Your guesses won't always be right, but that doesn't matter. Making predictions can help you enjoy reading more, because it keeps you engaged in the story.

As you read, use a chart to record your predictions, what actually happens, and whether your prediction was correct.

| My Prediction | Actual Event | Correct? (Yes or No) |
|---|---|---|
|  |  |  |

## ▲ VOCABULARY IN CONTEXT

The following words help W. W. Jacobs tell a frightening tale. Choose the word that best completes each sentence.

| WORD LIST | | |
|---|---|---|
| compensation | fate | peril |
| credulity | grimace | resignation |

1. The old woman's _____ allowed the stranger to trick her.
2. My creepy neighbor wanted _____ for his broken window.
3. The sailors faced great _____ as the storm approached.
4. His _____ scared the children.
5. Tom sighed with _____ upon realizing he was lost.
6. Had she not been saved, she could have met a terrible _____.

# Author Online

**Bored at the Bank**
William Wymark Jacobs grew up on the docks of London, where his father worked as a wharf manager. As a young man, Jacobs was employed at a bank, a job he hated, calling it his "days of captivity." To pass the time, he began writing humorous

**W. W. Jacobs**
**1863–1943**

short stories of ships and sailors. Eventually, he began publishing his stories in magazines and soon became one of the most popular and respected writers of his time.

**A Frightening Classic** Though most of Jacobs's stories were humorous, he is most famous for his horror classic "The Monkey's Paw," which has been adapted numerous times for the stage, film, and television. The story's "steady, relentlessly building tension" makes it one of the most widely read horror stories in history.

 **MORE ABOUT THE AUTHOR**
For more on W. W. Jacobs, visit the **Literature Center** at **ClassZone.com.**

## Background

**The British in India** Like most of Jacobs's stories, "The Monkey's Paw" is set in Britain. One of the characters is an officer in the British Army and served in India during the British occupation of the country. The British first arrived in India in the 1600s, when the British East India Company established trading. Their role changed dramatically after the Sepoy Mutiny of 1857–1858, in which Indian soldiers of the British Army revolted. From then on, the British government controlled India through a system of governors and military outposts. As a result, young men went to India to serve in the army. British rule of India ended in 1947, and today, India is an independent nation.

# THE MONKEY'S PAW

## W. W. Jacobs

**W**ithout, the night was cold and wet, but in the small parlor of Laburnum Villa the blinds were drawn and the fire burned brightly. Father and son were at chess; the former, who possessed ideas about the game involving radical changes, putting his king into such sharp and unnecessary **perils** that it even provoked comment from the white-haired old lady knitting placidly by the fire.

"Hark at the wind," said Mr. White, who, having seen a fatal mistake after it was too late, was amiably[1] desirous of preventing his son from seeing it.

"I'm listening," said the latter, grimly surveying the board as he stretched
10 out his hand. "Check."

"I should hardly think that he'd come tonight," said his father, with his hand poised over the board.

"Mate," replied the son.

"That's the worst of living so far out," bawled Mr. White, with sudden and unlooked-for violence; "of all the beastly, slushy, out-of-the-way places to live in, this is the worst. Pathway's a bog,[2] and the road's a torrent.[3] I don't know what people are thinking about. I suppose because only two houses in the road are let,[4] they think it doesn't matter." **A**

"Never mind, dear," said his wife soothingly; "perhaps you'll win the
20 next one."

---

1. **amiably** (ā′mē-ə-blē): in a friendly way.
2. **bog**: a swamp.
3. **torrent** (tôr′ənt): a swift-flowing stream.
4. **let**: rented.

---

**ANALYZE VISUALS**
What can you **infer** about the object in the photograph? Note the clues you use to make your inference.

**peril** (pĕr′əl) *n.* danger

**A** **MOOD**
Reread lines 1–18. Note words and phrases that describe the **setting**. What feelings do these suggest?

Mr. White looked up sharply, just in time to intercept a knowing glance between mother and son. The words died away on his lips, and he hid a guilty grin in his thin gray beard.

"There he is," said Herbert White, as the gate banged loudly and heavy footsteps came toward the door.

The old man rose with hospitable haste, and opening the door, was heard condoling[5] with the new arrival. The new arrival also condoled with himself, so that Mrs. White said, "Tut, tut!" and coughed gently as her husband entered the room, followed by a tall, burly man, beady of eye and rubicund of visage.[6]

30 "Sergeant-Major Morris," he said, introducing him.

The sergeant-major shook hands, and taking the proffered seat by the fire, watched contentedly while his host brought out drinks and stood a small copper kettle on the fire.

He began to talk, the little family circle regarding with eager interest this visitor from distant parts, as he squared his broad shoulders in the chair and spoke of wild scenes and doughty[7] deeds; of wars and plagues and strange peoples.

"Twenty-one years of it," said Mr. White, nodding at his wife and son. "When he went away, he was a slip of a youth in the warehouse. Now look 40 at him."

"He don't look to have taken much harm," said Mrs. White politely.

"I'd like to go to India myself," said the old man, "just to look round a bit, you know."

"Better where you are," said the sergeant-major, shaking his head. He put down the empty glass, and sighing softly, shook it again.

"I should like to see those old temples and fakirs and jugglers," said the old man. "What was that you started telling me the other day about a monkey's paw or something, Morris?"

"Nothing," said the soldier hastily. "Leastways nothing worth hearing."

50 "Monkey's paw?" said Mrs. White curiously.

"Well, it's just a bit of what you might call magic, perhaps," said the sergeant-major off-handedly.

His three listeners leaned forward eagerly. The visitor absent-mindedly put his empty glass to his lips and then set it down again. His host filled it for him.

"To look at," said the sergeant-major, fumbling in his pocket, "it's just an ordinary little paw, dried to a mummy."

He took something out of his pocket and proffered it. Mrs. White drew back with a **grimace,** but her son, taking it, examined it curiously.

60 "And what is there special about it?" inquired Mr. White as he took it from his son, and having examined it, placed it upon the table.

5. **condoling** (kən-dōl′ing): expressing sympathy.

6. **rubicund** (rōō′bĭ-kənd) **of visage** (vĭz′ĭj): with a ruddy complexion.

7. **doughty** (dou′tē): brave.

---

## VISUAL VOCABULARY

**fakir** (fə-kîr′) *n.* a Muslim or Hindu holy man

**grimace** (grĭm′ĭs) *n.* a facial expression of pain or disgust

"It had a spell put on it by an old fakir," said the sergeant-major, "a very holy man. He wanted to show that <u>fate</u> ruled people's lives, and that those who interfered with it did so to their sorrow. He put a spell on it so that three separate men could each have three wishes from it." **B**

His manner was so impressive that his hearers were conscious that their light laughter jarred somewhat.

"Well, why don't you have three, sir?" said Herbert White cleverly.

The soldier regarded him in the way that middle age is wont to regard
70 presumptuous youth. "I have," he said quietly, and his blotchy face whitened.

"And did you really have the three wishes granted?" asked Mrs. White.

"I did," said the sergeant-major, and his glass tapped against his strong teeth.

"And has anybody else wished?" persisted the old lady.

"The first man had his three wishes. Yes," was the reply; "I don't know what the first two were, but the third was for death. That's how I got the paw."

His tones were so grave that a hush fell upon the group.

"If you've had your three wishes, it's no good to you now, then, Morris," said the old man at last. "What do you keep it for?"

The soldier shook his head. "Fancy, I suppose," he said slowly. "I did have
80 some idea of selling it, but I don't think I will. It has caused enough mischief already. Besides, people won't buy. They think it's a fairy tale, some of them; and those who do think anything of it want to try it first and pay me afterward."

"If you could have another three wishes," said the old man, eyeing him keenly, "would you have them?"

"I don't know," said the other. "I don't know."

He took the paw, and dangling it between his forefinger and thumb, suddenly threw it upon the fire. White, with a slight cry, stooped down and snatched it off.

"Better let it burn," said the soldier solemnly.
90 "If you don't want it, Morris," said the other, "give it to me."

"I won't," said his friend doggedly. "I threw it on the fire. If you keep it, don't blame me for what happens. Pitch it on the fire again like a sensible man." **C**

The other shook his head and examined his new possession closely. "How do you do it?" he inquired.

"Hold it up in your right hand and wish aloud," said the sergeant-major, "but I warn you of the consequences."

"Sounds like the *Arabian Nights*,"[8] said Mrs. White, as she rose and began to set the supper. "Don't you think you might wish for four pairs of hands for me?"
100 Her husband drew the talisman[9] from his pocket, and then all three burst into laughter as the sergeant-major, with a look of alarm on his face, caught him by the arm.

"If you must wish," he said gruffly, "wish for something sensible." **D**

---

8. ***Arabian Nights:*** a famous collection of Asian stories.

9. **talisman** (tăl′ĭs-mən): an object thought to have magical powers.

---

**fate** (fāt) *n.* a power that is thought to determine the course of events

**B PREDICT**
Reread lines 62–65. What role will the monkey's paw play in the story? Describe your prediction in your chart.

**C MOOD**
What feeling do you get from the **dialogue** between the Whites and Sergeant-Major Morris?

**D PREDICT**
What, if anything, do you think Mr. White will wish for? Record your prediction.

Mr. White dropped it back in his pocket, and placing chairs, motioned his friend to the table. In the business of supper the talisman was partly forgotten, and afterward the three sat listening in an enthralled fashion to a second installment of the soldier's adventures in India.

"If the tale about the monkey's paw is not more truthful than those he has been telling us," said Herbert, as the door closed behind their guest, just in 110 time for him to catch the last train, "we shan't make much out of it."

"Did you give him anything for it, Father?" inquired Mrs. White, regarding her husband closely.

"A trifle," said he, coloring slightly. "He didn't want it, but I made him take it. And he pressed me again to throw it away."

"Likely," said Herbert, with pretended horror. "Why, we're going to be rich, and famous, and happy. Wish to be an emperor, Father, to begin with; then you can't be henpecked."

He darted round the table, pursued by the maligned Mrs. White armed with an antimacassar.[10]

120 Mr. White took the paw from his pocket and eyed it dubiously. "I don't know what to wish for, and that's a fact," he said slowly. "It seems to me I've got all I want."

"If you only cleared the house, you'd be quite happy, wouldn't you?" said Herbert, with his hand on his shoulder. "Well, wish for two hundred pounds, then; that'll just do it."

His father, smiling shamefacedly at his own **credulity,** held up the talisman, as his son, with a solemn face, somewhat marred by a wink at his mother, sat down at the piano and struck a few impressive chords.

"I wish for two hundred pounds," said the old man distinctly. **E**

130 A fine crash from the piano greeted the words, interrupted by a shuddering cry from the old man. His wife and son ran toward him.

"It moved," he cried, with a glance of disgust at the object as it lay on the floor. "As I wished, it twisted in my hand like a snake."

"Well, I don't see the money," said his son, as he picked it up and placed it on the table, "and I bet I never shall."

"It must have been your fancy, father," said his wife, regarding him anxiously.

He shook his head. "Never mind, though; there's no harm done, but it gave me a shock all the same."

They sat down by the fire again. Outside, the wind was higher than ever, 140 and the old man started nervously at the sound of a door banging upstairs. A silence unusual and depressing settled upon all three, which lasted until the old couple rose to retire for the night. **F**

"I expect you'll find the cash tied up in a big bag in the middle of your bed," said Herbert, as he bade them good-night, "and something horrible squatting up on top of the wardrobe[11] watching you as you pocket your ill-gotten gains."

**credulity** (krĭ-dōō′lĭ-tē) *n.* a disposition to believe too readily

**E PREDICT**
What do you think will happen as a result of Mr. White's first wish? Record your prediction.

**F MOOD**
Reread lines 130–142. Note the **imagery** in these lines. To what senses does it appeal? Explain how it contributes to the mood.

---

10. **antimacassar** (ăn′tĭ-mə-kăs′ər): a cloth placed over an arm or back of a chair.

11. **wardrobe:** a piece of furniture that serves as a closet.

He sat alone in the darkness, gazing at the dying fire, and seeing faces in it. The last face was so horrible and so simian[12] that he gazed at it in amazement. It got so vivid that, with a little uneasy laugh, he felt on the table for a glass containing a little water to throw over it. His hand grasped the monkey's paw, 150 and with a little shiver he wiped his hand on his coat and went up to bed.

## II

In the brightness of the wintry sun next morning as it streamed over the breakfast table he laughed at his fears. There was an air of prosaic[13] wholesomeness about the room which it had lacked on the previous night, and the dirty, shriveled little paw was pitched on the sideboard[14] with a carelessness which betokened no great belief in its virtues.[15] **G**

**ANALYZE VISUALS**
What do you see in the fire? How does this **compare** to what Herbert sees?

**G PREDICT**
Based on the **mood** of this paragraph, what do you think will happen in Part II? Add this to your chart.

---

12. **simian** (sĭm'ē-ən): monkey- or ape-like.

13. **prosaic** (prō-zā'ĭk): ordinary.

14. **sideboard:** a piece of furniture used to store linens and dishes.

15. **virtues:** powers.

"I suppose all old soldiers are the same," said Mrs. White. "The idea of our listening to such nonsense! How could wishes be granted in these days? And if they could, how could two hundred pounds hurt you, father?"

"Might drop on his head from the sky," said the frivolous[16] Herbert.

160 "Morris said the things happened so naturally," said his father, "that you might if you so wished attribute it to coincidence."

"Well, don't break into the money before I come back," said Herbert as he rose from the table. "I'm afraid it'll turn you into a mean, avaricious[17] man, and we shall have to disown you."

His mother laughed, and following him to the door, watched him down the road; and returning to the breakfast table, was very happy at the expense of her husband's credulity. All of which did not prevent her from scurrying to the door at the postman's knock, when she found that the post brought a tailor's bill.

170 "Herbert will have some more of his funny remarks, I expect, when he comes home," she said, as they sat at dinner.

"I dare say," said Mr. White, "but for all that, the thing moved in my hand; that I'll swear to."

"You thought it did," said the old lady soothingly.

"I say it did," replied the other. "There was no thought about it; I had just— What's the matter?"

His wife made no reply. She was watching the mysterious movements of a man outside, who, peering in an undecided fashion at the house, appeared to be trying to make up his mind to enter. In mental connection with the two 180 hundred pounds, she noticed that the stranger was well dressed, and wore a silk hat of glossy newness. Three times he paused at the gate, and then walked on again. The fourth time he stood with his hand upon it, and then with sudden resolution flung it open and walked up the path. Mrs. White at the same moment placed her hands behind her, and hurriedly unfastening the strings of her apron, put that useful article of apparel beneath the cushion of her chair.

She brought the stranger, who seemed ill at ease, into the room. He gazed at her furtively, and listened in a preoccupied fashion as the old lady apologized for the appearance of the room, and her husband's coat, a garment which he usually reserved for the garden. She then waited patiently for him to broach his 190 business, but he was at first strangely silent. **H**

"I—was asked to call," he said at last, and stooped and picked a piece of cotton from his trousers. "I come from Maw and Meggins."

The old lady started. "Is anything the matter?" she asked breathlessly. "Has anything happened to Herbert? What is it? What is it?"

Her husband interposed. "There, there, mother," he said hastily. "Sit down, and don't jump to conclusions. You've not brought bad news, I'm sure, sir;" and he eyed the other wistfully.

**H PREDICT**
Reread lines 177–190. Why do you think the man comes to see the Whites?

---

16. **frivolous** (frĭv'ə-ləs): inappropriately silly.

17. **avaricious** (ăv'ə-rĭsh'es): greedy.

"I'm sorry—" began the visitor.

"Is he hurt?" demanded the mother wildly.

200 The visitor bowed in assent. "Badly hurt," he said quietly, "but he is not in any pain."

"Oh!" said the old woman, clasping her hands. "Thank goodness for that! Thank—"

She broke off suddenly as the sinister meaning of the assurance dawned upon her and she saw the awful confirmation of her fears in the other's averted face. She caught her breath, and turning to her slower-witted husband, laid her trembling old hand upon his. There was a long silence. **Ⓘ**

"He was caught in the machinery," said the visitor at length in a low voice.

"Caught in the machinery," repeated Mr. White, in a dazed fashion, "yes."

210 He sat staring blankly out at the window, and taking his wife's hand between his own, pressed it as he had been wont to do in their old courting days nearly forty years before.

"He was the only one left to us," he said, turning gently to the visitor. "It is hard."

The other coughed, and rising, walked slowly to the window. "The firm wished me to convey their sincere sympathy with you in your great loss," he said, without looking round. "I beg that you will understand I am only their servant and merely obeying orders."

There was no reply; the old woman's face was white, her eyes staring, and 220 her breath inaudible; on the husband's face was a look such as his friend the sergeant might have carried into his first action.

"I was to say that Maw and Meggins disclaim all responsibility," continued the other. "They admit no liability at all, but in consideration of your son's services, they wish to present you with a certain sum as **compensation.**"

Mr. White dropped his wife's hand, and rising to his feet, gazed with a look of horror at his visitor. His dry lips shaped the words, "How much?"

"Two hundred pounds," was the answer.

Unconscious of his wife's shriek, the old man smiled faintly, put out his hands like a sightless man, and dropped, a senseless heap, to the floor. **Ⓙ**

## III

230 In the huge new cemetery, some two miles distant, the old people buried their dead, and came back to a house steeped in shadow and silence. It was all over so quickly that at first they could hardly realize it, and remained in a state of expectation as though of something else to happen—something else which was to lighten this load, too heavy for old hearts to bear.

But the days passed, and expectation gave place to **resignation**—the hopeless resignation of the old, sometimes miscalled apathy. Sometimes they hardly exchanged a word, for now they had nothing to talk about, and their days were long to weariness.

**Ⓘ MOOD**
Think about the news the stranger reveals during his conversation with the Whites. What emotions do you feel as a result of this news?

**compensation**
(kŏm′pən-sā′shən) *n.* something, such as money, received as payment

**Ⓙ PREDICT**
Did your prediction about what would result from Mr. White's first wish come true? Add your answer to your chart.

**resignation**
(rĕz′ĭg-nā′shən) *n.* acceptance of something that is inescapable

It was about a week after that the old man, waking suddenly in the night,
240 stretched out his hand and found himself alone. The room was in darkness,
and the sound of subdued weeping came from the window. He raised himself
in bed and listened.

"Come back," he said tenderly. "You will be cold."

"It is colder for my son," said the old woman, and wept afresh.

The sound of her sobs died away on his ears. The bed was warm, and his
eyes heavy with sleep. He dozed fitfully, and then slept until a sudden wild cry
from his wife awoke him with a start.

"*The paw!*" she cried wildly. "The monkey's paw!"

He started up in alarm. "Where? Where is it? What's the matter?"

250 She came stumbling across the room toward him. "I want it," she said
quietly. "You've not destroyed it?" **K**

"It's in the parlor, on the bracket," he replied, marveling. "Why?"

She cried and laughed together, and bending over, kissed his cheek.

"I only just thought of it," she said hysterically. "Why didn't I think of it
before? Why didn't *you* think of it?"

"Think of what?" he questioned.

"The other two wishes," she replied rapidly. "We've only had one."

"Was not that enough?" he demanded fiercely.

"No," she cried triumphantly; "we'll have one more. Go down and get it
260 quickly, and wish our boy alive again."

The man sat up in bed and flung the bedclothes from his quaking limbs.
"You are mad!" he cried, aghast.

"Get it," she panted; "get it quickly, and wish—Oh, my boy, my boy!"

Her husband struck a match and lit the candle. "Get back to bed," he said
unsteadily. "You don't know what you are saying."

"We had the first wish granted," said the old woman feverishly; "why not
the second?"

"A coincidence," stammered the old man.

"Go and get it and wish," cried his wife, quivering with excitement.

270 He went down in the darkness, and felt his way to the parlor, and then to
the mantelpiece. The talisman was in its place, and a horrible fear that the
unspoken wish might bring his mutilated son before him ere he could escape
from the room seized upon him, and he caught his breath as he found that he
had lost the direction of the door. His brow cold with sweat, he felt his way
round the table, and groped along the wall until he found himself in the small
passage with the unwholesome thing in his hand. **L**

Even his wife's face seemed changed as he entered the room. It was white
and expectant, and to his fears seemed to have an unnatural look upon it. He
was afraid of her.

280 "*Wish!*" she cried, in a strong voice.

"It is foolish and wicked," he faltered.

"*Wish!*" repeated his wife.

He raised his hand. "I wish my son alive again." **M**

**K** PREDICT
What do you think
Mrs. White plans to
do with the paw?

**L** MOOD
Reread lines 270–276.
What **imagery** does the
author use to establish
the mood in this
paragraph?

**M** PREDICT
Do you think the Whites'
wish will be granted?
Note the clues that
influence your answer.

The talisman fell to the floor, and he regarded it fearfully. Then he sank trembling into a chair as the old woman, with burning eyes, walked to the window and raised the blind.

He sat until he was chilled with the cold, glancing occasionally at the figure of the old woman peering through the window. The candle-end, which had burned below the rim of the china candlestick, was throwing pulsating shadows
290 on the ceiling and walls, until, with a flicker larger than the rest, it expired.

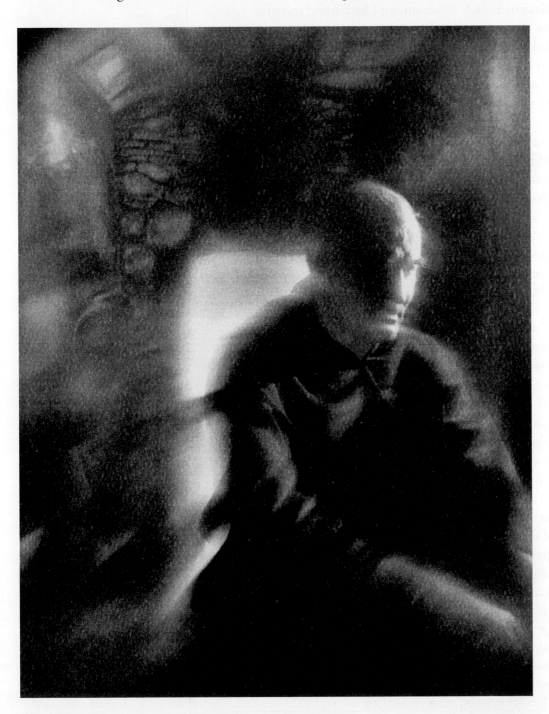

**ANALYZE VISUALS**
Describe the **mood** of this photograph. What details contribute to this mood?

The old man, with an unspeakable sense of relief at the failure of the talisman, crept back to his bed, and a minute or two afterward the old woman came silently and apathetically beside him.

Neither spoke, but lay silently listening to the ticking of the clock. A stair creaked, and a squeaky mouse scurried noisily through the wall. The darkness was oppressive, and after lying for some time gathering up his courage, he took the box of matches, and striking one, went downstairs for a candle.

At the foot of the stairs the match went out, and he paused to strike another; and at the same moment a knock, so quiet and stealthy as to be

300    scarcely audible, sounded on the front door. **N**

The matches fell from his hand. He stood motionless, his breath suspended until the knock was repeated. Then he turned and fled swiftly back to his room, and closed the door behind him. A third knock sounded through the house.

"*What's that?*" cried the old woman, starting up.

"A rat," said the old man in shaking tones— "a rat. It passed me on the stairs."

His wife sat up in bed listening. A loud knock resounded through the house.

"It's Herbert!" she screamed. "It's Herbert!"

She ran to the door, but her husband was before her, and catching her by the arm, held her tightly.

310    "What are you going to do?" he whispered hoarsely.

"It's my boy; it's Herbert!" she cried, struggling mechanically. "I forgot it was two miles away. What are you holding me for? Let go. I must open the door."

"Don't let it in," cried the old man, trembling.

"You're afraid of your own son," she cried, struggling. "Let me go. I'm coming, Herbert; I'm coming."

There was another knock, and another. The old woman with a sudden wrench broke free and ran from the room. Her husband followed to the landing, and called after her appealingly as she hurried downstairs. He heard the chain rattle back and the bottom bolt drawn slowly and stiffly from the

320    socket. Then the old woman's voice, strained and panting.

"The bolt," she cried loudly. "Come down. I can't reach it."

But her husband was on his hands and knees groping wildly on the floor in search of the paw. If he could only find it before the thing outside got in. A perfect fusillade[18] of knocks reverberated through the house, and he heard the scraping of a chair as his wife put it down in the passage against the door. He heard the creaking of the bolt as it came slowly back, and at the same moment he found the monkey's paw, and frantically breathed his third and last wish.

The knocking ceased suddenly, although the echoes of it were still in the house. He heard the chair drawn back, and the door opened. A cold wind

330    rushed up the staircase, and a long loud wail of disappointment and misery from his wife gave him courage to run down to her side, and then to the gate beyond. The streetlamp flickering opposite shone on a quiet and deserted road. **◡**

**N MOOD**
Reread lines 294–300. What sounds help create the mood in these paragraphs?

---

18. **fusillade** (fyōō′sə-läd′): discharge from many guns; a rapid outburst.

## Comprehension

1. **Recall** How does Mr. White get the monkey's paw?

2. **Recall** What power is the monkey's paw supposed to have?

3. **Clarify** Why does Sergeant-Major Morris throw the paw onto the fire?

## Literary Analysis

4. **Make Inferences** At the end of the story, why did the knocking stop so suddenly? Explain.

5. **Examine Predictions** Review the chart you created as you read. Did most of your predictions come true? Looking back at the places where your predictions were wrong, notice how W. W. Jacobs tried to surprise readers by giving false clues about what would happen.

6. **Analyze Mood** How would you describe this story's mood? Include your answer at the top of a chart like the one shown. Then provide examples of setting descriptions, conversations, and imagery that helped create the mood.

| Mood: | | |
|---|---|---|
| Setting Descriptions: | Conversations: | Imagery: |
| | | |

7. **Draw Conclusions** Reread lines 62–65, in which the sergeant-major explains how the monkey's paw supposedly got its power. Based on what you know from your reading of the story, do you think that the paw itself is powerful, or is its power dependent on the **superstitious** nature of the person who possesses it?

## Extension and Challenge

8. **Creative Response: Art** What words or images jumped out at you during your reading of "The Monkey's Paw"? Create a collage of words and images that show the story's mood. Combine pictures from newspapers or magazines with your own writing and sketches.

9. **Reader's Circle** Consider what would have happened if Mrs. White had opened the door before her husband made the final wish. Would you have liked to find out what was on the other side of the door? Or is it better for you as a reader not to know? In a small group, discuss your thoughts about the ending of "The Monkey's Paw."

**INDIANA STANDARDS**

**READING STANDARD**
**8.3.4** Analyze the importance of the setting to the mood, tone, and meaning of the text.

# Vocabulary in Context

## VOCABULARY PRACTICE

Choose the word in each group that is most nearly opposite in meaning to the boldfaced word.

1. **peril:** (a) safety, (b) risk, (c) hazard
2. **credulity:** (a) simplicity, (b) doubt, (c) openness
3. **resignation:** (a) respect, (b) resistance, (c) acceptance
4. **compensation:** (a) consideration, (b) reward, (c) loss
5. **fate:** (a) choice, (b) destiny, (c) luck
6. **grimace:** (a) frown, (b) scowl, (c) grin

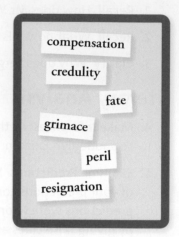

## VOCABULARY IN WRITING

If someone offered you a monkey's paw and claimed it had magical powers, how would you respond? Use at least two vocabulary words to write a one-paragraph answer. You might start like this.

**EXAMPLE SENTENCE**

*I don't believe a monkey's paw can change a person's **fate**.*

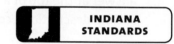

**INDIANA STANDARDS**

**READING STANDARD**
**8.1.3** Verify the meaning of a word in its context . . . .

## VOCABULARY STRATEGY: THE LATIN ROOT *cred*

The vocabulary word *credulity* contains the Latin root *cred*, meaning "to believe" or "to trust." A number of commonly used English words are formed using *cred*. To figure out the meanings of unfamiliar words containing *cred*, use your knowledge of the root as well as any context clues provided.

incredible     credence

**cred**

credentials     discredit

credo

***PRACTICE*** Choose a word from the web to complete each of the following sentences. Use context clues or, if necessary, consult a dictionary.

1. A person must get the proper _____ before he or she is able to teach.
2. Sharon didn't approve of the club's _____, so she didn't join.
3. I gave no _____ to his story, which changed each time he told it.
4. The violinist received several rounds of applause after her _____ performance.
5. They hoped to _____ the candidate by focusing on his lack of experience.

**VOCABULARY PRACTICE**
For more practice, go to the **Vocabulary Center** at ClassZone.com.

# Reading-Writing Connection

Broaden your understanding of "The Monkey's Paw" by responding to these prompts. Then complete the **Grammar and Writing** exercise.

| WRITING PROMPTS | SELF-CHECK |
|---|---|
| **A. Short Response: Examine the Message**<br>The fakir wanted to prove "that fate ruled people's lives." Do the events in "The Monkey's Paw" prove this, or is it just a **superstition?** Write **one paragraph** explaining your opinion. Support your ideas with evidence from the text. | *An effective response will . . .*<br>• offer a clear statement of opinion<br>• include examples from the story as support |
| **B. Extended Response: Rewrite the Ending**<br>Suppose Mr. White did not make that last wish. What would have happened when Mrs. White opened the door? In **two or three paragraphs,** write an alternate ending to "The Monkey's Paw." Be sure you use language that fits with the rest of the story. | *A well-written ending will . . .*<br>• provide an alternate ending that is believable and creative<br>• use a writing style that is similar to W.W. Jacobs's |

## GRAMMAR AND WRITING

**INDIANA STANDARDS**

**WRITING STANDARD**
**8.4.8** Edit and proofread one's own writing, as well as that of others . . . .

*MAINTAIN SUBJECT-VERB AGREEMENT* A **compound subject** is made up of two or more subjects joined by a conjunction, such as *and, or,* or *nor.* The conjunction determines whether you should use a singular or plural verb. If a compound subject is joined by *and,* then it usually takes a plural verb. If a compound subject is joined by *or* or *nor,* then the verb should agree in number with the part closest to it.

> *Original:* Neither Mr. White nor the two men before him finds happiness.

> *Revised:* Neither Mr. White nor the two men before him find happiness. (*The plural verb* find *is correct because the plural noun* men *is closer to it.*)

**PRACTICE** Choose the verb form that agrees with each compound subject.

1. Mr. and Mrs. White (has, have) different feelings about the paw.
2. Neither the paw nor the wishes (has, have) any effect on fate.
3. Herbert and his father (like, likes) to play chess.
4. Either fate or several coincidences (lead, leads) to Herbert's death and the company's compensation.

*For more help with subject-verb agreement with compound subjects, see page R65 in the* **Grammar Handbook.**

# Roll of Thunder, Hear My Cry

Historical Novel by Mildred D. Taylor

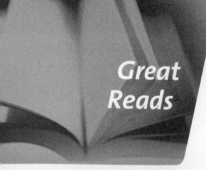

Mildred D. Taylor
born 1943

**Other Books by Mildred D. Taylor**

- *The Gold Cadillac*
- *The Land*
- *Let the Circle Be Unbroken*
- *The Road to Memphis*

## Meet Mildred D. Taylor

Mildred D. Taylor's personal exposure to segregation and bigotry has had a strong influence on her writing. Though Taylor was born in Mississippi, her family moved to the North when she was only three months old. Her father did not want his children to grow up in the racially segregated South. In the Ohio town where she was raised, Taylor was often the only African-American student in her class.

The Taylors returned to the South once a year, however, to visit relatives. The family tradition of sharing stories around bonfires led Taylor to imagine herself as a storyteller. Her father was considered one of the best storytellers in the family, and Taylor credits him for her success: "Without his teachings, without his words, my words would not have been."

## Try a Historical Novel

*Roll of Thunder, Hear My Cry* takes place in Mississippi in the 1930s. Blending fictional characters and events with facts about real places, people, and occurrences, Taylor's **historical novel** transports readers to that time and place.

It wasn't easy to be an African American in the South during the Great Depression. Jobs and food were scarce, and racial tension was high. Many white people viewed African Americans as inferior, and some whites committed acts of violence against them. Taylor creates a vivid picture of what life is like for an African-American family trying to remain united while their community is torn apart.

## Read a Great Book

Cassie Logan and her three brothers—Christopher-John, Stacey, and Little Man—often find themselves struggling to understand why some of the white people in their community treat them so badly. But after the Logan kids pull a prank on the white school's bus driver out of revenge for his mistreatment of them, they soon realize that their actions could have very serious consequences.

*from*

# Roll of THUNDER,
## Hear My Cry

MILDRED D. TAYLOR

The room grew quiet again, except for the earthy humming of Big Ma's rich alto voice, the crackle of the hickory fire, and the patter of rain on the roof. Engrossed in a mystery, I was startled when the comfortable sounds were shattered by three rapid knocks on the side door.

Rising quickly, Mama went to the door and called, "Who is it?"

"It's me, ma'am," came a man's gravelly voice. "Joe Avery."

Mama opened the door and Mr. Avery stepped dripping into the room.

"Why, Brother Avery," Mama said, "what are you doing out on a
10 night like this? Come on in. Take off your coat and sit by the fire. Stacey, get Mr. Avery a chair."

"No'm," said Mr. Avery, looking rather nervously over his shoulder into the night. "I ain't got but a minute." He stepped far enough into the room so that he could close the door, then nodded to the rest of us. "Evenin', Miz Caroline, how you t'night?"

"Oh, I'll do, I reckon," said Big Ma, still ironing. "How's Miz Fannie?"

"She's fine," he said without dwelling on his wife. "Miz Logan . . . uh, I come to tell you somethin' . . . somethin' important—Mr. Morrison 20 here?"

Mama stiffened. "David. You heard something about David?"

"Oh, no'm," replied Mr. Avery hastily. "Ain't heard nothin' 'bout yo' husband, ma'am."

Mama regarded him quizzically.

"It's . . . it's them again. They's ridin' t'night."

Mama, her face pale and frightened, glanced back at Big Ma; Big Ma held her iron in midair.

"Uh . . . children," Mama said, "I think it's your bedtime."

"But, Mama—" we chorused in protest, wanting to stay and hear 30 who was riding.

"Hush," Mama said sternly. "I said it was time to go to bed. Now go!"

Groaning loudly enough to voice our displeasure, but not loudly enough to arouse Mama's anger, we stacked our books upon the study table and started toward the boys' room.

"Cassie, I said go to bed. That's not your room."

"But, Mama, it's cold in there," I pouted. Usually, we were allowed to build small fires in the other rooms an hour before bedtime to warm them up.

"You'll be warm once you're under the covers. Stacey, take the 40 flashlight with you and light the lantern in your room. Cassie, take the lamp from the desk with you."

I went back and got the kerosene lamp, then entered my bedroom, leaving the door slightly ajar.

"Close that door, Cassie!"

Immediately, the door was closed.

I put the lamp on the dresser, then silently slid the latch off the outside door and slipped onto the wet front porch. I crossed to the boys' room. Tapping lightly, I whispered, "Hey, let me in."

The door creaked open and I darted in. The room was bathed in 50 darkness.

"What they say?" I asked.

"Shhhhh!" came the answer.

I crept to the door leading into Mama's room and huddled beside the boys.

The rain softened upon the roof and we could hear Mama asking, "But why? Why are they riding? What's happened?"

"I don't rightly know," said Mr. Avery. "But y'all knows how they is. Anytime they thinks we steppin' outa our *place,* they feels like they gotta stop us. You know what some of 'em done to the Berrys." He paused,
60 then went on bitterly, "It don't take but a little of nothin' to set them devilish night men off."

"But somethin' musta happened," Big Ma said. "How you know 'bout it?"

"All's I can tell ya, Miz Caroline, is what Fannie heard when she was leavin' the Grangers' this evenin'. She'd just finished cleanin' up the supper dishes when Mr. Granger come home with Mr. Grimes—ya know, that white school's bus driver—and two other mens. . . ."

A clap of deafening thunder drowned Mr. Avery's words, then the rain quickened and the conversation was lost.

70 I grabbed Stacey's arm. "Stacey, they're coming after *us!*"

"What!" squeaked Christopher-John.

"Hush," Stacey said harshly. "And Cassie, let go. That hurts."

"Stacey, somebody musta seen and told on us," I persisted.

"No . . ." Stacey replied unconvincingly. "It couldn't be."

"Couldn't be?" cried Christopher-John in a panic. "Whaddaya mean it couldn't be?"

"Stacey," said Little Man excitedly, "whaddaya think they gonna do to us? Burn us up?"

"Nothin'!" Stacey exclaimed, standing up suddenly. "Now why don't
80 y'all go to bed like y'all s'pose to?"

We were stunned by his attitude. He sounded like Mama and I told him so.

He collapsed in silence by the door, breathing hard, and although I could not see him, I knew that his face was drawn and that his eyes had taken on a haggard look. I touched his arm lightly. "Ain't no call to go blaming yourself," I said. "We all done it."

"But I got us into it," he said listlessly.

"But we all wanted to do it," I comforted.

"Not me!" denied Christopher-John. "All I wanted to do was eat my
90 lunch!"

"Shhhhh," hissed Little Man. "I can hear 'em again."

"I'd better go tell Mr. Morrison," Mr. Avery was saying. "He out back?"

"I'll tell him," said Mama.

We could hear the side door open and we scrambled up.

"Cassie, get back to your room quick," Stacey whispered. "They'll probably come check on us now."

"But what'll we do?"

"Nothin' now, Cassie. Them men probably won't even come near here."

"Ya really believe that?" asked Christopher-John hopefully.

100 "But shouldn't we tell Mama?" I asked.

"No! We can't ever tell nobody!" declared Stacey adamantly. "Now go on, hurry!"

Footsteps neared the door. I dashed onto the porch and hastened back to my own room, where I jumped under the bedcovers with my clothes still on. Shivering, I pulled the heavy patchwork quilts up to my chin.

A few moments later Big Ma came in, leaving the door to Mama's room open. Knowing that she would be suspicious of such an early surrender to sleep, I sighed softly and, making sleepy little sounds, turned onto my stomach, careful not to expose my shirt sleeves.

110 Obviously satisfied by my performance, Big Ma tucked the covers more closely around me and smoothed my hair gently. Then she stooped and started fishing for something under our bed.

I opened my eyes. Now what the devil was she looking for down there? While she was searching, I heard Mama approaching and I closed my eyes again.

"Mama?"

"Stacey, what're you doing up?"

"Let me help."

"Help with what?"

120 "With . . . with whatever's the matter."

Mama was silent a moment, then said softly, "Thank you, Stacey, but Big Ma and I can handle it."

"But Papa told me to help you!"

"And you do, more than you know. But right now you could help me most by going back to bed. It's a school day tomorrow, remember?"

"But, Mama—"

"If I need you, I'll call you. I promise."

I heard Stacey walk slowly away, then Mama whispering in the doorway, "Cassie asleep?"

130  "Yeah, honey," Big Ma said. "Go on and sit back down. I'll be out in a minute."

Then Big Ma stood up and turned down the wick of the kerosene lamp. As she left the room, my eyes popped open again and I saw her outlined in the doorway, a rifle in her hands. Then she closed the door and I was left to the darkness.

For long minutes I waited, wide awake, wondering what my next move should be. Finally deciding that I should again consult with the boys, I swung my legs over the edge of the bed, but immediately had to swing them back again as Big Ma reentered the room. She passed the

140  bed and pulled a straight-backed chair up to the window. Parting the curtains so that the blackness of the night mixed with the blackness of the room, she sat down without a sound.

I heard the door to the boys' room open and close and I knew that Mama had gone in. I waited for the sound of the door opening again, but it did not come. Soon the chill of the cotton sheets beneath me began to fade and as Big Ma's presence lulled me into a security I did not really feel, I fell asleep.

When I awoke, it was still nightly dark. "Big Ma?" I called. "Big Ma, you there?" But there was no reply from the chair by the window.

150  Thinking that Big Ma had fallen asleep, I climbed from the bed and felt my way to her chair.

She wasn't there. ❧

## Keep Reading

You've just gotten a sense of the tense situation the Logan family is in. As one of the few landowning African-American families in the community, the Logans face resentment from many of their white neighbors. Will they be able to hold on to their land through these tough times? Continue reading *Roll of Thunder, Hear My Cry* to find out.

## Going Where I'm Coming From

Memoir by Naomi Shihab Nye

# Can you BELONG *in two places?*

**KEY IDEA** Have you ever heard someone say, "This is where I belong"? What is it about a place that makes you feel a sense of **belonging?** If you spend a lot of time in two different places, such as home and your best friend's house, you may feel equally comfortable in both. The author of the memoir you are about to read discovered that during a year of being away from the United States, she developed a sense of belonging in her new home as well.

**QUICKWRITE** Think of one or two places where you feel a sense of belonging. What kinds of things make you feel that way—the people, the food, the sights and sounds, the routine? Record your thoughts in your journal.

## LITERARY ANALYSIS: SETTING IN NONFICTION

You might think of **setting,** the time and place in which events occur, as an element of fiction. But setting can be important in nonfiction, too. For example, details about people's customs, beliefs, and day-to-day life are all important to setting. In a memoir, a writer might discuss how these aspects of her childhood home influenced the adult she became.

As you read "Going Where I'm Coming From," notice how the author's identity is shaped by her experiences in her father's homeland.

## READING STRATEGY: CONNECT

Sometimes the experiences of people you read about will remind you of events from your own life. When you relate the content of literature to your own experience, you are **connecting** with what you read. By making connections, you can gain new insights into your life and the lives of others around you.

As you read the selection, compare Naomi Shihab Nye's thoughts and experiences with your own. How does this help you better understand her feelings? Take notes in a chart like the one shown.

| Author's Experiences | My Experiences | Insights |
|---|---|---|
| She doesn't feel love for her grandmother the first time she meets her. | I felt shy around my grandmother the first time I visited her in China. | Even family bonds can take time to develop. |

## ▲ VOCABULARY IN CONTEXT

Nye uses the boldfaced words to help tell her story of living in a new land. Use the context of the numbered sentences to figure out what each word means.

1. The fabric contained a complex and **intricate** design.
2. Mom allowed me to join the team with the **stipulation** that I keep my grades up.
3. In a **valiant** act of bravery, I entered my new classroom.
4. Her father often talked about what it was like to **emigrate** from Mexico to the United States.

# Author Online

**Combining Cultures**
Naomi Shihab Nye learned about both Palestinian and American cultures as she was growing up; her mother was born in the United States and her father was born in Palestine. She says that when the other Girl Scouts brought iced cupcakes for treats, she brought

**Naomi Shihab Nye
born 1952**

dates, apricots, and almonds. In the mid-1960s, Nye and her family moved to a home just outside of Jerusalem. Nye has said that her year there "altered my perception of the universe irrevocably." "Going Where I'm Coming From" is one of many works she's written about her experiences there.

**Building Bridges** In her poetry, novels, and essays, Nye encourages people from different cultures to learn to relate to each other. She believes that writers who belong to more than one culture can "build bridges between worlds."

## Background

**A City Among Valleys** Jerusalem is an ancient Middle Eastern city located between the Mediterranean Sea and the Dead Sea. Surrounded by valleys, Jerusalem experiences warm, dry summers and cool winters. Also known as The Holy City, Jerusalem is home to over 700,000 people from a variety of national, religious, and socioeconomic backgrounds. Today, Jerusalem is the capital of the State of Israel. One of the most ancient sections of Jerusalem, the Old City, is divided into four quarters: Armenian, Christian, Jewish, and Muslim.

**MORE ABOUT THE AUTHOR AND BACKGROUND**
To learn more about Naomi Shihab Nye and Jerusalem, visit the **Literature Center** at **ClassZone.com.**

# Going Where I'm Coming From

## Naomi Shihab Nye

Shortly after we arrived in Jerusalem, our relatives came to see us at a hotel. Sitti, our grandmother, was very short. She wore a long, thickly embroidered Palestinian dress, had a musical, high-pitched voice and a low, guttural laugh. She kept touching our heads and faces as if she couldn't believe we were there. I had not yet fallen in love with her. Sometimes you don't fall in love with people immediately, even if they're your own grandmother. Everyone seemed to think we were all too thin.

We moved into a second-story flat in a stone house eight miles north of the city, among fields and white stones and wandering sheep. My brother was enrolled
10 in the Friends Girls School and I was enrolled in the Friends Boys School in the town of Ramallah a few miles farther north—it all was a little confused. But the Girls School offered grades one through eight in English and high school continued at the Boys School. Most local girls went to Arabic-speaking schools after eighth grade.

I was a freshman, one of seven girl students among two hundred boys, which would cause me problems a month later. I was called in from the schoolyard at lunchtime, to the office of our counselor who wore shoes so pointed and tight her feet bulged out pinkly on top. **Ⓐ**

"You will not be talking to them anymore," she said. She rapped on the desk
20 with a pencil for emphasis.

"To whom?"

"All the boy students at this institution. It is inappropriate behavior. From now on, you will speak only with the girls."

**ANALYZE VISUALS**
What do the colors in this painting suggest about the **setting**?

**Ⓐ** **SETTING IN NONFICTION**
Reread lines 1–18. What details help you understand what life was like in Jerusalem?

*Jerusalem* (1984), Tamam Al-Akhal. Palestine. Oil on canvas, 50 cm × 70 cm. Private collection.

"But there are only six other girls! And I like only one of them!" My friend was Anna, from Italy, whose father ran a small factory that made matches. I'd visited it once with her. It felt risky to walk the aisles among a million filled matchboxes. Later we visited the factory that made olive oil soaps and stacked them in giant pyramids to dry.

"No, thank you," I said. "It's ridiculous to say that girls should only talk to
30 girls. Did I say anything bad to a boy? Did anyone say anything bad to me? They're my friends. They're like my brothers. I won't do it, that's all."

The counselor conferred with the headmaster[1] and they called a taxi. I was sent home with a little paper requesting that I transfer to a different school. The charge: insolence. My mother, startled to see me home early and on my own, stared out the window when I told her.

My brother came home from his school as usual, full of whistling and notebooks. "Did anyone tell you not to talk to girls?" I asked him. He looked at me as if I'd gone goofy. He was too young to know the troubles of the world. He couldn't even imagine them. **B**

40 "You know what I've been thinking about?" he said. "A piece of cake. That puffy white layered cake with icing like they have at birthday parties in the United States. Wouldn't that taste good right now?" Our mother said she was thinking about mayonnaise. You couldn't get it in Jerusalem. She'd tried to make it and it didn't work. I felt too gloomy to talk about food.

My brother said, "Let's go let Abu Miriam's chickens out." That's what we always did when we felt sad. We let our fussy landlord's red-and-white chickens loose to flap around the yard happily, puffing their wings. Even when Abu Miriam shouted and waggled his cane and his wife waved a dishtowel, we knew the chickens were thanking us.

50 My father went with me to the St. Tarkmanchatz Armenian School, a solemnly ancient stone school tucked deep into the Armenian Quarter of the Old City of Jerusalem. It was another world in there. He had already called the school officials on the telephone and tried to enroll me, though they didn't want to. Their school was for Armenian students only, kindergarten through twelfth grade. Classes were taught in three languages: Armenian, Arabic and English, which was why I needed to go there. Although most Arab students at other schools were learning English, I needed a school where classes were actually taught in English—otherwise I would have been staring out the windows triple the usual amount.

The head priest wore a long robe and a tall cone-shaped hat. He said, "Excuse
60 me, please, but your daughter, she is not an Armenian, even a small amount?"

"Not at all," said my father. "But in case you didn't know, there is a **stipulation** in the educational code books of this city that says no student may be rejected solely on the basis of ethnic background, and if you don't accept her, we will alert the proper authorities."

They took me. But the principal wasn't happy about it. The students, however, seemed glad to have a new face to look at. Everyone's name ended in *-ian,*

**B** CONNECT
Note Nye's reaction to the school's rule about boys and girls. How do you respond to rules you think are unfair?

SOCIAL STUDIES CONNECTION

Jerusalem was built around 3000 B.C. Its original name, *Urr Salem,* meant "the land of peace."

**stipulation**
(stĭp′yə lā′shən) *n.* the act of laying down a condition or agreement

---

1. **headmaster:** principal of a private school.

the beautiful, musical Armenian ending—Boghossian, Minassian, Kevorkian, Rostomian. My new classmates started calling me Shihabian. We wore uniforms, navy blue pleated skirts for the girls, white shirts, and navy sweaters. I waited during the lessons for the English to come around, as if it were a channel on television. While other students were on the other channels, I scribbled poems in the margins of my pages, read library books, and wrote a lot of letters filled with exclamation points. All the other students knew all three languages with three entirely different alphabets. How could they carry so much in their heads? I felt humbled by my ignorance. One day I felt so frustrated in our physics class—still another language—that I pitched my book out the open window. The professor made me go collect it. All the pages had let loose at the seams and were flapping free into the gutters along with the white wrappers of sandwiches. **C**

Every week the girls had a hands-and-fingernails check. We had to keep our nails clean and trim, and couldn't wear any rings. Some of my new friends would invite me home for lunch with them, since we had an hour-and-a-half break and I lived too far to go to my own house.

Their houses were a thousand years old, clustered beehive-fashion behind ancient walls, stacked and curled and tilting and dark, filled with pictures of unsmiling relatives and small white cloths dangling crocheted[2] edges. We ate spinach pies and white cheese. We dipped our bread in olive oil, as the Arabs did. We ate small sesame cakes, our mouths full of crumbles. They taught me to say "I love you" in Armenian, which sounded like *yes-kay-see-goo-see-rem*. I felt I had left my old life entirely. **D**

Every afternoon I went down to the basement of the school where the kindergarten class was having an Arabic lesson. Their desks were pint-sized, their full white smocks tied around their necks. I stuffed my fourteen-year-old self in beside them. They had rosy cheeks and shy smiles. They must have thought I was a very slow learner.

More than any of the lessons, I remember the way the teacher rapped the backs of their hands with his ruler when they made a mistake. Their little faces puffed up with quiet tears. This pained me so terribly I forgot all my words. When it was my turn to go to the blackboard and write in Arabic, my hand shook. The kindergarten students whispered hints to me from the front row, but I couldn't understand them. We learned horribly useless phrases: "Please hand me the bellows[3] for my fire." I wanted words simple as tools, simple as *food* and *yesterday* and *dreams*. The teacher never rapped my hand, especially after I wrote a letter to the city newspaper, which my father edited, protesting such harsh treatment of young learners. I wish I had known how to talk to those little ones, but they were just beginning their English studies and didn't speak much yet. They were at the same place in their English that I was in my Arabic.

From the high windows of St. Tarkmanchatz, we could look out over the Old City, the roofs and flapping laundry and television antennas, the pilgrims and churches and mosques, the olivewood prayer beads and fragrant *falafel*[4] lunch

**C** CONNECT
Reread lines 69–78. Think of a time when you felt frustrated in class. What did you do to solve the problem?

**D** SETTING IN NONFICTION
What details help you to picture the Armenian houses and to understand Armenian customs?

---

2. **crocheted** (krō-shād′): needlework made by looping thread with a hooked needle.

3. **bellows** (bĕl′ōz): an apparatus used for producing a strong current of air.

4. *falafel* (fə-lä′fəl): fried balls of ground, spiced chickpeas.

stands, the **intricate** interweaving of cultures and prayers and songs and holidays.
110 We saw the barbed wire separating Jordan from Israel then, the bleak, uninhabited strip of no-man's land reminding me how little education saved us after all. People who had differing ideas still came to blows, imagining fighting could solve things. Staring out over the quiet roofs of afternoon, I thought it so foolish. I asked my friends what they thought about it and they shrugged.

"It doesn't matter what we think about it. It just keeps happening. It happened in Armenia too,[5] you know. Really, really bad in Armenia. And who talks about it in the world news now? It happens everywhere. It happens in *your* country one by one, yes? Murders and guns. What can we do?" **E**

**E CONNECT**
Think of a serious conversation you have had with friends. Based on how you felt afterward, how do you think Nye might have felt after having this conversation?

---

5. **It happened in Armenia, too:** Refers to the Armenian massacres of 1915–1923. In response to Russia's use of Armenian troops against the Ottomans in World War I, the Ottoman empire ordered the deportation of 1.75 million Armenians. During the deportation, around a million Armenians were killed or died of starvation.

*The Olive Tree* (2005), Ismail Shammout. Palestine. Oil on canvas, 60 cm × 80 cm. Private collection.

**ANALYZE VISUALS**
What can you **infer** about this family from the way they are posed in this painting?

Sometimes after school, my brother and I walked up the road that led past
120 the crowded refugee camp of Palestinians who owned even less than our modest
relatives did in the village. The little kids were stacking stones in empty tin cans
and shaking them. We waved our hands and they covered their mouths and
laughed. We wore our beat-up American tennis shoes and our old sweatshirts
and talked about everything we wanted to do and everywhere else we wished
we could go.

"I want to go back to Egypt," my brother said. "I sort of feel like I missed it.
Spending all that time in bed instead of exploring—what a waste."

"I want to go to Greece," I said. "I want to play a violin in a symphony
orchestra in Austria." We made up things. I wanted to go back to the United
130 States most of all. Suddenly I felt like a patriotic citizen. One of my friends,
Sylvie Markarian, had just been shipped off to Damascus, Syria to marry a man
who was fifty years old, a widower. Sylvie was exactly my age—we had turned
fifteen two days apart. She had never met her future husband before. I thought
this was the most revolting thing I had ever heard of. "Tell your parents no
thank you," I urged her. "Tell them you *refuse.*"

Sylvie's eyes were liquid, swirling brown. I could not see clearly to the bottom
of them.

"You don't understand," she told me. "In United States you say no. We don't
say no. We have to follow someone's wishes. This is the wish of my father. Me, I
140 am scared. I never slept away from my mother before. But I have no choice. I am
going because they tell me to go." She was sobbing, sobbing on my shoulder. And
I was stroking her long, soft hair. After that, I carried two fists inside, one for Sylvie
and one for me. **ⓕ**

Most weekends my family went to the village to sit with the relatives. We sat
and sat and sat. We sat in big rooms and little rooms, in circles, on chairs or on
woven mats or brightly covered mattresses piled on the floor. People came in and
out to greet my family. Sometimes even donkeys and chickens came in and out.
We were like movie stars or dignitaries.[6] They never seemed to get tired of us.

My father translated the more interesting tidbits of conversation, the funny
150 stories my grandmother told. She talked about angels and food and money and
people and politics and gossip and old memories from my father's childhood,
before he **emigrated** away from her. She wanted to make sure we were going to
stick around forever, which made me feel very nervous. We ate from mountains of
rice and eggplant on large silver trays—they gave us little plates of our own since
it was not our custom to eat from the same plate as other people. We ripped the
giant wheels of bread into triangles. Shepherds passed through town with their
flocks of sheep and goats, their long canes and cloaks, straight out of the Bible.
My brother and I trailed them to the edge of the village, past the lentil fields to
the green meadows studded with stones, while the shepherds pretended we weren't
160 there. I think they liked to be alone, unnoticed. The sheep had differently colored
dyed bottoms, so shepherds could tell their flocks apart. **ⓖ**

---

6. **dignitaries** (dĭg′nĭ-tĕr′ēz): people of high rank or position.

**ⓕ SETTING IN NONFICTION**
Note Nye's reaction to her friend's problem. In what ways is she being affected by her experiences in Jerusalem?

**emigrate** (ĕm′ĭ-grāt′) *v.*
to leave one country and settle in another

**ⓖ SETTING IN NONFICTION**
Reread lines 144–161. What details help create a sense of place?

*In Jerusalem* (1997), Ismail Shammout. Palestine. Oil on canvas, 50 cm × 60 cm. Private collection.

During these long, slow, smoke-stained weekends—the men still smoked cigarettes a lot in those days, and the old *taboon,* my family's mounded bread-oven, puffed billowy clouds outside the door—my crying jags began. I cried without any warning, even in the middle of a meal. My crying was usually noiseless but dramatically wet—streams of tears pouring down my cheeks, onto my collar or the back of my hand.

Everything grew quiet.

Someone always asked in Arabic, "What is wrong? Are you sick? Do you wish 170 to lie down?"

My father made **valiant** excuses in the beginning. "She's overtired," he said. "She has a headache. She is missing her friend who moved to Syria. She is homesick just now."

My brother stared at me as if I had just landed from Planet X.

**ANALYZE VISUALS**
Nye describes the "stony splendor" of Jerusalem. How does this painting fit that description?

**valiant** (văl′yənt) *adj.* brave

Worst of all was our drive to school every morning, when our car came over the rise in the highway and all Jerusalem lay sprawled before us in its golden, stony splendor pockmarked with olive trees and automobiles. Even the air above the city had a thick, religious texture, as if it were a shining brocade[7] filled with broody incense. I cried hardest then. All those hours tied up in school lay just 180 ahead. My father pulled over and talked to me. He sighed. He kept his hands on the steering wheel even when the car was stopped and said, "Someday, I promise you, you will look back on this period in your life and have no idea what made you so unhappy here."

"I want to go home." It became my anthem. "This place depresses me. It weighs too much. . . . I hate the way people stare at me here." Already I'd been involved in two street skirmishes with boys who stared a little too hard and long. I'd socked one in the jaw and he socked me back. I hit the other one straight in the face with my purse. **H**

"You could be happy here if you tried just a little harder," my father said. 190 "Don't compare it to the United States all the time. Don't pretend the United States is perfect. And look at your brother—he's not having any problems!"

"My brother is eleven years old."

I had crossed the boundary from uncomplicated childhood when happiness was a good ball and a horde of candy-coated Jordan almonds. **I**

One problem was that I had fallen in love with four different boys who all played in the same band. Two of them were even twins. I never quite described it to my parents, but I wrote reams and reams of notes about it on loose-leaf paper that I kept under my sweaters in my closet.

Such new energy made me feel reckless. I gave things away. I gave away my 200 necklace and a whole box of shortbread cookies that my mother had been saving. I gave my extra shoes away to the gypsies. One night when the gypsies camped in a field down the road from our house, I thought about their mounds of white goat cheese lined up on skins in front of their tents, and the wild *oud*[8] music they played deep into the black belly of the night, and I wanted to go sit around their fire. Maybe they could use some shoes.

I packed a sack of old loafers that I rarely wore and walked with my family down the road. The gypsy mothers stared into my shoes curiously. They took them into their tent. Maybe they would use them as vases or drawers. We sat with small glasses of hot, sweet tea until a girl bellowed from deep in her throat, threw 210 back her head, and began dancing. A long bow thrummed across the strings. The girl circled the fire, tapping and clicking, trilling a long musical wail from deep in her throat. My brother looked nervous. He was remembering the belly dancer in Egypt, and her scarf. I felt invisible. I was pretending to be a gypsy. My father stared at me. Didn't I recognize the exquisite oddity of my own life when I sat right in the middle of it? Didn't I feel lucky to be here? Well, yes I did. But sometimes it was hard to be lucky.

**H** SETTING IN NONFICTION
Reread lines 175–188. What is it about Jerusalem that makes Nye feel sad and angry?

**I** CONNECT
Which of your own experiences can help you understand what Nye is feeling?

---

7. **brocade** (brō-kād′): a heavy fabric with a raised design.

8. *oud* (o͞od): a musical instrument resembling a lute.

**W**hen we left Jerusalem, we left quickly. Left our beds in our rooms and our car in the driveway. Left in a plane, not sure where we were going. The rumbles of fighting with Israel had been growing louder and louder. In the
220 barbed-wire no-man's land visible from the windows of our house, guns cracked loudly in the middle of the night. We lived right near the edge. My father heard disturbing rumors at the newspaper that would soon grow into the infamous Six Day War of 1967. We were in England by then, drinking tea from thin china cups and scanning the newspapers. Bombs were blowing up in Jerusalem. We worried about the village. We worried about my grandmother's dreams, which had been getting worse and worse, she'd told us. We worried about the house we'd left, and the chickens, and the children at the refugee camp. But there was nothing we could do except keep talking about it all.

My parents didn't want to go back to Missouri because they'd already said
230 goodbye to everyone there. They thought we might try a different part of the country. They weighed the virtues of different states. Texas was big and warm. After a chilly year crowded around the small gas heaters we used in Jerusalem, a warm place sounded appealing. In roomy Texas, my parents bought the first house they looked at. My father walked into the city newspaper and said, "Any jobs open around here?"

I burst out crying when I entered a grocery store—so many different kinds of bread. **J**

A letter on thin blue airmail paper reached me months later, written by my classmate, the bass player in my favorite Jerusalem band. "Since you left," he said,
240 "your empty desk reminds me of a snake ready to strike. I am afraid to look at it. I hope you are having a better time than we are."

Of course I was, and I wasn't. *Home* had grown different forever. *Home* had doubled. Back *home* again in my own country, it seemed impossible to forget the place we had just left: the piercing call of the *muezzin*[9] from the mosque[10] at prayer time, the dusky green tint of the olive groves, the sharp, cold air that smelled as deep and old as my grandmother's white sheets flapping from the line on her roof. What story hadn't she finished?

Our father used to tell us that when he was little, the sky over Jerusalem crackled with meteors and shooting stars almost every night. They streaked and
250 flashed, igniting the dark. Some had long golden tails. For a few seconds, you could see their whole swooping trail lit up. Our father and his brothers slept on the roof to watch the sky. "There were so many of them, we didn't even call out every time we saw one."

During our year in Jerusalem, my brother and I kept our eyes cast upwards whenever we were outside at night, but the stars were different since our father was a boy. Now the sky seemed too orderly, stuck in place. The stars had learned where they belonged. Only people on the ground kept changing. ∾

**J** SETTING IN
NONFICTION
Reread lines 217–237.
How is Texas different
from Jerusalem?

---

9. *muezzin* (myōō-ĕz′ĭn): a crier who calls the Muslim faithful to prayer.

10. **mosque** (mŏsk): a Muslim house of worship.

# My Father and the Figtree

Naomi Shihab Nye

For other fruits my father was indifferent.
He'd point at the cherry trees and say,
"See those? I wish they were figs."
In the evenings he sat by our beds
5 weaving folktales like vivid little scarves.
They always involved a figtree.
Even when it didn't fit, he'd stick it in.
Once Joha was walking down the road
and he saw a figtree.
10 Or, he tied his camel to a figtree and went to sleep.
Or, later when they caught and arrested him,
his pockets were full of figs.

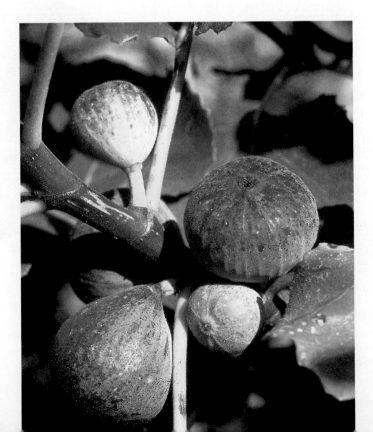

At age six I ate a dried fig and shrugged.
"That's not what I'm talking about!" he said,

15  "I'm talking about a fig straight from the earth—
gift of Allah!—on a branch so heavy
it touches the ground.
I'm talking about picking the largest, fattest,
    sweetest fig
in the world and putting it in my mouth."

20  (Here he'd stop and close his eyes.)

Years passed, we lived in many houses,
none had figtrees.
We had lima beans, zucchini, parsley, beets.
"Plant one!" my mother said,

25  but my father never did.
He tended garden half-heartedly, forgot to water,
let the okra get too big.
"What a dreamer he is. Look how many
things he starts and doesn't finish."

30  The last time he moved, I had a phone call,
my father, in Arabic, chanting a song
I'd never heard. "What's that?"
He took me out to the new yard.
There, in the middle of Dallas, Texas,

35  a tree with the largest, fattest,
sweetest figs in the world.
"It's a figtree song!" he said,
plucking his fruits like ripe tokens,
emblems, assurance

40  of a world that was always his own.

# Comprehension

**INDIANA STANDARDS**

**READING STANDARD**
**8.3.9** Analyze the relevance of setting (places, times, customs) to mood, tone, and meaning of text.

1.  **Recall** Why was it necessary for Naomi Shihab Nye to attend the Armenian school after being expelled from her first school?

2.  **Clarify** Reread lines 130–143. Why was the author angry about her friend's being sent to Damascus?

3.  **Clarify** Why did the family leave Jerusalem?

# Critical Analysis

4.  **Make Connections** Look at the chart you filled in as you read. Which two connections best helped you understand what the author experienced in Jerusalem? Explain.

5.  **Examine Setting** Use a web diagram to identify descriptive details that helped convey the **setting** of this selection. Then expand your web to include insights on how this setting affected the author.

6.  **Analyze Memoir** At what point in the selection does the author become aware of a sense of **belonging** in Jerusalem? Support your answer with examples from the memoir.

7.  **Compare Literary Works** Nye's father encouraged her to try to be happy in Jerusalem and to learn to appreciate the "exquisite oddity" of her life. What does the poem "My Father and the Figtree" on page 391 reveal about her father's feelings toward living in different places?

# Extension and Challenge

8.  **Creative Project: Music** Naomi Shihab Nye belongs to two cultures. If this memoir were to be made into a television show or a documentary, an appropriate soundtrack might feature American music as well as music from the Middle East. Divide this selection into parts and note which type of music should accompany each part.

9.   SOCIAL STUDIES CONNECTION Learn more about Jerusalem— its history, geographical setting, and culture. Present your information in the form of a colorful poster.

> **RESEARCH LINKS**
> For more on Jerusalem, visit the **Research Center** at **ClassZone.com**.

# Vocabulary in Context

## VOCABULARY PRACTICE

Show that you understand the vocabulary words by deciding if each statement is true or false.

1. A **valiant** action is a coward's way out.
2. If a pattern is **intricate,** it has a complicated design.
3. If you are given a **stipulation,** a condition of some kind is involved.
4. People who **emigrate** live in the same country their whole lives.

## VOCABULARY IN WRITING

Have you ever moved to a new country? If not, imagine what it must be like. Write a paragraph describing your experience, using two or more vocabulary words. You could start like this.

> **EXAMPLE SENTENCE**
>
> I made a **valiant** attempt to speak a few words to my new classmates.

## VOCABULARY STRATEGY: RECOGNIZING BASE WORDS

To understand an unfamiliar word with affixes (prefixes and suffixes), it helps to identify the base word first. Look within the word for a word that is familiar to you, though the spelling might be different. For example, in the word *emigrate,* you might notice the base word *migrate.* In cases where you do not recognize a base word, you may need to use context clues to figure out the meaning.

*PRACTICE* Define each boldfaced word. Then give the base word and affixes. Use a dictionary if necessary.

1. The heavy rainfall was causing **erosion** of the soil.
2. He admired the professor for her **wisdom** and knowledge.
3. The most difficult part of the journey was the **navigation** of the river rapids.
4. It was her turn in the **rotation** to take the dog for a walk.
5. Did she accept his **proposal** of marriage?

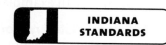

**INDIANA STANDARDS**

READING STANDARD
**8.1.3** Verify the meaning of a word in its context . . . .

**VOCABULARY PRACTICE**
For more practice, go to the **Vocabulary Center** at ClassZone.com.

# Reading-Writing Connection

Increase your understanding of "Going Where I'm Coming From" by responding to these prompts. Then complete the **Grammar and Writing** exercise.

| WRITING PROMPTS | SELF-CHECK |
|---|---|
| **A. Short Response: Analyze the Message**<br>Based on Nye's experience, do you think a person can truly **belong** in two places? In **one paragraph,** explain your opinion by citing from the memoir. | *A convincing response will . . .*<br>• state your position<br>• use details from the text |
| **B. Extended Response: Write a Letter**<br>When in Jerusalem, Nye wrote letters to her friends in the U.S. What do you think she said about life in her new country? Write a **two- or three-paragraph letter** that she might have sent. | *A realistic letter will . . .*<br>• be written in the first-person point of view<br>• contain details about people, places, and events |

## GRAMMAR AND WRITING

*MAINTAIN SUBJECT-VERB AGREEMENT* Pronouns that do not refer to a specific person, place, thing, or idea are called **indefinite pronouns.** Some indefinite pronouns are always singular, some are always plural, and some can be either singular or plural. Here are some common indefinite pronouns.

**INDIANA STANDARDS**

**WRITING STANDARD**
**8.4.8** Edit and proofread one's own writing, as well as that of others . . . .

| Singular | | Plural | | Singular or Plural | |
|---|---|---|---|---|---|
| anyone | neither | both | many | any | none |
| each | something | few | several | most | some |

If the pronoun can be singular or plural, use context clues to help you determine what verb to use with it. If the noun that the pronoun refers to is singular, use a singular verb; if it is plural, use a plural verb.

*Original:* Most of the students in the school was boys.

*Revised:* Most of the students in the school were boys.

**PRACTICE** Choose the verb form that agrees with each indefinite pronoun.

1. Both children (misses, miss) their favorite foods from back home.
2. Several students at the Armenian school (likes, like) Naomi.
3. According to dress code, each child (wear, wears) a white smock.
4. Though many of the shepherds are shy, some (wants, want) to talk to people.

*For more help with subject-verb agreement with indefinite pronouns, see page R66 in the **Grammar Handbook**.*

**The Story of an Eyewitness**
Magazine Article by Jack London

**Letter from New Orleans: Leaving Desire**
Magazine Article by Jon Lee Anderson

# What is the role of a
# WITNESS?

**INDIANA STANDARDS**

**READING STANDARDS**
**8.2.3** Find similarities and differences between texts in the treatment, amount of coverage, or organization of ideas.

**8.2.7** Analyze the structure, format, and purpose of informational materials (such as textbooks, newspapers, instructional or technical manuals, and public documents).

**KEY IDEA** When events such as natural disasters, crimes, and wars occur, it's important that a **witness** describe what happened so that others can learn from these events. Witnesses have played an important role in reporting everything from local sports to the events in your history textbook. The authors of the accounts you are about to read each witnessed natural disasters. Their writing allowed people from around the world to share in their experiences.

**ROLE-PLAY** Picture the tornadoes, hurricanes, floods, and snow storms you have seen in the news. Imagine that one of these disasters has just struck your community. With a partner, role-play an evening news broadcast on the disaster. Decide who will be the news reporter and who will be the eyewitness. Then conduct an interview. Remember that your audience will want to know what the disaster looked, sounded, and felt like, as well as how people got hurt or stayed safe.

## ● ELEMENTS OF NONFICTION: SCOPE

When writers choose how much of a subject to focus on, they're deciding on the **scope** of their accounts. The scope can be broad or narrow. For example, an article about Austin, Texas, that focuses on the city's history, economy, and residents has a broad scope. An article that focuses only on the music scene in Austin has a narrow scope.

The following eyewitness accounts describe two different natural disasters. As you read each one, try to determine its scope by considering these questions:

- How well do you get to know the people you meet?
- How much of the disaster area does the writer cover?
- How many events do you learn about? How much time do these events span?

## ● READING STRATEGY: SET A PURPOSE FOR READING

When you **set a purpose** for reading, you identify what you want to accomplish as you read. Your purpose for reading the following articles is to compare and contrast their scopes. As you read the first account, begin filling in the chart.

|  | *"The Story of an Eyewitness"* | *"Letter from New Orleans: Leaving Desire"* |
|---|---|---|
| *What is the topic?* |  |  |
| *Whom does the writer focus on?* |  |  |
| *How much of the disaster area does the writer cover?* |  |  |
| *Which events does the writer focus on?* |  |  |

## ▲ VOCABULARY IN CONTEXT

These words help the authors capture the impact of a disaster. Create a chart and place each word in the appropriate column.

| WORD LIST | | |
|---|---|---|
| compel | intermittently | menace |
| disconcert | lavishly | vigilantly |

| *Know Well* | *Think I Know* | *Don't Know at All* |
|---|---|---|
|  |  |  |

---

# Author On[line]

**Jack London: Nature Enthusiast** Inspired by his experiences as an outdoorsman, sailor, and war correspondent, Jack London became the most popular novelist of his time. He is still known throughout the world for *The Call of the Wild* and *The Sea Wolf.*

**Jack London
1876–1916**

**Jon Lee Anderson: Investigative Journalist** Jon Lee Anderson always wanted to be an explorer. Now, as a correspondent for *The New Yorker,* he travels around the world reporting on war, politics, and international affairs.

**Jon Lee Anderson
born 1957**

**MORE ABOUT THE AUTHOR**
For more about the authors, visit the **Literature Center** at **ClassZone.com.**

## Background

**San Francisco Earthquake** At 5:12 A.M. on April 18, 1906, a massive earthquake shook San Francisco, setting in motion events that would eventually destroy most of the city. Historians estimate that around 3,000 people died and 250,000 people were left homeless.

**Hurricane Katrina** Hurricane Katrina hit the Gulf Coast on the morning of August 29, 2005. New Orleans suffered some of the worst damage of the Gulf Coast cities. Heavy flooding there destroyed entire neighborhoods, forced thousands of people to flee the city, and stranded many others in dangerous and unsanitary conditions until they, too, could get out.

# The Story of an Eyewitness

## JACK LONDON

People on Russian Hill look toward San Francisco's downtown.

**ANALYZE VISUALS**
How much of San Francisco is captured in this image? Based on the **scope** of this photograph, make a **prediction** about the scope of this article.

*Upon receipt of the first news of the earthquake, Collier's telegraphed to Mr. Jack London—who lives only forty miles from San Francisco—requesting him to go to the scene of the disaster and write the story of what he saw. Mr. London started at once, and he sent the following dramatic description of the tragic events he witnessed in the burning city.*

The earthquake shook down in San Francisco hundreds of thousands of dollars worth of walls and chimneys. But the conflagration[1] that followed burned up hundreds of millions of dollars' worth of property. There is no estimating within hundreds of millions the actual damage wrought. Not in history has a modern imperial city been so completely destroyed.

---

1. **conflagration** (kŏn'flə-grā'shən): a large destructive fire.

San Francisco is gone. Nothing remains of it but memories and a fringe of dwelling houses on its outskirts. Its industrial section is wiped out. Its business section is wiped out. Its social and residential section is wiped out. The factories and warehouses, the great stores and newspaper buildings, the hotels and the palaces of the nabobs,[2] are all gone. Remains only the fringe of dwelling houses on the outskirts of what was once San Francisco. **Ⓐ**

Within an hour after the earthquake shock the smoke of San Francisco's burning was a lurid[3] tower visible a hundred miles away. And for three days and nights this lurid tower swayed in the sky, reddening the sun, darkening the day, and filling the land with smoke.

On Wednesday morning at a quarter past five came the earthquake. A minute later the flames were leaping upward. In a dozen different quarters south of Market Street, in the working-class ghetto, and in the factories, fires started. There was no opposing the flames. There was no organization, no communication. All the cunning adjustments of a twentieth century city had been smashed by the earthquake. The streets were humped into ridges and depressions, and piled with the debris of fallen walls. The steel rails were twisted into perpendicular and horizontal angles. The telephone and telegraph systems were disrupted. And the great water-mains had burst. All the shrewd contrivances[4] and safeguards of man had been thrown out of gear by thirty seconds' twitching of the earth-crust.

### The Fire Made Its Own Draft

By Wednesday afternoon, inside of twelve hours, half the heart of the city was gone. At that time I watched the vast conflagration from out on the bay. It was dead calm. Not a flicker of wind stirred. Yet from every side wind was pouring in upon the city. East, west, north, and south, strong winds were blowing upon the doomed city. The heated air rising made an enormous vacuum. Thus did the fire of itself build its own colossal chimney through the atmosphere. Day and night this dead calm continued, and yet, near to the flames, the wind was often half a gale, so mighty was the vacuum.

Wednesday night saw the destruction of the very heart of the city. Dynamite was **lavishly** used, and many of San Francisco's proudest structures were crumbled by man himself into ruins, but there was no withstanding the onrush of the flames. Time and again successful stands were made by the fire-fighters, and every time the flames flanked[5] around on either side or came up from the rear, and turned to defeat

Lines: 10, 20, 30, 40

**Ⓐ SCOPE**
How much of the city is Jack London describing in this paragraph?

**lavishly** (lăv'ĭsh-lē) *adv.* extravagantly

---

2. **nabobs** (nā'bŏbz'): people of wealth and prominence.
3. **lurid** (lŏŏr'ĭd): glowing with the glare of fire through a haze.
4. **contrivances** (kən-trī'vən-sĕz): acts of clever planning.
5. **flanked** (flăngk'd): placed at the side of.

ANALYZE VISUALS
What can you **infer** from this photo about the strength of the San Francisco earthquake?

**B SCOPE**
What aspects of the disaster is London describing?

**C SCOPE**
So far, has London described individuals or crowds? Tell what this suggests about the scope of his account.

the hard-won victory. An enumeration[6] of the buildings destroyed would be a directory of San Francisco. An enumeration of the buildings undestroyed would be a line and several addresses. An enumeration of the deeds of heroism would stock a library and bankrupt 50 the Carnegie medal fund. An enumeration of the dead will never be made. All vestiges[7] of them were destroyed by the flames. The number of the victims of the earthquake will never be known. South of Market Street, where the loss of life was particularly heavy, was the first to catch fire. **B**

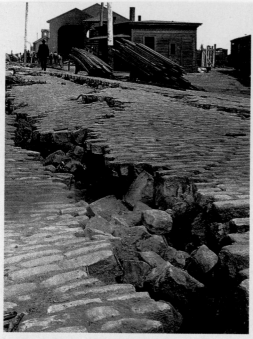

A street along San Francisco's waterfront, cracked during the earthquake

60   Remarkable as it may seem, Wednesday night while the whole city crashed and roared into ruin, was a quiet night. There were no crowds. There was no shouting and yelling. There was no hysteria, no disorder. I passed Wednesday night in the path of the advancing flames, and in all those terrible hours I saw not one woman who wept, not one man who was excited, not one person who was in the slightest degree panic stricken.

   Before the flames, throughout the night, fled tens of thousands of homeless ones. Some were wrapped in blankets. Others carried bundles of bedding and dear household treasures. Sometimes a whole family was harnessed to a carriage or delivery wagon that was weighted down with 70 their possessions. Baby buggies, toy wagons, and go-carts were used as trucks, while every other person was dragging a trunk. Yet everybody was gracious. The most perfect courtesy obtained. Never in all San Francisco's history were her people so kind and courteous as on this night of terror.

### A Caravan of Trunks

All night these tens of thousands fled before the flames. Many of them, the poor people from the labor ghetto, had fled all day as well. They had left their homes burdened with possessions. Now and again they lightened up, flinging out upon the street clothing and treasures they had dragged for miles. **C**

---

6. **enumeration** (ĭ-nōo′mə-rā′shŭn): the act of counting or listing one by one.

7. **vestiges** (vĕs′tĭj-əs): visible signs that something once existed.

Troops walk east along Market Street as the Call Building burns in the distance.

ANALYZE VISUALS
Which **detail** from this photograph best helps you understand the devastation to the city?

I went inside with the owner of the house on the steps of which I sat. He
150 was cool and cheerful and hospitable. "Yesterday morning," he said, "I was
worth six hundred thousand dollars. This morning this house is all I have
left. It will go in fifteen minutes. He pointed to a large cabinet. "That is my
wife's collection of china. This rug upon which we stand is a present. It cost
fifteen hundred dollars. Try that piano. Listen to its tone. There are few like
it. There are no horses. The flames will be here in fifteen minutes." **F**

Outside the old Mark Hopkins residence a palace was just catching fire.
The troops were falling back and driving the refugees before them. From
every side came the roaring of flames, the crashing of walls, and the
detonations of dynamite.

### The Dawn of the Second Day

160 I passed out of the house. Day was trying to dawn through the smoke-pall.[11]
A sickly light was creeping over the face of things. Once only the sun broke
through the smoke-pall, blood-red, and showing a quarter its usual size.
The smoke-pall itself, viewed from beneath, was a rose color that pulsed and
fluttered with lavender shades. Then it turned to mauve and yellow and dun.[12]
There was no sun. And so dawned the second day on stricken San Francisco.

An hour later I was creeping past the shattered dome of the City Hall.
Than it there was no better exhibit of the destructive force of the
earthquake. Most of the stone had been shaken from the great dome,
leaving standing the naked framework of steel. Market Street was piled
170 high with the wreckage, and across the wreckage lay the overthrown pillars
of the City Hall shattered into short crosswise sections.

**F** SCOPE
Reread lines 129–155.
What do you notice about how these people are described?

---

11. **pall** (pôl): a covering that darkens or covers.
12. **dun** (dŭn): dull brownish gray.

This section of the city, with the exception of the Mint and the Post-Office, was already a waste of smoking ruins. Here and there through the smoke, creeping warily under the shadows of tottering walls, emerged occasional men and women. It was like the meeting of the handful of survivors after the day of the end of the world.

### Beeves Slaughtered and Roasted

On Mission Street lay a dozen steers, in a neat row stretching across the street just as they had been struck down by the flying ruins of the earthquake. The fire had passed through afterward and roasted them.
180 The human dead had been carried away before the fire came. At another place on Mission Street I saw a milk wagon. A steel telegraph pole had smashed down sheer through the driver's seat and crushed the front wheels. The milk cans lay scattered around.

All day Thursday and all Thursday night, all day Friday and Friday night, the flames still raged on.

Friday night saw the flames finally conquered, though not until Russian Hill and Telegraph Hill had been swept and three-quarters of a mile of wharves and docks had been licked up. **G**

### The Last Stand

The great stand of the fire-fighters was made Thursday night on Van Ness
190 Avenue. Had they failed here, the comparatively few remaining houses of the city would have been swept. Here were the magnificent residences of the second generation of San Francisco nabobs, and these, in a solid zone, were dynamited down across the path of the fire. Here and there the flames leaped the zone, but these fires were beaten out, principally by the use of wet blankets and rugs. **H**

San Francisco, at the present time, is like the crater of a volcano, around which are camped tens of thousands of refugees. At the Presidio[13] alone are at least twenty thousand. All the surrounding cities and towns are jammed with the homeless ones, where they are being cared for by the relief
200 committees. The refugees were carried free by the railroads to any point they wished to go, and it is estimated that over one hundred thousand people have left the peninsula on which San Francisco stood. The government has the situation in hand, and, thanks to the immediate relief given by the whole United States, there is not the slightest possibility of a famine. The bankers and business men have already set about making preparations to rebuild San Francisco. **I**

---

13. **Presidio** (prĭ-sē′dē-ō′): a historic military post in San Francisco.

**G** SCOPE
What is the main event London tracked from beginning to end?

**H** SCOPE
How much do you learn about what took place Thursday and Friday?

**I** SCOPE
What information about the disaster does London provide in this last paragraph?

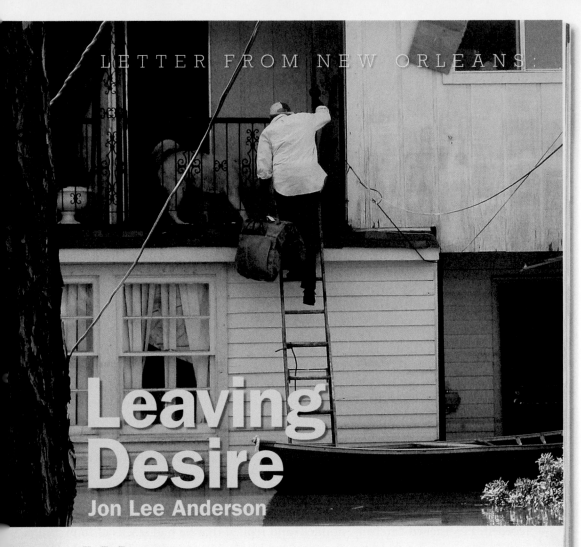

LETTER FROM NEW ORLEANS:

# Leaving Desire
## Jon Lee Anderson

**W**hen I first saw Lionel Petrie, he was standing on the second-story porch of his house, at the junction of Desire Street and North Bunny Friend, in the Ninth Ward of New Orleans. The house was built of wood, with white siding and peach trim. Petrie, an African-American with salt-and-pepper hair and a mustache, appeared to be in his sixties. A large Akita[1] was standing next to him, ears perked **vigilantly.** The two of them looked out from across the fenced-in expanse of the front yard. Petrie was clearly an organized man: a painter's ladder was dangling from the railing of the porch, and a clutch of orange life vests hung within reach of a fibreglass canoe that was tethered to the house. The canoe bobbed on the surface of the stinking black water that filled the street and had engulfed most of the first floor of the house. The spiked parapet of a wrought-iron fence poked up about eight inches above the waterline, etching out a formal square that separated the house from the street. **A**

**vigilantly**
(vĭj′ə-lənt-lē) *adv.* in a state of alertness; watchfully

**A SCOPE**
What is this paragraph about? Note the kind of details provided about the subject.

---

1. **Akita** (ä-kē′tə): a breed of Japanese hunting dog.

Petrie's house was different from those of his neighbors, most of which were small brick row houses, or rundown clapboard houses that had deep porches flush with the street. His was set far back in the lot, and had a self-possessed air about it. Near the fence, in what must have been the driveway, the hoods of two submerged cars and a truck could be seen.

20　　I was seated in the back of a four-person Yamaha WaveRunner that was piloted by Shawn Alladio, an energetic woman in her forties, with long blond hair, from Whittier, California. Eight days had passed since Hurricane Katrina made landfall, and Alladio was out on a search for trapped survivors and for what rescuers were calling "holdouts"—residents who didn't want to leave their homes—in one of the poorest and worst-hit parts of the city, the Ninth Ward, in eastern New Orleans.

Alladio maneuvered the WaveRunner so that we were alongside Petrie's fence, and, after calling out a greeting to him, she asked him if he wanted to leave; he waved politely in response, but shook his head. She told him

30　that the floodwater was toxic and that he would soon become sick. He said something in reply, but we couldn't hear him because of the rumble of the WaveRunner's idling engine. Alladio turned the ignition key off.

Petrie explained that his wife and son and daughter had left the city by car, heading for Baton Rouge, the day before Katrina hit. He didn't know where his family was now, and, if he left, they wouldn't know where he was. He said that he intended to wait for them to come back, and for the waters to go down.

Alladio told him that the authorities were not allowing people to return to this part of New Orleans, and that it might be a month before the waters

40　receded. He listened carefully, nodded, and replied that he had stocks of food and some water; that he'd be all right—he'd wait. He patted his dog's head. "Thank you, but I'll be fine," he said. Alladio tried again. "I can promise you that you will *not* see your family if you stay here," she told him; it was much likelier that he would pass out and die from the fumes from the water. ❸

He asked whether she would promise that he would be able to join his family.

Alladio paused, and said to me quietly, "I can't promise him that. If I turn him over to the authorities, like the other evacuees, he could end up anywhere in the country."

50　Turning back to Petrie, she asked, "If I drive you to Baton Rouge myself, will you come with me?"

"You would take me yourself?" he asked.

"Yes," she said. "I promise. Today, when I am done with my work, I will take you there."

Petrie took a step back on his porch. He raised his head thoughtfully and asked, "Can I take my dog with me?"

❸ **SCOPE**
What do you learn about Petrie's situation and his attitude toward it?

"Oh, God," Alladio said under her breath. "I hate this." Then she said to him, "I am so sorry, Mr. Petrie, but, no, they won't allow us to take out animals. You will have to leave him here."

60 Petrie gripped the railing of the porch and leaned over again, in a kind of slow, sustained forward lurch, his head down. Then he nodded and said, "O.K."

Alladio told Petrie to prepare a small bag with his essential belongings, to say goodbye to his dog and, if he wanted, put out some food and water for him. She would be back in an hour to pick him up; in the meantime, she needed to see if there were more people who needed evacuating. He said, "O.K.," and waved, and went back inside the house. The dog followed him. **C**

Alladio had arrived in New Orleans on Saturday, September 3rd, with a team of California rescue workers and a small flotilla[2] of donated 70 WaveRunners. She and her team were loosely attached to a task force sent by the State of California, but were mostly on their own. We had met at a staging area underneath an elevated section of Interstate 10. As I arrived, evacuees were being brought out of the water to a slightly raised stretch of land where railroad tracks ran under the highway. A boat came up and deposited an elderly black couple. Rescuers carried the woman, who was wearing a denim skirt, a T-shirt, and gold earrings, and sat her down on a fallen telephone pole. She rocked back and forth, with one hand raised, and murmured, "I just want to tell you—thank you, Jesus." Her husband walked over unsteadily to join her. They had stayed at home until just 80 before the hurricane, and then gone to their church. As the water rose, they took refuge in the choir loft. They stayed there for eight days, drinking the water the storm washed in. "We were down to our last two crackers," she said. Another man was brought over, shaking, and speaking incoherently. The only words I could make out were "I'm still alive."

After putting on chest waders to protect ourselves from the fetid[3] floodwaters—which Alladio warned me were "really gnarly"—we set off by boat from Interstate 10. . . .

We passed cargo yards, electrical pylons,[4] and houses with tar-paper roofs that had water halfway up the windows, and other houses that 90 were completely submerged. When we came to the intersection of Louisa Street and Higgins Boulevard, the street signs were at eye level and the traffic lights were barely above the surface of the water. We passed a house with a shattered plate-glass window. Peering down into the living room,

**C SCOPE**
Reread lines 50–67. What does the conversation between Alladio and Petrie reveal about the kind of person Alladio is?

---

2. **flotilla** (flō-tĭl′ə): a small fleet of ships.
3. **fetid** (fĕ′tĭd): having an offensive odor.
4. **electrical pylons** (pī′lŏnz′): steel towers supporting electrical wires.

I saw a sofa floating near a framed photo of Muhammad Ali standing triumphantly over Sonny Liston. At a community swimming pool, a lifeguard seat poked just above the waters. We passed a rowboat carrying two white men and being towed by a black man with dreadlocks, up to his neck in water. Later, we saw them again; all three were in the boat now, and were paddling with broken street signs.

100    It was a clear, hot day, and the floodwater smelled strongly of oil and raw sewage, and stung the eyes. There were other smells, from islands of rotting garbage, and, **intermittently,** as elsewhere in the city, the smell of death. Helicopters had been clattering overhead all morning, some of them dumping buckets of water on house fires that had broken out everywhere. Scudding[5] columns of brown and gray smoke shot up from half a dozen points around the city. The towers of downtown New Orleans were visible in the distance. **Ⓓ**

A New Orleans neighborhood lies under several feet of water.

Until the nineteenth century, the Ninth Ward was a swamp, and, even after it became home to a black and immigrant white community, and
110 was drained (in that order), it was periodically devastated by flooding. During Hurricane Betsy, in 1965, it was hit harder than most of the city, and was underwater for days. The neglect of the Ninth Ward by the city government was notorious; well into the twentieth century, it lacked adequate sewers and clean water. The Norman Rockwell image that the Ninth Ward inspired was that of the first grader Ruby Bridges, a tiny black

---

5. **scudding** (skŭd´ĭng): skimming along swiftly.

**intermittently**
(ĭn´tər-mĭt´nt-lē) *adv.* stopping and starting at intervals

**Ⓓ SCOPE**
What sights, sounds, and smells does the author describe?

**ANALYZE VISUALS**
In what way does this image help you understand the seriousness of Lionel Petrie's situation?

girl in a white dress, who was led to school by federal marshals past jeering white crowds—a chapter in a violent desegregation struggle that divided the city in the nineteen-sixties. In the next decades, many of the white residents of the Ninth Ward left; by the time Katrina hit, almost all the
120 students in the school that Ruby Bridges integrated were black.

At 2037 Desire, a block past Petrie's home, three people stood on the second-floor porch of a large wooden house: a bulky young woman in a white blouse, with dyed orange hair, and tattoos on one arm; a young man with copper skin in a lilac polo shirt . . . and an old man who was bare-chested except for a pair of red suspenders. The ground floor was flooded and a sign above it said, "Winner Supermarket—ATM Inside." Alladio hailed them and repeated the argument that she had made to Petrie. The young man said that his name was Theron Green, and that he and his father, Alfred Green, the old man, and his fiancée—Trinell Sanson, the tattooed woman—
130 were fine, and were planning to stay. They also had a friend inside the house, they said. Theron Green spoke in a thick local accent, and his eyes were alert and suspicious. He was clearly anxious for us to leave. "We feel comfortable, safe in our own house here," he said. "Anyway, I don't want no looters coming here." Alladio told him that there would soon be forced evacuations, but Green was adamant. "I'll wait till they force me out, then," he said. Trinell Sanson said, "We're fine. If it gets too bad, we'll catch the helicopter.". . .

Alladio warned me not to get spattered by the floodwater. "The people who have been in this are going to get sick," she said. The Environmental Protection Agency had teams out taking water samples to check for toxins,
140 and the rumor—apparently unfounded—was that entire districts were so contaminated that they would have to be razed, along with hundreds of thousands of vehicles. The people who lived there might not realize it, she said, "but once they leave they are never going to see their homes again.". . .

When we returned to Petrie's house, he was packed and waiting for us on the second-floor porch, dressed in slacks, a fresh unbuttoned shirt over a T-shirt, and a Marine Corps baseball cap. He leaned down to his dog, took both its ears in his hands and caressed them, and then told the dog to go inside. Petrie climbed into the canoe and began paddling over to us. The dog reemerged on the balcony, appearing **disconcerted** and watchful.
150 Petrie did not look back. He came alongside the fence and we helped him first with a bag and then with a little black case that he said had his wife's Bible in it. "I know she'd want me to bring that," he said. He climbed onto the WaveRunner behind me. Alladio gave the vessel a little power, and we began moving off. **E**

**disconcert** (dĭs′kən-sûrt′) *v.* to ruffle; to frustrate by throwing into disorder

**E** SCOPE
What event has this article focused on so far?

As we made our way down Desire, Petrie looked around him at the devastation, his neighbors' houses submerged in water. He said, "Oh, my God. I had no idea."

I asked him why he hadn't left earlier. "You tell yourself that the waters are going to recede, and when they don't one day you say maybe they will 160 the next," he answered.

The waters had subsided somewhat after the initial surge, he said. Then he had noticed, as the days went by, that there was an ebb and flow to them, as if a tide were moving in and out. To his mind, the city had become part of Lake Pontchartrain. He had heard on the radio about the levees breaking. When the electricity went out, he had listened to the radio each night, but had turned it off after a little while, to save his batteries.

As we spoke, he seemed to be trying to make sense of his own reaction to the catastrophe. He had understood logically that he was stranded and in danger, and yet he had decided that his first priority was to remain and 170 prepare the house for his family's return: "Pretty crazy, huh? I even started repairing my roof." About a third of the roof had been torn away by the hurricane, and he had worked for several days patching it up while the city lay underwater. . . .

When we passed Theron Green's house, he and his father and his fiancée waved and smiled at Petrie. . . .

Petrie told me that he was worried about his aunt Willa Mae Butler: "She's about eighty-two, and lives on Bartholomew Street. I'm worried that she's dead, because this time she said she wasn't going."

As we travelled slowly back toward Interstate 10, avoiding debris and 180 downed electrical lines, Petrie began calling out landmarks. He had lived in the neighborhood his entire life. As a child, he had lived on Louisa Street. He pointed to a building that he said was the primary school he had attended from kindergarten through eighth grade. . . . **F**

By now, he was reconciled to his rescue. "I think the good Lord sent you to me," he said. "I am looking forward to seeing my wife!" Her name was Mildred. He was sixty-four and Mildred was sixty-one. They had married when she was seventeen and he was twenty. "Everyone said we wouldn't last, but we've been together forty-five years, and this is the first time we have been apart.". . .

190 After we landed, Shawn Alladio went out on one more tour of the neighborhood to see if there was anyone else to bring in. While we waited for her to return, Petrie and I sat in my rented van in the shade under Interstate 10. Nearby, rescuers stripped down and washed in solutions of water and bleach. . . .

**F SCOPE**
How much of New Orleans is this article covering? Tell how you know.

A man crosses a flooded New Orleans street.

**ANALYZE VISUALS**
What **details** in this photograph help you understand how deep the water is?

Petrie told me about his own children. Lionel, his namesake, forty-three years old, had been in the Marine Corps for fifteen years and served in the first Gulf War. He had been an aviation mechanic, but when he got out he couldn't get a job, so he went back to school, at the University of New Orleans, where he was pursuing an undergraduate degree when the
200  hurricane arrived. Lionel owned two houses, one just blocks away from Petrie's, which he rented out. Petrie's second son, Bruce, who was thirty-eight, had also been a marine, had an accounting degree, and worked as a shelter supervisor for Girls and Boys Town. Bruce had driven out of the city with his wife and children before Katrina. Petrie smiled when he spoke of his daughter, Crystal, who was twenty-one. She was studying nursing in New Orleans. Lionel had driven her and their mother out of the city. **G**

Petrie hadn't gone to college; he got hired at a shipyard right after high school. After a couple of years, he decided to train as a welder. "For a year, I went to welders' school from 8 A.M. to noon and worked at American
210  Marine from 6 P.M. until 6 A.M. Got my certificate as a certified welder around 1962. I went to several places looking for a job as a welder, but never got hired." When, in 1965, Petrie went to apply for a job at Equitable Equipment, near his home, he saw white welders being hired even as he was told that the only openings were for laborers. He contacted the local N.A.A.C.P. and filed a complaint with the newly formed Equal Employment Opportunity Commission. "They took an interest in my case, and I was the first black to be hired as a skilled worker by Equitable," he said. "I would sit down to eat my lunch and the white guys would go

**G** **SCOPE**
What do you learn about Petrie in this paragraph?

sit somewhere else. I didn't care—I was just there to do my job." After
220 working for a decade at Equitable, and then at Kaiser Aluminum until
1983, when it shut down its Louisiana operations, he decided to set up his
own business, Petrie Iron and Construction. He didn't have insurance,
though, and he figured that he'd lost everything.

Later that evening, Alladio drove Petrie and me to Baton Rouge in a
rented pickup, towing her WaveRunner behind her. She had been told
that forced evacuations would begin soon, and that the operation would
shift toward law enforcement. She was leaving the next day. **Ⓗ**

In his exhaustion, Petrie had not been able to remember any telephone
numbers, but, as we drove along, cell-phone numbers for his son Bruce and
230 his daughter came back to him. I handed him my phone, and a minute
later I heard him say, "They're in Memphis!"

When he hung up, he said that his wife and daughter were staying in
Memphis at a cousin's house. Lionel had already found some temporary
factory work. Bruce was staying with his wife's family, in Kentucky. Willa
Mae Butler, Petrie's aunt, was alive and in Texas. Bruce was going to look
on the Internet for a flight for his father from Baton Rouge to Memphis.

A little while later, as we drove into the night, Petrie said reflectively,
"I don't know if I want to go back to New Orleans—seeing it how it was,
I don't think I do." He doubted, from what he had seen, that much of
240 it could ever be rebuilt. "The first thing I picture now is the water I saw
when I was coming out," he said.

A few minutes afterward, Bruce called back to say that the next available
flight was in three days' time. Alladio suggested that we try the Greyhound
station instead. It was already late when we arrived at the scruffy little
bus station in Baton Rouge, full of refugees from New Orleans. I joined a
long line of people waiting for information and tickets. Half an hour later,
it had barely moved. A man and a woman were arguing, and when the
stationmaster called for passengers for Houston, I heard the man tell her, "I
don't care what you say—I'm getting on that bus." After he left, the woman
250 leaned against a pillar and wiped her eyes. A tall man with a stack of religious
tracts was reciting Psalms from memory, and a woman made subdued sounds
of agreement or said, "That's right," in a rhythmic cadence. Two policemen
patrolled the station; there were a number of young men who looked street-
wise and seemed to be loitering among the waiting passengers.

Around midnight, Bruce called again. He had resolved to drive down
from Kentucky to get his father. He would leave shortly with his wife,
Donna. Lionel Petrie would wait for them in the Greyhound station. Bruce
thought that if he and Donna took turns driving they could make the trip
in twelve hours. They were there by noon the next day. **Ⓘ**

**Ⓗ** SCOPE
What information do
you get about Alladio?

**Ⓘ** SCOPE
Over what span of time
did the events in this
account take place?

## Comprehension

**INDIANA STANDARDS**

**READING STANDARD**
**8.2.7** Analyze the structure, format, and purpose of informational materials . . . .

1. **Recall** In "The Story of an Eyewitness," how much of San Francisco does Jack London say was destroyed by the earthquake and the fire that came afterward?

2. **Clarify** What span of time does London's account cover?

3. **Clarify** In "Letter from New Orleans," why is Lionel Petrie reluctant to leave his home?

## Critical Analysis

4. **Examine Scope** Which passage in "The Story of an Eyewitness" best helped you understand the extent of the tragedy that struck San Francisco? Explain.

5. **Evaluate Objectivity** An **objective** report is one that is fair, neutral, and evenhanded. Do you think that Jack London's account is objective? Cite evidence from the text to support your opinion.

6. **Make Judgments** The authorities forced thousands of people to leave behind their pets during the evacuation of New Orleans. Was it right to ask people to abandon their pets? Why or why not?

7. **Evaluate Accounts** Think about the two articles you have just read. Which account do you think is more powerful? Explain your opinion.

## Comparing Articles

Now that you've read both articles, finish filling in your chart. Then add the final question, and answer it, too.

| | *"The Story of an Eyewitness"* | *"Letter from New Orleans: Leaving Desire"* |
|---|---|---|
| *What is the topic?* | the San Francisco earthquake of 1906 | |
| *Whom does the writer focus on?* | | |
| *How much of the disaster area does the writer cover?* | | |
| *Which events does the writer focus on?* | | |
| *How would you describe the scope of the account?* | | |

# Vocabulary in Context

## VOCABULARY PRACTICE

Answer each question to show your understanding of the vocabulary words.

1. Would a **lavishly** decorated home be simple or elegant?
2. Is a **menace** something to avoid or to look forward to?
3. If you **disconcert** people, do you confuse them or calm them?
4. If you **compel** people to do something, are you forcing them or inviting them?
5. Would a person who watches **vigilantly** be alert or distracted?
6. Which sound would be heard **intermittently**—thunder or a steady siren?

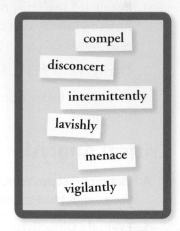

compel

disconcert

intermittently

lavishly

menace

vigilantly

## VOCABULARY IN WRITING

Imagine you volunteered to help in New Orleans after the hurricane. Using at least two vocabulary words, describe what you might have experienced. Here is a sample beginning.

> **EXAMPLE SENTENCE**
>
> *The hurricane was a **menace** to the city.*

## VOCABULARY STRATEGY: THE PREFIX *inter-*

A prefix is a word part attached to the beginning of a base word or root word. When a prefix is added, a new word is formed. The vocabulary word *intermittently* contains the prefix *inter-*, which means "between," added to the Latin word meaning "to let go." If you know the meaning of a prefix, it can help you figure out the meaning of an unfamiliar word, especially if you consider the word's context.

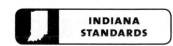

**INDIANA STANDARDS**

**READING STANDARD**
**8.1.3** Verify the meaning of a word in its context ....

*PRACTICE* The boldfaced words all contain the prefix *inter-*. Use your knowledge of this prefix and the base word to write a definition for each word. Remember to use context clues or a dictionary if you need help.

1. The twins looked so similar, they could be **interchanged** and no one would know.
2. The puzzle pieces **interlock** so that they won't come apart.
3. An **international** commission was established to study world hunger.
4. I have to pass the **intermediate** course before I can move on to the advanced level.
5. We took the **interstate** highway on our drive from New York to Ohio.

**VOCABULARY PRACTICE**
For more practice, go to the **Vocabulary Center** at ClassZone.com.

# Writing for Assessment

## 1. READ THE PROMPT

The two articles you've just read cover similar subjects in different ways. In writing assessments, you might be asked to compare such selections.

---

**PROMPT**

"The Story of an Eyewitness" and "Letter from New Orleans: Leaving Desire" are both eyewitness accounts of natural disasters. In four or five paragraphs, contrast the scope, or range of focus, of each article's disaster coverage. Use details from the articles to explain the differences between how people, places, and events are covered. Also explain how you think the scope affects the reader.

---

◀ **STRATEGIES IN ACTION**

1. I need to **identify the range of focus** of each article.
2. I need to **state the differences** between the articles' scopes.
3. I need to **support my statement with examples** about people, places, and events.
4. I need to **explain the effect** of each article's scope on the reader.

## 2. PLAN YOUR WRITING

To identify the scope of each reporter's disaster coverage, review the chart you completed. Write a thesis statement that tells how each article's scope differs. Then think about how you will set up the body of your response.

I. Introduction
II. Scope of first article
III. Scope of second article
IV. Conclusion

- Option A: In one paragraph, describe the scope of the first article's coverage of people, places, and events. In the next paragraph, describe the other article's scope.

- Option B: In one paragraph, contrast the way each article covers people. In the next paragraph, contrast the way each covers places. In the third, contrast the number of events covered.

Once you have decided on your approach, create an outline to organize your details.

## 3. DRAFT YOUR RESPONSE

**Introduction** Provide the titles and authors of both articles, a brief description of what each article is about, and your thesis statement.

**Body** With your outline as a guide, discuss the differences in the scope of each article, using details about the writers' coverage of people, places, and events as support.

**Conclusion** Restate your thesis statement, and leave your reader with a final thought about the role that scope plays in each of these articles.

**Revision** Double-check to make sure your thesis statement clearly presents the ideas you develop in your body paragraphs.

## Mi Madre
Poem by Pat Mora

## Canyon de Chelly
Poem by Simon J. Ortiz

# *What gifts does the* EARTH *provide?*

**INDIANA STANDARDS**

**READING STANDARDS**
**8.3.1** Determine and articulate the relationship between the purposes and characteristics of different forms of poetry (including ballads, lyrics, couplets, epics, elegies, odes, and sonnets).

**8.3.6** Identify significant literary devices . . . .

*KEY IDEA* It's not hard to appreciate nature when you're taking a walk on a sunny day or swimming at a scenic beach. But the **earth** gives us many gifts that we may not always recognize. The gas that warms our homes, the concrete we use to pave our sidewalks, even the paper we write on—these things are all precious resources provided to us by the earth. The poets whose works you're about to read share their appreciation for the earth's gifts through words.

*LIST IT* The earth's resources can be used in multiple ways. In a small group, choose one of the resources shown, and brainstorm at least five ways we can use it. Did you discover any new uses for these resources? Share your list with the class.

dirt          trees

plants        water

rocks         wind

sunlight

## ● LITERARY ANALYSIS: IMAGERY

The use of description that makes something seem real or easy to imagine is called **imagery.** Poets create imagery by using words and phrases that appeal to our senses of sight, hearing, smell, taste, and touch. Paying attention to imagery can enable you to "experience" a poem as if you were there. For example, look at the following lines from "Mi Madre":

*I say tease me.*
*She sprinkles raindrops in my face on a sunny day.*

The image "sprinkles raindrops" appeals to the sense of touch, while "sunny day" appeals to the sense of sight. If you combine these images in your mind, you can almost share in this scene. As you read "Mi Madre" and "Canyon de Chelly," use a word web to keep track of these and other examples of imagery.

## ◑ READING SKILL: UNDERSTAND SPEAKER

In poetry, the **speaker** is the voice that "talks" to the reader and relates the ideas presented in the poem from a specific point of view. It is important to understand that the speaker is not the same as the poet. For example, a poet may choose to write about a subject from the perspective of a child. In that case, the ideas that are expressed are those of the child, not necessarily the poet. As you read "Mi Madre" and "Canyon de Chelly," look for clues that will help you decide who each speaker is and how he or she feels about the subject of the poem.

# Author Online

**Pat Mora: Literacy Advocate** The granddaughter of Mexican immigrants, Pat Mora realized early in her writing career that her cultural heritage was "a source of pride." Her books celebrate family, the desert in which she grew up, and the Mexican-American experience. Her children's books frequently feature Latino characters, because she believes that children of all backgrounds should see themselves reflected in the books they read.

**Pat Mora**
**born 1942**

**Simon J. Ortiz: Native New Mexican** Raised on New Mexico's Acoma Pueblo, Simon Ortiz is regarded as one of today's greatest Native-American writers. His work frequently focuses on having a sense of place. "You have to have it," Ortiz says. "Otherwise you are drifting." Ortiz hopes that all people can learn from his poetry. "I tell you about me and my world," he says, "so you may be able to see yourself."

**Simon J. Ortiz**
**born 1941**

 **MORE ABOUT THE AUTHOR**
For more on Pat Mora and Simon J. Ortiz, visit the **Literature Center** at **ClassZone.com.**

## *Background*

Arizona's Canyon de Chelly (pronounced *shā*) is home to a Navajo tribal community that has preserved this sacred land for centuries. The canyon, now a national park, is known for its stunning landscapes, tribal artifacts, and rock paintings.

# MI MADRE[1]

## Pat Mora

I say feed me.
She serves red prickly pear on a spiked cactus.

I say tease me.
She sprinkles raindrops in my face on a sunny day.

5 I say frighten me.
She shouts thunder, flashes lightning. **Ⓐ**

I say comfort me.
She invites me to lay on her firm body.

I say heal me.
10 She gives me *manzanilla, orégano, dormilón.*[2]

I say caress me.
She strokes my skin with her warm breath. **Ⓑ**

I say make me beautiful.
She offers turquoise for my fingers, a pink blossom for my hair. **Ⓒ**

15 I say sing to me.
She chants lonely women's songs of femaleness.

I say teach me.
She endures: glaring heat
             numbing cold
20           frightening dryness.

She: the desert
She: strong mother.

---

1. **Mi Madre** (mē mä′drā) *Spanish:* my mother.

2. *manzanilla, orégano, dormilón* (mǎn′zə-nē′yə, ə-rĕg′ə-nō′, dôr-mē-lŏn′) *Spanish:* sweet-smelling herbs that can be used to make home medicines.

*Prickly Pear*, Isabel Bronson Cartwright. Oil on canvas. Private collection. © Peter Harholt/SuperStock.

**ANALYZE VISUALS**
**Compare** this painting with your own mental image of the desert. Are the images similar or different?

**Ⓐ IMAGERY**
Reread lines 1–6. To what senses do these images appeal? Record your answers in your word web.

**Ⓑ IMAGERY**
Reread lines 11–12. What feelings does this image suggest?

**Ⓒ SPEAKER**
What type of person is the speaker? How do you know?

# CANYON DE CHELLY

## Simon J. Ortiz

Lie on your back on stone,
the stone carved to fit
the shape of yourself.
Who made it like this,
5 knowing that I would be along
in a million years and look
at the sky being blue forever?

My son is near me. He sits
and turns on his butt
10 and crawls over to stones,
picks one up and holds it,
and then puts it into his mouth.
The taste of stone.
What is it but stone,
15 the earth in your mouth.
You, son, are tasting forever. **D**

**ANALYZE VISUALS**
Is this a photograph or
a painting? Tell what
led you to your answer,
and why others might
**conclude** differently.

**D SPEAKER**
What do you know about
the speaker of this poem?

© George H. H. Huey/Corbis.

We walk to the edge of cliff
and look down into the canyon.
On this side, we cannot see
20 the bottom cliff edge but looking
further out, we see fields,
sand furrows, cottonwoods.
In winter, they are softly gray.
The cliffs' shadows are distant,
25 hundreds of feet below;
we cannot see our own shadows.
The wind moves softly into us.
My son laughs with the wind;
he gasps and laughs. **E**

30 We find gray root, old wood,
so old, with curious twists
in it, curving back into curves,
juniper, piñon, or something
with hard, red berries in spring.
35 You taste them, and they are sweet
and bitter, the berries a delicacy
for bluejays. The plant rooted
fragilely into a sandy place
by a canyon wall, the sun bathing
40 shiny, pointed leaves.

My son touches the root carefully,
aware of its ancient quality.
He lays his soft, small fingers on it
and looks at me for information.
45 I tell him: wood, an old root,
and around it, the earth, ourselves. **F**

**E IMAGERY**
Reread lines 27–29.
Add the images in these
lines to your web. What
emotions do these
images suggest?

**F SPEAKER**
Reread lines 41–46. Why
do you think the speaker
brings his son to the
canyon?

# Comprehension

1. **Recall** In "Mi Madre," how does the desert heal the speaker?

2. **Recall** In "Canyon de Chelly," what two things does the speaker's son taste?

3. **Represent** Reread lines 13–14 from "Mi Madre" and lines 17–22 from "Canyon de Chelly." Choose one of these groups of lines and sketch the image created in your mind.

**INDIANA STANDARDS**

**READING STANDARD**
**8.3.1** Determine and articulate the relationship between . . . different forms of poetry . . . .

# Literary Analysis

4. **Interpret Poem** In "Mi Madre," the speaker refers to the desert as a "strong mother." How is the desert in the poem like a mother?

5. **Make Inferences** Reread the first three lines of "Canyon de Chelly." To whom do you think the speaker is talking? Why do you think so?

6. **Compare and Contrast Speakers** Using a Y-chart like the one shown, fill in the top part with what you know about each speaker's relationship to the **earth**. Include the gifts he or she receives from it and how he or she feels about it. How are these relationships similar? Then cross out the similarities and write them in the bottom part.

7. **Evaluate Imagery** Both "Mi Madre" and "Canyon de Chelly" are about real places the poets have visited. Review the imagery webs you created. Which poem's imagery best helped you to picture the subject of the poem?

# Extension and Challenge

8. **Creative Project: Poetry** Think of a place in the outdoors that you enjoy. Jot down notes about how the place looks, smells, feels, sounds, or tastes. Then write a poem about the place. Be sure to include **imagery** that appeals to at least three of the five senses.

9.  **SOCIAL STUDIES CONNECTION** The Navajo, or Diné, make up the largest Native American nation in the United States. Research their history and traditions, including their preservation of Canyon de Chelly as a national landmark. Share your findings with a group.

> **RESEARCH LINKS**
> For more on the Navajo, visit the **Research Center** at **ClassZone.com**.

# Comparison-Contrast Essay

In Unit 3 and in your own life, you have encountered people and situations that almost beg to be compared. To write an essay that compares or contrasts two real or fictional people, places, or events, start with the **Writer's Road Map**.

## WRITER'S ROAD MAP

### Comparison-Contrast Essay

### WRITING PROMPT 1

**Writing from Literature** Write an essay that compares or contrasts two selections that you have read this year. Concentrate on key aspects such as setting, people or characters, events, or the writer's style. Your essay should give your reader a new understanding of the selections.

**Selections to Compare**

• "The Monkey's Paw" and "The Tell-Tale Heart"

• "Going Where I'm Coming From" and "My First Free Summer"

• "Mi Madre" and "My Father and the Fig Tree"

### WRITING PROMPT 2

**Writing from Your Life** Write a comparison-contrast essay about two places, people, or events that are familiar, important, or interesting to you. Explain why you chose those two subjects.

**Subjects to Compare**

• two after-school hangouts

• two people who are important to you

• family rituals from two different cultures

 **WRITING TOOLS**
For prewriting, revision, and editing tools, visit the **Writing Center** at **ClassZone.com**.

### KEY TRAITS

#### 1. IDEAS

• Identifies the **subjects** being compared and contrasted

• Presents a **thesis statement** that identifies similarities or differences

• Supports key points with **examples**

#### 2. ORGANIZATION

• Includes an **introduction** that holds the reader's attention

• Has a clear **organizational pattern**

• Uses **transitions** to show how ideas are related

• Sums up the key points in a **conclusion** that also explains why the subjects are important

#### 3. VOICE

• Consistently uses language that is **appropriate** for the audience and purpose

#### 4. WORD CHOICE

• Uses **precise words** to explain similarities and differences

#### 5. SENTENCE FLUENCY

• Varies **sentence beginnings**

#### 6. CONVENTIONS

• Uses **correct grammar, spelling, and punctuation**

# Part 1: Analyze a Student Model

**WRITING STANDARD**
**8.5.7** Write for different purposes and to a specific audience . . . .

Tyler Kurcewski
West Fairview
Intermediate School

### Different Worlds, Similar Challenges

Nobody ever said life was easy. In fact, it's really about proving that you can face challenges. This is clear in the short stories "The Drummer Boy of Shiloh" by Ray Bradbury and "Hallucination" by Isaac Asimov. Although the main characters of these stories live on different planets

5 during different centuries, both successfully face tremendous challenges.

The settings of these two stories are completely different. "The Drummer Boy of Shiloh" takes place during the Civil War. It begins with a description that sounds almost like a poem: "In the April night, more than once, blossoms fell from the orchard trees and lighted with

10 rustling taps on the drumskin." The exact place is a field where a major battle will be fought the next day. "Hallucination," on the other hand, is set on Energy Planet—somewhere in the universe, sometime far in the future. To make things more like home, the Earth people have built a "transparent dome overhead. It was quite high, perhaps a thousand

15 meters high, and it stretched in all directions farther than he could clearly see." Young Earthlings get specialized training on this planet.

Although the two main characters are in totally different places and times, they are similar in several key ways. Both are young teenagers. The drummer boy, Joby, has just turned 14, and we

20 learn that he is too young to shave. We learn in the first sentence of "Hallucination" that Sam is 15. Both boys are also away from home: Joby has run away to join the army, and Sam is on Energy Planet because Central Computer sent him there. In addition, they both have difficult challenges to deal with. Joby may die in battle the next day.

25 Sam must solve the mystery of the hallucinations that nobody wants to talk about.

**KEY TRAITS IN ACTION**

Appealing, straightforward **introduction** states the **subjects** of the comparison. Highlighted **thesis statement** spells out the main similarities and differences.

**Organizational pattern** is logical, discussing setting in both stories and then moving on to characters in both stories. Quotations and other **examples** help the reader understand how the settings differ.

The way these two characters handle their challenges is very different, though. Joby seems weak and frightened. He's afraid to die and lies crying in the dark. There's not much he can do except
30  worry and wait for morning to come and the battle to begin. In sharp contrast, Sam is confident and determined. He ignores the assignment he's been sent to work on and investigates the hallucinations on his own.

By the end of the stories, though, both Joby and Sam accept their
35  challenges and face them with courage. In "The Drummer Boy of Shiloh," the general gives Joby the confidence he needs, telling him he is "the heart of the army. . . . the general of the army when the General's left behind." The story ends before the battle begins, but we know that Joby's attitude has changed. Turning his drum to face the sky shows that he is no longer
40  afraid of the sound of blossoms falling on it. Calmly and bravely, he has decided to march to war. In "Hallucination," Sam uses his intuition and almost superhuman intelligence to solve the mystery. He quickly learns how to communicate with the planet's insect-like creatures and realizes that "previous attempts at communication had failed because
45  the people . . . had been frightened." In the end, he discovers how these beings create the hallucinations. Making this discovery helps to cure the Commander and save the power station.

The settings of the short stories "The Drummer Boy of Shiloh" and "Hallucination" span history and the universe. The main characters in
50  the stories are very much alike, however. Both of them learn to face the challenges in their lives. Their courage inspires us and encourages us to face our own challenges.

A **transition** alerts the reader to an important difference between the characters.

Uses a variety of **sentence beginnings** to hold the reader's interest.

**Precise words** are clear and **appropriate** for the writer's purpose and for his audience (his classmates and teacher).

**Conclusion** summarizes the main points. The highlighted phrase explains the importance of the stories.

2

# Part 2: Apply the Writing Process

**WRITING STANDARD**
**8.4.9** Revise writing for word choice; appropriate organization ....

**PREWRITING**

| *What Should I Do?* | *What Does It Look Like?* |
|---|---|

### *What Should I Do?*

**1. Analyze the prompt.**
Choose a prompt from page 424 and study it carefully. Draw a (circle) around the type of writing it asks you to do. Underline the purpose of your writing. If the prompt doesn't tell you who your audience is, assume that you are writing for your teacher and classmates.

**2. Note similarities and differences.**
Use a Venn diagram or a chart to keep track of comparisons and contrasts.

**TIP** If you have trouble thinking of interesting, important similarities and differences, choose two other subjects.

**3. List your key points and find examples that support them.**
Write down the main similarities and differences between your subjects. Then look for facts, examples, and quotations to back up your ideas. If you use quotations, be sure to copy the words exactly.

**4. Draft a thesis statement.**
Tell your reader which subjects you're comparing, and then briefly describe their main similarities and differences. You can change your thesis statement as you draft and revise.

### *What Does It Look Like?*

**WRITING PROMPT**  Write an (essay) that compares or contrasts two selections that you have read this year. Concentrate on key aspects such as setting, people or characters, events, or the writer's style. Your essay should give your reader a new understanding of the selections.

> I liked the stories about the drummer boy and the kid on the alien planet. I think my teacher and classmates would enjoy reading more about them, too.

**"Drummer Boy"**
- set during the Civil War
- Joby is scared.

**Both**
- teenage boys
- facing challenges

**"Hallucination"**
- set in the future
- Sam is confident.

> Key point: Both characters meet their challenges.
> Support:
> - Joby bravely waits for battle. He knows he is "the heart of the army."
> - Sam figures out what the hallucinations are. He's really smart.

> I am comparing "The Drummer Boy of Shiloh" by Ray Bradbury and "Hallucination" by Isaac Asimov. The stories seem totally different at first, but it turns out that both main characters have to face bad situations.

## DRAFTING

### What Should I Do?

**1. Organize your ideas.**
Here are two ways to organize your essay. The writer of the model used point-by-point organization.

**Subject by subject**—Discuss all the points about one subject and then all the points about the other.

**Point by point**—Discuss your key points one by one, showing how they relate to each subject.

**TIP** Try out each organization and use the one that works better for your essay.

### What Does It Look Like?

**SUBJECT-BY-SUBJECT ORGANIZATION**

**Subject A: "Drummer Boy"**
**Setting:** U.S. during Civil War
**Main character:** Joby, a frightened teen
**Challenge:** to face a battle
**Subject B: "Hallucination"**
**Setting:** on Energy Planet in future
**Main character:** Sam, a confident teen
**Challenge:** to solve a mystery

**POINT-BY-POINT ORGANIZATION**

**Point 1: Setting**
"Drummer Boy": U.S. during Civil War
"Hallucination": Energy Planet, the future
**Point 2: Main Character**
"Drummer Boy": teen Joby at war, afraid
"Hallucination": teen Sam away from Earth, confident
**Point 3: Challenge**
"Drummer Boy": a battle
"Hallucination": a mystery

---

**2. Back up your key points.**
Instead of just telling readers "Sam is really smart," show them by giving details and quotations from the story.

Sam uses his intuition and almost superhuman intelligence to solve the mystery. ⎤ Key point

He quickly learns to communicate with the planet's insect-like creatures and realizes that "previous attempts at communication had failed because the people . . . had been frightened." ⎦ Details and quotation

---

**3. Use transitions to link ideas.**
Use words such as *both* and *similarly* to show how ideas are alike. Try *however, though,* or *on the other hand* to show differences. Placing some transitions at the beginning of your sentences will help give your writing variety.

**See page 430:** Add Transitions

The way these two characters handle their challenges is very different, though. Joby seems weak and frightened. He's afraid to die and lies crying in the dark. There's not much he can do except worry and wait for morning to come and the battle to begin. In sharp contrast, Sam is confident and determined.

## REVISING AND EDITING

| *What Should I Do?* | *What Does It Look Like?* |
|---|---|

**1. Create a thought-provoking introduction.**
- Reread the first sentence of your introduction. Ask yourself if it makes you want to read on.
- If not, add a question, an interesting detail, or a surprising quotation.

▶

> Nobody ever said life was easy. In fact, it's really about proving that you can face challenges. This is clear in
> ~~I am comparing~~ the short stories "The Drummer Boy of Shiloh" by Ray Bradbury and "Hallucination" by Isaac Asimov.

**2. Clarify your thesis.**
- [Bracket] the statement that explains the main similarities and differences of your subjects.
- Revise it if necessary so that it clearly and concisely states the key points of your essay.

▶

> [~~The stories seem totally different at first, but it turns out that both main characters have to face bad situations.~~]
> Although the main characters of these stories live on different planets during different centuries, both successfully face tremendous challenges.

**3. Be precise.**
- <u>Underline</u> any vague words, such as *nice*, *really*, *bad*, and *thing*.
- Replace those words with specific terms that tell your reader exactly what you mean.

> **TIP** Try replacing boring verbs (*ran* and *talk*) with precise ones (*fled* and *chatter*).

▶

>        assignment
> He ignores the ~~thing~~ he's been sent to work on and
> ~~does the research~~ on his own.
>       investigates the hallucinations

**4. Make your conclusion memorable.**
- Ask a peer reader to read your conclusion and tell you why you chose those two subjects to compare and contrast.
- If the reason isn't clear, add details to make sure readers understand the subjects' importance to you.

**See page 430:** Ask a Peer Reader

▶

> The settings of the short stories "The Drummer Boy of Shiloh" and "Hallucination" span history and the universe. The main characters in the stories are very much alike, however. Both of them learn to face the challenges in their lives. Their courage inspires us and encourages us to face our own challenges.

# Comparison-Contrast Essay

## Apply the Rubric

**A strong comparison-contrast essay . . .**

- ☑ has an attention-getting introduction that names the subjects being compared or contrasted

- ☑ points out the main similarities and differences of the subjects in a thesis statement

- ☑ Supports key points with quotations and other examples

- ☑ uses transitions to print out important comparisons or contrasts

- ☑ is logically organized

- ☑ varies sentence beginnings

- ☑ uses precise words and language suited to the audience and purpose

- ☑ concludes by summarizing key points and telling why the subjects are important

## Ask a Peer Reader

- What is the strongest and clearest point that I made?

- Do any points need more explanation? If so, which ones?

- Why do you think I chose these subjects?

## Add Transitions

| To Compare | To Contrast |
|---|---|
| also | although |
| by comparison | in contrast |
| in addition to | nevertheless |
| likewise | on the other hand |
| similarly | unlike |

## Check Your Grammar

- To correct a sentence fragment, add whatever the sentence is missing—a subject, a verb, or both.

> *He discovers*
> ∧*How these beings create the hallucinations.*

**See page R64:** Correcting Fragments

- Add punctuation to separate run-ons into individual sentences.

> *Joby seems weak and frightened○he's afraid to die and lies crying in the dark.*

**See pages R64–R65:** Correcting Run-on Sentences

## Writing On|ine

**PUBLISHING OPTIONS**
For publishing options, visit the **Writing Center** at **ClassZone.com**.

**ASSESSMENT PREPARATION**
For writing and grammar assessment practice, go to the **Assessment Center** at **ClassZone.com**.

**LISTENING/SPEAKING STANDARD**
**8.7.2** Match the message, vocabulary
…and tone to the audience and
purpose.

**PUBLISHING WITH TECHNOLOGY**

## Producing a Power Presentation

You can turn your essay into a power presentation. In other words, use a computer to create slides of the main points you made, and then present your work to an audience.

### Planning the Presentation

1. **Focus on your most important ideas.** Use a software program to make a slide for your introduction and another for your conclusion. Then create a slide for each of the key points you made in your essay. Each slide should have a headline and two to four short bullet points.

2. **Decide how you want your presentation to look.**
   You can select a template of preset fonts and colors or choose your own. Make sure the type is easy to read, even from the back of the room. You can add graphics or animations to make your slides more appealing, but be sure that the main focus stays on the words.

   > ## Contrast in Settings
   >
   > - **"Drummer Boy of Shiloh":** battlefield during the Civil War
   >
   > - **"Hallucination":** Energy Planet sometime in the future

3. **Try it out.** Work with the projection equipment until you're comfortable using it. Practice glancing at the slides and using the words like an outline to help you expand on your ideas.

### Delivering the Presentation

1. **Make it lively and interesting.** Don't just read the words on your slides. Instead, add examples and explanations that will interest your audience and help them understand your ideas. Look at people in various parts of the room as you speak.

2. **Ask for feedback.** When you have finished, ask for feedback and constructive criticism. Think about what you might do differently for your next presentation.

# Reading Comprehension

**DIRECTIONS** *Read these selections and answer the questions that follow.*

## *from* The Apprentice

### Dorothy Canfield Fisher

And now, this afternoon, when he was six months old, tall, rangy, powerful, standing up far above her knee, nearly to her waist, she didn't know where he was. But of course he must be somewhere around. He always was. She composed her face to look natural and went downstairs to search the house. He was probably asleep somewhere. She looked every room over carefully. Her mother was nowhere visible. It was safe to call him again, to give the special piercing whistle which always brought him racing to her, the white-feathered plume of his tail waving in elation that she wanted him.

But he did not answer. She stood still on the front porch to think.

10 Could he have gone up to their special place in the edge of the field where the three young pines, their branches growing close to the ground, made a triangular, walled-in space, completely hidden from the world? Sometimes he went up there with her. When she lay down on the dried grass to dream, he too lay down quietly, his head on his paws, his beautiful eyes fixed adoringly on her. He entered into her every mood. If she wanted to be quiet, all right, he did too.

It didn't seem as though he would have gone alone there. Still—She loped up the steep slope of the field rather fast, beginning to be anxious.

No, he was not there. She stood, irresolutely, in the roofless, green-walled 20 triangular hide-out, wondering what to do next.

Then, before she knew what thought had come into her mind, its emotional impact knocked her down. At least her knees crumpled under her. Last Wednesday the Wilsons had brought their sheep down to the home farm from the upper pasture! She herself had seen them on the way to school, and like an idiot had not thought of Rollie. She had seen them grazing on the river meadow.

She was off like a racer at the crack of the starting pistol, her long, strong legs stretched in great leaps, her pigtails flying. She took the short cut down to the upper edge of the meadow, regardless of the brambles. Their thorn-spiked, 30 wiry stems tore at her flesh, but she did not care. She welcomed the pain. It was something she was doing for Rollie, for her Rollie.

She was tearing through the pine woods now, rushing down the steep, stony path, tripping over roots, half-falling, catching herself just in time, not slackening her speed. She burst out on the open knoll above the river meadow, calling wildly, "Rollie, here, Rollie, here, boy! here! here!" She tried to whistle, but she was crying too hard to pucker her lips. She had not, till then, known she was crying.

There was nobody to see or hear her. Twilight was falling over the bare knoll. The sunless evening wind slid down the mountain like an invisible river,
40 engulfing her in cold. Her teeth began to chatter. "Here, Rollie, here, boy, here!" She strained her eyes to look down into the meadow to see if the sheep were there. She could not be sure. She stopped calling him as if he were a dog, and called out his name despairingly, as if he were her child, "Rollie! oh, *Rollie,* where are you!"

# *from* Year of the Black Pony
### Walt Morey

I was late. I took off from the house running fast as I could. I rounded the barn, crossed the pasture, and started up the long slope that led to the top of Christmas Ridge. I ran until my throat was dry and my heart felt like it was about to jump from my rib cage. Then the slope turned steep. I quit running and climbed the rest of the way.

The spine of Christmas Ridge is about fifty feet wide. It stretches for miles splitting the valley almost down the middle. There's an odd nest of big rocks up there about thirty feet high. I climbed to the topmost one and stretched out on my stomach. The valley rolled away beneath me, a spring-green carpet
10 of new grass speckled with clumps of trees and brush. In the middle stood our typical homesteader's board-and-bat cabin, the two outbuildings, and the pattern of fences and gates.

My breathing gradually settled back to normal and my heart stopped pounding. I kept listening and looking. There was nothing. I was too late. I was about to get up and leave when I heard it. A faint rumble rode the morning silence like the roll of distant thunder. It swelled in volume. I got to my knees in excitement. My heart was hammering again.

They burst around a shoulder of the ridge a hundred yards away—fifteen or twenty horses running hard. They were Sam Fletcher's young stock that
20 he let run loose on the open range. They followed the ridge every morning to feed in some distant part of the valley. At night a hired hand rode out and drove them home.

I had eyes for only one. The black pony in the lead. He ran like he loved being free. His head was up, sharp ears forward, black mane and tail flying in the wind. The sun made his black coat glisten like satin. The big muscles across shoulders and legs rippled like light flashes on water. They pounded past right under the rock where I crouched. I watched until they were out of sight. The whole thing took maybe two minutes.

30 Every Saturday since the winter weather had broken I'd climbed up here to watch that pony pass. The sight of him did something to me I've never quite been able to explain. He was more than tremendous strength and speed and beauty of motion. He set me dreaming.

# Comprehension

**DIRECTIONS** *Answer these questions about the excerpt from "The Apprentice."*

1. From the descriptive details used in this excerpt, you can tell that the story's setting is a
   ○ landscaped suburban community with grassy yards
   ○ large city park with trees and meadows
   ○ tropical forest with dense undergrowth
   ○ mountainous area of fields, forests, and farms

2. Which phrases contribute to the tense mood in the excerpt?
   ○ "probably asleep somewhere"; "completely hidden from the world"
   ○ "safe to call him"; "special piercing whistle"
   ○ "beginning to be anxious"; "She stood, irresolutely"
   ○ "on the way to school"; "grazing on the river"

3. Which phrase helps you visualize the girl running frantically in search of Rollie?
   ○ "the special piercing whistle" (lines 6–7)
   ○ "wondering what to do next" (line 20)
   ○ "tripping over roots, half-falling" (line 33)
   ○ "strained her eyes to look down" (line 41)

4. Reread lines 10–16. The description of the special place where the girl and Rollie like to go helps create a mood of
   ○ eeriness
   ○ peacefulness
   ○ nervousness
   ○ tenderness

5. Which image appeals to the reader's sense of touch?
   ○ "steep slope of the field" (line 18)
   ○ "crack of the starting pistol" (line 27)
   ○ "thorn-spiked wiry stems" (lines 29–30)
   ○ "the open knoll" (line 34)

6. The description of the setting in lines 38–42 creates a mood that is
   ○ calm
   ○ fearful
   ○ weary
   ○ lighthearted

**DIRECTIONS** *Answer these questions about the excerpt from* Year of the Black Pony.

7. The setting for this excerpt is
   ○ the top of Christmas Ridge
   ○ a valley far from Christmas Ridge
   ○ a pasture near Christmas Ridge
   ○ the barn at the foot of Christmas Ridge

**8.** The event described in the excerpt takes place on a

- ○ fall afternoon
- ○ summer night
- ○ winter evening
- ○ spring morning

**9.** In line 1, the narrator says, "I was late. I took off from the house running fast as I could." These statements create a mood of

- ○ playfulness
- ○ suspense
- ○ despair
- ○ confidence

**10.** The imagery in lines 15–17 appeals to the reader's sense of

- ○ hearing
- ○ sight
- ○ smell
- ○ taste

**11.** Which description helps you visualize the black pony running with the herd?

- ○ "Sam Fletcher's young stock" (line 19)
- ○ "mane and tail flying in the wind" (lines 24–25)
- ○ "big muscles across shoulders and legs" (lines 25–26)
- ○ "more than tremendous strength" (line 31)

**12.** The words *burst, flashes,* and *pounded* are used in the excerpt to help create feelings of

- ○ confusion
- ○ excitement
- ○ panic
- ○ terror

**DIRECTIONS** *Answer these questions about both selections.*

**13.** Imagery in both excerpts helps you visualize

- ○ untamed animals
- ○ mysterious characters
- ○ hilly, countryside settings
- ○ destructive forces in nature

**14.** The authors help you picture the characters mainly through

- ○ detailed descriptions of their actions
- ○ conversations between characters
- ○ words that name the characters' feelings
- ○ the animals' awareness of the characters

## Constructed Response

**SHORT ANSWER** *Write two or three sentences to answer these questions.*

**15.** Identify two sensory details in lines 6–12 in the excerpt from *Year of the Black Pony* that help you visualize the setting. To which of your senses do they appeal?

**16.** Which sensory details in the excerpt help you visualize Rollie's appearance in "The Apprentice"? Give two quotations from the excerpt to support your answer.

**ESSAY** *Write a paragraph to answer this question.*

**17.** Describe how the mood of the excerpt from "The Apprentice" changes as the girl looks for Rollie.

**GO ON** ▶

# Vocabulary

DIRECTIONS *Use context clues and your knowledge of idioms to answer the following questions.*

1. In line 5 of "The Apprentice," the girl "looked every room over carefully." The idiom *looked over* means
   - ○ tried to remember
   - ○ failed to notice
   - ○ described
   - ○ examined

2. In line 1 of *Year of the Black Pony*, the idiom *took off* means
   - ○ subtracted from
   - ○ became popular
   - ○ moved quickly
   - ○ imitated humorously

3. In line 21 of *Year of the Black Pony*, the idiom *hired hand* refers to a
   - ○ family member
   - ○ young horse
   - ○ manager
   - ○ paid laborer

4. In line 23 of *Year of the Black Pony*, the narrator says, "I had eyes for only one." The idiom *had eyes for* means that the narrator
   - ○ could afford to buy just one horse
   - ○ was interested in one particular horse
   - ○ needed glasses to see the herd
   - ○ watched the horses every day

DIRECTIONS *Use context clues and your knowledge of homographs to answer the following questions.*

> She was <u>tearing</u> though the pine woods now, rushing down the <u>steep</u>, stony path, tripping over roots, half-falling, catching herself just in time, not slackening her speed.

5. Which sentence uses *tearing* as it is used in line 32 of "The Apprentice"?
   - ○ Jake began tearing the wrapping paper from his birthday gift.
   - ○ Nora was tearing around her room in a great hurry.
   - ○ Jealousy was tearing their friendship apart.
   - ○ Madison blinked her eyes to stop them from tearing.

6. Which sentence uses *steep* as it is used in line 32 of "The Apprentice"?
   - ○ Raising a child is a steep undertaking.
   - ○ The price of those sneakers seems steep.
   - ○ Steep the tea bag in boiling water.
   - ○ The steep cliffs were impossible to climb.

> The sunless evening <u>wind</u> slid down the mountain like an invisible river, engulfing her in cold.

7. Which sentence uses *wind* as it is used in line 39 of "The Apprentice"?
   - ○ She had to wind a path through the dense forest.
   - ○ The plunge into icy water knocked the wind out of him.
   - ○ As he stepped outside, the gentle wind lingered on his face.
   - ○ Trumpets and saxophones are wind instruments.

# Writing & Grammar

**DIRECTIONS** *Read the passage and answer the questions that follow.*

(1) Ancient Egyptians regarded the cat as a sacred animal. (2) Cats <u>was</u> the protectors of grain, killing any rats or other animals that might eat this staple of the Egyptian diet. (3) Anyone who either purposely or accidentally killed a cat <u>were</u> put to death. (4) Egyptians so revered the animal that many Egyptian goddesses took the form of a cat. (5) Mafdet, Sekhmet, and Bastet <u>is</u> examples of ancient Egyptian cat goddesses. (6) Neither Mafdet nor Sekhmet <u>were</u> quite as celebrated as Bastet, though. (7) Beauty, fertility, and motherhood <u>was</u> three of the qualities for which Egyptians worshipped Bastet. (8) In the city of Bubastis, Egyptians would hold a yearly festival to celebrate her. (9) There and in Memphis, large cemeteries <u>was</u> devoted to the burial of mummified cats.

**1.** To maintain subject-verb agreement in sentence 2, change the underlined verb to

○ were
○ has been
○ am
○ is

**2.** To maintain subject-verb agreement in sentence 3, change the underlined verb to

○ are
○ was
○ have been
○ am

**3.** To maintain subject-verb agreement in sentence 5, change the underlined verb to

○ was
○ am
○ are
○ has been

**4.** To maintain subject-verb agreement in sentence 6, change the underlined verb to

○ was
○ am
○ are
○ have been

**5.** To maintain subject-verb agreement in sentence 7, change the underlined verb to

○ were
○ is
○ has been
○ am

**6.** To maintain subject-verb agreement in sentence 9, change the underlined verb to

○ am
○ is
○ has been
○ were

**STOP**

# UNIT 3

## More Great Reads

### Ideas for Independent Reading

Which questions from Unit 3 made an impression on you? Continue exploring them with these books.

## How do you find your purpose?

### The Boxer
*by Kathleen Karr*

In 1880s New York, 15-year-old Johnny is the one who has to work to feed his family. One night he sees a sign promising five dollars to anyone willing to fight, and suddenly he's a boxer. Will he win enough to get his family out of the tenements?

### Full Tilt
*by Neal Shusterman*

Focused, steady Blake has had one purpose his whole life: to keep his impulsive brother Quinn out of trouble. When Quinn steals Blake's ticket for a mysterious carnival, Blake goes to save his brother—again. But maybe Blake is the one who needs help.

### Olive's Ocean
*by Kevin Henkes*

Soon after Olive's death, Martha is given a page from Olive's journal. The two girls were never friends, but when Martha realizes they had a lot in common, she begins to see life differently. She spends the summer at the ocean, trying to fulfill Olive's dream.

## What is the role of a witness?

### Run, Boy, Run
*by Uri Orlev*

Srulik is only eight when he manages to escape from the Nazi-controlled ghetto into the Polish countryside. His father tells him he must forget who he is and do anything necessary to fit in and survive. But forgetting comes at a cost.

### Iqbal
*by Francesco D'Adamo*

Everything changes at the carpet factory when 13-year-old Iqbal is chained to a loom next to Fatima. Iqbal tells the children their owner will never release them, but he promises to escape. If Iqbal does get free, should he try to help his friends and risk recapture?

### Fish
*by L. S. Matthews*

Tiger's family moved from their home country to a drought-stricken village to run a clinic. They stay until the civil war forces them to leave, but the borders have closed, and only a treacherous trip over the mountains will bring them to safety.

## What gifts does the earth provide?

### Four Wings and a Prayer
*by Sue Halpern*

Every fall, millions of butterflies form an orange and black wave that rolls down from Canada or New York all the way to Mexico. Every spring a new generation of butterflies returns to their parents' homes. How do the butterflies know where to go?

### Saving the Planet and Stuff
*by Gail Gauthier*

As an intern at an environmental magazine in Vermont, Michael must live without a car, TV, or air conditioning. He thinks about quitting, but instead he stays and learns about business, composting, and himself.

### Tofu and T. rex
*by Greg Leitich Smith*

Freddie was protesting the treatment of her new school's mascot, a live bull, when the football field caught fire. She's been sent back to Chicago to live with her cousin and grandfather. Can a vegetarian survive life with two meat-eaters?

# A World of Meaning

## THEME AND SYMBOL

- In Fiction
- In Poetry
- In Drama
- In Media

# Share What You Know

## *What are life's hidden* MESSAGES?

What's the best story you've ever read? Chances are you enjoyed the story not just for its characters or plot but for its **theme,** or message about life and human nature. All great stories have a theme, whether it's about the value of friendship, the bonds of a family's love, or the triumph of good over evil. A story's characters grow and change because of what they learn through their experiences. As the characters learn these life lessons, you as a reader grow, too.

***ACTIVITY*** You may not have given it much thought, but your favorite movies have probably offered you valuable messages. Recall a movie that you love, and then answer these questions to help you identify its theme.

- What lessons, if any, do the characters learn?

- If there is a battle or struggle, who wins and who loses? Why?

- What did you learn from this movie that you can apply to your own life?

**INDIANA STANDARDS**

# Preview Unit Goals

**LITERARY ANALYSIS**
- Identify and interpret symbols in poetry
- Identify and analyze theme
- Identify, analyze, and compare universal themes
- Use a story map to analyze plot development

**READING**
- Make inferences and draw conclusions
- Synthesize information and make generalizations
- Set a purpose for reading

**WRITING AND GRAMMAR**
- Write a short story
- Use active voice
- Capitalize proper names correctly

**SPEAKING, LISTENING, AND VIEWING**
- Identify and analyze the elements of a documentary
- Compare and contrast information and events in print and nonprint sources
- Produce a video

**VOCABULARY**
- Use reference aids to find synonyms
- Use knowledge of root words and affixes to determine meanings of words

**ACADEMIC VOCABULARY**
- symbol
- theme
- universal theme
- synthesize

# Theme and Symbol

What makes a story memorable? Long after you've forgotten the names of the characters and the events of the plot, you'll likely remember the theme—the big idea at the heart of the story. A **theme** is a message about life or human nature that a writer wants you to understand. In this unit, you'll discover that themes in literature can give you insights into events, issues, and relationships in your life.

## Part 1: What's the Big Idea?

Friendship, war, and family are subjects that people of all ages and in all parts of the world think about. Writers—past and present—have considered these subjects too, exploring them in stories, poems, and plays. Some writers communicate unique themes, messages that are specific to a particular time, place, or situation. Others express **universal themes**—big ideas that show up again and again in literature of all time periods and cultures. "Friends help each other through tough times" and "People must learn from their mistakes" are two universal themes.

Whether it is universal or one of a kind, a theme is often communicated through different elements in a story, such as the characters, setting, and conflict. A writer may also use symbols to hint at a theme. A **symbol** is an object, activity, place, or person that stands for something beyond itself.

Notice how the theme is communicated in the following example.

**INDIANA STANDARDS**

**READING STANDARDS**
**8.3.5** Identify and analyze recurring themes (such as good versus evil) that appear frequently across traditional and contemporary works.

**8.3.6** Identify significant literary devices, such as metaphor, symbolism, dialect or quotations, and irony, which define a writer's style and use those elements to interpret the work.

**THEME**
**LIVE IN THE PRESENT, NOT THE PAST.**

### Character

The main character is **14-year-old Eva,** who has recently moved with her family to a new city. **Sullen and angry,** Eva desperately misses her friends back home.

### Setting

Eva can't stand the thought of exploring an **unfamiliar city** and an **intimidating school.** Being in this new setting reminds her of what she left behind.

### Symbol

Eva shuts herself in her room all day, looking through old yearbooks and e-mailing her friends. **Eva's room symbolizes the past,** where she remains trapped and isolated from the world.

### Conflicts

**Eva gets upset** when her parents suggest that she make new friends. She also feels hurt when **her friends don't e-mail very often.**

**Resolution:** Eventually, Eva realizes that she must move on. While she can hold onto the past in her memories, she has to live in the present.

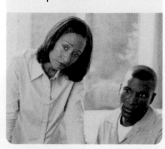

**MODEL: THEME AND SYMBOL**

Alfred is a high-school dropout who is barely staying out of trouble with the law. One night after getting beaten up, he steps into a gym to see if he can join the neighborhood boxing club. As he talks to Mr. Donatelli, the gym owner, about the challenges of training as a fighter, Alfred realizes Mr. Donatelli may be talking about more than just boxing.

*from*

# THE CONTENDER

Novel by **Robert Lipsyte**

"How far did you go in school?"

"Eleventh grade."

"What happened?"

"I quit."

5 "Why?"

"Didn't seem like any reason to stay."

"What makes you think you won't quit here too?"

Alfred swallowed. He suddenly wished he hadn't come up the steps, that he was somewhere else, anywhere. He thought of the cave.

10 "Well?"

"I want to be somebody."

"Everybody is somebody."

"Somebody special. A champion."

Donatelli's thin lips tightened. "Everybody wants to be a champion. That's 15 not enough. You have to start by wanting to be a contender, the man coming up, the man who knows there's a good chance he'll never get to the top, the man who's willing to sweat and bleed to get up as high as his legs and his brains and his heart will take him. That must sound corny to you."

"No."

20 "It's the climbing that makes the man. Getting to the top is an extra reward."

"I want to try."

Donatelli shrugged. "Boxing is a dying sport. People aren't much interested anymore. They want easy things like television, bowling, car rides. Get yourself a good job. Finish high school. Go at night if you have to."

25 "I'll try hard."

"Talk it over with your parents."

"I don't have any. I live with my aunt."

The pale blue eyes came around again. They seemed softer now. But the voice was still cold and flat. "It's not easy trying to become a contender. It's never any 30 fun in the beginning. It's hard work, you'll want to quit at least once every day. If you quit before you really try, that's worse than never starting at all."

**Close Read**

1. Reread the boxed text. What conflict is set up?

2. What is Alfred's goal? What does Mr. Donatelli think about that goal?

3. Given what Mr. Donatelli says in lines 14–20, what do you think boxing might symbolize to him?

4. Reread lines 29–31. What lesson might Alfred learn from training as a boxer? State this lesson as a theme.

# Part 2: Identifying Theme

Sometimes the theme of a story is stated directly by the narrator or a character. More often, the theme is implied, which means you have to do some digging to uncover it. It helps to look closely at the characters, the plot, and other clues when you're trying to identify a story's theme. The questions in the chart, as well as these reminders, can help you discover the message.

- The theme is not the topic of a story, but the writer's message *about* the topic. While a topic can be described in a word or two, it can take one or two sentences to express a theme. For example, "first impressions" is a topic. "First impressions aren't always right" is a theme.

- Some works of literature have multiple themes, but one may stand out more than the others.

- Different people can interpret the same story differently.

## CLUES TO THEME

### TITLE
The title of a story can suggest an important idea or symbol. Ask:

- What in the story does the title refer to?
- What idea or symbol does the title highlight?
- Could the title have more than one meaning?

### CHARACTERS
Characters can reflect theme by how they act or what they learn. Ask:

- What do the main character's actions and thoughts tell you about him or her?
- How does the character change?
- What lessons does the character learn?

### PLOT AND CONFLICT
A story revolves around conflicts that are central to the theme. Ask:

- What conflicts do the characters face?
- How are the conflicts resolved?

### SETTING
Setting can connect to a theme because of what it means to the characters or to readers. Ask:

- How does the setting affect the characters or influence their actions?
- What might the setting represent to readers?

### IMPORTANT STATEMENTS
The narrator or a character may make statements that hint at the theme. Ask:

- What key statements are made in the story?
- Could any statement be reworded as an overall theme?

### SYMBOLS
A symbol can convey a theme because of what it means to the main character. Ask:

- Does anything seem to stand for something beyond itself?
- What might the symbol mean to the main character? What might it represent to readers?

# Part 3: Analyze the Literature

Connie is not crazy about spending time with her Puerto Rican grandmother—
her *abuela*. What lesson will Connie learn when her grandmother comes to
visit? As you read, use what you've learned to uncover the theme of this story.

## *Abuela* INVENTS THE *Zero*

Short story by **Judith Ortiz Cofer**

"You made me feel like a zero, like a nothing," she says in Spanish, *un cero,*
*nada.* She is trembling, an angry little old woman lost in a heavy winter coat
that belongs to my mother. And I end up being sent to my room, like I was a
child, to think about my grandmother's idea of math.

5   It all began with Abuela coming from the Island[1] for a visit—her first
time in the United States. My mother and father paid her way here so that
she wouldn't die without seeing snow, though if you asked me, and nobody
has, the dirty slush in this city is not worth the price of a ticket. But I guess
she deserves some kind of award for having had ten kids and survived to tell
10   about it. My mother is the youngest of the bunch. Right up to the time when
we're supposed to pick up the old lady at the airport, my mother is telling me
stories about how hard times were for la familia on la isla,[2] and how *la abuela*
worked night and day to support them after their father died of a heart attack.
I'd die of a heart attack too if I had a troop like that to support. Anyway, I
15   had seen her only three or four times in my entire life, whenever we would go
for somebody's funeral. I was born here and I have lived in this building all
my life. But when Mami says, "Connie, please be nice to Abuela. She doesn't
have too many years left. Do you promise me, Constancia?"—when she uses
my full name, I know she means business. So I say, "Sure." Why wouldn't I be
20   nice? I'm not a monster, after all.

So we go to Kennedy[3] to get la abuela and she is the last to come out of the
airplane, on the arm of the cabin attendant, all wrapped up in a black shawl.
He hands her over to my parents like she was a package sent airmail. It is
January, two feet of snow on the ground, and she's wearing a shawl over a thin
25   black dress. That's just the start.

Ø   nce home, she refuses to let my mother buy her a coat because it's a
waste of money for the two weeks she'll be in *el Polo Norte,* as she calls
New Jersey, the North Pole. So since she's only four feet eleven inches tall, she
walks around in my mother's big black coat looking ridiculous. I try to walk
30   far behind them in public so that no one will think we're together. I plan to

---

1. **the Island:** Puerto Rico.
2. **la familia on la isla:** the family on the island.
3. **Kennedy:** John F. Kennedy International Airport.

**Close Read**

1. Examine the title of the story and reread the first paragraph. What symbol do you predict will be central to the theme?

2. Reread the boxed details, in which Connie shares her thoughts about her grandmother. Based on these details, how would you describe Connie?

3. What conflicts do you think might arise for Connie during her grandmother's visit?

stay very busy the whole time she's with us so that I won't be asked to take her anywhere, but my plan is ruined when my mother comes down with the flu and Abuela absolutely *has* to attend Sunday mass. . . . My father decides that he should stay home with my mother and that I should escort la abuela
35 to church. He tells me this on Saturday night as I'm getting ready to go out to the mall with my friends.

"No way," I say.

I go for the car keys on the kitchen table: he usually leaves them there for me on Friday and Saturday nights. He beats me to them.

40 "No way," he says, pocketing them and grinning at me.

Needless to say, we come to a compromise very quickly. I do have a responsibility to Sandra and Anita, who don't drive yet. There is a Harley-Davidson fashion show at Brookline Square that we *cannot* miss.

"The mass in Spanish is at ten sharp tomorrow morning, *entiendes?*" My
45 father is dangling the car keys in front of my nose and pulling them back when I try to reach for them. He's really enjoying himself.

"I understand. Ten o'clock. I'm out of here." I pry his fingers off the key ring. He knows that I'm late, so he makes it just a little difficult. Then he laughs. I run out of our apartment before he changes his mind. I have no idea
50 what I'm getting myself into.

*S*unday morning I have to walk two blocks on dirty snow to retrieve the car. I warm it up for Abuela as instructed by my parents, and drive it to the front of our building. My father walks her by the hand in baby steps on the slippery snow. The sight of her little head with a bun on top of it sticking
55 out of that huge coat makes me want to run back into my room and get under the covers. I just hope that nobody I know sees us together. I'm dreaming, of course. The mass is packed with people from our block. It's a holy day of obligation and everyone I ever met is there.

I have to help her climb the steps, and she stops to take a deep breath after
60 each one, then I lead her down the aisle so that everybody can see me with my bizarre grandmother. If I were a good Catholic, I'm sure I'd get some purgatory[4] time taken off for my sacrifice. She is walking as slow as Captain Cousteau[5] exploring the bottom of the sea, looking around, taking her sweet time. Finally she chooses a pew, but she wants to sit in the *other* end. It's like
65 she had a spot picked out for some unknown reason, and although it's the most inconvenient seat in the house, that's where she has to sit. So we squeeze by all the people already sitting there, saying, "Excuse me, please, *con permiso,* pardon me," getting annoyed looks the whole way. By the time we settle in, I'm drenched in sweat. I keep my head down like I'm praying so as not to see
70 or be seen. She is praying loud, in Spanish, and singing hymns at the top of her creaky voice.

---

4. **purgatory:** spiritual place in which souls purify themselves of sin before going to heaven.

5. **Captain Cousteau:** Jacques Yves Cousteau (zhäk ēv kōō-stō′) (1910–1997), a French underwater explorer, film producer, and author.

**Close Read**

4. How would you describe Connie's attitude toward and treatment of her grandmother? Support your answer.

I ignore her when she gets up with a hundred other people to go take communion.[6] I'm actually praying hard now—that this will all be over soon. But the next time I look up, I see a black coat dragging around and around

75 the church, stopping here and there so a little gray head can peek out like a periscope on a submarine. There are giggles in the church, and even the priest has frozen in the middle of a blessing, his hands above his head like he is about to lead the congregation in a set of jumping jacks.

I realize to my horror that my grandmother is lost. She can't find her way

80 back to the pew. I am so embarrassed that even though the woman next to me is shooting daggers at me with her eyes, I just can't move to go get her. I put my hands over my face like I'm praying, but it's really to hide my burning cheeks. I would like for her to disappear. I just know that on Monday my friends, and my enemies, in the barrio[7] will have a lot of senile-grandmother

85 jokes to tell in front of me. I am frozen to my seat. So the same woman who wants me dead on the spot does it for me. She makes a big deal out of getting up and hurrying to get Abuela.

*T*he rest of the mass is a blur. All I know is that my grandmother kneels the whole time with her hands over *her* face. She doesn't speak to me on the

90 way home, and she doesn't let me help her walk, even though she almost falls a couple of times.

When we get to the apartment, my parents are at the kitchen table, where my mother is trying to eat some soup. They can see right away that something is wrong. Then Abuela points her finger at me like a judge passing a sentence

95 on a criminal. She says in Spanish, "You made me feel like a zero, like a nothing." Then she goes to her room.

I try to explain what happened. "I don't understand why she's so upset. She just got lost and wandered around for a while," I tell them. But it sounds lame, even to my own ears. My mother gives me a look that makes me cringe and goes in to

100 Abuela's room to get her version of the story. She comes out with tears in her eyes.

"Your grandmother says to tell you that of all the hurtful things you can do to a person, the worst is to make them feel as if they are worth nothing."

I can feel myself shrinking right there in front of her. But I can't bring myself to tell my mother that I think I understand how I made Abuela feel. I

105 might be sent into the old lady's room to apologize, and it's not easy to admit you've been a jerk—at least, not right away with everybody watching. So I just sit there not saying anything.

My mother looks at me for a long time, like she feels sorry for me. Then she says, "You should know, Constancia, that if it wasn't for this old woman whose

110 existence you don't seem to value, you and I would not be here."

That's when *I'm* sent to *my* room to consider a number I hadn't thought much about—until today.

---

6. **communion:** the part of a Christian service in which bread and wine are consumed in memory of Christ's sacrifice.

7. **barrio:** Spanish-speaking community or neighborhood.

## Close Read

5. Why do you think the author chose a church as the setting for this scene? How might she want you to react to Connie's behavior there?

6. What lesson has Connie learned from the conflict with her grandmother? Where on this page do you see this lesson directly stated as a theme?

7. What new understanding of the word *zero* does Connie now have? What understanding do you have of the story's title?

## Gil's Furniture Bought & Sold

Anecdote by Sandra Cisneros

# *What makes something* PRICELESS?

**INDIANA STANDARDS**

**READING STANDARDS**

**8.2.9** Make reasonable statements and draw conclusions about a text, supporting them with accurate examples.

**8.3.6** Identify significant literary devices, such as metaphor, symbolism, dialect or quotations, and irony, which define a writer's style and use those elements to interpret the work.

**KEY IDEA** Perhaps you've heard a painting or antique described as **priceless.** In many cases, this means that the item is worth so much money that the amount can't be guessed at. But sometimes an object is priceless because it is worth more than money to the person who owns it. The anecdote you are about to read is a short account of a priceless object turning up in an unexpected place.

**QUICKWRITE** Describe your most prized possession and tell why it is special to you. Then consider if there are any circumstances under which you might give away or sell this object.

## ● LITERARY ANALYSIS: SYMBOL

When you see an American flag, you probably think of more than the fabric it's made of and its pattern of stars and stripes. The flag represents something much bigger—the United States of America. When a person, place, or thing stands for something beyond itself, it is called a **symbol.**

Writers often use symbols to quickly communicate complex ideas. For example, a sunrise can symbolize a new beginning, or a rose can stand for love. To recognize a symbol in literature, ask yourself questions such as these:

• What object appears repeatedly?

• How do the characters react to this object?

• What big ideas does the story address, and how does this object relate to them?

As you read "Gil's Furniture Bought & Sold," consider how an important object is used as a symbol.

## ● READING SKILL: MAKE INFERENCES

Skilled readers know they must "read between the lines" to make logical guesses about what a writer means but does not say directly. This process is called **making inferences,** and it can help you to understand the characters in a story. Follow these steps to make an inference:

• Gather details or evidence from the story.

• Consider your own experience and knowledge.

• Form an opinion based on both.

As you read, use a chart like the one shown to make inferences about the three characters in the selection.

| Details from Story | What I Know | Inference About Character |
|---|---|---|
| | | |
| | | |

# Author On|ine

**Sandra Cisneros
born 1954**

**A Bilingual Beginning**
Sandra Cisneros grew up in Chicago, the only daughter in a Mexican-American family with seven children. She spoke English to her mother and Spanish to her father, and she even thought the two languages were the same when she was very young. She was fascinated with the sound of words, especially those found in fairy tales and fantasy stories, such as *Alice in Wonderland*. The strange and fancy words in the pages of these books were quite different from those she heard every day at home and in her poor neighborhood. Cisneros dreamed of escaping her neighborhood and becoming a writer. She credits her mother with helping her achieve this goal.

**"I've Followed My Gut and My Heart"**
In order to earn a living, Cisneros decided she should work as an English teacher and write in her free time. The poetry and short fiction she produced revealed her unique voice, created from the influences of Latino and American culture. Her first novel, *The House on Mango Street,* was published in 1984 and helped make her a best-selling author. Her work often deals with struggles, such as alienation, poverty, and dual cultural loyalties. Cisneros's stories and poems have won many awards. She has said of her success, "In everything I've done in my life, including all the choices I've made as a writer, I've followed my gut and my heart."

 **MORE ABOUT THE AUTHOR**
For more on Sandra Cisneros, visit the **Literature Center** at **ClassZone.com.**

# Gil's Furniture
# BOUGHT & SOLD

## Sandra Cisneros

There is a junk store. An old man owns it. We bought a used refrigerator from him once, and Carlos sold a box of magazines for a dollar. The store is small with just a dirty window for light. He doesn't turn the lights on unless you got money to buy things with, so in the dark we look and see all kinds of things, me and Nenny. Tables with their feet upside-down and rows and rows of refrigerators with round corners and couches that spin dust in the air when you punch them and a hundred T.V.'s that don't work probably. Everything is on top of everything so the whole store has skinny aisles to walk through. You can get lost easy. **A**

10     The owner, he is a black man who doesn't talk much and sometimes if you didn't know better you could be in there a long time before your eyes notice a pair of gold glasses floating in the dark. Nenny who thinks she is smart and talks to any old man, asks lots of questions. Me, I never said nothing to him except once when I bought the Statue of Liberty for a dime. **B**

But Nenny, I hear her asking one time how's this here and the man says, This, this is a music box, and I turn around quick thinking he means a *pretty* box with flowers painted on it, with a ballerina inside. Only there's nothing like that where this old man is pointing, just a wood box that's old and got a big brass record in it with holes. Then he starts it up and all sorts of things 20 start happening. It's like all of a sudden he let go a million moths all over the dusty furniture and swan-neck shadows and in our bones. It's like drops of water. Or like marimbas only with a funny little plucked sound to it like if you were running your fingers across the teeth of a metal comb.

And then I don't know why, but I have to turn around and pretend I don't care about the box so Nenny won't see how stupid I am. But Nenny, who is stupider, already is asking how much and I can see her fingers going for the quarters in her pants pocket. **C**

This, the old man says shutting the lid, this ain't for sale. ✺

**ANALYZE VISUALS**
Look at the way objects are arranged in the store pictured on page 451. What can you **infer** about what it would be like to shop there?

**A** **MAKE INFERENCES**
Why do you think the narrator and Nenny shop at a junk store?

**B** **MAKE INFERENCES**
Reread lines 10–14. What can you assume about each character's personality from the details in this paragraph?

**C** **SYMBOL**
How do the narrator and Nenny react to the music box?

# Comprehension

1. **Recall** What item did the narrator's family buy from the junk store in the past?

2. **Clarify** Why is it sometimes hard to know that the owner is in the store?

3. **Summarize** In your own words, describe the appearance of the junk store.

**INDIANA STANDARDS**

READING STANDARD
8.3.6 Identify significant literary devices . . . .

# Literary Analysis

4. **Make Inferences** Review the chart you created as you read the anecdote. Based on these inferences, why do you think each character reacted to the music box the way he or she did? Give details from the anecdote to support your answer.

5. **Interpret a Symbol** What does the music box **symbolize?** Explain why you think so.

6. **Draw Conclusions** What do you think the narrator means when she says, "I have to turn around and pretend I don't care about the box so Nenny won't see how stupid I am"? Consider what this tells you about her personality.

7. **Compare and Contrast Characters** Using a Venn diagram like the one shown, compare and contrast the narrator and Nenny. As you fill in the diagram, note how they interact with the storeowner.

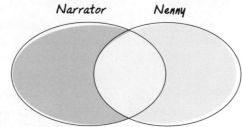

8. **Evaluate a Setting** A story's **setting** can affect your expectations about what is going to happen. Reread lines 1–9. In what ways is the junk store an appropriate setting for the characters to discover something **priceless?** In what ways is the setting surprising?

# Extension and Challenge

9. **Creative Project: Art** Think about the description of the junk store and the various items for sale there. Then make a collage of items you would expect to find in the store. You can cut out pictures from magazines and newspapers or include your own sketches.

10. **Inquiry and Research** Music boxes were once popular objects for people to have in their homes. The music box described in this story is a disc music box. Research more about disc music boxes and how they work. Also research how the popularity of the phonograph affected the music box industry in the early 1900s. Present your findings to the class.

**RESEARCH LINKS**
For more on music boxes, visit the **Research Center** at ClassZone.com.

# Reading-Writing Connection

Show your understanding of the characters in "Gil's Furniture Bought & Sold" by responding to these prompts. Then complete the **Grammar and Writing** exercise.

| WRITING PROMPTS | SELF-CHECK |
|---|---|
| **A. Short Response: Write a Dialogue**<br>Imagine what the narrator and Nenny talked about after they left the junk store. Write a **half-page dialogue** that captures what they may have said. Be sure to use language that matches the personalities of the characters. | *A creative dialogue will . . .*<br>• include details about their experience in the store<br>• reveal differences between the two characters through what they say |
| **B. Extended Response: Analyze a Character**<br>What did you learn about the junk store's owner based on his store, his behavior, and his words? Write **two or three paragraphs** describing the type of man he seems to be. Be sure to consider why the music box is **priceless** to him. | *A detailed analysis will . . .*<br>• support general statements about the man with evidence from the anecdote<br>• make inferences about why he values the music box |

## GRAMMAR AND WRITING

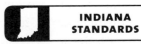

**INDIANA STANDARDS**

**WRITING STANDARD**
**8.4.8** Edit and proofread one's own writing, as well as that of others . . . .

***MAINTAIN SUBJECT-VERB AGREEMENT*** You may recall that subjects and verbs must agree in number. That rule remains true even when a subject and a verb have a **prepositional phrase** between them. The subject of a sentence is never found in a prepositional phrase. If you are having a problem deciding whether to use a singular or plural verb in a sentence that contains a prepositional phrase, mentally block out the phrase. This will help you determine what the subject of the sentence is and whether it needs a singular or plural verb.

> *Example:* The items in the junk shop are too numerous to count.
> (*The subject is* items, *not* shop, *so the sentence needs the plural verb* are.)

**PRACTICE** Choose the verb form that agrees with the subject in each sentence.

1. A box of books (was, were) one item that got sold to the owner of the store.
2. Refrigerators in the aisle (create, creates) a problem.
3. The owner's impression of the kids (are, is) that they aren't actually going to buy anything.
4. A handful of quarters (are, is) all that Nenny has to spend.

*For more help with subject-verb agreement, see page R65 in the **Grammar Handbook.***

## Pandora's Box

Greek Myth Retold by Louis Untermeyer

# *Is* CURIOSITY
## *a gift or a curse?*

**INDIANA STANDARDS**

**READING STANDARD**
**8.3.5** Identify and analyze recurring themes (such as good versus evil) that appear frequently across traditional and contemporary works.

**KEY IDEA** Have you ever heard the saying "Curiosity killed the cat"? This statement implies that **curiosity** can be dangerous. But curiosity has also led scientists to discover cures for diseases and journalists to ask important questions that inform the public. As you read the following myth, decide whether curiosity is presented as a desirable trait to have.

**LIST IT** Does curiosity lead to more benefits than it does problems? Or is it the other way around? With a small group of classmates, choose a side. In two minutes, come up with as many examples as possible to illustrate your point. Then see which side has more responses.

## ● LITERARY ANALYSIS: THEME

Writers often share with their readers messages about life or human nature—for example, love may come when you least expect it. This type of message is called a **theme.** Writers can either state a theme directly or allow readers to figure it out on their own. To infer a selection's theme, readers can look at important details or symbols. In the myth you are about to read, pay attention to a mysterious box and its contents to help you determine the theme.

## ● READING STRATEGY: READING A MYTH

Thousands of years ago, before anyone had microscopes or even books, people explained the world through stories called **myths.** Most myths

- were passed along through word of mouth
- feature gods or other supernatural beings who often show such human characteristics as anger and love
- reveal the consequences of human errors
- explain how something came to be

In order to understand a myth's significance, think beyond its basic story and consider what the characters, their actions, and the objects represent. As you read "Pandora's Box," take notes in a chart like the one shown.

| | |
|---|---|
| What human qualities do the gods display? | |
| What kind of behavior does Pandora demonstrate? | |
| What do the contents of the box represent? | |

## ▲ VOCABULARY IN CONTEXT

The boldfaced words help Louis Untermeyer tell the story of Pandora. Using context clues in each sentence, try to figure out what each word means.

1. The gods **adorn** her with special gifts.
2. She could no longer **restrain** her curiosity.
3. Zeus' **subtle** punishment was not immediately obvious.
4. Her beauty and charm helped **ensnare** his attention.

# Author Online

**Jeweler and Poet**
Louis Untermeyer, son of a wealthy jewelry manufacturer, dreamed of becoming a concert pianist. At age 15, however, he dropped out of high school and went to work for his father. He spent the next 22 years in the family business, working as a salesman, designer, and then vice president. During this time he also wrote and published many poems and puns.

**Louis Untermeyer**
**1885–1977**

**Translator and Anthologist** In 1923, Untermeyer quit the jewelry business and went to Europe for two years to study. After he returned to the United States, he became a writer, lecturer, and teacher. One of his friends was American poet Robert Frost. Untermeyer edited many poetry anthologies that became popular textbooks in schools. He also became a respected translator, adapting myths and stories for the contemporary American audience.

 **MORE ABOUT THE AUTHOR**
For more on Louis Untermeyer, visit the **Literature Center** at ClassZone.com.

## Background

**The Gods' Soap Opera** Many of the best-known myths, such as "Pandora's Box," come from ancient Greece. The Greek gods were a lively, passionate bunch. Zeus, king of the gods, ruled the heavens and earth from Mount Olympus. In one myth, Prometheus, a lesser god, gives humans fire against Zeus' will. Furious, Zeus condemns Prometheus to be chained for eternity to a rock. But as you'll see in the myth you're about to read, Zeus wasn't done punishing Prometheus yet. Now he's going to pick on Prometheus' brother, Epimetheus.

# Pandora's BOX

## Retold by Louis Untermeyer

Prometheus had thought about mankind with such sympathy that he had dared to steal the needed fire from Olympus,[1] and for this he was grievously punished by Zeus.[2] But the lord of Olympus did not think this cruelty was enough. Prometheus had a brother, Epimetheus, and though he was harmless and slow-witted, Zeus extended his displeasure to him. He did not punish Epimetheus as brutally as he had done his brother; he had a more **subtle** plan. It was a scheme which would not only affect Epimetheus but also the whole race of human beings whom Prometheus had dared to help and who were living happily and untroubled. **A**

10    Zeus ordered Hephaestus, the smith and artisan of the gods, to make a woman out of the materials of earth. Hephaestus took some river clay that had flakes of gold in it and began to make a lovely girl. In with the clay he mixed the fragrance of a river rose, the sweetness of Hymettus[3] honey, the smoothness of a silver dolphin, the voices of larks and lake-water, the color of sunrise on snow, the warmth of a sunny morning in May. Then he summoned

**subtle** (sŭt'l) *adj.* slight; difficult to detect

**A** **READING A MYTH**
Think about the gods you have met so far. What human characteristics do they have? Add this information to your chart.

**ANALYZE VISUALS**
Based on the woman's expression and body language, what can you **infer** about her attitude toward the box?

---

1. **Olympus** (ə-lǐm'pəs): home of the mythical Greek gods.
2. **Zeus** (zoōs): father of the Greek gods; ruler of the heavens.
3. **Hymettus** (hī-mĕt'əs): a mountain ridge near Athens, Greece.

*Pandora*, Helen Stratton. From *A Book of Myths* by Jean Lang. Mary Evans/Edwin Wallace.

the Four Winds to breathe life into the new creation. Finally he called upon the goddesses to complete the work and grant the glowing figure a touch of their own powers.

"Hephaestus has given her beauty," said Aphrodite,[4] "but I shall make
20 her more beautiful by adding the spark of love. It will shine in her eyes, and everyone that looks on her will be enchanted."

"I shall make her wise," said Athene.[5] "She shall be able to choose between false and true, between what men value and what she must know is worthless."

"I shall make her a woman, a puzzle to every man," said Hera, the wife of Zeus. "I shall make her a real woman, for I shall give her the gift of curiosity." **B**

Smiling, the goddesses **adorned** her, and when Zeus beheld her grace, her garland of gold, and the glory of her endowments, he was as charmed as though he had been a mortal. "We will call her Pandora," he said, "Pandora,
30 the All-Gifted. She shall become the bride of Epimetheus. But she shall not go empty-handed. She shall bring with her a casket, a box of magic as her dowry.[6] And Hermes, my messenger, shall conduct her to earth."

Epimetheus could not understand why the gods had become concerned about him. He was dazzled by Hermes, and it was some time before he could believe that the exquisite creature brought by the messenger god was meant for him. Even after Hermes departed in a flashing cloud and Pandora stood blushing beside him, he was perturbed. He remembered how often his brother Prometheus had warned him, "Do not trust the gods. And beware especially of Zeus and anything he may send you." However, when Pandora looked in his
40 eyes and smiled, he was, as Aphrodite had predicted, enchanted and **ensnared.** Yet, even as he took her in his arms, he cautioned her.

"We have reason to fear the gods," said Epimetheus, "and also their gifts," he added, pointing to the casket.

"But this is my dowry," murmured Pandora. "Zeus himself filled it with magic as a present for us. See how beautifully it is carved and painted. Look at the silver hinges and the great gold clasp that fastens it." **C**

"Keep it well fastened," said Epimetheus, "otherwise I shall never rest easy. I do not know what the casket may contain, and I do not want to know. Promise me one thing. Never open the box. It is, I grant, a beautiful thing, too
50 beautiful to destroy, and we will keep it. But hide it. Put it not only out of your sight but out of your mind. Then we shall both be content."

Happy that she could keep her dowry, Pandora put it under the bed and turned to her husband with love. And so for a long time nothing disturbed their married life and their continual joy in each other.

But, though Pandora benefited from the goddesses' gifts of beauty and wisdom, the gift of Hera had not been given in vain. For quite a while,

**B** READING A MYTH
What supernatural beings were involved in the creation of Pandora?

**adorn** (ə-dôrn') v. to enhance or decorate

**ensnare** (ĕn-snâr') v. to take or catch in something

**C** THEME
What can you **infer** about the contents of the box based on Zeus' desire for revenge?

---

4. **Aphrodite** (ăf'rə-dī'tē): Greek goddess of love and beauty.

5. **Athene** (ə-thē'nē): Greek goddess of wisdom; sometimes spelled *Athena*.

6. **dowry** (dou'rē): money or property a bride brings to a marriage.

Pandora **restrained** her curiosity about the wonderful casket. But with the passing of time she could not help wondering what it might contain. After all, it was *her* dowry, and she had a right to see what the greatest of the gods had
60  conferred upon her. Then, ashamed of her weakness, she put the idea from her, and thought only of her delight in her home with Epimetheus.

One day, however, the curiosity, so long stifled, overmastered her. "I shall only lift the lid," she said to herself, "and snatch a moment's glimpse of what may be inside. No matter what I see, I won't touch a thing. Surely there can be no harm in that." **D**

Anxiously, as though she were being watched, she tiptoed to her room. Gently getting down on her hands and knees, she drew the casket from under the bed. Half fearfully and half eagerly she lifted the lid. It was only a moment and the lid was up only an inch, but in that moment a swarm of horrible
70  things flew out. They were noisome,[7] abominably colored, and evil-looking, for they were the spirits of all that was evil, sad, and hurtful. They were War and Famine, Crime and Pestilence, Spite and Cruelty, Sickness and Malice, Envy, Woe, Wickedness, and all the other disasters let loose in the world.

Hearing Pandora's scream, Epimetheus rushed in. But it was too late. He and Pandora were set upon and stung, and the evil spirits flew off to attack the rest of mankind. **E**

"It is all my fault," cried Pandora. "If I had thought more about your warning and less about my own desires, I could have controlled my curiosity."

"The fault is mine," said Epimetheus. "I should have burned the box." Then
80  he added, for the poison of Malice was already taking effect, "After all, you are what you are—only a woman—and what else could one expect of a woman."

Disconsolate[8] that she had brought so harmful a dowry to Epimetheus as well as to all other men and women, Pandora wept. It was hours before she let her husband comfort her. Finally, after she grew quiet, they heard a faint sound inside the box.

"Lift the lid again," said Epimetheus. "I think you have released the worst. Perhaps something else, something better, is still there."

He was right. At the bottom of the box was a quivering thing. Its body was small; its wings were frail; but there was a radiance about it. Somehow Pandora
90  knew what it was, and she took it up, touched it carefully, and showed it to Epimetheus. "It is Hope," she said.

"Do you think it will live?" asked Epimetheus.

"Yes," answered Pandora. "I am sure it will. Somehow I know that it will outlive War and Sickness and all the other evils. And," she added, watching the shining thing rise and flutter about the room, "it will never leave us for long. Even if we lose sight of it, it will be there." **F**

She was no longer downhearted as Hope spread its wings and went out into the world. ❧

---

7. **noisome** (noiʹsəm): offensive.

8. **disconsolate** (dĭs-kŏnʹsə-lĭt): gloomy.

**restrain** (rĭ-strānʹ) *v.* to hold back; to control

**D** READING A MYTH
What prompts Pandora to look inside the box?

**E** READING A MYTH
What happens to humanity as a result of Pandora's actions?

**F** THEME
How does the winged creature relate to the other things in the box?

## Comprehension

1. **Recall** Why does Zeus punish Epimetheus?

2. **Clarify** Why does Pandora open the box with a mixture of fear and eagerness?

3. **Represent** Create a drawing that represents what happens when Pandora opens the box.

**INDIANA STANDARDS**

**READING STANDARD**
**8.3.5** Identify and analyze recurring themes . . . .

## Literary Analysis

4. **Interpret a Line** Reread lines 25–26. Why does having **curiosity** make Pandora "real"?

5. **Identify Theme** What is the theme of this myth? Consider the message about life the author conveys through events surrounding the box.

6. **Compare and Contrast Symbols** Use a Y-chart like the one shown to compare and contrast the box in "Pandora's Box" to the music box in "Gil's Furniture Bought & Sold." Think about the role the boxes play in the myth and the anecdote.

Music Box      Pandora's Box

Similarities

7. **Examine a Myth** Review the chart you made as you read. Based on the information you collected, what do you think the people of ancient Greece were trying to explain through this myth?

## Extension and Challenge

8.  **SOCIAL STUDIES CONNECTION** The phrase "Pandora's box" is widely used in the English language to describe an action that can have many negative consequences. Research why the atomic bomb developed by the United States has been called a "Pandora's box," and explain the connection to the myth. Present your findings to the class.

A mushroom cloud rises into the sky after a 1954 test of a nuclear device.

> **RESEARCH LINKS**
> For more on the atomic bomb, visit the **Research Center** at **ClassZone.com**.

# Vocabulary in Context

## VOCABULARY PRACTICE

Choose the word from the list that makes the most sense in each sentence.

1. Zeus had a _____ plan for Epimetheus.
2. The goddesses wanted to _____ Pandora with gold garlands.
3. Aphrodite predicted that Pandora would _____ Epimetheus.
4. Epimetheus warned Pandora to _____ her interest in the casket.

adorn

ensnare

restrain

subtle

## VOCABULARY IN WRITING

Why did Zeus decide to get back at Prometheus by picking on Epimetheus? Using two or more vocabulary words, write a paragraph describing what might have been going through his mind. You might start like this.

**EXAMPLE SENTENCE**

*Zeus could not **restrain** his desire for revenge.*

## VOCABULARY STRATEGY: USING REFERENCE AIDS

**Synonyms** are words with similar meanings. For example, a synonym for *restrain* is *stifle*. When you're writing, you can use the following reference aids to help you find a more precise or powerful word to express an idea:

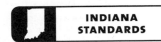

**INDIANA STANDARDS**

**READING STANDARD**
**8.1.3** Verify the meaning of a word in its context . . . .

- a **thesaurus**—a book that lists words related to each other in meaning. An electronic thesaurus tool is also found on many word processing programs.

  **restrain** *verb* check, detain, stifle, suppress

- a **dictionary**—a book that lists words in alphabetical order and gives their definitions and pronunciations. Synonyms are listed after the definition of some words.

  **restrain** (rĭ-strān′) *v.* **-strained, -strain•ing, -strains** to hold back or keep in check; control: *couldn't restrain the tears.* **syn** CHECK, DETAIN, STIFLE, SUPPRESS

*PRACTICE* Use a reference aid to find a synonym for each word. Note the synonym as well as the reference aid you used to find it. Then use each synonym in a sentence that matches its shade of meaning.

1. frail    2. methodical    3. scheme    4. invigorate

**VOCABULARY PRACTICE**
For more practice, go to the **Vocabulary Center** at ClassZone.com.

# The Old Grandfather and His Little Grandson
Russian Folk Tale Retold by Leo Tolstoy

# The Wise Old Woman
Japanese Folk Tale Retold by Yoshiko Uchida

# *How well do we treat our* ELDERS?

**INDIANA STANDARDS**

**READING STANDARDS**
**8.3.3** Compare and contrast the motivations and reactions of literary characters from different historical eras ....

**8.3.5** Identify and analyze recurring themes (such as good versus evil) that appear frequently across traditional and contemporary works.

**KEY IDEA** Think about all the things the elderly people you know have done in their long lives. They've probably cared for their families, made contributions on the job or in the community, and witnessed events that are now part of history. Do you think they get the **respect** they deserve from younger generations? The two folk tales you are about to read explore reasons why our elders have earned special treatment.

**LIST IT** Create a list of three to five things that you can do to honor the wisdom and experience of someone from an older generation. Remember that a small gesture can have a big impact.

> 1. Visit an elderly neighbor
> 2.
> 3.

## ● LITERARY ANALYSIS: UNIVERSAL THEME

Almost every culture has its **folk tales,** simple stories passed down through generations by word of mouth. Even though the cultures themselves may be different in many ways, the tales often focus on the same basic ideas about life and how to behave. As a result, many folk tales have a **universal theme,** or a message that is meaningful to people living in any country and at any time.

The two folk tales in this lesson come from different countries and cultures, yet they express a similar theme. To identify their universal theme, pay attention to the characters, their actions, and the consequences of their actions.

## ● READING STRATEGY: SET A PURPOSE FOR READING

In this lesson, your **purpose for reading** is to compare two folk tales and to identify the universal theme they share. To do this, as you read take notes in a chart like the one shown. Later on, you will be asked to do more with this chart.

|  | "The Old Grandfather and His Little Grandson" | "The Wise Old Woman" |
|---|---|---|
| Who are the important characters? | elderly character:<br><br>unkind characters:<br><br>other characters: | elderly character:<br><br>unkind characters:<br><br>other characters: |
| How is the elderly character mistreated? |  |  |
| What motivates characters to stop this mistreatment? |  |  |

## ▲ VOCABULARY IN CONTEXT

In "The Wise Old Woman," Yoshiko Uchida uses these words to describe a cruel lord and the people who suffer under his rule. Test your knowledge of each word by matching it with the numbered term closest in meaning.

| WORD LIST | arrogant | bewilderment | deceive | haughtily |
|---|---|---|---|---|

1. proudly    2. superior    3. astonishment    4. mislead

# Author On|ine

**Leo Tolstoy: Russian Novelist** Russian writer Leo Tolstoy wanted to produce literature that would help people adopt simple, religious lives. Tolstoy created some of the world's best-known novels, including *War and Peace* and *Anna Karenina.* He also wrote short stories,

**Leo Tolstoy**
**1828–1910**

dramas, essays, and adaptations. As he grew older, Tolstoy imposed increasingly strict rigors on himself in order to live what he saw as a good life. He became isolated from his wife and 13 children. In 1910, while escaping his family by train, Tolstoy developed pneumonia and died. His works live on as literary classics.

**Yoshiko Uchida: Japanese-American Author** The daughter of Japanese immigrants, Yoshiko Uchida grew up in California feeling different from her white classmates. This difference became more obvious after the bombing of Pearl Harbor in 1941. Government

**Yoshiko Uchida**
**1921–1992**

officials sent her father to an internment camp. Uchida and her family were later interned with him. She wrote many books for children that drew on her experience. She said, "I want to dispel the stereotypic image still held by many non-Asians about the Japanese and write about them as real people."

 **MORE ABOUT THE AUTHOR**
For more on Leo Tolstoy and Yoshiko Uchida, visit the **Literature Center** at **ClassZone.com.**

# The Old Grandfather and His Little Grandson

## Retold by Leo Tolstoy

The grandfather had become very old. His legs would not carry him, his eyes could not see, his ears could not hear, and he was toothless. When he ate, bits of food sometimes dropped out of his mouth. His son and his son's wife no longer allowed him to eat with them at the table. He had to eat his meals in the corner near the stove.

One day they gave him his food in a bowl. He tried to move the bowl closer; it fell to the floor and broke. His daughter-in-law scolded him. She told him that he spoiled everything in the house and broke their dishes, and she said that from now on he would get his food in a wooden dish. The old man sighed
10 and said nothing. **A**

A few days later, the old man's son and his wife were sitting in their hut, resting and watching their little boy playing on the floor. They saw him putting together something out of small pieces of wood. His father asked him, "What are you making, Misha?"

The little grandson said, "I'm making a wooden bucket. When you and Mamma get old, I'll feed you out of this wooden dish."

The young peasant and his wife looked at each other and tears filled their eyes. They were ashamed because they had treated the old grandfather so meanly, and from that day they again let the old man eat with them at the
20 table and took better care of him. ◆ **B**

**ANALYZE VISUALS**
How does color affect the **mood** of this picture?

**A** UNIVERSAL THEME
How do the man and his wife treat the grandfather?

**B** UNIVERSAL THEME
What have the man and his wife realized about themselves?

*Beggar and a Boy* (1903), Pablo Picasso. Oil on canvas, 125 cm × 92 cm. Pushkin Museum, Moscow. © Bridgeman Art Library. © 2007 Estate of Pablo Picasso/Artists Rights Society (ARS), New York.

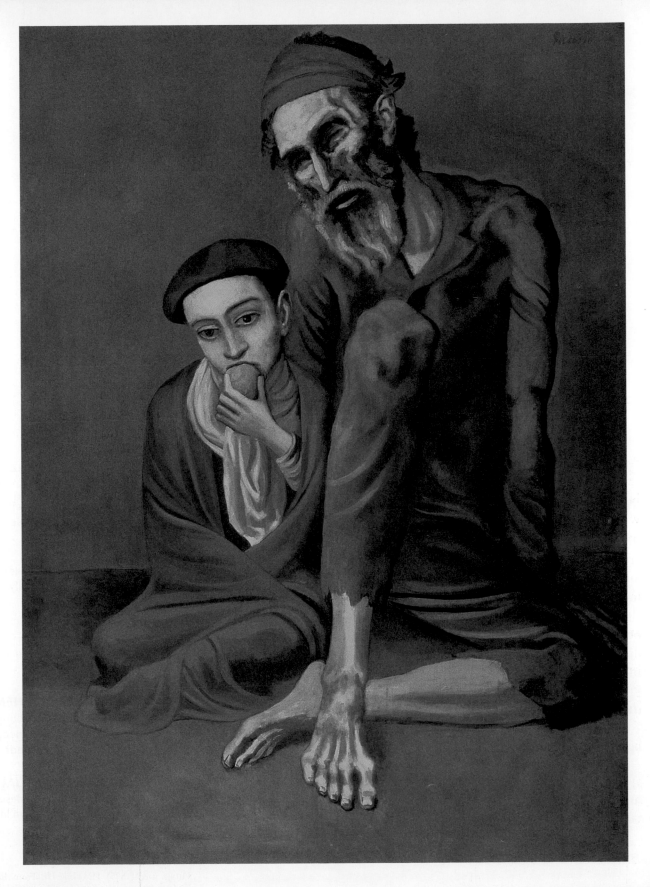

THE OLD GRANDFATHER AND HIS LITTLE GRANDSON    **465**

# THE WISE OLD WOMAN

## Retold by Yoshiko Uchida

Many long years ago, there lived an **arrogant** and cruel young lord who ruled over a small village in the western hills of Japan.

"I have no use for old people in my village," he said **haughtily.** "They are neither useful nor able to work for a living. I therefore decree[1] that anyone over seventy-one must be banished[2] from the village and left in the mountains to die."

"What a dreadful decree! What a cruel and unreasonable lord we have," the people of the village murmured. But the lord fearfully punished anyone who disobeyed him, and so villagers who turned seventy-one were tearfully carried
10 into the mountains, never to return.

Gradually there were fewer and fewer old people in the village and soon they disappeared altogether. Then the young lord was pleased.

"What a fine village of young, healthy and hard-working people I have," he bragged. "Soon it will be the finest village in all of Japan." **C**

**arrogant** (ăr′ə-gənt) *adj.* displaying a sense of self-importance

**haughtily** (hô′tə-lē) *adv.* proudly; scornfully

**C UNIVERSAL THEME**
Why does the young lord decide that old people must be banished?

**ANALYZE VISUALS**
How would you describe the **setting** shown in this picture?

---

1. **decree** (dĭ-krē′): to make an order; an order that has the force of law.
2. **banished:** forced to leave a country or a place.

*Village Street* (1875), Hiroshige III. From the series *Famous Places on the Tokaido: a Record of the Process of Reform.* © Asian Art & Archaeology, Inc./Corbis.

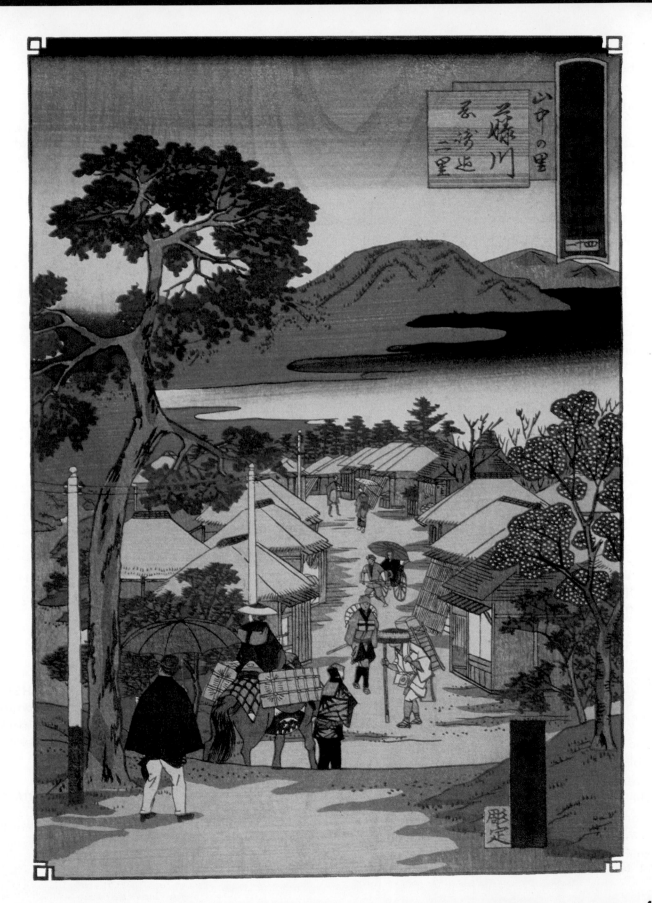

Now there lived in this village a kind young farmer and his aged mother. They were poor, but the farmer was good to his mother, and the two of them lived happily together. However, as the years went by, the mother grew older, and before long she reached the terrible age of seventy-one.

"If only I could somehow **deceive** the cruel lord," the farmer thought. 20 But there were records in the village books and every one knew that his mother had turned seventy-one.

Each day the son put off telling his mother that he must take her into the mountains to die, but the people of the village began to talk. The farmer knew that if he did not take his mother away soon, the lord would send his soldiers and throw them both into a dark dungeon to die a terrible death.

"Mother—" he would begin, as he tried to tell her what he must do, but he could not go on.

Then one day the mother herself spoke of the lord's dread decree. "Well, my son," she said, "the time has come for you to take me to the mountains. 30 We must hurry before the lord sends his soldiers for you." And she did not seem worried at all that she must go to the mountains to die.

"Forgive me, dear mother, for what I must do," the farmer said sadly, and the next morning he lifted his mother to his shoulders and set off on the steep path toward the mountains. Up and up he climbed, until the trees clustered close and the path was gone. There was no longer even the sound of birds, and they heard only the soft wail of the wind in the trees. The son walked slowly, for he could not bear to think of leaving his old mother in the mountains. On and on he climbed, not wanting to stop and leave her behind. Soon, he heard his mother breaking off small twigs from the trees 40 that they passed.

"Mother, what are you doing?" he asked.

"Do not worry, my son," she answered gently. "I am just marking the way so you will not get lost returning to the village."

The son stopped. "Even now you are thinking of me?" he asked, wonderingly.

The mother nodded. "Of course, my son," she replied. "You will always be in my thoughts. How could it be otherwise?"

At that, the young farmer could bear it no longer. "Mother, I cannot leave you in the mountains to die all alone," he said. "We are going home and no matter what the lord does to punish me, I will never desert you again." **D**

50 So they waited until the sun had set and a lone star crept into the silent sky. Then in the dark shadows of night, the farmer carried his mother down the hill and they returned quietly to their little house. The farmer dug a deep hole in the floor of his kitchen and made a small room where he could hide his mother. From that day, she spent all her time in the secret room and the farmer carried meals to her there. The rest of the time, he was careful to work in the fields and act as though he lived alone. In this way, for almost two years, he kept his mother safely hidden and no one in the village knew that she was there.

**deceive** (dǐ-sēv´) v. to cause to believe what is not true; to mislead

SOCIAL STUDIES CONNECTION

Japan is a string of several thousand islands off the east coast of the continent of Asia. Much of Japan consists of hills and mountains.

**D** UNIVERSAL THEME
Why does the son decide to disobey the decree even though he might be punished?

**ANALYZE VISUALS**
Based on this picture, what can you **conclude** about the journey up the mountain?

*The Moon and the Abandoned Old Woman* (1891), Yoshitoshi. © Asian Art & Archaeology, Inc./Corbis.

*Moon*, Tsukioka Yoshitoshi. From the *Snow, Moon and Flower* Series. © Christie's Images Ltd.

Then one day there was a terrible commotion among the villagers for Lord
60 Higa of the town beyond the hills threatened to conquer their village and
make it his own.

"Only one thing can spare you," Lord Higa announced. "Bring me a box
containing one thousand ropes of ash and I will spare your village."

The cruel young lord quickly gathered together all the wise men of his
village. "You are men of wisdom," he said. "Surely you can tell me how to meet
Lord Higa's demands so our village can be spared."

But the wise men shook their heads. "It is impossible to make even one rope
of ash, sire," they answered. "How can we ever make one thousand?"

"Fools!" the lord cried angrily. "What good is your wisdom if you cannot
70 help me now?"

And he posted a notice in the village square offering a great reward of gold
to any villager who could help him save their village.

But all the people in the village whispered, "Surely, it is an impossible thing,
for ash crumbles at the touch of the finger. How could anyone ever make
a rope of ash?" They shook their heads and sighed, "Alas, alas, we must be
conquered by yet another cruel lord."

The young farmer, too, supposed that this must be, and he wondered what
would happen to his mother if a new lord even more terrible than their own
came to rule over them.

80 When his mother saw the troubled look on his face, she asked, "Why are
you so worried, my son?"

**ANALYZE VISUALS**
What **details** about the
man's appearance affect
your impression of his
personality?

So the farmer told her of the impossible demand made by Lord Higa if the village was to be spared, but his mother did not seem troubled at all. Instead she laughed softly and said, "Why, that is not such an impossible task. All one has to do is soak ordinary rope in salt water and dry it well. When it is burned, it will hold its shape and there is your rope of ash! Tell the villagers to hurry and find one thousand pieces of rope."

The farmer shook his head in amazement. "Mother, you are wonderfully wise," he said, and he rushed to tell the young lord what he must do. **E**

90 "You are wiser than all the wise men of the village," the lord said when he heard the farmer's solution, and he rewarded him with many pieces of gold. The thousand ropes of ash were quickly made and the village was spared.

In a few days, however, there was another great commotion in the village as Lord Higa sent another threat. This time he sent a log with a small hole that curved and bent seven times through its length, and he demanded that a single piece of silk thread be threaded through the hole. "If you cannot perform this task," the lord threatened, "I shall come to conquer your village."

The young lord hurried once more to his wise men, but they all shook their heads in **bewilderment.** "A needle cannot bend its way through such curves," 100 they moaned. "Again we are faced with an impossible demand."

"And again you are stupid fools!'" the lord said, stamping his foot impatiently. He then posted a second notice in the village square asking the villagers for their help.

Once more the young farmer hurried with the problem to his mother in her secret room.

"Why, that is not so difficult," his mother said with a quick smile. "Put some sugar at one end of the hole. Then, tie an ant to a piece of silk thread and put it in at the other end. He will weave his way in and out of the curves to get to the sugar and he will take the silk thread with him."

110 "Mother, you are remarkable!" the son cried, and he hurried off to the lord with the solution to the second problem.

Once more the lord commended the young farmer and rewarded him with many pieces of gold. "You are a brilliant man and you have saved our village again," he said gratefully.

But the lord's troubles were not over even then, for a few days later Lord Higa sent still another demand. "This time you will undoubtedly fail and then I shall conquer your village," he threatened. "Bring me a drum that sounds without being beaten."

"But that is not possible," sighed the people of the village. "How can anyone 120 make a drum sound without beating it?"

This time the wise men held their heads in their hands and moaned, "It is hopeless. It is hopeless. This time Lord Higa will conquer us all."

**E UNIVERSAL THEME**
What do you learn about the old woman from the way she solves the village's problem?

**bewilderment**
(bĭ-wĭl′dər-mənt) *n.* the state of being confused or astonished

The young farmer hurried home breathlessly. "Mother, Mother, we must solve another terrible problem or Lord Higa will conquer our village!" And he quickly told his mother about the impossible drum.

His mother, however, smiled and answered, "Why, this is the easiest of them all. Make a drum with sides of paper and put a bumblebee inside. As it tries to escape, it will buzz and beat itself against the paper and you will have a drum that sounds without being beaten." **F**

130     The young farmer was amazed at his mother's wisdom. "You are far wiser than any of the wise men of the village," he said, and he hurried to tell the young lord how to meet Lord Higa's third demand.

When the lord heard the answer, he was greatly impressed. "Surely a young man like you cannot be wiser than all my wise men," he said. "Tell me honestly, who has helped you solve all these difficult problems?"

The young farmer could not lie. "My lord," he began slowly, "for the past two years I have broken the law of the land. I have kept my aged mother hidden beneath the floor of my house, and it is she who solved each of your problems and saved the village from Lord Higa."

140     He trembled as he spoke, for he feared the lord's displeasure and rage. Surely now the soldiers would be summoned to throw him into the dark dungeon. But when he glanced fearfully at the lord, he saw that the young ruler was not angry at all. Instead, he was silent and thoughtful, for at last he realized how much wisdom and knowledge old people possess.

"I have been very wrong," he said finally. "And I must ask the forgiveness of your mother and of all my people. Never again will I demand that the old people of our village be sent to the mountains to die. Rather, they will be treated with the respect and honor they deserve and share with us the wisdom of their years." **G**

150     And so it was. From that day, the villagers were no longer forced to abandon their parents in the mountains, and the village became once more a happy, cheerful place in which to live. The terrible Lord Higa stopped sending his impossible demands and no longer threatened to conquer them, for he too was impressed. "Even in such a small village there is much wisdom," he declared, "and its people should be allowed to live in peace."

And that is exactly what the farmer and his mother and all the people of the village did for all the years thereafter. ❧

**F** UNIVERSAL THEME
Why do you think the old woman is able to solve all the problems created by Lord Higa's demands?

**G** UNIVERSAL THEME
What lesson does the young lord learn?

# Comprehension

1. **Recall** In "The Old Grandfather and His Little Grandson," whose action shames the couple into treating the grandfather better?

2. **Recall** In "The Wise Old Woman," what is the young lord's decree?

3. **Clarify** What causes Lord Higa to spare the village?

**INDIANA STANDARDS**

**READING STANDARD**
**8.3.3** Compare and contrast the motivations and reactions of literary characters ....

# Literary Analysis

4. **Analyze Motives** In "The Old Grandfather and His Little Grandson," why do you think the son and his wife react so negatively to the grandfather's accident?

5. **Compare and Contrast Characters** Reread lines 1–49 of "The Wise Old Woman." How are the young lord and the young farmer different? In your answer, be sure to describe each character's traits.

6. **Identify Parallel Episodes** In folk tales, events often happen in threes. There may be three wishes or three tasks, for example. These repeated events are called **parallel episodes.** What parallel episodes can you find in "The Wise Old Woman"?

# Comparing Universal Theme

Now that you have read both tales, finish filling in your chart. Finally, add the question about universal theme to your chart and write your answer.

|  | "The Old Grandfather and His Little Grandson" | "The Wise Old Woman" |
|---|---|---|
| Who are the important characters? | elderly character: <br><br> unkind characters: <br><br> other characters: | elderly character: <br><br> unkind characters: <br><br> other characters: |
| How is the elderly character mistreated? |  |  |
| What motivates characters to stop this mistreatment? |  |  |
| What is the universal theme? |  |  |

# Vocabulary in Context

## VOCABULARY PRACTICE

Choose the word in each group that is most nearly opposite in meaning to the boldfaced word.

1. **haughtily:** (a) snobbishly, (b) modestly, (c) indifferently
2. **bewilderment:** (a) understanding, (b) confusion, (c) shock
3. **arrogant:** (a) smug, (b) humble, (c) aloof
4. **deceive:** (a) outsmart, (b) scam, (c) guide

## VOCABULARY IN WRITING

Write a paragraph from the young lord's perspective, explaining the lesson he learned. Include at least two vocabulary words. Here is a sample of how you might begin.

> **EXAMPLE SENTENCE**
>
> *When I learned how wise the old woman was, I felt truly ashamed I had been so **arrogant**.*

## VOCABULARY STRATEGY: THE SUFFIX -*ly*

A suffix is a word part that can be added to the end of a root or base word. Sometimes a suffix is used to change a word's part of speech. For example, when the suffix -*ly* is added to the end of the word *haughty*, it forms the adverb *haughtily*. When an adjective ends in -*y*, as *haughty* does, the *y* changes to *i* before -*ly* is added.

*PRACTICE* Change each boldfaced adjective to an adverb by adding the suffix -*ly*. Then rephrase each sentence so it makes sense.

1. In the beginning of the story, the young lord was **cruel.**
2. The **tearful** son had to take his mother into the mountains.
3. The **angry** lord asked the villagers for help.
4. The old woman was **happy** to provide her son with the answers.

**VOCABULARY PRACTICE**
For more practice, go to the **Vocabulary Center** at **ClassZone.com.**

# Writing for Assessment

## 1. READ THE PROMPT

In writing assessments, you will often be asked to compare and contrast
two works that share a similar theme.

**PROMPT**

The folk tales "The Old Grandfather and His
Little Grandson" and "The Wise Old Woman"
express the same universal theme in different
ways. In four to five paragraphs, compare and
contrast the ways in which the folk tales convey
their message. Include details from the tales to
support your response.

◀ **STRATEGIES IN ACTION**

*1. I have to make sure I understand the*
***message*** *expressed by these folk tales.*

*2. I need to identify the* ***similarities and***
***differences*** *in how the tales get*
*the message across.*

*3. I should support my ideas using*
***information*** *from the two tales.*

## 2. PLAN YOUR WRITING

Review your chart to identify the universal theme and the way
each folk tale expresses it. Then think about how you will set
up the body of your response.

*I. Introduce tales and*
*thesis statement*
*II. How first tale*
*expresses theme*
*III. How second tale*
*expresses theme*
*IV. Comparison of tales*
*V. Conclusion*

- Option A: In one paragraph, describe how the universal
  theme is conveyed in the first folk tale; in the next paragraph,
  describe how this theme is conveyed in the second folk tale;
  in a third paragraph, discuss similarities and differences.

- Option B: In one paragraph, compare the elderly characters;
  in a second paragraph, compare the mistreatment of
  the elderly characters; in a third paragraph, compare the
  motivations for ending the mistreatment.

Once you have decided on the organization, outline your essay.
Then write a thesis statement that describes the main idea of your essay.

## 3. DRAFT YOUR RESPONSE

**Introduction** Give the titles and authors of the tales. Provide a sentence telling what
each tale is about. State the universal theme and include your thesis statement.
**Body** Using your outline as a guide, discuss how each folk tale conveys the universal
theme. Use details from the tales to support your ideas.
**Conclusion** End each essay by restating the universal theme and your thesis statement.
Explain whether the values conveyed by these tales are still important.
**Revision** Make sure you clearly identify the tale you are discussing in each paragraph.

## My Mother Pieced Quilts
Poem by Teresa Palomo Acosta

## quilting
Poem by Lucille Clifton

# *What gives* MEANING *to simple things?*

**KEY IDEA** Is there a song that reminds you of a particular time or place in your life? Perhaps there is a food that makes you think of a special person or holiday. Simple things like these can have a unique **meaning** when they represent something more. In the poems you are about to read, you'll see how simple things can have personal significance.

**SURVEY** Take an informal survey of five to ten classmates to find out what simple things have the most meaning for them. What types of things come up most often? As a class, create an answer to the question "What gives meaning to simple things?"

## ● LITERARY ANALYSIS: SYMBOL IN POETRY

**Symbols** are people, places, and things that stand for something beyond themselves. Writers often use them to convey complex ideas in a few words. For example, in the poems you are about to read, quilts and quilting represent something more significant than an object or activity. To understand these symbols, use the following tips:

- Think about the big ideas each line or stanza expresses. Ask: *What message about families, art, or other big topics is the poem communicating?*

- Pay attention to the poet's word choice. Ask: *Which words have positive associations? Which have negative associations?*

- Notice how the symbol relates to the big ideas in the poem. Ask: *In what way do quilts or quilting help convey the poem's message?*

As you read, use graphics like the ones shown to write down clues that help you understand each symbol. You'll finish filling in the graphics later.

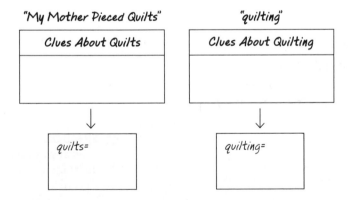

"My Mother Pieced Quilts"

| Clues About Quilts |
|---|
|  |

quilts=

"quilting"

| Clues About Quilting |
|---|
|  |

quilting=

## ● READING SKILL: DRAW CONCLUSIONS

You often must **draw conclusions** to understand the message a poet is trying to share. A conclusion is a belief you arrive at or a logical judgment you make by combining your inferences about the poem with your personal knowledge and experience.

To help you draw a conclusion, you can fill in a statement like this: "I believe _____ because _____ and _____." For example, "I believe the daughter respects her mother because she seems awed by her mother's talent and because I know from experience how important adult role models are." As you read "My Mother Pieced Quilts" and "quilting," fill in your own statements to draw conclusions about the value of quilting.

# Author On<sup>line</sup>

**Teresa Palomo Acosta: Women's Advocate**
Teresa Palomo Acosta grew up in central Texas, where she enjoyed listening to her grandfather tell colorful stories about her family's history in Mexico and Texas. Acosta's work as a writer springs from her desire to tell stories about people  who don't usually appear in literature. In particular, she writes about the lives and struggles of Mexican-American women in the past and present. Widely recognized for her efforts in support of women, she's been named an Outstanding Woman in the Arts.

**Teresa Palomo Acosta
born 1949**

**Lucille Clifton: Creating Beautiful Poems** Lucille Clifton grew up in the state of New York and was the first in her family to finish high school and attend college. Her poetry often deals with her African-American roots and having strength through difficult times. She  believes writing poetry explores what it means to be human. "Poetry doesn't have to be pretty," she said, "but it must be beautiful." Clifton has won many awards for her work, including the National Book Award and an Emmy Award.

**Lucille Clifton
born 1936**

 **MORE ABOUT THE AUTHOR**
For more on Teresa Palomo Acosta and Lucille Clifton, visit the **Literature Center** at **ClassZone.com**.

# My Mother Pieced Quilts

### Teresa Palomo Acosta

they were just meant as covers
in winters
as weapons
against pounding january winds

5 but it was just that every morning I awoke to these
october ripened canvases
passed my hand across their cloth faces
and began to wonder how you pieced
all these together
10 these strips of gentle communion cotton and flannel nightgowns
wedding organdies
dime store velvets **A**

how you shaped patterns square and oblong and round
positioned
15 balanced
then cemented them
with your thread
a steel needle
a thimble

20 how the thread darted in and out
galloping along the frayed edges, tucking them in
as you did us at night
oh how you stretched and turned and re-arranged
your michigan spring faded curtain pieces
25 my father's santa fe work shirt
the summer denims, the tweeds of fall **B**

**ANALYZE VISUALS**
What recognizable objects can you find in this quilt? Tell what each might **symbolize** to the quiltmaker.

**A** **SYMBOL**
In what ways are the quilts more than covers?

**B** **DRAW CONCLUSIONS**
How does the mother's skill in making the quilt mirror her role in the family?

*American Childhood* (1995), Jane Burch Cochran. Fabric, beads, buttons, paint, baby dress, gloves, 53" × 42".

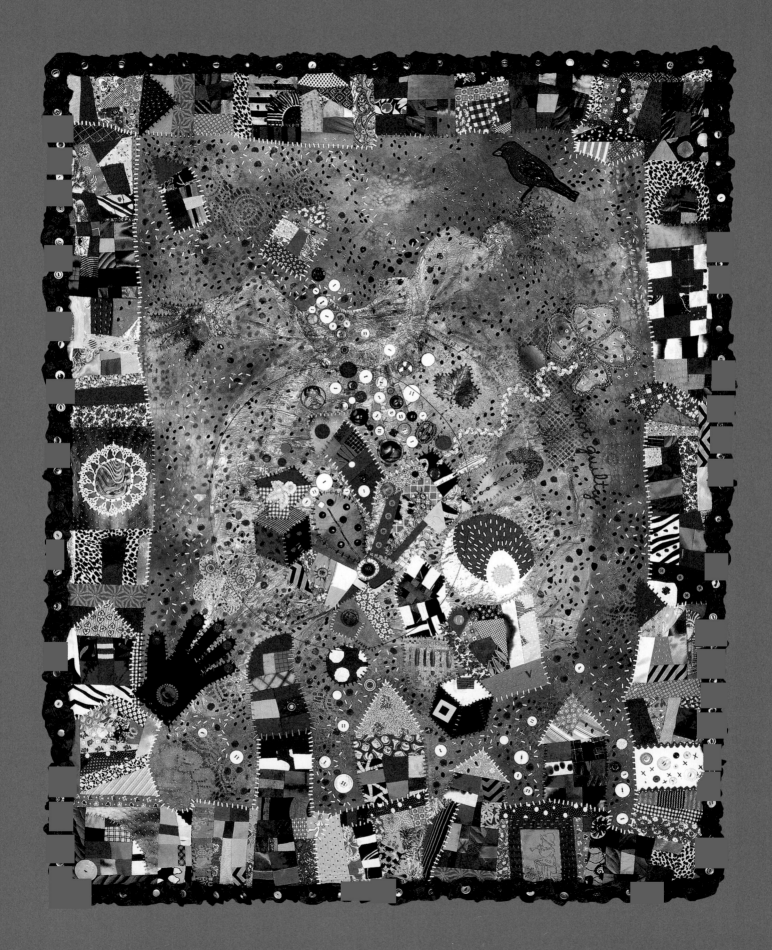

in the evening you sat at your canvas
—our cracked linoleum floor the drawing board
me lounging on your arm
30  and you staking out the plan:
whether to put the lilac purple of easter against the red plaid
      of winter-going-
into-spring
whether to mix a yellow with blue and white and paint the
35  corpus christi noon when my father held your hand
whether to shape a five-point star from the
somber black silk you wore to grandmother's funeral **C**

you were the river current
carrying the roaring notes
40  forming them into pictures of a little boy reclining
a swallow flying
you were the caravan master at the reins
driving your threaded needle artillery[1] across the mosaic[2]
      cloth bridges
45  delivering yourself in separate testimonies.[3]

oh mother you plunged me sobbing and laughing
into our past
into the river crossing at five
into the spinach fields
50  into the plainview cotton rows
into tuberculosis wards
into braids and muslin[4] dresses
sewn hard and taut to withstand the thrashings of twenty-five years **D**

stretched out they lay
55  armed/ready/shouting/celebrating

knotted with love
the quilts sing on **E**

**C  SYMBOL**
Reread lines 31–37. What parts of life do the fabrics in the quilt represent?

**D  DRAW CONCLUSIONS**
Think about the images the **speaker** uses as she describes her mother. What is the speaker's attitude toward her mother?

**E  SYMBOL**
What does the **speaker** mean when she says "the quilts sing on"? Consider how the quilt represents the family itself.

1. **artillery** (är-tǐl′ə-rē): large weapons that are operated by crews.
2. **mosaic** (mō-zā′ǐk): a picture or design created when small colored pieces of stone or tile are set into a surface.
3. **testimonies** (tĕs′tə-mō′nēz): declarations.
4. **muslin** (mǔz′lǐn): sturdy cotton fabric.

# quilting
## Lucille Clifton

*Crossing Borders* (1995), Deidre Scherer. Fabric and thread. © Deidre Scherer.

somewhere in the unknown world
a yellow eyed woman
sits with her daughter
quilting.

5 some other where
alchemists[1] mumble over pots.
their chemistry stirs
into science. their science
freezes into stone. **F**

10 in the unknown world
the woman
threading together her need
and her needle
nods toward the smiling girl
15 *remember*
*this will keep us warm.* **G**

how does this poem end?
do the daughters' daughters quilt?
do the alchemists practice their tables?
20 do the worlds continue spinning
away from each other forever?

---

1. **alchemist** (ăl′kə-mĭst): a chemist who tries to turn
   metals into gold.

**ANALYZE VISUALS**
What might the gesture
in this picture **symbolize?**

**F DRAW CONCLUSIONS**
Does the **speaker**
present the place where
the alchemists are in a
positive or negative way?
Tell what words in this
stanza make you think so.

**G SYMBOL**
How is the world where
the mother and daughter
quilt different from the
alchemists' world?

## Comprehension

1. **Recall** What were the quilts in "My Mother Pieced Quilts" meant for?

2. **Recall** In "My Mother Pieced Quilts," what does the mother consider doing with the black silk from the grandmother's funeral?

3. **Summarize** Describe the alchemists' work in "quilting."

**INDIANA STANDARDS**

**READING STANDARD**
**8.3.6** Identify significant literary devices . . . .

## Literary Analysis

4. **Visualize** In "My Mother Pieced Quilts," the poet uses vivid language to create a picture of the fabrics, patterns, and colors of the quilts. What three descriptive phrases best help you visualize the quilts?

5. **Clarify a Line** In "quilting," the mother threads together "her need and her needle." What need might quilting fulfill for the mother? Think about why it's important for her to share the experience with her daughter.

6. **Interpret a Question** In "quilting," the poem ends with the following question: "do the worlds continue spinning away from each other forever?" Think about how the worlds are contrasted in the poem. Why might they be moving apart? Explain your answer.

7. **Analyze Symbols** Finish filling in your graphics with any additional clues to the meanings of "quilts" and "quilting" in the two poems. In "My Mother Pieced Quilts," what do the quilts symbolize? In "quilting," what does the act of quilting symbolize? Write the answers in your graphic.

8. **Draw Conclusions** In a chart like the one shown, list examples from the poems of the practical, creative, and social reasons for quilting. Based on this list, what can you conclude about the value in making quilts?

|  | Reasons for Quilting |
|---|---|
| Practical | |
| Creative | |
| Social | |

## Extension and Challenge

9. **Creative Project: Art** If you were to make a quilt to represent your life, what would it look like? Think about the fabrics, colors, and designs you would choose and their **meaning** to you. Then make a collage of your quilt.

# Reading-Writing Connection

Delve deeper into "My Mother Pieced Quilts" and "quilting" by responding to these prompts. Then complete the **Grammar and Writing** exercise.

| WRITING PROMPTS | | SELF-CHECK |
|---|---|---|

**A. Short Response: Describe a Relationship**
In what way is the mother-daughter relationship central to the message in the poem "quilting"? In a **one-paragraph description,** explain why the mother wants to quilt with her daughter.

*An effective description will . . .*
- explain the importance of quilting to the mother
- reveal how quilting connects the generations

**B. Extended Response: Write a Speech**
Imagine a museum has decided to show the quilts described in "My Mother Pieced Quilts." The speaker of the poem has been asked to discuss her mother's work. Write a **one-page speech** in which the speaker explains to the audience how the quilts were created and what they **mean** to her.

*A successful speech will . . .*
- include details about how the quilts were made and what some of the squares represent
- reflect the relationship between the mother and daughter

## GRAMMAR AND WRITING

*USE THE ACTIVE VOICE* Verbs can be in either the active voice or passive voice. In a sentence that uses the **active voice,** the subject *performs* the verb's action. In a sentence that uses the **passive voice,** the subject *receives* the verb's action. The passive voice tends to make sentences dull and weak, so you should use the active voice whenever possible.

> *Passive:* The quilt was sewn together by my mother. (*The subject quilt receives the action of the verb phrase* was sewn.)
>
> *Active:* My mother sewed the quilt together. (*The subject* mother *performs the action of the verb* sewed.)

**INDIANA STANDARDS**

WRITING STANDARD
**8.4.8** Edit and proofread one's own writing, as well as that of others . . . .

*PRACTICE* Rewrite each of these sentences in the active voice.

1. The quilts were worked on every night by my mother.
2. I am reminded of my fifth birthday by this piece of pink satin.
3. The denim that's used in the quilt was worn by my father.
4. Our family was warmed and comforted by my mother's quilts.

*For more help with active and passive voice, see page R57 in the **Grammar Handbook.***

## The Diary of Anne Frank

Drama by Frances Goodrich and Albert Hackett

# What **IMPACT** will you have on the world?

**INDIANA STANDARDS**

**READING STANDARDS**
**8.3.2** Evaluate the structural elements of the plot, such as subplots, parallel episodes, and climax; the plot's development; and the way in which conflicts are (or are not) addressed and resolved.

**8.3.5** Identify and analyze recurring themes … that appear frequently across traditional and contemporary works.

**KEY IDEA** Everyone makes an **impact** on the world in some way. National leaders or sports heroes may inspire millions, while the rest of us can influence a smaller circle of friends and family through our actions, our beliefs, or our commitments. Whether you make your mark quietly or boldly, a life well lived can be a guide to others. In the play you're about to read, a young girl doesn't realize that the thoughts she expresses in her diary will later influence readers all over the world.

**QUICKWRITE** People of all ages make important contributions to the world. What impact do you now have on others? What impact do you hope to have later in your life? Write your ideas in a brief journal entry. Think about how education and life experience might affect your goals for the future.

## ● LITERARY ANALYSIS: THEME

The play you are about to read is based on a diary written by Anne Frank, a teenager who spent more than two years hiding from the Nazis. When Anne's diary was published, readers around the world were profoundly touched that, despite all she had been through, she still believed people were good at heart.

When the playwrights adapted Anne's diary, they used her belief in the essential goodness of people as one of the work's **themes,** or messages about life. As you read, notice how Anne's thoughts and feelings, as well as the characters' relationships with each other, work together to express this theme.

## ● READING SKILL: STORY MAPPING

As you know, a road map can be a useful tool to help you get someplace. Similarly, a **story map** can help you understand what you're reading. It shows how a story's parts fit together and how the action moves from one event to another. As you read *The Diary of Anne Frank,* complete a story map like the one shown.

*The Diary of Anne Frank*

Setting: _____

Characters: _____  _____
            _____  _____
            _____  _____

Problem: _____

Events: _____  _____
        _____  _____
        _____  _____

Resolution: _____

## ▲ VOCABULARY IN CONTEXT

The following words help the playwrights capture Anne's experiences. To see how many you know, try to match each word from the list with the word or phrase closest in meaning.

| WORD LIST | | |
|---|---|---|
| apprehension | fortify | remorse |
| disgruntled | indignantly | unabashed |
| foreboding | pandemonium | |

1. wild uproar
2. displeased
3. worry
4. angrily
5. strengthen
6. sinking feeling
7. bold
8. sorrow

# Author Online

**From Comedies to Drama** Screenwriting team Frances Goodrich and Albert Hackett were a married couple known for their upbeat comedies and musicals. In the late 1940s, they began working on a drama that would take eight years to complete. Their play, *The Diary of Anne Frank,* was based on Anne Frank's diary entries. As part of their research, the couple traveled to Amsterdam to interview Anne's father and to see the family's hiding place. Their play adaptation won a Pulitzer Prize in 1956.

**Frances Goodrich**
1890–1984

**Albert Hackett**
1900–1995

## *Background*

**Anne Frank's Diary** Anne Frank and her family were Jewish citizens of Germany. When the Nazi party, led by Adolf Hitler, came to power in 1933, the Nazis blamed the country's problems on the Jews. Jews were stripped of their rights. Many were eventually sent to concentration camps where more than 6 million Jews died in what became known as the Holocaust. The Franks moved to the Netherlands to escape persecution, but the Nazis invaded that country in 1940. In order to survive, Anne's family went into hiding when she was 13 years old. They hid in attic rooms behind Mr. Frank's office, and several other Jews joined them. In this "Secret Annex," Anne kept a diary about her life in hiding. More than two years later, the group's worst fears came true when the Nazis found them. Everyone who had been living there was sent to concentration camps. Anne's diary was discovered later.

> **MORE ABOUT THE AUTHOR AND BACKGROUND**
> To learn more about the authors and the Holocaust, visit the **Literature Center** at ClassZone.com.

# THE Diary OF Anne Frank

*Frances Goodrich
and Albert Hackett*

## CHARACTERS

**SECRET ANNEX RESIDENTS**

| | | |
|---|---|---|
| **Anne Frank** | **Mrs. Frank** | **Mrs. Van Daan** |
| **Margot Frank** | **Peter Van Daan** | **Mr. Dussel** |
| **Mr. Frank** | **Mr. Van Daan** | |

**WORKERS IN MR. FRANK'S BUSINESS**

**Miep Gies** (mēp gēs)

**Mr. Kraler** (krä'lər)

**The Time.** *July 1942–August 1944, November 1945*
**The Place.** *Amsterdam, the Netherlands*

*The scene remains the same throughout the play. It is the top floor of a warehouse and office building in Amsterdam, Holland. The sharply peaked roof of the building is outlined against a sea of other rooftops, stretching away into the distance. Nearby is the belfry of a church tower, the Westertoren, whose carillon rings out the hours. Occasionally faint sounds float up from below: the voices of children playing in the street, the tramp of marching feet, a boat whistle from the canal.*

*The three rooms of the top floor and a small attic space above are exposed to our view. The largest of the rooms is in the center, with two small rooms, slightly raised, on either side. On the right is a bathroom, out of sight. A narrow steep flight of stairs at the back leads up to the attic. The rooms are sparsely furnished with a few chairs, cots, a table or two. The windows are painted over, or covered with makeshift blackout curtains. In the main room there is a sink, a gas ring for cooking and a wood-burning stove for warmth.*

*The room on the left is hardly more than a closet. There is a skylight in the sloping ceiling. Directly under this room is a small steep stairwell, with steps leading down to a door. This is the only entrance from the building below. When the door is opened we see that it has been concealed on the outer side by a bookcase attached to it.*

*The Diary of Anne Frank,* starring Natalie Portman as Anne, ran on Broadway at the Music Box Theatre from December 1997 to June 1998.

## ACT ONE
### Scene 1

*The curtain rises on an empty stage. It is late afternoon November, 1945.*

*The rooms are dusty, the curtains in rags. Chairs and tables are overturned.*

*The door at the foot of the small stairwell swings open.* Mr. Frank *comes up the steps into view. He is a gentle, cultured European in his middle years. There is still a trace of a German accent in his speech.*

*He stands looking slowly around, making a*
10 *supreme effort at self-control. He is weak, ill. His clothes are threadbare.*

*After a second he drops his rucksack on the couch and moves slowly about. He opens the door to one of the smaller rooms, and then abruptly closes it again, turning away. He goes to the window at the back, looking off at the Westertoren as its carillon strikes the hour of six, then he moves restlessly on.*

*From the street below we hear the sound of a barrel organ and children's voices at play. There is a*
20 *many-colored scarf hanging from a nail.* Mr. Frank *takes it, putting it around his neck. As he starts back for his rucksack, his eye is caught by something lying on the floor. It is a woman's white glove. He holds it in his hand and suddenly all of his self-control is gone. He breaks down, crying.*

*We hear footsteps on the stairs.* Miep Gies *comes up, looking for* Mr. Frank. Miep *is a Dutch girl of about twenty-two. She wears a coat and hat, ready to go home. She is pregnant. Her attitude toward*
30 Mr. Frank *is protective, compassionate.*

**Miep.** Are you all right, Mr. Frank?

**Mr. Frank** (*quickly controlling himself*). Yes, Miep, yes.

**Miep.** Everyone in the office has gone home . . . It's after six. (*then pleading*) Don't stay up here, Mr. Frank. What's the use of torturing yourself like this?

**Mr. Frank.** I've come to say good-bye . . . I'm leaving here, Miep.

40 **Miep.** What do you mean? Where are you going? Where?

**Mr. Frank.** I don't know yet. I haven't decided.

**Miep.** Mr. Frank, you can't leave here! This is your home! Amsterdam is your home. Your business is here, waiting for you . . . You're needed here . . . Now that the war is over, there are things that . . .

**Mr. Frank.** I can't stay in Amsterdam, Miep. It has too many memories for me. Everywhere there's something . . . the house we lived in . . . the
50 school . . . that street organ playing out there . . . I'm not the person you used to know, Miep. I'm a bitter old man. (*breaking off*) Forgive me. I shouldn't speak to you like this . . . after all that you did for us . . . the suffering . . .

**Miep.** No. No. It wasn't suffering. You can't say we suffered. (*As she speaks, she straightens a chair which is overturned.*)

**Mr. Frank.** I know what you went through, you and Mr. Kraler. I'll remember it as long as I live.
60 (*He gives one last look around.*) Come, Miep.

(*He starts for the steps, then remembers his rucksack, going back to get it.*)

**Miep** (*hurrying up to a cupboard*). Mr. Frank, did you see? There are some of your papers here. (*She brings a bundle of papers to him.*) We found them in a heap of rubbish on the floor after . . . after you left.

**Mr. Frank.** Burn them.

(*He opens his rucksack to put the glove in it.*)

70 **Miep.** But, Mr. Frank, there are letters, notes . . .

**Mr. Frank.** Burn them. All of them.

**Miep.** Burn *this*?

(*She hands him a paperbound notebook.*)

**Mr. Frank** (*quietly*). Anne's diary. (*He opens the diary and begins to read.*) "Monday, the sixth of July, nineteen forty-two." (*to* Miep) Nineteen

forty-two. Is it possible, Miep? . . . Only three years ago. (*As he continues his reading, he sits down on the couch.*) "Dear Diary, since you and I are going to be great friends, I will start by telling you about myself. My name is Anne Frank. I am thirteen years old. I was born in Germany the twelfth of June, nineteen twenty-nine. As my family is Jewish, we emigrated to Holland when Hitler came to power."

(*As* Mr. Frank *reads on, another voice joins his, as if coming from the air. It is* Anne's Voice.)

**Mr. Frank and Anne.** "My father started a business, importing spice and herbs. Things went well for us until nineteen forty. Then the war came, and the Dutch capitulation, followed by the arrival of the Germans. Then things got very bad for the Jews."

(Mr. Frank's Voice *dies out.* Anne's Voice *continues alone. The lights dim slowly to darkness. The curtain falls on the scene.*)

**Anne's Voice.** You could not do this and you could not do that. They forced Father out of his business. We had to wear yellow stars.[1] I had to turn in my bike. I couldn't go to a Dutch school any more. I couldn't go to the movies, or ride in an automobile, or even on a streetcar, and a million other things. But somehow we children still managed to have fun. Yesterday Father told me we were going into hiding. Where, he wouldn't say. At five o'clock this morning Mother woke me and told me to hurry and get dressed. I was to put on as many clothes as I could. It would look too suspicious if we walked along carrying suitcases. It wasn't until we were on our way that I learned where we were going. Our hiding place was to be upstairs in the building where Father used to have his business. Three other people were coming in with us . . . the Van Daans and their son Peter . . . Father knew the Van Daans but we had never met them . . .

(*During the last lines the curtain rises on the scene. The lights dim on.* Anne's Voice *fades out.*)

*It is early morning, July, 1942. The rooms are bare, as before, but they are now clean and orderly.*

Mr. Van Daan, *a tall, portly man in his late forties, is in the main room, pacing up and down, nervously smoking a cigarette. His clothes and overcoat are expensive and well cut.*

Mrs. Van Daan *sits on the couch, clutching her possessions, a hatbox, bags, etc. She is a pretty woman in her early forties. She wears a fur coat over her other clothes.*

Peter Van Daan *is standing at the window of the room on the right, looking down at the street below. He is a shy, awkward boy of sixteen. He wears a cap, a raincoat, and long Dutch trousers, like "plus fours." At his feet is a black case, a carrier for his cat.*

*The yellow Star of David is conspicuous on all of their clothes.*

**Mrs. Van Daan** (*rising, nervous, excited*). Something's happened to them! I know it!

**Mr. Van Daan.** Now, Kerli!

**Mrs. Van Daan.** Mr. Frank said they'd be here at seven o'clock. He said . . .

**Mr. Van Daan.** They have two miles to walk. You can't expect . . .

**Mrs. Van Daan.** They've been picked up. That's what's happened. They've been taken . . .

(Mr. Van Daan *indicates that he hears someone coming.*)

**Mr. Van Daan.** You see?

(Peter *takes up his carrier and his schoolbag, etc., and goes into the main room as* Mr. Frank *comes up the stairwell from below.* Mr. Frank *looks much younger now. His movements are brisk, his manner confident. He wears an overcoat and carries his hat and a small cardboard box. He crosses to the* Van Daans, *shaking hands with each of them.*)

**Mr. Frank.** Mrs. Van Daan, Mr. Van Daan, Peter. (*then, in explanation of their lateness*) There were

---

1. **yellow stars:** the six-pointed Stars of David that the Nazis ordered all Jews to wear for identification.

too many of the Green Police[2] on the streets . . . we had to take the long way around.

(*Up the steps come* Margot Frank, Mrs. Frank, Miep [*not pregnant now*] *and* Mr. Kraler. *All of them carry bags, packages, and so forth. The Star of David is conspicuous on all of the* Franks' *clothing.* Margot *is eighteen, beautiful, quiet, shy.* Mrs. Frank *is a young mother, gently bred, reserved. She, like* Mr. Frank, *has a slight German accent.* Mr. Kraler *is a Dutchman, dependable, kindly.*

*As* Mr. Kraler *and* Miep *go upstage to put down their parcels,* Mrs. Frank *turns back to call* Anne.)

**Mrs. Frank.** Anne?

(Anne *comes running up the stairs. She is thirteen, quick in her movements, interested in everything, mercurial in her emotions. She wears a cape, long wool socks and carries a schoolbag.*)

**Mr. Frank** (*introducing them*). My wife, Edith. Mr. and Mrs. Van Daan (Mrs. Frank *hurries over, shaking hands with them.*) . . . their son, Peter . . . my daughters, Margot and Anne.

(Anne *gives a polite little curtsy as she shakes* Mr. Van Daan's *hand. Then she immediately starts off on a tour of investigation of her new home, going upstairs to the attic room.* Miep *and* Mr. Kraler *are putting the various things they have brought on the shelves.*)

**Mr. Kraler.** I'm sorry there is still so much confusion.

**Mr. Frank.** Please. Don't think of it. After all, we'll have plenty of leisure to arrange everything ourselves.

**Miep** (*to* Mrs. Frank). We put the stores of food you sent in here. Your drugs are here . . . soap, linen here.

**Mrs. Frank.** Thank you, Miep.

**Miep.** I made up the beds . . . the way Mr. Frank and Mr. Kraler said. (*She starts out.*) Forgive me. I have to hurry. I've got to go to the other side of town to get some ration books[3] for you.

**Mrs. Van Daan.** Ration books? If they see our names on ration books, they'll know we're here.

**Mr. Kraler.** There isn't anything . . .

**Miep.** Don't worry. Your names won't be on them. (*as she hurries out*) I'll be up later. } *Together*

**Mr. Frank.** Thank you, Miep.

**Mrs. Frank** (*to* Mr. Kraler). It's illegal, then, the ration books? We've never done anything illegal.

**Mr. Frank.** We won't be living here exactly according to regulations. (*As* Mr. Kraler *reassures* Mrs. Frank, *he takes various small things, such as matches, soap, etc., from his pockets, handing them to her.*)

**Mr. Kraler.** This isn't the black market,[4] Mrs. Frank. This is what we call the white market . . . helping all of the hundreds and hundreds who are hiding out in Amsterdam.

(*The carillon is heard playing the quarter-hour before eight.* Mr. Kraler *looks at his watch.* Anne *stops at the window as she comes down the stairs.*)

**Anne.** It's the Westertoren!

**Mr. Kraler.** I must go. I must be out of here and downstairs in the office before the workmen get here. (*He starts for the stairs leading out.*) Miep or I, or both of us, will be up each day to bring you food and news and find out what your needs are. Tomorrow I'll get you a better bolt for the door at the foot of the stairs. It needs a bolt that you can throw yourself and open only at our signal. (*to* Mr. Frank) Oh . . . You'll tell them about the noise?

**Mr. Frank.** I'll tell them.

**Mr. Kraler.** Good-bye then for the moment. I'll come up again, after the workmen leave.

**Mr. Frank.** Good-bye, Mr. Kraler.

**Mrs. Frank** (*shaking his hand*). How can we thank you? (*The others murmur their good-byes.*)

---

2. **Green Police:** the Nazi police who wore green uniforms.

3. **ration books:** books of stamps or coupons issued by the government in wartime. With these coupons, people could purchase scarce items, such as food, clothing, and gasoline.

4. **black market:** a system for selling goods illegally, in violation of rationing and other restrictions.

**Mr. Kraler.** I never thought I'd live to see the day when a man like Mr. Frank would have to go into hiding. When you think—(*He breaks off, going out.* Mr. Frank *follows him down the steps, bolting the door after him. In the interval before he returns,* Peter *goes over to* Margot, *shaking hands with her. As* Mr. Frank *comes back up the steps,* Mrs. Frank *questions him anxiously.*)

240 **Mrs. Frank.** What did he mean, about the noise?

**Mr. Frank.** First let us take off some of these clothes. (*They all start to take off garment after garment. On each of their coats, sweaters, blouses, suits, dresses, is another yellow Star of David.* Mr. *and* Mrs. Frank *are underdressed quite simply. The others wear several things, sweaters, extra dresses, bathrobes, aprons, nightgowns, etc.*)

**Mr. Van Daan.** It's a wonder we weren't arrested, walking along the streets . . . Petronella with a fur 250 coat in July . . . and that cat of Peter's crying all the way.

**Anne** (*as she is removing a pair of panties*). A cat?

**Mrs. Frank** (*shocked*). Anne, please!

**Anne.** It's all right. I've got on three more. (*She pulls off two more. Finally, as they have all removed their surplus clothes, they look to* Mr. Frank, *waiting for him to speak.*)

**Mr. Frank.** Now. About the noise. While the men are in the building below, we must have complete 260 quiet. Every sound can be heard down there, not only in the workrooms, but in the offices too. The men come at about eight-thirty, and leave at about five-thirty. So, to be perfectly safe, from eight in the morning until six in the evening we must move only when it is necessary, and then in stockinged feet. We must not speak above a whisper. We must not run any water. We cannot use the sink, or even, forgive me, the w.c.[5] The pipes go down through the workrooms. It would be heard. No 270 trash . . . (Mr. Frank *stops abruptly as he hears the sound of marching feet from the street below. Everyone is motionless, paralyzed with fear.* Mr. Frank *goes*

quietly into the room on the right to look down out of the window. Anne *runs after him, peering out with him. The tramping feet pass without stopping. The tension is relieved.* Mr. Frank, *followed by* Anne, *returns to the main room and resumes his instructions to the group.*) . . . No trash must ever be thrown out which might reveal that someone is living up 280 here . . . not even a potato paring. We must burn everything in the stove at night. This is the way we must live until it is over, if we are to survive.

(*There is silence for a second.*)

**Mrs. Frank.** Until it is over.

**Mr. Frank** (*reassuringly*). After six we can move about . . . we can talk and laugh and have our supper and read and play games . . . just as we would at home. (*He looks at his watch.*) And now I think it would be wise if we all went to our 290 rooms, and were settled before eight o'clock. Mrs. Van Daan, you and your husband will be upstairs. I regret that there's no place up there for Peter. But he will be here, near us. This will be our common room, where we'll meet to talk and eat and read, like one family.

**Mr. Van Daan.** And where do you and Mrs. Frank sleep?

**Mr. Frank.** This room is also our bedroom.

**Mrs. Van Daan.** That isn't right. We'll
300 sleep here and you take the room } *Together*
upstairs.

**Mr. Van Daan.** It's your place.

**Mr. Frank.** Please. I've thought this out for weeks. It's the best arrangement. The only arrangement.

**Mrs. Van Daan** (*to* Mr. Frank). Never, never can we thank you. (*then to* Mrs. Frank) I don't know what would have happened to us, if it hadn't been for Mr. Frank.

**Mr. Frank.** You don't know how your husband 310 helped me when I came to this country . . . knowing no one . . . not able to speak the language. I can never repay him for that. (*going to* Van Daan) May I help you with your things?

---

5. **w.c.:** water closet; toilet.

**Mr. Van Daan.** No. No. (*to* Mrs. Van Daan) Come along, *liefje.*[6]

**Mrs. Van Daan.** You'll be all right, Peter? You're not afraid?

**Peter** (*embarrassed*). Please, Mother.

(*They start up the stairs to the attic room above.*
320 Mr. Frank *turns to* Mrs. Frank.)

**Mr. Frank.** You too must have some rest, Edith. You didn't close your eyes last night. Nor you, Margot.

**Anne.** I slept, Father. Wasn't that funny? I knew it was the last night in my own bed, and yet I slept soundly.

**Mr. Frank.** I'm glad, Anne. Now you'll be able to help me straighten things in here. (*to* Mrs. Frank *and* Margot) Come with me . . . You and Margot rest in this room for the time being. (*He picks up
330 their clothes, starting for the room on the right.*)

**Mrs. Frank.** You're sure . . . ? I could help . . . And Anne hasn't had her milk . . .

**Mr. Frank.** I'll give it to her. (*to* Anne *and* Peter) Anne, Peter . . . it's best that you take off your shoes now, before you forget. (*He leads the way to the room, followed by* Margot.)

**Mrs. Frank.** You're sure you're not tired, Anne?

**Anne.** I feel fine. I'm going to help Father.

**Mrs. Frank.** Peter, I'm glad you are to be with us.

340 **Peter.** Yes, Mrs. Frank.

(Mrs. Frank *goes to join* Mr. Frank *and* Margot.)

(*During the following scene* Mr. Frank *helps* Margot *and* Mrs. Frank *to hang up their clothes. Then he persuades them both to lie down and rest. The* Van Daans *in their room above settle themselves. In the main room* Anne *and* Peter *remove their shoes.* Peter *takes his cat out of the carrier.*)

**Anne.** What's your cat's name?

**Peter.** Mouschi.[7]

350 **Anne.** Mouschi! Mouschi! Mouschi! (*She picks up the cat, walking away with it. To* Peter.) I love cats.

I have one . . . a darling little cat. But they made me leave her behind. I left some food and a note for the neighbors to take care of her . . . I'm going to miss her terribly. What is yours? A him or a her?

**Peter.** He's a tom. He doesn't like strangers.

(*He takes the cat from her, putting it back in its carrier.*)

**Anne** (<u>*unabashed*</u>). Then I'll have to stop being
360 a stranger, won't I? Is he fixed?

**Peter** (*startled*). Huh?

**Anne.** Did you have him fixed?

**Peter.** No.

**Anne.** Oh, you ought to have him fixed—to keep him from—you know, fighting. Where did you go to school?

**Peter.** Jewish Secondary.

**Anne.** But that's where Margot and I go! I never saw you around.

370 **Peter.** I used to see you . . . sometimes . . .

**Anne.** You did?

**Peter.** . . . in the school yard. You were always in the middle of a bunch of kids. (*He takes a penknife from his pocket.*)

**Anne.** Why didn't you ever come over?

**Peter.** I'm sort of a lone wolf. (*He starts to rip off his Star of David.*)

**Anne.** What are you doing?

**Peter.** Taking it off.

380 **Anne.** But you can't do that. They'll arrest you if you go out without your star.

(*He tosses his knife on the table.*)

**Peter.** Who's going out?

**Anne.** Why, of course! You're right! Of course we don't need them any more. (*She picks up his knife and starts to take her star off.*) I wonder what our friends will think when we don't show up today?

**Peter.** I didn't have any dates with anyone.

---

6. *liefje* (lēf′yə) *Dutch:* little darling.

7. **Mouschi** (mo͞o′shē)

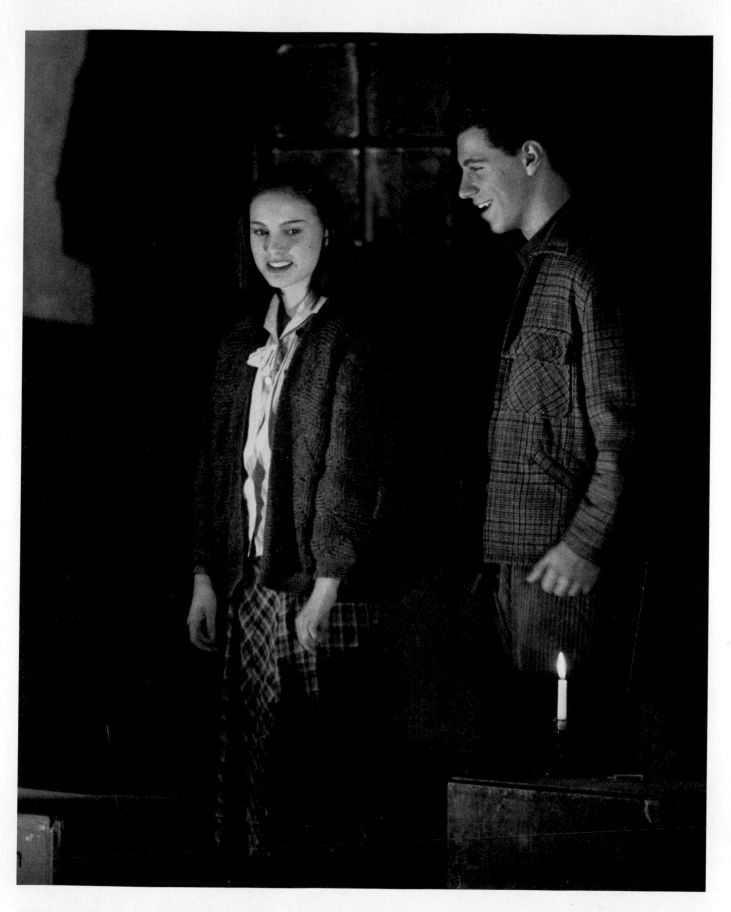

**Anne.** Oh, I did. I had a date with Jopie to go and
390 play ping-pong at her house. Do you know Jopie
de Waal?[8]

**Peter.** No.

**Anne.** Jopie's my best friend. I wonder what
she'll think when she telephones and there's no
answer? . . . Probably she'll go over to the house . . .
I wonder what she'll think . . . we left everything
as if we'd suddenly been called away . . . breakfast
dishes in the sink . . . beds not made . . . (*As she
pulls off her star, the cloth underneath shows clearly*
400 *the color and form of the star.*) Look! It's still there!
(Peter *goes over to the stove with his star.*) What're
you going to do with yours?

**Peter.** Burn it.

**Anne** (*She starts to throw hers in, and cannot.*) It's
funny, I can't throw mine away. I don't know why.

**Peter.** You can't throw . . . ? Something they
branded you with . . . ? That they made you wear
so they could spit on you?

**Anne.** I know. I know. But after all, it *is* the Star
410 of David, isn't it?

(*In the bedroom, right,* Margot *and* Mrs. Frank
*are lying down.* Mr. Frank *starts quietly out.*)

**Peter.** Maybe it's different for a girl.

(Mr. Frank *comes into the main room.*)

**Mr. Frank.** Forgive me, Peter. Now let me see.
We must find a bed for your cat. (*He goes to a
cupboard.*) I'm glad you brought your cat. Anne
was feeling so badly about hers. (*getting a used
small washtub*) Here we are. Will it be comfortable
420 in that?

**Peter** (*gathering up his things*). Thanks.

**Mr. Frank** (*opening the door of the room on the left*).
And here is your room. But I warn you, Peter, you
can't grow any more. Not an inch, or you'll have
to sleep with your feet out of the skylight. Are you
hungry?

**Peter.** No.

**Mr. Frank.** We have some bread and butter.

**Peter.** No, thank you.

430 **Mr. Frank.** You can have it for luncheon then.
And tonight we will have a real supper . . .
our first supper together.

**Peter.** Thanks. Thanks.

(*He goes into his room. During the following scene
he arranges his possessions in his new room.*)

**Mr. Frank.** That's a nice boy, Peter.

**Anne.** He's awfully shy, isn't he?

**Mr. Frank.** You'll like him, I know.

**Anne.** I certainly hope so, since he's the only boy
440 I'm likely to see for months and months.

(Mr. Frank *sits down, taking off his shoes.*)

**Mr. Frank.** Annele,[9] there's a box there. Will you
open it? (*He indicates a carton on the couch.* Anne
*brings it to the center table. In the street below there
is the sound of children playing.*)

**Anne** (*as she opens the carton*). You know the way
I'm going to think of it here? I'm going to think
of it as a boarding house. A very peculiar summer
boarding house, like the one that we—(*She breaks
450 off as she pulls out some photographs.*) Father! My
movie stars! I was wondering where they were!
I was looking for them this morning . . . and
Queen Wilhelmina! How wonderful!

**Mr. Frank.** There's something more. Go on.
Look further. (*He goes over to the sink, pouring
a glass of milk from a thermos bottle.*)

**Anne** (*pulling out a pasteboard-bound book*).
A diary! (*She throws her arms around her father.*)
I've never had a diary. And I've always longed for
460 one. (*She looks around the room.*) Pencil, pencil,
pencil, pencil. (*She starts down the stairs.*) I'm
going down to the office to get a pencil.

**Mr. Frank.** Anne! No! (*He goes after her, catching
her by the arm and pulling her back.*)

**Anne** (*startled*). But there's no one in the
building now.

---

8. **Jopie de Waal** (yō′pē də väl′)

9. **Annele/Anneke:** a nickname for Anne.

**Mr. Frank.** It doesn't matter. I don't want you ever to go beyond that door.

**Anne** (*sobered*). Never . . . ? Not even at nighttime, when everyone is gone? Or on Sundays? Can't I go down to listen to the radio?

**Mr. Frank.** Never. I am sorry, Anneke. It isn't safe. No, you must never go beyond that door.

(*For the first time* Anne *realizes what "going into hiding" means.*)

**Anne.** I see.

**Mr. Frank.** It'll be hard, I know. But always remember this, Anneke. There are no walls, there are no bolts, no locks that anyone can put on your mind. Miep will bring us books. We will read history, poetry, mythology. (*He gives her the glass of milk.*) Here's your milk. (*With his arm about her, they go over to the couch, sitting down side by side.*) As a matter of fact, between us, Anne, being here has certain advantages for you. For instance, you remember the battle you had with your mother the other day on the subject of overshoes? You said you'd rather die than wear overshoes. But in the end you had to wear them? Well now, you see, for as long as we are here you will never have to wear overshoes! Isn't that good? And the coat that you inherited from Margot, you won't have to wear that any more. And the piano! You won't have to practice on the piano. I tell you, this is going to be a fine life for you!

(Anne*'s panic is gone.* Peter *appears in the doorway of his room, with a saucer in his hand. He is carrying his cat.*)

**Peter.** I . . . I . . . I thought I'd better get some water for Mouschi before . . .

**Mr. Frank.** Of course.

(*As he starts toward the sink the carillon begins to chime the hour of eight. He tiptoes to the window at the back and looks down at the street below. He turns to* Peter, *indicating in pantomime that it is too late.* Peter *starts back for his room. He steps on a creaking board. The three of them are frozen for a minute in fear. As* Peter *starts away again,* Anne *tiptoes over*

to him and pours some of the milk from her glass into the saucer for the cat. Peter *squats on the floor, putting the milk before the cat.* Mr. Frank *gives* Anne *his fountain pen, and then goes into the room at the right. For a second* Anne *watches the cat, then she goes over to the center table, and opens her diary.*

*In the room at the right,* Mrs. Frank *has sat up quickly at the sound of the carillon.* Mr. Frank *comes in and sits down beside her on the settee, his arm comfortingly around her.*

*Upstairs, in the attic room,* Mr. *and* Mrs. Van Daan *have hung their clothes in the closet and are now seated on the iron bed.* Mrs. Van Daan *leans back exhausted.* Mr. Van Daan *fans her with a newspaper.*

Anne *starts to write in her diary. The lights dim out, the curtain falls.*

*In the darkness* Anne's Voice *comes to us again, faintly at first, and then with growing strength.*)

**Anne's Voice.** I expect I should be describing what it feels like to go into hiding. But I really don't know yet myself. I only know it's funny never to be able to go outdoors . . . never to breathe fresh air . . . never to run and shout and jump. It's the silence in the nights that frightens me most. Every time I hear a creak in the house, or a step on the street outside, I'm sure they're coming for us. The days aren't so bad. At least we know that Miep and Mr. Kraler are down there below us in the office. Our protectors, we call them. I asked Father what would happen to them if the Nazis found out they were hiding us. Pim said that they would suffer the same fate that we would . . . Imagine! They know this, and yet when they come up here, they're always cheerful and gay as if there were nothing in the world to bother them . . . Friday, the twenty-first of August, nineteen forty-two. Today I'm going to tell you our general news. Mother is unbearable. She insists on treating me like a baby, which I loathe. Otherwise things are going better. The weather is . . .

(*As* Anne's Voice *is fading out, the curtain rises on the scene.*)

## Scene 3

*It is a little after six o'clock in the evening, two months later.*

*Margot is in the bedroom at the right, studying. Mr. Van Daan is lying down in the attic room above.*

*The rest of the "family" is in the main room. Anne and Peter sit opposite each other at the center table, where they have been doing their lessons. Mrs. Frank*
560 *is on the couch. Mrs. Van Daan is seated with her fur coat, on which she has been sewing, in her lap. None of them are wearing their shoes.*

*Their eyes are on Mr. Frank, waiting for him to give them the signal which will release them from their day-long quiet. Mr. Frank, his shoes in his hand, stands looking down out of the window at the back, watching to be sure that all of the workmen have left the building below.*

*After a few seconds of motionless silence,*
570 Mr. Frank *turns from the window.*

**Mr. Frank** (*quietly, to the group*). It's safe now. The last workman has left. (*There is an immediate stir of relief.*)

**Anne** (*Her pent-up energy explodes.*) WHEE!

**Mrs. Frank** (*startled, amused*). Anne!

**Mrs. Van Daan.** I'm first for the w.c. (*She hurries off to the bathroom. Mrs. Frank puts on her shoes and starts up to the sink to prepare supper. Anne sneaks Peter's shoes from under the table and hides them*
580 *behind her back. Mr. Frank goes in to Margot's room.*)

**Mr. Frank** (*to Margot*). Six o'clock. School's over.

(*Margot gets up, stretching. Mr. Frank sits down to put on his shoes. In the main room Peter tries to find his.*)

**Peter** (*to Anne*). Have you seen my shoes?

**Anne** (*innocently*). Your shoes?

**Peter.** You've taken them, haven't you?

**Anne.** I don't know what you're talking about.

**Peter.** You're going to be sorry!

590 **Anne.** Am I? (Peter *goes after her.* Anne, *with his shoes in her hand, runs from him, dodging behind her mother.*)

**Mrs. Frank** (*protesting*). Anne, dear!

**Peter.** Wait till I get you!

**Anne.** I'm waiting! (Peter *makes a lunge for her. They both fall to the floor.* Peter *pins her down, wrestling with her to get the shoes.*) Don't! Don't! Peter, stop it. Ouch!

**Mrs. Frank.** Anne! . . . Peter!

600 (*Suddenly* Peter *becomes self-conscious. He grabs his shoes roughly and starts for his room.*)

**Anne** (*following him*). Peter, where are you going? Come dance with me.

**Peter.** I tell you I don't know how.

**Anne.** I'll teach you.

**Peter.** I'm going to give Mouschi his dinner.

**Anne.** Can I watch?

**Peter.** He doesn't like people around while he eats.

**Anne.** Peter, please.

610 **Peter.** No! (*He goes into his room.* Anne *slams his door after him.*)

**Mrs. Frank.** Anne, dear, I think you shouldn't play like that with Peter. It's not dignified.

**Anne.** Who cares if it's dignified? I don't want to be dignified.

(Mr. Frank *and* Margot *come from the room on the right.* Margot *goes to help her mother.* Mr. Frank *starts for the center table to correct* Margot's *school papers.*)

620 **Mrs. Frank** (*to Anne*). You complain that I don't treat you like a grownup. But when I do, you resent it.

**Anne.** I only want some fun . . . someone to laugh and clown with . . . After you've sat still all day and hardly moved, you've got to have some fun. I don't know what's the matter with that boy.

**Mr. Frank.** He isn't used to girls. Give him a little time.

**Anne.** Time? Isn't two months time? I could cry. 630 (*catching hold of* Margot) Come on, Margot . . . dance with me. Come on, please.

**Margot.** I have to help with supper.

**Anne.** You know we're going to forget how to dance . . . When we get out we won't remember a thing.

(*She starts to sing and dance by herself.* Mr. Frank *takes her in his arms, waltzing with her.* Mrs. Van Daan *comes in from the bathroom.*)

**Mrs. Van Daan.** Next? (*She looks around as she starts* 640 *putting on her shoes.*) Where's Peter?

**Anne** (*as they are dancing*). Where would he be!

**Mrs. Van Daan.** He hasn't finished his lessons, has he? His father'll kill him if he catches him in there with that cat and his work not done. (Mr. Frank *and* Anne *finish their dance. They bow to each other with extravagant formality.*) Anne, get him out of there, will you?

**Anne** (*at* Peter's *door*). Peter? Peter?

**Peter** (*opening the door a crack*). What is it?

650 **Anne.** Your mother says to come out.

**Peter.** I'm giving Mouschi his dinner.

**Mrs. Van Daan.** You know what your father says. (*She sits on the couch, sewing on the lining of her fur coat.*)

**Peter.** For heaven's sake, I haven't even looked at him since lunch.

**Mrs. Van Daan.** I'm just telling you, that's all.

**Anne.** I'll feed him.

**Peter.** I don't want you in there.

660 **Mrs. Van Daan.** Peter!

**Peter** (*to* Anne). Then give him his dinner and come right out, you hear? (*He comes back to the table.* Anne *shuts the door of* Peter's *room after her and disappears behind the curtain covering his closet.*)

**Mrs. Van Daan** (*to* Peter). Now is that any way to talk to your little girl friend?

**Peter.** Mother . . . for heaven's sake . . . will you please stop saying that?

**Mrs. Van Daan.** Look at him blush! Look at him!

670 **Peter.** Please! I'm not . . . anyway . . . let me alone, will you?

**Mrs. Van Daan.** He acts like it was something to be ashamed of. It's nothing to be ashamed of, to have a little girl friend.

**Peter.** You're crazy. She's only thirteen.

**Mrs. Van Daan.** So what? And you're sixteen. Just perfect. Your father's ten years older than I am. (*to* Mr. Frank) I warn you, Mr. Frank, if this war lasts much longer, we're going to be related and then . . .

680 **Mr. Frank.** *Mazeltov!*[10]

**Mrs. Frank** (*deliberately changing the conversation*). I wonder where Miep is. She's usually so prompt.

(*Suddenly everything else is forgotten as they hear the sound of an automobile coming to a screeching stop in the street below. They are tense, motionless in their terror. The car starts away. A wave of relief sweeps over them. They pick up their occupations again.* Anne *flings open the door of* Peter's *room, making a dramatic entrance. She is dressed in* Peter's *clothes.* 690 Peter *looks at her in fury. The others are amused.*)

**Anne.** Good evening, everyone. Forgive me if I don't stay. (*She jumps up on a chair.*) I have a friend waiting for me in there. My friend Tom. Tom Cat. Some people say that we look alike. But Tom has the most beautiful whiskers, and I have only a little fuzz. I am hoping . . . in time . . .

**Peter.** All right, Mrs. Quack Quack!

**Anne** (*outraged—jumping down*). Peter!

**Peter.** I heard about you . . . How you talked 700 so much in class they called you Mrs. Quack Quack. How Mr. Smitter made you write a composition . . . "'Quack, quack,' said Mrs. Quack Quack."

---

10. **Mazeltov!** (mä′zəl tôf′) *Hebrew:* Congratulations!

**Anne.** Well, go on. Tell them the rest. How it was so good he read it out loud to the class and then read it to all his other classes!

**Peter.** Quack! Quack! Quack . . . Quack . . . Quack . . .

(Anne *pulls off the coat and trousers.*)

710 **Anne.** You are the most intolerable, insufferable boy I've ever met!

(*She throws the clothes down the stairwell.* Peter *goes down after them.*)

**Peter.** Quack, quack, quack!

**Mrs. Van Daan** (*to* Anne). That's right, Anneke! Give it to him!

**Anne.** With all the boys in the world . . . Why I had to get locked up with one like you! . . .

**Peter.** Quack, quack, quack, and from now on stay 720 out of my room!

(*As* Peter *passes her,* Anne *puts out her foot, tripping him. He picks himself up, and goes on into his room.*)

**Mrs. Frank** (*quietly*). Anne, dear . . . your hair. (*She feels* Anne's *forehead.*) You're warm. Are you feeling all right?

**Anne.** Please, Mother. (*She goes over to the center table, slipping into her shoes.*)

**Mrs. Frank** (*following her*). You haven't a fever, have you?

730 **Anne** (*pulling away*). No. No.

**Mrs. Frank.** You know we can't call a doctor here, ever. There's only one thing to do . . . watch carefully. Prevent an illness before it comes. Let me see your tongue.

**Anne.** Mother, this is perfectly absurd.

**Mrs. Frank.** Anne, dear, don't be such a baby. Let me see your tongue. (*As* Anne *refuses,* Mrs. Frank *appeals to* Mr. Frank.) Otto . . . ?

**Mr. Frank.** You hear your mother, Anne. (Anne 740 *flicks out her tongue for a second, then turns away.*)

**Mrs. Frank.** Come on—open up! (*as* Anne *opens her mouth very wide*) You seem all right . . . but perhaps an aspirin . . .

**Mrs. Van Daan.** For heaven's sake, don't give that child any pills. I waited for fifteen minutes this morning for her to come out of the w.c.

**Anne.** I was washing my hair!

**Mr. Frank.** I think there's nothing the matter with our Anne that a ride on her bike, or a 750 visit with her friend Jopie de Waal wouldn't cure. Isn't that so, Anne?

(Mr. Van Daan *comes down into the room. From outside we hear faint sounds of bombers going over and a burst of ack-ack.*)

**Mr. Van Daan.** Miep not come yet?

**Mrs. Van Daan.** The workmen just left, a little while ago.

**Mr. Van Daan.** What's for dinner tonight?

**Mrs. Van Daan.** Beans.

760 **Mr. Van Daan.** Not again!

**Mrs. Van Daan.** Poor Putti! I know. But what can we do? That's all that Miep brought us.

(Mr. Van Daan *starts to pace, his hands behind his back.* Anne *follows behind him, imitating him.*)

**Anne.** We are now in what is known as the "bean cycle." Beans boiled, beans en casserole, beans with strings, beans without strings . . .

(Peter *has come out of his room. He slides into his place at the table, becoming immediately absorbed* 770 *in his studies.*)

**Mr. Van Daan** (*to* Peter). I saw you . . . in there, playing with your cat.

**Mrs. Van Daan.** He just went in for a second, putting his coat away. He's been out here all the time, doing his lessons.

**Mr. Frank** (*looking up from the papers*). Anne, you got an excellent in your history paper today . . . and very good in Latin.

**Anne** (*sitting beside him*). How about algebra?

780 **Mr. Frank.** I'll have to make a confession. Up until now I've managed to stay ahead of you in algebra. Today you caught up with me. We'll leave it to Margot to correct.

**Anne.** Isn't algebra *vile,* Pim!

**Mr. Frank.** Vile!

**Margot** (*to* Mr. Frank). How did I do?

**Anne** (*getting up*). Excellent, excellent, excellent, excellent!

**Mr. Frank** (*to* Margot). You should have used the subjunctive here . . .

**Margot.** Should I? . . . I thought . . . look here . . . I didn't use it here . . . (*The two become absorbed in the papers.*)

**Anne.** Mrs. Van Daan, may I try on your coat?

**Mrs. Frank.** No, Anne.

**Mrs. Van Daan** (*giving it to* Anne). It's all right . . . but careful with it. (Anne *puts it on and struts with it.*) My father gave me that the year before he died. He always bought the best that money could buy.

**Anne.** Mrs. Van Daan, did you have a lot of boy friends before you were married?

**Mrs. Frank.** Anne, that's a personal question. It's not courteous to ask personal questions.

**Mrs. Van Daan.** Oh I don't mind. (*to* Anne) Our house was always swarming with boys. When I was a girl we had . . .

**Mr. Van Daan.** Oh, God. Not again!

**Mrs. Van Daan** (*good-humored*). Shut up! (*Without a pause, to* Anne. Mr. Van Daan *mimics* Mrs. Van Daan, *speaking the first few words in unison with her.*) One summer we had a big house in Hilversum. The boys came buzzing round like bees around a jam pot. And when I was sixteen! . . . We were wearing our skirts very short those days and I had good-looking legs. (*She pulls up her skirt, going to* Mr. Frank.) I still have 'em. I may not be as pretty as I used to be, but I still have my legs. How about it, Mr. Frank?

**Mr. Van Daan.** All right. All right. We see them.

**Mrs. Van Daan.** I'm not asking you. I'm asking Mr. Frank.

**Peter.** Mother, for heaven's sake.

**Mrs. Van Daan.** Oh, I embarrass you, do I? Well, I just hope the girl you marry has as good. (*then to* Anne) My father used to worry about me, with so many boys hanging round. He told me, if any of them gets fresh, you say to him . . . "Remember, Mr. So-and-So, remember I'm a lady."

**Anne.** "Remember, Mr. So-and-So, remember I'm a lady." (*She gives* Mrs. Van Daan *her coat.*)

**Mr. Van Daan.** Look at you, talking that way in front of her! Don't you know she puts it all down in that diary?

**Mrs. Van Daan.** So, if she does? I'm only telling the truth!

(Anne *stretches out, putting her ear to the floor, listening to what is going on below. The sound of the bombers fades away.*)

**Mrs. Frank** (*setting the table*). Would you mind, Peter, if I moved you over to the couch?

**Anne** (*listening*). Miep must have the radio on.

(Peter *picks up his papers, going over to the couch beside* Mrs. Van Daan.)

**Mr. Van Daan** (*accusingly, to* Peter). Haven't you finished yet?

**Peter.** No.

**Mr. Van Daan.** You ought to be ashamed of yourself.

**Peter.** All right. All right. I'm a dunce. I'm a hopeless case. Why do I go on?

**Mrs. Van Daan.** You're not hopeless. Don't talk that way. It's just that you haven't anyone to help you, like the girls have. (*to* Mr. Frank) Maybe you could help him, Mr. Frank?

**Mr. Frank.** I'm sure that his father . . . ?

**Mr. Van Daan.** Not me. I can't do anything with him. He won't listen to me. You go ahead . . . if you want.

**Mr. Frank** (*going to* Peter). What about it, Peter? Shall we make our school coeducational?

**Mrs. Van Daan** (*kissing* Mr. Frank). You're an angel, Mr. Frank. An angel. I don't know why I didn't meet you before I met that one there.

Here, sit down, Mr. Frank . . . (*She forces him down on the couch beside* Peter.) Now, Peter, you listen to Mr. Frank.

**Mr. Frank.** It might be better for us to go into Peter's room. (Peter *jumps up eagerly, leading the way.*)

**Mrs. Van Daan.** That's right. You go in there, Peter.
870 You listen to Mr. Frank. Mr. Frank is a highly educated man. (*As* Mr. Frank *is about to follow* Peter *into his room,* Mrs. Frank *stops him and wipes the lipstick from his lips. Then she closes the door after them.*)

**Anne** (*on the floor, listening*). Shh! I can hear a man's voice talking.

**Mr. Van Daan** (*to* Anne). Isn't it bad enough here without your sprawling all over the place? (Anne *sits up.*)

880 **Mrs. Van Daan** (*to* Mr. Van Daan). If you didn't smoke so much, you wouldn't be so bad-tempered.

**Mr. Van Daan.** Am I smoking? Do you see me smoking?

**Mrs. Van Daan.** Don't tell me you've used up all those cigarettes.

**Mr. Van Daan.** One package. Miep only brought me one package.

**Mrs. Van Daan.** It's a filthy habit anyway. It's a good time to break yourself.

890 **Mr. Van Daan.** Oh, stop it, please.

**Mrs. Van Daan.** You're smoking up all our money. You know that, don't you?

**Mr. Van Daan.** Will you shut up? (*During this,* Mrs. Frank *and* Margot *have studiously kept their eyes down. But* Anne, *seated on the floor, has been following the discussion interestedly.* Mr. Van Daan *turns to see her staring up at him.*) And what are you staring at?

**Anne.** I never heard grownups quarrel before.
900 I thought only children quarreled.

**Mr. Van Daan.** This isn't a quarrel! It's a discussion. And I never heard children so rude before.

**Anne** (*rising,* **_indignantly_**). I, rude!

**Mr. Van Daan.** Yes!

**Mrs. Frank** (*quickly*). Anne, will you get me my knitting? (Anne *goes to get it.*) I must remember, when Miep comes, to ask her to bring me some more wool.

**Margot** (*going to her room*). I need some hairpins
910 and some soap. I made a list. (*She goes into her bedroom to get the list.*)

**Mrs. Frank** (*to* Anne). Have you some library books for Miep when she comes?

**Anne.** It's a wonder that Miep has a life of her own, the way we make her run errands for us. Please, Miep, get me some starch. Please take my hair out and have it cut. Tell me all the latest news, Miep.

(*She goes over, kneeling on the couch beside* Mrs. Van Daan.) Did you know she was engaged? His name is Dirk, and Miep's afraid the Nazis will ship him off to Germany to work in one of their war plants. That's what they're doing with some of the young Dutchmen . . . they pick them up off the streets—

**Mr. Van Daan** (*interrupting*). Don't you ever get tired of talking? Suppose you try keeping still for five minutes. Just five minutes. (*He starts to pace again. Again* Anne *follows him, mimicking him.* Mrs. Frank *jumps up and takes her by the arm up to the sink, and gives her a glass of milk.*)

**Mrs. Frank.** Come here, Anne. It's time for your glass of milk.

**Mr. Van Daan.** Talk, talk, talk. I never heard such a child. Where is my . . . ? Every evening it's the same, talk, talk, talk. (*He looks around.*) Where is my . . . ?

**Mrs. Van Daan.** What're you looking for?

**Mr. Van Daan.** My pipe. Have you seen my pipe?

**Mrs. Van Daan.** What good's a pipe? You haven't got any tobacco.

**Mr. Van Daan.** At least I'll have something to hold in my mouth! (*opening* Margot's *bedroom door*) Margot, have you seen my pipe?

**Margot.** It was on the table last night. (Anne *puts her glass of milk on the table and picks up his pipe, hiding it behind her back.*)

**Mr. Van Daan.** I know. I know. Anne, did you see my pipe? . . . Anne!

**Mrs. Frank.** Anne, Mr. Van Daan is speaking to you.

**Anne.** Am I allowed to talk now?

**Mr. Van Daan.** You're the most aggravating . . . The trouble with you is, you've been spoiled. What you need is a good old-fashioned spanking.

**Anne** (*mimicking* Mrs. Van Daan). "Remember, Mr. So-and-So, remember I'm a lady." (*She thrusts the pipe into his mouth, then picks up her glass of milk.*)

**Mr. Van Daan** (*restraining himself with difficulty*). Why aren't you nice and quiet like your sister Margot? Why do you have to show off all the time? Let me give you a little advice, young lady. Men don't like that kind of thing in a girl. You know that? A man likes a girl who'll listen to him once in a while . . . a domestic girl, who'll keep her house shining for her husband . . . who loves to cook and sew and . . .

**Anne.** I'd cut my throat first! I'd open my veins! I'm going to be remarkable! I'm going to Paris . . .

**Mr. Van Daan** (*scoffingly*). Paris!

**Anne.** . . . to study music and art.

**Mr. Van Daan.** Yeah! Yeah!

**Anne.** I'm going to be a famous dancer or singer . . . or something wonderful. (*She makes a wide gesture, spilling the glass of milk on the fur coat in* Mrs. Van Daan's *lap.* Margot *rushes quickly over with a towel.* Anne *tries to brush the milk off with her skirt.*)

**Mrs. Van Daan.** Now look what you've done . . . you clumsy little fool! My beautiful fur coat my father gave me . . .

**Anne.** I'm so sorry.

**Mrs. Van Daan.** What do you care? It isn't yours . . . So go on, ruin it! Do you know what that coat cost? Do you? And now look at it! Look at it!

**Anne.** I'm very, very sorry.

**Mrs. Van Daan.** I could kill you for this. I could just kill you! (Mrs. Van Daan *goes up the stairs, clutching the coat.* Mr. Van Daan *starts after her.*)

**Mr. Van Daan.** Petronella . . . *liefje! Liefje!* . . . Come back . . . the supper . . . come back!

**Mrs. Frank.** Anne, you must not behave in that way.

**Anne.** It was an accident. Anyone can have an accident.

**Mrs. Frank.** I don't mean that. I mean the answering back. You must not answer back. They are our guests. We must always show the greatest courtesy to them. We're all living under terrible tension. (*She stops as* Margot *indicates that* Van Daan *can hear. When he is gone, she continues.*) That's why we must control ourselves . . . You don't hear Margot getting into arguments with them, do you? Watch Margot. She's always courteous with them. Never familiar. She keeps her distance. And they respect her for it. Try to be like Margot.

**Anne.** And have them walk all over me, the way they do her? No, thanks!

**Mrs. Frank.** I'm not afraid that anyone is going to walk all over you, Anne. I'm afraid for other people, that you'll walk on them. I don't know what happens to you, Anne. You are wild, self-willed. If I had ever talked to my mother as you talk to me . . .

**Anne.** Things have changed. People aren't like that any more. "Yes, Mother." "No, Mother." "Anything you say, Mother." I've got to fight things out for myself! Make something of myself!

**Mrs. Frank.** It isn't necessary to fight to do it. Margot doesn't fight, and isn't she . . . ?

**Anne** (*violently rebellious*). Margot! Margot! Margot! That's all I hear from everyone . . . how wonderful Margot is . . . "Why aren't you like Margot?"

**Margot** (*protesting*). Oh, come on, Anne, don't be so . . .

**Anne** (*paying no attention*). Everything she does is right, and everything I do is wrong! I'm the goat around here! . . . You're all against me! . . . And you worst of all!

(*She rushes off into her room and throws herself down on the settee, stifling her sobs.* Mrs. Frank *sighs and starts toward the stove.*)

**Mrs. Frank** (*to* Margot). Let's put the soup on the stove . . . if there's anyone who cares to eat. Margot, will you take the bread out? (Margot *gets the bread from the cupboard.*) I don't know how we can go on living this way . . . I can't say a word to Anne . . . she flies at me . . .

**Margot.** You know Anne. In half an hour she'll be out here, laughing and joking.

**Mrs. Frank.** And . . . (*She makes a motion upwards, indicating the* Van Daans.) . . . I told your father it wouldn't work . . . but no . . . no . . . he had to ask them, he said . . . he owed it to him, he said. Well, he knows now that I was right! These quarrels! . . . This bickering!

**Margot** (*with a warning look*). Shush. Shush.

(*The buzzer for the door sounds.* Mrs. Frank *gasps, startled.*)

**Mrs. Frank.** Every time I hear that sound, my heart stops!

**Margot** (*starting for* Peter's *door*). It's Miep. (*She knocks at the door.*) Father?

(Mr. Frank *comes quickly from* Peter's *room.*)

**Mr. Frank.** Thank you, Margot. (*as he goes down the steps to open the outer door*) Has everyone his list?

**Margot.** I'll get my books. (*giving her mother a list*) Here's your list. (Margot *goes into her and* Anne's *bedroom on the right.* Anne *sits up, hiding her tears, as* Margot *comes in.*) Miep's here.

(Margot *picks up her books and goes back.* Anne *hurries over to the mirror, smoothing her hair.*)

**Mr. Van Daan** (*coming down the stairs*). Is it Miep?

**Margot.** Yes. Father's gone down to let her in.

**Mr. Van Daan.** At last I'll have some cigarettes!

**Mrs. Frank** (*to* Mr. Van Daan). I can't tell you how unhappy I am about Mrs. Van Daan's coat. Anne should never have touched it.

**Mr. Van Daan.** She'll be all right.

**Mrs. Frank.** Is there anything I can do?

**Mr. Van Daan.** Don't worry.

(*He turns to meet* Miep. *But it is not* Miep *who comes up the steps. It is* Mr. Kraler, *followed by* Mr. Frank. *Their faces are grave.* Anne *comes from the bedroom.* Peter *comes from his room.*)

**Mrs. Frank.** Mr. Kraler!

**Mr. Van Daan.** How are you, Mr. Kraler?

**Margot.** This is a surprise.

**Mrs. Frank.** When Mr. Kraler comes, the sun begins to shine.

**Mr. Van Daan.** Miep is coming?

**Mr. Kraler.** Not tonight.

(Kraler *goes to* Margot *and* Mrs. Frank *and* Anne, *shaking hands with them.*)

**Mrs. Frank.** Wouldn't you like a cup of coffee? . . . Or, better still, will you have supper with us?

**Mr. Frank.** Mr. Kraler has something to talk over with us. Something has happened, he says, which demands an immediate decision.

**Mrs. Frank** (*fearful*). What is it?

(Mr. Kraler *sits down on the couch. As he talks he takes bread, cabbages, milk, etc., from his briefcase, giving them to* Margot *and* Anne *to put away.*)

**Mr. Kraler.** Usually, when I come up here, I try to bring you some bit of good news. What's the use of telling you the bad news when there's nothing that you can do about it? But today something has happened . . . Dirk . . . Miep's Dirk, you know, came to me just now. He tells me that he has a Jewish friend living near him. A dentist. He says he's in trouble. He begged me, could I do anything for this man? Could I find him a hiding place? . . . So I've come to you . . . I know it's a terrible thing to ask of you, living as you are, but would you take him in with you?

**Mr. Frank.** Of course we will.

**Mr. Kraler** (*rising*). It'll be just for a night or two . . . until I find some other place. This happened so suddenly that I didn't know where to turn.

**Mr. Frank.** Where is he?

**Mr. Kraler.** Downstairs in the office.

**Mr. Frank.** Good. Bring him up.

**Mr. Kraler.** His name is Dussel . . . Jan Dussel.

**Mr. Frank.** Dussel . . . I think I know him.

**Mr. Kraler.** I'll get him. (*He goes quickly down the steps and out.* Mr. Frank *suddenly becomes conscious of the others.*)

**Mr. Frank.** Forgive me. I spoke without consulting you. But I knew you'd feel as I do.

**Mr. Van Daan.** There's no reason for you to consult anyone. This is your place. You have a right to do exactly as you please. The only thing I feel . . . there's so little food as it is . . . and to take in another person . . .

(Peter *turns away, ashamed of his father.*)

**Mr. Frank.** We can stretch the food a little. It's only for a few days.

**Mr. Van Daan.** You want to make a bet?

**Mrs. Frank.** I think it's fine to have him. But, Otto, where are you going to put him? Where?

**Peter.** He can have my bed. I can sleep on the floor. I wouldn't mind.

**Mr. Frank.** That's good of you, Peter. But your room's too small . . . even for *you.*

**Anne.** I have a much better idea. I'll come in here with you and Mother, and Margot can take Peter's room and Peter can go in our room with Mr. Dussel.

**Margot.** That's right. We could do that.

**Mr. Frank.** No, Margot. You mustn't sleep in that room . . . neither you nor Anne. Mouschi has caught some rats in there. Peter's brave. He doesn't mind.

**Anne.** Then how about *this?* I'll come in here with you and Mother, and Mr. Dussel can have my bed.

**Mrs. Frank.** No. No. *No!* Margot will come in here with us and he can have her bed. It's the only way. Margot, bring your things in here. Help her, Anne.

(Margot *hurries into her room to get her things.*)

**Anne** (*to her mother*). Why Margot? Why can't I come in here?

**Mrs. Frank.** Because it wouldn't be proper for Margot to sleep with a . . . Please, Anne. Don't argue. Please. (Anne *starts slowly away.*)

**Mr. Frank.** (*to* Anne). You don't mind sharing your room with Mr. Dussel, do you, Anne?

**Anne.** No. No, of course not.

**Mr. Frank.** Good. (Anne *goes off into her bedroom,* helping Margot. Mr. Frank *starts to search in the cupboards.*) Where's the cognac?

**Mrs. Frank.** It's there. But, Otto, I was saving it in case of illness.

**Mr. Frank.** I think we couldn't find a better time to use it. Peter, will you get five glasses for me?

(Peter *goes for the glasses.* Margot *comes out of her bedroom, carrying her possessions, which she hangs behind a curtain in the main room.* Mr. Frank *finds the cognac and pours it into the five glasses that* Peter *brings him.* Mr. Van Daan *stands looking on sourly.* Mrs. Van Daan *comes downstairs and looks around at all the bustle.*)

**Mrs. Van Daan.** What's happening? What's going on?

**Mr. Van Daan.** Someone's moving in with us.

**Mrs. Van Daan.** In here? You're joking.

**Margot.** It's only for a night or two . . . until Mr. Kraler finds him another place.

**Mr. Van Daan.** Yeah! Yeah!

(Mr. Frank *hurries over as* Mr. Kraler *and* Dussel *come up.* Dussel *is a man in his late fifties, meticulous, finicky . . . bewildered now. He wears a raincoat. He carries a briefcase, stuffed full, and a small medicine case.*)

**Mr. Frank.** Come in, Mr. Dussel.

**Mr. Kraler.** This is Mr. Frank.

**Dussel.** Mr. Otto Frank?

**Mr. Frank.** Yes. Let me take your things. (*He takes the hat and briefcase, but* Dussel *clings to his medicine case.*) This is my wife Edith . . .

Mr. and Mrs. Van Daan . . . their son, Peter . . . and my daughters, Margot and Anne. (Dussel *shakes hands with everyone.*)

**Mr. Kraler.** Thank you, Mr. Frank. Thank you all. Mr. Dussel, I leave you in good hands. Oh . . . Dirk's coat.

(Dussel *hurriedly takes off the raincoat, giving it to Mr. Kraler. Underneath is his white dentist's jacket, with a yellow Star of David on it.*)

**1200 Dussel** (*to Mr. Kraler*). What can I say to thank you . . . ?

**Mrs. Frank** (*to Dussel*). Mr. Kraler and Miep . . . They're our life line. Without them we couldn't live.

**Mr. Kraler.** Please. Please. You make us seem very heroic. It isn't that at all. We simply don't like the Nazis. (*to Mr. Frank, who offers him a drink*) No, thanks. (*then going on*) We don't like their methods. We don't like . . .

**1210 Mr. Frank** (*smiling*). I know. I know. "No one's going to tell us Dutchmen what to do with our damn Jews!"

**Mr. Kraler** (*to Dussel*). Pay no attention to Mr. Frank. I'll be up tomorrow to see that they're treating you right. (*to Mr. Frank*) Don't trouble to come down again. Peter will bolt the door after me, won't you, Peter?

**Peter.** Yes, sir.

**Mr. Frank.** Thank you, Peter. I'll do it.

**1220 Mr. Kraler.** Good night. Good night.

**Group.** Good night, Mr. Kraler. We'll see you tomorrow, (*etc., etc.*)

(Mr. Kraler *goes out with Mr. Frank. Mrs. Frank gives each one of the "grownups" a glass of cognac.*)

**Mrs. Frank.** Please, Mr. Dussel, sit down.

(Mr. Dussel *sinks into a chair. Mrs. Frank gives him a glass of cognac.*)

**Dussel.** I'm dreaming. I know it. I can't believe my eyes. Mr. Otto Frank here! (*to Mrs. Frank*)
**1230** You're not in Switzerland then? A woman told

me . . . She said she'd gone to your house . . . the door was open, everything was in disorder, dishes in the sink. She said she found a piece of paper in the wastebasket with an address scribbled on it . . . an address in Zurich. She said you must have escaped to Zurich.

**Anne.** Father put that there purposely . . . just so people would think that very thing!

**Dussel.** And you've been here all the time?

**1240 Mrs. Frank.** All the time . . . ever since July.

(Anne *speaks to her father as he comes back.*)

**Anne.** It worked, Pim . . . the address you left! Mr. Dussel says that people believe we escaped to Switzerland.

**Mr. Frank.** I'm glad . . . And now let's have a little drink to welcome Mr. Dussel. (*Before they can drink, Mr. Dussel bolts his drink. Mr. Frank smiles and raises his glass.*) To Mr. Dussel. Welcome. We're very honored to have you with us.

**1250 Mrs. Frank.** To Mr. Dussel, welcome.

(*The* Van Daans *murmur a welcome. The "grown-ups" drink.*)

**Mrs. Van Daan.** Um. That was good.

**Mr. Van Daan.** Did Mr. Kraler warn you that you won't get much to eat here? You can imagine . . . three ration books among the seven of us . . . and now you make eight.

(Peter *walks away, humiliated. Outside a street organ is heard dimly.*)

**1260 Dussel** (*rising*). Mr. Van Daan, you don't realize what is happening outside that you should warn me of a thing like that. You don't realize what's going on . . . (*As Mr. Van Daan starts his characteristic pacing, Dussel turns to speak to the others.*) Right here in Amsterdam every day hundreds of Jews disappear . . . They surround a block and search house by house. Children come home from school to find their parents gone. Hundreds are being deported . . . people
**1270** that you and I know . . . the Hallensteins . . . the Wessels . . .

**Mrs. Frank** (*in tears*). Oh, no. No!

**Dussel.** They get their call-up notice . . . come to the Jewish theatre on such and such a day and hour . . . bring only what you can carry in a rucksack. And if you refuse the call-up notice, then they come and drag you from your home and ship you off to Mauthausen.[11] The death camp!

1280 **Mrs. Frank.** We didn't know that things had got so much worse.

**Dussel.** Forgive me for speaking so.

**Anne** (*coming to* Dussel). Do you know the de Waals? . . . What's become of them? Their daughter Jopie and I are in the same class. Jopie's my best friend.

**Dussel.** They are gone.

**Anne.** Gone?

**Dussel.** With all the others.

1290 **Anne.** Oh, no. Not Jopie!

(*She turns away, in tears.* Mrs. Frank *motions to* Margot *to comfort her.* Margot *goes to* Anne, *putting her arms comfortingly around her.*)

**Mrs. Van Daan.** There were some people called Wagner. They lived near us . . . ?

**Mr. Frank** (*interrupting, with a glance at* Anne). I think we should put this off until later. We all have many questions we want to ask . . . But I'm sure that Mr. Dussel would like to get settled
1300 before supper.

**Dussel.** Thank you. I would. I brought very little with me.

**Mr. Frank** (*giving him his hat and briefcase*). I'm sorry we can't give you a room alone. But I hope you won't be too uncomfortable. We've had to make strict rules here . . . a schedule of hours . . . We'll tell you after supper. Anne, would you like to take Mr. Dussel to his room?

**Anne** (*controlling her tears*). If you'll come with
1310 me, Mr. Dussel? (*She starts for her room.*)

**Dussel** (*shaking hands with each in turn*). Forgive me if I haven't really expressed my gratitude to all of you. This has been such a shock to me. I'd always thought of myself as Dutch. I was born in Holland. My father was born in Holland, and my grandfather. And now . . . after all these years . . . (*He breaks off.*) If you'll excuse me.

(Dussel *gives a little bow and hurries off after* Anne. Mr. Frank *and the others are subdued.*)

1320 **Anne** (*turning on the light*). Well, here we are.

(Dussel *looks around the room. In the main room* Margot *speaks to her mother.*)

**Margot.** The news sounds pretty bad, doesn't it? It's so different from what Mr. Kraler tells us. Mr. Kraler says things are improving.

**Mr. Van Daan.** I like it better the way Kraler tells it.

(*They resume their occupations, quietly.* Peter *goes off into his room. In* Anne's *room,* Anne *turns to* Dussel.)

1330 **Anne.** You're going to share the room with me.

**Dussel.** I'm a man who's always lived alone. I haven't had to adjust myself to others. I hope you'll bear with me until I learn.

**Anne.** Let me help you. (*She takes his briefcase.*) Do you always live all alone? Have you no family at all?

**Dussel.** No one. (*He opens his medicine case and spreads his bottles on the dressing table.*)

**Anne.** How dreadful. You must be terribly lonely.

1340 **Dussel.** I'm used to it.

**Anne.** I don't think I could ever get used to it. Didn't you even have a pet? A cat, or a dog?

**Dussel.** I have an allergy for fur-bearing animals. They give me asthma.

**Anne.** Oh, dear. Peter has a cat.

**Dussel.** Here? He has it here?

**Anne.** Yes. But we hardly ever see it. He keeps it in his room all the time. I'm sure it will be all right.

---

11. **Mauthausen** (mout'hou′zən): a Nazi concentration camp in Austria.

**Dussel.** Let us hope so.

1350 (*He takes some pills to __fortify__ himself.*)

**Anne.** That's Margot's bed, where you're going to sleep. I sleep on the sofa there. (*indicating the clothes hooks on the wall*) We cleared these off for your things. (*She goes over to the window.*) The best part about this room . . . you can look down and see a bit of the street and the canal. There's a houseboat . . . you can see the end of it . . . a bargeman lives there with his family . . . They have a baby and he's just beginning to walk and

1360 I'm so afraid he's going to fall into the canal some day. I watch him . . .

**Dussel** (*interrupting*). Your father spoke of a schedule.

**Anne** (*coming away from the window*). Oh, yes. It's mostly about the times we have to be quiet. And times for the w.c. You can use it now if you like.

**Dussel** (*stiffly*). No, thank you.

**Anne.** I suppose you think it's awful, my talking about a thing like that. But you don't know

1370 how important it can get to be, especially when you're frightened . . . About this room, the way Margot and I did . . . she had it to herself in the afternoons for studying, reading . . . lessons, you know . . . and I took the mornings. Would that be all right with you?

**Dussel.** I'm not at my best in the morning.

**Anne.** You stay here in the mornings then. I'll take the room in the afternoons.

**Dussel.** Tell me, when you're in here, what

1380 happens to me? Where am I spending my time? In there, with all the people?

**Anne.** Yes.

**Dussel.** I see. I see.

**Anne.** We have supper at half past six.

**Dussel** (*going over to the sofa*). Then, if you don't mind . . . I like to lie down quietly for ten minutes before eating. I find it helps the digestion.

**Anne.** Of course. I hope I'm not going to be too much of a bother to you. I seem to be able to get

1390 everyone's back up.

(Dussel *lies down on the sofa, curled up, his back to her.*)

**Dussel.** I always get along very well with children. My patients all bring their children to me, because they know I get on well with them. So don't you worry about that.

(Anne *leans over him, taking his hand and shaking it gratefully.*)

**Anne.** Thank you. Thank you, Mr. Dussel.

1400 (*The lights dim to darkness. The curtain falls on the scene. Anne's Voice comes to us faintly at first, and then with increasing power.*)

**Anne's Voice.** . . . And yesterday I finished Cissy Van Marxvelt's latest book. I think she is a first-class writer. I shall definitely let my children read her. Monday the twenty-first of September, nineteen forty-two. Mr. Dussel and I had another battle yesterday. Yes, Mr. Dussel! According to him, nothing, I repeat . . .

1410 nothing, is right about me . . . my appearance, my character, my manners. While he was going on at me I thought . . . sometime I'll give you such a smack that you'll fly right up to the ceiling! Why is it that every grownup thinks he knows the way to bring up children? Particularly the grownups that never had any. I keep wishing that Peter was a girl instead of a boy. Then I would have someone to talk to. Margot's a darling, but she takes everything too seriously.

1420 To pause for a moment on the subject of Mrs. Van Daan. I must tell you that her attempts to flirt with Father are getting her nowhere. Pim, thank goodness, won't play.

(*As she is saying the last lines, the curtain rises on the darkened scene. Anne's Voice fades out.*)

## Scene 4

*It is the middle of the night, several months later. The stage is dark except for a little light which comes through the skylight in* Peter's *room.*

*Everyone is in bed.* Mr. *and* Mrs. Frank *lie on*
1430 *the couch in the main room, which has been pulled out to serve as a makeshift double bed.*

Margot *is sleeping on a mattress on the floor in the main room, behind a curtain stretched across for privacy. The others are all in their accustomed rooms.*

*From outside we hear two drunken soldiers singing "Lili Marlene." A girl's high giggle is heard. The sound of running feet is heard coming closer and then fading in the distance. Throughout the*
1440 *scene there is the distant sound of airplanes passing overhead.*

*A match suddenly flares up in the attic. We dimly see* Mr. Van Daan. *He is getting his bearings. He comes quickly down the stairs, and goes to the cupboard where the food is stored. Again the match flares up, and is as quickly blown out. The dim figure is seen to steal back up the stairs.*

*There is quiet for a second or two, broken only by the sound of airplanes, and running feet on the*
1450 *street below.*

*Suddenly, out of the silence and the dark, we hear* Anne *scream.*

**Anne** (*screaming*). No! No! Don't . . . don't take me!

(*She moans, tossing and crying in her sleep. The other people wake, terrified.* Dussel *sits up in bed, furious.*)

**Dussel.** Shush! Anne! Anne, for God's sake, shush!

**Anne** (*still in her nightmare*). Save me! Save me!

(*She screams and screams.* Dussel *gets out of bed,*
1460 *going over to her, trying to wake her.*)

**Dussel.** For God's sake! Quiet! Quiet! You want someone to hear?

(*In the main room* Mrs. Frank *grabs a shawl and pulls it around her. She rushes in to* Anne, *taking her in her arms.* Mr. Frank *hurriedly gets up, putting on his overcoat.* Margot *sits up, terrified.* Peter's *light goes on in his room.*)

**Mrs. Frank** (*to* Anne, *in her room*). Hush, darling, hush. It's all right. It's all right. (*over her shoulder*
1470 *to* Dussel) Will you be kind enough to turn on the light, Mr. Dussel? (*back to* Anne) It's nothing, my darling. It was just a dream.

(Dussel *turns on the light in the bedroom.* Mrs. Frank *holds* Anne *in her arms. Gradually* Anne *comes out of her nightmare, still trembling with horror.* Mr. Frank *comes into the room, and goes quickly to the window, looking out to be sure that no one outside had heard* Anne's *screams.* Mrs. Frank *holds* Anne, *talking softly to her. In*
1480 *the main room* Margot *stands on a chair, turning on the center hanging lamp. A light goes on in the* Van Daan's *room overhead.* Peter *puts his robe on, coming out of his room.*)

**Dussel** (*to* Mrs. Frank, *blowing his nose*). Something must be done about that child, Mrs. Frank. Yelling like that! Who knows but there's somebody on the streets? She's endangering all our lives.

**Mrs. Frank.** Anne, darling.

**Dussel.** Every night she twists and turns. I don't
1490 sleep. I spend half my night shushing her. And now it's nightmares!

(Margot *comes to the door of* Anne's *room, followed by* Peter. Mr. Frank *goes to them, indicating that everything is all right.* Peter *takes* Margot *back.*)

**Mrs. Frank** (*to* Anne). You're here, safe, you see? Nothing has happened. (*to* Dussel) Please, Mr. Dussel, go back to bed. She'll be herself in a minute or two. Won't you, Anne?

**Dussel** (*picking up a book and a pillow*). Thank
1500 you, but I'm going to the w.c. The one place where there's peace! (*He stalks out.* Mr. Van Daan, *in underwear and trousers, comes down the stairs.*)

**Mr. Van Daan** (*to* Dussel). What is it? What happened?

**Dussel.** A nightmare. She was having a nightmare!

**Mr. Van Daan.** I thought someone was murdering her.

**Dussel.** Unfortunately, no.

(*He goes into the bathroom. Mr. Van Daan goes* 1510 *back up the stairs. Mr. Frank, in the main room, sends* Peter *back to his own bedroom.*)

**Mr. Frank.** Thank you, Peter. Go back to bed.

(*Peter goes back to his room. Mr. Frank follows him, turning out the light and looking out the window. Then he goes back to the main room, and gets up on a chair, turning out the center hanging lamp.*)

**Mrs. Frank** (*to* Anne). Would you like some water? (Anne *shakes her head.*) Was it a very bad dream? Perhaps if you told me . . . ?

1520 **Anne.** I'd rather not talk about it.

**Mrs. Frank.** Poor darling. Try to sleep then. I'll sit right here beside you until you fall asleep. (*She brings a stool over, sitting there.*)

**Anne.** You don't have to.

**Mrs. Frank.** But I'd like to stay with you . . . very much. Really.

**Anne.** I'd rather you didn't.

**Mrs. Frank.** Good night, then. (*She leans down to kiss* Anne. Anne *throws her arm up over her face,* 1530 *turning away.* Mrs. Frank, *hiding her hurt, kisses* Anne's *arm.*) You'll be all right? There's nothing that you want?

**Anne.** Will you please ask Father to come.

**Mrs. Frank** (*after a second*). Of course, Anne dear. (*She hurries out into the other room. Mr. Frank comes to her as she comes in.*) Sie verlangt nach Dir![12]

**Mr. Frank** (*sensing her hurt*). Edith, *Liebe, schau . . .*[13]

**Mrs. Frank.** *Es macht nichts! Ich danke dem lieben* 1540 *Herrgott, dass sie sich wenigstens an Dich wendet, wenn sie Trost braucht! Geh hinein, Otto, sie ist ganz hysterisch vor Angst.*[14] (*as* Mr. Frank *hesitates*) *Geh zu ihr.*[15] (*He looks at her for a second and then goes to get a cup of water for* Anne. Mrs. Frank *sinks down on the bed, her face in her hands, trying to keep from sobbing aloud.* Margot *comes over to her, putting her arms around her.*) She wants nothing of me. She pulled away when I leaned down to kiss her.

**Margot.** It's a phase . . . You heard Father . . . 1550 Most girls go through it . . . they turn to their fathers at this age . . . they give all their love to their fathers.

**Mrs. Frank.** You weren't like this. You didn't shut me out.

**Margot.** She'll get over it . . . (*She smooths the bed for* Mrs. Frank *and sits beside her a moment as* Mrs. Frank *lies down. In* Anne's *room* Mr. Frank *comes in, sitting down by* Anne. Anne *flings her arms around him, clinging to him. In the distance* 1560 *we hear the sound of ack-ack.*)

**Anne.** Oh, Pim. I dreamed that they came to get us! The Green Police! They broke down the door and grabbed me and started to drag me out the way they did Jopie.

**Mr. Frank.** I want you to take this pill.

**Anne.** What is it?

**Mr. Frank.** Something to quiet you.

(*She takes it and drinks the water. In the main room* Margot *turns out the light and goes back* 1570 *to her bed.*)

**Mr. Frank** (*to* Anne). Do you want me to read to you for a while?

---

12. **Sie verlangt nach Dir** (zē fer-längt′ näĸʜ dîr) *German:* She is asking for you.

13. **Liebe, schau** (lē′bə shou′) *German:* Dear, look.

14. **Es macht . . . vor Angst** (ĕs mäĸʜt′ nĭĸʜts′! ĭĸʜ dängk′ə däm lē′bən hĕr′gôt, däs zē zĭĸʜ′ vān′ĭĸʜ-shtənz än dĭĸʜ′ vĕn′dət, vĕn zē trôst′ brouĸʜt! gä hĭn-īn′, ôt′tô; zē ĭst gänts hü-stĕr′ĭsh fôr ängst′) *German:* It's all right. I thank dear God that at least she turns to you when she needs comfort. Go in, Otto; she is hysterical with fear.

15. **Geh zu ihr** (gä′ tsoo îr′) *German:* Go to her.

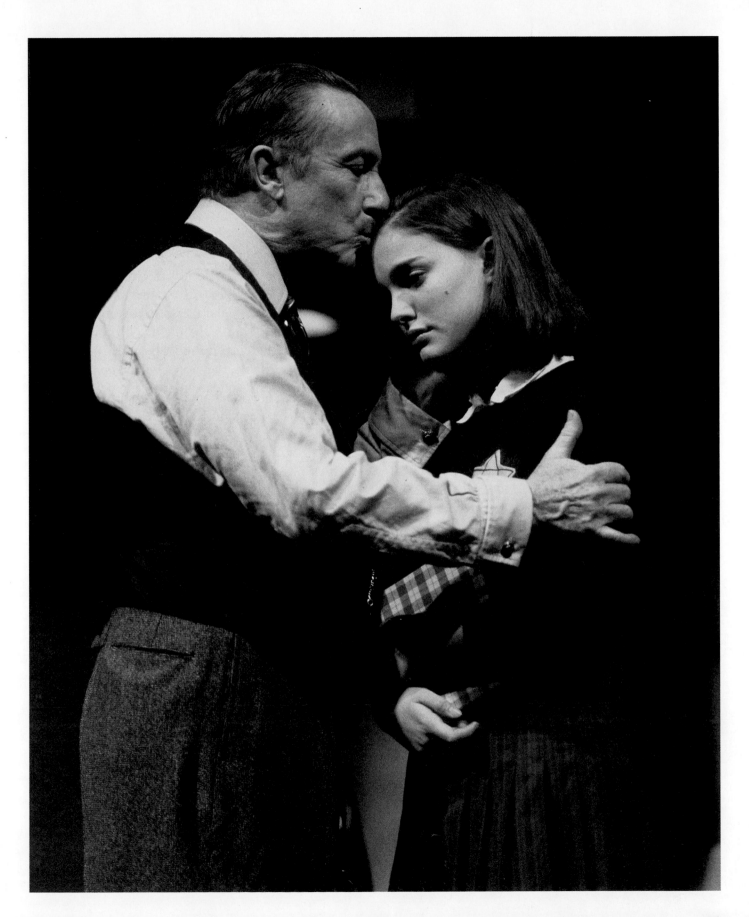

**Anne.** No. Just sit with me for a minute. Was I awful? Did I yell terribly loud? Do you think anyone outside could have heard?

**Mr. Frank.** No. No. Lie quietly now. Try to sleep.

**Anne.** I'm a terrible coward. I'm so disappointed in myself. I think I've conquered my fear . . . I think I'm really grown-up . . . and then something 1580 happens . . . and I run to you like a baby . . . I love you, Father. I don't love anyone but you.

**Mr. Frank** (*reproachfully*). Annele!

**Anne.** It's true. I've been thinking about it for a long time. You're the only one I love.

**Mr. Frank.** It's fine to hear you tell me that you love me. But I'd be happier if you said you loved your mother as well . . . She needs your help so much . . . your love . . .

**Anne.** We have nothing in common. She doesn't 1590 understand me. Whenever I try to explain my views on life to her she asks me if I'm constipated.

**Mr. Frank.** You hurt her very much just now. She's crying. She's in there crying.

**Anne.** I can't help it. I only told the truth. I didn't want her here . . . (*then, with sudden change*) Oh, Pim, I was horrible, wasn't I? And the worst of it is, I can stand off and look at myself doing it and know it's cruel and yet I can't stop doing it. What's the matter with me? Tell me. Don't say it's 1600 just a phase! Help me.

**Mr. Frank.** There is so little that we parents can do to help our children. We can only try to set a good example . . . point the way. The rest you must do yourself. You must build your own character.

**Anne.** I'm trying. Really I am. Every night I think back over all of the things I did that day that were wrong . . . like putting the wet mop in Mr. Dussel's bed . . . and this thing now with Mother. I say to myself, that was wrong. I make up my 1610 mind, I'm never going to do that again. Never!

Of course I may do something worse . . . but at least I'll never do *that* again! . . . I have a nicer side, Father . . . a sweeter, nicer side. But I'm scared to show it. I'm afraid that people are going to laugh at me if I'm serious. So the mean Anne comes to the outside and the good Anne stays on the inside, and I keep on trying to switch them around and have the good Anne outside and the bad Anne inside and be what I'd like to be . . . and might be . . . if 1620 only . . . only . . . (*She is asleep.* Mr. Frank *watches her for a moment and then turns off the light, and starts out. The lights dim out. The curtain falls on the scene.* Anne's Voice *is heard dimly at first, and then with growing strength.*)

**Anne's Voice.** . . . The air raids are getting worse. They come over day and night. The noise is terrifying. Pim says it should be music to our ears. The more planes, the sooner will come the end of the war. Mrs. Van Daan pretends to be a fatalist. 1630 What will be, will be. But when the planes come over, who is the most frightened? No one else but Petronella! . . . Monday, the ninth of November, nineteen forty-two. Wonderful news! The Allies have landed in Africa. Pim says that we can look for an early finish to the war. Just for fun he asked each of us what was the first thing we wanted to do when we got out of here. Mrs. Van Daan longs to be home with her own things, her needle-point chairs, the Beckstein piano her father gave her . . . 1640 the best that money could buy. Peter would like to go to a movie. Mr. Dussel wants to get back to his dentist's drill. He's afraid he is losing his touch. For myself, there are so many things . . . to ride a bike again . . . to laugh till my belly aches . . . to have new clothes from the skin out . . . to have a hot tub filled to overflowing and wallow in it for hours . . . to be back in school with my friends . . .

(*As the last lines are being said, the curtain rises on the scene. The lights dim on as* Anne's Voice *fades* 1650 *away.*)

## Scene 5

*It is the first night of the Hanukkah[16] celebration. Mr. Frank is standing at the head of the table on which is the Menorah.[17] He lights the Shamos, or servant candle, and holds it as he says the blessing. Seated listening is all of the "family," dressed in their best. The men wear hats,* Peter *wears his cap.*

**Mr. Frank** (*reading from a prayer book*). "Praised be Thou, oh Lord our God, Ruler of the universe, who has sanctified us with Thy commandments
1660 and bidden us kindle the Hanukkah lights. Praised be Thou, oh Lord our God, Ruler of the universe, who has wrought wondrous deliverances for our fathers in days of old. Praised be Thou, oh Lord our God, Ruler of the universe, that Thou has given us life and sustenance and brought us to this happy season." (Mr. Frank *lights the one candle of the Menorah as he continues.*) "We kindle this Hanukkah light to celebrate the great and wonderful deeds wrought through
1670 the zeal with which God filled the hearts of the heroic Maccabees, two thousand years ago. They fought against indifference, against tyranny and oppression, and they restored our Temple to us. May these lights remind us that we should ever look to God, whence cometh our help." Amen. [Pronounced O-mayn.]

**All.** Amen.

(Mr. Frank *hands* Mrs. Frank *the prayer book.*)

**Mrs. Frank** (*reading*). "I lift up mine eyes unto
1680 the mountains, from whence cometh my help. My help cometh from the Lord who made heaven and earth. He will not suffer thy foot to be moved. He that keepeth thee will not slumber. He that keepeth Israel doth neither slumber nor sleep. The Lord is thy keeper. The Lord is thy shade upon thy right hand. The sun shall not smite thee by day,

nor the moon by night. The Lord shall keep thee from all evil. He shall keep thy soul. The Lord shall guard thy going out and thy coming in, from this
1690 time forth and forevermore." Amen.

**All.** Amen.

(Mrs. Frank *puts down the prayer book and goes to get the food and wine.* Margot *helps her.* Mr. Frank *takes the men's hats and puts them aside.*)

**Dussel** (*rising*). That was very moving.

**Anne** (*pulling him back*). It isn't over yet!

**Mrs. Van Daan.** Sit down! Sit down!

**Anne.** There's a lot more, songs and presents.

**Dussel.** Presents?

1700 **Mrs. Frank.** Not this year, unfortunately.

**Mrs. Van Daan.** But always on Hanukkah everyone gives presents . . . everyone!

**Dussel.** Like our St. Nicholas' Day.[18] (*There is a chorus of "no's" from the group.*)

**Mrs. Van Daan.** No! Not like St. Nicholas! What kind of a Jew are you that you don't know Hanukkah?

**Mrs. Frank** (*as she brings the food*). I remember particularly the candles . . . First one, as we have
1710 tonight. Then the second night you light two candles, the next night three . . . and so on until you have eight candles burning. When there are eight candles it is truly beautiful.

**Mrs. Van Daan.** And the potato pancakes.

**Mr. Van Daan.** Don't talk about them!

**Mrs. Van Daan.** I make the best *latkes*[19] you ever tasted!

**Mrs. Frank.** Invite us all next year . . . in your own home.

1720 **Mr. Frank.** God willing!

**Mrs. Van Daan.** God willing.

---

16. **Hanukkah** (hä′nə-kə): a Jewish holiday, celebrated in December and lasting eight days.

17. **Menorah** (mə-nôr′ə): a candleholder with nine branches, used in the celebration of Hanukkah.

18. **St. Nicholas's Day:** December 6, the day that Christian children in the Netherlands receive gifts.

19. **latkes** (lät′kəz): potato pancakes.

**Margot.** What I remember best is the presents we used to get when we were little . . . eight days of presents . . . and each day they got better and better.

**Mrs. Frank** (*sitting down*). We are all here, alive. That is present enough.

**Anne.** No, it isn't. I've got something . . .

(*She rushes into her room, hurriedly puts on a little*
1730 *hat improvised from the lamp shade, grabs a satchel bulging with parcels and comes running back.*)

**Mrs. Frank.** What is it?

**Anne.** Presents!

**Mrs. Van Daan.** Presents!

**Dussel.** Look!

**Mr. Van Daan.** What's she got on her head?

**Peter.** A lamp shade!

**Anne** (*She picks out one at random*). This is for Margot. (*She hands it to* Margot, *pulling her to*
1740 *her feet.*) Read it out loud.

**Margot** (*reading*).

"You have never lost your temper.
You never will, I fear,
You are so good.
But if you should,
Put all your cross words here."

(*She tears open the package.*)

A new crossword puzzle book! Where did you get it?

1750 **Anne.** It isn't new. It's one that you've done. But I rubbed it all out, and if you wait a little and forget, you can do it all over again.

**Margot** (*sitting*). It's wonderful, Anne. Thank you. You'd never know it wasn't new.

(*From outside we hear the sound of a streetcar passing.*)

**Anne** (*with another gift*). Mrs. Van Daan.

**Mrs. Van Daan** (*taking it*). This is awful . . . I haven't anything for anyone . . . I never
1760 thought . . .

**Mr. Frank.** This is all Anne's idea.

**Mrs. Van Daan** (*holding up a bottle*). What is it?

**Anne.** It's hair shampoo. I took all the odds and ends of soap and mixed them with the last of my toilet water.

**Mrs. Van Daan.** Oh, Anneke!

**Anne.** I wanted to write a poem for all of them, but I didn't have time. (*offering a large box to* Mr. Van Daan) Yours, Mr. Van Daan, is *really*
1770 something . . . something you want more than anything. (*as she waits for him to open it*) Look! Cigarettes!

**Mr. Van Daan.** Cigarettes!

**Anne.** Two of them! Pim found some old pipe tobacco in the pocket lining of his coat . . . and we made them . . . or rather, Pim did.

**Mrs. Van Daan.** Let me see . . . Well, look at that! Light it, Putti! Light it.

(Mr. Van Daan *hesitates.*)

1780 **Anne.** It's tobacco, really it is! There's a little fluff in it, but not much.

(*Everyone watches intently as* Mr. Van Daan *cautiously lights it. The cigarette flares up. Everyone laughs.*)

**Peter.** It works!

**Mrs. Van Daan.** Look at him.

**Mr. Van Daan** (*spluttering*). Thank you, Anne. Thank you.

(Anne *rushes back to her satchel for another*
1790 *present.*)

**Anne** (*handing her mother a piece of paper*). For Mother, Hanukkah greeting. (*She pulls her mother to her feet.*)

**Mrs. Frank** (*She reads.*) "Here's an I.O.U. that I promise to pay. Ten hours of doing whatever you say. Signed, Anne Frank." (Mrs. Frank, *touched, takes* Anne *in her arms, holding her close.*)

**Dussel** (*to* Anne). Ten hours of doing what you're told? *Anything* you're told?

1800 **Anne.** That's right.

**Dussel.** You wouldn't want to sell that, Mrs. Frank?

**Mrs. Frank.** Never! This is the most precious gift I've ever had!

(*She sits, showing her present to the others.* Anne *hurries back to the satchel and pulls out a scarf, the scarf that* Mr. Frank *found in the first scene.*)

**Anne** (*offering it to her father*). For Pim.

**Mr. Frank.** Anneke . . . I wasn't supposed to have
1810 a present! (*He takes it, unfolding it and showing it to the others.*)

**Anne.** It's a muffler . . . to put round your neck . . . like an ascot, you know. I made it myself out of odds and ends . . . I knitted it in the dark each night, after I'd gone to bed. I'm afraid it looks better in the dark!

**Mr. Frank** (*putting it on*). It's fine. It fits me perfectly. Thank you, Annele.

(Anne *hands* Peter *a ball of paper, with a string*
1820 *attached to it.*)

**Anne.** That's for Mouschi.

**Peter** (*rising to bow*). On behalf of Mouschi, I thank you.

**Anne** (*hesitant, handing him a gift*). And . . . this is yours . . . from Mrs. Quack Quack. (*as he holds it gingerly in his hands*) Well . . . open it . . . Aren't you going to open it?

**Peter.** I'm scared to. I know something's going to jump out and hit me.

1830 **Anne.** No. It's nothing like that, really.

**Mrs. Van Daan** (*as he is opening it*). What is it, Peter? Go on. Show it.

**Anne** (*excitedly*). It's a safety razor!

**Dussel.** A what?

**Anne.** A razor!

**Mrs. Van Daan** (*looking at it*). You didn't make that out of odds and ends.

**Anne** (*to* Peter). Miep got it for me. It's not new. It's second-hand. But you really do need a razor

1840 now.

**Dussel.** For what?

**Anne.** Look on his upper lip . . . you can see the beginning of a mustache.

**Dussel.** He wants to get rid of that? Put a little milk on it and let the cat lick it off.

**Peter** (*starting for his room*). Think you're funny, don't you.

**Dussel.** Look! He can't wait! He's going in to try it!

1850 **Peter.** I'm going to give Mouschi his present! (*He goes into his room, slamming the door behind him.*)

**Mr. Van Daan** (*disgustedly*). Mouschi, Mouschi, Mouschi.

(*In the distance we hear a dog persistently barking.* Anne *brings a gift to* Dussel.)

**Anne.** And last but never least, my roommate, Mr. Dussel.

**Dussel.** For me? You have something for me?

1860 (*He opens the small box she gives him.*)

**Anne.** I made them myself.

**Dussel** (*puzzled*). Capsules! Two capsules!

**Anne.** They're ear-plugs!

**Dussel.** Ear-plugs?

**Anne.** To put in your ears so you won't hear me when I thrash around at night. I saw them advertised in a magazine. They're not real ones . . . I made them out of cotton and candle wax. Try them . . . See if they don't work . . .

1870 see if you can hear me talk . . .

**Dussel** (*putting them in his ears*). Wait now until I get them in . . . so.

**Anne.** Are you ready?

**Dussel.** Huh?

**Anne.** Are you ready?

**Dussel.** Good God! They've gone inside! I can't get them out! (*They laugh as* Mr. Dussel *jumps about, trying to shake the plugs out of his ears. Finally he gets them out. Putting them away.*)

1880 Thank you, Anne! Thank you!

**Mr. Van Daan.** A real Hanukkah!

**Mrs. Van Daan.** Wasn't it cute of her?

**Mrs. Frank.** I don't know when she did it.

*Together*

**Margot.** I love my present.

**Anne** (*sitting at the table*). And now let's have the song, Father . . . please . . . (*to* Dussel) Have you heard the Hanukkah song, Mr. Dussel? The song is the whole thing! (*She sings.*) "Oh, Hanukkah!

1890 Oh Hanukkah! The sweet celebration . . . "

**Mr. Frank** (*quieting her*). I'm afraid, Anne, we shouldn't sing that song tonight. (*to* Dussel) It's a song of jubilation, of rejoicing. One is apt to become too enthusiastic.

**Anne.** Oh, please, please. Let's sing the song. I promise not to shout!

**Mr. Frank.** Very well. But quietly now . . . I'll keep an eye on you and when . . .

(*As* Anne *starts to sing, she is interrupted by* Dussel,

1900 *who is snorting and wheezing.*)

**Dussel** (*pointing to* Peter). You . . . You! (Peter *is coming from his bedroom, ostentatiously holding a bulge in his coat as if he were holding his cat, and*

*dangling* Anne's *present before it.*) How many times . . . I told you . . . Out! Out!

**Mr. Van Daan** (*going to* Peter). What's the matter with you? Haven't you any sense? Get that cat out of here.

**Peter** (*innocently*). Cat?

1910 **Mr. Van Daan.** You heard me. Get it out of here!

**Peter.** I have no cat. (*Delighted with his joke, he opens his coat and pulls out a bath towel. The group at the table laugh, enjoying the joke.*)

**Dussel** (*still wheezing*). It doesn't need to be the cat . . . his clothes are enough . . . when he comes out of that room . . .

**Mr. Van Daan.** Don't worry. You won't be bothered any more. We're getting rid of it.

**Dussel.** At last you listen to me. (*He goes off into*
1920 *his bedroom.*)

**Mr. Van Daan** (*calling after him*). I'm not doing it for you. That's all in your mind . . . all of it! (*He starts back to his place at the table.*) I'm doing it because I'm sick of seeing that cat eat all our food.

**Peter.** That's not true! I only give him bones . . . scraps . . .

**Mr. Van Daan.** Don't tell me! He gets fatter every day! Damn cat looks better than any of us. Out
1930 he goes tonight!

**Peter.** No! No!

**Anne.** Mr. Van Daan, you can't do that! That's Peter's cat. Peter loves that cat.

**Mrs. Frank** (*quietly*). Anne.

**Peter** (*to* Mr. Van Daan). If he goes, I go.

**Mr. Van Daan.** Go! Go!

**Mrs. Van Daan.** You're not going and the cat's not going! Now please . . . this is Hanukkah . . . Hanukkah . . . this is the time to celebrate . . .
1940 What's the matter with all of you? Come on, Anne. Let's have the song.

**Anne** (*singing*). "Oh, Hanukkah! Oh, Hanukkah! The sweet celebration."

**Mr. Frank** (*rising*). I think we should first blow out the candle . . . then we'll have something for tomorrow night.

**Margot.** But, Father, you're supposed to let it burn itself out.

**Mr. Frank.** I'm sure that God understands
1950 shortages. (*before blowing it out*) "Praised be Thou, oh Lord our God, who hast sustained us and permitted us to celebrate this joyous festival."

(*He is about to blow out the candle when suddenly there is a crash of something falling below. They all freeze in horror, motionless. For a few seconds there is complete silence. Mr. Frank slips off his shoes. The others noiselessly follow his example. Mr. Frank turns out a light near him. He motions to Peter to turn off the center lamp. Peter tries to reach it,*
1960 *realizes he cannot and gets up on a chair. Just as he is touching the lamp he loses his balance. The chair goes out from under him. He falls. The iron lamp shade crashes to the floor. There is a sound of feet below, running down the stairs.*)

**Mr. Van Daan** (*under his breath*). God Almighty! (*The only light left comes from the Hanukkah candle. Dussel comes from his room. Mr. Frank creeps over to the stairwell and stands listening. The dog is heard barking excitedly.*) Do you hear
1970 anything?

**Mr. Frank** (*in a whisper*). No. I think they've gone.

**Mrs. Van Daan.** It's the Green Police. They've found us.

**Mr. Frank.** If they had, they wouldn't have left. They'd be up here by now.

**Mrs. Van Daan.** I know it's the Green Police. They've gone to get help. That's all. They'll be back!

**Mr. Van Daan.** Or it may have been the Gestapo,[20]
1980 looking for papers . . .

---

20. **Gestapo** (gə-stä′pō): the Nazi secret police force, known for its terrorism and brutality.

**Mr. Frank** (*interrupting*). Or a thief, looking for money.

**Mrs. Van Daan.** We've got to do something . . . Quick! Quick! Before they come back.

**Mr. Van Daan.** There isn't anything to do. Just wait.

(*Mr. Frank holds up his hand for them to be quiet. He is listening intently. There is complete silence as they all strain to hear any sound from below.*
1990 *Suddenly Anne begins to sway. With a low cry she falls to the floor in a faint. Mrs. Frank goes to her quickly, sitting beside her on the floor and taking her in her arms.*)

**Mrs. Frank.** Get some water, please! Get some water!

(*Margot starts for the sink.*)

**Mr. Van Daan** (*grabbing* Margot). No! No! No one's going to run water!

**Mr. Frank.** If they've found us, they've found us.
2000 Get the water. (*Margot starts again for the sink. Mr. Frank, getting a flashlight*) I'm going down.

(*Margot rushes to him, clinging to him. Anne struggles to consciousness.*)

**Margot.** No, Father, no! There may be someone there, waiting . . . It may be a trap!

**Mr. Frank.** This is Saturday. There is no way for us to know what has happened until Miep or Mr. Kraler comes on Monday morning. We cannot live with this uncertainty.

2010 **Margot.** Don't go, Father!

**Mrs. Frank.** Hush, darling, hush. (*Mr. Frank slips quietly out, down the steps and out through the door below.*) Margot! Stay close to me.

(*Margot goes to her mother.*)

**Mr. Van Daan.** Shush! Shush!

(*Mrs. Frank whispers to Margot to get the water. Margot goes for it.*)

**Mrs. Van Daan.** Putti, where's our money? Get our money. I hear you can buy the Green Police

2020 off, so much a head. Go upstairs quick! Get the money!

**Mr. Van Daan.** Keep still!

**Mrs. Van Daan** (*kneeling before him, pleading*). Do you want to be dragged off to a concentration camp? Are you going to stand there and wait for them to come up and get you? Do something, I tell you!

**Mr. Van Daan** (*pushing her aside*). Will you keep still! (*He goes over to the stairwell to listen. Peter*
2030 *goes to his mother, helping her up onto the sofa. There is a second of silence, then Anne can stand it no longer.*)

**Anne.** Someone go after Father! Make Father come back!

**Peter** (*starting for the door*). I'll go.

**Mr. Van Daan.** Haven't you done enough?

(*He pushes* Peter *roughly away. In his anger against his father* Peter *grabs a chair as if to hit him with it, then puts it down, burying his face in his hands.*
2040 Mrs. Frank *begins to pray softly.*)

**Anne.** Please, please, Mr. Van Daan. Get Father.

**Mr. Van Daan.** Quiet! Quiet!

(*Anne is shocked into silence. Mrs. Frank pulls her closer, holding her protectively in her arms.*)

**Mrs. Frank** (*softly, praying*). "I lift up mine eyes unto the mountains, from whence cometh my help. My help cometh from the Lord who made heaven and earth. He will not suffer thy foot to be moved . . . He that keepeth thee will not slumber . . ." (*She*
2050 *stops as she hears someone coming. They all watch the door tensely. Mr. Frank comes quietly in. Anne rushes to him, holding him tight.*)

**Mr. Frank.** It was a thief. That noise must have scared him away.

**Mrs. Van Daan.** Thank God.

**Mr. Frank.** He took the cash box. And the radio. He ran away in such a hurry that he didn't stop to shut the street door. It was swinging wide

open. (*A breath of relief sweeps over them.*) I think
2060 it would be good to have some light.

**Margot.** Are you sure it's all right?

**Mr. Frank.** The danger has passed. (Margot *goes to light the small lamp.*) Don't be so terrified, Anne. We're safe.

**Dussel.** Who says the danger has passed? Don't you realize we are in greater danger than ever?

**Mr. Frank.** Mr. Dussel, will you be still!

(Mr. Frank *takes* Anne *back to the table, making her sit down with him, trying to calm her.*)

2070 **Dussel** (*pointing to* Peter). Thanks to this clumsy fool, there's someone now who knows we're up here! Someone now knows we're up here, hiding!

**Mrs. Van Daan** (*going to* Dussel). Someone knows we're here, yes. But who is the someone? A thief! A thief! You think a thief is going to go to the Green Police and say . . . I was robbing a place the other night and I heard a noise up over my head? You think a thief is going to do that?

**Dussel.** Yes. I think he will.

2080 **Mrs. Van Daan** (*hysterically*). You're crazy! (*She stumbles back to her seat at the table.* Peter *follows protectively, pushing* Dussel *aside.*)

**Dussel.** I think some day he'll be caught and then he'll make a bargain with the Green Police . . . if they'll let him off, he'll tell them where some Jews are hiding!

(*He goes off into the bedroom. There is a second of appalled silence.*)

**Mr. Van Daan.** He's right.

2090 **Anne.** Father, let's get out of here! We can't stay here now . . . Let's go . . .

**Mr. Van Daan.** Go! Where?

**Mrs. Frank** (*sinking into her chair at the table*). Yes. Where?

**Mr. Frank** (*rising, to them all*). Have we lost all faith? All courage? A moment ago we thought that they'd come for us. We were sure it was the end. But it wasn't the end. We're alive, safe. (Mr. Van Daan *goes to the table and sits.* Mr. Frank
2100 *prays.*) "We thank Thee, oh Lord our God, that in Thy infinite mercy Thou hast again seen fit to spare us." (*He blows out the candle, then turns to* Anne.) Come on, Anne. The song! Let's have the song! (*He starts to sing.* Anne *finally starts falteringly to sing, as* Mr. Frank *urges her on. Her voice is hardly audible at first.*)

**Anne** (*singing*). "Oh, Hanukkah! Oh, Hanukkah! The sweet . . . celebration . . ." (*As she goes on singing, the others gradually join in, their voices
2110 still shaking with fear.* Mrs. Van Daan *sobs as she sings.*)

**Group.** "Around the feast . . . we . . . gather
In complete . . . jubilation . . .
Happiest of sea . . . sons
Now is here.
Many are the reasons for good cheer."

(Dussel *comes from the bedroom. He comes over to the table, standing beside* Margot, *listening to them as they sing.*)

2120 "Together
We'll weather
Whatever tomorrow may bring."

(*As they sing on with growing courage, the lights start to dim.*)

"So hear us rejoicing
And merrily voicing
The Hanukkah song that we sing.
Hoy!"

(*The lights are out. The curtain starts slowly
2130 to fall.*)

"Hear us rejoicing
And merrily voicing
The Hanukkah song that we sing."

(*They are still singing, as the curtain falls.*)
*The Curtain Falls.*

**DIARY ENTRY** Anne Frank's diary entries give readers an intimate understanding of what was going through her mind while she was in hiding. This entry from December 1943 describes her conflicting emotions about life in the Annex.

28

**Friday, December 24, 1943**

Dear Kitty,

As I've written you many times before, moods have a tendency to affect us quite a bit here, and in my case it's been getting worse lately. *"Himmelhoch jauchzend, zu Tode betrübt"*[1] certainly applies to me. I'm "on top of the world" when I think of how fortunate we are and compare myself to other Jewish children, and "in the depths of despair" when, for example, Mrs. Kleiman comes by and talks about Jopie's hockey club, canoe trips, school plays and afternoon teas with friends.

I don't think I'm jealous of Jopie, but I long to have a really good time for once and to laugh so hard it hurts. We're stuck in this house like lepers, especially during winter and the Christmas and New Year's holidays. Actually, I shouldn't even be writing this, since it makes me seem so ungrateful, but I can't keep everything to myself, so I'll repeat what I said at the beginning: "Paper is more patient than people."

Whenever someone comes in from outside, with the wind in their clothes and the cold on their cheeks, I feel like burying my head under the blankets to keep from thinking, "When will we be allowed to breathe fresh air again?" I can't do that—on the

contrary, I have to hold my head up high and put a bold face on things, but the thoughts keep coming anyway. Not just once, but over and over.

Believe me, if you've been shut up for a year and a half, it can get to be too much for you sometimes. But feelings can't be ignored, no matter how unjust or ungrateful they seem. I long to ride a bike, dance, whistle, look at the world, feel young and know that I'm free, and yet I can't let it show. Just imagine what would happen if all eight of us were to feel sorry for ourselves or walk around with the discontent clearly visible on our faces. Where would that get us? . . .

Yours, Anne

---

1. *"Himmelhoch jauchzend, zu Tode betrübt":* A famous line from Goethe: "On top of the world, or in the depths of despair."

## Comprehension

**INDIANA STANDARDS**

**READING STANDARD**
**8.3.2** Evaluate the structural elements of the plot....

1. **Recall** How do the people in the Annex get food and other supplies?

2. **Recall** Why do some of the people in the Annex complain about Anne?

3. **Clarify** Why does Mr. Frank say that the loud air raids should be music to the ears of those hiding in the attic?

## Literary Analysis

4. **Interpret a Character's Words** What does Anne mean when she writes in her diary, "Paper is more patient than people"? Cite specific examples from the play that explain Anne's attitude.

5. **Examine Your Story Map** Look over your story map and make sure it's complete so far. What is the last major event in this act? What do you predict might happen in Act Two as a result of this event?

6. **Understand Conflicts** A conflict in literature is a struggle between two opposing forces. An **external conflict** is a struggle between a character and society, another character, or a force of nature. An **internal conflict** is a struggle within a character's mind. In a chart like the one shown, include the external and internal conflicts you notice so far in the play. Circle the one or two conflicts you think are the main ones.

| External Conflicts | Internal Conflicts |
|---|---|
|  |  |

7. **Identify Subplot** A **subplot** is an additional, or secondary, plot in a work of literature. The subplot contains its own conflict, often separate from the main conflicts of the story. What is one subplot that has been introduced in Act One?

8. **Analyze Theme** Which characters help the most to develop the theme that people are good at heart? Consider actions of people both inside and outside the Secret Annex. Do any other characters make you question the play's theme? Explain.

## Extension and Challenge

9. **Readers' Circle** Review the diary entry included on page 520. Anne admits she sometimes feels like burying her head under the blankets. Yet she holds her head up high and puts a "bold face on things." What **impact** do you think her behavior had on those around her? Discuss this question with a small group.

## ACT TWO
### Scene 1

*In the darkness we hear* Anne's Voice, *again reading from the diary.*

**Anne's Voice.** Saturday, the first of January, nineteen forty-four. Another new year has begun and we find ourselves still in our hiding place. We have been here now for one year, five months and twenty-five days. It seems that our life is at a standstill.

*The curtain rises on the scene. It is late afternoon.*
10 *Everyone is bundled up against the cold. In the main room* Mrs. Frank *is taking down the laundry which is hung across the back.* Mr. Frank *sits in the chair down left, reading.* Margot *is lying on the couch with a blanket over her and the many-colored knitted scarf around her throat.* Anne *is seated at the center table, writing in her diary.* Peter, Mr. *and* Mrs. Van Daan, *and* Dussel *are all in their own rooms, reading or lying down.*

*As the lights dim on,* Anne's Voice *continues,*
20 *without a break.*

**Anne's Voice.** We are all a little thinner. The Van Daans' "discussions" are as violent as ever. Mother still does not understand me. But then I don't understand her either. There is one great change, however. A change in myself. I read somewhere that girls of my age don't feel quite certain of themselves. That they become quiet within and begin to think of the miracle that is taking place in their bodies. I think that what is happening
30 to me is so wonderful . . . not only what can be seen, but what is taking place inside. Each time it has happened I have a feeling that I have a sweet secret. (*We hear the chimes and then a hymn being played on the carillon outside.*) And in spite of any pain, I long for the time when I shall feel that secret within me again.

(*The buzzer of the door below suddenly sounds. Everyone is startled,* Mr. Frank *tiptoes cautiously to the top of the steps and listens. Again the buzzer*
40 *sounds, in* Miep's *V-for-Victory signal.*)

**Mr. Frank.** It's Miep! (*He goes quickly down the steps to unbolt the door.* Mrs. Frank *calls upstairs to the* Van Daans *and then to* Peter.)

**Mrs. Frank.** Wake up, everyone! Miep is here! (Anne *quickly puts her diary away.* Margot *sits up, pulling the blanket around her shoulders.* Mr. Dussel *sits on the edge of his bed, listening,* **disgruntled.** Miep *comes up the steps, followed by* Mr. Kraler. *They bring flowers, books, newspapers,*
50 *etc.* Anne *rushes to* Miep, *throwing her arms affectionately around her.*) Miep . . . *and* Mr. Kraler . . . What a delightful surprise!

**Mr. Kraler.** We came to bring you New Year's greetings.

**Mrs. Frank.** You shouldn't . . . you should have at least one day to yourselves. (*She goes quickly to the stove and brings down teacups and tea for all of them.*)

**Anne.** Don't say that, it's so wonderful to see them!
60 (*sniffing at* Miep's *coat*) I can smell the wind and the cold on your clothes.

**Miep** (*giving her the flowers*). There you are. (*then to* Margot, *feeling her forehead*) How are you, Margot? . . . Feeling any better?

**Margot.** I'm all right.

**Anne.** We filled her full of every kind of pill so she won't cough and make a noise. (*She runs into her room to put the flowers in water.* Mr. *and* Mrs. Van Daan *come from upstairs. Outside there is the sound*
70 *of a band playing.*)

**Mrs. Van Daan.** Well, hello, Miep. Mr. Kraler.

**Mr. Kraler** (*giving a bouquet of flowers to* Mrs. Van Daan). With my hope for peace in the New Year.

**Peter** (*anxiously*). Miep, have you seen Mouschi? Have you seen him anywhere around?

**Miep.** I'm sorry, Peter. I asked everyone in the neighborhood had they seen a gray cat. But they said no.

(Mrs. Frank *gives* Miep *a cup of tea.* Mr. Frank
80 *comes up the steps, carrying a small cake on a plate.*)

**Mr. Frank.** Look what Miep's brought for us!

**Mrs. Frank** (*taking it*). A cake!

**Mr. Van Daan.** A cake! (*He pinches* Miep's *cheeks gaily and hurries up to the cupboard.*) I'll get some plates.

(Dussel, *in his room, hastily puts a coat on and starts out to join the others.*)

**Mrs. Frank.** Thank you, Miepia. You shouldn't have done it. You must have used all of your sugar
90 ration for weeks. (*giving it to* Mrs. Van Daan) It's beautiful, isn't it?

**Mrs. Van Daan.** It's been ages since I even saw a cake. Not since you brought us one last year. (*without looking at the cake, to* Miep) Remember? Don't you remember, you gave us one on New Year's Day? Just this time last year? I'll never forget it because you had "Peace in nineteen forty-three" on it. (*She looks at the cake and reads.*) "Peace in nineteen forty-four!"

100 **Miep.** Well, it has to come sometime, you know. (*as* Dussel *comes from his room*) Hello, Mr. Dussel.

**Mr. Kraler.** How are you?

**Mr. Van Daan** (*bringing plates and a knife*). Here's the knife, *liefje.* Now, how many of us are there?

**Miep.** None for me, thank you.

**Mr. Frank.** Oh, please. You must.

**Miep.** I couldn't.

**Mr. Van Daan.** Good! That leaves one . . . two . . . three . . . seven of us.

110 **Dussel.** Eight! Eight! It's the same number as it always is!

**Mr. Van Daan.** I left Margot out. I take it for granted Margot won't eat any.

**Anne.** Why wouldn't she!

**Mrs. Frank.** I think it won't harm her.

**Mr. Van Daan.** All right! All right! I just didn't want her to start coughing again, that's all.

**Dussel.** And please, Mrs. Frank should cut the cake.

**Mr. Van Daan.** What's the difference? ⎫
120 **Mrs. Van Daan.** It's not Mrs. Frank's cake, is it, Miep? It's for all of us. ⎬ *Together*
⎭

**Dussel.** Mrs. Frank divides things better.

**Mrs. Van Daan** (*going to* Dussel). What are you trying to say? ⎫
**Mr. Van Daan.** Oh, come on! Stop wasting time! ⎬ *Together*
⎭

**Mrs. Van Daan** (*to* Dussel). Don't I always give everybody exactly the same? Don't I?

**Mr. Van Daan.** Forget it, Kerli.

130 **Mrs. Van Daan.** No. I want an answer! Don't I?

**Dussel.** Yes. Yes. Everybody gets exactly the same . . . except Mr. Van Daan always gets a little bit more.

(Mr. Van Daan *advances on* Dussel, *the knife still in his hand.*)

**Mr. Van Daan.** That's a lie!

(Dussel *retreats before the onslaught of the* Van Daans.)

**Mr. Frank.** Please, please! (*then to* Miep) You see
140 what a little sugar cake does to us! It goes right to our heads!

**Mr. Van Daan** (*handing* Mrs. Frank *the knife*). Here you are, Mrs. Frank.

**Mrs. Frank.** Thank you. (*then to* Miep *as she goes to the table to cut the cake*) Are you sure you won't have some?

**Miep** (*drinking her tea*). No, really, I have to go in a minute.

(*The sound of the band fades out in the distance.*)

150 **Peter** (*to* Miep). Maybe Mouschi went back to our house . . . they say that cats . . . Do you ever get over there . . . ? I mean . . . do you suppose you could . . . ?

**Miep.** I'll try, Peter. The first minute I get I'll try. But I'm afraid, with him gone a week . . .

**Dussel.** Make up your mind, already someone has had a nice big dinner from that cat!

(Peter *is furious, inarticulate. He starts toward* Dussel *as if to hit him.* Mr. Frank *stops him.*
160 Mrs. Frank *speaks quickly to ease the situation.*)

**Mrs. Frank** (*to* Miep). This is delicious, Miep!

**Mrs. Van Daan** (*eating hers*). Delicious!

**Mr. Van Daan** (*finishing it in one gulp*). Dirk's in luck to get a girl who can bake like this!

**Miep** (*putting down her empty teacup*). I have to run. Dirk's taking me to a party tonight.

**Anne.** How heavenly! Remember now what everyone is wearing, and what you have to eat and everything, so you can tell us tomorrow.

170 **Miep.** I'll give you a full report! Good-bye, everyone!

**Mr. Van Daan** (*to* Miep). Just a minute. There's something I'd like you to do for me. (*He hurries off up the stairs to his room.*)

**Mrs. Van Daan** (*sharply*). Putti, where are you going? (*She rushes up the stairs after him, calling hysterically.*) What do you want? Putti, what are you going to do?

**Miep** (*to* Peter). What's wrong?

**Peter** (*his sympathy is with his mother*). Father says 180 he's going to sell her fur coat. She's crazy about that old fur coat.

**Dussel.** Is it possible? Is it possible that anyone is so silly as to worry about a fur coat in times like this?

**Peter.** It's none of your darn business . . . and if you say one more thing . . . I'll, I'll take you and I'll . . . I mean it . . . I'll . . .

(*There is a piercing scream from* Mrs. Van Daan *above. She grabs at the fur coat as* Mr. Van Daan 190 *is starting downstairs with it.*)

**Mrs. Van Daan.** No! No! No! Don't you dare take that! You hear? It's mine! (*Downstairs* Peter *turns away, embarrassed, miserable.*) My father gave me that! You didn't give it to me. You have no right. Let go of it . . . you hear?

(Mr. Van Daan *pulls the coat from her hands and hurries downstairs.* Mrs. Van Daan *sinks to the floor, sobbing. As* Mr. Van Daan *comes into the main room the others look away, embarrassed for him.*)

200 **Mr. Van Daan** (*to* Mr. Kraler). Just a little—discussion over the advisability of selling this coat. As I have often reminded Mrs. Van Daan, it's very selfish of her to keep it when people outside are in such desperate need of clothing . . . (*He gives the coat to* Miep.) So if you will please to sell it for us? It should fetch a good price. And by the way, will you get me cigarettes. I don't care what kind they are . . . get all you can.

210 **Miep.** It's terribly difficult to get them, Mr. Van Daan. But I'll try. Good-bye.

(*She goes.* Mr. Frank *follows her down the steps to bolt the door after her.* Mrs. Frank *gives* Mr. Kraler *a cup of tea.*)

**Mrs. Frank.** Are you sure you won't have some cake, Mr. Kraler?

**Mr. Kraler.** I'd better not.

**Mr. Van Daan.** You're still feeling badly? What does your doctor say?

**Mr. Kraler.** I haven't been to him.

220 **Mrs. Frank.** Now, Mr. Kraler! . . .

**Mr. Kraler** (*sitting at the table*). Oh, I tried. But you can't get near a doctor these days . . . they're so busy. After weeks I finally managed to get one on the telephone. I told him I'd like an appointment . . . I wasn't feeling very well. You know what he answers . . . over the telephone . . . Stick out your tongue! (*They laugh. He turns to* Mr. Frank *as* Mr. Frank *comes back.*) I have some contracts here . . . I wonder if you'd look over 230 them with me . . .

**Mr. Frank** (*putting out his hand*). Of course.

**Mr. Kraler** (*He rises.*) If we could go downstairs . . . (Mr. Frank *starts ahead,* Mr. Kraler *speaks to the others.*) Will you forgive us? I won't keep him but a minute. (*He starts to follow* Mr. Frank *down the steps.*)

**Margot** (*with sudden __foreboding__*). What's happened? Something's happened! Hasn't it, Mr. Kraler?

(Mr. Kraler *stops and comes back, trying to reassure* 240 Margot *with a pretense of casualness.*)

**Mr. Kraler.** No, really. I want your father's advice . . .

**Margot.** Something's gone wrong! I know it!

**Mr. Frank** (*coming back, to* Mr. Kraler). If it's something that concerns us here, it's better that we all hear it.

**Mr. Kraler** (*turning to him, quietly*). But . . . the children . . . ?

250 **Mr. Frank.** What they'd imagine would be worse than any reality.

(*As* Mr. Kraler *speaks, they all listen with intense* **apprehension.** Mrs. Van Daan *comes down the stairs and sits on the bottom step.*)

**Mr. Kraler.** It's a man in the storeroom . . . I don't know whether or not you remember him . . . Carl, about fifty, heavy-set, near-sighted . . . He came with us just before you left.

**Mr. Frank.** He was from Utrecht?

**Mr. Kraler.** That's the man. A couple of weeks ago,
260 when I was in the storeroom, he closed the door and asked me . . . how's Mr. Frank? What do you hear from Mr. Frank? I told him I only knew there was a rumor that you were in Switzerland. He said he'd heard that rumor too, but he thought I might know something more. I didn't pay any attention to it . . . but then a thing happened yesterday . . . He'd brought some invoices to the office for me to sign. As I was going through them, I looked up. He was standing staring at the bookcase . . . your
270 bookcase. He said he thought he remembered a door there . . . Wasn't there a door there that used to go up to the loft? Then he told me he wanted more money. Twenty guilders[1] more a week.

**Mr. Van Daan.** Blackmail!

**Mr. Frank.** Twenty guilders? Very modest blackmail.

**Mr. Van Daan.** That's just the beginning.

**Dussel** (*coming to* Mr. Frank). You know what I think? He was the thief who was down there that night. That's how he knows we're here.

280 **Mr. Frank** (*to* Mr. Kraler). How was it left? What did you tell him?

**Mr. Kraler.** I said I had to think about it. What shall I do? Pay him the money? . . . Take a chance on firing him . . . or what? I don't know.

**Dussel** (*frantic*). For God's sake don't fire him! Pay him what he asks . . . keep him here where you can have your eye on him.

**Mr. Frank.** Is it so much that he's asking? What are they paying nowadays?

290 **Mr. Kraler.** He could get it in a war plant. But this isn't a war plant. Mind you, I don't know if he really knows . . . or if he doesn't know.

**Mr. Frank.** Offer him half. Then we'll soon find out if it's blackmail or not.

**Dussel.** And if it is? We've got to pay it, haven't we? Anything he asks we've got to pay!

**Mr. Frank.** Let's decide that when the time comes.

**Mr. Kraler.** This may be all my imagination. You get to a point, these days, where you suspect
300 everyone and everything. Again and again . . . on some simple look or word, I've found myself . . .

(*The telephone rings in the office below.*)

**Mrs. Van Daan** (*hurrying to* Mr. Kraler). There's the telephone! What does that mean, the telephone ringing on a holiday?

**Mr. Kraler.** That's my wife. I told her I had to go over some papers in my office . . . to call me there when she got out of church. (*He starts out.*) I'll offer him half then. Good-bye . . . we'll hope for
310 the best!

(*The group call their good-byes half-heartedly. Mr. Frank follows* Mr. Kraler, *to bolt the door below. During the following scene, Mr. Frank comes back up and stands listening, disturbed.*)

**Dussel** (*to* Mr. Van Daan). You can thank your son for this . . . smashing the light! I tell you, it's just a question of time now. (*He goes to the window at the back and stands looking out.*)

**Margot.** Sometimes I wish the end would come
320 . . . whatever it is.

**Mrs. Frank** (*shocked*). Margot!

(Anne *goes to* Margot, *sitting beside her on the couch with her arms around her.*)

**Margot.** Then at least we'd know where we were.

---

1. **guilders** (gĭl′dərz): the basic monetary unit of the Netherlands at the time.

**Mrs. Frank.** You should be ashamed of yourself! Talking that way! Think how lucky we are! Think of the thousands dying in the war, every day. Think of the people in concentration camps.

**Anne** (*interrupting*). What's the good of that?
330 What's the good of thinking of misery when you're already miserable? That's stupid!

**Mrs. Frank.** Anne!

(*As* Anne *goes on raging at her mother,* Mrs. Frank *tries to break in, in an effort to quiet her.*)

**Anne.** We're young, Margot and Peter and I! You grownups have had your chance! But look at us . . . If we begin thinking of all the horror in the world, we're lost! We're trying to hold onto some kind of ideals . . . when everything . . .
340 ideals, hopes . . . everything, are being destroyed! It isn't our fault that the world is in such a mess! We weren't around when all this started! So don't try to take it out on us!

(*She rushes off to her room, slamming the door after her. She picks up a brush from the chest and hurls it to the floor. Then she sits on the settee, trying to control her anger.*)

**Mr. Van Daan.** She talks as if we started the war! Did we start the war? (*He spots* Anne's *cake. As he*
350 *starts to take it,* Peter *anticipates him.*)

**Peter.** She left her cake. (*He starts for* Anne's *room with the cake. There is silence in the main room. Mrs. Van Daan goes up to her room, followed by Van Daan. Dussel stays looking out the window. Mr. Frank brings Mrs. Frank her cake. She eats it slowly, without relish. Mr. Frank takes his cake to* Margot *and sits quietly on the sofa beside her.* Peter *stands in the doorway of* Anne's *darkened room, looking at her, then makes a little movement to let*
360 *her know he is there.* Anne *sits up, quickly, trying to hide the signs of her tears.* Peter *holds out the cake to her.*) You left this.

**Anne** (*dully*). Thanks.

(Peter *starts to go out, then comes back.*)

**Peter.** I thought you were fine just now. You know just how to talk to them. You know just how to say it. I'm no good . . . I never can think . . . especially when I'm mad . . . That Dussel . . . when he said that about Mouschi . . . someone eating him . . . all
370 I could think is . . . I wanted to hit him. I wanted to give him such a . . . a . . . that he'd . . . That's what I used to do when there was an argument at school . . . That's the way I . . . but here . . . And an old man like that . . . it wouldn't be so good.

**Anne.** You're making a big mistake about me. I do it all wrong. I say too much. I go too far. I hurt people's feelings . . .

(Dussel *leaves the window, going to his room.*)

**Peter.** I think you're just fine . . . What I want to
380 say . . . if it wasn't for you around here, I don't
know. What I mean . . .

(Peter *is interrupted by* Dussel's *turning on the light.*
Dussel *stands in the doorway, startled to see* Peter.
Peter *advances toward him forbiddingly.* Dussel *backs
out of the room.* Peter *closes the door on him.*)

**Anne.** Do you mean it, Peter? Do you really mean it?

**Peter.** I said it, didn't I?

**Anne.** Thank you, Peter!

(*In the main room* Mr. *and* Mrs. Frank *collect the*
390 *dishes and take them to the sink, washing them.*
Margot *lies down again on the couch.* Dussel, *lost,
wanders into* Peter's *room and takes up a book,
starting to read.*)

**Peter** (*looking at the photographs on the wall*).
You've got quite a collection.

**Anne.** Wouldn't you like some in your room?
I could give you some. Heaven knows you spend
enough time in there . . . doing heaven knows
what . . .

400 **Peter.** It's easier. A fight starts, or an argument . . .
I duck in there.

**Anne.** You're lucky, having a room to go to.
His lordship is always here . . . I hardly ever get a
minute alone. When they start in on me, I can't
duck away. I have to stand there and take it.

**Peter.** You gave some of it back just now.

**Anne.** I get so mad. They've formed their
opinions . . . about everything . . . but we . . .
we're still trying to find out . . . We have problems
410 here that no other people our age have ever
had. And just as you think you've solved them,
something comes along and bang! You have to
start all over again.

**Peter.** At least you've got someone you can talk to.

**Anne.** Not really. Mother . . . I never discuss
anything serious with her. She doesn't understand.
Father's all right. We can talk about everything . . .
everything but one thing. Mother. He simply
won't talk about her. I don't think you can be

420 really intimate with anyone if he holds something
back, do you?

**Peter.** I think your father's fine.

**Anne.** Oh, he is, Peter! He is! He's the only one
who's ever given me the feeling that I have any
sense. But anyway, nothing can take the place of
school and play and friends of your own age . . .
or near your age . . . can it?

**Peter.** I suppose you miss your friends and all.

**Anne.** It isn't just . . . (*She breaks off, staring up
430 at him for a second.*) Isn't it funny, you and I?
Here we've been seeing each other every minute
for almost a year and a half, and this is the first
time we've ever really talked. It helps a lot to have
someone to talk to, don't you think? It helps you
to let off steam.

**Peter** (*going to the door*). Well, any time you want
to let off steam, you can come into my room.

**Anne** (*following him*). I can get up an awful lot of
steam. You'll have to be careful how you say that.

440 **Peter.** It's all right with me.

**Anne.** Do you mean it?

**Peter.** I said it, didn't I?

(*He goes out.* Anne *stands in her doorway looking
after him. As* Peter *gets to his door he stands for a
minute looking back at her. Then he goes into his
room.* Dussel *rises as he comes in, and quickly passes
him, going out. He starts across for his room.* Anne
*sees him coming, and pulls her door shut.* Dussel
*turns back toward* Peter's *room.* Peter *pulls his door*
450 *shut.* Dussel *stands there, bewildered, forlorn.*

*The scene slowly dims out. The curtain falls on the
scene.* Anne's Voice *comes over in the darkness . . .
faintly at first, and then with growing strength.*)

**Anne's Voice.** We've had bad news. The people
from whom Miep got our ration books have been
arrested. So we have had to cut down on our food.
Our stomachs are so empty that they rumble and
make strange noises, all in different keys. Mr. Van
Daan's is deep and low, like a bass fiddle. Mine is
460 high, whistling like a flute. As we all sit around

waiting for supper, it's like an orchestra tuning up. It only needs Toscanini[2] to raise his baton and we'd be off in the Ride of the Valkyries.[3] Monday, the sixth of March, nineteen forty-four. Mr. Kraler is in the hospital. It seems he has ulcers. Pim says we are his ulcers. Miep has to run the business and us too. The Americans have landed on the southern tip of Italy. Father looks for a quick finish to the war. Mr. Dussel is waiting every day
470 for the warehouse man to demand more money. Have I been skipping too much from one subject to another? I can't help it. I feel that spring is coming. I feel it in my whole body and soul. I feel utterly confused. I am longing . . . so longing . . . for everything . . . for friends . . . for someone to talk to . . . someone who understands . . . someone young, who feels as I do . . .

(*As these last lines are being said, the curtain rises on the scene. The lights dim on.* Anne's Voice *fades out.*)

## Scene 2

480    *It is evening, after supper. From outside we hear the sound of children playing. The "grownups," with the exception of* Mr. Van Daan, *are all in the main room.* Mrs. Frank *is doing some mending,* Mrs. Van Daan *is reading a fashion magazine.* Mr. Frank *is going over business accounts.* Dussel, *in his dentist's jacket, is pacing up and down, impatient to get into his bedroom.* Mr. Van Daan *is upstairs working on a piece of embroidery in an embroidery frame.*

*In his room* Peter *is sitting before the mirror,*
490 *smoothing his hair. As the scene goes on, he puts on his tie, brushes his coat and puts it on, preparing himself meticulously for a visit from* Anne. *On his wall are now hung some of* Anne's *motion picture stars.*

*In her room* Anne *too is getting dressed. She stands before the mirror in her slip, trying various ways of dressing her hair.* Margot *is seated on the sofa, hemming a skirt for* Anne *to wear.*

*In the main room* Dussel *can stand it no longer. He comes over, rapping sharply on the door of his and*
500 Anne's *bedroom.*

**Anne** (*calling to him*). No, no, Mr. Dussel! I am not dressed yet. (Dussel *walks away, furious, sitting down and burying his head in his hands.* Anne *turns to* Margot.) How is that? How does that look?

**Margot** (*glancing at her briefly*). Fine.

**Anne.** You didn't even look.

**Margot.** Of course I did. It's fine.

**Anne.** Margot, tell me, am I terribly ugly?

**Margot.** Oh, stop fishing.

510 **Anne.** No. No. Tell me.

**Margot.** Of course you're not. You've got nice eyes . . . and a lot of animation, and . . .

**Anne.** A little vague, aren't you?

(*She reaches over and takes a brassière out of* Margot's *sewing basket. She holds it up to herself, studying the effect in the mirror. Outside,* Mrs. Frank, *feeling sorry for* Dussel, *comes over, knocking at the girls' door.*)

**Mrs. Frank** (*outside*). May I come in?

520 **Margot.** Come in, Mother.

**Mrs. Frank** (*shutting the door behind her*). Mr. Dussel's impatient to get in here.

**Anne** (*still with the brassière*). Heavens, he takes the room for himself the entire day.

**Mrs. Frank** (*gently*). Anne, dear, you're not going in again tonight to see Peter?

**Anne** (*dignified*). That is my intention.

**Mrs. Frank.** But you've already spent a great deal of time in there today.

530 **Anne.** I was in there exactly twice. Once to get the dictionary, and then three-quarters of an hour before supper.

**Mrs. Frank.** Aren't you afraid you're disturbing him?

**Anne.** Mother, I have some intuition.

---

2. **Toscanini** (tŏs'kə-nē'nē): Arturo Toscanini, a famous Italian orchestral conductor.

3. **Ride of the Valkyries** (văl-kîr'ēz): a moving passage from an opera by Richard Wagner, a German composer.

**Mrs. Frank.** Then may I ask you this much, Anne. Please don't shut the door when you go in.

**Anne.** You sound like Mrs. Van Daan! (*She throws the brassière back in* Margot's *sewing basket and picks up her blouse, putting it on.*)

540 **Mrs. Frank.** No. No. I don't mean to suggest anything wrong. I only wish that you wouldn't expose yourself to criticism . . . that you wouldn't give Mrs. Van Daan the opportunity to be unpleasant.

**Anne.** Mrs. Van Daan doesn't need an opportunity to be unpleasant!

**Mrs. Frank.** Everyone's on edge, worried about Mr. Kraler. This is one more thing . . .

**Anne.** I'm sorry, Mother. I'm going to Peter's
550 room. I'm not going to let Petronella Van Daan spoil our friendship.

(Mrs. Frank *hesitates for a second, then goes out, closing the door after her. She gets a pack of playing cards and sits at the center table, playing solitaire. In* Anne's *room* Margot *hands the finished skirt to* Anne. *As* Anne *is putting it on,* Margot *takes off her high-heeled shoes and stuffs paper in the toes so that* Anne *can wear them.*)

**Margot** (*to* Anne). Why don't you two talk in the
560 main room? It'd save a lot of trouble. It's hard on Mother, having to listen to those remarks from Mrs. Van Daan and not say a word.

**Anne.** Why doesn't she say a word? I think it's ridiculous to take it and take it.

**Margot.** You don't understand Mother at all, do you? She can't talk back. She's not like you. It's just not in her nature to fight back.

**Anne.** Anyway . . . the only one I worry about is you. I feel awfully guilty about you.

570 (*She sits on the stool near* Margot, *putting on* Margot's *high-heeled shoes.*)

**Margot.** What about?

**Anne.** I mean, every time I go into Peter's room, I have a feeling I may be hurting you. (Margot *shakes her head.*) I know if it were me, I'd be wild. I'd be desperately jealous, if it were me.

**Margot.** Well, I'm not.

**Anne.** You don't feel badly? Really? Truly? You're not jealous?

580 **Margot.** Of course I'm jealous . . . jealous that you've got something to get up in the morning for . . . But jealous of you and Peter? No.

(Anne *goes back to the mirror.*)

**Anne.** Maybe there's nothing to be jealous of. Maybe he doesn't really like me. Maybe I'm just taking the place of his cat . . . (*She picks up a pair of short white gloves, putting them on.*) Wouldn't you like to come in with us?

**Margot.** I have a book.

590 (*The sound of the children playing outside fades out. In the main room* Dussel *can stand it no longer. He jumps up, going to the bedroom door and knocking sharply.*)

**Dussel.** Will you please let me in my room!

**Anne.** Just a minute, dear, dear Mr. Dussel. (*She picks up her* Mother's *pink stole and adjusts it elegantly over her shoulders, then gives a last look in the mirror.*) Well, here I go . . . to run the gauntlet.[4] (*She starts out, followed by* Margot.)

600 **Dussel** (*as she appears—sarcastic*). Thank you so much.

(Dussel *goes into his room.* Anne *goes toward* Peter's *room, passing* Mrs. Van Daan *and her parents at the center table.*)

**Mrs. Van Daan.** My God, look at her! (Anne *pays no attention. She knocks at* Peter's *door.*) I don't know what good it is to have a son. I never see him. He wouldn't care if I killed myself. (Peter *opens the door and stands aside for* Anne *to come in.*) Just a minute,
610 Anne. (*She goes to them at the door.*) I'd like to say a few words to my son. Do you mind? (Peter *and* Anne *stand waiting.*) Peter, I don't want you staying up till all hours tonight. You've got to have your sleep. You're a growing boy. You hear?

---

4. **to run the gauntlet:** to endure a series of troubles or difficulties.

**Mrs. Frank.** Anne won't stay late. She's going to bed promptly at nine. Aren't you, Anne?

**Anne.** Yes, Mother . . . (*to* Mrs. Van Daan) May we go now?

**Mrs. Van Daan.** Are you asking me? I didn't know 620 I had anything to say about it.

**Mrs. Frank.** Listen for the chimes, Anne dear.

(*The two young people go off into* Peter's *room, shutting the door after them.*)

**Mrs. Van Daan** (*to* Mrs. Frank). In my day it was the boys who called on the girls. Not the girls on the boys.

**Mrs. Frank.** You know how young people like to feel that they have secrets. Peter's room is the only place where they can talk.

630 **Mrs. Van Daan.** Talk! That's not what they called it when I was young.

(Mrs. Van Daan *goes off to the bathroom.* Margot *settles down to read her book.* Mr. Frank *puts his papers away and brings a chess game to the center table. He and* Mrs. Frank *start to play. In* Peter's *room,* Anne *speaks to* Peter, *indignant, humiliated.*)

**Anne.** Aren't they awful? Aren't they impossible? Treating us as if we were still in the nursery.

(*She sits on the cot.* Peter *gets a bottle of pop and* 640 *two glasses.*)

**Peter.** Don't let it bother you. It doesn't bother me.

**Anne.** I suppose you can't really blame them . . . they think back to what *they* were like at our age. They don't realize how much more advanced we are . . . When you think what wonderful discussions we've had! . . . Oh, I forgot. I was going to bring you some more pictures.

**Peter.** Oh, these are fine, thanks.

**Anne.** Don't you want some more? Miep just 650 brought me some new ones.

**Peter.** Maybe later. (*He gives her a glass of pop and, taking some for himself, sits down facing her.*)

**Anne** (*looking up at one of the photographs*). I remember when I got that . . . I won it. I bet Jopie that I could eat five ice-cream cones. We'd

all been playing ping-pong . . . We used to have heavenly times . . . we'd finish up with ice cream at the Delphi, or the Oasis, where Jews were allowed . . . there'd always be a lot of boys . . . 660 we'd laugh and joke . . . I'd like to go back to it for a few days or a week. But after that I know I'd be bored to death. I think more seriously about life now. I want to be a journalist . . . or something. I love to write. What do you want to do?

**Peter.** I thought I might go off some place . . . work on a farm or something . . . some job that doesn't take much brains.

**Anne.** You shouldn't talk that way. You've got the most awful inferiority complex.

670 **Peter.** I know I'm not smart.

**Anne.** That isn't true. You're much better than I am in dozens of things . . . arithmetic and algebra and . . . well, you're a million times better than I am in algebra. (*with sudden directness*) You like Margot, don't you? Right from the start you liked her, liked her much better than me.

**Peter** (*uncomfortably*). Oh, I don't know.

(*In the main room* Mrs. Van Daan *comes from the bathroom and goes over to the sink, polishing* 680 *a coffee pot.*)

**Anne.** It's all right. Everyone feels that way. Margot's so good. She's sweet and bright and beautiful and I'm not.

**Peter.** I wouldn't say that.

**Anne.** Oh, no, I'm not. I know that. I know quite well that I'm not a beauty. I never have been and never shall be.

**Peter.** I don't agree at all. I think you're pretty.

**Anne.** That's not true!

690 **Peter.** And another thing. You've changed . . . from at first, I mean.

**Anne.** I have?

**Peter.** I used to think you were awful noisy.

**Anne.** And what do you think now, Peter? How have I changed?

**Peter.** Well . . . er . . . you're . . . quieter.

(*In his room* Dussel *takes his pajamas and toilet articles and goes into the bathroom to change.*)

**Anne.** I'm glad you don't just hate me.

700 **Peter.** I never said that.

**Anne.** I bet when you get out of here you'll never think of me again.

**Peter.** That's crazy.

**Anne.** When you get back with all of your friends, you're going to say . . . now what did I ever see in that Mrs. Quack Quack.

**Peter.** I haven't got any friends.

**Anne.** Oh, Peter, of course you have. Everyone has friends.

710 **Peter.** Not me. I don't want any. I get along all right without them.

**Anne.** Does that mean you can get along without me? I think of myself as your friend.

**Peter.** No. If they were all like you, it'd be different.

(*He takes the glasses and the bottle and puts them away. There is a second's silence and then* Anne *speaks, hesitantly, shyly.*)

**Anne.** Peter, did you ever kiss a girl?

720 **Peter.** Yes. Once.

**Anne** (*to cover her feelings*). That picture's crooked. (Peter *goes over, straightening the photograph.*) Was she pretty?

**Peter.** Huh?

**Anne.** The girl that you kissed.

**Peter.** I don't know. I was blindfolded. (*He comes back and sits down again.*) It was at a party. One of those kissing games.

**Anne** (*relieved*). Oh. I don't suppose that really 730 counts, does it?

**Peter.** It didn't with me.

**Anne.** I've been kissed twice. Once a man I'd never seen before kissed me on the cheek when he picked me up off the ice and I was crying. And the other was Mr. Koophuis, a friend of Father's who kissed my hand. You wouldn't say those counted, would you?

**Peter.** I wouldn't say so.

**Anne.** I know almost for certain that Margot 740 would never kiss anyone unless she was engaged to them. And I'm sure too that Mother never touched a man before Pim. But I don't know . . . things are so different now . . . What do you think? Do you think a girl shouldn't kiss anyone except if she's engaged or something? It's so hard to try to think what to do, when here we are with the whole world falling around our ears and you think . . . well . . . you don't know what's going to happen tomorrow and . . . What do you think?

750 **Peter.** I suppose it'd depend on the girl. Some girls, anything they do's wrong. But others . . . well . . . it wouldn't necessarily be wrong with them. (*The carillon starts to strike nine o'clock.*) I've always thought that when two people . . .

**Anne.** Nine o'clock. I have to go.

**Peter.** That's right.

**Anne** (*without moving*). Good night.

(*There is a second's pause, then* Peter *gets up and moves toward the door.*)

760 **Peter.** You won't let them stop you coming?

**Anne.** No. (*She rises and starts for the door.*) Sometime I might bring my diary. There are so many things in it that I want to talk over with you. There's a lot about you.

**Peter.** What kind of things?

**Anne.** I wouldn't want you to see some of it. I thought you were a nothing, just the way you thought about me.

**Peter.** Did you change your mind, the way I 770 changed my mind about you?

**Anne.** Well . . . You'll see . . .

(*For a second* Anne *stands looking up at* Peter, *longing for him to kiss her. As he makes no move he turns away. Then suddenly* Peter *grabs her awkwardly in his arms, kissing her on the cheek.* Anne *walks out dazed. She stands for a minute, her back to the people in the main room. As she regains her poise she goes to her mother and father and* Margot, *silently kissing them. They murmur their good nights to her. As she*

780 *is about to open her bedroom door, she catches sight of* Mrs. Van Daan. *She goes quickly to her, taking her face in her hands and kissing her first on one cheek and then on the other. Then she hurries off into her room.* Mrs. Van Daan *looks after her, and then looks over at* Peter's *room. Her suspicions are confirmed.*)

**Mrs. Van Daan** (*She knows.*) Ah hah!

(*The lights dim out. The curtain falls on the scene. In the darkness* Anne's Voice *comes faintly at first and then with growing strength.*)

790 **Anne's Voice.** By this time we all know each other so well that if anyone starts to tell a story, the rest can finish it for him. We're having to cut down still further on our meals. What makes it worse, the rats have been at work again. They've carried off some of our precious food. Even Mr. Dussel wishes now that Mouschi was here. Thursday, the twentieth of April, nineteen forty-four. Invasion fever is mounting every day. Miep tells us that people outside talk of nothing else. For myself,
800 life has become much more pleasant. I often go to Peter's room after supper. Oh, don't think I'm in love, because I'm not. But it does make life more bearable to have someone with whom you can exchange views. No more tonight. P.S. . . . I must be honest. I must confess that I actually live for the next meeting. Is there anything lovelier than to sit under the skylight and feel the sun on your cheeks and have a darling boy in your arms? I admit now that I'm glad the Van Daans had a son and not a
810 daughter. I've outgrown another dress. That's the third. I'm having to wear Margot's clothes after all. I'm working hard on my French and am now reading *La Belle Nivernaise.*

(*As she is saying the last lines—the curtain rises on the scene. The lights dim on, as* Anne's Voice *fades out.*)

## Scene 3

*It is night, a few weeks later. Everyone is in bed. There is complete quiet. In the* Van Daans' *room a match flares up for a moment and then is quickly put out.* Mr. Van Daan, *in bare feet, dressed in underwear*
820 *and trousers, is dimly seen coming stealthily down the stairs and into the main room, where* Mr. *and* Mrs.

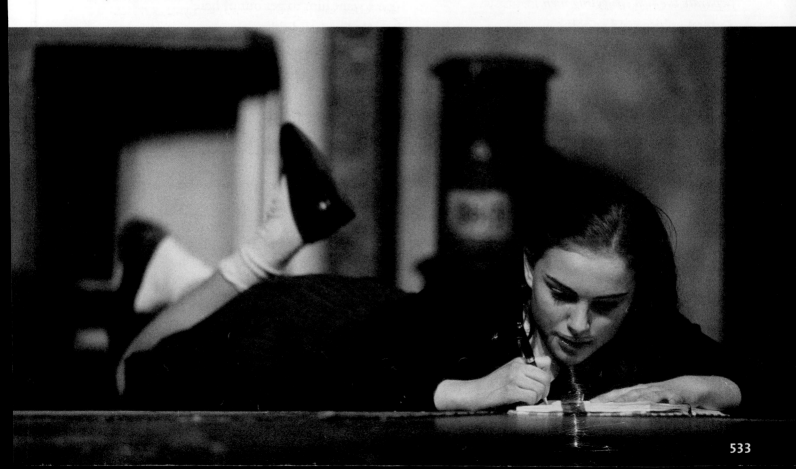

Frank *and* Margot *are sleeping. He goes to the food safe and again lights a match. Then he cautiously opens the safe, taking out a half-loaf of bread. As he closes the safe, it creaks. He stands rigid.* Mrs. Frank *sits up in bed. She sees him.*

**Mrs. Frank** (*screaming*). Otto! Otto! *Komme schnell!*[5]

(*The rest of the people wake, hurriedly getting up.*)

**Mr. Frank.** *Was ist los? Was ist passiert?*[6]

830 (Dussel, *followed by* Anne, *comes from his room.*)

**Mrs. Frank** (*as she rushes over to* Mr. Van Daan). *Er stiehlt das Essen!*[7]

**Dussel** (*grabbing* Mr. Van Daan). You! You! Give me that.

**Mrs. Van Daan** (*coming down the stairs*). Putti . . . Putti . . . what is it?

**Dussel** (*his hands on* Van Daan's *neck*). You dirty thief . . . stealing food . . . you good-for-nothing . . .

840 **Mr. Frank.** Mr. Dussel! For God's sake! Help me, Peter!

(Peter *comes over, trying, with* Mr. Frank, *to separate the two struggling men.*)

**Peter.** Let him go! Let go!

(Dussel *drops* Mr. Van Daan, *pushing him away. He shows them the end of a loaf of bread that he has taken from* Van Daan.)

**Dussel.** You greedy, selfish . . . !

(Margot *turns on the lights.*)

850 **Mrs. Van Daan.** Putti . . . what is it?

(*All of* Mrs. Frank's *gentleness, her self-control, is gone. She is outraged, in a frenzy of indignation.*)

**Mrs. Frank.** The bread! He was stealing the bread!

**Dussel.** It was you, and all the time we thought it was the rats!

**Mr. Frank.** Mr. Van Daan, how could you!

**Mr. Van Daan.** I'm hungry.

**Mrs. Frank.** We're all of us hungry! I see the children getting thinner and thinner. Your own son Peter . . . 860 I've heard him moan in his sleep, he's so hungry. And you come in the night and steal food that should go to them . . . to the children!

**Mrs. Van Daan** (*going to* Mr. Van Daan *protectively*). He needs more food than the rest of us. He's used to more. He's a big man.

(Mr. Van Daan *breaks away, going over and sitting on the couch.*)

**Mrs. Frank** (*turning on* Mrs. Van Daan). And you . . . you're worse than he is! You're a mother, 870 and yet you sacrifice your child to this man . . . this . . . this . . .

**Mr. Frank.** Edith! Edith!

(Margot *picks up the pink woolen stole, putting it over her mother's shoulders.*)

**Mrs. Frank** (*paying no attention, going on to* Mrs. Van Daan). Don't think I haven't seen you! Always saving the choicest bits for him! I've watched you day after day and I've held my tongue. But not any longer! Not after this! Now I want him to go! 880 I want him to get out of here!

**Mr. Frank.** Edith!

**Mr. Van Daan.** Get out of here? ⎫

**Mrs. Van Daan.** What do you mean? ⎭ *Together*

**Mrs. Frank.** Just that! Take your things and get out!

**Mr. Frank** (*to* Mrs. Frank). You're speaking in anger. You cannot mean what you are saying.

**Mrs. Frank.** I mean exactly that!

(Mrs. Van Daan *takes a cover from the* Franks' *bed, pulling it about her.*)

890 **Mr. Frank.** For two long years we have lived here, side by side. We have respected each other's rights . . . we have managed to live in peace. Are we now going to throw it all away? I know this will never happen again, will it, Mr. Van Daan?

---

5. *Komme schnell!* (kôm'e shnĕl') *German:* Come quickly!

6. *Was ist los? Was ist passiert?* (väs ĭst lôs'? väs ĭst päsērt'?) *German:* What's the matter? What has happened?

7. *Er stiehlt das Essen!* (ĕr shtēlt' däs ĕs'ən) *German:* He is stealing food!

**Mr. Van Daan.** No. No.

**Mrs. Frank.** He steals once! He'll steal again!

(Mr. Van Daan, *holding his stomach, starts for the bathroom. Anne puts her arms around him, helping him up the step.*)

900 **Mr. Frank.** Edith, please. Let us be calm. We'll all go to our rooms . . . and afterwards we'll sit down quietly and talk this out . . . we'll find some way . . .

**Mrs. Frank.** No! No! No more talk! I want them to leave!

**Mrs. Van Daan.** You'd put us out, on the streets?

**Mrs. Frank.** There are other hiding places.

**Mrs. Van Daan.** A cellar . . . a closet. I know. And we have no money left even to pay for that.

910 **Mrs. Frank.** I'll give you money. Out of my own pocket I'll give it gladly. (*She gets her purse from a shelf and comes back with it.*)

**Mrs. Van Daan.** Mr. Frank, you told Putti you'd never forget what he'd done for you when you came to Amsterdam. You said you could never repay him, that you . . .

**Mrs. Frank** (*counting out money*). If my husband had any obligation to you, he's paid it, over and over.

**Mr. Frank.** Edith, I've never seen you like this 920 before. I don't know you.

**Mrs. Frank.** I should have spoken out long ago.

**Dussel.** You can't be nice to some people.

**Mrs. Van Daan** (*turning on Dussel*). There would have been plenty for all of us, if *you* hadn't come in here!

**Mr. Frank.** We don't need the Nazis to destroy us. We're destroying ourselves.

(*He sits down, with his head in his hands. Mrs. Frank goes to Mrs. Van Daan.*)

930 **Mrs. Frank** (*giving Mrs. Van Daan some money*). Give this to Miep. She'll find you a place.

**Anne.** Mother, you're not putting *Peter* out. Peter hasn't done anything.

**Mrs. Frank.** He'll stay, of course. When I say I must protect the children, I mean Peter too.

(Peter *rises from the steps where he has been sitting.*)

**Peter.** I'd have to go if Father goes.

(Mr. Van Daan *comes from the bathroom. Mrs. Van Daan hurries to him and takes him to the couch.* 940 *Then she gets water from the sink to bathe his face.*)

**Mrs. Frank** (*while this is going on*). He's no father to you . . . that man! He doesn't know what it is to be a father!

**Peter** (*starting for his room*). I wouldn't feel right. I couldn't stay.

**Mrs. Frank.** Very well, then. I'm sorry.

**Anne** (*rushing over to* Peter). No, Peter! No! (Peter *goes into his room, closing the door after him. Anne turns back to her mother, crying.*) I don't care 950 about the food. They can have mine! I don't want it! Only don't send them away. It'll be daylight soon. They'll be caught . . .

**Margot** (*putting her arms comfortingly around* Anne). Please, Mother!

**Mrs. Frank.** They're not going now. They'll stay here until Miep finds them a place. (*to* Mrs. Van Daan) But one thing I insist on! He must never come down here again! He must never come to this room where the food is stored! We'll divide 960 what we have . . . an equal share for each! (Dussel *hurries over to get a sack of potatoes from the food safe. Mrs. Frank goes on, to* Mrs. Van Daan.) You can cook it here and take it up to him.

(Dussel *brings the sack of potatoes back to the center table.*)

**Margot.** Oh, no. No. We haven't sunk so far that we're going to fight over a handful of rotten potatoes.

**Dussel** (*dividing the potatoes into piles*). Mrs. Frank, 970 Mr. Frank, Margot, Anne, Peter, Mrs. Van Daan, Mr. Van Daan, myself . . . Mrs. Frank . . .

(*The buzzer sounds in* Miep's *signal.*)

**Mr. Frank.** It's Miep! (*He hurries over, getting his overcoat and putting it on.*)

**Margot.** At this hour?

**Mrs. Frank.** It is trouble.

**Mr. Frank** (*as he starts down to unbolt the door*). I beg you, don't let her see a thing like this!

**Mr. Dussel** (*counting without stopping*). . . . Anne, 980 Peter, Mrs. Van Daan, Mr. Van Daan, myself . . .

**Margot** (*to* Dussel). Stop it! Stop it!

**Dussel.** . . . Mr. Frank, Margot, Anne, Peter, Mrs. Van Daan, Mr. Van Daan, myself, Mrs. Frank . . .

**Mrs. Van Daan.** You're keeping the big ones for yourself! All the big ones . . . Look at the size of that! . . . And that! . . .

(Dussel *continues on with his dividing.* Peter, *with his shirt and trousers on, comes from his room.*)

**Margot.** Stop it! Stop it!

990 (*We hear* Miep's *excited voice speaking to* Mr. Frank *below.*)

**Miep.** Mr. Frank . . . the most wonderful news! . . . The invasion has begun!

**Mr. Frank.** Go on, tell them! Tell them!

(Miep *comes running up the steps, ahead of* Mr. Frank. *She has a man's raincoat on over her nightclothes and a bunch of orange-colored flowers in her hand.*)

**Miep.** Did you hear that, everybody? Did you hear 1000 what I said? The invasion has begun! The invasion!

(*They all stare at* Miep, *unable to grasp what she is telling them.* Peter *is the first to recover his wits.*)

**Peter.** Where?

**Mrs. Van Daan.** When? When, Miep?

**Miep.** It began early this morning . . .

(*As she talks on, the realization of what she has said begins to dawn on them. Everyone goes crazy. A wild demonstration takes place.* Mrs. Frank *hugs* Mr. Van Daan.)

1010 **Mrs. Frank.** Oh, Mr. Van Daan, did you hear that?

(Dussel *embraces* Mrs. Van Daan. Peter *grabs a frying pan and parades around the room, beating on it, singing the Dutch National Anthem.* Anne *and* Margot *follow him, singing, weaving in and out among the excited grownups.* Margot *breaks away to take the flowers from* Miep *and distribute them to everyone. While this* **pandemonium** *is going on*

Mrs. Frank *tries to make herself heard above the excitement.*)

1020 **Mrs. Frank** (*to* Miep). How do you know?

**Miep.** The radio . . . The B.B.C.! They said they landed on the coast of Normandy!

**Peter.** The British?

**Miep.** British, Americans, French, Dutch, Poles, Norwegians . . . all of them! More than four thousand ships! Churchill spoke, and General Eisenhower! D-Day they call it!

**Mr. Frank.** Thank God, it's come!

**Mrs. Van Daan.** At last!

1030 **Miep** (*starting out*). I'm going to tell Mr. Kraler. This'll be better than any blood transfusion.

**Mr. Frank** (*stopping her*). What part of Normandy did they land, did they say?

**Miep.** Normandy . . . that's all I know now . . . I'll be up the minute I hear some more! (*She goes hurriedly out.*)

**Mr. Frank** (*to* Mrs. Frank). What did I tell you? What did I tell you?

(Mrs. Frank *indicates that he has forgotten to bolt* 1040 *the door after* Miep. *He hurries down the steps.* Mr. Van Daan, *sitting on the couch, suddenly breaks into a convulsive sob. Everybody looks at him, bewildered.*)

**Mrs. Van Daan** (*hurrying to him*). Putti! Putti! What is it? What happened?

**Mr. Van Daan.** Please. I'm so ashamed.

(Mr. Frank *comes back up the steps.*)

**Dussel.** Oh, for God's sake!

**Mrs. Van Daan.** Don't, Putti.

1050 **Margot.** It doesn't matter now!

**Mr. Frank** (*going to* Mr. Van Daan). Didn't you hear what Miep said? The invasion has come! We're going to be liberated! This is a time to celebrate!

(*He embraces* Mrs. Frank *and then hurries to the cupboard and gets the cognac and a glass.*)

**Mr. Van Daan.** To steal bread from children!

**Mrs. Frank.** We've all done things that we're ashamed of.

1060 **Anne.** Look at me, the way I've treated Mother . . . so mean and horrid to her.

**Mrs. Frank.** No, Anneke, no.

(Anne *runs to her mother, putting her arms around her.*)

**Anne.** Oh, Mother, I was. I was awful.

**Mr. Van Daan.** Not like me. No one is as bad as me!

**Dussel** (*to* Mr. Van Daan). Stop it now! Let's be happy!

**Mr. Frank** (*giving* Mr. Van Daan *a glass of cognac*).
1070 Here! Here! *Schnapps! L'chaim!*[8]

(Van Daan *takes the cognac. They all watch him. He gives them a feeble smile.* Anne *puts up her fingers in a V-for-Victory sign. As* Van Daan *gives an answering V-sign, they are startled to hear a loud sob from behind them. It is* Mrs. Frank, *stricken with* **remorse.** *She is sitting on the other side of the room.*)

**Mrs. Frank** (*through her sobs*). When I think of the terrible things I said . . .

1080 (Mr. Frank, Anne, *and* Margot *hurry to her, trying to comfort her.* Mr. Van Daan *brings her his glass of cognac.*)

**Mr. Van Daan.** No! No! You were right!

**Mrs. Frank.** That I should speak that way to you! . . . Our friends! . . . Our guests! (*She starts to cry again.*)

**Dussel.** Stop it, you're spoiling the whole invasion!

(*As they are comforting her, the lights dim out. The curtain falls.*)

1090 **Anne's Voice** (*faintly at first and then with growing strength*). We're all in much better spirits these days. There's still excellent news of the invasion. The best part about it is that I have a feeling that friends are coming. Who knows? Maybe I'll be back in school by fall. Ha, ha! The joke is on us! The warehouse man doesn't know a thing and we are paying him all that money! . . . Wednesday,
the second of July, nineteen forty-four. The invasion seems temporarily to be bogged down.
1100 Mr. Kraler has to have an operation, which looks bad. The Gestapo have found the radio that was stolen. Mr. Dussel says they'll trace it back and back to the thief, and then, it's just a matter of time till they get to us. Everyone is low. Even poor Pim can't raise their spirits. I have often been downcast myself . . . but never in despair. I can shake off everything if I write. But . . . and that is the great question . . . will I ever be able to write well? I want to so much. I want to go
1110 on living even after my death. Another birthday has gone by, so now I am fifteen. Already I know what I want. I have a goal, an opinion.

(*As this is being said—the curtain rises on the scene, the lights dim on, and* Anne's Voice *fades out.*)

### Scene 4

*It is an afternoon a few weeks later . . . Everyone but* Margot *is in the main room. There is a sense of great tension.*

*Both* Mrs. Frank *and* Mr. Van Daan *are nervously pacing back and forth,* Dussel *is standing*
1120 *at the window, looking down fixedly at the street below.* Peter *is at the center table, trying to do his lessons.* Anne *sits opposite him, writing in her diary.* Mrs. Van Daan *is seated on the couch, her eyes on* Mr. Frank *as he sits reading.*

*The sound of a telephone ringing comes from the office below. They all are rigid, listening tensely.* Mr. Dussel *rushes down to* Mr. Frank.

**Dussel.** There it goes again, the telephone! Mr. Frank, do you hear?

1130 **Mr. Frank** (*quietly*). Yes. I hear.

**Dussel** (*pleading, insistent*). But this is the third time, Mr. Frank! The third time in quick succession! It's a signal! I tell you it's Miep, trying to get us! For some reason she can't come to us and she's trying to warn us of something!

---

8. *Schnapps!* (shnäps) *German:* Brandy! *L'chaim!* (lə кнä′yĭm) *Hebrew:* To life!

**Mr. Frank.** Please. Please.

**Mr. Van Daan** (*to* Dussel). You're wasting your breath.

**Dussel.** Something has happened, Mr. Frank.
1140 For three days now Miep hasn't been to see us! And today not a man has come to work. There hasn't been a sound in the building!

**Mrs. Frank.** Perhaps it's Sunday. We may have lost track of the days.

**Mr. Van Daan** (*to* Anne). You with the diary there. What day is it?

**Dussel** (*going to* Mrs. Frank). I don't lose track of the days! I know exactly what day it is! It's Friday, the fourth of August. Friday, and not a man at
1150 work. (*He rushes back to* Mr. Frank, *pleading with him, almost in tears.*) I tell you Mr. Kraler's dead. That's the only explanation. He's dead and they've closed down the building, and Miep's trying to tell us!

**Mr. Frank.** She'd never telephone us.

**Dussel** (*frantic*). Mr. Frank, answer that! I beg you, answer it!

**Mr. Frank.** No.

**Mr. Van Daan.** Just pick it up and listen. You don't
1160 have to speak. Just listen and see if it's Miep.

**Dussel** (*speaking at the same time*). For God's sake . . . I ask you.

**Mr. Frank.** No. I've told you, no. I'll do nothing that might let anyone know we're in the building.

**Peter.** Mr. Frank's right.

**Mr. Van Daan.** There's no need to tell us what side you're on.

**Mr. Frank.** If we wait patiently, quietly, I believe that help will come.

1170 (*There is silence for a minute as they all listen to the telephone ringing.*)

**Dussel.** I'm going down. (*He rushes down the steps.* Mr. Frank *tries ineffectually to hold him.* Dussel *runs to the lower door, unbolting it. The telephone stops ringing.* Dussel *bolts the door and comes slowly back*

*up the steps.*) Too late. (Mr. Frank *goes to* Margot *in* Anne's *bedroom.*)

**Mr. Van Daan.** So we just wait here until we die.

**Mrs. Van Daan** (*hysterically*). I can't stand it! I'll
1180 kill myself! I'll kill myself!

**Mr. Van Daan.** For God's sake, stop it!

(*In the distance, a German military band is heard playing a Viennese waltz.*)

**Mrs. Van Daan.** I think you'd be glad if I did! I think you want me to die!

**Mr. Van Daan.** Whose fault is it we're here? (Mrs. Van Daan *starts for her room. He follows, talking at her.*) We could've been safe somewhere . . . in America or Switzerland. But no! No! You
1190 wouldn't leave when I wanted to. You couldn't leave your things. You couldn't leave your precious furniture.

**Mrs. Van Daan.** Don't touch me!

(*She hurries up the stairs, followed by* Mr. Van Daan. Peter, *unable to bear it, goes to his room.* Anne *looks after him, deeply concerned.* Dussel *returns to his post at the window.* Mr. Frank *comes back into the main room and takes a book, trying to read.* Mrs. Frank *sits near the sink, starting to peel*
1200 *some potatoes.* Anne *quietly goes to* Peter's *room, closing the door after her.* Peter *is lying face down on the cot.* Anne *leans over him, holding him in her arms, trying to bring him out of his despair.*)

**Anne.** Look, Peter, the sky. (*She looks up through the skylight.*) What a lovely, lovely day! Aren't the clouds beautiful? You know what I do when it seems as if I couldn't stand being cooped up for one more minute? I *think* myself out. I think myself on a walk in the park where I used to go with
1210 Pim. Where the jonquils and the crocus and the violets grow down the slopes. You know the most wonderful part about *thinking* yourself out? You can have it any way you like. You can have roses and violets and chrysanthemums all blooming at the same time . . . It's funny . . . I used to take it all for granted . . . and now I've gone crazy about everything to do with nature. Haven't you?

**Peter.** I've just gone crazy. I think if something doesn't happen soon . . . if we don't get out of here . . . I can't stand much more of it!

**Anne** (*softly*). I wish you had a religion, Peter.

**Peter.** No, thanks! Not me!

**Anne.** Oh, I don't mean you have to be Orthodox[9] . . . or believe in heaven and hell and purgatory and things . . . I just mean some religion . . . it doesn't matter what. Just to believe in something! When I think of all that's out there . . . the trees . . . and flowers . . . and seagulls . . . when I think of the dearness of you, Peter . . . and the goodness of the people we know . . . Mr. Kraler, Miep, Dirk, the vegetable man, all risking their lives for us every day . . . When I think of these good things, I'm not afraid any more . . . I find myself, and God, and I . . .

(Peter *interrupts, getting up and walking away.*)

**Peter.** That's fine! But when I begin to think, I get mad! Look at us, hiding out for two years. Not able to move! Caught here like . . . waiting for them to come and get us . . . and all for what?

**Anne.** We're not the only people that've had to suffer. There've always been people that've had to . . . sometimes one race . . . sometimes another . . . and yet . . .

**Peter.** That doesn't make me feel any better!

**Anne** (*going to him*). I know it's terrible, trying to have any faith . . . when people are doing such horrible . . . But you know what I sometimes think? I think the world may be going through a phase, the way I was with Mother. It'll pass, maybe not for hundreds of years, but some day . . . I still believe, in spite of everything, that people are really good at heart.

**Peter.** I want to see something now . . . Not a thousand years from now! (*He goes over, sitting down again on the cot.*)

**Anne.** But, Peter, if you'd only look at it as part of a great pattern . . . that we're just a little minute in the life . . . (*She breaks off.*) Listen to us, going at each other like a couple of stupid grownups! Look at the sky now. Isn't it lovely? (*She holds out her hand to him.* Peter *takes it and rises, standing with her at the window looking out, his arms around her.*) Some day, when we're outside again, I'm going to . . .

(*She breaks off as she hears the sound of a car, its brakes squealing as it comes to a sudden stop. The people in the other rooms also become aware of the sound. They listen tensely. Another car roars up to a screeching stop.* Anne *and* Peter *come from* Peter's *room.* Mr. *and* Mrs. Van Daan *creep down the stairs.* Dussel *comes out from his room. Everyone is listening, hardly breathing. A doorbell clangs again and again in the building below.* Mr. Frank *starts quietly down the steps to the door.* Dussel *and* Peter *follow him. The others stand rigid, waiting, terrified.*

*In a few seconds* Dussel *comes stumbling back up the steps. He shakes off* Peter's *help and goes to his room.* Mr. Frank *bolts the door below, and comes slowly back up the steps. Their eyes are all on him as he stands there for a minute. They realize that what they feared has happened.* Mrs. Van Daan *starts to whimper.* Mr. Van Daan *puts her gently in a chair, and then hurries off up the stairs to their room to collect their things.* Peter *goes to comfort his mother. There is a sound of violent pounding on a door below.*)

**Mr. Frank** (*quietly*). For the past two years we have lived in fear. Now we can live in hope.

(*The pounding below becomes more insistent. There are muffled sounds of voices, shouting commands.*)

**Men's Voices.** *Auf machen! Da drinnen! Auf machen! Schnell! Schnell! Schnell! etc., etc.*[10]

(*The street door below is forced open. We hear the heavy tread of footsteps coming up.* Mr. Frank *gets two school bags from the shelves, and gives one to* Anne *and the other to* Margot. *He goes to get a bag for* Mrs. Frank. *The sound of feet coming up grows*

---

9. **Orthodox:** Orthodox Jews who strictly observe Jewish laws and traditions.

10. **Auf machen! . . . Schnell!** (ouf′ mäzкн′ən! dä drĭn′ən! ouf′ mäкн′ən! shnĕl! shnĕl! shnĕl!) *German:* Open up! Inside there! Open up! Quick! Quick! Quick!

*louder.* Peter *comes to* Anne, *kissing her good-bye, then he goes to his room to collect his things. The* 1300 *buzzer of their door starts to ring.* Mr. Frank *brings* Mrs. Frank *a bag. They stand together, waiting. We hear the thud of gun butts on the door, trying to break it down.*

Anne *stands, holding her school satchel, looking over at her father and mother with a soft, reassuring smile. She is no longer a child, but a woman with courage to meet whatever lies ahead.*

*The lights dim out. The curtain falls on the scene. We hear a mighty crash as the door is shattered.* 1310 *After a second* Anne's Voice *is heard.)*

**Anne's Voice.** And so it seems our stay here is over. They are waiting for us now. They've allowed us five minutes to get our things. We can each take a bag and whatever it will hold of clothing. Nothing else. So, dear Diary, that means I must leave you behind. Good-bye for a while. P.S. Please, please, Miep, or Mr. Kraler, or anyone else. If you should find this diary, will you please keep it safe for me, because some day 1320 I hope . . .

*(Her voice stops abruptly. There is silence. After a second the curtain rises.)*

## Scene 5

*It is again the afternoon in November, 1945. The rooms are as we saw them in the first scene.* Mr. Kraler *has joined* Miep *and* Mr. Frank. *There are coffee cups on the table. We see a great change in* Mr. Frank. *He is calm now. His bitterness is gone. He slowly turns a few pages of the diary. They are blank.*

**Mr. Frank.** No more. *(He closes the diary and puts it* 1330 *down on the couch beside him.)*

**Miep.** I'd gone to the country to find food. When I got back the block was surrounded by police . . .

**Mr. Kraler.** We made it our business to learn how they knew. It was the thief . . . the thief who told them.

*(Miep goes up to the gas burner, bringing back a pot of coffee.)*

**Mr. Frank** *(after a pause).* It seems strange to say this, that anyone could be happy in a 1340 concentration camp. But Anne was happy in the camp in Holland where they first took us. After two years of being shut up in these rooms, she could be out . . . out in the sunshine and the fresh air that she loved.

**Miep** *(offering the coffee to* Mr. Frank). A little more?

**Mr. Frank** *(holding out his cup to her).* The news of the war was good. The British and Americans were sweeping through France. We felt sure 1350 that they would get to us in time. In September we were told that we were to be shipped to Poland . . . The men to one camp. The women to another. I was sent to Auschwitz. They went to Belsen. In January we were freed, the few of us who were left. The war wasn't yet over, so it took us a long time to get home. We'd be sent here and there behind the lines where we'd be safe. Each time our train would stop . . . at a siding, or a crossing . . . we'd all get out and go from 1360 group to group . . . Where were you? Were you at Belsen? At Buchenwald? At Mauthausen? Is it possible that you knew my wife? Did you ever see my husband? My son? My daughter? That's how I found out about my wife's death . . . of Margot, the Van Daans . . . Dussel. But Anne . . . I still hoped . . . Yesterday I went to Rotterdam. I'd heard of a woman there . . . She'd been in Belsen with Anne . . . I know now.

*(He picks up the diary again, and turns the pages* 1370 *back to find a certain passage. As he finds it we hear* Anne's Voice.)

**Anne's Voice.** In spite of everything, I still believe that people are really good at heart.

(Mr. Frank *slowly closes the diary.)*

**Mr. Frank.** She puts me to shame. *(They are silent.)* *The Curtain Falls.*

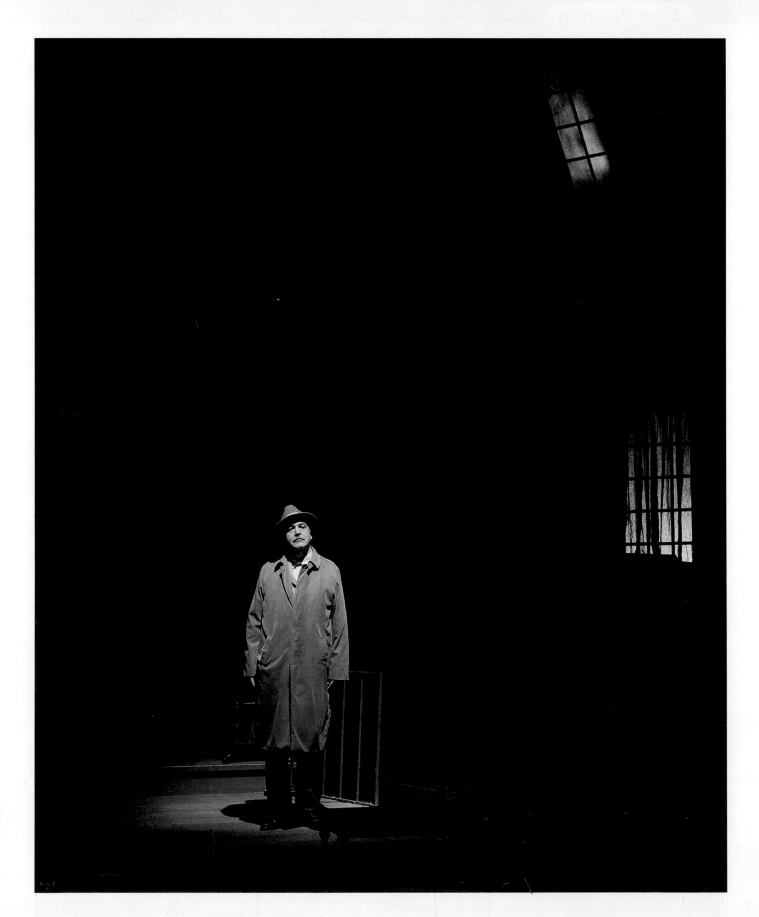

THE DIARY OF ANNE FRANK: ACT TWO

# Comprehension

1. **Recall** Who was stealing the bread in the Annex?

2. **Clarify** According to Margot, why don't Anne and her mother get along?

3. **Summarize** Why does the man from the storeroom request extra money?

# Literary Analysis

4. **Complete Your Story Map** Review your story map and make sure you're satisfied. Then circle the event you consider to be the climax of the play, and add the play's resolution. Remember the **climax** is the point of highest action, and the **resolution** is the point at which the conflict is resolved.

5. **Draw Conclusions** Mrs. Van Daan doesn't need her fur coat in the attic. Why does she react so strongly when Mr. Van Daan wants to sell it?

6. **Interpret Characters' Actions** Why do Anne and Mrs. Frank apologize to each other after hearing about the invasion of Normandy? Think about what **impact** the circumstances might have had on their attitudes.

7. **Analyze Flashback** A flashback is a scene from an earlier time that interrupts the ongoing action of a story. Most of the play takes place during the war years, but the first and last scene take place after the war. Make a timeline like the one shown that clarifies the order in which important events happen. How does reading about the events out of order affect your understanding?

*Arrive at Annex*

*July 1942*

8. **Evaluate Theme** At the end of Act Two, Anne shares with Peter her ideas about the tragic events they have been hearing about. She says, "I think the world may be going through a phase . . . . It'll pass." How do Anne's ideas illustrate the theme of the play? How does Peter react to her ideas?

# Extension and Challenge

9. **Creative Project: Drama** With a small group of classmates, choose a scene that supports the play's theme and practice acting it out. When you perform for the class, explain why you chose the scene you did.

10.  **SOCIAL STUDIES CONNECTION** Many Jews in Europe escaped their countries or went into hiding when the Nazis came to power. Research one of the following people to find out how ordinary people tried to save themselves from the Nazis: Yettie Mendels, Erika Van Hesteren, Alfred Lessing, and Joseph Heinrich. Present your findings to the class.

> **RESEARCH LINKS**
> For more on the Holocaust, visit the **Research Center** at ClassZone.com.

**INDIANA STANDARDS**

**READING STANDARD**
**8.3.5** Identify and analyze recurring themes . . . .

# Reading-Writing Connection

Increase your understanding of *The Diary of Anne Frank* by responding to these prompts. Then complete the **Grammar and Writing** exercise.

| WRITING PROMPTS | SELF-CHECK |
|---|---|
| **A. Short Response: Describe a Relationship**<br>Anne's relationship with Peter is an important subplot in the play. Write a **one-paragraph description** that summarizes her changing feelings toward Peter. Consider how having a peer to talk to helped Anne cope with conflict both inside and outside the Annex. | *An effective description will...*<br>• describe Anne's feelings toward Peter at different points in the play<br>• support statements with quotations from the characters |
| **B. Extended Response: Evaluate a Legacy**<br>Why do you think Anne Frank's diary has made an **impact** on countless readers around the world? Write **two or three paragraphs** explaining why readers might identify with Anne and draw inspiration from her life. | *An insightful evaluation will...*<br>• describe Anne's personality<br>• convey your ideas about why Anne's outlook on life is inspiring and unique |

## GRAMMAR AND WRITING

***CAPITALIZE CORRECTLY*** Languages, nationalities, ethnicities, political parties, and religions should always be capitalized. Here are some examples:

**INDIANA STANDARDS**

**WRITING STANDARD**
**8.6.6** Use correct capitalization.

**Languages**—English, Spanish, Russian, Chinese

**Countries and Nationalities**—Mexico, Canada, Irish, South African

**Ethnicities**—Hispanic, Native American, Caucasian, Asian

**Political Parties**—Democrats, Republicans, Socialists, Nazis

**Religions**—Judaism, Islam, Christianity, Buddhism

> *Example:* Although the Franks lived in Holland, their first language was German.

***PRACTICE*** Rewrite the following sentences, correcting any errors in capitalization. A sentence may contain more than one error.

1. Not all germans wanted the nazis to be in control.
2. For many europeans, it was dangerous to practice judaism.
3. Because they were jewish, the Franks fled to holland to escape persecution.
4. Anne Frank's diary was translated into many languages, including english.

*For more help with capitalization, see page R51 in the **Grammar Handbook.***

# Beyond *The Diary of Anne Frank*

- Newspaper Article, page 545
- Interview, page 547

Use with *The Diary of Anne Frank*, page 486.

**INDIANA STANDARDS**

**READING STANDARDS**
**8.2.3** Find similarities and differences between texts in the treatment, amount of coverage, or organization of ideas.

**8.2.9** Make reasonable statements and draw conclusions about a text, supporting them with accurate examples.

## What's the Connection?

In *The Diary of Anne Frank,* you learned what life in hiding was like for Anne and her family. Now you will read accounts from two Holocaust survivors that will tell you more about Anne, Nazi-occupied Amsterdam, and the concentration camp where the Franks were sent.

## Skill Focus: Synthesize

Reading a play, diary, or book about a topic can teach you a great deal. However, you can seldom get a complete picture from any one source. To fully understand something, you have to **synthesize,** or connect facts, details, and ideas from different sources in order to form new ideas about the topic.

In this lesson, you will synthesize what you have already learned from *The Diary of Anne Frank* and one of Anne's diary entries (page 520) with information and impressions from two more sources. Your goal is to develop a fuller picture of what life was like for Jewish families in Nazi-occupied Amsterdam and in the Bergen-Belsen concentration camp.

To begin, use a chart like the one shown to record what you've learned from the play and from Anne's diary entry. Then read the next selections to add to your knowledge and fill in gaps in your understanding. Continue filling in the chart with what you learn about life under the Nazis.

|  | Life for a Jewish family hiding in Amsterdam | Life for a Jewish family living openly in Amsterdam | Life in a German concentration camp | Impressions of Anne Frank |
|---|---|---|---|---|
| *The Diary of Anne Frank* & Anne's December 1943 diary entry |  |  |  |  |
| "A Diary from Another World" |  |  |  |  |
| from *The Last Seven Months of Anne Frank* |  |  |  |  |

# A Diary from Another World

## Gerda Weissmann Klein

"On Friday, June 12, I woke up at 6 A.M. and—small wonder—it was my birthday. I received a warm welcome from my cat and masses of things from Mummy and Daddy . . ."

Any 13-year-old girl could have written that on her birthday. As it happens these words appear in a diary which was one of the "masses of things" and in which Anne Frank wrote: "I hope I shall be able to confide in you completely, as I have never been able to do in anyone before . . ."

She thought that what she would write in her diary would be for her eyes alone, so she committed her innermost thoughts to it. She thought that perhaps in the very distant future—when she might have children, or even grandchildren, that they might on a rainy afternoon find their grandmother's old diary. . . .

Alas, Anne Frank died as a young girl, for no other reason than that she was Jewish. The Nazis invaded Holland, as they did most other European countries, and anyone who loved freedom and equality and was free of prejudice became an enemy of the Nazi regime. . . .

I visited Anne Frank's house the other day. Actually, I visited it twice—once alone at night when it was tightly closed, the inside shrouded in darkness. It conveyed then the eerie feeling of a tomb in which Anne's unfulfilled dreams had been dreamed during many lonely nights. . . .

Then I returned during the daytime, as the sun shone brightly and the carillon[1] from the nearby clock tower, of which Anne had written, was just playing a merry tune. In the bright sunlight, I heard music playing, saw boats moving on the canal and observed people walking by.

Across the canal I noticed a boutique, saw some young people looking at sweaters. Two kids in jeans rode on bicycles. Life was going on, even as it must have gone on while she lived there. **A**

---

1. **carillon** (kăr′ə-lŏn′): set of tuned bells in a tower.

Front of Anne Frank House, Amsterdam, the Netherlands

**A SYNTHESIZE**
What are Gerda Weissmann Klein's impressions of Anne Frank's house and neighborhood?

Actually, I found it sadder during the daytime, for the night at least seemed to shut out the rest of the world, whereas during the day everything revolved around the silent, subdued girl who so desperately wanted to be a part of that stream of life.

60 What did she think about in those tiny rooms where shutters had to be closed in the daytime? She tells us that often the heat became oppressive from the tiny stove on which the families cooked their meals. We know that the toilet could not be flushed in the daytime, lest the neighbors would be alerted to the existence of the hiding place.

70 What did Anne Frank think about as she sat on her bed during those perilous days looking at the pictures of American movie stars and a picture of a chimpanzee's birthday party which still hangs there today?

Her diary tells us that she thought not of fame, nor wealth, nor greatness. She thought rather how much she would want to run downstairs into the tiny 80 garden where sunflowers now bloom against the fence, instead of having to glimpse them from far above.

She thought of touching them and running through a meadow in the spring, of buying an ice cream cone from a vendor on a hot summer afternoon.

She thought of ordinary things, such as going to school with other kids. She thought of dressing up and being 90 able to go to the movies.

In short, she thought of all the things which millions of kids do every day and find boring. But to Anne, who occasionally dared to climb to the roof to see the sky and the patch of world below, that world was as remote as the evening star. **B**

This is the legacy she left us, the understanding of things all of us take 100 for granted. Through understanding, let us assure that all people everywhere can live in freedom so that a book like *The Diary of Anne Frank* will never be written again as a true story.

**B** SYNTHESIZE
Reread lines 76–97. What new insights about Anne's thoughts do you get from this article?

Anne Frank's diary

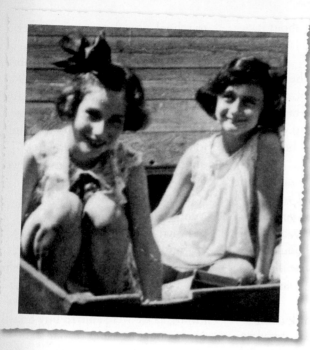

Hannah Elisabeth
Pick-Goslar and
Anne Frank

*from*

# The Last Seven Months of Anne Frank

## Interview with Hannah Elisabeth Pick-Goslar

*Willy Lindwer*

**M**r. Frank's factory, Opekta, produced a substance for making jam. My mother always got the old packages as a gift. Soon after school let out, my mother sent me to the Franks' house to get the scale because she wanted to make jam. It was a beautiful day.

I went as usual to the Franks'
10 house and rang and rang and rang, but no one opened the door. I didn't know why no one answered. I rang again, and finally, Mr. Goudsmit, a tenant, opened the door. **C**

"What do you want? What have you come for?" he asked in astonishment.

"I've come to borrow the scale."

"Don't you know that the entire Frank family has gone to
20 Switzerland?"

**F OCUS ON FORM**
An **interview** is a meeting in which one person asks another about his or her thoughts, feelings, insights, or experiences. In this interview, which was conducted for a television documentary about Anne Frank, the questions asked by Willy Lindwer have been omited. Only Pick-Goslar's answers are printed.

**C** **INTERVIEW**
On the basis of the photograph and what you've read so far, what do you think might be the relationship between Hannah and Anne?

I didn't know anything about it. "Why?" I asked.

He didn't know either.

This was a bolt out of the blue. Why had they gone to Switzerland? The only connection the Frank family had with Switzerland was that Otto Frank's mother lived there.

But later it appeared that, in fact, 30 the family had always reckoned that it would get worse for Jews. They had been preparing for a whole year to go into hiding. We didn't know anything about this. You can't talk about something like that. Because if anyone talked, then the whole affair would go amiss. . . .

I believe that Anne was the first girlfriend that I lost. It was, of course, 40 very frightening, but we began to get used to the idea. When I went back to school after the summer, fewer children came to class every day.

We stayed in Amsterdam almost a full year longer, until June 20, 1943, and all this time things were getting worse and worse. Jews had to wear a yellow star. We had an *Ausweis* (an identification card), with a large "J" 50 on it—for Jew. People were stopped on the street: "May I see your *Ausweis?*" If you were Jewish, you were taken away and you never returned home. And a mother waiting for her child would ask herself: Where is my child? Have they taken her away? . . . **D**

So far, my family had been lucky insofar as we were able to buy South 60 American citizenship through an uncle in Switzerland. We were expatriates. That's why it was

**D** SYNTHESIZE
After the Franks went into hiding, what happened to other Jews in Amsterdam?

A Dutch Jewish star with the word *Jood* (Jew) on it

A household identification card (*Ausweis*) that identified families as Jewish possible. We got passports from Paraguay. Laughing, my father said, "You'd better know something about Paraguay in case they ask." So I learned the name of the capital, Asunción. I didn't know anything else, but no one ever asked me 70 anything.

Because of these passports we could still go out for a while longer without trembling in fear, but you never knew what would happen tomorrow. . . .

So we continued to live, with little to eat and with a great deal of fear, but at least we were at home. In October, my mother died during 80 childbirth. The baby was born dead. That was in Anne's diary. Someone told Anne that our baby had died, but not that my mother had died too. They probably didn't have the heart to tell her. . . . **E**

Everything went along fine until June 20, 1943, when there was the big roundup in Amsterdam-South. On that day, the Germans started

90 something new. At five o'clock in the morning while everyone was asleep they blocked off all the southern part of Amsterdam. They went from door to door, rang, and asked:

"Do Jews live here?"

"Yes."

"You have fifteen minutes; take a backpack, put a few things in it, and get outside quickly."

100 That was our neighborhood, so we had to pack too. A passport no longer helped. We had a quarter of an hour, and we had to go with them. . . .

So we were taken to Westerbork. My father ended up in a very large barracks. My sister and I were put in an orphanage, where, they said, there was more to eat. My father had 110 known the director of the orphanage when he was in Germany. My little sister wasn't there very long. She became seriously ill and had to have operations on both ears. She was in the hospital for almost the entire time that we were in Westerbork. . . .

**E SYNTHESIZE**
Reread lines 58–85. What strategies did Jews living openly use to survive? What hardships did they endure?

```
5                    3 September              4 ' Blatt
    JUDENTRANSPORT AUS DEN NIEDERLANDEN - LAGER WESTERBORK
                        Haeftlinge

301. ✓Engers          Isidor — ✓30.4. 93 — Kaufmann
302 ✓ Engers          Leonard   15.6. 20 — Lamdarbeiter
303 ✓ Franco          Manfred - ✓1.5.  05 — Verleger
304.  Frank           Arthur    22.8. 81   Kaufmann
305.  Frank ✗         Isaac    ✓29.11.87   Installateur
306.  Frank           Margot .  16.2. 26   ohne
307.  Frank      ✓    Otto    ✓12.5. 89   Kaufmann
308.✓ Frank-Hollaender Edith    16.1. 00   ohne
309.  Frank           Anneliese 12.6. 29   ohne
310.  v.Franck        Sara —    27.4. 02 — Typistin
311.  Franken         Rozanna   16.5. 96 — Landarbeiter
312.✓ Franken-Weyand  Johanna   24.12.96 ✓ Landbauer
313.  Franken         Hermann — ✓12.5.34   ohne
314.  Franken         Louis     10.8. 17 — Gaertner
315.  Franken R       Rosalina  29.3. 27   Landbau
316.  Frankfort       Alex      14.11.19 — Dr.i.d.Oekonomie
```

The Franks' names on a transport list from the Westerbork transit camp

**F** SYNTHESIZE

Reread lines 148–162. What is the relationship between this incident and the **theme** of the play?

On February 15, 1944, we were transported to Bergen-Belsen. . . . When we arrived, our clothes weren't
120 taken away and families weren't separated. My father and my sister stayed with me. We slept in different places, but we could see each other every evening. The trip took—I don't remember precisely—two or three days to get to Bergen-Belsen. . . .

In Bergen-Belsen, it was very cold in the winter. We soon found that out. Because we had been arrested in
130 June we hadn't thought about winter clothes. Especially me, a young girl, who had to do her own packing. But what I had brought, I kept.

My sister had a large bandage on her head because she had had surgery on her ears in Westerbork. The first day we arrived in Bergen-Belsen, I got jaundice. The policy of the Germans was: whoever got sick
140 had to go to the hospital; otherwise, all the others could be infected. I didn't know what to do with my little sister. My father was confined in another barracks and I couldn't take her to him. He also had to work, so that wouldn't have worked out.

So there I was and didn't know what to do. This situation showed me
150 that there were very special people in that camp. I told an old lady that I was at my wits' end: "Tomorrow morning, I have to go to the hospital and my little sister is sick."

Two hours later, a woman came, who said, "My name is Abrahams. Mrs. Lange told me that you were here and that you don't know what to do with your sister. I have seven
160 children; give her to me; then we'll just have one more little child with us." **F**

And that's how it worked out. The next morning her daughter, who seemed to be about my age, came and took the little girl with her. Meanwhile, my father was able to visit me. We were together with that family until the end. To this day we
170 have stayed on friendly terms with them. . . .

One day, we looked in the direction where there hadn't been any barracks and saw that tents had suddenly appeared there. . . . Then a barbed-wire fence was built through the middle of the camp and filled with straw so that we couldn't see the other side. But we were, of course,
180 very close to each other, because the camp wasn't large. All those people from the tents were taken to the barracks on the other side. In spite of the German guards on the high watchtowers, we tried to make contact. . . .

One of my acquaintances, an older woman, came up to me one day. "Do you know, there are some Dutch
190 people there. I spoke to Mrs. Van Daan." The woman had known her from before, and she told me that Anne was there. She knew that I knew Anne.

"Go over to the barbed-wire fence and try to talk to her." And, of course, I did. In the evening, I stood by the barbed-wire fence and began to call out. And quite by chance Mrs.
200 Van Daan was there again. I asked her, "Could you call Anne?"

She said, "Yes, yes, wait a minute, I'll go to get Anne. I can't get Margot; she is very, very ill and is in bed."

THIS IS THE SITE OF
THE INFAMOUS BELSEN CONCENTRATION CAMP
*Liberated by the British on 15 April 1945.*

10,000 UNBURIED DEAD WERE FOUND HERE,
ANOTHER 13,000 HAVE SINCE DIED,
ALL OF THEM VICTIMS OF THE
GERMAN NEW ORDER IN EUROPE,
AND AN EXAMPLE OF NAZI KULTUR.

A sign posted by the British army outside the Bergen-Belsen concentration camp

But naturally I was much more interested in Anne, and I waited there a few minutes in the dark.

Anne came to the barbed-wire fence—I couldn't see her. The fence 210 and the straw were between us. There wasn't much light. Maybe I saw her shadow. It wasn't the same Anne. She was a broken girl. I probably was, too, but it was so terrible. She immediately began to cry, and she told me, "I don't have any parents anymore."

I remember that with absolute certainty. That was terribly sad,

220 because she couldn't have known anything else. She thought that her father had been gassed right away. But Mr. Frank looked very young and healthy, and of course the Germans didn't know how old everybody was who they wanted to gas, but selected them on the basis of their appearance. Someone who looked healthy had to work, but 230 another who might even be younger, but who was sick or looked bad, went directly to the gas chamber. **G**

I always think, if Anne had known that her father was still alive, she

**G** **SYNTHESIZE**
What happened to Jewish people in the concentration camps who looked healthy? What happened to those who were sick or looked ill?

might have had more strength to survive, because she died very shortly before the end—only a few days before [liberation]. But maybe it was all predestined.

240 So we stood there, two young girls, and we cried. I told her about my mother. She hadn't known that; she only knew that the baby had died. And I told her about my little sister. I told her that my father was in the hospital. He died two weeks later; he was already very sick. She told me that Margot was seriously ill and she told me about going into hiding
250 because I was, of course, extremely curious.

"But what are you doing here? You were supposed to be in Switzerland, weren't you?" And then she told me what had happened. That they didn't go to Switzerland at all and why they had said that; so that everyone should think that they had gone to her grandmother's.

260 Then she said, "We don't have anything at all to eat here, almost nothing, and we are cold; we don't have any clothes and I've gotten very thin and they shaved my hair." That was terrible for her. She had always been very proud of her hair. It may have grown back a bit in the meantime, but it certainly wasn't the long hair she'd had before, which she playfully curled
270 around her fingers. It was much worse for them than for us. I said, "They didn't take away our clothes." That was our first meeting. **H**

Then for the first time—we had already been in the camp for more than a year; we arrived in February 1944, and this was February 1945—we received a very small Red Cross

package: my sister, my father, and I.
280 A very small package, the size of a book, with *knäckebrot* (Scandinavian crackers), and a few cookies. You can't imagine how little that was. My son always says, "But Mama, that was something really very special." But in those days we really collected everything, half a cookie, a sock, a glove—anything that gave a little warmth or something to eat. My
290 friends also gave me something for Anne. I certainly couldn't have thrown a large package over the barbed-wire fence; not that I had one, but that wouldn't have been possible at all.

We agreed to try to meet the next evening at eight o'clock—I believe I still had a watch. And, in fact, I succeeded in throwing the package
300 over.

But I heard her screaming, and I called out, "What happened?"

And Anne answered, "Oh, the woman standing next to me caught it, and she won't give it back to me."

Then she began to scream.

I calmed her down a bit and said, "I'll try again but I don't know if I'll be able to." We arranged to meet
310 again, two or three days later, and I was actually able to throw over another package. She caught it; that was the main thing.

After these three or four meetings at the barbed-wire fence in Bergen-Belsen, I didn't see her again, because the people in Anne's camp were transferred to another section in Bergen-Belsen. That happened
320 around the end of February. **I**

That was the last time I saw Anne alive and spoke to her.

**H** SYNTHESIZE
What do you learn about Anne's circumstances from this first meeting?

**I** SYNTHESIZE
By the end of this account, what have you learned about life in Bergen-Belsen?

## Comprehension

1. **Recall** For what occasion does Anne Frank receive her diary?

2. **Summarize** Briefly describe Hannah Elisabeth Pick-Goslar's experiences in Bergen-Belsen before she reconnects with Anne.

## Critical Analysis

3. **Evaluate a Source** Gerda Weissmann Klein, the author of "A Diary from Another World," is Jewish. When she was 15, Nazis invaded her home country, Poland. She was forced to work as a slave laborer in German factories. Her entire family was killed in the Holocaust. What effect does Klein's background have on the way you view the information in the article?

4. **Analyze an Interview** Pick-Goslar has a unique view of Anne. Explain why that is. What new information about Anne and her family do you learn from Pick-Goslar's account?

5. **Synthesize** What were the physical and emotional effects of living in a Nazi-occupied country as a Jew? What survival techniques allowed people to withstand the hardships they did? Refer to the chart you filled in as you read, and support your answer with evidence from at least three selections.

**INDIANA STANDARDS**

**READING STANDARDS**
**8.2.3** Find similarities and differences between texts in the treatment, amount of coverage, or organization of ideas.

**8.2.9** Make reasonable statements and draw conclusions about a text, supporting them with accurate examples.

## Read for Information: Make a Generalization

**WRITING PROMPT**

Identify an important life lesson you take away from these Jewish families' experiences. Support your response with evidence from the selections.

To respond to this prompt, you will have to make a generalization. A **generalization** is a broad statement about a topic that follows logically from solid evidence. To arrive at your generalization, follow these steps:

1. Review the information you gathered in your chart, jotting down any general statements about life or human nature that this information suggests to you.

2. Pick the most convincing statement you have jotted down and rephrase it as a life lesson. To do this, begin with a phrase such as "It is human nature to . . ."

3. Review the evidence for your generalization to make sure it comes from more than one source and supports your statement.

4. In a paragraph, state the life lesson you've identified. Then present evidence for this generalization.

Broad Statements
1.
2.

Life Lesson

Evidence

*from* **Anne Frank Remembered**

Film Clips on  *MediaSmart* DVD

# Can films make HISTORY *fresh?*

**INDIANA STANDARDS**

**LISTENING/SPEAKING STANDARD**
**8.7.9** Interpret and evaluate the various ways in which visual image makers (such as graphic artists, illustrators, and news photographers) communicate information and affect impressions and opinions.

*KEY IDEA* Have you ever wanted to meet a famous figure from **history?** We can learn the facts about a famous person's life, but we can't know what it would be like to sit down and talk to him or her. In this lesson, you'll watch a biographical documentary about Anne Frank. You'll explore how the filmmakers try to bring you into Anne's world and give you a sense of what she was really like.

## Background

**Behind the Symbol** Anne Frank's diary has sold over 31 million copies in approximately 67 languages. She has become an enduring symbol of the tragedy of the Holocaust. But behind that symbol was a real girl, a teenager trapped for two years in a small hiding place with seven other people.

*Anne Frank Remembered* is a documentary that explores the life and death of the girl behind the symbol. The film takes viewers inside the Franks' hidden annex, revealing what it was like to live in such cramped quarters. It also tells the story of Anne's diary, and how her private thoughts became the book that has touched readers throughout the world.

# Media Literacy: Documentary

A **documentary** is a nonfiction film that often presents social, political, or historical subject matter. Famous historical figures make good subjects for documentaries, because the filmmakers can tell the story of both the individual and the time period. To create a documentary, filmmakers often gather **primary sources,** firsthand information such as diaries, photographs, and eyewitness accounts. They then combine these materials with **voice-over narration** and, often, a **re-enactment** of scenes or settings to re-create the times for viewers.

## FEATURES OF A DOCUMENTARY

**Footage** is recorded material that gives information about a subject. It includes film clips, photographs, news reports, and interviews. Footage from a particular time period can show viewers what life was like back then.

**Voice-over narration** is the voice of an unseen speaker that is heard in a documentary. The voice-over tells the subject's story and explains the footage. **Primary sources,** such as diary entries, can also be read as part of the voice-over narration.

**Re-enactment** is the re-creation of key events or important settings. Filmmakers shoot scenes or settings using sets, props, actors, and costumes. They try to re-create the subject's story as realistically as possible.

### STRATEGIES FOR VIEWING

- Identify the different types of **footage.** Notice how the filmmakers combine primary source footage with footage they shoot themselves, such as interviews and re-enactments, to tell the whole story.
- Think about the purpose of the **voice-over narration.** Different narrators can present different sides of someone's personality.
- Notice the type of information you learn from any **re-enactments.** Re-enactments are often used in historical documentaries. Think about why the filmmakers might have chosen to present the information in this way.

### MediaSmart DVD

- **Film:** *Anne Frank Remembered*
- **Director:** Jon Blair
- **Voice-over Narrators:** Kenneth Branagh and Glenn Close
- **Genre:** Documentary
- **Running Time:** 4 minutes

## *Viewing Guide for*
# Anne Frank Remembered

You'll view three clips from *Anne Frank Remembered*. They reveal the Franks' secret annex in Amsterdam, the story of the publication of the diary, and the only known moving footage of Anne Frank. As you view the clips, think about how the documentary features add a freshness to her story. You'll hear two different **voice-over narrators.** Notice the different types of information you learn from each. Watch for different types of **footage** and any **re-enactment** of setting the film provides. Before answering these questions, you may want to view the clip more than once.

### NOW VIEW

#### *FIRST VIEWING:* Comprehension

1. **Recall** After Otto Frank had such trouble getting Anne's diary published, what finally caused a publisher to step forward?

2. **Clarify** Give two examples of **primary source** material used in the clips you viewed.

#### *CLOSE VIEWING:* Media Literacy

3. **Examine the Visuals** Think about the **re-enactment** of the setting of the secret annex. Why do you think the filmmakers show the food and furniture fading away to leave empty rooms?

4. **Analyze Voice-over Narration** Think about the different types of information the two **voice-over narrators** provide. Why might the filmmakers have decided to use two narrators rather than one?

5. **Determine Filmmakers' Purpose** The clip of Anne Frank standing at the window is from the end of the documentary. What effect do you think the filmmakers intended this clip to have on viewers?

## Write or Discuss

**Compare the Texts** Think about the impression you had of Anne Frank from the play you read. Now think about the documentary clips you viewed. Write a brief comparison of the Anne you read about in the play and the Anne described in the film. Which is most effective at going beyond the symbol and revealing what you believe to be the real Anne Frank? Think about the following:

- the documentary footage of the actual secret annex where the Franks hid
- how the play portrays Anne's personality
- the footage of Anne at the window, and the voice-over reading of her diary

## Produce Your Own Media

**Create a Visual Timeline** When filmmakers plan a biographical documentary, they look closely at their subject's entire life story. They decide what events to include in the documentary and what to leave out. Imagine you're planning a documentary about a friend's life. Choose five or six events in that person's life, and create a visual timeline depicting these events. Your timeline should include a photograph or drawing and a caption for each event.

*HERE'S HOW* Here are a few suggestions for preparing your visual timeline:

- Start by choosing the events you want to show. Choose the most exciting and interesting things that have happened to your friend.
- Collect or take photographs to illustrate each event. You might want to have your friend **re-enact** a favorite event, such as a time he or she won a contest.
- Write a brief sentence for each picture that describes the event depicted.
- Arrange your pictures on a board in chronological order.

**MEDIA TOOLS**

For help with creating a timeline, visit the **Media Center** at **ClassZone.com.**

**STUDENT MODEL**

Age 1 — Joel celebrates his first birthday.

Age 6 — At age six, a new friend enters Joel's life. He names the puppy Buster.

Age 10 — After a rough start, Joel finds his way at Frontier Middle School.

Age 11 — He takes second at the spelling bee, after missing the "h" in "gherkin."

Age 13 — Joel's competitive nature shows through, both on the mantel . . .

Age 13 — . . . and on the basketball court.

**Tech Tip**

If available, use a computer software program to present your timeline.

## Writing Workshop

# Short Story

What did you like best about the stories you read this year—the characters, the suspense, or maybe the satisfying endings? In this workshop, you will weave your own tale of adventure, mystery, triumph, or woe. Follow the **Writer's Road Map** to learn how.

### WRITER'S ROAD MAP

*Short Story*

#### WRITING PROMPT 1

**Writing from Your Imagination** Write a short story that has an interesting plot. Make sure that your story includes a conflict and at least two characters.

**Plots to Consider:**

- Two people adopt an unusual dog.
- An alien lands on the school football field.
- A family gets locked in at the local natural history museum.

#### WRITING PROMPT 2

**Writing from Literature** Choose a "big question" from this unit that really made you think. Then write a short story inspired by that question. Create a plot, conflict, setting, and at least two characters to hold your reader's attention.

**Questions to Make You Think:**

- What makes something priceless? ("Gil's Furniture Bought and Sold")
- Is curiosity a gift or a curse? ("Pandora's Box")
- What impact will you have on the world? (*The Diary of Anne Frank*)

 **WRITING TOOLS**
Go to the **Writing Center** at **Classzone.com** for interactive models, publishing ideas, and other support for this workshop.

#### KEY TRAITS

**1. IDEAS**

- Has an intriguing **plot** and at least two **characters**
- Develops and resolves a **central conflict**
- Includes **descriptive details** that reveal the setting and characters
- Uses **dialogue** to show characters' personalities

**2. ORGANIZATION**

- **Introduces** the characters, setting, or action in a way that gets the reader's attention
- Follows a clear **sequence of events**
- Resolves the conflict in a convincing **conclusion**

**3. VOICE**

- Shows the writer's unique **style**

**4. WORD CHOICE**

- Includes **sensory language** to help readers imagine the fictional world

**5. SENTENCE FLUENCY**

- Varies **sentence lengths**

**6. CONVENTIONS**

- Uses **correct grammar, spelling, and punctuation**

# Part 1: Analyze a Student Model

**WRITING STANDARD**
**8.5.1** Write biographies, autobiographies, and short stories....

**James Pickford**
**Eldridge Middle School**

### Flight Patterns

Working with Joe on the science project hadn't been Samuel's idea. Joe was a good kid, but he was the school soccer star, not the school science star. Samuel loved science but didn't think he was any good at sports. So when Ms. Krunkner shouted, "Joe and Samuel, you're up!"
5  Samuel wondered for the twentieth time why she had ever put them on the same team.

Samuel, who hated standing in front of the class, shuffled to the front of the room as Joe walked confidently to the starting line that Ms. Krunkner had taped on the floor. Joe was holding the paper
10  airplane that Samuel had designed.

"Joe, are you launching it?" Ms. Krunkner asked.

"Yeah. Is that okay, Samuel?" Joe asked.

After Samuel nodded a timid yes, Ms. Krunkner gave Samuel the tape measure so he could measure how far the plane flew.
15  "You have three tries, but all of them will count toward your average," Ms. Krunkner said.

Joe cranked his arm back and threw the plane fast—it looped straight up, back toward Joe, and then forward only a few feet before it hit the ground. Samuel measured the distance. It was barely five feet.
20  The class started laughing. Samuel brought the plane back to Joe, who looked embarrassed.

"Throw it as level to the ground as you can," Samuel said.

"That's what I'm trying to do," Joe said.

Joe threw it again, and again it did a dramatic loop and crashed six
25  feet away. Samuel picked it up and smoothed the nose, which had gotten a little crunched, and made sure the wings were evenly folded.

**KEY TRAITS IN ACTION**

**Introduces** three **characters** and a **central conflict** (Samuel is nervous about working with Joe).

**Develops** an interesting **plot** with a clear **sequence of events.**

"Samuel, you do it this time," Joe said.

"What?" Samuel said, panicking.

"You throw it!" Joe whispered, refusing to take the plane out of
30 Samuel's hands.

"Come on, boys," Ms. Krunkner said.

Samuel's heart was racing as he stepped up to the line. As he raised
the plane up above his shoulder, he paused for an instant to imagine
it flying smoothly in a straight line. Then he pulled his arm back and
35 launched the plane gently forward. It sailed smoothly to the opposite
wall. When Samuel heard his classmates cheering, he let out the breath
that he realized he'd been holding.

"Very nice, Samuel," Ms. Krunkner said. As the boys returned to
their places, some kids high-fived them.
40 Samuel was in a great mood for the rest of the day. He felt as if
people were looking at him with admiration.

At the end of the day, as Samuel walked by the soccer field, Joe
called out, "Hey Samuel! Come and play Frisbee with us." Samuel
started to say he wasn't good at sports, but Joe just smiled.
45 A second later, someone threw the Frisbee right at Samuel. Samuel
put his hands up and caught it. He looked at the Frisbee and realized
that making it fly would be all about getting it to spin and stay level. He
held it flat and flicked his wrist to throw the Frisbee back. It soared over
the grass and straight into waiting hands. He didn't even have to think
50 about it; it just felt right. It was a good day for new flight patterns.

**Descriptive details** (highlighted) and lots of **dialogue** are important parts of this writer's **style.**

Highlighted **sensory language** helps the reader understand Samuel's emotions. Varied **sentence lengths** add interest and sophistication.

Satisfying, thoughtful **conclusion** shows how Samuel is changing.

2

# Part 2: Apply the Writing Process

**WRITING STANDARD**
**8.4.1** Discuss ideas for writing . . . and use graphic organizers to plan writing.

## PREWRITING

| What Should I Do? | What Does It Look Like? |
|---|---|

**1. Find an idea.**
Start with a list. Jot down any story elements that come to mind, such as characters (two brothers?), settings (a dark cave?), and conflicts (a longstanding feud?). Put a star next to one or more that interest you.

**TIP** You can also get started by asking "what if" questions. See page 564 for some examples.

▶

| Characters | Settings | Conflicts |
|---|---|---|
| Jill and her dad | Griffin Park | different personalities* |
| Samuel and Joe* | the cafeteria | the MVP award |
| Billy and his team | Avon Beach | conscience and peer pressure |
| my sister and me | science class* | |

**2. Create a story map.**
A successful story has characters, setting, and a **plot**—a sequence of events that leads to a climax. To make sure that your idea is truly a story rather than just a description, make a story map, an outline, or a flow chart.

**See page 24:** Plot and Conflict

▶

**Characters:** Samuel and Joe    **Setting:** science class

**Conflict:** different personalities; also Samuel's insecurity

↓

**Event 1:** Ms. Krunkner calls on Joe and Samuel to demonstrate their project.

**Event 2:** Joe messes up twice.

**Event 3:** Samuel succeeds.

**Event 4:** Joe invites Samuel to play Frisbee, and Samuel succeeds again.

↓

**Solution or Ending:** Samuel has new confidence.

**3. Add interest to your characters.**
Jot down some details about your characters, such as what they say, how they look, and how they act.

▶

| Samuel | Joe |
|---|---|
| • shy, good student, quiet | • confident and strong |
| • hates being in front of the class | • soccer star |
| • smart, likes science | • nice guy, no attitude |

| What Should I Do? | What Does It Look Like? |
|---|---|

**1. Grab your reader's attention.**
Write an opening that says, "Read me!" Try starting with a surprising statement, a bit of dialogue, sensory language, or a conflict.

> **A surprising statement**
> *"Get me out of here!" Samuel thought.*
>
> **Sensory details**
> *Samuel's cheeks and the tips of his ears burned with embarrassment.*
>
> **A conflict**
> *Working with Joe on the science project hadn't been Samuel's idea.*

**2. Choose your point of view.**
Some stories are told from the third-person point of view by someone outside the story. The third-person point of view uses pronouns such as *he, she,* and *they.* Other stories are told in the first-person point of view. The narrator is a character in these stories and uses the pronoun *I.*

> **Third-person point of view**
> *Samuel nodded a timid yes.*
>
> **First-person point of view**
> *I nodded a timid yes.*

**3. Bring your characters to life.**
Realistic dialogue and precise descriptive details can give your reader clues about the characters' ages, thoughts, interests, and personalities.

> *"Samuel, you do it this time," Joe said.*
> *"What?" Samuel said, panicking.*
> *"You throw it!" Joe whispered, refusing to take the plane out of Samuel's hands.*

**4. Make the conflict clear.**
If you haven't got a conflict, you haven't got a story. Be sure the problem or conflict is clear and that the plot centers on how it is resolved.

**TIP** Before you revise, look back at the **key traits** on page 558 and the **rubric** and **peer-reader questions** on page 564.

> *Samuel wondered for the twentieth time why she had ever put them on the same team.*

> *The class started laughing. Samuel brought the plane back to Joe, who looked embarrassed.*

## REVISING AND EDITING

| **What Should I Do?** | **What Does It Look Like?** |
| --- | --- |

**1. Check the sequence.**

- Remember to show or tell your reader how one event leads to the next.

- <u>Underline</u> places where you should add transitional or other words and phrases to help your reader follow the sequence of events.

▶

*After*
~~Samuel nodded a timid yes.~~ Ms. Krunkner gave Samuel the tape measure. ~~He could measure how far the plane flew.~~   *so*

**2. Improve the dialogue.**

- Ask a peer reader to [bracket] dialogue that sounds too formal or so slangy that your audience may not understand it.

- Revise the dialogue until it is realistic and convincing. You can include fragments and grammatical errors if that's how your characters would actually talk.

**See page 564:** Ask a Peer Reader

▶

~~"Joe, [will you be the one who will launch the paper airplane that you have made?"] Ms. Krunkner asked.~~

~~["Yes, if that is all right with Samuel,"] Joe said.~~

"Joe, are you launching it?" Ms. Krunkner asked.

"Yeah. Is that okay, Samuel?" Joe asked.

**3. Focus on the details.**

- Put a box around your strongest details, whether those are sensory or descriptive.

- Add or revise details to tell your reader more about the setting, characters, and events.

▶

Samuel's heart was racing as he stepped up to the line.

~~It was a good throw, so Samuel felt relief.~~

When Samuel heard his classmates cheering, he let out the breath that he realized he'd been holding.

**4. Solve the conflict.**

- Reread your last few paragraphs. Did you resolve the central conflict?

- Create an ending that solves the problem and satisfies the reader. For example, you might show how a character has changed.

▶

He looked at the Frisbee and realized that making it fly would be all about getting it to spin and stay level. He held it flat and flicked his wrist to throw the Frisbee back. It soared over the grass and straight into waiting hands. He didn't even have to think about it; it just felt right. It was a good day for new flight patterns.

## Apply the Rubric

**A strong short story . . .**

- ☑ creates interest starting with the first sentence
- ☑ has a well-developed plot with a logical sequence of events
- ☑ presents, develops, and resolves a central conflict
- ☑ uses descriptive details, sensory language, and dialogue to enliven the characters, setting, and events
- ☑ varies sentence lengths
- ☑ shows the writer's distinctive style
- ☑ has a satisfying, believable conclusion

## Ask a Peer Reader

- What is the conflict in my story? How is it resolved?
- Is the dialogue believable? If not, how could I improve it?
- Is the sequence unclear at any point? If so, where?
- How would you describe the main character or characters?

## "What If" Questions

What if a character got lost in the woods, in a city, or in a huge amusement park?

What if a game or a field trip didn't go as planned because of a conflict between two characters?

What if someone discovered a secret that could change a life?

What if two people had to race against time to reach safety?

What if a character woke up one morning as a different person, an animal, or a space alien?

## Check Your Grammar

- Most stories use the past tense to tell what happened.

  > Samuel shuffled to the front of the room.
  > Joe was the school's soccer star.

- Most dialogue uses some form of the present tense.

  > "Joe, are you launching it?"
  > "That's what I'm trying to do," said Joe.

# Writing On**line**

**PUBLISHING OPTIONS**
For publishing options, visit the **Writing Center** at **ClassZone.com**.

**ASSESSMENT PREPARATION**
For writing and grammar assessment practice, go to the **Assessment Center** at **ClassZone.com**.

## Producing a Video

You can make a video of the story you wrote or of any story or scene from this unit.

### Planning the Video

1. **Write a script.** Turning a story into a script almost always involves adding dialogue. Often, it also means adding a narrator who supplies background information. Remember that a script also includes stage directions as well as ideas for sound effects (sometimes abbreviated as *SFX*) and music.

2. **Create a storyboard.** Plan your video by making simple sketches of each scene.

3. **Find actors and props.** Ask classmates to act in and narrate your video. Gather any props you will need.

**Ms. Krunkner:** *Joe and Samuel, you're up!*
**SFX:** *sound of a beating heart*

**Narrator:** *Samuel's heart is racing.*
**SFX:** *sound of heart grows louder*

### Producing the Video

1. **Shoot the footage.** Include different kinds of shots, such as close-ups, medium shots, and long shots. Try using different camera angles. Your goal is to tell a story that it is both clear and interesting.

2. **Wrap it up.** Use editing software to put the scenes in the right order and to add a title screen and credits. Remember, it's more important to tell a good story that your audience can follow easily than to stay close to the original. Don't hesitate to cut or to add.

3. **Show your masterpiece.** Screen your video for your classmates and invited guests. If you wish, hold a comments and questions session afterward. Ask your audience for feedback on what they liked and didn't like about your video.

# Reading Comprehension

**DIRECTIONS** *Read this selection and answer the questions that follow.*

# A Blind Man Catches a Bird

**Alexander McCall Smith**

A young man married a woman whose brother was blind. The young man was eager to get to know his new brother-in-law and so he asked him if he would like to go hunting with him.

"I cannot see," the blind man said. "But you can help me see when we are out hunting together. We can go."

The young man led the blind man off into the bush. At first they followed a path that he knew and it was easy for the blind man to tag on behind the other. After a while, though, they went off into thicker bush, where the trees grew closely together and there were many places for the animals to hide. The blind
10 man now held on to the arm of his sighted brother-in-law and told him many things about the sounds that they heard around them. Because he had no sight, he had a great ability to interpret the noises made by animals in the bush.

"There are warthogs around," he would say, "I can hear their noises over there."

Or: "That bird is preparing to fly. Listen to the sound of its wings unfolding."

To the brother-in-law, these sounds were meaningless, and he was most impressed at the blind man's ability to understand the bush although it must have been for him one great darkness.

20 They walked on for several hours, until they reached a place where they could set their traps. The blind man followed the other's advice, and put his trap in a place where birds might come for water. The other man put his trap a short distance away, taking care to disguise it so that no bird would know that it was there. He did not bother to disguise the blind man's trap, as it was hot and he was eager to get home to his new wife. The blind man thought that he had disguised his trap, but he did not see that he had failed to do so and any bird could tell that there was a trap there.

They returned to their hunting place the next day. The blind man was excited at the prospect of having caught something, and the young man had
30 to tell him to keep quiet, or he would scare all the animals away. Even before they reached the traps, the blind man was able to tell that they had caught something.

"I can hear birds," he said. "There are birds in the traps."

When he reached his trap, the young man saw that he had caught a small bird. He took it out of the trap and put it in a pouch that he had brought with him. Then the two of them walked towards the blind man's trap.

"There is a bird in it," he said to the blind man. "You have caught a bird too."

As he spoke, he felt himself filling with jealousy. The blind man's bird was marvelously colored, as if it had flown through a rainbow and been stained by
40 the colors. The feathers from a bird such as that would make a fine present for his new wife, but the blind man had a wife too, and she would also want the feathers.

The young man bent down and took the blind man's bird from the trap. Then, quickly substituting his own bird, he passed it to the blind man and put the colored bird into his own pouch.

"Here is your bird," he said to the blind man. "You may put it in your pouch."

The blind man reached out for the bird and took it. He felt it for a moment, his fingers passing over the wings and the breast. Then, without saying
50 anything, he put the bird into his pouch and they began the trip home.

On their way home, the two men stopped to rest under a broad tree. As they sat there, they talked about many things. The young man was impressed with the wisdom of the blind man, who knew a great deal, although he could see nothing at all.

"Why do people fight with one another?" he asked the blind man. It was a question which had always troubled him and he wondered if the blind man could give him an answer.

The blind man said nothing for a few moments, but it was clear to the young man that he was thinking. Then the blind man raised his head, and it
60 seemed to the young man as if the unseeing eyes were staring right into his soul. Quietly he gave his answer.

"Men fight because they do to each other what you have just done to me."

The words shocked the young man and made him ashamed. He tried to think of a response, but none came. Rising to his feet, he fetched his pouch, took out the brightly colored bird and gave it back to the blind man.

The blind man took the bird, felt over it with his fingers, and smiled.

"Do you have any other questions for me?" he asked.

"Yes," said the young man. "How do men become friends after they have fought?"
70 The blind man smiled again.

"They do what you have just done," he said. "That's how they become friends again."

**GO ON**

# Comprehension

DIRECTIONS *Answer these questions about "A Blind Man Catches a Bird."*

1. Which statement expresses the overall theme of the story?
   - ○ People cheat others because it makes them feel smart.
   - ○ People should rely more on their hearing than on their sight.
   - ○ True friendship depends on respect and fairness.
   - ○ Hunting is a good way to learn about animal behavior.

2. Which quotation conveys one of the story's themes?
   - ○ "At first they followed a path that he knew and it was easy for the blind man to tag on behind the other." (lines 6–7)
   - ○ "The blind man followed the other's advice, and put his trap in a place where birds might come for water." (line 21–22)
   - ○ "When he reached his trap, the young man saw that he had caught a small bird." (lines 34–35)
   - ○ "The young man was impressed with the wisdom of the blind man, who knew a great deal, although he could see nothing at all." (lines 52–54)

3. The hunting trip could be a symbol of the
   - ○ wisdom of a person who is blind
   - ○ search for what is important in life
   - ○ human struggle to control nature
   - ○ difficulty of living without sight

4. The sounds in the bush are meaningless to the young man because
   - ○ his ability to see limits his ability to listen
   - ○ he cannot speak the language of the animals
   - ○ a thick growth of trees muffles every sound
   - ○ the blind man is talking in a loud voice

5. The disguised trap might symbolize the young man's
   - ○ carelessness
   - ○ foolishness
   - ○ laziness
   - ○ deceitfulness

6. From the two questions that he asks the blind man in lines 55 and 68–69, you can conclude that the young man is
   - ○ trying to understand human nature
   - ○ having problems with his new wife
   - ○ testing the blind man's intelligence
   - ○ looking for something to argue about

7. Which theme is suggested by the blind man's answer to the question about why people fight?
   - ○ Dishonesty ruins people's relationships.
   - ○ Friends must be willing to forgive.
   - ○ People should think before they speak.
   - ○ Compromise will solve most problems.

8. Which quality might the blind man symbolize?
   - ○ wisdom
   - ○ strength
   - ○ courage
   - ○ jealousy

9. You can conclude that the young man is eager to please his new wife when he
   - ○ does not help the blind man disguise his bird trap
   - ○ is impressed that the blind man can understand the animals' sounds
   - ○ steals the colorful bird so that she can have its feathers
   - ○ asks his brother-in-law why people fight

**10.** Why is the blind man silent when he realizes that the young man has cheated him by switching the birds?

○ He plans to catch another bird to replace the small one.

○ He is waiting for the right moment to talk calmly with his brother-in-law.

○ He knows that the young man will be punished later.

○ He plans to tell the young man's wife what happened.

**11.** Reread lines 55–64. You can conclude that the young man is shocked at the response to his question because he

○ thinks the blind man doesn't know that the young man cheated him

○ expects the blind man to politely ignore his question

○ knows the blind man doesn't understand his question

○ believes that he has a right to take the beautiful bird

**12.** What does the colorful bird symbolize to the men in the story?

○ bad luck

○ a valued prize

○ a happy memory

○ broken promises

**13.** You can conclude that the young man gives the colorful bird to the blind man in order to

○ restore their friendship

○ show his generosity

○ please his new wife

○ avoid an argument

# Constructed Response

**SHORT ANSWER** *Write two or three sentences to answer each question.*

**14.** Even though he doesn't know how to set a trap, the blind man catches a beautiful bird. What conclusion can you draw from that incident?

**15.** What might the blindness in the story symbolize? In what ways are the two characters blind?

**ESSAY** *Write a paragraph to answer this question.*

**16.** Explain the connection between one symbol and one theme in the story.

GO ON ➡

# Vocabulary

**DIRECTIONS** *Use context clues and the thesaurus entries to answer the following questions.*

> **tag:** *verb.* call, identify, brand, label, follow, trail, chase

1. Which word could be substituted for the word *tag* as it is used in line 7?
   - ○ chase
   - ○ identify
   - ○ follow
   - ○ call

> **distance:** *noun.* space, coldness, separation, gap, length, remoteness

2. Which word could be substituted for the word *distance* as it is used in line 23?
   - ○ length
   - ○ separation
   - ○ remoteness
   - ○ coldness

> **prospect:** *noun.* customer, chance, hope, possibility, scene, view

3. Which word could be substituted for the word *prospect* as it is used in line 29?
   - ○ customer
   - ○ possibility
   - ○ scene
   - ○ view

**DIRECTIONS** *Use context clues and your knowledge of suffixes to answer the following questions.*

4. The word *able* means "having the power or skill to do something." What is the most likely meaning of the word *ability* as it is used in line 12?
   - ○ feeling
   - ○ desire
   - ○ talent
   - ○ intelligence

5. The word *meaning* refers to "something that one wishes to convey, especially by language." What is the most likely meaning of the word *meaningless* as it is used in line 17?
   - ○ easily overlooked
   - ○ beautifully melodic
   - ○ not worth listening to
   - ○ impossible to understand

6. The word *marvel* means "one that inspires admiration." What is the most likely meaning of the word *marvelously* as it is used in line 39?
   - ○ in a lighthearted manner
   - ○ with a reddish tint
   - ○ in a way that causes wonder
   - ○ with unattractive colors

# Writing & Grammar

**DIRECTIONS** *Read this passage and answer the questions that follow.*

(1) South Africa's current population descends from african, asian, and european settlers. (2) More than 1,500 years ago, the Transvaal region of South Africa was settled by members of the Bantu language group. (3) In 1652, the Dutch became the first Europeans to settle in South Africa. (4) Though dutch was the dominant language throughout the 1700s, english and a new language, known as afrikaans, later became the official languages of south africa. (5) Today, 11 official languages are recognized by the government. (6) The Zulu, the Xhosa, and the Sotho are just some of the African ethnic groups who speak these languages. (7) Respect for the many other languages spoken in the country is encouraged in the constitution.

**1.** Which words should be capitalized in sentence 1?
- ○ african, european
- ○ asian
- ○ european, settlers
- ○ african, asian, european

**2.** Choose the correct way to rewrite sentence 2 in the active voice.
- ○ The Transvaal region of South Africa was settled by members of the Bantu language group more than 1,500 years ago.
- ○ The Transvaal region of South Africa was settled more than 1,500 years ago by members of the Bantu language group.
- ○ More than 1,500 years ago, members of the Bantu language group settled the Transvaal region of South Africa.
- ○ The Transvaal region of South Africa was first settled by members of the Bantu language group more than 1,500 years ago.

**3.** Which words should be capitalized in sentence 4?
- ○ dutch, english
- ○ dutch, english, afrikaans, south africa
- ○ afrikaans, south africa
- ○ english

**4.** Choose the correct way to rewrite sentence 5 in the active voice.
- ○ Today, 11 official languages are being recognized by the government.
- ○ Eleven official languages are now recognized by the government.
- ○ Today, the government recognizes 11 official languages.
- ○ A total of 11 official languages are recognized today by the government.

**5.** Choose the correct way to rewrite sentence 7 in the active voice.
- ○ Respect is encouraged in the constitution for the many other languages spoken in the country.
- ○ The constitution encourages respect for the many other languages spoken in the country.
- ○ In the constitution, respect is encouraged for the many other languages spoken in the country.
- ○ Use of the many other languages spoken in the country is respected in the constitution.

STOP

# More Great Reads

## Ideas for Independent Reading

Which questions from Unit 4 made an impression on you?
Continue exploring them with these books.

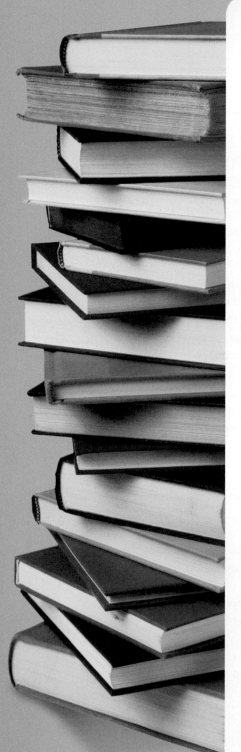

## Is curiosity a gift or a curse?

### East
**by Edith Pattou**

Rose was born curious. When a white bear shows up and asks her to go with him so her family can prosper, teenaged Rose agrees. She doesn't realize that living with a bear is only the beginning of a longer journey.

### Mable Riley: A Reliable Record of Humdrum, Peril, and Romance
**by Marthe Jocelyn**

The year is 1901, and Mable hopes she'll have an adventure when she moves away with her sister. At first, life remains boring. But everything changes when Mable meets the neighbor.

### The Thief Lord
**by Cornelia Funke**

Prosper and Bo have run away to Venice to escape their aunt and uncle. They are taken in by the Thief Lord, a masked boy who leads a band of children. When the Thief Lord accepts a mysterious assignment, the adventures of the band get complicated.

## How well do we treat our elders?

### The Cay
**by Theodore Taylor**

Phillip and his mother escape the German invasion of Curaçao on a freighter, but the boat is torpedoed. Phillip wakes up on a life raft with a cat and a West Indian named Timothy. Will Phillip be able to survive with only an old man for support?

### A Step from Heaven
**by An Na**

Young Ju is only four when her family moves to the U.S. from Korea. At first, everyone is happy, but then her parents start fighting again. Young Ju has been raised to respect her elders, but she knows that sometimes her father isn't right. What should she do?

### The Not-So-Star-Spangled Life of Sunita Sen
**by Mitali Perkins**

When Sunita's grandparents visit from India, her life changes. For one thing, she can't have boys over anymore. She has to find a way to accept her family and still fit in.

## What impact will you have on the world?

### The Book Thief
**by Markus Zusak**

Liesel is a little girl the first time she meets Death in Nazi Germany. The second time, she's a book thief, stealing books and reading them to anyone who needs to listen. Later, she writes her own story. This is the book Death wants you to hear.

### The Merlin Conspiracy
**by Diana Wynne Jones**

Roddy and Grundo are just teenagers in the Royal Court. No one but an outsider will believe them when they warn of a conspiracy against the king. Can three young magicians win a battle to keep the magic in the multiverse?

### Be the Difference: A Beginner's Guide to Changing the World
**by Danny Seo**

At 12, Danny Seo inspired thousands of students to join him in an environmental movement. Ten years later, he wrote this book. Read his advice about how teenagers can improve the world.

# Painting with Words

**POETRY**

# What makes a POEM?

Have you ever tried to write a **poem?** If so, you probably had to think about what a poem is. Is it lines that rhyme? Pictures painted with words? Toe-tapping rhythms? A poem can be all of these things—or none of them.

**ACTIVITY** Poetry is everywhere—in our favorite songs, the nursery rhymes we read as children, and even in some television commercials. With a partner, make a list of poems that you have read or heard. Then answer the following questions:

- Did you find poetry in any unexpected places?

- What do these poems have in common?

- How do the words create mental pictures?

- Do these poems rhyme, or have rhythm?

Once you've answered these questions, see if you can define a poem.

**INDIANA STANDARDS**

# Preview Unit Goals

| | |
|---|---|
| **LITERARY ANALYSIS** | • Identify and analyze figurative language |
| | • Identify, analyze, and compare length and meaning of stanzas |
| | • Identify and analyze sound devices |
| | • Identify, analyze, and compare rhyme schemes |
| | • Analyze repetition in poetry |
| | • Identify and analyze rhythm and meter and their effects |
| | • Identify and analyze speaker |
| **READING** | • Develop strategies for reading, including visualizing, clarifying, and setting a purpose for reading |
| | • Paraphrase lines in poetry |
| | • Outline information |
| | • Support an opinion |
| **WRITING AND GRAMMAR** | • Write a personal response to a poem |
| | • Use commas and other punctuation correctly |
| **SPEAKING, LISTENING, AND VIEWING** | • Give an oral interpretation of a poem |
| **VOCABULARY** | • Use knowledge of word roots and word origins to help determine word meaning |
| **ACADEMIC VOCABULARY** | • figurative language   • stanza |
| | • sound devices   • rhyme scheme |

# Appreciating Poetry

The poet Robert Frost once said that a poem "begins in delight and ends in wisdom." While many poems are entertaining, a poem can also have the power to change how you see the world. Whether it follows a set pattern or bends all the rules, each poem uses language in a new way to communicate its message.

**INDIANA STANDARDS**

**READING STANDARDS**
**8.3.1** Determine and articulate the relationship between the purposes and characteristics of different forms of poetry . . . .

**8.3.6** Identify significant literary devices, such as metaphor, symbolism, dialect or quotations, and irony, which define a writer's style and use those elements to interpret the work.

## Part 1: The Basics

What do you see when you look at a poem? One difference between a poem and a short story is the **form,** or the structure of the writing. All poems are broken up into **lines.** The length of each line and where it breaks, or ends, contribute to the poem's meaning and sound. Lines often appear in groups, or **stanzas.** The stanzas work together to convey the overall message of the poem.

Some poems follow the rules of a traditional form. For example, a poem might have a specific number of lines and stanzas or a regular pattern of rhythm and rhyme. Other poems are unconventional, with no recognizable patterns. A poet might even choose to use incorrect grammar or spelling to create a particular sound or to emphasize meaning.

Just as a story has a narrator, a poem has a voice that "talks" to readers. This voice, or **speaker,** is sometimes a fictional character rather than the poet.

Take a look at the following poems. Which is traditional? Which is unconventional? Which one has a distinct speaker?

**EXAMPLE 1**

*from* **"The Geese"**
Poem by **Richard Peck**

My father was the first to hear
The passage of the geese each fall,
Passing above the house so near
He'd hear within his heart their call.

And then at breakfast time he'd say:
"The geese were heading south last
    night,"
For he had lain awake till day,
Feeling his earthbound soul take flight.

**EXAMPLE 2**

*from* **"Street Corner Flight"**
Poem by **Norma Landa Flores**

From this side . . .
    of their concrete barrio
    two small boys hold
        fat white pigeons
trapped in their trembling hands.

Then,
    gently,
        not disturbing
            their powers of flight,
                release them
into the air.

## MODEL 1: TRADITIONAL FORM

In this traditional poem, the speaker reflects on the return of night at the end of a day. Read it aloud to help you identify the characteristics of its form.

*from*

# Good-Night

Poem by **Robert Louis Stevenson**

When the bright lamp is carried in,
The sunless hours again begin;
O'er all without, in field and lane,
The haunted night returns again.

5   Now we behold the embers flee
About the firelit hearth; and see
Our faces painted as we pass,
Like pictures, on the window-glass.

**Close Read**

1. How many lines are in each stanza?

2. In the first stanza, rhyming pairs are highlighted. Identify the rhyming words in the second stanza. What pattern do you see?

## MODEL 2: FREE VERSE

In this unconventional poem—called a **free verse** poem—the poet lets the ideas drive where each line breaks and when each stanza ends.

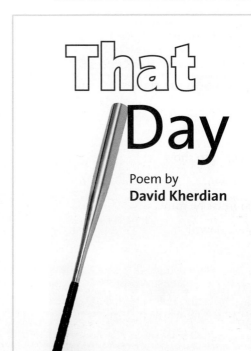

# That Day

Poem by
**David Kherdian**

Just once
my father stopped on the way
into the house from work
and joined in the softball game
5   we were having in the street,
and attempted to play in *our*
game that *his* country had never
known.

Just once
10   and the day stands out forever
in my memory
as a father's living gesture
to his son,
that in playing even the fool
15   or clown, he would reveal
that the lines of their lives
were sewn from a tougher fabric
than the son had previously known.

**Close Read**

1. How does the form of this poem differ from that of "Good-Night"?

2. Notice the short lengths of the boxed lines. What might the poet be trying to emphasize by isolating and repeating this phrase?

3. What do you learn about the speaker of this poem?

# Part 2: Poetic Elements

Like different colors of paint or the notes on a musical scale, language can be arranged to create a desired effect. For example, short, choppy lines can produce a fast-paced pounding beat, while long, rhythmic lines can create a soothing melody. Poets manipulate the words and lines in their writing, fully conscious of how their work will sound when read aloud and how it will make readers feel. Sound devices, imagery, and figurative language are important tools of the trade.

## SOUND DEVICES

Poets choose words not only for their meaning, but also for their sounds. The sound of a word or line can help emphasize meaning or create a musical quality. Here are some examples of sound devices poets use.

| SOUND DEVICES | EXAMPLE |
|---|---|
| **RHYTHM**<br>the pattern of stressed ( ˊ ) and unstressed ( �‿ ) syllables in each line. A regular pattern of rhythm is called **meter**. | **"Afternoon on a Hill"**<br>Poem by **Edna St. Vincent Millay** |
| | I will be the gladdest thing ⟶ *a* |
| | Under the sun! ⟶ *b* |
| **RHYME**<br>the repetition of sounds at the ends of words, as in *sun* and *one*. **Rhyme scheme** is the pattern that the end-rhyming words follow. To identify rhyme scheme, assign a letter to each sound, as shown here. | I will touch a hundred flowers ⟶ *c* |
| | And not pick one. ⟶ *b* |
| | I will look at cliffs and clouds ⟶ *d* |
| | With quiet eyes, ⟶ *e* |
| **REPETITION**<br>the use of a word, phrase, line, or sound more than once, such as the repeated use of the phrase *I will* | Watch the wind bow down the grass, ⟶ *f* |
| | And the grass rise. ⟶ *e* |
| | And when lights begin to show ⟶ *g* |
| **ALLITERATION**<br>the repetition of consonant sounds at the beginning of words, such as the *m* in *mark*, *must*, and *mine* | Up from the town, ⟶ *h* |
| | I will mark which must be mine, ⟶ *i* |
| | And then start down! ⟶ *h* |
| **ASSONANCE**<br>the repetition of vowel sounds in words that don't end with the same consonant, such as the *ow* sound in *bow* and *down* | |

## MODEL 1: RHYTHM AND RHYME

Read this traditional poem aloud, listening for its rhythm and rhyme.

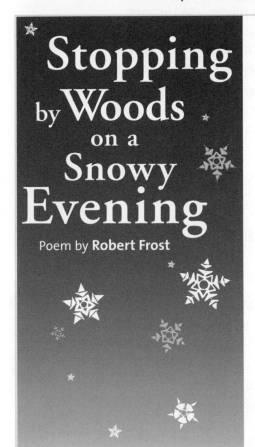

# Stopping by Woods on a Snowy Evening

Poem by **Robert Frost**

Whose woods these are I think I know.
His house is in the village, though;
He will not see me stopping here
To watch his woods fill up with snow.

5   My little horse must think it queer
To stop without a farmhouse near
Between the woods and frozen lake
The darkest evening of the year.

He gives his harness bells a shake
10  To ask if there is some mistake.
The only other sound's the sweep
Of easy wind and downy flake.

The woods are lovely, dark and deep,
But I have promises to keep,
15  And miles to go before I sleep,
And miles to go before I sleep.

**Close Read**

1. Stressed (ʹ) and unstressed (˘) syllables are marked in the first stanza. Read the second stanza out loud. Does it follow the same pattern as the first stanza?

2. The end rhymes in the first stanza are highlighted. Examine the end rhymes in the other stanzas to figure out the rhyme scheme.

## MODEL 2: ALLITERATION AND REPETITION

This unconventional poem uses alliteration and repetition to help emphasize meaning. Make sure to read the lines all the way across.

*from* **Chrysalis** *Diary*

Poem by **Paul Fleischman**

                              November 13:

Cold told me
to fasten my feet
to this branch,
5                              to dangle upside down
                              from my perch,
to shed my skin,
                              to cease being a caterpillar
and I have obeyed.             and I have obeyed.

**Close Read**

1. The alliteration in the boxed line helps to create a sense of the caterpillar's strong grip. Find another example of alliteration.

2. What does the repetition in the last line help emphasize?

3. Who is the speaker of the poem?

# IMAGERY AND FIGURATIVE LANGUAGE

In addition to sound devices, poets use **imagery,** or language that appeals to one or more of your senses—sight, hearing, smell, taste, and touch. Vivid images help readers to more clearly understand what a poet describes. In "Stopping by Woods on a Snowy Evening," for example, images like "the sweep / Of easy wind and downy flake" help you to visualize the scene and hear the sounds of winter.

One way poets create imagery is by using **figurative language,** or imaginative descriptions that are not literally true. Notice how these examples of figurative language help you to picture ordinary things in new ways.

## SIMILE

**a comparison of two things using the word *like* or *as***

The sun spun like
a tossed coin.
It whirled on the azure sky,
it clattered into the horizon,
it clicked in the slot,
and neon-lights popped
and blinked "Time expired,"
as on a parking meter.

—"Sunset"
by Oswald Mbuyiseni Mtshali

## PERSONIFICATION

**a description of an object, animal, or idea as if it has human qualities and emotions**

When I opened the door
I found the vine leaves
speaking among themselves in abundant
whispers.
        My presence made them
hush their green breath,
embarrassed, the way
humans stand up, buttoning their jackets,
acting as if they were leaving anyway, as if
the conversation had ended
just before you arrived.

—from "Aware"
by Denise Levertov

## METAPHOR

**a comparison of two things that does not include the word *like* or *as***

In the pond in the park
all things are doubled:
Long buildings hang and
wriggle gently. Chimneys
are bent legs bouncing
on clouds below.

—from "Water Picture"
by May Swenson

# Part 3: Analyze the Literature

In "Lineage," Margaret Walker uses many different poetic elements to describe the speaker's admiration for her ancestors. Using what you've learned in this workshop, analyze the form, sound devices, and language in this poem. Notice how all these elements work together to communicate a powerful message.

# LINEAGE

Poem by **Margaret Walker**

My grandmothers were strong.
They followed plows and bent to toil.
They moved through fields sowing seed.
They touched earth and grain grew.
5   They were full of sturdiness and singing.
My grandmothers were strong.

My grandmothers are full of memories
Smelling of soap and onions and wet clay
With veins rolling roughly over quick hands
10   They have many clean words to say.
My grandmothers were strong.
Why am I not as they?

## Close Read

1. What is traditional about the form of this poem?

2. One example of alliteration is boxed. Find two more examples.

3. The poem's first line is repeated two more times and helps to emphasize an important message. How is strength defined in the poem?

4. Find four images that help you picture the grandmothers. What sense does each image appeal to?

5. How would you describe the speaker of this poem? Think about the qualities she admires in her grandmothers and how she sees herself in relation to them.

## Simile: Willow and Ginkgo
Poem by Eve Merriam

## Introduction to Poetry
Poem by Billy Collins

# *How can* WORDS *create pictures?*

**INDIANA STANDARDS**

**READING STANDARDS**
**8.3.1** Determine and articulate the relationship between the purposes and characteristics of different forms of poetry . . . .

**8.3.6** Identify significant literary devices, such as metaphor, symbolism, dialect or quotations, and irony, which define a writer's style and use those elements to interpret the work.

**KEY IDEA** Have you ever seen the movie version of a book you've already read? Then you probably have had the experience of being surprised when a character didn't look the way you had pictured him or her. **Words** can create such distinct and powerful images that what you imagine while reading can seem as "real" as what you see. The poems you are about to read might help you see words themselves in a fresh, new way.

**QUICKWRITE** Choose a photograph from a magazine. Try to think of the way the pictured item might feel, sound, smell, or taste, in addition to how it appears. In a brief paragraph, create a vivid description of the image. Read your paragraph to a partner and ask which words best help him or her picture what you're describing. Then show the image.

582

## ● POETIC FORM: STANZA

Many poems are divided into **stanzas,** or groupings of two or more lines that form a unit. In poetry, a stanza serves a similar purpose to a paragraph in prose. Stanzas may be used to separate ideas, add emphasis, or create a certain appearance on the page.

## ● LITERARY ANALYSIS: METAPHOR AND SIMILE

Have you ever heard an expression that didn't mean exactly what it said? The expression probably contained figurative language. **Figurative language** consists of words used in an imaginative way to communicate meaning beyond their strict definition. Two types of figurative language are

- **Similes,** which use *like* or *as* to compare two unlike things. For example: *The frozen lake is like glass.*

- **Metaphors,** which make comparisons without the words *like* or *as.* For example: *All the world is a stage.*

As you read the following poems, look for examples of metaphors and similes and note how the poets use them to create an emotional response, present vibrant images, or express complex ideas with a few words.

## ● READING STRATEGY: VISUALIZE

One way to help yourself enjoy the richness of a poem is to take the time to **visualize** the words, or form pictures in your mind. To visualize, pay attention to details that help you imagine how something looks, sounds, smells, feels, or even tastes. Combine these details with your own knowledge and experiences. As you read these poems, keep track of what you visualize in a chart like the one shown.

| What I Visualize | Words and Phrases That Helped |
|---|---|
| dark, jerky lines | "crude sketch" |

# Author On|ine

**Eve Merriam: Always a Poet** Eve Merriam began writing poetry when she was about eight years old, and she never considered any other career. "It's like . . . oxygen," she said, "when I hear rhymes and word play." Although at times during her life she was forced to take other jobs, she

**Eve Merriam
1916–1992**

continued writing poetry. Her first collection of poetry for adults, *Family Circle,* won the 1946 Yale Younger Poets Prize. Later in her career, Merriam focused on sharing her love of language with children, eventually publishing 24 books of poetry for young readers.

**Billy Collins: America's Most Popular Poet**
In the United States, even the top poets can be unknown to most of the public. Billy Collins, however, is well known and well loved. His rise to fame began when Collins became a regular guest on radio programs, where his humor

**Billy Collins
born 1941**

and welcoming manner won him a loyal following. He has since become one of the best-selling poets of his generation and regularly attracts standing-room-only crowds to his poetry readings. When he served as the Poet Laureate of the United States from 2001 to 2003, he created the 180 Project, which provided high schools across the country with poems to be read along with daily announcements. His goal was to make poetry part of everyday life for young people.

 **MORE ABOUT THE AUTHOR**
For more on these poets, visit the **Literature Center** at ClassZone.com.

# Simile: *Willow and Ginkgo*

## EVE MERRIAM

**ANALYZE VISUALS**
What **motif**, or repeated element, do you notice in this image?

The willow is like an etching,
Fine-lined against the sky.
The ginkgo is like a crude sketch,
Hardly worthy to be signed.

5 The willow's music is like a soprano,
Delicate and thin.
The ginkgo's tune is like a chorus
With everyone joining in.

The willow is sleek as a velvet-nosed calf;
10 The ginkgo is leathery as an old bull.
The willow's branches are like silken thread;
The ginkgo's like stubby rough wool. Ⓐ

Ⓐ **METAPHOR AND SIMILE**
In lines 9–12, what similes are used to describe the willow? What similes describe the ginkgo?

The willow is like a nymph with streaming hair;
Wherever it grows, there is green and gold and fair.
15 The willow dips to the water,
Protected and precious, like the king's favorite daughter.

The ginkgo forces its way through gray concrete;
Like a city child, it grows up in the street.
Thrust against the metal sky,
20 Somehow it survives and even thrives. Ⓑ

Ⓑ **STANZA**
Why do you think the poet started a new stanza at line 17?

*My eyes feast upon the willow,*
*But my heart goes to the ginkgo.*

*Light–1* (1992), Atsuko Kato.
Oil on board, 100 cm × 70 cm.

# Introduction *to* Poetry

### BILLY COLLINS

*Wednesday 6: Rain, slowly clearing eastwards* (2001), Ben McLaughlin. Oil on
board, 20.3 cm × 20.3 cm. Private collection. © Bridgeman Art Library.

I ask them to take a poem
and hold it up to the light
like a color slide

or press an ear against its hive. **C**

5 I say drop a mouse into a poem
and watch him probe his way out,

or walk inside the poem's room
and feel the walls for a light switch.

I want them to waterski
10 across the surface of a poem
waving at the author's name on the shore.

But all they want to do
is tie the poem to a chair with rope
and torture a confession out of it. **D**

15 They begin beating it with a hose
to find out what it really means.

**C** VISUALIZE
Reread lines 1–4. What
words help you visualize
what the poet describes?
To which senses do the
details appeal?

**D** METAPHOR AND
SIMILE
In lines 12–14, what
metaphor is used to
describe the poem?

## Comprehension

1. **Recall** In "Simile: Willow and Ginkgo," which tree does the speaker think is more beautiful?

2. **Recall** What does the speaker in "Introduction to Poetry" want readers to do on the surface of a poem?

**INDIANA STANDARDS**

**READING STANDARD**
**8.3.6** Identify significant literary devices . . . .

## Literary Analysis

3. **Visualize** Review the chart you made as you read. Select two examples that were especially effective in helping you make visualizations. What **words** helped you "see" images in your mind?

4. **Identify Simile and Metaphor** For each poem, identify as many figurative comparisons as you can. In a chart like the one shown, list what is being described and what it is compared to. Then identify whether the comparison is a simile or a metaphor.

| "Introduction to Poetry" | | | |
|---|---|---|---|
| Line(s) | What Is Being Described | What It Is Compared To | Simile or Metaphor |
| 2–3 | poem | color slide | simile |

5. **Interpret a Line** Reread the last two lines of "Simile: Willow and Ginkgo." Why do you think the speaker's "heart goes to the ginkgo"? Support your answer with words and phrases from the poem.

6. **Compare Stanzas** Look back at the stanzas in "Introduction to Poetry." How are the poem's stanzas alike? How are they different? Consider their length as well as their content.

7. **Analyze Tone** In "Introduction to Poetry," the **tone,** or the expression of a writer's attitude toward the subject, changes partway through the poem. Identify where this change occurs. How do the poet's word choice and imagery signal the change?

## Extension and Challenge

8. **Literary Criticism** Billy Collins has described his poetry as "reader-friendly, hospitable, congenial, welcoming." Do you agree? Use details from "Introduction to Poetry" to support your opinion.

9. **Creative Project: Poem** Write your own short poem describing what the experience of reading poetry is like for you. Include at least one **metaphor** and one **simile.**

## Macavity: The Mystery Cat
Poem by T. S. Eliot

## Vermin
Poem by E. B. White

# *What's the smartest* ANIMAL?

**KEY IDEA** Cats can escape from peculiar places. Dogs can learn tricks. Chimpanzees can communicate in sign language. All **animals** can appear to be intelligent at times. In the poems that follow, you will read about a couple of animals that are too clever to be caught— no matter how hard people try.

**LIST IT** Certain qualities are often associated with specific **animals.** For example, loyalty is a trait displayed by dogs. With a group, identify what the animals listed are known for. Did other groups come up with similar ideas?

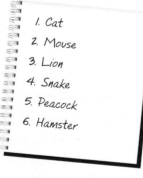

1. Cat
2. Mouse
3. Lion
4. Snake
5. Peacock
6. Hamster

## ● LITERARY ANALYSIS: COUPLET

"Macavity: The Mystery Cat" is written in **couplets,** or rhymed pairs of lines. The lines in each couplet usually have the same or a similar number of syllables. As you read, use a chart like the one shown to record the rhymes T. S. Eliot uses to construct a poem made up entirely of couplets.

| Stanza | Rhymes |
|--------|--------|
| 1 | Paw, Law |
|   | despair, there |
| 2 | |

## ● READING SKILL: ANALYZE FIGURATIVE LANGUAGE

You may recall that **figurative language** refers to words used in an imaginative rather than literally true way to express ideas. The following poems contain these types of figurative language:

- **Personification** gives human qualities to an animal, object, or idea.

- **Extended metaphors** develop a comparison of two unlike things throughout several lines, multiple stanzas, or an entire poem.

As you read, identify the type of figurative language used in each poem and consider the ideas it conveys.

## ▲ VOCABULARY IN CONTEXT

The words in Column A help T. S. Eliot and E. B. White portray memorable animals in their poems. Match each word in Column A to the word in Column B that is closest in meaning.

| Column A | Column B |
|----------|----------|
| **1.** bafflement | **a.** pest |
| **2.** depravity | **b.** courtesy |
| **3.** fiend | **c.** immorality |
| **4.** levitation | **d.** confusion |
| **5.** suavity | **e.** rising |
| **6.** vermin | **f.** monster |

# MACAVITY:
## The Mystery Cat

## T. S. Eliot

Macavity's a Mystery Cat: he's called the Hidden Paw—
For he's the master criminal who can defy the Law.
He's the **bafflement** of Scotland Yard,[1] the Flying Squad's[2] despair:
For when they reach the scene of crime—*Macavity's not there!*

5 Macavity, Macavity, there's no one like Macavity,
He's broken every human law, he breaks the law of gravity.
His powers of **levitation** would make a fakir[3] stare,
And when you reach the scene of crime—*Macavity's not there!*
You may seek him in the basement, you may look up in the air—
10 But I tell you once and once again, *Macavity's not there!*

Macavity's a ginger cat, he's very tall and thin;
You would know him if you saw him, for his eyes are sunken in.
His brow is deeply lined with thought, his head is highly domed;
His coat is dusty from neglect, his whiskers are uncombed.
15 He sways his head from side to side, with movements like a snake;
And when you think he's half asleep, he's always wide awake. **A**

**ANALYZE VISUALS**
What **traits** might the cat in the photograph possess?

**bafflement** (băf'əl-mənt) *n.* confusion; puzzlement

**levitation** (lĕv'ĭ-tā'shŭn) *n.* the act of rising into the air and floating

**A** **FIGURATIVE LANGUAGE**
What human physical qualities does the poet give to Macavity?

---

1. **Scotland Yard:** police headquarters in London, England.
2. **the Flying Squad:** a group of highly skilled detectives in London's police force.
3. **fakir** (fə-kîr'): a Muslim or Hindu holy person who may perform magic tricks.

Macavity, Macavity, there's no one like Macavity,
For he's a **fiend** in feline shape, a monster of **depravity.**
You may meet him in a by-street, you may see him in the square—
20 But when a crime's discovered, then *Macavity's not there!*

He's outwardly respectable. (They say he cheats at cards.)
And his footprints are not found in any file of Scotland Yard's.
And when the larder's[4] looted, or the jewel-case is rifled,[5]
Or when the milk is missing, or another Peke's[6] been stifled,[7]
25 Or the greenhouse glass is broken, and the trellis past repair—
Ay, there's the wonder of the thing! *Macavity's not there!* **B**

And when the Foreign Office find a Treaty's gone astray,
Or the Admiralty[8] lose some plans and drawings by the way,
There may be a scrap of paper in the hall or on the stair—
30 But it's useless to investigate—*Macavity's not there!*
And when the loss has been disclosed, the Secret Service say:
"It *must* have been Macavity!"—but he's a mile away.
You'll be sure to find him resting, or a-licking of his thumbs,
Or engaged in doing complicated long division sums.

35 Macavity, Macavity, there's no one like Macavity,
There never was a Cat of such deceitfulness and **suavity.**
He always has an alibi, and one or two to spare:
At whatever time the deed took place—MACAVITY WASN'T THERE!
And they say that all the Cats whose wicked deeds are widely known
40 (I might mention Mungojerrie, I might mention Griddlebone)
Are nothing more than agents for the Cat who all the time
Just controls their operations: the Napoleon[9] of Crime! **C**

**B COUPLET**
How many couplets
make up the fifth stanza?
What rhyming words end
each pair of lines? Record
them in your chart.

**C FIGURATIVE
LANGUAGE**
What human personality
traits does Macavity have?

---

4. **larder** (lär′dər): a food storage cupboard.

5. **rifled** (rī′fəld): robbed; plundered.

6. **Peke** (pēk): a Pekinese dog.

7. **stifled** (stī′fəld): killed by smothering.

8. **Admiralty** (ăd′mər-əl-tē): the British government department that once was in charge of Britain's navy.

9. **Napoleon** (nə-pō′lē-ən): a French emperor (1804–1814/1815) who conquered much of Europe.

# VERMIN

## E. B. White

The mouse of Thought infests[1] my head.
He knows my cupboard and the crumb.
   **Vermin!** I despise[2] vermin.
I have no trap, no skill with traps,
5 No bait, no hope, no cheese, no bread—
I fumble with the task to no avail.[3]
I've seen him several times lately.
He is too quick for me,
I see only his tail. **D**

**vermin** (vûr′mĭn) *n., pl.*
destructive and annoying
insects and small animals,
such as cockroaches
and rats

**D FIGURATIVE
LANGUAGE**
What two things are
compared in this poem?

---

1. **infests** (ĭn-fĕstz′): lives in or overruns in large
   numbers.
2. **despise** (dĭ-spīz′): dislike intensely.
3. **to no avail:** without success; uselessly.

## Comprehension

1. **Recall** Who does Macavity fool and confuse?

2. **Recall** What part of the mouse does the speaker see in "Vermin"?

3. **Represent** Reread lines 11–14 of "Macavity: the Mystery Cat." Based on this description, make a sketch of Macavity. Label your sketch to show what details from the poem you included.

**INDIANA STANDARDS**

**READING STANDARD**
**8.3.1** Determine and articulate the...characteristics of different forms of poetry....

## Literary Analysis

4. **Examine Couplets** Review the chart you used to record the rhymes in "Macavity: The Mystery Cat." Does T. S. Eliot repeat any rhymes?

5. **Analyze Personification** What do you learn about Macavity from the personification used in the poem? Use a web like the one shown to collect details about the cat's human appearance, behavior, and personality.

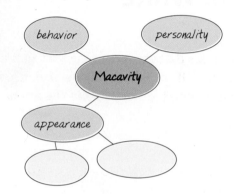

6. **Interpret a Line** In poetry, a word or line can have more than one meaning. In "Vermin," the speaker says "I fumble with the task to no avail." What different ways can you interpret this?

7. **Draw Conclusions from Extended Metaphor** In "Vermin," identify two similarities between the speaker's thoughts and a mouse. What does this comparison suggest about the speaker's attitude toward his own thoughts?

## Extension and Challenge

8. **Big Question Activity** Review the list you created on page 588. How do the traits you assigned to cats and mice compare with the traits displayed by the **animals** in the poems? Write your own poem about one of the animals on the list. Make sure you use either **personification** or **metaphor** to explore ideas or add humor.

# Vocabulary in Context

## VOCABULARY PRACTICE

Decide whether the words in each pair are synonyms (words with similar meanings) or antonyms (words with opposite meanings).

1. depravity/saintliness
2. levitation/ascent
3. bafflement/puzzlement
4. suavity/awkwardness
5. vermin/pest
6. fiend/beast

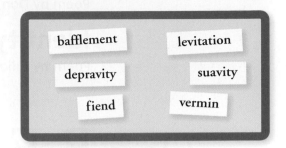

bafflement    levitation

depravity    suavity

fiend    vermin

## VOCABULARY IN WRITING

Do you know any creatures that share qualities with either the cat or mouse described in these poems? If not, imagine one. Use at least two vocabulary words to write a **one-paragraph description** of the animal. You could start this way.

> **EXAMPLE**
>
> My cat Katrina is a **fiend** and a thief. She is always stealing small items such as hair clips and rubber bands.

## VOCABULARY STRATEGY: WORD ORIGINS

Like people and countries, words have their own histories. A good way to understand a word's current meaning is to learn about its history, or **etymology**. For example, the word *suavity*, which means "graceful politeness" comes from the Latin word *suvis*, which means "delightful, sweet."

A word's origin can be found in most dictionaries and can reveal a great deal about a word's meaning. For example, look at the etymology in this dictionary entry:

> **neighbor** (nā′bər) *n.* One who lives near or next to another [from Old English *nēahgebūr: nēah*, near + *gebūr*, dweller]

*PRACTICE* Look up the etymology of each of these words in the dictionary. Write the word's origin and explain how knowing the word's history can help you remember its meaning.

1. hippopotamus
2. hybrid
3. dinosaur
4. sports
5. calendar

**INDIANA STANDARDS**

**READING STANDARD**
**8.1.2** Understand the influence of historical events on English word meaning and vocabulary expansion.

**VOCABULARY PRACTICE**

For more practice, go to the **Vocabulary Center** at **ClassZone.com**.

## the lesson of the moth
Poem by Don Marquis

## Identity
Poem by Julio Noboa

# Does B E A U T Y matter?

**INDIANA STANDARDS**

**READING STANDARD**
8.3.1 Determine and articulate the relationship between the purposes and characteristics of different forms of poetry ....

**KEY IDEA** What is our standard of **beauty?** A recent study found that people judged the beauty of strangers differently than they judged the beauty of people they knew. With strangers, people took into account only physical appearance. With familiar faces, the participants considered characteristics such as intelligence, courage, and dependability. The speakers in the poems you're about to read have their own ideas about beauty.

**SURVEY** Survey your classmates to find out what five or six characteristics they think make someone beautiful. List the ten answers that were given most often, and then separate them into internal and external characteristics. According to your survey, is beauty only skin deep?

## ● POETIC FORM: FREE VERSE

It is often said that to write poetry, you first have to learn the rules—then you can break them. **Free verse** is poetry that "breaks the rules" because it does not contain regular patterns of rhythm or rhyme. However, writers of free verse often use repetition and other sound devices to emphasize meaning. As you read, notice the way the poems sound like everyday speech.

## ● LITERARY ANALYSIS: SPEAKER

In a poem, the voice that "talks" to the reader is called the **speaker.** Readers often assume that the speaker and the poet are the same, but this is not always true. The speaker may be a character created by the poet. For example, the speaker in "the lesson of the moth" is a cockroach named Archy. As you read each poem, think about the speaker's point of view.

## ● READING SKILL: CLARIFY MEANING

Just as poets use words, rhythm, and rhyme to create certain effects, they also use line breaks, stanzas, and punctuation to help emphasize ideas. For example, look at the way the punctuation and line and stanza breaks in the first stanza of "Identity" affect meaning.

*Let them be as flowers,*
*always watered, fed, guarded, admired,*
*but harnessed to a pot of dirt.*

In the first two lines, commas cause you to pause and linger on words that are associated with positive feelings. However, the third line, which ends with a period, abruptly undercuts the comforting words the speaker associates with flowers. Because the stanza ends with this line, it emphasizes that the speaker sees confinement where others see beauty. As you study each poem, think about the way the line breaks, stanzas, and punctuation affect the way you read and understand it. Use a graphic organizer like the one shown to note these elements and the effects they create.

| Elements | Used? | Effect |
|---|---|---|
| line and stanza breaks | yes | separate positive and negative ideas |
| commas | | |
| end marks (question marks, periods, etc.) | | |

# the lesson of the moth

## Don Marquis

i was talking to a moth
the other evening
he was trying to break into
an electric light bulb
5 and fry himself on the wires **A**

why do you fellows
pull this stunt i asked him
because it is the conventional[1]
thing for moths or why
10 if that had been an uncovered
candle instead of an electric
light bulb you would
now be a small unsightly cinder[2]
have you no sense **B**

15 plenty of it he answered
but at times we get tired
of using it
we get bored with the routine

---

---

1. **conventional:** customary; usual; accepted.
2. **cinder:** a piece of burned material.

and crave beauty
20 and excitement
fire is beautiful
and we know that if we get
too close it will kill us
but what does that matter
25 it is better to be happy
for a moment
and be burned up with beauty
than to live a long time
and be bored all the while
30 so we wad all our life up
into one little roll
and then we shoot the roll
that is what life is for
it is better to be a part of beauty
35 for one instant and then to cease to
exist than to exist forever
and never be a part of beauty
our attitude toward life
is to come easy go easy
40 we are like human beings
used to be before they became
too civilized to enjoy themselves **C**

and before i could argue him
out of his philosophy
he went and immolated[3] himself
on a patent[4] cigar lighter
i do not agree with him
myself i would rather have
half the happiness and twice
50 the longevity[5] **D**

but at the same time i wish
there was something i wanted
as badly as he wanted to fry himself

—archy

---

3. **immolated** (ĭm′ə-lātd′): killed as a sacrifice.

4. **patent** (păt′nt): patented; covered by a lawful grant that gives the inventor the exclusive right to manufacture an item for a certain time period.

5. **longevity** (lŏn-jĕv′ĭ-tē): length of life.

# IDENTITY

## Julio Noboa

*The Mountain* (1991), Albert Herbert. Oil on canvas, 50.8 cm × 61 cm. Private collection. © Bridgeman Art Library.

Let them be as flowers,
always watered, fed, guarded, admired,
but harnessed to a pot of dirt.

I'd rather be a tall, ugly weed,
5 clinging on cliffs, like an eagle
wind-wavering above high, jagged rocks. **E**

To have broken through the surface of stone
to live, to feel exposed to the madness
of the vast, eternal sky.
10 To be swayed by the breezes of an ancient sea,
carrying my soul, my seed beyond the mountains
    of time
or into the abyss[1] of the bizarre.

I'd rather be unseen, and if,

then shunned[2] by everyone
15 than to be a pleasant-smelling flower,
growing in clusters in the fertile valley
where they're praised, handled, and plucked
by greedy, human hands. **F**

I'd rather smell of musty, green stench
20 than of sweet, fragrant lilac.
If I could stand alone, strong and free,
I'd rather be a tall, ugly weed.

**E SPEAKER**
Reread lines 1–6. How does the speaker's view of himself or herself contrast with the way the speaker views "them"?

**F CLARIFY MEANING**
Reread lines 13–18, paying attention to the commas. What effect do they have on the way you read this stanza?

---

1. **abyss:** a seemingly bottomless space.
2. **shunned:** deliberately avoided; shut out.

# Comprehension

1. **Recall** According to "the lesson of the moth," why do moths fly toward light?

2. **Represent** Create a sketch that shows the differences between the flower and the weed described in "Identity." Make sure your sketch reflects at least two specific details from the poem.

**INDIANA STANDARDS**

**READING STANDARD**
**8.3.1** Determine and articulate the…characteristics of different forms of poetry….

# Literary Analysis

3. **Make Inferences** What does the **speaker** learn about himself in "the lesson of the moth"? Support your response with evidence from the poem.

4. **Examine Stanza** In "the lesson of the moth," how does the poet use **stanzas** to help you follow the conversation between the cockroach and the moth?

5. **Analyze Metaphor** What kind of person does the speaker in "Identity" want to be? What kind of person does he not want to be?

6. **Clarify Meaning** Refer to the charts you created as you read. For each poem, tell whether the line breaks, the stanzas, or the punctuation did the most to help you understand the poem's meaning. Explain what and how that element helped you understand.

7. **Compare and Contrast Views** In "the lesson of the moth," what is the moth's attitude about the price of **beauty?** In "Identity," what is the speaker's attitude about the price of beauty? Explain whether you think their views are more similar or more different.

8. **Evaluate Free Verse** Use a chart like the one shown to list examples of rhyme, repetition, or other sound devices, such as **alliteration** (the repetition of consonant sounds at the beginning of words). What images or ideas do these devices emphasize?

| | "the lesson of the moth" | "Identity" |
|---|---|---|
| Rhyme | | |
| Repetition | | |
| Sound Devices | | |

# Extension and Challenge

9.  **SCIENCE CONNECTION** How do the qualities of real cockroaches and moths correspond to the poetic creations Don Marquis presents in "the lesson of the moth"? Research to find out about each creature's habits and life span. Display your findings in a poster, and be ready to explain how the poem does—or does not—relate to reality.

Cockroach

**RESEARCH LINKS**
For more on cockroaches and moths, visit the **Research Center** at **ClassZone.com.**

# Reading-Writing Connection

Continue to explore the meaning of "the lesson of the moth" and "Identity" by responding to these prompts. Then complete the **Grammar and Writing** exercise.

| WRITING PROMPTS | SELF-CHECK |
|---|---|
| **A. Short Response: Answer the Big Question** <br> Choose one of the "characters" from the poems— Archy, the moth, or the speaker in "Identity." Write **a paragraph** answering the question, "Does **beauty** matter?" from the point of view of this character. | ***An effective answer will . . .*** <br> • use the first person pronoun "I" <br> • express the character's personality and perspective |
| **B. Extended Response: Identify Emotions** <br> A critic once wrote that Don Marquis was "remarkable for his ability to intertwine the humorous and the melancholy [sad]." How does "the lesson of the moth" display this ability? Write a **two- or three-paragraph response.** | ***A strong response will . . .*** <br> • show an understanding of the poem's meaning <br> • cite both funny and serious lines and images |

## GRAMMAR AND WRITING

***USE COMMAS CORRECTLY*** By using commas properly, you can avoid confusing your readers. When writing a sentence that lists **items in a series,** insert a comma after every item except the last one. (A series consists of three or more items.) Also insert a comma between two or more **adjectives** of equal rank that modify the same noun.

**INDIANA STANDARDS**

**WRITING STANDARD**
**8.6.5** Use correct punctuation.

> *Original:* Both the moth in "the lesson of the moth" and the speaker in "Identity" find beauty in unusual surprising places.
>
> *Revised:* Both the moth in "the lesson of the moth" and the speaker in "Identity" find beauty in unusual, surprising places.

***PRACTICE*** Insert commas where needed in the following sentences.

1. The moth would rather take risks get injured and die young than be bored.
2. He thinks that the dangerous exciting heat of fire is beautiful.
3. I wouldn't mind being unseen shunned and alone like a weed.
4. Unlike flowers, weeds are strong free and independent.

*For more help with using commas correctly, see page R49 in the **Grammar Handbook**.*

**It's all I have to bring today—**
Poem by Emily Dickinson

**We Alone**
Poem by Alice Walker

# *Can you be* R I C H *without money?*

**INDIANA STANDARDS**

**READING STANDARDS**
**8.3.5** Identify and analyze recurring themes (such as good versus evil) that appear frequently across traditional and contemporary works.

**8.3.7** Analyze a work of literature, showing how it reflects the heritage, traditions, attitudes, and beliefs of its author.

*KEY IDEA* If you hear that people are wealthy, you probably think they have a lot of money. Perhaps you imagine that they own expensive things like jewels, antiques, and designer goods. But does **wealth** always have to refer to material objects? The poets whose works you are about to read would like us to find riches in more common places.

*QUICKWRITE* What types of non-material things do you consider part of your wealth? Family? Friends? Pets? With a small group, discuss the everyday things that can lend richness to your life.

## LITERARY ANALYSIS: RECURRING THEME

You already know that the message of a literary work is called the theme. When the same message is found in different works, it is called a **recurring theme**. The following poems were written in different centuries by poets of different cultures and backgrounds, but they express a similar idea: common things should be considered valuable. As you read, notice how each poet develops this recurring theme. Pay attention to

- the speaker's feelings and beliefs
- important statements the speaker makes
- images and details that stand out
- repeated words and phrases

## READING STRATEGY: SET A PURPOSE FOR READING

Your **purpose for reading** the two poems is to compare the way the poets communicate the recurring theme. After you've read the poems once, go back and read them again. This time, take notes in a chart like the one shown.

| Recurring Theme: *Common things should be considered valuable.* | | |
|---|---|---|
| | *"It's all I have to bring today—"* | *"We Alone"* |
| What strong feelings or beliefs does the speaker express? | | |
| Which images and details stand out? | | |
| Which words and phrases are repeated? | | |

# It's all I have to bring today—

*Emily Dickinson*

It's all I have to bring today—
This, and my heart beside—
This, and my heart, and all the fields—
And all the meadows wide—
5 Be sure you count—should I forget
Some one the sum could tell—
This, and my heart, and all the Bees
Which in the Clover dwell. **Ⓐ**

**ANALYZE VISUALS**
How might you feel if you were in the **setting** depicted in this picture?

**Ⓐ RECURRING THEME**
What images of nature do you find in the poem?

# We Alone

*Alice Walker*

We alone can devalue gold
by not caring
if it falls or rises
in the marketplace.
5 Wherever there is gold
there is a chain, you know,
and if your chain
is gold
so much the worse
10 for you. **B**

Feathers, shells
and sea-shaped stones
are all as rare.

This could be our revolution:
15 To love what is plentiful
as much as
what is scarce. **C**

**ANALYZE VISUALS**
To what objects does the
light draw attention?

**B RECURRING THEME**
How does the speaker
feel about the value
of gold?

**C RECURRING THEME**
Reread lines 14–17 and
paraphrase the speaker's
statement.

# Comprehension

1. **Recall** In "It's all I have to bring today—," what does the speaker bring?

2. **Recall** According to the speaker in "We Alone," how can people decrease the value of gold?

3. **Recall** In "We Alone," what items in nature are as rare as gold?

**INDIANA STANDARDS**

**READING STANDARD**
8.3.5 Identify and analyze recurring themes....

# Literary Analysis

4. **Visualize** What mental pictures did you create as you read "It's all I have to bring today—"? Describe how you visualized the speaker, the setting, and the situation in this poem.

5. **Interpret Poetry** In "It's all I have to bring today—," the word *this* is repeated in lines 2, 3, and 7. What do you think *this* might refer to—the speaker, the poem, or something else? Support your ideas.

6. **Make Inferences** Do you think the speaker in "It's all I have to bring today—" feels **wealthy?** Explain your answer.

7. **Analyze Symbol** A symbol is a person, place, or thing that stands for something beyond itself. In "We Alone," what ideas does the chain represent? Support your response.

8. **Draw Conclusions** Reread the last stanza of "We Alone." What are some "plentiful" things that we should love as much as or more than the scarce things?

9. **Evaluate Tone** The tone of a poem is the poet's or speaker's attitude toward the subject. Do the two poems have the same tone or different tones? Support your answer with details from each poem.

# Comparing Recurring Theme

Now that you've read both poems, finish filling in your chart. Then start thinking about the similarities and differences in how the poems express the theme.

| Recurring Theme: Common things in life should be considered valuable. | | |
|---|---|---|
| | "It's all I have to bring today—" | "We Alone" |
| What strong feelings or beliefs does the speaker express? | She offers only her heart and nature's beauty. | The worth of gold is determined by people. |
| Which images and details stand out? | | |
| Which words and phrases are repeated? | | |

# Writing for Assessment

## 1. READ THE PROMPT

You've just read two poems that express similar ideas about wealth. In writing assessments, you will often be asked to compare literary selections that differ in some ways but share a recurring theme.

**PROMPT**

"It's all I have to bring today—" and "We Alone" express this theme: common things should be considered valuable. In four or five paragraphs, compare and contrast how this theme is expressed in the poems. Focus on the speakers, images, and use of repetition in each poem. Use details from the poems to support each point.

◀ **STRATEGIES IN ACTION**

1. I should make sure I understand how each poem expresses the **message**.

2. I need to identify the **similarities and differences** in how the poems develop the message.

3. I must support my ideas using **quotations** from the poems.

## 2. PLAN YOUR WRITING

Review your chart, thinking about the way each poem conveys the theme. Make sure you can cite words and phrases to support your notes. Then think about how you will set up your response.

- Option A: In one paragraph, describe how the recurring theme is developed in the first poem; in the next paragraph, describe how this theme is developed in the second poem; in a third paragraph, discuss similarities and differences in how the poems develop the theme.

- Option B: In one paragraph, compare how the speakers contribute to the theme; in a second paragraph, compare the use of imagery; in a third paragraph, compare the use of repetition.

Now, outline your essay. Then write a thesis statement that describes your main idea.

I. Introduce poems and thesis statement
II. How Emily Dickinson develops theme
III. How Alice Walker develops theme
IV. Compare and contrast elements
V. Conclusion

## 3. DRAFT YOUR RESPONSE

**Introduction** Include the titles and the poets' names. State the theme and your thesis.
**Body** Using your outline and the details in your chart, describe how each poem develops the recurring theme. Include details from the poems to support your ideas.
**Conclusion** End your essay by restating the recurring theme and your thesis. Include a final thought about why this theme is important.
**Revision** Make sure the poem details you cite truly support your ideas. Gather additional support from the poems if necessary.

# Speech to the Young
# Speech to the Progress-Toward

Poem by Gwendolyn Brooks

# Mother to Son

Poem by Langston Hughes

# *What is good* ADVICE?

**INDIANA STANDARDS**

**READING STANDARDS**
**8.3.1** Determine and articulate the relationship between the purposes and characteristics of different forms of poetry ....

**8.3.6** Identify significant literary devices, such as metaphor, symbolism, dialect or quotations, and irony, which define a writer's style and use those elements to interpret the work.

*KEY IDEA* Suggestions about how to improve your grades or how to approach the new guy at school can be welcome, but how do you know if it's good **advice?** Sometimes it depends on who gives it. Is it someone who has been there and learned from his or her own experience? Is it someone who cares about you or has a stake in the outcome? In the two poems you are about to read, the speakers share what they have learned with a younger generation.

*DISCUSS* Imagine you need to bring up your grade in science class. In a small group, brainstorm a list of three people you would ask for advice on how to improve your study habits and grade and tell why you consider these people a good source for advice.

( 38 ) ADVICE

## stella says....

Dear Stella,
My best friend isn't speaking to me anymore, and I don't know why. We've been friends since kindergarten, but lately, she ignores me and spends all her time with these other girls who are more popular than me. I really want to be friends with her again, but I don't know how to get her to like me. What should I do?
—Confused, 14

Dear Confused,
That's a tough question! You have a right to be confused. Sometimes friendships fall apart, and it's hard to tell why. But don't bl...
like your frie...

## ● POETIC FORM: LYRIC POETRY

If you're a poet and you want to share your deepest feelings on a topic such as love, death, or the power of nature, what kind of poem would you write? A good choice would be a **lyric poem.** Lyric poems

- are short
- have a single speaker who expresses personal thoughts and feelings
- focus on a single, strong idea

## ● LITERARY ANALYSIS: SOUND DEVICES

Writers use sound devices to create a musical quality and to call attention to certain words. **Alliteration** is the repetition of consonant sounds at the beginning of words. Notice the repeated *w* sound in the following example:

*When the wind whispers*

Another sound device based on repetition is **assonance**, in which a vowel sound is repeated in two or more syllables.

*Poetry is old, ancient, goes back far.*

As you read the following poems, notice the alliteration and assonance and think about the effect of these sound devices.

## ● READING SKILL: MAKE INFERENCES

As you try to understand the speakers and the advice they give in these two poems, look for clues that hint at their experiences, attitudes, and personality. Combine these clues with your own knowledge or experience to **make inferences,** logical guesses about what the poet doesn't state directly. Use inference equations like the one shown to record your inferences about the speakers.

| The title of the poem is "Speech to the Young." | + | Older people like to give advice. | = | Speaker is an older person. |

# Author Online

**Gwendolyn Brooks: Young Talent** As a budding young poet, Gwendolyn Brooks went to hear Langston Hughes give a speech at her church. Brooks's mother insisted that she show some of her work to Hughes. He read her poems on the spot and told her she had talent. "That did mean a lot to a sixteen-year-old girl," Brooks later said. Brooks went on to achieve great fame as a poet. As Poet Laureate of Illinois, she used her own money to fund literary awards for young writers.

**Gwendolyn Brooks**
**1917–2000**

**Langston Hughes: World Traveler** Langston Hughes was voted "class poet" at his high school in Cleveland, Ohio. After graduation, Hughes visited his father, who was living in Mexico. During the trip, Hughes wrote "The Negro Speaks of Rivers." It remains one of his best-known works. Hughes continued to see the world, traveling extensively in Africa and Europe. The poetry he sent home helped build his literary reputation. Hughes described the people he wrote about as "beaten and baffled, but determined not to be wholly beaten." Some African-American critics disapproved of his choice of subject matter, but Hughes felt that "the masses of our people had as much in their lives to put into books as did those more fortunate ones."

**Langston Hughes**
**1902–1967**

> **MORE ABOUT THE AUTHOR**
> For more on these poets, visit the **Literature Center** at ClassZone.com.

# Speech to the Young Speech to the Progress-Toward

## (Among them Nora and Henry III)

*Gwendolyn Brooks*

Say to them,
say to the down-keepers,
the sun-slappers,
the self-soilers,
5 the harmony-hushers,
"Even if you are not ready for day
it cannot always be night."
You will be right.
For that is the hard home-run. **A**

10 Live not for battles won.
Live not for the-end-of-the-song.
Live in the along. **B**

**ANALYZE VISUALS**
What can you **infer** about the relationship between the girl and the woman in the picture?

**A** **SOUND DEVICES**
How many examples of **alliteration** can you find in the first stanza?

**B** **MAKE INFERENCES**
What attitude does the speaker express in lines 10–12?

*New Dreams* (2002), Ernest Crichlow. Lithograph, 24¾″ × 16¾″. Photo by Maureen Turci, Mojo Portfolio. Courtesy of the Estate of Ernest Crichlow.

# Mother to Son

*Langston Hughes*

*Lady,* Ernest Crichlow. Etching, 22″ × 18″.
Courtesy of the Estate of Ernest Crichlow.

Well, son, I'll tell you:
Life for me ain't been no crystal stair.
It's had tacks in it,
And splinters,
5 And boards torn up,
And places with no carpet on the floor—
Bare.
But all the time
I'se been a-climbin' on,
10 And reachin' landin's,
And turnin' corners,
And sometimes goin' in the dark
Where there ain't been no light.
So boy, don't you turn back. **C**
15 Don't you set down on the steps
'Cause you finds it's kinder hard.
Don't you fall now—
For I'se still goin', honey,
I'se still climbin',
20 And life for me ain't been no crystal stair. **D**

**ANALYZE VISUALS**
What personality **traits** would you expect the woman in the painting to have?

**C SOUND DEVICES**
Notice the **assonance** created by the use of the long *o* sound in lines 12–14. What words contain this sound?

**D LYRIC POETRY**
What is the main idea the speaker is expressing about her life?

## Comprehension

1. **Recall** In "Speech to the Young," what does the speaker tell the young to say?

2. **Recall** What two things does the speaker in "Speech to the Young" say we should *not* live for?

3. **Represent** Create a sketch of the stairway described by the speaker in "Mother to Son."

## Literary Analysis

4. **Interpret Meaning** What does the speaker in "Speech to the Young" mean by "Even if you are not ready for the day/it cannot always be night"?

5. **Examine Dialect** In "Mother to Son," words such as *ain't* and *kinder* are examples of **dialect,** the particular way language is used in a certain place or by a certain group of people. What does Hughes's use of dialect help you to understand about the speaker?

6. **Identify Figurative Language** What **metaphor** is used throughout "Mother to Son"? What does it tell you about the mother's life and how she has responded to it?

7. **Make Inferences About the Speakers** In your own words, describe how you picture the speaker in each poem. Use the inference equations you made as you read to help you.

8. **Analyze Sound Devices** For each poem, use a chart like the one shown to record the instances of **alliteration** and **assonance.** Which poem makes greater use of these sound devices?

| "Speech to the Young" | |
|---|---|
| *Alliteration* | *Assonance* |
| say/sun-slappers/self-soilers | |

9. **Evaluate Lyric Poetry** Which lyric poem gives you a more hopeful feeling? Explain your choice.

## Extension and Challenge

10. **Readers' Circle** In a group, discuss the **advice** each speaker gives. Which speaker's advice do you think is best? Why?

**INDIANA STANDARDS**

**READING STANDARD**
**8.3.6** Identify significant literary devices . . . .

# On the Grasshopper and Cricket
Poem by John Keats

# Ode on Solitude
Poem by Alexander Pope

# When does **FORM** *matter?*

**INDIANA STANDARDS**

**READING STANDARD**
**8.3.1** Determine and articulate the relationship between the purposes and characteristics of different forms of poetry (including ballads, lyrics, couplets, epics, elegies, odes, and sonnets).

**KEY IDEA** "Bend from the waist." "Lift your chin." "Hold your arms like this." Learning almost any new skill—swinging a bat or a tennis racket, swimming and diving, cartwheeling or dancing—involves learning **form.** In the poems you are about to read, two of the most well-respected poets in the English language use traditional poetic forms to create meaning.

**LIST IT** Make a list of activities that involve **form.** Rank them in order of which requires the most attention to form.

1. Ballroom dancing
2. Baseball
3. Writing
4. Painting

## POETIC FORM: TRADITIONAL FORMS

The poems that follow are examples of two traditional **forms,** or types. Both are **lyric poems,** or short poems in which a speaker expresses personal thoughts and feelings.

- "On the Grasshopper and Cricket" is a **sonnet**—a lyric poem with 14 lines and regular patterns of rhyme and rhythm.
- "Ode on Solitude" is an **ode,** a type of lyric poem that deals with an important topic.

## LITERARY ANALYSIS: RHYME SCHEME

**Rhyme scheme** is the pattern of rhyming words at the ends of a poem's lines. You can use letters to identify rhyme scheme. Write the letter *a* next to the first rhyming word and all words that rhyme with it. Then write the letter *b* next to the second rhyming word and the words that rhyme with it, and so on.

| | |
|---|---|
| *Happy the man, whose wish and <u>care</u>* | *a* |
| *A few paternal acres <u>bound</u>,* | *b* |
| *Content to breathe his native <u>air</u>* | *a* |
| *In his own <u>ground</u>.* | *b* |

The letter *a* identifies all the words at the ends of lines that rhyme with *care.* The letter *b* indicates all the words that rhyme with *bound.* After your first reading of each of these poems, read it a second time and note the rhyme scheme in a chart.

| "On the Grasshopper and Cricket" | |
|---|---|
| Line | Rhyme Scheme |
| 1 | a |
| 2 | |

## READING STRATEGY: PARAPHRASE

Since these poems use language in a way that is seldom heard today, they can be challenging to read. One good way to make sure you understand what you read is to **paraphrase** it, or restate it in your own words.

As you read the poems, look for punctuation marks that show where a thought begins and ends. Then check your understanding by paraphrasing the idea. If you still find a thought difficult to "translate," reread the lines slowly and use the context and a dictionary to decode important words that you don't know.

# Author Online

**John Keats: A Short, Creative Life** John Keats lost both his parents when he was a child. His guardian wanted him to be a doctor, but when Keats went to London to study, he met a group of young writers and abandoned a medical career to pursue his poetry. He was

**John Keats**
**1795–1821**

remarkably creative, writing four of his most famous poems in a single month. In 1818, Keats's brother died of tuberculosis. The following year, Keats began to show the same symptoms and soon became too ill to write. He died at the age of 25. In his three-year writing career, Keats created a body of work whose quality is greater than that of Shakespeare or Wordsworth at the same age.

**Alexander Pope: Living on Poetry** Alexander Pope suffered from severe headaches, and later in life, asthma. In addition, he was Catholic, which at that time meant that he could not attend universities. None of this stopped him from his studies. Pope mostly educated

**Alexander Pope**
**1688–1744**

himself, learning Latin and Greek. His translations were so successful they made Pope the first English poet able to live off of his work. He is famous for his poetry, essays, and satires. Lines from his essays—such as "To err is human, to forgive, divine"—have become part of the English language.

 **MORE ABOUT THE AUTHOR**
For more on these poets, visit the **Literature Center** at ClassZone.com.

# ON THE
# Grasshopper
## AND Cricket

### John Keats

The poetry of earth is never dead:
   When all the birds are faint with the hot sun,
   And hide in cooling trees, a voice will run
From hedge to hedge about the new-mown mead; **Ⓐ**
5 That is the Grasshopper's—he takes the lead
   In summer luxury,—he has never done
   With his delights; for when tired out with fun
He rests at ease beneath some pleasant weed.
The poetry of earth is ceasing never:
10    On a lone winter evening, when the frost
      Has wrought[1] a silence, from the stove there shrills
The Cricket's song, in warmth increasing ever,
   And seems to one in drowsiness half lost,
      The Grasshopper's among some grassy hills. **Ⓑ**

**Ⓐ RHYME SCHEME**
How would you describe the rhyme scheme in lines 1–4? Note that *mead* is a shortened form of *meadow,* so is pronounced mĕd.

**Ⓑ PARAPHRASE**
How would you paraphrase lines 10–12? Now read lines 13–14. What does the cricket's song remind the speaker of?

**ANALYZE VISUALS**
What **mood** does this image suggest?

---

1. **wrought** (rôt): made; produced.

# Ode
## ON Solitude
### Alexander Pope

*Barn at Cove, Oregon* (2005),  Gary Ernest Smith. Oil on canvas, 30″ × 40″.

Happy the man whose wish and care
   A few paternal[1] acres bound,
Content to breathe his native[2] air,
      In his own ground.

5 Whose herds with milk, whose fields with bread,
   Whose flocks supply him with attire,
Whose trees in summer yield him shade,
      In winter fire. **C**

Blest, who can unconcern'dly find
10   Hours, days, and years slide soft away,
In health of body, peace of mind,
      Quiet by day,

Sound sleep by night; study and ease,
   Together mixt; sweet recreation;
15 And Innocence, which most does please
      With meditation.

Thus let me live, unseen, unknown,
   Thus unlamented[3] let me die,
Steal from the world, and not a stone
20      Tell where I lie. **D**

**C PARAPHRASE**
In the second stanza, what do the speaker's herds, fields, flocks, and trees provide for him? State the answer in your own words.

**D TRADITIONAL FORMS**
What words and phrases in the last stanza help develop the theme of solitude?

---

1. **paternal** (pə-tûr′nəl): received from a father.
2. **native:** being one's own because of one's birthplace.
3. **unlamented** (ŭn-lə-mĕnt′ĕd): not missed; not mourned for.

## Comprehension

**INDIANA STANDARDS**

**READING STANDARD**
**8.3.1** Determine and articulate the...characteristics of different forms of poetry....

1. **Recall** In "On the Grasshopper and Cricket," which insect represents summer? Which insect represents winter?

2. **Recall** Name three of the things that, according to the speaker in "Ode on Solitude," make man happy.

## Literary Analysis

3. **Examine Imagery** You remember that imagery consists of words or phrases that appeal to the senses. Use a web to record imagery from "On the Grasshopper and Cricket." To which senses does the poet appeal?

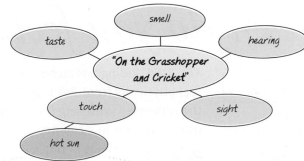

4. **Identify Soft Rhyme** Sometimes a poet cannot find words that fit a poem's rhyme scheme *and* express the correct meaning. In such a case, a poet might use a **soft rhyme,** words that share one or more sounds but do not actually rhyme. What example of a soft rhyme do you find in "Ode on Solitude"?

5. **Paraphrase Poetry** Choose two especially challenging lines from each poem and "translate" them in your own words. What does each paraphase help you to understand about the poem?

6. **Understand Traditional Forms** According to the bulleted definitions on page 619, what characteristics of its form does each poem show?

7. **Compare and Contrast Rhyme Scheme** Look back at the chart you made for each poem's rhyme scheme. Which poem's rhyme scheme is more complex? Explain.

## Extension and Challenge

8. **Readers' Circle** Alexander Pope wrote the first draft of "Ode on Solitude" around 1700. How do you think the speaker's idea of happiness might be different if the poem were rewritten today? Explain.

## One More Round
Poem by Maya Angelou

## Not My Bones
Poem by Marilyn Nelson

# *When do you feel most* FREE?

**INDIANA STANDARDS**

**READING STANDARDS**
**8.3.1** Determine and articulate the relationship between the purposes and characteristics of different forms of poetry . . . .

**8.3.6** Identify significant literary devices, such as metaphor, symbolism, dialect or quotations, and irony, which define a writer's style and use those elements to interpret the work.

**KEY IDEA** Riding a skateboard or a bike or a horse makes many people feel physically **free.** Reading a book can liberate the mind to explore the universe. Watching fireworks on the Fourth of July might remind us that we live in a country of many freedoms. The following poems convey the feelings of those who have found freedom at long last.

**QUICKWRITE** When have you felt most free? Think of two or three times and either describe them or sketch them in your journal. Try to explain why these situations gave you a sense of freedom.

## ● LITERARY ANALYIS: WORD CHOICE

To express complicated thoughts and feelings in just a few lines, poets must make every word count. So a poet's **word choice,** or use of words, is particularly important.

For example, in "Not My Bones," Marilyn Nelson writes "The soul runs free. It roams the night sky's mute geometry." Why did she choose these words when she could have written, "The soul flies among the stars in the sky"? Perhaps because the words *mute geometry* suggests a quiet order to the universe.

As you read each poem, look for similarly interesting, unusual, or striking words, and consider why the poet might have chosen them. Record your thoughts on a chart like the one shown.

| Striking Words | Why Poet Might Have Chosen |
|----------------|----------------------------|
| mute geometry | to suggest a quiet, planned universe |

## ● READING STRATEGY: READ POETRY

One way poems can make an impact is through their use of **repetition,** a technique in which a sound, word, phrase, or line is repeated to emphasize an important idea or to create a pattern throughout the poem. Repetition also helps to reinforce meaning and to create an appealing rhythm. For example, look at the first lines of "Not My Bones":

*I was not this body,*
*I was not these bones.*

By repeating *I was not,* the speaker emphasizes her strong feelings. Try reading the poems aloud to get a better sense of how repetition helps create meaning and rhythm.

## ▲ VOCABULARY IN CONTEXT

The following words help poet Marilyn Nelson explain how an enslaved person can find freedom. To see how many you know, use the words to complete the sentences.

| WORD LIST | converge | cosmic | essential | incarnation |
|-----------|----------|--------|-----------|-------------|

1. Abolitionist groups ____ to fight slavery.
2. Some believe that each soul has more than one ____.
3. Freedom of speech is ____ to a democracy.
4. Astronomers' work is to understand the ____ order.

# Author Online

**Maya Angelou: Silence to Star**
At the age of seven, Maya Angelou went through a difficult time and stopped talking for five years. A family friend not only taught her the importance of the spoken word but also encouraged her to write. Since then, Angelou has written poetry, autobiographies, plays, screenplays, children's books, and even a cookbook. As her fame has grown, she has become an important public figure, mixing with presidents, television and movie stars, and other internationally recognized artists.

Maya Angelou
born 1928

**Marilyn Nelson: Early Promise**
Marilyn Nelson's sixth-grade teacher predicted that Nelson would become a famous writer. The teacher was right. Nelson's books of poetry have won many awards, including the Newbery Honor. The poem "Not My Bones" comes from the book *Fortune's Bones: The Manumission Requiem,* which Nelson wrote to honor the memory of Fortune, an enslaved person who died in 1798. Nelson was commissioned to write the book by the Mattatuck Museum in Connecticut after the descendents of Fortune's owners donated his skeleton to the institution. Nelson has said she is motivated by the desire "to talk about finding pride . . . in people who triumphed over slavery."

Marilyn Nelson
born 1946

**MORE ABOUT THE AUTHOR**
For more on these poets, visit the **Literature Center** at ClassZone.com.

# ONE MORE ROUND

## Maya Angelou

There ain't no pay beneath the sun
As sweet as rest when a job's well done.
I was born to work up to my grave
But I was not born
5 To be a slave.

One more round
And let's heave it down,
One more round
And let's heave it down.

10 Papa drove steel and Momma stood guard,
I never heard them holler 'cause the work was hard.
They were born to work up to their graves
But they were not born
To be worked-out slaves. Ⓐ

15 One more round
And let's heave it down,
One more round
And let's heave it down.

Brothers and sisters know the daily grind,[1]
20 It was not labor made them lose their minds.
They were born to work up to their graves
But they were not born
To be worked-out slaves.

Ⓐ **WORD CHOICE**
Reread the third stanza.
What words stand out
to you? Note what these
words and phrases make
you think of and then add
them to your chart.

---

1. **grind:** a labor-intensive routine.

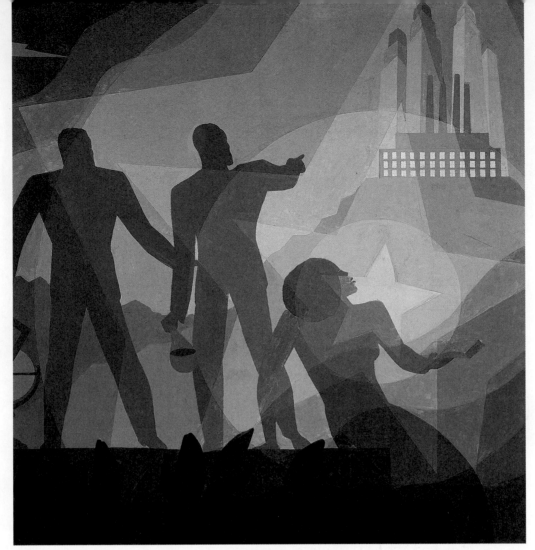

*Aspiration* (1936), Aaron Douglas. Oil on canvas, 60″ × 60″.
© Fine Arts Museums of San Francisco.

One more round
25 And let's heave it down,
One more round
And let's heave it down.

And now I'll tell you my Golden Rule,[2]
I was born to work but I ain't no mule.
30 I was born to work up to my grave
But I was not born
To be a slave.

One more round
And let's heave it down,
35 One more round
And let's heave it down. **B**

**ANALYZE VISUALS**
What **symbols** do you
see in this painting?

**B** **READ POETRY**
This poem is modeled
after songs workers sang
as they labored. What
stanzas remind you of
a song?

2. **Golden Rule:** the biblical teaching that one should behave towards
others as one wants others to behave towards oneself.

# Not My Bones

## Marilyn Nelson

*Fortune* (2001), William B. Westwood.
© William B. Westwood.

I was not this body,
I was not these bones.
This skeleton was just my
temporary home.
5 Elementary molecules[1] **converged** for a breath,
then danced on beyond my individual death.
And I am not my body,
I am not my body.

We are brief **incarnations,**
10 we are clouds in clothes.
We are water respirators,
we are how earth knows.
I bore[2] light passed on from an original flame;
while it was in my hands it was called by my name.
15 But I am not my body,
I am not my body. **C**

---

1. **elementary molecules:** the smallest, most basic particles of
   substances.
2. **bore:** carried; transported.

**converge** (kən-vûrj′) *v.*
to come together in one
place; meet

**incarnation**
(ĭn′-kär-nā′-shən) *n.* a
bodily form

**C** **WORD CHOICE**
Reread lines 3–6. What
are they saying about
our physical bodies?
What words in lines 9–14
suggest the same ideas?
Add these to your chart.

You can own a man's body,
but you can't own his mind.
That's like making a bridle
20 to ride on the wind.
I will tell you one thing, and I'll tell you true:
Life's the best thing that can happen to you.
But you are not your body,
you are not your body.

25 You can own someone's body,
but the soul runs free.
It roams the night sky's
mute geometry.
You can murder hope, you can pound faith flat,
30 but like weeds and wildflowers, they grow right back.
For you are not your body,
you are not your body.

You are not your body,
you are not your bones.
35 What's **essential** about you
is what can't be owned.
What's essential in you is your longing to raise
your itty-bitty voice in the **cosmic** praise.
For you are not your body,
40 you are not your body.

Well, I woke up this morning just so glad to be free,
glad to be free, glad to be free.
I woke up this morning in restful peace.
For I am not my body,
45 I am not my bones.
I am not my body,
glory hallelujah, not my bones,
I am not my bones. **D**

**essential** (ĭ-sĕn′shəl) *adj.*
having the qualities that
give something its true
identity

**cosmic** (kŏz′mik) *adj.*
universal; infinitely large

**D READ POETRY**
What lines in this poem
have been most often
repeated?

## Comprehension

1  **Recall**  In "One More Round," what is the speaker's "Golden Rule"?

2. **Recall**  According to the speaker in "Not My Bones," what happens when hope is murdered and faith is pounded flat?

**INDIANA STANDARDS**

**READING STANDARD**
**8.3.6** Identify significant literary devices....

## Literary Analysis

3. **Interpret Poetry**  Using a word web like the one shown, note important phrases about work associated with the people mentioned in "One More Round." What distinction does the speaker draw between work and slavery?

parents

speaker

"I ain't no mule."

"drove steel"

Work

siblings

4. **Make Inferences**  Why does the speaker in "Not My Bones" feel that a person's mind and soul cannot be owned?

5. **Analyze Repetition**  For each poem, identify the two phrases or sections that are repeated most frequently.  How do these repeated words contribute to the poems' meaning?

6. **Compare Word Choice**  Review the charts you made as you read the poems. Make a generalization, or overall statement, about each poet's word choice. What is different about the words chosen for each poem?

7. **Evaluate Theme**  Which poem's theme do you think conveys a greater sense of **freedom?**  Support your response with details from the poem.

8. **Draw Conclusions**  Do you think the people mentioned in "One More Round" would agree with the speaker of "Not My Bones" that "you are not your body"?  Explain why or why not.

## Extension and Challenge

9. **Creative Project: Music**  Work with a small group to create a song from "One More Round." Practice reading the poem aloud, using desks, pencils, or other classroom materials as drums to keep the rhythm.  Perform your piece for the class.

# Vocabulary in Context

## VOCABULARY PRACTICE

Choose the letter of the word that means the same, or nearly the same, as the boldfaced word.

1. two streams **converge:** (a) rise, (b) separate, (c) meet, (d) flow
2. **cosmic** ideas: (a) fascinating, (b) universal, (c) mistaken, (d) weird
3. **essential** elements: (a) dissimilar, (b) toxic, (c) similar, (d) basic
4. a brief **incarnation:** (a) meeting, (b) lifetime, (c) quarrel, (d) vacation

**INDIANA STANDARDS**

**READING STANDARD**
**8.1.3** Verify the meaning of a word in its context . . . .

## VOCABULARY IN WRITING

Do you think Marilyn Nelson is right when she says that people are not their bodies? Write a paragraph explaining your opinion. Use at least two vocabulary words in your paragraph. You could start this way.

> **EXAMPLE SENTENCE**
>
> I agree with Nelson when she says that each person's soul is an **essential** part of him or her.

## VOCABULARY STRATEGY: THE LATIN ROOT *carn*

The vocabulary word *incarnation* comes from the Latin root *carn*, which means "flesh." *Carn* (combined with other word parts) appears in a number of English words. To determine the meaning of a word that contains this root, use context clues—the words and sentences around the word—as well as your knowledge of the root's meaning.

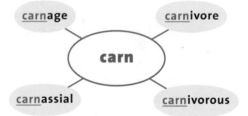

**PRACTICE** Choose the word from the web that best completes each sentence. Be ready to explain how the root *carn* helps to give each word its meaning.

1. Tyrannosaurus Rex was a huge _____ that devoured other dinosaurs.
2. The wolf is a _____ mammal that lives and hunts in a pack.
3. Drunk drivers cause _____ on U.S. highways.
4. Molars are _____ teeth, because they are adapted for chewing meat.

**VOCABULARY PRACTICE**
For more practice, go to the **Vocabulary Center** at **ClassZone.com.**

# Fortune's Bones
Book Excerpt

## What's the Connection?

The poem "Not My Bones" was inspired by the real life of Fortune, an enslaved person. Now learn more about this man and about what happened to his bones after he died.

## Skill Focus: Outline

When you read nonfiction, do you find it hard to remember the main facts and ideas? Taking notes in the form of an outline can help you.

An **outline** is a way of summarizing the main topics, subtopics, and details in a text. If the text has headings and subheadings, those will probably tell you the main topics and subtopics to cover. If, as in "Fortune's Bones," there are no headings, see if you can use the topic sentence of each paragraph to identify the main topics. Next, follow these steps:

- Write the main topics as short phrases or sentences beside Roman numerals, leaving plenty of space below each Roman numeral entry.
- Underneath each Roman numeral entry, jot down related subtopics, using capital letters to order them.
- Continue adding information according to the level of its importance. Use Arabic numbers for entries below the capital letters. If necessary, use lowercased letters for details beneath the numbers.

As you read the following book excerpt, complete the outline started here.

Use with "Not My Bones,"
page 628.

**INDIANA
STANDARDS**

**READING STANDARDS**
**8.2.5** Use information from a variety of consumer and public documents to explain a situation or decision and to solve a problem.

**8.2.7** Analyze the structure, format, and purpose of informational materials (such as textbooks, newspapers, instructional or technical manuals, and public documents).

---

### Fortune

I. Fortune before he was bones in a Connecticut museum
   A. Status: A husband, father, baptized Christian, and a slave
      1. Husband to Dinah
      2. Father of two sons and two daughters
         a.
         b.
      3.
      4.
   B. Circumstances: When and where he lived and what he did
      1.
      2.
      3.
   C. Death: Fortune died in 1798 at about the age of 60.
II. Fortune's bones
   A. Dr. Porter preserved Fortune's bones to study the human skeleton.
   B.

# from Fortune's Bones

Notes by Pamela Espeland

**FOCUS ON FORM**

You're about to read the notes that accompany "Not My Bones" and Marilyn Nelson's other poems about Fortune. These **notes** provide facts and additional information about Fortune's life and his bones.

A sculptor used information about Fortune's bones to create this reconstruction of Fortune's face.

Before Fortune was bones in a Connecticut museum, he was a husband, a father, a baptized Christian, and a slave.

His wife's name was Dinah. His sons were Africa and Jacob. His daughters were Mira and Roxa. He was baptized in an Episcopal church, which did not make him free. His master was Dr. Preserved Porter, a physician who specialized in setting broken bones. **A**

They lived in Waterbury, Connecticut, in the late 1700s. Dr. Porter had a 75-acre farm, which Fortune probably ran. He planted and harvested corn, rye, potatoes, onions, apples, buckwheat, oats, and hay. He cared for the cattle
10  and hogs.

Unlike many slaves, who owned little or nothing and were often separated from their families, Fortune owned a small house near Dr. Porter's home. He and Dinah and their children lived together. **B**

When Dr. Porter died in 1803, he left an estate that was worth about $7,000— a lot of money for the time. The estate included Fortune's widow, Dinah, and their son Jacob. Fortune had died in 1798.

According to Connecticut's Act of Gradual Emancipation, children born to enslaved parents after March 1, 1784, were to be freed when they reached age 21. Jacob was 18. By law, he could be enslaved for another three years.
20  In Dr. Porter's will, he left Dinah to his wife, Lydia. He gave Jacob to his daughter Hannah. **C**

No one knows what happened to Africa, Mira, and Roxa.

**A OUTLINE**
What information do you learn about Fortune's sons? About his daughters? Add these details next to lowercase letters *a* and *b* on your outline.

**B OUTLINE**
When and where did Fortune live? Under subtopic *B*, note this information next to numbers *1* and *2*. Next to number *3*, include information about the work Fortune did.

**C NOTES**
What facts about slavery in the northern United States do you learn from these notes?

Most slaves who died in Waterbury in the 1700s were buried in one of the town's cemeteries. When Fortune died, he wasn't buried. Instead, Dr. Porter preserved Fortune's skeleton to further the study of human anatomy.

Dr. Porter had been a bonesetter for many years, but he'd never had a skeleton to study. He had two sons who were also doctors. They could learn from the skeleton, too.

Fortune was about 60 at the time of his death and, in spite of his injuries, 30 in relatively good health. His skeleton was sturdy and complete. . . .

Four more generations of Porters became physicians, and the skeleton stayed in the family. Porter children, grandchildren, and great-grandchildren used it to learn the names of the bones. This was their earliest medical training.

Sally Porter Law McGlannan, the last Porter doctor, remembered playing with the skeleton as a young girl. . . . Another family member, Leander Law, once brought part of Fortune's skeleton to a college physiology class.

At some point—no one knows exactly when—"Larry" was written on the skull. Fortune's name was forgotten for nearly a century. **D**

Over the years, the skeleton was lost and found. It was boarded up in an attic, 40 then discovered by a crew of workers hired to renovate an old building.

In 1933, Sally Porter Law McGlannan gave the bones to the Mattatuck Museum. The museum sent the bones to Europe to be assembled for display. The skeleton hung in a glass case in the museum for decades, fascinating adults and frightening children.

Many stories were invented about the skeleton. Some said that "Larry" was a Revolutionary War hero—maybe even George Washington. Some said he fell to his death. Some said he drowned. Some said he was killed trying to escape. Some thought he had been hanged.

One Waterbury resident remembers, "Larry was the thing to see when you 50 go to the museum. I don't think anybody ever envisioned that this was truly a human being." **E**

In 1970, the skeleton, still called "Larry," was taken out of its case and put into storage. Times had changed. The museum now believed that displaying the skeleton was disrespectful. It wasn't just a bunch of bones. It was the remains of someone's son, maybe someone's father.

The skeleton rested for more than 25 years. Then, in the 1990s, historians searched local records and found a slave named Fortune. Archaeologists and anthropologists studied the bones, which started giving up their secrets. The bones told how Fortune labored, suffered, and died: A quick, sudden injury, 60 like whiplash, may have snapped a vertebra in his neck. He did not drown or fall from a cliff. He was not hanged. **F**

But he was free.

---

**D OUTLINE**
Reread lines 26–38. What else happened to the skeleton while it stayed in the family? Add these details under section *II*, letter *A*. Number each detail you include.

**E OUTLINE**
Reread lines 39–51, and note the topic sentences. Turn the topic sentences of the first two paragraphs in this section into capital-lettered entries *B* and *C*. Then, beneath *C*, add details about the skeleton's "life" as museum property.

**F OUTLINE**
When did scholars learn more about the bones? Include this information on your outline next to the letter *D*. Underneath, number the details about what scholars learned.

# Comprehension

1. **Recall** Where did Fortune live?

2. **Recall** Who gave Fortune's skeleton to the museum? What was her relationship to Fortune?

3. **Clarify** How did the museum learn how Fortune died?

# Critical Analysis

4. **Refine Your Outline** Review your outline. If it's missing any important topics or details, add them now. What could someone learn about Fortune just from reading the capital letter headings of your outline?

5. **Evaluate Notes** Reread "Not My Bones" on pages 628–629. Compare the understanding of Fortune that you get from this poem with the understanding of him that you get from the accompanying notes. What might be the strengths of a book that combines poems with historical notes?

**INDIANA STANDARDS**

**READING STANDARDS**
**8.2.5** Use information from a variety of consumer and public documents to explain a situation or decision and to solve a problem.

**8.2.7** Analyze the structure, format, and purpose of informational materials (such as textbooks, newspapers, instructional or technical manuals, and public documents).

# Read for Information: Support an Opinion

### WRITING PROMPT

In the afterword of *Fortune's Bones,* Marie Galbraith, the executive director of the Mattatuck Museum, writes:

> "When the Fortune Project began, the committee members felt strongly that Fortune's remains should be buried. Now they are divided on this issue, as are visitors to the museum's exhibit 'Fortune's Story/Larry's Legacy.'"

What do you think should be done with Fortune's bones? Should the skeleton be buried, or should it be kept on display? Support your opinion with reasons and evidence, including details from the poem and the notes.

To answer this prompt, first decide what your opinion is. Then follow these steps:

1. Briefly state your opinion of what should be done with Fortune's skeleton.

2. Jot down the reasons for your opinion and gather evidence to support those reasons, including information from the poem and notes.

3. In a paragraph, state your opinion in a sentence or two. Then support it with clearly stated reasons and evidence.

# Boots of Spanish Leather
Poem by Bob Dylan

# *from* The Song of Hiawatha
Poem by Henry Wadsworth Longfellow

# *When do poems tell a* STORY?

**KEY IDEA** When you hear the word **story,** you might think of plots that unfold in short stories, novels, or movies. But some of the first stories that people told to each other took on the form of poetry. Ever since, some writers have used the stanzas, rhythm, and rhyme of poetry to tell about characters, setting, and conflict. The following two works are examples of stories told in poetic form.

**DISCUSS** Think of a poem or song you know that tells a story. For your group, summarize the story in your own words. How many of your classmates can guess the original work?

## ● POETIC FORM: NARRATIVE POETRY

The two poems that follow are examples of specific types of **narrative poetry,** or poetry that tells a story.

- "Boots of Spanish Leather" is a **ballad,** a narrative poem that is meant to be sung and focuses on a single tragic event.
- *The Song of Hiawatha* is an **epic,** a long narrative poem about the life of a hero whose actions reflect the values of the group he or she belongs to.

Like all narrative poems, ballads and epics contain characters, plot, and setting.

## ● LITERARY ANALYSIS: RHYTHM AND METER

One way that poetry differs from prose is the extent to which it features rhythm and meter. **Rhythm** is the pattern of stressed (ˊ) and unstressed (˘) syllables in a line of poetry. Narrative poetry often has a regular, repeated pattern of rhythm, which is called **meter.**

   Rhythm and meter create the overall tempo or pace of a poem. They give poems their musical sound and help poets to emphasize certain words or phrases. For example, notice the soothing, regular rhythm in the following lines from *The Song of Hiawatha:*

Bý thĕ shóres ŏf Gítchĕ Gúmĕe,

Bý thĕ shíning Bíg-Sĕa-Wáter,

As you read the poems, listen for the way rhythm and meter create emphasis and add a musical effect.

## ● READING STRATEGY: SUMMARIZE

When you **summarize,** you briefly retell the main ideas and most important details of a piece of writing in your own words. Summarizing narrative poetry can help you make sure you understand the characters' feelings, thoughts, and actions. As you read each poem, use a graphic organizer like the one shown to help yourself identify the most important ideas of each stanza or section.

| Stanza/Section | Main Idea | Detail(s) |
|---|---|---|
| 1 | A woman lives in the forest by the water. | Her name is Nokomis. |

# Author Online

**Bob Dylan: A Poet of His Times** In the 1960s, Bob Dylan burst onto the folk music scene in New York City. He quickly became famous as the voice of his generation. But the young man, who was born Robert Zimmerman in a Minnesota mining town, was not content to be labeled. He disappointed many of his early fans when he began to play rock music. He confused others when he left the rock scene to pursue a religious path. And all the while, drawing from both classic literature and traditional American music, he wrote lyrics widely recognized as important poems.

**Bob Dylan born 1941**

**Henry Wadsworth Longfellow: American Legend** Henry Wadsworth Longfellow introduced American landscapes, history, and culture to a wide readership. Many of his works draw from the history of European Americans; *The Song of Hiawatha* was one of the first literary works in English to treat Native-American themes with respect. The real Hiawatha was a Native American chief credited with helping to make peace among warring tribes. Longfellow's hero was a combination of this historical figure and other people the poet learned about through researching the traditions of various Native American groups.

**Henry Wadsworth Longfellow 1807–1882**

**MORE ABOUT THE AUTHOR**
For more on these poets, visit the **Literature Center** at ClassZone.com.

# Boots of Spanish Leather

*Bob Dylan*

Oh, I'm sailin' away my own true love,
I'm sailin' away in the morning.
Is there something I can send you from across the sea,
From the place that I'll be landing?

5 No, there's nothin' you can send me, my own true love,
There's nothin' I wish to be ownin'.
Just carry yourself back to me unspoiled,
From across that lonesome ocean. **Ⓐ**

Oh, but I just thought you might want something fine
10 Made of silver or of golden,
Either from the mountains of Madrid[1]
Or from the coast of Barcelona.[2]

Oh, but if I had the stars from the darkest night
And the diamonds from the deepest ocean,
15 I'd forsake[3] them all for your sweet kiss,
For that's all I'm wishin' to be ownin'. **Ⓑ**

That I might be gone a long time
And it's only that I'm askin',
Is there something I can send you to remember me by,
20 To make your time more easy passin'.

---

1. **Madrid** (mə-drĭd): the capital of Spain, located in the central part of the country.
2. **Barcelona** (bär'-sə-lōnə): a northeastern Spanish city, located on the Mediterranean Sea coast.
3. **forsake** (fôr-sāk'): to give up (something that was formerly precious).

**ANALYZE VISUALS**
What is the **mood** of this painting? Explain how the colors contribute to that mood.

**Ⓐ NARRATIVE POETRY**
Reread the first two stanzas. What do you know about the speaker in the first stanza? Who is the speaker in the second?

**Ⓑ SUMMARIZE**
What is this speaker's attitude toward the offered gift?

*La Promenade en Mer* (1988), Jean Plichart. Copper engraving. © SuperStock.

Oh, how can, how can you ask me again,
It only brings me sorrow.
The same thing I want from you today,
I would want again tomorrow. **C**

25  I got a letter on a lonesome day,
It was from her ship a-sailin',
Saying I don't know when I'll be comin' back again,
It depends on how I'm a-feelin'.

Well, if you, my love, must think that-a-way,
30  I'm sure your mind is roamin'.
I'm sure your heart is not with me,
But with the country to where you're goin'.

So take heed, take heed of the western wind,
Take heed of the stormy weather.
35  And yes, there's something you can send back to me,
Spanish boots of Spanish leather. **D**

**C** NARRATIVE POETRY
What is the **conflict** between the two speakers, or characters?

**D** RHYTHM AND METER
Reread lines 33–36 aloud. Which words are emphasized by the repetition and rhythm?

# The Song of Hiawatha

*Henry Wadsworth Longfellow*

By the shores of Gitche Gumee,
By the shining Big-Sea-Water,
Stood the wigwam of Nokomis,
Daughter of the Moon, Nokomis.
5 Dark behind it rose the forest,
Rose the black and gloomy pine trees,
Rose the firs with cones upon them;
Bright before it beat the water,
Beat the clear and sunny water,
10 Beat the shining Big-Sea-Water. **E**
  There the wrinkled old Nokomis
Nursed the little Hiawatha,
Rocked him in his linden[1] cradle,
Bedded soft in moss and rushes,
15 Safely bound with reindeer sinews;
Stilled his fretful wail by saying,
"Hush! the Naked Bear will hear thee!"
Lulled him into slumber, singing,
"Ewa-yea! my little owlet!
20 Who is this, that lights the wigwam?
With his great eyes lights the wigwam?
Ewa-yea! my little owlet!"
  Many things Nokomis taught him
Of the stars that shine in heaven;
25 Showed him Ishkoodah, the comet,

**ANALYZE VISUALS**
What is the attitude of the person in this painting?

**E** **NARRATIVE POETRY**
What is the **setting** of this poem?

---

1. **linden** (lĭn′dən): made of wood from a linden tree.

*Communion*, Joe Geshick. © Joe Geshick.

Ishkoodah, with fiery tresses;[2]
Showed the Death-Dance of the spirits,
Warriors with their plumes and war-clubs,
Flaring far away to northward
30 In the frosty nights of Winter;
Showed the broad white road in heaven,
Pathway of the ghosts, the shadows,
Running straight across the heavens,
Crowded with the ghosts, the shadows. **F**

35    At the door on summer evenings
Sat the little Hiawatha;
Heard the whispering of the pine-trees,
Heard the lapping of the waters,
Sounds of music, words of wonder;
40 "Minne-wawa!" said the pine-trees,
"Mudway-aushka!" said the water.

    Saw the firefly, Wah-wah-taysee,
Flitting through the dusk of evening,
With the twinkle of its candle
45 Lighting up the brakes[3] and bushes,
And he sang the song of children,
Sang the song Nokomis taught him:
"Wah-wah-taysee, little firefly,
Little, flitting, white-fire insect,
50 Little, dancing, white-fire creature,
Light me with your little candle,
Ere upon my bed I lay me,
Ere in sleep I close my eyelids!" **G**

    Saw the moon rise from the water
55 Rippling, rounding from the water,
Saw the flecks and shadows on it,
Whispered, "What is that, Nokomis?"
And the good Nokomis answered:
"Once a warrior, very angry,
60 Seized his grandmother, and threw her
Up into the sky at midnight;
Right against the moon he threw her;
'Tis her body that you see there."

    Saw the rainbow in the heaven,
65 In the eastern sky, the rainbow,
Whispered, "What is that, Nokomis?"

**F SUMMARIZE**
Each new section of this poem begins with an indented line. What is the main idea of this section? Add it to your chart.

**G RHYTHM AND METER**
Read lines 42–53 aloud, tapping your pencil to their rhythm. Is the rhythm regular?

---

2. **tresses:** long locks or ringlets of hair.

3. **brakes:** areas overgrown with dense bushes; thickets.

And the good Nokomis answered:
"'Tis the heaven of flowers you see there
All the wildflowers of the forest,
70 All the lilies of the prairie,
When on earth they fade and perish,
Blossom in that heaven above us."
      When he heard the owls at midnight,
Hooting, laughing in the forest,
75 "What is that?" he cried in terror,
"What is that," he said, "Nokomis?"
And the good Nokomis answered:
"That is but the owl and owlet,
Talking in their native language,
80 Talking, scolding at each other." ⓗ
      Then the little Hiawatha
Learned of every bird its language,
Learned their names and all their secrets:
How they built their nests in Summer,
85 Where they hid themselves in Winter;
Talked with them whene'er he met them,
Called them "Hiawatha's Chickens."
      Of all beasts he learned the language,
Learned their names and all their secrets:
90 How the beavers built their lodges,
Where the squirrels hid their acorns,
How the reindeer ran so swiftly,
Why the rabbit was so timid,
Talked with them whene'er he met them,
95 Called them "Hiawatha's Brothers." ⓘ
      Then Iagoo, the great boaster,
He the marvelous storyteller,
He the traveler and the talker,
He the friend of old Nokomis,
100 Made a bow for Hiawatha;
From a branch of ash he made it,
From an oak bough made the arrows,
Tipped with flint,[4] and winged with feathers
And the cord he made of deerskin.
105      Then he said to Hiawatha:
"Go, my son, into the forest,
Where the red deer herd together.

ⓗ **NARRATIVE POETRY**
Nokomis, Hiawatha's grandmother, raises him as her own. What kind of relationship do the woman and boy seem to have?

ⓘ **SUMMARIZE**
Reread lines 81–95. What does Hiawatha learn in this section?

---

4. **flint:** a hard, gray or black quartz.

*Deer Spirit Helper*, Joe Geshick. Oil. © Joe Geshick.

Kill for us a famous roebuck,
Kill for us a deer with antlers!"
110  Forth into the forest straightway
All alone walked Hiawatha
Proudly, with his bow and arrows;
And the birds sang round him, o'er him,
"Do not shoot us, Hiawatha!"
115  Sang the robin, the Opechee,
Sang the bluebird, the Owaissa,
"Do not shoot us, Hiawatha!"
Up the oak tree, close beside him,
Sprang the squirrel, Adjidaumo,
120  In and out among the branches,
Coughed and chattered from the oak tree,
Laughed, and said between his laughing,
"Do not shoot me, Hiawatha!"
And the rabbit from his pathway
125  Leaped aside, and at a distance
Sat erect upon his haunches,
Half in fear and half in frolic,
Saying to the little hunter,
"Do not shoot me, Hiawatha!"
130  But he heeded⁵ not, nor heard them,
For his thoughts were with the red deer;
On their tracks his eyes were fastened,

**ANALYZE VISUALS**
What does the painting
suggest about the
relationship between
people and animals?

---

5. **heeded:** listened to and considered; paid attention to.

Leading downward to the river,
To the ford across the river,
135 And as one in slumber walked he.
    Hidden in the alder bushes,
There he waited till the deer came,
Till he saw two antlers lifted,
Saw two eyes look from the thicket,
140 Saw two nostrils point to the windward,
And a deer came down the pathway,
Flecked with leafy light and shadow.
And his heart within him fluttered,
Trembled like the leaves above him,
145 Like the birch leaf palpitated,
As the deer came down the pathway. **J**
    Then, upon one knee uprising,
Hiawatha aimed an arrow;
Scarce a twig moved with his motion,
150 Scarce a leaf was stirred or rustled,
But the wary roebuck started,
Stamped with all his hooves together,
Listened with one foot uplifted,
Leaped as if to meet the arrow;
155 Ah! the singing, fatal arrow,
Like a wasp it buzzed and stung him!
    Dead he lay there in the forest,
By the ford across the river,
Beat his timid heart no longer;
160 But the heart of Hiawatha
Throbbed and shouted and exulted,[6]
As he bore the red deer homeward,
And Iagoo and Nokomis
Hailed his coming with applauses.
165     From the red deer's hide Nokomis
Made a cloak for Hiawatha,
From the red deer's flesh Nokomis
Made a banquet to his honor.
All the village came and feasted,
170 All the guests praised Hiawatha,
Called him Strong-Heart, Soan-ge-taha!
Called him Loon-Heart, Mahn-go-taysee! **K**

**J RHYTHM AND METER**
Reread lines 136–146.
How does the meter help
convey the **suspense** of
a hunt?

**K NARRATIVE POETRY**
What **conflict** does
Hiawatha face? How
is it resolved?

---

6. **exulted** (ĭg-zŭltd′): rejoiced; felt jubilant and triumphant.

# Comprehension

1. **Recall** What does the speaker who is left behind in "Boots of Spanish Leather" want at the beginning of the poem? At the end?

2. **Recall** Who raises Hiawatha?

3. **Clarify** What does the village celebrate at the end of *The Song of Hiawatha*?

INDIANA STANDARDS

READING STANDARD
**8.3.1** Determine and articulate the...characteristics of different forms of poetry....

# Literary Analysis

4. **Summarize Poetry** Look back at the graphic organizers you made as you read. Which stanzas or sections contain the most important information? Summarize each poem in a few sentences.

5. **Identify Onomatopoeia** When the sound of a word suggests its meaning, such as "splat," it is called onomatopoeia. Find three examples of onomatopoeia in *The Song of Hiawatha*.

6. **Make Inferences** In "Boots of Spanish Leather," why does the speaker change his mind about wanting a gift? What may he have realized?

7. **Examine Rhythm and Meter** Copy lines 31–34 of *The Song of Hiawatha* and mark the stressed and unstressed syllables as in the example on page 637. What pattern does the rhythm follow? Note whether the rest of the poem follows the same rhythm or different ones.

8. **Draw Conclusions about an Epic** The heroes in epic poems often represent values important to the culture they come from. What values does Hiawatha stand for? Note them on a graphic like the one shown. Also give examples that support each value.

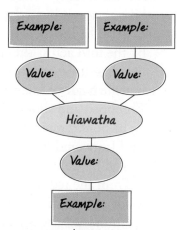

9. **Evaluate Narrative Poems** Did the **stories** these poems told satisfy you in the same way a good short story does? Explain your answer, making sure to consider whether the poems created memorable characters, suspenseful plots, and rewarding resolutions.

# Extension and Challenge

10. **Literary Criticism** In his diary, Longfellow wrote, "I have at length hit upon a plan for a poem on the American Indians which seems to me the right one, and the only. It is to weave together their beautiful traditions into a whole...." Do you think it was a good idea for him to blend different tribal traditions to create his epic? With a group, discuss the value of this poem.

# Reading-Writing Connection

Increase your appreciation of "Boots of Spanish Leather" and *The Song of Hiawatha* by responding to these prompts. Then complete the **Grammar and Writing** exercise.

| WRITING PROMPTS | SELF-CHECK |
| --- | --- |
| **A. Short Response: Analyze a Character**<br>How does Hiawatha change during this part of the epic? Write a **one-paragraph response** in which you compare the traits of the very young Hiawatha in the beginning of the excerpt to those of the growing boy at the end. | *A well-written response will . . .*<br>• include a clear statement about how Hiawatha changes over the course of the poem<br>• cite words, phrases, and events from the poem that reveal Hiawatha's traits |
| **B. Extended Response: Write a Short Story**<br>Choose one of these poems and rewrite it as a **one-or-two page short story** that would appeal to teenagers today. Change or add details about the setting, characters, and conflict. Consider using dialogue to make the events seem real. | *An engaging short story will . . .*<br>• contain interesting characters<br>• present a problem that the characters face |

## GRAMMAR AND WRITING

INDIANA
STANDARDS

WRITING STANDARD
8.6.5 Use correct punctuation.

*PUNCTUATE TITLES CORRECTLY* A title is punctuated according to the type of work it is. Use **quotation marks** for the titles of shorter works, such as articles, short stories, essays, and songs. Use **italics** (or underlining) for the titles of longer works, such as books, plays, magazines, newspapers, and movies. Note that the titles of short poems receive quotation marks, while the titles of epic poems like *The Song of Hiawatha* receive italics.

> *Example:* Longfellow's research for his epic poem *The Song of Hiawatha* came from the book *The Hiawatha Legends*.

**PRACTICE** Rewrite each sentence, correctly punctuating the titles.

1. Bob Dylan's song Boots of Spanish Leather talks about the pain of separation.
2. Longfellow wrote another epic poem entitled Evangeline: A Tale of Acadie.
3. Longfellow also wrote the short poem Paul Revere's Ride.
4. Let Us Read Longfellow is an article from the newspaper The Wall Street Journal.

*For more help with punctuating titles, see page R50 in the **Grammar Handbook**.*

# Personal Response to a Poem

Laughter, sadness, confusion, anger—the poems in this unit may have made you feel all these emotions and more. A good way to share your personal response is to put it in writing. The **Writer's Road Map** can show you how.

## WRITER'S ROAD MAP

### Personal Response to a Poem

**WRITING PROMPT 1**

**Writing from Literature** Choose a poem that you liked, disliked, or found puzzling. Write a personal response that explains why the poem made you react so strongly. Briefly describe the poem so readers will understand your response.

**Poems to Explore**

- "Stopping by Woods on a Snowy Evening"
- "Mother to Son"

**WRITING PROMPT 2**

**Writing for the Real World** Write an essay about a song lyric that has special meaning for you. Include explanations and quotations from the lyric so readers will understand why the song matters to you.

**Types of Music to Explore**

- love songs
- rap
- traditional songs of a culture

**WRITING TOOLS**
For prewriting, revision, and editing tools, visit the **Writing Center at ClassZone.com.**

### KEY TRAITS

**1. IDEAS**
- Clearly presents an **overall response** to the poem or song
- Supports key points with **explanations and quotations**

**2. ORGANIZATION**
- **Identifies** the poem or song in the introduction
- Provides enough **information** about the work so readers can understand the response
- Uses **transitional words and phrases** to connect ideas
- **Summarizes** the response in a conclusion

**3. VOICE**
- Maintains a **tone** that shows the writer's honest response

**4. WORD CHOICE**
- Uses **precise literary terms** when describing the poem or song

**5. SENTENCE FLUENCY**
- Varies **sentence lengths**

**6. CONVENTIONS**
- Uses **correct grammar, spelling, and punctuation**

# Part 1: Analyze a Student Model

**WRITING STANDARD**
**8.5.2** Write responses to literature . . . .

**Susan Liang**
**Martin Luther King, Jr. Middle School**

### What "Identity" Taught Me

    "I'd rather be a tall, ugly weed." These words shocked me when I first read them in Julio Noboa's poem "Identity." Why would anybody choose to be something that people want to destroy? By the time I finished reading the poem, though, I understood the poet's message.

5  The clear, powerful imagery in the poem helped me see that the speaker just wants to be himself, no matter what other people think. I realized that I want to be independent, too.

    The first stanza of the poem is an unusual simile that compares people and plants: "Let them be as flowers," beautiful but "harnessed to

10  a pot of dirt." Using the pronoun *them* shows that the speaker doesn't identify with these people—he is setting himself apart from them. He doesn't want to be fussed over and admired like some flowers in a pot. I had never thought about flowers as dependent before. What kind of plant would the speaker want to be? I wondered.

15     The second and third stanzas of the poem answered my question. The speaker tells us that he would rather be a weed. I always thought of weeds as ugly and unwanted, but his descriptions helped me think about them differently. He describes weeds as free and strong—"clinging on cliffs" and able to break through rocks. Unlike potted flowers, weeds

20  aren't bound by anything. They face "the vast eternal sky" and are "beyond the mountains of time." That's total, unlimited freedom. The speaker is saying that being independent is much better than being admired. I agree.

### KEY TRAITS IN ACTION

Appealing introduction **identifies** the poem's title and author.

The rest of the opening paragraph clearly states a positive **overall response** to the poem.

Uses **precise literary terms** (highlighted) and gives extensive **information** about the poem to help the reader understand the response.

**Transitional words** signal important contrasts. Varied **sentence lengths** give the writing a pleasing rhythm.

The next stanza gave me even more reasons to agree with the

25  speaker. He points out that flowers aren't left alone. They are smelled, "praised, handled, and plucked / by greedy, human hands." This description made me remember how I felt when my parents or teachers nagged at me to do this or that. People ignore weeds, however, because they don't think weeds are worth anything. The speaker doesn't seem to

30  mind being ignored. In fact, he says he'd "rather be unseen."

In the next stanza, the speaker admits that weeds can smell bad. He doesn't seem to think that's a problem, though. It's important to be who you are, he explains, no matter what other people think. I can remember so many times when I wanted to do one thing, but I did something else

35  just to make people like me. It sounds as if the speaker doesn't do that. He insists that being himself matters more to him than anything else. All he wants to do is "stand alone, strong and free."

Reading "Identity" made me think about who I am and who I want to be. By comparing different kinds of people with flowers and weeds,

40  Noboa made me see the plants and myself in a new way. The poem made me envy the speaker's strength and want to be like him. It helped me realize that I care too much about other people's opinions. I, too, would rather be a tall, ugly weed than a pampered flower.

> **Explanations and quotations** from the poem support the key point about flowers not being left alone. Sharing responses this way creates an open, honest **tone.**

> Conclusion **summarizes** how the student reacted to the poem and what she learned from reading it.

2

# Part 2: Apply the Writing Process

**WRITING STANDARD**
**8.4.2** Create compositions that have a clear message . . . .

## PREWRITING

### What Should I Do?

### What Does It Look Like?

**1. Choose a poem or song.**
Reread the prompts on page 648 and decide whether you will write about a poem or a song. Once you have a poem or song in mind, read it or listen to it several times. Then make a chart that lists quotations from the work and your reactions, questions, and comments.

| Lines from "Identity" | Questions and Comments |
|---|---|
| "I'd rather be a tall, ugly weed" | Huh? Who wants to be a weed? |
| flowers "praised, handled, and plucked / by greedy, human hands" | This reminds me of when Mom nags me— too much attention. |
| "If I could stand alone, strong, and free" | I think this means that it's better to be independent than admired. |

**2. Freewrite about your reactions.**
Write down thoughts and feelings about the poem or song as they occur to you.

**TIP** If your reactions to this song or poem are too personal to share with your classmates and teacher, go back to step 1 and choose another work.

"Identity" made me realize how much I try to please other people even though I know I shouldn't worry so much about what others think of me.

Why can't I just be free to be whoever I am?

If that means being ugly and smelly, oh well.

Flowers = pretty but helpless, dependent on others to take care of them

I never thought that I would want to be like a weed! It sure is a different way of looking at things.

**3. Find support for your ideas.**
Keep your reactions in mind as you read the poem or listen to the song again. List specific quotations and examples that support those reactions.

Main idea:

Weeds are free and independent.

Support:

• not "harnessed to a pot of dirt" like flowers

• "beyond the mountains of time"

• "unseen" or "shunned by everyone" (that means totally ignored)

| **What Should I Do?** | **What Does It Look Like?** |
|---|---|

**1. Make your introduction surprising or appealing.**
Try to get your reader interested right away. Then give the title and author of the work and state your overall response to it.

**TIP** You may need to try two or three different introductions before you find the right one.

▶

**Ask a question**
*Why would anybody want to be a weed?*

**Include a surprising quotation**
*"I'd rather be a tall, ugly weed." These words shocked me.*

**Provide an imaginative description**
*Imagine a tall weed growing on the edge of a rocky, isolated cliff.*

---

**2. Organize your ideas.**
An informal outline can help you plan your essay. You can begin with the most important idea and then write about the next most important idea, and so on. You can also discuss ideas as they appear in the work, from beginning to end.

▶

*Main message: The speaker just wants to be himself.*

*First stanza: simile: other people are like flowers, "harnessed to a pot of dirt" (So what kind of plant would the speaker be?)*

*Second and third stanzas: Speaker is free like a weed.*

*Fourth stanza: Flowers get "praised, handled, and plucked."*

*Fifth stanza: Weeds smell bad, and people ignore them; speaker would "rather be unseen."*

*Conclusion: The poem helped me realize that I want to be more like the speaker—less concerned with what other people think of me.*

---

**3. Explain why you reacted the way you did.**
Don't just tell readers your response to the work. Show them by including specific examples and quotations.

**See page 654:** Check Your Grammar

**TIP** Before you revise, look back at the **key traits on page 648** and the **rubric and peer-reader questions on page 654.**

▶

*The first part of the poem is an unusual simile that compares people and plants: "Let them be as flowers," beautiful but "harnessed to a pot of dirt."* ⎤ Key idea

*Using the pronoun them shows that the man doesn't identify with these people— he is setting himself apart from them. He doesn't want to be fussed over and admired like some flowers in a pot.* ⎤ Support

## REVISING AND EDITING

| What Should I Do? | What Does It Look Like? |
|---|---|

**1. Strengthen your introduction.**
- Does your introduction reach out and grab readers, name the work, and state your overall response?
- If not, rewrite your opening and add any missing information.

▶

*in Julio Noboa's poem "Identity."*

"I'd rather be a tall, ugly weed." These words shocked me when I first read them. Why would anybody choose to be something that people want to destroy? By the time I finished reading the poem, though, I understood the poet's message. The clear, powerful imagery in the poem helped me see that the speaker just wants to be himself, no matter what other people think. I realized that I want to be independent, too.

**2. Use correct literary terms.**
- (Circle) the literary terms you included.
- If you have few or no circles, add terms such as *speaker, stanza, rhythm, imagery, simile,* and *metaphor*.

**See page 654:** Literary Terms

▶

*stanza*

The first ~~part~~ of the poem is an unusual (simile) that compares people and plants: "Let them be as flowers," beautiful but "harnessed to a pot of dirt." Using the pronoun <u>them</u> shows that the ~~man~~ doesn't identify with these people—he is setting himself apart from them.

*speaker*

**3. Pay attention to sentence length.**
- Find the longest and the shortest sentences in your response. Count the number of words in each.
- If most of your sentences are about the same length, divide or combine some to give your reader some variety.

▶

~~He describes weeds as free and strong. They are "clinging on cliffs." They can even break through rocks.~~

He describes weeds as free and strong—"clinging on cliffs" and able to break through rocks.

**4. Make logical connections.**
- Ask a peer reader to draw a box around sentences that are not connected logically.
- Add transitions as needed to make the relationship between the ideas clear.

**See page 654:** Ask a Peer Reader

▶

Reading "Identity" made me think about who I am and who I want to be. Noboa made me see the plants and myself in a new way.

By comparing different kinds of people with flowers and weeds,

# Personal Response to a Poem

## Apply the Rubric

**A strong personal response to a poem . . .**

- ☑ introduces the essay by identifying the poem or song
- ☑ presents an overall response to the work
- ☑ gives readers enough information so they can understand the writer's reaction
- ☑ includes quotations that support the key ideas
- ☑ uses literary terms accurately
- ☑ maintains a tone that matches the writer's honest response
- ☑ uses transitions to connect the ideas
- ☑ varies sentence lengths
- ☑ concludes with a concise summary

## Ask a Peer Reader

- In your own words, what was my overall response to this poem or song?
- Where could I add transitions to connect ideas?
- Which of my points is most memorable? Why?

## Literary Terms

**free verse**—poetry without regular patterns of rhyme and rhythm

**imagery**—words and phrases that appeal to the reader's five senses

**metaphor**—a comparison that does not use *like* or *as*

**rhythm**—beat caused by stressed and unstressed syllables

**simile**—a comparison that uses *like* or *as*

**speaker**—the voice that "talks" to the reader, similar to a narrator in fiction

**stanza**—group of two or more lines that form a unit in a poem

## Check Your Grammar

When you quote poems or songs, copy the words exactly and put quotation marks at the beginning and end. Show where one line ends and another begins by using a slash (/).

> *They are smelled, "praised, handled, and plucked / by greedy, human hands."*

## Writing Online

**PUBLISHING OPTIONS**
For publishing options, visit the **Writing Center** at ClassZone.com.

**ASSESSMENT PREPARATION**
For writing and grammar assessment practice, go to the **Assessment Center** at ClassZone.com.

# Oral Interpretation of a Poem

Part of the power of poetry is the sound of the spoken words. Giving an oral interpretation of your poem will let your audience hear that power for themselves.

## Planning the Oral Interpretation

1. **Practice reciting the poem aloud.** Try pausing, speeding up, or speaking more softly or loudly to stress the deeper meaning of the poem. Appropriate gestures or facial expressions also may help your audience understand the words. For example, for the line, "I'd rather be a tall, ugly weed," you might stand up as tall as you can.

2. **Mark up a copy of the poem.** Leave extra space between the lines so you can add notes about using gestures or facial expressions. Highlight places where you plan to change your volume or speed.

> I'd rather be a tall, ugly weed, ⟵ Stand tall.
>
> clinging on cliffs, like an eagle ⟵ Spread arms.
>
> wind-wavering above high, jagged rocks. ⟵ Speed up pace.

3. **Refine your delivery.** Run through your presentation several times in front of a mirror or with an audience of friends or family members. Ask for feedback on how well you convey the message of the poem.

## Giving the Oral Interpretation

1. **Show your audience that you enjoy sharing this poem.** Speak normally, but loudly enough to be heard at the back of the room. If you use gestures, make them seem as natural as possible.

2. **Make eye contact.** Don't keep your eyes on your script. Instead, look up frequently and focus on people in various parts of the room.

3. **Get your audience involved.** Ask for questions or comments on your oral interpretation. This information can help you improve your next presentation.

**See page R82:** Evaluate an Oral Interpretation

# Reading Comprehension

**DIRECTIONS** *Read these poems and answer the questions that follow.*

# An Indian Summer Day on the Prairie

### Vachel Lindsay

IN THE BEGINNING

The sun is a huntress young,
The sun is a red, red joy,
The sun is an Indian girl,
Of the tribe of the Illinois.

MID-MORNING

5   The sun is a smoldering fire,
That creeps through the high gray plain,
And leaves not a bush of cloud
To blossom with flowers of rain.

NOON

The sun is a wounded deer,
10  That treads pale grass in the skies,
Shaking his golden horns,
Flashing his baleful eyes.

SUNSET

The sun is an eagle old,
There in the windless west.
15  Atop of the spirit-cliffs
He builds him a crimson nest.

# The Sunflowers

**Mary Oliver**

Come with me
     into the field of sunflowers.
          Their faces are burnished disks,
             their dry spines

5    creak like ship masts,
     their green leaves,
          so heavy and many,
             fill all day with the sticky

sugars of the sun.
10         Come with me
          to visit the sunflowers,
            they are shy

but want to be friends;
     they have wonderful stories
15         of when they were young—
            the important weather,

the wandering crows.
     Don't be afraid
          to ask them questions!
20            Their bright faces,

which follow the sun,
     will listen, and all
          those rows of seeds—
            each one a new life!—

25   hope for a deeper acquaintance;
     each of them, though it stands
         in a crowd of many,
           like a separate universe,

is lonely, the long work

30      of turning their lives

        into a celebration

        is not easy. Come

and let us talk with those modest faces,

        the simple garments of leaves,

35      the coarse roots in the earth

        so uprightly burning.

## Comprehension

**DIRECTIONS** *Answer these questions about*
*"An Indian Summer Day on the Prairie."*

**1.** In the first stanza, the sun is personified as
- a tribe from Illinois
- three red planets
- a girl who is hunting
- the beginning of the day

**2.** With each stanza in this poem, the poet develops
- one idea in a single sentence
- an unusual appearance on the page
- several images in four sentences
- a list of unrelated ideas in five lines

**3.** Which statement is the best paraphrase of lines 5–8?
- The sun's strong rays set the plain on fire during midmorning.
- By midmorning, the fiery sun is so hot that it burns away the rain clouds.
- The sun at noon is so red that it looks like a fire in the sky.
- The midmorning sun is drying up the bushes on the plain.

**4.** The pattern of rhyming words in every stanza of this poem is
- *abba*        - *abab*
- *abcb*        - *abcc*

**5.** The extended metaphor in lines 9–12 compares the sun to
- a wounded deer        - the noon sky
- pale grass            - golden horns

**6.** In lines 13–16, the eagle building his nest is a metaphor for the
- western sky        - wild deer
- setting sun        - prairie hunters

**7.** Which line from the poem contains an example of assonance?
- "The sun is a huntress young"
- "The sun is a smoldering fire"
- "And leaves not a bush of cloud"
- "Shaking his golden horns"

**8.** Which line from the poem contains an example of alliteration?
- "The sun is an Indian girl"
- "There in the windless west"
- "Atop of the spirit-cliffs"
- "The sun is an eagle old"

**DIRECTIONS** *Answer these questions about* *"The Sunflowers."*

9. By giving the sunflowers human qualities, the speaker in the poem is
   ○ creating a humorous image
   ○ emphasizing human weaknessses
   ○ expressing a connection with nature
   ○ making the poem more lyrical

10. The poem's speaker is asking readers to
    ○ go along on a visit to the sunflowers
    ○ learn about the different parts of a sunflower
    ○ be strong, like sunflowers in a field
    ○ celebrate life, like each seed of a sunflower

11. The simile in lines 1–7 compares the sound of the sunflower stalks to the
    ○ shape of human faces
    ○ sight of burnished disks
    ○ noise made by ship masts
    ○ smell of green leaves

12. The speaker's exclamation in lines 18–19, "Don't be afraid to ask them questions!" is directed to the
    ○ sunflowers          ○ crows
    ○ readers             ○ sun

13. The simile in lines 26–29 compares each sunflower to a "separate universe" to emphasize its
    ○ isolation           ○ short life
    ○ loyalty             ○ weakness

14. Which statement is the best paraphrase of lines 29–32: "the long work / of turning their lives / into a celebration / is not easy"?
    ○ Water helps sunflower seeds grow.
    ○ Sunflowers are beautiful and useful.
    ○ It takes time for seeds to become sunflowers.
    ○ Sunflowers can teach us about having fun.

15. Which statement best describes the four-line stanzas in this poem?
    ○ The pattern of indented lines connects the ideas from stanza to stanza.
    ○ Each stanza contains a single idea that is unrelated to the ideas of the other stanzas.
    ○ The stanzas have a simple rhyme scheme that emphasizes the rhythm of the poem.
    ○ The length of every line follows the same pattern in each stanza.

**DIRECTIONS** *Answer this question about both* *selections.*

16. To give their descriptions of a bright summer day a musical quality, both poets use
    ○ metaphors and similes
    ○ assonance and alliteration
    ○ rhyming lines
    ○ free verse

## Constructed Response

**SHORT ANSWER** *Write two or three sentences* *to answer each question.*

17. Paraphrase the speaker's invitation in lines 10–17 of "The Sunflowers."

18. What can you tell about the speaker of "The Sunflowers" from the statements made in the poem?

**ESSAY** *Write a paragraph to answer* *this question.*

19. What do the stanza titles tell you about "An Indian Summer Day on the Prairie"? What story is told by the four stanzas together?

**GO ON** ➡

# Vocabulary

**DIRECTIONS** *Use context clues and the explanations of word origins to answer the following questions.*

1. Which word in "An Indian Summer Day on the Prairie" comes from *qirmiz,* the Arabic word for an insect that is used to produce a red dye?

   ○ sun      ○ pale
   ○ golden      ○ crimson

2. Which word in "An Indian Summer Day on the Prairie" comes from *smorian,* an Old English word that means "to smoke"?

   ○ shaking      ○ smoldering
   ○ flashing      ○ spirit

3. Which word in "An Indian Summer Day on the Prairie" comes from *bealu,* an Old English word that means "misery"?

   ○ baleful      ○ young
   ○ wounded      ○ bush

4. Which word in "The Sunflowers" comes from *brun,* a Germanic word that means "brown, polished"?

   ○ sunflower      ○ burnished
   ○ bright      ○ burning

5. Which word in "The Sunflowers" comes from *garnir,* a Old French word that means "to equip, adorn"?

   ○ green      ○ coarse
   ○ garment      ○ modest

**DIRECTIONS** *Use your knowledge of Latin words and roots to answer the following questions.*

6. Which word in "The Sunflowers" comes from *accognoscere,* a Latin word that means "to know perfectly"?

   ○ visit
   ○ friends
   ○ celebration
   ○ acquaintance

7. Which word in "The Sunflowers" comes from *separare,* a Latin word that means "apart"?

   ○ rows
   ○ uprightly
   ○ separate
   ○ wandering

8. Which word in "The Sunflowers" comes from the Latin words *unus,* which means "one," and *vertere,* which means "to turn"?

   ○ lonely
   ○ rotating
   ○ universe
   ○ wonderful

# Writing & Grammar

**DIRECTIONS** *Read this passage and answer the questions that follow.*

(1) Last winter I read the article Bringing Back the Prairie in Audubon magazine.
(2) I told my mom dad and brother that I wanted to plant a prairie in our backyard.
(3) I hoped to plant yellow foxtail, prairie cordgrass and cattail sedge. (4) My brother offered to build a pond after he read Carl Sandburg's short poem Young Bullfrogs.
(5) He wanted big green bullfrogs to visit our backyard! (6) Before we began planting our small prairie, we all read the book Where the Sky Began: Land of the Tallgrass Prairie to learn as much as we could about what to plant.

**1.** Choose the correct way to punctuate the article and magazine titles in sentence 1.

○ *Bringing Back the Prairie* in *Audubon*

○ "Bringing Back the Prairie" in *Audubon*

○ *Bringing Back the Prairie* in "Audubon"

○ "Bringing Back the Prairie" in "Audubon"

**2.** Choose the correct way to punctuate sentence 2 with commas.

○ I told, my mom dad and brother that I wanted, to plant a prairie in our backyard.

○ I told my mom, dad, and brother that I wanted to plant a prairie in our backyard.

○ I told my mom, dad, and brother, that I wanted to plant a prairie in our backyard.

○ I told my mom dad and brother that I wanted to plant a prairie, in our backyard.

**3.** Choose the correct way to punctuate sentence 3 with commas.

○ I hoped to plant yellow foxtail, prairie cordgrass and cattail, sedge.

○ I hoped to plant yellow foxtail prairie cordgrass and, cattail sedge.

○ I hoped to plant, yellow foxtail prairie cordgrass and cattail sedge.

○ I hoped to plant yellow foxtail, prairie cordgrass, and cattail sedge.

**4.** Choose the correct way to punctuate the title of the poem in sentence 4.

○ *Young Bullfrogs*

○ *"Young Bullfrogs"*

○ "Young Bullfrogs"

○ "Young" Bullfrogs

**5.** Choose the correct way to punctuate sentence 5 with commas.

○ He wanted big, green bullfrogs to visit our backyard!

○ He wanted, big green bullfrogs to visit our backyard!

○ He wanted big, green, bullfrogs to visit our backyard!

○ He wanted big green bullfrogs, to visit our backyard!

**6.** Choose the correct way to punctuate the book title in sentence 6.

○ "Where the Sky Began: Land of the Tallgrass Prairie"

○ *Where the Sky Began:* Land of the Tallgrass Prairie

○ *Where the Sky Began: Land of the Tallgrass Prairie*

○ "*Where the Sky Began: Land of the Tallgrass Prairie*"

## Ideas for Independent Reading

Which questions from Unit 5 made an impression on you?
Continue exploring them with these books.

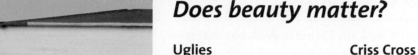

# Does beauty matter?

### Uglies
*by Scott Westerfeld*

In the future, all 16-year-olds have an operation that makes them "beautiful." Most of the younger Uglies can't wait until it's their turn for the operation, but a girl named Shay rebels against being the same as everyone else. Will her friend Tally help her or betray her?

### Criss Cross
*by Lynne Rae Perkins*

Debbie and Hector are 14 years old, and they'd like their appearance to reflect the interesting people they hope they're becoming. How will these important changes happen? It's not always clear, but by the end of the summer, a great deal will be different.

### Margaux with an X
*by Ronald Koertge*

Margaux is dazzlingly beautiful and very popular. She's also miserable. Most of the boys in school have crushes on her, but she's only interested in Danny. A shabby-looking outcast, Danny shares her love of language and helps her cope with problems at home.

# Can you be rich without money?

### Colibrí
*by Ann Cameron*

Years ago, a fortune teller told Uncle that Rosa would make him rich. They have been traveling through Guatemala ever since, begging and cheating people to get money and food. Now that Rosa is older, lying to people is harder, and Uncle is getting impatient.

### The Black Pearl
*by Scott O'Dell*

When Ramon finds the Pearl of Heaven, everyone comes to look at it, and his father gives the pearl to the church. Some people think the jewel brings bad luck because it belongs to the Manta Diable. When misfortune hits the village, only Ramon can fix it.

### A Year Down Yonder
*by Richard Peck*

It's the Depression, and people are broke. Mary Alice is sent to live in rural Illinois with her eccentric Grandma Dowdell. Grandma has habits, like "borrowing" the Sheriff's boat or Old Man Nyquist's apples, which seem to make life a little easier.

# When do you feel most free?

### The Upstairs Room
*by Johanna Reiss*

Annie is only six when Hitler comes to power in Germany and starts making laws that punish the Jews. Annie is glad she lives in Holland so her family is safe, but as the German army gets stronger, how long will Annie's safety last?

### Let Me Play: The Story of Title IX, the Law That Changed the Future of Girls in America
*by Karen Blumenthal*

Before 1972, many girls weren't able join a soccer team or enter medical school. Finally, the people fighting against this injustice won, and the law was changed.

### The Warrior Heir
*by Cinda Williams Chima*

Every day Jack takes medicine for his heart condition. One day he forgets, and it's the best day of his life. Suddenly, he's faster and stronger. He finds out he's really a magical warrior and his "medicine" was hiding him from people who want to kill him.

# A Unique Imprint

## STYLE, VOICE, AND TONE

- In Fiction
- In Nonfiction
- In Poetry

# What's in STYLE?

How do you decide what clothes to put on in the morning, or how to arrange your hair? You might follow current trends, or you might draw on the fashions of years past to create a unique look. Whatever you choose, your appearance reflects your personal **style,** the way you express yourself to others. Writers, filmmakers, songwriters, and artists have their own ways of expressing themselves, too. Their style includes the way they use elements of their craft to communicate ideas.

*ACTIVITY* With a partner, think of an author, actor, singer, or artist whose style you and your partner both like. What about this person's work makes it unique? Answer the following questions:

• What three things come to mind first when you think of this person's creations?

• What sets this person apart?

• What words would you use to describe his or her style?

After answering these questions, discuss whether this person's style has influenced your own style, and how.

INDIANA STANDARDS

# Preview Unit Goals

**LITERARY ANALYSIS**
- Identify, analyze, and evaluate style, including diction, imagery, and sentence structure
- Compare and contrast style
- Identify and analyze voice, irony, and tone

**READING**
- Evaluate information and opinions
- Use and interpret graphic aids
- Synthesize information
- Identify sequence using signal words

**WRITING AND GRAMMAR**
- Write a literary analysis essay
- Write concisely by using appositives and appositive phrases
- Form compound and complex sentences

**SPEAKING, LISTENING, AND VIEWING**
- Create an online database

**VOCABULARY**
- Use context to help determine meaning of idioms and multiple-meaning words
- Understand connotative and denotative meanings of words
- Use knowledge of Latin word roots to help determine word meaning

**ACADEMIC VOCABULARY**
- style
- tone
- literary analysis
- synthesize
- voice
- irony

# Reader's Workshop

# Style, Voice, and Tone

Think about the last time you read an e-mail from a friend. Could you almost "hear" that friend talking to you? Perhaps the e-mail contained phrases your friend often uses, or expressed an attitude that is typical of him or her. The personality that comes across in any piece of writing—whether it's a friend's e-mail or a classic novel—is the **voice**. The voice can belong to the writer or to a narrator. Either way, it is created through the writer's one-of-a-kind style.

## Part 1: What Is Style?

"The rosy fingertips of dawn spread delicately across the sky." "The sun bounced into view like a giant rubber ball." *How* something is said often affects a reader as much as *what* is being said. In literature, how something is said is called the **style**. A writer's style can be described using such words as *formal*, *conversational*, or *journalistic*. Style is created through a combination of elements, including word choice, sentence structure, and imagery.

**INDIANA STANDARDS**

**READING STANDARDS**
**8.3.7** Analyze a work of literature, showing how it reflects the heritage, traditions, attitudes, and beliefs of its author.

**8.3.6** Identify significant literary devices, such as metaphor, symbolism, dialect or quotations, and irony, which define a writer's style and use those elements to interpret the work.

| ELEMENTS OF STYLE | EXAMPLES | |
|---|---|---|
| **Word Choice**<br>Is the writing packed with conversational words and slang, or elegant, formal phrases? Precise, vivid, casual, formal—the kinds of words a writer uses can help to create style. | The simple, informal language in this sentence helps to create a conversational style.<br><br>I didn't try to shout over the helicopters; they chopped up sound and the air, and whupped up heartbeats.<br><br>—from *The Fifth Book of Peace* by Maxine Hong Kingston |  |
| **Sentence Structure**<br>One element of style is **sentence structure**, the lengths and types of sentences a writer uses. Some writers are noted for crafting long, complex sentences. Others are noted for using short, simple ones. | This long sentence reflects a flowing, descriptive style and gives you a sense of the character's energy.<br><br>Miranda gave her mother a quick smile and bounded forward in great skipping leaps up the ramp, across the red and gold carpet in the lobby, down the long side aisle and up the steps onto the stage.<br><br>—from "Dancing Miranda" by Diane de Anda |  |
| **Imagery**<br>Words and phrases that appeal to readers' senses create memorable **images**. The kinds and amount of images a writer uses can help to define his or her style. | This writer layers on image after image, creating a poetic style that reflects the rhythm of the sea.<br><br>Beyond the sails stretched the sky itself, as blue as a baby's bluest eyes, while the greenish sea, crowned with lacy caps of foaming white, rushed by with unrelenting speed.<br><br>—from *The True Confessions of Charlotte Doyle* by Avi |  |

## MODEL 1: COMPARING STYLE

In this excerpt, Rita Williams-Garcia uses a conversational, humorous style to convey the narrator's dread of a family meal. As you read, look closely at the author's word choice—the element that helps to create this style.

### *from* **Food** from the **Outside**

Short story by **Rita Williams-Garcia**

My sister, brother, and I didn't have a dog, but we sure could have used one around dinnertime. Our dog would never have had to beg for table scraps, for we promised sincerely in our mealtime prayers always to feed Rover the main course. It wouldn't have been so much for love of dog, but for survival. You
5 see, our mother, known throughout the neighborhood as "Miss Essie," was still refining her cooking skills. Until we could persuade our parents to let us have a dog, we sat at the dinner table with wax sandwich bags hidden in our pockets, especially when Miss Essie served "Hackensack," our code word for mystery stew.

**Close Read**

1. Find two examples of words and phrases in this excerpt that sound like casual conversation.

2. Reread the boxed details. Would you describe the narrator's voice as humorous, sincere, sarcastic, or something else? Explain.

## MODEL 2: COMPARING STYLE

C. S. Lewis uses a more formal, descriptive style to write about an elaborate feast in the enchanted world of Narnia.

### *from* The Voyage of the *Dawn Treader*

Novel by **C. S. Lewis**

On the table itself there was set out such a banquet as had never been seen, not even when Peter the High King kept his court at Cair Paravel. There were turkeys and geese and peacocks, there were boars' heads and sides of venison, there were pies shaped like ships under full sail or like dragons and elephants,
5 there were ice puddings and bright lobsters and gleaming salmon, there were nuts and grapes, pineapples and peaches, pomegranates and melons and tomatoes. There were flagons[1] of gold and silver and curiously-wrought[2] glass; and the smell of the fruit and the wine blew toward them like a promise of all happiness.

---

1. **flagons:** vessels used for holding wine; flasks.

2. **curiously-wrought:** strangely crafted.

**Close Read**

1. How would you describe the structure of the author's sentences?

2. One element of Lewis's style is his use of imagery. Two examples have been boxed. Find three more examples.

3. What is the most striking stylistic difference between how the two authors describe a meal? Support your answer.

# Part 2: Tone

Another important element of style is **tone**—a writer's attitude toward a subject. The tone of a piece of writing might be described using words such as *humorous, sarcastic, mocking, admiring, serious,* or *sympathetic.* One way to determine a writer's tone is to look at the specific words, phrases, and details he or she chooses to include.

Take a look at these two excerpts. In each, the writer conveys a very specific attitude toward sports.

## COMPARING TONE

**Walter Dean Myers**

> By the time I was eleven, basketball had entered my life. I knew I was going to be a star and I could dream about myself playing in the NBA. My strength was my outside shot and in my dreams I always made the last, desperate shot that swished through the net just as the buzzer sounded.
>
> —from "Daydreams"

▶ Myers uses an **optimistic, confident tone** to express his attitude toward his basketball abilities.

- Myers's choice of words reveals his dreamy optimism.
- Details convey the author's confidence.

**William Sleator**

> I was always the last one picked for teams. I was so used to it that it didn't bother me. I was always way out in left field or right field or whichever field it is that balls hardly ever go to, and I lived in fear that a ball would come my way and I'd have to try to catch the thing and it would hit me on the head or I'd drop it. PE was the worst thing about school.
>
> —from "The Masque of the Red Death"

▶ Sleator uses a **negative, yet humorous tone** to express his attitude toward PE class.

- Words and phrases let readers know exactly how Sleator felt about playing baseball in PE class.
- The details reveal the author's sense of humor about his experience, as well as explain *why* PE class was so terrible.

## MODEL 1: COMPARING TONE

The narrator of this novel, a teenaged boy, thinks back on helping a neighbor with her lawn. Read on to find out how he felt about this experience.

---

### *from* Bird

Novel by **Angela Johnson**

I used to mow old Mrs. Pritchard's lawn when I was eight. She had one of those old mowers that was hard as anything to push through all the grass in her backyard. She said she didn't like the gas mowers because they stunk and scared all the birds away.

5   I wouldn't have done it for anybody else, but she always had lemonade out for me, then she'd feed me the best peach cobbler I ever tasted. I didn't tell her, but I'd have mowed that big yard for nothing but some of that cobbler. I'm easy that way.

---

**Close Read**

1. What words and phrases in the boxed lines help you to understand the boy's feelings about helping Mrs. Pritchard?

2. Which word pair best describes the tone revealed in the boxed lines?

   **a.** warm, nostalgic
   **b.** resentful, bitter
   **c.** biting, sarcastic

---

## MODEL 2: COMPARING TONE

In her memoir, Haven Kimmel recalls a time in her childhood when she was strongly encouraged to do good deeds for other people. As you read about Kimmel's first attempt to do something good, think about how you would describe her attitude, or tone.

### *from* A Girl Named ZIPPY

Nonfiction by **Haven Kimmel**

I spent every afternoon stalking good works. My first victim was Agnes Johnson who was 164 years old. Her skin, impatient for her to get it over with and die, appeared to be sliding down off her body into a pool around her ankles. She was older than dirt, but feisty. She insisted on cutting her

5 own grass every week with an ancient push mower. For years I'd seen her out there, pushing against the mower as if it were a huge rock, her skinny arms quivering, her lips trembling, a thin film of sweat shining on the place most people had an upper lip. I'd never paid her much mind, but on this particular day I realized I'd hit the jackpot. Ordinarily I'd have rather run naked into

10 a rose bush than cut grass; at my own house I suggested a few times a week that we get a goat or some other furry grazing thing to live in the backyard. (I thought a goat was an especially clever choice because they could also eat our empty tin cans.) So if I mowed Agnes Johnson's yard, I could probably avoid doing any more good deeds until I myself was flat-out old.

---

**Close Read**

1. Examine the boxed words. Are these words you would typically associate with doing good deeds? Explain.

2. Identify three details that help you understand Kimmel's feelings about helping Agnes Johnson.

3. What word would you use to describe the author's tone, or attitude, toward doing good deeds?

---

# Part 3: Analyze the Literature

Both of the following selections are about romance and the anxiety that it can spark. Though the excerpts share a similar topic, each reveals its writer's distinct personality.

The first excerpt is from an essay Lloyd Alexander wrote about his earliest experience with dating—or, rather, not dating. As you read, look for examples of the elements of style that you have studied in this workshop.

*from* THE **Truth** ABOUT THE WORLD

Essay by **Lloyd Alexander**

My first date never happened. When I finally built up enough nerve, I dared to ask one of the girls in my ninth-grade class to go to some kind of dance or other—I don't remember exactly; it was long ago. To my amazement, she accepted. For myself, I always thought in large, long-range terms. We
5   would, I imagined, become sweethearts, get engaged, eventually marry, and live happily ever after.

Friday afternoon, the day before the glorious event, our gym teacher ordered us outdoors to play soccer. I usually preferred loitering around the fringes of the action, but when the ball bounded straight at me, I seized the
10   moment to give it the mightiest kick in school history.

I noticed a couple of things. For one, I glimpsed the ball rocketing across the field, missing the goal by what looked like about half a mile; for another, I saw an expression of despondency and long suffering on the face of the gym teacher. By then, I was on the grass, trying to hold my left foot in both hands
15   and giving my full attention to learning the nature of agony.

A couple of classmates hauled me to the nurse's office. My mother had to be summoned. She took me home in our ancient Plymouth and phoned the doctor (they made house calls in those days). He examined my foot, now swollen to the size of a baked ham. He assured me I would live. I was sorry to
20   hear that.

The date, of course, was off. My mother took charge of canceling it; I hadn't the heart to do it myself. In those days, pain was supposed to build character. After nearly a week of character-building, I limped back to school. I was too ashamed even to look at my might-have-been date. And she, very
25   properly, decided the right thing to do was never to speak to me again.

## Close Read

1. One element of Alexander's style is his use of imagery. Find two examples of imagery in the excerpt.

2. The boxed details help to create a humorous, self-mocking tone. Identify two other details that reflect this tone.

3. Based on the voice you "heard" as you read, how would you describe the author's personality?

The following excerpt is from a novel, so the voice you "hear" belongs to the narrator—a teenager named Leo. Here, Leo describes an awkward early encounter with his future girlfriend, who calls herself Stargirl. As you read, consider what elements help to create the author's style.

*from*

# Stargirl

Novel by **Jerry Spinelli**

At first it was enough just to see the house. Then I began to wonder if she was inside. I wondered what she could be doing. Light came from every window I could see. There was a car in the driveway. The longer I hung around, the closer I wanted to be. I crossed the street and practically dashed
5 past the house. As I went by, I scooped up a stone from the yard. I went up the street, turned, and looked at her house in the distance.

I whispered to the salt-sprinkled sky, "That's where Stargirl Caraway lives. She likes me."

I headed back toward the house. The street, the sidewalks were deserted.
10 The stone was warm in my hand. This time I walked slowly as I approached. I felt strange. My eyes fixed on a triangle of light in a curtained window. I saw a shadow on a yellow wall. I seemed to be drifting, footless, into the light.

Suddenly the front door opened. I dived behind the car in the driveway and crouched by the rear fender. I heard the door close. I heard steps. The steps
15 matched the movement of a long shadow cast down the driveway. My breath stopped. The shadow stopped. I felt both ridiculous and weirdly, perfectly placed, as if crouching by that car was precisely what life had in store for me at that moment.

Her voice came from beyond the shadow. "Remember when you followed
20 me into the desert that day after school?"

Absurdly, I debated whether to answer, as if doing so would—what? Give me away? I leaned into the smooth metal of the fender. It never occurred to me to stand, to show myself. Hours seemed to pass before I finally croaked, "Yes."

"Why did you turn around and go back?"

25 Her tone was casual, as if she held conversations every night with people crouching behind the car in the driveway.

## Close Read

1. Spinelli's writing includes rich imagery that helps readers to visualize the setting. Find three examples.

2. Describe the structures of the boxed sentences. What effect do you think Spinelli was trying to achieve through this stylistic choice?

3. Which word pair best describes the tone revealed in lines 7–12 and 16–18?
   **a.** sarcastic and bitter
   **b.** romantic and dreamy
   **c.** sad and serious

4. Compare Spinelli's writing with Alexander's. How are the authors' styles similar or different?

## New York Day Women

Short Story by Edwidge Danticat

# Who is the REAL you?

**INDIANA STANDARDS**

**READING STANDARDS**
**8.2.9** Make reasonable statements and draw conclusions about a text, supporting them with accurate examples.

**8.3.6** Identify significant literary devices, such as metaphor, symbolism, dialect or quotations, and irony, which define a writer's style and use those elements to interpret the work.

**KEY IDEA** At first, it might seem silly to wonder who you really are. But do you act the same around your teachers as you do around your friends? And do your grandparents **perceive** the same person your friends see? We all have different sides to ourselves. In the story you are about to read, a young woman discovers a side of her mother she never knew existed.

**QUICKWRITE** Think of three or four people who know you in different ways—for example, your best friend, a teacher, a parent, and an enemy. What adjectives would each person use to describe you? How would you describe yourself? Jot down your thoughts about whether anyone perceives the real you.

## LITERARY ANALYSIS: STYLE

Each of us has a unique style, or way of dressing, acting, and speaking. In literature, **style** is a writer's way of expressing himself or herself. Style does not refer to what is said, but rather how it is said. Writers show style through the choices they make about the following things:

- Word choice and **imagery**—descriptive words and phrases that appeal to the senses. Notice Edwidge Danticat's descriptions.
- Presentation—the way the story appears on the page. Notice Danticat's use of line spacing, italics, and typographical symbols.
- Sentence structure. Notice Danticat's purposeful use of sentence fragments.

## READING SKILL: IDENTIFY SEQUENCE

**Sequence** is the order in which events occur in a story. To help yourself keep track of the order, look for signal words and phrases, such as *today, that morning, as, now, an hour later, then,* and *before.*

In the story you are about to read, the narrator relates present-day events while reflecting on conversations and incidents from the past. Keep track of the sequence of present-day events by recording them in a sequence chart like the one shown.

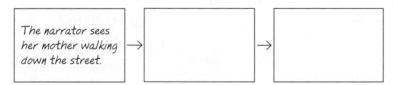

| The narrator sees her mother walking down the street. | → | | → | |

## ▲ VOCABULARY IN CONTEXT

The following boldfaced words help Danticat show how people sometimes don't really understand each other. To see how many words you know, restate each sentence, using a different word or phrase for the boldfaced word.

1. Pablo can **mesmerize** people with his charm, so they forget he isn't reliable.
2. Jenny's only **offense** is that she brags too much.
3. My **pursuit** of the truth only left me more confused.
4. I **contemplate** joining the game, but no one expects me to, so I don't.
5. I doubt that the feisty Emily will **surrender** easily.

# Author Online

**A New Home in New York** Writer Edwidge Danticat (ĕd'wēj dän'tē-kä) emigrated from Haiti to Brooklyn, New York, when she was 12. Danticat had a hard time adjusting to life in New York. Her classmates made fun of her clothing, hairstyle, and Haitian accent. To escape from the loneliness

**Edwidge Danticat born 1969**

she felt during this time, Danticat wrote stories about her home country. Over her career, Danticat has published several novels and short story collections, most of which involve Haitian culture and characters.

**Krik? Krak!** During her childhood, Danticat heard many Haitian stories. Storytellers begin their tales by asking the audience, "Krik?" If the audience is ready, they will respond with an excited "Krak!" This exchange of words became the title of Danticat's first collection of short stories, in which "New York Day Women" appears.

 **MORE ABOUT THE AUTHOR**
For more on Edwidge Danticat, visit the **Literature Center** at ClassZone.com.

## Background

**A Haven for Haitians** Danticat's homeland is one of the most densely populated and least developed countries in the Western hemisphere. This small country in the West Indies has been ruled by brutal dictators for much of its history. Hundreds of thousands of Haitians, including Danticat's family, have fled to the United States. Many have settled in Brooklyn, a borough of New York City. According to the 2000 census, over 200,000 Haitians and Haitian Americans live there. In some Brooklyn schools, Haitian children make up 75 percent of the population.

# NEW YORK DAY WOMEN

## Edwidge Danticat

Today, walking down the street, I see my mother. She is strolling with a happy gait, her body thrust toward the DON'T WALK sign and the yellow taxicabs that make forty-five-degree turns on the corner of Madison and Fifty-seventh Street.

I have never seen her in this kind of neighborhood, peering into Chanel and Tiffany's and gawking at the jewels glowing in the Bulgari[1] windows. My mother never shops outside of Brooklyn. She has never seen the advertising office where I work. She is afraid to take the subway, where you may meet those young black militant street preachers who curse black women for straightening their hair.

10     Yet, here she is, my mother, who I left at home that morning in her bathrobe, with pieces of newspapers twisted like rollers in her hair. My mother, who accuses me of random **offenses** as I dash out of the house. **A**

❖

*Would you get up and give an old lady like me your subway seat? In this state of mind, I bet you don't even give up your seat to a pregnant lady.*

❖

My mother, who is often right about that. Sometimes I get up and give my seat. Other times, I don't. It all depends on how pregnant the woman is and whether or not she is with her . . . husband and whether or not *he* is sitting down. **B**

    As my mother stands in front of Carnegie Hall,[2] one taxi driver yells to another, "What do you think this is, a dance floor?"

20     My mother waits patiently for this dispute to be settled before crossing the street.

❖

*In Haiti when you get hit by a car, the owner of the car gets out and kicks you for getting blood on his bumper.*

❖

---

1. **Chanel** (shə-nĕl'); **Tiffany's**; **Bulgari** (bŏŏl' gä-rē): very expensive shops that sell luxury goods such as designer clothing, perfume, glassware, and jewelry.
2. **Carnegie Hall** (kär'nə-gē hôl): a famous concert hall in New York City.

**offense** (ə-fĕns') *n.* a violation of a moral or social code; a sin

**A** SEQUENCE
Reread lines 10–12. When did the mother accuse the narrator of "random offenses"? Tell how you know.

**B** STYLE
Reread lines 10–17. Note any **repetition** of words or phrases. Based on this repetition, what do you think will be the subject of this story?

*The Promenade, Fifth Avenue* (1986), Bill Jacklin. Oil on canvas, 243.6 cm × 182.7 cm. Private collection. © Bill Jacklin/Bridgeman Art Library.

My mother who laughs when she says this and shows a large gap in her mouth where she lost three more molars to the dentist last week. My mother, who at fifty-nine, says dentures are okay.

❖

*You can take them out when they bother you. I'll like them. I'll like them fine.*

❖

Will it feel empty when Papa kisses you?

❖

*Oh no, he doesn't kiss me that way anymore.*

❖

My mother, who watches the lottery drawing every night on channel 11
30 without ever having played the numbers.

❖

*A third of that money is all I would need. We would pay the mortgage, and your father could stop driving that taxicab all over Brooklyn.*

❖

I follow my mother, **mesmerized** by the many possibilities of her journey. Even in a flowered dress, she is lost in a sea of pinstripes[3] and gray suits, high heels and elegant short skirts, . . . sneakers, dashing from building to building.
    My mother, who won't go out to dinner with anyone.

❖

*If they want to eat with me, let them come to my house, even if I boil water and give it to them.*

❖

My mother, who talks to herself when she peels the skin off poultry.

❖

40 *Fat, you know, and cholesterol. Fat and cholesterol killed your aunt Hermine.* **C**

❖

My mother, who makes jam with dried grapefruit peel and then puts in cinnamon bark that I always think is cockroaches in the jam. My mother, whom I have always bought household appliances for, on her birthday. A nice rice cooker, a blender.
    I trail the red orchids in her dress and the heavy faux[4] leather bag on her shoulders. Realizing the ferocious pace of my **pursuit**, I stop against a wall to rest. My mother keeps on walking as though she owns the sidewalk under her feet.
    As she heads toward the Plaza Hotel,[5] a bicycle messenger swings so close to her that I want to dash forward and rescue her, but she stands dead in her
50 tracks[6] and lets him ride around her and then goes on.

---

3. **pinstripes:** fabrics with very thin stripes, usually used to make business suits.
4. **faux** (fō): artificial but meant to look genuine.
5. **Plaza Hotel:** a world-renowned hotel located near Central Park in New York City.
6. **dead in her tracks:** perfectly still.

⬤ **SOCIAL STUDIES CONNECTION**

New York City is divided into five boroughs, or municipalities. The family in the story lives in Brooklyn. The narrator and her mother are now in Manhattan.

**mesmerize** (měz′mə-rīz′) *v.* to spellbind; to enthrall

**C** **STYLE**
Why do you think Danticat chooses to show the mother's words in italics?

**pursuit** (pər-soōt′) *n.* the act of chasing

My mother stops at a corner hot-dog stand and asks for something. The vendor hands her a can of soda that she slips into her bag. She stops by another vendor selling sundresses for seven dollars each. I can tell that she is looking at an African print dress, **contemplating** my size. I think to myself, Please Ma, don't buy it. It would be just another thing I would bury in the garage or give to Goodwill.

❖

*Why should we give to Goodwill when there are so many people back home who need clothes? We save our clothes for the relatives in Haiti.*

❖

Twenty years we have been saving all kinds of things for the relatives in Haiti. I need the place in the garage for an exercise bike.

❖

60 *You are pretty enough to be a stewardess. Only dogs like bones.*

❖

This mother of mine, she stops at another hot-dog vendor's and buys a frankfurter that she eats on the street. I never knew that she ate frankfurters. With her blood pressure, she shouldn't eat anything with sodium.[7] She has to be careful with her heart, this day woman.[8]

❖

*I cannot just swallow salt. Salt is heavier than a hundred bags of shame.*

❖

She is slowing her pace, and now I am too close. If she turns around, she might see me. I let her walk into the park before I start to follow again. **D**

My mother walks toward the sandbox in the middle of the park. There a woman is waiting with a child. The woman is wearing a leotard with biker's
70 shorts and has small weights in her hands. The woman kisses the child good-bye and **surrenders** him to my mother, then she bolts off, running on the cemented stretches in the park.

The child given to my mother has frizzy blond hair. His hand slips into hers easily, like he's known her for a long time. When he raises his face to look at my mother, it is as though he is looking at the sky.

My mother gives this child the soda that she bought from the vendor on the street corner. The child's face lights up as she puts . . . a straw in the can for him. This seems to be a conspiracy just between the two of them. **E**

My mother and the child sit and watch the other children play in the sandbox.
80 The child pulls out a comic book from a knapsack with Big Bird on the back. My mother peers into his comic book. My mother, who taught herself to read as a little girl in Haiti from the books that her brothers brought home from school.

My mother, who has now lost six of her seven sisters in Ville Rose[9] and has never had the strength to return for their funerals.

❖

---

7. **sodium** (sō′dē-əm): salt.

8. **day woman:** a woman who is employed as a housekeeper or babysitter but does not live in her employer's home.

9. **Ville Rose** (vĭl rōz): a fictional Haitian town.

---

**contemplate**
(kŏn′təm-plāt′) *v.*
to consider carefully
and at length

**D** SEQUENCE
Reread lines 66–67.
What words help you
understand the sequence
of events?

**surrender** (sə-rĕn′dər) *v.*
to give up possession or
control to another

**E** STYLE
Reread lines 68–78.
Danticat uses vivid
**imagery** in this passage.
Which images do you
think best illustrate
the special relationship
between the narrator's
mother and the boy?

*Many graves to kiss when I go back. Many graves to kiss.*

❖

She throws away the empty soda can when the child is done with it. I wait and watch from a corner until the woman in the leotard and biker's shorts returns, sweaty and breathless, an hour later. My mother gives the woman back her child and strolls farther into the park.

90    I turn around and start to walk out of the park before my mother can see me. My lunch hour is long since gone. I have to hurry back to work. I walk through a cluster of joggers, then race to a *Sweden Tours* bus. I stand behind the bus and take a peek at my mother in the park. She is standing in a circle, chatting with a group of women who are taking other people's children on an afternoon outing. They look like a Third World[10] Parent-Teacher Association meeting.

I quickly jump into a cab heading back to the office. Would Ma have said hello had she been the one to see me first? **F**

As the cab races away from the park, it occurs to me that perhaps one day I would chase an old woman down a street by mistake and that old woman
100  would be somebody else's mother, who I would have mistaken for mine.

❖

*Day women come out when nobody expects them.*

❖

Tonight on the subway, I will get up and give my seat to a pregnant woman or a lady about Ma's age.

My mother, who stuffs thimbles in her mouth and then blows up her cheeks like Dizzy Gillespie[11] while sewing yet another Raggedy Ann[12] doll that she names Suzette after me. **G**

❖

*I will have all these little Suzettes in case you never have any babies, which looks more and more like it is going to happen.*

❖

My mother, who sews lace collars on my company softball T-shirts when she
110  does my laundry.

❖

*Why, you can't look like a lady playing softball?*

❖

My mother, who never went to any of my Parent-Teacher Association meetings when I was in school.

❖

*You're so good anyway. What are they going to tell me? I don't want to make you ashamed of this day woman. Shame is heavier than a hundred bags of salt.* ◔

**F** SEQUENCE
How long has the narrator been watching her mother? Tell how you know.

**G** STYLE
Reread lines 104–106. In what way does the structure of this sentence represent Danticat's style?

---

10. **Third World:** the developing nations of Africa, Asia, and Latin America.

11. **Dizzy Gillespie** (dĭz′ē gə-lĕs′pē): an American trumpet player, bandleader, and composer (1917–1993) whose cheeks ballooned out when he played.

12. **Raggedy Ann:** a red-haired rag doll and fictional character who was the subject of several children's books.

# Comprehension

**INDIANA STANDARDS**

READING STANDARD
**8.3.6** Identify significant literary devices . . . .

1. **Recall** What does the narrator's mother do for a living?

2. **Clarify** Why is the narrator, Suzette, surprised to see her mother?

3. **Clarify** Why doesn't Suzette go up to greet her mother?

# Literary Analysis

4. **Examine Characterization** How does Edwidge Danticat bring the mother's character to life? Using a character map like the one shown, record details from the story that describe the mother's appearance, beliefs and values, and actions.

*Mother*

*Appearance*   *Beliefs and Values*   *Actions*

5. **Examine Sequence** Review the sequence chart you made while reading. Under each square, note what Suzette seems to feel about her mother at that point in the story. In what way does Suzette's **perception** of her mother change from the beginning to the end of the story?

6. **Draw Conclusions** In the beginning of the story Suzette admits that she might not give up her seat on a bus to an older or pregnant woman. Yet by the story's end, she changes her mind. What do you think causes this change?

7. **Make Judgments** Reread lines 114–115. Do you think Suzette is ashamed of her mother? Why or why not? Support your answer with examples from the story.

8. **Evaluate Style** Choose a passage from the story that you think is a good example of Danticat's style. You may wish to look for a passage in which Danticat uses **imagery,** unique sentence structures, or **repetition.** Why did you pick the passage that you did?

# Extension and Challenge

9. **Readers' Circle** Should Suzette have approached her mother, and if so, what should she have said? Why do you think the mother never told Suzette about her trips to Manhattan? Discuss these questions with a small group.

10.  **SOCIAL STUDIES CONNECTION** Although the action in "New York Day Women" occurs in Manhattan, Suzette and her mother actually live in Brooklyn. Research the people, landmarks, geography, and history of these two boroughs, and create a poster contrasting the two. Present your poster to your class.

**RESEARCH LINKS**
For more on Brooklyn and Manhattan, visit the **Research Center** at **ClassZone.com.**

# Vocabulary in Context

## VOCABULARY PRACTICE

Choose the letter of the word or phrase that means the same, or nearly the same, as the boldfaced word or phrase.

1. **contemplate** a decision: (a) disregard, (b) consider, (c) ignore, (d) avoid
2. **mesmerize** an audience: (a) fascinate, (b) bore, (c) puzzle, (d) disappoint
3. **pursuit** of a criminal: (a) arrest, (b) imprisonment, (c) chasing, (d) pardon
4. **surrender** her valuables: (a) purchase, (b) give up, (c) hide, (d) hold
5. a minor **offense**: (a) wrongdoing, (b) injury, (c) argument, (d) accomplishment

contemplate

mesmerize

offense

pursuit

surrender

## VOCABULARY IN WRITING

What do you think you would learn if you followed someone you knew for a day? Write a paragraph explaining your answer. Use at least two vocabulary words in your paragraph. You could start this way.

> **EXAMPLE SENTENCE**
>
> *As my mother enters the coffee shop, I **contemplate** following her, but I decide to stay outside instead.*

## VOCABULARY STRATEGY: MULTIPLE-MEANING WORDS

Many English words have more than one meaning. For example, you might know that *offense* is a term used in sports that means "those players whose primary responsibility it is to score." But you might not be familiar with its meaning in this selection: "a violation of a moral or social code."

   If a word does not make sense to you, look at the words around it for clues to other possible meanings. For example:

*My mother, who accuses me of random offenses as I dash out of the house.*

Would the mother be more likely to accuse the narrator of a sports-related move, or of a moral or social mistake? Based on the context of the sentence, you can conclude that the second definition is correct. For further help with multiple-meaning words, check a dictionary.

*PRACTICE* Define the boldfaced words. Identify context clues that helped you understand the meaning of each.

1. The bus stops suddenly, and the motion **jerks** me out of a deep sleep.
2. Although we were tired, Michael and I decided to play one more **round** of chess.
3. Please **book** me a seat on the next plane to Washington, D.C.
4. I think we need to **table** this issue for now. Let's put it aside until next week.
5. These new circumstances open a **window** of opportunity for us.

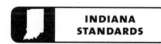

**INDIANA STANDARDS**

**READING STANDARD**
**8.1.3** Verify the meaning of a word in its context....

**VOCABULARY PRACTICE**
For more practice, go to the **Vocabulary Center** at **ClassZone.com**.

# Reading-Writing Connection

Get to know the characters in "New York Day Women" better by responding to these prompts. Then complete the **Grammar and Writing** exercise.

| WRITING PROMPTS | SELF-CHECK |
|---|---|
| **A. Short Response: Write a Character Sketch**<br>What do you learn about Suzette as she pursues her mother? Make inferences about her age, appearance, occupation, and personality. Then write a **one-paragraph character sketch** of her. | ***A thorough description will . . .***<br>• include details about Suzette's life and personality<br>• cite specific details from the story that helped you make inferences about her |
| **B. Extended Response: Write A Scene**<br>Imagine that Suzette tells her mother what she saw and how her **perceptions** of her mother have changed as a result of this experience. How does the mother respond? Is she upset? surprised? relieved? Write a **two- or three-paragraph scene** about the encounter. | ***An engaging scene will . . .***<br>• be based on details about both characters<br>• use words and phrases appropriate to each character |

## GRAMMAR AND WRITING

**WRITE CONCISELY** An **appositive** is a noun or pronoun that identifies or renames another noun or pronoun. An **appositive phrase** is made up of an appositive and its modifiers. You can make your writing more concise by using an appositive or appositive phrase to combine two sentences into one.

INDIANA STANDARDS

WRITING STANDARD
**8.6.3** Use subordination, coordination, noun phrases that function as adjectives . . . .

   *Original:*   The mother works in Manhattan. She is a native of Haiti.

   *Revised:*   The mother, a native of Haiti, works in Manhattan. (A native of Haiti *is an appositive phrase that identifies* mother.)

Place commas before and after an appositive phrase when it adds extra, nonessential information about the noun or pronoun that precedes it, as in the example above.

**PRACTICE** In each item, combine the two sentences by changing the second sentence to an appositive phrase.

1. Suzette works in Manhattan. She is a resident of Brooklyn.
2. Suzette doesn't give her subway seat to older passengers. She is the narrator.
3. The mother babysits children. She is a day woman.
4. The mother waits to cross the street. She is a patient woman.

*For more help with appositive phrases, see page R61 in the* **Grammar Handbook.**

## The Lady, or the Tiger?

Short Story by Frank R. Stockton

# *How do you make* DECISIONS?

**KEY IDEA** How we make **decisions** depends on the situation. A simple coin toss can help you decide who goes first when playing a video game. But you wouldn't want to flip a coin when making a more important choice, such as which sport to play or which high school to attend. In the story you are about to read, a decision has life-or-death consequences.

**SURVEY** Working with a small group, create a list of ways people commonly make decisions. Survey the class to learn how others choose what course to follow. Add more methods to the list as people mention them. What methods come up most often? Which do you think are most effective?

| How Do You Make Decisions? | |
|---|---|
| List Pros and Cons | )) |
| Talk to Parents | )))) |

## ● LITERARY ANALYSIS: TONE

Writers often express an attitude, or **tone,** toward the subject, setting, or characters they're writing about. A tone can often be described with one word, such as angry, proud, or playful. Just as knowing a friend's attitude can help you decide whether she's serious or joking, knowing a writer's tone can help you grasp his or her message. To help you determine Frank R. Stockton's tone, pay attention to the words and details he uses to describe

- the **characters**—Do his descriptions of them suggest whether he thinks they're smart or foolish, kind or cruel?
- the **setting**—Does he admire the society's customs?
- the **plot events**—Does his language show that he takes the events seriously, or not?

## ● READING STRATEGY: PARAPHRASE

One good way to understand and remember what you read is to **paraphrase** it, or restate the writer's language in your own words. To paraphrase, follow these steps:

- Reread the passage, looking for the main ideas.
- Define unfamiliar words using context clues or a dictionary.
- Restate important ideas and details in your own words. A good paraphrase should be about as long as the original text.

As you read, paraphrase difficult sections in your notebook.

| Line Numbers | Paraphrase |
|---|---|
| 1–4 | Long ago, there lived a rough, cruel king. He had been influenced by forward-thinking cultures, but he was still uncivilized. |

## ▲ VOCABULARY IN CONTEXT

The following words help reveal Stockton's opinion of his characters. How many do you know? Make a chart like the one shown, putting each word in the appropriate column.

| WORD LIST | | |
|---|---|---|
| anguished | conventional | progressiveness |
| aspire | devious | subordinate |
| assert | impartial | waver |

| Know Well | Think I Know | Don't Know at All |
|---|---|---|
|  |  |  |

# Author Online

**Full of Fairy Tales**
Though today Frank R. Stockton's most popular story is "The Lady, or the Tiger?" many of his other works were widely read during his lifetime. Born near Philadelphia, Pennsylvania, Stockton began writing fairy tales as a child, later claiming that he did so because "my mind was full of them."

**Frank R. Stockton
1834–1902**

**Literary Sensation** While still in high school, Stockton won a short story contest sponsored by a magazine. Later on in life, Stockton wrote stories for both adults and children. "The Lady, or the Tiger?" caused a sensation among the American public. The ending was debated in high schools, and Stockton received hundreds of letters from people seeking the solution. Unfortunately, Stockton did not like the story as much as his readers did; he felt it did not represent his best work.

 **MORE ABOUT THE AUTHOR**
For more on Frank R. Stockton, visit the **Literature Center** at ClassZone.com.

## Background

**Historic Arena** Much of the action in "The Lady, or the Tiger?" takes place in an amphitheater. One of the most famous amphitheaters in history is the Colosseum, built during the Roman empire in the year A.D. 72. Capable of seating 50,000 people, this massive structure featured three levels of seating, wood floors, and an innovative canvas roof that brought in cool air from the outside. The Colosseum was the scene of gruesome "games" involving slaves, prisoners, or animals fighting gladiators (professionally trained swordsmen) to the death. Although lightning and earthquakes destroyed large parts of the Colosseum over the years, much of it still stands today.

# The *Lady,* or the *Tiger?*

## Frank R. Stockton

I n the very olden time, there lived a semi-barbaric king, whose ideas, though somewhat polished and sharpened by the **progressiveness** of distant Latin neighbors, were still large, florid,[1] and untrammeled,[2] as became the half of him which was barbaric.[3] He was a man of exuberant fancy, and, withal, of an authority so irresistible that, at his will, he turned his varied fancies into facts. He was greatly given to self-communing;[4] and, when he and himself agreed upon anything, the thing was done. When every member of his domestic and political systems moved smoothly in its appointed course, his nature was bland and genial; but whenever there was a little hitch, and 10 some of his orbs got out of their orbits, he was blander and more genial still, for nothing pleased him so much as to make the crooked straight, and crush down uneven places. **A**

Among the borrowed notions by which his barbarism had become semifixed was that of the public arena, in which, by exhibitions of manly and beastly valor, the minds of his subjects were refined and cultured.

---

1. **florid** (flôr'ĭd): very ornate; flowery.
2. **untrammeled** (ŭn-trăm'əld): not limited or restricted.
3. **barbaric** (bär-bâr'ĭk): marked by crudeness or lack of restraint in taste, style, or manner.
4. **self-communing:** the act of "talking" things over with oneself only.

**progressiveness**
(prə-grĕs'ĭv-nĭs) *n.* the state of advancing toward better conditions or new policies, ideas, or methods

**A** **TONE**
Based on the words he uses to describe the king, how do you think Stockton feels about this character?

**ANALYZE VISUALS**
What do the details in this painting help you **infer** about the kingdom and its people?

*Spring* (1894), Lawrence Alma-Tadema. Oil on canvas, 70¼″ × 31½″. The J. Paul Getty Museum, Los Angeles. (72.PA.3). © J. Paul Getty Trust.

But even here the exuberant and barbaric fancy **asserted** itself. The arena of the king was built, not to give the people an opportunity of hearing the rhapsodies of dying gladiators, nor to enable them to view the inevitable conclusion of a conflict between religious opinions and hungry jaws, but for
20 purposes far better adapted to widen and develop the mental energies of the people. This vast amphitheater, with its encircling galleries, its mysterious vaults, and its unseen passages, was an agent of poetic justice, in which crime was punished, or virtue rewarded, by the decrees of an impartial and incorruptible chance.

When a subject was accused of a crime of sufficient importance to interest the king, public notice was given that on an appointed day the fate of the accused person would be decided in the king's arena—a structure which well deserved its name; for, although its form and plan were borrowed from afar, its purpose emanated solely from the brain of this man, who, every barleycorn
30 a king,[5] knew no tradition to which he owed more allegiance than pleased his fancy, and who ingrafted on every adopted form of human thought and action the rich growth of his barbaric idealism. **B**

When all the people had assembled in the galleries and the king, surrounded by his court, sat high up on his throne of royal state on one side of the arena, he gave a signal, a door beneath him opened, and the accused subject stepped out into the amphitheater. Directly opposite him, on the other side of the enclosed space, were two doors, exactly alike and side by side. It was the duty and the privilege of the person on trial to walk directly to these doors and open one of them. He could open either door he pleased; he was subject to no guidance or
40 influence but that of the aforementioned **impartial** and incorruptible chance. If he opened the one, there came out of it a hungry tiger, the fiercest and most cruel that could be procured, which immediately sprang upon him and tore him to pieces, as a punishment for his guilt. The moment that the case of the criminal was thus decided, doleful iron bells were clanged, great wails went up from the hired mourners posted on the outer rim of the arena, and the vast audience, with bowed heads and downcast hearts, wended slowly their homeward way, mourning greatly that one so young and fair, or so old and respected, should have merited so dire a fate.

But if the accused person opened the other door, there came forth from
50 it a lady, the most suitable to his years and station that his majesty could select among his fair subjects; and to this lady he was immediately married, as a reward for his innocence. It mattered not that he might already possess a wife and family, or that his affections might be engaged upon an object of his own selection: the king allowed no such **subordinate** arrangements to interfere with his great scheme of retribution and reward. The exercises, as in the other instance, took place immediately and in the arena. Another door opened beneath the king, and a priest, followed by a band of choristers

**assert** (ə-sûrt′) *v.* to act forcefully; to take charge

**VISUAL VOCABULARY**

**amphitheater** (ăm′fə-thē′ə-tər) *n.* an arena where contests and spectacles are held

**B** **PARAPHRASE**
Reread lines 25–32. Paraphrase this passage. Was the amphitheater used in the same way in this kingdom as it was elsewhere? Explain.

**impartial** (ĭm-pär′shəl) *adj.* not partial or biased; unprejudiced

**subordinate** (sə-bôr′dn-ĭt) *adj.* secondary; belonging to a lower rank

---

5. **every barleycorn a king:** a playful exaggeration of the expression "every ounce a king," meaning "thoroughly kingly." (Grains of barley were formerly used as units of measurement.)

and dancing maidens blowing joyous airs on golden horns and treading an epithalamic measure,[6] advanced to where the pair stood, side by side; and
60 the wedding was promptly and cheerily solemnized.[7] Then the gay brass bells rang forth their merry peals, the people shouted glad hurrahs, and the innocent man, preceded by children strewing flowers on his path, led his bride to his home.

This was the king's semi-barbaric method of administering justice. Its perfect fairness is obvious. The criminal could not know out of which door would come the lady: he opened either he pleased, without having the slightest idea whether, in the next instant, he was to be devoured or married. On some occasions the tiger came out of one door and on some out of the other. The decisions of this tribunal[8] were not only fair, they were positively
70 determinate: the accused person was instantly punished if he found himself guilty; and, if innocent, he was rewarded on the spot, whether he liked it or not. There was no escape from the judgments of the king's arena. **C**

**C PARAPHRASE**
Reread lines 64–72. How would you explain the king's "perfect" system of justice? Add this to your notebook.

---

6. **treading an epithalamic** (ĕp′ə-thə-lā′mĭk) **measure:** dancing to wedding music.

7. **solemnized** (sŏl′əm-nīzd′): celebrated or observed with dignity.

8. **tribunal** (trī-byōō′nəl): something that has the power to determine guilt or innocence.

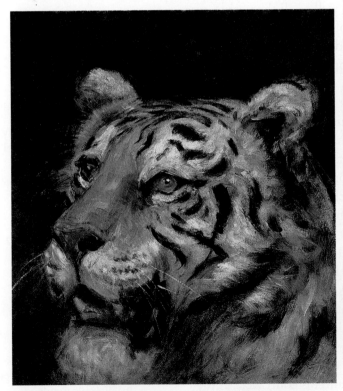

*Head Study of a Tiger,* Roland Wheelwright. Oil on board, 49.5 cm × 60.9 cm. Private collection. © Roland Wheelwright/Bridgeman Art Library.

Detail of *Study of a Lady,* Frederic Leighton. Oil on canvas, 25.5 cm × 19 cm. Private collection. © Bridgeman Art Library.

The institution was a very popular one. When the people gathered together on one of the great trial days, they never knew whether they were to witness a bloody slaughter or a hilarious wedding. This element of uncertainty lent an interest to the occasion which it could not otherwise have attained. Thus, the masses were entertained and pleased, and the thinking part of the community could bring no charge of unfairness against this plan; for did not the accused person have the whole matter in his own hands?

80     This semi-barbaric king had a daughter as blooming as his most florid fancies, and with a soul as fervent[9] and imperious[10] as his own. As is usual in such cases, she was the apple of his eye and was loved by him above all humanity. Among his courtiers was a young man of that fineness of blood and lowness of station common to the **conventional** heroes of romance who love royal maidens. This royal maiden was well satisfied with her lover, for he was handsome and brave to a degree unsurpassed in all this kingdom; and she loved him with an ardor that had enough of barbarism in it to make it exceedingly warm and strong. This love affair moved on happily for many months, until one day the king happened to discover its existence. He did not hesitate nor **waver** in

90 regard to his duty in the premises. The youth was immediately cast into prison, and a day was appointed for his trial in the king's arena. This, of course, was an especially important occasion; and his majesty, as well as all the people, was greatly interested in the workings and development of this trial. Never before had such a case occurred; never before had a subject dared to love the daughter of a king. In after-years such things became commonplace enough, but then they were, in no slight degree, novel and startling. **D**

    The tiger-cages of the kingdom were searched for the most savage and relentless beasts, from which the fiercest monster might be selected for the arena; and the ranks of maiden youth and beauty throughout the land were

100 carefully surveyed by competent judges, in order that the young man might have a fitting bride in case fate did not determine for him a different destiny. Of course, everybody knew that the deed with which the accused was charged had been done. He had loved the princess, and neither he, she, nor any one else thought of denying the fact; but the king would not think of allowing any fact of this kind to interfere with the workings of the tribunal, in which he took such great delight and satisfaction. No matter how the affair turned out, the youth would be disposed of; and the king would take an aesthetic[11] pleasure in watching the course of events, which would determine whether or not the young man had done wrong in allowing himself to love the princess. **E**

110     The appointed day arrived. From far and near the people gathered, and thronged the great galleries of the arena, and crowds, unable to gain admittance, massed themselves against its outside walls. The king and his court were in their places, opposite the twin doors,—those fateful portals, so terrible in their similarity.

---

9. **fervent** (fûr'vənt): having or showing great emotion or zeal.

10. **imperious** (ĭm-pîr'ē-əs): arrogantly domineering or overbearing.

11. **aesthetic** (ĕs-thĕt'ĭk): concerning the artistic appreciation of beauty.

---

**conventional**
(kən-vĕn'shə-nəl) *adj.* conforming to established practice or accepted standards; traditional

**waver** (wā'vər) *v.* to exhibit indecision; to hesitate

**D** TONE
Reread lines 91–96. Stockton describes the citizens as being "greatly interested" in the "novel and startling" events that are unfolding. In what way might this description be **ironic**, stating the opposite of what Stockton believes?

**E** PARAPHRASE
Reread lines 102–109. What is the young man's fate? Rewrite this passage in your own words.

All was ready. The signal was given. A door beneath the royal party opened, and the lover of the princess walked into the arena. Tall, beautiful, fair, his appearance was greeted with a low hum of admiration and anxiety. Half the audience had not known so grand a youth had lived among them. No wonder the princess loved him! What a terrible thing for him to be there!

As the youth advanced into the arena, he turned, as the custom was, to
120 bow to the king: but he did not think at all of that royal personage; his eyes were fixed upon the princess, who sat to the right of her father. Had it not been for the moiety[12] of barbarism in her nature, it is probable that lady would not have been there; but her intense and fervid[13] soul would not allow her to be absent on an occasion in which she was so terribly interested. From the moment that the decree had gone forth, that her lover should decide his fate in the king's arena, she had thought of nothing, night or day, but this great event and the various subjects connected with it. Possessed of more power, influence, and force of character than any one who had ever before been interested in such a case, she had done what no other person had done—she
130 had possessed herself of the secret of the doors. She knew in which of the two rooms, that lay behind those doors, stood the cage of the tiger, with its open front, and in which waited the lady. Through these thick doors, heavily curtained with skins on the inside, it was impossible that any noise or suggestion should come from within to the person who should approach to raise the latch of one of them; but gold, and the power of a woman's will, had brought the secret to the princess. **F**

And not only did she know in which room stood the lady ready to emerge, all blushing and radiant, should her door be opened, but she knew who the lady was. It was one of the fairest and loveliest of the damsels of the court
140 who had been selected as the reward of the accused youth, should he be proved innocent of the crime of **aspiring** to one so far above him; and the princess hated her. Often had she seen, or imagined that she had seen, this fair creature throwing glances of admiration upon the person of her lover, and sometimes she thought these glances were perceived and even returned. Now and then she had seen them talking together; it was but for a moment or two, but much can be said in a brief space; it may have been on most unimportant topics, but how could she know that? The girl was lovely, but she had dared to raise her eyes to the loved one of the princess; and, with all the intensity of the savage blood transmitted to her through long lines of
150 wholly barbaric ancestors, she hated the woman who blushed and trembled behind that silent door. **G**

When her lover turned and looked at her, and his eyes met hers as she sat there paler and whiter than anyone in the vast ocean of anxious faces about her, he saw, by that power of quick perception which is given to those whose souls are one, that she knew behind which door crouched the tiger, and behind

**F** TONE
Reread lines 119–136. What is Stockton's attitude toward the princess? Tell what words and details in the passage reveal this attitude.

**aspire** (ə-spīr′) v. to have a great ambition or an ultimate goal; to desire strongly

**G** TONE
Stockton frequently refers to barbarism in this story. What does this reveal about his attitude toward the characters?

---

12. **moiety** (moi′ĭ-tē): a portion.

13. **fervid** (fûr′vĭd): passionate.

which stood the lady. He had expected her to know it. He understood her nature, and his soul was assured that she would never rest until she had made plain to herself this thing, hidden to all other lookers-on, even to the king. The only hope for the youth in which there was any element of certainty was 160 based upon the success of the princess in discovering this mystery; and the moment he looked upon her, he saw she had succeeded, as in his soul he knew she would succeed.

Then it was that his quick and anxious glance asked the question: "Which?" It was as plain to her as if he shouted it from where he stood. There was not an instant to be lost. The question was asked in a flash; it must be answered in another.

*Cleopatra* (about 1888), John W. Waterhouse. Oil on canvas, 65.4 cm × 56.8 cm. © 2002 Christie's Images Limited.

**ANALYZE VISUALS**
Does the person in this painting match your idea of the princess in the story? Explain why or why not.

Her right arm lay on the cushioned parapet[14] before her. She raised her hand and made a slight, quick movement toward the right. No one but her lover saw her. Every eye but his was fixed on the man in the arena.

170 He turned, and with a firm and rapid step he walked across the empty space. Every heart stopped beating, every breath was held, every eye was fixed immovably upon that man. Without the slightest hesitation, he went to the door on the right and opened it.

Now, the point of the story is this: Did the tiger come out of that door, or did the lady?

The more we reflect upon this question, the harder it is to answer. It involves a study of the human heart which leads us through **devious** mazes of passion, out of which it is difficult to find our way. Think of it, fair reader, not as if the decision of the question depended upon yourself, but upon that hot-blooded, 180 semi-barbaric princess, her soul at a white heat beneath the combined fires of despair and jealousy. She had lost him, but who should have him? Ⓗ

How often, in her waking hours and in her dreams, had she started in wild horror, and covered her face with her hands as she thought of her lover opening the door on the other side of which waited the cruel fangs of the tiger!

But how much oftener had she seen him at the other door! How in her grievous reveries[15] had she gnashed her teeth, and torn her hair, when she saw his start of rapturous[16] delight as he opened the door of the lady! How her soul had burned in agony when she had seen him rush to meet that woman, with her flushing cheek and sparkling eye of triumph; when she had seen him lead her forth, his 190 whole frame kindled with the joy of recovered life; when she had heard the glad shouts from the multitude, and the wild ringing of the happy bells; when she had seen the priest, with his joyous followers, advance to the couple, and make them man and wife before her very eyes; and when she had seen them walk away together upon their path of flowers, followed by the tremendous shouts of the hilarious multitude, in which her one despairing shriek was lost and drowned!

Would it not be better for him to die at once, and go to wait for her in the blessed regions of semi-barbaric futurity?

And yet, that awful tiger, those shrieks, that blood!

Her decision had been indicated in an instant, but it had been made after 200 days and nights of **anguished** deliberation. She had known she would be asked, she had decided what she would answer, and, without the slightest hesitation, she had moved her hand to the right.

The question of her decision is one not to be lightly considered, and it is not for me to presume to set myself up as the one person able to answer it. And so I leave it with all of you: Which came out of the opened door—the lady, or the tiger? ❧

---

14. **parapet** (păr'ə-pĭt): a low railing at the edge of a balcony.

15. **reveries** (rĕv'ə-rēz): daydreams.

16. **rapturous** (răp'chər-əs): filled with great joy; ecstatic.

**devious** (dē'vē-əs) *adj.* departing from the straight or direct course

Ⓗ **PARAPHRASE**
Reread lines 176–181. What is Stockton saying to his readers? Paraphrase this passage in your notebook.

**anguished** (ăng'gwĭsht) *adj.* tormented; distressed

## Comprehension

1. **Recall** How do the citizens of the kingdom feel about the king's method of justice?

2. **Recall** What "crime" has the young man committed?

3. **Represent** Reread lines 21–24 and 33–63. Create a diagram of the arena. Use information from the story to include at least three labels in your diagram.

**INDIANA STANDARDS**

**READING STANDARD**
**8.3.2** Evaluate the structural elements of the plot . . . .

## Literary Analysis

4. **Examine a Story's Ending** What was surprising about the way "The Lady, or the Tiger?" ended? Why did you expect something different?

5. **Identify Tone** Choose the one word from the following list that you think best describes the tone of the story: *sarcastic, sad, serious, playful, bitter, anxious, sentimental,* or *curious.* Write the word in the top of a chart like the one shown. Fill in your chart with words and details about the characters, setting, and situation in the story that support your choice.

6. **Explore Paraphrasing** Choose two of the passages you paraphrased in your notebook. What crucial information did you gain from paraphrasing these passages that helped you understand the story?

7. **Evaluate** Describe the king's system of "justice." Is there anything just, or fair, about it? Explain.

8. **Draw Conclusions** Based on what you know about the princess, which door do you think she **decides** on? Use details from the selection to support your response.

## Extension and Challenge

9. **Literary Criticism** Frank R. Stockton once said, "If you decide which it was— the lady or the tiger—you find out what kind of person you are yourself." What might your interpretation of the story show you about yourself and your view of human nature?

10. **Creative Response: Writing** Why do you think the princess didn't stand up for her beloved? If she had done so, what might she have said to her father? Write a scene in which the princess defends the man she loves against the king's accusations.

# Vocabulary in Context

## VOCABULARY PRACTICE

Choose the word in each group that is most nearly opposite in meaning to the boldfaced word.

1. **impartial:** (a) unbiased, (b) fair, (c) prejudiced, (d) objective
2. **assert:** (a) deny, (b) claim, (c) declare, (d) stress
3. **subordinate:** (a) beneath, (b) second-in-command, (c) presiding, (d) assisting
4. **conventional:** (a) customary, (b) unusual, (c) accepted, (d) traditional
5. **waver:** (a) hesitate, (b) falter, (c) pause, (d) continue
6. **devious:** (a) straightforward, (b) cunning, (c) sneaky, (d) deceitful
7. **aspire:** (a) plan, (b) hope, (c) attempt, (d) fail
8. **anguished:** (a) tormented, (b) pained, (c) miserable, (d) pleased
9. **progressiveness:** (a) narrow-mindedness, (b) forward-thinking, (c) acceptance, (d) tolerance

## VOCABULARY IN WRITING

What makes the princess in this tale different from most fairy-tale princesses that you have read about? Write a paragraph explaining your answer. Use at least two vocabulary words in your paragraph. You could start this way.

> **EXAMPLE SENTENCE**
>
> Unlike most fairy-tale heroines, this princess is **devious** in nature.

## VOCABULARY STRATEGY: CONNOTATION AND DENOTATION

A **denotation** is the literal meaning of a word—that is, the definition found in a dictionary. A word's **connotation** is a feeling or attitude linked with a word. Connotations have a big impact on the meaning a word conveys. For example, the vocabulary word *conventional* means "traditional." But it also connotes "old-fashioned" or "unimaginative." Recognizing connotations will help you identify the tone of what you read.

**PRACTICE** Show the difference in the connotations of the word pairs by writing a sentence for each word.

1. bland/simple
2. youthful/immature
3. fierce/strong
4. disagree/clash
5. cunning/smart
6. adventurous/reckless
7. smell/stench
8. grueling/challenging

**INDIANA STANDARDS**

**READING STANDARD**
**8.1.3** Verify the meaning of a word in its context ....

**VOCABULARY PRACTICE**
For more practice, go to the **Vocabulary Center** at ClassZone.com.

Use with "The Lady, or the Tiger?" page 684.

**INDIANA STANDARDS**

**READING STANDARDS**
**8.2.5** Use information from a variety of consumer and public documents to explain a situation or decision and to solve a problem.

**8.2.9** Make reasonable statements and draw conclusions about a text, supporting them with accurate examples.

# The Monty Hall Debate
Newspaper Article

## What's the Connection?

In "The Lady, or the Tiger?" you read about a man who had to make a life-or-death choice between two doors. The following article is about a similar (though far less serious) decision faced by contestants of "Let's Make a Deal," a television game show popular in the 1960s and 1970s.

## Skill Focus: Use a Graphic Aid

"Let's Make a Deal," host Monty Hall became famous for asking contestants to guess which of three doors hid a big prize. After a contestant picked a door, Hall would open one of the other two doors to show that the prize wasn't behind it. Then he'd give the contestants a choice: Do you want to change your guess to the other door or stick to the door you originally picked?

The article you're about to read explains why one choice is better than the other. The explanation is somewhat complicated, but the diagram shown here can help you understand it. Like other **graphic aids,** this diagram provides a visual representation of ideas. Copy it into your notebook, so you can write on it if you want to. Then refer to the diagram as you read the article, and use these tips to help you interpret it:

- Use symbols such as arrows to help you follow the diagram.
- Pay attention to labels that identify specific details, and relate them to what you read in the article.
- Look for patterns in the use of shading. For example, does one type of information always get shaded a certain way?

### The New York Times

*SUNDAY, JULY 21, 1991*                                           C3

# The Monty Hall Debate

**John Tierney**

**M**arilyn vos Savant, a magazine columnist who is listed in the *Guinness Book of World Records* for highest IQ, was once asked this question:

Suppose you're on a game show, and you're given the choice of three doors: Behind one door is a car; behind the others, goats. You pick a 10 door, say No. 1, and the host, who knows what's behind the other doors, opens another door, say No. 3, which has a goat. He then says to you, "Do you want to stick with your original choice or pick door No. 2?" Is it to your advantage to take the switch?

Ms. vos Savant's answer was that you should always change and pick 20 the other door, because the chances are two in three that there will be a car behind that door. Since she gave her answer, Ms. vos Savant estimates she has received 10,000 letters, the great majority disagreeing with her. . . . Of the critical letters she received, close to 1,000 carried signatures with Ph.D.'s, and many were on letterheads of mathematics 30 and science departments. . . .

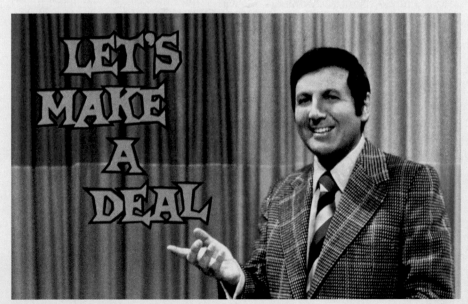

Monty Hall hosted "Let's Make A Deal" from 1963 to 1976.

**A GRAPHIC AID**
Notice how the description in lines 6–13 is represented in the diagram you copied. What do the first and second rows of the diagram show? What do the third and fourth rows show?

**B** GRAPHIC AID
Reread lines 64–71.
What does the
shading on the
chart on page 694
indicate?

Robert Sachs, a professor of mathematics at George Mason University in Fairfax, Va., expressed the prevailing view that there was no reason to switch doors.

"You blew it!" he wrote. "Let me explain: If one door is shown to be a loser, that information changes the probability of either remaining 40 choice—*neither of which has any reason to be more likely*—to ½. As a professional mathematician, I'm very concerned with the general public's lack of mathematical skills. Please help by confessing your error and, in the future, being more careful.". . .

Monty Hall, the game show host who actually gave contestants this 50 choice on "Let's Make a Deal," said he was not surprised at the experts' insistence that the probability was one out of two. "That's the same assumption contestants would make on the show after I showed them there was nothing behind one door," he said. "They'd think the odds on their door had now gone up to one in two, so they hated to give up the 60 door no matter how much money I offered.[1] By opening one of the other doors we were applying pressure.". . .

Mr. Hall said he realized the contestants were wrong, because the odds on Door 1 were still only one in three even after he opened another door. Since the only other place the car could be was behind Door 2, the 70 odds on that door must now be two in three. **B**

Sitting at his dining room table, Mr. Hall quickly conducted ten rounds of the game as this contestant tried the non-switching strategy. The result was four cars and six goats. Then for the next ten rounds the contestant tried switching doors, and there was a dramatic 80 improvement: eight cars and two goats. A pattern was emerging.

"So her answer's right: you should switch," Mr. Hall said, reaching the same conclusion as the tens of thousands of students who conducted similar experiments at Ms. vos Savant's suggestion. That conclusion was also reached eventually by many of her critics in academia, although most did 90 not bother to write letters of retraction. Dr. Sachs, whose letter was published in her column, was one of the few with the grace to concede his mistake.

"I wrote her another letter," Dr. Sachs said, "telling her that after removing my foot from my mouth I'm now eating humble pie.[2] I vowed as penance to answer all the 100 people who wrote to castigate[3] me. It's been an intense professional embarrassment.". . .

---

1. **how much money I offered:** Monty Hall would sometimes increase the drama of the show by offering contestants money to change their minds about whether to switch doors.

2. **after removing my foot . . . eating humble pie:** after making a careless comment I'm now forced to make an embarrassing apology.

3. **castigate** (kăs′tĭ-gāt′): severely criticize.

## Comprehension

1. **Recall** Who is Marilyn vos Savant?

2. **Recall** Did most people who wrote to Ms. vos Savant agree or disagree with her answer to the Monty Hall problem?

3. **Clarify** Reread lines 36–41. According to Robert Sachs, what does Ms. vos Savant fail to realize?

## Critical Analysis

4. **Understand a Graphic Aid** How does the shading on the diagram help you understand that a contestant has a two-in-three chance of getting a car if he or she changes doors? Also explain how the shading reveals what the chance of getting the car is if the contestant sticks with his or her original choice.

## Read for Information: Synthesize

**INDIANA STANDARDS**

**READING STANDARDS**
**8.2.5** Use information from a variety of consumer and public documents to explain a situation or decision and to solve a problem.

**8.2.9** Make reasonable statements and draw conclusions about a text, supporting them with accurate examples.

> **WRITING PROMPT**
>
> Imagine your best friend is about to go on a game show like "Let's Make a Deal." Since you have seen the show before, you understand that the host knows which door the car is behind. Sometimes he offers contestants money to influence their decision. What advice should you give your friend so that he or she chooses the winning door? Synthesize what you've learned about decision-making from the short story, this article, and your life to answer this question. Then write a letter in which you present your friend with guidelines about making the right decision. Be sure to support your advice with details and examples.

When you **synthesize,** you combine information from various sources to gain a better understanding of a subject. Following these steps can help you synthesize:

1. Reflect on what you learned about decision-making from the story, the article, and your life.

2. Jot down the most important considerations about decision-making that you found in these sources.

3. Write a letter in which you present these considerations as guidelines for choosing the winning door. Support each guideline you offer with an example from your life, the article, or "The Lady, or the Tiger?"

# Kira-Kira

Coming-of-Age Novel by Cynthia Kadohata

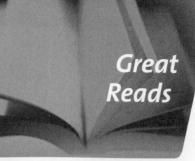

**Cynthia Kadohata**
**born 1956**

**Other Books by**
**Cynthia Kadohata**

- *The Floating World*
- *The Glass Mountains*

## Meet Cynthia Kadohata

Like the main character's family in *Kira-Kira*, Cynthia Kadohata's family moved often so that her parents could seek work. They lived in Illinois, Arkansas, Georgia, and Michigan before finally settling in California. Kadohata, a Japanese American, often did not feel like she fit in during her childhood. "I remember a little girl asking me something like, 'Are you black or white?'" she says. "I really stumbled for an answer. I said, 'I don't know.'" But since then, Kadohata has come to embrace her cultural identity. Today, she is often viewed as one of the great voices in Asian-American writing.

Although she majored in journalism in college, in her early 20s Kadohata began to appreciate the power of fiction. "I had always thought that nonfiction represented the 'truth,'" she explains, "but . . . I realized you could say things with fiction that you couldn't say any other way." Kadohata set out to become a fiction writer and was determined to succeed. She received 25 rejection letters before *The New Yorker* finally published one of her stories, launching her career as an award-winning author. *Kira-Kira* is her first young-adult novel.

## Try a Coming-of-Age Novel

At what point do you leave your childhood fears behind and boldly take on greater responsibilities? When a child is faced with a challenging situation or difficult decision, he or she often has to grow up very quickly. A novel that centers on a young person's path to greater maturity is called a **coming-of-age novel**. *Kira-Kira*, which follows the life of its young narrator, is an example of this type of novel.

## Read a Great Book

Katie Takeshima thinks her older sister, Lynn, is a genius—partly because Lynn sees the world in such a unique way. Lynn finds beauty in ordinary things and teaches Katie to see them *kira-kira,* or glittering, too. The family business is far from being a shining success, however; and when Katie's parents get down to their last $600, they decide it's time to move on. As the family prepares to leave Iowa in order for Mr. and Mrs. Takeshima to pursue better job opportunities in Georgia, Katie wonders how their lives will change.

*from*

# KIRA-KIRA

*cynthia kadohata*

We were poor, but in the way Japanese are poor, meaning we never borrowed money from anyone, period. Meaning once a year we bought as many fifty-pound bags of rice as we could afford, and we didn't get nervous again about money until we reached our last bag. Nothing went to waste in our house. For breakfast my parents often made their *ochazuke*—green tea mixed with rice—from the crusty old rice at the bottom of the pot. For our move to Georgia, Dad and Uncle loaded up the truck with all the bags of rice that we hadn't sold at the store. I watched my parents look at the rice in the truck, and I could see that
10 the rice made them feel good. It made them feel safe.

   I liked to see them that way, especially my mother, who never seemed to feel safe. My mother was a delicate, rare, and beautiful flower. Our father told us that. She weighed hardly more than Lynn. She was so delicate that if you bumped into her accidentally, you could bruise her. She fell down a single stair once, and she broke her leg. To her that was proof even a single stair could present peril. When I would approach even a single stair, she would call out, "Be careful!"

Our mother didn't like us to run or play or climb, because it was dangerous. She didn't like us to walk in the middle of our empty street, because you never knew. She didn't want us to go to college someday, because we might get strange ideas. She liked peace and quiet. My father used to say, "Shhhh. Your mother is taking a bath." Or, "Quiet down, girls, your mother is drinking tea." We never understood why we couldn't make noise while our mother was doing anything at all. My mother's favorite thing to tell us, in her iron-rimmed singsong voice, was *"Shizukani!"* That means "Hush!"

She never said *"Shizukani!"* to my father. She made him food and rubbed his feet, and for this he let her handle all the money. Lynn said our mother probably knew a special foot-rubbing technique that made men silly. My father loved my mother a lot. That made *me* feel safe.

The night before we moved, my father and uncle sat on a tree stump across the road. Lynn and I peeked out at them before we got in bed. My uncle talked and talked, and my father listened and listened. Sometimes they both laughed loudly.

"What are they talking about?" I said.

"Women," Lynn said knowingly.

"What are they saying about women?"

"That the pretty ones make them giggle."

"Oh. Good night."

"Good night!"

Our mother came into the bedroom in the middle of the night, the way she always did, to make sure we were asleep. As usual, Lynn was asleep and I was awake. If I was awake, I usually pretended to be asleep so as not to get in trouble. But tonight I said, "Mom?"

"It's late, why are you up?"

"I can't sleep without Bera-Bera." Bera-Bera was my favorite stuffed animal, which my mother had packed in a box. Bera-Bera talked too much, laughed too loudly, and sometimes sassed me, but still I loved him.

"Someday you won't even remember Bera-Bera." She said this gently, and as if the thought made her a little sad. The thought made me a little sad too. She kissed my forehead and left. Outside I could hear noises: "Yah! Ooooh-YAH!" Et cetera. Lynn was sound asleep. I got up and watched Uncle Katsuhisa spit. My father no longer sat on the tree stump. It was just Uncle Katsuhisa out there. He was a madman, for sure.

We left Iowa at dusk the next evening. We had meant to leave in the morning but got a little behind schedule for several reasons:

60

1. I couldn't find the box with Bera-Bera, and I was convinced he was lost. Naturally, I had to have hysterics.
2. My parents misplaced their six hundred dollars.
3. Lynn couldn't find her favorite sweater with embroidered flowers. Naturally, she had to have hysterics.
4. Uncle Katsuhisa fell asleep, and we thought it would be rude to wake him.

Uncle woke up on his own. My parents found their money. But Lynn and I didn't find our items, so naturally, we continued our hysterics. Finally, my mother said, "We must leave or I don't know what!" She looked at Lynn and me crying. "Maybe you girls should keep your uncle
70 company while he drives."

"Oh, no," said Uncle. "I wouldn't want to deprive you of their delightful company."

"No," said my mother. "I wouldn't want you to be lonely."

So we climbed into the noisy truck with our noisy uncle. Then we cried so much that our uncle refused to drive with us anymore. He pulled to the side of the highway. Then we got in our parents' car and cried so much that they pulled over and flipped a coin with Uncle Katsuhisa. Uncle lost, so we got back in the truck with him.

Lynn and I were perfectly happy in Iowa. I did not see why we had
80 to move to a new job that my father had told us would be the hardest work he had ever done. I did not see why we had to move to a southern state where my father said you could not understand a word people said

because of their southern accents. I did not see why we had to leave our house for a small apartment.

After awhile Lynn and I ran out of tears and sat glumly in the truck with Uncle Katsuhisa. I knew if I thought of Bera-Bera, I would cry. But I had nothing else to do, so I thought of him. He was half dog, half rabbit, and he had orange fur. He was my best friend next to Lynn. "I want Bera-Bera!" I cried out.

90    Lynn cried out, "I want my sweater!" We both burst into tears.

It was a warm night. Whenever we paused in our crying, the only other sound inside the truck was the sound of my uncle smacking his chewing tobacco. I dreaded to know what would happen when he spit out that tobacco. Now he rolled down the window, and I thought the Great Spit was about to come. Instead, he looked at us slyly.

"I could teach you girls how to spit like a master," he said.

My sister squinted at him. She stopped crying. So did I. I could tell she thought it might be fun to learn how to spit like a master. So did I. Our mother would kill us. Lynn said, "Maybe."

100    He belched very loudly, then glanced at us. I realized his belch was preparation for spitting. I swallowed some air and burped. So did Lynn. Then Uncle Katsuhisa's throat rumbled. The rumbling got louder and louder. Even over the sound of the motor, it seemed like a war was going on in his throat. Lynn and I tried to rumble our throats like him.

"Hocka-hocka-hocka!" he said.

Lynn and I copied him: "Hocka-hocka-hocka!"

"Geh-geh-geh!"

"Geh-geh-geh!"

He turned to his open window, and an amazing wad of brown juice

110 flew from his mouth. The brown juice was like a bat bursting out of a cave. We turned around to watch it speed away. A part of me hoped it would hit the car behind us, but it didn't. I leaned over Lynn and out the passenger window. "Hyaaahhhh!" I said, and a little trickle of saliva fell down my chin.

No one spoke. For some reason the silence made me start crying again. As if Uncle Katsuhisa couldn't restrain himself, he started singing my name over and over, "Katie, Katie, Katie . . ." Then he sang

Katie songs to the tunes of "Row, Row, Row Your Boat," "America the Beautiful," "Kookaburra," and some songs I didn't recognize. For 120 instance, he sang, "Oh, Katie, Kate, for spacious skies, for Katie Katie Kate." He made me giggle. It was almost as if someone were tickling me. For a while I forgot about Bera-Bera.

Lynn smiled with satisfaction. I knew this was because she liked for me to be happy. The wind hit our hair as Uncle Katsuhisa continued to sing Katie songs. I looked outside over a field and tried to find the *Sode Boshi,* the kimono sleeve in the sky where Uncle Katsuhisa said westerners see the constellation Orion. Then my uncle began to sing Lynnie songs.

She laughed and laughed and laughed. ❧

## Keep Reading

The Takeshimas are on their way to a new life in a small Georgia town, where there are very few other Japanese Americans. How different will things be for them there? As you continue to read *Kira-Kira,* you will see the family through times of great joy and times of deep sorrow. Through it all, Katie continues to follow her sister's example by looking for beauty in the world around her. Read along as Katie's experiences in Georgia help her to grow into a thoughtful young woman.

## *from* **Roughing It**
Memoir by Mark Twain

# *Why do we* EXAGGERATE?

**INDIANA STANDARDS**

**READING STANDARDS**
**8.3.6** Identify significant literary devices, such as metaphor, symbolism, dialect or quotations, and irony, which define a writer's style and use those elements to interpret the work.

**8.2.9** Make reasonable statements and draw conclusions about a text, supporting them with accurate examples.

*KEY IDEA* "It takes me forever to walk to school." "I have about a million hours of homework to do." "My backpack must weigh two hundred pounds." Have you ever found yourself saying something like this, even when you know it's not accurate? We all **exaggerate** at times. In the memoir you are about to read, Mark Twain uses exaggeration not only to make us laugh, but also to make us think.

*DISCUSS* How good are you at exaggerating? Choose a simple event—your trip to the grocery store, or yesterday's band practice. Tell the story in its basic form, with no exaggeration. Then tell the story again, this time exaggerating the events and descriptive details. Did your exaggeration make the second version more fun to hear? Or did it push the limits of believability too far? Share your stories with your group and let them decide.

**Peanuts**                                                                 by Charles Schulz

*Peanuts*, Charles Schulz. August 5, 1983. © United Feature Syndicate, Inc.

## ● LITERARY ANALYSIS: VOICE

In literature, **voice** refers to a writer's unique use of language. The way a writer chooses words, constructs sentences, and expresses ideas makes his or her personality come through on the page. As you read, look for the ways Mark Twain achieves his humorous voice through

- complex sentences containing amusing descriptions
- **hyperbole,** or exaggeration
- **understatement,** or downplaying something's importance

## ● READING STRATEGY: MONITOR

Twain uses long sentences and old-fashioned vocabulary. To make sure you understand what he's saying, **monitor** yourself, or pause to check your understanding. If you're not clear about what you just read, try these strategies:

- **Adjust your reading rate** by slowing down when you get to long, complicated sentences and passages.
- **Use context clues** or a dictionary to figure out the meaning of archaic (old-fashioned) vocabulary.
- **Note descriptive details** to help you picture characters, events, and settings.
- **Reread difficult passages** to help clarify information.

As you read, use a chart to note the line numbers of difficult passages and the strategies you used to understand them.

| Confusing Lines | What They Mean | How I Figured It Out |
|---|---|---|
| | | |

## ▲ VOCABULARY IN CONTEXT

Twain uses the following words in a humorous way. To see how many you know, match each word with its synonym, the word closest to it in meaning.

| WORD LIST | array | legitimate | sensational |
|---|---|---|---|
| | conspicuous | livelihood | tolerable |
| | contrive | rigid | yield |

1. occupation
2. inflexible
3. shocking
4. surrender
5. assortment
6. valid
7. invent
8. adequate
9. obvious

# Author **On⃝line**

**Mark Twain**
**1835–1910**

**Growing Up on the River** When Samuel Clemens was four years old, his family moved to Hannibal, Missouri, a small town on the Mississippi River. Clemens grew up fascinated by the river, traveling its waters in homemade rafts, playing in swimming holes, and exploring nearby woods and caves. His carefree childhood days ended at 11, however, when his father died of pneumonia. In order to support his family, Clemens left school and worked for a newspaper and printing firm.

**Looking for Adventure** In 1853, Clemens left Hannibal to seek his fortune mining along the Amazon River. But Clemens never made it to the Amazon. On his journey south he befriended a steamboat captain, and for four years he sailed the Mississippi River. After a brief stint in the Confederate Army during the Civil War, Clemens moved to Nevada and began writing for a local paper. It was during this time that he assumed the pen name "Mark Twain," a term that means "two fathoms deep," or water that is deep enough for a riverboat to navigate safely.

**The Start of a Legend** Mark Twain made a name for himself traveling around the world and writing newspaper columns about his adventures. His humorous voice captured the hearts of American readers, and before long, Twain was a household name. His book *Roughing It* contains essays about his travels and work experiences, all told in his signature way.

 **MORE ABOUT THE AUTHOR**
For more on Mark Twain, visit the **Literature Center** at ClassZone.com.

# ROUGHING IT

**Mark Twain**

What to do next?

It was a momentous question. I had gone out into the world to shift for myself,[1] at the age of thirteen (for my father had indorsed[2] for friends, and although he left us a sumptuous legacy of pride in his fine Virginian stock and its national distinction, I presently found that I could not live on that alone without occasional bread to wash it down with). **A**
I had gained a **livelihood** in various vocations, but had not dazzled anybody with my successes; still the list was before me, and the amplest liberty in the matter of choosing, provided I wanted to work—which I did not, after being
10 so wealthy. I had once been a grocery clerk, for one day, but had consumed so much sugar in that time that I was relieved from further duty by the proprietor;[3] said he wanted me outside, so that he could have my custom. I had studied law an entire week, and then given it up because it was so prosy and tiresome. I had engaged briefly in the study of blacksmithing, but wasted so much time trying to fix the bellows so that it would blow itself, that the master turned me adrift in disgrace, and told me I would come to no good. I had been a bookseller's clerk for a while, but the customers bothered me so much I could not read with any comfort, and so the proprietor gave me a furlough and forgot

**A** MONITOR
Why did Twain need to support himself at a young age? Rephrase the information in parenthesis to find out.

**livelihood** (līv′lē-ho͝od′) *n.* a means of support; a way of making a living

**ANALYZE VISUALS**
What does this image of Mark Twain suggest about his **writing process**?

---

1. **shift for myself:** take care of myself.
2. **indorsed** (ĭn-dôrsd′): endorsed; signed financial documents; perhaps this means that Twain's father backed up friends' unwise financial schemes, and lost all of his own money as a result.
3. **proprietor** (prə-prī′ĭ-tər): one who owns and manages a business.

to put a limit to it. I had clerked in a drug store part of a summer, but my
20 prescriptions were unlucky, and we appeared to sell more stomach-pumps than
soda-water. So I had to go. I had made of myself a **tolerable** printer, under the
impression that I would be another Franklin some day, but somehow had missed
the connection thus far. There was no berth⁴ open in the Esmeralda *Union,* and
besides I had always been such a slow compositor⁵ that I looked with envy upon
the achievements of apprentices of two years' standing; and when I took a "take,"
foremen were in the habit of suggesting that it would be wanted "some time
during the year." I was a good average St. Louis and New Orleans pilot and by
no means ashamed of my abilities in that line; wages were two hundred and fifty
dollars a month and no board⁶ to pay, and I did long to stand behind a wheel
30 again and never roam any more—but I had been making such a fool of myself
lately in grandiloquent letters home about my blind lead and my European
excursion that I did what many and many a poor disappointed miner had done
before; said, "It is all over with me now, and I will never go back home to be
pitied—and snubbed." I had been a private secretary, a silver-miner and a
silver-mill operative, and amounted to less than nothing in each, and now— **B**

   **W**hat to do next?

   I **yielded** to Higbie's appeals and consented to try the mining once more.
We climbed far up on the mountainside and went to work on a little rubbishy
claim of ours that had a shaft on it eight feet deep. Higbie descended into it
40 and worked bravely with his pick till he had loosened up a deal of rock and
dirt, and then I went down with a long-handled shovel (the most awkward
invention yet **contrived** by man) to throw it out. You must brace the shovel
forward with the side of your knee till it is full, and then, with a skillful toss,
throw it backward over your left shoulder. I made the toss, and landed the
mess just on the edge of the shaft and it all came back on my head and down
the back of my neck. I never said a word, but climbed out and walked home.
I inwardly resolved that I would starve before I would make a target of myself
and shoot rubbish at it with a long-handled shovel. I sat down, in the cabin,
and gave myself up to solid misery—so to speak. Now in pleasanter days I
50 had amused myself with writing letters to the chief paper of the territory, the
Virginia *Daily Territorial Enterprise,* and had always been surprised when they
appeared in print. My good opinion of the editors had steadily declined; for
it seemed to me that they might have found something better to fill up with
than my literature. I had found a letter in the post-office as I came home from
the hillside, and finally I opened it. Eureka! [I never did know what Eureka
meant, but it seems to be as proper a word to heave in as any when no other
that sounds pretty offers.] It was a deliberate offer to me of Twenty-five Dollars
a week to come up to Virginia and be city editor of the *Enterprise.* **C**

---

4. **berth:** job.

5. **compositor** (kəm-pŏz′ĭ-tər): a worker who sets type for a printing business.

6. **board:** meals.

**tolerable** (tŏl′ər-ə-bəl)
*adj.* fairly good; passable

**B VOICE**
Reread lines 19–21.
Where does Twain use
**understatement** in this
passage?

**yield** (yēld) *v.* to give in
to another

**contrive** (kən-trīv′) *v.*
to invent or fabricate,
especially by improvisation

**C MONITOR**
How did Twain get a job
offer from the *Enterprise?*
Note the strategy you
used to find this answer.

I would have challenged the publisher in the "blind lead" days—I wanted
60 to fall down and worship him, now. Twenty-five Dollars a week—it looked
like bloated luxury—a fortune, a sinful and lavish waste of money. But
my transports[7] cooled when I thought of my inexperience and consequent
unfitness for the position—and straightway, on top of this, my long **array** of
failures rose up before me. Yet if I refused this place I must presently become
dependent upon somebody for my bread, a thing necessarily distasteful to a
man who had never experienced such a humiliation since he was thirteen years
old. Not much to be proud of, since it is so common—but then it was all I had
to *be* proud of. So I was scared into being a city editor. I would have declined,
otherwise. Necessity is the mother of "taking chances." I do not doubt that
70 if, at that time, I had been offered a salary to translate the Talmud[8] from the
original Hebrew, I would have accepted—albeit with diffidence and some
misgivings—and thrown as much variety into it as I could for the money. **D**

**array** (ə-rā′) *n.* a large
number of items

**D** VOICE
Reread lines 69–72.
Where is **hyperbole** used
in this passage?

---

7. **transports:** joyful excitement.
8. **Talmud** (täl′mŏŏd): a collection of ancient writings by rabbis; this is the basis of Orthodox Jewish law.

**ANALYZE VISUALS**
Identify which man in the
illustration is Mark Twain.
How does the drawing of
him **compare** with your
mental image?

I went up to Virginia and entered upon my new vocation. I was a rusty-looking city editor, I am free to confess—coatless, slouch hat, blue woolen shirt, pantaloons stuffed into boot-tops, whiskered half down to the waist, and the universal navy revolver slung to my belt. But I secured a more
80 conservative costume and discarded the revolver. I had never had occasion to kill anybody, nor ever felt a desire to do so, but had worn the thing in deference to popular sentiment, and in order that I might not, by its absence, be offensively **conspicuous,** and a subject of remark. But the other editors, and all the printers, carried revolvers. I asked the chief editor and proprietor (Mr. Goodman, I will call him, since it describes
90 him as well as any name could do) for some instructions with regard to my duties, and he told me to go all over town and ask all sorts of people all sorts of questions, make notes of the information gained, and write them out for publication. And he added: **E**

"Never say 'We learn' so-and-so, or 'It is reported,' or 'It is rumored,' or 'We understand' so-and-so, but go to headquarters and get the absolute facts,
100 and then speak out and say 'It *is* so-and-so.' Otherwise, people will not put confidence in your news. Unassailable[9] certainty is the thing that gives a newspaper the firmest and most valuable reputation."

It was the whole thing in a nutshell; and to this day, when I find a reporter commencing his article with "We understand," I gather a suspicion that he has not taken as much pains to inform himself as he ought to have done. I moralize well, but I did not always practise well when I was a city editor; I let fancy get the upper hand of fact too often when there was a dearth[10] of news. I can never
110 forget my first day's experience as a reporter. I wandered about town questioning everybody, boring everybody, and finding out that nobody knew anything. At the end of five hours my note-book was still barren. I spoke to Mr. Goodman. He said:

"Dan used to make a good thing out of the hay-wagons in a dry time when there were no fires or inquests. Are there no hay-wagons in from the Truckee?

**conspicuous**
(kən-spĭk′yōō-əs) *adj.*
easy to notice; obvious

**E MONITOR**
Reread lines 73–95.
Do you find any of these sentences difficult to understand? If so, choose a strategy to help you clarify their meaning.

---

9. **unassailable** (ŭn′ə-sā′lə-bəl): impossible to dispute or disprove; undeniable.

10. **dearth** (dûrth): a scarce supply; a lack.

If there are, you might speak of the renewed activity and all that sort of thing, in the hay business, you know. It isn't **sensational** or exciting, but it fills up and looks business-like."

120     I canvassed the city again and found one wretched old hay-truck dragging in from the country. But I made affluent use of it. I multiplied it by sixteen, brought it into town from sixteen different directions, made sixteen separate items of it, and got up such another sweat about hay as Virginia City had never seen in the world before.

    This was encouraging. Two nonpareil[11] columns had to be filled, and I was getting along. Presently, when things began to look dismal again, a desperado killed a man in a saloon and joy returned once more. I never was so glad over any mere trifle before in my life. I said to the murderer:

    "Sir, you are a stranger to me, but you have done me a kindness this day which I can never forget. If whole years of gratitude can be to you any slight

130 compensation, they shall be yours. I was in trouble and you have relieved me nobly and at a time when all seemed dark and drear. Count me your friend from this time forth, for I am not a man to forget a favor." **F**

    If I did not really say that to him I at least felt a sort of itching desire to do it. I wrote up the murder with a hungry attention to details, and when it was finished experienced but one regret—namely, that they had not hanged my benefactor on the spot, so that I could work him up too.

    Next I discovered some emigrant-wagons[12] going into camp on the plaza and found that they had lately come through the hostile Indian country and had fared rather roughly. I made the best of the item that the circumstances

140 permitted, and felt that if I were not confined within **rigid** limits by the presence of the reporters of the other papers I could add particulars that would make the article much more interesting. However, I found one wagon that was going on to California, and made some judicious inquiries of the proprietor. When I learned, through his short and surly answers to my cross-questioning, that he was certainly going on and would not be in the city next day to make trouble, I got ahead of the other papers, for I took down his list of names and added his party to the killed and wounded. Having more scope here, I put this wagon through an Indian fight that to this day has no parallel in history. **G**

    My two columns were filled. When I read them over in the morning I felt that

150 I had found my **legitimate** occupation at last. I reasoned within myself that news, and stirring news, too, was what a paper needed, and I felt that I was peculiarly endowed[13] with the ability to furnish it. Mr. Goodman said that I was as good a reporter as Dan. I desired no higher commendation. With encouragement like that, I felt that I could take my pen and murder all the immigrants on the plains if need be, and the interests of the paper demanded it. ꝏ

---

11. **nonpareil** (nŏn′pə-rĕl′): unequalled; peerless.

12. **emigrant-wagons** (ĕm′ĭ-grənt): wagons in which pioneers rode on their way to settle in the West.

13. **peculiarly endowed**(pĭ-kyōōl′yər-lē ĕn-doud′): specifically supplied with a talent or quality.

**sensational**
(sĕn-sā′shə-nəl) *adj.*
intended to arouse strong curiosity or interest, especially through exaggerated details

**F** VOICE
Do you think Twain really responded to the murder in this way? Explain your answer.

**rigid** (rĭj′ĭd) *adj.*
inflexible; strict

**G** VOICE
Reread lines 137–148. What **amusing descriptions** does Twain use to explain his article about the emigrant-wagons?

**legitimate** (lə-jĭt′ə-mĭt) *adj.* genuine; authentic

# Comprehension

**INDIANA STANDARDS**

**READING STANDARD**
**8.2.9** Make reasonable statements and draw conclusions....

1. **Recall** Why does Mark Twain lose his jobs at the grocery store, bookstore, and drugstore?

2. **Recall** What does Twain decide about mining as an occupation?

3. **Clarify** How does Twain fill up his two newspaper columns?

# Literary Analysis

4. **Make Inferences** Although an **exaggeration** may be misleading, it often contains a grain of truth. Skim the selection for three examples of exaggeration that provide information about the author. In a diagram like the one shown, present the examples and tell what you can infer from each one.

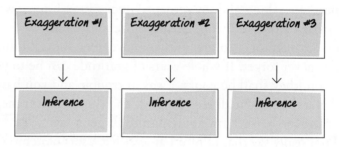

5. **Analyze Voice** Long sentences containing amusing descriptions, hyperbole, and understatement are typical of Twain's unique voice. Find three sentences that you think are particularly funny or effective. Then, rewrite each sentence in a more straightforward way. Which version do you like better?

6. **Examine Monitoring** Review the list you kept while reading. Which monitoring strategy helped you best understand and enjoy *Roughing It?* Explain, and give examples.

7. **Draw Conclusions About Style** Reread lines 2–10. Based on what you know about Twain, why do you think he uses such long, complicated sentences?

8. **Make Judgments** A **memoir** is a form of autobiographical nonfiction in which an author shares part of his or her life story. Memoirs are assumed to be based on fact. Given Twain's generous use of exaggeration, do you think it is fair to label *Roughing It* a memoir? Why or why not?

# Extension and Challenge

9. **Creative Response: Art** If *Roughing It* were made into a movie, which parts would draw viewers to the theater? Design a movie poster that illustrates the scenes or characters most likely to attract an audience. Be sure to create an interesting slogan to entice people to see the movie.

10. **Speaking and Listening** With a partner, create a mock interview with Mark Twain. First, brainstorm a list of questions a reporter would ask Twain, based on the information he provides in *Roughing It*. Then, with one person acting as the reporter and one as Twain, conduct the interview in front of the rest of the class. Try to stay true to the selection, and to Twain's voice, by adding humor and **exaggeration** to Twain's responses.

# Vocabulary in Context

## VOCABULARY PRACTICE

**Synonyms** have a similar meaning, and **antonyms** have opposite or nearly opposite meanings. Decide whether the words in each pair are synonyms or antonyms.

1. rigid/permissive
2. tolerable/acceptable
3. conspicuous/noticeable
4. livelihood/occupation
5. legitimate/wrong
6. yield/resist
7. array/variety
8. sensational/understated
9. contrive/invent

array
conspicuous
contrive
legitimate
livelihood
rigid
sensational
tolerable
yield

## VOCABULARY IN WRITING

Sometimes we exaggerate to make dull stories more interesting. Think of a boring chore that you are required to do. Write an exaggerated description of how you handle this task. Use at least two vocabulary words in your paragraph. You could start this way.

**EXAMPLE SENTENCE**

*Although it's been several years since I cleaned my room, I find the mess* **tolerable**.

**INDIANA STANDARDS**

**READING STANDARD**
**8.1.3** Verify the meaning of a word in its context....

## VOCABULARY STRATEGY: THE LATIN ROOT *leg*

The vocabulary word *legitimate* comes from the Latin root *leg*, which means "law." *Leg* (combined with other word parts) appears in a number of English words. To understand the meaning of a word that contains this root, use context clues and your knowledge of the root's meaning.

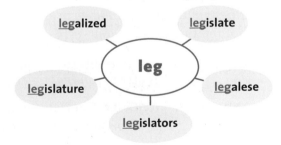

legalized    legislate

**leg**

legislature    legalese

legislators

**PRACTICE** Choose the word from the web that best completes each sentence. Then explain how the root *leg* helps to give each word its meaning.

1. The document was written in _____, but I finally figured out what it meant.
2. Each region's voters elect one member of our state _____.
3. Dad e-mailed Representative Lee and asked her to help _____ some tough new environmental laws.
4. Senators are _____ who propose laws in Congress.
5. California abolished the death penalty and then _____ it again.

**VOCABULARY PRACTICE**
For more practice, go to the **Vocabulary Center** at **ClassZone.com**.

# Reading-Writing Connection

Broaden your understanding of *Roughing It* by responding to these prompts. Then complete the **Grammar and Writing** exercise.

| WRITING PROMPTS | SELF-CHECK |
|---|---|
| **A. Short Response: Explore Author's Attitude** <br> A writer's voice reveals his or her unique attitudes and beliefs. Based on your reading of *Roughing It,* how do you think Mark Twain feels about work? In **one paragraph,** describe Twain's attitude toward work. | ***A strong response will . . .*** <br> • use examples from the selection <br> • contain a clear statement of opinion |
| **B. Extended Response: Write an Evaluation** <br> Imagine that John McCandlish Phillips, author of "The Simple Commandments of Journalistic Ethics" on page 715, is Twain's teacher. How would he evaluate Twain's reporting techniques, including his use of **exaggeration?** Write a **half-page evaluation** of Twain's news articles from Phillips's point of view. | ***An effective evaluation will . . .*** <br> • include a statement of opinion about Twain's work as a reporter <br> • provide Twain with advice on how to write ethically |

## GRAMMAR AND WRITING

***FORM COMPOUND SENTENCES*** An **independent clause** is a group of words that contains a subject and a verb and can stand alone as a sentence. A **simple sentence** contains one independent clause. A **compound sentence** contains two or more independent clauses that are joined either by a comma and a coordinating conjunction, such as *and, but, or, so,* or *yet,* or by a semicolon.

INDIANA STANDARDS

**WRITING STANDARD**
**8.6.1** Use correct and varied sentence types....

> Original: Mark Twain is creative. He's a good writer. (*Each simple sentence contains one independent clause.*)

> Revised: Mark Twain is creative, and he's a good writer. (*The compound sentence contains two independent clauses that are joined by a comma and a coordinating conjunction.*)

***PRACTICE*** Create a compound sentence by joining the two simple sentences with either a comma and a coordinating conjunction or a semicolon.

1. Twain is not interested in hard work. He needs a job to support himself.

2. Twain has an interesting way with words. He tells too many tall tales.

3. Twain will not pass his journalism class. He does not follow the rules of ethical writing.

4. Twain should conduct better research. He should not exaggerate his articles for the sake of selling newspapers.

*For more help with independent clauses and simple and compound sentences, see pages R62 and R63 in the **Grammar Handbook.***

# The Simple Commandments of Journalistic Ethics

**John McCandlish Phillips**

. . . Long after my years in news reporting, I have had repeated occasions to speak to young or aspiring journalists. With rare exceptions, the matter they have wanted most to hear about is reportorial ethics. . . .

Here is the core of what I tell aspiring journalists about the question they so reliably pose:

In journalistic usage, you shall be as accurate and balanced and fair, and as faithful to pinned-down facts, as you possibly can be. The right does not exist to put anything whatever between quotation marks that are not words as

Students design a school newspaper.

they were spoken, to 97 percent word accuracy. Misquotation or fabricated quotation is lying in print—a terrible disservice to those abused by the license taken. It does not help when the act is careless rather than deceitful.

You will not lie. You will not distort. You will not make things up.

You will not embroider your story for effect.

If you get into investigative reporting, never let your suspicions run one-eighth of an inch ahead of your facts—solid, fully ascertained evidence that conclusively verifies the suspicions that promoted the investigation.

Newspapers and broadcast news must—and they do—report accusations made by public figures against other such figures. When the newspaper itself levels the accusation, and presents its supporting case, it is much more deeply hurtful to the accused than the former is.

Always remember that, in public accusation, the irreducible, primary, essential requirement is that it be factually accurate. If it truly is, you have every right to take it to print or on air, and things will likely be better for it.

## Us and Them
Personal Essay by David Sedaris

# What's really NORMAL?

**INDIANA STANDARDS**

**READING STANDARDS**
**8.3.6** Identify significant literary devices, such as metaphor, symbolism, dialect or quotations, and irony, which define a writer's style and use those elements to interpret the work.

**8.3.7** Analyze a work of literature, showing how it reflects the heritage, traditions, attitudes, and beliefs of its author.

**KEY IDEA** Imagine a town where everyone dyes his or her hair purple and spends free time either at puppet shows or raising ferrets. If someone moves in who has brown hair and loves video games and soccer, would he or she be considered **normal?** What we mean by that word often depends on where we are and who we're with. In the selection you are about to read, a young boy is fascinated by a family that doesn't seem normal.

**DISCUSS** How do you define *normal?* Think about things like the way you and your friends and family dress, the music you listen to, and the activities you participate in. Create a definition for the word *normal* based on these observations, and compare it with classmates' definitions. Is everyone's view of *normal* the same?

## LITERARY ANALYSIS: IRONY

Have you ever stayed up late to study for a test, only to find out that the test was postponed? Many people would call this turn of events ironic. **Irony** is a contrast between what is expected and what actually exists or happens. Irony can make a piece of literature tragic, thoughtful, or funny, depending upon the writer's goal. Types of irony include

- **situational irony,** which is a contrast between what is expected to happen and what actually does happen
- **verbal irony,** which occurs when someone states one thing and means another
- **dramatic irony,** which happens when readers know more about a situation or a character in a story than the characters do

As you read, record examples of irony in a chart as shown.

| Example | Type of Irony | Why It's Ironic |
|---------|---------------|-----------------|
|         |               |                 |

*Review:* **Tone**

## READING SKILL: EVALUATE

When you **evaluate,** you make judgments about the author's opinions, actions, or statements. Forming opinions on what you read makes you think about what's right and wrong, and why. As you read, judge whether the young David Sedaris's thoughts and actions seem sensible, fair, and accurate.

## ▲ VOCABULARY IN CONTEXT

The way Sedaris uses the following boldfaced words helps create the ironic **tone** of his story. Use context clues in each sentence to figure out the meaning of the boldfaced terms.

1. Lucy doesn't **merit** an invitation to my party.
2. Don't **imply** that you believe me if you really don't.
3. Carmen, don't **inflict** your terrible music on me!
4. Although I disagree, I won't **interfere** with your decision.
5. I **attribute** John's grades to hard work and dedication.
6. Taylor tosses her papers **indiscriminately** into her bag.
7. There's no way Mom can **accommodate** all of us in her tiny car.
8. If you **provoke** me, I will likely argue with you.

# Author On|ine

**A Man of Many Jobs**
David Sedaris has had several odd jobs over the years, including apple picking, house painting, performance art, and apartment cleaning. But a humorous essay he wrote about his experiences working as an elf in a department store's holiday display

**David Sedaris
born 1957**

launched his writing career. After reading "The SantaLand Diaries" on National Public Radio, Sedaris became an instant hit, and since then his books have sold millions of copies. His inspiration comes from the diaries he has kept for over 30 years, in which he records his intelligent, funny, and emotional observations on everyday life.

**Literary Rock Star** Sedaris frequently tours the U.S. and Europe, reading his essays and short stories to sold-out concert halls. These appearances give Sedaris a chance to meet his fans and also to improve his writing. He often reads unpublished essays, revising them based on the crowd's reaction.

**Family Secrets** Many of Sedaris's essays are about the people in his life. His book *Dress Your Family in Corduroy and Denim,* from which this essay was taken, contains thoughts on his family and childhood. In one essay, he writes that his family is afraid to tell him anything important for fear that their stories will end up in his next book. Most of their conversations, he says, begin with the words "You have to swear you will never repeat this." Fortunately for his readers, Sedaris doesn't make those promises.

 **MORE ABOUT THE AUTHOR**
For more on David Sedaris, visit the **Literature Center** at ClassZone.com.

# Us and Them

## David Sedaris

**W**hen my family first moved to North Carolina, we lived in a rented
house three blocks from the school where I would begin the third
grade. My mother made friends with one of the neighbors, but one seemed
enough for her. Within a year we would move again and, as she explained,
there wasn't much point in getting too close to people we would have to say
good-bye to. Our next house was less than a mile away, and the short journey
would hardly **merit** tears or even good-byes, for that matter. It was more of a
"see you later" situation, but still I adopted my mother's attitude, as it allowed
me to pretend that not making friends was a conscious[1] choice. I could if I
10  wanted to. It just wasn't the right time. **Ⓐ**

   Back in New York State, we had lived in the country, with no sidewalks or
streetlights; you could leave the house and still be alone. But here, when you
looked out the window, you saw other houses, and people inside those houses.
I hoped that in walking around after dark I might witness a murder, but
for the most part our neighbors just sat in their living rooms, watching TV.
The only place that seemed truly different was owned by a man named Mr.
Tomkey, who did not believe in television. This was told to us by our mother's
friend, who dropped by one afternoon with a basketful of okra.[2] The woman
did not editorialize[3]—rather, she just presented her information, leaving her
20  listener to make of it what she might. Had my mother said, "That's the craziest
thing I've ever heard in my life," I assume that the friend would have agreed,
and had she said, "Three cheers for Mr. Tomkey," the friend likely would have
agreed as well. It was a kind of test, as was the okra.

---

1.  **conscious:** deliberate.

2.  **okra** (ō′krə): edible pods used in soups and as a vegetable.

3.  **editorialize** (ĕd′ĭ-tôr′ē-əl-īz′): to give one's own opinions on a topic.

**merit** (mĕr′ĭt) *v.*
to deserve

**Ⓐ IRONY**
Reread lines 6–10.
When Sedaris says he
could make friends if he
wanted to, what does
he actually mean?

**ANALYZE VISUALS**
Note the colors used in
this painting. Why do you
think the artist chose to
**contrast** the inside and
outside of the house in
this way?

Detail of *Outside In* (2004), Ryan Kapp. Oil on
canvas on panel, 18″ × 24″. © Ryan Kapp.

To say that you did not believe in television was different from saying that you did not care for it. Belief **implied** that television had a master plan and that you were against it. It also suggested that you thought too much. When my mother reported that Mr. Tomkey did not believe in television, my father said, "Well, good for him. I don't know that I believe in it, either."

"That's exactly how I feel," my mother said, and then my parents watched
30 the news, and whatever came on after the news. **B**

**W**ord spread that Mr. Tomkey did not own a television, and you began hearing that while this was all very well and good, it was unfair of him to **inflict** his beliefs upon others, specifically his innocent wife and children. It was speculated that just as the blind man develops a keener sense of hearing, the family must somehow compensate for their loss. "Maybe they read," my mother's friend said. "Maybe they listen to the radio, but you can bet your boots they're doing *something*."

I wanted to know what this something was, and so I began peering through the Tomkeys' windows. During the day I'd stand across the street from their
40 house, acting as though I were waiting for someone, and at night, when the view was better and I had less chance of being discovered, I would creep into their yard and hide in the bushes beside their fence.

Because they had no TV, the Tomkeys were forced to talk during dinner. They had no idea how puny their lives were, and so they were not ashamed that a camera would have found them uninteresting. They did not know what attractive was or what dinner was supposed to look like or even what time people were
50 supposed to eat. Sometimes they wouldn't sit down until eight o'clock, long after everyone else had finished doing the dishes. During the meal, Mr. Tomkey would occasionally pound the table and point at his children with a fork, but the moment he finished, everyone would start laughing. I got the idea that he was imitating someone else, and wondered if he spied on us while we were eating.

When fall arrived and school began, I saw
60 the Tomkey children marching up the hill with paper sacks in their hands. The son was one grade lower than me, and the daughter was one grade higher. We never spoke, but I'd pass them in the halls from time to time and attempt to view the world through their eyes. What must it be like to be so ignorant and alone? Could a normal person even imagine it? Staring at an

imply (ĭm-plī′) *v.* to express indirectly

**B** **IRONY**
Reread lines 29–30. What's the difference between what the mother says and what she does?

inflict (ĭn-flĭkt′) *v.* to deal out something unpleasant or burdensome; to impose

Elmer Fudd[4] lunch box, I tried to divorce myself from[5] everything I already knew: Elmer's inability to pronounce the letter *r*, his constant pursuit of an
70 intelligent and considerably more famous rabbit. I tried to think of him as just a drawing, but it was impossible to separate him from his celebrity. **C**

One day in class a boy named William began to write the wrong answer on the blackboard, and our teacher flailed her arms, saying, "Warning, Will. Danger, danger." Her voice was synthetic and void of emotion, and we laughed, knowing that she was imitating the robot in a weekly show about a family who lived in outer space. The Tomkeys, though, would have thought she was having a heart attack. It occurred to me that they needed a guide, someone who could accompany them through the course of an average day and point out all the things they were unable to understand. I could have done it on weekends, but
80 friendship would have taken away their mystery and **interfered** with the good feeling I got from pitying them. So I kept my distance.[6] **D**

In early October the Tomkeys bought a boat, and everyone seemed greatly relieved, especially my mother's friend, who noted that the motor was definitely secondhand. It was reported that Mr. Tomkey's father-in-law owned a house on the lake and had invited the family to use it whenever they liked. This explained why they were gone all weekend, but it did not make their absences any easier to bear. I felt as if my favorite show had been canceled.

Halloween fell on a Saturday that year, and by the time my mother took us to the store, all the good costumes were gone. My sisters dressed as witches
90 and I went as a hobo. I'd looked forward to going in disguise to the Tomkeys' door, but they were off at the lake, and their house was dark. Before leaving, they had left a coffee can full of gumdrops on the front porch, alongside a sign reading DON'T BE GREEDY. In terms of Halloween candy, individual gumdrops were just about as low as you could get. This was evidenced by the large number of them floating in an adjacent dog bowl. It was disgusting to think that this was what a gumdrop might look like in your stomach, and it was insulting to be told not to take too much of something you didn't really want in the first place. "Who do these Tomkeys think they are?" my sister Lisa said.
100 The night after Halloween, we were sitting around watching TV when the doorbell rang. Visitors were infrequent at our house, so while my father stayed behind, my mother, sisters, and I ran downstairs in a group, opening the door to discover the entire Tomkey family on our front stoop. The parents looked as they always had, but the son and daughter were dressed in costumes—she as a ballerina and he as some kind of a rodent with terry-cloth ears and a tail made from what looked to be an extension cord. It seemed they had spent the previous evening isolated at the lake and had missed the opportunity

**C** **TONE**
Reread lines 43–71. What words and images reveal Sedaris's attitude toward the Tomkeys?

**interfere** (ĭn'tər-fîr') *v.* to create an obstacle

**D** **EVALUATE**
Do you think Sedaris is right to keep his distance? Explain.

---

4. **Elmer Fudd** (ĕl'mər fŭd): a cartoon character who is always chasing after Bugs Bunny; Fudd mispronounces the *r* sound as *w*, as in "wascally wabbit."

5. **divorce myself from:** separate myself from.

6. **kept my distance:** kept myself emotionally distant.

to observe⁷ Halloween. "So, well, I guess we're trick-or-treating *now,* if that's okay," Mr. Tomkey said.

110    I **attributed** their behavior to the fact that they didn't have a TV, but television didn't teach you everything. Asking for candy on Halloween was called trick-or-treating, but asking for candy on November first was called begging, and it made people uncomfortable. This was one of the things you were supposed to learn simply by being alive, and it angered me that the Tomkeys didn't understand it. **E**

**attribute** (ə-trĭb′yo͞ot) *v.* to relate to a certain cause

**E** **EVALUATE**
Is Sedaris's reaction to the late trick-or-treaters appropriate?

"Why, of course it's not too late," my mother said. "Kids, why don't you . . . run and get . . . the candy."

"But the candy is gone," my sister Gretchen said. "You gave it away last night."

"Not *that* candy," my mother said. "The other candy. Why don't you run and

120 go get it?"

"You mean *our* candy?" Lisa said. "The candy that we *earned?*"

This was exactly what our mother was talking about, but she didn't want to say this in front of the Tomkeys. In order to spare their feelings, she wanted them to believe that we always kept a bucket of candy lying around the house, just waiting for someone to knock on the door and ask for it. "Go on, now," she said. "Hurry up."

My room was situated right off the foyer, and if the Tomkeys had looked in that direction, they could have seen my bed and the brown paper bag marked MY CANDY. KEEP OUT. I didn't want them to know how much I had, and so I

130 went into my room and shut the door behind me. Then I closed the curtains and emptied my bag onto the bed, searching for whatever was the crummiest. All my life chocolate has made me ill. I don't know if I'm allergic or what, but even the smallest amount leaves me with a blinding headache. Eventually, I learned to stay away from it, but as a child I refused to be left out. The brownies were eaten, and when the pounding began I would blame the grape juice or my mother's cigarette smoke or the tightness of my glasses—anything but the chocolate. My candy bars were poison but they were brand-name, and so I put them in pile no. 1, which definitely would not go to the Tomkeys.

Out in the hallway I could hear my mother straining for something to talk

140 about. "A boat!" she said. "That sounds marvelous. Can you just drive it right into the water?"

"Actually, we have a trailer," Mr. Tomkey said. "So what we do is back it into the lake."

"Oh, a trailer. What kind is it?"

"Well, it's a *boat* trailer," Mr. Tomkey said.

"Right, but is it wooden or, you know . . . I guess what I'm asking is what *style* trailer do you have?"

Behind my mother's words were two messages. The first and most obvious was "Yes, I am talking about boat trailers, but also I am dying." The second,

150 meant only for my sisters and me, was "If you do not immediately step forward

---

7. **observe:** to celebrate.

**ANALYZE VISUALS**
What's the first thing you notice in this photograph? Now look at the photo more carefully and tell what new **details** you see.

with that candy, you will never again experience freedom, happiness, or the possibility of my warm embrace."

I knew that it was just a matter of time before she came into my room and started collecting the candy herself, grabbing **indiscriminately,** with no regard to my rating system. Had I been thinking straight, I would have hidden the most valuable items in my dresser drawer, but instead, panicked by the thought of her hand on my doorknob, I tore off the wrappers and began cramming the candy bars into my mouth, desperately, like someone in a contest. Most were miniature, which made them easier to **accommodate,** but still there was only
160 so much room, and it was hard to chew and fit more in at the same time. The headache began immediately, and I chalked it up to[8] tension. **F**

My mother told the Tomkeys she needed to check on something, and then she opened the door and stuck her head inside my room. "What . . . are you doing?" she whispered, but my mouth was too full to answer. "I'll just be a moment," she called, and as she closed the door behind her and moved toward my bed, I began breaking the wax lips and candy necklaces pulled from pile no. 2. These were the second-best things I had received, and while it hurt to destroy them, it would have hurt even more to give them away. I had just started to mutilate a miniature box of Red Hots when my mother pried them from my hands, accidentally
170 finishing the job for me. BB-size pellets clattered onto the floor, and as I followed them with my eyes, she snatched up a roll of Necco wafers. **G**

**indiscriminately**
(ĭn'dĭ-skrĭm'ə-nĭt-lē) *adv.* without making careful distinctions or choices

**accommodate**
(ə-kŏm'ə-dāt) *v.* to make room for

**F IRONY**
What actually causes Sedaris's headache? Tell why this is ironic.

**G EVALUATE**
What positive or negative qualities is Sedaris displaying?

---

8. **chalked it up to:** identified its cause or source as.

"Not those," I pleaded, but rather than words, my mouth expelled chocolate, chewed chocolate, which fell onto the sleeve of her sweater. "Not those. Not those."

She shook her arm, and the mound of chocolate dropped . . . upon my bedspread. "You should look at yourself," she said. "I mean, *really* look at yourself."

Along with the Necco wafers she took several Tootsie Pops and half a dozen caramels wrapped in cellophane. I heard her apologize to the Tomkeys for her absence, and then I heard my candy hitting the bottom of their bags.

"What do you say?" Mrs. Tomkey asked.

And the children answered, "Thank you."

W hile I was in trouble for not bringing my candy sooner, my sisters were in more trouble for not bringing theirs at all. We spent the early part of the evening in our rooms, then one by one we eased our way back upstairs, and joined our parents in front of the TV. I was the last to arrive, and took a seat on the floor beside the sofa. The show was a Western, and even if my head had not been throbbing, I doubt I would have had the wherewithal[9] to follow it. A posse of outlaws crested a rocky hilltop, squinting at a flurry of dust advancing from the horizon, and I thought again of the Tomkeys and of how alone and out of place they had looked in their dopey costumes. "What was up with that kid's tail?" I asked.

"Shhhh," my family said.

For months I had protected and watched over these people, but now, with one stupid act, they had turned my pity into something hard and ugly. The shift wasn't gradual, but immediate, and it **provoked** an uncomfortable feeling of loss. We hadn't been friends, the Tomkeys and I, but still I had given them the gift of my curiosity. Wondering about the Tomkey family had made me feel generous, but now I would have to shift gears and find pleasure in hating them. The only alternative was to do as my mother had instructed and take a good look at myself. This was an old trick, designed to turn one's hatred inward, and while I was determined not to fall for it, it was hard to shake the mental picture snapped[10] by her suggestion: here is a boy sitting on a bed, his mouth smeared with chocolate. He's a human being, but also he's a pig, surrounded by trash and gorging himself so that others may be denied. Were this the only image in the world, you'd be forced to give it your full attention, but fortunately there were others. This stagecoach, for instance, coming round the bend with a cargo of gold. This shiny new Mustang convertible. This teenage girl, her hair a beatiful mane, sipping Pepsi through a straw, one picture after another, on and on until the news, and whatever came on after the news. ꩜ **H**

**provoke** (prə-vōk′) *v.* to cause; to bring up

**H** IRONY
Reread lines 198–210. Why is it ironic for Sedaris to say he felt generous toward the Tomkeys?

---

9. **wherewithal** (wâr′wĭth-ôl′): ability.

10. **mental picture snapped:** an imagined picture brought quickly to mind, like a snapshot, a quickly taken photograph.

## Comprehension

**INDIANA STANDARDS**

**READING STANDARD**
**8.3.6** Identify significant literary devices....

1. **Recall** Why did the young Sedaris begin spying on the Tomkeys?

2. **Recall** Why were the Tomkeys unable to trick-or-treat on Halloween?

3. **Clarify** Why did Mrs. Sedaris want to give her children's candy to the Tomkey children?

## Literary Analysis

4. **Identify Judgments** The young Sedaris had strong opinions about many things that the Tomkeys did or said. Look through the essay and find at least three places where he makes a positive or negative statement about the family. What do you learn about Sedaris from the judgments he makes? Is his behavior toward the Tomkeys fair? Explain your answer using examples from the selection.

5. **Analyze Irony** This essay was written by an adult looking back on his childhood. Review the chart you made while reading. Which examples of irony show that Sedaris is making fun of himself and his family? Explain.

6. **Draw Conclusions** Reread lines 164–168. Why is it so difficult for Sedaris to share his candy with the Tomkeys? What might have happened if he had chosen to share?

7. **Evaluate Attitudes** Review the passages in which Sedaris mentions television. What are the good and bad things about the role it plays in his and his family's lives? Note them on a scale like the one shown. Then explain whether you think there's anything wrong with the way the Sedarises use TV.

| | |
|---|---|
| 3. _____ | 3. _____ |
| 2. _____ | 2. _____ |
| 1. _____ | 1. _____ |
| *Good* | *Bad* |

## Extension and Challenge

8. **Speaking and Listening** David Sedaris has said that he likes to "paint mental pictures" for the people who listen to his essays on the radio. In a small group, take turns reading portions of "Us and Them" out loud. As one person reads, the others should listen for images that particularly stand out to them. Then discuss whether it's more fun to read the essay or hear it, and why.

9. **Readers' Circle** Comedian Joe Ancis once said, "The only **normal** people are the ones you don't know very well." Do you think that Sedaris would agree with this quote? Do you agree? Share your conclusions with the class.

# Vocabulary in Context

## VOCABULARY PRACTICE

Show that you understand the meaning of each boldfaced word by deciding *true* or *false* for each statement.

1. A small car can easily **accommodate** six passengers.
2. Moving away can **provoke** homesickness.
3. Winning a competition does not **merit** congratulations.
4. If someone looks tired, we might **attribute** this to lack of sleep.
5. To **imply** that someone is wrong means to tell that person, "You are wrong."
6. Work experience and confidence usually **interfere** with a successful job search.
7. Someone who buys shoes **indiscriminately** may not try them on first.
8. If you **inflict** your views on others, you are forcing people to listen to you.

accommodate
attribute
imply
indiscriminately
inflict
interfere
merit
provoke

## VOCABULARY IN WRITING

How many people have you formed the wrong opinion about? Write a paragraph explaining how your first impression of someone was wrong. Use at least two vocabulary words in your paragraph. You could start this way.

> **EXAMPLE SENTENCE**
>
> The first time I met Richard, I **_attributed_** his unusual style to his being strange.

## VOCABULARY STRATEGY: IDIOMS

An **idiom** is an expression that has a different meaning from its literal meaning. For example, in this essay Sedaris says that when he got a headache, he "chalked it up to tension." *Chalked it up to* is an idiomatic expression that means "identified the cause as." There is no actual chalk or chalkboard involved.

If you encounter an unfamiliar idiom, you can often use context clues to figure out its meaning. Otherwise, look up the first word of the expression in a dictionary, where you will often find idioms explained in the entry.

**PRACTICE** Identify the idiom in each sentence and give a definition for it.

1. We expected her to be shy, but she'd tell you her life story at the drop of a hat.
2. Josh is definitely up to something—I can tell by the expression on his face.
3. Although I was tired during practice, my coach told me to hang in there.
4. Cynthia was unhappy with the store's service, but her complaints fell on deaf ears.
5. In order to get the exhausted cast through the last hour of rehearsal, the director told them to take five.

**INDIANA STANDARDS**

**READING STANDARD**
**8.1.1** Analyze idioms and comparisons … to infer the literal and figurative meanings of phrases.

**VOCABULARY PRACTICE**
For more practice, go to the **Vocabulary Center** at ClassZone.com.

# Reading-Writing Connection

Continue exploring "Us and Them" by responding to the prompts. Then complete the **Grammar and Writing** exercise.

| **WRITING PROMPTS** | **SELF-CHECK** |
|---|---|
| **A.** **Short Response: Write a Journal** <br> Sedaris often wondered what life must have been like for the Tomkeys. What did they do since they didn't watch TV? Write a **one-paragraph journal entry** from the perspective of one of the Tomkey children, describing a **normal** day in your household. | *A creative journal entry will . . .* <br> • describe the members of the Tomkey family <br> • use information from the essay to add details to the narrative |
| **B.** **Extended Response: Analyze the Message** <br> What do you think Sedaris learned from his experience with the Tomkeys? What might he want others to learn? In **two or three paragraphs,** analyze the message of "Us and Them," using examples from the selection. | *An effective analysis will . . .* <br> • clearly state the message of the essay <br> • refer to specific scenes, lines, and details |

## GRAMMAR AND WRITING

*FORM COMPLEX SENTENCES* A **complex sentence** contains one independent clause and one or more dependent clauses. An **independent clause** can stand alone as a sentence. A **dependent clause** is a group of words that contains a subject and a verb but cannot stand alone as a sentence. Dependent clauses begin with words such as *after, because, even though, since, until, where,* and *who.* By adding one of these words or phrases to an independent clause, you make it dependent. The dependent clause can then be combined with an independent clause to form a complex sentence.

**INDIANA STANDARDS**

**WRITING STANDARD**
**8.6.1** Use correct and varied sentence types . . . .

> *Original:*  We don't own a television. My family still has fun together.
>
> *Revised:*  Even though we don't own a television, my family still has fun together. (*This is now one complex sentence.*)

**PRACTICE** In each item, change one independent clause to a dependent clause. Then combine the clauses to form a complex sentence.

1. My family doesn't have a TV. We spend more time talking to each other.
2. We also spend time at the lake house. My brother catches a lot of fish.
3. Sometimes I wish we had a TV. The kids at school make fun of us.
4. We moved to this neighborhood last year. I've made a few friends.

*For more help with dependent clauses and complex sentences, see page R64 in the **Grammar Handbook.***

# O Captain! My Captain!
# I Saw Old General at Bay

Poems by Walt Whitman

# *What is the* C O S T *of victory?*

**KEY IDEA** Triumph often comes with consequences. For example, the Union victory in the Civil War preserved the United States and ended slavery, but these outcomes came at a **cost**. Almost 700,000 people died, countless others suffered, and enormous amounts of property were destroyed. In the two poems you are about to read, Walt Whitman reflects on the great cost of victory in the Civil War.

**QUICKWRITE** Wars are not the only events in which winning takes a toll. We all have had personal victories that cost us in one way or another. For example, suppose you and your best friend have an argument over an issue that is very important to both of you. You might win the argument, but lose your friend in the process. In your journal, write about a time in your life when victory had a price. Was what you won worth the cost? Explain.

## LITERARY ANALYSIS: STYLE IN POETRY

Walt Whitman is known for his uniquely American **style,** or way of using language to express ideas. One thing that makes Whitman's style stand out is his unconventional use of language. He often didn't follow traditional rules of line length and rhyme as other poets of his time did. In addition, Whitman often wrote about politics and current events, topics the poets who came before him tended to avoid. The following elements are also part of Whitman's style:

- strong **imagery,** or words and phrases that appeal to the reader's five senses
- **repetition** of a sound, word, phrase, or line for emphasis
- **irony,** or a contrast between what is expected and what actually happens

As you read "O Captain! My Captain!" and "I Saw Old General at Bay," use a chart like the one shown to help you identify these elements of the legendary poet's style.

|  | *"O Captain! My Captain!"* | *"I Saw Old General at Bay"* |
|---|---|---|
| Imagery |  |  |
| Repetition |  |  |
| Irony |  |  |

## READING SKILL: UNDERSTAND HISTORICAL CONTEXT

As with other works of literature, Whitman's poems become easier to understand once you know their **historical context,** the real events and people that influenced them. Whitman wrote "O Captain! My Captain!" and "I Saw Old General at Bay" as a way of expressing his thoughts and feelings about the Civil War. Before you begin the two poems, read the **Background** on this page. The information can help you better appreciate Whitman's message.

# Author Online

**An American Voice**
Poet Walt Whitman is considered one of America's most beloved and original writers. The poems in his collection *Leaves of Grass* were the first to be written in free verse, which means they did not contain regular patterns of rhythm and rhyme. Whitman's poetry

**Walt Whitman
1819–1892**

was praised by a few critics in his lifetime, but many others did not like it. As a result, his work did not become popular until after his death.

## Background

**The "Good Gray Poet"** When his brother George, a Union soldier, was injured in battle in 1862, Whitman went to Virginia to care for him. Whitman was moved by the sight of the injured soldiers and decided to stay in Washington, D.C., volunteering in army hospitals. Friends often referred to Whitman as the "Good Gray Poet" because of his charity toward the troops.

**A Poet in Mourning** On April 14, 1865, only five days after the end of the Civil War, President Abraham Lincoln was assassinated because of his antislavery beliefs. Whitman was a great admirer of Lincoln's. He wrote "O Captain! My Captain!" to capture the sense of tragedy that overwhelmed the nation upon Lincoln's death. The poem "I Saw Old General at Bay" was published in a collection called *Drum Taps,* which included many poems expressing Whitman's feelings about the war.

**MORE ABOUT THE AUTHOR AND BACKGROUND**
To learn more about Walt Whitman and the Civil War, visit the **Literature Center** at **ClassZone.com.**

# O Captain! My Captain!

## Walt Whitman

O Captain! my Captain! our fearful trip is done,
The ship has weather'd every rack,[1] the prize we sought[2] is won, **A**
The port is near, the bells I hear, the people all exulting,
While follow eyes the steady keel,[3] the vessel grim and daring:
5      But O heart! heart! heart!
          O the bleeding drops of red,
              Where on the deck my Captain lies,
                  Fallen cold and dead. **B**

O Captain! my Captain! rise up and hear the bells;
10 Rise up—for you the flag is flung[4]—for you the bugle trills,
For you bouquets and ribbon'd wreaths—for you the shores
     a-crowding,
For you they call, the swaying mass, their eager faces turning;
          Here Captain! dear father!
              This arm beneath your head!
15          It is some dream that on the deck,
                  You've fallen cold and dead. **C**

My Captain does not answer, his lips are pale and still,
My father does not feel my arm, he has no pulse nor will,
The ship is anchor'd safe and sound, its voyage closed and done,
20 From fearful trip the victor ship comes in with object won;
          Exult O shores, and ring O bells!
              But I with mournful tread,[5]
                  Walk the deck my Captain lies,
                      Fallen cold and dead.

---

1. **rack:** a mass of wind-driven clouds.
2. **sought** (sôt): searched for; tried to gain.
3. **keel:** the main part of a ship's structure.
4. **flung:** suddenly put out.
5. **tread** (trĕd): footsteps.

**A** HISTORICAL CONTEXT
Given what you read in the Background on page 729, who do you think is the captain, and what is his ship?

**B** STYLE IN POETRY
Reread lines 1–8. In what way does the description of the rejoicing crowds help emphasize the tragedy and **irony** of the captain's death?

**C** STYLE IN POETRY
Reread lines 9–16. What **imagery** does Whitman use to convey the people's adoration of their leader? Add these images to your chart.

**ANALYZE VISUALS**
What words would you use to describe the **mood** of this painting?

*Lincoln 2*, Wendy Allen. Oil on canvas. © Wendy Allen.

# I Saw Old General at Bay

## Walt Whitman

I saw old General at bay,
(Old as he was, his gray eyes yet shone out in battle like stars,) **D**
His small force was now completely hemm'd[1] in, in his works,
He call'd for volunteers to run the enemy's lines, a desperate
    emergency,
5 I saw a hundred and more step forth from the ranks, but two
    or three were selected,
I saw them receive their orders aside, they listen'd with care,
    the adjutant[2] was very grave,
I saw them depart with cheerfulness, freely risking their lives. **E**

---

1. **hemm'd:** hemmed; surrounded or enclosed.

2. **adjutant** (ăj′ə-tənt): a staff officer who helps a commanding officer with
administrative affairs.

**D STYLE IN POETRY**
Reread line 2. What descriptive words and details help you understand what the general looks like?

**E HISTORICAL CONTEXT**
Reread the last line. Which of Whitman's experiences best helps you interpret it?

Detail of *Major General John Sedgwick Monument,* Wendy Allen. Oil on canvas, 40″ × 30″.
© Wendy Allen.

# Comprehension

**INDIANA STANDARDS**

**READING STANDARD**
**8.3.6** Identify significant literary devices....

1. **Recall** What does the speaker of "O Captain! My Captain!" see on the deck of the ship?

2. **Clarify** What "desperate emergency" did the old general face?

3. **Clarify** For what did the general need volunteers?

# Literary Analysis

4. **Apply Historical Context** Knowing the historical context of a poem often helps you understand the figurative language that is used. In "O Captain! My Captain!" Walt Whitman uses an **extended metaphor,** a comparison of two unlike things that unfolds throughout several lines or stanzas, or even an entire poem. How does knowing about Whitman's life and times help you identify the metaphor? Create a chart to list the elements of the metaphor and what each element represents.

| Element | What It Represents |
|---|---|
| captain | President Lincoln |
| fearful trip | |
| ship | |
| prize | |
| storm | |
| arrival of the ship at port | |

5. **Make Inferences** Reread the last line of "I Saw Old General at Bay." What do the volunteers' attitudes say about the general?

6. **Understand Elegy** An **elegy** is an extended, thoughtful poem in which the speaker reflects upon death—often in tribute to a person who has died recently. Which of the two poems best fits this definition? Support your answer with examples from the poem you chose.

7. **Analyze Style** Review the chart you made while reading. Note the places Whitman uses imagery, repetition, and irony. How do these elements emphasize both the **cost** of the war and the greatness of those who led the Union to victory?

# Extension and Challenge

8. **Creative Project: Art** What pictures might help others to understand these poems? Choose one of the poems and look online for pictures or clip art that help capture its **mood.** Assemble the images in the form of a collage.

9.  **SOCIAL STUDIES CONNECTION** Find out more about the Civil War. Create a poster showing the causes, benefits, and cost of the war, and present your poster to the class.

**RESEARCH LINKS**
For more on the Civil War, visit the **Research Center** at **ClassZone.com.**

## Western Wagons
Poem by Rosemary and Stephen Vincent Benét

## The Other Pioneers
Poem by Roberto Félix Salazar

# *What makes a* PIONEER?

**KEY IDEA** Many of us are satisfied with where we live and what we do. Others have a more restless spirit. They want to build a path toward new ways of living or thinking. What are these **pioneers** searching for? The poems you're about to read describe two different groups that broke new ground.

**LIST IT** Who do you think of as a pioneer? Maybe it's someone you've met in real life, or someone you've read about in a history book or news article. Brainstorm with your group to create a list of pioneers—in science, art, sports, and other fields—who have made discoveries or developed new ways of thinking. Next to each name, tell why you included him or her.

Pioneers
1. Neil Armstrong:
first person to
walk on the moon
2.
3.

## ● LITERARY ANALYSIS: TONE

Poems tell about all kinds of subjects—love, nature, and memorable people, to name a few. The **tone** of a poem is the poet's attitude toward the subject. All literary elements can contribute to tone. For example, word choice, imagery, sound devices, and the choice of speaker (or voice that tells the poem) can suggest a tone that is optimistic, gloomy, or proud.

The poems in this lesson describe two different groups of pioneers. Use the following strategies to identify each poet's attitude toward the pioneers:

- Notice the **language** the poet uses. Do the images and descriptive words seem sad, joyful, or something else?

- Think about the **speaker**. How does he or she seem to feel about the subject?

- Consider any **sound devices**. How does the use of repetition, rhyme, or rhythm affect the poem?

## ■ READING STRATEGY: SET A PURPOSE FOR READING

Your **purpose for reading** "Western Wagons" and "The Other Pioneers" is to identify the tone of each poem and then to compare and contrast the tones. First, read the poems all the way through to understand what they are about. What's your first impression of each poet's attitude toward the subject? Now reread the poems, using a chart like the one shown to note any clues to the tone. Later you will add to this chart.

| *Shared Subject:* Pioneers in Early America | | |
|---|---|---|
| | "Western Wagons" | "The Other Pioneers" |
| What images, words, and phrases tell about the pioneers and their actions? | | |
| How does the speaker feel? | | |
| What sound devices, if any, does the poet use? How do they affect the poem? | | |

# Author Online

**Rosemary and Stephen Vincent Benét: A Literary Family**
Stephen Vincent Benét grew up in a family of writers. He published his first book when he was just 17. In 1920, Benét met Rosemary Carr, a journalist. Stephen and Rosemary often combined their writing talents, especially in children's books that brought American history to life.

**Rosemary Carr Benét 1898?–1962**

**Stephen Vincent Benét 1898–1943**

**Roberto Félix Salazar: Paying Tribute**
Salazar was born in Laredo, Texas, a town close to the border between Mexico and the United States. In "The Other Pioneers" he celebrates his heritage and honors the contributions of his Spanish ancestors.

**Roberto Félix Salazar born 1913–1996**

## *Background*

**O Pioneers!** Between 1840 and 1861, over 300,000 people headed west toward California and Oregon, some looking for gold, others for the perfect spot of land. Even before this, Spanish pioneers came to North America looking for good farming land and the promise of a better life.

**MORE ABOUT THE AUTHOR AND BACKGROUND**
To learn more about the authors and the American frontier, visit the **Literature Center** at ClassZone.com.

# Western Wagons

## Rosemary and Stephen Vincent Benét

They went with axe and rifle, when the trail was still to blaze,[1]
They went with wife and children, in the prairie-schooner[2] days,
With banjo and with frying pan—Susanna, don't you cry![3]
For I'm off to California to get rich out there or die!

5 We've broken land and cleared it, but we're tired of where we are.
They say that wild Nebraska is a better place by far.
There's gold in far Wyoming, there's black earth in Ioway,
So pack up the kids and blankets, for we're moving out today!

The cowards never started and the weak died on the road,
10 And all across the continent the endless campfires glowed.
*We'd taken land and settled—but a traveler passed by—*
*And we're going West tomorrow—Lordy, never ask us why!* **Ⓐ**

We're going West tomorrow, where the promises can't fail.
O'er the hills in legions, boys, and crowd the dusty trail!
15 We shall starve and freeze and suffer. We shall die, and tame
the lands.
But we're going West tomorrow, with our fortune in our hands. **Ⓑ**

---

1. **blaze:** to show a trail by cutting marks into trees.
2. **prairie schooner** (prâr′ē skōō′nər): a covered wagon, which looks like a schooner (ship) sailing across the prairie.
3. **Susanna, don't you cry:** lyrics from a traditional song.

**ANALYZE VISUALS**
What feeling does this **setting** evoke for you? Tell what elements of the painting contribute to that feeling.

**Ⓐ TONE**
How does the speaker seem to feel about the pioneers and the decisions they made? Tell which words and phrases help you know.

**Ⓑ TONE**
Reread the poem aloud, paying attention to the **rhyme** and **rhythm**. What adjectives would you use to describe them?

Detail of *Covered Wagons Heading West*, N. C. Wyeth. Oil on canvas. © Bridgeman Art Libarary.

# The *Other* Pioneers

### Roberto Félix Salazar

Now I must write
Of those of mine who rode these plains
Long years before the Saxon[1] and the Irish came.
Of those who plowed the land and built the towns
5 And gave the towns soft-woven Spanish names.
Of those who moved across the Rio Grande[2]
Toward the hiss of Texas snake and Indian yell.
Of men who from the earth made thick-walled homes
And from the earth raised churches to their God.
10 And of the wives who bore them sons
And smiled with knowing joy. **C**

They saw the Texas sun rise golden-red with promised wealth
And saw the Texas sun sink golden yet, with wealth unspent.
"Here," they said. "Here to live and here to love."
15 "Here is the land for our sons and the sons of our sons."
And they sang the songs of ancient Spain
And they made new songs to fit new needs.
They cleared the brush and planted the corn
And saw green stalks turn black from lack of rain.
20 They roamed the plains behind the herds
And stood the Indian's cruel attacks.
There was dust and there was sweat.
And there were tears and the women prayed. **D**

**C TONE**
Reread lines 1–11.
What words and **images** describe the pioneers and their actions? Tell which qualities of the pioneers are highlighted by this description.

**D TONE**
Which words and phrases help you understand the speaker's feelings toward the pioneers?

---

1. **Saxon** (săk'sən): British.
2. **Rio Grande** (rē'ō grănd'): a river that flows through Colorado, New Mexico, and Texas, and forms part of the United States/Mexican border; its name means "big river."

*The Vaquero* (about 1851), Hugo Wilhelm Arthur Nahl. Oil on canvas mounted on masonite.
Courtesy of the Oakland Museum of California Kahn Collection (A65.57).

And the years moved on.
25   Those who were first placed in graves
     Beside the broad mesquite and the tall nopal.[3]
     Gentle mothers left their graces and their arts
     And stalwart fathers pride and manly strength.
     Salinas, de la Garza, Sánchez, García,
30   Uribe, Gonzálaz, Martinez, de León:
     Such were the names of the fathers.
     Salinas, de la Garza, Sánchez, García,
     Uribe, Gonzálaz, Martinez, de León:
     Such are the names of the sons. **E**

**ANALYZE VISUALS**
How do you think the artist feels about the subject of this painting?

**E TONE**
Reread lines 29–34. What idea is emphasized by the **repetition** in these lines?

---

3.  **mesquite** (mĕ-skēt′), **nopal** (nō′pəl): plants native to the southwestern United States.

## Comprehension

1. **Recall** In "Western Wagons," what things are the pioneers taking with them?

2. **Clarify** Who were the "other pioneers"?

## Literary Analysis

3. **Make Inferences about Speaker** What do you know about the feelings and situation of the speaker in "Western Wagons"? Cite specific lines from the poem to support your answer.

4. **Analyze Repetition** Look for examples of repetition in "Western Wagons." What ideas are emphasized through the use of repetition?

5. **Interpret Poetry** Reread lines 12–15 of "The Other Pioneers." What were the people hoping for from their new home?

6. **Draw Conclusions about Purpose** What might have been Salazar's purpose for writing "The Other Pioneers"?

7. **Compare and Contrast** Compare and contrast the **pioneers** in "Western Wagons" and "The Other Pioneers." How are the pioneers' traits and attitudes the same? How are they different? Consider their ideas about home, moving, and future generations.

## Comparing Tone

Now that you've read both poems, finish filling in your chart. Then add—and answer—the final question.

| Shared Subject: Pioneers in Early America | | |
|---|---|---|
| | "Western Wagons" | "The Other Pioneers" |
| What images, words, and phrases tell about the pioneers and their actions? | | |
| How does the speaker feel? | | |
| What sound devices, if any, does the poet use? How do they affect the poem? | | |
| What is the tone of the poem? | | |

INDIANA STANDARDS

**READING STANDARD**
**8.3.7** Analyze a work of literature, showing how it reflects ... beliefs of its author.

# Writing for Assessment

## 1. READ THE PROMPT

You just read two poems about pioneers. In writing assessments, you may be asked to compare and contrast the tone of selections such as these that share a similar subject.

**PROMPT**

"Western Wagons" and "The Other Pioneers" both tell about pioneers, but the tone of the poems is not identical. In four or five paragraphs, compare and contrast the tone of each poem and describe how this tone is developed through imagery, word choice, sound devices, and speakers. Use quotations from the poems to support your ideas.

◀ **STRATEGIES IN ACTION**

1. I need to describe the **attitude** toward pioneers expressed in each poem and tell how this attitude is shown.

2. I need to tell how the attitudes are **similar and different**.

3. I must support my ideas using **examples** from the poems.

## 2. PLAN YOUR WRITING

Review the chart you filled out and note the similarities and differences between the tones of the two poems and the way they're conveyed. Make sure you have enough quotations and examples to support your ideas. Then think about how you will set up the body of your response.

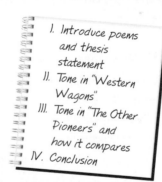

I. Introduce poems and thesis statement
II. Tone in "Western Wagons"
III. Tone in "The Other Pioneers" and how it compares
IV. Conclusion

- Option A: In one paragraph, describe the tone of the first poem and explain how it was created. In the next paragraph, describe the tone of the second poem and explain how it is similar and different from the tone of the first.

- Option B: In one paragraph, compare how speaker and word choice contribute to the tone. In a second paragraph, compare how sound devices and imagery contribute to the tone.

Choose an option. Then outline your essay and write a thesis statement.

## 3. DRAFT YOUR RESPONSE

**Introduction** Give the titles of the poems, the poets' names, and your thesis statement.
**Body** Follow your outline to describe the tone of each poem and explain the similarities and differences between the poems. Include details from the poems to support your ideas.
**Conclusion** End your essay by restating your thesis statement. You might also include your thoughts about which poem's tone made the strongest impression on you and why.
**Revision** Make sure the quotations you cite are correctly punctuated with quotation marks.

## Writing Workshop

# Literary Analysis

In this unit, you looked closely at style, voice, and other literary elements that make writing distinctive. In this workshop, you will examine literary elements that make a work especially meaningful or enjoyable to you. Use the **Writer's Road Map** as your guide.

### WRITER'S ROAD MAP

#### Literary Analysis

**WRITING PROMPT 1**

**Writing from Literature** Choose a selection from this unit and write an essay that helps a reader understand it more deeply. Focus on one or two literary elements, such as plot, characters, setting, or mood.

**Selections to Consider**

- "The Lady, or the Tiger?"
- "New York Day Women"
- "Us and Them"

**WRITING PROMPT 2**

**Writing from the Real World** Think of a memorable story you have viewed or read. Write an essay in which you describe the story and analyze the reasons that it is meaningful to you.

**Sources of Stories**

- television shows with particular settings, such as a police station or a hospital
- movies with exciting or surprising plots
- magazine articles that describe real-life adventures

 **WRITING TOOLS**
For prewriting, revision, and editing tools, visit the **Writing Center** at ClassZone.com.

#### KEY TRAITS

**1. IDEAS**
- Presents a **thesis statement** that identifies the main idea of the analysis
- Supports key points with **evidence,** such as quotations and details

**2. ORGANIZATION**
- **Identifies the title and author** of the work in a thought-provoking introduction
- Provides **details** as needed to give the reader background information
- Uses **transitions** to connect ideas
- **Summarizes** the analysis in a conclusion and makes a broad judgment about the work

**3. VOICE**
- Uses language that is **appropriate** for the audience and purpose

**4. WORD CHOICE**
- Uses **precise words** to examine the work

**5. SENTENCE FLUENCY**
- Varies **sentence structures**

**6. CONVENTIONS**
- Uses **correct grammar, spelling, and punctuation**

# Part 1: Analyze a Student Model

**WRITING STANDARD**
**8.5.2** Write responses to literature....

**Ramón Cepero**
**Oxford Charter School**

### Fancy Is Funnier Than Fact

"I let fancy get the upper hand of fact too often," Mark Twain explains in *Roughing It.* What he means is that he likes to tell a few tall tales. He also likes to skip over or change some of the facts, which makes his writing style surprising and funny. In *Roughing It,* Twain uses
5  irony and exaggeration to create humor.

Twain begins by listing several jobs that he has already tried and lost. Each failure is funny because Twain uses irony to describe what really happened. For instance, Twain remembers working in a bookstore. He says he spent all his time there reading. He adds that the
10  customers "bothered" him by interrupting his reading. It's funny to think of someone who is bothered by having to work at his job. When Twain tells about being a clerk in a drug store, he says his "prescriptions were unlucky." He adds that, as a result, "we appeared to sell more stomach-pumps than soda-water." This description is humorous, even
15  though readers probably feel sorry for the customers who got sick taking medicine that was supposed to make them better.

The way Twain describes his time as a reporter is laugh-out-loud funny. For example, his boss tells Twain to write about hay-wagons that come into the city. Twain finds only one hay-wagon, but he turns it into
20  a whopping sixteen news stories. He explains how he did it this way: "I multiplied [the one hay-wagon] by sixteen, brought it into town from sixteen different directions, made sixteen separate items of it, and got up such another sweat about hay as Virginia City had never seen in the world before." One story about a hay-wagon sounds boring, but Twain's
25  sixteen stories, as well as the big "sweat about hay" in Virginia City, sound funny.

---

**KEY TRAITS IN ACTION**

Begins with a thought-provoking introduction that identifies the work's **title and author,** as well as a clear **thesis statement.**

Varies **sentence structures** and uses **appropriate** language.

Provides **details** that add needed background information. Supports the thesis with **evidence.**

Later in the narrative, Twain tells another tall tale about his work as a reporter. He explains that one day he was desperate because there was nothing to write about. Then he found out that an outlaw had killed

30 a man in a saloon. Twain says that "joy returned once more. I never was so glad." This is funny because it's so ridiculous. Twain might have been a little relieved that there was news to write about, but he couldn't have been joyful. Then Twain surprises the reader by explaining how he wrote a letter to the outlaw. He told the man, "You have done me

35 a kindness this day which I can never forget." Twain can't really be thinking of murder as a kindness or a personal favor. He is just glad to get some news, but the irony about his "joy" makes it funny.

In *Roughing It,* Twain turns his experiences with work into a funny narrative about failing at jobs, getting fired, inventing "news," and

40 finally finding a "legitimate occupation" as a writer. He uses irony and exaggeration and lets "fancy get the upper hand of fact too often" as he tells about his work life. Twain's many exaggerations make *Roughing It* a hilarious and worthwhile read.

> Uses **transitions** effectively.

> **Precise words** help to make the analysis clear and logical.

> Lively conclusion **summarizes** the analysis and makes a broad judgment about the work.

2

# Part 2: Apply the Writing Process

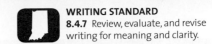

**WRITING STANDARD**
**8.4.7** Review, evaluate, and revise writing for meaning and clarity.

**PREWRITING**

| *What Should I Do?* | *What Does It Look Like?* |
|---|---|

**1. Reread or re-view the work you chose.**
One way to find an idea or focus is to go back over the piece you have chosen and examine its literary elements, such as its characters, dialogue, setting, or style. List examples of each element.

▶

| Element | Examples |
|---|---|
| Repetition | "What to do next?"; repeated failures at various jobs |
| Language | long sentences; fancy words (proprietor, dearth, excursion) |
| Exaggeration | the drugstore sold more stomach pumps than soda water; one hay-wagon turns into sixteen hay-wagons |

**2. Develop a working thesis.**
For Prompt 1, your thesis should name one or two literary elements and explain how they affect the meaning of the work. For Prompt 2, your thesis should tell the reader why the work matters to you.

▶

*Working thesis:*
Twain exaggerates a lot, and that makes a funny narrative.

**3. Craft a strong introduction.**
Your opening paragraph should grab the reader's attention and state the thesis clearly and completely.

**TIP** Strong introductions include quotations, surprising statements, or questions.

▶

**Start with a question:**
*Why is Mark Twain's writing so funny?*
**Start with a quotation:**
*"I let fancy get the upper hand of fact too often."*
**Start with a surprising statement:**
*One hay-wagon can become sixteen news stories in the hand of a clever and devious reporter.*

**4. Find evidence to support your thesis.**
Prove your thesis by referring directly to the details of the work. For example, the writer of the student model wanted to figure out what made *Roughing It* so funny. He analyzed the work and found several examples of irony.

▶

*Key point:* Twain uses irony.
*Supporting evidence:*
- *doesn't like working in a bookstore because customers bother him instead of letting him read*
- *reacts to murder with "joy" and says, "I was never so glad"*

| What Should I Do? | What Does It Look Like? |
|---|---|

**1. Plan your analysis.**
The writer of the student model discussed each key point in the order it appeared in Twain's narrative. If you prefer, you could discuss your key points in order of importance—putting the most important key point either first or last.

▶

*Order of appearance in the narrative:*

1. Jobs Twain tried and failed at
2. Early event in Twain's career as a newspaperman
3. Later event in Twain's career as a newspaperman

*Order of importance:*

1. Greatest example: response to saloon killing
2. Another example: stories about hay-wagons
3. Another example: early jobs

**2. Consider your audience.**
Your audience may not be familiar with the work you are analyzing. Remember to add background information to help readers follow your points.

▶

*Twain is a good storyteller, and he is so funny. For example, his boss tells Twain to write about hay-wagons that come into the city. Twain finds only one hay-wagon, but he turns it into a whopping sixteen news stories. He explains how he did it this way: "I multiplied [the one hay-wagon] by sixteen, brought it into town from sixteen different directions, made sixteen separate items of it, and got up such another sweat about hay as Virginia City had never seen in the world before." One story about a hay-wagon sounds boring, but Twain's sixteen stories, as well as the big "sweat about hay" in Virginia City, sound funny.*

**3. Back up your points with evidence.**
You need to prove each key point that you make. You can do this with evidence, such as a few well-chosen details or quoted words.

**TIP** Before you revise, look back at the key traits on page 742 and the rubric and peer-reader questions on page 748.

▶

*Each failure is funny. That's because Twain uses exaggeration and irony.* ⎤ —Key point

*For instance, Twain remembers working in a bookstore. He says he spent all his time there reading. He adds that the customers "bothered" him by interrupting his reading. It's funny to think of someone who is bothered by having to work at his job.* ⎤ —Support

## REVISING AND EDITING

| *What Should I Do?* | *What Does It Look Like?* |
|---|---|

**1. Improve how you start.**
- Reread your opening sentence. Ask yourself: Will this interest my reader?
- (Circle) the author's name and the title of the work. **Add this information** if it is missing.
- [Bracket] your thesis. Make it as **clear and specific** as possible.

▶ (Mark Twain) ~~likes to tell tall tales. He also likes to change some of the facts in his story. [Twain exaggerates a lot, and that makes a funny narrative.]~~
"I let fancy get the upper hand of fact too often," Mark Twain explains in <u>Roughing It</u>. What he means is that he likes to tell a few tall tales. He also likes to skip over or change some of the facts, which makes his writing style surprising and funny. In <u>Roughing It</u>, Twain uses exaggeration to create humor.

**2. Use exact, specific words.**
- Consider replacing some of your weak, state-of-being verbs, such as *is* and *might be*, with action verbs.
- Also, think about **replacing dull, tired modifiers**, such as *really*, *very*, and *so*, with more specific words.

▶ ~~Twain is a good storyteller, and he is so funny.~~ The way Twain describes his time as a reporter is laugh-out-loud funny.

**3. Vary your sentences.**
- **Highlight** places where you have used several simple sentences in a row.
- Revise to include a mix of sentence structures that make your analysis more sophisticated.

▶ ~~Twain lists several jobs. He has already tried and lost each one. Each failure is funny. That's because Twain uses exaggeration and irony.~~
Twain begins by listing several jobs that he has already tried and lost. Each failure is funny because Twain uses exaggeration and irony to tell what really happened.

**4. Tell why it matters.**
- Ask a peer reader to point out statements in your conclusion that discuss the meaning or impact of the work.
- Add a reflection on the work if one is needed.

**See page 748:** Ask a Peer Reader

▶ Twain turns his experiences with work into a funny narrative about failing at jobs, getting fired, inventing "news," and finally finding a "legitimate occupation" as a writer. He exaggerates and lets "fancy get the upper hand of fact too often" as he tells about his work life. Twain's many exaggerations make <u>Roughing It</u> a hilarious and worthwhile read.

# Literary Analysis

## Apply the Rubric

**A strong literary analysis . . .**

☑ has an attention-getting introduction that identifies the title and author of the work being analyzed

☑ presents a clear, specific thesis

☑ supports key points with evidence

☑ provides background information so the reader can understand the analysis

☑ varies sentence structures

☑ uses transitions, appropriate language, and precise words

☑ concludes by summarizing the key ideas and reflecting on the work's effect or importance

## Ask a Peer Reader

• What is my thesis?

• How well do I support each main point I make? Do I need to add details or quotations?

• Where in my conclusion do I explain what effect the work had on me?

## Check Your Grammar

• Make sure that elements in your sentences are parallel. For example, phrases that serve the same purpose in a sentence should take the same form.

> Twain likes to tell tall tales, skip over some of the facts, and ~~exaggerating~~ *exaggerate* some of the details.

> *Roughing It* is a funny narrative about failing at jobs, getting fired, inventing "news," and ~~how he finds~~ *finding* work.

**See page R64:** Parallel Structure

• Do not misplace modifiers. Remember to follow the modifying phrase directly with the noun or pronoun it modifies.

> ~~In a saloon, Twain found out that an outlaw had killed a man.~~
> Twain found out that an outlaw had killed a man in a saloon.

**See page R59:** Misplaced Modifiers

## Writing Onine

**PUBLISHING OPTIONS**
For publishing options, visit the **Writing Center** at **ClassZone.com.**

**ASSESSMENT PREPARATION**
For writing and grammar assessment practice, go to the **Assessment Center** at **ClassZone.com.**

## Creating an Online Database

You and your classmates can publish your work by building an online database. The database you create could house your literary analyses as well as other reviews that give your opinions on books, movies, video games, or restaurants.

### Preparing the Scene

1. **Decide on the content.** Determine what your database will include.
2. **Plan the organization of the database.** Decide how you will organize the database—perhaps by type of review or by keyword. Will you provide an index, a FAQ (that's a Frequently Asked Questions section), or a way for users to submit feedback?
3. **Sketch your home page.** Be sure that your home page shows the name of your site and has clear, easy-to-use navigation buttons. Add interest to your home page with graphics and color.
4. **Create credits.** On your home page, provide a link that says "About This Site" or otherwise signals information about site contents. Then list the site's creators, including all authors, as well as credits for all visuals.

> **TIP** Remember to get permission for anything you include on the site. This includes your classmates' permission to upload their work, as well as permission for any visuals, sound effects, or other items you import.

### Producing the Database

1. **Use an authoring program.** Find out what software your school offers for building Web sites. Your school's computer specialist may offer a quick lesson in how to use it to import text and visuals. Otherwise, consult the Help menu, the manual, or an online tutorial for guidance.
2. **Ask peers to try out an early version of the database.** Find out what works well and what needs revising. Be sure to proofread the text, too.
3. **Upload it.** Work with the computer specialist at your school to make your database available on the Web.

# Reading Comprehension

**DIRECTIONS** *Read this selection and answer the questions that follow.*

# A Hike in New York City

### Sam Levenson

At least once each summer we kids went off on a hike, but never without strong opposition from Mama. When it came to the open road, Mama had a closed mind.

Her method of discouraging us from venturing into the unknown was to make the entire project appear ridiculous:

"You're going on a what?"

"We're going on a hike."

"What's a hike?" Mama would ask.

When we started to explain it, the whole idea did in fact become ridiculous.

10 "We go walking, Ma."

"Walking? For that you have to leave home? What's the matter with walking right here? You walk; I'll watch."

"You don't understand, Ma. We take lunch along."

"I'll give you lunch here, and you can march right around the table," and she would start singing a march, clapping her hands rhythmically.

"Ma, we climb mountains in the woods."

She couldn't understand why it was so much more enjoyable to fall off a mountain than off a fire escape.

"And how about the wild animals in the woods?"

20 "Wild animals? What kind of wild animals?"

"A bear, for instance. A bear could eat you up."

"Ma, bears don't eat little children."

"Okay. So he won't eat you, but he could take a bite and spit it out! I'm telling you now, if a wild animal eats you up don't come running to me. And who's going with you?"

"Well, there's Georgie—"

"Georgie! Not him! He's a real wild animal!" She then went on to list all the conditions for the trip. "And remember one thing, don't tear your pants, and remember one thing, don't eat wild berries and bring me home the cramps, and

30 remember one thing, don't tell me tomorrow morning that you're too tired to go to school, and remember one thing, wear boots, a sweater, warm underwear, and an umbrella, and a hat, and remember one thing, if you should get lost in the jungle, call up so I'll know you're all right. And don't dare come home without color in your cheeks. I wish I was young and free like you. Take soap."

Since the consent was specifically granted for the next day only, that night none of us slept. There was always a chance that it might rain. Brother Albert stayed at the crystal set[1] all night like a ship's radio operator with his earphones on, listening to weather bulletins and repeating them aloud for the rest of us. "It's clearing in Nebraska. Hot air masses coming up from the Gulf. They say
40 it's good for planting alfalfa. Storm warning off the coast of Newfoundland. It's drizzling in Montreal."

At 6:00 A.M. we were ready for Operation Hike, rain or shine, but we had to wait for Papa to get up. We didn't need his permission, but we did need his blanket.

Into the valley of Central Park we marched, bowed down with knapsacks, flashlights, a compass-mirror (so you could tell not only where you were lost but who was lost), a thermos bottle (semi-automatic—you had to fill it but it emptied by itself), and an ax. Onward! Forward! Upward! Philip was always the leader. He was the one to get lost first. Jerry was the lookout. He would yell,
50 "Look out!" and fall off the cliff. None of us knew how long we were supposed to march. We went on because we didn't know what to do if we stopped. One brave coward finally spoke up. "I can't go on anymore. The heat is killing me. Let's start the fire here."

No hike was complete without Georgie and his Uncle Bernie's World War I bugle. This kid had lungs like a vacuum cleaner. With him outside the walls of Jericho, they could have sent the rest of the army home. He used to stand on a hill and let go a blast that had the Staten Island ferries running into each other.

Lunch, naturally, had been packed in a shoe box—sandwiches, fruit, cheese, and napkins all squashed together neatly. The lid would open by itself every
60 twenty minutes for air.

It happened every time, the Miracle of the Sandwiches. One kid always got a "brilliant idea." "Hey, I got a brilliant idea. I'm tired of my mother's sandwiches. Let's everybody trade sandwiches." All the kids exchanged sandwiches, and miraculously we all ended up with salami.

Albert was the true nature lover. "You know, you can learn a lot about human nature from the ants," he always said as he lifted up rock after rock to study his favorite insects. And he was right. While he was studying the ants, someone swiped his apple.

We came home with color in our cheeks—green. To make sure we could go
70 again, we didn't forget Mama. We brought her a bouquet. She took one whiff and broke out in red blotches.

**GO ON** ➤

---

1. **crystal set:** a radio.

# Comprehension

**DIRECTIONS** *Answer these questions about "A Hike in New York City."*

1. When do the children set out on their hike?
   ○ before Albert hears the weather report
   ○ at six o'clock in the morning
   ○ after they get Papa's blanket
   ○ as soon as they eat lunch

2. Which words and phrases from the passage help the reader follow the order of events?
   ○ at least, in the woods
   ○ on a hike, right here
   ○ that night, at 6:00 A.M.
   ○ open road, rain or shine

3. One element of the author's style is his use of
   ○ mostly short sentences
   ○ mostly long sentences
   ○ all short sentences
   ○ a mix of long and short sentences

4. Which one of the first four sentences in the passage tells you this will be a funny story?
   ○ sentence 1
   ○ sentence 2
   ○ sentence 3
   ○ sentence 4

5. The author sets the tone by using
   ○ long sentences
   ○ ironic comments
   ○ specialized vocabulary
   ○ detailed descriptions

6. In lines 28–32, the repetition of the phrase "and remember one thing" has the effect of
   ○ creating an angry tone
   ○ clarifying the sequence of events
   ○ building excitement for the hike
   ○ emphasizing Mama's many worries

7. In lines 32–33, Mama says "if you should get lost in the jungle, call up so I'll know you're all right." This statement is ironic because
   ○ it is easy to get lost in a big city park
   ○ Mama is afraid that the children will get lost
   ○ the children are not all right if they are lost
   ○ the New York City park is not a jungle

8. Which image appeals to the reader's sense of sight and hearing?
   ○ Mama "singing a march, clapping her hands rhythmically"(line 15)
   ○ Albert at the crystal set "with his earphones on" (lines 37–38)
   ○ the children "bowed down with knapsacks" (line 45)
   ○ lunch items "squashed together neatly" in a shoe box (line 59)

9. The phrases "Operation Hike" and "the Miracle of the Sandwiches" are funny because they

   ○ express a child's innocent point of view
   ○ show Mama's concern for her children
   ○ can be interpreted in different ways
   ○ make everyday events seem important

10. Which words in the passage help to create an informal style?

    ○ opposition, ridiculous, rhythmically
    ○ kids, swiped, squashed
    ○ hike, walk, marched
    ○ coward, insects, bouquet

11. With the exclamations "Onward! Forward! Upward!" in line 48, the author emphasizes the boys'

    ○ excitement about the hike
    ○ fear of getting lost
    ○ need for their mother
    ○ interest in climbing a hill

12. In line 55, the image that compares Georgie's lungs to a vacuum cleaner shows that he

    ○ has strong lungs
    ○ speaks very loudly
    ○ likes to play the bugle
    ○ has dirt in his lungs

13. In line 62, the quotation marks around "brilliant idea" suggest that this phrase is an example of

    ○ understatement
    ○ verbal irony
    ○ vivid imagery
    ○ symbolism

14. Reread lines 69–71. What is ironic about the children's gift to Mama?

    ○ The children bring Mama a gift so that she will let them go hiking again.
    ○ The children find flowers in Central Park to bring to Mama.
    ○ Mama has an allergic reaction to the bouquet.
    ○ Mama is surprised by the children's gift.

15. Which event happens last in the passage?

    ○ The children exchange sandwiches.
    ○ Someone steals Albert's apple.
    ○ Mama breaks out in red blotches.
    ○ Georgie plays his uncle's bugle.

## Constructed Response

**SHORT ANSWER**  *Write two or three sentences to answer this question.*

16. Find two examples of irony in the passage and identify each as situational, verbal, or dramatic irony.

**ESSAY**  *Write a paragraph to answer this question.*

17. The author's writing style turns his remembrance into a funny story. Give two examples of his humor, and explain how the words, images, or sentences in the examples contribute to the humor.

GO ON

# Vocabulary

**DIRECTIONS** *Use context clues and your knowledge of idioms to answer the following questions.*

1. In line 1, the narrator says that the children in his family went hiking "at least once each summer." The idiom *at least* means
   - as much as
   - not less than
   - more than
   - roughly

2. In lines 2–3, the narrator says, "When it came to the open road, Mama had a closed mind." The idiom *when it came to* means
   - in addition to
   - because of
   - with regard to
   - upon arriving at

3. In line 57, Georgie "let go a blast" on his uncle's bugle. The idiom *let go* means
   - was scared by
   - forgot about
   - left alone
   - blew forcefully

4. In line 71, the narrator says that his mother "broke out" when she sniffed the bouquet. The idiom *broke out* means
   - developed a rash
   - tried to avoid
   - worried about
   - scratched at

**DIRECTIONS** *Use context clues and your understanding of Latin words and roots to answer the following questions.*

5. The prefix *ob-* means "against," and the Latin word *ponere* means "to put." What is the meaning of the word *opposition* in line 2?
   - punishment
   - resistance
   - influence
   - approval

6. The Latin word *ridere* means "to laugh." What is the meaning of the word *ridiculous* in line 5?
   - enjoyable
   - silly
   - realistic
   - unusual

7. The Latin word *mirari* means "to wonder at." What is the meaning of the word *miraculously* in line 64?
   - with great curiosity
   - without even trying
   - by any means possible
   - in a way that cannot be explained

# Writing & Grammar

**DIRECTIONS** *Read this passage and answer the questions that follow.*

(1) Central Park occupies 843 acres of land in New York City. (2) It is the most visited park in the nation. (3) When the city bought the land in the mid 1800s, it had to be cleared of farms, livestock, and open sewers. (4) The city held a competition for the new park's design. (5) Officials chose a plan. (6) The completed park looked natural. (7) It consisted of artificial lakes and imported trees and shrubs. (8) Now the park is a popular spot for bird watching. (9) It is an oasis for migrating birds.

1. How might you use an appositive phrase to combine sentences 1 and 2?
   - ○ Central Park is the most visited park in the nation and occupies 843 acres of land in New York City.
   - ○ The most visited park in the nation is Central Park, and it occupies 843 acres of land in New York City.
   - ○ Central Park, the most visited park in the nation, occupies 843 acres of land in New York City.
   - ○ Occupying 843 acres of land in New York City, Central Park is the most visited park in the nation.

2. How might you combine sentences 4 and 5 to form one compound sentence?
   - ○ The city held a competition for the new park's design, choosing a plan.
   - ○ The city held a competition for the new park's design, and officials chose a plan.
   - ○ After the city held a competition for the new park's design, officials chose a plan.
   - ○ The city held a competition for the new park's design and chose a plan.

3. How might you combine sentences 6 and 7 to form one complex sentence?
   - ○ The completed park looked natural, but it consisted of artificial lakes and imported trees and shrubs.
   - ○ Though the completed park looked natural, it consisted of artificial lakes and imported trees and shrubs.
   - ○ The completed park looked natural but consisted of artificial lakes and imported trees and shrubs.
   - ○ The completed park looked natural, consisting of artificial lakes and imported trees and shrubs.

4. How might you use an appositive phrase to combine sentences 8 and 9?
   - ○ Migrating birds now make the park an oasis and a popular spot for bird watching.
   - ○ Because it is an oasis for migrating birds, the park is now a popular spot for bird watching.
   - ○ The park, an oasis for migrating birds, is now a popular spot for bird watching.
   - ○ The park is an oasis for migrating birds, so now it is a popular spot for bird watching.

# UNIT 6
# More Great Reads

## Ideas for Independent Reading

Which questions from Unit 6 made an impression on you?
Continue exploring them with these books.

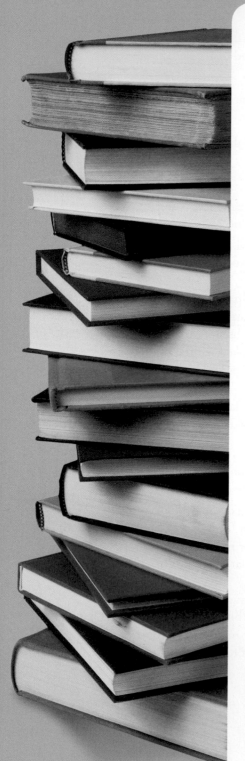

## How do you make decisions?

### Cheating Lessons
*by Nan Willard*

Wickham High will finally compete against fancy Pinehurst at the State Quiz Bowl. Bernadette can't wait to crush the other team until she realizes there's no way her school honestly aced the test. She has to decide between telling a lie or hurting friends.

### Good Brother, Bad Brother: The Story of Edwin Booth and John Wilkes Booth
*by James Cross Giblin*

Two brothers grow up together. Both become well-known actors like their father, but one goes on to kill the President of the United States. What happened?

### Princess Academy
*by Shannon Hale*

The king's priests have decreed that the next princess will come from tiny Mount Eskel. Suddenly, all the girls in the village have to go to school. Miri decides she has to be the best student. But what will Miri do if the prince chooses her?

## What's really normal?

### Act I, Act II, Act Normal
*by Martha Weston*

Topher has been waiting for three years to be the lead in the 8th grade play. Too bad this year's production is Rumpelstiltskin, the Musical, written by geeky Samantha. Topher takes the role, but will the school bully and the touchy leading lady ruin it for him?

### Sweetgrass Basket
*by Marlene Carvell*

In the early 1900s, Mattie and Sarah are forced to go to a boarding school for Native American children. They're told it's their best chance for a "normal" life. Now far from home, the two girls have to figure out how to survive and keep their traditions.

### Hans Christian Andersen: His Fairy Tale Life
*by Hjordis Varmer and Lilian Brogger*

Everyone knows Andersen's fairy tales, but did you know he was obsessed with fame? He begged rich men, a princess, and even the king, until someone would support his dream to write and act.

## What makes a pioneer?

### China's Son: Growing Up in the Cultural Revolution
*by Da Chen*

Da Chen suffers in 1960s China, which is run by communists. His father is often in labor camps and his brothers and sisters work in the fields. Then Da gets the chance to apply for college. Will life finally get better?

### Guinea Pig Scientists
*by Leslie Dendy and Mel Boring*

Scientists who experiment on themselves are brave and sometimes foolhardy. We wouldn't know how the digestive system worked, what animal spread yellow fever, or how to build safer cars without these people.

### O Pioneers!
*by Willa Cather*

Alexandra is only 16 when her father dies and leaves her in charge of their failing homestead on the Nebraska prairies. Her brothers agree to listen to her advice, but will they let her put the farm deeper in debt to chase her father's dream?

# 7

# Our Place in the World

## HISTORY, CULTURE, AND THE AUTHOR

- In Fiction
- In Nonfiction
- In Media
- In Poetry

# What SHAPES
## *who we are?*

If you were to write a book about your life, where would you begin? If you're like many authors and artists, what you say would probably reflect the influence of your family, friends, and **culture.** Although you can't always see it, culture plays an important part in shaping your world. The language you speak, the holidays you celebrate, the games you play, and the music you listen to are all part of your culture.

***ACTIVITY*** What parts of your history and culture influence you the most? Think about the important people, places, and events in your life. Then reflect on your family's traditions and your own taste in entertainment. Make a collage out of images and mementos that symbolize what shapes you.

**INDIANA STANDARDS**

# Preview Unit Goals

**LITERARY ANALYSIS**
- Identify and analyze influence of writer's background
- Identify and analyze historical and cultural context of selections
- Identify and analyze author's perspective
- Identify and analyze characteristics of an autobiography

**READING**
- Make inferences
- Identify and analyze cause-and-effect relationships
- Identify and analyze treatment of an idea
- Compare and contrast

**WRITING AND GRAMMAR**
- Write a cause-and-effect essay
- Combine sentences to form a compound-complex sentence
- Use colons and semicolons correctly

**SPEAKING, LISTENING, AND VIEWING**
- Identify visual aspects of illustrations
- Compare different points of view in nonprint media sources
- Deliver a multimedia presentation

**VOCABULARY**
- Use context to determine the meaning of homographs
- Distinguish between connotative and denotative meanings of words

**ACADEMIC VOCABULARY**
- author's background
- author's perspective
- historical context
- cultural context
- cause-and-effect
- treatment

# History, Culture, and the Author

Have you ever heard the lyrics to a song and wondered what motivated the musician to write them? If you found out that an athlete had once overcome a serious illness, would that make his or her best season even more impressive? What about a work of literature—do you ever wonder what inspired its creation? In this workshop, you'll learn about different factors that can affect writers. By examining the layers of a writer's experience, you can "read into" literature with far more insight.

## Part 1: A Writer's Background

You are the unique product of many factors, including your heritage, family life, national identity, and economic status. Just as all these factors shape your ideas and beliefs, they influence writers as well. Writers may not consciously realize it, but their personal backgrounds affect not only what they choose to write about but how they express their ideas.

For instance, consider "Eating Together," a poem that paints a touching picture of a close-knit family. First, read the poem itself. Then go back and read the background on Li-Young Lee to discover how knowledge about the author's family adds extra meaning to the poem.

**INDIANA STANDARDS**

**READING STANDARDS**
**8.3.1** Determine and articulate the relationship between the purposes and characteristics of different forms of poetry (including ballads, lyrics, couplets, epics, elegies, odes, and sonnets).

**8.3.7** Analyze a work of literature, showing how it reflects the heritage, traditions, attitudes, and beliefs of its author.

# Eating Together

Poem by **Li-Young Lee**

**BACKGROUND** Li-Young Lee was born to Chinese parents in Jakarta, Indonesia, in 1957. The family moved many times during Lee's childhood—often to avoid anti-Chinese sentiments—before settling in the United States. Lee's poetry frequently focuses on his close-knit, traditional Chinese family, and many poems express the poet's grief over his father's death.

In the steamer is the trout
seasoned with slivers of ginger,
two sprigs of green onion, and sesame oil.
We shall eat it with rice for lunch,
5  brothers, sister, my mother who will
taste the sweetest meat of the head,
holding it between her fingers
deftly, the way my father did
weeks ago. Then he lay down
10  to sleep like a snow-covered road
winding through pines older than him,
without any travelers, and lonely for no one.

**QUESTIONS TO ASK**

**What evidence of the author's heritage and customs do I see?**
The Asian family described in the poem seems close-knit and traditional, much like Lee's own family.

**What might have been the author's motivation for writing this poem?**
Lee may have wanted to express his feelings about his father's death and to reflect on how his father's absence has affected his family.

## MODEL 1: ANALYZING A POEM

Read this poem a first time, without knowing anything about the author behind the words and ideas. How would you describe the speaker?

**Dusting**

Poem by **Julia Alvarez**

Each morning I wrote my name
on the dusty cabinet, then crossed
the dining table in script, scrawled
in capitals on the backs of chairs,
5  practicing signatures like scales
while Mother followed, squirting
linseed[1] from a burping can
into a crumpled-up flannel.

She erased my fingerprints
10  from the bookshelf and rocker,
polished mirrors on the desk
scribbled with my alphabets.
My name was swallowed in the towel
with which she jeweled the table tops.
15  The grain surfaced in the oak
and the pine grew luminous.
But I refused with every mark
to be like her, anonymous.

---

1. **linseed:** yellowish oil made from flax seeds, often used to help preserve the shine of natural wood furniture.

**Close Read**

1. What images does Alvarez use to help you visualize the actions of the speaker and her mother? Find three examples.

2. Think about what the speaker means by what she says in the [boxed] lines. How is she different from her mother?

## MODEL 2: THE WRITER'S BACKGROUND

Read this background information about Julia Alvarez. Then go back and read the poem a second time.

Julia Alvarez was born in New York in 1950. When she was three months old, her parents returned with her to their native country, the Dominican Republic. However, the family came back to the
5  United States for political reasons when Alvarez was ten years old. Alvarez grew up speaking Spanish, with English as a second language. Her mother worked as a housekeeper and, as a young girl, Alvarez would
10  often go with her mother to work. Alvarez has said, "As I followed my mother cleaning house, washing and ironing clothes, rolling dough, I was using the material of my housebound girl life to claim my woman's legacy." Alvarez later became a writer and continues to share her childhood experiences in her works.

**Close Read**

1. In what way does the background information help you to better understand the poem?

2. What connection can you draw between the last two lines of the poem and Alvarez's career?

# Part 2: Historical and Cultural Influences

Knowing about a writer's personal background can help you to appreciate his or her work more fully. Similarly, knowing the **historical and cultural contexts** in which the work was written can help you interpret and analyze that work more accurately. **Historical and cultural contexts** refer to the events, social problems, traditions, and values that may have influenced the author and the writing. For example, what events and issues of the time was the author concerned about? How are those concerns reflected in the writing?

Take a look at this excerpt from a story by James Baldwin. Notice how reading the background and answering some questions can give you new insights into Baldwin's vivid descriptions.

# *from* Sonny's Blues

### Short story by **James Baldwin**

**BACKGROUND** In the early 1900s, African Americans were encouraged to move to Manhattan's Harlem neighborhood, partly to shelter them from emerging racial conflicts in other neighborhoods. By 1920, Harlem was populated almost exclusively by African Americans. Though the 1920s became known as the Harlem Renaissance because of the blossoming of jazz music, writing, and art in the African-American community, it was also a time of economic hardship. Since many landlords in other areas refused to rent apartments to African Americans, landlords in Harlem often took advantage of their tenants by charging high rents.

"Sonny's Blues" was published in 1957, reflecting James Baldwin's firsthand knowledge of the neighborhood in which he grew up. Throughout most of the twentieth century, Harlem was known for being troubled by crime and poverty as well as being a prominent African-American cultural community.

*The narrator and his brother are returning to the neighborhood of their youth:*

Houses exactly like the houses of our past yet dominated the landscape, boys exactly like the boys we once had been found themselves smothering in these houses, came down into the streets for light and air and found themselves encircled by disaster. Some escaped the trap, most didn't. Those
5   who got out always left something of themselves behind, as some animals amputate a leg and leave it in the trap. It might be said, perhaps, that I had escaped, after all, I was a schoolteacher; or that Sonny had, he hadn't lived in Harlem for years. Yet, as the cab moved uptown through streets which seemed, with a rush, to darken with dark people, and as I covertly studied
10  Sonny's face, it came to me that what we both were seeking through our separate cab windows was that part of ourselves which had been left behind.

*QUESTIONS TO ASK*

**What social problems are reflected in the writing?**
Baldwin uses words and phrases like "smothering," "encircled by disaster," and "the trap" to describe the poverty-stricken Harlem neighborhood of his youth.

**What might have prompted the author to write this story?**
Baldwin may have wanted to explore why former residents of Harlem who "escaped the trap" still feel so connected to the neighborhood in which they grew up.

## MODEL 1: ANALYZING FICTION

In this story, a British pilot wakes up in a French hospital during World War II. Find out what he's thinking about as a nurse tends to him. First, read this excerpt and answer the **Close Read** questions. Then read the background that follows.

*from* # Beware of the Dog

### Short story by **Roald Dahl**

"I believe there's someone coming down to see you from the Air Ministry after breakfast," she went on. "They want a report or something. I expect you know all about it. How you got shot down and all that. I won't let him stay long, so don't worry."

5     He did not answer. She finished washing him and gave him a toothbrush and some toothpowder. He brushed his teeth, rinsed his mouth, and spat the water out into the basin.

    Later she brought him his breakfast on a tray, but he did not want to eat. He was still feeling weak and sick and he wished only to lie still and think
10  about what had happened. And there was a sentence running through his head. It was a sentence which Johnny, the Intelligence Officer of his squadron, always repeated to the pilots every day before they went out. He could see Johnny now, leaning against the wall of the dispersal hut with his pipe in his hand, saying, "And if they get you, don't forget, just your name, rank, and
15  number. Nothing else. For God's sake, say nothing else."

**Close Read**

1. What do you learn about the pilot in this passage?

2. The hospital staff is being kind to the pilot, but he believes they are only trying to get information from him. Which words and phrases convey his anxiety?

## MODEL 2: HISTORICAL AND CULTURAL CONTEXT

The following background helps to explain why a British pilot would be nervous about waking up in a French hospital.

    World War II began with Germany's 1939 invasion of Poland, which caused Britain and France to declare war on Germany. By 1941, German forces had occupied France and much of Western Europe, but Great Britain was still fighting back. Other countries joined the war on both sides of the
5  conflict, dividing into the Axis forces and the Allies. France was not liberated from German occupation until 1944.

    Roald Dahl joined the British Royal Air Force in 1939. He became a fighter pilot and flew missions over North Africa, Greece, and the Middle East during the war. After his plane crashed in Egypt, he spent six
10  months in a hospital, recovering from a head injury. When he was asked later to share his experiences, Dahl's career as a writer began. "Beware of the Dog" was published in 1944.

**Close Read**

1. What exactly is the pilot worried about? Explain how the background helps you to understand his situation.

2. In your opinion, is Dahl's tone in the story sympathetic to the pilot? Explain.

# Part 3: Analyze the Literature

Before reading "Origami," read the following background information about the author, Susan K. Ito, and the topics mentioned in her story.

## BACKGROUND
## Crafting Words and Mending Old Wounds

### Seeking to Belong

As a child, Susan K. Ito often struggled with her sense of
5  identity. She says, "I felt like I was the only one of my kind: mixed-race, adopted, only child." She often found
10  herself envying women who were full-blooded Japanese, since she was only part Japanese. When she began taking literature and creative writing classes in graduate school, Ito felt like
15  she had found where she belonged: "I was finally immersing myself in the world that I'd longed to be in forever: the world of words." Life as a Japanese American and the struggle for a sense
20  of belonging have been the focus of much of her writing.

Susan K. Ito

### Peace Cranes

"Origami" is named after a paper-folding
25  craft that has been practiced for centuries in
Japan. Its popularity has now spread to many other countries. One of the
30  most popular paper designs is the crane—a type of bird. In many Asian countries, the crane is a symbol of peace. Many people from around the world send paper cranes to a memorial
35  in Hiroshima, Japan, every year. It is done in memory of those who died there during World War II and as an expression of the senders' wish for world peace.

40  **Japanese Internment**  During World War II, nations were divided between the Axis and Allied forces. In 1941 Japan—a member of the Axis powers—bombed the U.S.
45  military base at Pearl Harbor in Honolulu, Hawaii, prompting the United States to declare war on Japan. Four years later, the United States dropped atomic bombs on
50  two Japanese cities: Hiroshima and Nagasaki.

Americans were fearful of another attack within their borders. As a precaution, Japanese immigrants and
55  Americans of Japanese ancestry were sent to and held in facilities called internment camps in order to isolate them from the rest of the American public. The largest camp was the
60  Tule Lake Segregation Center in California. At the time, limiting the rights of one ethnic group was viewed as being done in service of the greater good of the American
65  public. The last internment camp closed in 1948. However, it was not until 1988 that the U.S. government issued its first official apology for its treatment of Japanese Americans
75  during World War II.

**Japanese internment camp in Santa Anita, California**

The narrator of this short story views herself as an outsider struggling to prove that she belongs. As you read this excerpt, consider how the background information enhances your understanding of the story.

*from* ORIGAMI

Short story by **Susan K. Ito**

I take my place, hesitantly, among the group of Japanese women, smile back at the ones who look up from their task to nod at me. Their words float around me like alphabet soup, familiar, comforting, but nothing that I clearly understand. The long cafeteria table blooms with folded paper birds of all
5  colors: royal purple, light gray, a small shimmering silver one. They're weaving an origami wreath for Sunday's memorial service, a thousand cranes for the souls of those who died at Tule Lake's internment camp.

I spread the square of sky-blue paper flat under my hands, then fold it in half. So far, this is easy. I'm going to follow all the directions. It's going to be
10  a perfect crane, *tsuru,* flying from my palm. Fold again, then flip that side of the triangle under to make a box. Oh no. What? I didn't get that. I'm lost. The women around me keep creasing, folding, spreading, their fingers moving with easy grace. My thumbs are huge, thick, in the way of these paper wings that are trying to unfold but can't.

15  My heart rises and flutters, beating against its cage in panic, in confusion. I try to retrace my steps, turn the paper upside down, in reverse. It's not working. I want to crumple the paper into a blue ball, an origami rock.

But instead I unfold the paper with damp, shaking fingers. I persevere. *Gambaro.* Don't give up. I'm going to make this crane if it kills me. I'm going
20  to prove that I can do this thing, this Japanese skill. I'm going to pull the coordination out of my blood, make it flow into my fingers. I have to.

But what if I can't? Then it only proves the thing that I fear the most, don't want to believe. That I'm not really Japanese. That I'm just an imposter, a fake, a watered-down, inauthentic K-mart version of the real thing.

**Close Read**

1. Reread the boxed text. How does the background enhance your reading of this passage?

2. Why does the narrator feel insecure in this situation? Support your answer.

3. Does Ito seem to sympathize with the narrator? Explain.

4. Which details show you that the narrator admires people who are Japanese?

5. Which details in the background help you understand why Ito might have chosen to write this story?

## The Snapping Turtle
Short Story by Joseph Bruchac

# *Where do we get our* VALUES?

**KEY IDEA** Do you remember where you learned that honesty is the best policy? Or that hard work pays off? We get our **values** from a patchwork of different sources, including important people in our lives, the communities around us, and mass media. The boy in the story you're about to read gets many of his values from his grandparents, but as you'll see, these values are put to the test.

**LIST IT** Take one minute to list some of the values that are important to you. Circle the value that most influences how you live your life. Then, as a class, generate a list that reflects the group's responses, and discuss where you learned these values.

1. loyalty
2.
3.

## ● LITERARY ANALYSIS: INFLUENCE OF AUTHOR'S BACKGROUND

An author's background, including life experiences and cultural heritage, shapes his or her way of looking at the world and often affects what he or she writes. For example, Joseph Bruchac was raised by his grandparents, one of whom was Native American. Many of his stories, in turn, have Native American characters and reflect Native American values.

Before you read, learn more about Bruchac from the biography on this page. Then, as you read, notice how Bruchac's characters reflect his own cultural heritage, beliefs and values, and life story.

## ● READING SKILL: COMPARE AND CONTRAST

When you **compare** two or more things, you identify ways in which they are alike. When you **contrast** them, you find ways in which they are different. Thinking about characters' similarities and differences can help you recognize their qualities and values. In "The Snapping Turtle," you will compare and contrast

- the narrator and other boys
- the narrator's grandmother and grandfather

As you read, use Venn diagrams to compare and contrast these characters' attitudes, backgrounds, and values.

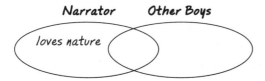

Narrator     Other Boys

loves nature

## ▲ VOCABULARY IN CONTEXT

The boldfaced words help Bruchac tell about a boy's relationship with nature. Try restating each sentence, using a different word or phrase for the boldfaced word.

1. My **philosophy** is "Leave nothing but footprints."
2. The memorial garden seemed to give the hero **immortality.**
3. Amy and I like to **traipse** around the meadow.
4. I have no **inclination** to go indoors when it's nice outside.
5. It takes **craftiness** to successfully trick a raccoon.
6. I **cache** my camping gear behind a tree while I hike.
7. Following their **migration** route, the geese flew north.
8. The thick undergrowth made the forest **impregnable.**
9. The **basking** sunbather enjoyed the afternoon breeze.
10. **Undaunted,** the bird flew on in search of food.

# THE SNAPPING TURTLE

## Joseph Bruchac

My grandmother was working in the flower garden near the road that morning when I came out with my fishing pole. She was separating out the roots of iris. As far as flowers go, she and I were agreed that iris had the sweetest scent. Iris would grow about anywhere, shooting up green sword-shaped leaves like the mythical soldiers that sprang from the planted teeth of a dragon. But iris needed some amount of care. Their roots would multiply so thick and fast that they could crowd themselves right up out of the soil. Spring separating and replanting were, as my grandmother put it, just the ticket.[1]

10 Later that day, I knew, she would climb into our blue 1951 Plymouth to drive around the back roads of Greenfield, a box of iris in the back seat. She would stop at farms where she had noticed a certain color of iris that she didn't have yet. Up to the door she would go to ask for a root so that she could add another splash of color to our garden. And, in exchange, she would give that person, most often a flowered-aproned and somewhat elderly woman like herself, some of her own iris.

It wasn't just that she wanted more flowers herself. She had a **philosophy**. If only one person keeps a plant, something might happen to it. Early frost, insects, animals, Lord knows what. But if many have that kind of plant, then it 20 may survive. Sharing meant a kind of **immortality**. I didn't quite understand it then, but I enjoyed taking those rides with her, carrying boxes and cans and flowerpots with new kinds of iris back to the car. **A**

"Going fishing, Sonny?" she said now.

Of course, she knew where I was going. Not only the evidence of the pole in my hand, but also the simple facts that it was a Saturday morning in late May and I was a boy of ten, would have led her to that natural conclusion. But she had to ask. It was part of our routine.

---

**ANALYZE VISUALS**
What **effect** does the artist's use of color have on what you notice in this painting?

**philosophy** (fĭ-lŏs′ə-fē) *n.* a system of values or beliefs

**immortality** (ĭm′ôr-tăl′ĭ-tē) *n.* the condition of having an endless life

**A** **AUTHOR'S BACKGROUND**
Which of the grandmother's thoughts and actions show that she believes in treating the earth with respect?

---

1. **just the ticket:** the perfect solution.

*Child Fishing* (1989), Lincoln Seligman. Private collection. © Bridgeman Art Library.

"Un-hun," I answered, as I always did. "Unless you and Grampa need some help." Then I held my breath, for though my offer of aid had been sincere enough, I really wanted to go fishing.

Grama thrust her foot down on the spading[2] fork, carefully levering out a heavy clump of iris marked last fall with a purple ribbon to indicate the color. She did such things with half my effort and twice the skill, despite the fact I was growing, as she put it, like a weed. "No, you go on along. This afternoon Grampa and I could use some help, though."

"I'll be back by then," I said, but I didn't turn and walk away. I waited for the next thing I knew she would say.

"You stay off of the state road, now."

In my grandmother's mind, Route 9N, which came down the hill past my grandparents' little gas station and general store on the corner, was nothing less than a Road of Death. If I ever set foot on it, I would surely be as doomed as our four cats and two dogs that met their fates there.

"Runned over and kilt," as Grampa Jesse put it.

Grampa Jesse, who had been the hired man for my grandmother's parents before he and Grama eloped, was not a person with book learning like my college-educated grandmother. His family was Abenaki Indian, poor but honest hill people who could read the signs in the forest, but who had never **traipsed** far along the trails of schoolhouse ways. Between Grama's books and Grampa's practical knowledge, some of which I was about to apply to bring home a mess of[3] trout, I figured I was getting about the best education a ten-year-old boy could have. I was lucky that my grandparents were raising me. **B**

"I'll stay off the state road," I promised. "I'll just follow Bell Brook."

Truth be told, the state road made me a little nervous, too. It was all too easy to imagine myself in the place of one of my defunct pets, stunned by the elephant bellow of a tractor-trailer's horn, looking wild-eyed up to the shiny metal grill; the thud, the lightning-bolt flash of light, and then the eternal dark. I imagined my grandfather shoveling the dirt over me in a backyard grave next to that of Lady, the collie, and Kitty-kitty, the gray cat, while my grandmother dried her eyes with her apron and said, "I told him to stay off that road!"

I was big on knowledge but very short on courage in those years. I mostly played by myself because the other kids my age from the houses and farms scattered around our rural township regarded me as a Grama's boy who would tell if they were to tie me up and threaten to burn my toes with matches, a ritual required to join the local society of pre-teenage boys. A squealer. And they were right.

I didn't much miss the company of other kids. I had discovered that most of them had little interest in the living things around them. They were noisier than Grampa and I were, scaring away the rabbits that we could creep right

traipse (trāps) v. to walk or tramp around

**B** COMPARE AND CONTRAST
Reread lines 44–51. What differences does the narrator point out between Grama and Grampa?

---

2. **spading:** digging.

3. **a mess of:** an amount of (food).

70　up on. Instead of watching the frogs catching flies with their long, gummy tongues, those boys wanted to shoot them with their BB guns. I couldn't imagine any of them having the patience or **inclination** to hold out a hand filled with sunflower seeds, as Grampa had showed me I could, long enough for a chickadee to come and light on an index finger.

Even fishing was done differently when I did it Grampa's way. I knew for a fact that most of those boys would go out and come home with an empty creel. They hadn't been watching for fish from the banks as I had in the weeks before the trout season began, so they didn't know where the fish lived. They didn't know how to keep low, float your line in, wait for that first tap, and
80　then, after the strike that bent your pole, set the hook. And they never said thank-you to every fish they caught, the way I remembered to do. **C**

Walking the creek edge, I set off downstream. By mid-morning, my bait can of moss and red earthworms that Grampa and I had dug from the edge of our manure pile was near empty. I'd gone half a mile and had already caught seven trout. All of them were squaretails, native brook trout whose sides were patterned with a speckled rainbow of bright circles—red, green, gold. I'd only kept the ones more than seven inches long, and I'd remembered to wet my hand before taking the little ones off the hook. Grasping a trout with a dry hand would abrade the slick coat of natural oil from the skin and leave it open
90　for infection and disease.

As always, I'd had to keep the eyes in the back of my head open just as Grampa had told me to do whenever I was in the woods.

"Things is always hunting one another," he'd said.

And he was right. Twice, at places where Bell Brook swung near Mill Road I'd had to leave the stream banks to take shelter when I heard the ominous crunch of bicycle tires on the gravel. Back then, when I was ten, I was smaller than the other boys my age. I made up for it by being harder to catch. Equal parts of **craftiness** and plain old panic at being collared by bullies I viewed as close kin to Attila the Hun[4] kept me slipperier than an eel.

100　From grapevine tangles up the bank, I'd watched as Pauly Roffmeier, Ricky Holstead, and Will Backus rolled up to the creek, making more noise than a herd of hippos, to plunk their own lines in. Both times, they caught nothing. It wasn't surprising, since they were talking like jaybirds, scaring away whatever fish might have been within half a mile. And Will kept lighting matches and throwing them down to watch them hiss out when they struck the water. Not to mention the fact that I had pulled a ten-inch brook trout out of the first hole and an eleven incher out of the second before they even reached the stream. **D**

I looked up at the sky. I didn't wear a watch then. No watch made by man
110　seemed able to work more than a few days when strapped to my wrist. It was a common thing on my Grampa's side of the family. "We jest got too much 'lectricity in us," he explained.

---

4. **Attila the Hun:** a barbarian leader who successfully invaded the Roman Empire in the A.D. 400s.

**inclination**
(ĭn-klə-nā′shən) *n.* a tendency to prefer one thing over another

VISUAL VOCABULARY

**creel:** a basket used to carry caught fish

**C AUTHOR'S BACKGROUND**
Reread lines 67–81. Which of the narrator's habits and attitudes reflect his Abenaki heritage?

**craftiness** (krăf′tē-nĕs) *n.* deviousness or deception

**D COMPARE AND CONTRAST**
Reread lines 100–108. How is the boys' approach to fishing different from that of the narrator?

Without a watch, I could measure time by the sun. I could see it was about ten. I had reached the place where Bell Brook crossed under the state road. Usually I went no further than this. It had been my boundary for years. But somewhere along the way I had decided that today would be different. I think perhaps a part of me was ashamed of hiding from the other boys, ashamed of always being afraid. I wanted to do something that I'd always been afraid to do. I wanted to be brave.

120    I had no need to fish further. I had plenty of trout for our supper. I'd cleaned them all out with my Swiss Army knife, leaving the entrails⁵ where the crows and jays could get them. If you did that, the crows and jays would know you for a friend and not sound the alarm when they saw you walking in the woods. I sank the creel under water, wedged it beneath a stone. The water of the brook was deep and cold and I knew it would keep the flesh of the trout fresh and firm. Then I **cached** my pole and bait can under the spice bushes. As I looked up at the highway, Grama's words came back to me:

"Stay off the state road, Sonny."

"*Under,*" I said aloud, "is not *on.*"

130    Then, taking a deep breath, bent over at the waist, I waded into the culvert⁶ that dove under the Road of Death. I had gone no more than half a dozen steps before I walked into a spider web so strong that it actually bounced me back. I splashed a little water from the creek up onto it and watched the beads shape a pattern of concentric circles. The orb-weaver sat unmoving in a corner, one leg resting on a strand of the web. She'd been waiting for the vibration of some flying creature caught in the sticky strands of her net. Clearly, I was much more than she had hoped for. She sat there without moving. Her wide back was patterned with a shape like that of a red and gold hourglass. Her compound eyes, jet black on her head, took in my giant shape. Spiders gave
140  some people the willies.⁷ I knew their bite would hurt like blue blazes, but I still thought them graced with great beauty.

"Excuse me," I said. "Didn't mean to bother you."

The spider raised one front leg. A nervous reaction, most likely, but I raised one hand back. Then I ducked carefully beneath the web, entering an area where the light was different. It was like passing from one world into another. I sloshed through the dark culvert, my fingertips brushing the rushing surface of the stream, the current pushing at my calves. My sneakered feet barely held their purchase⁸ on the ridged metal, slick with moss. **E**

When I came out the other side, the sunlight was blinding. Just ahead of
150  me the creek was overarched with willows. They were so thick and low that there was no way I could pass without either going underwater or breaking a way through the brush. I wasn't ready to do either. So I made my way up the

---

cache (kăsh) *v.* to store in a hiding place

**E** **AUTHOR'S BACKGROUND**
What effect might the narrator's heritage have on his reaction to the spider? Explain.

---

5. **entrails** (ĕn'trālz'): the internal organs.

6. **culvert** (kŭl'vərt): a drain that passes under a road.

7. **the willies:** a feeling of fear and/or disgust.

8. **held their purchase:** gripped; refrained from slipping.

*Bridge Over Weekeepeemee* (1974), Mark Potter. Oil on canvas. Private collection. © Bridgeman Art Library.

bank, thinking to circle back and pick up the creek farther down. For what purpose, I wasn't sure, aside from just wanting to do it. I was nervous as a hen yard when a chicken hawk is circling overhead. But I was excited, too. This was new ground to me, almost a mile from home. I'd gone farther from home in the familiar directions of north and west, into the safety of the woods, but this was different: Across the state road, in the direction of town; someone else's hunting territory. I stayed low to the ground and hugged the edges of the
160 brush as I moved. Then I saw something that drew me away from the creek: The glint of a wider expanse of water. The Rez, the old Greenfield Reservoir.

I'd never been to the Rez, though I knew the other boys went there. As I'd sat alone on the bus, my bookbag clasped tightly to my chest, I'd heard them talk about swimming there, fishing for bass, spearing bullfrogs five times as big as the little frogs in Bell Brook.

I knew I shouldn't be there, yet I was. Slowly I moved to the side of the wide trail that led to the edge of the deep water, and it was just as well that I did: Their bikes had been stashed in the brush down the other side of the path. They'd been more quiet than usual. I might have walked up on them if I
170 hadn't heard a voice. . . .

**ANALYZE VISUALS**
**Compare** the scene in this painting with the way you picture the culvert in the story. What are the similarities and differences?

I picked up some of the dark mud with my fingertips and drew lines across my cheeks. Grampa had explained it would make me harder to see. Then I slid to a place where an old tree leaned over the bank, cloaked by the cattails that grew from the edge of the Rez. I made my way out on the trunk and looked. . . .

"It's not gonna come up," Ricky said. He picked up something that looked like a makeshift spear. "You lied."

"I did not. It was over there. The biggest snapper I ever saw." Will shaded his eyes with one hand and looked right in my direction without seeing me.
180 "If we catch it, we could sell it for ten dollars to that man on Congress Street. They say snapping turtles have seven different kinds of meat in them."

"Hmph," Pauly said, throwing his own spear aside. "Let's go find something else to do."

One by one, they picked up their fishing poles and went back down the path. I waited without moving, hearing their heavy feet on the trail and then the rattle of their bike chains. . . . All I could think of was that snapping turtle.

I knew a lot about turtles. There were mud turtles and map turtles. There was the smart orange-legged wood turtle and the red-eared slider with its cheeks painted crimson as if it was going to war. Every spring Grama and
190 Grampa and I would drive around, picking up those whose old **migration** routes had been cut by the recent and lethal ribbons of road. Spooked by a car, a turtle falls into that old defense of pulling head and legs and tail into its once **impregnable** fortress. But a shell does little good against the wheels of a Nash or a DeSoto.[9]

Some days we'd rescue as many as a dozen turtles, taking them home for a few days before releasing them back into the wild. Painted turtles, several as big as two hands held together, might nip at you some, but they weren't really dangerous. And the wood turtles would learn in a day or so to reach out for a strawberry or a piece of juicy tomato and then leave their heads out for a
200 scratch while you stroked them with a finger.

Snappers though, they were different. Long-tailed, heavy-bodied and short-tempered, their jaws would gape wide and they'd hiss when you came up on them ashore. Their heads and legs were too big to pull into their shells and they would heave up on their legs and lunge forward as they snapped at you. They might weigh as much as fifty pounds, and it was said they could take off a handful of fingers in one bite. There wasn't much to recommend a snapping turtle as a friend. **F**

Most people seemed to hate snappers. Snappers ate the fish and the ducks; they scared swimmers away. Or I should say that people hated them alive.
210 Dead, they were supposed to be the best-eating turtle of all. *Ten dollars,* I thought. *Enough for me to send away to the mail-order pet place and get a pair of real flying squirrels.* I'd kept that clipping from *Field and Stream* magazine

**migration** (mī-grā'shən) *n.* the act of changing location seasonally (used here as an adjective)

**impregnable** (ĭm-prĕg'nə-bəl) *adj.* impossible to enter by force

**F** AUTHOR'S BACKGROUND
Do you think Bruchac has had experiences similar to those the narrator describes here? Explain your answer.

---

9. **Nash . . . DeSoto:** car brands that were popular during the 1950s.

thumbtacked over my bed for four months now. A sort of plan was coming into my mind. **G**

People were afraid of getting bit by snappers when they were swimming. But from what I'd read, and from what Grampa told me, they really didn't have much to worry about.

"Snapper won't bother you none in the water," Grampa said. If you were even to step on a snapping turtle resting on the bottom of a pond, all it would
220 do would be to move away. On land, all the danger from a snapper was to the front or the side. From behind, a snapper couldn't get you. Get it by the tail, you were safe. That was the way.

And as I thought, I kept watch. And as I kept watch, I kept up a silent chant inside my mind.

*Come here, I'm waiting for you.*
*Come here, I'm waiting for you.*

Before long, a smallish log that had been sticking up farther out in the pond began to drift my way. It was, as I had expected, no log at all. It was a turtle's head. I stayed still. The sun's heat beat on my back, but I lay there like
230 a **basking** lizard. Closer and closer the turtle came, heading right into water less than waist deep. It was going right for shore, for the sandy bank bathed in sun. I didn't think about why then, just wondered at the way my wanting seemed to have called it to me.

When it was almost to shore, I slid into the water on the other side of the log I'd been waiting on. The turtle surely sensed me, for it started to swing around as I moved slowly toward it, swimming as much as walking. But I lunged and grabbed it by the tail. Its tail was rough and ridged, as easy to hold as if coated with sandpaper. I pulled hard and the turtle came toward me. I stepped back, trying not to fall and pull it on top of me. My feet found the
240 bank, and I leaned hard to drag the turtle out, its clawed feet digging into the dirt as it tried to get away. A roaring hiss like the rush of air from a punctured tire came out of its mouth, and I stumbled, almost losing my grasp. Then I took another step, heaved again, and it was mine.

Or at least it was until I let go. I knew I could not let go. I looked around, holding its tail, moving my feet to keep it from walking its front legs around to where it would snap at me. It felt as if it weighed a thousand pounds. I could only lift up the back half of its body. I started dragging it toward the creek, fifty yards away. It seemed to take hours, a kind of dance between me and the great turtle, but I did it. I pulled it back through the roaring culvert, water
250 gushing over its shell, under the spider web, and past my hidden pole and creel. I could come back later for the fish. Now there was only room in the world for Bell Brook, the turtle, and me.

The long passage upstream is a blur in my memory. I thought of salmon leaping over falls and learned a little that day how hard such a journey must be.

**G** COMPARE AND CONTRAST
What does the narrator have in common with Will, one of the other boys?

basking (băsk'ĭng) *adj.* warming oneself pleasantly, as in sunlight

When I rounded the last bend and reached the place where the brook edged our property, I breathed a great sigh. But I could not rest. There was still a field and the back yard to cross.

My grandparents saw me coming. From the height of the sun it was now mid-afternoon, and I knew I was dreadful late.

260    "Sonny, where have you . . . ?" began Grama.

Then she saw the turtle.

"I'm sorry. It took so long because of . . ." I didn't finish the sentence because the snapping turtle, **<u>undaunted</u>** by his backward passage, took that opportunity to try once more to swing around and get me. I had to make three quick steps in a circle, heaving at its tail as I did so.

**undaunted** (ŭn-dôn′tĭd) *adj.* not discouraged; courageous

**ANALYZE VISUALS**
What **details** on the snapping turtle do you notice most? What details are difficult to see?

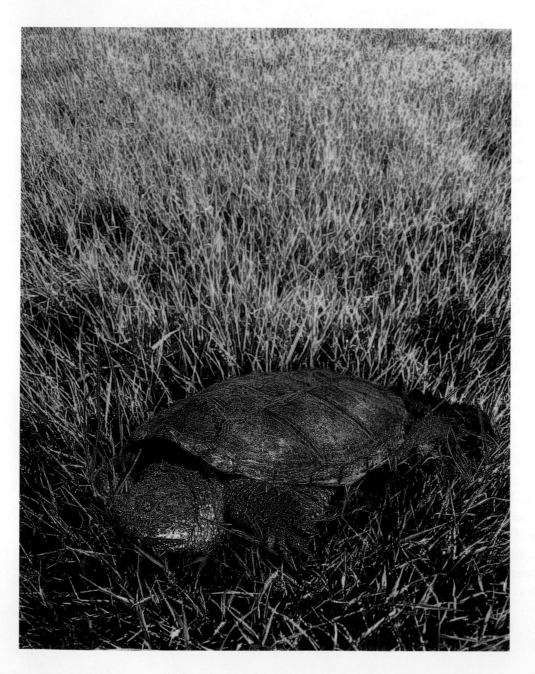

"Nice size turtle," Grampa Jesse said.

My grandmother looked at me. I realized then I must have been a sight. Wet, muddy, face and hands scratched from the brush that overhung the creek.

"I caught it at the reservoir," I said. I didn't think to lie to them about where 270 I'd been. I waited for my grandmother to scold me. But she didn't.

"Jesse," she said, "Get the big washtub."

My grandfather did as she said. He brought it back and then stepped next to me.

"Leave go," he said.

My hands had a life of their own, grimly determined never to let loose of that all-too-familiar tail, but I forced them to open. The turtle flopped down Before it could move, my grandfather dropped the big washtub over it. All was silent for a minute as I stood there, my arms aching as they hung by my side. Then the washtub began to move. My grandmother sat down on it and it 280 stopped.

She looked at me. So did Grampa. It was wonderful how they could focus their attention on me in a way that made me feel they were ready to do whatever they could to help. Ⓗ

"What now?" Grama said.

"I heard that somebody down on Congress Street would pay ten dollars for a snapping turtle."

"Jack's," Grampa said.

My grandmother nodded. "Well," she said, "if you go now you can be back in time for supper. I thought we were having trout." She raised an 290 eyebrow at me.

"I left them this side of the culvert by 9N," I said. "Along with my pole."

"You clean up and put on dry clothes. Your grandfather will get the fish."

"But I hid them."

My grandmother smiled. "Your grandfather will find them." And he did.

An hour later, we were on the way to Congress Street. . . . In the 1950s, Congress Street was like a piece of Harlem[10] dropped into an upstate town. We pulled up in front of Jack's, and a man who looked to be my grandfather's age got up and walked over to us. His skin was only a little darker than my grandfather's, and the two nodded to each other.

300 My grandfather put his hand on the trunk of the Plymouth.

"What you got there?" Jack said.

"Show him, Sonny."

I opened the trunk. My snapping turtle lifted up its head as I did so.

"I heard you might want to buy a turtle like this for ten dollars," I said.

Jack shook his head. "Ten dollars for a little one like that? I'd give you two dollars."

I looked at my turtle. Had it shrunk since Grampa wrestled it into the trunk?

**Ⓗ COMPARE AND CONTRAST**
Reread lines 266–283. What similar qualities do Grama and Grampa display?

---

10. **Harlem:** a New York City neighborhood that was and is largely African American.

"That's not enough," I said.

"Three dollars. My last offer."

310 I looked at Grampa. He shrugged his shoulders.

"I guess I don't want to sell it," I said.

"All right," Jack said. "You change your mind, come on back." He touched his hat with two fingers and walked back over to his chair in the sun.

As we drove back toward home, neither of us said anything for a while. Then my grandfather spoke.

"Would five dollars've been enough?"

"No," I said.

"How about ten?"

I thought about that. "I guess not."

320 "Why you suppose that turtle was heading for that sandbank?" Grampa said.

I thought about that, too. Then I realized the truth of it.

"It was coming out to lay its eggs."

"Might be."

I thought hard then. I'd learned it was never right for a hunter to shoot a mother animal, because it hurt the next generation to come. Was a turtle any different? ❶

"Can we take her back?" I asked.

"Up to you, Sonny."

And so we did. Gramp drove the Plymouth right up the trail to the edge of

330 the Rez. He held a stick so the turtle would grab onto it as I hauled her out of the trunk. I put her down and she just stayed there, her nose a foot from the water but not moving.

"We'll leave her," Grampa said. We turned to get into the car. When I looked back over my shoulder, she was gone. Only ripples on the water, widening circles rolling on toward other shores like generations following each other, like my grandmother's flowers still growing in a hundred gardens in Greenfield, like the turtles still seeking out that sandbank, like this story that is no longer just my own but belongs now to your memory, too. ❧

❶ AUTHOR'S BACKGROUND
What lesson does the narrator learn? Tell how this lesson relates to Bruchac's values.

## Comprehension

1. **Recall** What actions does the narrator take to make sure he fishes responsibly?

2. **Recall** Why does the narrator decide to cross under the state road?

3. **Represent** How does the narrator get the snapping turtle out of the water? Reread lines 234–243, and sketch the scene.

## Literary Analysis

4. **Visualize** How well does Joseph Bruchac help you visualize the characters, events, and settings in the story? Choose a passage that you find visually descriptive and explain what words and phrases help you picture the scene.

5. **Make Inferences About Relationships** Describe the narrator's relationship with his grandparents. Do you think the other boys in the story would have similar relationships with the adults in their lives? Explain your answer.

6. **Compare and Contrast Characters** What are the similarities and differences between Grama and Grampa? Consider their backgrounds, **values,** and traits. Use the notes from one of your Venn diagrams to help you answer the question, and cite evidence from the story.

7. **Analyze Influence of Author's Background** Reread Bruchac's biography on page 767 to remind you of his Abenaki beliefs. In what ways does "The Snapping Turtle" reflect these values? In a graphic like the one shown, give examples from the story.

8. **Evaluate the Ending** Reread the last paragraph of the story. How well do you think it wraps up the **plot** and summarizes the **theme?** Refer to specific phrases in the paragraph as you explain your answer.

## Extension and Challenge

9. **Inquiry and Research** In Native American cultures, stories are often used to teach children. Find a retelling of a Native American story, perhaps from one of Joseph Bruchac's collections, and present it to the class. Explain what lesson it is meant to teach.

**RESEARCH LINKS**
For more on Abenaki stories, visit the **Research Center** at **ClassZone.com.**

INDIANA STANDARDS

READING STANDARD
**8.3.7** Analyze a work of literature, showing how it reflects the ... beliefs of its author.

# Vocabulary in Context

## VOCABULARY PRACTICE

Choose the word in each group that is closest in meaning to the boldfaced word.

1. **craftiness:** (a) intelligence, (b) slyness, (c) dishonesty
2. **traipse:** (a) stroll, (b) slither, (c) bounce
3. **cache:** (a) spend, (b) waste, (c) conceal
4. **migration:** (a) relocation, (b) nesting, (c) settlement
5. **impregnable:** (a) frightening, (b) unguarded, (c) impenetrable
6. **inclination:** (a) wisdom, (b) desire, (c) strength
7. **basking:** (a) sunbathing, (b) swimming, (c) cooking
8. **undaunted:** (a) unhurt, (b) unafraid, (c) uncaring
9. **immortality:** (a) birth, (b) death, (c) permanence
10. **philosophy:** (a) belief, (b) style, (c) story

basking · inclination · cache · migration · craftiness · philosophy · immortality · traipse · impregnable · undaunted

## VOCABULARY IN WRITING

Using at least two vocabulary words, write a paragraph telling about your own views on nature. You may want to compare yourself with the boys in the story. You could start this way.

> **EXAMPLE SENTENCE**
>
> Unlike the narrator, I don't have an **inclination** toward fishing.

**INDIANA STANDARDS**

**READING STANDARD**
**8.1.1** Analyze idioms and comparisons ... to infer the literal and figurative meanings of phrases.

## VOCABULARY STRATEGY: ANALOGIES

An analogy compares similar aspects of two or more different things. Analyzing an analogy is one way of figuring out the meanings of unfamiliar words in context. For example, you can determine the meaning of the word *generations* from the thing it is compared to in this passage:

> *Only ripples on the water, widening circles rolling on toward other shores like* **generations** *following each other* .... (lines 334–336)

**PRACTICE** Use the comparison in each sentence to help you understand the boldfaced word.

1. **Defunct** Web sites are like ghost towns that once bustled with life.
2. Like a **makeshift** shelter, a flimsy excuse soon falls apart.
3. Carmina **tended** to the mold she was growing for the science fair the way a mother bird looks after her nest.
4. Like a baseball player stealing second base, Tomás **sprinted** down the hall and slid into his seat just as the bell finished ringing.

**VOCABULARY PRACTICE**
For more practice, go to the **Vocabulary Center** at ClassZone.com.

# Reading-Writing Connection

Demonstrate your understanding of "The Snapping Turtle" by responding to these prompts. Then complete the **Grammar and Writing** exercise.

| WRITING PROMPTS | SELF-CHECK |
|---|---|

**A. Short Response: Write a Letter**
Think about the narrator's relationship with his grandparents. Then imagine the narrator as an adult. Write a **one-paragraph letter** in which the grown-up narrator expresses his appreciation to his grandparents for raising him.

*A well-written letter will . . .*
- sound like it's written by an adult
- use details to show why the narrator is appreciative

**B. Extended Response: Examine Values**
Do you think that modern American society respects the Native American **values** described in Joseph Bruchac's story? Explain why or why not in a **two- or three-paragraph response.**

*An insightful response will . . .*
- include a clear position statement
- demonstrate an understanding of Abenaki values

## GRAMMAR AND WRITING

**INDIANA STANDARDS**

**WRITING STANDARD**
**8.6.1** Use correct and varied sentence types . . . .

*FORM COMPOUND-COMPLEX SENTENCES* A **compound-complex sentence** contains two or more independent clauses and one or more dependent clauses. (Recall that a dependent clause cannot stand alone as a sentence and is introduced by words such as *after, because, if,* and *though*.) Compound-complex sentences can help add variety to writing by allowing short, related sentences to be combined.

*Original:* I did something wrong. You were ready to help. You made me feel safe.

*Revised:* Though I did something wrong, you were ready to help, and you made me feel safe.

*PRACTICE* In each item, combine the sentences to form one compound-complex sentence. Use the first word in parentheses to join two independent clauses. Use the second word to change one sentence to a dependent clause.

1. You wanted to add a new color to both your garden and hers. You'd ask the woman for her iris roots. You'd give her some of your own. (*and, if*)
2. I was going to sell the turtle. I didn't. I remembered your lessons. (*but, after*)
3. We'd catch turtles. Then we'd release them. You didn't want them to die. (*and, because*)
4. The other boys couldn't catch fish. We could. We were quiet. (*but, because*)

*For more help with compound-complex sentences, see page R64 in the* **Grammar Handbook.**

## Out of Bounds

Short Story by Beverley Naidoo

# *How do you know what's* RIGHT?

**INDIANA STANDARDS**

**READING STANDARDS**

**8.2.9** Make reasonable statements and draw conclusions about a text, supporting them with accurate examples.

**8.3.7** Analyze a work of literature, showing how it reflects the heritage, traditions, attitudes, and beliefs of its author.

**KEY IDEA** Can you think of a situation when you weren't sure what to do? If so, you know that it's not always easy to tell **right** from wrong. Sometimes you must rely on your internal compass to guide your behavior. In this story, a boy decides to disobey a rule in order to help someone in need.

**DISCUSS** What purpose do rules serve in families and society? When might rules have to be changed? Discuss these questions with a small group.

## LITERARY ANALYSIS: CULTURAL CONFLICT

When you read a story set in another country, knowing about the area's history and culture can be important background. It can help you to understand the characters' behavior and the cultural conflicts that unfold. A **cultural conflict** is a struggle that arises because of the differing values, customs, or circumstances between groups of people. For example, if a story is set in a place where one religious group has been fighting against another, parents might be angry if their child becomes friends with someone from outside their group.

"Out of Bounds" takes place in South Africa. As you read the selection, think about how South Africa's history and culture affect the conflicts. The background on this page will provide you with some of the information you need.

## READING SKILL: MAKE INFERENCES

Fiction writers do not always make direct statements about characters or the cultures in which they live. Instead, writers provide certain details and expect readers to combine these details with their own knowledge to "read between the lines" of a story. This process of forming logical guesses is called **making inferences.** As you read, use a chart like the one shown to record your inferences about the characters and their culture.

| Evidence from Story | My Knowledge | Inference |
|---|---|---|
| Father tops wall with wire. | | |

## VOCABULARY IN CONTEXT

The boldfaced words help Beverley Naidoo describe a society influenced by its history of racial injustice. Using context clues, try to write a definition for each word.

1. Afraid to go to a school where they would be teased, the boys **straggle** behind their older brother.
2. The flood could **maroon** many people on rooftops.
3. Members of the newer **sect** didn't agree with people from the orthodox church.
4. The Africans fought **vigorously** for equality.
5. The peace talks gave people a **glimmer** of hope.
6. The evening news was interesting enough to **engross** him.
7. We watched the energized boy **bound** up the hill.
8. Poor communication will **hamper** efforts to get along.

# Author Online

**Writing for Justice**
Beverley Naidoo grew up in Johannesburg, South Africa, when the country was racially segregated. It wasn't until she went to college that she recognized the injustice of the laws. After she moved to England, she decided to write children's books that speak

**Beverley Naidoo
born 1943**

honestly about South African society. She published her first book, *Journey to Jo'burg*, in 1984. It was banned in her home country until 1991.

## Background

**Apartheid** South Africa is the southernmost country on the African continent. The nation is ethnically diverse, with whites forming the smallest group. However, up until 1994, whites ruled the country under a system called apartheid (apartness). Apartheid was based on segregation between the races. The white government classified non-whites into three groups. Africans made up the largest group but had the fewest rights. "Coloureds" (people of mixed race) and those of Indian descent were granted limited rights in 1984. The government decided where each group could live, conduct business, or own land. The effects of apartheid continue to influence South African society today. Africans, on average, remain poorer and have less access to education than other groups.

**Storms and Floods** "Out of Bounds" is set in 2000. That year, severe storms devastated southern Africa. Floods swept away schools, roads, crops, and livestock. About 540,000 people were left homeless.

**MORE ABOUT THE AUTHOR AND BACKGROUND**
To learn more about Beverley Naidoo and South Africa, visit the **Literature Center** at ClassZone.com.

# OUT OF BOUNDS

Beverley Naidoo

**O**ut of bounds.

That's what his parents said as soon as the squatters[1] took over the land
below their house. Rohan's dad added another meter of thick concrete bricks to
their garden wall and topped it with curling barbed wire. He certainly wasn't
going to wait for the first break-in and be sorry later. They lived on the ridge
of a steep hill with the garden sloping down. Despite the high wall, from his
bedroom upstairs, Rohan could see over the spiked-wire circles down to the
place where he and his friends used to play. The wild fig trees under which
they had made their hideouts were still there. They had spent hours dragging
10  planks, pipes, sheets of metal and plastic—whatever might be useful—up
the hill from rubbish tipped in a ditch below. The first squatters pulled their
hideouts apart and used the same old scraps again for their own constructions.
Rohan could still see the "ski slope"—the red earth down which he and
his friends had bumped and flown on a couple of old garbage can lids. The
squatters used it as their road up the hill. Now it looked like a crimson scar cut
between the shacks littering the hillside.

"There's only one good thing about this business," Ma said after the back
wall was completed. "We won't have to wash that disgusting red dust out of
your clothes any more!" **A**

**ANALYZE VISUALS**
**Compare** the house at
the top of the hill with
the buildings below.
What similarities and
differences do you notice?

**A  CULTURAL CONFLICT**
In lines 1–19, what do you
learn about the family's
feelings toward the
squatters?

---

1.  **squatters:** people who occupy public land in order to gain ownership of it.

20  Rohan said nothing. How could he explain what he had lost?

At first, some of the squatter women and children came up to the houses with buckets asking for water. For a couple of weeks his mother opened the gate after checking that no men were hanging around in the background. She allowed the women to fill their buckets at the outside tap. Most of her neighbors found themselves doing the same. Torrential rains and floods had ushered in the new millennium by sweeping away homes, animals and people in the north of the country. The television was awash with pictures of homeless families and efforts to help them. No one knew from where exactly the squatters had come. But as Ma said, how could you refuse a woman or
30  child some water?

It wasn't long before all that changed. The first complaint of clothes disappearing off the washing line came from their new neighbors. The first African family, in fact, to move in among the Indians on Mount View. No one had actually seen anyone but everyone was suspicious including the neighbor, Mrs. Zuma.

"You can't really trust these people, you know," Mrs. Zuma tutted[2] when she came to ask if Ma had seen anyone hanging around. However, it was when thieves broke into old Mrs. Pillay's house, grabbed the gold thali from around her neck, and left her with a heart attack that views hardened. Young
40  men could be seen hanging around the shacks. Were some of them not part of the same gang? Mrs. Pillay's son demanded the police search through the settlement immediately. But the police argued they would need more evidence and that the thieves could have come from anywhere. **B**

A new nervousness now gripped the house owners on top of the hill. Every report of theft, break-in, or car hijacking, anywhere in the country, led to another conversation about the squatters on the other side of their garden walls.

At night Rohan peered through the bars of his window before going to sleep. Flickering lights from candles and lamps were the only sign that people
50  were living out there in the thick darkness. In the daytime, when Ma heard the bell and saw that it was a woman or child with a bucket, she no longer answered the call.

All the neighbors were agreed. Why should private house owners be expected to provide water for these people? That was the Council's job. If the squatters were refused water, then perhaps they would find somewhere else to put up their shacks. A more suitable place. Or even, go back to where they came from. **C**

The squatters did not go away. No one knew from where they managed to get their water or how far they had to walk. On the way to school, Rohan
60  and his dad drove past women walking with buckets on their heads.

---

2. **tutted:** made a "tut tut" sound with the tongue to express annoyance.

**VISUAL VOCABULARY**

**thali** *n.* necklace given by a groom to his bride at a Hindu wedding ceremony

**B** **MAKE INFERENCES**
What ethnicity is Rohan's family?

**C** **MAKE INFERENCES**
How does crime affect the residents' attitude toward the squatters?

"These people are tough as ticks! You let them settle and it's impossible to get them out," complained Dad. "Next thing they'll be wanting our electricity."

But Rohan wasn't really listening. He was scanning the line of African children who **straggled** behind the women and who wore the black and white uniform of Mount View Primary, his old school. He had been a pupil there until his parents had moved him to his private school in Durban[3] with its smaller classes, cricket pitch, and its own rugby ground.[4] Most of the African children at Mount View had mothers who cleaned, washed, and ironed for the families on top of the hill. But since the New Year they had been joined by the 70 squatter children and each week the line grew longer.

The queue[5] of traffic at the crossroads slowed them down, giving Rohan more time to find the "wire car" boy. He was looking for a boy who always steered a wire car in front of him with a long handle. He was about his own age—twelve or thirteen perhaps—and very thin and wiry himself. What interested Rohan was that the boy never had the same car for more than two or three days. Nor had he ever seen so many elaborate designs simply made out of wire, each suggesting a different make of car. They were much more complicated than the little wire toys in the African Crafts shop at the mall. **D**

**straggle** (străg′əl) *v.* to spread out in a scattered group

**D** CULTURAL CONFLICT
What differences between Rohan's life and the life of the "wire car" boy are illustrated in lines 63–78?

---

3. **Durban** (dûr′bən): a city in South Africa.
4. **cricket pitch** and **rugby ground:** playing fields for ballgames that originated in England.
5. **queue** (kyo͞o): a waiting line.

"Hey, cool!" Rohan whistled. "See that, Dad?" The boy must have heard
80 because he glanced toward them. His gaze slid across the silver hood of their
car toward the trunk but didn't rise up to look at Rohan directly.

"It's a Merc[6]—like ours, Dad! What a beaut! Do you think—"

"*Don't* think about it, son! You want us to stop and ask how much he wants,
don't you?"

Rohan half frowned, half smiled. How easily his father knew him!

"No way! If we start buying from these people, we'll be encouraging them!
That's not the message we want them to get now, is it?"

Rohan was quiet. He couldn't argue with his dad's logic. If the squatters
moved away, he and his friends could get their territory back again. **E**

90 **R**ohan returned home early from school. A precious half day. In the past
he would have spent it in his hideout. Instead he flicked on the television.
News. As his finger hovered over the button to switch channels, the whirr of a
helicopter invaded the living room.

"Hey, Ma! Look at this!"

Ma appeared from the kitchen, her hands cupped, white and dusty with
flour. On the screen, a tight human knot swung at the end of a rope above a
valley swirling with muddy water.

"A South African Air Force rescue team today saved a baby from certain
death just an hour after she was born in a tree. Her mother was perched in the
100 tree over floodwaters that have devastated Mozambique. The mother and her
baby daughter were among the lucky few. Many thousands of Mozambicans
are still waiting to be lifted to safety from branches and rooftops. They have
now been **marooned** for days by the rising water that has swallowed whole
towns and villages."

"Those poor people! What a place to give birth!" Ma's floury hands almost
looked ready to cradle a baby.

Rohan was watching how the gale from the rotors[7] forced the leaves and
branches of the tree to open like a giant flower until the helicopter began to
lift. Members of the mother's family still clung desperately to the main trunk.
110 Rohan saw both fear and determination in their eyes.

He and Ma listened to the weather report that followed. Although Cyclone
Eline was over, Cyclone Gloria[8] was now whipping up storms across the Indian
Ocean and heading toward Mozambique. Where would it go next? Durban
was only down the coast. Rohan had seen a program about a **sect** who believed
the new millennium would mark the end of the world. They were convinced
that the floods were a sign that The End was beginning.

"What if the cyclone comes here, Ma?"

**E** **CULTURAL CONFLICT**
Reread lines 83–89. How
is Rohan's reason for
wanting the squatters to
leave different from that
of his father?

**SOCIAL STUDIES
CONNECTION**

Racial tension in South
Africa and Mozambique
affected the response to
the flooding.

**maroon** (mə-rōōn') *v.*
to leave behind in a place
from which there is little
hope of escape

**sect** (sĕkt) *n.* a religious
group

---

6. **Merc:** short for Mercedes, a brand of car.

7. **rotors** (rō'tərz): helicopter blades.

8. **Cyclone Eline, Cyclone Gloria:** tropical storms that struck in 2000.

"No, we'll be all right son. But that lot out there will get it. The government really should do something." Ma nodded in the direction of the squatters.

120     "Now, let me finish these *rotis*[9] for your sister!"

Ma returned to her bread making. When she had finished, she wanted Rohan to come with her to his married sister's house. He pleaded to stay behind.

"I've got homework to do, Ma! I'll be fine."

"You won't answer the door unless it's someone we know, will you?"

"No, Ma!" he chanted. Ma said the same thing every time.

**A**lone in the house, Rohan daydreamed at his desk. He was close enough to the window to see down the hill. What if there was so much rain that a river formed along the road below! As the water rose, people would have to abandon their shacks to climb higher up. They would be trapped between the flood
130 below and the torrents above. In assembly they had heard the story of Noah building the ark. Perhaps it wasn't just a story after all. Perhaps the people had tried to cling on to the tops of trees as tightly as those they had seen on television.

*Tough as ticks.*

The phrase popped into his mind. Wasn't that what his dad had said about the squatters? Yet the one sure way to get rid of ticks was to cover them in liquid paraffin.[10] Drown them. A terrible thought. He should push it right away. **F**

Rohan was about to stretch out for his math book when a figure caught his eye on the old ski slope. It was the thin wiry boy, but he wasn't pushing a
140 car this time. He was carrying two large buckets, one on his head, the other by his side. He descended briskly down the slope and turned along the road in the opposite direction to that taken by the women who carried buckets on their heads. Rohan followed the figure until he went out of sight, then forced himself to open his book.

The bell rang just as he was getting interested in the first question. Nuisance! He hurried to the landing. If someone was standing right in front of the gate, it was possible to see who it was from the window above the stairs. He stood back, careful not to be seen himself. It was the same boy, an empty container on the ground each side of him! Didn't he know not to come to
150 the house up here? But he was only a child, and it looked as if he just wanted some water. It would be different if it were an adult or a complete stranger. Rohan's daydream also made him feel a little guilty. He could see the boy look anxiously through the bars, his hand raised as if wondering whether to ring the bell again. Usually when the boy was pushing his wire car on the way to school, he appeared relaxed and calm.

By the time the bell rang a second time, Rohan had decided. He hurried downstairs but slowed himself as he walked outside toward the gate.

**F** MAKE INFERENCES
Note the change in Rohan's attitude toward the squatters. What has caused this change?

---

9. *rotis* (rō′tēs): Indian flatbreads that are cooked on a griddle.

10. **paraffin** (păr′ə-fĭn): wax.

"What do you want?" Rohan tried not to show that he recognized the boy.

"I need water for my mother. Please." The boy held his palms out in front of him as if asking for a favor. "My mother—she's having a baby—it's bad—there's no more water. Please."

This was an emergency. Not on television but right in front of him. Still Rohan hesitated. His parents would be extremely cross that he had put himself in this situation by coming to talk to the boy. Weren't there stories of adults who used children as decoys to get people to open their gates so they could storm in? He should have stayed inside. Should he tell the boy to go next door where there would at least be an adult? But the boy had chosen to come here. Perhaps he had seen Rohan watching him from the car and knew this was his house.

"We stay there." The boy pointed in the direction of the squatter camp. "I go to school there." He pointed in the direction of Mount View Primary. He was trying to reassure Rohan that it would be OK to open the gate. He was still in his school uniform but wore a pair of dirty-blue rubber sandals. His legs were as thin as sticks.

"Isn't there a doctor with your mother?" It was such a silly question that as soon as it was out, Rohan wished he could take it back. If they could afford a doctor, they wouldn't be squatters on a bare hillside. The boy shook his head **vigorously.** If he thought it was stupid, he didn't let it show on his troubled face.

"Wait there!" Rohan returned to the house. The button for the electric gate was inside the front door. The boy waited while the wrought-iron bars slowly rolled back. **G**

"OK. Bring your buckets over here." Rohan pointed to the outside tap. The buckets clanked against each other as the boy jogged toward him.

"Thank you," he said quietly.

The unexpected softness in his voice had a strange effect on Rohan. It sounded so different from his own bossy tone. Suddenly he felt a little ashamed. This was the same boy whose wire cars he admired! If he were still at Mount View Primary they would probably be in the same class. They might even have been friends, and he would be learning how to make wire cars himself. Why had he spoken so arrogantly? It was really only a small favor that was being asked for. The water in the bucket gurgling and churning reminded Rohan of the water swirling beneath the Mozambican woman with her baby. *Her* rescuer had been taking a really big risk but hadn't looked big headed.[11] He had just got on with the job.

When both buckets were full, the boy stooped to lift one on to his head. Rohan saw his face and neck muscles strain under the weight. How would he manage to keep it balanced and carry the other bucket too?

"Wait! I'll give you a hand." Rohan's offer was out before he had time to think it through properly. If the boy was surprised, he didn't show it. All his energy seemed to be focused on his task. Rohan dashed into the kitchen to grab the spare set of keys. Ma would be away for another hour at least. He

vigorously (vĭg′ər-əs-lē) *adv.* energetically

**G MAKE INFERENCES**
Why do you think Rohan decides to open the gate?

---

11. **big headed:** conceited.

would be back soon, and she need never know. It was only after the gate clicked behind them that Rohan remembered the neighbors. If anyone saw him, they were bound to ask Ma what he was doing with a boy from the squatter camp. He crossed the fingers of one hand. **H**

At first Rohan said nothing. Sharing the weight of the bucket, he could feel the strain all the way up from his fingers to his left shoulder. When they reached the corner and set off down the hill, the bucket seemed to propel them forward. It was an effort to keep a steady pace. Rohan glanced at the container on the boy's head, marveling at how he kept it balanced. He caught the boy's eye.

210 "How do you do that? You haven't spilled a drop!"

The boy gave a **glimmer** of a smile.

"You learn."

Rohan liked the simple reply. He should ask the boy about the cars. This was his chance, before they turned into the noisy main road and reached the squatter camp.

"I've seen you with wire cars. Do you make them yourself?"

"Yes—and my brother."

"You make them together? Do you keep them all?"

"My brother—he sells them at the beach." The boy waved his free hand in 220 the direction of the sea. "The tourists—they like them." **I**

"Your cars are better than any I've seen in the shops! Do you get lots of money for them?"

*"Mmhh!"* The boy made a sound something between a laugh and a snort. Rohan realized that he had asked another brainless question. Would they be staying in a shack if they got lots of money? Rohan had often seen his own father bargaining to get something cheaper from a street hawker.[12] He tried to cover his mistake.

"There's a shop in the mall where they sell wire cars. They charge a lot and yours are a hundred times better!"

230 "We can't go there. The guards—they don't let us in."

Rohan knew the security guards at the entrance to the mall. Some of them even greeted his parents with a little salute. Rohan had seen poor children hanging around outside. They offered to push your trolley,[13] to clean your car—anything for a few cents. Sometimes Ma gave an orange or an apple from her shopping bag to a child. Other times she would just say "No thank you" and wave a child away. Ma never gave money. . . . Rohan had never thought what it would be like to be chased away. How did the guards decide who could enter? How could the boy and his brother go and show the lady in the African Crafts shop his cars if they weren't allowed in? **J**

240 Rohan was quiet as they reached the main road and turned toward the squatter camp. The noise of vehicles roaring past was deafening. He never normally walked down here. Not by himself nor with anyone else. His family

---

12. **hawker:** seller.
13. **trolley:** shopping cart.

went everywhere by car. With all the locks down, of course. The only people who walked were poor people. His eyes were drawn to a group of young men walking toward them. They were still some distance away, but already Rohan began to feel uneasy. They were coming from the crossroads that his dad always approached on full alert. Rohan knew how his father jumped the red lights when the road was clear, especially at night. Everyone had heard stories of gangs who hijacked cars waiting for the lights to change.

250    The handle had begun to feel like it was cutting into his fingers. The boy must have sensed something because he signaled to Rohan to lower the bucket. For a few seconds they each stretched their fingers.

"It's too far? You want to go?" The boy was giving him a chance to change his mind. To leave and go back home. He had already helped carry the water more than half the way. He could make an excuse about the time. But the thought of running back to the house along the road on his own now worried him.

"No, it's fine. Let's go." Rohan heard a strange brightness in his own voice. He curled his fingers around the handle again. **K**

260    As they drew nearer the men, Rohan felt their gaze on him and suddenly his head was spinning with questions. Why on earth had he offered to help carry the water? What did he think he was doing coming down here? And he hadn't even yet entered the squatter camp itself!

"We go here." The boy's voice steadied him a little.

Rohan turned and stared up at his old ski slope. He felt the force of the young men's eyes on his back as he and the boy began to ascend the rough track. Someone behind called out something in Zulu[14] and, without turning, the boy shouted back.

The words flew so quickly into one another that Rohan didn't pick up any
270 even though he was learning Zulu in school. They must be talking about him, but he was too embarrassed—and frightened—to ask. He could feel his heart pumping faster and told himself it was because of the stiff climb. He needed to concentrate where he put each foot. The track was full of holes and small stones. A quick glance over his shoulder revealed that the young men had also entered the squatter camp but seemed to be heading for a shack with a roof covered in old tires on the lower slope. A couple of them were still watching. He must just look ahead and control his fear. As long as he was with the boy, he was safe, surely? **L**

A bunch of small children appeared from nowhere, giggling and staring. He
280 couldn't follow their chatter but heard the word *"iNdiya!"* The boy ignored them until a couple of children started darting back and forth in front of them, sweeping up the red dust with their feet.

*"Hambani!"* Rohan could hear the boy's irritation as he waved them away. But the darting and dancing continued just out of reach.

**K** MAKE INFERENCES
What do you think gives Rohan renewed determination to help?

**L** MAKE INFERENCES
Reread lines 269–278. What is Rohan afraid of?

---

14. **Zulu** (zōō'lōō): the language of the Zulu, a Bantu people of South Africa.

*"Hambani-bo!"* This time the boy's voice deepened to a threat, and the cluster of children pulled aside with one or two mischievous grins. Beads of sweat had begun trickling down the boy's face. With his own skin prickling with sticky heat, Rohan wondered at the wiry strength of the boy whose back, head, and bucket were still perfectly upright as they mounted the hill.

290     "It's that one—we stay there." The boy, at last, pointed to a structure of corrugated iron,[15] wood, and black plastic a little further up. It was not far from the old fig trees. For a moment Rohan thought he would say something about his hideout which the first squatters had pulled down. But he stopped himself. Maybe the boy had even been one of them!

As they drew nearer, they heard a woman moaning and a couple of other women's voices that sounded as if they were comforting her. The boy lowered the bucket swiftly from his head and pushed aside a plywood sheet, the door to his home.

**ANALYZE VISUALS**
What do you think life is like in the **setting** pictured?

---

15. **corrugated** (kôr′ə-gā′tĭd) **iron:** sheet iron with parallel ridges.

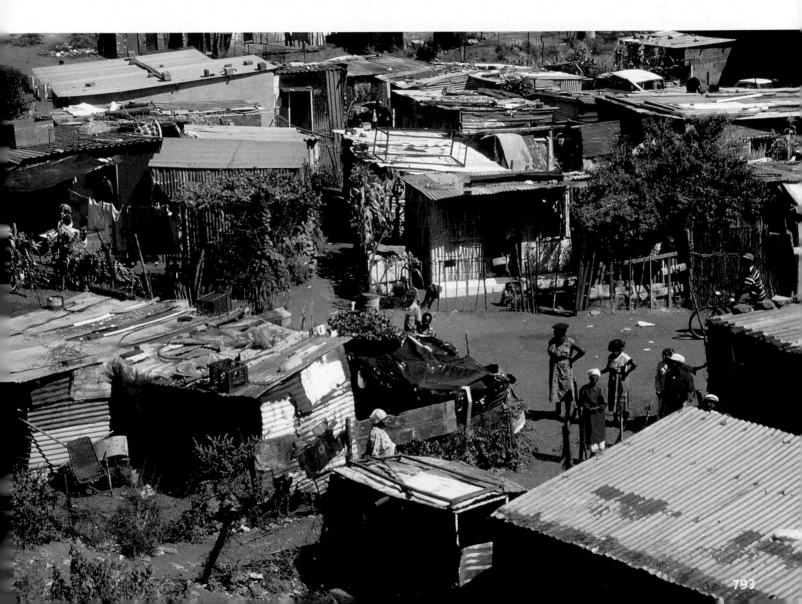

Rohan wasn't sure what to do. He knew he couldn't follow. The sounds from
300 within scared him. The moans were rapid and painful. . . .

Rohan folded his arms tightly, trying not to show how awkward he felt.
The little children were still watching but keeping their distance. They could
probably also hear the cries. It would be hard to keep anything private here. The
only other people nearby were two gray-haired men sitting on boxes a little lower
down the hill. One of them was bent over an old-fashioned sewing machine
placed on a metal drum, a makeshift table. Normally Rohan would have been
very curious to see what he was stitching, but now he was just grateful that both
men were **engrossed** in talking and didn't seem interested in him.

He turned to look up the hill—toward his house and the others at the top
310 protected by their walls with wires, spikes, and broken bottles. When he had
hidden in his hideout down here, he had always loved the feeling of being safe
yet almost in his own separate little country. But that had been a game and
he could just hop over the wall to return to the other side. Surrounded now
by homes made out of scraps and other people's leftovers, this place seemed a
complete world away from the houses on the hill. In fact, how was he going to
get home? If he didn't leave soon, Ma would be back before him. Would the
boy at least take him part of the way through the squatter camp? He needed
him to come outside so that he could ask him.

"What do you want here?"

320 Rohan spun around. A man with half-closed eyes and his head tilted to one
side stood with his hands on his hips, surveying Rohan from head to foot. His
gaze lingered for a moment on Rohan's watch.

"I . . . I brought water with . . . with . . ." Rohan stammered. He hadn't asked
the boy his name! Panic-stricken, he pointed to the door of the shack. The man
stepped forward, and Rohan stumbled back against the wall of corrugated iron.
The clattering brought the boy to the door. The man immediately switched into
loud, fast Zulu. The boy spoke quietly at first, but when the man's voice didn't
calm down, the boy's began to rise too. Even when he pointed to the bucket
and Rohan, the man's face remained scornful. Rohan was fully expecting to be
330 grabbed when a sharp baby's cry interrupted the argument. The boy's face lit up,
and the man suddenly fell silent. Rohan's heart thumped wildly as the man's eyes
mocked him before he turned and walked away. **Ⓜ**

Rohan folded his arms tightly, trying not to shake. Before he could say
anything, a lady appeared behind the boy, placing a hand on his shoulder.

"You have a little sister!" She smiled at the boy and then at Rohan. She
looked friendly but tired. Her cheeks shone as if she too had been perspiring.
It was obviously hard work helping to deliver a baby.

"Tell your mother thank you for the water. You really helped us today."
Rohan managed to smile back.

340 "It's OK." His voice came out strangely small.

"Solani will take you back now—before it gets dark."

Rohan felt a weight lifting. He did not need to ask.

engross (ĕn-grōs´) v.
to completely occupy

**Ⓜ CULTURAL CONFLICT**
Why do you think the man
is scornful and mocks
Rohan with his eyes?

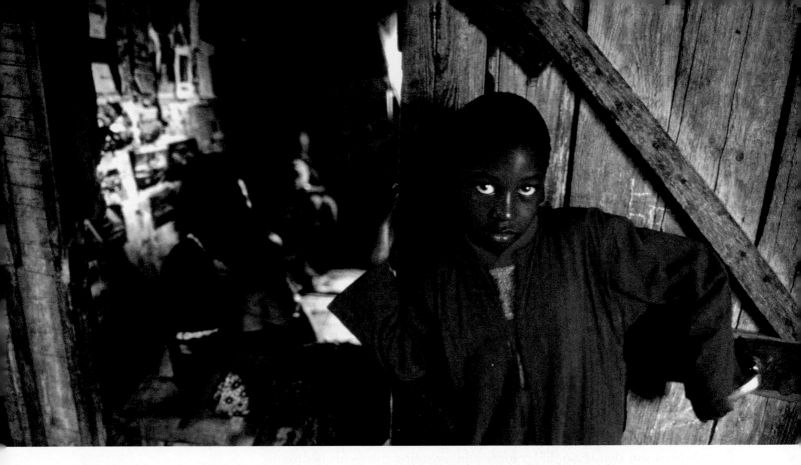

The sun was getting lower and made long rodlike shadows leap beside them as they scrambled down the slope. Knowing the boy's name made Rohan feel a little easier, and he wondered why he hadn't asked him earlier. He told Solani his own, and the next thing he was telling him about riding on garbage can lids down the ski slope. Solani grinned.

"It's good! But this place—it's a road now. We can't do it. The people will be angry if we knock someone down."

350 Rohan understood that. But what he didn't understand was why the man with scornful eyes had been so angry with him. And why had those other young men looked at him so suspiciously? He decided to ask Solani.

"They don't know you. Sometimes people come and attack us. So if a stranger comes, they must always check first."

When they reached the road, neither spoke. The hometime traffic would have drowned their voices anyway. Rohan thought about what Solani had said about him being a stranger. Surely they knew that he was from one of the houses on top of the hill. The houses that also did not welcome strangers. Like the squatters.

360 They parted at the top of the hill. Rohan was anxious to reach the house before his mother returned, and Solani was eager to see his baby sister. Opening the electronic gates, Rohan was relieved that his mother's car was neither in the yard nor the garage. He dashed upstairs to his room and peered out of the window over to the squatter camp. The evening was falling very rapidly. His mother would be home any minute—and his dad. Neither liked to drive in the dark if they could help it.

**ANALYZE VISUALS**
Note the boy's expression and body language. What can you **infer** about his mood?

**N CULTURAL CONFLICT**
What do Rohan's neighborhood and the squatters' camp have in common?

Rohan fixed his eyes on the deep crimson scar, hoping to see Solani climbing the slope. How strange to think that he had been there himself less than half an hour ago. In that other world. Yes! There was Solani! A tiny, wiry figure
370 **bounding** up the hill. Not **hampered** this time with a container of water on his head. Rohan watched Solani weave through other figures traveling more slowly until three quarters of the way up the hill, he darted off and disappeared into the darkening shadow that was his home.

Rohan surprised his parents by joining them for the eight o'clock news. The story about the rescue of mother and baby from the floods in Mozambique was repeated.

"Sophia Pedro and her baby daughter Rositha were among the lucky few. Many thousands of Mozambicans are still waiting to be lifted to safety. . . ."

This time the reporter added their names. Rohan observed the mother
380 more closely. Had she also cried and moaned like Solani's mother? With the roaring waters underneath, how many people had heard her? 🔘

"It's nice to see these South African soldiers doing some good," said Ma when the news was finished.

Rohan wished he could say what he too had done that afternoon. But he feared the storm that it would let loose and went upstairs to his bedroom. Before slipping between his sheets, he peered out once again through the bars at the hill swallowed up by the night. He thought he saw a light still flickering in Solani's home and wondered how many people were tucked inside the sheets of iron, plastic, and wood. He prayed that Cyclone Gloria
390 would keep well away.

Next morning, the glint of metal beside the gate caught his eye from the front door. His dad was reversing the car out of the garage. Rohan ran across the drive. There, just inside the gate, was a wire car. A small, perfect Merc! Who could it be from, except Solani? He must have slipped it through the bars of the gate in the early morning. Quickly Rohan pushed it behind a cluster of scarlet gladioli. If his parents saw it, they would want to know from where it had come. They would discover he had gone out of bounds. . . . Well, so had Solani! Each of them had taken a risk. He needed time to think. In the meantime, the car would have to be his secret. Their secret.
400 His and Solani's. ❧

**bound** (bound) *v.* to leap forward

**hamper** (hăm′pər) *v.* to prevent the free movement of

🔘 **MAKE INFERENCES**
Why has Rohan become more interested in the news?

## Comprehension

1. **Recall** Why doesn't Rohan go to his hideout anymore?

2. **Recall** Where has Rohan seen Solani before Solani comes to his house?

3. **Represent** Make a sketch showing Rohan's house and the squatters' camp. Think about what these places look like and where they are in relation to one another. Use descriptions in the story to guide you.

**INDIANA STANDARDS**

**READING STANDARD**
**8.2.9** Make reasonable statements and draw conclusions . . . .

## Literary Analysis

4. **Make Inferences About Characters** Review your chart of inferences about the characters and their culture. Why does Rohan think it's the **right** decision to help Solani? Name three reasons why these two boys might be drawn together.

5. **Analyze Cultural Conflict** What causes the residents of Mount View to discriminate against the squatters? Consider what you know about the history and culture of South Africa as well as events in the story's plot. Record your response in a diagram like the one shown.

6. **Evaluate Attitudes** Describe the attitudes of Rohan's mother and father toward the squatters. Do you think they are prejudiced against Africans? Then consider Rohan's experience in the squatters' camp. Do you think the Africans are prejudiced against him? Explain your responses, citing evidence from the story.

7. **Make Judgments** Who do you think took the greater risk by going out of bounds—Rohan or Solani? Explain your answer.

8. **Predict** Do you think that Rohan and Solani will be able to maintain their friendship? Why or why not?

## Extension and Challenge

9. **Literary Criticism** As a child, Beverley Naidoo didn't notice that she lived in an unfair society. "It was like being brought up to be a horse with blinkers," she has said. "Luckily when I left school, I met people who challenged me . . . and I was able to take off the blinkers." How do Rohan's experiences in "Out of Bounds" reflect the author's background?

10.  **SOCIAL STUDIES CONNECTION** Research Nelson Mandela's role in ending the system of apartheid in South Africa. Why is he considered an inspirational leader?

> **RESEARCH LINKS**
> For more on Nelson Mandela, visit the **Research Center** at **ClassZone.com**.

Nelson Mandela

# Vocabulary in Context

## VOCABULARY PRACTICE

For each item, choose the word that differs most in meaning from the other words. Refer to a dictionary if you need help.

1. (a) bound, (b) leap, (c) spring, (d) stroll
2. (a) engross, (b) distract, (c) involve, (d) interest
3. (a) glimmer, (b) trace, (c) fraction, (d) excess
4. (a) hamper, (b) free, (c) prevent, (d) hinder
5. (a) maroon, (b) rescue, (c) save, (d) retrieve
6. (a) sect, (b) denomination, (c) group, (d) everyone
7. (a) straggle, (b) lead, (c) scatter, (d) dawdle
8. (a) vigorously, (b) energetically, (c) enthusiastically, (d) weakly

## VOCABULARY IN WRITING

Using at least two vocabulary words, write a paragraph from Solani's point of view telling how he felt as he approached Rohan's house to ask for water.

**EXAMPLE SENTENCE**

*I was afraid, but I couldn't let that **hamper** me because my mother needed water.*

## VOCABULARY STRATEGY: HOMOGRAPHS

**Homographs** are words that look the same but have different meanings, origins, and sometimes pronunciations. For example, in the phrase "out of bounds," *bounds* means "boundaries." However, in the sentence "Solani bounds up the hill," *bounds* means "springs forward."

If a familiar-looking word does not make sense to you, look at the words around it for context clues to other possible meanings. For further help, check a dictionary.

*PRACTICE* Use context clues to define the boldfaced words. Then check your definitions in a dictionary and note the word's origin.

1. She said goodbye to him in front of a **bank** of elevators.
2. The goatherd **drove** his flock up the hill.
3. Great-Grandma's **lined** face shows her age.
4. Your **pupils** grow tiny when you step into bright sunlight.
5. Cowhands herded longhorn **steers** into a corral.

**INDIANA STANDARDS**

READING STANDARD
**8.1.3** Verify the meaning of a word in its context . . . .

**VOCABULARY PRACTICE**
For more practice, go to the **Vocabulary Center** at **ClassZone.com**.

# Reading-Writing Connection

Demonstrate your understanding of "Out of Bounds" by responding to these prompts. Then complete the **Grammar and Writing** exercise.

| WRITING PROMPTS | SELF-CHECK |
| --- | --- |
| **A. Short Response: Write a Journal Entry**<br><br>How has reading this story affected your beliefs about whether it's **right** to go "out of bounds" to help another person? Write a **one-paragraph journal entry** explaining how the story changed your thinking or confirmed your beliefs. | **A well-written entry will . . .**<br><br>• state your original ideas about whether it's ever good to go out of bounds<br><br>• use examples from the story to explain why your thinking changed or stayed the same |
| **B. Extended Response: Create a Community Plan**<br><br>How could the residents of Mount View improve their relationship with the squatters? Write a **two- or three-paragraph plan** to help the two communities better understand one another. | **A strong plan will . . .**<br><br>• reflect an understanding of the relationship between the communities in the story<br><br>• present several ideas to bring the two communities together |

## GRAMMAR AND WRITING

**WRITING STANDARD**
**8.6.5** Use correct punctuation.

**USE COLONS CORRECTLY** A **colon** should be placed after a formal greeting in a business letter (*To Whom It May Concern:*) and before a list of items (*I had the following foods for breakfast: eggs, toast, and cereal*). When using a colon to introduce a list, avoid placing it directly after a verb or a preposition. Instead, insert the colon after a noun or after the words *the following*.

> *Original:* The squatters suffer from: poverty, homelessness, and a lack of water.

> *Revised:* The squatters suffer from the following: poverty, homelessness, and a lack of water. (*Inserting* the following *after the preposition* from *makes use of the colon correct.*)

**PRACTICE** Rewrite the following letter, correcting the colon errors.

Dear Mount View residents
To improve our relationship with the squatters, we are recommending that residents provide squatters with: food, water, and blankets. Also, we request that these professionals offer aid to the squatters, doctors, nurses, and teachers. From the walls, please remove: wire, spikes, and broken glass.

*For more help with using colons correctly, see page R50 in the **Grammar Handbook**.*

## Pecos Bill
Tall Tale Retold by Mary Pope Osborne

# What is a
# FOLK HERO?

**INDIANA STANDARDS**

**READING STANDARDS**
**8.3.2** Evaluate the structural elements of the plot ....
**8.3.6** Identify significant literary devices, such as metaphor, symbolism, dialect or quotations, and irony, which define a writer's style and use those elements to interpret the work.

***KEY IDEA*** A steel-driving man who defeats a machine through hard work and perseverance. An outlaw who steals from the rich to give to the poor. A cowgirl who can circle the moon. Every culture has its **folk heroes,** characters whose courage, generosity, or accomplishments inspire ordinary people. Some folk heroes are real people or are based on the lives of real people; others are invented to symbolize the values of a particular culture. In the tall tale you are about to read, you will meet a fictional American folk hero known for his strength and bravery.

***DISCUSS*** Imagine you were on a committee to select a folk hero to speak at your school. In small groups, choose a real person or a character you've read about who would inspire you and your classmates. What qualities does this person possess that make him or her a folk hero? What topics would you like to see this person address at your school?

## LITERARY ANALYSIS: TALL TALE

Folk heroes often appear in **tall tales,** which are humorous stories about impossible events. Many of these stories were originally passed down from generation to generation by being told out loud. Some of them even started off with a kernel of truth, but as you'll see, they aren't exactly realistic. Tall tales have these characteristics:

- The hero or heroine is often larger than life, which means he or she is bigger, louder, stronger, or stranger than any real person could be.
- Problems are solved in humorous ways.
- **Hyperbole,** or exaggeration, is used to emphasize the main character's qualities and create humor.

As you read, note how these characteristics apply to "Pecos Bill."

## READING STRATEGY: VISUALIZE

Tall tales are funny and action-packed. To enjoy them fully, it helps to **visualize,** or picture in your mind, the incredible events in the story as you read about them. To visualize, focus on descriptions that appeal to your senses, especially those of sight, sound, and touch. Use these sensory details to form a mental picture of the characters and action. As you read, use a chart like the one shown to note descriptive words and phrases that help you visualize the tall tale.

| Character or Event | Descriptive Words or Phrases |
|---|---|
| Little Bill falls out of the wagon. | "sat there in the dirt" "rattle off in a cloud of dust" |

# Author Online

### Finding Her Way

After graduating from college, Mary Pope Osborne decided to explore the world. She traveled around Europe, the Middle East, and southern Asia. She slept outdoors and bathed in rivers in Iraq, Afghanistan, and India. And, she says, she was "terrified"

**Mary Pope Osborne**
**born 1949**

almost the whole time. She survived an earthquake and a riot, only to end up sick in a hospital, all alone and far from home. While she rested, she read J. R. R. Tolkien's *The Lord of the Rings* series. She identified with Tolkien's hero, Frodo, whose dangerous journey seemed to resemble her own. Says Osborne, "Ultimately Frodo's courage and powers of endurance became mine," which helped her recover from her illness and make her way home. Eventually, she began writing children's stories for fun and discovered her new career.

 **MORE ABOUT THE AUTHOR**
For more on Mary Pope Osborne, visit the **Literature Center** at **ClassZone.com.**

## Background

**Tall Tales and the American Frontier**
Tall tales are often set on the American frontier—large parts of the West and Southwest that had small populations in the 19th century. Life on the frontier was often adventurous and free-spirited, and sharing stories became an important social activity. Tall tales may have started as bragging contests held by ranch hands on the frontier. As they tried to outdo each other, they exaggerated stories about their abilities more and more. The achievements described in tall tales often center around the characteristics of courage, determination, and cleverness, all of which were needed to survive on the frontier.

# Pecos Bill

## RETOLD BY MARY POPE OSBORNE

Illustrations by Michael McCurdy.

Ask any coyote near the Pecos River in western Texas who was the best cowboy who ever lived, and he'll throw back his head and howl, "Ah-hooo!" If you didn't know already, that's coyote language for *Pecos Bill*.

When Pecos Bill was a little baby, he was as tough as a pine knot. He teethed on horseshoes instead of teething rings and played with grizzly bears instead of teddy bears. He could have grown up just fine in the untamed land of eastern Texas. But one day his pappy ran in from the fields, hollering, "Pack up, Ma! Neighbors movin' in fifty miles away! It's gettin' too crowded!"

Before sundown Bill's folks loaded their fifteen kids and all their belongings
10 into their covered wagon and started west. Ⓐ

As they clattered across the desolate land of western Texas, the crushing heat nearly drove them all crazy. Baby Bill got so hot and cross that he began to wallop[1] his big brothers. Pretty soon all fifteen kids were going at one another tooth and nail.[2] Before they turned each other into catfish bait, Bill fell out of the wagon and landed *kerplop* on the sun-scorched desert. Ⓑ

The others were so busy fighting that they didn't even notice the baby was missing until it was too late to do anything about it.

Well, tough little Bill just sat there in the dirt, watching his family rattle off in a cloud of dust, until an old coyote walked over and sniffed him.
20 "Goo-goo!" Bill said.

Now it's an amazing coincidence, but "Goo-goo" happens to mean something similar to "Glad to meet you" in coyote language. Naturally the old coyote figured he'd come across one of his own kind. He gave Bill a big lick and picked him up by the scruff of the neck and carried him home to his den.

---

1. **wallop** (wŏl´əp): to beat up.
2. **tooth and nail:** very fiercely.

Ⓐ **TALL TALE**
Which of young Bill's and his father's qualities are exaggerated?

Ⓑ **VISUALIZE**
Reread lines 11–15. What words and phrases help you picture the scene?

Bill soon discovered the coyote's kinfolk were about the wildest, roughest bunch you could imagine. Before he knew it, he was roaming the prairies with the pack. He howled at the moon, sniffed the brush, and chased lizards across the sand. He was having such a good time, scuttling about naked and dirty on all fours, that he completely forgot what it was like to be a
30 human. **C**

Pecos Bill's coyote days came to an end about seventeen years later. One evening as he was sniffing the sagebrush, a cowpoke[3] came loping by on a big horse. "Hey, you!" he shouted. "What in the world are you?"

Bill sat on his haunches and stared at the feller.

"What *are* you?" asked the cowpoke again.

"Varmint,"[4] said Bill hoarsely, for he hadn't used his human voice in seventeen years.

"No, you ain't!"

"Yeah, I am. I got fleas, don't I?"

40 "Well, that don't mean nothing. A lot of Texans got fleas. The thing varmints got that you ain't got is a tail."

"Oh, yes, I do have a tail," said Pecos Bill.

"Lemme see it then," said the cowpoke.

Bill turned around to look at his rear end, and for the first time in his life he realized he didn't have a tail.

"Dang," he said. "But if I'm not a varmint, what am I?"

"You're a cowboy! So start acting like one!"

Bill just growled at the feller like any coyote worth his salt[5] would. But deep down in his heart of hearts he knew the cowpoke was right. For the last
50 seventeen years he'd had a sneaking suspicion that he was different from that pack of coyotes. For one thing, none of them seemed to smell quite as bad as he did. **D**

So with a heavy heart he said good-bye to his four-legged friends and took off with the cowpoke for the nearest ranch.

Acting like a human wasn't all that easy for Pecos Bill. Even though he soon started dressing right, he never bothered to shave or comb his hair. He'd just throw some water on his face in the morning and go around the rest of the day looking like a wet dog. Ignorant cowpokes claimed Bill wasn't too smart. Some of the meaner ones liked to joke that he wore a ten-dollar hat on a
60 five-cent head.

The truth was Pecos Bill would soon prove to be one of the greatest cowboys who ever lived. He just needed to find the kind of folks who'd appreciate him. One night when he was licking his dinner plate, his ears perked up. A couple of ranch hands were going on about a gang of wild cowboys.

**C TALL TALE**
Baby Bill gets separated from his family. What's humorous about the way this problem gets solved?

**D TALL TALE**
Reread lines 39–52. Which lines, if any, are funny to you? Explain why.

---

3. **cowpoke:** cowhand; cattle herder.

4. **varmint:** wild and/or vicious animal.

5. **worth his salt:** worthy of respect.

"Yep. Those fellas are more animal than human," one ranch hand was saying.

"Yep. Them's the toughest bunch I ever come across. Heck, they're so tough, they can kick fire out of flint rock[6] with their bare toes!"

"Yep. 'N' they like to bite nails in half for fun!"

"Who are these fellers?" asked Bill.

70 "The Hell's Gate Gang," said the ranch hand. "The mangiest, meanest, most low-down bunch of low-life varmints that ever grew hair."

"Sounds like my kind of folks," said Bill, and before anyone could holler whoa, he jumped on his horse and took off for Hell's Gate Canyon.

Bill hadn't gone far when disaster struck. His horse stepped in a hole and broke its ankle.

"Dang!" said Bill as he stumbled up from the spill. He draped the lame critter around his neck and hurried on.

After he'd walked about a hundred more miles, Bill heard some mean rattling. Then a fifty-foot rattlesnake reared up its ugly head and stuck out its
80 long, forked tongue, ready to fight.

"Knock it off, you scaly-hided fool. I'm in a hurry," Bill said.

The snake didn't give a spit for Bill's plans. He just rattled on.

Before the cussed varmint could strike, Bill had no choice but to knock him cross-eyed. "Hey, feller," he said, holding up the dazed snake. "I like your spunk. Come go with us." Then he wrapped the rattler around his arm and continued on his way.

After Bill had hiked another hundred miles with his horse around his neck and his snake around his arm, he heard a terrible growl. A huge mountain lion was crouching on a cliff, getting ready to leap on top of him.
90 "Don't jump, you mangy bobtailed[7] fleabag!" Bill said.

Well, call any mountain lion a mangy bobtailed fleabag, and he'll jump on your back for sure. After this one leaped onto Bill, so much fur began to fly that it darkened the sky. Bill wrestled that mountain lion into a headlock, then squeezed him so tight that the big cat had to cry uncle.[8] **E**

When the embarrassed old critter started to slink off, Bill felt sorry for him. "Aw, c'mon, you big silly," he said. "You're more like me than most humans I meet."

He saddled up the cat, jumped on his back, and the four of them headed for the canyon, with the mountain lion screeching, the horse neighing, the rattler
100 rattling, and Pecos Bill hollering a wild war whoop. **F**

When the Hell's Gate Gang heard those noises coming from the prairie, they nearly fainted. They dropped their dinner plates, and their faces turned as white as bleached desert bones. Their knees knocked and their six-guns shook.

"Hey, there!" Bill said as he sidled up to their campfire, grinning. "Who's the boss around here?"

---

**E TALL TALE**
What can you **infer** about Bill's abilities from the feats he performs in lines 76–94?

**F VISUALIZE**
Reread lines 98–100. What words help you see and hear the action?

---

6. **flint rock:** a very hard, fine-grained quartz that sparks when struck with steel.

7. **bobtailed:** having a very short tail or one that has been bobbed (cut short).

8. **cry uncle:** give up fighting; admit that one has been beaten.

A nine-foot feller with ten pistols at his sides stepped forward and in a shaky voice said, "Stranger, I was. But from now on, it'll be you."

"Well, thanky, pardner," said Bill. "Get on with your dinner, boys. Don't let me interrupt."

110     Once Bill settled down with the Hell's Gate Gang, his true genius revealed itself. With his gang's help, he put together the biggest ranch in the southwest. He used New Mexico as a corral and Arizona as a pasture. He invented tarantulas and scorpions as practical jokes. He also invented roping. Some say his rope was exactly as long as the equator; others argue it was two feet shorter. **G**

Things were going fine for Bill until Texas began to suffer the worst drought in its history. It was so dry that all the rivers turned as powdery as biscuit flour. The parched grass was catching fire everywhere. For a while Bill and his gang managed to lasso water from the Rio Grande.[9] When that river 120 dried up, they lassoed water from the Gulf of Mexico.

No matter what he did, though, Bill couldn't get enough water to stay ahead of the drought. All his horses and cows were starting to dry up and blow away like balls of tumbleweed. It was horrible.

Just when the end seemed near, the sky turned a deep shade of purple. From the distant mountains came a terrible roar. The cattle began to stampede, and a huge black funnel of a cyclone appeared, heading straight for Bill's ranch.

The rest of the Hell's Gate Gang shouted, "Help!" and ran.

But Pecos Bill wasn't scared in the least. "Yahoo!" he hollered, and he 130 swung his lariat and lassoed that cyclone around its neck.

Bill held on tight as he got sucked up into the middle of the swirling cloud. He grabbed the cyclone by the ears and pulled himself onto her back. Then he let out a whoop and headed that twister across Texas.

The mighty cyclone bucked, arched, and screamed like a wild bronco. But Pecos Bill just held on with his legs and used his strong hands to wring the rain out of her wind. He wrung out rain that flooded Texas, New Mexico, and Arizona, until finally he slid off the shriveled-up funnel and fell into California. The earth sank about two hundred feet below sea level in the spot where Bill landed, creating the area known today as Death Valley. **H**

140     "There. That little waterin' should hold things for a while," he said, brushing himself off.

After his cyclone ride, no horse was too wild for Pecos Bill. He soon found a young colt that was as tough as a tiger and as crazy as a streak of lightning. He named the colt Widow Maker and raised him on barbed wire and dynamite. Whenever the two rode together, they back-flipped and somersaulted all over Texas, loving every minute of it.

**G** **TALL TALE**
Which of Bill's characteristics and achievements are exaggerated in lines 110–115?

**H** **TALL TALE**
Tall tales sometimes explain how natural phenomena came to be. What do lines 134–139 explain?

---

9. **Rio Grande** (rē'ō gränd'): a river that forms part of the U.S.-Mexican border.

One day when Bill and Widow Maker were bouncing around the Pecos River, they came across an awesome sight: a wild-looking, red-haired woman riding on the back of the biggest catfish Bill had ever seen. The woman looked like she was having a ball, screeching, "Ride 'em, cowgirl!" as the catfish whipped her around in the air.

"What's your name?" Bill shouted.

"Slue-foot[10] Sue! What's it to you?" she said. Then she war-whooped away over the windy water.

Thereafter all Pecos Bill could think of was Slue-foot Sue. He spent more and more time away from the Hell's Gate Gang as he wandered the barren cattle-lands, looking for her. When he finally found her lonely little cabin, he was so love-struck he reverted to some of his old coyote ways. He sat on his haunches in the moonlight and began a-howling and ah-hooing.

150

**❶ TALL TALE**
What **traits** do Bill and the woman have in common?

---

10. **slue** (slōō): to rotate, turn sharply, or pivot.

160     Well, the good news was that Sue had a bit of coyote in her too, so she completely understood Bill's language. She stuck her head out her window and ah-hooed back to him that she loved him, too. Consequently Bill and Sue decided to get married.

    On the day of the wedding Sue wore a beautiful white dress with a steel-spring bustle,[11] and Bill appeared in an elegant buckskin suit.

    But after a lovely ceremony, a terrible catastrophe occurred. Slue-foot Sue got it into her head that she just had to have a ride on Bill's wild bronco, Widow Maker.

    "You can't do that, honey," Bill said. "He won't let any human toss a leg
170 over him but me."

    "Don't worry," said Sue. "You know I can ride anything on four legs, not to mention what flies or swims." **J**

    Bill tried his best to talk Sue out of it, but she wouldn't listen. She was dying to buck on the back of that bronco. Wearing her white wedding dress with the bustle, she jumped on Widow Maker and kicked him with her spurs.

    Well, that bronco didn't need any thorns in his side to start bucking to beat the band. He bounded up in the air with such amazing force that suddenly Sue was flying high into the Texas sky. She flew over plains and mesas,[12] over
180 canyons, deserts, and prairies. She flew so high that she looped over the new moon and fell back to earth.

    But when Sue landed on her steel-spring bustle, she rebounded right back into the heavens! As she bounced back and forth between heaven and earth, Bill whirled his lariat[13] above his head, then lassoed her. But instead of bringing Sue back down to earth, he got yanked into the night sky alongside her!

    Together Pecos Bill and Slue-foot Sue bounced off the earth and went flying to the moon. And at that point Bill must have gotten some sort of foothold in a moon crater—because neither he nor Sue returned to earth.
190 Not ever.

    Folks figure those two must have dug their boot heels into some moon cheese and raised a pack of wild coyotes just like themselves. Texans'll tell you that every time you hear thunder rolling over the desolate land near the Pecos River, it's just Bill's family having a good laugh upstairs. When you hear a strange ah-hooing in the dark night, don't be fooled—that's the sound of Bill howling *on* the moon instead of *at* it. And when lights flash across the midnight sky, you can bet it's Bill and Sue riding the backs of some white-hot shooting stars. ❧ **K**

**J TALL TALE**
Do you think Sue will succeed in riding Widow Maker? Why or why not?

**K VISUALIZE**
Reread lines 191–198. Note the descriptive details in this passage. What do they help you picture?

---

11. **bustle** (bŭs′əl): a springy steel framework worn under the back of a woman's skirt to make it puff out.

12. **mesas** (mā′səs): high, flat-topped areas of land.

13. **lariat** (lăr′ē-ət): a rope with a slip-knotted loop at one end that a cowhand throws over an animal's head or body and pulls tight.

## Comprehension

1. **Recall** Why does a coyote decide to take care of Bill?

2. **Clarify** How does Bill become the leader of the Hell's Gate Gang?

3. **Summarize** How do Bill and Sue end up leaving Earth and living in the sky?

**INDIANA STANDARDS**

**READING STANDARD**
**8.3.2** Evaluate the structural elements of the plot . . . .

## Literary Analysis

4. **Examine a Tall Tale** In what ways does "Pecos Bill" exhibit the characteristics of a tall tale? Review the characteristics on page 801. Give examples from the story to support each one.

5. **Visualize** Review the chart you filled in as you read. What person or event did you picture most clearly? Tell what descriptions and sensory details helped you. Overall, how well do you think the author helped you visualize the story? Explain.

6. **Analyze Characterization** How does the author help you get to know what Pecos Bill is like? Use a character map to show what you learn about Bill through each of the four methods of characterization.

Appearance:
never bothered to shave or comb his hair

Bill's Words, Thoughts, and Actions:

Pecos Bill

Other Comments:

Narrator's Comments:

7. **Draw Conclusions** Why do you think Pecos Bill became a **folk hero** in American culture? Consider what his personal characteristics and achievements might represent to people.

## Extension and Challenge

8. **Creative Project: Comic Strip** The incredible characters and events in tall tales have much in common with cartoons. Choose one of the events described in "Pecos Bill." Create a three- to four-panel comic strip that illustrates this event.

9. **SOCIAL STUDIES CONNECTION** What were the lives of cowboys in the 19th century really like? Research the topic, and then compare your findings with the life of Pecos Bill in the story. Are there similarities?

**RESEARCH LINKS**
For more on 19th-century cowboys, visit the **Research Center** at **ClassZone.com**.

# The Pearl

Novella by John Steinbeck

## Meet John Steinbeck

John Steinbeck grew up in Salinas, California. Some of his earliest jobs were in sugar factories and ranches in this fertile area of the state. He worked alongside many Mexican Americans, and he gained respect for their culture and sympathized with their tough living and working conditions. Later, he lived in Mexico for a time, which made him even more aware of how poverty affects people's lives. Even after achieving success, he never flaunted his wealth. He lived simply and traveled often.

Steinbeck wrote stories about the poor at a time when many people preferred not to think about such things. Though Steinbeck won many prominent awards, including the 1962 Nobel Prize in literature, he also received hate mail from some readers, and some of his work was even banned.

John Steinbeck
1902–1968

### Other Books by John Steinbeck

- *Cannery Row*
- *The Grapes of Wrath*
- *The Red Pony*
- *Travels with Charley*

## Try a Novella

Some stories are too short to be called novels but too long to be called short stories. These fall into the category of the **novella,** a story ranging from about 50 to 100 pages in length. Being limited in length, a novella usually focuses on a particular situation or conflict and has fewer characters than a novel.

Some of John Steinbeck's best-known works are novellas. The brief form allows his stories to seem simple while conveying powerful themes. He based his novella *The Pearl* on a Mexican parable, a traditional story that is meant to teach a lesson. He heard it while traveling around the Gulf of California, also known as the Sea of Cortez.

## Read a Great Book

*"If this story is a parable, perhaps everyone takes his own meaning from it and reads his own life into it."* So begins the story of Kino, the poor fisherman, his wife, Juana, their baby, Coyotito, and the great pearl that was found and lost again. When Coyotito is stung by a scorpion, Kino and Juana travel from their village to take him to the nearest doctor. However, being poor, they are unable to pay for treatment and are turned away. But once they have a large pearl in their possession, the greedy doctor makes a house call, hoping to get a share of the profits.

*from*

# The *Pearl*

"It is as I thought," he said. "The poison has gone inward and it will strike soon. Come look!" He held the eyelid down. "See—it is blue." And Kino, looking anxiously, saw that indeed it was a little blue. And he didn't know whether or not it was always a little blue. But the trap was set. He couldn't take the chance.

The doctor's eyes watered in their little hammocks. "I will give him something to try to turn the poison aside," he said. And he handed the baby to Kino.

Then from his bag he took a little bottle of white powder and a
10  capsule of gelatine. He filled the capsule with the powder and closed it, and then around the first capsule he fitted a second capsule and closed it. Then he worked very deftly. He took the baby and pinched its lower lip until it opened its mouth. His fat fingers placed the capsule far back on the baby's tongue, back of the point where he could spit it out, and then from the floor he picked up the little pitcher of pulque and gave Coyotito a drink, and it was done. He looked again at the baby's eyeball and he pursed his lips and seemed to think.

At last he handed the baby back to Juana, and he turned to Kino.
20 "I think the poison will attack within the hour," he said. "The medicine may save the baby from hurt, but I will come back in an hour. Perhaps I am in time to save him." He took a deep breath and went out of the hut, and his servant followed him with the lantern.

Now Juana had the baby under her shawl, and she stared at it with anxiety and fear. Kino came to her, and he lifted the shawl and stared at the baby. He moved his hand to look under the eyelid, and only then saw that the pearl was still in his hand. Then he went to a box by the wall, and from it he brought a piece of rag. He wrapped the pearl in the rag, then went to the corner of the brush house and dug a little
30 hole with his fingers in the dirt floor, and he put the pearl in the hole and covered it up and concealed the place. And then he went to the fire where Juana was squatting, watching the baby's face.

The doctor, back in his house, settled into his chair and looked at his watch. His people brought him a little supper of chocolate and sweet cakes and fruit, and he stared at the food discontentedly.

In the houses of the neighbors the subject that would lead all conversations for a long time to come was aired for the first time to see how it would go. The neighbors showed one another with their thumbs how big the pearl was, and they made little caressing gestures
40 to show how lovely it was. From now on they would watch Kino and Juana very closely to see whether riches turned their heads, as riches turn all people's heads. Everyone knew why the doctor had come. He was not good at dissembling and he was very well understood.

Out in the estuary a tight woven school of small fishes glittered and broke water to escape a school of great fishes that drove in to eat them. And in the houses the people could hear the swish of the small ones and the bouncing splash of the great ones as the slaughter went on. The dampness arose out of the Gulf and was deposited on bushes and cacti and on little trees in salty drops. And the night mice
50 crept about on the ground and the little night hawks hunted them silently.

The skinny black puppy with flame spots over his eyes came to Kino's door and looked in. He nearly shook his hind quarters loose when Kino glanced up at him, and he subsided when Kino looked away. The puppy did not enter the house, but he watched with frantic interest while Kino ate his beans from the little pottery dish and wiped it clean with a corncake and ate the cake and washed the whole down with a drink of pulque.

Kino was finished and was rolling a cigarette when Juana spoke
60 sharply. "Kino." He glanced at her and then got up and went quickly to her for he saw fright in her eyes. He stood over her, looking down, but the light was very dim. He kicked a pile of twigs into the fire hole to make a blaze, and then he could see the face of Coyotito. The baby's face was flushed and his throat was working and a little thick drool of saliva issued from his lips. The spasm of the stomach muscles began, and the baby was very sick.

Kino knelt beside his wife. "So the doctor knew," he said, but he said it for himself as well as for his wife, for his mind was hard and suspicious and he was remembering the white powder. Juana rocked from side to
70 side and moaned out the little Song of the Family as though it could ward off the danger, and the baby vomited and writhed in her arms. Now uncertainty was in Kino, and the music of evil throbbed in his head and nearly drove out Juana's song.

The doctor finished his chocolate and nibbled the little fallen pieces of sweet cake. He brushed his fingers on a napkin, looked at his watch, arose, and took up his little bag.

The news of the baby's illness traveled quickly among the brush houses, for sickness is second only to hunger as the enemy of poor people. And some said softly, "Luck, you see, brings bitter friends."
80 And they nodded and got up to go to Kino's house. The neighbors scuttled with covered noses through the dark until they crowded into Kino's house again. They stood and gazed, and they made little comments on the sadness that this should happen at a time of joy, and they said, "All things are in God's hands." The old women squatted down beside Juana to try to give her aid if they could and comfort if they could not.

Then the doctor hurried in, followed by his man. He scattered the old women like chickens. He took the baby and examined it and felt its head. "The poison it has worked," he said. "I think I can defeat
90 it. I will try my best." He asked for water, and in the cup of it he put three drops of ammonia, and he pried open the baby's mouth and poured it down. The baby spluttered and screeched under the

treatment, and Juana watched him with haunted eyes. The doctor spoke a little as he worked. "It is lucky that I know about the poison of the scorpion, otherwise—" and he shrugged to show what could have happened.

But Kino was suspicious, and he could not take his eyes from the doctor's open bag, and from the bottle of white powder there. Gradually the spasms subsided and the baby relaxed under the doctor's hands. And then Coyotito sighed deeply and went to sleep, for he was very tired with vomiting.

The doctor put the baby in Juana's arms. "He will get well now," he said. "I have won the fight." And Juana looked at him with adoration.

The doctor was closing his bag now. He said, "When do you think you can pay this bill?" He said it even kindly.

"When I have sold my pearl I will pay you," Kino said.

"You have a pearl? A good pearl?" the doctor asked with interest.

And then the chorus of the neighbors broke in. "He has found the Pearl of the World," they cried, and they joined forefinger with thumb to show how great the pearl was.

"Kino will be a rich man," they clamored. "It is a pearl such as one has never seen."

The doctor looked surprised. "I had not heard of it. Do you keep this pearl in a safe place? Perhaps you would like me to put it in my safe?"

Kino's eyes were hooded now, his cheeks were drawn taut. "I have it secure," he said. "Tomorrow I will sell it and then I will pay you."

The doctor shrugged, and his wet eyes never left Kino's eyes. He knew the pearl would be buried in the house, and he thought Kino might look toward the place where it was buried. "It would be a shame to have it stolen before you could sell it," the doctor said, and he saw Kino's eyes flick involuntarily to the floor near the side post of the brush house.

When the doctor had gone and all the neighbors had reluctantly returned to their houses, Kino squatted beside the little glowing coals in the fire hole and listened to the night sound, the soft sweep of the little waves on the shore and the distant barking of dogs, the creeping of the breeze through the brush house roof and the soft speech of his neighbors in their houses in the village. For these people do not sleep

130  soundly all night; they awaken at intervals and talk a little and then go to sleep again. And after a while Kino got up and went to the door of his house.

He smelled the breeze and he listened for any foreign sound of secrecy or creeping, and his eyes searched the darkness, for the music of evil was sounding in his head and he was fierce and afraid. After he had probed the night with his senses he went to the place by the side post where the pearl was buried, and he dug it up and brought it to his sleeping mat, and under his sleeping mat he dug another little hole in the dirt floor and buried the pearl and covered it up again.

140  And Juana, sitting by the fire hole, watched him with questioning eyes, and when he had buried his pearl she asked, "Who do you fear?" ◌

## Keep Reading

Is Kino right to fear that something bad is going to happen now that he has the "Pearl of the World"? As you continue to read the novella, you'll follow Kino and Juana as they seek their fortune, dodging danger at every turn. Discover how finding the pearl will change their lives forever.

## One Last Time
Memoir by Gary Soto

# What can you learn from a JOB?

**INDIANA STANDARDS**

**READING STANDARDS**
**8.3.6** Identify significant literary devices . . . .

**8.3.7** Analyze a work of literature, showing how it reflects the heritage, traditions, attitudes, and beliefs of its author.

*KEY IDEA* Does the thought of taking out the trash make you groan? Would you rather stay in bed than deliver newspapers on a rainy morning? Lots of times, **jobs** don't sound fun. But they can teach important lessons and help you figure out your goals for the future. In this memoir, the author discovers that finding out what he doesn't want to do is almost as important as finding out what he does want to do.

*QUICKWRITE* What have you learned from a job? Whether it was inside or outside your home, describe a job you've had or a chore you've done and the lessons you took away from it.

## ● LITERARY ANALYSIS: AUTHOR'S PERSPECTIVE

Your view of the world is based on the people you know, the places you've lived, and the experiences you've had. Similarly, an **author's perspective**—the way a writer looks at a topic—is shaped by his or her experiences, environment, and values.

In his memoir, Gary Soto describes his teenage years working as a field laborer. As you read, look for clues to help you identify Soto's perspective on his work.

## ● READING STRATEGY: ANALYZE SENSORY DETAILS

Does it ever feel like you're actually seeing or hearing the experiences described on the page? If so, it's probably because of the author's expert use of sensory details. **Sensory details** are words and phrases that appeal to a reader's five senses. By using such details, a writer helps the reader create vivid mental pictures of settings, people, and events.

For example, in "One Last Time" Soto describes a bus that "started off in slow chugs"—a detail that helps you "hear" the rickety old bus. As you read, look for two or three details that appeal to each sense and record them in a web.

## ▲ VOCABULARY IN CONTEXT

The words in Column A help Soto describe his jobs. See how many you know by matching each word to the word or phrase in Column B that is closest in meaning.

| Column A | Column B |
|---|---|
| **1.** ramble | **a.** weak |
| **2.** foreman | **b.** angry |
| **3.** grope | **c.** workers' boss |
| **4.** stoop | **d.** bend over at the waist |
| **5.** contractor | **e.** unpleasant situation |
| **6.** irate | **f.** awkwardly grab for |
| **7.** feeble | **g.** talk on and on |
| **8.** predicament | **h.** one who provides services for a price |

# One Last Time

GARY SOTO

Yesterday I saw the movie *Gandhi*[1] and recognized a few of the people—
not in the theater but in the film. I saw my relatives, dusty and thin as
sparrows, returning from the fields with hoes balanced on their shoulders.
The workers were squinting, eyes small and veined, and were using their
hands to say what there was to say to those in the audience with popcorn. . . .
I didn't have any, though. I sat thinking of my family and their years in the
fields, beginning with Grandmother who came to the United States after the
Mexican revolution[2] to settle in Fresno where she met her husband and bore
children, many of them. She worked in the fields around Fresno, picking
10 grapes, oranges, plums, peaches, and cotton, dragging a large white sack like
a sled. She worked in the packing houses, Bonner and Sun-Maid Raisin, where
she stood at a conveyor belt passing her hand over streams of raisins to pluck
out leaves and pebbles. For over twenty years she worked at a machine that
boxed raisins until she retired at sixty-five. **Ⓐ**

Grandfather worked in the fields, as did his children. Mother also found
herself out there when she separated from Father for three weeks. I remember
her coming home, dusty and so tired that she had to rest on the porch before
she trudged inside to wash and start dinner. I didn't understand the complaints
about her ankles or the small of her back, even though I had been in the grape
20 fields watching her work. With my brother and sister I ran in and out of the
rows; we enjoyed ourselves and pretended not to hear Mother scolding us to
sit down and behave ourselves. A few years later, however, I caught on when
I went to pick grapes rather than play in the rows.

1. **Gandhi** (gän′dē): a 1982 film biography of Mohandas Gandhi (1869–1948), an Indian spiritual and
   political leader who, through nonviolent struggle, forced England to grant India's independence.

2. **Mexican revolution** (1910–1920): an armed conflict during which revolutionaries overthrew Mexico's
   longtime dictator and reformed the government.

**ANALYZE VISUALS**
What can you **infer** about
the boys based on their
posture and clothing?

**Ⓐ AUTHOR'S
PERSPECTIVE**
What does Soto think
about when he sees the
working people in the
movie? As you continue
reading, notice how his
family history affects his
view of field work.

Detail of *Los Comaradas del
Barrio* (1976), Jesse Treviño. Acrylic on
canvas, 36″ × 48″. Collection of the artist.

Mother and I got up before dawn and ate quick bowls of cereal. She drove in silence while I **rambled** on how everything was now solved, how I was going to make enough money to end our misery and even buy her a beautiful copper tea pot, the one I had shown her in Long's Drugs. When we arrived I was frisky and ready to go, self-consciously aware of my grape knife dangling at my wrist. I almost ran to the row the **foreman** had pointed out, but I returned
30 to help Mother with the grape pans and jug of water. She told me to settle down and reminded me not to lose my knife. I walked at her side and listened to her explain how to cut grapes; bent down, hands on knees, I watched her demonstrate by cutting a few bunches into my pan. She stood over me as I tried it myself, tugging at a bunch of grapes that pulled loose like beads from a necklace. "Cut the stem all the way," she told me as last advice before she walked away, her shoes sinking in the loose dirt, to begin work on her own row.

I cut another bunch, then another, fighting the snap and whip of vines. After ten minutes of **groping** for grapes, my first pan brimmed with bunches. I poured them on the paper tray, which was bordered by a wooden frame that
40 kept the grapes from rolling off, and they spilled like jewels from a pirate's chest. The tray was only half filled, so I hurried to jump under the vines and begin groping, cutting, and tugging at the grapes again. I emptied the pan, raked the grapes with my hands to make them look like they filled the tray, and jumped back under the vine on my knees. I tried to cut faster because Mother, in the next row, was slowly moving ahead. I peeked into her row and saw five trays gleaming in the early morning. I cut, pulled hard, and stopped to gather the grapes that missed the pan; already bored, I spat on a few to wash them before tossing them like popcorn into my mouth. **B**

So it went. Two pans equaled one tray—or six cents. By lunchtime I had
50 a trail of thirty-seven trays behind me while Mother had sixty or more. We met about halfway from our last trays, and I sat down with a grunt, knees wet from kneeling on dropped grapes. I washed my hands with the water from the jug, drying them on the inside of my shirt sleeve before I opened the paper bag for the first sandwich, which I gave to Mother. I dipped my hand in again to unwrap a sandwich without looking at it. I took a first bite and chewed it slowly for the tang of mustard. Eating in silence I looked straight ahead at the vines, and only when we were finished with cookies did we talk.

"Are you tired?" she asked.

"No, but I got a sliver from the frame," I told her. I showed her the web of
60 skin between my thumb and index finger. She wrinkled her forehead but said it was nothing.

"How many trays did you do?"

I looked straight ahead, not answering at first. I recounted in my mind the whole morning of bend, cut, pour again and again, before answering a **feeble** "thirty-seven." No elaboration, no detail. Without looking at me she told me how she had done field work in Texas and Michigan as a child. But I had a difficult time listening to her stories. I played with my grape knife, stabbing it

**ramble** (răm′bəl) *v.* to talk at length and aimlessly

**foreman** (fôr′mən) *n.* the leader of a work crew

**grope** (grōp) *v.* to reach about with uncertainty

**B** **SENSORY DETAILS**
What details in lines 37–48 help you understand the experience of cutting grapes? Add this information to your web.

**feeble** (fē′bəl) *adj.* weak or faint

into the ground, but stopped when Mother reminded me that I had better not lose it. I left the knife sticking up like a small, leafless plant. She then talked about school, the junior high I would be going to that fall, and then about Rick and Debra, how sorry they would be that they hadn't come out to pick grapes because they'd have no new clothes for the school year. She stopped talking when she peeked at her watch, a bandless one she kept in her pocket. She got up with an *"Ay, Dios,"*[3] and told me that we'd work until three, leaving me cutting figures in the sand with my knife and dreading the return to work.

Finally I rose and walked slowly back to where I had left off, again kneeling under the vine and fixing the pan under bunches of grapes. By that time, 11:30, the sun was over my shoulder and made me squint and think of the pool at the Y.M.C.A. where I was a summer member. I saw myself diving face first into the water and loving it. I saw myself gleaming like something new, at the edge of the pool. I had to daydream and keep my mind busy because boredom was a terror almost as awful as the work itself. My mind went dumb with stupid things, and I had to keep it moving with dreams of baseball and would-be girlfriends. I even sang, however softly, to keep my mind moving, my hands moving. **C**

I worked less hurriedly and with less vision. I no longer saw that copper pot sitting squat on our stove or Mother waiting for it to whistle. The wardrobe that I imagined, crisp and bright in the closet, numbered only one pair of jeans and two shirts because, in half a day, six cents times thirty-seven trays was two dollars and twenty-two cents. It became clear to me. If I worked eight hours, I might make four dollars. I'd take this, even gladly, and walk downtown to look into store windows on the mall and long for the bright madras[4] shirts from Walter Smith or Coffee's, but settling for two imitation ones from Penney's.

That first day I laid down seventy-three trays while Mother had a hundred and twenty behind her. On the back of an old envelope, she wrote out our numbers and hours. We washed at the pump behind the farm house and walked slowly to our car for the drive back to town in the afternoon heat. That evening after dinner I sat in a lawn chair listening to music from a transistor radio while Rick and David King played catch. I joined them in a game of pickle, but there was little joy in trying to avoid their tags because I couldn't get the fields out of my mind: I saw myself dropping on my knees under a vine to tug at a branch that wouldn't come off. In bed, when I closed my eyes, I saw the fields, yellow with kicked up dust, and a crooked trail of trays rotting behind me. **D**

The next day I woke tired and started picking tired. The grapes rained into the pan, slowly filling like a belly, until I had my first tray and started my second. So it went all day, and the next, and all through the following week, so that by the end of thirteen days the foreman counted out, in tens mostly, my pay of fifty-three dollars. Mother earned one hundred and forty-eight dollars. She wrote this on her envelope, with a message I didn't bother to ask her about.

**C AUTHOR'S PERSPECTIVE**
What do Soto's statements about work in lines 75 and 81–82 tell you about his attitude toward field work?

**D AUTHOR'S PERSPECTIVE**
What effect does the author's work environment have on his life away from work?

---

3. **Ay, Dios** (ī dē-ōs´) *Spanish*: "Oh, God."

4. **madras** (măd´rəs): cotton cloth, usually with a plaid pattern.

*La Calle Cuatro* (2001), Emigdio Vasquez. Oil on canvas, 22″ × 28″. © Emigdio Vasquez.

**ANALYZE VISUALS**
Why might a **setting** like that in the picture be a difficult place for Soto to spend time?

The next day I walked with my friend Scott to the downtown mall where
110 we drooled over the clothes behind fancy windows, bought popcorn, and sat at a tier of outdoor fountains to talk about girls. Finally we went into Penney's for more popcorn, which we ate walking around, before we returned home without buying anything. It wasn't until a few days before school that I let my fifty-three dollars slip quietly from my hands, buying a pair of pants, two shirts, and a maroon T-shirt, the kind that was in style. At home I tried them on while Rick looked on enviously; later, the day before school started, I tried them on again wondering not so much if they were worth it as who would see me first in those clothes.

Along with my brother and sister I picked grapes until I was fifteen,
120 before giving up and saying that I'd rather wear old clothes than **stoop** like a Mexican. Mother thought I was being stuck-up, even stupid, because there would be no clothes for me in the fall. I told her I didn't care, but when Rick and Debra rose at five in the morning, I lay awake in bed feeling that perhaps I had made a mistake but unwilling to change my mind. That fall Mother bought me two pairs of socks, a packet of colored T-shirts, and underwear. The T-shirts would help, I thought, but who would see that I had new underwear and socks? I wore a new T-shirt on the first day of school, then an old shirt on Tuesday, then another T-shirt on Wednesday, and on Thursday an old Nehru shirt[5] that was embarrassingly out of style. On Friday I changed
130 into the corduroy pants my brother had handed down to me and slipped into my last new T-shirt. I worked like a magician, blinding my classmates, who were all clothes conscious and small-time social climbers, by arranging my wardrobe to make it seem larger than it really was. But by spring I had to do something—my blue jeans were almost silver and my shoes had lost their form, puddling like black ice around my feet. That spring of my sixteenth year,

**stoop** (sto͞op) *v.* to bend forward and down from the waist or the middle of the back

---

5. **Nehru** (nā′ro͞o) **shirt:** an Indian-style shirt with a stand-up collar.

Rick and I decided to take a labor bus to chop cotton. In his old Volkswagen, which was more noise than power, we drove on a Saturday morning to West Fresno—or Chinatown as some call it—parked, walked slowly toward a bus, and stood gawking at the . . . blacks, Okies,[6] *Tejanos*[7] with gold teeth, . . .
140 Mexican families, and labor **contractors** shouting "Cotton" or "Beets," the work of spring. **E**

We boarded the "Cotton" bus without looking at the contractor who stood almost blocking the entrance. . . . We boarded scared. . . . We sat . . . looking straight ahead, and only glanced briefly at the others who boarded, almost all of them broken and poorly dressed in loudly mismatched clothes. Finally when the contractor banged his palm against the side of the bus, the young man at the wheel, smiling and talking in Spanish, started the engine, idled it for a moment while he adjusted the mirrors, and started off in slow chugs. Except for the windshield there was no glass in the windows, so as soon as we
150 were on the rural roads outside Fresno, the dust and sand began to be sucked into the bus, whipping about like **irate** wasps as the gravel ticked about us. We closed our eyes, clotted up our mouths that wanted to open with embarrassed laughter because we couldn't believe we were on that bus with those people and the dust attacking us for no reason. **F**

When we arrived at a field we followed the others to a pickup where we each took a hoe and marched to stand before a row. Rick and I, self-conscious and unsure, looked around at the others who leaned on their hoes or squatted in front of the rows, almost all talking in Spanish, joking . . . all waiting for the foreman's whistle to begin work. Mother had explained how to chop cotton by
160 showing us with a broom in the backyard.

"Like this," she said, her broom swishing down weeds. "Leave one plant and cut four—and cut them! Don't leave them standing or the foreman will get mad."

The foreman whistled and we started up the row stealing glances at other workers to see if we were doing it right. But after awhile we worked like we knew what we were doing, neither of us hurrying or falling behind. But slowly the clot of men, women, and kids began to spread and loosen. Even Rick pulled away. I didn't hurry, though. I cut smoothly and cleanly as I walked at a slow pace, in a sort of funeral march. My eyes measured each space of cotton
170 plants before I cut. If I missed the plants, I swished again. I worked intently, seldom looking up, so when I did I was amazed to see the sun, like a broken orange coin, in the east. It looked blurry, unbelievable, like something not of this world. I looked around in amazement, scanning the eastern horizon that was a taut line jutted with an occasional mountain. The horizon was beautiful, like a snapshot of the moon, in the early light of morning, in the quiet of no cars and few people. **G**

---

6. **Okies** (ō'kēz): people from Oklahoma and other midwestern states who moved to California to find work during the Great Depression of the 1930s.

7. *Tejanos* (tā-hä'nōs): Texans of Mexican ancestry.

**contractor** (kŏn'trăk'tər) *n.* one who agrees to provide services for a specific price

**E** AUTHOR'S PERSPECTIVE
Reread lines 119–141. What reasons does Soto give for rejecting field work? Tell why his views change.

**irate** (ī-rāt') *adj.* very angry

**F** SENSORY DETAILS
Reread lines 142–154. What words and phrases help you feel, hear, and see what it was like to ride the "Cotton" bus?

**G** SENSORY DETAILS
What sensory details does Soto use to help you see the beauty of his surroundings?

The foreman trudged in boots in my direction, stepping awkwardly over the plants, to inspect the work. No one around me looked up. We all worked steadily while we waited for him to leave. When he did leave, with a feeble
180 complaint addressed to no one in particular, we looked up smiling under straw hats and bandanas.

By 11:00, our lunch time, my ankles were hurting from walking on clods[8] the size of hardballs. My arms ached and my face was dusted by a wind that was perpetual, always busy whipping about. But the work was not bad, I thought. It was better, so much better, than picking grapes, especially with the hourly wage of a dollar twenty-five instead of piece work. Rick and I walked sorely toward the bus where we washed and drank water. Instead of eating in the bus or in the shade of the bus, we kept to ourselves by walking down to the irrigation canal[9] that ran the length of the field, to open our lunch of
190 sandwiches and crackers. We laughed at the crackers, which seemed like a cruel joke from our Mother, because we were working under the sun and the last thing we wanted was a salty dessert. We ate them anyway and drank more water before we returned to the field, both of us limping in exaggeration. Working side by side, we talked and laughed at our **predicament** because our Mother had warned us year after year that if we didn't get on track in school we'd have to work in the fields and then we would see. We mimicked Mother's whining voice and smirked at her smoky view of the future in which we'd be trapped by marriage and screaming kids. We'd eat beans and then we'd see. **H**

Rick pulled slowly away to the rhythm of his hoe falling faster and
200 smoother. It was better that way, to work alone. I could hum made-up songs or songs from the radio and think to myself about school and friends. At the time I was doing badly in my classes, mainly because of a difficult stepfather, but also because I didn't care anymore. All through junior high and into my first year of high school there were those who said I would never do anything, be anyone. They said I'd work like a donkey and marry the first Mexican girl that came along. I was reminded so often, verbally and in the way I was treated at home, that I began to believe that chopping cotton might be a lifetime job for me. If not chopping cotton, then I might get lucky and find myself in a car wash or restaurant or junkyard. But it was clear; I'd work, and work hard. **I**
210 I cleared my mind by humming and looking about. The sun was directly above with a few soft blades of clouds against a sky that seemed bluer and more beautiful than our sky in the city. Occasionally the breeze flurried and picked up dust so that I had to cover my eyes and screw up my face. The workers were hunched, brown as the clods under our feet, and spread across the field that ran without end—fields that were owned by corporations, not families.

I hoed trying to keep my mind busy with scenes from school and pretend girlfriends until finally my brain turned off and my thinking went fuzzy with boredom. I looked about, no longer mesmerized by the beauty of the

**predicament**
(prĭ-dĭk′ə-mənt) *n.* an unpleasant situation from which it is difficult to free oneself

**H** SENSORY DETAILS
Which detail in lines 182–198 most helps you feel what it was like to be with Soto and Rick that day?

**I** AUTHOR'S PERSPECTIVE
How might Soto's experiences at school and home affect his expectations for himself?

---

8. **clods:** hardened clumps of soil.

9. **irrigation canal:** a ditch that brings water to crops.

landscape, . . . no longer dreaming of the clothes I'd buy with my pay. My
eyes followed my chopping as the plants, thin as their shadows, fell with each
strike. I worked slowly with ankles and arms hurting, neck stiff, and eyes
stinging from the dust and the sun that glanced off the field like a mirror.

By quitting time, 3:00, there was such an excruciating pain in my ankles
that I walked as if I were wearing snowshoes. Rick laughed at me and I
laughed too, embarrassed that most of the men were walking normally and I
was among the first timers who had to get used to this work. "And what about
you . . ." I came back at Rick. His eyes were meshed red and his long hippie
hair was flecked with dust and gnats and bits of leaves. We placed our hoes in
the back of a pickup and stood in line for our pay, which was twelve fifty. I
was amazed at the pay, which was the most I had ever earned in one day, and
thought that I'd come back the next day, Sunday. This was too good.

Instead of joining the others in the labor bus, we jumped in the back of
a pickup when the driver said we'd get to town sooner and were welcome to
join him. We scrambled into the truck bed to be joined by a heavy-set and
laughing *Tejano* whose head was shaped like an egg, particularly so because the
bandana he wore ended in a point on the top of his head. He laughed almost
demonically as the pickup roared up the dirt path, a gray cape of dust rising
behind us. On the highway, with the wind in our faces, we squinted at the
fields as if we were looking for someone. The *Tejano* had quit laughing but was
smiling broadly, occasionally chortling tunes he never finished. I was scared of
him, though Rick, two years older and five inches taller, wasn't. If the *Tejano*
looked at him, Rick stared back for a second or two before he looked away to
the fields. **J**

I felt like a soldier coming home from war when we rattled into Chinatown.
People leaning against car hoods stared, their necks following us, owl-like; . . .
Chinese grocers stopped brooming their storefronts to raise their cadaverous
faces at us. We stopped in front of the Chi Chi Club where Mexican music
blared from the juke box and cue balls cracked like dull ice. The *Tejano,* who
was dirty as we were, stepped awkwardly over the side rail, dusted himself off
with his bandana, and sauntered into the club. **K**

Rick and I jumped from the back, thanked the driver who said *de nada*[10]
and popped his clutch, so that the pickup jerked and coughed blue smoke. We
returned smiling to our car, happy with the money we had made and pleased
that we had, in a small way, proved ourselves to be tough; that we worked as
well as other men and earned the same pay.

We returned the next day and the next week until the season was over and
there was nothing to do. I told myself that I wouldn't pick grapes that summer,
saying all through June and July that it was for Mexicans, not me. When August
came around and I still had not found a summer job, I ate my words, sharpened
my knife, and joined Mother, Rick, and Debra for one last time. ॐ

**J SENSORY DETAILS**
Reread lines 234–243.
What details help you
understand what the
*Tejano* looks like and
sounds like as he rides
in the truck?

**K AUTHOR'S PERSPECTIVE**
Why does Soto feel like
"a soldier coming home
from war"?

---

10. *de nada* (də nä′də) *Spanish:* "You're welcome—it's nothing."

# How Things Work

## GARY SOTO

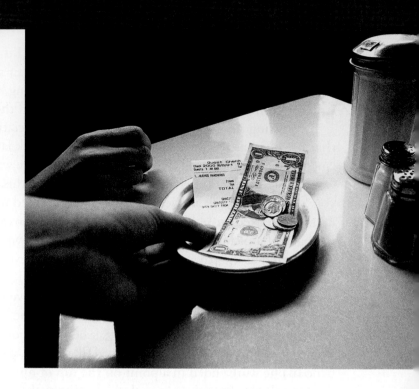

Today it's going to cost us twenty dollars
To live. Five for a softball. Four for a book,
A handful of ones for coffee and two sweet rolls,
Bus fare, rosin[1] for your mother's violin.
5 We're completing our task. The tip I left
For the waitress filters down
Like rain, wetting the new roots of a child
Perhaps, a belligerent cat that won't let go
Of a balled sock until there's chicken to eat.
10 As far as I can tell, daughter, it works like this:
You buy bread from a grocery, a bag of apples
From a fruit stand, and what coins
Are passed on helps others buy pencils, glue,
Tickets to a movie in which laughter
15 Is thrown into their faces.
If we buy a goldfish, someone tries on a hat.
If we buy crayons, someone walks home with a broom.
A tip, a small purchase here and there,
And things just keep going. I guess.

---

1. **rosin** (rŏz′ĭn): a substance derived from tree sap that is used
   to increase sliding friction on stringed instruments' bows.

## Comprehension

**INDIANA STANDARDS**

**READING STANDARD**
**8.3.7** Analyze a work of literature, showing how it reflects the . . . beliefs of its author.

1. **Recall** What does Gary Soto dream of buying his mother?

2. **Recall** What does Soto think about when he is bored at work?

3. **Summarize** Describe Soto's first day chopping cotton.

## Literary Analysis

4. **Make Inferences** How might Soto's family history affect his thoughts and feelings about working in the fields? Cite evidence from the story and the biography on page 817 to support your response.

5. **Analyze Sensory Details** Review the sensory details you noted in your web. What single detail best captures for you what it was like to pick grapes or chop cotton?

6. **Compare and Contrast** Which does Soto like more, picking grapes or chopping cotton? Note the similarities and differences between the two jobs. Then explain why Soto prefers the one he does.

7. **Examine Author's Perspective** In what ways does Gary Soto's perspective toward work change throughout the selection? Consider what happens to Soto's dreams the longer he works in the fields. Track his attitude toward his jobs on a timeline like the one shown. Record his positive feelings above the line and negative feelings below the line.

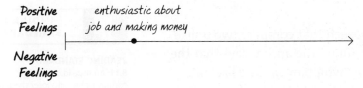

Positive Feelings — enthusiastic about job and making money

Negative Feelings

8. **Compare Literary Works** Think about Gary Soto's childhood experiences as a field laborer. What effect might they have had on the view of money he expresses in his poem "How Things Work" on page 826? Explain.

## Extension and Challenge

9. **Big Question Activity** What might Soto say he learned from his **jobs** working in the fields? Respond to the Quickwrite activity on page 816 as if you were Soto.

10. **Readers' Circle** Writers choose titles for their selections very carefully. Why do you think Gary Soto titled this memoir "One Last Time"? Reread the last paragraph of the memoir and think about the ideas Soto emphasizes. Then, in small groups, brainstorm other possible titles. Share your best idea with the class.

# Vocabulary in Context

## VOCABULARY PRACTICE

Show that you understand the vocabulary words by telling whether each statement is true or false.

1. Someone who **rambles** on about a topic gets right to the point.
2. It is a **foreman**'s job to tell workers what to do.
3. Someone who **gropes** for an item finds it right away.
4. If you drop something on the floor, you can **stoop** to pick it up.
5. **Contractors** supply labor and materials for a project.
6. Most people feel **irate** on their birthdays.
7. A **feeble** voice is difficult to hear.
8. Having two appointments at the same time might be called a **predicament**.

## VOCABULARY IN WRITING

What is the worst summer job you can imagine? Using at least two vocabulary words, write a paragraph describing your first day.

> **EXAMPLE SENTENCE**
>
> The labor **_contractor_** hired us to work.

## VOCABULARY STRATEGY: SIMILES

Writers sometimes use **similes,** or figures of speech that compare two unlike things using the words *like* or *as*. In "One Last Time," the author says that the dust and sand flying into their moving bus was "whipping around like irate wasps." This simile helps readers imagine what it would feel like to be riding in the bus.

Similes can also provide context clues to help you figure out unfamiliar word meanings. If you know that "whipping around" implies fast, curving motion and that *wasps* move more quickly when they're angered, then you can figure out that *irate* means "very angry."

*PRACTICE* Use the simile in each sentence as a context clue to help you define the boldfaced word.

1. His **elaborate** story was as layered as a wedding cake.
2. The **idling** engine purred like a lazy kitten.
3. She stared at me as **intently** as a cat watches a bird.
4. The lightning **illuminated** the sky like a fireworks display.
5. Her **excruciating** sense of homesickness felt like physical pain.

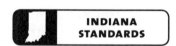

**INDIANA STANDARDS**

**READING STANDARD**
**8.1.1** Analyze idioms and comparisons ... to infer the literal and figurative meanings of phrases.

**VOCABULARY PRACTICE**
For more practice, go to the **Vocabulary Center** at ClassZone.com.

# Reading-Writing Connection

Deepen your appreciation of "One Last Time" by responding to the prompts. Then complete the **Grammar and Writing** exercise.

## WRITING PROMPTS

**A. Short Response: Write a Letter to the Editor**
Do you think children under the age of 16 should be allowed to work **jobs** harvesting crops? Write a **one-paragraph letter to the editor** of a newspaper, expressing your opinion.

**B. Extended Response: Compare Narrators**
Gary Soto in "One More Time" and the narrator in "The Snapping Turtle" (page 766) are both deeply affected by their cultural heritage. In a **two- or three-paragraph response,** compare and contrast how their heritages influence their actions.

## SELF-CHECK

*A strong letter will . . .*
- clearly state your position for or against the issue
- give reasons that support your opinion

*An effective comparison will . . .*
- identify each person's heritage and how he feels about it
- support your points with evidence from the selections

## GRAMMAR AND WRITING

**USE SEMICOLONS CORRECTLY** When there are commas within parts of a series, you must use a **semicolon** to separate the parts.

INDIANA STANDARDS

**WRITING STANDARD**
**8.6.5** Use correct punctuation.

*Original:* Some children need to earn money to buy bus tokens, clothing, and school supplies, such as pencils, paper, and notebooks.

*Revised:* Some children need to earn money to buy bus tokens; clothing; and school supplies, such as pencils, paper, and notebooks. (*Because one part of the series contains commas, a semicolon should separate the parts.*)

**PRACTICE** In the following sentences, insert semicolons as needed.

1. Not all parents can afford to buy food, clothing, and other necessities, pay for their children's education, and maintain a roof over their heads.

2. Hard work teaches children responsibility, independence, and self-respect, enables them to earn a living, and instructs them in the value of money.

3. Children should be able to work on farms if they attend school, don't handle pesticides, machinery, or dangerous animals, and are paid a decent wage.

4. A job harvesting crops provides children with exercise, sunshine, and clean air, gets them away from TV, and teaches them to appreciate their food.

*For more help with semicolons, see page R49 in the **Grammar Handbook.***

## *from* **Dreams from My Father**
Autobiography by Barack Obama

# *What makes you* PROUD?

**INDIANA STANDARDS**

**READING STANDARDS**
**8.3.7** Analyze a work of literature, showing how it reflects the heritage, traditions, attitudes, and beliefs of its author.

**8.3.8** Contrast points of view ... in narrative text and explain how they affect the overall theme of the work.

***KEY IDEA*** No other person in the world is exactly like you. Even identical twins develop distinct personalities and interests. But so often, instead of being **proud** of their uniqueness, people want to "fit in" by trying to be like everyone else. In this autobiography, Barack Obama describes how, as a child, he began to take pride in his family heritage—the very thing that made him feel different from most of his classmates.

***SKETCH IT*** What has been your proudest moment? It doesn't have to involve something others recognize as a major accomplishment. It just has to be meaningful to you. Make a sketch that reflects details of this moment and how you felt. If you're struggling to think of an example, make a drawing of a goal you have for yourself and what it might be like to achieve it.

## ● LITERARY ANALYSIS: AUTOBIOGRAPHY

An **autobiography** is the true story of a person's life, told by that person. Autobiographies share the following characteristics:

- They are told from the first-person point of view.
- They focus on significant people and events in the writer's life.
- They express the ways those people and events affected the writer.

This excerpt from Barack Obama's autobiography describes a visit from his father. As you read, pay attention to the details that reveal the relationship between father and son.

## ● READING SKILL: RECOGNIZE CAUSE-AND-EFFECT RELATIONSHIPS

Why do people do the things they do? Why do they feel the way they feel? Understanding **cause-and-effect relationships** between actions, events, and feelings can give you greater insight into the people you read about. In Barack Obama's autobiography, not every cause-and-effect relationship is stated directly. Sometimes you will have to look deeper to notice when one or more things are responsible for causing another.

As you read, notice how Obama's emotions affect his actions. For each important cause-and-effect relationship, create a graphic like the one shown.

| Cause | | Effect |
|---|---|---|
| Obama feels isolated at school. | → | He spends most of his free time watching TV with his grandfather. |

## ▲ VOCABULARY IN CONTEXT

Barack Obama uses the following words to tell about his boyhood visit with his father. How well do you know these words? Place each one in the correct column of a chart like the one shown.

| WORD LIST | dowdy | novelty | refuge |
|---|---|---|---|
| | inevitable | opaque | volatile |
| | irretrievably | recuperation | |

| Know Well | Think I Know | Don't Know at All |
|---|---|---|
| | | |

# Author Online

**A Cultural Mix**
Barack Obama once described himself as a "skinny kid with a funny name." *Barack* means "blessing" in Swahili, a language spoken in Kenya and other African countries. Obama was named after his father, who was Kenyan. Obama's parents met at the

**Barack Obama born 1961**

University of Hawaii. There, Obama Sr. was the first-ever African student. Obama's mother, who is white, was originally from Kansas. Their marriage was short-lived, and Obama's father eventually moved back to Kenya. His mother remarried and took Obama to live with her new husband in Indonesia for four years. At age ten, Obama returned to Hawaii, where his grandparents helped raise him.

**A Life of Service** After graduating from Columbia University in New York City, Obama worked as a community organizer in Chicago, helping people affected by unemployment. He then attended Harvard Law School. He was offered jobs working for an important judge and in high-powered law firms, but instead he chose to return to Chicago to practice civil-rights law. In 1997, Obama entered politics, becoming an Illinois state senator representing Chicago's south side. In 2004, Obama was elected to the United States Senate. That same year, he wrote and presented the keynote speech at the Democratic National Convention, an important meeting at which the Democratic Party declares its candidate for president. The speech and Obama's delivery of it were widely praised.

 **MORE ABOUT THE AUTHOR**
For more on Barack Obama, visit the **Literature Center** at ClassZone.com.

# Dreams *from* My *Father*

## BARACK OBAMA

As the summer drew to a close, I became increasingly restless to start school. My main concern was finding companions my own age; but for my grandparents, my admission into Punahou Academy heralded the start of something grand, an elevation in the family status that they took great pains to let everyone know. Started by missionaries[1] in 1841, Punahou had grown into a prestigious prep school, an incubator for island elites. Its reputation had helped sway my mother in her decision to send me back to the States: It hadn't been easy to get me in, my grandparents told her; there was a long waiting list, and I was considered only because of the intervention of Gramps's boss, who
10 was an alumnus (my first experience with affirmative action,[2] it seems, had little to do with race). . . . **Ⓐ**

With my admission notice had come a thick packet of information that Toot[3] set aside to pore over one Saturday afternoon. "Welcome to the Punahou family," the letter announced. A locker had been assigned to me; I was enrolled in a meal plan unless a box was checked; there was a list of things to buy—a uniform for physical education, scissors, a ruler, number two pencils, a calculator (optional). Gramps spent the evening reading the entire school catalog, a thick book that listed my expected progression through the next seven years—the college prep courses, the extracurricular activities, the traditions of well-rounded excellence.
20 With each new item, Gramps grew more and more animated; several times he got up, with his thumb saving his place, and headed toward the room where Toot was reading, his voice full of amazement: "Madelyn, get a load of this!"

**ANALYZE VISUALS**
Look at Obama's actual class picture. What **details** about Obama and his classmates stand out the most?

**Ⓐ AUTOBIOGRAPHY**
What makes starting school such an important event for Obama and his family?

---

1. **missionaries:** people who travel to distant places and spread their religion.
2. **affirmative action:** a system in which employers and schools give preference to members of minority groups in order to make up for past discrimination.
3. **Toot:** Obama's name for his grandmother.

So it was with a great rush of excitement that Gramps accompanied me on my first day of school. He had insisted that we arrive early, and Castle Hall, the building for the fifth and sixth graders, was not yet opened. A handful of children had already arrived, busy catching up on the summer's news. We sat beside a slender Chinese boy who had a large dental retainer strapped around his neck.

"Hi there," Gramps said to the boy. "This here's Barry. I'm Barry's
30 grandfather. You can call me Gramps." He shook hands with the boy, whose name was Frederick. "Barry's new."

"Me too," Frederick said, and the two of them launched into a lively conversation. I sat, embarrassed, until the doors finally opened and we went up the stairs to our classroom. At the door, Gramps slapped both of us on the back.

"Don't do anything I would do," he said with a grin.

"Your grandfather's funny," Frederick said as we watched Gramps introduce himself to Miss Hefty, our homeroom teacher.

"Yeah. He is."

40 We sat at a table with four other children, and Miss Hefty, an energetic middle-aged woman with short gray hair, took attendance. When she read my full name, I heard titters break across the room. Frederick leaned over to me.

"I thought your name was Barry."

"Would you prefer if we called you Barry?" Miss Hefty asked. "Barack is such a beautiful name. Your grandfather tells me your father is Kenyan. I used to live in Kenya, you know. Teaching children just your age. It's such a magnificent country. Do you know what tribe your father is from?"

Her question brought on more giggles, and I remained speechless for a moment. When I finally said "Luo," a sandy-haired boy behind me repeated
50 the word in a loud hoot, like the sound of a monkey. The children could no longer contain themselves, and it took a stern reprimand from Miss Hefty before the class would settle down and we could mercifully move on to the next person on the list.

I spent the rest of the day in a daze. A redheaded girl asked to touch my hair and seemed hurt when I refused. A ruddy-faced boy asked me if my father ate people. When I got home, Gramps was in the middle of preparing dinner.

"So how was it? Isn't it terrific that Miss Hefty used to live in Kenya? Makes the first day a little easier, I'll bet."

I went into my room and closed the door.

60 The **novelty** of having me in the class quickly wore off for the other kids, although my sense that I didn't belong continued to grow. The clothes that Gramps and I had chosen for me were too old-fashioned; the Indonesian sandals that had served me so well in Djakarta⁴ were **dowdy.** Most of my

**SOCIAL STUDIES CONNECTION**

Kenya is a country of great ethnic diversity.

**novelty** (nŏv′əl-tē) *n.* the quality of being new

**dowdy** (dou′dē) *adj.* out of style; shabby

---

4. **Djakarta** (jə-kär′tə): the capital city of Indonesia, an island nation in Southeast Asia; sometimes spelled *Jakarta.*

classmates had been together since kindergarten; they lived in the same neighborhoods, in split-level homes with swimming pools; their fathers coached the same Little League teams; their mothers sponsored the bake sales. Nobody played soccer or badminton or chess, and I had no idea how to throw a football in a spiral or balance on a skateboard. **B**

70   A ten-year-old's nightmare. Still, in my discomfort that first month, I was no worse off than the other children who were relegated to the category of misfits—the girls who were too tall or too shy, the boy who was mildly hyperactive, the kids whose asthma excused them from PE.

There was one other child in my class, though, who reminded me of a different sort of pain. Her name was Coretta, and before my arrival she had been the only black person in our grade. She was plump and dark and didn't seem to have many friends. From the first day, we avoided each other but watched from a distance, as if direct contact would only remind us more keenly of our isolation.

Finally, during recess one hot, cloudless day, we found ourselves occupying
80   the same corner of the playground. I don't remember what we said to each other, but I remember that suddenly she was chasing me around the jungle gyms and swings. She was laughing brightly, and I teased her and dodged this way and that, until she finally caught me and we fell to the ground breathless. When I looked up, I saw a group of children, faceless before the glare of the sun, pointing down at us.

"Coretta has a boyfriend! Coretta has a boyfriend!"

The chants grew louder as a few more kids circled us.

"She's not my g-girlfriend," I stammered. I looked to Coretta for some assistance, but she just stood there looking down at the ground. "Coretta's
90   got a boyfriend! Why don't you kiss her, mister boyfriend?"

"I'm not her boyfriend!" I shouted. I ran up to Coretta and gave her a slight shove; she staggered back and looked up at me, but still said nothing. "Leave me alone!" I shouted again. And suddenly Coretta was running, faster and faster, until she disappeared from sight. Appreciative laughs rose around me. Then the bell rang, and the teachers appeared to round us back into class. **C**

For the rest of the afternoon, I was haunted by the look on Coretta's face just before she had started to run: her disappointment, and the accusation. I wanted to explain to her somehow that it had been nothing personal; I'd just never had
100  a girlfriend before and saw no particular need to have one now. But I didn't even know if that was true. I knew only that it was too late for explanations, that somehow I'd been tested and found wanting; and whenever I snuck a glance at Coretta's desk, I would see her with her head bent over her work, appearing as if nothing had happened, pulled into herself and asking no favors.

**B CAUSE AND EFFECT**
What are some of the causes of Obama's discomfort around his classmates?

**C CAUSE AND EFFECT**
Reread lines 91–96. What causes Obama to push Coretta away?

My act of betrayal bought me some room from the other children, and like Coretta, I was mostly left alone. I made a few friends, learned to speak less often in class, and managed to toss a wobbly football around. But from that day forward, a part of me felt trampled on, crushed, and I took **refuge** in the life that my grandparents led. After school let out, I would walk the five blocks to our apartment; if I had any change in my pockets, I might stop off at a newsstand run by a blind man, who would let me know what new comics had come in. Gramps would be at home to let me into the apartment, and as he lay down for his afternoon nap, I would watch cartoons and sitcom reruns. At four-thirty, I would wake Gramps and we would drive downtown to pick up Toot. My homework would be done in time for dinner, which we ate in front of the television. There I would stay for the rest of the evening, negotiating with Gramps over which programs to watch, sharing the latest snack food he'd discovered at the supermarket. At ten o'clock, I went to my room (Johnny Carson came on at that time, and there was no negotiating around that), and I would fall asleep to the sounds of Top 40 music on the radio. **D**

Nested in the soft, forgiving bosom of America's consumer culture, I felt safe; it was as if I had dropped into a long hibernation. I wonder sometimes how long I might have stayed there had it not been for the telegram Toot found in the mailbox one day.

"Your father's coming to see you," she said. "Next month. Two weeks after your mother gets here. They'll both stay through New Year's."

She carefully folded the paper and slipped it into a drawer in the kitchen. Both she and Gramps fell silent, the way I imagine people react when the doctor tells them they have a serious, but curable, illness. For a moment the air was sucked out of the room, and we stood suspended, alone with our thoughts.

"Well," Toot said finally, "I suppose we better start looking for a place where he can stay."

Gramps took off his glasses and rubbed his eyes.

"Should be one heck of a Christmas."

Over lunch, I explained to a group of boys that my father was a prince. "My grandfather, see, he's a chief. It's sort of like the king of the tribe, you know . . . like the Indians. So that makes my father a prince. He'll take over when my grandfather dies."

"What about after that?" one of my friends asked as we emptied our trays into the trash bin. "I mean, will you go back and be a prince?"

"Well . . . if I want to, I could. It's sort of complicated, see, 'cause the tribe is full of warriors. Like Obama . . . that means 'Burning Spear.' The men in our tribe all want to be chief, so my father has to settle these feuds before I can come." **E**

**refuge** (rĕf'yōōj) *n.* a source of comfort in times of trouble

**D** **AUTOBIOGRAPHY**
What role do television and radio play in Obama's daily life as a child?

**E** **CAUSE AND EFFECT**
Why might Obama tell exaggerated or untrue stories about his father?

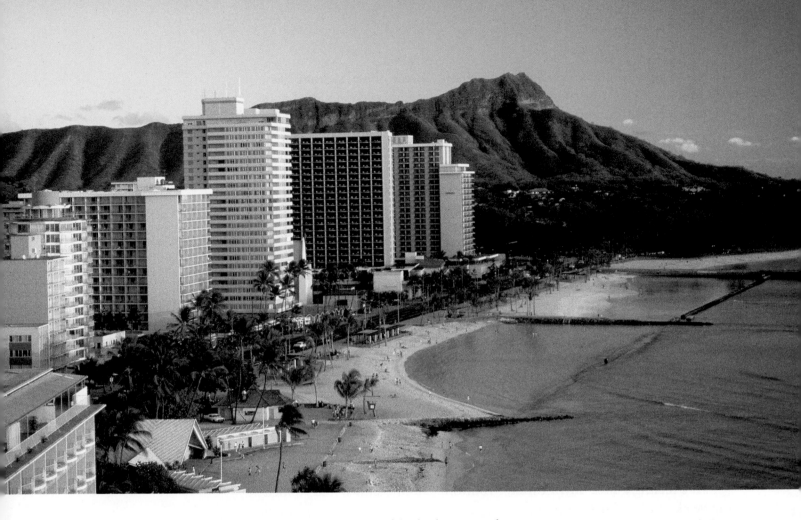

As the words tumbled out of my mouth, and I felt the boys re-adjust to me, more curious and familiar as we bumped into each other in the line back to class, a part of me really began to believe the story. But another part of me knew that what I was telling them was a lie, something I'd constructed from the scraps of information I'd picked up from my mother. After a week of my father in the flesh, I had decided that I preferred his more distant image, an image I could alter on a whim—or ignore when convenient. If my father hadn't exactly disappointed me, he remained something unknown, something **volatile** and vaguely threatening.

My mother had sensed my apprehension in the days building up to his arrival—I suppose it mirrored her own—and so, in between her efforts to prepare the apartment we'd sublet for him, she would try to assure me that the reunion would go smoothly. She had maintained a correspondence with him throughout the time we had been in Indonesia, she explained, and he knew all about me. Like her, my father had remarried, and I now had five brothers and one sister living in Kenya. He had been in a bad car accident, and this trip was part of his **recuperation** after a long stay in the hospital.

"You two will become great friends," she decided. . . .

150
160

**ANALYZE VISUALS**
Look at this picture of Honolulu in 1972. What are some features of the **setting** where Obama grew up?

**volatile** (vŏl′ə-tl) *adj.* difficult to define or pin down; unpredictable

**recuperation** (rĭ-koō′pə-rā′shən) *n.* a return to health or strength; recovery

The big day finally arrived, and Miss Hefty let me out early from class, wishing me luck. I left the school building feeling like a condemned man. My legs were heavy, and with each approaching step toward my grandparents' apartment, the thump in my chest grew louder. When I entered the elevator, I stood without pressing the button. The door closed, then reopened, and an older Filipino man who lived on the fourth floor got on.

170  "Your grandfather says your father is coming to visit you today," the man said cheerfully. "You must be very happy." **F**

When—after standing in front of the door and looking out across the Honolulu skyline at a distant ship, and then squinting at the sky to watch sparrows spiral through the air—I could think of no possible means of escape, I rang the doorbell. Toot opened the door.

"There he is! Come on, Bar . . . come meet your father."

And there, in the unlit hallway, I saw him, a tall, dark figure who walked with a slight limp. He crouched down and put his arms around me, and I let my arms hang at my sides. Behind him stood my mother, her chin trembling as usual.

180  "Well, Barry," my father said. "It is a good thing to see you after so long. Very good."

He led me by the hand into the living room, and we all sat down.

"So, Barry, your grandmama has told me that you are doing very well in school."

I shrugged.

"He's feeling a little shy, I think," Toot offered. She smiled and rubbed my head.

"Well," my father said, "you have no reason to be shy about doing well. Have I told you that your brothers and sister have also excelled in their

190  schooling? It's in the blood, I think," he said with a laugh.

I watched him carefully as the adults began to talk. He was much thinner than I had expected, the bones of his knees cutting the legs of his trousers in sharp angles; I couldn't imagine him lifting anyone off the ground. Beside him, a cane with a blunt ivory head leaned against the wall. He wore a blue blazer, and a white shirt, and a scarlet ascot.[5] His horn-rimmed glasses reflected the light of the lamp so that I couldn't see his eyes very well, but when he took the glasses off to rub the bridge of his nose, I saw that they were slightly yellow, the eyes of someone who's had malaria[6] more than once. There was a fragility about his frame, I thought, a caution. . . . After an hour or so, my mother suggested

200  that he looked tired and should take a nap, and he agreed. He gathered up his travel bag, then stopped in mid-stride and began to fish around in it, until he finally pulled out three wooden figurines—a lion, an elephant, and an ebony[7] man in tribal dress beating a drum—and handed them to me. **G**

**F** AUTOBIOGRAPHY
How does Obama feel about seeing his father? Compare this with how other people think he feels.

**G** AUTOBIOGRAPHY
What are Obama's first impressions of his father?

---

5. **ascot** (ăs'kət): a neck scarf worn knotted so that its ends lie flat, one upon the other.

6. **malaria** (mə-lâr'ē-ə): a serious disease that is spread by mosquitoes and causes fever and chills.

7. **ebony** (ĕb'ə-nē): a hard, black wood grown in Africa.

"Say thank you, Bar," my mother said.

"Thank you," I muttered.

My father and I both looked down at the carvings, lifeless in my hands. He touched my shoulder.

"They are only small things," he said softly. Then he nodded to Gramps, and together they gathered up his luggage and went downstairs to the other
210 apartment.

A month. That's how long we would have together, the five of us in my grandparents' living room most evenings, during the day on drives around the island or on short walks past the private landmarks of a family: the lot where my father's apartment had once stood; the remodeled hospital where I had been born; my grandparents' first house in Hawaii, before the one on University Avenue, a house I had never known. There was so much to tell in that single month, so much explaining to do; and yet when I reach back into my memory for the words of my father, the small interactions or conversations we might have had, they seem **irretrievably** lost. Perhaps they're imprinted
220 too deeply, his voice the seed of all sorts of tangled arguments that I carry on with myself, as impenetrable now as the pattern of my genes, so that all I can perceive is the worn-out shell. My wife offers a simpler explanation—that boys and their fathers don't always have much to say to each other unless and until they trust—and this may come closer to the mark, for I often felt mute before him, and he never pushed me to speak. I'm left with mostly images that appear and die off in my mind like distant sounds: his head thrown back in laughter at one of Gramps's jokes as my mother and I hang Christmas ornaments; his grip on my shoulder as he introduces me to one of his old friends from college; the narrowing of his eyes, the stroking of his sparse goatee, as he reads his
230 important books. **H**

Images, and his effect on other people. For whenever he spoke—his one leg draped over the other, his large hands outstretched to direct or deflect attention, his voice deep and sure, cajoling and laughing—I would see a sudden change take place in the family. Gramps became more vigorous and thoughtful, my mother more bashful; even Toot, smoked out of the foxhole of her bedroom, would start sparring with him about politics or finance, stabbing the air with her blue-veined hands to make a point. It was as if his presence had summoned the spirit of earlier times and allowed each of them to reprise his or her old role; as if Dr. King had never been shot, and the
240 Kennedys continued to beckon the nation, and war and riot and famine were nothing more than temporary setbacks, and there was nothing to fear but fear itself. **I**

It fascinated me, this strange power of his, and for the first time I began to think of my father as something real and immediate, perhaps even permanent.

**irretrievably**
(ĭr'ĭ-trē'və-blē) *adv.*
permanently; in a manner
that cannot be reversed

**H** AUTOBIOGRAPHY
Reread lines 211–230.
Why is this month with
his father so important
to Obama? Note the
memories of his father
that are most vivid to him.

**I** CAUSE AND EFFECT
What effect does
Obama's father have on
members of the family?

After a few weeks, though, I could feel the tension around me beginning to build. Gramps complained that my father was sitting in his chair. Toot muttered, while doing the dishes, that she wasn't anybody's servant. My mother's mouth pinched, her eyes avoiding her parents, as we ate dinner. One evening, I turned on the television to watch a cartoon special—*How the* 250 *Grinch Stole Christmas*—and the whispers broke into shouts.

"Barry, you have watched enough television tonight," my father said. "Go in your room and study now, and let the adults talk."

Toot stood up and turned off the TV. "Why don't you turn the show on in the bedroom, Bar."

"No, Madelyn," my father said, "that's not what I mean. He has been watching that machine constantly, and now it is time for him to study."

My mother tried to explain that it was almost Christmas vacation, that the cartoon was a Christmas favorite, that I had been looking forward to it all week. "It won't last long."

260 "Anna, this is nonsense. If the boy has done his work for tomorrow, he can begin on his next day's assignments. Or the assignments he will have when he returns from the holidays." He turned to me. "I tell you, Barry, you do not work as hard as you should. Go now, before I get angry at you."

**ANALYZE VISUALS**
**Compare** the scene in the photograph with the way you imagine Toot and Gramps' apartment. What are the similarities?

I went to my room and slammed the door, listening as the voices outside grew louder, Gramps insisting that this was his house, Toot saying that my father had no right to come in and bully everyone, including me, after being gone all this time. I heard my father say that they were spoiling me, that I needed a firm hand, and I listened to my mother tell her parents that nothing ever changed with them. We all stood accused, and even after my father left and Toot came in to say that I could watch the last five minutes of my show, I felt as if something had cracked open between all of us, goblins rushing out of some old, sealed-off lair. Watching the green Grinch on the television screen, intent on ruining Christmas, eventually transformed by the faith of the doe-eyed creatures who inhabited Whoville, I saw it for what it was: a lie. I began to count the days until my father would leave and things would return to normal. **J**

The next day, Toot sent me down to the apartment where my father was staying to see if he had any laundry to wash. I knocked, and my father opened the door, shirtless. Inside, I saw my mother ironing some of his clothes. Her hair was tied back in a ponytail, and her eyes were soft and dark, as if she'd been crying. My father asked me to sit down beside him on the bed, but I told him that Toot needed me to help her, and left after relaying the message. Back upstairs, I had begun cleaning my room when my mother came in.

"You shouldn't be mad at your father, Bar. He loves you very much. He's just a little stubborn sometimes."

"Okay," I said without looking up. I could feel her eyes follow me around the room until she finally let out a slow breath and went to the door.

"I know all this stuff is confusing for you," she said. "For me, too. Just try to remember what I said, okay?" She put her hand on the doorknob. "Do you want me to close the door?"

I nodded, but she had been gone for only a minute when she stuck her head back into the room.

"By the way, I forgot to tell you that Miss Hefty has invited your father to come to school on Thursday. She wants him to speak to the class."

I couldn't imagine worse news. I spent that night and all of the next day trying to suppress thoughts of the **inevitable**: the faces of my classmates when they heard about mud huts, all my lies exposed, the painful jokes afterward. Each time I remembered, my body squirmed as if it had received a jolt to the nerves. **K**

I was still trying to figure out how I'd explain myself when my father walked into our class the next day. Miss Hefty welcomed him eagerly, and as I took my seat I heard several children ask each other what was going on. I became more desperate when our math teacher, a big, no-nonsense Hawaiian named Mr. Eldredge, came into the room, followed by thirty confused children from his homeroom next door.

**J** CAUSE AND EFFECT
What causes tension in the family?

**inevitable**
(ĭn-ĕv'ĭ-tə-bəl) *n.*
that which cannot be avoided or prevented

**K** AUTOBIOGRAPHY
Why is Obama afraid to have his father visit his class?

"We have a special treat for you today," Miss Hefty began. "Barry Obama's father is here, and he's come all the way from Kenya, in Africa, to tell us about his country."

310 The other kids looked at me as my father stood up, and I held my head stiffly, trying to focus on a vacant point on the blackboard behind him. He had been speaking for some time before I could finally bring myself back to the moment. He was leaning against Miss Hefty's thick oak desk and describing the deep gash in the earth where mankind had first appeared. He spoke of the wild animals that still roamed the plains, the tribes that still required a young boy to kill a lion to prove his manhood. He spoke of the customs of the Luo, how elders received the utmost respect and made laws for all to follow under great-trunked trees. And he told us of Kenya's struggle to be free, how the British had wanted to stay and unjustly rule the people, just as they had in

320 America; how many had been enslaved only because of the color of their skin, just as they had in America; but that Kenyans, like all of us in the room, longed to be free and develop themselves through hard work and sacrifice.

When he finished, Miss Hefty was absolutely beaming with pride. All my classmates applauded heartily, and a few struck up the courage to ask questions, each of which my father appeared to consider carefully before answering. The bell rang for lunch, and Mr. Eldredge came up to me.

"You've got a pretty impressive father."

The ruddy-faced boy who had asked about cannibalism said, "Your dad is pretty cool."

330 And off to one side, I saw Coretta watch my father say good-bye to some of the children. She seemed too intent to smile; her face showed only a look of simple satisfaction. **L**

Two weeks later he was gone. In that time, we stand together in front of the Christmas tree and pose for pictures, the only ones I have of us together, me holding an orange basketball, his gift to me, him showing off the tie I've bought him ("Ah, people will know that I am very important wearing such a tie"). At a Dave Brubeck[8] concert, I struggle to sit quietly in the dark auditorium beside him, unable to follow the spare equations of sound that the performers make, careful to clap whenever he claps. For brief spells in the day

340 I will lie beside him, the two of us alone in the apartment sublet from a retired old woman whose name I forget, the place full of quilts and doilies and knitted seat covers, and I read my book while he reads his. He remains **opaque** to me, a present mass; when I mimic his gestures or turns of phrase, I know neither their origins nor their consequences, can't see how they play out over time. But I grow accustomed to his company. **M**

The day of his departure, as my mother and I helped him pack his bags, he unearthed two records, forty-fives, in dull brown dust jackets.

**L CAUSE AND EFFECT**
What effect does Obama's father's talk have on the class?

**opaque** (ō-pāk') *adj.* hidden; difficult or impossible to understand

**M AUTOBIOGRAPHY**
In what ways has Obama's relationship with his father changed during their visit?

---

8. **Dave Brubeck** (brōō'bĕk): an American jazz pianist and composer whose music was very popular during the 1960s.

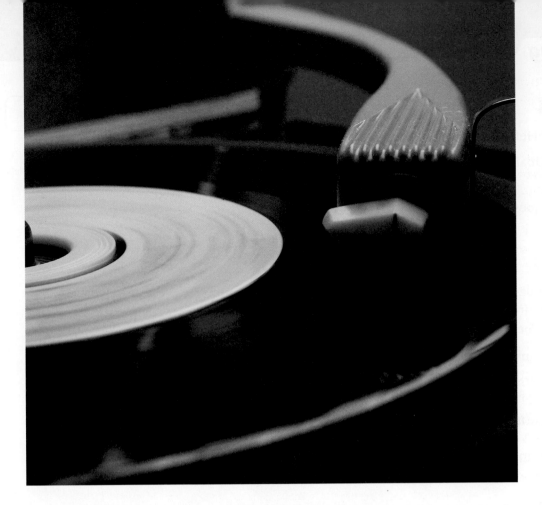

ANALYZE VISUALS
What **details** of
this stereo does the
photographer focus on?

"Barry! Look here—I forgot that I had brought these for you. The sounds of your continent."

350 It took him a while to puzzle out my grandparents' old stereo, but finally the disk began to turn, and he gingerly placed the needle on the groove. A tinny guitar lick opened, then the sharp horns, the thump of drums, then the guitar again, and then the voices, clean and joyful as they rode up the back beat, urging us on.

"Come, Barry," my father said. "You will learn from the master." And suddenly his slender body was swaying back and forth, the lush sound was rising, his arms were swinging as they cast an invisible net, his feet wove over the floor in off-beats, his bad leg stiff but his rump high, his head back, his hips moving in a tight circle. The rhythm quickened, the horns sounded, and

360 his eyes closed to follow his pleasure, and then one eye opened to peek down at me and his solemn face spread into a silly grin, and my mother smiled, and my grandparents walked in to see what all the commotion was about. I took my first tentative steps with my eyes closed, down, up, my arms swinging, the voices lifting. And I hear him still: As I follow my father into the sound, he lets out a quick shout, bright and high, a shout that leaves much behind and reaches out for more, a shout that cries for laughter. ∾ N

N **CAUSE AND EFFECT**
Reread lines 355–366.
What feelings does
his father's music and
dancing create in Obama?

# Comprehension

1. **Recall** Why is Miss Hefty interested in Obama's Kenyan heritage?

2. **Clarify** Why does Obama's father object to the young Obama watching television?

3. **Summarize** What does Obama's father discuss in his speech to Obama's class?

INDIANA
STANDARDS

READING STANDARD
**8.3.7** Analyze a work of literature, showing how it reflects the ... beliefs of its author.

# Literary Analysis

4. **Identify Cultural Values** Note things about American culture that Obama values as a child. As an adult looking back on his life, do you think Obama is critical of the way he spent his own time? Explain why or why not.

5. **Interpret Autobiography** Do you think Obama grows close to his father during their one-month visit? Cite details from the autobiography to support your opinion about their relationship.

6. **Examine Cause-and-Effect Relationships** Review the cause-and-effect graphics you created as you read. Create one more that shows the overall effect Obama's father's visit had on Obama.

Cause    Effect

Obama's father visits. →

7. **Analyze a Symbolic Event** Reread lines 73–104. Obama calls his rejection of Coretta a "betrayal." What might this event symbolize, beyond Obama's desire to be left alone by the other students?

8. **Draw Conclusions** How does the title *Dreams from My Father* relate to this selection? What dreams do you think Obama's father inspired in Obama? Consider how Obama's feelings of **pride** changed during the visit.

# Extension and Challenge

9. **Literary Criticism** Barack Obama has said of *Dreams from My Father*, "I see my book as part of my politics. . . . Policy [official government planning] has to be guided by facts, but to move people you have to tell stories." Why might people be moved by Obama's personal story? Why might they relate to him?

10.  **SOCIAL STUDIES CONNECTION** Research more about the history, beliefs, and culture of the Luo tribe in Kenya. Then make a poster that summarizes the key points of what you learned.

> **RESEARCH LINKS**
> For more on the Luo tribe in Kenya, visit the **Research Center** at **ClassZone.com**.

# Vocabulary in Context

## VOCABULARY PRACTICE

Answer each question to show your understanding of the vocabulary words.

1. Are **dowdy** clothes stylish or unstylish?
2. If you try to change the **inevitable,** are you likely to succeed?
3. If an item is **irretrievably** lost, is it possible or impossible to find?
4. If having guests over is a **novelty,** is it typical or unusual?
5. If an idea seems **opaque** to you, is that idea easy or difficult to understand?
6. During a **recuperation,** do you get better or worse?
7. Is a rabbit more likely to take **refuge** in its burrow or in an open field?
8. If someone has a **volatile** personality, are the person's actions difficult or easy to predict?

dowdy

inevitable

irretrievably

novelty

opaque

recuperation

refuge

volatile

## VOCABULARY IN WRITING

Using at least two vocabulary words, write a paragraph from young Obama's point of view that explains how he feels when his family argues about his television habits.

> **EXAMPLE SENTENCES**
>
> *After a tense evening at the apartment, I want to take **refuge** in the comfort of my room.*

## VOCABULARY STRATEGY: DENOTATION AND CONNOTATION

A word's **denotation** is its dictionary definition, but many words have additional ideas and feelings associated with them. These associations, or shades of meaning, are called **connotations**. Connotations can be positive or negative. For example, the words *clever* and *conniving* have different connotations. *Clever* describes someone who is creative and smart, while *conniving* implies the person is manipulative and dishonest. To fully understand what you read, it is important to recognize word connotations.

**PRACTICE** Each pair of phrases uses words with similar meanings but different connotations. Use each phrase in a sentence that reflects the word's connotation.

1. a unique gift
   a bizarre gift

2. the stubborn child
   the persistent child

3. a rowdy audience
   a lively audience

4. to control a situation
   to manipulate a situation

**INDIANA STANDARDS**

**READING STANDARD**
**8.1.3** Verify the meaning of a word in its context . . . .

**VOCABULARY PRACTICE**
For more practice, go to the **Vocabulary Center** at **ClassZone.com.**

# Out of Many, One
Speech

## What's the Connection?

The autobiography you just read provides insight into what Barack Obama's family life was like when he was growing up. Now see how Obama describes his family background in the beginning of a keynote political speech he gave at the 2004 Democratic National Convention.

## Skill Focus: Identify Treatment

Three writers know they have to write about the first day of middle school. One writer writes a funny newspaper column about an embarrassing moment she had when she started sixth grade. Another writer describes the first day of sixth grade in a letter to her grandmother. A third writer creates an e-mail that gives students tips on how to find their way around the new middle school. How can such a variety of writings come from the same topic? It's because writers can handle the same subject matter in very different ways.

The way a topic is handled is called its treatment. The writer's purpose, or reason for writing, helps determine a work's treatment. So does the form the writing takes and the tone, or attitude the writer expresses about the topic. In order to identify a writer's treatment, ask yourself the following questions:

- **What form does the writing take?** For example, is it a newspaper column, a personal letter, or a business memo?

- **For what purpose(s) is the selection written?** Is it written to entertain, to express ideas and feelings, to inform, or to inspire? If there is more than one purpose, which is primary?

- **What is the writer's tone, or attitude toward the subject?** For example, the tone of a selection might be described as mocking, optimistic, or serious.

In the following excerpt of "Out of Many, One," Obama's topic is his family background. As you read, identify Obama's treatment of this topic by completing a chart such as the one begun here.

|  | *"Out of Many, One"* |
|---|---|
| *What form does the writing take?* | *speech* |
| *For what purpose(s) is the selection written?* *What is the writer's primary purpose?* |  |
| *What is the writer's tone?* |  |

Use with *Dreams from My Father*, page 832.

**INDIANA STANDARDS**

**READING STANDARDS**
**8.2.3** Find similarities and differences between texts in the treatment, amount of coverage, or organization of ideas.

**8.2.7** Analyze the structure, format, and purpose of informational materials (such as textbooks, newspapers, instructional or technical manuals, and public documents).

# from Out of Many, One

### by Barack Obama

Barack Obama at the 2004 Democratic National Convention

**F**OCUS ON FORM
A **speech** is a talk or public address that is meant to be heard by an audience. A **keynote speech** is one that reflects the key points of a group's ideas and policies.

On behalf of the great state of Illinois, crossroads of a nation, Land of Lincoln, let me express my deepest gratitude for the privilege of addressing this convention. **Ⓐ**

Tonight is a particular honor for me because—let's face it—my presence on this stage is pretty unlikely. My father was a foreign student, born and raised in a small village in Kenya. He grew up herding goats, went to school in a tin-roof shack. His father—my grandfather—was a cook, a domestic servant to the British.

But my grandfather had larger dreams for his son. Through hard work and
10 perseverance my father got a scholarship to study in a magical place, America, that shone as a beacon of freedom and opportunity to so many who had come before.

**Ⓐ SPEECH**
What words or phrases help you know that this is a speech?

While studying here, my father met my mother. She was born in a town on the other side of the world, in Kansas. Her father worked on oil rigs and farms through most of the Depression. The day after Pearl Harbor my grandfather signed up for duty; joined Patton's army, marched across Europe. Back home, my grandmother raised their baby and went to work on a bomber assembly line. After the war, they studied on the G.I. Bill, bought a house through F.H.A., and later moved west all the way to Hawaii in search of opportunity.

20 And they, too, had big dreams for their daughter. A common dream, born of two continents.

My parents shared not only an improbable love, they shared an abiding faith in the possibilities of this nation. They would give me an African name, Barack, or "blessed," believing that in a tolerant America your name is no barrier to success. They imagined me going to the best schools in the land, even though they weren't rich, because in a generous America you don't have to be rich to achieve your potential. **B**

They are both passed away now. And yet, I know that, on this night, they look down on me with great pride.

30 I stand here today, grateful for the diversity of my heritage, aware that my parents' dreams live on in my two precious daughters. I stand here knowing that my story is part of the larger American story, that I owe a debt to all of those who came before me, and that, in no other country on Earth, is my story even possible. **C**

Tonight, we gather to affirm the greatness of our nation—not because of the height of our skyscrapers, or the power of our military, or the size of our economy. Our pride is based on a very simple premise, summed up in a declaration made over two hundred years ago: "We hold these truths to be self-evident, that all men are created equal. That they are endowed by their

40 Creator with certain inalienable rights. That among these are life, liberty, and the pursuit of happiness."

That is the true genius of America—a faith in simple dreams, an insistence on small miracles. That we can tuck in our children at night and know that they are fed and clothed and safe from harm. That we can say what we think, write what we think, without hearing a sudden knock on the door. That we can have an idea and start our own business without paying a bribe. That we can participate in the political process without fear of retribution, and that our votes will be counted, at least most of the time.

This year, in this election, we are called to reaffirm our values and our

50 commitments, to hold them against a hard reality and see how we are measuring up to the legacy of our forbearers and the promise of future generations.

**B** IDENTIFY TREATMENT

How would you describe Obama's **tone** as he talks about his parents?

**C** IDENTIFY TREATMENT

Reread lines 30–34. What do these lines suggest about Obama's main purpose for sharing his family background?

# Comprehension

1. **Recall** According to Obama, why was it "pretty unlikely" that he would end up giving an important speech at a national political convention?

2. **Clarify** What do Obama's parents and grandparents all have in common?

# Critical Analysis

3. **Identify Treatment** Review the chart you completed as you read. In your own words, define Obama's treatment of his family in this speech.

4. **Identify Repetition** Identify one important word, phrase, or idea that Obama repeats in his speech. What does the repetition help Obama emphasize?

5. **Evaluate a Speech** In your opinion, was it appropriate for Obama to share so much about his personal history in his **keynote speech?** Support your answer.

## Read for Information: Compare and Contrast

> **WRITING PROMPT**
>
> In a paragraph, compare and contrast Barack Obama's portrayal of his family in this speech with the portrayal in his autobiography.

Remember that when you **compare and contrast,** you identify the ways in which two or more things are alike and different. To get started, follow these steps:

1. Review each selection and note the main points and most important details Obama includes about each family member.

2. Identify the similarities and differences between the way the family members are portrayed in the speech and autobiography.

3. In a sentence, make a general statement about the similarities and differences in the portrayals. Support your statement with specific examples. Then draw a conclusion about the differences you have noticed.

**INDIANA STANDARDS**

**READING STANDARDS**
**8.2.3** Find similarities and differences between texts in the treatment, amount of coverage, or organization of ideas.

**8.2.7** Analyze the structure, format, and purpose of informational materials (such as textbooks, newspapers, instructional or technical manuals, and public documents).

## Political Cartoons

Image Collection on  **MediaSmart** DVD

# Can CARTOONS
*have a point?*

**INDIANA STANDARDS**

**LISTENING/SPEAKING STANDARD**
**8.7.9** Interpret and evaluate the various ways in which visual image makers (such as graphic artists, illustrators, and news photographers) communicate information and affect impressions and opinions.

**KEY IDEA** In the United States, everyone can express an opinion, and there are countless ways opinions are expressed. In this lesson, you'll look at how images and words can be carefully combined to make timely **statements** about American life.

## Background

**Cartoon Comments** A **political cartoon** is a humorous drawing that makes a comment about a political issue or an event. Political cartoons usually appear on the editorial pages of newspapers, alongside writings that express opinions. These cartoons can reflect current topics in a funny or serious way.

The following cartoon presents two characters who might look familiar. In political cartoons, the elephant often appears as the symbol of the Republican Party and the donkey stands for the Democratic Party. These characters often represent two sides of an issue. In this case, though, does the cartoonist seem to think that either side is correct?

# Media Literacy: Messages in Political Cartoons

For any cartoon, the cartoonist's aim is to include images and details that help you figure out his or her message. One of the most enduring images in political cartoons is the figure of Uncle Sam. Political cartoonists use him as a symbol for the United States. His appearance may vary from cartoon to cartoon. However, he's usually easy to recognize, and the message he communicates is tied to a national issue. Use the following strategies to analyze political cartoons.

## STRATEGIES FOR ANALYZING A POLITICAL CARTOON

FRANK EVERS
Courtesy New York Daily News

© Frank Evers/Courtesy New York Daily News.

**Identify the subject.**

Look for labels. Any words you see might be used to identify people, groups, or events. What label appears in this cartoon?

**Identify symbols and specific details.**

Almost every detail in a political cartoon is carefully chosen to communicate part of the message. What key symbols and images appear in this cartoon?

**Look for exaggeration.**

Just as in ordinary comics, the humor in political cartoons is delivered often through exaggeration. In this political cartoon, what details appear to be extreme or unusual?

**Figure out the point of view.**

In any political cartoon, look for clues to the cartoonist's point of view. Are characters portrayed positively or negatively? Are their actions admirable, foolish, or criminal?

**Notice how the art elements are used to catch the eye and to create certain effects.**

- Political cartoons usually appear in black and white. When you spot any other color, consider what the cartoonist is highlighting and what message he or she is communicating.

- **Lines** convey certain moods. Straight lines can signal an issue is serious. Curvy lines convey playfulness.

- To get your attention, cartoonists exaggerate **shapes,** often making objects appear to be larger than life. Most often, cartoonists exaggerate by changing the **sizes** of familiar objects or of labels.

**MediaSmart DVD**

- **Selection 1:** "Acid Rain"
- **Cartoonist:** Frank Evers
- **Selection 2:** "The Silver Sun of Prosperity"
- **Cartoonist:** Bernard Gillam
- **Genre:** Political Cartoons

# *Viewing Guide for*
# Political Cartoons

Use the DVD to see larger versions of the political cartoons. As you examine each one, think about when it was created and the issue it comments on. The political cartoon on page 851 was published at a time when the effects of acid rain first became a topic in the news. The cartoon here first appeared in 1890, when the U.S. Congress passed the Sherman Silver Purchase Act. This act called for the government to put more money into circulation by purchasing more silver than ever before.

Think about the way Uncle Sam is drawn in each political cartoon and the images and words each cartoonist uses to make a comment. Use these questions to help you interpret the messages.

## NOW VIEW

### *FIRST VIEWING:* Comprehension

1. **Identify** Name any object that appears unusually large in size in the "Acid Rain" political cartoon.

2. **Clarify** Apart from the title, "The Silver Sun of Prosperity," what helps you to understand the subject of this political cartoon?

### *CLOSE VIEWING:* Media Literacy

3. **Identify Exaggeration** In the "Acid Rain" political cartoon, what looks exaggerated about the appearance of Uncle Sam and the rain?

4. **Analyze the Message** In "Acid Rain," Uncle Sam seems to be a bit confused. What comment might the political cartoonist be making by drawing Uncle Sam in this way?

5. **Analyze the Message** The political cartoonist of "The Silver Sun of Prosperity" was in favor of the Sherman Silver Act. What evidence do you see of this in the political cartoon? Think about

   - Uncle Sam's action in the cartoon and what he symbolizes
   - the color choices and the use of text and exaggeration
   - the specific objects the cartoonist chose to depict

## Write or Discuss

**Compare Political Cartoons** You've seen how the image of Uncle Sam has spanned generations. The political cartoons in this lesson were created at different times to address different issues. How else are they alike or different? Write a brief comparison-contrast paragraph that describes at least two more differences. Think about

- whether the political cartoon includes many details or only a few
- the message of each political cartoon
- whether each cartoonist uses color

## Produce Your Own Media

**Create a Political Cartoon** Choose an issue that you think would make a good subject for your own **political cartoon.** This issue may be something that affects your school, your neighborhood, or the entire nation. The basic rule is to choose an issue that's familiar to your audience and that is important enough for them to care about. It may help you to briefly discuss your ideas with your teacher.

*HERE'S HOW* Use these suggestions in making your political cartoon:

- What details could you use to represent the issue?
- What might you exaggerate in the image to highlight your point?
- Draw attention to the most important part of your image through the use of art elements. For example, make the person or object that matters most larger in size than the other objects.
- Draw or label the people or objects in the political cartoon so that they're easy to recognize. You can also use speech balloons to show what a character is saying. Make sure there are reasons for using any words you include.

**STUDENT MODEL**

Big Oil Rules

**MEDIA TOOLS**

For help with creating a political cartoon, visit the **Media Center** at **ClassZone.com.**

**Tech Tip**

If available, use a software program to make a slideshow of the cartoons in your class.

## I Want to Write

## Sit-Ins

Poems by Margaret Walker

# How can we fight
# INJUSTICE?

**INDIANA STANDARDS**

**READING STANDARDS**
**8.3.6** Identify significant literary devices . . . .

**8.3.7** Analyze a work of literature, showing how it reflects the heritage, traditions, attitudes, and beliefs of its author.

*KEY IDEA* A girl is blamed for someone else's mistake. A boy is accused because of the color of his skin. People are denied rights because of the group they belong to, or they are put into danger because of what they believe. Witnessing **injustice** can make you feel angry, powerless, or even physically sick. But there are ways to fight back. In the poems you're about to read, Margaret Walker celebrates working for what's right.

*LIST IT* How can people fight injustice? With a small group, brainstorm a list of ways people can help make the world a fairer place. Then compare your lists with those of other groups. Who came up with the most examples? Who came up with ideas no one else did?

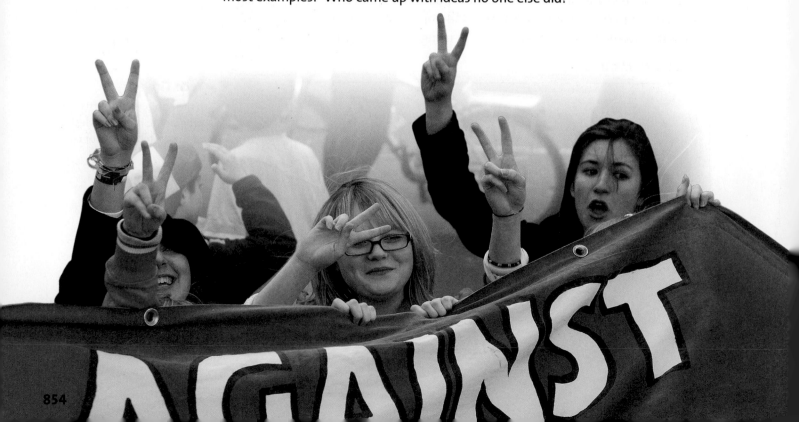

## LITERARY ANALYSIS: HISTORICAL CONTEXT

Just as a writer's cultural background can affect his or her work, the time period in which a writer lives also can influence his or her subject matter and attitude. When you look at literature in its **historical context,** you consider what was happening in society at the time a piece of writing was created.

Margaret Walker wrote the two poems you are about to read in different decades. She wrote "I Want to Write" in the 1930s and "Sit-Ins" in the 1960s. First study the background on this page, and read the excerpt from *A Dream of Freedom* on page 859. Then, as you read the poems, try to connect historical events with Margaret Walker's words.

## READING SKILL: ANALYZE REPETITION

Sound devices can add interest and appeal to all types of poems, whether long, short, funny, or serious. One of the sound devices used in Walker's poems is **repetition,** in which a sound, word, phrase, or line is repeated for emphasis or unity. To understand the effect of repetition in a poem, follow these steps:

- Write down repeated words, phrases, or lines.
- Think about what ideas these repeated elements emphasize.
- Notice how the repetition relates to the poem's overall message.

As you read each poem, record examples of repetition in a chart like the one shown, and describe the effect each has on your understanding of Walker's ideas.

| Repetition | Effect |
|---|---|
|  |  |

# Author Online

**Privilege and Pain**
Margaret Walker had a middle-class upbringing in the South at a time when many African Americans weren't so lucky. Her parents' jobs provided a nice income, but the family still suffered from discrimination. In an interview, she recalled the effects of racial

**Margaret Walker**
**1915–1998**

prejudice: "Before I was 10, I knew what it was to step off the sidewalk to let a white man pass; otherwise he might knock me off. . . ."

**For Her People** While Walker was growing up in the 1920s, an African-American cultural movement called the Harlem Renaissance was flourishing in New York City. Walker discovered the works of these new writers when she was 11 years old. Already showing a gift for writing, Walker knew that she, too, wanted to tell the stories of African Americans. Encouraged by poet Langston Hughes, Walker went to college in the North in 1932. Ten years later, Yale University published her first collection of poetry, *For My People.*

## Background

**Civil Rights** In the South, "Jim Crow" laws kept blacks and whites separated in public places, such as schools and restaurants. In the 1960s, Martin Luther King Jr. and other leaders organized nonviolent protests against segregation. Tactics included boycotts (refusing to buy products from companies that supported segregation) and sit-ins (peacefully demanding service at segregated businesses).

 **MORE ABOUT THE AUTHOR AND BACKGROUND**
To learn more about Margaret Walker and the civil rights movement, visit the **Literature Center** at **ClassZone.com.**

Illustration by Jérôme Lagarrigue.

# I Want to Write

## Margaret Walker

I want to write
I want to write the songs of my people.
I want to hear them singing melodies in the dark.
I want to catch the last floating strains¹ from their sob-torn throats.
5 I want to frame their dreams into words; their souls into notes.
I want to catch their sunshine laughter in a bowl;
fling dark hands to a darker sky
and fill them full of stars
then crush and mix such lights till they become
10 a mirrored pool of brilliance in the dawn. **Ⓐ**

**ANALYZE VISUALS**
Look at the image on this page. **Describe** the expression on the girl's face. What do you think her personality is like?

**Ⓐ REPETITION**
Note the phrase in this poem that is repeated. What idea does it emphasize?

---

1. **strains:** tunes.

Illustration by Jérôme Lagarrigue.

# *Sit-Ins*
## Margaret Walker

*Greensboro, North Carolina, in the Spring of 1960*

You were our first brave ones to defy their dissonance of hate
With your silence
With your willingness to suffer
Without violence
5 Those first bright young to fling your names across pages
Of new southern history
With courage and faith, convictions, and intelligence **B**
The first to blaze a flaming path for justice
And awaken consciences
10 Of these stony ones.

*Come, Lord Jesus, Bold Young Galilean*[1]
*Sit Beside this Counter, Lord, with Me!* **C**

**ANALYZE VISUALS**
What can you **infer** about why the woman and child might be walking away from the counter?

**B** **REPETITION**
Reread lines 1–7. What does the repetition help you to understand about the people Walker is describing?

**C** **HISTORICAL CONTEXT**
What historical details does Walker cite in the poem?

---

1. **Galilean** (găl'ə-lē'ən): According to the Bible, Jesus lived near the Sea of Galilee, in Israel.

# Comprehension

1. **Recall** In "I Want to Write," what does the speaker want to write about?

2. **Recall** In "Sit-Ins," what qualities do the people participating in the sit-ins have?

**INDIANA STANDARDS**

**READING STANDARD**
**8.3.6** Identify significant literary devices . . . .

# Literary Analysis

3. **Understand Imagery** Recall that imagery consists of words and phrases that appeal to readers' senses. In a chart like the one shown, note the images in "I Want to Write" that appeal to the senses of hearing, sight, and touch. What do these images help you to understand about the people Walker wants to write about?

| Hearing | Sight | Touch |
|---|---|---|
| "singing melodies" | | |

4. **Examine Historical Context** Margaret Walker writes, "I want to write the songs of my people." Tell what you know about conditions and events that affected African Americans in the 1930s. How might Walker have been trying to protest racial **injustice** in "I Want to Write"? Support your answer with quotations from the poem.

5. **Interpret a Passage** In "Sit-Ins," Walker describes those participating in the sit-ins as "The first to blaze a flaming path for justice/And awaken consciences/Of these stony ones." Who might the "stony ones" be? Think about the qualities the word *stony* suggests.

6. **Compare Texts** What information in the excerpt from *A Dream of Freedom* does the most to help you understand the poem "Sit-Ins"? What details do you get in the poem that help you understand the book excerpt? Explain.

7. **Analyze Repetition** Look at the chart you completed as you read. Decide which poem makes greater use of repetition. What is the overall effect of this repetition on your understanding of Walker's ideas?

# Extension and Challenge

8. **Big Question Activity** Review the list you came up with on page 854. After reading the poems and the book excerpt, do you have anything you want to add to the list? With your group, decide which method you think would be most effective in achieving justice.

9.  **SOCIAL STUDIES CONNECTION** Research another major event in the civil rights movement, such as the Montgomery Bus Boycott or the March on Washington. How did people participating in these events hope to achieve justice? In a presentation to the class, explain the event and its significance.

**RESEARCH LINKS**
For more on the civil rights movement, visit the **Research Center** at **ClassZone.com**.

**BOOK EXCERPT** In 1960, four African-American college students decided to protest racial segregation in a new way. This book excerpt describes their bold actions and how the students inspired others to join their cause.

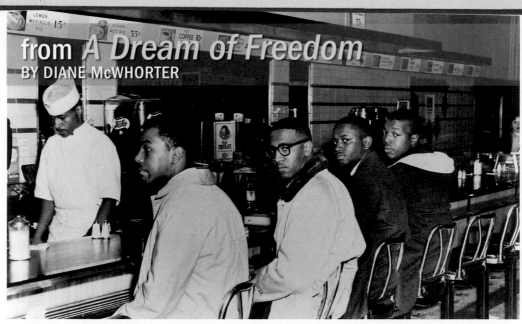

# from *A Dream of Freedom*
## BY DIANE McWHORTER

Four protesters sit at a whites-only lunch counter at Woolworth's.

On the last day of January 1960, a North Carolina teenager named Ezell Blair Jr. announced to his mother, "Mom, we are going to do something tomorrow that may change history, that might change the world." Blair attended a black college in Greensboro called North Carolina Agricultural and Technical. On Monday afternoon, February 1, he and three A&T classmates, Franklin McCain, David Richmond, and Joseph McNeil, went downtown to Woolworth's department store, took a seat at the lunch counter, and ordered a doughnut and coffee.

"I'm sorry," said the waitress, "we don't serve you here."

Though white-only lunch counters were a fact of southern life, one of the students replied, "We just beg to disagree with you." Before sitting down, they had deliberately bought some school supplies. Holding up a receipt, they pointed out that they had just been served at a nearby cash register. One of the most insulting hypocrisies of segregation was that stores in the South, as Franklin McCain put it, "don't separate your money in this cash register, but, no, please don't step down to the hot dog stand."

The youths sat at the counter for an hour. They were heckled by a black dishwasher, and stared at by a white policeman. An elderly white woman cheered in a loud whisper: "You should have done it ten years ago!"

The store manager turned off the lights at five-thirty, half an hour before closing time. "By then," McCain recalled, "we had the confidence, my goodness, of a Mack truck." In a week, the Greensboro Four had grown to hundreds. Within two months, protests had taken place in 125 cities in nine states. . . .

The sit-ins, as the lunch counter campaign became known, sparked a freedom flame.

# Cause-and-Effect Essay

In this unit, you learned the effects that some early experiences had on Gary Soto, Barack Obama, and other writers. Check out the **Writer's Road Map** and begin writing about a cause-and-effect relationship that is important to you.

## WRITER'S ROAD MAP

### Cause-and-Effect Essay

**WRITING PROMPT 1**

**Writing from the Real World** Write an essay about a cause-and-effect relationship that you think is important or interesting. Make sure you can show clearly how one event caused another event to happen.

**Topics to Consider**

- a natural event, such as a hurricane or a storm
- a historical event, such as the California gold rush
- a community event, such as building a skate park

**WRITING PROMPT 2**

**Writing from Literature** Literature can be full of cause-and-effect relationships. Write an essay that traces a cause-and-effect relationship in a literary work.

**Literature to Consider**

- experiencing how others live ("Out of Bounds")
- the effects of political protest ("Sit-Ins")
- the power of dreams ("Out of Many, One")

**WRITING TOOLS**
For prewriting, revision, and editing tools, visit the **Writing Center** at ClassZone.com.

### KEY TRAITS

**1. IDEAS**

- Identifies a true **cause-and-effect relationship**
- Presents a **thesis statement** that explains the connection between causes and effects
- Uses facts, examples, and other **details** to **support** each cause and effect

**2. ORGANIZATION**

- Presents causes and effects in a sensible **order**
- Uses **transitions** to show the relationship between effects and causes
- Has an attention-getting **introduction** and a **conclusion** that summarizes the cause-and-effect relationship

**3. VOICE**

- Uses a **tone** that is appropriate for the audience and purpose

**4. WORD CHOICE**

- Uses **precise language** to explain each cause and effect

**5. SENTENCE FLUENCY**

- Uses a variety of **sentence types** (statements, questions, and exclamations)

**6. CONVENTIONS**

- Uses **correct grammar, spelling, and punctuation**

# Part 1: Analyze a Student Model

**WRITING STANDARD**
**8.5.7** Write for different purposes and to a specific audience or person....

**Chris Hawkins**
**Danvers Intermediate School**

### Why Is It So Noisy?

One afternoon last week, I was sitting in the park, trying to relax. I had gone there because I thought the sound of the wind in the trees and the waves on the shore of the lake would help get my mind off a problem that was bothering me. What I heard instead wasn't soothing natural
5  sounds, but noise, noise, and more noise. The blaring car horns, beeping trucks, squealing bus brakes, shrieking ambulance sirens, and barking dogs made me even more nervous than I was before. "I can't even hear myself think!" I shouted. This kind of noise pollution is everywhere, and it's not just annoying—it's harmful because it may lead to hearing loss.

10  Traffic sounds like the ones I heard in the park are the major cause of noise pollution. Just think how much noise a passing car, truck, bus, train, or motorcycle makes. Can you imagine hearing dozens of them at once? It doesn't take much imagination, because we actually experience that racket every time we go outside. Don't look up for relief, either. According to the
15  Council on the Environment of New York City, an airplane 2,000 feet away makes a noise as loud as a car blowing its horn just a step away. The sound of a jet taking off can actually cause buildings near an airport to vibrate, so just imagine what it does to our bodies.

Another cause of noise pollution is machinery like jackhammers,
20  bulldozers, leaf blowers, and lawnmowers. As anyone who lives in the city or suburbs knows, the annoying vibrations from these machines can have immediate and dramatic effects. The noise interrupts our thoughts, makes conversations difficult, and can even be painful to our ears.

## KEY TRAITS IN ACTION

**Introduction** includes an anecdote that gets the reader interested.

**Thesis** states a **cause-and-effect relationship:** excessive noise leads to harm.

Specific **details** and a fact **support** the idea that noise pollution is a serious issue. The writer varies **sentence types** by including a question.

Entire essay follows a logical **order.** The writer has already discussed the major cause of noise pollution and moves on to other sources in this paragraph. Use of the words *cause* and *effect* help to make the ideas clear.

When it's loud, music becomes noise, too. The noise level at concerts,
25  arcades, parties, and other events can be almost deafening. We have
actually gotten so used to blaring music that it doesn't even seem loud
to us. As a result, when we listen to music at home, or even through
headphones, we turn the volume way up.

The effects of all this noise pollution are frightening. According to an
30  article I read in the *Danvers Ledger*, "Loud noises can actually destroy the
cells inside our ears." The longer we're exposed to the noise and the louder
it is, the worse the damage will be. If these cells are destroyed, there is no
way to restore them or our hearing. The House Ear Institute estimates
that almost 10 million Americans suffer from hearing loss caused by noise.

35  Living in the world means dealing with noise. However, since we
understand the causes of noise pollution, we can try to prevent its harmful
effects. We can avoid noisy environments as much as possible and wear
earplugs or earmuffs when we're in construction zones or at the airport. We
can turn down our TVs, DVD and CD players, computers, and personal
40  music players. Finally, we need to tell other people about the dangers of
noise pollution and start doing what we can to prevent it—now.

Highlighted **precise language** makes the causes and effects clear.

Highlighted **transition** brings attention to one effect that loud music has on people.

The word *we* helps to create a **tone** that makes the reader feel comfortable. **Conclusion** summarizes the causes of noise pollution and suggests ways to minimize its harmful effects.

2

# Part 2: Apply the Writing Process

**WRITING STANDARD**
**8.4.10** Create an organizational structure that balances all aspects of the composition....

## PREWRITING

| **What Should I Do?** | **What Does It Look Like?** |
|---|---|

**1. Decide on the right topic for you.**
Think of events in your life or the world that made you ask yourself "Why did that happen?" or "What happened after that?" List the ideas that come to mind. (Circle) the topic that interests you most.

> **TIP** Grouping your ideas into categories can help you focus.

▶

| My World | The Wider World |
|---|---|
| • Sid's skateboarding accident | • melting glaciers |
| • Leslie wanting to get a dog | • noise pollution |
| • getting lost during school field trip | • lowering the voting age to 16 |
| • earning my blue belt in judo | • stereotypes of teenagers |

**2. Use a flow chart to explore causes and effects.**
Ask yourself if the events are true causes and effects. One event may follow another but not be caused by it. "I went out without drying my hair and caught pneumonia" is an example of a **false cause.** Germs cause illness; wet hair does not.

▶

Causes
Traffic noise ⟶
Machinery noise ⟶ Effect
Loud music ⟶ Hearing loss

**3. Draft a thesis statement.**
Write a sentence explaining the main points you want to make about the cause-and-effect relationship.

▶

**Working thesis statement**
Our world is definitely not a quiet place, and the noise pollution we experience every day is annoying and can also cause hearing problems.

**4. Collect details in support of your key points.**
Look for facts, statistics, quotations, and anecdotes to support the statements you make about causes and effects.

▶

**Key point:** Noise pollution is damaging.
**Evidence:**
• <u>Danvers Ledger</u> reports, "Loud noises can actually destroy the cells inside our ears."
• According to the House Ear Institute, almost 10 million Americans have loss of hearing due to noise.

| What Should I Do? | What Does It Look Like? |
|---|---|

**1. Organize your thoughts with an informal outline.**

This writer described the major causes of noise pollution and then discussed its most significant effect. You can also present the effects first and then analyze their causes.

**TIP** Try different ways of organizing your essay and choose the one that works best for you.

> **Introduction**
> *Discuss how noise affects my life*
> *Thesis: Noise pollution annoying and damaging*
>
> **Most important cause: Traffic**
> *Cars, buses, trains, airplanes*
>
> **Second most important cause: Machinery**
> *Jackhammers, bulldozers, leaf blowers, lawnmowers*
>
> **Third most important cause: Music**
> *Concerts, parties, personal music players*
>
> **Most important effect: Hearing loss**
> *Permanent damage to ear cells; 10 million Americans affected*
>
> **Conclusion**
> *Need to take action to prevent harmful effects of noise pollution*

**2. Clearly explain how and why things happen.**

Remember the details you collected in step 4 on the previous page? Include those and other specific, relevant details to help your reader understand the cause-and-effect relationship.

> *Another cause of noise pollution is machinery like jackhammers, bulldozers, leaf blowers, and lawnmowers. As anyone who lives in the city or suburbs knows, the annoying vibrations from these machines can interrupt our thoughts, make conversations difficult, and even be painful to our ears.*

**3. Leave your reader with something to think about.**

Your conclusion should use fresh, new language to summarize the causes and effects. If possible, it should also show how the topic is important to the reader's life or suggest what the reader can do to change the situation.

**TIP** Before revising, look back at the **key traits** on page 860 and the **rubric and peer-reader questions** on page 866.

> *We understand the causes of noise pollution, so we can try to prevent its harmful effects. We can avoid noisy environments as much as possible and turn down our personal music players. Finally, we need to tell other people about the dangers of noise pollution and start doing what we can to prevent it—now.*

## REVISING AND EDITING

| *What Should I Do?* | *What Does It Look Like?* |
|---|---|
| **1. Have a classmate review your introduction.**<br>• Ask a peer reader if the first few sentences of your essay make him or her want to read on.<br>• If the answer is no, try eliminating sentences that give little information or adding an interesting detail, quotation, question, or anecdote.<br><br>**See page 866:** Ask a Peer Reader | ▶ My essay is about noise pollution because I think it is very important. This issue is getting worse.<br><br>One afternoon last week, I was sitting in the park, trying to relax. I had gone there because I thought the sound of the wind in the trees and the waves on the shore of the lake would help get my mind off a problem that was bothering me. What I heard instead wasn't soothing natural sounds, but noise, noise, and more noise. |
| **2. Evaluate your supporting information.**<br>• [Bracket] the facts and examples that illustrate your key points.<br>• Consider adding quotations, statistics, or other details that make your statements easy to understand. | ▶ Don't look up for relief, either. [Jet planes make a terrible racket.] According to the Council on the Environment of New York City, an airplane 2,000 feet away makes a noise as loud as a car blowing its horn just a step away. |
| **3. Use transitions wisely.**<br>• <u>Underline</u> the transitional words and phrases you used to make the relationship between causes and effects clear.<br>• Think about **adding transitions** such as *however, since,* and *as a result* to show how ideas are connected.<br><br>**See page 866:** Add Transitional Words | ▶ We understand the causes of noise pollution, so we can try to prevent its harmful effects. Living in the world means dealing with noise. However, since we understand the causes of noise pollution, we can try to prevent its harmful effects. |
| **4. Add a question or exclamation where appropriate.**<br>• Reread your essay. Do all your sentences end with periods?<br>• Consider including an exclamation or a question for a change of pace.<br><br>**TIP** Use exclamations and questions sparingly to avoid sounding overexcited or confused. | ▶ Just think how much noise a passing car, truck, bus, train, or motorcycle makes. Then imagine hearing dozens of them at once.? Can you |

# Cause-and-Effect Essay

## Apply the Rubric

**A strong cause-and-effect essay . . .**

☑ has an intriguing introduction

☑ explains an actual cause-and-effect relationship rather than simply showing how one event follows another

☑ includes a thesis statement

☑ uses transitions to signal important causes and effects

☑ supports key ideas with examples, quotations, or other details

☑ is organized logically

☑ uses precise words to help readers understand the causes and effects

☑ includes an occasional question or exclamation for variety

☑ maintains an appropriate tone

☑ summarizes the causes and effects in a compelling conclusion

## Ask a Peer Reader

• How can I improve my introduction?

• Which causes or effects need more explanation?

• Which point that I made was most interesting, surprising, or disturbing? Why?

## Add Transitional Words

| Cause | Effect |
|---|---|
| because | as a result |
| if | consequently |
| provided that | so |
| since | then |
| | therefore |

## Check Your Grammar

Use a comma to set off an introductory word or phrase.

> One afternoon last week, I was sitting in the park.

> As a result, we turn the volume way up when we listen to music at home.

> However, we can try to prevent the harmful effects of noise pollution.

**See page R49:** Quick Reference: Punctuation

## Writing On|ine

**PUBLISHING OPTIONS**
For publishing options, visit the **Writing Center** at ClassZone.com.

**ASSESSMENT PREPARATION**
For writing and grammar assessment practice, go to the **Assessment Center** at ClassZone.com.

## Creating a Multimedia Presentation

Now that you have traced a cause-and-effect relationship, share that information with others by creating a multimedia presentation.

### Planning the Presentation

1. **Decide on your technology.** Ask your school's media specialist about doing a power presentation, a slide show, or an interactive display.

2. **Think about the visuals and audio.** You may be able to present supporting evidence through spoken words, video clips, photographs, animations, maps, charts, or graphs. Consider adding music or sound effects to get your message across.

*Sound effect:* loud jet engines
*Voiceover:* What does this sound do to your ears?

3. **Create a storyboard.** Sketch exactly what your audience will see and hear. Include details about text, voiceovers, music, effects, and other images and sounds.

### Delivering the Presentation

1. **Put it all together.** Scan or download all of your images and sounds onto a computer. Record voiceovers and insert them in the proper places. Create title screens, text, and any other elements you want to include.

   **TIP** Be sure to get permission for words, images, or audio that you did not create yourself.

2. **Share your results.** Deliver your presentation to an audience or invite small groups to explore it on their own.

3. **Find out what others thought.** Ask your audience for positive and negative comments on your presentation. Use the feedback to improve your next presentation.

**DIRECTIONS** Caught by the Sea *is an autobiography, and* The Voyage of the *Frog* *is a novel. Read these excerpts and answer the questions that follow.*

## *from* Caught by the Sea

### Gary Paulsen

The motor suddenly became an intrusion, an ugly sound, and as soon as I was past the jetties and was in open ocean I killed it. For a few seconds, half a minute, we moved on in silence by inertia, coasting from the energy the motor had given us, and then it died and I felt the breeze again on my face as I looked to the rear. It was pushing at the back edge of the sail and I pulled the tiller over to steer off the wind a bit and felt the sail fill. The boat moved differently now, started the dance with the wind and water and moonlight as she heeled slightly and took on life, personality. We glided along in near silence, the only sound the soft gurgle of water along the hull.

10    I did not dare to walk forward in the dark and put up the jib, having never done it before, but she sailed pretty well on the mainsail alone and we kept our course, moving at three or four knots by the speedometer in the cockpit, until daylight some four hours away, when the wind stopped, entirely, and left the dawning ocean as still as a pond and me marooned some twelve miles offshore.

I didn't care. I was completely enraptured by what had happened to me. I lowered the mainsail and sat peacefully drifting around in circles, feeling at home, truly at home.

For the entire morning there was no wind, and while I might have had enough gas to motor partway back to the harbor, there was something wrong about using 20   it on such a beautiful morning. I made a small pot of oatmeal on the little stove and some instant coffee and ate breakfast in the cockpit, letting the morning sun warm me; then I pulled my sleeping bag out of the cabin and laid it in the cockpit and took a small sleep while the boat rocked gently on the swells.

A sound awakened me an hour or so later and I looked over the side to see the boat surrounded by swarms of small fish, maybe anchovies or herring. No sooner did I spot them than pelicans came in and began crash-diving around the boat and then other seabirds arrived, and within minutes a huge pod of dolphins, hundreds of them, showed up. The dolphins began working the school of bait fish, sweeping back and forth like happy wolves, thrashing the water with their 30   tails, perhaps to stun the fish. Then they ate them by the thousands.

While I lay in the calm, all around the boat the sea seethed with life. After the dolphins came some sharks, three or four on call to clean up the debris from the slaughter. In half an hour they were gone, moving off, following the schools of small fish and dolphins and flocks of seabirds.

"Amazing," I said aloud. It was amazing that I would be greeted on the sea with such enthusiasm, amazing that on one of the most populated coasts in the world, near a metropolis that stretched nearly two hundred miles from San Diego to Santa Barbara, where nearly eighteen million people jammed the freeways and sidewalks, I would be completely alone with the sea and my boat; 40 amazing that the planet still held such a place.

# *from* The Voyage of the *Frog*

**Gary Paulsen**

And at two in the morning he saw the light in the water. He saw it first to the stern. In his wake, in the silent bubbles left by the *Frog* moving through the water, there was a rippled, dotted line of eerie light glowing up from the water. It was blue-green, seemed to come from down in the water, and at first it startled and frightened him. But then he remembered hearing about it.

Small animals in the water, microscopic organisms, sometimes phosphoresced—gave off light almost like lightning bugs—when disturbed. He must be going through a mass of them. In back of the *Frog* was a long line of blue light, fading as the water settled down again.

10 He tied the tiller off, leaned over the side, and looked toward the front where the bow cut a wave that curled over.

"Ohhh . . ." It slipped out of his mouth unbidden, almost a sigh of amazement. The boat was moving through blue fire, blue fire in the night. The bow wave was a rolling curve of blue light, sparkled with bits of green that seemed to want to crawl up the side of the boat and then fold back and over, splashing out in ripples and droplets of light.

It could not be as beautiful as it was—not be that beautiful and be real. It was so bright and shining a thing that the *Frog* seemed to be moving through, a lake of cold fire, and as he watched he saw a form move beneath 20 the boat, caught in the blue glow of the bow wave, a torpedo form that shot forward with an incredible burst of speed. He saw first the glowing curved line around the head of the creature and the line showed him that it was the front of a dolphin. All in seconds, in short parts of seconds, he saw the head and the body moving forward beneath the boat and then it exploded—the dolphin blew out of the water in front of the boat.

It rose in a clean curve just in front of the bowsprit, five, six feet out of the water in a leap of joy that only dolphins can make, carrying with it a shroud of splashing blue-green fire that whirled and spiraled in the darkness to follow

the dolphin up, over and down, back into the water and plunging in green light
30 back to the depths beneath the *Frog.*

David was frozen with it, did not know how long he stayed with one hand reaching up as if to touch where the dolphin had been, touch the curve of blue fire. It was all there and gone—just as suddenly gone as if it had never been— and his breath burst suddenly out into the night.

He looked back, expecting to see the dolphin as the boat went over it but there was nothing.

## Comprehension

**DIRECTIONS** *Answer these questions about the excerpt from* Caught by the Sea.

1. Which characteristic of an autobiography can you identify in this excerpt?
   - ○ It shows how Paulsen was affected by the people in his life.
   - ○ It focuses on a memorable event in Paulsen's life.
   - ○ It reveals what other people think about Paulsen.
   - ○ It explains why Paulsen decided to become a writer.

2. One clue that this excerpt is from an autobiography is that the author
   - ○ does not reveal his thoughts
   - ○ stresses how alone he is on his boat
   - ○ uses the first person point of view
   - ○ discusses his childhood experiences

3. Which sentence tells you that Paulsen enjoys his sailing experience?
   - ○ "I lowered the mainsail and sat peacefully drifting around in circles, feeling at home, truly at home."
   - ○ "I made a small pot of oatmeal on the little stove and some instant coffee and ate breakfast in the cockpit. . . . "
   - ○ "I did not dare to walk forward in the dark and put up the jib. . . ."
   - ○ "While I lay in the calm, all around the boat the sea seethed with life."

4. Reread lines 1–5. Paulsen turns off the motor of his boat because he
   - ○ has to save fuel
   - ○ is bothered by its noise
   - ○ senses danger ahead
   - ○ doesn't want to scare the fish

5. In lines 19–20, Paulsen writes that there is "something wrong" about using the motor on a beautiful morning. What can you infer about him from this statement?
   - ○ He worries about disturbing others.
   - ○ He enjoys the peaceful setting.
   - ○ He is learning how to operate the boat.
   - ○ He is hiding from someone.

6. What attracts the seabirds, dolphins, and sharks to the waters around the boat?
   - ○ light from the moon
   - ○ the smell of a human
   - ○ swarms of small fish
   - ○ the sound of the boat's motor

7. If *Caught by the Sea* were a biography instead of an autobiography, the excerpt might have left out
   - ○ Paulsen's expression of his feelings
   - ○ facts about weather conditions
   - ○ information on the boat's location
   - ○ a description of the animals that surround the boat

**DIRECTIONS** *Answer these questions about the excerpt from* The Voyage of the *Frog.*

8. Paulsen's experience as an outdoorsman is reflected in the story's
   ○ point of view
   ○ conflict
   ○ setting
   ○ chronology

9. At first, the "eerie light glowing up from the water" in lines 3–5 causes David to feel
   ○ scared
   ○ giddy
   ○ alone
   ○ confused

10. Reread lines 6–9. Why are the small animals in the water giving off light?
    ○ Their bright light helps them locate food.
    ○ The movement of the boat stirs them up.
    ○ They sense that predators are nearby.
    ○ They are signaling to other fish in the water.

11. Reread lines 26–34. You can infer that David holds his breath when he sees the dolphin because he
    ○ plans to capture the dolphin
    ○ does not want to disturb the dolphin
    ○ is amazed at the sight of the dolphin
    ○ thinks that the dolphin might hurt him

12. When he sees the leaping dolphin and the glowing water around it, David
    ○ tries to sail after the dolphin
    ○ reaches out as if to touch what he sees
    ○ hides in the bow of the boat
    ○ shouts out in disbelief

13. The presence of a dolphin suggests that the *Frog* is sailing in
    ○ an ocean
    ○ a stream
    ○ a pond
    ○ a river

**DIRECTIONS** *Refer to both selections to answer this question.*

14. The excerpt from *The Voyage of the* Frog reflects which experience in Paulsen's background?
    ○ staying up all night to watch the sunrise
    ○ getting an unexpected glimpse of sea animals
    ○ cooking and sleeping on a boat
    ○ learning how to operate a sailboat

# Constructed Response

**SHORT ANSWER** *Write two or three sentences to answer the questions.*

15. Name two things Paulsen finds amazing in the excerpt from *Caught by the Sea.* Use quotations from the excerpt to support your answer.

16. Choose one experience described in *The Voyage of the* Frog that is similar to Paulsen's experiences in *Caught by the Sea,* and explain the similarity between the two.

**ESSAY** *Write a paragraph to answer this question.*

17. Reread lines 1–9 and 15–17 in *Caught by the Sea.* What effect does his sailing experience have on Paulsen? Support your answer with examples from the excerpt.

**GO ON** ➡

# Vocabulary

**DIRECTIONS** *Use context clues and your knowledge of homographs to answer the following questions.*

1. Which sentence uses *pod* as it is used in line 27 of the excerpt from *Caught by the Sea?*

   ". . . within minutes a huge <u>pod</u> of dolphins, hundreds of them, showed up."

   ○ The divers descended to the ocean floor in a small pod.

   ○ A pod of gray whales was visible from the shore.

   ○ The pod separated from the spacecraft during reentry.

   ○ Some insects lay eggs in clusters that are called pods.

2. Which sentence uses *wake* as it is used in line 2 of the excerpt from *The Voyage of the* Frog?

   "In his <u>wake</u>, in the silent bubbles left by the *Frog* moving through the water. . . ."

   ○ The floodwaters ruined every house and barn in their wake.

   ○ After the admiral died, the sailors held his wake at sea.

   ○ A small boat can be swamped in the wake of a larger ship.

   ○ Some of the passengers on the cruise ship did not wake up until noon.

3. Which sentence uses *bow* as it is used in line 11 of the excerpt from *The Voyage of the* Frog?

   "He tied the tiller off, leaned over the side, and looked toward the front where the <u>bow</u> cut a wave that curled over."

   ○ The pianist took a bow after her performance.

   ○ He wrapped a big blue bow across the boat.

   ○ It is hard to catch fish with a bow and arrow.

   ○ I saw the sunrise from the bow of the ship.

4. Which sentence uses *fold* as it is used in line 15 of the excerpt from *The Voyage of the* Frog?

   "The bow wave was a rolling curve of blue light, sparkled with bits of green that seemed to want to crawl up the side of the boat and then <u>fold</u> back and over. . . ."

   ○ You can fold the newspaper so it will fit into your backpack.

   ○ The owner had to fold his company because he was leaving the city.

   ○ The farmer kept his sheep in a large fold behind the barn.

   ○ The grandparents welcomed the new baby into the fold.

**DIRECTIONS** *Use context clues and your knowledge of denotation and connotation to answer the following questions.*

5. The word *thrashing* in line 29 of the excerpt from *Caught by the Sea* has a connotation of

   ○ sadness          ○ forcefulness

   ○ intelligence     ○ rudeness

6. The denotation of the word *seethed* in line 31 of the excerpt from *Caught by the Sea* is "bubbled or foamed." What is its connotation?

   ○ secrecy          ○ movement

   ○ gentleness       ○ happiness

7. The word *exploded* in line 24 of the excerpt from *The Voyage of the* Frog has a connotation of

   ○ speed            ○ heaviness

   ○ hardness         ○ clumsiness

# Writing & Grammar

**DIRECTIONS** *Read this passage and answer the questions that follow.*

(1) Dolphins live in water. (2) Many people think of them as fish. (3) They are actually mammals. (4) The following are different types of dolphins the bottle-nosed dolphin, the common dolphin, and the white-sided dolphin. (5) All dolphins share the following characteristics smooth skin, flippers, and a blowhole. (6) Dolphins have no sense of smell. (7) They have a keen sense of hearing. (8) They can detect sounds that humans cannot. (9) Dolphins have been trained to perform in amusement parks, zoos, and aquariums, to retrieve objects, and to guard military ships.

**1.** Choose the correct way to combine sentences 1, 2, and 3 into one compound-complex sentence.

- ○ Dolphins live in water, so many people think of them as fish, but they are actually mammals.
- ○ Dolphins live in water, and many people think of them as fish, but they are actually mammals.
- ○ Because dolphins live in water, many people think of them as fish, but they are actually mammals.
- ○ Dolphins are actually mammals living in water, although many people think of them as fish.

**2.** In sentence 4, a colon should be placed after which word?

- ○ following
- ○ are
- ○ of
- ○ dolphins

**3.** In sentence 5, a colon should be placed after which word?

- ○ share
- ○ following
- ○ characteristics
- ○ skin

**4.** Choose the correct way to combine sentences 6, 7, and 8 into one compound-complex sentence.

- ○ Though dolphins have no sense of smell, they have a keen sense of hearing, and they can detect sounds that humans cannot.
- ○ Having no sense of smell but a keen sense of hearing, dolphins can detect sounds that humans cannot.
- ○ Dolphins have no sense of smell but a keen sense of hearing, enabling them to detect sounds that humans cannot.
- ○ Despite having no sense of smell, dolphins have a keen sense of hearing, detecting sounds that humans cannot.

**5.** In sentence 9, a semicolon should be placed after which words?

- ○ to, aquariums, objects
- ○ parks, zoos, aquariums, objects
- ○ perform, retrieve, guard
- ○ aquariums, objects

**STOP**

## Ideas for Independent Reading

Which questions from Unit 7 made an impression on you?
Continue exploring them with these books.

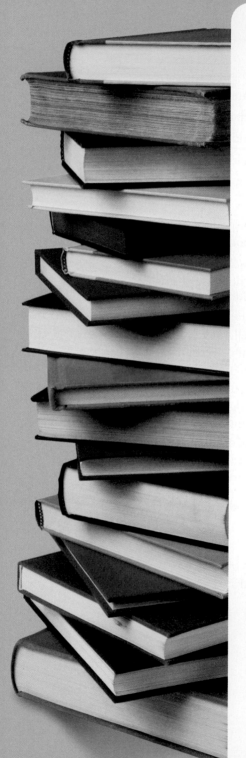

# *Where do we get our values?*

### Betsy and the Emperor
*by Staton Rabin*

After years at boarding school, 14-year-old Betsy is back home on St. Helena. Her family is hosting a special "guest": Napoleon, the former emperor of France, is a prisoner at Betsy's house. What can an ex-emperor and a rebellious teenager have in common?

### Lizzie Bright and the Buckminster Boy
*by Gary D. Schmidt*

People in Phippsburg, Maine, don't like it when Turner befriends Lizzie Bright, who lives in a nearby African-American settlement. When the town evicts Lizzie's community, Turner helps fight back.

### Part of Me
*by Kimberly Willis Holt*

Raised in Louisiana during the Great Depression, Rose never gets to college, but she tries to pass on her love of books to her children and grandchildren. Although not all of them follow in her footsteps, the family stories help each generation stay strong.

# *What can you learn from a job?*

### Code Talker
*By Joseph Bruchac*

World War II is raging, and Ned wants to help. He joins the Marines and becomes a secret Navajo code talker. He helps create a code that can't be cracked, and then uses it to send and receive messages in the midst of battle. Will Ned survive the fighting?

### Gathering Blue
*by Lois Lowry*

In the future, when society is in ruins from disasters, a crippled orphan like Kira is often destined to die. But Kira's weaving skills are discovered, and suddenly she's important. If only her new job didn't bring with it serious problems.

### Ghost Boy
*Iain Lawrence*

Harold is an albino, and in his small town he's an outcast. When the circus comes to town, Harold leaves with it, immediately accepted by members of the sideshow. He soon finds out that even in the circus, he and his friends are considered strange.

# *How can we fight injustice?*

### Stop The Train!
*by Geraldine McCaughrean*

In 1893, people came to Florence, Oklahoma, searching for a stake in a new prairie town. Now the Red Rock Railroad Company refuses to stop in Florence. The new town is sure to die unless the settlers can find a way to get the train to stop.

### The Outcasts of 19 Schuyler Place
*by E.L. Konigsburg*

Margaret Rose is happy to be rescued from Camp Talequa by her uncles. But they seem to accept that the town wants to destroy the three beautiful towers they built in the backyard. Someone has to save these works of art.

### Warriors Don't Cry
*by Melba Pattillo Beals*

Melba Pattillo Beals was one of the nine African-American teenagers who integrated the Little Rock Central High School in 1957. In this memoir, she describes both the violent protesters she faced as well as the people and ideals that gave her courage and hope.

# UNIT 8

# Believe It or Not

## FACTS AND INFORMATION

- In Nonfiction
- In Media

# Where do you get your FACTS?

You don't go a single day without needing to gather some **facts.** With message boards, magazines, books, and directories all offering you information, where do you turn when you need an answer you can count on? It depends on what kind of facts you're looking for, and what you need to know.

*ACTIVITY* Work with a partner to analyze where you get your information.

- Make a list of five or six facts that you might look for in a typical day.

- Next to each fact, write one or more sources in which you might find it.

- Share your list with others. Do you get most of your facts from printed material, from the Internet, or from somewhere else?

- Discuss which of these sources are most trustworthy and which are easiest to use.

**1000 GREAT RAIL-TRAILS**
A COMPREHENSIVE DIRECTORY
**Third Edition**

THE OFFICIAL RAILS-TO-TRAILS CONSERVANCY DIRECTORY

## Preview Unit Goals

 **INDIANA STANDARDS**

**READING**
- Identify main idea and supporting details
- Identify and analyze author's purpose
- Distinguish between fact and opinion
- Adjust reading rate to purpose
- Summarize main ideas in an article
- Take notes
- Use text features to comprehend and locate information
- Interpret and evaluate graphic aids

**WRITING AND GRAMMAR**
- Write a problem-solution essay
- Capitalize titles correctly
- Use commas correctly after introductory words and phrases

**SPEAKING, LISTENING, AND VIEWING**
- Interpret how events and information are presented in the news
- Compare how different media cover the same event
- Deliver an oral report

**VOCABULARY**
- Apply knowledge of base words, affixes, and root words to determine the meaning of words
- Use word origins to help understand how other languages have influenced English word meaning

**ACADEMIC VOCABULARY**
- main idea
- supporting details
- summarize
- text features
- graphic aids

# Reading Informational Text

You are living in an age of information. In a matter of minutes, you can find magazine articles, Web sites, and blogs on just about any topic, from global warming to cell-phone technology. But how can you be sure you're getting the most out of what you're reading? What's the best way to wade through all those facts and figures? Learning a few strategies can help you navigate through a sea of information, find answers to your questions, and remember what you've learned.

## Part 1: Text Features

Time is money in the fast-paced, modern world. So, it's important to be able to find information quickly when you're searching through Web sites, books, and magazines. One way to locate useful information at a glance is to notice the text features writers use. **Text features** include titles, subheadings, captions, sidebars, boldfaced words, bulleted lists, and links. These elements allow you to see the most important ideas without having to read every word.

Consider the following article from the back of a "Fun Facts" pamphlet. By scanning the text features, you can anticipate what information the article include before deciding to read further.

INDIANA STANDARDS

**READING STANDARD**
**8.2.7** Analyze the structure, format, and purpose of informational materials (such as textbooks, newspapers, instructional or technical manuals, and public documents).

**❶** The **title** reveals the topic of the article— the history of hot dogs.

**❷** **Subheadings** highlight what each section of the article is about.

**❸** A **sidebar** provides more information.

**❹** A **bulleted list** presents information in an easy-to-read format.

---

# The History of ❶ Hot Dogs

## Hot Dogs in Europe ❷

There are several different theories about the origin of the hot dog. Traditionally, Frankfurt-am-Main, Germany, is credited with originating the frankfurter.

### Hot Dog Specialties ❸

- ❹ In the South, people like their hot dogs "dragged through the garden" with a cole-slaw type topping.
- New Yorkers like their hot dogs served with steamed onions and pale yellow mustard.
- Folks in Kansas City enjoy hot dogs with sauerkraut and Swiss cheese.

## All-American Dogs

Another story points to the Louisiana Purchase Exposition in 1904. A concessionaire sold hot dogs as plain sausages, and provided customers with white gloves for easier eating. After the gloves were not returned, he consulted a baker, who designed the "hot dog bun" to protect eaters' fingers.

One of the more credible stories comes from Barry Popick, a prominent hot dog historian at Roosevelt University. He claims the term began appearing in college magazines in the 1890s. Yale students kept referring to wagons selling hot sausages in buns outside their dorms as "dog wagons." It didn't take long for the use of the word *dog* to become "hot dog."

## MODEL: TEXT FEATURES

Skim the text features in this Web article. What information do you think the article will provide? Now read the full article and answer the questions.

BACK  FORWARD  STOP  REFRESH  HOME  PRINT

| Articles | Games | Fun Facts | Home |

# DANGER from the Sky

That's not Swiss cheese up there. The <u>craters</u> that cover much of the Moon's surface were caused by collisions with space objects billions of years ago. In 1953 an astronomer even caught on film
5  the bright flash of an object hitting the Moon. With so much evidence of objects hitting our nearest neighbor, scientists wonder when another large object from space will strike our planet.

<u>See More Photos</u>

## Impacts on Earth

10  Earth's <u>atmosphere</u> protects us from collisions with small objects, which burn up in the air. However, when a large object strikes Earth, the atmosphere can spread the effects of the impact far beyond the crater. A large collision may throw dust high into the air, where it can be carried around the globe. The dust can block sunlight for months and sharply lower global temperatures.

15      About 65 million years ago, a large space object struck Earth. At about the same time, most species of organisms died out, including the dinosaurs. Many scientists think that the results of this collision caused the global devastation.

## Risk of a Meteorite Collision

When will the next space object hit Earth?
20  A collision is probably occurring as you read this sentence. Tiny particles hit Earth's atmosphere all the time. Some of these particles have enough mass to make it through the atmosphere.

Objects that reach Earth's surface are called
25  <u>meteorites.</u> Most meteorites splash harmlessly into the ocean or hit unpopulated areas. However, every few years a meteorite damages a home or other property.

—by Miguel Lopez

**TRACKING ASTEROIDS**
Although Earth is unlikely to have a major collision with a space object anytime soon, scientists feel the danger is too great to ignore. They are using telescopes to find large, rocky space objects called <u>asteroids</u>. After locating an asteroid, they use computer models to predict its path.

### Close Read

1. If you were doing a report on meteorites, would this article be useful to you? Explain which text feature helped you find the answer.

2. Summarize the information that appears under the subheading *Impacts on Earth*. Write another subheading that the author could have used.

3. What additional information does the sidebar provide?

# Part 2: Main Idea and Supporting Details

After you preview a text, you're ready to examine it more closely. The following strategies can help you to better understand what you are reading and gather the information you need.

## IDENTIFYING MAIN IDEAS

The **topic** of a piece of nonfiction is what the text is about. A topic can usually be stated in a word or two, such as *pets* or *dog training*. The **main idea** is the most important idea that a writer wants to share about a topic. The main idea might be the focus of a single paragraph, a section, or the entire article. For example, a main idea might be "The most important factor in dog training is consistent communication."

| | LENGTH | EXAMPLE |
|---|---|---|
| **TOPIC** | one or two words | dog training |
| **MAIN IDEA** | sentence | The most important factor in dog training is consistent communication. |

Often, the main idea of a paragraph or section is directly stated in a **topic sentence,** which is usually the first or the last sentence in that paragraph or section. The facts and examples the writer provides as support for the main idea are called **supporting details.** Sometimes, the main idea is implied, which means it's not directly stated. In that case, you need to **infer** the main idea by looking for what the supporting details add up to. Identifying the main idea of each section or paragraph can help you determine the main idea of the entire article.

Examine this paragraph from "Danger from the Sky." Notice how the main idea and supporting details work together to form a paragraph. The main idea of this paragraph can help you figure out the main idea of the entire article—that our risk of a major collision with space objects is low.

Although Earth is unlikely to have a major collision with a space object anytime soon, scientists feel the danger is too great to ignore. They are using telescopes to find large, rocky space objects called asteroids. After locating an asteroid, they use computer models to predict its path.

Notice that the **main idea** is directly stated: The danger of a major collision between Earth and a space object, though unlikely, is too great to ignore.

These facts **support** the main idea by explaining what scientists are doing to predict dangerous collisions.

## MODEL 1: MAIN IDEA AND DETAILS

Read this article about a lifelike robot created by a Korean scientist.

# Female Android Debuts

Article by **Victoria Gilman**

These school-age tots seem to be making friends with EveR-1, a female android that made her debut in South Korea. The robot was built by
5 Baeg Moon-hong, a senior researcher with the Division for Applied Robot Technology at the Korea Institute of Industrial Technology in Ansan, just south of Seoul.
10 **Meet EveR-1** EveR-1 is designed to resemble a Korean female in her early 20s. Fifteen motors underneath her silicon skin allow her to express a limited range of emotions, and a 400-
15 word vocabulary enables her to hold a simple conversation. The android weighs 110 pounds and would stand 5

**Children check out Korean android EveR-1.**

feet, 3 inches tall—if she could stand.
20 EveR-1 can move her arms and hands, but her lower half is immobile.

**Not Alone** Researchers at Osaka University in Japan unveiled their own life-size female android, Repliee Q1. That robot could "speak," and gesture
25 and even appeared to breathe but, like EveR-1, was only mobile from the waist up.

**Close Read**

1. The main idea of the *Meet EveR-1* section is boxed. Identify the details that support it.

2. What is the main idea of the section with the subheading *Not Alone?*

## MODEL 2: MAIN IDEA AND DETAILS

This article is about deadly poisons. Skim the title and the subheading, and answer the first **Close Read** question. Then read the article more closely to help you answer the second question.

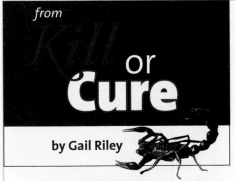

from
# Kill or Cure
by Gail Riley

Night falls in an Israeli desert. A cockroach skitters across the sand. Suddenly, a scorpion grabs the cockroach in its pincers. It
5 injects searing venom into its victim through its stinger. The venom causes paralysis. The cockroach cannot move. It can do nothing to fend off the scorpion's attack.

10 **Toxic Treatments**
It's hard to believe, but the deadly venom that paralyzed the cockroach can be used to heal rather than harm. Scientists are experimenting with the Israeli scorpion's venom. Some of them believe it has the power to shrink brain tumors. For hundreds of years, scientists have been experimenting
15 with poisons extracted from animals and plants. They have found that the same toxins that can injure or kill can also be used to treat health problems.

**Close Read**

1. Based on the title and the subheading, what do you think the main idea of the article will be?

2. Identify the main idea that the boxed sentences are supporting.

## TAKING NOTES

Have you ever read an article on a fascinating subject—talking robots or life-saving poisons, for example—and later realized that you couldn't recall a single thing about it? Taking notes as you read can help you retain the main ideas and imprint them on your memory. There's something about finding, organizing, and recording the most critical information that can really help you learn.

Your notes can take any number of forms, including an outline, a bulleted list, or a graphic organizer, such as a word web or a Y-chart. The form you use isn't as important as the information you include. As you read, try to determine what information is most important, then restate it in your own words.

Notice how information from one of the articles you just read can be organized in two different ways.

*OUTLINE*

I. EveR-I resembles a Korean female in her 20s.
  A. Made in South Korea
  B. Can show emotion, talk, and move her arms
  C. Can only move the top half of her body

II. Repliee QI is another life-size female android.
  A. Made in Japan
  B. Can talk, move her arms, and looks like she's breathing
  C. Can only move the top half of her body

*GRAPHIC ORGANIZER*

**EveR-I**
- made in South Korea
- shows emotion

**Repliee QI**
- made in Japan
- looks like she's breathing

**Both**
- female android
- can talk
- moves her arms
- only top half moves

If you own the book, newspaper, or magazine you are reading, you might use a highlighter to mark the main ideas and supporting details. If you don't own the text, you can use colored sticky notes to flag important information. Just make sure to remove them after you've finished organizing your notes.

Both South Korea and Japan have developed life-like female androids. Only the top half of each android moves. (from Science News, B20)

* I wonder if other robots are in development. What will new advances in technology bring?

## Part 3: Analyze the Text

Preview this article and answer the first **Close Read** question. Then read the article more closely, using the other questions to help you take notes.

# THE
# *Great Chicago Fire*
## OF 1871

Magazine article
by **Michael Burgan**

$R$ECIPE FOR DISASTER Chicago in 1871 was already a big city, bustling with more than 334,000 residents. Its streets, sidewalks, and most of its buildings were made of wood. Hay and straw were inside every barn. To make the situation worse, people used candles and oil lamps.

5    Fires had been common that year because of the dry weather. The Chicago Fire Department was overworked and underequipped. On Saturday, October 7, firefighters began putting out a fire that wiped out four city blocks. It took them 16 hours. By Sunday evening the men were exhausted. Then around 8:45 P.M., a fire began in the barn of Patrick and Catherine O'Leary.

10 **"EVERYTHING WENT WRONG"**

Human error then made a bad situation worse. One firefighter later said, "From the beginning of that fatal fire, everything went wrong!" A watchman atop the 15 courthouse saw smoke rising from the O'Leary barn, but he assumed it was coming from the previous fire. When he finally realized a new fire was blazing, he misjudged its location. His assistant 20 sent a message to the fire stations, but he mistakenly directed horse-drawn fire wagons to a location about a mile from the burning barn. When the fire department finally reached the barn, its equipment 25 was no match for the blaze. The new fire raged on.

**OUT OF CONTROL**

As the fire blazed, there arose a deafening roar—wood crackling as flames devoured 30 it, cries for help, explosions from oil and gas tanks, the crash of falling buildings. The fire department could do nothing to stop the fire. Around 4 A.M. the next day, the fire destroyed the city's waterworks, 35 shutting off water to the fire hydrants. Firefighters had to drag water in buckets from Lake Michigan and the Chicago River. City officials made a desperate call for help to other cities, but their forces 40 arrived too late. The fire kept burning— totally out of control.

**THE AFTERMATH**

The Great Fire burned until October 10, when rain finally fell. Thousands of 45 buildings had been destroyed. About 300 people had died in the blaze, and more than 100,000 were left homeless.

### Close Read

1. Preview the title and subheadings. What information do you think this article will provide?

2. Describe the main idea that the boxed details support. Copy the main idea and details into your notebook. Add letters as necessary.

> I.
>   A.
>   B.

3. The main idea of the second section is listed here. Copy it into your notebook, along with the supporting details.

> II. *Human error made a bad situation even worse.*
>   A.
>   B.

4. Identify the main idea and details in the third and fourth sections. Add the information to your outline.

> III.
>   A.
>   B. *The fire destroyed the city's waterworks.*
> IV.
>   A. *300 people died.*
>   B.

## The Spider Man Behind *Spider-Man*
Feature Article by Bijal P. Trivedi

# *What is your*
# DREAM JOB?

**INDIANA STANDARDS**

**READING STANDARDS**
**8.2.7** Analyze the structure, format, and purpose of informational materials (such as textbooks, newspapers, instructional or technical manuals, and public documents).

**8.3.2** Evaluate the structural elements of the plot . . . .

**KEY IDEA** Ever since you were little, people have probably asked you what you want to be when you grow up. Now that you're older and know yourself better, your dream job might be coming into focus. Is it a job that would take you outdoors? Onto a movie set? Into a sports arena? Your ideal **career** probably reflects your individual talents, interests, and personality. In the following article, you'll read about a man who turned his passion into a dream job.

**SURVEY** Interview several classmates to find out what their dream jobs would be. Ask these students why they chose the jobs they did. How do their dream careers compare to your own?

| Name | Dream Job | Why? |
|------|-----------|------|
| Kayla | Veterinarian | 1. Likes taking care of animals<br>2. Gets good grades in science<br>3. Enjoys learning about animals |

## ● ELEMENTS OF NONFICTION: TEXT FEATURES

Nonfiction articles often contain **text features,** design elements that help organize the material and identify key ideas. Common text features include

- **headings**—the title of the article
- **subheadings**—headings that signal the beginning of a new topic or section within a written piece
- **sidebars**—additional information set in a box alongside, below, or within an article
- **bulleted lists**—lists of items of equal value or importance. This list of text features is an example of a bulleted list.

Recognizing text features can help you find information. As you read "The Spider Man Behind *Spider-Man,*" notice how the text features clue you in to the topics and key ideas.

## ● READING STRATEGY: SUMMARIZE

Have you ever told a friend about a movie you just saw? If so, you probably gave your friend a summary. When you **summarize** a piece of writing, you briefly retell the main ideas or key points. Summarizing is a way to check your understanding, and it can help you remember information. As you read "The Spider Man Behind *Spider-Man,*" use a chart to take notes on the key points. Later, you'll use these notes to summarize the article.

| What Steven Kutcher Does | His Training and Background | His Spider-Man Experience |
|---|---|---|
| | | |

## ▲ VOCABULARY IN CONTEXT

The boldfaced words help the author describe one man's interesting career. Try using context clues to figure out what each word means.

1. He has the **perseverance** necessary to finish the job.
2. Bill is an **engaging** person whom everyone likes.
3. Maria has the **potential** to become a first-rate scientist.
4. Ashley's watercolor **rendition** of her dream earned praise from her art teacher.

# Author Online

**A Love of Science**
Bijal Trivedi (bĭj′əl trē-vä′dē) became fascinated with dinosaurs at the age of nine. Soon after, she transferred her interest to the space shuttle and astronomy. From an early age, it was clear that Trivedi's dream job would involve science.

**Bijal P. Trivedi
born 1970**

**Exciting Places and Discoveries** Trivedi studied science in college and earned master's degrees in both biology and science journalism. Because Trivedi didn't want to work in a lab, she became a science writer. She has written for magazines such as *National Geographic, Popular Science,* and *Wired.* She says, "Being a science writer is a bit like being Indiana Jones—you get to travel with lots of smart scientists to exciting places and then write stories about their discoveries." Trivedi has won several awards for her journalism.

**MORE ABOUT THE AUTHOR**
For more on Bijal P. Trivedi, visit the **Literature Center** at **ClassZone.com.**

## *Background*

**The Amazing Spider-Man** In 1962, writer Stan Lee and artist Steve Ditko created the character of Peter Parker, a teenager who gains spider-like powers through the bite of a radioactive spider and becomes Spider-Man. Spider-Man first appeared in an issue of *Amazing Fantasy* by Marvel Comics and then gained a comic book series all his own. *The Amazing Spider-Man* comics have been popular ever since. In the movies about the superhero, CGI, or computer-generated imagery, made it appear that Peter Parker could swing from one tall building to another, stick to walls, and do other incredible feats that only a Spider-Man could do.

# THE SPIDER MAN
# BEHIND
# SPIDER-MAN

### Bijal P. Trivedi

**E**ntomologist Steven Kutcher is the spider man behind *Spider-Man*. "He's the guy to call in Hollywood when you need insects—he is the ultimate insect trainer," says Robin Miller, property master for the movie *Spider-Man*.

"I know how to get a cockroach to run across the floor and flip onto its back. I can get cockroaches, beetles, and spiders to crawl to a quarter four feet away on cue. I can make bees swarm indoors and I can repair butterfly wings," says Kutcher. He has even made a live wasp fly into an actor's mouth. "I study insect behavior, and learn what they do and then adapt the behavior to what the director wants," says Kutcher. **A**

## Passion for Bugs **B**

Kutcher's love of insects began as a toddler when he collected fireflies in New York. But he was also influenced by very "positive early childhood experiences in nature" when his family would spend summers in the Catskills.[1] "Something about seeing fish, catching butterflies, lit a fire within me," says Kutcher.

Kutcher followed his passion for bugs and studied entomology in college, receiving his B.S. from the University of California, Davis, and later an M.A. in biology—with an emphasis on entomology,[2] insect behavior, and ecology[3] from the California State University in Long Beach.
20 He had planned to pursue a Ph.D.,[4] but when he wasn't accepted at the graduate school of his choice he decided to reevaluate his career options.

---

1. **Catskills** (kăt'skĭlz'): the Catskill Mountain region in New York state. It is a popular vacation area.
2. **entomology** (ĕn'tə-mŏl'ə-jē): the study of insects.
3. **ecology** (ĭ-kŏl'ə-jē): the study of relationships among living things and their environment.
4. **B.S.; M.A.; Ph.D.:** Bachelor of Science, an undergraduate degree; Master of Arts, a graduate degree; Doctor of Philosophy, a graduate degree that is usually more time-consuming and difficult to earn than a master's degree.

---

**A** **SUMMARIZE**
What are some of Kutcher's unique skills? Record them in your chart.

**B** **TEXT FEATURES**
On the basis of this **subheading** and what you've read so far, what information do you expect to find in this section?

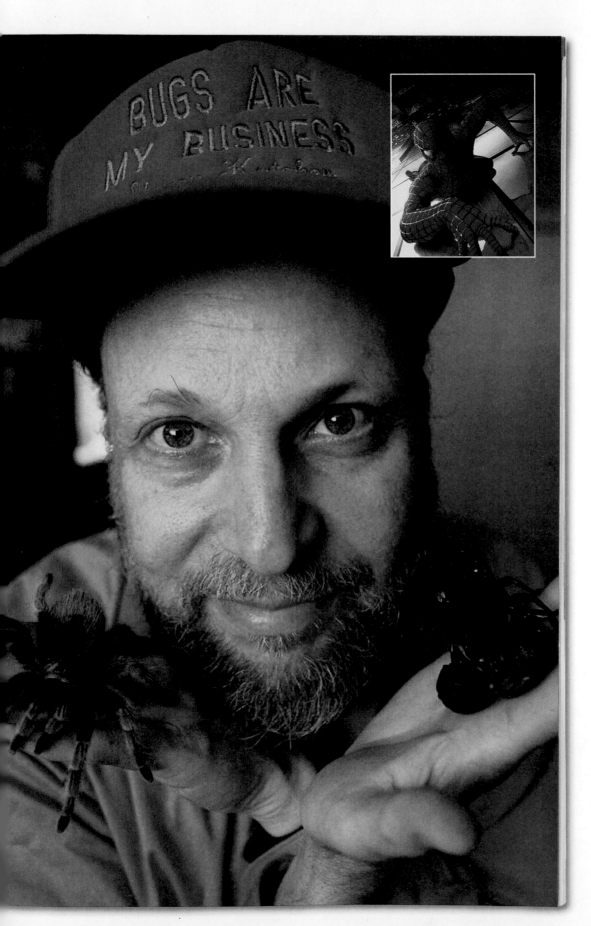

**ANALYZE VISUALS**
Based on this photo of Steven Kutcher, what can you **infer** about his interests and personality?

**potential** (pə-tĕn'shəl)
*n.* the ability to grow or
develop

One day he received a call from his former academic advisor asking him to baby-sit 3,000 locusts that were to be used for the movie *Exorcist 2.* Kutcher had to place the locusts wherever they were needed, including on the stars Richard Burton and Linda Blair. That was his first job, and it has been Hollywood creepy crawlies ever since.

After doing a long survey of movies Kutcher found that about one third of all movies had an insect in it. "I saw immediate job **potential,**" Kutcher says.

30 Almost 25 years after his first job Kutcher now holds an impressive list of movie, television, music video, and commercial credits that include his biggest movie, *Arachnophobia,* the comedy-thriller in which a California town is overrun with deadly spiders. He also supervised the bug and spider stunts in *Alien, Contact, Jurassic Park, Pacific Heights,* and *Wild Wild West.*

**engaging** (ĕn-gāj'ĭng) *adj.*
charming; likeable

"He is a very observant and **engaging** guy," says Lucinda Strub, a special effects person who worked with Kutcher on *Arachnophobia.* "One of his main goals is to educate the public about how fascinating and interesting insects are. He is really out to teach people about bugs," says Strub, who then . . . clarified that "of course spiders are not bugs, they are arachnids."

# So You Want to Be an Entomologist?

**D**o you get grossed out when you see a spider or earwig[5] crawling up your wall? Or does the spider's web and the inchworm's movement fascinate you? If the latter question describes you, then entomology could be the perfect career for you.

Entomologists study the classification, life cycle, and habits of insects and related life forms, and plan and implement insect surveys and pest management programs. They also investigate ways to control insect pests and manage beneficial insects such as plant pollinators,[6] insect parasites, and insect predators.

**Interests and Skills**
Entomologists need the intellect, curiosity, creativity, patience, and **perseverance** required to pursue answers to complex research questions about bugs. Because there are thousands and thousands of insect species, entomologists must also have a good memory. Entomologists must be able to work well both independently and as part of a team.

**perseverance**
(pûr'sə-vîr'əns) *n.* steady
persistence in sticking to
a course of action

---

5. **earwig** (îr-wĭg'): an insect that has two pincers protruding from the rear of its abdomen.

6. **pollinators** (pŏl'ə-nāt'tərs): animals that carry pollen from one plant to another, causing the plants to produce fruit.

40    Even with his busy filmmaking schedule, Kutcher still finds time to teach once a week at a local community college. He also started the annual Insect Fair at the Los Angeles Arboretum. **C**

## The Perfect Match

Kutcher's most recent challenge has been finding the perfect spider for the movie *Spider-Man. . . .* The concept designer for the movie produced a computer **rendition** that combined traits of up to four arachnids to create an image of the mutant spider that bites Peter Parker (a.k.a. Spider-Man) and endows him with spider powers. **D**

50    "I was given this drawing of a spider that didn't exist and told to find a real spider that matched it," says Miller, whose responsibilities include assembling all the props in the entire film. The spider resembled a black widow, which wasn't an option because its bite is too dangerous.

    Miller contacted Steven Kutcher and showed him the picture. Kutcher then arranged a "spider Olympics" for *Spider-Man* director Sam Raimi. Kutcher brought in different types of spiders to showcase the talents of each, says Miller. "He literally had the spiders doing tricks." One spider

**C** SUMMARIZE
Reread lines 22–42. What are two of the most important pieces of information you get from these paragraphs? Add them to your chart.

**rendition** (rĕn-dĭsh′ən) *n.* a pictorial representation; an interpretation

**D** TEXT FEATURES
Reread the **subheading** and first sentence of this section. What "perfect match" does the subheading refer to?

## Typical Tasks

- Study the evolution of insects
- Discover and describe new species of insects
- Conduct research into the impact and control of insect pest problems
- Conduct field and laboratory tests of pesticides to evaluate their effect on different species of insects under different conditions
- Curate museum insect collections
- Prepare publications that make it possible to identify insect, spider, mite, and tick species
- Coordinate public awareness and education programs **E**

**AVERAGE EARNINGS**

**Maximum Salary: $71,270**

**Average Salary: $47,740**

**Entry Level Salary: $29,260**

## Educational Paths

Students interested in a career working with insects should prepare for college by taking a variety of science classes. Many students get a general undergraduate degree in biology or zoology[7] and then specialize in entomology at the post-graduate level. For those wishing to lead research teams or teach at the university level, a Ph.D. is a requirement. **F**

**E** TEXT FEATURES
What does this **bulleted list** help you better understand?

**F** TEXT FEATURES
What does the information presented in the blue **sidebar** add to your understanding of Steven Kutcher and his career?

---

7. **zoology** (zōō-ŏl′ə-jē): the study of animals.

could jump, another was able to spin webs very quickly, and yet another was able to produce a drag line and essentially swing out of the way—all activities that Spider-Man can do.

The spider that Raimi selected was *Steatoda grossa,* a brown spider with a smooth, swollen body and thin twiggy legs. The problem was that the color was wrong, "we needed a spider that had metallic blue and a radioactive[8] red-orange color to it," says Miller.

The answer was spider make-up. Originally Kutcher wanted to make an entire costume for the spider, but the timing came down to the wire and he finally settled on body paint. "I had to find a non-toxic[9] paint, design a little harness to hold the spider as he was painted, and supervise the artist painting *Steatoda.*"

The *Steatoda grossa* spider

"I need the spider to go from A to B to C and Steve can train it to do that," says Miller, who has worked with Kutcher on several movies. "He is very creative; he can figure out how to get the creature to do what he wants while being very delicate," says Strub.

Why, in this age of computer-generated special effects, did the director simply not animate the spider? "The real thing always looks best, especially when it fills the whole movie screen," says Miller. And computer-generated graphics are very expensive, although the scene where the mutant spider bites Peter Parker is computer-generated.

"People find me, and I'm off on these adventures," says Kutcher, "problem solving, and exploring, and teaching, and educating people about insects." But Steven Kutcher's hat best describes his life, his love, and his philosophy: "Bugs are my business." **G**

**G** **SUMMARIZE**
What crucial jobs did Kutcher perform in the making of *Spider-Man?* Add these to the appropriate section of your chart.

---

8. **radioactive** (rā′dē-ō-ăk′tĭv): exhibiting radiation emissions that possibly result from a nuclear explosion.

9. **non-toxic:** not poisonous or otherwise life-threatening.

## Comprehension

1. **Recall** What was Steven Kutcher's first experience on a movie set?

2. **Recall** Why did the makers of *Spider-Man* want to use a real spider instead of a computer-generated spider for most of the spider scenes?

3. **Clarify** Why was it such a challenge for Kutcher to find the perfect spider for the movie *Spider-Man?*

INDIANA STANDARDS

**READING STANDARD**
**8.2.7** Analyze the structure, format, and purpose of informational materials ....

## Critical Analysis

4. **Examine Text Features** Which text features help you find the following pieces of information? Note your answers in a chart like the one shown.

| Information | Text Feature That Helps You Find It |
|---|---|
| Broad focus of the article | |
| Kutcher's interest in bugs | |
| Typical tasks performed by entomologists | |
| General information about entomologists | |

5. **Compare Summaries** Using the chart you made as you read, write a summary of the entire article. Next, trade summaries with a classmate. Compare the summary you received with the article to see if the summary is complete. Share your findings with your classmate, and then revise your own summary as needed.

6. **Make Generalizations** A generalization is a broad statement about a group of people or a topic. Based on the information given in the article and the sidebar, what's one generalization you can make about the kind of people who become entomologists?

7. **Draw Conclusions** Reread lines 11–15 and 35–42. Why do you think Kutcher wants other people to have a better understanding of insects?

## Extension and Challenge

8. **Big Question Activity** What was your answer to the big question on page 884? Using books or the Internet, find out what skills or education you might need for this **career.** Present this information in a format similar to the sidebar on pages 888–889.

9. **Creative Project: Music** Alone or in a small group, create a song or rap from the point of view of an insect who "works" for Steven Kutcher. Look back at the article to help you recall some of the things these creatures have been trained to do and Kutcher's attitude toward what some people call "creepy crawlies." Share your song or rap with the class.

# Vocabulary in Context

## VOCABULARY PRACTICE

Decide whether the words in each pair are synonyms (words with similar meanings) or antonyms (words with opposite meanings).

1. perseverance/laziness
2. rendition/interpretation
3. engaging/disagreeable
4. potential/promise

## VOCABULARY IN WRITING

Imagine that you are applying for a job as Steven Kutcher's assistant. What makes you a good candidate? Using at least two vocabulary words, write a paragraph telling Kutcher why he should hire you. You might start this way.

> **EXAMPLE SENTENCE**
>
> *Because of my **perseverance**, I earned top grades in school.*

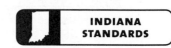

**INDIANA STANDARDS**

**READING STANDARD**
**8.1.3** Verify the meaning of a word in its context....

## VOCABULARY STRATEGY: RECOGNIZING BASE WORDS

To understand an unfamiliar word that has affixes (prefixes and suffixes), it helps to identify the base word first. Look within the word for a word that is familiar to you, even though the spelling may be different. For example, in the word *engaging*, you might notice the base word *engage*. In cases where you do not recognize a base word, using context clues may help you to figure out the meaning.

**PRACTICE** Find the base word in each boldfaced word. Think about its meaning. Then try to define the whole word. Use a dictionary if necessary.

1. If you do not understand an idea, ask your teacher for **clarification.**
2. President Lincoln spoke to a small **assemblage.**
3. My **classification** system is based on size, shape, and color.
4. Mayor Diaz will give a speech about the city's high **unemployment** rate.
5. What **adaptations** help desert plants to cope with their environment?

**VOCABULARY PRACTICE**
For more practice, go to the **Vocabulary Center** at **ClassZone.com.**

# Reading-Writing Connection

Explore Steven Kutcher's career further by responding to these prompts. Then complete the **Grammar and Writing** exercise.

| WRITING PROMPTS | SELF-CHECK |
|---|---|

**A. Short Response: Describe the Subject**
In the article "The Spider Man Behind *Spider-Man*," Steven Kutcher is described by several people who have worked with him on movie sets. Using your own words, combine these accounts into a **one-paragraph description** of Kutcher.

*A thorough description will . . .*
- not include direct quotes but will restate the information given
- give details about Kutcher's talents, skills, and interests

**B. Extended Response: Write a Job Advertisement**
Imagine that you are a movie director looking to hire someone to train insects for your next film. What type of person do you want to hire? Write a **two- or three-paragraph advertisement** giving the education, skills, and interests needed for this **career.** Include a subheading for each section.

*A strong advertisement will . . .*
- incorporate details from the article and sidebar about the education and skills needed
- give a description of the job, including the name of the movie and a brief summary of its plot

## GRAMMAR AND WRITING

 INDIANA STANDARDS

**WRITING STANDARD**
**8.6.6** Use correct capitalization.

***CAPITALIZE CORRECTLY*** The **titles** of books, movies, articles, songs, magazines, and other works should be correctly capitalized. When writing titles, always capitalize the first and last words and all other important words within the title. Unless they appear as the first or last words in the title, articles, coordinating conjunctions, and prepositions of fewer than five letters should not be capitalized.

> Original:   the Top Careers For Science Majors
>
> Revised:   The Top Careers for Science Majors

***PRACTICE*** Rewrite each title, correcting the capitalization errors.

1. The amazing spider-Man
2. Field Guide To North American Insects And Spiders
3. Movie magic: Creating Special Effects For The Big Screen
4. National geographic

*For more help with capitalizing titles, see page R51 in the **Grammar Handbook.***

# Over the Top: The True Adventures of a Volcano Chaser

Magazine Article by Renee Skelton

# *Why do people seek* DANGER?

**INDIANA STANDARDS**

**READING STANDARD**
**8.2.7** Analyze the structure, format, and purpose of informational materials (such as textbooks, newspapers, instructional or technical manuals, and public documents).

*KEY IDEA* Most people avoid **danger.** They buckle their seat belts when they fly on a plane. They take care not to anger mean dogs, not to swim where there are sharks, not to walk on thin ice. But then there are other people—the ones who dream of skydiving and who soar through half-pipes on their skateboards. The man featured in the article you're about to read belongs to this group. He's willing to risk his life to photograph mysteries of the earth.

*WEB IT* What dangerous activities are also popular pastimes? What is it about these activities that makes people willing to risk their safety? Use a web to explore the reasons why these activities can be viewed as both fun and dangerous.

## ● ELEMENTS OF NONFICTION: GRAPHIC AIDS

If you've read a magazine article lately, chances are you've come across a **graphic aid,** a visual representation of information. Writers use graphic aids to highlight or summarize important concepts and to explain things in fewer words. Common graphic aids include photographs, maps, diagrams, graphs, and timelines.

As you read "Over the Top: The True Adventures of a Volcano Chaser," note the graphic aids that are included. What do they help you understand? Take notes in a chart like the one shown.

| Type of Graphic Aid | What It Explains |
|---|---|
|  |  |

*Review:* **Text Features**

## ● READING STRATEGY: ADJUST READING RATE TO PURPOSE

Effective readers change the speed at which they read to suit their purpose. Try this as you read the following article.

| When your purpose is to | Adjust your rate like this |
|---|---|
| Get an overview of the article | **Skim** before you begin. This involves **quickly** reading the title, subheadings, and any graphic aids. |
| Find key words or particular information | **Scan** the text. This involves moving your eyes **quickly** over the text, looking for the words or information you need. |
| Gain a full understanding of something, or clarify information | Read the material at a **slower** pace, and **reread** if necessary. |

To use the best strategy for your purpose, stay mindful of why you're reading and whether you need to adjust your rate.

## ▲ VOCABULARY IN CONTEXT

The following vocabulary words help Renee Skelton tell about a man with a dangerous job. To see how many you know, match each word with its numbered synonym.

| WORD LIST | cavernous | pinnacle | searing |
|---|---|---|---|
|  | labyrinth | scale | straddle |

**1.** climb    **3.** top    **5.** maze
**2.** vast    **4.** span    **6.** hot

# Background

**Renee Skelton: A Well-Versed Writer**
Freelance writer Renee Skelton has written books and articles on topics ranging from American history to climate change. She lives in New Jersey and is a frequent contributor to *National Geographic Kids*.

## *Background*

**Sharing Science**
*National Geographic,* first published in 1888, is one of the world's best-known magazines. It's especially known for its colorful, detailed photographs of geographic regions and the people who live there. The

photos are taken by some of the world's best photojournalists, people who present a news story primarily through photographs. These men and women travel the globe with their cameras, seeking out fascinating and sometimes dangerous locations.

**Exploring the Unknown** In the article you are about to read, photojournalist Carsten Peter visits an active volcano and chambers beneath glacial ice. No stranger to dangerous situations, Peter has captured stunning images of glaciers, caves, and tornadoes for the pages of *National Geographic*. Why is he so attracted to the dangerous natural wonders he photographs? "I'm most interested in the unknown," he says.

 **BUILDING BACKGROUND**
To learn more about Carsten Peter and *National Geographic*, visit the **Literature Center** at ClassZone.com.

# Over the Top

## The True Adventures of a Volcano Chaser

Renee Skelton

**A ADJUST READING RATE**
What can you expect to learn from this article? Take a minute to **skim** the selection and make some predictions about what you'll be reading.

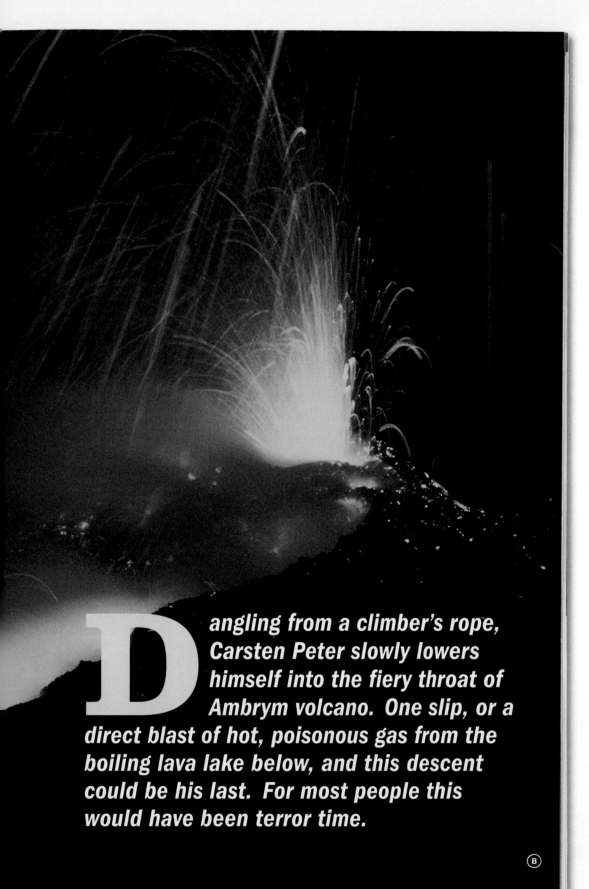

**D**angling from a climber's rope, Carsten Peter slowly lowers himself into the fiery throat of Ambrym volcano. One slip, or a direct blast of hot, poisonous gas from the boiling lava lake below, and this descent could be his last. For most people this would have been terror time.

Ⓑ

**Ⓑ GRAPHIC AIDS**
What does this **photograph** suggest about what the article will focus on?

scale (skāl) *v.* to climb up or over; ascend

**C** **GRAPHIC AIDS**
Look carefully at the **map** and its caption. What facts does it offer that you don't get from the text?

**D** **ADJUST READING RATE**
What is the tallest volcano on Earth? **Scan** these captions to find the answer.

But for Peter it was
10 all in a day's work. The daredevil photographer roams the world, <u>scaling</u> mountains and dropping into erupting volcanoes to photograph these fiery mountains at their most frightening—and most beautiful. Does he get scared? "Sure," Peter
20 says. "You wouldn't be normal if you didn't get scared." But volcanoes are a window into Earth's scorching center. And for Peter, peering through that window with his camera is worth the risk.

Peter's adventures keep him globe-trotting. The map shows a few of the places he has explored volcanoes. **C**

## Into a Boiling Pit

Ambrym is a tiny South Pacific island that consists of a flat-topped volcano. The volcano erupted violently about 2,000 years ago. The explosion left the

◄ **Long Ago**
Mount Vesuvius's[1] eruption in A.D. 79 buried two Roman cities, killing 16,000 people.

**Ring**
Most volcanoes are concentrated around the edge of the Pacific Ocean, in the "Ring of Fire."

**Out There** ▶
The biggest volcano in our solar system is Olympus Mons on Mars. It is 17 miles high. **D**

**Loud**
The 1883 explosion of Krakatoa, a volcano in Indonesia,[2] was heard 3,000 miles away.

**Blown Away** ▶
In mere seconds, whole forests of trees around Mount St. Helens,[3] Washington, were flattened in 1980. Trees 165 feet tall were blown down like toothpicks by the force of the volcano's eruption.

**Up There**
Mauna Kea, in Hawaii, is the world's tallest volcano. It is 30,000 feet high.

---

1. **Mount Vesuvius** (vĭ-sōō′vē-əs): a volcano located in southern Italy.
2. **Indonesia** (ĭn-dō-nē′zhə): an island nation located in Southeast Asia.
3. **Mount St. Helens:** volcano located in southern Washington state.

seven-and-one-half-mile-wide caldera, or wide crater, that now forms its top. Peter hoped to use one of the vent openings in Ambrym's caldera as a porthole into the volcano's fiery center.

30 When Peter arrived at Ambrym, the volcano was rumbling, its craters belching steam, gas, and ash. He and his group set out right away, hacking through dense jungle and climbing 4,000 feet up the side of the volcano. They emerged from the jungle onto the caldera's rim—a moonscape of boulders and gray-black ash.

After several days of exploring the caldera's surface, Peter decided to descend into Marum, one of Ambrym's pitlike craters. Wearing protective gear, he attached one end of a climbing rope to an anchor hammered into the ground and the other end to his descent device. Peter then disappeared over the edge of Marum's clifflike rim, camera equipment mounted on his helmet and tethered to his back and waist. Peter descended 1,000 feet down the face of the crater's steep walls,
40 as heat rising from the **searing** lava lake blasted him. Pockets of gas and water trapped in the lava expanded and exploded, sending out booms that echoed and shook the crater walls. "The Earth was trembling all around me," Peter says. "And I felt the vibrations all through my body." **E**

Peter had to be careful. A sharp rock could have cut his rope, dropping him into the **cavernous** pit. Tremors[4] could have pried boulders from the cliff above, sending them crashing down on an arm or leg. Peter paused partway down, clutching the rope as volcanic ash stung his eyes and intense heat and sound from the blasting lava rose around him. "If the volcano had exploded then, it would have been the last eruption I ever saw," he says. He drew as close as possible to the spitting, belching lava lake at
50 the bottom. Glowing lava bombs were bursting like fireworks from its surface as Peter snapped photos all night.

---

4. **tremors** (trĕm'ərz): shaking or vibrating of the earth.

**E** **ADJUST READING RATE**
What steps did Peter take to safely descend into the crater? Reread lines 34–40 and note Peter's process.

Peter captures images of the 2002 eruption of Mount Etna in Sicily.

The next morning, exhausted, Peter attached his rope and pulled himself up to safety on Marum's rim. It was time to leave Ambrym for new adventures.

## Fire and Ice **F**

60 Half a world away in Iceland,[5] the challenge was more ice than fire. Because of Iceland's location, many volcanoes are hidden below its thick glacial ice. Iceland <u>straddles</u> the mid-Atlantic ridge, where two of the plates that form Earth's crust are pulling apart. The results are frequent tremors and volcanic eruptions. When volcanoes under Iceland's glaciers erupt, they burn through ice at the glacier's base. Escaping heat carves out spectacular formations under the ice.

**Signs That "It's Gonna Blow!"**

1. In and around a volcano, the frequency and intensity of earthquakes increase.
2. The ground at the eruption site deforms or bulges.
3. The amount of gas released by the volcano increases.

**G**

---

5. **Iceland:** an island nation located in the North Atlantic Ocean near the Arctic Circle.

**F TEXT FEATURES**
Based on this **subheading**, what can you predict about the content of this section?

**G GRAPHIC AIDS**
What does this **diagram** add to your understanding of the danger Peter faces while photographing Ambrym?

**straddle** (străd'l) *v.* to be on both sides of

**H GRAPHIC AIDS**
What do these **photos** and captions add to your understanding of Peter's career?

**H** Intense heat from a volcano created this ice cave inside a glacier in Iceland.

70 Peter's goal was to photograph these underground wonders. After a jolting jeep ride over part of the glacier, Peter continued on foot—leaping crevasses, sloshing through icy rivers of meltwater, and scrambling over jagged ice <u>pinnacles</u>. "The heat created chambers inside the ice we were passing over," says Peter. "We had to be very careful." Peter found that out the hard way. Crossing an area of ice that looked solid, Peter stepped on a thin section and crashed through into a hidden river of icy water. He struggled to keep his head and cameras above water. The cameras didn't make it. Luckily Peter did, thanks to two friends who pulled him out of the frigid water.

Exploring the surface ice, Peter discovered a collapsed ice chamber that led to a <u>labyrinth</u> of ice caves and tunnels inside the glacier. "It was beautiful, but we
80 were in potential danger because the chamber could have collapsed at any time," Peter says. "Also, we were in a region where earthquakes and floods are common occurrences." But using carbide[6] lights to illuminate the dark tunnels, Peter took incredible photos of the formations in the glacier's frozen heart. **❶**

As you read this, Peter is probably perched on the rim of another volcano, camera in hand. He's withstanding heat from 2,200 degrees Fahrenheit lava flows and dodging deadly clouds of gas to get close to nature at its most extreme. Earth's geology continues to fascinate him. "Volcanoes are very powerful," he says. "When you feel these eruptions, it's the greatest experience you can have."

---

6. **carbide** (kär'bīd'): a very hard material made partly of carbon.

Peter lowers himself through a heat vent in Iceland's Grímsvötn volcano.

# Comprehension

**INDIANA STANDARDS**

**READING STANDARD**
**8.2.7** Analyze the structure, format, and purpose of informational materials . . . .

1. **Recall** What could have killed or injured Carsten Peter as he photographed inside the Ambrym volcano?

2. **Recall** What did Peter go to Iceland to photograph?

3. **Represent** Using the information provided by the captions on page 898, draw a simple timeline that shows the order in which three famous volcanoes erupted.

# Critical Analysis

4. **Analyze Reading Rate** What part of the article did you read most quickly? When did you have to change your reading rate? Explain which strategy you found most useful as you read.

5. **Draw Conclusions** Why do you think Carsten Peter feels it is important to photograph volcanoes in spite of the **danger** involved?

6. **Compare and Contrast** In what ways are the careers of Steven Kutcher ("The Spider Man Behind *Spider-Man*," page 886) and Carsten Peter alike? In what ways are they different? Complete a Y-chart like the one shown to compare and contrast the two men and their careers. Record the differences in the top part of the Y, and the similarities in the bottom.

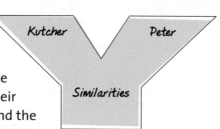

7. **Evaluate Graphic Aids** Look back at the chart you made as you read. What information do you get from the graphic aids? Would this information have been more or less clear if it had been included with the main text but without any visuals? Explain.

# Extension and Challenge

8. **Readers' Circle** Carsten Peter obviously believes that the risks he takes are worth the results. Imagine that he is a member of your family, such as your brother, uncle, or father. Would you support his choices, or would you urge him to find a safer career? Discuss your ideas.

9. **SCIENCE CONNECTION** How are volcanoes formed? What causes them to erupt? Research these questions about volcanoes, and ask one additional question of your own. Present your findings to the class in the form of a "slide show," either on paper or the computer.

> **RESEARCH LINKS**
> For more on volcanoes, visit the **Research Center** at **ClassZone.com**.

# Vocabulary in Context

## VOCABULARY PRACTICE

For each item, choose the word that differs most in meaning from the other words. Refer to a dictionary if you need help.

1. (a) searing, (b) scorching, (c) frigid, (d) sweltering
2. (a) descend, (b) scale, (c) climb, (d) ascend
3. (a) slant, (b) tilt, (c) straddle, (d) lean
4. (a) maze, (b) labyrinth, (c) network, (d) beeline
5. (a) gaping, (b) shallow, (c) deep, (d) cavernous
6. (a) pinnacle, (b) bottom, (c) base, (d) foot

cavernous
labyrinth
pinnacle
scale
searing
straddle

## VOCABULARY IN WRITING

Using at least two vocabulary words, write a paragraph about a daring sport or exciting hobby that you've tried or want to try. You might start like this.

> **EXAMPLE SENTENCE**
>
> I was terrified as we climbed slowly to the **_pinnacle_** of the mountain.

## VOCABULARY STRATEGY: WORD ORIGINS

Many common words in the English language have interesting histories. For example, the vocabulary word *scale* comes from the Latin word *scalae*, meaning "ladder." It makes sense, then, that to scale something means to climb it.

You can find a word's **etymology,** or the history of the word, in most dictionaries. Understanding etymologies can help you connect the word's meaning to something you already know. Here is an example of an etymology:

> **expand** (ĭk-spănd′) *v.* to become greater in size, quantity, volume, or scope [Middle English *expanden,* to spread out, from Latin *expandere: ex-* + *pandere,* to spread]

*PRACTICE* Look up the etymology of each word in the dictionary. Write the word's origin, and tell how knowing the word's history can help you remember its meaning.

1. intense      3. sparse      5. danger
2. grief        4. glacier

**INDIANA STANDARDS**

READING STANDARD
**8.1.2** Understand the influence of historical events on English word meaning and vocabulary expansion.

**VOCABULARY PRACTICE**

For more practice, go to the **Vocabulary Center** at ClassZone.com.

## News Reports

TV Newscast Clip/Magazine Article on  **MediaSmart** DVD

# What's the SOURCE?

**INDIANA STANDARDS**

**READING STANDARD**
**8.2.7** Analyze the structure, format, and purpose of informational materials (such as textbooks, newspapers, instructional or technical manuals, and public documents).

*KEY IDEA* Recall a time you watched a TV news report in which someone was making statements to a reporter. What was the circumstance? Did the statements appear to be ones you could trust? In news reporting, it's not just the events that matter but what people have to say about them. In this lesson, you'll see how **quotes** can help you fully understand a news event.

## Background

**Fireworks in Space** July 4, 2005, was a day of celebration at the National Aeronautics and Space Administration (NASA). As part of a major mission called "Deep Impact," NASA launched a space probe that hit a comet so hard, it burrowed through its surface—then exploded. Scientists and engineers cheered as the probe's nearby mother ship transmitted images of the spectacular event. NASA realized it had gathered a wealth of scientific data about the comet that would help in future research.

To explore how news reporters gather and support their facts, you'll watch a TV newscast and read a magazine article that cover this remarkable event.

# Media Literacy: Sources in the News

In the world of news, a **source** is a person who provides information for a news report. A reporter usually uses one or more sources while creating a news report. In printed news, the reporter includes **quotations,** the words spoken by the sources to the reporter. In a TV or radio newscast, the quoted statements are called **sound bites,** which are edited from interviews with the sources. Here are the types of sources usually quoted in the news.

## TYPES OF SOURCES

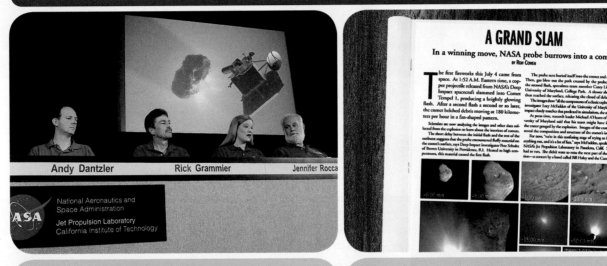

### Witnesses

These are the people who are present at the time of an event or who are directly affected by it.

### Experts

Often experts are quoted after an event occurs. They're qualified to share their knowledge about what happened.

### Officials

These sources are authority figures, those who represent the government, a business, and so on.

### Sources as Counterpoints

One source may give one side of an event or an issue. In the same report, another source may have a very different view.

### STRATEGIES FOR ANALYZING SOURCES

- Identify a source by name and determine his or her role.
- Question why a source is included in a news report. Ask yourself: What is this source helping me to understand about the event?
- Be aware that what you're hearing or reading is not the entire interview. Think about how the sound bites or quotations support certain facts.
- In reports that include countering or opposing sources, check to see that the two sides are **balanced** or are represented equally. It's important that a news report be neutral and fair to all sides.

*Viewing Guide for*
# News Reports

You'll watch the CBS network news report that first aired at the time of the event. Then you'll read an article that appeared a few days later in the weekly newsmagazine *Science News.* As you examine each one, look for the people who make statements. Take notes about the sources or about any striking feature of each format. Answer these questions to help analyze the news reports.

## NOW VIEW

### FIRST VIEWING: Comprehension

1. **Clarify** NASA had created an animated model, or simulation, of the comet explosion. According to the TV newscast, what makes the simulation remarkable?

2. **Recall** Which one of the sources is an investigator from Brown University?

### CLOSE VIEWING: Media Literacy

3. **Analyze TV Sources** In the "Deep Impact" news report, each **sound bite** is included after a certain amount of factual information is presented. Why do you think the news report is edited in this way?

4. **Analyze Print Sources** The sources who are quoted in the magazine article are quoted directly or are **paraphrased.** This means the reporter has restated what he was told in his own words. In a science-related article, why might he have chosen to paraphrase?

5. **Compare News Sources** Use a chart like this to identify and compare the types of sources of both news reports.

|  | Sources |
|---|---|
| "Deep Impact" |  |
| "A Grand Slam" |  |

# Write or Discuss

**Evaluate Sources** You encountered a number of sources in the TV newscast and in the magazine article. Now choose one of the news reports and make your own statement. In a short paragraph, tell how effectively you think the sources are used. Consider:

- what types of individuals are used as sources
- your basic impressions of these sources
- what the sources helped you to understand in the news report

# Produce Your Own Media

**Create an Interview Plan** In small groups, brainstorm at least three possible news stories to cover in your school or neighborhood. Once these are determined, imagine you're a team of reporters preparing to interview different sources for the news reports. Use your ideas to help you create an **interview plan.** This plan will help you to determine the most likely people to contact for an interview. It can also help you prepare interview questions.

*HERE'S HOW* To help you devise your interview plan, use these tips.

- For this planning stage, list the possible sources. Jot down a detail that describes that person's connection to the news story.
- For each source, jot down questions that you think would clearly relate to the news story.
- Try to create questions that are open-ended. The best sound bites start with questions like these. Avoid questions that lead to a simple "yes" or "no" response.

**STUDENT MODEL**

| |
|---|
| *Possible News Stories:* |
| • the opening of a school's time capsule from 1990 |
| • the new neighborhood garden project |
| |
| *Sources:* |
| *Mr. Camacho—He originally installed the time capsule.* |
| *Ms. Evans—School principal* |
| *Tara Sebring and Jamal Humphrey—They've assembled a new capsule.* |
| |
| *Possible Questions:* |
| • *Why now for opening the capsule?* |
| • *Will there be some sort of ceremony to mark the opening?* |
| • *What does the new capsule contain?* |
| |

**MEDIA TOOLS**

For help with creating a interview plan, visit the **Media Center** at **ClassZone.com.**

**Tech Tip**

If available, record your interview plans as electronic files.

## Interview with a Songcatcher
Interview by Brian Handwerk

# *What does* MUSIC *say about us?*

**INDIANA STANDARDS**

**READING STANDARDS**
**8.2.7** Analyze the structure, format, and purpose of informational materials (such as textbooks, newspapers, instructional or technical manuals, and public documents).

**8.2.9** Make reasonable statements and draw conclusions about a text, supporting them with accurate examples.

**KEY IDEA** Imagine someone you've never met, who knows nothing about you but your three favorite songs. What could she guess about you based on this information? Could she tell what you think is important? what makes you happy? what makes you sad? In the following interview, journalist Brian Handwerk talks to a woman who has made a career of learning about other people through their **music.**

**CHART IT** Copy this chart in a notebook. Then decide whether you agree or disagree with each statement. After you read "Interview with a Songcatcher," you'll revisit this chart.

| Anticipation Guide | | |
|---|---|---|
| | Before Reading | After Reading |
| People with different tastes in music probably don't have much else in common. | | |
| The words of a song are not as important as the melody. | | |
| Politics and social conditions have little impact on a culture's music. | | |

## ● ELEMENTS OF NONFICTION: INTERVIEW

If you've ever read an entertainment magazine, you have probably read an interview. An **interview** is a conversation between two people in which one person asks questions and the other responds. An interview

- often includes both the reporter's questions and the interviewee's responses
- typically provides long, uninterrupted quotations that give readers a sense of the person speaking

As you read "Interview with a Songcatcher," notice how the format of the interview helps you follow who is speaking.

## ● READING SKILL: DISTINGUISH FACT AND OPINION

A **fact** is a statement that can be proved true from personal observations, by consulting a reliable source such as an encyclopedia, or even by conducting an experiment. An **opinion** is a statement that cannot be proved because it expresses a person's feelings, thoughts, or beliefs.

> Fact: *The Chicago White Sox won the 2005 World Series.*
>
> Opinion: *The Chicago White Sox are a great team.*

When you read nonfiction, it's important to distinguish between facts that you can rely on and opinions about which people could disagree. To practice telling the difference, use a chart to note at least four facts and four opinions as you read this interview.

| Statement | Fact or Opinion? |
|-----------|------------------|
|           |                  |

## ▲ VOCABULARY IN CONTEXT

The words in column A help one woman tell how she's learned about people's music. Match each word with the word in column B that you think is closest in meaning.

**Column A**
1. circumstance
2. composer
3. informant
4. intimate
5. primitive
6. remote

**Column B**
a. undeveloped
b. innermost
c. situation
d. distant
e. songwriter
f. speaker

# Author Online

**Writing That Travels the Globe** Freelance writers like Brian Handwerk don't work for one particular newspaper or magazine. They get to write for a variety of publications on a range of topics. For example, Handwerk has written articles on the environment, politics, and scientific

**Brian Handwerk born 1970**

discoveries. His articles have been printed in publications around the globe. He says, "One of the best parts of the job is being able to interview amazing people like Henrietta Yurchenco . . . I'm lucky to be able to meet people like her through my writing."

## *Background*

**Ethnomusicology** Each culture has a unique way of expressing itself through music. The study of ethnomusicology (ĕth'nō-myōō'zǐ-kŏl'ə-jē) is dedicated to preserving the music of all the world's cultures. Ethnomusicologists—also called songcatchers—travel to remote areas to record music from different groups. In addition to studying songs and instruments, songcatchers also study the ideas and methods that lead to the creation of music. For example, Henrietta Yurchenco (hĕn-re-ĕt'ə yûr-chĕn'kō), the songcatcher featured in this interview, spent two years studying and recording music in isolated areas of Mexico and Guatemala. Today, a number of universities and colleges offer courses in ethnomusicology.

> **MORE ABOUT THE AUTHOR AND BACKGROUND**
> To learn more about Brian Handwerk and songcatching, visit the **Literature Center** at **ClassZone.com**.

BACK   FORWARD   STOP   REFRESH   HOME   PRINT

# Interview with a Songcatcher

### Brian Handwerk

Ethnomusicologist Henrietta Yurchenco spent over 60 years traveling the world in search of the unrecorded music of small cultural groups. Yurchenco recorded the music of various groups and tribes in Mexico, Central and South America, Spain, and Morocco. Her collection of world music is now housed in the United States Library of Congress, preserved for future generations of music lovers.

**A** **INTERVIEW**
Who is asking this question? Tell how you know.

**circumstance**
(sûr′kəm-stăns′) *n.*
a condition that affects or relates to an event or series of events

*You've had such an incredible career, how did it all begin?* **A**

To tell you the truth, I think that most of the things that happened to me in life happened with absolutely no plan whatsoever—just a set of funny **circumstances**.

When I was working at WNYC [radio station] I was introduced to music from around the world, because everyone came to WNYC. I played artists like Woody Guthrie, Leadbelly, Pete Seeger,[1] and I also played music from all around the world. I was curious, you know, just plain curiosity.

One of our friends, the great Mexican painter Rufino Tamayo, called
10 my husband and I and said "We're driving to Mexico, do you want to go?" We did. We drove from New York to Mexico and it changed my life.

---

1. **Woody Guthrie; Leadbelly; Pete Seeger:** American folksingers and composers.

Henrietta Yurchenco shows off her early recording equipment.

**ANALYZE VISUALS**
What do the **details** in this photograph suggest about Henrietta Yurchenco's interests and personality?

*It was in Mexico where you first began field recording of remote tribes?*

Yes, because of a chance letter from the Library of Congress. I was doing radio programs for the Inter-American Indian Institute. . . . Dr. [Manuel] Gamio, the head of that institute, said, "We've received a letter from the Library of Congress. They'll send equipment and a little money. Are you interested?" **B**

20   I almost bit his hand off. I said, "I'll do it!" He was telling me about sleeping on the ground, long trips by animals, deadly scorpions, et cetera, but I wasn't listening. I didn't care. That's what I did for the next two years in Mexico and Guatemala.[2]

*Were the practical aspects as difficult as advertised? Dealing with cumbersome early equipment, for example?*

It was a horror.... People have asked me, "You went so far into those **remote** areas with just one recording machine?" One machine? I was thankful

---

2. **Guatemala** (gwä′tə-mä′lə): a country in northern Central America.

**B FACT AND OPINION**
Yurchenco states that the Library of Congress offered money and equipment to the Inter-American Indian Institute to record tribes in Mexico. Is this a fact or an opinion? Explain.

**remote** (rĭ-mōt′) *adj.* located far away

Yurchenco poses with Tzotzil Maya musicians in 1942.

to have one. . . . At one point the cord broke when we were way into the mountains. My photographer was with me on that trip and he just held it together with his hands. He stayed absolutely still, didn't move an inch, 30 and it was a perfect recording.

On most of the trips we had a big car motor for power. We had to carry gasoline, the machine, and the aluminum or even steel discs. That's all we had so we just hauled it everywhere. The only thing that really terrified me was deadly scorpions. It's not comfortable sleeping on the ground when you know those things are around—but it was a great adventure. **C**

Some places I had help from missionaries,[3] some places I was alone with 200 pounds of equipment. Don't ask me how it worked sometimes. **D**

**How difficult was it for you to understand the culture of these remote communities?**

40 When I was in Mexico I visited some very **primitive** and isolated people who had had no contact with mainstream society for many years. I swear I saw animal sacrifices and curing ceremonies that were thousands of years old. I discovered what there was of pre-Hispanic[4]

---

3. **missionaries** (mĭsh′ə-nĕr′ēz): people who are sent to do religious work in foreign countries.

4. **pre-Hispanic** (prē-hĭ-spăn′ĭk): related to an era before Spanish conquerors arrived in the Americas.

**C** **INTERVIEW**
Reread lines 33–35. What do they reveal about Yurchenco's personality?

**D** **FACT AND OPINION**
Reread lines 36–37. What might you do to verify these statements as facts?

**primitive** (prĭm′ĭ-tĭv) *adj.* of or relating to a nonindustrial, often tribal, culture music and dance at that time among 14 different tribes. After some of the recordings these people died and the younger people did not really learn the stuff. . . .

People in the field have to be very careful because they're told things but shouldn't believe them. You have to look behind the words. **Informants** might tell you what you want to hear, or not tell you something that the
50 community won't want you to hear. So you have to be very careful, and really observe. . . .

*How are you able to do that as an outsider with a lot of recording equipment?*

First of all it was easy because, as you've no doubt noticed, I'm a woman. So I'm not threatening and they did not regard a woman as threatening. Secondly, I never asked direct questions. Anthropologists[5] go into the field with questions. I didn't, I just went with hugs and kisses and asked "Will you please sing for me?" When you ask about music it means, "She's interested, she likes me, she respects me." And I've never met a people
60 who didn't respond to that.

The Yaquis,[6] for example, who were known as a very warlike tribe, were absolutely marvelous. They were poets; their stuff was gorgeous. I said to the chieftain, "I want to get the words for all these songs"; he said, "We'll come together before you leave and we'll write it all down so you get it right." Well, the entire tribe came to this little community center, babies, women, grandparents, everyone. We sweltered in there, it was 100 degrees, but we got it all down. **E**

You had to be a good listener. I've sat on many, many a porch with women of all kinds and colors and just asked "So what happened after that?"

70 *Was the lack of a common language a problem?*

I never found that there was a distance between them and me because I didn't understand their language. To this day I travel to one area of Mexico that has a rich musical heritage. I've been going there since 1942, and the

---

5. **anthropologists** (ăn'thrə-pŏl'ə-jĭsts): scientists who study the origin, behavior, and cultural development of humans.

6. **Yaquis** (yä'kēs): a native people of Sonora, Mexico, who settled mainly along the Yaqui River.

**informant** (ĭn-fôr'mənt) *n.* one who gives information

**E** **FACT AND OPINION**
What two opinions does Yurchenco express about the Yaquis? Tell what words led you to this conclusion.

**composer** (kəm-pō'zər) *n.* one who creates musical pieces

**F INTERVIEW**
What does this response to the question reveal about Yurchenco's approach to her work?

**G FACT AND OPINION**
Reread the first sentence of this paragraph. Can you verify this statement as fact?

wife of the main Indian **composer** there doesn't speak Spanish. Every time she sees me we just hug, and she kisses me and cries. They know whether you respect them and you don't need words. **F**

It's better to use music than bombs to win friendships. When we were in Morocco[7] the last time most of the Jews had left for other countries. We were sitting in Tangier[8] in a café, and a little ensemble
80 was playing Arabic music. I went up to them and I said, "We are musicians from New York." They got up, gave us hugs and kisses, and said, "Please sit down and we'll play for you." It's a wonderful bond. There's nothing more emotional than the arts and music. **G**

***There's a voice to be heard through that emotion as well?***

The song to me is the basic human expression. It tells you things, or avoids telling you things, or disguises things, but you have to look at what it means.

There's so much study of folk music and typically there's not much study of the words. It's like going to the opera for many people, and they
90 don't have the ghost of an idea what it's about. They just hear the music. But if that's what the composer had meant he would have just written, you know, "Blah, blah, blah." Music itself tells you things but so do the words. You have to look at the meaning. . . .

***You've always been attuned to the political aspect of music as well.***

I'm concerned with more than music. I'm concerned with the society, with the people more than anything. When I hear popular music I have to consider the social and political things that are going on in order to understand it. It's the same with any music around the world, but that
100 fact is very often neglected.

I'm not a romantic; I'm political. These romantics say "We must preserve the precious culture." But at the cost of poverty and ignorance? Is that what you want? That's what it means. Life changes, and with modern communications, roads, and infrastructure a lot of things will

7. **Morocco** (mə-rŏk'ō): a country in northwest Africa. It has coastlines on the Mediterranean Sea and the Atlantic Ocean.
8. **Tangier** (tăn-jîr'): a northern Moroccan city.

disappear, of course. But maybe people's lives will be better—I don't just talk about music as if it were surrounded by a moat[9] or something.

**Why is the work of field recordings important, and why is it important to preserve and distribute these voices of the past 100-odd years?**

110 It's our history. We have a written history. There are books for political history, the formation of nations, political and social struggles. But music is one of the most **intimate** expressions. Through music you become knowledgeable of the intimate aspects of life that aren't told in books. It's important because the people themselves tell you; it's not someone's interpretation. History books are written by the victors, but songs are the people's own words and melodies. That's what makes music a very powerful tool to understand people.

---

9. **moat** (mōt): a water-filled ditch that surrounds and protects a castle, fortress, or town.

**intimate** (ĭn′tə-mĭt) *adj.* relating to one's deepest nature

**H FACT AND OPINION**
Find one fact and one opinion in this paragraph. How were you able to identify each?

**ANALYZE VISUALS**
What can you **infer** from this photo about the way Yurchenco relates to the people she meets?

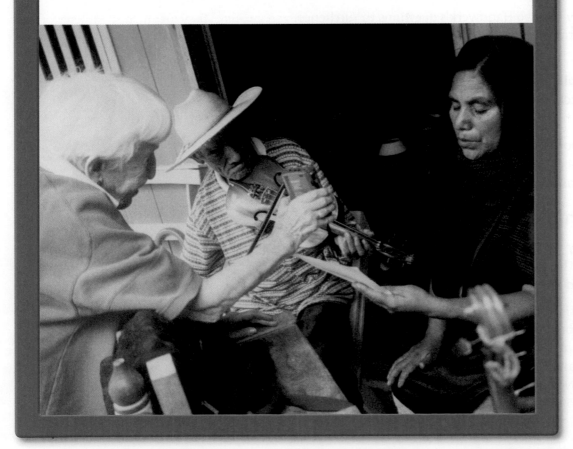

## Comprehension

1. **Recall** How did Henrietta Yurchenco begin recording tribal music?

2. **Clarify** Why does Yurchenco think music can tell more about a culture than history books?

3. **Summarize** Reread lines 70–83. How is Yurchenco able to communicate with people who don't speak her language?

**READING STANDARD**
**8.2.7** Analyze the structure, format, and purpose of informational materials ....

## Critical Analysis

4. **Describe a Songcatcher** What type of person is Henrietta Yurchenco? Using a chart like the one shown, write three adjectives that describe Yurchenco's personality. Expand your chart using one statement from the interview that supports each adjective.

5. **Analyze an Interview** Reread Handwerk's questions to Yurchenco. What do these questions tell you about his interest in or prior knowledge of songcatching?

6. **Evaluate Fact and Opinion** Look back at the facts and opinions you recorded as you read. Then exchange your list with a partner. Does he or she agree with you about which statements are facts and which are opinions?

7. **Make Judgments** Look again at the questions Handwerk asked Yurchenco. Were they good choices? Why or why not? If you were to continue the **interview,** what are another two questions you would ask?

## Extension and Challenge

8. **Big Question Activity** Go back to the anticipation guide you started before reading. Now, fill in the "After Reading" column. Have any of your opinions about **music** changed after reading this interview? Explain.

9. **Creative Project: Music** Imagine that Henrietta Yurchenco came to your class. What music would you play for her to let her know what it's like to be a student your age in the United States today? With a group, come up with a list of five songs. They can be songs written by recording artists, or songs written by one or all of you. Next to each song, explain why you chose it.

# Vocabulary in Context

## VOCABULARY PRACTICE

Show that you understand the boldfaced vocabulary words by telling whether each statement is true or false.

1. A **remote** village is far away from other communities.
2. A **composer** is someone who writes plays.
3. Most European cultures are **primitive.**
4. An **informant** is the same as a liar.
5. Most people share **intimate** details about their lives with no one but family members and friends.
6. A **circumstance** is a person who bosses others around.

circumstance
composer
informant
intimate
primitive
remote

## VOCABULARY IN WRITING

If Henrietta Yurchenco were to write the story of her career as a songcatcher, what might she say? Write the introductory paragraph of Yurchenco's memoir. You might start like this.

> **EXAMPLE SENTENCE**
>
> My first trip was to a **remote** village in Mexico.

## VOCABULARY STRATEGY: DENOTATION AND CONNOTATION

A word's **denotation** is the basic definition found in a dictionary. Its **connotation** is a feeling or attitude linked with that word. Connotations can influence the meaning a word conveys. For example, the vocabulary word *primitive* means "of or relating to a nonindustrial, often tribal, culture." But the word has also come to mean "unsophisticated" or "crude." Recognizing connotations can help you understand the opinions of the people you read about.

*PRACTICE* Replace each boldfaced word with another word with a similar meaning, but a negative connotation.

1. Marcus's dog is **overweight** because the family feeds it too much.
2. Even after she left the room, Lia's perfume left an odd **scent** in the air.
3. The **elderly** woman moved slowly as she crossed the street.
4. Michael is so **clever.** He always gets his way.
5. I can't be friends with Cynthia. Her attitude is **unpleasant.**

**INDIANA STANDARDS**

**READING STANDARD**
8.1.3 Verify the meaning of a word in its context . . . .

**VOCABULARY PRACTICE**

For more practice, go to the **Vocabulary Center** at **ClassZone.com.**

## Kabul's Singing Sensation
Magazine Article by Tim McGirk

# *Why do we* S I N G ?

**KEY IDEA** Think about the last time you **sang.** Was it at a birthday party? during choir practice? on the street with a group of friends? Whether it's to celebrate, lift someone's spirits, or express joy, almost everyone belts out a tune at some point or another. In the article you're about to read, you'll meet a boy whose singing helps relieve the suffering of his country.

**WEB IT** People sing for a variety of reasons. Fill in a web like the one shown with places and events where people sing or hear singing. What do you think is the most common reason to sing?

to entertain — for pleasure — **Reasons for Singing** — for money — to inspire — in a recording studio

918

## ● ELEMENTS OF NONFICTION: FEATURE ARTICLE

What was the last article you read in a magazine or newspaper? If it was a piece about a favorite celebrity or about skate parks around the country, what you read was probably a feature article. A **feature article** is an article that

- focuses on a person or topic of human interest, rather than a current news event
- often includes language and imagery that appeal to emotions
- often gives only one perspective on a story

As you read "Kabul's Singing Sensation," notice how the author helps you understand the difficult life of one young Afghan singer.

## ● READING SKILL: IDENTIFY MAIN IDEA AND DETAILS

Nonfiction writers usually organize their writing around **main ideas,** the most important ideas they want to share about a topic. Sometimes these main ideas are stated directly, often at the beginning of a section or paragraph. Other times they may merely be implied, or suggested. **Supporting details,** such as facts or examples, help to illustrate main ideas.

The article you are about to read contains several main ideas supported by details. Use an outline like the one shown to record supporting details for each main idea.

> I. History and politics of Afghanistan
>    A.
>    B.
> II. Difficulties faced by Mirwais and his family
>    A.
>    B.

## ▲ VOCABULARY IN CONTEXT

Tim McGirk uses the following words to describe the challenges faced by a young musician. How many words do you know? Make a chart like the one shown, putting each vocabulary word in the appropriate column.

| WORD LIST | | |
|---|---|---|
| edict | immaculate | transcendent |
| exile | puritanical | virtuoso |

| Know Well | Think I Know | Don't Know at All |
|---|---|---|
| | | |

# Author On|ine

**Danger and Determination**
Reporters who travel to dangerous areas of the world often have difficult decisions to make. How bold or how careful should they be in order to get information? Tim McGirk, a reporter for *Time* magazine, has had to answer this question himself.

**Tim McGirk born 1952**

In 2001, McGirk had to decide whether to visit an island in the Philippines where rebels held kidnapped tourists and journalists and sometimes killed them. Because of the dangers involved, he chose not go to the island. However, since 1976, McGirk has covered his share of difficult assignments, including reporting on the people and situations in Latin America and in war-torn areas of the Middle East.

## Background

**Turbulent Times** The late 20th century saw years of civil unrest in Afghanistan, a landlocked country in southern Asia. The Taliban, a violent Muslim extremist group, captured control of the country in the 1990s. The group imposed strict rules on the Afghan people, based on its extreme interpretation of Islam. Under the Taliban's rule, Afghan girls lost their right to an education, art and sports were outlawed, and even music was banned. Those who violated the Taliban's rules were often brutally punished. The Taliban fell out of power after a 2001 invasion by the United States and its allies. A new government was created, and people in certain parts of the country again enjoyed some of the freedoms they had missed for years.

**MORE ABOUT THE AUTHOR AND BACKGROUND**
To learn more about Tim McGirk and Afghanistan, visit the **Literature Center** at ClassZone.com.

**ANALYZE VISUALS**
This photograph shows Mirwais Najrabi singing at a wedding in Kabul, Afghanistan. How would you describe the expression on his face?

# Kabul's Singing Sensation

## TIM MᶜGIRK

It's midnight, long past bedtime for most children. But in a poor, war-ravaged neighborhood of Kabul,[1] more than 300 men are gathered at a wedding party to listen to the singing of Mirwais Najrabi, a pale, chestnut-haired 13-year-old. He performs in an open courtyard, under the night sky, to an audience that has endured so much suffering and grief over years of oppression, war, and mayhem. Yet for this brief, **transcendent** moment, their burden is lifted by the exquisite purity of the boy's voice. **Ⓐ**

With his jaunty, Bollywood-style[2] haircut and white embroidered
10 tunic, Mirwais looks as though he would warble like a pretty songbird, but his singing is forceful and worldly, as if he has already seen it all. And he has. Tonight, he croons folksongs of impossible love, betrayal, and heroism that flow from the depths of Afghanistan's tragic history. . . . Two men leap up to dance, circling each other like angry cobras. They turn aggressive and are pulled apart. . . . When performances get wild, says Mirwais, he tells himself: "I must not be scared, never."

---

1. **Kabul** (käʹbŏŏl): Afghanistan's capital city.
2. **Bollywood** (bŏlʹē-wŏŏdʹ): the Indian film industry. The name combines the names *Hollywood* (center of the U.S. film industry) and *Bombay* (the former name for Mumbai, a large Indian city).

**transcendent**
(trăn-sĕnʹdənt) *adj.* being above the material world

**Ⓐ FEATURE ARTICLE**
Reread lines 1–8. What words and phrases suggest that you are reading a feature article?

Note that Afghanistan is a mountainous country.

**B** MAIN IDEA

What details help you understand the difficulties Mirwais has faced? Add these details to your outline.

puritanical

(pyŏŏr-ĭ-tăn'ĭ-kəl) *adj.* strictly observant of religious practices; sternly moral

edict (ē'dĭkt') *n.* a command from those in power

The soulful melancholy in Mirwais's voice is the product of hard times. He may be only 13, but he has already suffered greatly, and this, he says, may have helped him capture the anguish that many Afghans have endured
20 in the last 25 years of scorching battle and **exile.** "I sing what I feel," he says with a child's simplicity. His father was a famous musician who died when Mirwais was only five years old. The family had the misfortune of living in the Char-Deh neighborhood of Kabul on the front line between two warring commanders; as mortars and rockets exploded around them, Mirwais and his brothers risked their lives every day just to draw water from a communal well. **B**

Boy vocalists, long a part of Afghan tradition, were once silenced completely by the **puritanical** Taliban regime, which regarded song as un-Islamic and had many musicians arrested and beaten. When
30 the Taliban seized power, one of their first **edicts** was to ban music. They ransacked the Afghan Radio and Television station, decorating nearby trees and rosebushes with streamers of ripped-out audiotape. (Brave technicians, however, sealed thousands of Afghan records and tapes behind a false wall at the studio, which the Taliban never found.) "We were afraid that the Taliban would kill us," recalls Mirwais's older

brother Nur-ul-Haq, a tabla[3] player who says dozens of artists were beaten in public by Taliban zealots. So the family buried their musical instruments under a chicken coop in the garden. Another brother left to sell flowers in Iran, while Nur-ul-Haq hawked carpets in Pakistan.
40  Mirwais, who was just five years old when the Taliban took over, stayed in Kabul with his mother. **C**

As a toddler, Mirwais showed no interest in music. It wasn't until he was six, a year after his father's death, that anyone even heard him sing. According to Nur-ul-Haq, Mirwais had never hummed or whistled until the day when he climbed a pomegranate tree in the garden and sang to his mother. His voice was a revelation. She immediately apprenticed him to a music teacher, Ustaad Amin Jan Mazari, who listened to him and took him on for free. In the South Asian tradition of gurus and disciples,[4] Mirwais lived with his teacher "like a son," recalls Mazari. He did
50  household chores and spent hours each day practicing the broad range of vocal scales found in classical Afghan music. Mirwais came to revere his master. Today, when they meet, the boy's face glows, and he bows to touch his teacher's feet. "He has good talent," says Mazari, "and, by the kindness of Allah, when Mirwais is 40 years old or so, with practice, he will become great."

. . . After the Taliban were defeated, singers began wandering back from exile in Europe and the U.S. to a tumultuous welcome, and Kabul's **virtuosos** unearthed the instruments they buried in their gardens. Songs now blast from Kabul shops, and more than a dozen
60  radio stations flourish around the country. Mirwais, one of the first to sing in public after the Taliban's ouster,[5] is at the front of this revival. Despite his youth, he recognizes the enormity of the change. In the old days, he says, "If the Taliban caught me, they would have shaved my head. And only Allah knows what other punishments I would have faced." **D**

Remaining a singer until adulthood may be a challenge. Already, Mirwais works punishing hours, often singing until 3:00 A.M. and then rising late to ride his bicycle—whose handlebars have sprouted a bouquet of artificial flowers—to a dirt-floor schoolhouse that has no doors or
70  windows to ward off the icy winter winds. Mirwais sits there with other drably uniformed boys, a bright kid with a sad smile. The schoolyard is full of toughs, and he knows better than to show off his one luxury, a new cell phone in which he's stored dozens of jangling tunes. **E**

---

3. **tabla** (tä´bla): a small hand drum of northern India.

4. **gurus and disciples** (go͝o-ro͞oz´, dī-sī´pəls): spiritual or religious teachers and their students, who respect them very much.

5. **ouster** (ous´tər): the state of being ejected or forced out.

**C MAIN IDEA**
How did the Taliban enforce the ban on music? Note the details that helped you answer this question.

**virtuoso** (vûr´cho͞o-ō´sō) *n.* a musician with excellent abilities, techniques, and/or an attractive personal style

**D MAIN IDEA**
Reread lines 56–65. How did Kabul change with the Taliban out of power? Add these details to your outline.

**E FEATURE ARTICLE**
Identify two examples of strong **imagery** used in this paragraph. What do they help you better understand about Mirwais's daily life?

Young artists like Mirwais have several advantages over their older rivals. The . . . clarity of their voices blends harmoniously with the Afghan rabab, an ancient, 19-stringed instrument that is a cross between a sitar and a mandolin.⁶ And because he is still a boy, Mirwais is allowed at weddings to sing for both men and women, whose parties are strictly segregated. This will last until Mirwais turns 15 and is considered a man, no longer to be
80 trusted around unveiled women.⁷

Among the boy singers, Mirwais is tops, though he has a 14-year-old rival, Wali Fateh Ali Khan, a favorite of former King Zahir Shah. But among the common folk, Mirwais is considered the best. He and his three-piece band—a tabla drummer and rabab and harmonium⁸ players—were booked every night during the three-month wedding season prior to the holy month of Ramadan, when the partying stops. His crowning achievement came last September, when he won a famous singing contest at Kabul's Park Cinema. That day, Mirwais appeared in an **immaculate** white suit, handling the audience with the casual manner of a mite-sized Sinatra.⁹ His performance
90 blew the other contestants off the stage. **F**

---

6. **sitar** (sĭ-tär′)**; mandolin** (măn′də-lĭn′)**:** two guitarlike string instruments.

7. **unveiled women:** Some Muslims (followers of Islam) believe that women should wear veils to hide themselves from all men except close family members.

8. **harmonium** (här-mo′nē-əm)**:** an organlike keyboard instrument.

9. **Sinatra** (sə-nä′trə)**:** Frank Sinatra (1915–1998). American singer and actor known for his beautiful voice.

Mirwais practices with his music teacher, Ustaad Mazari (center).

**immaculate** (ĭ-măk′yə-lĭt) *adj.* spotless; very clean

**F** **FEATURE ARTICLE**
Identify one **opinion** given in this paragraph. Does the author try to be objective, or unbiased, in this article?

## Comprehension

1. **Recall** When did Mirwais first sing?

2. **Recall** From whom did Mirwais receive his musical training?

3. **Recall** What advantages do younger singers have over older singers in Afghanistan?

**INDIANA STANDARDS**

**READING STANDARD**
**8.2.7** Analyze the structure, format, and purpose of informational materials....

## Critical Analysis

4. **Summarize Main Ideas and Details** Look back at the outline you created while reading "Kabul's Singing Sensation." Based on the main ideas and details you noted, summarize the article.

5. **Examine Word Choice** What does Mirwais's voice sound like? Look back at the article and find words and **imagery** that help you "hear" Mirwais's voice.

6. **Analyze Quotations** A quotation is a direct statement made by someone. Lines 16, 20, and 63–65 contain three quotations from Mirwais. What do these quotations tell you about the young singer?

7. **Evaluate a Feature Article** Do you think Mirwais Najrabi is a good subject for a human-interest piece? Explain why most people would—or would not—be interested in reading about him.

## Extension and Challenge

8. **Readers' Circle** What if **singing** were banned in this country? How would you react to this decision? What would you be willing to risk to preserve music? Consider how Mirwais and his family reacted to life under the Taliban as you discuss these and other questions.

9.  **SOCIAL STUDIES CONNECTION** What is the current state of Afghanistan? What is life like for those who live there? Research the social and political climate of Afghanistan. Share your findings with the class.

> **RESEARCH LINKS**
> For more on Afghanistan, visit the **Research Center** at **ClassZone.com**.

A family rides on horseback through the mountains of Afghanistan.

# Vocabulary in Context

## VOCABULARY PRACTICE

Note the letter of the item that you might associate with each boldfaced word.

1. **edict:** (a) a friend's suggestion, (b) a king's order, (c) a polite request
2. **exile:** (a) being sent away, (b) being imprisoned, (c) having to pay a fine
3. **immaculate:** (a) without decorations, (b) without wrinkles, (c) without dirt
4. **puritanical:** (a) like a new school principal, (b) like a group with strict rules, (c) like a popular athletic coach
5. **transcendent:** (a) sinking down, (b) rising above, (c) solving problems
6. **virtuoso:** (a) a beginning violinist, (b) an off-key singer, (c) a musical star

## VOCABULARY IN WRITING

Tim McGirk used emotional language and imagery to describe Mirwais's voice. How would you describe your favorite singer? Using at least two vocabulary words, write a one-paragraph review of his or her music. You might start like this.

> **EXAMPLE SENTENCE**
>
> *Although he's only 16 years old, Chris is already a hip-hop* **virtuoso.**

**INDIANA STANDARDS**

**READING STANDARD**
**8.1.3** Verify the meaning of a word in its context . . . .

## VOCABULARY STRATEGY: SUFFIXES THAT FORM ADJECTIVES

A **suffix** is a word part that can be added to a root or base word to form a new word. Some suffixes, such as *-ical* in *puritanical,* can be added to nouns to form adjectives. Others, such as *-ent* in *transcendent,* can be added to verbs to form adjectives. If you can recognize the root or base word in a word with a suffix, you can often figure out the entire word's meaning. Consult the chart for common adjective suffixes and their meanings.

| Suffix | Meaning |
|---|---|
| *-ant, -ate, -ent, -ic, -ical, -ous* | like; having to do with; showing; causing |

**PRACTICE** Identify the base word in each boldfaced adjective. Then define the adjective.

1. Yesterday I received the **joyous** news that my grandmother will be coming to visit.
2. Like the earth, the moon is roughly **spherical.**
3. As he waits for his food, our dog wears an **expectant** expression.
4. Can you solve **algebraic** problems?
5. Mrs. Pine is a **considerate** host who makes sure that her guests are comfortable.

**VOCABULARY PRACTICE**
For more practice, go to the **Vocabulary Center** at **ClassZone.com.**

# Reading-Writing Connection

Demonstrate your understanding of "Kabul's Singing Sensation" by responding to these prompts. Then complete the **Grammar and Writing** exercise.

| WRITING PROMPTS | SELF-CHECK |
|---|---|
| **A.  Short Response: Write an Explanation**<br>Why do you think Mirwais and other Afghan musicians were willing to risk their lives for music? Write a **one-paragraph explanation** of Mirwais's possible motivation. | *A clear explanation will . . .*<br>• show an understanding of Mirwais's background and personality<br>• consider the role music plays in culture |
| **B.  Extended Response: Write a Letter**<br>Music can connect people across distance and culture.  Write a **two- or three-paragraph letter** to Mirwais expressing your reactions to the article you just read.  Then share with him some of your own experiences and thoughts about **singing** and music. | *A successful letter will . . .*<br>• clearly state your opinion about what you read in the article<br>• make connections between yourself and Mirwais |

## GRAMMAR AND WRITING

***USE COMMAS CORRECTLY***  Be sure to insert commas after **introductory words and phrases** to avoid possible confusion.  Place commas immediately after introductory words, such as *finally* and *afterwards,* and after introductory phrases.

**INDIANA STANDARDS**

**WRITING STANDARD**
**8.6.5** Use correct punctuation.

> *Original:*   In Afghanistan the Taliban ransacked the Afghan Radio and Television station.
>
> *Revised:*   In Afghanistan, the Taliban ransacked the Afghan Radio and Television station.

***PRACTICE***  In each sentence, add commas where they are needed.

1. Since the age of four I've played the trumpet.
2. Over the summer my friends and I formed a singing group.
3. After reading the article I wanted to hear your music.
4. Fortunately you were not harmed by the Taliban.

*For more help with commas, see page R49 in the **Grammar Handbook.***

## Robo-Legs
Magazine Article by Michel Marriott

## Eureka: Scientific Twists of Fate
Online Article

# *How has* SCIENCE *changed our lives?*

**INDIANA STANDARDS**

**READING STANDARD**
**8.2.7** Analyze the structure, format, and purpose of informational materials (such as textbooks, newspapers, instructional or technical manuals, and public documents).

*KEY IDEA* The next time you answer a cell phone, turn on a light, or take your asthma medicine, think about the knowledge that was needed to create these things. **Science** has made it possible for doctors, engineers, and inventors to develop technologies and medicines that make our lives healthier and more convenient. In the following articles, you'll read about some of the amazing scientific breakthroughs that have allowed people to lead longer, better lives.

*QUICKWRITE* What is one scientific development that you feel you could not live without? Think beyond obvious technological gadgets such as your computer or cell phone. Write one paragraph telling what a day might be like if this discovery had never taken place.

## ● ELEMENTS OF NONFICTION: AUTHOR'S PURPOSE

When you write an e-mail to a friend, you often do so with a purpose—to tell him or her about your day, or to inquire about this weekend's plans. An **author's purpose** is his or her reason for writing a certain piece. That reason might be to persuade, to entertain, to inform or explain, or to express his or her thoughts and feelings. Although a writer may have more than one reason for writing, usually one purpose stands out.

You can figure out an author's purpose by examining the author's subject, **tone,** and words. For example, a serious piece about the environment is probably meant to inform or persuade. Your reaction to a piece is also a good indicator. If you laugh out loud while reading an essay, then the author's purpose is probably to entertain. As you read the following articles, try to identify each author's purpose.

## ● READING STRATEGY: MONITOR

When you **monitor** your reading, you pause to check your comprehension of the material. To monitor effectively, pause frequently and try the following strategies:

- **Ask questions** about the information presented.
- **Visualize,** or picture, events and details described.
- **Reread** passages that you find confusing.

Use a chart like the one shown to help you monitor.

| Where I Paused | What Confused Me | How I Clarified the Information |
|---|---|---|
|  |  |  |

## ▲ VOCABULARY IN CONTEXT

How many of the boldfaced words do you know? Use context clues to figure out a definition for each.

1. People who lose an **appendage** can still exercise.
2. The pollution could **contaminate** the water supply.
3. **Infectious** diseases can be transmitted quickly.
4. I need **keener** eyesight to thread the needle.
5. Roberto gains **mobility** by using a wheelchair.
6. The infection was **pervasive** throughout her body.
7. Mrs. Blake needed **rehabilitation** following knee surgery.
8. The scientist's **serendipitous** discovery led to a cure.

# Author Online

**A Born Communicator**
Michel Marriott says that he was "practically born talking." As a child, he talked all the time, and eventually he began writing out his thoughts on paper. Through his work at his school newspaper, Marriott realized that journalism was a good career choice.

**Michel Marriott**
**born 1954**

Since then, Marriott has worked for the *Washington Post, Newsweek,* and *The New York Times,* covering a variety of topics, including technology, fashion, and urban crime. In 1995, director Spike Lee produced *New Jersey Drive,* a film based on Marriott's series of articles about the desperate lives of young car thieves. The series was nominated for a Pulitzer Prize.

**MORE ABOUT THE AUTHOR**
For more on Michel Marriott, visit the **Literature Center** at **ClassZone.com.**

## *Background*

**Marvelous Medical Inventions** Throughout history, scientists and inventors have worked to make life better for those with physical disabilities. The first eyeglasses were created in the 1200s. The first hearing aids, called "trumpets," were invented in the early 1800s. Prosthetics, used to replace missing arms and legs, were made of wood or metal as long ago as the days of ancient Rome. In medieval times, a knight who lost an arm could be fitted with a metal prosthetic that held a shield during battle. In the 1800s, wooden legs were fashioned to resemble real legs. They included springs and sockets to allow movement. Today, scientists draw on robotics and a better understanding of the human body to create prosthetics that are very similar to real limbs.

# Robo-Legs

## Michel Marriott

**ANALYZE VISUALS**
This photo shows Cameron Clapp competing at the 2005 Endeavor Games. Based on his body language and facial expression, what can you **conclude** about Clapp's personality?

*New prosthetic limbs[1] are providing increased* **mobility** *for many amputees—and blurring the line between humans and machines*

**W**ith his blond hair, buff torso, and megawatt smile, Cameron Clapp is in many ways the typical California teenager. There are, however, a few things that set him apart: For starters, this former skater boy is now making his way through life on a pair of shiny, state-of-the-art[2] robotic legs. **A**

"I make it look easy," he says.

Clapp, 19, lost both his legs above the knee and his right arm just short of his shoulder after getting hit by a train almost five years ago near his home in Grover Beach, California. Following years of **rehabilitation** and
10   a series of prosthetics, each more technologically advanced than the last, he has become part of a new generation of people who are embracing breakthrough technologies as a means of overcoming their own bodies' limitations.

"I do have a lot of motivation and self-esteem," Clapp says, "but I might look at myself differently if technology was not on my side."

The technology he's referring to is the C-Leg. Introduced by Otto Bock HeathCare, a German company that makes advanced prosthetics, the C-Leg combines computer technology with hydraulics. Sensors monitor how the leg is being placed on the ground, and microprocessors[3] guide the
20   limb's hydraulic system, enabling it to imitate a natural step. It literally does the walking for the walker. The technology, however, is not cheap; a single C-Leg can cost more than $40,000. **B**

The C-Leg is one of the examples of how blazing advancements, including tiny programmable microprocessors, lightweight materials, and **keener** sensors, are restoring remarkable degrees of mobility to amputees, says William Hanson, president of . . . a Massachusetts company that specializes in developing and distributing advanced prosthetic arms and hands.

**A AUTHOR'S PURPOSE** Reread lines 1–5. Based on the information presented so far, what one or two purposes do you think the author has for writing?

**B MONITOR** Examine lines 16–21. What words and phrases help you **visualize** Clapp's legs? Compare your mental image with the photo on page 930.

---

1. **prosthetic limbs** (prŏs-thĕt′ĭk lĭmz): artificial arms and legs.
2. **state-of-the-art**: made using the newest technology available.
3. **microprocessors**: tiny computer parts that operators can program, or give new instructions to.

Clapp's prosthetic legs feature several attachments to suit different purposes.

**C** AUTHOR'S PURPOSE
Why do you think the author included facts about Clapp's three sets of prosthetic legs?

**D** MONITOR
What **questions** do you have after reading this paragraph? Decide whether to reread or read on for answers.

### Three Sets of Legs

For example, Clapp, who remains very involved in athletics despite his
30 condition, has three different sets of specialized prosthetic legs: one for walking, one for running, and one for swimming. He put all of them to use at the Endeavor Games in Edmond, Oklahoma—an annual sporting event for athletes with disabilities—where he competed in events like the 200-meter dash and the 50-yard freestyle swim. **C**

### Man or Machine?

But increased mobility is only part of the story. Something more subtle, and possibly far-reaching, is also occurring: The line that has long separated human beings from the machines that assist them is blurring, as complex technologies become a visible part of the people who depend upon them. **D**

40     Increasingly, amputees, especially young men like Clapp, and soldiers who have lost limbs in Afghanistan and Iraq, are choosing not to hide their

prosthetics under clothing as previous generations did. Instead, some of the estimated 1.2 million amputees in the United States—more than two-thirds of whom are men—proudly polish and decorate their electronic limbs for all to see. . . .

Many young people, especially those who have been using personal electronics since childhood, are comfortable recharging their limbs' batteries in public and plugging their prosthetics into their computers to adjust the software, Hanson says.

50 Nick Springer, 20, a student at Eckerd College in St. Petersburg, Florida, who lost his arms and legs to meningitis when he was 14, recalls doing just that at a party when the lithium-ion batteries[4] for his legs went dead.

"I usually get 30 hours out of them before I have to charge them again," he says. "But I didn't charge them up the day before."

### Terminator Legs

When his legs ran out of power, he spent most of his time sitting on a couch talking to people while his legs were plugged into an electrical outlet nearby. According to Springer, no one at the party seemed to care, and his faith in his high-tech **appendages** appears unfazed. "I love my Terminator[5] legs," he says. **E**

60 Springer also remembers going to see *Star Wars: Episode III—Revenge of the Sith* with his father. While he liked the movie, he found the final scenes—in which Anakin Skywalker loses his arms and legs in a light-saber battle and is rebuilt with fully functional prosthetics to become the infamous Darth Vader—a little far-fetched.

70 "We have a long way to go before we get anything like that," he says. "But look how far humanity has come in the past decade. Who knows? The hardest part is getting the ball rolling. We pretty much got it rolling."

Nick Springer plays hockey with the help of specially-made prosthetics. © Dith Pran/New York Times/Redux.

---

4. **lithium-ion batteries** (lĭth′ē-əm-ī′ŏn′ băt′ə-rēz): very light, small batteries with a great deal of energy packed into a small space.

5. **Terminator:** a robotic character in a 1984 film, *The Terminator*.

**appendage** (ə-pĕn′dĭj) *n.* a body part, such as an arm or leg, that is attached to the main part of the body

**E** **AUTHOR'S PURPOSE**
Reread lines 55–59. What do you think is Marriott's attitude toward the subject of today's prosthetics and the people who use them?

PBS

# Eureka:
## Scientific Twists of Fate

. . . We are all familiar with the tale of Newton's apple. While sitting in his orchard one day in 1665, Isaac Newton's[1] curiosity was sparked by a falling apple, leading him to "discover" the law of gravity. As doubtful as the story sounds, writings by Newton and his contemporaries verify the incident. Though science often seems an orderly and methodical process, history is dotted with surprising discoveries such as these. Were they merely luck? Or the results of a gifted mind? Actually, a bit of both. Sometimes scientific discoveries come from the most unexpected places, when talented people are watching out for them. Here are two examples of similarly **serendipitous** finds. **Ⓐ**

### The Smallpox Cure

In the late 1700s, Edward Jenner, a young English doctor-in-training, was told by a local
10  milkmaid that she was safe from smallpox[2] because she had already had cowpox. Like its deadly cousin, cowpox also produced painful blisters, yet doctors had not made a connection between the two diseases. After extensive research, Jenner discovered that what she said was true—milkmaids exposed to a common strain of cowpox almost never contracted smallpox.

Jenner's supervising physicians took little interest in his findings. Then, in 1796, he injected a young boy named James Phipps with tissue taken from a cowpox blister on a milkmaid's hand. He then exposed the boy to the deadly smallpox virus. So **pervasive** and devastating was this disease at the time that the boy's family was willing to take this unimaginable risk. But their gamble paid off. Young James remained completely healthy,
20  and the vaccination process was born.

Jenner's idea opened the door not only to the eradication of smallpox but to the subsequent perfection of the immunization procedure by Louis Pasteur.[3] The modern

---

1. **Isaac Newton:** mathematician and scientist (1642–1727) who developed the theory of gravity.
2. **smallpox:** a highly infectious, often fatal disease characterized by high fevers and blisters that leave pockmarks on the skin.
3. **Louis Pasteur** (lōō'ē păs-tûr'): French chemist (1822–1895) who founded modern microbiology and developed several life-saving vaccines.

**Ⓐ AUTHOR'S PURPOSE**
Based on the tone of this paragraph and the information presented, what do you think might be the purpose or purposes of this article?

**serendipitous**
(sĕr'ən-dĭp'ĭ-təs) *adj.*
found by fortunate accident

**pervasive** (pər-vā'sĭv) *adj.*
present throughout

term "vaccine," from the Latin word for "cow," honors Jenner and his life-saving inspiration. . . . **B**

### Penicillin

Arguably the most important medical discovery of the 20th century came about purely by accident. Throughout the 1920s, Scottish scientist Alexander Fleming was

30 searching for a cure for **infectious** disease, the major cause of death throughout much of human history. As part of his research, Fleming was cultivating several species of bacteria in separate petri dishes.

Alexander Fleming

One day, Fleming noticed that a mold had **contaminated** the petri dish containing the bacteria *Staphylococcus,* a common microbe responsible for a variety of ailments ranging from the earaches to deadly post-operative infections. But before tossing away the moldy dish, Fleming realized that the intruder had actually killed off much of the bacteria culture.

40 The tiny, wind-born mold spore must have landed in the *Staphylococcus* colony during a brief moment Fleming had uncovered the dish. Fleming isolated the mold and identified it as a member of the genus *Penicillium.* He called the antibiotic substance it secreted penicillin.

Fleming's further investigation found that penicillin killed off several, but not all, strains of the disease-causing microbes he was growing in his lab. Had the penicillium contaminated a different dish, Fleming might never have discovered its medicinal benefits.

Additionally, Fleming found penicillin was non-toxic to humans and animals. Realizing the strategic advantage in possessing the world's first antibiotic, the U.S. and Britain joined forces to mass-produce the drug, and treated thousands of Allied troops wounded

50 in the D-Day invasion of Europe. It has saved countless lives ever since. In 1945, Fleming shared the Nobel Prize in Medicine for his work on the "Wonder Drug" penicillin. . . . **C**

### Serendipity or Smarts?

Each of these examples of serendipity helped advance the scope of human knowledge by great leaps and bounds. But these accidents and twists of fate are not quite as random as they seem. Each discovery occurred in the presence of a well-trained intellect. . . . As Louis Pasteur once said, "In the fields of observation, chance favors only the prepared mind."

**B MONITOR**
Reread the subheading of this section. Based on this, what question about smallpox should you be able to answer? If you can't answer this question for yourself, **reread** lines 9–25.

**infectious** (ĭn-fĕk′shəs) *adj.* capable of being transmitted by infection

**contaminate** (kən-tăm′ə-nāt′) *v.* to make impure or unclean through contact

**C MONITOR**
Why is penicillin important? Reread this section if you don't know the answer.

# Comprehension

**INDIANA STANDARDS**

**READING STANDARD**
**8.2.7** Analyze the structure, format, and purpose of informational materials....

1. **Recall** How does the C-Leg described in "Robo-Legs" work?

2. **Summarize** According to "Robo-Legs," what is different about the way young amputees feel about their prosthetic limbs?

3. **Clarify** James Phipps is mentioned in "Eureka: Scientific Twists of Fate." Why was his family willing to risk his exposure to the smallpox virus?

# Critical Analysis

4. **Examine the Message** Reread the first paragraph of "Robo-Legs" as well as lines 23–28 and 35–39. Based on the information stated and the descriptive words and phrases used, what do you think is the message the author wants to share about **science** and technology?

5. **Interpret Quotation** "Eureka: Scientific Twists of Fate" contains this quote from Louis Pasteur: "In the fields of observation, chance favors only the prepared mind." What does he mean? Use examples from the article to support your answer.

6. **Evaluate Monitoring Techniques** Look back at the chart you created as you read. Which strategy best helped you understand the articles? Explain.

7. **Analyze Authors' Purposes** Reflect back on your reading of both articles. What's the author's main purpose in "Robo-Legs"? What is the main purpose of "Eureka: Scientific Twists of Fate"? Give examples from each selection to support your answers.

8. **Compare Texts** Use a Venn diagram like the one shown to record similarities and differences between the articles. Consider the subject matter, purpose, and tone of each article. Why do you think these two articles were presented together in a single lesson?

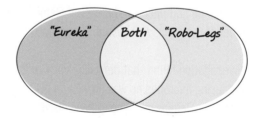

"Eureka"  Both  "Robo-Legs"

# Extension and Challenge

9. **Readers' Circle** Both "Robo-Legs" and "Eureka: Scientific Twists of Fate" describe medical advancements that have helped people lead better lives. What problems would you like science to solve? Discuss your answer with a small group.

10.  **SCIENCE CONNECTION** Robotics has become an exciting and popular field of scientific study. Other than prosthetics, what is another way robotics is being used today? Research to find an answer. Then present your findings to the class.

> **RESEARCH LINKS**
> For more on robotics, visit the **Research Center** at **ClassZone.com.**

# Vocabulary in Context

## VOCABULARY PRACTICE

Answer each question to show your understanding of the vocabulary words.

1. Which is an **appendage,** a boy's back or his leg?
2. Which can **contaminate** your dinner, bacteria or salt?
3. Which are **infectious,** colds or injuries?
4. If your eyesight gets **keener,** does it get better or worse?
5. Which provides **mobility,** an armchair or a car?
6. If an attitude is **pervasive,** do many people share it or just a few?
7. Would you need **rehabilitation** to recover from a broken leg, or from a cold?
8. If you make a **serendipitous** discovery, are you lucky or unlucky?

| appendage | mobility |
|---|---|
| contaminate | pervasive |
| infectious | rehabilitation |
| keener | serendipitous |

## VOCABULARY IN WRITING

How has medical technology helped you or someone you know? Write a paragraph describing the way medical advancements improve people's quality of life. You might start like this.

> **EXAMPLE SENTENCE**
>
> My grandmother's wheelchair provides her with **mobility**.

**INDIANA STANDARDS**

READING STANDARD
**8.1.3** Verify the meaning of a word in its context . . . .

## VOCABULARY STRATEGY: THE LATIN ROOT *pend*

The vocabulary word *appendage* contains the Latin root *pend*, which means "hang." Many English words contain this root. To figure out the meaning of words with this root, use context clues and your knowledge of the root's meaning.

*PRACTICE* Choose the word from the web that best completes each sentence. Then explain how the root *pend* relates to the meaning of the word.

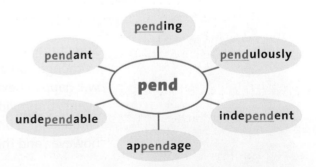

1. If an employee is ____, he will not keep his job very long.
2. Dogs are pack animals, so they hate being left alone; however, cats are fairly ____ creatures.
3. She wore a diamond____ around her neck.
4. The detective has several cases ____, but none of them are resolved.
5. The elephant's trunk swung ____ from side to side.

**VOCABULARY PRACTICE**
For more practice, go to the **Vocabulary Center** at ClassZone.com.

# An American Plague:
## The True and Terrifying Story of the Yellow Fever Epidemic of 1793

History Book by Jim Murphy

**Jim Murphy**
**born 1947**

## Other Books by Jim Murphy

- *Blizzard!: The Storm That Changed America*
- *The Great Fire*
- *A Young Patriot: The American Revolution as Experienced by One Boy*

## Meet Jim Murphy

Jim Murphy didn't read much as a child. It wasn't until a high school teacher told his class that they weren't allowed to read a particular novel that Murphy became inspired to read. At first, he did it just to be rebellious. Murphy says that as he continued to read, he developed a love of history, because it enabled him to "visit many different times and places in the past."

Today, Murphy is the award-winning author of over 25 books about American history. He finds his work rewarding, and he especially enjoys the research stage of each project. He seeks out eyewitness accounts of events and loves to uncover the vivid details that add drama and emotion to his work. "One of my goals in writing about events from the past is to show that children weren't just observers of our history," Murphy says. "They were actual participants and sometimes did amazing and heroic things."

## Try a History Book

Sometimes a nonfiction book can be so enthralling, it's almost as though you are reading a suspense novel, wondering what will happen next. History books tell about a series of important events or provide details about one major event, often in chronological order. Some history books start with the outcome, however, and then back up to show readers how it came about.

## Read a Great Book

In 1793, Philadelphia, Pennsylvania, was the nation's capital. It was also a city at the mercy of an invisible enemy. In this vivid account of the yellow fever epidemic, Jim Murphy highlights some of the conditions in Philadelphia at that time and shows how those conditions contributed to the spread of a deadly disease.

*from*

# An American Plague:

## *The True and Terrifying Story of the Yellow Fever Epidemic of 1793*

*Saturday, August 3, 1793.* The sun came up, as it had every day since the end of May, bright, hot, and unrelenting. The swamps and marshes south of Philadelphia had already lost a great deal of water to the intense heat, while the Delaware and Schuylkill Rivers had receded to reveal long stretches of their muddy, root-choked banks. Dead fish and gooey vegetable matter were exposed and rotted, while swarms of insects droned in the heavy, humid air.

In Philadelphia itself an increasing number of cats were dropping dead every day, attracting, one Philadelphian complained, "an amazing
10 number of flies and other insects." Mosquitoes were everywhere, though their high-pitched whirring was particularly loud near rain barrels, gutters, and open sewers.

These sewers, called "sinks," were particularly ripe this year. Most streets in the city were unpaved and had no system of covered sewers and pipes to channel water away from buildings. Instead, deep holes were dug at various street corners to collect runoff water and anything else that might be washed along. Dead animals were routinely tossed into this soup, where everything decayed and sent up noxious bubbles to foul the air.

Down along the docks lining the Delaware, cargo was being loaded
onto ships that would sail to New York, Boston, and other distant ports.
The hard work of hoisting heavy casks into the hold was accompanied
by the stevedores' usual grunts and muttered oaths.

The men laboring near Water Street had particular reason to curse.
The sloop *Amelia* from Santo Domingo had anchored with a cargo
of coffee, which had spoiled during the voyage. The bad coffee was
dumped on Ball's Wharf, where it putrefied in the sun and sent out a
powerful odor that could be smelled over a quarter mile away. Benjamin
Rush, one of Philadelphia's most celebrated doctors and a signer of the
Declaration of Independence, lived three long blocks from Ball's Wharf,
but he recalled that the coffee stank "to the great annoyance of the
whole neighborhood."

Despite the stench, the streets nearby were crowded with people that
morning—ship owners and their captains talking seriously, shouting
children darting between wagons or climbing on crates and barrels, well-
dressed men and women out for a stroll, servants and slaves hurrying
from one chore to the next. Philadelphia was then the largest city in
North America, with nearly 51,000 inhabitants; those who didn't
absolutely have to be indoors working had escaped to the open air to
seek relief from the sweltering heat.

Many of them stopped at one of the city's 415 shops, whose doors
and windows were wide open to let in light and any hint of a cooling
breeze. The rest continued along, headed for the market on High Street.

Here three city blocks were crowded with vendors calling their wares
while eager shoppers studied merchandise or haggled over weights and
prices. Horse-drawn wagons clattered up and down the cobblestone
street, bringing in more fresh vegetables, squawking chickens, and
squealing pigs. People commented on the stench from Ball's Wharf, but
the market's own ripe blend of odors—of roasting meats, strong cheeses,
days-old sheep and cow guts, dried blood, and horse manure—tended
to overwhelm all others.

One and a half blocks from the market was the handsomely
refurbished mansion of Robert Morris, a wealthy manufacturer who
had used his fortune to help finance the Revolutionary War. Morris was
lending this house to George and Martha Washington and had moved
himself into another, larger one he owned just up the block. Washington
was then president of the United States, and Philadelphia was the
temporary capital of the young nation and the center of its federal
government. Washington spent the day at home in a small, stuffy office

seeing visitors, writing letters, and worrying. It was the French problem
60 that was most on his mind these days.

Not so many years before, the French monarch, Louis XVI, had sent
money, ships, and soldiers to aid the struggling Continental Army's
fight against the British. The French aid had been a major reason why
Washington was able to surround and force General Charles Cornwallis
to surrender at Yorktown in 1781. This military victory eventually led
to a British capitulation three years later and to freedom for the United
States—and lasting fame for Washington.

Then, in 1789, France erupted in its own revolution. The common
people and a few nobles and churchmen soon gained complete power
70 in France and beheaded Louis XVI in January 1793. Many of France's
neighbors worried that similar revolutions might spread to their
countries and wanted the new French republic crushed. Soon after
the king was put to death, revolutionary France was at war with Great
Britain, Holland, Spain, and Austria.

Naturally, the French republic had turned to the United States for
help, only to have President Washington hesitate. Washington knew that
he and his country owed the French an eternal debt. He simply wasn't
sure that the United States had the military strength to take on so many
formidable foes.

80 Many citizens felt Washington's Proclamation of Neutrality was
a betrayal of the French people. His own secretary of state, Thomas
Jefferson, certainly did, and he argued bitterly with Treasury Secretary
Alexander Hamilton over the issue. Wasn't the French fight for
individual freedom, Jefferson asked, exactly like America's struggle
against British oppression? . . .

While Washington worried, the city's taverns, beer gardens, and
coffeehouses—all 176 of them—were teeming with activity that
Saturday. There men, and a few women, lifted their glasses in toasts and
singing and let the hours slip away in lively conversation. Business and
90 politics and the latest gossip were the favorite topics. No doubt the heat,
the foul stink from Ball's Wharf, and the country's refusal to join with
France were discussed and argued over at length.

In all respects it seemed as if August 3 was a very normal day, with
business and buying and pleasure as usual.

Oh, there were a few who felt a tingle of unease. For weeks an
unusually large supply of wild pigeons had been for sale at the market.
Popular folklore suggested that such an abundance of pigeons always
brought with it unhealthy air and sickness.

Dr. Rush had no time for such silly notions, but he, too, sensed
that something odd was happening. His concern focused on a series of
illnesses that had struck his patients throughout the year—the mumps
in January, jaw and mouth infections in February, scarlet fever in March,
followed by influenza in July. "There was something in the heat and
drought," the good doctor speculated, "which was uncommon, in their
influence upon the human body."

The Reverend J. Henry C. Helmuth of the Lutheran congregation,
too, thought something was wrong in the city, though it had nothing to
do with sickness of the body. It was the souls of its citizens he worried
about. "Philadelphia . . . seemed to strive to exceed all other places in
the breaking of the Sabbath," he noted. . . .

Rush and Helmuth would have been surprised to know that their
worries were turning to reality on August 3. For on that Saturday a young
French sailor rooming at Richard Denny's boarding house, over on North
Water Street, was desperately ill with a fever. Eighteenth-century record
keeping wasn't very precise, so no one bothered to write down his name.
Besides, this sailor was poor and a foreigner, not the sort of person who
would draw much attention from the community around him. All we
know is that his fever worsened and was accompanied by violent seizures,
and that a few days later he died.

Other residents at Denny's would follow this sailor to the grave—a
Mr. Moore fell into a stupor and passed away, Mrs. Richard Parkinson
expired on August 7, next the lodging house owner and his wife, Mary,
and then the first sailor's roommate. Around the same time, two people
in the house next to Denny's died of the same severe fever.

Eight deaths in the space of a week in two houses on the same
street . . . but the city did not take notice. Summer fevers were
common visitors to all American cities in the eighteenth century, and
therefore not headline news. Besides, Denny's was located on a narrow
out-of-the-way street—really more an alley than a street. "It is much
confined," a resident remarked, "ill-aired, and, in every respect, is a
disagreeable street." Things happened along this street all the time—
sometimes very bad things—that went unnoticed by the authorities
and the rest of the population.

So the deaths did not disrupt Philadelphia much at all. Ships came
and went; men and women did chores, talked, and sought relief from
the heat and insects; the markets and shops hummed with activity;
children played; and the city, state, and federal governments went about
their business.

No one noticed that the church bells were tolling more often than
140  usual to announce one death, and then another. They rang for Dr. Hugh
Hodge's little daughter, for Peter Aston, for John Weyman, for Mary
Shewell, and for a boy named McNair. No one knew that a killer was
already moving through their streets with them, an invisible stalker that
would go house to house until it had touched everyone, rich or poor, in
some terrible way.  ∾

## Keep Reading

You've just read about the start of the 1793 yellow fever
outbreak. Thousands of people in Philadelphia will die before
the cause of the numerous deaths is discovered, and the public's
fear is spreading even faster than the fever. Keep reading to
learn about the heroic efforts of many citizens to care for the
sick and search for a cure.

# Problem-Solution Essay

In this unit, you learned how scientists, inventors, and many other people face problems. One good way to resolve situations that bother you is to write a problem-solution essay. To learn more, consult the **Writer's Road Map**.

## WRITER'S ROAD MAP

### Problem-Solution Essay

**WRITING PROMPT 1**

**Writing for the Real World** Choose a problem that really interests you. Write an essay in which you explain the problem, examine its causes, and explore possible solutions.

**Problems to Explore**

- stereotypes of teenagers
- environmental issues
- overcrowding in the school lunchroom
- cheating in professional sports

**WRITING PROMPT 2**

**Writing from Literature** Every selection in this unit deals with solving a problem. Choose one of the problems you read about in the unit. Write an essay identifying the problem and describing a solution.

**Selections to Explore**

- "The Spider Man Behind *Spider-Man*" (training insects)
- "Interview with a Songcatcher" (recording and preserving world music)
- "Robo-Legs" (providing mobility for amputees)

 **WRITING TOOLS**
For prewriting, revision, and editing tools, visit the **Writing Center at ClassZone.com.**

### KEY TRAITS

**1. IDEAS**
- **States the problem** in a clearly worded thesis
- Explains the **causes and effects** of the problem
- Discusses different **solutions**
- Gives **details** to help explain the solution to the problem

**2. ORGANIZATION**
- Makes the importance of the problem clear in the **introduction**
- Uses **transitions** to connect ideas
- **Concludes** by summing up the best solution

**3. VOICE**
- Maintains a **tone** that is suited to topic, audience, and purpose

**4. WORD CHOICE**
- Uses **precise words** to express the problem and solution

**5. SENTENCE FLUENCY**
- Varies **sentence beginnings**

**6. CONVENTIONS**
- Uses **correct grammar, spelling, and punctuation**

# Part 1: Analyze a Student Model

**WRITING STANDARD**
**8.5.7** Write for different purposes and to a specific audience or person....

**Alicia M. Fiore**
**LaSalle Academy**

### Our Public Pool: Problem or Solution?

I always look forward to summer vacation, but this year, I'm even more excited than usual. Swimming is my favorite sport, and I just learned that the new public pool in Madison Park will be finished ahead of schedule. Best of all, it will open the day after school closes.

5   I was really excited until I learned that users have to pay an expensive membership fee. Unless we can find a way to make the pool available to the whole community, many of my friends and I will have a long, hot summer vacation.

According to the dictionary, the word *public* means "relating to
10   people in general." To me, that definition means that a public pool should be open to everybody, not just to everybody who can pay the membership fee. The problem is not just what the pool is called, though. What the community needs is a pool that really is available to every citizen.

15   I know that building a pool is expensive. Once it is built, it has to be treated with chemicals and cleaned regularly to make sure the water is safe for people to swim in. Someone has to water and mow the grass in the sunbathing area. Then there are lifeguards, locker-room attendants, and snack-bar workers who must be paid. Our community needs to find
20   money to cover these expenses. However, charging the public a large fee to cover these expenses prevents many citizens from enjoying the pool.

A solution to this problem will have to satisfy both the people who want to use the pool and the ones who run it. One possibility would be for the town to raise taxes to cover the costs of operating the pool. If other
25   people are like my parents, though, they think their taxes are already much too high. For this reason, raising taxes probably wouldn't work.

---

**KEY TRAITS IN ACTION**

**Introduction** shows the importance of the topic. Highlighted thesis **states the problem.**

Varies **sentence beginnings** to hold the reader's interest.

Describes the **causes** of the problem (having a pool is expensive) and an important **effect** (the community must find a way to pay for it).

Presents a possible **solution.** Highlighted **transitions** help connect the ideas showing the disadvantages of this option.

Another option would be for the community government to sponsor fundraising events like car washes, bake sales, cleanup days, and concerts. People like to get together and donate their time for a good cause, so these

30  fundraisers could be successful. They would be one-time events, however, and the pool would need money coming in regularly to stay open.

Here's a better solution. The town could still charge a membership fee for those who can pay, but open the pool to everyone at certain times. Free swims could be scheduled one or two days a week, a few hours every

35  day, or any time the temperature rises above a certain point. Community members who can afford the fee would probably feel good about giving other people the chance to use the pool, too. I know my friends and I would be thrilled.

There is a simple, effective solution to the problem of the new public

40  pool—free swims. With your support, I know it will work. Just sign the petition posted outside the town hall and give everyone the chance to kick back, cool off, and float through the summer.

> Proposes a second possible solution and gives **details** about its advantages and disadvantages.

> **Precise words** make the third possible solution easy to understand. Matter-of-fact, honest **tone** is suited to the audience—the writer's classmates and neighbors.

> **Concludes** by summarizing the best solution, telling the reader how to help make it happen, and describing how enjoyable using the pool will be for everyone.

2

# Part 2: Apply the Writing Process

**WRITING STANDARD**
**8.4.1** Discuss ideas for writing . . . .

## PREWRITING

| *What Should I Do?* | *What Does It Look Like?* |
|---|---|

**1. Choose a prompt.**
Reread the prompts on page 944. Pick the one that interests you. Look it over carefully, circling all the details you need to cover in your essay.

▶ **WRITING PROMPT** *Choose a problem that really interests you. Write an (essay) in which you (explain) (the problem,) (examine its causes) and (explore possible) (solutions.)*

> *I can think of many interesting problems, but I need to write about one that really can be solved.*

**2. Focus on a problem.**
Make a list of problems from your life or from something that you have read. Group them in categories to help you come up with ideas. <u>Underline</u> the problem that will be the focus of your essay.

▶

| *Family* | *Community* | *Environment* |
|---|---|---|
| • arguments with parents | • <u>new public pool requires fee</u> | • litter in parks |
| • too many chores | • ban on certain dog breeds | • West Nile virus |

**3. Try out a variety of solutions.**
Think about the problem you have chosen. Alone or with a friend, brainstorm possible solutions. Consider the advantages and disadvantages of each.

**TIP** If you have trouble thinking of solutions that will work, choose another problem to write about.

▶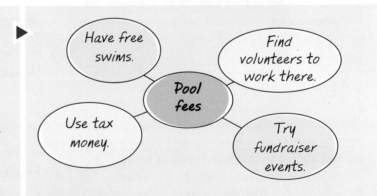

**4. Find support for your best solution.**
It's not enough to tell your reader, "I'm sure my solution will work." For Prompt 1, list facts, reasons, and other details that show why the solution you propose is the best one. For Prompt 2, find evidence in the literature that explains why the solution was successful or unsuccessful.

▶ **Have free swims at certain times.**
- Town will get the fees it needs from people who can pay.
- People will feel good about helping others.
- Everybody will be able to enjoy the pool.
- BUT . . . how would free swims work?

## DRAFTING

| What Should I Do? | What Does It Look Like? |
|---|---|
| **1. Spell out the problem and its importance.**<br>Before you can propose a solution, you need to make sure that your reader understands exactly what the problem is and why it matters. | ▶ *I was really excited about the new public pool until I learned that users have to pay an expensive membership fee. Unless we can find a way to make the pool available to the whole community, many of my friends and I will have a long, hot summer vacation.* |
| **2. Explain the problem's causes and effects.**<br>Write about factors that led to the problem and results of those factors. Make sure that there are logical connections between causes and effects. | ▶ *Building and maintaining a pool is expensive. As a result, our community needs to find money to cover those expenses. However, charging the public a large fee prevents many citizens from enjoying the pool.* |
| **3. Describe several possible solutions.**<br>Think about the solutions you came up with when you were brainstorming. Choose two or three and describe them for your reader. | ▶ *One possibility would be for the town to raise taxes to cover the costs of operating the pool.* — Possible solution<br><br>*If other people are like my parents, though, they think their taxes are already much too high.* — Why it won't work |
| **4. Decide on a structure for your essay.**<br>Make an informal outline of your key points. Describe the problem first. Then you can discuss possible solutions and end with the one you think is best, as this writer did. Or, if you prefer, explain the best solution first and then address the ones that you believe are not as strong. | ▶ ***Problem:*** *Fee prevents everybody from using public pool.*<br><br>***Possible solution A:*** *Raise taxes (but they are too high already).*<br><br>***Possible solution B:*** *Hold fund-raisers (but they wouldn't be a regular source of money).*<br><br>***Proposed solution C:*** *Have free swims (the best solution because money comes in from people who can afford it, and everybody gets a chance to use the pool).* |

## REVISING AND EDITING

| *What Should I Do?* | *What Does It Look Like?* |
|---|---|
| **1. Clarify with transitions.**<br>• Ask a peer reader to <u>underline</u> sentences that don't seem to be connected logically.<br>• If your essay has underlines, add a transition or other information to show the logical relationship between ideas.<br>**See page 950:** Ask a Peer Reader | <u>People like to get together and donate their time for a good cause,</u> ~~and also~~ <sup>so</sup> <u>these fund-raisers could be successful.</u> They would be one-time events, and the pool would need money coming in regularly to stay open.<br><br>however, |
| **2. Strengthen supporting details.**<br>• Draw a box around statements that lack details or that contain information not connected to your key ideas.<br>• Replace with information that makes your case stronger. | ~~Lots of people work at the pool.~~<br>The pool has to be treated with chemicals and cleaned regularly to make sure the water is safe for people to swim in. Someone has to water and mow the grass in the sunbathing area. Then there are lifeguards, locker-room attendants, and snack-bar workers who must be paid. Our community needs to find money to cover these expenses. |
| **3. Be on the lookout for vague statements.**<br>• Circle statements such as "Something has to be done," "This is really important," or "It's a serious problem."<br>• Revise using specific words that explain your ideas clearly. | ~~It just doesn't make sense.~~<br>What the community needs is a pool that really is available to every citizen. |
| **4. Make your conclusion complete.**<br>• Be sure that your conclusion sums up the problem and reiterates the solution that you believe is best.<br>• Depending on your topic, you may want to add a call to action. That's when you tell your reader what to do about the problem. | There is a simple, effective solution to the problem of the new public pool—free swims. With your support, I know it will work. Just sign the petition posted outside the town hall and give everyone the chance to kick back, cool off, and float through the summer. |

# Problem-Solution Essay

## Apply the Rubric

**A strong problem-solution essay . . .**

☑ begins by describing the problem and why it matters

☑ presents a logical thesis statement

☑ explains the causes and effects of the problem

☑ proposes several solutions

☑ supports the best solution with details and explanations

☑ connects ideas with transitions

☑ has a tone that suits the audience and purpose

☑ uses precise words to express ideas

☑ varies sentence beginnings

☑ concludes with a summary of the problem and the best solution

## Ask a Peer Reader

• Why is this problem important to me?

• Which of my ideas need better logical connections?

• What other solutions to this problem can you think of?

## Avoid Logical Fallacies

**Circular reasoning**—supporting a statement merely by repeating it in different words ("Access to the pool is crucial because it is really, really important.")

**Either/or fallacy**—suggesting that there are only two choices in a situation that really offers more options ("Either the pool is free for everyone or our summer vacation is ruined.")

**Overgeneralization**—a generalization that is too broad to be valid ("Everyone loves to swim, so the pool should be free to all.")

## Check Your Grammar

Use correct singular or plural verb forms with indefinite pronoun subjects.

Everyone is excited about the pool. (singular)

Most of the pool <u>area</u> is paved. (singular)

Most of the <u>swimmers</u> pay the fee. (plural)

Many of the <u>swimmers</u> pay the fee. (plural)

**See page R66:** Indefinite Pronouns as Subjects

## Writing On**l**ine

**PUBLISHING OPTIONS**
For publishing options, visit the **Writing Center** at ClassZone.com.

**ASSESSMENT PREPARATION**
For writing and grammar assessment practice, go to the **Assessment Center** at ClassZone.com.

## Giving an Oral Report

In Unit 8, you read nonfiction that described a variety of problems, and you wrote a problem-solution essay. To inform people about a problem that bothers you—the one you wrote about or a different one—present it as an oral report.

### Planning the Oral Report

1. **Choose the points you will cover.** Find out to whom you will be speaking, what audience members already know about the problem, and how long you are expected to speak. Think about what questions your listeners might ask and how you will answer them.

2. **Find visuals to include.** Collect or create drawings, photographs, maps, charts, spreadsheets, or other graphics to make your report more interesting and informative.

> *Possible Solutions to Pool Fees*
>
> *Raise taxes.*
> * *Taxes are already high.*
> * *People will never agree.*

3. **Practice presenting your report.** Run through your report several times in front of a practice audience. This practice will help you weave your visuals into your presentation and smooth out your delivery.

### Delivering the Oral Report

1. **Relate to your audience.** Be relaxed and look directly at your audience when speaking. Move your eyes around the room so everyone feels included.

2. **Speak loudly and clearly at a natural speed.** Don't be afraid to pause to think or take a breath.

3. **Use gestures and facial expressions.** Move your arms, hands, and head to stress what you are saying. Facial expressions can also convince listeners that you care about the problem.

4. **Ask for feedback.** Invite listeners to tell you what they thought of your presentation. Listen carefully to their comments and use them to improve your next oral report.

# Reading Comprehension

**DIRECTIONS** *Read this selection and answer the questions that follow.*

## *from* Odd Couples

**Amy Sarver**

Living in the wild can be hard. Finding food and staying safe aren't easy. Each day, animals struggle to survive in their habitats. Not all animals get by on their own. Some animals form a close partnership with other kinds of animals. These pairings are called symbiotic relationships.

In a symbiotic relationship, the animals depend on each other. One animal helps the other meet its needs. Sounds good, right? Not always. Some animals are not very kind to their partners. In some cases, one animal meets its needs but hurts its partner. Sounds crazy, but it does happen. Take ticks, for example. These insects guzzle blood to live. To get blood, they attach themselves to
10 other kinds of animals. Ticks do not help their hosts. Instead, they can pass germs that cause disease. In other relationships, animals don't treat their partners so poorly. Both animals benefit, or get help, from living with the other animal. Check out how animals pair up to survive.

### Keeping Clean

Small animals called cleaner shrimps have found a way of helping fish at coral reefs. As their name suggests, the shrimps clean the fish. Here's how it works. The shrimps hang out at what scientists call a cleaning station. A fish stops by. Then a shrimp climbs onto the fish. The shrimp even steps into the fish's mouth. The shrimp uses its tiny claws to pick stuff off the fish's body.
20 That can include dead skin, tiny pieces of food, and wee creatures that can hurt the fish. The fish gets a nice cleaning. The shrimp enjoys a tasty meal of fish trash.

Small birds called plovers are also in the cleaning business. They have big customers—crocodiles. Crocs have long snouts filled with sharp teeth. Cleaning them is tricky. That's where the plover comes in. When a croc opens its mouth, the plover hops right in. The croc does not snap its snout shut. Instead, it lets the plover eat small, harmful animals attached to the crocodile's teeth. The plover gets an easy meal. The croc gets clean teeth.

### Sweet Success

30 Some animals need each other because they like the same food. Take the honeyguide bird and the ratel. They live on grasslands in Africa. Both animals love honey. Yet each has a problem getting some. The bird can find a beehive, but can't open it. The ratel can open a hive, but doesn't know how to find one.

So the two animals team up. The bird flies over the grasslands, looking for hives. When it spots one, it swoops down and makes noise. The sound tells the ratel to come eat. The ratel uses its sharp claws to tear apart the hive. It gobbles up most of the honey-covered mess. Then the honeyguide bird enjoys finishing off the leftovers.

## Clowning Around

40    Land and sky animals aren't the only ones that work together. So do some sea animals. One of the oddest couples is made up of the sea anemone and the clownfish. You might think sea anemones look like plants, but they are really hungry animals. They attach themselves to a rock or a coral reef. There they wait for a fish to swim by. Then they sting it with their tentacles. The stunned fish is then pulled into the sea anemone's hidden mouth. Still, one daring fish makes its home among sea anemones. It's the clownfish. This orange-and-white fish isn't kidding

50    around. Its body is shielded by a thick layer of mucus. The slime protects the clownfish from the sea anemone's dangerous, stinging tentacles. The clownfish is also a good neighbor. It helps the sea anemone by luring in fish. When a hungry fish spots a colorful clownfish, it darts toward it. The clownfish safely swims under the anemone's tentacles. If the hungry fish follows, it gets stung. Then it becomes the anemone's next meal. The brave clownfish not only reels in fish food, it chases away fish that might eat an anemone. So the clownfish and

60    anemone help keep each other fed and safe.

Instead of searching the sky for insects, the oxpecker bird catches a ride aboard large animals such as the antelope. In return, the bird picks ticks and other pests off the animal's body.

Clownfish live safely among sea anemones. They lure edible fish into the anemones' deadly tentacles and chase away harmful ones.

## A Different Way of Life

All animals want to do one thing—survive in the wild. Some do that by living alone. Others live in flocks, herds, hives, packs, or schools. Some animals, both large and small, know the best way to stay alive is to live with or near other kinds of animals. At first glance, these teammates don't seem to make sense. If you look more closely, you'll soon learn that these animals help one another find food, shelter, and safety. They make the most of their various differences. These unlikely partners pair up to get the most out of life.

| SYMBIOTIC INTERACTIONS | | |
|---|---|---|
| **Type of Relationship** | **Example** | **Interaction** |
| **Mutualism:** both species benefit | bees and flowers | Bees gather nectar from flowers; they spread pollen that the flowers need to reproduce. |
| | aphids and ants | Aphids provide ants with sweet liquid; ants protect aphids from predators. |
| **Commensalism:** one species benefits; the other is not affected | trumpetfish and soft coral | Coral gives the trumpetfish camouflage for hunting; coral is unharmed. |
| | lichens and trees | Lichens live on trees; trees are unharmed. |
| **Parasitism:** one species benefits; the other is harmed | tapeworms and pigs | The tapeworm lives in the intestines of a host, such as a pig; it causes sickness in the host. |
| | mistletoe and trees | Mistletoe takes food from trees; the trees are damaged. |

# Comprehension

**DIRECTIONS** *Answer these questions about the article "Odd Couples."*

1. Which statement best summarizes the information in lines 15–28?

   ○ Some animals set up cleaning stations where they get food from other animals that stop by.

   ○ There isn't much food in the ocean, so shrimp need to eat fish trash.

   ○ Birds such as plovers have learned from shrimp how to get food out of another animal's mouth.

   ○ Sometimes, one animal gets food by cleaning another animal, so both animals benefit.

2. Reread lines 30–38. The term "sweet success" in the subheading (line 29) refers to what happens when the

   ○ honeyguide bird finds a beehive

   ○ honeyguide bird makes loud noises to attract the ratel

   ○ honeyguide bird and the ratel work together to get honey

   ○ ratel tears up the beehive and eats most of the honey

3. Which fact in the article does the photograph of the clownfish help you understand?

   ○ Sea anemones look like plants.

   ○ The clownfish is shielded by a layer of mucus.

   ○ A hungry fish gets stung when it darts toward a clownfish.

   ○ The clownfish chases away fish that might eat the anemones.

**4.** Reread the definitions in the chart. Which animal mentioned in the article has a parasitic relationship with another animal?

○ shrimp

○ tick

○ ratel

○ clownfish

**5.** According to the article, an unlikely couple can form a relationship that helps both partners. Which two species described in the selection best illustrate that idea?

○ tick and antelope

○ tapeworm and pig

○ trumpetfish and soft coral

○ plover and crocodile

**6.** Which detail helps you understand the main idea of the article?

○ The honeyguide bird and the ratel both live on grasslands in Africa.

○ Many animals survive in the wild by living together in flocks or herds.

○ Crocodiles have longs snouts with sharp teeth that are difficult to clean.

○ The cleaner shrimp enjoys a meal while removing harmful creatures from a fish.

**7.** Which statement best summarizes lines 61–68?

○ Many animals live together in groups of their own species, such as flocks, herds, or schools.

○ The strongest animals survive in the wild by living alone.

○ Wild animal behavior is difficult to predict and often makes little sense.

○ Animals use different survival strategies, including teaming up with unlikely partners.

**8.** The relationship between the clownfish and the sea anemone supports the idea that

○ a few animals form partnerships to have fun together

○ in some symbiotic relationships, both animals benefit from forming a partnership

○ animals that form partnerships survive better than animals that get by on their own

○ in some symbiotic relationships, one animal meets its needs but hurts its partner

**9.** Reread the caption with the antelope photograph. Under which subheading in the article would you add a paragraph about the antelope and the oxpecker bird?

○ Keeping Clean

○ Sweet Success

○ Clowning Around

○ A Different Way of Life

## Constructed Response

**SHORT ANSWER** *Write two or three sentences to answer this question.*

**10.** Choose an animal pair from either photograph. Where would you place that pair in the chart: under mutualism, commensalism, or parasitism? Explain your answer.

**ESSAY** *Write a paragraph to answer this question.*

**11.** Summarize the key points presented in the chart. Give one example of each type of symbiotic interaction to support your answer.

**GO ON** ➡

# Vocabulary

**DIRECTIONS** *Use context clues and your knowledge of suffixes to answer the following questions.*

1. What is the meaning of the word *symbiotic* as it is used in line 4?
   - ○ staying alert to danger
   - ○ competing for food
   - ○ acting in an aggressive way
   - ○ having a close association

2. What is the meaning of the word *stunned* as it is used in line 46?
   - ○ confused
   - ○ paralyzed
   - ○ astonished
   - ○ bored

3. What is the meaning of the word *various* as it is used in line 67?
   - ○ many
   - ○ changing
   - ○ extreme
   - ○ consistent

4. What is the meaning of the word *edible* as it is used in the caption with the clownfish photograph?
   - ○ injured
   - ○ hungry
   - ○ safe to eat
   - ○ pleasant tasting

**DIRECTIONS** *Use context clues and your knowledge of base words to answer the following questions.*

5. What is the meaning of the word *creatures* in line 20?
   - ○ domestic animals
   - ○ living organisms
   - ○ imaginary beings
   - ○ artistic life forms

6. What is the meaning of the word *differences* as it is used in line 68?
   - ○ disagreements or arguments
   - ○ comparisons
   - ○ the ways of being unlike
   - ○ unsure reactions

7. What is the meaning of the word *reproduce* as it is used to describe the bee-pollen interaction in the chart?
   - ○ do something again
   - ○ imitate an action
   - ○ begin a process
   - ○ generate offspring

8. What is the meaning of the word *predators* as it is used to describe the aphid-ant interaction in the chart?
   - ○ organisms that live by hunting or catching others
   - ○ animals that lived before humans existed
   - ○ those that make their presence known in advance
   - ○ groups that help each other survive

# Writing & Grammar

**DIRECTIONS** *Read this passage and answer the questions that follow.*

> (1) In 1921 Margaret Bourke-White received her first camera. (2) She would go on to became a renowned photojournalist in the next decade. (3) During the Great Depression Bourke-White photographed the South. (4) Her haunting images later appeared in the book *You have seen their Faces.* (5) Bourke-White also photographed Russia during World War II, documenting it in her book *shooting the Russian war.* (6) In the late 1940s Bourke-White spent two years in India. (7) Her photographs from this trip appeared in the book *halfway to Freedom: A Report on the new India.*

**1.** Choose the correct way to punctuate sentence 1 with a comma.
- ○ In 1921, Margaret Bourke-White received her first camera.
- ○ In 1921 Margaret, Bourke-White received her first camera.
- ○ In 1921 Margaret Bourke-White received, her first camera.
- ○ In 1921 Margaret Bourke-White received her first, camera.

**2.** Choose the correct way to punctuate sentence 3 with a comma.
- ○ During the Great Depression Bourke-White, photographed the South.
- ○ During the Great Depression Bourke-White photographed, the South.
- ○ During the Great Depression, Bourke-White photographed the South.
- ○ During the Great, Depression Bourke-White photographed the South.

**3.** Choose the correct way to capitalize the title in sentence 4.
- ○ *You have seen Their Faces*
- ○ *You Have Seen their faces*
- ○ *You Have Seen their Faces*
- ○ *You Have Seen Their Faces*

**4.** Choose the correct way to capitalize the title in sentence 5.
- ○ *Shooting the Russian war*
- ○ *Shooting the Russian War*
- ○ *shooting the Russian War*
- ○ *Shooting The Russian War*

**5.** Choose the correct way to punctuate sentence 6 with a comma.
- ○ In the late 1940s, Bourke-White spent two years in India.
- ○ In the late 1940s Bourke-White, spent two years in India.
- ○ In the late 1940s Bourke-White spent two, years in India.
- ○ In the late 1940s Bourke-White spent two years, in India.

**6.** Choose the correct way to capitalize the title in sentence 7.
- ○ *Halfway to Freedom: A Report on the new India*
- ○ *Halfway To Freedom: A Report On The New India*
- ○ *Halfway to Freedom: A Report On the New India*
- ○ *Halfway to Freedom: A Report on the New India*

STOP

## Ideas for Independent Reading

Which questions from Unit 8 made an impression on you?
Continue exploring them with these books.

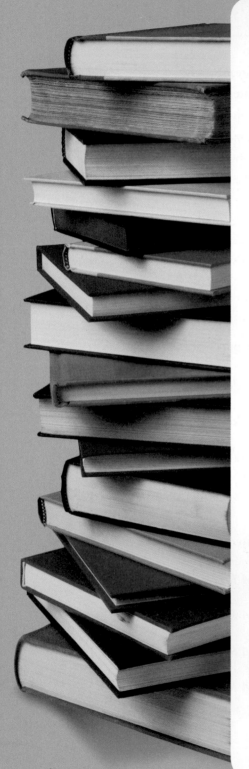

## *What is your dream job?*

**Dare to Dream!
25 Extraordinary Lives**
*by Sandra McLeod
Humphrey*

Some of the world's most
famous athletes, scientists,
artists, and politicians had to
overcome serious obstacles
to achieve success. This book
tells the real-life stories of
people who beat the odds.

**Come Back to
Afghanistan: A California
Teenager's Story**
*by Said Hyder Akbar and
Susan Burton*

After the fall of the Taliban
government, Said and
his father returned to
Afghanistan. Said tells what
it was like to be a teenager
working to rebuild a country.

**Stonecutter**
*by Leander Watts*

It's 1835, and 14-year-old
Albion is learning to be a
stonecutter. His big break
comes when he's hired
to do the stonework at a
new estate. When he gets
there, he finds a creepy,
half-finished mansion.
Something isn't right.

## *Why do people seek danger?*

**Mortal Engines**
*by Philip Reeve*

What could an assassin,
a third-class historian,
and a rich man's daughter
ever have in common?
They are all teenagers who
are willing to risk their safety
to solve the mystery that
threatens to destroy the
world.

**Eragon**
*by Christopher Paolini*

Eragon lives a quiet life on a
farm until he finds a dragon's
egg. After it hatches, Eragon's
peaceful childhood comes
to a violent end. He realizes
it's his fate to become a
dragon rider and join in the
war against the evil King
Galbatorix.

**The Gadget**
*by Paul Zindel*

Thirteen-year-old Stephen
escapes war-torn London to
live with his father, who is a
scientist on a secret military
base in New Mexico. Stephen
is determined to learn all he
can about the "gadget" his
father is working on, but at
what price?

## *What does music say about us?*

**The Black Canary**
*by Jane Louise Curry*

James's parents think he will
become a musician like them,
but that is the one thing he
knows he doesn't want. His
opinion changes when he
finds a portal to another time.
He's stuck in the 1600s, and
he can't go home until he
develops his musical gifts.

**Mountain Solo**
*by Jeanette Ingold*

Tess is a violin prodigy, but
after a disastrous concert she
vows to give up music. She
goes to live with her dad and
his new wife in Montana.
Can the mystery surrounding
a young musician from the
pioneer days help her figure
out her own truth?

**This Land Was Made for
You and Me: The Life and
Songs of Woody Guthrie**
*by Elizabeth Partridge*

Woody Guthrie was a
songwriter who traveled
the country, singing about
people struggling to get by.
His own life was difficult, too,
but he inspired people from
many generations.

# 9

# State Your Case

## ARGUMENT AND PERSUASION

- In Nonfiction
- In Media
- In Literature

# *Share What You Know*

## *Whom can you* BELIEVE?

As soon as you wake up in the morning, you're surrounded by people, groups, and corporations trying to influence the way you think or act. To **persuade** you to buy a brand of shoes, a company runs an ad showing a great athlete wearing the same pair as he sinks a jump shot. To encourage you to sell T-shirts for a fundraiser, the class president starts the morning announcements by offering a prize to the student who sells the most. Meanwhile, a friend begs you to work with her instead of with your usual partner. How can you be sure you're doing what's best for you?

***ACTIVITY*** Think about a time when an advertisement persuaded you to buy a product. What influenced your decision to believe that company's claims? Consider the following questions:

- Were you familiar with that company's products?

- What did the advertisement tell you that you did not hear from competing companies' ads?

- Did the company use celebrity endorsements, statistics, or other persuasive techniques to convince you to buy its product?

**INDIANA STANDARDS**

## Preview Unit Goals

**READING**
- Identify and analyze elements of an argument
- Identify and analyze persuasive techniques
- Analyze the effectiveness of persuasive techniques
- Distinguish between and evaluate facts and opinions
- Identify and analyze author's purpose
- Identify and analyze comparisons and contrasts
- Identify and analyze the historical context of a text
- Identify and analyze tone

**WRITING AND GRAMMAR**
- Write a persuasive essay
- Use parallelism to link related ideas
- Capitalize names correctly

**SPEAKING, LISTENING, AND VIEWING**
- Analyze and evaluate an ad campaign
- Recognize persuasive techniques in media messages
- Deliver a persuasive speech

**VOCABULARY**
- Use knowledge of word roots, base words, and affixes to help determine word meaning
- Use antonyms as context clues to determine word meaning

**ACADEMIC VOCABULARY**
- argument
- tone
- fact and opinion
- author's purpose
- historical context
- persuasive techniques

# Argument and Persuasion

Persuasive messages are everywhere—on buses and billboards, on television and the Web, even on cereal boxes and candy wrappers. Using direct or subtle techniques, these messages tell you what to wear, what to buy, and what to think. How can you sift through all the pitches, claims, and pizzazz, and make sure you figure out what's really important? In this workshop, you'll learn how to separate the substance of these messages from what's simply a sugar coating.

**INDIANA STANDARDS**

**READING STANDARDS**
**8.2.2** Analyze text that uses proposition (statement of argument) and support patterns.
**8.2.6** Evaluate the logic (inductive or deductive argument), internal consistency, and structural patterns of text.

## Part 1: Elements of an Argument

The word *argument* doesn't always refer to two people having a disagreement. In formal speaking and writing, an **argument** is a claim supported by reasons and evidence. Sound arguments appeal to logic, not to emotions. A strong argument

- presents a **claim,** or the writer's position on a problem or an issue. The claim might be stated directly ("Vitamins are good for you.") or indirectly ("Take your vitamins—feel the difference."). The claim often appears in the introduction, conclusion, or title of an argument.

- provides **support,** or the reasons and evidence that back up the claim. Support can include facts, statistics, examples, and quotations from experts.

- anticipates what people with the opposing viewpoint might say and counters their objections by offering further evidence to support the claim.

Look closely at the elements of an argument in this poster.

❶ **Claim:** The title of the poster states its claim: One person can make a difference.

❷ **Support 1:** Giving a few hours of your time will build a stronger community.

❸ **Support 2:** Volunteering will make you a better person.

❹ Notice that an opposing viewpoint is addressed and countered: No effort is a wasted effort.

❶ **ONE PERSON CAN MAKE A DIFFERENCE!**
*Want to make a difference? Volunteer!*

❷ **Public service builds a stronger community.** Consider volunteering a couple of hours each week—as a tutor, activities leader, or coach—to help others.

❸ **Serving others will give you a sense of self-satisfaction.** You'll also grow as an individual. Come see what you can do.

❹ **Don't let anyone convince you that one person can't make a difference.** No effort is a wasted effort!

## MODEL: ELEMENTS OF AN ARGUMENT

The author of this essay makes a case against junk food by focusing on one example. As you read this excerpt, try to identify the author's claim. What reasons and evidence does he provide as support for his position?

*from* # Why Can't I Live on *French Fries?*

Essay by **Richard J. Roberts**

So what's so bad about stuffing yourself with nothing but French fries all the time, anyway? Simple: Pretty soon you'll be missing important nutrients. Let's start with vitamins. The body does not need much of them, but in most cases, it cannot produce them. Potatoes contain mostly vitamin C and hardly
5  any other vitamin. No vitamin K, for example, which is needed to form a scab when you're bleeding so that the bleeding stops. And no vitamin A, needed for the eyes to function properly. Not enough vitamin A, and you'll see even less well at night than everyone else. Over the long run, a lack of vitamin A can even cause blindness. Many children in Africa suffer from it.
10    If you were to eat only French fries, your teeth would also slowly go bad and your bones would become brittle. That's because potatoes do not contain enough calcium, and your bones need calcium throughout your life, not just while you're growing. Besides, all those mountains of fries would overload you with sodium, because they're often too salty, and salt contains sodium.
15  It's important that your body maintain a good sodium balance, because otherwise, it can't regulate its body temperature very well, but too much sodium causes high blood pressure in some people.

    French fries also contain little protein. Proteins are critical. They are the true bearers of life. The cells from which most living creatures are built consist
20  mostly of proteins. Without proteins, for example, you would not have any muscles. . . .

    We chemists and doctors still know far too little about nutrition and its effects on health. This is why every person has to find out for him- or herself what's good for each. But one thing I can guarantee: You'll get into trouble
25  if you always eat nothing but French fries. By the way, I myself would love to wolf down French fries every day. But I, too, have to restrain myself and should stick to the advice that I've given you here.

### Close Read

1. Reread the title and lines 1–2. What is the author's claim?

2. In the ⬚boxed lines, the author explains that a person needs vitamins that are not found in French fries. What examples does he use to support this reason?

3. In lines 10–21, the author offers three other reasons to support his claim. Restate these reasons in your own words.

4. What does the author do in the last paragraph to strengthen his argument?

# Part 2: The Power of Persuasion

Who can ignore the pleading expression on the face of a starving child or a description of an injured animal whose survival depends on *you*? Effective writers, speakers, and advertisers know how to pull your heartstrings. They try to influence your feelings and actions using **persuasive techniques,** such as the ones shown here. While these techniques can enhance strong arguments, they can also mask the flaws in weak ones. That's why it's important for you to recognize these techniques for what they are. Use this chart as a guide.

| PERSUASIVE TECHNIQUES | EXAMPLES |
|---|---|
| **Appeals by Association** | |
| **Bandwagon Appeal**<br>Taps into people's desire to belong | Millions of teens have made City Jeanz part their wardrobe. What are you waiting for? |
| **Snob Appeal**<br>Taps into people's need to feel superior to others | Join the Brookside Club for Seasoned Skiiers—because you're *way beyond* the beginner slopes. |
| **Testimonial**<br>Relies on the backing of a celebrity, an expert, or a satisfied customer | As a supermodel, it's important for me to have a great smile. Brite Strips whiten your teeth without the wait. |
| **Transfer**<br>Connects a product, a candidate, or a cause with a positive image or idea | Vote for cleaner air. Vote for Tony Leonard. |
| **Appeal to Values** | |
| **Ethical Appeal**<br>Tries to gain moral support for a claim by linking the claim to a widely accepted value | If you believe that every child deserves a good education, support the Great Minds Organization. |
| **Emotional Appeals** | |
| **Appeal to Fear**<br>Makes people feel as if their safety, security, or health is in danger | How clean are the hotel rooms you're staying in? You'll be shocked by what our documentary reveals. |
| **Appeal to Pity**<br>Taps into people's compassion for others | For the cost of one cup of coffee a day, you could save a life. |
| **Word Choice** | |
| **Loaded Language**<br>Uses words with strongly positive or negative connotations to stir people's emotions | The alley next to the parking lot is dark and dangerous. Vote to increase the number of street lamps in our neighborhood. Residents deserve to feel safe and protected. |

**MODEL 1: PERSUASION IN TEXT**

This article challenges the positive concept of competition. What techniques does the author use to persuade you to adopt her position?

*from*

## Against Competition

Newspaper article by **Gayle Heaney**

Our society uses sports metaphors for almost every aspect of life: Gear up, go for the goal, score one for the team! But studies show that the competitive spirit we admire can also have negative effects on a person—especially if the pressure to compete is instilled at a young age.

5    Young children often place excessive value on how they perform and can be emotionally devastated if they fail. Consider, for example, if a boy feels pressured to succeed in a particular sport. If he is unable to improve his skills, his self-esteem will disintegrate. If anyone criticizes his performance, he magnifies the criticism and views himself as a failure in everything.

10    In adults, competition can cause a person's stress levels to skyrocket. High stress levels can have damaging and dangerous consequences because they often lead to high blood pressure or to uncontrollable outbursts of anger. Road rage is turning our nation's highways into battlefields. Sports events often turn into violent fistfights, either on the field or in the crowd.

15    Is this the kind of behavior we should be modeling for our children?

**Close Read**

1. Notice the highlighted examples of loaded language in the boxed sentence. Find two other examples of loaded language.

2. Reread lines 10–15. Which type of emotional appeal is the author using?

**MODEL 2: PERSUASION IN ADVERTISING**

Persuasion is a key factor in the advertisements you see on television, in magazines, and on product packaging. What techniques do you notice in this promotional poster?

**ANNUAL SPORTS CHALLENGE:**
June 20–26

Do *you* have what it takes
to be a champion? Let us show you.

"I DIDN'T HAVE THE NERVE TO TRY OUT FOR THE SOCCER TEAM LAST YEAR. BUT THE SPORTS CHALLENGE PROGRAM HELPED ME BUILD MY SKILLS IN A FUN, CHALLENGING ENVIRONMENT. NOW I HAVE THE CONFIDENCE I NEED TO COMPETE—AND SUCCEED."

**JEANNIE, AGE 14**

**Close Read**

1. Which type of appeal by association does this poster use?

2. Describe the intended effect of the poster on readers.

## Part 3: Analyze the Texts

Now you'll apply what you've learned in this workshop as you analyze two texts—an editorial and a poster. Both texts are about the legal driving age. As you read each text, try to identify the claim, the support, and any persuasive techniques that are used.

# Should the Driving Age Be Raised to 18?

**NO!**

Editorial by **Alex Koroknay-Palicz**
National Youth Rights Association

If your neighbor robs a bank, should you go to jail? No. If your classmate gets in an accident, should your driver's license be taken away? Of course not. Neither situation is fair. Raising the driving age will punish all young drivers for the mistakes of a few of their peers.

5 In this country we live by the principle of innocent until proven guilty. Those who want to raise the driving age have labeled teens guilty before they've gotten in an accident or before they've even stepped into a car. They believe that just because of your birth date, you are dangerous and must be punished by having your ability to drive taken from you.

10 Those who favor raising the driving age say that statistics show teenagers are more likely to get into accidents than adults. What they don't say is that statistics also show that men of all ages are 77 percent more likely to kill someone while driving than women. If people want to save lives by raising the driving age, then how about saving lives by allowing only women to drive?

15 Except raising the driving age won't save lives. Studies show that it is inexperience, not age, that causes accidents. Raising the driving age will just create inexperienced, accident-prone drivers at 18 instead of 16.

Teens need the ability to drive just as much as anyone else—to get to school, to get to work, to get to sports or band practice, or just to go out with 20 their friends. Cars are necessary for mobility in this country. Taking that away is a large disruption to the lives of teenagers—for no good reason.

**Close Read**

1. The title tells you which side of the issue the author falls on, but the claim of his argument is stated in the first paragraph. What is the author's claim?

2. What reasons and evidence does the author provide as support for his claim?

3. The author presents an opposing viewpoint in the boxed lines. In your own words, restate his response to this opposition.

The creators of this public-service poster offer a different viewpoint on the same issue. What techniques are used to get you to see their side?

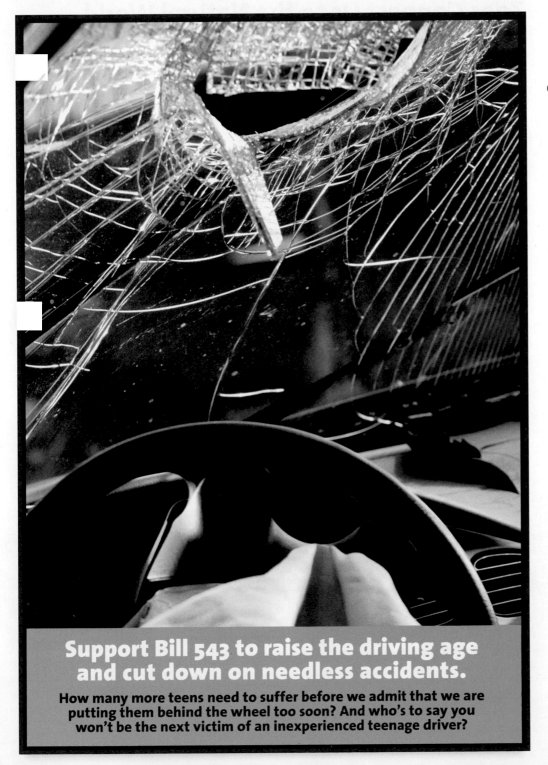

**Support Bill 543 to raise the driving age and cut down on needless accidents.**

How many more teens need to suffer before we admit that we are putting them behind the wheel too soon? And who's to say you won't be the next victim of an inexperienced teenage driver?

### Close Read

1. Examine the text and photograph used in this ad. What emotional appeal is being used?

2. In what way does this ad use the technique of transfer?

## Zoos: Myth and Reality
Online Article by Rob Laidlaw

## Zoos Connect Us to the Natural World
Opinion Piece by Michael Hutchins

# Should WILDLIFE stay wild?

**INDIANA STANDARDS**

**READING STANDARDS**
**8.2.2** Analyze text that uses proposition (statement of argument) and support patterns.

**8.2.6** Evaluate the logic (inductive or deductive argument), internal consistency, and structural patterns of text.

**KEY IDEA** Close your eyes and picture an elephant. Are you picturing it in the zoo or in the wild? As humans inhabit more and more of the earth's land, some species of **wildlife** are more likely to be found in captivity than in their natural habitat. But is this a good thing? The writers of the selections you're about to read have different views on whether or not zoos are good for humans and animals.

**LIST IT** With a group, make a list of the good things and bad things about zoos. Do the pros outnumber the cons, or vice versa? Tell whether you think zoos are a good idea.

| Pros | Cons |
|------|------|
| 1. They keep animals safe. | 1. |
| 2. | 2. |

## ● ELEMENTS OF NONFICTION: ARGUMENT

When you express an opinion on an issue or problem and support it with evidence and reasons, you are presenting an **argument.** An effective argument provides

- a **claim,** or the writer's position on the issue or problem
- **support,** or any material that helps to prove a claim
- a **counterargument,** or an argument made to disprove or answer another viewpoint.

As you read, notice how the authors build their arguments using claims, support, and counterarguments.

## ● READING SKILL: DISTINGUISH FACT AND OPINION

To decide if an argument is convincing, you need to be able to tell the difference between a statement of fact and a writer's opinion. A **fact** is a statement that can be proved through a personal observation, an eyewitness account, a reliable source, a scientific experiment, or a discussion with an expert. An **opinion** can vary from person to person. It cannot be proved because it expresses a belief, feeling, or thought. As you read each selection, list three important facts and three strong opinions.

| *"Zoos: Myth and Reality"* | |
| --- | --- |
| Facts: | Opinions: |
| 1. | 1. |
| 2. | 2. |

## ▲ VOCABULARY IN CONTEXT

The words in Column A help the authors develop arguments about zoos. See how many you know by matching each word to the item in Column B that comes closest to its meaning.

| Column A | Column B |
| --- | --- |
| 1. propaganda | a. unusual |
| 2. deprivation | b. corresponding position |
| 3. futility | c. stark |
| 4. sterile | d. uselessness |
| 5. languish | e. biased information |
| 6. counterpart | f. use for selfish reasons |
| 7. exotic | g. weaken |
| 8. exploit | h. a lack of |

## Author Online

**Rob Laidlaw: Wildlife Guardian**
Rob Laidlaw has dedicated himself to improving the conditions of animals in captivity. He is co-founder and Executive Director of Zoocheck Canada, an animal protection charity. Laidlaw has inspected close to 1,000 zoos, circuses, and wildlife displays throughout Canada and the United States. He has worked with Canada's government on establishing standards for zoos. Laidlaw also worked on developing a humane stray dog program, and he investigated Canada's role in the international pet reptile trade. Laidlaw shares his knowledge about animals through writing. He has published articles about all kinds of wildlife, from wild horses and polar bears to the red-eared slider and the black rhino.

**Rob Laidlaw**
**born 1959**

**Michael Hutchins: Animal Caretaker**
As the executive director of The Wildlife Society, Michael Hutchins has traveled to more than 33 countries. His efforts have involved trapping and tagging mountain goats in the Olympic Mountains, scuba diving with manta rays, and tracking jaguars. He has published many articles, books, and reports on the relationships between animals and their environments and on conservation.

**Michael Hutchins**
**born 1951**

 **MORE ABOUT THE AUTHOR**
For more on Rob Laidlaw and Michael Hutchins, visit the **Literature Center** at ClassZone.com.

# Zoos: Myth and Reality

**Rob Laidlaw**

**propaganda**
(prŏp′ə-găn′də) *n.* information that supports a certain cause

**deprivation**
(dĕp′rə-vā′shən) *n.* the condition of not having one's needs met; a lack of

Ⓐ **ARGUMENT**
What is the author's **claim** about zoos? Remember that a claim is a position or opinion, not a fact.

In recent years, zoos have become the target of intense public scrutiny and criticism. In response, many have tried to repackage themselves as institutions devoted to wildlife conservation, public education, and animal welfare. But most zoos fail to live up to their own **propaganda** and vast numbers of zoo animals continue to endure lives of misery and **deprivation.** Ⓐ

Nearly every zoo, from the smallest amateur operation to the largest professional facilities, claims to be making important contributions to conservation, usually through participation in endangered species captive
10 propagation initiatives and public education programming. The zoo world buzzword[1] of the moment is "conservation."

Yet, with an estimated 10,000 organized zoos worldwide, representing tens of thousands of human workers and billions of dollars in operating budgets, only a tiny percentage allocate the resources necessary to

---

1. **buzzword:** a word or phrase connected with a specialized field or group that sounds important or technical and is usually used to impress those outside the group.

participate in captive propagation initiatives, and fewer still provide any real support for the *in situ*[2] protection of wildlife and their natural habitat.

So far, the record on reintroductions to the wild is dismal. Only 16 species have established self-sustaining populations in the wild as a result of captive breeding efforts, and most of those programs were
20 initiated by government wildlife agencies—not zoos. The contribution of zoos in this regard has been minimal, and often involves supplementing existing wild populations with a small number of captive-born individuals who are ill-prepared for life in the wild. **B**

As the **futility** of captive breeding as a major conservation tool becomes evident to those in the industry, many zoos are now turning to education to justify themselves. Yet, zoos claim that they teach visitors about wildlife conservation and habitat protection, and their contention that they motivate members of the public to become directly involved in wildlife conservation work doesn't stand up to scrutiny. The truth is
30 that scant empirical evidence exists to prove that the primary vehicle for education in most zoos—the animal in the cage—actually teaches anyone anything. In fact, viewing animals in cages may be counterproductive educationally by conveying the wrong kinds of messages to the public. Also, the legions[3] of conservationists that zoos should have produced, if their claims were true, have never materialized. **C**

## Humane Treatment

But there is one issue about which there appears to be widespread agreement—at least in principle. So long as wild animals are kept in captivity, they ought to be treated humanely.

Studies have shown that animals can suffer physically, mentally, and
40 emotionally. For this reason, captive environments must be complex enough to compensate for the lack of natural freedom and choice, and they must facilitate expression of natural movement and behavior patterns. This principle has been widely espoused by the modern zoo community in various articles, books, and television documentaries. **D**

Yet despite the best of intentions or claims, most animals in zoos in North America are still consigned to lead miserable lives in undersized,

---

2. *in situ* (ĭn sē'tōō): a Latin phrase; in zoology, it refers to studying an animal without removing it from its natural habitat.

3. **legions** (lē'jənz): large numbers.

**B** FACT AND OPINION
Reread lines 17–23. Identify the opinion and the facts. Do the facts support the author's opinion?

**futility** (fyōō-tĭl'ĭ-tē) *n.* uselessness

**C** ARGUMENT
Reread lines 26–35. What **counterargument** does the author present against the zoos' claims?

**D** FACT AND OPINION
Reread lines 39–44. What sources does the author cite here? Explain whether these sources sound reliable to you.

impoverished enclosures, both old and new, that fail to meet their biological and behavioral needs. Many in the zoo industry will bristle[4] at this statement and point to numerous improvements in the zoo field.
50 They'll claim they've shifted from menagerie-style[5] entertainment centers where animals were displayed in barred, **sterile,** biologically irrelevant cages, to kinder, gentler, more scientifically-based kinds of institutions.

But many of the "advances" in zoo animal housing and husbandry are superficial and provide little benefit to the animals. For example, the many new, heavily promoted, Arctic "art deco" polar bear exhibits that are springing up in zoos across the continent consistently ignore the natural biology and behavior of these animals. The artificial rockwork and hard floor surfaces typically resemble a Flintstones movie set more than the natural Arctic ice and tundra habitat of polar bears. These exhibits
60 are made for the public and dupe them into believing things are getting better. What they really achieve is more misery and deprivation.

In addition, many new exhibits are hardly larger than the sterile, barred cages of days gone by. And one look at the prison-like, off-display holding and service areas in most zoos, where many animals spend a good portion of their lives, is proof of the hypocrisy of zoo claims that things are better for the animals than they were in the past. **E**

## Behind the Invisible Bars

If not all is well behind the invisible bars of North America's more luxurious zoos, a more transparent problem is found in the hundreds of substandard roadside zoos that dot the continent. These amateurish
70 operations fall far below any professional standard and do nothing but cause misery and death to thousands of animals.

My own investigations have revealed animals in visible distress lying unprotected from the full glare of the hot summer sun; primates in barren cages with no opportunity to climb; groups of black bears begging for marshmallows as they sit in stagnant moats of excrement-filled water, scarred and wounded from fighting; nocturnal[6] animals kept without shade or privacy; animals without water; and the list goes on and on.

---

4.  **bristle** (brĭs'əl): to show annoyance or anger.

5.  **menagerie** (mə-năj'ə-rē): a collection of live wild animals on display.

6.  **nocturnal** (nŏk-tûr'nəl): habitually active at night and asleep during the daytime.

---

**sterile** (stĕr'əl) *adj.*
barren; lacking vitality

**E** **FACT AND OPINION**
Reread the sentence that begins at line 63. Is this statement a fact or an opinion? Tell how you know.

Many zoos, including those that meet industry guidelines, also annually produce a predictable surplus in animals that often end up in the hands of
80 private collectors, animal auctions, circuses and novelty acts, substandard zoos, and even "canned hunt" operations where they're shot as trophies.

A look at compliance with the zoo industry's own standards (which in the author's view do not necessarily constitute adequate standards) demonstrates how bad the situation really is. Of the estimated 200 public display facilities in Canada, only 26—slightly more than 10 percent—have been deemed to meet the standards of the Canadian Association of Zoos and Aquariums (CAZA).

In the U.S., out of the 1,800–2,000 licensed exhibitors of wild animals (which includes biomedical research institutions, breeding facilities, small
90 exhibitors, travelling shows, educational programs using live animals, zoos and aquariums), about 175 are accredited by the American Zoo and Aquarium Association (AZA), equivalent to less than 10 percent of all facilities. **F**

Times are changing, and with them, public attitudes. Increasingly, members of the public find the confinement of animals in substandard conditions offensive. Zoos across the continent are feeling the pressure. They have to accept that if wild animals are to be kept in captivity, their needs must be met.

Are there good captive environments where the biological and
100 behavioral needs of animals are being satisfied? The answer is yes. A recent Zoocheck Canada survey of black bear and gray wolf facilities in North America revealed a number of outstanding exhibits where the animals displayed an extensive range of natural movements and behaviors. But they are few and far between.

Can zoos make a useful contribution to conservation and education? Again, the answer is yes. The Durrell Wildlife Conservation Trust (Jersey Zoo) in the U.K., for example, clearly shows that zoos can become leaders in conservation education and wildlife protection. But few actually do.

I can't understand why the more responsible segments of the
110 zoo industry have not come to their senses and acknowledged the obvious—the present state of zoos is untenable. Either zoos can voluntarily adopt humane policies and practices, push for the closure of substandard facilities, and participate in advocating for laws to help wildlife, or they can be dragged kicking and screaming into the new millennium. It's their choice.

**F** **ARGUMENT**
Explain whether these statistics prove the author's claim.

# Zoos Connect Us to the Natural World [G]

## Michael Hutchins

**G** **ARGUMENT**
You can often identify the writer's **claim** by reading the title. What do you think this opinion piece will argue?

**languish** (lăng'gwĭsh) *v.* to lose strength and vitality

**counterpart** (koun'tər-pärt') *n.* one that has the same functions and traits as another

**H** **FACT AND OPINION**
Reread lines 32–42. Can this information be verified? Once you decide whether this statement is a fact or opinion, add it to your chart.

The scene of Little Joe, the curious young gorilla out of his zoo exhibit wandering through Franklin Park,[1] certainly sold papers last month. But less well covered was the very real success that our nation's best zoos have had in nurturing the animals who live within their walls.

At the turn of the last century, gorillas—these strange, human-like creatures from "darkest Africa"—still flourished in the wild and thoroughly captivated the American public. But once relocated from their jungle habitat, gorillas **languished.** Zoos found it impossible to keep the animals alive for more than a few weeks since little was known about the natural history of gorillas. Even as late as the 1960s and '70s, most zoo gorillas were kept singly or in pairs in small, sterile concrete and tile cages and fed inappropriate foods. But things began to change as information from field and zoo biologists brought more understanding of both the physiological and psychological needs of these remarkable creatures.

Gorillas in today's zoos are typically kept in large, naturalistic exhibits, maintained in appropriate social groupings, fed nutritionally appropriate diets, and provided with excellent veterinary care. The result is that zoo gorillas exhibit behavior similar to their wild **counterparts,** reproduce consistently, and live longer on average than they do in nature. [H]

In fact, recent advances in exhibit design, animal nutrition, genetic management, and veterinary medicine have revolutionized animal welfare and care in our zoos. Today, more than 90 percent of mammals housed in accredited[2] facilities were born in zoos and not taken from the wild. They are under the charge of animal curators and caretakers who are trained professionals, with both academic and practical experience. Furthermore, accredited zoos have

---

1. **Franklin Park:** a Boston, Massachusetts, park that has a zoo in it.

2. **accredited** (ə-krĕd'ĭt-əd): meeting certain standards that have been set by a respected authority (in this case, the American Zoo and Aquarium Association).

ANALYZE VISUALS
What **conclusions** can you draw about the impact this encounter might have on the girl?

become "learning organizations" that constantly strive to improve the lives and health of the animals 60 in their care. ❶

So why should we have gorillas or any other wild animals in zoos today? Before speculating about the role of these institutions in contemporary society, I must first draw a distinction between accredited zoos and other kinds of facilities that keep wild animals for public display. All of my statements 70 are focused exclusively on the 213 facilities accredited by the American Zoo and Aquarium Association. AZA members undergo a detailed peer-review[3] process, which is more comprehensive than existing local, state, or federal regulations.

At a time when children learn more about the world around them from television and computers 80 than from personal experience, modern zoos—and aquariums, for that matter—offer fun, safe opportunities to view living wild animals up close and personal. In 2002, over 140 million people visited AZA zoos and aquariums, more than attended all professional baseball, football, basketball, and ice hockey games combined. 90 Modern zoological parks provide us a wonderful opportunity to build awareness and appreciation of wildlife in an increasingly urbanized populace—a group that is becoming progressively disconnected from the natural world. ❷

Only a small percentage of our nation's citizens can afford to travel to **exotic** locations to view wild 100 tigers, elephants, or giant pandas

❶ **ARGUMENT**
What criticisms is the author addressing in this paragraph? Paraphrase his **counterargument.**

❷ **ARGUMENT**
Reread lines 77–96. Which sentence provides support for the author's **claim?** Which is a restatement of his claim?

**exotic** (ĭg-zŏt′ĭk) *adj.* foreign; unusual; exciting

---

3. **peer-review:** evaluation by equals (in this case, other zoo officials).

or to dive with sharks or moray
eels. Zoos provide exhilarating
experiences that can't be replicated
on two-dimensional television or
computer screens. Seeing, smelling,
and in some cases even touching
real, live animals is a powerful
experience. **K**

110    The best zoos include
conservation, education, and
science among their core missions,[4]
and the animals in their collections
can be viewed as ambassadors for
their counterparts in the wild.
Many species are endangered or
threatened and would have little
chance of survival without human
intervention. Increasingly, zoos
are playing an important role in
120 those efforts. Last year alone, AZA
member institutions supported
1,400 field conservation[5] and
associated educational and
scientific projects in over 80
countries worldwide. These
ranged from restoring habitat
for endangered Karner blue
butterflies[6] in Ohio to attempting
to curb the illegal, commercial
130 harvest of wildlife for meat in
Africa to rehabilitating injured
marine mammals and sea turtles
and returning them to the sea. **L**
   Some critics have characterized
zoos and aquariums as "**exploiting**"
animals for personal financial
gain, but that's not true of the

professionals I know. As a curatorial
intern at New York's Bronx Zoo/
140 Wildlife Conservation Society in
the late 1980s, I went on rounds
with the staff veterinarians as
they cared for sick and injured
animals. They worked long hours
for comparatively little pay, and
their dedication was inspiring. I also
witnessed animal keepers weeping
over the loss of their favorite animals
and spending their own money to
150 attend training programs to improve
their knowledge and skills. **M**
   In my opinion, a society
that values wildlife and nature
should support our best zoos and
aquariums. Habitat conservation
is the key to saving endangered
species, and professionally
managed zoos and aquariums and
their expert, dedicated staffs play
160 a vital role by supporting on-the-
ground conservation efforts and by
encouraging people to care for and
learn about wildlife and nature.
   Zoos and aquariums are
reinventing themselves, but
while many are in the process
of rebuilding their aging
infrastructures, still others retain
vestiges of the past or have been hit
170 hard by recent state or local budget
cuts. Good zoos and aquariums
are invaluable community assets,
and they deserve our attention and
enthusiastic support.

**L** FACT AND OPINION
Find one statement of
fact and one opinion in
this paragraph.

**exploit** (ĕk′sploit′) *v.* to
use for selfish purposes

**M** ARGUMENT
What opposing viewpoint
does the author
present? What is his
**counterargument?**

---

4. **core missions:** central goals and beliefs.

5. **field conservation:** conservation of wild organisms in their natural habitats (not in zoos).

6. **Karner blue butterflies:** endangered butterflies of the northern U.S. and Canada.

## Comprehension

1. **Recall** According to "Zoos: Myth and Reality," what often happens to surplus animals from zoos?

2. **Recall** According to "Zoos Connect Us to the Natural World," how do zoos benefit people?

3. **Clarify** What kind of action does each author call for?

**INDIANA STANDARDS**

**READING STANDARD**
**8.2.2** Analyze text that uses proposition (statement of argument) and support patterns.

## Critical Analysis

4. **Analyze Arguments** For each selection, identify the author's **claim.** Note the claim in a graphic organizer like the one shown. Then list three reasons or pieces of evidence the author uses to support his claim.

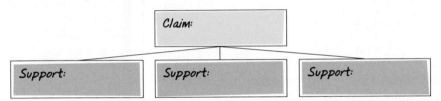

5. **Compare Scope** Tell whether the article or the opinion piece has the broadest scope, meaning the greatest range of coverage. Consider especially the number of zoos each selection refers to. Do you think the broader scope makes the selection more or less convincing? Explain.

6. **Evaluate Fact and Opinion** Review the lists you made of facts and opinions from the two selections. In your view, what is the single most convincing fact and the single most convincing opinion? Explain why you think so.

## Extension and Challenge

7. **Speaking and Listening** Form two teams, one representing Rob Laidlaw and one representing Michael Hutchins. Then, with your team, answer the question "Should wildlife stay wild?" from the perspective of your author. Debate the question with the other team, using support from the two selections.

8. **Inquiry and Research** Learn more about a zoo that you've visited or heard about. Is it accredited? What kind of background do the employees have? How are they trained? How are the animals housed and cared for? Research to find answers, and discuss your findings with the class. Share your opinions on whether the zoo is keeping **wildlife** safe.

**RESEARCH LINKS**
For more on zoos, visit the **Research Center** at **ClassZone.com.**

# Vocabulary in Context

## VOCABULARY PRACTICE

For each item, choose the word that differs most in meaning from the other words.

1. (a) suffer, (b) languish, (c) enjoy, (d) endure
2. (a) exploit, (b) aid, (c) help, (d) befriend
3. (a) hope, (b) uselessness, (c) futility, (d) meaninglessness
4. (a) unadorned, (b) desolate, (c) lush, (d) sterile
5. (a) suffering, (b) deprivation, (c) lack, (d) wealth
6. (a) persuasion, (b) truth, (c) propaganda, (d) bias
7. (a) boss, (b) equal, (c) peer, (d) counterpart
8. (a) ordinary, (b) exotic, (c) foreign, (d) extraordinary

counterpart

deprivation

exotic

exploit

futility

languish

propaganda

sterile

## VOCABULARY IN WRITING

Using at least two vocabulary words, write a surprising fact about zoos that you learned from the selections. You might start like this.

> **EXAMPLE SENTENCE**
>
> I learned that the majority of zoo animals **languish** in uncomfortable, inappropriate environments.

## VOCABULARY STRATEGY: THE GREEK ROOT *exo*

The vocabulary word *exotic* contains the Greek root *exo*, which means "outside" or "external." You can use your understanding of this root along with context clues to help you to figure out the meaning of other words formed from *exo*.

exodus    exoskeleton

**exo**

exocarp    exosphere

**PRACTICE** Use a dictionary to look up each word that appears in the web. Then decide which word best completes each sentence. Be ready to explain how the meaning of the root is reflected in each word.

1. The earth's _____ protects it from much of the sun's ultraviolet radiation.
2. A peach's fuzzy ____ holds in the juicy fruit.
3. There was a mass _____ of fans from the stadium after the concert.
4. A beetle's _____ is like armor, protecting it from predators and weather.

**VOCABULARY PRACTICE**
For more practice, go to the **Vocabulary Center** at ClassZone.com.

# Reading-Writing Connection

Demonstrate your understanding of the arguments in "Zoos: Myth and Reality" and "Zoos Connect Us to the Natural World" by responding to these prompts. Then complete the **Grammar and Writing** exercise.

| WRITING PROMPTS | SELF-CHECK |
|---|---|
| **A. Short Response: Letter to the Editor** <br> What argument would you make about **wildlife in captivity**? Write a **one-paragraph letter to the editor,** supporting or criticizing a zoo, circus, or other place that houses wild animals. | **A convincing letter to the editor will . . .** <br> • make your position clear <br> • include a call to action |
| **B. Extended Response: Compare Perspectives** <br> Look back at the authors' biographies on page 969. How do you think each author's experience has influenced his opinion of zoos? Write **two or three paragraphs** comparing the authors' perspectives, or the ideas and values that influence their viewpoints. | **A successful comparison will . . .** <br> • clearly state each author's opinion <br> • connect each author's experience to his opinion |

## GRAMMAR AND WRITING

**CAPITALIZE CORRECTLY** In your writing, remember to **capitalize** all the important words in the names of organizations, institutions, stores, and companies. Do not capitalize words such as *hospital, school, company, church,* and *college* when they are not used as parts of the official names.

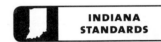
**WRITING STANDARD**
**8.6.6** Use correct capitalization.

> Original: The university of texas is one of the many Universities offering zoology classes.

> Revised: The University of Texas is one of the many universities offering zoology classes.

**PRACTICE** Correct the capitalization errors in the following sentences.

1. I believe the lincoln park zoo is teaching people to value wildlife.
2. The Zoo's habitats are safer for animals than the danger of the wild.
3. The durrell wildlife conservation trust actually protects wildlife.
4. Some circuses might not have high standards, but ringling brothers and barnum and bailey circus is trying to improve.

*For more help with capitalization, see page R51 in the* **Grammar Handbook.**

# How do ads create
# BUZZ?

**INDIANA STANDARDS**

**LISTENING/SPEAKING STANDARD 8.7.9** Interpret and evaluate the various ways in which visual image makers (such as graphic artists, illustrators, and news photographers) communicate information and affect impressions and opinions.

*KEY IDEA* Think about the last movie you just couldn't wait to see. How did you find out about it? Did you watch a preview that made it look exciting? Maybe you saw ads while surfing the Internet or passed billboards on the way to school. In this lesson, you'll explore how advertisers use these marketing techniques to build a sense of **anticipation** for an upcoming movie release.

## Background

**Coming Soon ...** Movie studios know that sometimes a commercial is not enough to persuade their target audience to see an upcoming film. They use a series of different types of ads to create excitement, so that not only will you run out to see the movie; you'll also tell your friends about it. In effect, you become part of the studio's ad campaign. This word of mouth is powerful, as people are more likely to trust the opinion of someone they know over the razzle-dazzle of a commercial. A movie is said to have **buzz** around it when it gets people excited enough to spread the word.

You'll look at advertisements for the movie *Star Wars: Episode III—Revenge of the Sith* to see how advertisers try to create buzz.

# Media Literacy: Persuasion in Ads

An **ad campaign** is a series of advertisements for a single product or brand. The ads appear over time and in several different forms. Movie studios use carefully chosen visual and sound techniques in each ad to persuade their target audience. The image you see in a **print ad** should evoke the movie's mood as much as the music that plays in a **trailer.** Here are some of the types of advertisements that studios use.

## FEATURES OF AN AD CAMPAIGN

> **Trailers** are movie ads that show selected scenes from a film. Trailers usually appear a few months before the movie opens. They persuade viewers to see the movie by showing the most exciting, funny, or touching moments from the film.

> **Teaser Trailers** are shorter, flashier trailers made to build anticipation. Teasers often come out long before the movie is released. They're short because they're designed to make you curious.

> **Print Ads** include billboards, posters, magazine, and newspaper ads. Print ads play a large role in many movie ad campaigns. They often persuade with a **tagline,** or memorable phrase that sums up the movie, and a single image meant to evoke a feeling about the film.

> **Promotional Web Site** is a Web site created to advertise the movie. Movie Web sites often include trailers, cast and crew information, games, and information about the making of the film. They're often designed to draw the audience's interest with an interactive experience.

### STRATEGIES FOR ANALYZING MOVIE ADS

Whether you're looking at a print ad, a trailer, or a promotional Web site, think about how the ad creates anticipation and excitement about the film.

- Determine the target audience. Think about who is most likely to see the movie and consider how the ad is directed at that group.
- Consider the visual and sound techniques used. Think about why each image or sound was chosen and the effect that each has on the viewer.
- Notice how the different ads work together to create an overall feeling about the film. The early ads are usually designed to spark curiosity. The later ads then build on that curiosity, providing more information about the film.

*Viewing Guide for*
# Movie Ad Campaign

View the DVD to examine the ad campaign used for the movie *Star Wars: Episode III—Revenge of the Sith.* You'll examine a **teaser trailer,** a full-length **trailer,** and the visuals and words of **print ads.** As you look at each selection, consider how it attempts to persuade you to see and talk about the film. Jot down the impressions you get of the movie from each selection. Then think about the overall effect of the ad campaign. Use these questions to help you analyze it.

## NOW VIEW

### FIRST VIEWING:  Comprehension

1. **Clarify**  What do you learn about the plot of the movie from the **teaser?**

2. **Identify**  According to the full-length **trailer,** who are the main characters in *Star Wars: Episode III?*

### CLOSE VIEWING:  Media Literacy

3. **Analyze Music**  What effect does the music in the **teaser** have on the viewer?

4. **Analyze Images**  What impressions do you get about *Star Wars: Episode III* from the images on the **posters?**

5. **Compare Trailers**  Compare and contrast the **teaser** and the full-length **trailer.**  How does your response to each differ?

6. **Interpret the Effect**  Think about the effect the **ad campaign** may have had on potential moviegoers when the movie was released.  Based on the materials you viewed, how do you think these people would have described the movie to their friends?

## Write or Discuss

**Evaluate the Ad Campaign** You've explored how advertisers attempt to create buzz. Think about the ads you examined for *Star Wars: Episode III—Revenge of the Sith*. What parts of the ad campaign did you find effective? Write an opinion statement describing whether or not you think the ad campaign would create buzz among you and your friends today. Think about

- whether the **teaser trailer** sparks your curiosity
- the details you learn about the movie from the full-length **trailer**
- your overall impression of the movie from all of the selections you viewed

## Produce Your Own Media

**Create Your Own Ad Campaign** Imagine your favorite short story or novel has just been made into a movie. You've been asked to plan an **ad campaign** that will get people buzzing about it. Working with one or two other students, draw **storyboards** for a **teaser trailer** and a full-length **trailer,** and draw a **poster** for the film.

*HERE'S HOW* Use these tips as you create your ad campaign:

- Remember that a storyboard is made up of drawings and brief descriptions of what happens in each shot.
- Think about the most exciting aspects of the story you choose. What will get people talking about the movie?
- For your poster, use an image that represents the overall feeling you want people to get from the film.
- Consider what music you want to play during your teaser trailer.

**MEDIA TOOLS**

For help with creating an ad campaign, visit the **Media Center** at ClassZone.com.

**STUDENT MODEL**

**Tech Tip**

If a camera is available, take photos of classmates dressed as characters and use a computer graphics program to create your poster.

## Position on Dodgeball in Physical Education
Position Statement by the National Association for Sport and Physical Education

## The Weak Shall Inherit the Gym
Opinion Piece by Rick Reilly

# Are all GAMES worth playing?

**INDIANA STANDARDS**

**READING STANDARDS**
**8.2.2** Analyze text that uses proposition (statement of argument) and support patterns.
**8.2.3** Find similarities and differences between texts in the treatment, amount of coverage, or organization of ideas.

**KEY IDEA** Games are supposed to be fun, right? But have you ever watched a customer at a carnival game spend 20 or 30 dollars trying to win a cheap stuffed animal? Seeing this might make you question not only how fun it is, but also whether or not all **games** are worth playing. You're about to read two very different opinions on whether the game of dodgeball is fun or torture for those who play it.

**LIST IT** Work with a group to make two lists. On the first, list five or more games you think are worth playing. On the second, list five or more games you think are not worth the time, money, or risk. Compare your lists with others'. Were there any games that appeared on both the good and not-so-good lists?

## ● ELEMENTS OF NONFICTION: PERSUASION

A logical, well-supported argument can be very persuasive. But writers often rely on more than facts to convince readers. Sometimes they express an attitude, or **tone** toward their subject, in order to win your support. Writers might also use **persuasive techniques** such as these:

- **Emotional appeals**—the use of words, descriptions, or images that call forth strong feelings, such as pity, fear, or anger.

  *If this law doesn't pass, innocent puppies will continue to be horribly mistreated in puppy mills.*

- **Ethical appeals**—attempts to gain moral support for a claim by linking the claim to a widely accepted value.

  *We need this law because animals deserve decent treatment.*

As you read, notice the ways the authors try to convince you.

## ● READING STRATEGY: SET A PURPOSE FOR READING

When you **set a purpose** for reading, you decide what you want to accomplish as you read. In this lesson, your purpose is to compare and contrast the persuasive techniques used in two selections. Filling in a chart like the one begun here can help. Use line numbers to tell where the appeals are.

|  | *"Position on Dodgeball in Physical Education"* | *"The Weak Shall Inherit the Gym"* |
|---|---|---|
| **What emotional appeals does the writer use?** | *Appeal to pity: lines 34–35* | |
| **What ethical appeals does the writer use?** | | |
| **What is the writer's tone? How does it affect you?** | | |

## ▲ VOCABULARY IN CONTEXT

The boldfaced words help to convey opinions about playing dodgeball. Try to figure out each word's meaning.

1. If you witness someone cheating, report the **impropriety.**
2. Students are not **adequately** prepared for competition.
3. We were able to **eliminate** the other players one by one.
4. One great player can **annihilate** an entire opposing team.
5. Is dodgeball a safe way to take out **aggression?**
6. The school is going to **ban** the game.

# Author Online

**Funny Man with Serious Talent** Many *Sports Illustrated* readers turn to the last page of their magazine first in order to read Rick Reilly's weekly column "Life of Reilly." The column, along with his novels and essay collections, has earned Reilly the reputation as "one of the funniest humans on the planet." Reilly has written about everything from ice-skating to the Iditarod, the Alaskan dog race. His adventures include facing fastballs from eight-time All-Star pitcher Nolan Ryan, cycling with seven-time Tour de France winner Lance Armstrong, and playing 108 holes of golf in one day. He began his sports writing career as a sophomore at the University of Colorado, taking phoned- in high-school volleyball scores for his hometown newspaper. After graduation, he moved on to stints at the *Denver Post* and the *Los Angeles Times*, eventually landing at *Sports Illustrated* in 1985. He has been voted National Sportswriter of the Year 10 times.

**Rick Reilly
born 1958**

**National Association for Sport and Physical Education** The NASPE is made up of gym teachers, coaches, athletic directors, athletic trainers, sport management professionals, researchers, and college faculty. The association provides a way for all of these professionals to help one another to improve physical education in schools. By researching, developing standards, and spreading information, NASPE helps students learn about fitness and stay active all their lives.

 **MORE ABOUT THE AUTHOR**
For more on Rick Reilly and the National Association for Sport and Physical Education, visit the **Literature Center** at ClassZone.com.

# Position on Dodgeball in Physical Education

### National Association for Sport and Physical Education

With the recent release of both a movie and television show about dodgeball, debate about the game's merits and **improprieties** has escalated in the media and on the NASPE listserv.[1] Thus, the National Association for Sport and Physical Education (NASPE) would like to reiterate its position about including dodgeball in school physical education programs.

NASPE believes that dodgeball is **not** an appropriate activity for K–12 school physical education programs. The purpose of physical education is to provide students with:

- The knowledge, skills, and confidence needed to be physically
10 active for a lifetime
- A daily dose of physical activity for health benefits
- Positive experiences so that kids want to be physically active outside of physical education class and throughout their lifetime

The goals of physical education can be obtained through a wide variety of appropriate physical activities. **Ⓐ**

Getting and keeping children and adolescents active is one of the biggest challenges facing parents and youth leaders.

- 61.5% of children aged 9–13 years do not participate in any organized physical activity during their non-school hours
20 and 22.6% do not engage in any free-time physical activity.
- One-third of high school students are not **adequately** active and over 10% do not participate in any physical activity at all.
- 16% of U.S. youth aged 6–19 are overweight—triple the proportion of 25 years ago. **Ⓑ**

According to NASPE's *Appropriate Practices for Elementary School Physical Education* (2000), "in a quality physical education class teachers involve ALL children in activities that allow them to participate actively, both physically and mentally. Activities such as relay races, dodgeball, and

---

1. **listserv** (lĭst-sûrv): an e-mail list that allows a group of people to hold a discussion by writing to each other via the Internet.

---

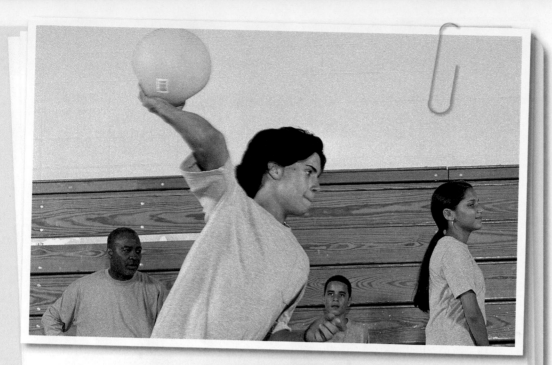

**ANALYZE VISUALS**
How many people pictured on this dodgeball team appear to be getting exercise?

elimination tag provide limited opportunities for everyone in the class,
30 especially the slower, less agile students who need the activity the most."

The students who are **eliminated** first in dodgeball are typically the ones who most need to be active and practice their skills. Many times these students are also the ones with the least amount of confidence in their physical abilities. Being targeted because they are the "weaker" players, and being hit by a hard-thrown ball, does not help kids to develop confidence.

**eliminate** (ĭ-lĭm′ə-nāt′)
*v.* to remove from consideration by defeating

The arguments most often heard in favor of dodgeball are that it allows for the practice of important physical skills—and kids like it.

- Dodgeball does provide a means of practicing some important physical skills—running, dodging, throwing, and catching.
40   However, there are many activities that allow practice of these skills without using human targets or eliminating students from play.
- Some kids may like it—the most skilled, the most confident. But many do not! Certainly not the student who gets hit hard in the stomach, head, or groin. And it is not appropriate to teach our children that you win by hurting others. **C**

**C PERSUASION**
Reread lines 42–45. What kind of **emotional appeal** is being made? What is the **ethical appeal?**

In a recent article about the new GSN (games network) TV show called "Extreme Dodgeball," there is talk of "developing and executing extreme strategies to **annihilate** opponents" and the use of terms such as "throw-to-kill ratios," and "headshots." NASPE asks, "Is this the type
50 of game that you want children to be exposed to?"

**annihilate** (ə-nī′ə-lāt′)
*v.* to completely destroy or defeat

# The Weak Shall Inherit the Gym

*Rick Reilly*

**Not to alarm you, but America is going softer than left-out butter. Exhibit 9,137: Schools have started banning dodgeball.**

I kid you not. Dodgeball has been outlawed by some school districts in New York, Texas, Utah and Virginia. Many more are thinking about it, like Cecil County, Md., where the school board wants to **ban** any game with "human targets." **D**

Human targets? What's tag? What's a snowball fight? What's a close play at second? Neil Williams, a physical education professor at Eastern
10 Connecticut State, says dodgeball has to go because it "encourages the best to pick on the weak." Noooo! You mean there's weak in the world? There's strong? Of course there is, and dodgeball is one of the first opportunities in life to figure out which one you are and how you're going to deal with it. **E**

We had a bully, Big Joe, in our seventh grade. Must have weighed 225 pounds, . . . We also had a kid named Melvin, who was so thin we could've faxed him from class to class. I'll never forget the dodgeball game in which Big Joe had a ball in each hand and one sandwiched

---

**ban** (băn) *v.* to prohibit

**D** **PERSUASION**
What words and phrases in the first sentence make Rick Reilly's **tone** immediately clear?

**E** **PERSUASION**
Why does Neil Williams object to dodgeball? Describe Reilly's response to this objection.

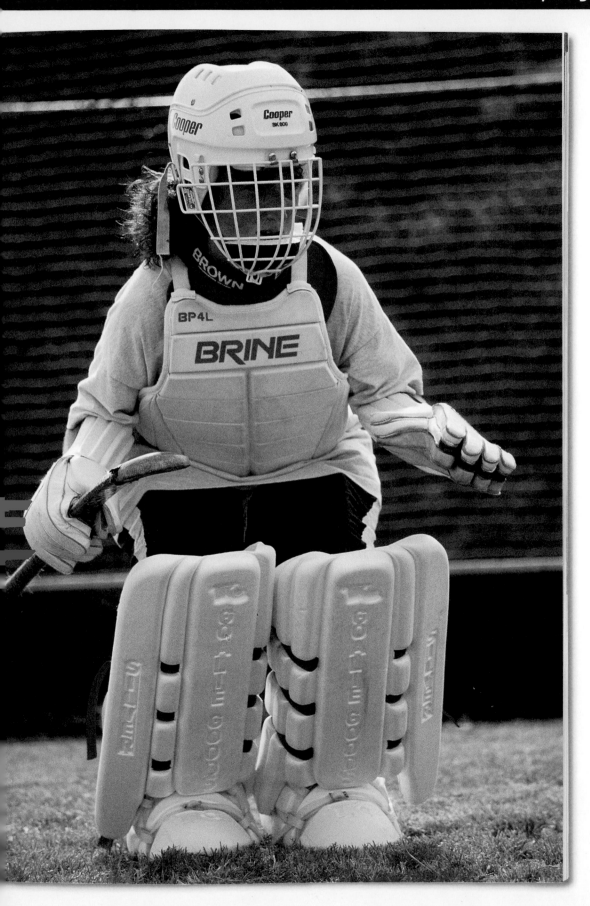

between his knees, firing at our side like a human tennis-ball machine, when, all of a sudden, he got plunked. . . . Joe whirled around to see who'd done it and saw that it was none other than Melvin, all 83 pounds of him, most of it smile.

Some of these . . . whiners say dodgeball is inappropriate in these violent times. Are you kidding? Dodgeball is one of the few times in life when you get to let out your **aggressions,** no questions asked. We don't need less dodgeball in schools, we need more!

I know what all these . . . parents want. They want their Ambers and their Alexanders to grow up in a cozy womb of noncompetition, where everybody shares tofu[1] and Little Red Riding Hood and the big, bad wolf set up a commune.[2] Then their kids will stumble out into the bright light of the real world and find out that, yes, there's weak and there's strong and teams and sides and winning and losing. You'll recognize those kids. They'll be the ones filling up chalupas.[3] Very noncompetitive. **F**

But Williams and his fellow whiners aren't stopping at dodgeball. In their Physical Education Hall of Shame they've also included duck-duck-goose and musical chairs. Seriously. So, if we give them dodgeball, you can look for these games to be banned next:

*Tag.* Referring to any child as *it* is demeaning and hurtful. Instead of the child hollering, "You're it!" we recommend, "You're special!"

*Baseball.* Involves wrong-headed notions of *stealing, errors* and gruesome *hit-and-run.* Players should always be safe, never out.

*Capture the flag.* Mimics war.

*Kick the can.* Unfair to the can.

If we let these PC twinkies[4] have their way, we'll be left with:

*Duck-duck-duck.* Teacher spends the entire hour patting each child softly on the head.

*Upsy down.* The entire class takes turns fluffing the gym teacher's pillow before her nap.

*Swedish baseball.* Players are allowed free passage to first, second or third, where they receive a relaxing two-minute massage from opposing players. **G**

---

1. **tofu** (to′foō): a protein-rich soybean curd that many vegetarians eat in place of meat.
2. **commune** (kŏm′yoōn′): a cooperative community in which a group of people who are not necessarily related live and work together.
3. **chalupas** (chə-lū′päs): fried tortillas filled with meat, a Mexican dish similar to tacos that is served at several U.S. fast-food chains.
4. **PC twinkies:** Reilly's expression for people who are too concerned (politically correct) with offending others by words or actions.

## Comprehension

1. **Recall**  What reason does the NASPE give for once again announcing its position on dodgeball in school physical education programs?

2. **Clarify**  Reread lines 15–22 of "The Weak Shall Inherit the Gym." What did dodgeball do for Melvin?

## Critical Analysis

3. **Identify Persuasive Technique**  Often writers use **loaded language,** or words with strong positive or negative associations, to influence readers.  Reread lines 46–50 of "Position on Dodgeball." Identify the loaded language used to create an **appeal to fear.**

4. **Examine Name-Calling**  Attempting to discredit a position or idea by attacking people associated with it is name-calling.  Find examples of name-calling in "The Weak Shall Inherit the Gym." Does it make Reilly's argument more or less convincing?  Give reasons for your answer.

5. **Analyze Tone**  What is Reilly's tone, or attitude toward opponents of dodgeball?  Explain how this tone might persuade readers to share his opinion of the **game.**

6. **Make Judgments**  A **stereotype** is an overgeneralization about a person or group.  In your opinion, is Reilly guilty of stereotyping?  Explain.

7. **Evaluate**  After reading these two positions on dodgeball, would you say it is a game worth playing?  Explain why or why not.

## Comparing Persuasive Techniques

Now that you've read "Position on Dodgeball in Physical Education" and "The Weak Shall Inherit the Gym," finish filling in your chart.  Then add and answer the final question.

|  | "Position on Dodgeball in Physical Eduction" | "The Weak Shall Inherit the Gym" |
|---|---|---|
| What emotional appeals does the writer use? | Appeal to pity: lines 34–35 |  |
| What ethical appeals does the writer use? |  |  |
| What is the writer's tone? How does it affect you? |  |  |
| What does the writer rely upon most to persuade—emotional appeals, ethical appeals, or tone? |  |  |

**INDIANA STANDARDS**

**READING STANDARD**
**8.2.2** Analyze text that uses proposition (statement of argument) and support patterns.

# Vocabulary in Context

## VOCABULARY PRACTICE

**Synonyms** are words that have similar meanings, and **antonyms** are words that have opposite meanings. Decide whether the words in each pair are synonyms or antonyms.

1. adequately—insufficiently
2. aggression—ferocity
3. annihilate—destroy
4. ban—legalize
5. eliminate—banish
6. impropriety—rudeness

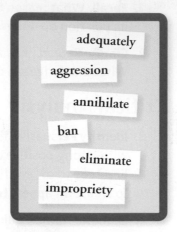

## VOCABULARY IN WRITING

What gym class activity would you like to see either added to or banned from your school? Using at least two vocabulary words, write a short paragraph in which you explain your opinion. You might start like this.

> **EXAMPLE SENTENCE**
>
> I would **ban** dodgeball from physical education classes.

**INDIANA STANDARDS**

**READING STANDARD**
**8.1.3** Verify the meaning of a word in its context . . . .

## VOCABULARY STRATEGY: THE LATIN WORD *gressus*

The vocabulary word *aggression* comes from the Latin word *gressus*, which means "to go." Many English words have the same origin. To figure out the meaning of words with this history, use context clues and your knowledge of the meaning of *gressus*.

*PRACTICE* Choose the word from the web that best completes each sentence. Then explain how the word *gressus* relates to the meaning of the word.

1. The trainer works with ____ dogs to make them gentler and more obedient.
2. Many dogs will ____ if they don't get constant social interaction.
3. Stealing a car is a serious _____, so car thieves receive harsh penalties.
4. Please stick to the topic and do not _____.
5. The Renaissance was a _____ time period in which the arts flourished and scientists made important discoveries.

**VOCABULARY PRACTICE**
For more practice, go to the **Vocabulary Center** at **ClassZone.com.**

# Writing for Assessment

## 1. READ THE PROMPT

The two selections you've just read support opposite sides of the same issue. In writing assessments, you might be asked to compare or contrast such selections.

**PROMPT**

"Position on Dodgeball in Physical Education" and "The Weak Shall Inherit the Gym" each express a position on whether dodgeball should be played in school. In four or five paragraphs, contrast the tone and persuasive techniques in each selection. Use details from the selections to explain the differences in how these techniques are used to persuade readers.

◀ **STRATEGIES IN ACTION**

1. I need to **identify the tone and types of appeals** used in each selection.

2. I need to **state the differences** in the writers' use of tone and persuasive techniques.

3. I need to **support my statements with examples** from the selections.

## 2. PLAN YOUR WRITING

To make sure you understand the persuasive techniques each writer uses, review the chart you completed. Write a thesis statement identifying the differences in their methods of persuasion. Then consider how to organize your response.

I. Introduction
II. Tone and persuasive techniques in first selection
III. Tone and persuasive techniques in second selection
IV. Conclusion

- **Option A:** In one paragraph, describe the tone and persuasive techniques the writer of the position paper relies upon. In the next paragraph, describe the tone and persuasive techniques the writer of the editorial relies upon.

- **Option B:** In one paragraph, contrast each writer's tone. In the next paragraph, contrast their emotional appeals. In a third, contrast their ethical appeals and any other techniques they use to persuade.

Once you have decided on your approach, create an outline to organize your details.

## 3. DRAFT YOUR RESPONSE

**Introduction** Provide the titles and authors of both selections, a brief description of each author's position, and your thesis statement.

**Body** Using your outline as a guide, compare the tone and persuasive techniques used in the two selections. Include details from the selections to illustrate your statements.

**Conclusion** Restate your thesis statement, and leave your reader with a final thought about the persuasion used in each of these selections.

**Revision** Double-check to make sure your thesis statement clearly presents the ideas you develop in your body paragraphs.

## The Sanctuary of School
Essay by Lynda Barry

# Why do we need SCHOOLS?

**INDIANA STANDARDS**

**READING STANDARDS**
**8.2.2** Analyze text that uses proposition (statement of argument) and support patterns.

**8.2.9** Make reasonable statements and draw conclusions about a text, supporting them with accurate examples.

**KEY IDEA** Traditionally, a school's most basic function was to teach the "three Rs": reading, writing, and 'rithmetic. More recently, Bill Gates, founder of the Microsoft Corporation, suggested that today's schools need to focus on three new "Rs": rigor, relevance, and **relationships**. In the essay you're about to read, Lynda Barry describes how the relationships made all the difference in her life.

**DISCUSS** With a small group, discuss what you think are a school's three most important tasks. Write them down and share them with your class. How many ideas have to do with the classroom and lessons? How many are tied to something less academic?

## ● ELEMENTS OF NONFICTION: AUTHOR'S PURPOSE

Writers usually have one or more **purposes** when they sit down to write, and they carefully select strategies to achieve these purposes. In this essay, Lynda Barry's purpose is to persuade us to value and support public schools. As you read, analyze the way that Barry uses a personal experience from her childhood to make her larger point. Pay attention to the effect that her words, details, and images have on you.

## ● READING SKILL: IDENTIFY CAUSE AND EFFECT

A **cause** is an event or action that directly results in another event. An **effect** is the direct outcome of an event or action. For example, if your school bus gets a flat tire, that could be the cause of your being late for school. Being late is the effect. Sometimes signal words will alert you to causes (*because, since*) and effects (*as a result, therefore*). Other times, you'll have to make the connection for yourself.

As you read this essay, look for the conditions in Barry's environment that cause her to behave the way she does. Each time you recognize a cause-and-effect relationship, create a diagram like the one shown.

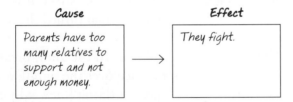

Cause

| Parents have too many relatives to support and not enough money. |

→

Effect

| They fight. |

## ▲ VOCABULARY IN CONTEXT

The boldfaced words help Lynda Barry to convey what she felt about school when she was a little girl. To see how many of them you know, restate each sentence, using a different word or phrase for the boldfaced term.

1. A **neglectful** student forgets to do her homework.
2. Children thrive in loving, **secure** homes.
3. Our school doesn't look unique or exciting on the outside, but inside it is anything but **nondescript**.
4. On a hot day, an air-conditioned classroom is a **sanctuary**.

### The New York Times

*SUNDAY, JANUARY 5, 1992*                                    A2

# The Sanctuary of School

### LYNDA BARRY

**sanctuary**
(săngk'chōō-ĕr'ē) *n.*
a place of refuge

I was seven years old the first time I snuck out of the house in the dark. It was winter and my parents had been fighting all night. They were short on money and long on relatives who kept "temporarily" moving into our house because they had nowhere else to go.

My brother and I were used to giving up our bedroom. We slept on the couch, something we actually liked because it put us that much closer to the light of our lives, our television.

At night when everyone was asleep, we lay on our pillows watching it with the sound off. We watched Steve Allen's[1] mouth moving. We watched Johnny Carson's[2] mouth moving. We watched movies filled with gangsters shooting machine guns into packed rooms, dying soldiers hurling a last grenade and beautiful women crying at windows. Then the sign-off finally came and we tried to sleep.

The morning I snuck out, I woke up filled with a panic about needing to get to school. The sun wasn't quite up yet but my anxiety was so fierce that I just got dressed, walked quietly across the kitchen and let myself out the back door.

It was quiet outside. Stars were still out. Nothing moved and no one was in the street. It was as if someone had turned the sound off on the world.

I walked the alley, breaking thin ice over the puddles with my shoes. I didn't know why I was walking to school in the dark. I didn't think about it. All I knew was a feeling of panic, like the panic that strikes kids when they realize they are lost. **Ⓐ**

That feeling eased the moment I turned the corner and saw the dark outline of my school at the top of the hill. My school was made up of about 15 **nondescript**

**Ⓐ AUTHOR'S PURPOSE**
What can you **infer** about Barry's reason for walking to school in the dark?

**nondescript**
(nŏn'dĭ-skrĭpt') *adj.*
lacking unique qualities

---

1. **Steve Allen:** (1921–2000) actor, comedian, songwriter, and author who hosted popular TV variety shows in the 1950s and 60s.
2. **Johnny Carson:** (1925–2005) comedian who hosted a late-night TV show, *The Tonight Show*, from 1962 to 1992.

portable classrooms set down on a fenced concrete lot in a rundown Seattle[3] neighborhood, but it had the most beautiful view of the Cascade Mountains. You could see them from anywhere on the playfield and you could see them from the windows of my classroom—Room 2. **B**

---

3. **Seattle:** a city in west central Washington state.

**B** CAUSE AND EFFECT
Reread lines 47–50. What causes Barry to feel less panicked?

**C CAUSE AND EFFECT**
What causes Barry's parents not to notice she is missing?

**D AUTHOR'S PURPOSE**
Reread lines 74–86. What connection does Barry make between herself, other children, and the importance of school?

**E AUTHOR'S PURPOSE**
What are your impressions of the janitor and the teachers, and of Barry's relationships with them?

**secure** (sĭ-kyŏŏr') *adj.* safe; protected; free from fear or anxiety

**F CAUSE AND EFFECT**
Reread lines 119–131. Describe the effect that being in school has on Barry.

60 I walked over to the monkey bars and hooked my arms around the cold metal. I stood for a long time just looking across Rainier Valley.[4] The sky was beginning to whiten and I could hear a few birds.

In a perfect world my absence at home would not have gone unnoticed. I would have had two parents in a panic to locate me, 70 instead of two parents in a panic to locate an answer to the hard question of survival during a deep financial and emotional crisis. **C**

But in an overcrowded and unhappy home, it's incredibly easy for any child to slip away. The high levels of frustration, depression and anger in my house made my brother and me invisible. 80 We were children with the sound turned off. And for us, as for the steadily increasing number of neglected children in this country, the only place where we could count on being noticed was at school. **D**

"Hey there, young lady. Did you forget to go home last night?" It was Mr. Gunderson, our janitor, 90 whom we all loved. He was nice and he was funny and he was old with white hair, thick glasses and an unbelievable number of keys. I could hear them jingling as he walked across the playfield. I felt incredibly happy to see him.

He let me push his wheeled garbage can between the different portables as he unlocked each 100 room. He let me turn on the lights and raise the window shades and I saw my school slowly come to life. I saw Mrs. Holman, our school secretary, walk into the office without her orange lipstick on yet. She waved.

I saw the fifth-grade teacher, Mr. Cunningham, walking under the breezeway eating a hard roll. 110 He waved.

And I saw my teacher, Mrs. Claire LeSane, walking toward us in a red coat and calling my name in a very happy and surprised way, and suddenly my throat got tight and my eyes stung and I ran toward her crying. It was something that surprised us both. **E**

It's only thinking about it now, 120 28 years later, that I realize I was crying from relief. I was with my teacher, and in a while I was going to sit at my desk, with my crayons and pencils and books and classmates all around me, and for the next six hours I was going to enjoy a thoroughly **secure,** warm and stable world. It was a world I absolutely relied on. Without it, 130 I don't know where I would have gone that morning. **F**

Mrs. LeSane asked me what was wrong and when I said, "Nothing," she seemingly left it at that. But she asked me if I would carry her purse for her, an honor above all honors, and she asked if I wanted to come into Room 2 early and paint.

---

4. **Rainier Valley:** a section of southeast Seattle.

She believed in the natural
healing power of painting
and drawing for troubled children.
In the back of her room there
was always a drawing table and
an easel with plenty of supplies,
and sometimes during the day
she would come up to you for
what seemed like no good reason
and quietly ask if you wanted to
go to the back table and "make
some pictures for Mrs. LeSane."
We all had a chance at it—to sit
apart from the class for a while to
paint, draw and silently work out
impossible problems on 11 × 17
sheets of newsprint.

Drawing came to mean
everything to me. At the back
table in Room 2, I learned to build
myself a life preserver that I could
carry into my home. **G**

We all know that a good
education system saves lives,
but the people of this country are
still told that cutting the budget for
public schools is necessary, that poor
salaries for teachers are all we can
manage and that art, music and all
creative activities must be the first
to go when times are lean.

Before- and after-school programs
are cut and we are told that public
schools are not made for baby-sitting
children. If parents are **neglectful**
temporarily or permanently, for
whatever reason, it's certainly sad,
but their unlucky children must

fend for themselves. Or slip through
the cracks.[5] Or wander in a dark
night alone.

We are told in a thousand
ways that not only are public
schools not important, but that
the children who attend them, the
children who need them most,
are not important either. We leave
them to learn from the blind eye
of a television, or to the mercy of
"a thousand points of light"[6] that
can be as far away as stars.

I was lucky. I had Mrs. LeSane.
I had Mr. Gunderson. I had an
abundance of art supplies. And I
had a particular brand of neglect
in my home that allowed me to
slip away and get to them. But
what about the rest of the kids
who weren't as lucky? What
happened to them?

By the time the bell rang
that morning I had finished my
drawing and Mrs. LeSane pinned
it up on the special bulletin board
she reserved for drawings from the
back table. It was the same picture
I always drew—a sun in the corner
of a blue sky over a nice house with
flowers all around it.

Mrs. LeSane asked us to please
stand, face the flag, place our right
hands over our hearts and say the
Pledge of Allegiance. Children
across the country do it faithfully.
I wonder now when the country
will face its children and say a
pledge right back. **H**

---

5. **slip through the cracks:** become lost or harmed due to negligence.
6. **"a thousand points of light":** volunteers and charities—a metaphor from a 1989 speech by then-President George H. W. Bush.

**G AUTHOR'S PURPOSE**
Reread lines 156–160.
What do you think Barry
means when she says she
learned to build herself
"a life preserver"?

**neglectful** (nǐ-glěkt'fəl)
*adj.* characterized by a
failure to properly care for
someone or something

**H AUTHOR'S PURPOSE**
Reread lines 161–215.
Which sentence best
sums up Barry's purpose?

## Comprehension

1. **Recall** Where does Lynda Barry go after she sneaks out of her house?

2. **Clarify** Why does Barry cry when she sees Mrs. LeSane?

## Critical Analysis

3. **Examine Cause and Effect** Look back at the cause-and-effect diagrams you created as you read. Which cause-and-effect relationship do you think is most important to Barry's argument in favor of public schools?

4. **Interpret Imagery** Skim pages 996 and 998, and note the three places where Barry describes someone or something as having "the sound turned off." In a graphic like the one shown, tell what she is referring to in each case. Why do you think the image is so powerful to Barry?

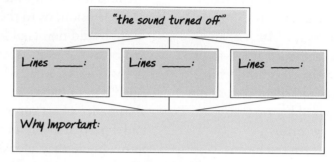

5. **Make Inferences** Reread the last paragraph of the essay. What is the "pledge" that Barry wants Americans to make to schoolchildren?

6. **Analyze Author's Purpose** The evidence Barry offers to persuade the reader comes from a single source—her personal experience. Generalizing from a single experience can be considered **overgeneralization.** Would you say Barry's argument is effective, or is her experience is too narrow to achieve her purpose? Explain.

7. **Draw Conclusions** How might Barry's life have been different if she hadn't had creative activities at school?

## Extension and Challenge

8. **Big Question Activity** Revisit the notes you took on page 994. With your group, discuss whether reading Lynda Barry's essay changed your opinion about schools' three most important tasks.

9. **Inquiry and Research** Lynda Barry's essay encourages us to support public schools for the education and important **relationships** they offer to all students. Find out about the purpose of public education in the United States. When were public schools established and why? How are they funded? On the basis of what you find out, decide whether Barry's expectations for schools are reasonable.

**RESEARCH LINKS**
For more on public education in the United States, visit the **Research Center** at **ClassZone.com.**

**INDIANA STANDARDS**

**READING STANDARD**
**8.2.9** Make reasonable statements and draw conclusions....

# Vocabulary in Context

## VOCABULARY PRACTICE

Choose the letter of the term that is most closely related to the boldfaced word.

1. **sanctuary**: (a) playground, (b) forest, (c) refuge
2. **nondescript:** (a) plain, (b) ugly, (c) beautiful
3. **secure:** (a) free, (b) safe, (c) loose
4. **neglectful:** (a) cruel, (b) bossy, (c) inattentive

## VOCABULARY IN WRITING

Using at least two vocabulary words, describe a place you consider a "sanctuary." You might start like this.

---

**EXAMPLE SENTENCE**

*The tree house my brothers and I built has become our* **sanctuary.**

---

## VOCABULARY STRATEGY: RELATED WORDS

One strategy that can help you figure out the meaning of an unfamiliar word is to look for a relationship between it and a word you already know. For example, if you don't know the meaning of the word *nondescript*, you might recognize a similarity between that word and the word *descriptive*. You can then guess that *nondescript* has something to do with how much there is to describe.

**PRACTICE** Identify a word you know that relates to each numbered word. Then guess at the definition for the numbered word. Check your definition in a dictionary, and write a sentence using the word.

1. criminology
2. humanitarian
3. logistical
4. inconsolable
5. disenchantment
6. elongation

**VOCABULARY PRACTICE**
For more practice, go to the **Vocabulary Center** at **ClassZone.com.**

# Educating Sons
Speech by Chief Canasatego

# The First Americans
Letter by the Grand Council Fire of American Indians

# *Who decides what's* IMPORTANT?

**KEY IDEA** Not everyone agrees on what we should teach or on how it should be taught. Often what is considered **important** to learn depends on where and when we're living. For example, the speech and letter that follow were written before Native American cultures received much respect from European Americans. Native American leaders have had to argue that their culture, language, history, and way of life are useful knowledge.

**SURVEY** As a class, make a list of the most **important** and useful things you've learned in school. Vote on the top four and post them in the four corners of your classroom. Then go stand under the one that you consider most important. Why did you choose what you did? Present your reasons to the class.

## ● ELEMENTS OF NONFICTION: HISTORICAL CONTEXT

You'll understand the following selections better if you consider their **historical context**. This means thinking about the conditions and events that caused the authors to say or write what they did. The Background information on this page provides some historical context. As you read the speech and letter that follow, keep this information in mind.

## ● READING SKILL: IDENTIFY COMPARISONS AND CONTRASTS

Writers often make their points by **comparing** and **contrasting** two subjects, pointing out the similarities and differences between them. For example, in the arguments you're about to read, the authors compare and contrast what is taught to young people with what the authors think should be taught. To help you keep track of the arguments, create a chart for each selection.

| *"Educating Sons"* | |
|---|---|
| *What Is Taught* | *What Should Be Taught* |
| | |

## ▲ VOCABULARY IN CONTEXT

The following words help convey some Native Americans' viewpoints on education in the United States. To see how many you know, use the words to complete the sentences.

| WORD LIST | | |
|---|---|---|
| decline | oratory | savage |
| esteem | sacred | treacherous |

1. For the Lakota people, the Black Hills region is a _____ place with deep religious significance.
2. Because of his famous speech "I will fight no more forever," Chief Joseph is known for his brilliant _____.
3. To call someone a _____ is to say that he is uncivilized.
4. Because the United States broke so many treaties, most Native Americans viewed the government as _____.
5. Many Cherokees chose to _____ offers by the government and were forcibly removed from their land.
6. In most Native cultures, grandparents are held in high _____ and treated with respect.

# Author Online

**A Man of Influence**
Chief Canasatego of the Onondaga Tribe was an influential leader in the Iroquois Confederacy, a group of tribes in the upper New York State area. Benjamin Franklin used Canasatego's ideas in his early plans for colonial union.

## *Background*

**A "No Thank You" Speech** In the 1700s, the British and the French were competing for land and resources in North America. English colonists thought that by offering Iroquois boys the chance to attend the university in Virginia, they would convince the Iroquois to support their side. The Iroquois, however, didn't want to send their sons to the school, for reasons made clear in Chief Canasatego's 1744 speech.

**The Grand Council Fire of American Indians** In 1927, Mayor William Hale Thompson of Chicago raised a protest against school textbooks he believed presented history in a way that was prejudiced in favor of Great Britain. The mayor wanted to revise textbooks to be what he called "100 percent American." The members of the Grand Council Fire of American Indians—led by its president Scott H. Peters, a Chippewa Indian—wanted to point out that the British were not the only group portrayed inaccurately in textbooks. They wrote a letter asking the mayor to change texts to reflect the perspectives and accomplishments of Native Americans. They wore full ceremonial dress and war paint when presenting the mayor with their letter.

 **MORE ABOUT THE AUTHOR AND BACKGROUND**
To learn more about Chief Canasatego and the Grand Council Fire of American Indians, visit the **Literature Center** at ClassZone.com.

# EDUCATING SONS

## Chief Canasatego

esteem (ĭ-stēm') v. to regard with respect

We know you highly **esteem** the kind of learning taught in these colleges. And the maintenance of our young men, while with you, would be very expensive to you. We're convinced, therefore, that you mean to do us good by your proposal, and we thank you heartily. But you who are so wise must know that different nations have different conceptions of things. And you will not, therefore, take it amiss[1] if our ideas of this kind of education happens not to be the same with yours.

We have had some experience of it. Several of our young people were formerly brought up in the colleges of the northern province. They were 10 instructed in all your sciences. But when they came back to us, they were bad runners, ignorant of every means of living in the woods, unable to bear either cold or hunger, knew neither how to build a cabin, take a deer, or kill an enemy, spoke our language imperfectly, and therefore were neither fit for hunters nor warriors nor councilors. They were totally good for nothing. Ⓐ

**Ⓐ HISTORICAL CONTEXT**
What can you **infer** about Chief Canasatego's Onondaga society?

We are, however, not the less obliged[2] for your kind offer, though we **decline** accepting. To show our grateful sense of it, if the gentlemen of Virginia will send us a dozen of their sons, we would take great care in their education, instruct them in all we know, and make men of them.

**decline** (dĭ-klīn') v. to politely refuse

---

1. **take it amiss:** be offended.
2. **obliged** (ə-blījd'): grateful or indebted.

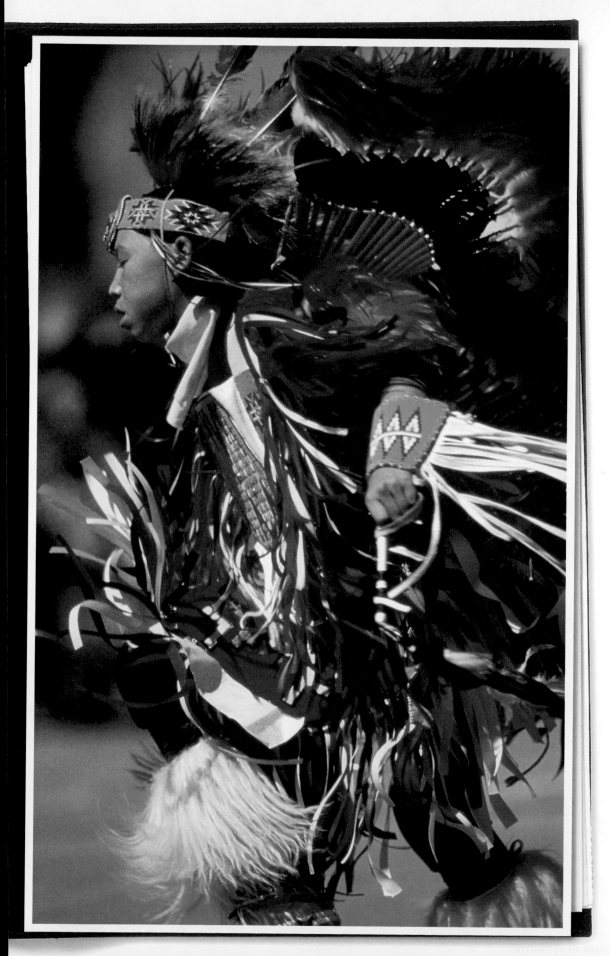

# The First Americans

## THE GRAND COUNCIL FIRE OF AMERICAN INDIANS

**DECEMBER I, 1927**

**TO THE MAYOR OF CHICAGO:—**

You tell all white men "America First." We believe in that. We are the only ones, truly, that are 100 percent. We therefore ask you while you are teaching school children about America First, teach them truth about the First Americans.

We do not know if school histories are pro-British, but we do know that they are unjust to the life of our people—the American Indian. They call all white victories, battles, and all Indian victories, massacres. The battle with Custer[1] has been taught to school children as a fearful massacre on 10 our part. We ask that this, as well as other incidents, be told fairly. If the Custer battle was a massacre, what was Wounded Knee?[2]

History books teach that Indians were murderers—is it murder to fight in self-defense? Indians killed white men because white men took their lands, ruined their hunting grounds, burned their forests, destroyed their buffalo. White men penned our people on reservations, then took away the reservations. White men who rise to protect their property are called patriots—Indians who do the same are called murderers.

White men call Indians **treacherous**—but no mention is made of broken treaties on the part of the white man. White men say that Indians 20 were always fighting. It was only our lack of skill in white man's warfare that led to our defeat. An Indian mother prayed that her boy be a great medicine man[3] rather than a great warrior. It is true that we had our own small battles, but in the main we were peace-loving and home-loving. **B**

White men called Indians thieves—and yet we lived in frail skin lodges and needed no locks or iron bars. White men call Indians **savages.** What is civilization? Its marks are a noble religion and philosophy, original arts, stirring music, rich history and legend. We had these. Then we were not savages, but a civilized race.

We made blankets that were beautiful that the white man with all 30 his machinery has never been able to duplicate. We made baskets that

---

1. **Custer:** George Armstrong Custer (1839–1876), a U.S. cavalry officer who fought Sioux and Cheyenne warriors at Little Bighorn; Custer was killed and his army was wiped out.
2. **Wounded Knee:** a creek in South Dakota where U.S. troops massacred about 200 Native Americans on December 29, 1890.
3. **medicine man:** a Native-American holy man and healer.

---

**treacherous** (trĕch′ər-əs) *adj.* not to be relied on; untrustworthy

**B COMPARISONS AND CONTRASTS**
Reread lines 6–23. According to the Grand Council Fire members, what do textbooks teach about Native Americans? Add this information to your chart.

**savage** (săv′ĭj) *n.* a person regarded as primitive or uncivilized

were beautiful. We wove in beads and colored quills, designs that were not just decorative motifs, but were the outward expression of our very thoughts. We made pottery—pottery that was useful and beautiful as well. Why not make school children
40 acquainted with the beautiful handicrafts in which we were skilled? Put in every school Indian blankets, baskets, pottery.

We sang songs that carried in their melodies all the sounds of nature— the running of waters, the sighing of winds, and the calls of the animals. Teach these to your children that they may come to love nature as we love it.

We had our statesmen—and their **oratory** has never been equalled. Teach the children some of these speeches of our people, remarkable for
50 their brilliant oratory.

We played games—games that brought good health and sound bodies. Why not put these in your schools? We told stories. Why not teach school children more of the wholesome proverbs and legends of our people? Tell them how we loved all that was beautiful. That we killed game only for food, not for fun. Indians think white men who kill for fun are murderers. **C**

Tell your children of the friendly acts of Indians to the white people who first settled here. Tell them of our leaders and heroes and their deeds. Tell them of Indians such as Black Partridge,[4] Shabbona,[5] and others who
60 many times saved the people of Chicago at great danger to themselves. Put in your history books the Indian's part in the World War.[6] Tell how the Indian fought for a country of which he was not a citizen, for a flag to which he had no claim, and for a people that have treated him unjustly. **D**

The Indian has long been hurt by these unfair books. We ask only that our story be told in fairness. We do not ask you to overlook what we did, but we do ask you to understand it. A true program of America First will give a generous place to the culture and history of the American Indian.

We ask this, Chief, to keep **sacred** the memory of our people.

---

4. **Black Partridge:** a Potawatomi chief who befriended white settlers.

5. **Shabbona** (shä′bō-nə): a member of the Ottawa people who befriended white settlers.

6. **World War:** World War I (1914–1918), in which Great Britain, France, the United States, and their allies defeated Germany, Austria-Hungary, and their allies.

**oratory** (ôr′ə-tôr′ē) *n.* the art of making speeches

**C** COMPARISONS AND CONTRASTS
Reread lines 39–54. What does the Grand Council suggest schools should teach?

**D** HISTORICAL CONTEXT
Why does the Grand Council mention Native Americans who helped the people of Chicago?

**sacred** (sā′krĭd) *adj.* holy; worthy of religious veneration or respect

# Comprehension

1. **Recall** Why does Chief Canasatego not want to send Iroquois sons to be educated by the colonists?

2. **Recall** According to the Grand Council Fire of American Indians, how do textbooks refer to "Indian victories"?

3. **Summarize** What cultural activities does the Grand Council Fire of American Indians think should be emphasized in textbooks?

# Critical Analysis

4. **Analyze Irony** Irony occurs when what the speaker says is different from what he or she actually means. Reread lines 16–19 of "Educating Sons." What is the irony in these closing remarks? Explain your answer.

5. **Examine Historical Context** In the 1920s, Native Americans began to receive better treatment and greater rights from the federal government. In 1924, Native Americans were finally granted citizenship, which meant that for the first time, many could vote. How do you think these changes might have affected the Grand Council's decision to speak up?

6. **Identify Comparisons and Contrasts** Review the chart you completed as you read "The First Americans." Summarize the difference between what was being taught to children and what the Grand Council thought should be taught.

7. **Draw Conclusions About Values** In a Y-chart like the one shown, list three values that Chief Canasatego and the Grand Council each argue are **important** in their cultures. List the values that are common to both cultures in the stem of the Y. What conclusion can you draw about how Native American values changed over time?

Chief Canasatego
1.
2.
3.

Grand Council
1.
2.
3.

Common Values

# Extension and Challenge

8. **Readers' Circle** With a group, decide what each author would say is the most important thing for young people to learn. Cite lines from the speech and letter to support your views. Then discuss whether these things are still important to learn today.

9.  **SOCIAL STUDIES CONNECTION** Research the Battle of Little Bighorn or the Battle of Wounded Knee. What does this information add to your understanding of the Grand Council's argument?

> **RESEARCH LINKS**
> For more on the Battle of Little Big Horn and the Battle of Wounded Knee, visit the **Research Center** at **ClassZone.com**.

**INDIANA STANDARDS**

**READING STANDARD**
**8.3.7** Analyze a work of literature, showing how it reflects the … beliefs of its author.

George Custer, who led American forces at Little Bighorn

# Vocabulary in Context

## VOCABULARY PRACTICE

For each item, choose the word that differs most in meaning from the other words. Refer to a dictionary if you need help.

1. (a) esteem, (b) revere, (c) admire, (d) scorn
2. (a) decline, (b) accept, (c) invite, (d) welcome
3. (a) loyal, (b) treacherous, (c) traitorous, (d) unreliable
4. (a) savage, (b) aristocrat, (c) scholar, (d) intellectual
5. (a) speeches, (b) oratory, (c) proclamations, (d) chitchat
6. (a) holy, (b) sacred, (c) sanctified, (d) profane

decline
esteem
oratory
sacred
savage
treacherous

## VOCABULARY IN WRITING

Imagine that a friend's family offers to teach you the traditions from their culture, which is different from yours. Using at least two vocabulary words, write a short speech in which you accept or decline the offer. You might start like this.

> **EXAMPLE SENTENCE**
>
> *I hope you know, I hold your culture in the highest **esteem**. I understand you have so much to teach me.*

## VOCABULARY STRATEGY: ANTONYMS AND CONTEXT CLUES

You can often find **context clues** in the words and phrases that surround an unfamiliar word. **Antonyms,** or words with opposite meanings, provide one kind of context clue. For example, a passage in "The First Americans" reads: "White men call Indians savages.... We had [religion, philosophy, arts, music, history, and legend]. Then we were not savages, but a civilized race." The words *not* and *but* signal that *savages* is an antonym for *civilized race*.

**PRACTICE** In each sentence, identify an antonym for each boldfaced word. Then define the boldfaced word.

1. Although I am **ignorant** of many things, I am very knowledgeable about cats.
2. I should feel **obliged** to her for the invitation, but I'm actually feeling ungrateful.
3. He was certainly not a patriot; in fact, he was a **traitor** to his country.
4. Please stop eating unhealthy food; eat something **wholesome** for a change!
5. My parents **overlooked** my untidy bedroom but punished me for lying.

**INDIANA STANDARDS**

**READING STANDARD**
8.1.3 Verify the meaning of a word in its context ....

**VOCABULARY PRACTICE**
For more practice, go to the **Vocabulary Center** at ClassZone.com.

## St. Crispian's Day Speech

Drama excerpt from *Henry V* by William Shakespeare

# *What* INSPIRES *you?*

**INDIANA STANDARDS**

**READING STANDARDS**

**8.2.2** Analyze text that uses proposition (statement of argument) and support patterns.

**8.2.6** Evaluate the logic (inductive or deductive argument), internal consistency, and structural patterns of text.

**KEY IDEA** Nursing a baby bird to health might make you want to learn more about nature. Watching a classmate work for a worthy cause could cause you to volunteer, too. **Inspiration**—a strong emotion or desire to take action—can come from many places. You might find it in songs or pictures, or in people's words or deeds. In the speech you are about to read, a king uses words to inspire courage in the face of almost certain death.

**QUICKWRITE** In your journal, write a paragraph about an experience, person, event, or work of art that has **inspired** you. Has the source of your inspiration caused you to change your behavior or take action in some way?

## ● LITERARY ANALYSIS: PERSUASION IN LITERATURE

Playwrights often have their characters use the same persuasive techniques that nonfiction authors do. In this dramatic speech, King Henry's goal is to get his men to fight against a much stronger enemy. To do this he uses an age-old persuasive technique. This technique, now called **snob appeal,** is often used in advertising to appeal to a person's desire to be special or to think that he or she is "better than everyone else." For example, to convince you to buy designer jeans, an ad might say, "You're not ordinary, so why should you wear ordinary jeans?" As you read the speech, pay attention to how King Henry "sells" the idea of joining in the battle.

## ● READING STRATEGY: PARAPHRASE

When you **paraphrase,** you restate something in your own words. Paraphrasing is different than summarizing. A summary covers only the work's most important points. A paraphrase covers all the content and should be about the same length as or longer than the original. If you can accurately restate the meaning of a written work in your own words, you can be certain that you understand it.

As you read "St. Crispian's Day Speech," watch for where each idea begins and ends. Paying attention to punctuation marks such as commas and dashes, as well as line breaks, will help you. Figure out the meaning of important terms by looking at footnotes, context clues, or the dictionary. Then paraphrase each idea in a chart like the one shown.

| Lines | Paraphrase |
|-------|------------|
| 1–4   | It's St. Crispian's Day. The men who survive today's battle will stand above others and feel proud every year when St. Crispian's Day comes around. |

# Author Online

**Writer, Actor, Businessman**
William Shakespeare played many roles. He was the main playwright for a theater troupe called Lord Chamberlain's Men. As part owner, Shakespeare shared in the company's profits. He was also a frequent performer on stage. While he

**William Shakespeare 1564–1616**

was popular during his time, with each passing century his fame has grown. His plays are still performed and adapted for the stage and screen, and his poetry is constantly quoted and taught. He is now considered one of the finest writers in the English language.

> **MORE ABOUT THE AUTHOR**
> For more on William Shakespeare, visit the **Literature Center** at **ClassZone.com.**

## Background

**Henry V** Shakespeare's play describes the adventures of Henry V, king of England from 1413 to 1422. His reign occurred during the Hundred Years' War, in which the English and French fought for control of France. The Battle of Agincourt, a turning point in the war, is the setting for the following speech. It was 1415, and the English troops were attempting to return to England from France, where they had lost a lot of men. Their route was blocked by 20,000 to 30,000 French soldiers. King Henry had only about 6,000 men under his command. St. Crispian's Day dawned with the two armies preparing for battle. Thanks to Henry's brilliant leadership and France's poor choice of battlefields, the English were able to defeat a much larger enemy force. In 1420, Henry was recognized as the heir to the French throne.

# St Crispian's Day Speech

*William Shakespeare*

This day is call'd the feast of Crispian:[1]
He that outlives this day, and comes safe home,
Will stand a' tiptoe when this day is named,
And rouse him at the name of Crispian.
5 He that shall live this day, and see old age,
Will yearly on the vigil feast his neighbors,
And say, "To-morrow is Saint Crispian."
Then will he strip his sleeve and show his scars,
And say, "These wounds I had on Crispin's day."
10 Old men forget; yet all shall be forgot,
But he'll remember with advantages
What feats he did that day. Then shall our names,
Familiar in his mouth as household words,
Harry the King, Bedford and Exeter,
15 Warwick and Talbot, Salisbury and Gloucester,[2]
Be in their flowing cups freshly rememb'red. **Ⓐ**
This story shall the good man teach his son;
And Crispin Crispian shall ne'er go by,
From this day to the ending of the world,
20 But we in it shall be remembered—
We few, we happy few, we band of brothers;
For he to-day that sheds his blood with me
Shall be my brother; be he ne'er so vile,[3]
This day shall gentle his condition;
25 And gentlemen in England, now a-bed,
Shall think themselves accurs'd they were not here;
And hold their manhoods cheap[4] whiles any speaks
That fought with us upon Saint Crispin's day. **Ⓑ**

**ANALYZE VISUALS**
In this film still from *Henry V*, what can you **infer** about the relationship between King Henry and his troops?

**Ⓐ PERSUASION**
What does the king promise his men in lines 10–16?

**Ⓑ PARAPHRASE**
Restate lines 25–28 in your own words. Why might these lines inspire Henry's men?

---

1. **the feast of Crispian** (krĭs'pē-ən): religious day honoring two martyred brothers (Crispian and Crispin). It falls on October 25, the day of the Battle of Agincourt.

2. **Bedford and Exeter** (ĕk'sĭ-tər), **Warwick** (wôr'ĭk) and Talbot, Salisbury (sôlz'bĕr'ē) and Gloucester (glŏs'tər): noblemen who fought with the king at the Battle of Agincourt.

3. **be he ne'er so vile:** no matter how humble or lowborn he is.

4. **hold their manhoods cheap:** not consider themselves very strong or brave.

## Comprehension

**INDIANA STANDARDS**

**READING STANDARD**
**8.2.2** Analyze text that uses proposition (statement of argument) and support patterns.

1. **Recall** According to King Henry, on future St. Crispian's Days, how will men prove they fought at the Battle of Agincourt?

2. **Recall** What relationship does the king offer to any man who "sheds his blood" with Henry?

3. **Clarify** According to Henry, what effect will fighting in the battle have on men who are "vile"?

## Literary Analysis

4. **Analyze Character** King Henry V is often cited as an example of someone who is a strong leader. What leadership qualities does Shakespeare's Henry show in the "St. Crispian's Day Speech"? Support your response with evidence from the text.

5. **Analyze Persuasion in Literature** Create a list of all the examples of **snob appeal** in the speech. Then, beside each example, tell what Henry is promising his men. Which of King Henry's appeals do you find most persuasive? Why?

| Snob Appeal | Promise |
|---|---|
| Will stand a' tiptoe | Will be better than others |

6. **Evaluate Paraphrase** Select one of the paraphrases you recorded in your chart. Compare it with Shakespeare's original words. Which version do you think would be more **inspirational** to people today? Why?

7. **Compare Across Texts** Members of the Grand Council Fire of American Indians clearly state how their people should be remembered in "The First Americans" (pages 1006–1007). Compare this with King Henry's vision of how his men will be remembered. What is similar and different about what the two groups want to be known for? What might help explain the differences?

## Extension and Challenge

8. **Literary Criticism** The king's speech in *Henry V* is one of Shakespeare's most famous passages. What do you think gives this speech its power and continuing appeal? Support your answer.

9. **SOCIAL STUDIES CONNECTION** The skillful tactics employed by King Henry were a major factor in the English victory at Agincourt. Research how the battle was fought, and create a poster depicting the movements and strategies of Henry's troops and the French troops.

**RESEARCH LINKS**
For more on the Battle of Agincourt, visit the **Research Center** at **ClassZone.com**.

# Reading-Writing Connection

Show your understanding of the "St. Crispian's Day Speech" by responding to these prompts. Then complete the **Grammar and Writing** exercise.

| WRITING PROMPTS | SELF-CHECK |
|---|---|
| **A. Short Response: Persuade Your Classmates** Think of a cause that you support. Write **one paragraph** that will **inspire** your classmates to sacrifice something in order to help your cause. Use the technique of **snob appeal** in your response. | *A strong response will . . .* <br> • motivate readers to take action <br> • demonstrate an understanding of snob appeal |
| **B. Extended Response: Analyze a Speech** In the "St. Crispian's Day Speech," Henry V makes an appeal to his men to follow him into battle. In **two or three paragraphs**, explain the way he convinces his men to fight a battle in which they are outnumbered. | *A well-written analysis will . . .* <br> • explain how Henry tries to convince his audience <br> • use examples to illustrate your points |

## GRAMMAR AND WRITING

**INDIANA STANDARDS**

**WRITING STANDARD**
**8.6.2** Identify and use parallelism . . . .

*USE CORRECT SENTENCE STRUCTURE* **Parallelism** is the use of similar grammatical structures to link related ideas. Parts of a sentence that have parallel meanings should have parallel structure. For example, if you're listing various activities, use the same sentence part to describe each activity—nouns with nouns, verbs with verbs, or phrases with phrases. A typical error occurs when *and* is used to join different sentence parts.

> *Original:* Volunteering is fun, easy, and rewards you. (*The construction is not parallel because two adjectives are joined to a verb.*)
>
> *Revised:* Volunteering is fun, easy, and rewarding. (*The construction is now parallel because three adjectives are joined.*)

**PRACTICE** Rewrite each of these sentences to make its structure parallel.

1. Volunteers are kind and sympathize with people.
2. Donating clothing, volunteering at a food bank, and work at a homeless shelter are all ways you can help others.
3. Food banks are important for people who are unemployed, disabled, or don't have a home.
4. Don't spend all your time playing video games, watching movies, and at the mall.

*For more help with parallelism, see page R64 in the **Grammar Handbook.***

## Writing Workshop

# Persuasive Essay

Which of the arguments in this unit did you find most persuasive? You can take a stand on an issue that matters to you by putting your beliefs in writing and backing them up with facts. To get started on your own persuasive essay, check out the **Writer's Road Map.**

### WRITER'S ROAD MAP

#### Persuasive Essay

**WRITING PROMPT 1**

**Writing for the Real World** Choose an issue you feel strongly about. Write a persuasive essay in which you explain the issue and convince your readers to agree with your point of view.

**Issues to Explore**

- school dress codes
- locker searches
- restrictions on leaving school grounds at lunch

**WRITING PROMPT 2**

**Writing from Literature** Something you read may make you aware of an injustice. Using a selection in this unit as a springboard, write a persuasive essay about an issue that interests you.

**Issues to Explore**

- whether parents and teachers are overprotective ("Position on Dodgeball in Physical Education" and "The Weak Shall Inherit the Gym")
- treatment of zoo animals ("Zoos: Myth and Reality" and "Zoos Connect Us to the Natural World")

 **WRITING TOOLS**
For prewriting, revision, and editing tools, visit the **Writing Center** at ClassZone.com.

**KEY TRAITS**

**1. IDEAS**

- Presents a **thesis statement** taking a position on a clearly identified issue
- Uses **convincing details** to support the position
- Answers **opposing arguments** and counterclaims

**2. ORGANIZATION**

- **Introduces** the issue in an attention-getting way
- Uses **transitions** to create a consistent organizational pattern
- **Concludes** by summarizing the position and issuing a call to action or call to agreement

**3. VOICE**

- Reflects the **writer's strong belief** in his or her opinion

**4. WORD CHOICE**

- Uses **persuasive language** effectively

**5. SENTENCE FLUENCY**

- Varies **sentence lengths and structures**

**6. CONVENTIONS**

- Uses **correct grammar, spelling, and punctuation**

# Part 1: Analyze a Student Model

**WRITING STANDARD**
**8.5.4** Write persuasive compositions.

**Michael Vickers**
**Arlington Middle School**

### Raise Your Hand for Helping Hands

Are you tired of being treated like a little kid? Do you wish you could prove to other people that you're responsible and mature and have a lot to offer to others? Well, a new program proposed by a school board member could make that wish come true. Helping Hands would give
5  all eighth graders a chance to volunteer our services to the community. This program would benefit everyone involved, and it deserves everyone's enthusiastic support.

The Helping Hands program would require every eighth grader to do some kind of community service for four hours a month. Reading
10  to children or senior citizens, helping out at day camps and recreation facilities, working at after-school art and sports programs, cleaning up parks and beaches—these are just some of the activities students could do. The school administrators would post a list of volunteer positions available, and each student would be able to choose a job that interested
15  him or her. Teachers or workers at the facilities would supervise our activities and report our hours directly to the school.

The community would benefit from this program because we would provide important services at no cost. In addition, we students would gain many advantages from taking part in this program. First of
20  all, we would be able to use skills we already have and learn new ones. Also, we would become better members of the community and get to know many different people, occupations, and work situations. This information would help us discover our interests and strengths; it might even give us ideas about future careers.

## KEY TRAITS IN ACTION

**Introduces** the essay with a question that concerns the writer's audience of eighth graders.

**Thesis statement** presents the issue and the writer's position on it.

Different **sentence lengths and structures** help to make the details interesting and memorable.

Highlighted **transition** helps the reader understand the organization of the essay.

Some students might oppose this program because they think they already spend too much time on school-related activities. Besides the actual hours spent in class, there are sports practices and games, club meetings, and homework. Most students also have chores to do at home, and many take music or other lessons. They don't want to give up what little free time they have.

Students are very busy, of course. However, Helping Hands would require only four hours a month. That's just an hour a week. Most of us spend three or four times that much time talking on the telephone. We also waste even more time just sitting around or putting off what we're supposed to be doing. These few hours of community service wouldn't interfere with any of our other activities and would still leave us plenty of time to relax. In fact, needing to work this service into our schedules might even help us become more organized and efficient with our time.

There's no question that this proposed program benefits the community, the school, and the students. Support it now by attending the school board meeting next week, raising your hand, and saying a rousing "Yes!" to Helping Hands.

> Describes an **opposing argument.**

> Effectively uses **persuasive language** to answer the opposition and express the writer's **strong belief** in the program.

> **Concludes** persuasively by restating the writer's support for the program and telling readers exactly what they should do.

2

# Part 2: Apply the Writing Process

**WRITING STANDARD**
**8.4.7** Review, evaluate, and revise writing for meaning and clarity.

## PREWRITING

| What Should I Do? | What Does It Look Like? |
|---|---|

**1. Analyze the prompt.**
Read the prompts on page 1016. Choose the one that appeals to you. Then (circle) the type of writing you will be doing and <u>underline</u> details about your purpose and audience.

▶ **WRITING PROMPT** Choose an issue you feel strongly about. Write a (persuasive essay) in which you <u>explain the issue and convince your readers to agree with your point of view.</u>

*This is a class assignment, so I should choose a topic that will interest other eighth graders.*

**2. Find an issue that you believe deserves attention.**
List issues that concern you, adding your questions or comments about each. Put a star by the issue that will be the focus of your essay.

**TIP** Make sure the issue you choose has two sides.

▶ *School Issues*
- *backpack searches—are they legal?*
- *Helping Hands program—a great way to prove our maturity and responsibility* ✱

*Community Issues*
- *violence (one-sided issue—nobody supports violence)*
- *helmet law for cyclists—how can we get one passed?*

**3. Create a working thesis statement.**
Write a sentence or two summarizing the issue and your stand on it. You can rewrite your thesis statement as you draft, so don't worry about making it perfect at this stage.

▶ *Working thesis statement*

*Helping Hands is great because it would give all eighth graders a chance to serve the community.*

**4. Collect information that supports your position.**
You'll need solid logic as well as specific facts, statistics, and reliable opinions to persuade your reader. Check books, local and national newspapers and magazines, and the Internet for information.

**TIP** Think about opposing arguments and look for details you can use to refute them.

▶ *Services we could provide*
- *reading to little kids or senior citizens*
- *working at day camps and after-school programs*
- *cleaning up litter at parks and beaches*
- *others? (Check with school officials and at town hall.)*

| **What Should I Do?** | **What Does It Look Like?** |
|---|---|

**1. Organize your facts and ideas.**
Here are two ways of organizing a persuasive essay:

**Pattern 1**—Discuss all points on one side of the issue, then all points on the other side. This is the pattern the writer of the student model used.

**Pattern 2**—Present the arguments for and against one key point. Then do the same for another key point, and so on.

**PATTERN 1**

Introduction and description of program

**For Helping Hands**

- serves community
- helps students develop talents, learn about careers

**Against Helping Hands**

- students too busy
- need free time

Conclusion and call to action

**PATTERN 2**

Introduction and description of program

**Opposing Argument 1:**
students too busy

**Counterargument 1:**
only four hours per month

**Opposing Argument 2:**
need free time

**Counterargument 2:**
teaches organization and efficiency

Conclusion and call to action

**2. Support each key point you make.**
Why do you believe what you believe? Back up your statements with strong examples and reasons.

We students would gain many advantages from taking part in this program.  ⎤ Key point

We would be able to use the skills we already have and learn new ones. Also, we would get to know many different people, occupations, and work situations.  ⎦ Support

**3. Rebut each opposing argument.**
Address each point on the other side of the issue and explain why it doesn't make sense.

**TIP** Before revising, review the key traits on page 1016 and the rubric and peer-reader questions on page 1022.

Some students might oppose this program because they think they already spend too much time on school-related activities....

Students are very busy, of course. However, Helping Hands would require only four hours a month. These few hours of community service wouldn't interfere with any of our other activities and would still leave us plenty of time to relax.

## REVISING AND EDITING

| What Should I Do? | What Does It Look Like? |
|---|---|

**1. Use emotional appeals wisely.**
- Reread your draft. Put a box around words or phrases that use so much flattery, pity, or fear that they may cause your reader to dismiss your entire message.
- Replace these statements with appeals that include sound reasoning and evidence.

**See page 1022:** Emotional Appeals

▶ ~~Join Helping Hands to show that you are the smartest, most responsible student in this school.~~

Are you tired of being treated like a little kid? Do you wish you could prove to other people that you're responsible and mature and have a lot to offer to others? Well, a new program proposed by a school board member could make that wish come true.

**2. Strengthen your supporting details.**
- Underline details that support and explain your points. Is your support clear and relevant?
- If your essay has only a few underlines, add details. If the underlined parts are confusing, replace them with clear explanations.

▶ ~~There are all kinds of things we could do.~~

Reading to children or senior citizens, helping out at day camps and recreation facilities, working at after-school art and sports programs, cleaning up parks and beaches—these are just some of the activities students could do.

**3. Sharpen imprecise language.**
- Have a peer reader (circle) vague phrases like *a good idea* and *might be helpful.*
- Replace these words with specific terms that persuade your reader.

**See page 1022:** Ask a Peer Reader

▶ ~~It seems like a (pretty good) idea, so you (might want to think about) joining.~~

This program would benefit everyone involved, and it deserves everyone's enthusiastic support.

**4. Make your conclusion complete.**
- End by summarizing your position on the issue and issuing a **call to action** or **call to agreement.** In other words, tell your reader what to do or what to think.
- Reread your conclusion and add or revise information as needed.

▶ ~~In conclusion, joining Helping Hands is the right thing to do.~~

There's no question that this proposed program benefits the community, the school, and the students. Support it now by attending the school board meeting next week, raising your hand, and saying a rousing "Yes!" to Helping Hands.

## Apply the Rubric

**A strong persuasive essay . . .**

☑ captures the reader's attention from the first paragraph

☑ presents a thesis that describes the issue and the writer's opinion

☑ supports that opinion with convincing details

☑ explains opposing arguments and answers them effectively with counterclaims

☑ uses precise, persuasive language

☑ uses transitions to show how ideas are related

☑ varies sentence lengths and structures

☑ ends by restating the writer's position and calling for action or agreement

## Ask a Peer Reader

• How can I make my introduction more lively?

• Which of my statements was most convincing? Why?

• Were any words or phrases weak, vague, or confusing? If so, which?

## Emotional Appeals

It's fine to try to create strong feelings when you write your essay. However, make sure your appeals don't make your reader feel manipulated.

• **Overemotional appeal to pity**—How can you cruelly ignore those sad little kids who have nobody to read to them?!

• **Effective appeal to pity**—It's a chance to help the people in our community who most need and deserve our attention.

## Check Your Grammar

Use the active voice whenever possible to clarify who or what is doing the action. This will help make your statements as strong and persuasive as they can be.

> School administrators would post
> ∧A list of volunteer positions₀ ~~would be posted.~~
>   Helping Hands would require
> ∧Only three or four hours a month₀ ~~would be~~
> ~~required by Helping Hands.~~

**See page R57:** Active and Passive Voice

## Writing Online

**PUBLISHING OPTIONS**
For publishing options, visit the **Writing Center** at ClassZone.com.

**ASSESSMENT PREPARATION**
For writing and grammar assessment practice, go to the **Assessment Center** at ClassZone.com.

# Delivering a Persuasive Speech

Turning your essay into a persuasive speech can help you reach a wider audience and get your ideas across even more effectively.

## Planning the Speech

1. **Mark up your essay.** Highlight or underline the points you want to include in your speech.
2. **Write a script.** Start with a strong introduction. You can use the introduction from your essay or get your listeners' attention by telling a story, perhaps including actions or gestures.
3. **Create a visual.** Put the points you want to make on a flip chart, on transparencies, in a power presentation, or in some other visual format. Create one page for each main point and add supporting details in short bullet points. Be sure the text is large enough to be readable at the back of the room.

> *Choose your own volunteer work.*
> * *What skills do you already have?*
> * *What skills would you like to learn?*
> * *What jobs are available?*

4. **Be clear and specific.** Use precise words that tell your listeners exactly how you feel about the issue and what you want them to do.

## Delivering the Speech

1. **Read the guidelines in the Speaking and Listening Handbook (page R79).** These guidelines explain the keys to a successful persuasive speech. Learn them, and then practice your speech until you feel comfortable delivering it. Present it in front of a mirror first, and then ask your family or friends to watch.
2. **Put your visuals to work.** Make sure everyone in the audience can see the visual that you are using. Help listeners follow along by using your finger or a laser pointer to indicate which point you are talking about.

# Reading Comprehension

**DIRECTIONS** *Read this selection and answer the questions that follow.*

# Nuclear Energy: Does It Make Sense for the Environment?

**After decades of wariness, interest in nuclear power is picking up. Do the benefits outweigh the risks?**

### YES

Nuclear power is the largest source of emission-free energy generation in the United States. One of every five American homes and businesses gets its electricity from a nuclear plant.

Meeting tighter limits on air pollution is an ambitious task—one that would be virtually impossible without the clean-air benefits of nuclear power. The Department of Energy recognizes nuclear energy's essential role, identifying it as the single most effective strategy for reducing air pollution.

Nuclear power is the only expandable, large-scale energy source that avoids air pollution and can meet the electricity demands of our growing economy.
10 Nuclear plants do not emit carbon dioxide or other greenhouse gases linked to global warming, nor do they emit pollutants that contribute to haze or smog.

Here's another way to look at nuclear energy's positive impact: Based on 1999 figures, if nuclear plants had to be replaced with oil- or coal-burning plants, the United States would have to eliminate 135 million passenger cars (about half of all cars!) just to keep our carbon dioxide emissions at current levels.

With regard to security, the nation's 103 nuclear power plants are among the best-defended industrial facilities in the United States. And today's nuclear plants have state-of-the-art safety features to prevent accidents.
20 Several notable environmentalists have recently endorsed nuclear energy. They believe global warming is increasingly our most pressing environmental concern, and recognize nuclear energy is a key part of the solution.

—Scott Peterson, Vice President
Nuclear Energy Institute

**NO**

Nuclear energy is not the answer to global warming. It makes no sense to solve one set of environmental problems by creating a bigger and more serious set of problems. And nuclear energy is full of very big and very serious problems.

Although new nuclear power plants would certainly be safer than older plants, the consequences of a major accident are still the same: widespread and long-lasting radiation pollution affecting several generations. An explosion at
30 the Chernobyl nuclear reactor in the Soviet Union in 1986 killed 31 people and caused hundreds of thousands of cases of delayed illnesses.

In addition, nuclear power plants make attractive targets for terrorists. A disaster caused by sabotage or attack would cause great harm to people and the environment. Another problem for the environment is the spent fuel from nuclear power plants, which remains toxic for thousands of years. The United States still has no operational long-term repository to store this spent fuel safely.

The process of turning uranium into fuel for nuclear reactors can be easily modified to produce uranium for nuclear bombs. Pakistan's and India's nuclear
40 bombs were made this way. The potential use of these weapons—possibly by terrorists—would be catastrophic to our environment.

Instead of investing in nuclear power, which just trades one set of problems for another, let's invest in renewable energy sources like wind and solar energy. They may cost a little more now, but they don't cause any harm—and they don't run out.

—Kelly Kissock, Associate Professor of Engineering
University of Dayton, Ohio

# Comprehension

**DIRECTIONS** *Answer these questions about "Nuclear Energy: Does It Make Sense for the Environment?"*

1. The author's main purpose in writing the "Yes" response is to
   - ○ warn people about global warming
   - ○ report on oil- and coal-burning plants
   - ○ prove that cars emit pollutants
   - ○ promote the use of nuclear power

2. Which statement from the "Yes" response is an opinion?
   - ○ "Nuclear power is the largest source of emission-free energy generation in the United States." (lines 1–2)
   - ○ "Meeting tighter limits on air pollution is an ambitious task. . . ." (line 4)
   - ○ "Nuclear plants do not emit carbon dioxide or other greenhouse gases linked to global warming. . . ." (lines 10–11)
   - ○ "Several notable environmentalists have recently endorsed nuclear energy." (line 20)

3. What claim does the author of the "Yes" response make in lines 8–11?
   - ○ Nuclear plants are a clean source of energy.
   - ○ It is impossible to eliminate air pollution.
   - ○ Nuclear power improves the nation's economy.
   - ○ All types of energy have risks and benefits.

4. In line 11, the author claims that nuclear power plants do not contribute to haze or smog. This is an example of which persuasive technique?
   - ○ appeal by association
   - ○ ethical appeal
   - ○ emotional appeal
   - ○ appeal to authority

5. In lines 12–16, the author makes a comparison between
   - ○ past and current figures on carbon dioxide emissions
   - ○ passenger cars and other forms of transportation
   - ○ nuclear plants and oil- and coal-burning plants
   - ○ emissions in the United States and other parts of the world

6. What ethical issue does the author raise in the "Yes" response?
   - ○ finding an alternative to cars
   - ○ cutting energy costs
   - ○ protecting the environment
   - ○ creating convenient energy sources

7. The "Yes" response claims that "today's nuclear plants have state-of-the-art safety features to prevent accidents." Which statement in the "No" response is a counterargument to that claim?
   - ○ "Another problem for the environment is the spent fuel from nuclear power plants, which remains toxic for thousands of years." (lines 34–35)
   - ○ "In addition, nuclear power plants make attractive targets for terrorists. A disaster caused by sabotage or attack would cause great harm. . . ." (lines 32–34)
   - ○ "An explosion at the Chernobyl nuclear reactor in the Soviet Union in 1986 killed 31 people and caused hundreds of thousands of cases of delayed illness." (lines 29–31)
   - ○ "Although new nuclear power plants would certainly be safer than older plants, the consequences of a major accident are still the same: widespread and long-lasting radiation pollution. . . ." (lines 27–29)

**8.** The author's main purpose in writing the "No" response is to

○ explain how uranium is converted into fuel for nuclear reactors

○ document the consequences of the accident at Chernobyl

○ prove that terrorists can attack nuclear power plants in the United States

○ convince people that nuclear energy is not worth the risks it presents

**9.** What is the author's claim in the "No" response?

○ New nuclear power plants are no safer than the old ones.

○ Global warming is our most urgent environmental concern.

○ Nuclear energy creates as many problems as it solves.

○ Scientists are looking for ways to store spent nuclear fuel.

**10.** To which emotion does the argument in lines 32–34 appeal?

○ anger        ○ pity
○ fear         ○ pride

**11.** Which words in the "No" response convey the author's attitude toward nuclear energy?

○ widespread, nuclear, uranium

○ power, potential, operational

○ sabotage, catastrophic, disaster

○ delayed, targets, repository

**12.** In lines 42–45, the author contrasts forms of energy to show that

○ it makes sense to use renewable energy sources

○ nuclear energy costs more than renewable energy

○ the world has a variety of energy sources

○ it is possible to run out of nuclear resources

**13.** Which statement is a fact presented in both arguments?

○ Meeting tighter air pollution limits is virtually impossible without nuclear energy.

○ Uranium for fuel can easily be turned into uranium for nuclear bombs.

○ Newer nuclear power plants are safer than older nuclear power plants.

○ The nation's nuclear power plants are well defended against terrorist attacks.

**14.** Which opinion do the authors share?

○ Global warming is a threat to the environment.

○ Nuclear energy is a source of serious problems.

○ The uranium used for fuel can easily be processed for nuclear bombs.

○ The use of nuclear power effectively reduces air pollution.

## Constructed Response

**SHORT ANSWER**   *Write two or three sentences to answer each question.*

**15.** Reread lines 8–11 of the "Yes" response. What evidence does the author cite to support his claim that nuclear plants are a clean source of energy?

**16.** Reread lines 42–45 of the "No" response. Name two of the comparisons that the author makes between nuclear energy and energy from the wind and the sun.

**ESSAY**   *Write a paragraph to answer this question.*

**17.** Identify the author's purpose in writing the "No" response and discuss the reasons given to support that argument.

# Vocabulary

**DIRECTIONS** *Use context clues and your knowledge of related words to answer the following questions.*

1. Use what you know about the word *essence* to define the related word *essential* in line 6.
   - ○ enjoyable
   - ○ helpful
   - ○ necessary
   - ○ lasting

2. Use what you know about the word *emit* to define the related word *emissions* in line 15.
   - ○ costs of labor and materials
   - ○ substances released into the air
   - ○ chances of explosion
   - ○ dangers to the environment

3. Use what you know about the word *ray* to define the related word *radiation* in line 29.
   - ○ a colorless, odorless gas
   - ○ a system of pipes for heating or cooling
   - ○ waves or particles of radioactive energy
   - ○ a device that transmits radio signals

4. Use what you know about the word *position* to define the related word *repository* in line 36.
   - ○ a place to put things
   - ○ an electrical outlet for a plug
   - ○ something hidden for safekeeping
   - ○ one who acts on behalf of another

**DIRECTIONS** *Use context clues and your knowledge of Greek and Latin words and roots to answer the following questions.*

5. The word *economy* comes from the Greek word *oikonomos*, meaning "one who runs a household." What is the meaning of *economy* in line 9?
   - ○ the system or range of financial activity in a country
   - ○ a nation's air, water, and other natural resources
   - ○ a family's management of its resources
   - ○ the least expensive accommodations for travelers

6. The word *pollutants* comes from the root *per*, meaning "through," and the Latin word *lutum*, meaning "mud." What is the meaning of *pollutants* in line 11?
   - ○ areas of low-lying, soggy ground
   - ○ masses of rocks left by glaciers
   - ○ tiny particles that live in swamps
   - ○ waste material that contaminates the air

7. The word *catastrophic* comes from the root *kat*, meaning "down," and the Greek word *strephein*, meaning "to turn." What is the meaning of *catastrophic* in line 41?
   - ○ going against the laws of nature
   - ○ producing lower air temperatures
   - ○ moving in an opposite direction
   - ○ causing great suffering or damage

# Writing & Grammar

**DIRECTIONS** *Read this passage and answer the questions that follow.*

(1) In 1970, the government established the environmental protection agency to safeguard the country's land, water, and air. (2) For almost 40 years, the agency has conducted research, set standards, and enforcing activities to prevent pollution. (3) In 1975, the united nations designated the agency as an information center for environmental data. (4) Its information is reliable, complete, and offers access to everyone. (5) The agency works with organizations such as Habitat for Humanity to make land safe for housing. (6) The agency's mission has always been to give Americans an environment that is clean, healthy, and can be sustained.

1. Which words should be capitalized in sentence 1?
   ○ environmental, agency
   ○ environmental, protection, agency
   ○ government, protection, agency
   ○ land, water, air

2. How would you rewrite sentence 2 to make its structure parallel?
   ○ For almost 40 years, the agency has conducted research, set standards, and enforced activities to prevent pollution.
   ○ For almost 40 years, the agency has conducted research, set standards, and it enforces activities to prevent pollution.
   ○ For almost 40 years, the agency has conducted research, set standards, and to enforce activities to prevent pollution.
   ○ For almost 40 years, the agency has conducted research, set standards, and will enforce activities to prevent pollution.

3. Which words should be capitalized in sentence 3?
   ○ united, nations
   ○ nations, agency
   ○ information, environmental
   ○ environmental, data

4. How would you rewrite sentence 4 to make its structure parallel?
   ○ Its information is reliable, complete, and lacking in secrecy.
   ○ Its information is reliable, complete, and accessible to everyone.
   ○ Its information is reliable, complete, and offering everyone an opportunity to educate himself or herself.
   ○ Its information is reliable, complete, and without boundaries in its accessibility.

5. How would you rewrite sentence 6 to make its structure parallel?
   ○ The agency's mission has always been to give Americans an environment that is clean, healthy, and that has sustainability.
   ○ The agency's mission has always been to give Americans an environment that is clean, healthy, and that won't decay.
   ○ The agency's mission has always been to give Americans an environment that is clean, healthy, and wanting to be sustained.
   ○ The agency's mission has always been to give Americans an environment that is clean, healthy, and sustainable.

STOP

## UNIT 9
# More Great Reads

## Ideas for Independent Reading

Which questions from Unit 9 made an impression on you?
Continue exploring them with these books.

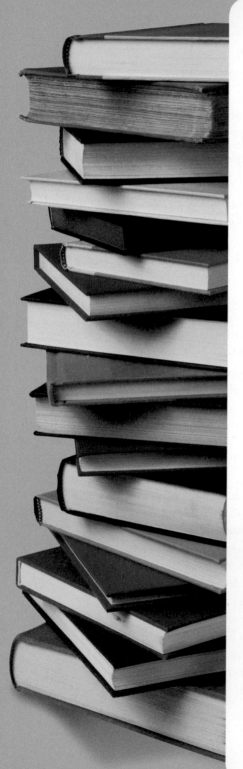

## Should wildlife stay wild?

### The Exchange Student
*by Kate Gilmore*

One hundred years after the crash, Daria is the youngest animal breeder working with endangered animals on Earth. The last thing she needs is to host an alien exchange student named Fen who is obsessed with Daria's zoo but who won't say why.

### Frightful's Mountain
*by Jean Craighead George*

Frightful is a peregrine falcon that has lived with Sam since she was around 10 days old. When Sam is forced to let her go, she must learn to live in the wild on her own. Will her instincts be enough to guide her?

### The Wilderness Family: At Home with Africa's Wildlife
*by Kobie Krüger*

When Kobie moves to the African bush with her husband and three daughters, she becomes a foster mother to a lion named Leo. Can a human mother teach a young lion about life in the wild?

## Are all games worth playing?

### Heat
*by Mike Lupica*

Mike's team is sure to make it to the Little League World Series until Mike, their best pitcher, isn't allowed to play. The authorities want proof of his age, and they are asking questions about other things Mike and his brother don't want anyone to know about.

### Surviving Antarctica: Reality TV 2083
*by Andrea White*

In 2083, five teens are chosen to reenact a historic trip to the South Pole for a television audience. They might die in the process, but they have no other way to improve their lives. Will society tolerate the way they're treated?

### Game Design for Teens
*by Les Pardew and Alpine Studios*

How do you create a computer game? This book shows you how to take an idea for a game and make it a reality. You'll learn the skills you need and meet people who have invented successful games.

## Who decides what's important?

### Our Eleanor
*by Candace Fleming*

Until Eleanor Roosevelt came along, most first ladies didn't try to affect government policy. But Eleanor was different. She persuaded her husband President Roosevelt to make the needs of poor people, women, and children a priority.

### Photo by Brady: A Picture of the Civil War
*by Jennifer Armstrong*

The Civil War was the first war to be photographed. The images captured by the photographers who went to the battlegrounds affected the way those on the home front viewed the war.

### Quicksilver
*by Stephanie Spinner*

Zeus, the ruler of the Greek gods, decides the fate of everyone. This book is told from the point of view of Hermes, Zeus' favorite errand boy. Hermes is quick and funny, but can he change Zeus's mind when people's lives are on the line?

# The Power of Research

## RESEARCH WORKSHOPS

- Research Strategies
- Writing Research Reports

# *Share What You Know*

## *How can* RESEARCH *help me?*

Doing research means locating, analyzing, and understanding information in order to answer a question. You may already be skilled at tracking down some types of information, such as movie times and sports statistics. However, there are always new resources to find and ways to improve your search. In this unit, you will learn to find, use, and evaluate sources of information. You will also learn how to improve your ability to search for sources and judge the sources you already use.

***ACTIVITY*** What do you research at school, at home, while shopping, or while doing homework? Work with a partner to list examples.

|  | What I Research | Where I Find Answers |
|---|---|---|
| at school |  |  |
| at home |  |  |
| other places |  |  |

**INDIANA STANDARDS**

# Preview Unit Goals

| | |
|---|---|
| **DEVELOPING RESEARCH SKILLS** | • Find and narrow a topic |
| | • Search the Internet |
| | • Use library and media center resources |
| | • Choose nonfiction sources |
| | • Evaluate information and sources, including nonfiction books, periodicals, and Web sites |
| | • Conduct your own research |
| | |
| **WRITING** | • Write a research report |
| | • Narrow your research topic |
| | • Locate and evaluate sources |
| | • Take notes |
| | • Make source cards |
| | • Summarize and paraphrase |
| | • Quote directly and avoid plagiarism |
| | • Document sources |
| | • Prepare a Works Cited list |
| | • Format your paper |
| | |
| **SPEAKING, LISTENING, AND VIEWING** | • Create a Web site |
| | |
| **ACADEMIC VOCABULARY** | • research topic • sources • documentation |
| | • research report • source cards • Works Cited |
| | • resources • plagiarism |

# What is the research PROCESS?

*KEY IDEA* Researching a fact or two usually isn't challenging. Researching a topic, however, is a complex process that involves using several sources to find many—and sometimes conflicting—facts and opinions. Furthermore, finding the information is only the beginning of the research process. Research also requires you to evaluate the sources you find.

*QUICKWRITE* In this unit, you will follow a student who is interested in entering a competition for young inventors. If you were this student, how could you find information that would help you accomplish your goals? Try creating a cluster diagram like this one with questions you could ask.

Young Inventors' Competition

What inventions have teens submitted?

Who sponsors contests for young inventors?

## CREATIVE THINKING ZONE

**invites all teen inventors to a contest for the *BEST NEW INVENTION* by a teenager!**

Go to our Web site for details.

# Finding and Narrowing Your Topic

Before you begin the research process, take a few minutes to set a research goal and to develop a clearer idea of your topic.

## SET RESEARCH GOALS

First, write down a few goals for your research. Here is how one student listed a set of goals related to the topic of competitions for young inventors.

> **General goal:** I want to enter a contest for young inventors.
>
> **Questions:**
>
> - **What are the requirements?** Are the few simple things I've invented suitable to enter in a contest?
>
> - **What are the contests like?** I'd like a chance to meet other inventors and learn more about inventing in general.
>
> **Specific goals:** I want to learn more about how a young inventor like me can compete in contests, meet other inventors, and learn more about inventing.

## LEARN ABOUT YOUR TOPIC

Once you have decided on some specific goals, it's time to start your search. You can use any or all of these methods.

- **Use the Internet.** Type words related to your topic, such as *teen inventors*, into a search engine. Select one or two Web pages from the search results. Then visit them to get ideas about your topic.

- **Talk with people.** Find someone who knows about your topic or shares your interest in it. Present your research goals and ask for ideas.

- **Use print resources.** Read an article on your topic or skim a nonfiction book.

- **Talk with a librarian.** Ask for suggestions for sources and ways to improve your research focus.

## NARROW YOUR TOPIC

A more specific topic is easier to research than a broad topic. Here's how one student narrowed her topic after reading.

| Topic | More Specific | Even More Specific |
|-------|---------------|--------------------|
| inventions | competitions for young inventors | competitions for young inventors of robots |

## DEVELOP RESEARCH QUESTIONS

After you have narrowed the focus of your topic, the next step is to ask research questions about it. Notice how these research questions can't be answered with just yes or no. Instead, they require rich, full answers.

- Which kinds of inventions have teens submitted?
- How do I find a contest that will accept my new game?
- How can I protect my idea?

After you write your research questions, highlight the **keywords,** or words that clearly identify your topic. You will use keywords to search library catalogs and databases and to get information from search engines.

## PREPARE TO TAKE NOTES

Getting and staying organized helps you keep track of details, credit sources correctly, and do more in less time. One way to be sure you are organized is to take careful notes. If you are doing research for a report, consider using note cards. See pages 1059–1060 to learn more about this note-taking method.

For other kinds of research, try using lists and charts. Think about what kinds of information you are looking for and which format would be best for that information. Here is how one student kept track of contests she found.

| Name of Competition | Type | Requirements | Notes and Important Dates |
|---|---|---|---|
| Creative Thinking Zone | toys | fully working prototype | Grades 6–8 March 1 online registration |
| Staples Invention Quest | office products | idea described in detailed drawings and itemized specifications | Grades 8–12 October 15 mail-in registration form |
| Craftsman NSTA Young Inventors Award | tools | description and drawings—no physical prototypes | Grades 6–8 February 15 online registration |
| Wizardkids.net | all kinds of inventions | working models or drawings | Grades 6–12 March 15 online registration |

Many researchers start their searches online. Read on to learn how to find the best sites.

# Searching the Internet

The **Internet** is a system of connected computers. The World Wide Web is part of the Internet. The nickname *Web* comes from the hundreds of millions of connections, or links, from site to site. These links can lead users to billions of Web pages.

## SELECT SEARCH ENGINES

**Search engines** are Web sites that organize information based on keywords, headings, popularity among Web users, and other criteria. You can choose from many search engines. Each returns different choices because each selects and organizes information in slightly different ways. To get the best results, learn the rules for the specific search engine you are using. You might also try using the advanced search forms that most search engines offer.

## USE SPECIFIC KEYWORDS AND SEARCH LIMITERS

To get the best results from a search, be specific. Try combining keywords and using search modifiers or limiters like these.

- **Use quotation marks.** Put related words together in quotation marks. A search for "young inventors" will give you results that mention both terms, in that order, right next to each other.

- **Combine terms.** Some search engines allow you to use the term AND or a plus sign to combine terms. For example, *"young inventors" AND toys* will return only pages that contain all those terms.

- **Exclude terms.** Some search engines let you exclude terms from your results by typing NOT or a minus sign. For instance, *"inventions by young people" –computers* will return all pages with the phrase "inventions by young people" except the ones that also mention computers.

This chart shows how using search limiters can give you more useful results.

| YOU TYPE IN... | YOU GET... | THIS IS... |
|---|---|---|
| *young inventors* | 1,090,000 results | far too many results, so you make your keywords more specific |
| *"young inventor" competition* | 104 results | much better, but you can tell from the descriptions that many of the results are unrelated to your topic |
| *+"young inventor" +toys +competition* | 10 results | best, because the results are closest to the research goal |

**TIP** Identifying the best search terms is a multi-step process. Keep changing and refining your terms until you get the results you want.

## EVALUATE SEARCH ENGINE RESULTS

Searches often return far more results, also called *hits*, than you can examine. Follow these guidelines for deciding which results to click on.

1. **Don't just click on the first result.** It may not be the right one for you.

2. **Focus first on the Web address.** Sites with *.com* and *.net* in their address are usually personal or commercial sites and may contain sales pitches or biased information. Sites with *.org* and *.gov* in their address are usually the work of government agencies or institutions such as museums and nonprofit organizations. Be aware, however, that organizations such as political parties also have *.org* addresses.

3. **Next, read the brief description the search engine provides.** If the address appears promising and the description matches your goal or keywords, click on the result. If not, you can go to the next result or the next page of results. You can also change or refine your search terms and try again.

4. **Read the page.** Print only those pages that provide information that is closely related to your topic and your research goals.

**TIP** In general, *.gov* and *.org* sites are more reliable than other sites because they are usually the work of large, reputable groups, and their purpose is often only to inform.

**TRY IT OUT!** *Choose Search Engine Results*

This page shows the first four results from an online search.

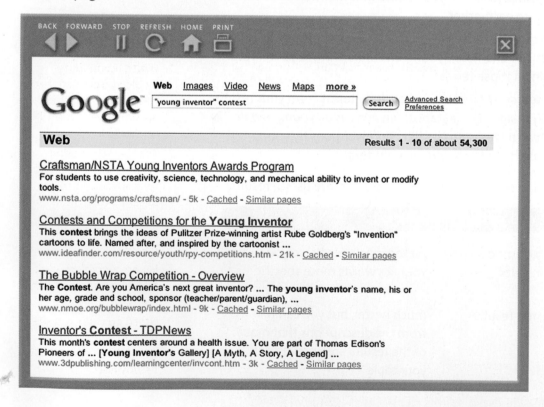

**Close Read**

1. What terms did the searcher use? How do you know?

2. Do you think these results would be useful to a student searching for contests for young inventors? Explain your answer.

3. How would you modify this search to find out about contests for young inventors of robots? Write your new search terms exactly as you would type them into a search box.

**EXPLORE A WEB SITE**

When you click on a search result, a Web page will come up.

- **Home page**—A **home page** is the main page of a Web site. It welcomes you to the site and gives a general overview.

- **Menus and Hyperlinks**—**Menus** show the main categories of information on a Web site. Another option for finding information is **hyperlinks,** sometimes referred to simply as links. Hyperlinks and links are underlined or highlighted words, terms, URLs (Web addresses), or Web site names. Click on hyperlinks to move to another page or another site.

- **Icons**—These are small pictures or symbols that you can click on to find information. On the Web site below, clicking on the beanie icon brings up information on Jerome Lemelson's invention of a mechanical beanie.

- **Credits and Sponsor**—The **credits** tell who produced the site, when the site was created, and when it was last updated. A **sponsor** is an organization, agency, or individual that owns the site and controls its content. Knowing about the credits and sponsor helps you evaluate the site for accuracy and reliability. Look for a link that says "About This Site" or "About Us."

**TRY IT OUT!** *Examine a Web Page*

This Web page contains the kinds of information shown on many home pages.

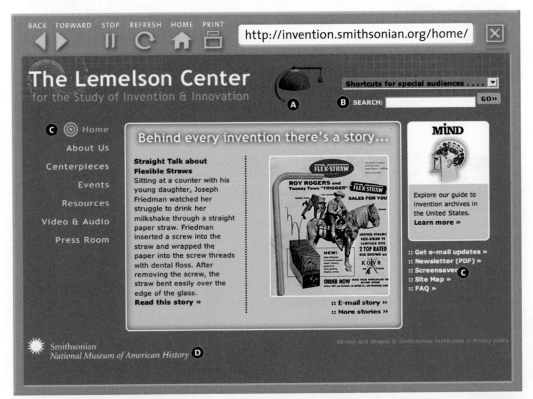

Ⓐ **Icon**   Ⓑ **Search Options**   Ⓒ **Menus**   Ⓓ **Sponsor**

**Close Read**

1. Which menu item would you click on if you wanted to be notified of upcoming events at the Lemelson Center?

2. The "Search" option (item B) lets you search for a specific term or terms within the Lemelson Center site. Why is this a useful option?

3. Where would you click to find out more about who owns this site?

4. Based on what you see here, do you judge this site to be reliable? Why or why not?

# Using Library Resources

**ACADEMIC VOCABULARY FOR THE LIBRARY**

These terms will come in handy as you use the library or media center:

- fiction
- nonfiction
- reference work
- library catalog
- primary source
- secondary source
- table of contents
- bibliography
- glossary
- index

The Internet isn't the only place to find information. Your local public library and your school's media center are also storehouses of information. Furthermore, these places offer access to online information that you cannot get by using most search engines.

Before you start your research, learn how your library or media center is organized and what it offers. Most libraries have different sections for adults, young adults, and children. There may also be special sections devoted to business, local history, or genealogy (tracing your family tree). Many libraries and media centers offer space for quiet study. Computer terminals throughout the library allow you to find out about the library or media center's holdings, use other online sources, send e-mail, and create reports.

## LIBRARY AND MEDIA CENTER RESOURCES

**BOOKS**

**Fiction**—Novels and short stories are examples of fiction. Fictional works come from the writer's imagination, but they may be based on real people, places, and events.

**Nonfiction**—Nonfiction works present facts and tell about real people, places, and events. Newspaper and magazine articles, scientific works, essays, speeches, history books, instructional and procedural manuals, and biographies are nonfiction.

**REFERENCE**

**Reference desk**—This is the place to ask for help with identifying and locating library materials.

**Reference works**—The reference section of the library includes almanacs, dictionaries, atlases, encyclopedias, and statistical abstracts. These are for use only in the library—you can't check them out and take them home.

**NEWSPAPERS AND PERIODICALS**

**Newspapers and magazines**—Most libraries and media centers carry current issues. Some also have past issues in print, on microfilm, on microfiche, or in a digitized format.

**AUDIO AND VIDEO RESOURCES**

**DVDs**—Many libraries lend documentaries, instructional films, and filmed performances.

**Audio**—Libraries also lend CD recordings of books, music, speeches, poems, and plays.

**E-RESOURCES**

**Electronic collections**—You can access and print out articles from databases. You can also download e-books, e-audiobooks, CD-ROMs, podcasts, and MP3s.

**TIP** To access e-resources from a home or other remote computer, all you need is a library card barcode, which you can get when you apply for a library card.

## UNDERSTAND THE LIBRARY CATALOG

The **library catalog** is a complete index of the library's or library network's holdings. Consult the reference librarian or the online search tips for the best and fastest ways to search it.

Library catalogs provide many options for searching. The most common methods are by author, title, and keyword or subject.

- **Author**—Type the author's last name first, like this: *Twain, Mark.* If no results appear, check the spelling, or try the first name first: *Mark Twain.*

- **Title**—Type in the full title or any part of it you know. Leave out unimportant first words such as *the* and *a.*

- **Subject or Keyword**—Type in a word or phrase that names your subject, such as *inventor.* If the results are too broad, then add to your keyword, such as by typing *teen inventor.* Keep in mind that you may need to try several words and phrases before the catalog returns results you can use. For instance, you might find that the phrase *young inventor* or *patent invention* produces better results.

### TRY IT OUT! *Search a Library Catalog*

A student typed in the phrase *inventor's contests* to get to the catalog page below.

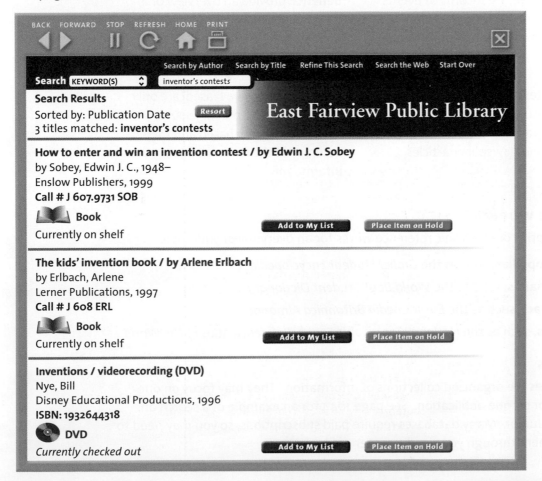

**Close Read**

1. How are the results on this page arranged?

2. Name five types of information the page gives for each result.

3. Name three options the user has for getting different search results.

# Choosing Nonfiction Sources

Understanding different types of nonfiction sources can help you decide which ones to choose as sources.

## PRIMARY AND SECONDARY SOURCES

Every nonfiction work is either a primary source or a secondary source.

| TYPE OF SOURCE | BENEFITS AND DRAWBACKS |
| --- | --- |
| **Primary sources:** materials written or created by people who took part in or witnessed the events they recorded ▼ | **Benefits:** supply interesting firsthand information and details ▼ |
| **Examples:** autobiographies, public documents such as birth certificates, advertisements, speeches, letters, e-mails, diaries and journals, editorials, political cartoons, first-person newspaper and magazine articles | **Drawbacks:** may be biased because they give just one person's limited point of view; may require specialized knowledge to interpret |
| **Secondary sources:** records of events created by people who were not directly involved in or present at the events ▼ | **Benefits:** provide an overview or a broad understanding; often synthesize many points of view ▼ |
| **Examples:** textbooks, encyclopedias, reviews, documentaries, most history books, biographies, third-person magazine and newspaper articles | **Drawbacks:** may be biased; are only as reliable as the primary sources on which they are based and the accuracy of the writer gathering the information |

## REFERENCE WORKS

Consult print or electronic reference works for an overview of your topic.

- **Encyclopedias,** such as the *Grolier Student Encyclopedia*
- **Dictionaries,** such as the *World Book Student Dictionary*
- **Almanacs,** such as the *Encyclopedia Britannica Almanac*
- **Atlases,** such as the *National Geographic Family Reference Atlas of the World*

## DATABASES

**Databases** are organized collections of information. They may focus on one subject or on one publication. See page 1044 for an example of a search on InfoTrac Junior. Many databases require paid subscriptions, so you may need to access them through your media center or library.

## NONFICTION BOOKS

For in-depth information on a topic, be sure to consult nonfiction books. To decide whether a specific book is right for your research goal, follow these steps:

1. Read the **title** and **subtitle** to get a general idea of what the book is about.

2. Examine the **copyright page.** Find the latest copyright date shown. This will tell you how recent the information is.

3. Read the **table of contents.** The titles of parts and chapters will give you an overview of the book's contents. This page also often lists other useful features, such as a **bibliography** (a list of sources used), a list of suggested **further reading,** and a **glossary** (a section that lists and defines specialized terms the author uses).

4. Check the **index** for specific topics or terms that interest you. Single page numbers can signal that there is no more than a brief mention of the topic.

**TRY IT OUT!** *Examine the Parts of a Book*

Notice the features of the book shown below.

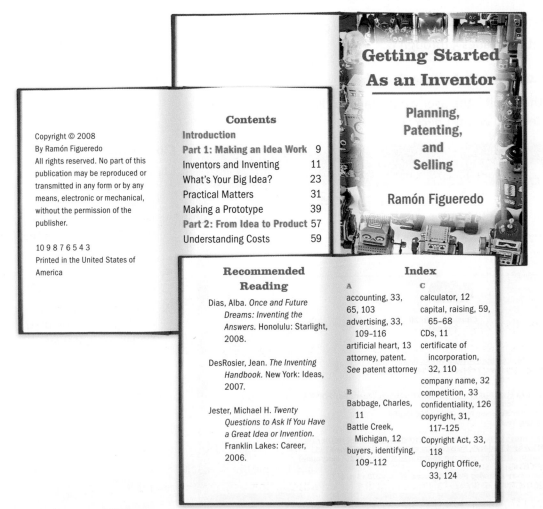

**Contents**

Copyright © 2008
By Ramón Figueredo
All rights reserved. No part of this publication may be reproduced or transmitted in any form or by any means, electronic or mechanical, without the permission of the publisher.

10 9 8 7 6 5 4 3
Printed in the United States of America

**Getting Started As an Inventor**

Planning, Patenting, and Selling

Ramón Figueredo

**Recommended Reading**

Dias, Alba. *Once and Future Dreams: Inventing the Answers.* Honolulu: Starlight, 2008.

DesRosier, Jean. *The Inventing Handbook.* New York: Ideas, 2007.

Jester, Michael H. *Twenty Questions to Ask If You Have a Great Idea or Invention.* Franklin Lakes: Career, 2006.

**Index**

A
accounting, 33, 65, 103
advertising, 33, 109–116
artificial heart, 13
attorney, patent. *See* patent attorney

B
Babbage, Charles, 11
Battle Creek, Michigan, 12
buyers, identifying, 109–112

C
calculator, 12
capital, raising, 59, 65–68
CDs, 11
certificate of incorporation, 32, 110
company name, 32
competition, 33
confidentiality, 126
copyright, 31, 117–125
Copyright Act, 33, 118
Copyright Office, 33, 124

**Close Read**

1. Is this book recent enough to be helpful? How do you know?

2. Does this book give practical advice about both creating and selling an invention? Explain how you arrived at your answer.

3. Does this book contain information on making a prototype? How about on patent attorneys? Tell where you found this information.

# Newspapers and Periodicals

**Newspapers** are publications that contain news and advertising. Many newspapers include other features as well, such as editorials, letters to the editor, cartoons, and puzzles. Newspapers are published daily, weekly, or very frequently. Most daily newspapers have online versions that are updated throughout the day.

Like newspapers, **periodicals** are publications issued on a regular basis. They contain news, advice, fiction, research findings, or a combination of these. Periodicals called magazines are published for the general public. Periodicals called journals are published for academic and scholarly audiences. Online versions of periodicals often include corrections, updates, and previously published articles.

Researchers often turn to recent newspaper and magazine articles for up-to-date information presented in understandable language. Older newspaper and magazine articles can offer some perspective on a particular time period.

- **Examples of Newspapers:** *Washington Post, San Francisco Chronicle, Denver Post*
- **Examples of Magazines:** *Time, Consumer Reports, Odyssey, Teen Ink, Next Step*

To find articles on your topic, use a database. The page below comes from InfoTrac Junior, a database for students in grades 5 through 12.

**TRY IT OUT!** *Examine an Articles Database Search*

To see each article listed in the results, the user would have to click on the underlined title of the article or the underlined words *Check Out*.

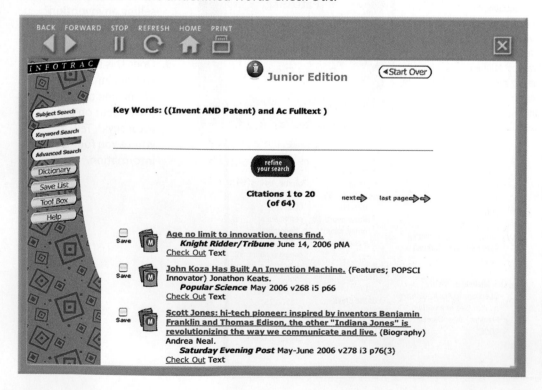

**Close Read**

1. What three options does this database provide for searching? (Hint: See the menu on the left-hand side of the page.)
2. Which two keywords did the researcher use?
3. Which of these results would you click on first? Explain your answer.

# Evaluating Sources

Sources vary widely in purpose, authorship, and the care with which they were created. Therefore, always carefully evaluate the sources you use. **Evaluating** means asking and answering questions like the ones below about the trustworthiness of every book, magazine, newspaper, Web site, and other source you use. Refer to pages 1046–1048 for questions about specific types of sources.

| QUESTION | REASONS TO ASK |
|---|---|
| **What is the publication date?** | Up-to-date information is important, especially in medicine, technology, sports, and politics. Even when you are researching an event that happened many years ago, up-to-date sources usually present the latest findings and insights. |
| **Who is the author?** | In general, look for sources of information written by people who are experts in their field. The author's profession, other publications, and awards are additional guides to his or her knowledge of the subject. |
| **Who published the source?** | Some publishers take more care to ensure accuracy than others do. Magazines and newspapers that feature articles about fads and celebrities can be unreliable. Instead, look for well-known publishers and university presses. If you're in doubt, ask a librarian for help. |
| **What is the author's or publisher's purpose?** | Many Web sites and publications have a political or commercial purpose. Some may present **biased,** or one-sided, views of topics, leaving out information that does not suit their purposes. Determine the source's intended purpose before you decide whether to use it. |
| **Is this information useful to me?** | Make sure the source is written at a level that's appropriate for you—not too childish or too scholarly. Also, study the table of contents or menus for your keywords or for other words and phrases that relate specifically to your research goals. |

## EVALUATE WEB SITES

A book is often the result of teamwork: it has an author as well as editors and reviewers. On the other hand, a Web site may be the work of just one individual. In many cases, no one has checked or reviewed personal Web sites.

To evaluate a Web site, ask and answer these questions:

- **Who created the site?** Is the author an expert? What does the site tell you about the author(s)?

- **Why was the site created?** Consider whether the creators want to sell you something—either a product or an idea.

- **Are there problems on the site?** Watch for mistakes in facts, grammar, or spelling, which may mean that the source is unreliable.

- **Are there credits?** Look for a bibliography of the site's creator, the name of a sponsoring organization, and a "last updated" reference.

- **Could you consult a more reliable source to find coverage of the same topic?** Use a variety of sources, such as encyclopedias, almanacs, magazines, newspapers, documentaries, and interviews with experts.

### TRY IT OUT! *Examine a Personal Web Site*

What is useful about this site? What errors or problems do you see?

**Close Read**

1. What is the purpose of this site?

2. What is missing from this site that could help you evaluate it?

3. Name two other problems with this site.

## EVALUATE A NONFICTION BOOK

Once you have found a book with information on your topic, how do you evaluate it? Ask and answer these questions:

- **What is the copyright date?** Look for the most recent date on the copyright page. If you see many dates, that is a good sign because it means that the book has been through many updates and printings. The book jacket may also say *revised, updated,* or *new.*

- **Is the book carefully researched?** Look for a **bibliography,** a list of works the author referred to when writing. Also, look for **footnotes** and **end notes** that help you understand where the author found specific information. Check the back of the book for an **appendix** with additional information, such as maps, charts, or tables.

- **Who is the author?** Look for an author biography on the book jacket or at the end of the book. Use the biography to learn more about the author's education, profession, and other publications.

**TRY IT OUT!** *Examine a Nonfiction Book*

Decide whether this book is a reliable source for someone who is researching the topic of teen inventors who got patents. Use what you have learned about nonfiction books and about the parts of a book (page 1043).

### Kids Create

*New for 1992! 3rd Edition*

America's Youngest Inventors

**Ilana Brodsky**

### About the Author

The author of ten books and numerous articles for young readers, Ilana Brodsky has written on topics that range from lasers to artificial turf to the poet Emily Dickinson. The idea for *Kids Create* was born when Brodsky stumbled into a competition for teen inventors in Omaha. "This fascinating story just screamed to be told," Brodsky explained.

Ms. Brodsky lives in Buffalo, New York, with her two cats.

### Close Read

1. What is this book about?

2. Is the author an expert on this topic? What are her qualifications?

3. How up to date is this book? Is it new or revised?

4. What other parts of this book would provide information about its reliability and usefulness? (Hint: See page 1043.)

## EVALUATE NEWSPAPERS AND PERIODICALS

Periodicals are a good source of recent information. Your library may offer some of them in print and many others online or on microfilm. Once you find a periodical article, you should evaluate it before you use it. Ask and answer these questions:

- **Is this magazine or newspaper well-known and respected?** Many national magazines and newspapers with large circulation numbers are reliable. If a publication prints rumors about celebrities, stories about space aliens, or miracle weight-loss cures, avoid it.

- **When was it published?** Up-to-date sources are best unless you're looking for details or insights from a particular period. For example, if you are researching a particular inventor from the past, a magazine or newspaper article from when he or she was alive and inventing could be among your best sources.

- **Who is the author?** Look for information about the writer. Assume that staff writers are as reliable as the publication in which they appear.

- **Can you verify the facts?** You should be able to verify every fact in at least one other source.

**TRY IT OUT!** *Examine a Newspaper Article*

Ask questions about the periodical, the author, the facts, and other content to evaluate this article.

---

*from the* **Warren Star**

# Warren Teen Wins Inventors' Competition

BY DERONE SANDAGE, STAFF WRITER

Judges at the Young Inventors' Convention in Buffalo have awarded first prize to a local teenager.

"Shoveling snow is nobody's favorite chore," says Warren Middle School student Alex Heisner, "so I thought I would make it a little easier."

Heisner invented the Shovel-L, a sturdy, wheeled shovel that makes snow removal less of a strain on the back and shoulders. "It works on heavy, wet snow and on the dry, powdery kind," explained the 13-year-old, who has applied for a patent. "It isn't so great with leaves, though. They mostly just blow away."

### HELP FOR YOUNG INVENTORS

- The Young Inventors Convention will meet in Baltimore next October. Other area and national conventions exist.

- Try calling local colleges and universities and asking for the school of business. Professors, instructors, or business clubs may offer advice.

- The local office of the Small Business Administration can offer tips and contacts.

When Heisner demonstrated his device at the convention, judges agreed that it really did work.

**See INVENTOR, page B7**

## Close Read

1. How well is this article related to the research topic "invention competitions for teens"?

2. Do you think the information in this article is reliable? Why or why not?

3. At the end of this article, the reporter included his e-mail address and the Web address for the Young Inventors' Convention. Why is this information important?

# Conducting Your Own Research

The Internet and the library aren't the only places you can find information on your topic. For example, you may be able to gather data by conducting a survey or doing another kind of field research or observation. You may even be able to locate experts to interview.

## OBSERVATION AND FIELD RESEARCH

Doing **field research** means observing with a specific research goal in mind. For example, you might attend a young inventors' competition and collect data about the entries and the people who submitted them. Here are the field notes that one student took.

*Notes on Visit to Young Inventors' Competition, Cincinnati, 4/26/2008*

- *128 participants, 128 inventions*

- *participants represent 22 counties in Ohio (78 participants, or 61 percent, from Hamilton County)*

- *28 household devices; 61 devices related to computer hardware or software; 4 industrial devices; 6 transportation-related items; 4 inventions related to pets and pet care; 25 miscellaneous*

- *Youngest participant: 12 years, 7 months; oldest participant, 17 years, 8 months*

- *Sources of inspiration: 16 percent friends; 10 percent parents; 42 percent media (movies, TV, Web sites, radio, books, podcasts); 12 percent teachers or school projects; 20 percent "out of the blue"/don't know*

## INTERVIEWS

Interviews can yield valuable information from primary sources. You can conduct an interview in person, by telephone, by e-mail, by instant message, or by letter. For the topic of young inventors, you might interview a successful inventor, someone who organizes inventors' competitions, or a patent attorney. Successful interviews depend on excellent preparation. See pages R83–R84 for tips and strategies.

*Questions for Competition Participants*

- *What does your invention do?*

- *How did you get the idea for it?*

- *What was your development process? Did you build a prototype, make sketches, or talk to experts as you made improvements to your invention?*

- *About how much did it cost to develop your invention?*

- *I would like to be an inventor. Do you have any advice for me?*

# Research Tips and Strategies

## Where to Search

Your options for finding information are constantly increasing. Be aware of your choices.

### Search Engines

There are many search engines. Always use more than one.

- Google (www.google.com)
- Yahoo! (www.yahoo.com)
- Ask (www.ask.com)

### Metasearch Tools

These tools access many search engines and combine the results.

- Dogpile (www.dogpile.com)
- Clusty (clusty.com)

### Directories

Directories put Internet resources into categories.

- About (about.com)
- Google Directory (dir.google.com)
- Yahoo! Kids (kids.yahoo.com)

### Virtual Libraries

Virtual libraries contain information in encyclopedias, directories, and indexes.

- Internet Public Library (www.ipl.org)
- Librarians' Internet Index (www.lii.org)

### Other Web Resources

- American Memory, Library of Congress (memory.loc.gov)
- The Tech Museum of Innovation (www.thetech.org)
- U.S. Government Portal (firstgov.gov)
- Databases: ProQuest K–12, InfoTrac Junior Edition

## Checklist for Evaluating a Source

- ☑ Is the information directly related to your topic?
- ☑ Is the information up to date?
- ☑ Is the author qualified to write about your topic?
- ☑ Can you determine the author's purpose?
- ☑ Is the writing at your level?
- ☑ Was the information provided by a reliable institution?
- ☑ Have experts reviewed or updated the information?
- ☑ Can you verify the facts in at least one other source?

## Understanding Web Addresses

Web addresses provide clues to the site's author and purpose.

### WEB ABBREVIATIONS AND MEANINGS

| | |
|---|---|
| .COM | commercial—businesses, products, and many personal Web sites |
| .EDU | education—schools, including teachers' and students' personal sites |
| .GOV | U.S. government—official U.S. government sites, such as whitehouse.gov, usmint.gov, nutrition.gov, and www.census.gov |
| .MIL | military—official U.S. armed forces and related sites |
| .NET | network—product information and sales |
| .ORG | organizations—museums, libraries, political parties, charities, and other nonprofit groups |

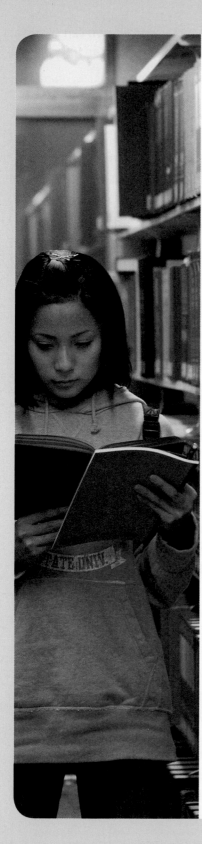

## Exploring the Library or Media Center

Fiction is always arranged alphabetically according to the author's last name. Systems for classifying nonfiction vary by library. Most high school and public libraries use the Dewey decimal system. Most university and research libraries use the Library of Congress system.

### DEWEY DECIMAL SYSTEM

| | |
|---|---|
| 000–099 | General works |
| 100–199 | Philosophy and psychology |
| 200–299 | Religion |
| 300–399 | Social sciences |
| 400–499 | Language |
| 500–599 | Natural sciences and mathematics |
| 600–699 | Technology (applied sciences) |
| 700–799 | Art and recreation |
| 800–899 | Literature and rhetoric |
| 900–999 | Geography and history |

### LIBRARY OF CONGRESS SYSTEM

| | | | | |
|---|---|---|---|---|
| A | General works | M | Music |
| B | Philosophy, psychology, religion | N | Fine arts |
| C–D | History | P | Language and literature |
| E–F | American history | Q | Science |
| G | Geography, anthropology, recreation | R | Medicine |
| | | S | Agriculture |
| H | Social sciences | T | Technology |
| J | Political science | U | Military science |
| K | Law | V | Naval science |
| L | Education | Z | Bibliography and library science |

## Writing Workshop

# Research Report

Now that you have learned how to find a variety of reliable sources, you can create a research report that showcases what you know. For the best route to an informative, interesting report, follow the **Writer's Road Map.**

---

### WRITER'S ROAD MAP

#### Research Report

**WRITING PROMPT 1**

**Writing from the Real World** Write a research report that investigates a topic that interests you. Your report should include information from at least four sources.

**Topics to Consider**
- What were the achievements of the Lewis and Clark expedition?
- Do dolphins have their own language?
- Who invented baseball?

**WRITING PROMPT 2**

**Writing from Literature** Write a research report that investigates a topic you discovered in a piece of literature you read. Your report should include data from at least four sources.

**Topics to Consider**
- Who started the Underground Railroad? ("Harriet Tubman: Conductor on the Underground Railroad")
- Who else rode with Paul Revere? ("Paul Revere's Ride")
- What makes a person smart? (*Flowers for Algernon*)

**WRITING TOOLS**
For prewriting, revision, and editing tools, visit the **Writing Center** at ClassZone.com.

**KEY TRAITS**

**1. IDEAS**
- Presents a **thesis statement** that clearly identifies the topic and controlling idea of the report
- Supports the thesis with **evidence,** such as examples, facts, statistics, and expert opinions
- Synthesizes information from **multiple sources** and includes **quotations** and **paraphrases**
- Includes the **writer's own ideas**

**2. ORGANIZATION**
- Follows a clear **organizational pattern**
- Connects ideas with **transitions**
- Includes an interesting **introduction** and a thoughtful **conclusion**

**3. VOICE**
- Maintains a serious, formal **tone**

**4. WORD CHOICE**
- Uses **precise words** to explain ideas

**5. SENTENCE FLUENCY**
- Varies the **lengths of sentences**

**6. CONVENTIONS**
- Uses **correct grammar, spelling, and punctuation**
- **Credits sources**
- Uses **correct formats and style**

# Part 1: Analyze a Student Model

**WRITING STANDARD**
**8.5.3** Write or deliver a research report....

Jess Chu

Mr. Kinsella

English 8

6 May 2008

### The Difficult Job of a Civil War Drummer Boy

When the Civil War broke out, many boys thought that going off to war would be an exciting adventure. When they tried to sign up, however, recruiters wouldn't let most of them become soldiers because they were too young (Murphy 8). In fact, the writer Stephen Currie
5  says that some of these boys were under the age of eleven (3). Civil War expert Jay Hoar lists some as young as age six (227). Instead of turning these young volunteers into soldiers, the armies of the North and the South used them as musicians, especially as drummer boys (Murphy 10). Yet even those jobs had many responsibilities and dangers. For the
10  most part, drummer boys were too young to do the difficult jobs they faced and much too young for war.

### The Drummer Boy's Jobs

Drummer boys for the North and South had similar duties. One important job of every drummer was to be a kind of human clock.
15  Drummers woke the troops up in the morning, called them to roll call and other duties, and sent them to bed (Wolfe 745; Heiser). This part of the job was not too difficult, but the day was very long for a child. It began as early as 5:45 A.M. (Wolfe 745).

A more difficult job was keeping time as the troops marched. This
20  job was clearly challenging for many young boys. Hoar points out that at least one drummer boy was just 40 inches tall, so the drums were very big in comparison to the little boys (116). Since marches went on for miles, it's likely that carrying a big drum was exhausting.

**KEY TRAITS IN ACTION**

Correct **formats and style** include the page numbers and header information that this teacher requires.

**Introduction** contains detailed, surprising information. Highlighted **thesis statement** makes the point that the writer will prove.

Examples of the **writer's own ideas** are highlighted. Formal **tone** is appropriate to the topic, purpose, and audience.

Drummers also called the men to battle, and some drummed
25  commands during battle. They had to drum with bullets and cannon
balls zooming all around them. They watched soldiers die. Sometimes,
drummer boys "found themselves the target of enemy fire" (Murphy
40). When drummer boy Delavan Miller was caught in the fighting, he
admitted, "I was never so scared in all my life" (quoted in Currie 6).

30  Sometimes drummers had to help care for injured soldiers
(Heiser). Drummers suffered in other ways, too. For example, hunger
was constant for many Confederates, and some wore ragged clothing
(Robertson 1024). Troops also faced bad weather and disease. They had
to deal with being bored and homesick, too.

35  **Dying for a Cause**

Many drummer boys did even more than drumming, helping with
the wounded, and other chores. Although they were very young, some
even gave their lives. A few were heroes.

For instance, a legend grew up about the drummer boy of Shiloh
40  ("Shiloh"). Stories vary, but the drummer boy is said to have kept
drumming even when the troops were retreating and bullets were flying
(Hoar 120). In the song called "The Drummer Boy of Shiloh" by Will
S. Hays, the drummer boy dies. As he dies, he says,

"I've loved my country as my God.
45  To serve them both I've tried."
He smiled, shook hands—death seized the boy,
Who prayed before he died (13–16, quoted in "Shiloh").
This song tells about a child who made the greatest sacrifice for his
country. Many drummer boys died in the war. Some, like William
50  Johnston at age 11, were so brave that they won the highest possible
medal, the Congressional Medal of Honor (Hoar 24, 234). Others, like
12-year-old Clarence McKenzie, died from a "stray bullet" (Hoar 3).

Well-chosen **evidence** from **multiple sources** supports the thesis.

**Transitions** and subheadings help to give this report a clear **organizational pattern.**

**Paraphrases** most sources but **quotes** when the source is especially descriptive. Correct **formats and style** include setting off and indenting quotations of four or more lines.

Varies **lengths of sentences** and uses **precise words** to hold the reader's interest.

Chu 3

How many drummer boys died during the Civil War? Murphy says that "hundreds were killed and thousands more wounded" (43). Giving

55 their lives was an enormous sacrifice for these children to make.

**The Last Drummer Boys**

The Civil War was the last war to use drummer boys on the battlefield. Later wars were noisier, with more rifles, more soldiers, and more cannons. Therefore, no one could hear the drummer boy anymore

60 (Murphy 41, 43). That seems like one of the few good things to come out of deadlier wars. Drummer boys of the Civil War were too young for the many challenges that they faced. Children today are lucky that this job no longer exists.

> Correctly **credits sources** throughout the report.

> Focused, thoughtful **conclusion** sums up the writer's findings and makes a final point.

Chu 4

**Works Cited**

Currie, Stephen. "Drummer Boys." <u>Cobblestone</u>. Dec. 1999: 3-7.

> Magazine

Heiser, John. "Music of the Civil War." <u>Gettysburg National Military Park Kidzpage</u>. Dec. 2003. National Park Service. 21 Apr. 2008 <http://www.nps.gov/archive/gett/gettkidz/music.htm>.

> Reliable Web site

Hoar, Jay S. <u>Callow, Brave and True: A Gospel of Civil War Youth</u>. Gettysburg: Thomas, 1999.

Murphy, Jim. <u>The Boys' War</u>. New York: Clarion, 1990.

> Books

Robertson, James I., Jr. "Soldiers." <u>The Confederacy</u>. New York: Simon, 1993.

> Reference book

"Shiloh Inspires Writers." <u>Shiloh</u>. 2 Dec. 2002. National Park Service. 18 Apr. 2008 <http://www.cr.nps.gov/history/online_books/hh/10/hh10h.htm>.

Wolfe, Charles K. "Music." <u>The Confederacy</u>. New York: Simon, 1993.

# Part 2: Apply the Writing Process

**WRITING STANDARD**
**8.4.11** Identify topics; ask and evaluate questions; and develop ideas....

## PREWRITING

| **What Should I Do?** | **What Does It Look Like?** |
|---|---|

**1. Select a topic and freewrite.**
Select a topic from page 1052, or focus on a topic or general subject area your teacher has assigned. Then begin freewriting about the topic. In other words, jot down ideas and associations that occur to you as you think about it. (Circle) ideas that you think might be interesting to research.

▶ *I liked that story we read about the Civil War. Where did Bradbury get the idea for it? What would it be like to be just a kid and in a war ... to know that a big battle is coming and have the general admit he is scared? (Were there really boys like this in the Civil War?)*

**2. Create research questions.**
Now decide what you really want to know about the idea or ideas you just circled. List questions you have. Make your questions as specific as possible.

**See page 1036:** Develop Research Questions

▶ *My Research Questions:*
- *How did young kids end up in the Civil War?*
- *What jobs did drummer boys do?*
- *Did drummer boys ever fight, too?*

**3. Find out more.**
Get a better sense of your topic by visiting Web sites or by reading an encyclopedia or magazine article about your topic. As you do so, look for answers to your research questions. Make some notes.

▶ *My Answers and Other Notes:*
- *Lots of boys wanted to fight in the war but were too young to be soldiers.*
- *Drummer boys kept time while the soldiers marched. They also called the men to their meals and duties.*
- *There's a lot of information about the work drummer boys did in camp and in battles. That might make a good focus.*

**4. Make your topic more specific.**
Think about the length of the report you have been assigned. If whole books have been written on your topic, then you probably need to find one narrow part of the topic to explore.

▶ *Narrowing My Topic:*
*Boys in the Civil War (too big a topic!)*
↓
*Drummer boys (still seems like a lot for a three-page report)*
↓
*The jobs drummer boys did (narrow topic)*

## RESEARCHING

| *What Should I Do?* | *What Does It Look Like?* |
|---|---|

**1. Identify sources.**

After you have narrowed your topic, you can begin the research process. The first step is to identify **keywords,** specific words or phrases that relate to your topic. You will need keywords to locate materials in the library or on the Internet. See pages 1037–1041 for help with searching for information in a library or on the Internet.

Make a chart like this one to record and analyze the sources you find.

**TIP** For best search results from a library catalog, read the library's online tips for searching the catalog, use the advanced search form, or ask a reference librarian for help.

| Sources | My Comments |
|---|---|
| **Library Reference Works** "Civil War," <u>World Book Encyclopedia</u> | nothing about boys who went to war |
| **Other Library Books** <u>The Boys' War</u> by Jim Murphy (J973.7 M978) | full of primary source material—has a whole chapter about drummer boys |
| <u>The Children's Civil War</u> by James Marten (973.7 M377) | chapters on war and society, the war in children's literature, and children responding to the war |
| **Web Sites** "Young Heroes of the Civil War" | no information about the author, and no links to a home page or other sources |
| "Music of the Civil War" (I bookmarked this on Ted's computer) | several good facts about my topic, and the sponsor is the National Park Service |

**2. Evaluate what you find.**

Determine whether you should actually use each source you find.

- Do not use a source if it is too difficult or too childish for you.

- Do not use a source that might not be accurate. For example, Web sites without an author, a sponsor, or working links might be the work of just one person who is not an expert.

**See pages 1045–1048:** Evaluating Sources

**Rejected Sources**

1. "Civil War," <u>World Book Encyclopedia</u> (no information on my narrowed topic)

2. <u>The Children's Civil War</u> by James Marten (not specifically about drummer boys; also too difficult for me)

3. "Young Heroes of the Civil War" (might not be an accurate source)

## What Should I Do?

## What Does It Look Like?

**3. Make one index card for each source.**
Number each card in the top right corner. Then record the following information so you will be able to cite your source correctly later.

**Online encyclopedia**
- author (if given) and title of the article
- date of publication (if given)
- name of publisher
- date you accessed the article
- complete URL (Web address)

**Print or CD-ROM encyclopedia**
- author (if given) and title of the article
- name and year of encyclopedia
- if a CD-ROM, the term *CD-ROM*, plus the publisher and the place of publication

**Web site**
- author (if given) and title of page or article
- name of Web site (if given)
- date of Web site (if given)
- site sponsor or creator (if given)
- date you accessed the article
- complete URL (Web address)
- if the site comes from a print publication, the publisher, place of publication, and year of publication

**Book**
- author and/or editor
- title
- publisher, place of publication, and year of publication
- library call number

**See page 1066:** Citing Sources

**Online encyclopedia**

①
"American Civil War." Encyclopaedia Britannica. 2006. Encyclopaedia Britannica Online. 31 Mar. 2008 ‹http://searchebcom/eb/article-9006104 ›.

**Print encyclopedia**

②
"Civil War." The World Book Encyclopedia. 2006 ed.

**Web site**

③
Heiser, John. "Music of the Civil War." Gettysburg National Military Park Kidzpage. Dec. 2003. National Park Service. 21 Apr. 2008 ‹http://www.nps.gov/gett/gettkidz/musichtm›.

**Book**

④
Hoar, Jay S. Callow, Brave and True: A Gospel of Civil War Youth. Gettysburg, PA: Thomas, 1999. 973.7 HOAR

## RESEARCHING

| **What Should I Do?** | **What Does It Look Like?** |
|---|---|

**4. Make note cards.**

Now you are ready to take notes. Start with a clean index card.

- Write the number of the source on it (the same number you put on the source card).
- Write a specific heading for the card. Use the same heading on cards with similar information.
- Write the fact or idea that interests you.
- Record the page number if there is one.

> *Jobs for a drummer* ③
>
> *Drummers woke the troops and called them to different duties, such as sick duty and work details (no page number)..*

> *Age of boys in Civil War* ④
>
> *The youngest boys were just six years old (227).*

**5. Take careful, responsible notes.**

Use these three ways to record information from a source.

- **Quote** the source by copying the important phrase, sentence, or paragraph word for word. Enclose the copied words in quotation marks.
- **Paraphrase** the source by using your own words to tell what the source says. Use about the same number of words as the source does.
- **Summarize** the source by recording only the most important ideas in your own words. Use fewer words than the source does.

**TIP** Quote only when you cannot restate the idea in the source as clearly, vividly, or forcefully as the source does. Most of your notes should be summaries and paraphrases.

**Original source**

> Many [boys from the North] joined because they wanted to take the defiant South and "set them straight." But most signed up for a simpler reason—to escape the boring routine of farm life and take part in an exciting adventure.
>
> *Murphy, Jim, The Boys' War*

**Paraphrase**

> *Reasons boys joined up* ⑥
>
> *Boys from the North wanted to punish the South for being rebellious. An even more important reason for joining was that boys thought they would have a thrilling life instead of a dull one spent on a farm (Murphy 8).*

**Summary**

> *Reasons boys joined up* ⑥
>
> *Northern boys wanted to beat the South and have an adventure (Murphy 8).*

**What Should I Do?**

**What Does It Look Like?**

6. **Avoid plagiarism.**
   Plagiarism occurs when you use someone else's words or ideas without correctly formatting and crediting them. Follow these guidelines to avoid plagiarism.

   - **Paraphrase and summarize as you take notes.** Take the time to think through and understand what you are reading. Put as much of your reading as you can into your own words.

   - **Don't rely heavily on a single source.** Even if you find one source that is clearly superior to all others, be sure you blend the facts, ideas, and opinions from at least four sources.

   - **Place quotation marks around every significant word, phrase, or sentence that you copy.** Even if you copy just a few key words while paraphrasing the majority of the passage, you must put quotation marks around those words.

   - **Put away your sources when you begin your draft.** Don't work from an open book. Never cut and paste chunks of information from an online source. Rely on your note cards instead.

   **TIP** When you paraphrase and summarize, you do not have to put quotation marks around common words from your source or around words that you use over and over, such as *Civil War, drummer,* and *battle.* You do have to put quotation marks around specific, descriptive words and phrases, such as in this example: *Drummer boys were often "unintended sacrifices," caught in enemy fire.*

**Original source**

When fighting appeared imminent, musicians were often ordered to the rear to assist surgeons and care for the wounded.

*Heiser, John, "Music of the Civil War"*

**Plagiarized paraphrase**

When a battle appeared imminent, musicians were often sent to care for the wounded.

**Correctly documented paraphrase**

Drummer boys often had to help care for injured soldiers (Heiser).

**Original source**

Since Shiloh was significant for the bravery of the young untrained men of the North and South alike, writers frequently wrote about the young and otherwise undistinguished soldiers rather than the . . . leaders. The drummer boy, often a mere lad who had run away from home to seek adventure in the ranks, became the subject of the most popular literature of the day.

*"Shiloh Inspires Writers"*

**Plagiarized summary**

The drummer boy of Shiloh became the subject of the most popular literature of the time.

**Correctly written and documented summary**

A legend grew up about the drummer boy of Shiloh ("Shiloh").

## RESEARCHING

| What Should I Do? | What Does It Look Like? |
| --- | --- |

**7. Write a thesis statement.**
A **thesis statement** is the main idea or controlling idea of your report. Everything in your report should relate to or prove your thesis statement.

Be sure your thesis statement names your writing topic and says something about it. Don't worry if your thesis isn't perfect now. You can—and should—revise it after you work on your first draft.

▶

**My topic:**
Drummer boys in the Civil War
↓
**What I will say about the topic:**
Drummer boys had many difficult jobs.
↓
**My working thesis statement:**
Drummer boys were too young for the jobs they were given and much too young for war.

**8. Organize your notes and make an outline.**
You can create a writing plan from your note cards by following these steps:

- Separate your cards into groups with similar or related headings.
- Decide on an order for the groups you created. You might organize information chronologically, in order of importance, or in any logical order that is appropriate to your thesis.
- Put your cards in the most appropriate order and create an outline based on that order.

**TIP** The outline on this page is a formal outline, but you can also make an informal outline or create a graphic organizer such as a flow chart or sequence chain.

▶

**Drummer Boys in the Civil War**

I. Who the drummer boys were
   A. Too young to be soldiers
   B. Had jobs that were too hard for them
II. Drummer boys' duties
   A. Acted as human clocks
   B. Drummed the beat of the march
   C. Drummed during battle
   D. Sometimes helped care for wounded
III. Dying for a cause
   A. Drummer Boy of Shiloh
   B. William Johnston
   C. Clarence McKenzie
   D. Number of deaths
IV. Last drummer boys
   A. Civil War the last time drummer boys used
   B. Later wars too noisy to hear drums

| What Should I Do? | What Does It Look Like? |
|---|---|

**1. Begin your first draft.**
Use your outline or other organizational plan in addition to your note cards to begin creating complete sentences and paragraphs.

**Outline**

> II. Drummer boys' duties
>     A. Acted as human clocks

**First draft**

> Drummer boys for the North and South had similar duties. One important job of every drummer was to be a kind of human clock. Drummers woke the troops up in the morning, called them to roll call and other duties, and sent them to bed.

**2. Stay focused on your thesis.**
Make sure each point you make relates to or proves your thesis. Sometimes it's a good idea to repeat some key words from your thesis in your topic sentences.

**TIP** Consider creating a chart, graph, timeline, or other visual. Be sure to give it a title that relates to your thesis. Add a source line at the bottom that tells where you found your information.

> **Thesis:** Drummer boys were too young to do the difficult jobs they faced.
>
> **Related topic sentence:** A more difficult job was keeping time as the troops marched.

**3. Weave in your sources.**
As you write, let your reader know where ideas are coming from. Try using introductory phrases like these:

- "According to Murphy, . . ."
- "Wolfe points out . . ."
- "In 'Drummer Boys and Fifers,' Stephen Currie writes . . ."

> The writer Stephen Currie says
> Some of these boys were under the age of eleven (Currie 3).

> Civil War expert Jay Hoar points out that
> At least one drummer was just 40 inches tall (Hoar 116).

**DRAFTING**

## What Should I Do?

## What Does It Look Like?

4. **Credit your sources.**
You have to **credit,** or document, each source you use at the end of the sentence or sentences in which it appears. Because this information appears in parentheses, it is called **parenthetical documentation.** It usually consists of the author's last name and a page number and looks like this: (Murphy 8). Here are some exceptions:

- **Web site:** Because a Web site has no page numbers, use only the author's name: (Heiser). If the site does not credit an author, use a short form of the title: ("Shiloh").

- **Author named in sentence:** Use only the page number: (8).

- **More than one source for a single idea:** List both sources and separate them with a semicolon: ("Shiloh"; Wolfe 745).

▶ Drummer boys also sometimes "found themselves the target of enemy fire" (Murphy 40).

> *Author and page number*

Hoar points out that some drummer boys were just 40 inches tall (116).

> *Author named in sentence*

Drummers woke the troops up in the morning, called them to roll call and other duties, and sent them to bed (Wolfe 745; Heiser).

> *Information from two sources*

5. **Make a Works Cited list.**
Alphabetize your source cards by the author's last name. If a source does not name an author, alphabetize by title. Some common types of sources are shown here. See page 1066 of this book or the *MLA Handbook for Writers of Research Papers* for other kinds of entries.

▶ **Works Cited**

Currie, Stephen. "Drummer Boys." <u>Cobblestone</u>. Dec. 1999: 3-7.

Heiser, John. "Music of the Civil War." <u>Gettysburg National Military Park Kidzpage</u>. Dec. 2003. National Park Service. 21 Apr. 2008 ‹http://www.nps.gov/gett/gettkidz/musichtm›.

Hoar, Jay S. <u>Callow, Brave & True: A Gospel of Civil War Youth</u>. Gettysburg, PA: Thomas, 1999.

| *What Should I Do?* | *What Does It Look Like?* |
|---|---|
| **1. Take another look at your introduction.**<br>• Highlight the sentences that help lead up to or explain your thesis.<br>• Do these sentences provide useful details and help to capture your reader's interest?<br>• Add background information to help your reader understand where you are heading. | ~~Armies of the North and South used drummer boys during the Civil War. These boys faced many responsibilities and dangers.~~<br>When the Civil War broke out, many boys thought that going off to war would be an exciting adventure. When they tried to sign up, however, recruiters wouldn't let most of them become soldiers because they were too young (Murphy 8). |
| **2. Improve your support.**<br>• Ask a peer reader to <u>underline</u> points you made that are hard to understand or that lack support.<br>• Add facts, explanations, reasons, or other support, as well as correct documentation.<br><br>**See page 1066:** Ask a Peer Reader | This song tells about a child who made the greatest sacrifice for his country. <u>He wasn't the only one.</u> Many drummer boys died in the war. For example, 12-year-old Clarence McKenzie died from a "stray bullet" (Hoar 3). |
| **3. Add your own insights and ideas.**<br>• Do your own ideas appear in your report, or have you merely repeated the opinions of others?<br>• Look for places to include your own reflections and insights on the facts or opinions. | Hoar points out that at least one drummer boy was just 40 inches tall, so the drums were very big in comparison to the little boys (116). Since marches went on for miles, it's likely that carrying a big drum was exhausting. |
| **4. Delete unnecessary details.**<br>• Check your report for ideas that do not relate to or prove the thesis.<br>• Delete any words, phrases, or sentences that interfere with clarity or unity. | *Dying for a Cause*<br>Many drummer boys did even more than drumming, helping with the wounded, and other chores. ~~Some also drummed deserters out of the unit (Wolfe).~~ Although they were young, some even gave their lives, and a few were heroes. |

## REVISING AND EDITING

| What Should I Do? | What Does It Look Like? |
|---|---|

**5. Add transitions.**
- Decide whether each sentence and each paragraph flows smoothly to the next. (Circle) connecting words.
- If you don't see many circles, add transitions to help your reader make connections between ideas.

▶

                                      , too. For example,
Drummers suffered in other ways/Hunger was constant for many Confederates, and some wore ragged clothing (Robertson 1024). Troops faced bad weather and disease.           also

**6. Notice sentence lengths.**
- Reread your report. If you have many short, choppy sentences, try combining some for a more graceful flow of ideas.
- If you have many long sentences, break them up with one or two short sentences to create interest and variety.

▶

When Drummer boy Delavan Miller was caught in the fighting, He admitted, "I was never so scared in all my life" (quoted in Currie 6).

Many drummer boys did even more than drumming, helping with the wounded, and other chores. Although they were very young, some even gave their lives, and a few were heroes.

**7. Make your conclusion memorable.**
- Decide whether your conclusion is thoughtful and interesting or just pointlessly repeats what you've already said.
- Consider ending with a memorable phrase or two.
- Don't overlook this opportunity to present your own thinking.

▶

~~As my report shows, drummer boys of the Civil War faced many challenges. They had to put in long days, carry big drums, and help with the wounded.~~

The Civil War was the last war to use drummer boys on the battlefield. Later wars were noisier, with more rifles, more soldiers, and more cannons. No one could hear the drummer boys anymore (Murphy 41, 43). That seems like one of the few good things to come out of deadlier wars. Drummer boys of the Civil Wars were too young for the many challenges that they faced. Children today are lucky that this job no longer exists.

## Apply the Rubric

**A strong research report . . .**

- ☑ has an appealing or thought-provoking introduction
- ☑ presents a clear thesis statement
- ☑ supports the thesis with evidence
- ☑ correctly summarizes, paraphrases, and quotes multiple sources
- ☑ includes the writer's own ideas and reflections
- ☑ follows a clear pattern of organization and uses transitions
- ☑ varies the lengths of sentences and uses precise words
- ☑ has a thoughtful, memorable conclusion

## Ask a Peer Reader

- What is my thesis? Do I need to clarify it? If so, how?
- Where should I add more support or background information?
- Which part of my report was most interesting? Why?
- What else would you like to know about this topic?

## Citing Sources

Follow these examples for citing different types of sources.

**CD-ROM encyclopedia**
"American Civil War." Encyclopaedia Britannica. 2004 ed. CD-ROM. Chicago: Encyclopaedia Britannica, 2006.

**Newspaper or magazine article**
Dolan, Sean, and Marina Hincapie. "The Real Drummer Boy of Shiloh." Pomona Herald. 6 Jan. 2008: C11+.

**Interview you conducted with an expert**
Shubert, William. Personal interview. 1 Apr. 2008.

**Book with an editor**
DeYoe, Veronica, ed. Boys Who Went to War. Chicago: Battlefield, 2008.

**Film or documentary**
Civil War Life. Dir. Mark Bussler. DVD. Inecom, 2003.

For more examples, see the *MLA Handbook for Writers of Research Papers.*

## Writing Online

**PUBLISHING OPTIONS**
For publishing options, visit the **Writing Center** at **ClassZone.com.**

**ASSESSMENT PREPARATION**
For writing and grammar assessment practice, go to the **Assessment Center** at **ClassZone.com.**

**WRITING STANDARD**
**8.4.6** Use a computer to create documents....

## Creating a Web Site

You have learned a great deal about your topic. Developing a Web site will give others an opportunity to learn about your topic, too.

### Planning the Web Site

1. **Think in screens or in key ideas.** For example, two key ideas from your report about drummer boys are "Jobs Drummer Boys Did" and "Drummer Boys in Battle." Next, think of images that will help illustrate your main ideas. You might use photographs, video clips, graphic organizers, maps, charts, databases, or timelines. In addition, you could create audio narration.

2. **Create a site plan.** List your ideas for pages. Then make a map with arrows showing how your pages might link up.

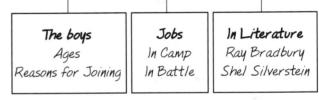

3. **Sketch the pages and write the text.** Draw rough sketches of how you want each page to look. Include images, buttons, and links. Then write the text that will appear on each page. Use short, bulleted lists instead of long paragraphs.

### Producing the Web Site

1. **Avoid plagiarism.** Items that you find on other Web sites may be copyrighted. Some site sponsors allow students to use their elements in school projects. Be sure to credit what you use.

2. **Choose an authoring program.** This type of program helps you combine media elements into a Web document. Your school's computer specialist can help you with this step, as well as with scanning and importing your materials.

3. **Make your site clear and attractive.** Label all elements in type that is 12 points or larger. Use the same font style and size for all your headings.

4. **Revise and upload.** Ask a classmate to try out your site and give you feedback. When you have fixed any problems, make your site available on your school's internal server or on the Web.

# Student Resource Bank

*Reading any text—whether it is a short story, poem, magazine article, newspaper, or Web page—requires the use of special strategies. For example, you might plot the events of a short story on a diagram, or use text features to spot main ideas in a magazine article. You also need to identify patterns of organization in the text. Using such strategies can help you read different texts with ease and also help you understand what you're reading.*

# 1 Reading Literary Texts

**Literary texts** include short stories, novels, poems, and dramas. Literary texts can also be biographies, autobiographies, and essays. To appreciate and analyze literary texts, you will need to understand the characteristics of each type of text.

## 1.1 READING A SHORT STORY
### Strategies for Reading

- Read the **title.** As you read the story, you may notice that the title has a special meaning.

- Keep track of **events** as they happen. Plot the events on a diagram like this one.

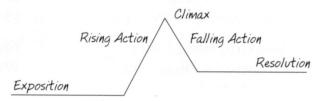

- From the details the writer provides, **visualize** the characters. **Predict** what they might do next.

- Look for specific adjectives that help you visualize the **setting**—the time and place in which events occur.

## 1.2 READING A POEM
### Strategies for Reading

- Notice the **form** of the poem, or the number of its lines and their arrangement on the page.

- Read the poem aloud a few times. Listen for **rhyme** and **rhythm.**

- **Visualize** the images and comparisons.

- **Connect** with the poem by asking yourself what message the poet is trying to send.

- Create a word web or other **graphic organizer** to record your reactions and questions.

## 1.3 READING A PLAY
### Strategies for Reading

- Read the stage directions to help you **visualize** the setting and characters.

- **Question** what the title means and why the playwright chose it.

- Identify the main conflict (struggle or problem) in the play. To **clarify** the conflict, make a chart that shows what the conflict is and how it is resolved.

- **Analyze** the characters. What do they want? How do they change during the play? You may want to make a chart that lists each character's name, appearance, and traits.

## 1.4 READING LITERARY NONFICTION
### Strategies for Reading

- If you are reading a biography, an autobiography, or another type of biographical writing (such as a diary, a memoir, or letters), use a family tree or word web to keep track of the people mentioned.

- When reading an essay, **evaluate** the writer's ideas. Is there a clear main idea? Does the writer use appropriate details to support a main idea?

## ❷ Reading Informational Texts: Text Features

An **informational text** is writing that provides factual information. Informational materials—such as chapters in textbooks and articles in magazines, encyclopedias, and newspapers—usually contain elements that help the reader recognize their purpose, organization, and key ideas. These elements are known as **text features.**

### 2.1 UNDERSTANDING TEXT FEATURES

**Text features** are design elements of a text that indicate its organizational structure or otherwise make its key ideas and information understandable. Text features include titles, headings, subheadings, boldface type, bulleted and numbered lists, and graphic aids, such as charts, graphs, illustrations, and photographs. Notice how the text features help you find key information on the textbook page shown.

**Ⓐ** The **title** identifies the topic.

**Ⓑ** A **subheading** indicates the start of a new topic or section and identifies the focus of that section.

**Ⓒ** **Questions** may be used to focus your understanding of the text.

**Ⓓ** A **bulleted list** shows items of equal importance.

**Ⓔ** **Graphic aids,** such as illustrations, photographs, charts, diagrams, maps, and timelines, often make ideas in the text clearer.

**Ⓕ** A **caption,** or the text that accompanies a graphic aid, gives information about the graphic aid that isn't necessarily obvious from the image itself.

#### PRACTICE AND APPLY

1. What is a surplus?

2. What facts do the photograph and caption add to the text?

3. What informational texts do you read outside of class? Why are they informational?

---

## Ⓐ The First Communities

**Ⓓ TERMS & NAMES**
- surplus
- specialization
- artisan
- social class
- government

**Build on What You Know** Do you live in the country, a small town, a city, or a suburb? In the distant past, simple farming villages developed, over hundreds of years, into more complex villages and eventually into cities.

### Villages Around the World Ⓑ

**Ⓒ ESSENTIAL QUESTION** How did farming villages develop?

When villages prospered, they were able to support more people. Their populations grew. People's skills became more specialized. Village economies became more varied.

**Surpluses Boost Development** As agricultural techniques improved, farmers sometimes produced **surpluses**—more than what they needed to survive. For example, farmers might grow more grain than their families or village could use. The extra was an economic surplus.

Surpluses in early farming villages were not limited to food. Surpluses also included materials for making cloth and other products. Sheep raisers, for example, may have had surplus wool. Surpluses of food and other materials in good seasons helped villages survive bad seasons.

**Moroccan Village**
This modern village in the Atlas Mountains of Morocco in North Africa continues a way of life that has lasted for thousands of years. ▼ Ⓕ

Ⓔ

65

## 2.2 USING TEXT FEATURES

You can use text features to locate information, to help you understand it, and to take notes. Just use the following strategies when you encounter informational text.

### Strategies for Reading

- **Preview** the text by looking at the title, headings, and subheadings to get an idea of the main concepts and the way the text is organized.

- Before you begin reading the text more thoroughly, **skim** it—read it quickly—to get an overview.

- Read any **questions** that appear at the end of a lesson or chapter. Doing this will help you set a purpose for your reading.

- Turn subheadings into questions. Then use the text below the subheadings to answer the questions. Your answers will be a **summary** of the text.

- **Take notes** by turning headings and subheadings into main ideas. You might use a chart like the following.

| The First Communities | | Main heading |
|---|---|---|
| Villages Around the World | 1. prosperity means growth | Subheading |
| | 2. specialized skills | |
| | 3. varied economies | |

- As you read to locate particular facts or details, **scan** the text. Look for key words and phrases as you move slowly down the page.

## 2.3 TURNING TEXT HEADINGS INTO OUTLINE ENTRIES

After you have read a selection at least once, you can use text features to take notes in outline form. The following outline shows how one student used text headings from the sample textbook page on page R3. Study the outline and use the strategies that follow to create an outline based on text features.

### Strategies for Using Text Headings

- Preview the headings and subheadings in the text to get an idea of what different kinds there are and what their positions might be in an outline.

- Be consistent. Note that subheadings that are the same size and color should be used consistently in Roman-numeral or capital-letter entries in the outline. If you decide that a chapter heading should appear with a Roman numeral, then that's the level at which all other chapter headings should appear.

- Write the headings and subheadings that you will use as your Roman-numeral and capital-letter entries first. As you read, fill in numbered details from the text under the headings and subheadings in your outline.

#### PRACTICE AND APPLY

Reread "So You Want to be an Entomologist?" pages 888–889. Use text features in the selection to take notes in outline form.

Preview the subheadings in the text to get an idea of the different kinds. Write the headings and subheadings you are using as your Roman numeral and capital letter entries first. Then fill in the details.

## 2.4 GRAPHIC AIDS

Information is communicated not only with words but also with graphic aids. **Graphic aids** are visual representations of verbal statements. They can be charts, webs, diagrams, graphs, photographs, or other visual representations of information.

Graphic aids usually make complex information easier to understand. For that reason, graphic aids are often used to organize, simplify, and summarize information for easy reference.

## Graphs

Graphs are used to illustrate statistical information. A **graph** is a drawing that shows the relative values of numerical quantities. Different kinds of graphs are used to show different numerical relationships.

## *Strategies for Reading*

**Ⓐ** Read the title.

**Ⓑ** Find out what is being represented or measured.

**Ⓒ** In a circle graph, compare the sizes of the parts.

**Ⓓ** In a line graph, study the slant of the line. The steeper the line, the faster the rate of change.

**Ⓔ** In a bar graph, compare the lengths of the bars.

A **circle graph,** or **pie graph,** shows the relationships of parts to a whole. The entire circle equals 100 percent. The parts of the circle represent percentages of the whole.

**MODEL: CIRCLE GRAPH**

Line graphs show changes in numerical quantities over time and are effective in presenting trends such as changes in life expectancy. A line graph is made on a grid. Here, the vertical axis indicates degrees Fahrenheit, and the horizontal axis shows dates. Points on the graph indicate data. The line that connects the points highlights a trend or pattern.

**MODEL: LINE GRAPH**

In a **bar graph,** vertical or horizontal bars are used to show or compare categories of information, such as the heights of different buildings. The lengths of the bars in this case indicate height.

**MODEL: BAR GRAPH**

**WATCH OUT!** Evaluate carefully the information presented in graphs. For example, circle graphs show major factors and differences well but tend to reduce the importance of smaller factors and differences.

## Diagrams

A **diagram** is a drawing that shows how something works or how its parts relate to one another. A **picture diagram** is a picture or drawing of the subject being discussed.

### Strategies for Reading

Ⓐ Read the title.

Ⓑ Read each label and look at the part it identifies.

Ⓒ Follow any arrows or numbers that show the order of steps in a process, and read any captions.

**MODEL: PICTURE DIAGRAM**

Ⓐ **Ancient Irrigation**

This model shows how an ancient irrigation system worked.

❶ Gates controlled how much water flowed from the river.

❷ Main canals led from the river. They sloped gently downward to keep the water flowing.

❸ Medium-sized branch canals led away from the main canals.

❹ Small feeder canals led water directly to the fields. Ⓒ

In a **schematic diagram,** lines, symbols, and words are used to help readers visualize processes or objects they cannot normally see. A **cutaway diagram** is a drawing or model of something with part of the outside removed, to show the inside.

**MODEL: SCHEMATIC DIAGRAM**

Ⓑ smooth paving stones

pebbles and gravel

slabs of stone

rubble

◀ **Roman Road** Ⓐ **Construction**

Roman roads were constructed in layers. The average width of a road was 15 to 18 feet. Ⓒ

## Charts and Tables

A **chart** presents information, shows a process, or makes comparisons, usually in rows or columns.

A **table** is a specific type of chart that presents a collection of facts in rows and columns and shows how the facts relate to one another.

### Strategies for Reading

Ⓐ Read the title to learn what information the chart or table covers.

Ⓑ Study column headings and row labels to determine the categories of information presented.

Ⓒ Look down columns and across rows to find specific information.

**MODEL: CHART**

| The Domestication of Animals Ⓐ | | |
|---|---|---|
| **Animal** | **Location** | **Use** Ⓑ |
| llama | South America | transport, meat |
| turkey | North America | meat |
| cattle | Europe, Asia, Africa | milk, meat |
| horse | Asia (southwest steppes) | transport Ⓒ |
| dog | Asia (possibly China) | guarding, herding, hunting |

**MODEL: TABLE**

| Light Rail Meadowview Route Monday–Friday A.M. | | | |
|---|---|---|---|
| **Meadowview** Ⓑ | **City College** | **Arden/ Del Paso** | **Watt/I-8o** |
| 6:05 | 6:14 | 6:42 | 6:53 |
| 7:05 | 7:14 | 7:42 | 7:53 |
| 7:20 | 7:29 Ⓒ | 7:57 | 8:08 |
| 7:50 | 7:59 | 8:27 | 8:38 |
| 8:05 | 8:14 | 8:42 | 8:53 |
| 8:35 | 8:44 | 9:12 | 9:23 |
| 9:05 | 9:14 | 9:42 | 9:53 |
| 9:50 | 9:59 | 10:27 | 10:38 |
| 10:05 | 10:14 | 10:42 | 10:53 |
| 11:05 | 11:14 | 11:42 | 11:53 |

## Maps

A **map** visually represents a geographic region, such as a state or country. It provides information about areas through lines, colors, shapes, and symbols. There are different kinds of maps.

- **Political maps** show political features, such as national borders.
- **Physical maps** show the landforms in areas.
- **Road or travel maps** show roads and highways.
- **Thematic maps** show information on a specific topic, such as climate, weather, or natural resources.

### Strategies for Reading

Ⓐ Read the title to find out what kind of map it is.

Ⓑ Read the labels to get an overall sense of what the map shows.

Ⓒ Look at the **key** or **legend** to find out what the symbols and colors on the map stand for.

**MODEL: PHYSICAL MAP**

**MODEL: THEMATIC MAP**

**PRACTICE AND APPLY**

1. According to the circle graph, how many days a week do most people exercise?

2. On which date was a temperature of 60° F recorded?

3. According to the bar graph, where is the world's tallest structure located?

4. How many kinds of canals were used in ancient irrigation?

5. What material formed the bottom layer of Roman roads?

6. According to the chart, which animal was domesticated in South America?

7. What time would you have to leave City College to get to the Watt/I-80 train station by 11:00?

8. What body of water is on the east coast of India?

9. What is the main economic activity of Afghanistan?

## 3 Reading Informational Texts: Patterns of Organization

Reading any type of writing is easier once you recognize how it is organized. Writers usually arrange ideas and information in ways that best help readers see how they are related. There are several common patterns of organization:

- main idea and supporting details
- chronological order
- cause-effect organization
- compare-and-contrast organization
- problem-solution organization

Writers also typically present arguments in ways that will help readers follow their reasoning.

*For more about deductive and inductive methods of organization, see Analyzing Logic and Reasoning, pages R22–R25.*

### 3.1 MAIN IDEA AND SUPPORTING DETAILS

**Main idea and supporting details** is a basic pattern of organization in which a central idea about a topic is supported by details. The **main idea** is the most important idea about a topic that a particular text or paragraph conveys. **Supporting details** are words, phrases, or sentences that tell more about the main idea. The main idea may be directly stated at the beginning and then followed by supporting details, or it may be merely implied by the supporting details. It may also be stated after it has been implied by supporting details.

### *Strategies for Reading*

- To find a stated main idea in a paragraph, identify the paragraph's topic. The topic is what the paragraph is about and can usually be summed up in one or two words. The word, or synonyms of it, will usually appear throughout the paragraph. Headings and subheadings are also clues to the topics of paragraphs.
- Look for the topic sentence, or the sentence that states the most important idea the paragraph conveys. It is often the first sentence in a paragraph; however, it may appear at the end.

- To find an implied main idea, ask yourself: Whom or what did I just read about? What do the details suggest about the topic?
- Formulate a sentence stating this idea and add it to the paragraph. Does your sentence convey the main idea?

Notice how the main idea is expressed in each of the following models.

---

**MODEL: MAIN IDEA AS THE FIRST SENTENCE**

On the second day of the heat wave, the temperature soared to a sweltering 110 degrees. [Main idea] The sun melted the tar of the newly paved driveway. It was almost impossible to escape the fumes, which caused him to hold his nose and breathe through his mouth. The air felt like a wet blanket smothering his lungs. Each breath was a struggle. [Supporting details]

---

**MODEL: MAIN IDEA AS THE LAST SENTENCE**

His body tried to maintain a healthy temperature by producing large amounts of sweat. Because the air was so humid and there was no breeze, the sweat didn't evaporate and cool him at all. It just dripped unpleasantly, and he grew even hotter as he angrily tried to wipe it away. Despite losing all that water, he wasn't even thirsty. [Supporting details] Though he didn't know it, he was in danger of becoming dehydrated. [Main idea]

---

**MODEL: IMPLIED MAIN IDEA**

As he walked along the street looking for something to drink, he began to feel light-headed. He ignored the feeling for a few minutes, but then became so dizzy that he had to sit down. Soon he started to feel sick to his stomach. As he stretched out, he began to shiver. "How can I be cold when it's 110 degrees?" he wondered before he fainted. [Implied main idea: He was dehydrated, which was a serious problem.]

Read each paragraph, and then do the following:

1. Identify the main idea in the paragraph, using one of the strategies discussed on the previous page. Tell whether it is stated or implied.

2. Evaluate the pattern of organization used in the paragraph. Does it express the main idea effectively?

> The earthquake shook down in San Francisco hundreds of thousands of dollars' worth of walls and chimneys. But the conflagration that followed burned up hundreds of millions of dollars' worth of property. There is no estimating within hundreds of millions the actual damage wrought. Not in history has a modern imperial city been so completely destroyed. San Francisco is gone. Nothing remains of it but memories and a fringe of dwelling houses on its outskirts.
> —Jack London, "The Story of an Eyewitness"

> They never saw him. Now and then they heard whispered rumors to the effect that he was in the neighborhood. The woods were searched. The roads were watched. There was never anything to indicate his whereabouts. But a few days afterward, a goodly number of slaves would be gone from the plantation. Neither the master nor the overseer had heard or seen anything unusual in the quarter. Sometimes one or the other would vaguely remember having heard a whippoorwill call somewhere in the woods, close by, late at night. Though it was the wrong season for whippoorwills.
> —Ann Petry, *Harriet Tubman: Conductor on the Underground Railroad*

## 3.2 CHRONOLOGICAL ORDER

**Chronological order** is the arrangement of events in the order in which they happen. This type of organization is used in many short stories and novels, historical writing, biographies, and autobiographies. To show the order of events, writers use order words such as *after, next,* and *later* and time words and phrases that identify specific times of day, days of the week, and dates, such as *the next morning, Tuesday,* and *March 13, 2007.*

### Strategies for Reading

- Scan the text for headings and subheadings that may indicate a chronological pattern of organization.

- Look for words and phrases that identify times, such as *in a year, three hours earlier, in A.D. 1066,* and *the next day.*

- Look for words that signal order, such as *first, afterward, then, during,* and *finally,* to see how events or steps are related.

- Note that a paragraph or passage in which ideas and information are arranged chronologically will have several words or phrases that indicate time order, not just one.

- Ask yourself: Are the events in the paragraph or passage presented in time order?

Notice the words and phrases that signal time order in the first two paragraphs of the following model.

**MODEL**

### The Life of Jack London

Jack London was born in San Francisco, California, in 1876. His family was poor and moved frequently in search of work. In 1881, the family began working on farms. London's dislike of farming drew him to literature as a way "to get beyond the sky lines of my narrow California valley."

The Londons were unlucky in farming. When they lost their land, they moved across the bay to Oakland. To help support his family, the 10-year-old London took his first job. By the time he was 15, he had quit school and was working long hours in a factory. London became a tough teenager who knew how to fight but who never lost his burning passion for books.

**Time words and phrases**

**Events**

Living by the sea, London became fascinated by the ships that promised contact with faraway places. At the age of 17, he joined the *Sophia Sutherland* on a seal-hunting voyage to Japan. This trip provided material for his first short story, "Story of a Typhoon off the Coast of Japan," for which he won first prize in a writing contest.

London then returned to California with a passion for travel. The next year, he "hopped a train" heading east and lived as a tramp. However, homelessness persuaded him to return to high school in Oakland. In 1896, with only one year of high school behind him, he passed the entrance exam for the University of California at Berkeley.

Unfortunately, London had to give up his university studies for lack of money. After working for a while in a laundry, he joined the rush north to Canada's Klondike River in search of gold. Although London never struck it rich, his Klondike experiences inspired his later writing.

**PRACTICE AND APPLY**

Reread the preceding model and then do the following:

1. List three words or phrases in the last three paragraphs that indicate time or order.

2. Describe how London became interested in books.

3. Explain why he returned home after living as a tramp.

## 3.3 CAUSE-EFFECT ORGANIZATION

**Cause-effect organization** is a pattern of organization that shows causal relationships between events, ideas, and trends. Cause-effect relationships may be directly stated or merely implied by the order in which the information is presented. Writers often use the cause-effect pattern in historical and scientific writing. Cause-effect relationships may have several forms.

**One cause with one effect**

Cause ▶ Effect

**One cause with multiple effects**

Cause ▶ Effect
      ▶ Effect

**Multiple causes with a single effect**

Cause ▶
Cause ▶ Effect

**A chain of causes and effects**

Cause ▶ Effect/Cause ▶ Effect

### *Strategies for Reading*

- Look for headings and subheadings that indicate a cause-effect pattern of organization, such as "Effects of Food Allergies."

- To find the effect or effects, read to answer the question "What happened?"

- To find the cause or causes, read to answer the question "Why did it happen?"

- Look for words and phrases that help you identify specific relationships between events, such as *because, since, had the effect of, led to, as a result, resulted in, for that reason, due to, therefore, if . . . then,* and *consequently.*

- Look closely at each cause-effect relationship. Do not assume that because one event happened before another, the first event caused the second event.

- Use graphic organizers like the diagrams shown to record cause-effect relationships as you read.

Notice the words that signal causes and effects in the following model.

**MODEL**

### We're Destroying Our Rain Forests

According to a study done by Brazilian scientists, nearly 5 million acres of rain forest are disappearing a year. That's equal to seven football fields a minute.

**Effect**

The cause of this destruction is simple—cutting down trees. Every minute, around 2,000 trees are felled to create highways, railroads, and farms. Some trees, such as mahogany and teak, are harvested for their beautiful hardwood.

**Signal words**

**Cause**

This destruction of the rain forests has wide-ranging effects on living things. About 30,000 plant species live in the Amazon rain forest alone. These plants provide important foods such as bananas, coffee, chocolate, and nuts, as well as medicinal compounds found nowhere else. Just four square miles of a rain forest shelters more than 550 species of birds, reptiles, and amphibians. Almost 100 species worldwide face extinction every day, many due to habitat loss in rainforests.

Rain forests also act as climate regulators, balancing the exchange of oxygen and carbon dioxide in the atmosphere and helping to offset global warming. The earth's well-being will suffer as a result of the rain forests' destruction.

It is crucial that steps be taken immediately to reduce the number of trees being cut down. If this destruction is not reversed, within 50 years, thriving rain forests will be no more than a memory.

### PRACTICE AND APPLY

Refer to the preceding model to do the following:

1. Use one of the graphic organizers on page R10 to show the multiple effects of cutting down trees described in the model.

2. List three words or phrases used to signal cause and effect in the last four paragraphs.

### 3.4 COMPARE-AND-CONTRAST ORGANIZATION

**Compare-and-contrast organization** is a pattern of organization that provides a way to look at similarities and differences in two or more subjects. A writer may use this pattern of organization to compare the important points or characteristics of two or more subjects. These points or characteristics are called **points of comparison.** There are two ways to develop compare-and-contrast organization:

**Point-by-point organization**—The writer discusses one point of comparison for both subjects, then goes on to the next point.

**Subject-by-subject organization**—The writer covers all points of comparison for one subject and then all points of comparison for the next subject.

## Strategies for Reading

- Look in the text for headings, subheadings, and sentences that may suggest a compare-and-contrast pattern of organization, such as "Common Behaviors of Different Pets," to help you identify where similarities and differences are addressed.

- To find similarities, look for words and phrases such as *like, all, both, every,* and *in the same way.*

- To find differences, look for words and phrases such as *unlike, but, on the other hand, more, less, in contrast,* and *however.*

- Use a graphic organizer, such as a Venn diagram or a compare-and-contrast chart, to record points of comparison and similarities and differences.

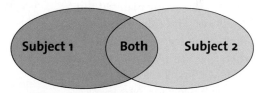

|  | **Subject 1** | **Subject 2** |
|---|---|---|
| Point 1 |  |  |
| Point 2 |  |  |
| Point 3 |  |  |

As you read the following models, use the signal words and phrases to identify the similarities and differences between the subjects and how the details are organized in each text.

**MODEL 1**
### Mr. Frank and Mr. Van Daan

Moving into a tiny apartment with people you have never met is a sure way to discover your differences. In the play *The Diary of Anne Frank,* Mr. Frank and Mr. Van Daan are in a similar situation, but have very different personalities, behaviors, and relationships with their families.

Both men are Jews living in Nazi-occupied Amsterdam during World War II. Both have children: Mr. Frank, two daughters; and Mr. Van Daan, a son. They try to hide

**Subjects**

**Comparison words and phrases**

their families from the Nazis in the same apartment.

Despite these similarities, there are many differences between the two men. First, they have nearly opposite personalities. Mr. Van Daan is very concerned with appearances and wears expensive clothes. He can be kind, but often loses his temper. He also has strong opinions about the roles of men and women. For example, he acts embarrassed that his son Peter likes his pet cat and disapproves of Anne's outspokenness. He tells her, "A man likes a girl who'll listen to him once in a while."

In contrast, Mr. Frank doesn't seem to care about material things. He always stays calm and has compassion for other people. Even when Mr. Van Daan is caught stealing food, Mr. Frank tries to understand the man's behavior. Mr. Frank's attitude about women differs from Mr. Van Daan's as well. Mr. Frank never criticizes Anne for being unladylike; instead, he encourages her to be herself. He gives her a diary because he knows she loves to write, and he is proud of her creativity when she makes Hanukkah presents for everyone. As Anne says about her father, "He's the only one who's ever given me the feeling that I have any sense."

The two men also respond differently to their situation. Mr. Van Daan is self-centered and believes he suffers more from hunger than the others. He even tries to take Anne's piece of cake. Mr. Frank, on the other hand, always puts the needs of others before his own. For example, he makes the newcomer, Dr. Dussel, feel welcome and gladly offers him food. He also risks his own safety to investigate when a robber enters the downstairs warehouse.

Mr. Frank and Mr. Van Daan relate differently with their families.

Although Mr. and Mrs. Van Daan are close, they quarrel often. Mr. Van Daan criticizes his son's slowness and threatens to get rid of his beloved cat. In contrast, Mr. Frank shows only love and respect for his wife and daughters. Even when he scolds Anne, he does it privately and gently. After Anne hurts her mother's feelings, Mr. Frank tells her that parents "can only try to set a good example. The rest you must do yourself."

The differences between Mr. Frank and Mr. Van Daan in *The Diary of Anne Frank* far outnumber their similarities. Mr. Van Daan's selfishness endangers both families, while Mr. Frank's compassion and consideration help them all make the best of a terrible situation.

**MODEL 2**

## Two for Tea

Next to water, tea is the most popular drink worldwide. Served hot or iced, it comes in a variety of flavors to suit every taste. Yerba maté and green tea are two varieties that seem to suit the tastes of increasing numbers of people of all ages and nationalities.

Yerba maté is native to South America. Made from the dried leaves of the yerba maté tree, it is traditionally brewed in hollow gourds, which are themselves called *matés*. The gourd is filled three-quarters full with leaves, and they are then covered with hot water. When the leaves have completely absorbed the moisture, more water is added. The brewed tea is then drunk through a tube with a strainer at one end called a *bombilla*. Yerba maté is sometimes served with milk, sugar, or lemon juice to cut its slight bitterness.

Yerba maté is thought to offer many health benefits. It is loaded with antioxidants that may boost

**Comparison words and phrases**

**Subject**

**Contrast words and phrases**

**Subject**

**Contrast words and phrases**

**Subjects**

**Comparison words and phrases**

the immune system and help prevent cancer. It also seems to aid digestion.

Green tea, on the other hand, is native to China and was exported to Japan in about A.D. 800. Unlike yerba maté, green tea usually is brewed in teapots. Only about a teaspoonful of leaves is used per pot. The leaves are steeped for only around two minutes—much less than the soaking time for yerba maté. Green tea has a very mild taste and generally is served plain in ceramic cups so the delicate taste can be savored.

**Contrast words and phrases**

Like yerba maté, green tea also is beneficial to health. Similarly rich in antioxidants, it has been reputed to lower cholesterol and blood sugar and also to relieve the pain of arthritis. So, the next time you have tea for two, try one of these two popular drinks—yerba maté and green tea.

**Comparison words and phrases**

### PRACTICE AND APPLY

Refer to the preceding models to answer the following questions:

1. Which model is organized by points of comparison? Which model is organized by subject?

2. For each model, list three words or phrases that signal comparisons or contrasts.

3. Identify two points in each model that the writer compares or contrasts.

4. Make a Venn diagram or compare-and-contrast graphic to show the similarities and differences in one of the models.

### 3.5 PROBLEM-SOLUTION ORGANIZATION

**Problem-solution organization** is a pattern of organization in which a problem is stated and analyzed and then one or more solutions are proposed and examined. This pattern of organization is often used in persuasive writing, such as editorials or proposals.

## Strategies for Reading

- Look for an explanation of the problem in the first or second paragraph.

- Look for words such as *problem* and *reason* that may signal an explanation of the problem.

- To find the solution, ask: What suggestion does the writer offer to solve the problem?

- Look for words such as *propose, conclude,* and *answer* that may signal a solution.

**MODEL**

Teachers, administrators, school board members, and parents have begun expressing concerns that the foreign language students aren't getting enough practice using their languages in conversation.

Students read dialogues from their textbooks and respond to questions. They also use the language lab to get more practice speaking the language. The facilities are limited, though, and have to be used after school, which conflicts with other activities. Also, the language lab doesn't give them real-life experience with using the new language to listen to others, either.

One solution to this problem would be to establish language tables in the lunchroom. Students taking a given language would eat lunch at a specific table one day a week. For that time, they would speak only the foreign language.

This plan has several advantages. First, it doesn't require any additional equipment, staff, or materials. Second, it wouldn't take time away from other classes or activities. Language students have to eat lunch just like everyone else, so why not make it an enjoyable learning experience?

Setting up language tables would let students supplement their language skills while nourishing their bodies. That's a recipe for success!

### PRACTICE AND APPLY

Reread the model and then answer the following questions:

1. According to the model, what is the cause of the problem?

2. What solution does the writer offer? What words are a clue?

# 4 Reading Informational Texts: Forms

Magazines, newspapers, Web pages, and consumer, public, and workplace documents are all examples of informational materials. To understand and analyze informational texts, pay attention to text features and patterns of organization.

## 4.1 READING A FEATURE ARTICLE

Because people often skim newspapers, newspaper publishers use devices to attract attention to articles. **Feature articles** usually address a single human-interest or lifestyle topic in-depth.

### Strategies for Reading

**A** Notice whether **text** or **graphic aids** attract your attention at first glance.

**B** Read the **title** and other **headings** to find out more about the article's topic and organization.

**C** Notice whether the article has a **byline,** a line naming the author.

**D** A **caption** accompanying a graphic aid may provide information that adds to the meaning of the article.

### PRACTICE AND APPLY

1. Who wrote this article?

2. What do your learn from the photograph and caption?

3. When was this birthday tribute to Poe started? By whom?

---

**MODEL: FEATURE ARTICLE**

Source: *The Washington Times*

## **B** Birthday Ritual a Grave Tradition

### New figure brings tribute to Poe

A raven on the top of Poe's grave recalls his famous poem.

**C** by Roger J. Hansen

BALTIMORE—A black-clad stranger carried on the half-century tradition here of placing three red roses and something to drink at the grave of Edgar Allan Poe in a pre-dawn visit on Jan. 19.

Because he was dressed in ordinary street clothes, the man slipped in unrecognized past two dozen people who had gathered at 3 A.M. at Westminster Church to watch the ritual.

Beginning in 1949, one man—his identity unknown—visited the grave on the poet and author's birthday. In recent years, a new man, dressed in black and wearing a hat, has sneaked into the small graveyard tucked in downtown Baltimore. . . .

Martha Womack, a high school literature teacher in Farmville, Va., was as thrilled to see the tribute this year as in her three prior visits.

"It's one of those mysteries we just don't want to lose," she said. "Every year it's a little bit different."

Ms. Womack said, "I think people are still interested in him because of the mystery surrounding his life and his death.". . .

And what would Poe make of the curious birthday tradition?

"He would love it," Ms. Womack said, her eyes lighting up. "Without a doubt, he would love it because he didn't get the attention he deserved in life. But he gets it now."

## 4.2 READING A TEXTBOOK

Each textbook that you use has its own system of organization based on the content in the book. Often an introductory unit will explain the book's organization and special features. If your textbook has such a unit, read it first.

### Strategies for Reading

**(A)** Before you begin reading the lesson or chapter, read any **questions** that appear at the beginning or end of it. Then use the questions to set your purpose for reading.

**(B)** Read slowly and carefully to better understand and remember the ideas presented in the text. When you come to an unfamiliar word, first try to figure out its meaning from **context clues.** If necessary, find the meaning of the word in a **glossary** in the textbook, or in a dictionary. Avoid interrupting your reading by constantly looking up words in a dictionary.

*For more information on context clues and glossaries, see the **Vocabulary and Spelling Handbook,** pages R68 and R74.*

**(C)** Use the book's special features, such as sidebars, to increase your understanding of the text. A **sidebar** is a short presentation of additional information. It is usually set off in a box on the page.

**(D)** Take notes as you read. Use text features such as **subheadings** and boldfaced terms to help you organize your notes. Record your notes in graphic organizers, such as cause-effect diagrams, to help you clarify relationships among ideas.

**MODEL: TEXTBOOK PAGE**

### Early Human Culture

**(A)** **ESSENTIAL QUESTION** What kind of culture did early humans create?

What sets humans apart from other creatures? Art, language, and religion are special to humans and help create their culture.

**(D)** **Language** Human language probably developed as a result of the need for people to work together. One theory suggests that the need for cooperation during the hunt spurred language development. Hunters needed to be able to talk to one another in order to outsmart, trap, and kill animals for food. Another theory suggests that the cooperation needed to gather and share food led to the development of language.

**(D)** **Religion** Religion is the worship of God, gods, or spirits. Early humans probably believed that everything in nature, including rocks, trees, and animals, had a spirit. Some archaeologists believe that early cave paintings of animals were made to honor the spirits of animals killed for food.

**Comparisons Across Cultures**

**(C)** **Prehistoric Cave Art**

Prehistoric people in different parts of the world painted scenes on cave walls. Such rock paintings are among the oldest art in the world.

The cave art on the top was done by a Native American artist in Utah. The painting shows a holy man holding a snake. Snakes were seen as links between the human and underground worlds.

The painting at the bottom was done by an Australian Aboriginal artist. It shows a dreamtime spirit. Dreamtime is a supernatural past in which ancestor spirits shaped the natural world.

**SKILLBUILDER**
**INTERPRETING VISUALS**
**Making Inferences** What do these examples tell you about early human art? On the basis of their art, how important does religion seem to have been in the lives of prehistoric peoples?

54 • Chapter 2

### PRACTICE AND APPLY

Reread the textbook page and answer the following questions:

1. Which subheading does the sidebar relate to?

2. What is a possible relationship between art and religion?

3. What is the answer to the Essential Question?

## 4.3 READING A CONSUMER DOCUMENT

**Consumer documents** are printed materials that accompany products and services. They usually provide information about the use, care, operation, or assembly of the products they accompany. Some common consumer documents are contracts, warranties, manuals, instructions, and schedules.

### Strategies for Reading

**A** Read the **heading** to see what information the document covers. Read the **subheadings** to learn what process each section of the instructions explains.

**B** Read the directions all the way through at least once.

**C** Look for **numbers** or **letters** that indicate the order in which the steps should be followed.

**D** If there is an **illustration** or **diagram,** try to match the words in the instructions to words or symbols in the graphic aid.

**E** Look for **verbs that describe actions** you should take, such as *turn, separate, place,* and *twist.*

---

**PRACTICE AND APPLY**

Read the assembly instructions and warranty for the portable kennel and the pet adoption contract. Then answer the following questions:

1. Which text features are found in the instructions but not in the contract?

2. What action should you take if the kennel is used frequently?

3. Why would someone not request a free replacement if his or her dog destroyed the kennel door?

4. What should you do if you have to find another home for your adopted animal?

---

**MODEL: ASSEMBLY INSTRUCTIONS AND WARRANTY**

# A Friend Fur Good  Puppy Kennel

**ASSEMBLY INSTRUCTIONS** **A**
The kennel consists of three parts:
(1) plastic top section; (2) plastic bottom section; (3) steel door.

**TO ASSEMBLE KENNEL** **A**
1. Separate the two kennel halves.
2. Turn bottom half of kennel over and place flat side on floor. Place top half of kennel onto the bottom half and align pieces.
3. Hold top section as shown and place metal door in opening so ends of hinge and latch rods fit in holes (A). Lower top section so hinge and latch rod fit into holes (B).
4. Secure the two halves together with the 8 kennel body fasteners. Place kennel body fastener in hole and turn. Fasteners are now in the locked position. Check the locks periodically to ensure that they are tightly fastened.

**D**
**E**

> LIMITED ONE-YEAR WARRANTY Warranted for one year from date of retail purchase against defects in material and workmanship.
>
> COVERED: Replacement of defective parts and labor, and product return to consumer.
>
> NOT COVERED: Damages caused by abuse or failure to perform normal maintenance. This warranty shall not apply to any defect or malfunction caused by damage due to unreasonable use.

---

**MODEL: CONTRACT**

# PET ADOPTION CONTRACT **A**

The Adopter agrees to adopt the following animal (referred to here as "Animal") from A Friend Fur Good Animal Shelters:

Name/Breed_____ Age_____
Color/Markings_____ Sex_____

As Adopter, I agree to the following:
1. To allow a representative of A Friend Fur Good Animal Shelters to visit my premises to ensure the terms of this agreement have been kept.
2. The Animal will be provided with adequate fresh food and water, clean, dry shelter when outside, and daily exercise.
3. To provide a safe collar with rabies and I.D. tags to be worn at all times.
4. To adopt the Animal only as a personal pet/companion and not as a guard dog.
5. If it becomes necessary to find the Animal another home, the Friend Fur Good Shelter will be contacted and the Animal shall be returned to them.

As Adopter, I accept full responsibility for the care of this animal, and I release A Friend Fur Good Animal Shelter and its representatives of any liability from this date forward.

This adoption contract is entered into this _____ day of _____, 2006, between A Friend Fur Good Animal Shelters and

Adopter's Full Name _____
Address_____
City, State, Zip_____
Home Phone_____ Work Phone_____

## 4.4 READING A PUBLIC DOCUMENT

**Public documents** are documents that are written for the public to provide information that is of general interest or concern. These documents are often free. They can be federal, state, or local government documents. They can be speeches or historical documents. They may even be laws, posted warnings, signs, or rules and regulations.

### Strategies for Reading

**A** Read the **title** to find out what the notice is about.

**B** Look for **subheadings** that indicate what categories of information are being discussed.

**C** Pay attention to **bulleted lists.** These show individual details of equal importance.

**MODEL: PUBLIC DOCUMENT**

**A** **Patron Code of Conduct**

A "Code of Conduct" is published to ensure that all users of the library can experience a pleasant and productive environment for study and research. Misuse of the library, whether by theft, mutilation, or vandalism of library materials or property, or by interference with the study and research of library users, shows disrespect for the institution and disregard of the rights of other patrons.

**B** **Examples of Unacceptable Behavior:**
- Disruptive behavior such as rowdiness, running, noise, vandalism, or such behavior that interferes with the normal use of the library.
**C**
- Harassment of library staff or other patrons.
- Entering an unauthorized area, remaining in the library after closing or when requested to leave during emergency situations.
- Mutilation of library materials by marking, underlining, removal of pages, removing electronic theft detection devices or in any way defacing library property.
- Removal of library materials without authorization.
- Tampering with or intentionally damaging computer hardware, software, printer, operating systems or other associated equipment.
- Smoking, consumption of food, and the use of smokeless tobacco within the library.
- Refusal to abide by library regulations regarding return of materials and payment of fines.
- Entering the library with uncovered beverages.

**In Addition:**
- Children under the age of eight may not be left unattended.
- Furniture may not be rearranged.
- Cellular phone usage is limited to the first floor vestibule.
- All users must comply with library policies, federal, state and local laws.

**PRACTICE AND APPLY**

Refer to the public notice to answer the following questions:

1. Where are cell phones permitted in the library?

2. Can you mark or highlight interesting passages in a book you have checked out?

3. If you are entering the library and you have an open bottle of soda, what should you do?

## 4.5 READING A WORKPLACE DOCUMENT

**Workplace documents** are materials that are produced or used within a workplace, usually to aid in the functioning of a business. These may be documents generated by a business to monitor itself, such as minutes of a meeting or a sales report. These documents may also explain company policies, organizational structures, and operating procedures. Workplace documents include memos, business letters, job applications, and résumés.

### Strategies for Reading

Ⓐ Read the **heading** in an e-mail or the **letterhead** in a business letter to determine the sender, the person who received it, and the date it was sent.

Ⓑ When reading an e-mail, check the **subject line** to identify what topics the e-mail will discuss.

Ⓒ Read the document slowly and carefully, as it may contain details that should not be overlooked.

Ⓓ Notice how to contact the creator of the document. You will need this information to reply or clear up anything you don't understand.

Ⓔ Take notes to help you remember what actions are required.

**MODEL: E-MAIL**

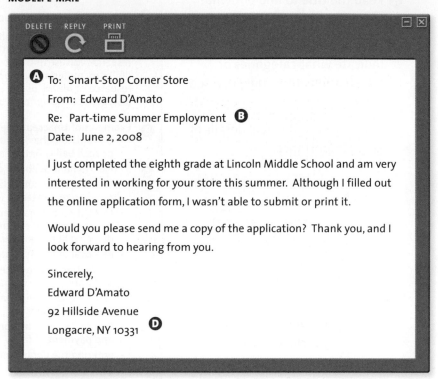

DELETE    REPLY    PRINT

Ⓐ To: Smart-Stop Corner Store
From: Edward D'Amato
Re: Part-time Summer Employment  Ⓑ
Date: June 2, 2008

I just completed the eighth grade at Lincoln Middle School and am very interested in working for your store this summer. Although I filled out the online application form, I wasn't able to submit or print it.

Would you please send me a copy of the application? Thank you, and I look forward to hearing from you.

Sincerely,
Edward D'Amato
92 Hillside Avenue
Longacre, NY 10331  Ⓓ

---

### PRACTICE AND APPLY

Read the business e-mail and letter and answer the following questions:

1. Why did Edward D'Amato write his e-mail?

2. What action does he want the store to take?

3. According to Darcie Grey's letter, what should Edward do if he doesn't receive the application forms within three working days?

**MODEL: BUSINESS LETTER**

Ⓐ Smart-Stop Corner Store
45 Blue Hill Avenue
Longacre, NY 10331

Edward D'Amato
92 Hillside Avenue
Longacre, NY 10331

June 3, 2008

Dear Edward:

I'm very sorry about the trouble you had using our website. Our main office will send you an application and instructions for completing and submitting it. If you don't receive these items within three working days, you can pick up the forms at the address shown above.

Yours Truly,
*Darcie Grey*
Darcie Grey, Manager

## 4.6 READING ELECTRONIC TEXT

**Electronic text** is any text that is in a form that a computer can store and display on a screen. Electronic text can be part of Web pages, CD-ROMs, search engines, and documents that you create with your computer software. Like books, Web pages often provide aids for finding information. However, each Web page is designed differently, and information is not in the same location on each page. It is important to know the functions of different parts of a Web page so that you can easily find the information you want.

### Strategies for Reading

**Ⓐ** Look at the **title** of a page to determine what topics it covers.

**Ⓑ** For an online source, such as a Web page or search engine, note the **Web address,** known as a **URL** (Universal Resource Locator). You may want to make a note of it in case you need to return to the page later.

**Ⓒ** Look for a **menu bar** along the top, bottom, or side of a Web page. Clicking on an item in a menu bar will take you to another part of the Web site.

**Ⓓ** Notice any hyperlinks to related pages. **Hyperlinks** are often underlined or highlighted in a contrasting color. You can click on a hyperlink to get to another page—one that may or may not have been created by the same person or organization.

**Ⓔ** For information that you want to keep for future reference, save documents on your computer or print them. For online sources, you can pull down the **Favorites** or **Bookmarks** menu and bookmark pages so that you can easily return to them. Printing the pages you need will allow you to highlight key ideas on a hard copy.

**MODEL: WEB PAGE**

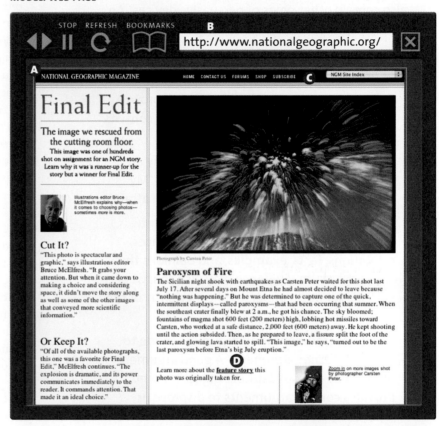

### PRACTICE AND APPLY

1. What is the URL of this Web page?

2. Which hyperlinks would you click on to find further information about the photograph?

3. How could you find information about subscribing to *National Geographic* magazine?

# 5 Reading Persuasive Texts

## 5.1 ANALYZING AN ARGUMENT

An **argument** expresses a position on an issue or problem and supports it with reasons and evidence. Being able to analyze and evaluate arguments will help you distinguish between claims you should accept and those you should not. A sound argument should appeal strictly to reason. However, arguments are often used in texts that also contain other types of persuasive devices. An argument includes the following elements:

- A **claim** is the writer's position on an issue or problem.

- **Support** is any material that serves to prove a claim. In an argument, support usually consists of reasons and evidence.

- **Reasons** are declarations made to justify an action, decision, or belief. For example: "My reason for walking so quickly is that I'm afraid I'll be late for class."

- **Evidence** consists of the specific references, quotations, facts, examples, and opinions that support a claim. Evidence may also consist of statistics, reports of personal experience, or the views of experts.

- A **counterargument** is an argument made to oppose another argument. A good argument anticipates the opposition's objections and provides counterarguments to disprove or answer them.

| Claim | I need a larger allowance. |
|---|---|
| Reason | I don't have enough money to pay for my school lunches, fees, and transportation. |
| Evidence | I had to borrow money from my friend two weeks in a row to buy lunch. |
| Counterargument | My parents say I just need to budget my allowance better, but they don't realize what my expenses are. |

Read the following book review and use a chart like the one shown to identify the claim, reason, evidence, and counterargument.

### Hatchet
#### Reviewed by Kristen Loos

What would you do if you suddenly found yourself in the middle of a wilderness with no one else around and only a hatchet to help you survive? That's what happens to Brian Robeson, a boy about my age, in Gary Paulsen's book *Hatchet.* Even if this sounds like a situation you'll never be in, *Hatchet* is worth reading for what it says about facing your fears.

After his parents get a divorce, Brian heads up to northern Canada to spend the summer with his dad. But the pilot flying the airplane has a heart attack, and Brian is forced to crash-land it by himself. From then on, he has to take charge of the situation, or he won't live to tell about it.

From the beginning all the way to the end of the book, Brian faces big problems just to survive. He's a city kid, so he's used to opening up the refrigerator any time he wants to eat. Now, at the edge of the woods, he has to figure out things like how to be safe from wild animals and how to make a fire without matches. At first, he panics. He doesn't even know what to drink or how to find and prepare food. Even so, he doesn't give up.

One of the things I like about the book is how Brian changes. At first, he hopes he will be rescued very soon. He thinks he can hold out for a few days until his parents or a search party finds him. During this part of the book, he starts to think things out for himself. But he still gets scared easily and feels sorry for himself a lot.

Then, when a plane flies over without seeing him, he realizes that he is really on his own. He learns to make tools to fish and hunt with and to depend on himself for everything he needs. In the end, he is able to confront all kinds of dangers and still hold out hope for himself. To him, this is "tough hope."

Some readers may not like the book because they think this is an unusual situation that most people will never have to face. I don't agree, though, because I think the real message is not just about being lost in the wilderness, but about bravely dealing with whatever challenges we face in our lives.

I'm not going to spoil the book for you by saying how it ends or whether Brian gets rescued. Read it yourself for an exciting adventure and some good lessons about surviving in the wilderness. I hope you enjoy it as much as I did.

## 5.2 RECOGNIZING PERSUASIVE TECHNIQUES

Persuasive texts typically rely on more than just the **logical appeal** of an argument to be convincing. They also rely on ethical and emotional appeals and other **persuasive techniques**—devices that can convince you to adopt a position or take an action.

**Ethical appeals** establish a writer's credibility and trustworthiness with an audience. When a writer links a claim to a widely accepted value, the writer not only gains moral support for that claim but also establishes himself or herself as a reputable, moral person readers can and should trust. For example, with the following appeal, the writer reminds readers of a value they should accept and suggests that if they share this value, then they should support the writer's position: "Most of us agree that we should protect our natural resources, but we don't invest enough time or money to preserve them."

The chart shown here explains several other means by which a writer may attempt to sway you to adopt his or her position. Learn to recognize these techniques, and you are less likely to be influenced by them.

| Persuasive Technique | Example |
|---|---|
| **Appeals by Association** | |
| **Bandwagon appeal** Suggests that a person should believe or do something because "everyone else" does | Join the millions of health-conscious people who've made Wonder Water their beverage of choice! |
| **Testimonial** Relies on endorsements from well-known people or satisfied customers | Now you can send your game over the top with Macon Ace—the racket designed and used by tennis legend Sonja Macon. |
| **Snob appeal** Taps into people's desire to be special or part of an elite group | The best deserve only the best—you deserve Beautiful Bubbles bath soap. |
| **Appeal to loyalty** Relies on people's affiliation with a particular group | Support the PTA and stand up for increased school funding. |
| **Emotional Appeals** | |
| **Appeals to pity, fear, or vanity** Use strong feelings, rather than facts, to persuade | Why go unnoticed when Pretty Face can make you the center of attention? |
| **Word Choice** | |
| **Glittering generality** A generalization that includes a word or phrase with positive connotations, to promote a product, person, or idea. | A vote for our candidate is a vote for honesty, integrity, and accountability. |

Identify the persuasive techniques used in this model.

### Face the Truth

Every thinking human being should be required to see *An Inconvenient Truth*. Featuring former Vice President Al Gore, this fact-filled, frightening, yet entertaining movie critically examines global temperature changes. It highlights Mr. Gore's extensive research and lobbying about this issue and is backed up by expert testimonies, statistics, graphs, and photographs.

This is a rare and important film that tells it like it is—and it isn't pretty. For starters, if we don't make changes soon, in less than 45 years, a million species of living things could become extinct. Far from being a statement of doom, though, the movie ends with a detailed list of steps each of us can take to help save our planet. If you consider yourself an aware, concerned citizen, you must see this movie!

## 5.3 ANALYZING LOGIC AND REASONING

While persuasive techniques may sway you to side with a writer, they should not be enough to convince you that an argument is sound. To determine the soundness of an argument, you really need to examine the argument's claim and support and the logic or reasoning that links them. To do this, it is helpful to identify the writer's mode of reasoning.

## The Inductive Mode of Reasoning

When a writer leads from specific evidence to a general principle or generalization, that writer is using **inductive reasoning.** A writer may even choose to organize all of the information in a text inductively—for example, the writer may present three paragraphs of evidence, followed by one paragraph explaining his or her conclusion. Here is an example of inductive reasoning.

**SPECIFIC FACTS**

**Fact 1** Wind and water wear away rocks over time.

**Fact 2** Earthquakes and volcanoes create immediate and drastic changes in the land.

**Fact 3** The slow movement of the continents and spreading of the sea floor create new landforms.

**GENERALIZATION**

Natural forces continually change the surface of the earth.

### Strategies for Determining the Soundness of Inductive Arguments

Ask yourself the following questions to evaluate an inductive argument:

- **Is the evidence valid and sufficient support for the conclusion?** Inaccurate facts lead to inaccurate conclusions.

- **Does the conclusion follow logically from the evidence?** From the facts listed above, the conclusion that Earth's *core* as well as its surface are constantly changing would be too broad.

- **Is the evidence drawn from a large enough sample?** These three facts are enough to support the claim. If you wanted to claim that these are the *only* forces that cause change, you would need more facts.

## The Deductive Mode of Reasoning

When a writer arrives at a conclusion by applying a general principle to a specific situation, the writer is using **deductive reasoning.** If a writer wishes to organize a text deductively, he or she may begin by stating a claim and then give evidence supporting the claim. Here's an example of deductive reasoning.

| Driving a car requires complete concentration. | General principle or premise |

| Talking on a cell phone divides the driver's attention. | Specific situation |

| People shouldn't talk on the phone while driving. | Specific conclusion |

### Strategies for Determining the Soundness of Deductive Arguments

Ask yourself the following questions to evaluate a deductive argument:

- **Is the general principle actually stated, or is it implied?** Note that writers often use deductive reasoning in arguments without stating the general principles. They just assume that readers will recognize and agree with the principles. So you may want to identify the general principle for yourself.

- **Is the general principle sound?** Don't just assume the general principle is sound. Ask yourself whether it is really true.

- **Is the conclusion valid?** To be valid, a conclusion in a deductive argument must follow logically from the general principle and the specific situation.

The following chart shows two conclusions drawn from the same general principle.

| All spiders have eight legs. | |
| --- | --- |
| **Accurate Deduction** | **Inaccurate Deduction** |
| The black widow is a spider, therefore it has eight legs. | An octopus has eight legs, therefore it is a spider. |

An octopus has eight legs, but it belongs to a different category of animals than the spider.

### PRACTICE AND APPLY

Identify the mode of reasoning used in the following paragraph.

> People do the most unexpected things. The other day when I was waiting at the stoplight on my bike, I noticed that the car in front of me was in the right lane and had its right turn signal on. Wouldn't you have assumed, just like I did, that the driver was going to turn right? Well, I was wrong, and you probably would've been, too. As soon as the light turned green, the car swerved across two lanes and turned left.
>
> Then there was the surprise birthday party the neighborhood kids and I had for one of our friends. We'd managed to keep it a secret, so we all expected her to be really surprised and pleased. Instead, she was upset because she wasn't dressed properly for a party and was embarrassed at being caught off-guard.
>
> I've finally learned to stop making assumptions about how other people will act. Now that seems like a logical thing to do!

## Identifying Faulty Reasoning

Sometimes an argument at first appears to make sense but isn't valid because it is based on a fallacy. A **fallacy** is an error in logic. Learn to recognize these common fallacies.

| TYPE OF FALLACY | DEFINITION | EXAMPLE |
|---|---|---|
| **Circular reasoning** | Supporting a statement by simply repeating it in different words | My mother is always busy because **she has too much to do.** |
| **Either/or fallacy** | A statement that suggests that there are only two choices available in a situation that really offers more than two options | **Either** I grow two inches this summer **or** I'll never make any friends at my new school. |
| **Oversimplification** | An explanation of a complex situation or problem as if it were much simpler than it is | **All you have to do to get good grades** is listen carefully in class. |
| **Overgeneralization** | A generalization that is too broad. You can often recognize overgeneralizations by the use of words such as *all, everyone, every time, anything, no one,* and *none*. | **Nobody** has as many chores as I do. |
| **Hasty generalization** | A conclusion drawn from too little evidence or from evidence that is biased | I sneezed after taking a bite of the salad, so **I must be allergic to something in it.** |
| **Stereotyping** | A dangerous type of overgeneralization. Stereotypes are broad statements about people on the basis of their gender, ethnicity, race, or political, social, professional, or religious group. | **Artists are emotional** and hard to get along with. |
| **Attacking the person or name-calling** | An attempt to discredit an idea by attacking the person or group associated with it. Candidates often engage in name-calling during political campaigns. | Only **selfish** people don't do volunteer work. |
| **Evading the issue** | Responding to an objection with arguments and evidence that do not address its central point | I forgot to get the milk, **but dairy products are hard to digest anyway.** |
| **False cause** | The mistake of assuming that because one event occurred after another event, the first event caused the second one to occur | It rained this afternoon, **because I left my umbrella at home.** |
| *Non sequitur* | A conclusion that does not follow logically from the "proof" offered to support it | Mrs. Lewis will make Steve the baseball team captain. **He is already the captain of the volleyball team.** |

Look for examples of logical fallacies in the following argument. Identify each one and explain why you identified it as such.

> Store clerks are so rude. A cashier was impatient with me in the supermarket the other day because I bought too much yogurt. They must train the employees to treat customers that way so more people will use the self-checkout lines. I need to budget more money for groceries.

### 5.4 EVALUATING PERSUASIVE TEXTS

Learning how to evaluate persuasive texts and identify bias will help you become more selective when doing research and also help you improve your own reasoning and arguing skills.

#### Strategies for Identifying Bias

**Bias** is an inclination for or against a particular opinion or viewpoint. A writer may reveal a strongly positive or negative bias on an issue by presenting only one way of looking at it or by heavily weighting the evidence on one side of the argument. The presence of the following is often a sign that a writer is biased:

- **unfairly weighted evidence,** which is weak or unproven evidence that a writer treats as more important or influential than it really is

- **loaded language,** which consists of words with strongly positive or negative connotations that are intended to influence a reader's attitude

EXAMPLE: *At the* Village Star, *we bring you the most relevant, up-to-the-minute news.* (Someone who works for the paper is making the claim. *Relevant* and *up-to-the-minute* have very positive connotations.)

#### Strategies for Identifying Propaganda

**Propaganda** is any form of communication that is so distorted that it conveys false or misleading information. Some politicians create and distribute propaganda. Logical fallacies such as name-calling, the either/or fallacy, and false causes are often used in propaganda. The following example shows false cause. The writer uses one fact to support a particular point of view but does not reveal another fact that does not support that viewpoint.

EXAMPLE: *Since Jack Carter was elected mayor, unemployment has decreased by 25%.* (The writer does not mention that it was the previous mayor, not Jack Carter, who was responsible for bringing in the new factory that provides the extra jobs.)

*For more information on logical fallacies, see **Identifying Faulty Reasoning,** page R24.*

### Strategies for Evaluating Evidence

It is important to have a set of standards by which you can evaluate persuasive texts. Use the questions below to help you critically assess facts and opinions that are presented as evidence.

- **Are the presented facts verifiable?** Facts can be proved by eyewitness accounts, authoritative sources such as encyclopedias and almanacs, experts, or research.

- **Are the presented opinions well informed?** Any opinions offered should be supported by facts, be based on research or eyewitness accounts, or be the opinions of experts on the topic.

- **Is the evidence thorough?** Thorough evidence leaves no reasonable questions unanswered. If a choice is offered, background for making the choice should also be provided. If taking a side is called for, all sides of the issue should be presented.

- **Is the evidence balanced?** Be alert to evidence that is weighted unfairly and contains loaded language or other signs of bias.

- **Is the evidence authoritative?** The people, groups, or organizations that provided the evidence should have credentials that support their authority.

- **Is it important that the evidence be current?** Where timeliness is crucial, as in the areas of medicine and technology, the evidence should reflect the latest developments in the areas.

Read the argument below. Identify the facts, opinions, and elements of bias.

Ultra Bars are the tastiest and most efficient way to get your daily requirement of important nutrients. Our bodies need a well-balanced combination of protein, carbohydrates, fats, vitamins, minerals, and trace elements to function most effectively and make us feel our best. The ingredients in Ultra Bars have been chosen in the perfect proportion to ensure you get the maximum benefit. Best of all, they taste terrific. And they aren't just for athletes—ordinary people should carry these bars with them, too, for a quick boost throughout the day!

## Strategies for Determining a Strong Argument

Make sure that all or most of the following statements are true:

- The argument presents a claim or thesis.

- The claim is connected to its support by a general principle that most readers would readily agree with. Valid general principle: *Doing your best will bring you personal pride.* Invalid general principle: *Doing your best will bring you success.*

- The reasons make sense.

- The reasons are presented in a logical and effective order.

- The claim and all reasons are adequately supported by sound evidence.

- The evidence is adequate, accurate, and appropriate.

- The logic is sound. There are no instances of faulty reasoning.

- The argument adequately anticipates and addresses readers' concerns and counterclaims with counterarguments.

Use the preceding criteria to evaluate the strength of the following proposal.

MODEL

**Summary of Proposal**

I propose that the city government create a park on the unused plot of land at the edge of town.

**Need**

We must preserve the natural beauty of the area for all to appreciate and enjoy.

**Proposed Solution**

The five-acre plot of land on the south side of town is now being considered for improvement.

Some people want to sell the land to a building developer. They say that doing this would be profitable for the town and also provide good housing for new residents.

It's true that the town could make money by developing the land. A park could also be a source of income, however.

The park would generate income in a number of ways. It could charge a small admission fee for summer concerts and other events. It also could lease the space to neighboring communities for their gatherings and to local food concessions and special-interest groups.

The cost of creating and maintaining a park is less than what it would bring in. Community groups already have agreed to donate plants, provide volunteers to landscape and take care of the grounds, create gazebos, and install benches, water fountains, and trashcans.

Without a park, we can't ensure the safety and health of our residents. It would have playgrounds and areas to bike, skate, picnic, and walk or jog. Unlike commercial and even residential buildings, parks do not encourage vandalism and graffiti. The chief of police has confirmed that parks are easier to supervise, too, because it isn't as hard to police them.

No one who cares about our community could fail to see how important it is to create this park.

# 6 Adjusting Reading Rate to Purpose

You may need to change the way you read certain texts in order to understand what you read. To adjust the way you read, you first need to be aware of what you want to get out of the text. Then you can adjust the speed at which you read in response to your purpose and the difficulty of the material.

## Determine Your Purpose for Reading

You read different types of materials for different purposes. You may read a novel for enjoyment. You may read a textbook unit to learn a new concept or to master the content for a test. When you read for enjoyment, you naturally read at a pace that is comfortable for you. When you read for information, you need to read more slowly and thoroughly. When you are being tested on material, you may think you have to read fast, especially if the test is being timed. However, you can actually increase your understanding of the material if you slow down.

## Determine Your Reading Rate

The rate at which you read most comfortably is called your **independent reading level.** It is the rate that you use to read materials that you enjoy. To learn to adjust your reading rate to read materials for other purposes, you need to be aware of your independent reading level. You can figure out your reading level by following these steps:

1. Select a passage from a book or story you enjoy.
2. Have a friend or classmate time you as you begin reading the passage silently.
3. Read at the rate that is most comfortable for you.
4. Stop when your friend or classmate tells you one minute has passed.
5. Determine the number of words you read in that minute and write down the number.
6. Repeat the process at least two more times, using different passages.
7. Add the numbers and divide the sum by the number of times your friend timed you.

## Reading Techniques for Informational Material

You can use the following techniques to adapt your reading for informational texts, to prepare for tests, and to better understand what you read:

- **Skimming** is reading quickly to get the general idea of a text. To skim, read only the title, headings, graphic aids, highlighted words, and first sentence of each paragraph. Also, read any introduction, conclusion, or summary. Skimming can be especially useful when taking a test. Before reading a passage, you can skim the questions that follow it in order to find out what is expected. This will help you focus on the important ideas in the text.

    When researching a topic, skimming can help you decide whether a source has information related to your topic. This will save time.

- **Scanning** is reading quickly to find a specific piece of information, such as a fact or a definition. When you scan, your eyes sweep across a page, looking for key words that may lead you to the information you want. Use scanning to review for tests and to find answers to questions.

- **Changing pace** is speeding up or slowing down the rate at which you read parts of a particular text. When you come across explanations of familiar concepts, you might be able to speed up without misunderstanding them. When you encounter unfamiliar concepts or material presented in an unpredictable way, however, you may need to slow down to understand the information.

**WATCH OUT!** Reading too slowly can affect your ability to understand what you read. Make sure you aren't just reading one word at a time. Practice reading phrases.

### PRACTICE AND APPLY

Find an article in a magazine or textbook. Skim the article. Then answer the following questions:

1. What did you notice about the organization of the article from skimming it?
2. What is the main idea of the article?

*Writing is a process through which you can explore your thoughts, experiment with ideas, and make connections. Through writing, you can record your thoughts, feelings, and ideas for yourself alone or you can choose to communicate them to an audience.*

**WRITING TOOLS**
Go to the **Writing Center** at **ClassZone.com** for interactive models, publishing ideas, and other support.

# 1 The Writing Process

The writing process consists of the following stages: prewriting, drafting, revising and editing, proofreading, and publishing. These are not stages that you must complete in a set order. Rather, you may return to an earlier stage at any time to improve your writing.

## 1.1 PREWRITING

In the prewriting stage, you explore what you want to write about, what your purpose for writing is, whom you are writing for, and what form you will use to express your ideas. Ask yourself the following questions to get started.

| Topic | • Is my topic assigned, or can I choose it?<br>• What would I be interested in writing about? |
|---|---|
| Purpose | • Am I writing to entertain, to inform, to persuade, or for some combination of these purposes?<br>• What effect do I want to have on my readers? |
| Audience | • Who is the audience?<br>• What might the audience members already know about my topic?<br>• What about the topic might interest them? |
| Format | • Which format will work best? Letter? Essay? Poem? Speech? Memoir? Short story? Article? Editorial? Review? Research paper? Instructions? |

### Find Ideas for Writing

• Look at magazines, newspapers, and Web sites.

• Start a log of articles you want to save for future reference.

• With a group, brainstorm as many ideas as you can. Compile your ideas into a list.

• Write down anything that comes into your head.

• Interview someone who is an expert on a particular topic.

• Use a graphic organizer, such as a cluster map, to explore secondary ideas related to a topic.

### Organize Ideas

Once you've chosen a topic, you will need to compile and organize your ideas. If you are writing a description, you may need to gather sensory details. For an essay or a research paper, you may need to record information from different sources. To record notes from sources you read or view, use any or all of these methods:

• **Summarize**—Briefly retell the main ideas of a piece of writing in your own words.

• **Paraphrase**—Restate all or almost all of the information in your own words.

• **Quote**—Record the author's exact words.

Depending on what form your writing takes, you may also need to arrange your ideas in a certain pattern.

*For more information, see the **Writing Handbook**, pages R34–R41.*

## 1.2 DRAFTING

In the drafting stage, you put your ideas on paper and allow them to develop as you write. You don't need to worry about correct grammar and spelling at this stage. There are two ways to draft:

**Discovery drafting** is a good approach when you are not sure what you think about your subject. Start writing and let your feelings and ideas lead you in developing the topic.

**Planned drafting** may work better if you know your ideas have to be arranged in a certain way, as in a research paper. Try making a writing plan or an informal outline before you begin drafting.

## 1.3 REVISING AND EDITING

The revising and editing stage allows you to polish your draft and make changes in its content, organization, and style. Asking questions will help you spot changes that would improve your work:

- Does my writing have a **main idea** or central focus? Is my thesis clear?

- Have I used **precise** nouns, verbs, and modifiers?

- Have I included **adequate details** and **evidence?** Have I left out any important information? Where might I add a vivid detail or example?

- Is my writing **unified?** Are all ideas and supporting details relevant to my main idea? Have I eliminated any repetitive information?

- Is my writing clear and **coherent?** Do sentences connect to one another smoothly and logically?

- Have I used a consistent **point of view?**

- Do I need to add **transitional words, phrases, or sentences** to explain relationships among ideas?

- Have I used a **variety of sentence types?** Are they well constructed? What sentences might I combine to improve the rhythm of my writing?

- Have I used a **tone** appropriate for my audience and purpose? Would informal or formal English be more appropriate?

## 1.4 PROOFREADING

After revising your paper, proofread it for mistakes. Ask the following questions:

- Have I corrected any errors in **subject-verb agreement** and **pronoun-antecedent agreement?**

- Have I checked for errors in **possessive forms** and in the **comparative and superlative forms** of adjectives and adverbs?

- Have I checked for errors in **confusing word pairs**, such as *it's/its, than/then,* and *too/to?*

- Have I corrected any **run-on sentences** and **sentence fragments?**

- Have I followed rules for **correct capitalization** and **punctuation marks?**

- Have I checked the dictionary for the **spellings of unfamiliar words?**

**TIP** If possible, don't begin proofreading right after you finish writing. Put your work away for at least a few hours. When you return to it, you will find it easier to identify and correct mistakes.

Use the proofreading symbols in the chart to mark changes on your draft.

*For more information, see the **Grammar Handbook** and the **Vocabulary and Spelling Handbook**, pages R46–R77.*

| Proofreading Symbols | |
|---|---|
| ∧ Add letters or words. | / Make a capital letter lowercase. |
| ⊙ Add a period. | ⌶ Begin a new paragraph. |
| ≡ Capitalize a letter. | ↗ Delete letters or words. |
| ⊃ Close up space. | ∿ Switch the positions of letters or words. |
| ∧ Add a comma. | |

## 1.5 PUBLISHING AND REFLECTING

Always consider sharing your finished writing with a wider audience. Reflecting on your writing is another good way to finish a project.

**Publishing Ideas**

- Post your writing on a Weblog.

- Create a multimedia presentation and share it with classmates.

- Publish your writing in a school newspaper, local newspaper, or literary magazine.

- Present your work orally in a report, speech, reading, or dramatic performance.

**Reflecting on Your Writing**

Think about your writing process and whether you will add what you have written to your portfolio. You might ask yourself questions like these:

- Which parts of the process did I find easiest?

- What problems did I face during the writing process? How did I solve the problems?

- What changes have occurred in my writing style?

- What features in the writing of published authors or my peers can I apply to my own work?

## 1.6 PEER RESPONSE

Peer response consists of the suggestions and comments you make about the writing of your peers and also the comments and suggestions they make about your writing. You can ask a peer reader for help at any time in the writing process.

### Using Peer Response as a Writer

- Indicate whether you are more interested in feedback about your ideas or about your presentation of them.

- Ask questions that require more than yes-or-no answers. These are more likely to give you specific information you can use as you revise.

- Encourage your readers to be honest, and give them plenty of time to respond thoughtfully to your writing.

### Being a Peer Reader

- Respect the writer's feelings. Offer positive reactions first.

- Make sure you understand what kind of feedback the writer is looking for, and then respond accordingly.

*For more information on the writing process, see the* **Introductory Unit,** *pages 1–19.*

## 2 Building Blocks of Good Writing

Whatever your purpose in writing, you need to capture your reader's interest and organize your thoughts clearly.

## 2.1 INTRODUCTIONS

An introduction should capture your reader's attention. It may also include a thesis statement or introduce a main idea.

### Kinds of Introductions

There are many different ways to write an introduction. The one you choose depends on who the audience is and on your purpose for writing.

**Make a Surprising Statement** Beginning with a startling statement or an interesting fact can arouse your reader's curiosity about a subject, as in this model.

> **MODEL**
>
> Imagine something only 15 to 20 inches long dropping out of the sky at 200 miles an hour! It would be nothing but a blur. That's exactly what makes the peregrine falcon such an effective bird of prey.

**Provide a Description** A vivid description sets a mood and brings a scene to life for your reader. Here, details about how a hot air balloon works set the tone for a narrative about a balloon ride.

> **MODEL**
>
> Whoosh! The red and yellow flame shot up into the great nylon cone. The warm air filled the balloon so that the cooler air below held the apparatus aloft. A soft breeze helped to push the balloon and basket along. The four passengers hardly noticed the noise or the heat as they stared in awe at the hilly farmland below.

**Ask a Question** Beginning with a question can make your reader want to read on to find out the answer. The following introduction asks about the reader's interest in exploring new places.

> **MODEL**
>
> Have you ever wanted to explore uncharted territory? The participants of the Lewis and Clark expedition of 1804–1806 did just that. Their purpose was to map a good water route from St. Louis and the Mississippi River to the Pacific Ocean.

**Relate an Anecdote** Beginning with an anecdote, or brief story, can hook your reader and help you make a point in a dramatic way. The following anecdote introduces a story about a family trip.

> **MODEL**
>
> When I was in fifth grade, a local bank held a competition with a grand prize of a trip to the Cayman Islands. My parents entered the contest, never dreaming they would win. They also never dreamed that entering a contest would put us all smack in the middle of a hurricane.

**Address the Reader** Speaking directly to your reader establishes a friendly, informal tone and involves the reader in your topic.

> **MODEL**
>
> Show your concern for our community by supporting the campaign of Jonas Wright. Come to our next meeting at the Community Center Wednesday evening at 6:30—and bring your friends!

**Begin with a Thesis Statement** A thesis statement expressing a main idea may be woven into both the beginning and the end of a piece of nonfiction writing.

> **MODEL**
>
> There are many similarities between Mahatma Gandhi and Martin Luther King Jr. Both believed in nonviolent resistance to laws they felt were unfair. Both drew millions of people to support their causes and met tragic ends.

**TIP** To write the best introduction for your paper, you may want to try more than one of the methods and then decide which is the most effective for your purpose and audience.

## 2.2 PARAGRAPHS

A paragraph is made up of sentences that work together to develop an idea or accomplish a purpose. Whether or not it contains a topic sentence stating the main idea, a good paragraph must have unity and coherence.

### Unity

A paragraph has unity when all the sentences support and develop one stated or implied idea. Use the following technique to create unity in your writing:

**Write a Topic Sentence** A topic sentence states the main idea of the paragraph; all other sentences in the paragraph provide supporting details. A topic sentence is often the first sentence in a paragraph, as shown in the model that follows. However, it may also appear later in a paragraph to reinforce or summarize the main idea.

> **MODEL**
>
> The ability to assemble complex social structures is one of the dolphins' most remarkable qualities. Dolphins live and travel in groupings called pods. These pods often show cooperative behavior and strong social bonding—separated pod-mates will still recognize one another six months later.

**TIP** Paying attention to topic sentences when you read literature can help you craft your own topic sentences. Notice the use of topic sentences in "Kabul's Singing Sensation" on pages 918–927. For example, the third paragraph on page 922 begins, "The soulful melancholy in Mirwais' voice is the product of hard times." The rest of the paragraph then describes some of those hard times in detail.

## Coherence

A paragraph is coherent when all its sentences are related to one another and each flows logically to the next. The following techniques will help you achieve coherence in your writing:

- Present your ideas in the most logical order.
- Use pronouns, synonyms, and repeated words to connect ideas.
- Use transitional words to show relationships among ideas.

In the model shown here, the writer used several techniques to create a coherent paragraph.

> **MODEL**
>
> According to the English colonist John Smith, Pocahontas saved his life. A few years later, she was kidnapped by other colonists. While living with them, she fell in love with John Rolfe, and they were married. Later, Pocahontas, her husband, and their infant son traveled to England, where Pocahontas was introduced to the king.

## 2.3 TRANSITIONS

Transitions are words and phrases that show connections between details. Clear transitions help show how your ideas relate to one another.

### Kinds of Transitions

The types of transitions you choose depend on the ideas you want to convey.

**Time or Sequence** Some transitions help to clarify the sequence of events over time. When you are telling a story or describing a process, you can connect ideas with such transitional words as *first, second, always, then, next, later, soon, before, finally, after, earlier, afterward,* and *tomorrow.*

> **MODEL**
>
> The first thing I did was make sure I wasn't dreaming. That was easy, because I knew my messy room wouldn't appear in anybody's dream. Before I got out of bed, though, I turned on the light and put on my glasses. Only then did I scream.

**Spatial Order** Transitional words and phrases such as *in front, behind, next to, along, nearest, lowest, above, below, underneath, on the left,* and *in the middle* can help your reader visualize a scene.

> **MODEL**
>
> On my mother's dresser, you can read the history of our family. On the left, a picture shows my parents' wedding. The picture in the middle is of my older brother as a baby, still toothless.

**Degree of Importance** Transitional words such as *mainly, strongest, weakest, first, second, most important, least important, worst,* and *best* may be used to rank ideas or to show degrees of importance.

> **MODEL**
>
> The most important quality I look for in a friend is whether he or she has interests similar to mine. Second, I want someone who can keep a secret. Least important, my new friend should get along with all my other friends.

**Compare and Contrast** Words and phrases such as *similarly, likewise, also, like, as, neither . . . nor,* and *either . . . or* show similarity between details. *However, by contrast, yet, but, unlike, instead, whereas,* and *while* show difference. Note how transitions show contrast in the model.

> **MODEL**
>
> Like the lawyer in "The Bet," Jerry in "A Mother in Mannville" spends much of his time alone. Both characters experience loneliness. As an orphan, however, Jerry never chooses to be alone, whereas the lawyer agrees to his solitary confinement.

**TIP** Both *but* and *however* can be used to join two independent clauses. When *but* is used as a coordinating conjunction, it is preceded by a comma. When *however* is used as a conjunctive adverb, it is preceded by a semicolon and followed by a comma.

**EXAMPLE**

Water is the best thirst quencher, but it should be cold.

Iced water can be very refreshing; however, drinking it too fast is not good for you and can cause stomach cramps.

**Cause-Effect** When you are writing about a cause-effect relationship, use transitional words and phrases such as *since, because, thus, therefore, so, due to, for this reason,* and *as a result* to help explain the relationship and make your writing coherent.

**MODEL**

My notebook might look tattered, but I treasure it because Silvio gave it to me. He was my best friend, and he moved to Texas. Since the notebook is all I have to remember him by, I will never throw it out.

## 2.4 CONCLUSIONS

A conclusion should leave readers with a strong final impression.

### Kinds of Conclusions

Good conclusions sum up ideas in a variety of ways. Here are some techniques you might try.

**Restate Your Thesis** A good way to conclude an essay is by restating your thesis, or main idea, in different words. The following conclusion restates the thesis introduced on page R31.

**MODEL**

It is ironic and tragic that the two similar leaders Mahatma Gandhi and Martin Luther King Jr. both inspired the world by preaching and practicing nonviolence, yet both died violent deaths.

**Ask a Question** Try asking a question that sums up what you have said and gives your reader something new to think about. This question concludes a piece of persuasive writing.

**MODEL**

So, if you care about your health and want to get in shape, shouldn't you talk to your doctor and begin a fitness program today?

**Make a Recommendation** When you are persuading your audience to take a position on an issue, you can conclude by recommending a specific course of action.

**MODEL**

Shawn, Maria, and Katie are real children. The next time you see a homeless person, remember these children and think about what you can do to help.

**Offer an Opinion** Leave your reader with something to think about by offering your personal opinion on the topic. The following model offers an opinion about homelessness.

**MODEL**

Any one of us could become homeless at any moment due to events we can't control. Remembering this frightening fact can help us take the problem of homelessness more seriously.

**End with the Last Event** If you're telling a story, you may end with the last thing that happens. Here, the ending includes the narrator's important realization.

**MODEL**

By the time the firefighters finally arrived, I had managed to get everyone out of the house and away from danger. Although we all were frightened and in shock, no one was badly hurt. As I watched the flames turn our home into ashes, I knew this was a night I'd never forget.

## 2.5 ELABORATION

Elaboration is the process of developing an idea by providing specific supporting details that are relevant and appropriate to the purpose and form of your writing.

**Facts and Statistics** A fact is a statement that can be verified, and a statistic is a fact expressed as a number. Make sure the facts and statistics you supply are from reliable, up-to-date sources.

> **MODEL**
>
> The heat wave this July broke all records. Temperatures rose above 100°F for 11 days in a row, and the scorching 113°F recorded at the airport on Wednesday was the highest reading ever measured here.

**Sensory Details** Details that show how something looks, sounds, tastes, smells, or feels can enliven a description, making readers feel they are actually experiencing what you are describing. Which senses does the writer appeal to in the following model?

> **MODEL**
>
> Opening the cabin door, she felt transported back to her childhood halfway across the country. The crisp air held the promise of frost, and the pine needles on the path were beginning to turn brown and curl up at the edges as if trying to stay warm.

**Incidents** From our earliest years, we are interested in hearing "stories." One way to illustrate a point powerfully is to relate an incident or tell a story, as shown in the example.

> **MODEL**
>
> Pedestrians, like drivers, should look both ways before crossing the street. I learned how dangerous it can be to break that rule when I was almost hit by a driver who was going the wrong way down a one-way street.

**Examples** An example can help make an abstract idea concrete or can serve to clarify a complex point for your reader.

> **MODEL**
>
> Narrative poetry tells a story in poetic form. "Paul Revere's Ride" by Henry Wadsworth Longfellow, for example, describes the dramatic events that took place in Massachusetts on April 18, 1775, the night before the battles of Lexington and Concord.

**Quotations** Choose quotations that clearly support your point, and be sure to copy each quotation word for word. Remember always to credit the source.

> **MODEL**
>
> In his short story "The Tell-Tale Heart," Edgar Allan Poe uses bizarre and frightening details to grip the reader with a sense of horror. "I saw it [the eye] with perfect distinctness—all a dull blue, with a hideous veil over it that chilled the very marrow in my bones . . . ."

## 3 Descriptive Writing

Descriptive writing allows you to paint word pictures about anything, from events of global importance to the most personal feelings. It is an essential part of almost every piece of writing.

> **RUBRIC: Standards for Writing**
>
> **Successful descriptive writing should**
>
> - have a clear focus and sense of purpose
> - use sensory details and precise words to create a vivid image, establish a mood, or express emotion
> - present details in a logical order

*For more information, see* **Writing Workshop: Describing a Person,** *pages 292–299.*

### 3.1 KEY TECHNIQUES

**Consider Your Goals** What do you want to accomplish with your description? Do you want to show why something is important to you? Do you want to make a person or scene more memorable? Do you want to explain an event?

**Identify Your Audience** Who will read your description? How familiar are they with your subject? What background information will they need? Which details will they find most interesting?

**Think Figuratively** What figures of speech might help make your description vivid and interesting? What simile or metaphor comes to mind? What imaginative comparisons can you make? What living thing does an inanimate object remind you of?

**Gather Sensory Details** Which sights, smells, tastes, sounds, and textures make your subject come alive? Which details stick in your mind when you observe or recall your subject? Which senses does your subject most strongly affect?

You might want to use a chart like the one shown here to collect sensory details about your subject.

| Sights | Sounds | Textures | Smells | Tastes |
|--------|--------|----------|--------|--------|
|        |        |          |        |        |

**Organize Your Details** Details that are presented in a logical order help the reader form a mental picture of the subject. Descriptive details may be organized chronologically, spatially, by order of impression, or by order of importance.

### 3.2 OPTIONS FOR ORGANIZATION

**Option 1: Spatial Order** Choose one of these options to show the spatial order of elements in a scene you are describing.

*For more information, see **Transitions**, page R32.*

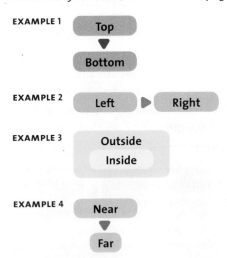

EXAMPLE 1
Top ▼ Bottom

EXAMPLE 2
Left ▶ Right

EXAMPLE 3
Outside / Inside

EXAMPLE 4
Near ▼ Far

**MODEL**

Thunder's nostrils quivered as he was led into the barn. How would this be as a place to spend nights from now on? In the stall to the left, the straw smelled fresh. Beyond that stall, a saddle hung from the rough boards. To the right of his stall was another from which a mare looked at him curiously. So far, so good. To the far right, beyond two empty stalls, a cat lay on its side.

**Option 2: Order of Impression** Order of impression is the order in which you notice details.

What first catches your attention
▼
What you notice next
▼
What you see after that
▼
What you focus on last

**TIP** Use transitions that help readers understand the order of the impressions you are describing. Some useful transitions are *after, next, during, first, before, finally,* and *then.*

**MODEL**

As I walked into the planetarium, I was struck by the total darkness. Gradually, my eyes adjusted, and I could see the rows of seats. Finally, daring to raise my eyes from the ground, I gasped in awe at the domed ceiling. Spangled with hundreds of glittering stars, it created the sensation of standing outside on a clear summer night.

**Option 3: Order of Importance** You can use order of importance as the organizing structure for a description.

More important
▼
More important
▼
Least important

*For more information, see **Transitions**, page R32.*

**Option 4: Chronological Order** You can use chronological order as the organizing structure for a description. See section 4.2 on this page for an example of how this is done.

# 4 Narrative Writing

Narrative writing tells a story. If you write a story from your imagination, it is a fictional narrative. A true story about actual events is a nonfictional narrative. Narrative writing can be found in short stories, novels, news articles, personal narratives, and biographies.

> **RUBRIC: Standards for Writing**
>
> **A successful narrative should**
> - begin with an attention-getting introduction
> - present a clear incident, event, or situation
> - include vivid, well-chosen details in describing characters, setting, and action
> - use strategies such as dialogue and comparison/contrast to support descriptions
> - explain the significance of the event for the writer
> - have a logical organization with a clear beginning, middle, and end
> - use language suited to the audience and purpose
> - keep a consistent tone and point of view

*For more information, see **Writing Workshop: Short Story**, pages 558–565, and **Writing Workshop: Personal Narrative**, pages 144–151.*

## 4.1 KEY TECHNIQUES

**Identify the Main Events** What are the most important events in your narrative? Is each event needed to tell the story?

**Describe the Setting** When do the events occur? Where do they take place? How can you use setting to create mood and suspense, and to set the stage for the characters and their actions?

**Depict Characters Vividly** What do your characters look like? What do they think and say? How do they act? What details can show what they are like?

**TIP** Dialogue is an effective means of developing characters in a narrative. As you write dialogue, choose words that express your characters' personalities and that show how the characters feel about one another and about the events in the plot.

## 4.2 OPTIONS FOR ORGANIZATION

**Option 1: Chronological Order** One way to organize a narrative is to arrange the events in chronological order, as shown.

> **EXAMPLE**
>
> Yukiko's alarm doesn't go off, and she wakes up late on the day of an important English test.
>
> Panic-stricken, she leaps out of bed, throws on her clothes, and grabs her books, ignoring her mother's pleas to eat breakfast.
>
> She dashes into the classroom just as the final bell rings. She feels light-headed from running and not having eaten anything.
>
> Her mind goes blank, and she can't answer any of the questions. She takes a few minutes to calm down and tells herself she'll just do the best she can.

**Introduction** *Characters and setting*

**Event 1**

▼

**Event 2**

▼

**End** *Perhaps showing the significance of the events*

**Option 2: Flashback** In narrative writing, it is also possible to introduce events that happened before the beginning of the story. You may want to hook your reader's interest by opening a story with an exciting event. After your introduction, you can use a flashback to show how past events led up to the present situation or to provide background about a character or event. Use clue words such as *last summer, as a young girl, the previous school year,* and *his earliest memories* to let your reader know that you are interrupting the main action to describe earlier events.

Notice how the flashback interrupts the action in the model.

**MODEL**

As Yukiko fidgeted in her chair, she remembered a story she once read about a woman with amnesia. The woman wandered around for weeks, not remembering that she had a husband and children. The fact that the woman eventually regained her memory gave Yukiko hope that the material she'd studied so hard eventually would come back to her.

**Option 3: Focus on Conflict** When a fictional narrative focuses on a central conflict, the story's plot may be organized as in the following example.

**EXAMPLE**

Yukiko is worried about an important English test and stays up late studying. When she finally goes to bed, she forgets to set her alarm. In the morning, she wakes up in a panic, realizing that school starts in only 20 minutes.

> **Describe main characters and setting.**

She wonders whether she should try to get to class on time or pretend she is sick and take a make-up test later.

> **Present conflict.**

- She tells her mother the situation and asks her advice.
- She decides to race to school and take the test, since she's already studied so hard.
- She begins to feel dizzy and weak.

> **Relate events that make conflict complex and cause characters to change.**

Yukiko gets to class just as the test is beginning. She's nervous and doesn't do as well as she could have, but she is proud of having made the right decision.

> **Present resolution or outcome of conflict.**

## ⑤ Expository Writing

Expository writing informs and explains. You can use it to explain how to cook spaghetti, to explore the origins of the universe, or to compare two pieces of literature. There are many types of expository writing. Think about your topic and select the type that will present the information most clearly.

### 5.1 COMPARISON AND CONTRAST

Compare-and-contrast writing examines the similarities and differences between two or more subjects. You might, for example, compare and contrast two short stories, the main characters in a novel, or two movies.

**RUBRIC: Standards for Writing**

**Successful compare-and-contrast writing should**

- hook the reader's attention with a strong introduction
- clearly identify the subjects that are being compared
- include specific, relevant details
- follow a clear plan of organization
- use language and details appropriate to the audience
- use transitional words and phrases to clarify similarities and differences

*For more information, see **Writing Workshop: Comparison-Contrast Essay**, pages 424–431, **Writing Workshop: Personal Response to a Poem**, pages 648–655, **Writing Workshop: Literary Analysis**, pages 742–749 and **Writing Workshop: Cause-and-Effect Essay**, pages 860–867.*

### Options for Organization

Compare-and-contrast writing can be organized in different ways. The examples that follow demonstrate point-by-point organization and subject-by-subject organization.

#### Option 1: Point-by-Point Organization

**EXAMPLE**

I. Similarities between older and newer childrens' books

> **Point 1**

  **Subject A.** Older books feature children as characters.

  **Subject B.** Today's books also often include children.

II. Differences between older and newer childrens' books

> **Point 2**

  **Subject A.** Older books tend to avoid racial and social conflicts.

  **Subject B.** Today's books are likely to describe realistic racial and social conflicts.

## Option 2: Subject-by-Subject Organization

**EXAMPLE**

I. Older childrens' books — **Subject A**

   **Point 1.** They focus on children as main characters.

   **Point 2.** They avoid discussing racial or social conflicts.

II. Today's childrens' books — **Subject B**

   **Point 1.** They focus on children and young people.

   **Point 2.** They describe realistic racial and social conflicts.

*For more information, see **Writing Workshop: Comparison-Contrast Essay**, pages 424–431.*

## 5.2 CAUSE AND EFFECT

Cause-effect writing explains why something happened, why certain conditions exist, or what resulted from an action or a condition. You might use cause-effect writing to explain a character's actions, the progress of a disease, or the outcome of a war.

### RUBRIC: Standards for Writing

**Successful cause-effect writing should**

- hook the reader's attention with a strong introduction
- clearly state the cause-and-effect relationship
- show clear connections between causes and effects
- present causes and effects in a logical order and use transitions effectively
- use facts, examples, and other details to illustrate each cause and effect
- use language and details appropriate to the audience

*For more information, see **Writing Workshop: Cause-and-Effect Essay**, pages 860–867.*

## Options for Organization

Your organization will depend on your topic and your purpose for writing.

**Option 1: Effect-to-Cause Organization** If you want to explain the causes of an event, such as the risk of not having enough energy to take a test, you might first state the effect and then examine its causes.

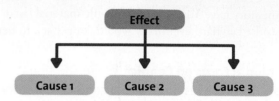

**Option 2: Cause-to-Effect Organization** If your focus is on explaining the effects of an event, such as the importance of eating a healthy breakfast, you might first state the cause and then explain the effects.

**Option 3: Cause-Effect Chain Organization**
Sometimes you'll want to describe a chain of cause-and-effect relationships to explore a topic such as how to do well on a test.

**TIP** Don't assume that a cause-effect relationship exists just because one event follows another. Look for evidence that the later event could not have happened if the first event had not caused it.

## 5.3 PROBLEM-SOLUTION

Problem-solution writing clearly states a problem, analyzes the problem, and proposes a solution to the problem. It can be used to identify and solve a conflict between characters, investigate global warming, or tell why the home team keeps losing.

> ### RUBRIC: Standards for Writing
> **Successful problem-solution writing should**
> - hook the reader's attention with a strong introduction
> - identify the problem and help the reader understand the issues involved
> - analyze the causes and effects of the problem
> - include quotations, facts, and statistics
> - explore possible solutions to the problem and recommend the best one(s)
> - use language, details, and a tone appropriate to the audience

### Options for Organization

Your organization will depend on the goal of your problem-solution piece, your intended audience, and the specific problem you have chosen to address. The organizational methods that follow are effective for different kinds of problem-solution writing.

### Option 1: Simple Problem-Solution

### Option 2: Deciding Between Solutions

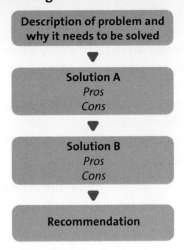

## 5.4 ANALYSIS

In writing an analysis, you explain how something works, how it is defined, or what its parts are.

> ### RUBRIC: Standards for Writing
> **A successful analysis should**
> - hook the reader's attention with a strong introduction
> - clearly define the subject and its parts
> - use a specific organizing structure to provide a logical flow of information
> - show connections among facts and ideas through transitional words and phrases
> - use language and details appropriate for the audience

### Options for Organization

Organize your details in a logical order appropriate to the kind of analysis you're writing. Use one of the following options: process analysis, definition analysis, or parts analysis.

**Option 1: Process Analysis** A process analysis is usually organized chronologically, with steps or stages in the order in which they occur. You might use a process analysis to explain how to program a cell phone or prepare for a test.

> **MODEL**
>
> Preparing for a test — Introduce process
>
> Doing well on a test requires careful preparation. — Give background
>
> **Step 1:** Reread the material that will be covered on the test and your class notes.
> **Step 2:** Outline the material.
> **Step 3:** Answer any questions in the text and make up and answer your own.
> **Step 4:** Get plenty of sleep the night before. — Explain steps

**Option 2: Definition Analysis** You can organize the details of a definition analysis in order of importance or impression. Use a definition analysis to explain the characteristics of a limerick, the characteristics of insects, or a quality (such as excellence).

> **MODEL**
>
> What is excellence? — Introduce term and definition
>
> Excellence is the quality of being first-rate, exceeding all others, and setting a standard of performance.
>
> **Feature 1:** being first-rate
>
> **Feature 2:** exceeding all others — Explain features
>
> **Feature 3:** setting a standard of performance

**Option 3: Parts Analysis** A parts analysis explains a subject by breaking it down into its main pieces.

> **MODEL**
>
> Test preparation consists of three main parts. — Introduce subject
>
> **Part 1:** Getting to know the material
>
> **Part 2:** Practicing the material — Explain parts
>
> **Part 3:** Resting and being healthy for the test

## 6 Persuasive Writing

Persuasive writing allows you to use the power of language to inform and influence others. It includes speeches, persuasive essays, newspaper editorials, advertisements, and critical reviews.

> **RUBRIC: Standards for Writing**
>
> **Successful persuasive writing should**
> - grab the reader's attention with a strong introduction
> - present a well-defined thesis that states the issue and the writer's position
> - support arguments with detailed evidence, examples, and reasons
> - clearly distinguish between fact and opinion
> - anticipate and answer counterarguments, or opposing views, with solid facts and reasons
> - use sound logic and persuasive language
> - conclude with a summary of points or a call to action

*For more information, see **Writing Workshop: Persuasive Essay,** pages 1016–1023.*

### 6.1 KEY TECHNIQUES

**Clarify Your Position** What do you believe about the issue? How can you express your opinion most clearly?

**Know Your Audience** Who will read your writing? What do they already know and believe about the issue? What objections to your position might they have? What additional information might they need? What tone and approach would be most effective?

**Support Your Opinion** Why do you feel the way you do about the issue? What facts, statistics, examples, quotations, anecdotes, or expert opinions support your view? What reasons will convince your readers? What evidence can answer their objections?

| Ways to Support Your Argument | |
|---|---|
| **Statistics** | facts that are stated in numbers |
| **Examples** | specific instances that explain points |
| **Observations** | events or situations you have seen firsthand |
| **Anecdotes** | brief stories that illustrate points |
| **Quotations** | direct statements from authorities |

*For more information, see **Identifying Faulty Reasoning**, page R24.*

**Begin and End with a Bang** How can you hook your readers and make a lasting impression? What memorable quotation, anecdote, or statistic will catch their attention at the beginning or stick in their minds at the end? What strong summary or call to action can you conclude with?

---

**MODEL**

**Beginning**

Have you ever enjoyed the antics of the orangutans or watched the polar bears swim at Green Park Zoo? Unless we make sure that public funding for the zoo continues, those experiences will be just memories.

**End**

In addition to being a place for relaxation and fun, Green Park Zoo is a scientific laboratory where professionals work to create educational programs and ensure the survival of endangered species. Don't let the zoo become an endangered species itself. Support public funding today.

---

## 6.2 OPTIONS FOR ORGANIZATION

In a two-sided persuasive essay, you want to show the weaknesses of other opinions as you explain the strengths of your own.

### Option 1: Reasons for Your Opinion

Introduction states issue and your position on it
▼
Reason 1 with evidence and support
▼
Reason 2 with evidence and support
▼
Reason 3 with evidence and support
▼
Objections to whole argument
▼
Response to objections
▼
Conclusion restates your position and recommends a course of action

### Option 2: Point-by-Point Basis

Introduction states issue and your position on it
▼
Reason 1 with evidence and support
▼
Objections and responses for reason 1
▼
Reason 2 with evidence and support
▼
Objections and responses for reason 2
▼
Reason 3 with evidence and support
▼
Objections and responses for reason 3
▼
Conclusion restates your position and recommends a course of action

# 7 Workplace and Technical Writing

Business writing is writing done in a workplace to support the work of a company or business. You may need to do business writing to request information or complain about a product or service. Several types of formats, such as memos, letters, e-mails, and applications, have been developed to make communication easier.

> **RUBRIC: Standards for Writing**
>
> **Successful business writing should**
>
> - clearly state the purpose of the communication in the opening paragraph
> - follow a standard format
> - use language that is precise and appropriate to the audience
> - have a formal, respectful tone
> - include only necessary information
> - present information in a logical order
> - conclude with a summary of important points

## 7.1 KEY TECHNIQUES OF WORKPLACE WRITING

**Think About Your Purpose** Why are you doing this writing? Do you want to order or complain about a product? If you know what you want, you're more likely to get the desired results.

**Identify Your Audience** Who will read your writing? What background information will they need? What tone or language is appropriate?

**Use a Pattern of Organization That Is Appropriate to the Content** If you have to compare and contrast two products in a letter, you can use the same compare-and-contrast organization that you would use in an essay.

**Support Your Points** What specific details might clarify your ideas? What reasons do you have for your statements?

**Finish Strongly** How can you best sum up your statements? What is your main point? What action do you want the recipients to take?

**Revise and Proofread Your Writing** Just as you are graded on the quality of an essay you write for a class, you will be judged on the quality of your writing in the workplace.

## 7.2 MATCHING THE FORMAT TO THE OCCASION

E-mail messages, memos, and letters have similar purposes but are used in different situations. The chart shows how each format can be used.

| Format | Occasion |
|---|---|
| **Memo** | use to send correspondence **inside** the workplace only |
| **E-mail message** | use to send correspondence **inside or outside** the company |
| **Letter** | use to send correspondence **outside** the company |

**TIP** Memos are often sent as e-mail messages in the workplace. Remember that both require formal language and standard spelling, capitalization, and punctuation.

Technical writing is used for detailed instructions or descriptions of items and processes. It is important to a variety of fields, such as science, government, and industry. Technical writing is used to present information in such a way that the reader can use it to complete a task, such as performing an experiment, assembling an object, or using a tool.

At work, at school, or in everyday life, you may have to use technical writing to leave instructions for another person.

> **RUBRIC: Standards for Writing**
>
> **Instructions should**
>
> - present no unnecessary information
> - include all essential information such as definitions of unfamiliar terms
> - explain all the steps in a logical order
> - use direct, precise language
> - use present-tense action verbs
> - use transitions and formatting, such as numbered steps, headings, and different fonts to aid understanding

## 7.3 KEY TECHNIQUES OF TECHNICAL WRITING

**Think About Your Organization** As you write, make sure you are presenting your information in a sensible order. For example, you would probably list any necessary tools and materials early on. Then you would present the steps in the order in which they should be followed.

**Keep Your Audience in Mind** Make sure you explain what readers unfamiliar with the activity or process will need to know. Sometimes making a comparison to something the reader is familiar with can help. Graphics, such as pictures and maps, can also help make instructions easier to understand.

**Use Transitions as Needed** Transitions such as *first, next, after,* and *last* and numbered steps can make the order of steps clear and guide your reader from one step to the next.

**Review Your Ending** You can simply end with the last step, or you can end by describing the result or outcome of following the directions.

**Evaluate Your Instructions** Have a friend follow your instructions to make sure they are clear.

## 7.4 FORMATS

Business letters usually have a formal tone and a specific format as shown here. The key to writing a business letter is to get to the point as quickly as possible and to present your information clearly.

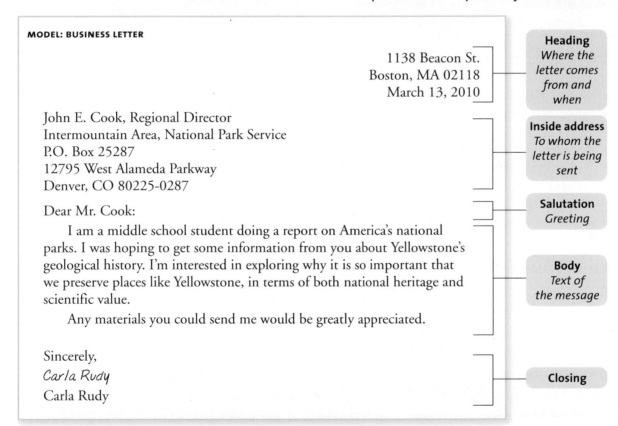

**MODEL: BUSINESS LETTER**

1138 Beacon St.
Boston, MA 02118
March 13, 2010

**Heading**
*Where the letter comes from and when*

John E. Cook, Regional Director
Intermountain Area, National Park Service
P.O. Box 25287
12795 West Alameda Parkway
Denver, CO 80225-0287

**Inside address**
*To whom the letter is being sent*

Dear Mr. Cook:

**Salutation**
*Greeting*

   I am a middle school student doing a report on America's national parks. I was hoping to get some information from you about Yellowstone's geological history. I'm interested in exploring why it is so important that we preserve places like Yellowstone, in terms of both national heritage and scientific value.

   Any materials you could send me would be greatly appreciated.

**Body**
*Text of the message*

Sincerely,
*Carla Rudy*
Carla Rudy

**Closing**

### PRACTICE AND APPLY

1. Draft a response to the letter. Then revise your letter as necessary according to the rubric at the beginning of page R42. Make sure you have included the necessary information and have written in an appropriate tone.

2. Proofread your letter for grammatical errors and spelling mistakes. Follow the format of the model and use appropriate spacing between parts.

Memos are often used in the workplace as a way of sending information in a direct and concise manner. They can be used to announce or summarize meetings and to request actions or specific information.

**MODEL: MEMO**

To: Joellen Snipes
From: John Cook
Subject: Informational brochures
Date: March 16, 2010

Joellen, please read the attached letter and send Carla our brochure packet. It's encouraging to receive inquiries from concerned young people, so please add a personal note of thanks for her interest.

**Heading**
*Receiver's name*
*Sender's name*
*Topic of memo*
*Complete date*

**Body**

### PRACTICE AND APPLY

Write a memo in response to the memo shown here. Tell the receiver what actions you have taken. Follow the format of the model.

**TIP** Don't forget to write the topic of your memo in the subject line. This will help the receiver determine the importance of your memo.

When filling out an application, pay special attention to any lines that require a response or a signature from you. Answer any questions accurately and completely.

---

**JIFFY JEANS**
**EMPLOYMENT APPLICATION**

Print clearly in black or blue ink. Answer all questions. Sign and date the form.

**PERSONAL INFORMATION:**

**Name:** Marquell Janek      **Social Security Number:** 555-77-5656

**Address:** 7218 University Place      **City:** Woodland   **State:** CA   **Zip:** 95659

**Phone Number:** (530) 667-7814

If you are under age 18, do you have an employment/age certificates? Yes _X_ No ___

**POSITION/AVAILABILITY:**

**Position Applied for:** Stockroom helper

**Days/Hours Available:** Monday _____ Tuesday _____ Wednesday 6–8 PM Thursday _____
                              Friday _____ , Saturday 8 AM–6 PM , Sunday 1 PM–6 PM

**What date are you available to start work?** June 19, 2010

**EDUCATION:**

**School:** Westleigh Middle School      **Highest Grade Completed:** 8

I certify that information contained in this application is true and complete. I understand that false information may be grounds for not hiring me or for immediate termination of employment at any point in the future if I am hired. I authorize the verification of any or all information listed above.

**Signature:** Marquell Janek      **Date:** 5/31/2010

When writing instructions, be sure to include any materials someone would need in order to complete the task. Number or letter each step to show order.

---

**MODEL: INSTRUCTIONS**

### How to Etch Glass by eHow.com

Turn a boring mirror or pane of glass into a work of art!

What you **need:**

- carbon paper
- clear contact paper
- crafts knife
- etching cream
- glass cleaner
- latex gloves
- soft, lint-free cloth
- piece of glass or mirror
- pencils
- paper towels

**Steps:**

1. Clean the surface you will be etching with glass cleaner and a soft cloth. Cover the surface with clear contact paper and press out all the bubbles.

2. Put the design you are using behind the glass.

3. Trace the design onto the contact paper if you are doing a mirror. Put carbon paper on top of the contact paper and then place your design on top of that. Trace the design, transferring it to the contact paper.

4. Use a crafts knife to cut the contact paper away from the areas that you want to etch. Make sure that all of the edges are stuck tight to the glass and that there are no bubbles at the edges.

5. Use a paper towel to smear a liberal layer of etching cream onto the design area.

6. Wait the amount of time required for the brand of etching cream you are using—usually 5 to 10 minutes.

7. Run cool water over the cream to rinse it off. Peel off the contact paper and rinse the glass under cool water again.

**Tips:**

Areas where the acid isn't thick enough will look streaked. Be sure to get a good coat of the etching cream onto the piece of glass.

**Warning:**

Wear latex gloves when working with etching cream. It's an acid. Apply the cream in a well-ventilated area.

**Courtesy of www.ehow.com: Clear instructions on how to do (just about) anything!**

---

**PRACTICE AND APPLY**

Think about something you might want someone else to do for you while you're at school, such as do your laundry or prepare dinner. Use the rubric at the bottom of page R42 to write instructions. Be sure to include the following:

- an opening statement that describes what needs to be done

- a list of tools and materials needed to perform the task

- the steps needed to perform the task, including transition words and/or numbered steps if order is important

- any special notes or warnings about a tool or step in the process

*Writing that is full of mistakes can confuse or even annoy a reader. Punctuation errors in a letter might lead to a miscommunication and delay a reply. Sentence fragments might lower your grade on an essay. Paying attention to grammar, punctuation, and capitalization rules can make your writing clearer and easier to read.*

# Quick Reference: Parts of Speech

| PART OF SPEECH | FUNCTION | EXAMPLES |
|---|---|---|
| Noun | names a person, a place, a thing, an idea, a quality, or an action | |
| Common | serves as a general name, or a name common to an entire group | shadow, harmonica, paw, mistake |
| Proper | names a specific, one-of-a-kind person, place, or thing | Chinatown, Switzerland, Jupiter, Herbert |
| Singular | refers to a single person, place, thing, or idea | earthquake, laboratory, medication, outcome |
| Plural | refers to more than one person, place, thing, or idea | chemicals, splinters, geniuses, soldiers |
| Concrete | names something that can be perceived by the senses | calendar, basketball, ocean, snow |
| Abstract | names something that cannot be perceived by the senses | democracy, authority, beauty, fame |
| Compound | expresses a single idea through a combination of two or more words | self-esteem, mountaintop, firefighters, light bulb |
| Collective | refers to a group of people or things | team, family, class, choir |
| Possessive | shows who or what owns something | Pandora's, Strauss's, Franks', women's |
| Pronoun | takes the place of a noun or another pronoun | |
| Personal | refers to the person making a statement, the person(s) being addressed, or the person(s) or thing(s) the statement is about | I, me, my, mine, we, us, our, ours, you, your, yours, she, he, it, her, him, hers, his, its, they, them, their, theirs |
| Reflexive | follows a verb or preposition and refers to a preceding noun or pronoun | myself, yourself, herself, himself, itself, ourselves, yourselves, themselves |
| Intensive | emphasizes a noun or another pronoun | (same as reflexives) |
| Demonstrative | points to one or more specific persons or things | this, that, these, those |
| Interrogative | signals a question | who, whom, whose, which, what |
| Indefinite | refers to one or more persons or things not specifically mentioned | both, all, most, many, anyone, everybody, several, none, some |
| Relative | introduces an adjective clause by relating it to a word in the clause | who, whom, whose, which, that |

| PART OF SPEECH | FUNCTION | EXAMPLES |
|---|---|---|
| Verb | Expresses an action, a condition, or a state of being | |
| Action | tells what the subject does or did, physically or mentally | find, know, clings, displayed, rises, crave |
| Linking | connects the subject to something that identifies or describes it | am, is, are, was, were, sound, taste, appear, feel, become, remain, seem |
| Auxiliary | precedes the main verb in a verb phrase | Be, have, can, do, could, will, would, may, might |
| Transitive | directs the action toward someone or something; always has an object | She <u>opened</u> the **door.** |
| Intransitive | does not direct the action toward someone or something; does not have an object | The door **opened.** |
| Adjective | modifies a noun or pronoun | **slight** groan, **dying** gladiators, **ancient** sea, **two** pigtails |
| Adverb | modifies a verb, an adjective, or another adverb | **always** closed, **very** patiently, **more** pleasant, ran **quickly** |
| Preposition | relates one word to another word | at, by, for, from, in, of, on, to, with |
| Conjunction | joins words or word groups | |
| Coordinating | joins words or word groups used the same way | and, but, or, for, so, yet, nor |
| Correlative | used as a pair to join words or word groups used the same way | both . . . and, either . . . or, neither . . . nor |
| Subordinating | introduces a clause that cannot stand by itself as a complete sentence | although, after, as, before, because, when, if, unless |
| Interjection | expresses emotion | wow, ouch, hooray |

# Quick Reference: The Sentence and Its Parts

The diagrams that follow will give you a brief review of the essentials of a sentence and some of its parts.

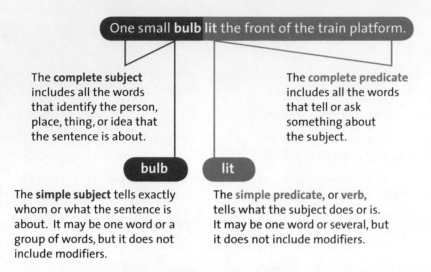

One small **bulb** **lit** the front of the train platform.

The **complete subject** includes all the words that identify the person, place, thing, or idea that the sentence is about.

The **complete predicate** includes all the words that tell or ask something about the subject.

**bulb**

**lit**

The **simple subject** tells exactly whom or what the sentence is about. It may be one word or a group of words, but it does not include modifiers.

The **simple predicate**, or **verb**, tells what the subject does or is. It may be one word or several, but it does not include modifiers.

Every word in a sentence is part of a complete subject or a complete predicate.

The train platform would give him shelter from the wind.

**subject**

Verbs often have more than one part. A verb may be made up of a **main verb**, like *give*, and one or more **auxiliary**, or **helping, verbs**, like *would*.

A **prepositional phrase** consists of a preposition, its object, and any modifiers of the object. In this phrase, *from* is the preposition and *wind* is its object.

An **indirect object** is a word or group of words that tells to whom or for whom or to what or for what the verb's action is performed. A sentence can have an indirect object only if it has a direct object. The indirect object always comes before the direct object.

A **direct object** is a word or group of words that tells who or what receives the action of the verb.

# Quick Reference: Punctuation

| MARK | FUNCTION | EXAMPLES |
|---|---|---|
| **End Marks**<br>period, question mark, exclamation point | ends a sentence | We can start now.<br>When would you like to leave?<br>What a fantastic hit! |
| period | follows an initial or abbreviation<br><br>**Exception:** postal abbreviations of states | Mrs. Dorothy Parker, McDougal Littell Inc., C. P. Cavafy, P.M., A.D., lb., oz., Blvd., Dr.<br>NE (Nebraska), NV (Nevada) |
| period | follows a number or letter in an outline | I. Volcanoes<br>  A. Central-vent<br>    1. Shield |
| **Comma** | separates part of a compound sentence | I had never disliked poetry, but now I really love it. |
| | separates items in a series | Her humor, grace, and kindness served her well. |
| | separates adjectives of equal rank that modify the same noun | The slow, easy route is best. |
| | sets off a term of address | Maria, how can I help you?<br>You must do something, soldier. |
| | sets off a parenthetical expression | Hard workers, as you know, don't quit.<br>I'm not a quitter, believe me. |
| | sets off an introductory word, phrase, or dependent clause | Yes, I forgot my key.<br>At the beginning of the day, I feel fresh.<br>While she was out, I was here.<br>Having finished my chores, I went out. |
| | sets off a nonessential phrase or clause | Ed Pawn, the captain of the chess team, won.<br>Ed Pawn, who is the captain, won.<br>The two leading runners, sprinting toward the finish line, finished in a tie. |
| | sets off parts of dates and addresses | Mail it by May 14, 2010, to the Hauptman Company, 321 Market Street, Memphis, Tennessee. |
| | follows the salutation and closing of a letter | Dear Jim, Sincerely yours, |
| | separates words to avoid confusion | By noon, time had run out.<br>What the minister does, does matter.<br>While cooking, Jim burned his hand. |
| **Semicolon** | separates items in a series that contain commas | We spent the first week of summer vacation in Chicago, Illinois; the second week in St. Louis, Missouri; and the third week in Albany, New York. |
| | separates parts of a compound sentence that are not joined by a coordinating conjunction | The last shall be first; the first shall be last. I read the Bible; however, I have not memorized it. |
| | separates parts of a compound sentence when the parts contain commas | After I ran out of money, I called my parents; but only my sister was home, unfortunately. |

| MARK | FUNCTION | EXAMPLES |
|---|---|---|
| **Colon** | introduces a list | Those we wrote to were the following: Dana, John, and Will. |
| | introduces a long quotation | Abraham Lincoln wrote: "Four score and seven years ago, our fathers brought forth on this continent a new nation . . . ." |
| | follows the salutation of a business letter | To Whom It May Concern: <br> Dear Leonard Atole: |
| | separates certain numbers | 1:28 P.M., Genesis 2:5 |
| **Dash** | indicates an abrupt break in thought | I was thinking of my mother—who is arriving tomorrow—just as you walked in. |
| **Parentheses** | enclose less important material | It was so unlike him (John is always on time) that I began to worry. The last World Series game (did you see it?) was fun. |
| **Hyphen** | joins parts of a compound adjective before a noun | The not-so-rich taxpayer won't stand for this! |
| | joins parts of a compound with *all-*, *ex-*, *self-*, or *-elect* | The ex-firefighter helped rescue him. <br> Our president-elect is self-conscious. |
| | joins parts of a compound number (to ninety-nine) | Today is the twenty-fifth of November. |
| | joins parts of a fraction | My cup is one-third full. |
| | joins a prefix to a word beginning with a capital letter | I'm studying the U.S. presidents pre-1900. It snowed in mid-October. |
| | indicates that a word is divided at the end of a line | How could you have any reasonable expect-ations of getting a new computer? |
| **Apostrophe** | used with *s* to form the possessive of a noun or an indefinite pronoun | my friend's book, my friends' books, anyone's guess, somebody else's problem |
| | replaces one or more omitted letters in a contraction or numbers in a date | don't (omitted *o*), he'd (omitted *woul*), the class of '99 (omitted *19*) |
| | used with *s* to form the plural of a letter | I had two A's on my report card. |
| **Quotation Marks** | set off a speaker's exact words | "That, I'll do," Lemon said. "That," Lemon said, "I'll do." Did Lemon say, "That I'll do"? Lemon said, "That I'll do!" |
| | set off the title of a story, an article, a short poem, an essay, a song, or a chapter | I recited Alice Walker's "We Alone" at the assembly. <br> Poe's "The Tell-Tale Heart" and Stockton's "The Lady or the Tiger?" held my interest. <br> I enjoyed Bob Dylan's "Boots of Spanish Leather." |
| **Ellipses** | replace material omitted from a quotation | "Her diary tells us that she . . . thought of ordinary things, such as going to school with other kids . . ." |
| **Italics** | indicate the title of a book, a play, a magazine, a long poem, an opera, a film, or a TV series, or the name of a ship | *Harriet Tubman: Conductor on the Underground Railroad, The Hitchhiker, TIME, The Magic Flute,* the *Iliad, Star Wars, 60 Minutes,* the *Mayflower* |

# Quick Reference: Capitalization

| CATEGORY | EXAMPLES |
|---|---|
| **People and Titles** | |
| Names and initials of people | Jack London, T.S. Eliot |
| Titles used before a name | Professor Holmes, Senator Long |
| Deities and members of religious groups | Jesus, Allah, Buddha, Zeus, Baptists, Roman Catholics |
| Names of ethnic and national groups | Hispanics, Jews, African Americans |
| **Geographical Names** | |
| Cities, states, countries, continents | Philadelphia, Kansas, Japan, Europe |
| Regions, bodies of water, mountains | the South, Lake Baikal, Mount Everest |
| Geographic features, parks | Great Basin, Yellowstone National Park |
| Streets and roads, planets | 318 East Sutton Drive, Charles Court, Jupiter, Mars |
| **Organizations, Events, Etc.** | |
| Companies, organizations, teams | Ford Motor Company, Boy Scouts of America, St. Louis Cardinals |
| Buildings, bridges, monuments | Empire State Building, Eads Bridge, Washington Monument |
| Documents, awards | Declaration of Independence, Stanley Cup |
| Special named events | Mardi Gras, World Series |
| Government bodies, historical periods and events | U.S. Senate, House of Representatives, Middle Ages, Vietnam War |
| Days and months, holidays | Thursday, March, Thanksgiving, Labor Day |
| Specific cars, boats, trains, planes | Porsche, Carpathia, Southwest Chief, Concorde |
| **Proper Adjectives** | |
| Adjectives formed from proper nouns | French cooking, Spanish omelet, Edwardian age, Western movie |
| **First Words and the Pronoun I** | |
| First word in a sentence or quotation | This is it. He said, "Let's go." |
| First word of sentence in parentheses that is not within another sentence | The spelling rules are covered in another section. (Consult that section for more information.) |
| First words in the salutation and closing of a letter | Dear Madam, Very truly yours, |
| First word in each line of most poetry<br>Personal pronoun I | Then am I<br>A happy fly<br>If I live<br>Or if I die. |
| First word, last word, and all important words in a title | "The Ransom of Red Chief," "Rules of the Game," *Roll of Thunder, Hear My Cry* |

# 1 Nouns

A **noun** is a word used to name a person, a place, a thing, an idea, a quality, or an action. Nouns can be classified in several ways.

*For more information on different types of nouns, see **Quick Reference: Parts of Speech,** page R46.*

## 1.1 COMMON NOUNS

**Common nouns** are general names, common to entire groups.

## 1.2 PROPER NOUNS

**Proper nouns** name specific, one-of-a-kind people, places, and things.

| Common | Proper |
|---|---|
| legend, canyon, girl, city | Pecos Bill, Canyon de Chelly, Anne, Amsterdam |

*For more information, see **Quick Reference: Capitalization,** page R51.*

## 1.3 SINGULAR AND PLURAL NOUNS

A noun may take a singular or a plural form, depending on whether it names a single person, place, thing, or idea or more than one. Make sure you use appropriate spellings when forming plurals.

| Singular | Plural |
|---|---|
| diary, valley, revolution, calf | diaries, valleys, revolutions, calves |

*For more information, see **Forming Plural Nouns,** page R76.*

## 1.4 POSSESSIVE NOUNS

A **possessive noun** shows who or what owns something.

*For more information, see **Forming Possessives,** page R76.*

# 2 Pronouns

A **pronoun** is a word that is used in place of a noun or another pronoun. The word or word group to which the pronoun refers is called its **antecedent.**

## 2.1 PERSONAL PRONOUNS

**Personal pronouns** change their form to express person, number, gender, and case. The forms of these pronouns are shown in the following chart.

| | Nominative | Objective | Possessive |
|---|---|---|---|
| **Singular** | | | |
| First person | I | me | my, mine |
| Second person | you | you | your, yours |
| Third person | she, he, it | her, him, it | her, hers, his, its |
| **Plural** | | | |
| First person | we | us | our, ours |
| Second person | you | you | your, yours |
| Third person | they | them | their, theirs |

## 2.2 AGREEMENT WITH ANTECEDENT

Pronouns should agree with their antecedents in number, gender, and person.

If an antecedent is singular, use a singular pronoun.
> **EXAMPLE:** *Rachel wrote a **detective story.** It has a surprise ending.*

If an antecedent is plural, use a plural pronoun.
> **EXAMPLES:** *The **characters** have their motives for murder.*
> *Javier loves **mysteries** and reads them all the time.*

The gender of a pronoun must be the same as the gender of its antecedent.
> **EXAMPLE:** *The **man** has to use all his wits to stay alive and solve the crime.*

The person of the pronoun must be the same as the person of its antecedent. As the chart in Section 2.1 shows, a pronoun can be in first-person, second-person, or third-person form.
> **EXAMPLE:** *You want a story to grab your attention.*

Rewrite each sentence so that the underlined pronoun agrees with its antecedent.

1. Lawrence Yep, author of "The Great Rat Hunt," had asthma when <u>it</u> was young.

2. The story's suspense keeps readers interested in <u>them</u>.

3. Yep and his father put out rat traps and place bait on <u>it</u>.

4. When the rat shows <u>their</u> teeth, Yep panics.

5. You and <u>her</u> friends should read the story sometime.

## 2.3 PRONOUN FORMS

Personal pronouns change form to show how they function in sentences. The three forms are the subject form, the object form, and the possessive form. For examples of these pronouns, see the chart in Section 2.1.

A **subject pronoun** is used as a subject in a sentence.

> EXAMPLE: *The poem "Mi Madre" compares the desert to a mother. It was written by Pat Mora.*

Also use the subject form when the pronoun follows a linking verb.

> EXAMPLE: *The person healed by the desert is she.*

An **object pronoun** is used as a direct object, an indirect object, or the object of a preposition.

SUBJECT    OBJECT
*We will give them to her.*
                OBJECT OF PREPOSITION

A **possessive pronoun** shows ownership. The pronouns *mine, yours, hers, his, its, ours,* and *theirs* can be used in place of nouns.

> EXAMPLE: *The desert's gifts are hers.*

The pronouns *my, your, her, his, its, our,* and *their* are used before nouns.

> EXAMPLE: *The poem changed my view of the desert.*

**WATCH OUT!** Many spelling errors can be avoided if you watch out for *its* and *their.* Don't confuse the possessive pronoun *its* with the contraction *it's,* meaning "it is" or "it has." The homonyms *they're* (a contraction of *they are*) and *there* ("in that place") are often mistakenly used for *their.*

**TIP** To decide which pronoun to use in a comparison, such as "He tells better tales than (I *or* me)," fill in the missing word(s): *He tells better tales than I tell.*

Write the correct pronoun form to complete each sentence.

1. The thunder and lightning frightens (her, she).

2. Has (him, he) ever eaten prickly pear?

3. The desert sings, but (its, it) songs are mysterious.

4. Raindrops in the desert would surprise (me, I).

5. The desert has lessons for all of (we, us).

## 2.4 REFLEXIVE AND INTENSIVE PRONOUNS

These pronouns are formed by adding *-self* or *-selves* to certain personal pronouns. Their forms are the same, and they differ only in how they are used.

A **reflexive pronoun** follows a verb or preposition and reflects back on an earlier noun or pronoun.

> EXAMPLES: *He likes himself too much.*
> *She is now herself again.*

**Intensive pronouns** intensify or emphasize the nouns or pronouns to which they refer.

> EXAMPLES: *They themselves will educate their children.*
> *You did it yourself.*

**WATCH OUT!** Avoid using *hisself* or *theirselves*. Standard English does not include these forms.

**NONSTANDARD:** *Colorful desert flowers offer theirselves to the poem's speaker.*

**STANDARD:** *Colorful desert flowers offer themselves to the poem's speaker.*

## 2.5 DEMONSTRATIVE PRONOUNS

**Demonstrative pronouns** point out things and persons near and far.

|        | Singular | Plural |
| ------ | -------- | ------ |
| Near   | this     | these  |
| Far    | that     | those  |

## 2.6 INDEFINITE PRONOUNS

**Indefinite pronouns** do not refer to specific persons or things and usually have no antecedents. The chart shows some commonly used indefinite pronouns.

| Singular | Plural | Singular or Plural | |
| -------- | ------ | --- | ---- |
| another  | both   | all | none |
| anybody  | few    | any | some |
| no one   | many   | more | most |
| neither  |        |     |      |

**TIP** Indefinite pronouns that end in *-one*, *-body*, or *-thing* are always singular.

**INCORRECT:** *Did everybody play their part well?*

If the indefinite pronoun might refer to either a male or a female, *his or her* may be used to refer to it, or the sentence may be rewritten.

**CORRECT:** *Did everybody play his or her part well?*
*Did all the students play their parts well?*

## 2.7 INTERROGATIVE PRONOUNS

An **interrogative pronoun** tells a reader or listener that a question is coming. The interrogative pronouns are *who, whom, whose, which,* and *what.*

**EXAMPLES:** *Who is going to rehearse with you?*
*From whom did you receive the script?*

**TIP** *Who* is used as a subject; *whom,* as an object. To find out which pronoun you need to use in a question, change the question to a statement.

**QUESTION:** *(Who/Whom) did you meet there?*
**STATEMENT:** *You met (?) there.*

Since the verb has a subject (*you*), the needed word must be the object form, *whom.*

**EXAMPLE:** *Whom did you meet there?*

**WATCH OUT!** A special problem arises when you use an interrupter, such as *do you think,* within a question.

**EXAMPLE:** *(Who/Whom) do you think will win?*

If you eliminate the interrupter, it is clear that the word you need is *who.*

## 2.8 RELATIVE PRONOUNS

**Relative pronouns** relate, or connect, adjective clauses to the words they modify in sentences. The noun or pronoun that a relative clause modifies is the antecedent of the relative pronoun. Here are the relative pronouns and their uses.

|               | Subject | Object | Possessive |
| ------------- | ------- | ------ | ---------- |
| Person        | who     | whom   | whose      |
| Thing         | which   | which  | whose      |
| Thing/Person  | that    | that   | whose      |

Often, short sentences with related ideas can be combined by using a relative pronoun to create a more effective sentence.

**SHORT SENTENCE:** *Louisa May Alcott wrote* Hospital Sketches

**RELATED SENTENCE:** Hospital Sketches *describes Alcott's experiences as a volunteer nurse.*

**COMBINED SENTENCE:** *Louisa May Alcott wrote* Hospital Sketches, *which describes her experiences as a volunteer nurse.*

Write the correct form of each incorrect pronoun.

1. Few would have volunteered her services like Alcott did.

2. For who did she risk her own life?

3. Everyone received their care from Alcott.

4. A wounded soldier proved hisself to be respectful.

5. Whom can read her diary without being moved?

## 2.9 PRONOUN REFERENCE PROBLEMS

The referent of a pronoun should always be clear. Avoid problems by rewriting sentences.

An **indefinite reference** occurs when the pronoun *it, you,* or *they* does not clearly refer to a specific antecedent.

UNCLEAR: *People appreciate it when they learn from an author's experiences.*

CLEAR: *People appreciate learning from an author's experiences.*

A **general reference** occurs when the pronoun *it, this, that, which,* or *such* is used to refer to a general idea rather than a specific antecedent.

UNCLEAR: *I picture myself in the author's situation. This helps me understand her reactions.*

CLEAR: *I picture myself in the author's situation. Putting myself in her position helps me understand her reactions.*

*Ambiguous* means "having more than one possible meaning." An **ambiguous reference** occurs when a pronoun could refer to two or more antecedents.

UNCLEAR: *Manuel urged Simon to edit his new film review.*

CLEAR: *Manuel urged Simon to edit Manuel's new film review.*

Rewrite the following sentences to correct indefinite, ambiguous, and general pronoun references.

1. Adams kept seeing the hitchhiker as he walked down the road.

2. Adams didn't pick the hitchhiker up, but it made him feel like a fool.

3. The car stalled on the railroad tracks with a train coming. That almost got Adams killed.

4. When Adams tells his story, they think he's crazy.

# 3 Verbs

A **verb** is a word that expresses an action, a condition, or a state of being.

*For more information, see **Quick Reference: Parts of Speech**, page R47.*

## 3.1 ACTION VERBS

**Action verbs** express mental or physical activity.

EXAMPLE: *Otto Frank comforted his family.*

## 3.2 LINKING VERBS

**Linking verbs** join subjects with words or phrases that rename or describe them.

EXAMPLE: *They were in hiding during the war.*

## 3.3 PRINCIPAL PARTS

Action and linking verbs typically have four principal parts, which are used to form verb tenses. The principal parts are the **present,** the **present participle,** the **past,** and the **past participle.**

Action verbs and some linking verbs also fall into two categories: regular and irregular. A **regular verb** is a verb that forms its past and past participle by adding *-ed* or *-d* to the present form.

| Present | Present Participle | Past | Past Participle |
|---------|--------------------|------|-----------------|
| jump | (is) jumping | jumped | (has) jumped |
| solve | (is) solving | solved | (has) solved |
| grab | (is) grabbing | grabbed | (has) grabbed |
| carry | (is) carrying | carried | (has) carried |

An **irregular verb** is a verb that forms its past and past participle in some other way than by adding -ed or -d to the present form.

| Present | Present Participle | Past | Past Participle |
|---------|--------------------|------|-----------------|
| begin | (is) beginning | began | (has) begun |
| break | (is) breaking | broke | (has) broken |
| go | (is) going | went | (has) gone |

## 3.4 VERB TENSE

The **tense** of a verb indicates the time of the action or the state of being. An action or state of being can occur in the present, the past, or the future. There are six tenses, each expressing a different range of time.

The **present tense** expresses an action or state that is happening at the present time, occurs regularly, or is constant or generally true. Use the present participle.

> NOW: *That snow looks deep.*
> REGULAR: *It snows every day.*
> GENERAL: *Snow falls.*

The **past tense** expresses an action that began and ended in the past. Use the past participle.

> EXAMPLE: *The storyteller finished his tale.*

The **future tense** expresses an action or state that will occur. Use *shall* or *will* with the present participle.

> EXAMPLE: *They will attend the next festival.*

The **present perfect tense** expresses an action or state that (1) was completed at an indefinite time in the past or (2) began in the past and continues into the present. Use *have* or *has* with the past participle.

> EXAMPLE: *Poetry has inspired many readers.*

The **past perfect tense** expresses an action in the past that came before another action in the past. Use *had* with the past participle.

> EXAMPLE: *He had built a fire before the dog ran away.*

The **future perfect tense** expresses an action in the future that will be completed before another action in the future. Use *shall have* or *will have* with the past participle.

> EXAMPLE: *They will have read the novel before they see the movie version of the tale.*

**TIP** A past-tense form of an irregular verb is not used with an auxiliary verb, but a past-participle main irregular verb is always used with an auxiliary verb.

> INCORRECT: *I have saw her somewhere before.* (*Saw* is the past-tense form of an irregular verb and shouldn't be used with *have.*)
> CORRECT: *I have seen her somewhere before.*
> INCORRECT: *I seen her somewhere before.* (*Seen* is the past participle of an irregular verb and shouldn't be used without an auxiliary verb.)

## 3.5 PROGRESSIVE FORMS

The progressive forms of the six tenses show ongoing actions. Use forms of *be* with the present participles of verbs.

> PRESENT PROGRESSIVE: *Anne is arguing her case.*
> PAST PROGRESSIVE: *Anne was arguing her case.*
> FUTURE PROGRESSIVE: *Anne will be arguing her case.*
> PRESENT PERFECT PROGRESSIVE: *Anne has been arguing her case.*
> PAST PERFECT PROGRESSIVE: *Anne had been arguing her case.*
> FUTURE PERFECT PROGRESSIVE: *Anne will have been arguing her case.*

**WATCH OUT!** Do not shift from tense to tense needlessly. Watch out for these special cases.

- In most compound sentences and in sentences with compound predicates, keep the tenses the same.

> INCORRECT: *She defied him, and he scolds her.*
> CORRECT: *She defied him, and he scolded her.*

- If one past action happens before another, do shift tenses.

> INCORRECT: *They wished they started earlier.*
> CORRECT: *They wished they had started earlier.*

## GRAMMAR PRACTICE

Rewrite each sentence, using a form of the verb in parentheses. Identify each form that you use.

1. Frederick Douglass (write) a letter to Harriet Tubman in which he (praise) her.

2. He (say) that she (do) much to benefit enslaved people.

3. People (remember) her work with the Underground Railroad forever.

4. Both Douglass and Tubman (appear) in the history books that kids study.

5. They (inspire) seekers of justice for many years to come.

Rewrite each sentence to correct an error in tense.

1. When she went to the plantations, Tubman's signal has been the spiritual "Go Down Moses."

2. She is leading the slaves all the way from Maryland to Canada, and brought them to freedom.

3. Although she never will have been to Canada, she went bravely on.

4. They arrived safe and sound, but Tubman leaves for the South again.

5. Her life's work for the next six years had began.

### 3.6 ACTIVE AND PASSIVE VOICE

The voice of a verb tells whether its subject performs or receives the action expressed by the verb. When the subject performs the action, the verb is in the **active voice.** When the subject is the receiver of the action, the verb is in the **passive voice.**

Compare these two sentences:

ACTIVE: *Anton Chekhov wrote "The Bet."*

PASSIVE: *"The Bet" was written by Anton Chekhov.*

To form the passive voice, use a form of *be* with the past participle of the verb.

WATCH OUT! Use the passive voice sparingly. It can make writing awkward and less direct.

AWKWARD: *"The Bet" is a short story that was written by Anton Chekhov.*

BETTER: *Anton Chekhov wrote the short story "The Bet."*

There are occasions when you will choose to use the passive voice because

- you want to emphasize the receiver: *The king was shot.*

- the doer is unknown: *My books were stolen.*

- the doer is unimportant: *French is spoken here.*

## 4 Modifiers

Modifiers are words or groups of words that change or limit the meanings of other words. Adjectives and adverbs are common modifiers.

### 4.1 ADJECTIVES

**Adjectives** modify nouns and pronouns by telling which one, what kind, how many, or how much.

WHICH ONE: *this, that, these, those*

EXAMPLE: *This poem uses no capital letters.*

WHAT KIND: *electric, bright, small, open*

EXAMPLE: *An open flame would kill the moth.*

HOW MANY: *one, several, both, none, each*

EXAMPLE: *The moth wants one moment of beauty.*

HOW MUCH: *more, less, enough, as much*

EXAMPLE: *I think the cockroach has more sense than the moth.*

### 4.2 PREDICATE ADJECTIVES

Most adjectives come before the nouns they modify, as in the examples above. A **predicate adjective,** however, follows a linking verb and describes the subject.

EXAMPLE: *My friends are very intelligent.*

Be especially careful to use adjectives (not adverbs) after such linking verbs as *look, feel, grow, taste,* and *smell.*

EXAMPLE: *The bread smells wonderful.*

### 4.3 ADVERBS

**Adverbs** modify verbs, adjectives, and other adverbs by telling where, when, how, or to what extent.

WHERE: *The children played outside.*

WHEN: *The author spoke yesterday.*

HOW: *We walked slowly behind the leader.*

TO WHAT EXTENT: *He worked very hard.*

Adverbs may occur in many places in sentences, both before and after the words they modify.

EXAMPLES: *Suddenly the wind shifted.*

*The wind suddenly shifted.*

*The wind shifted suddenly.*

### 4.4 ADJECTIVE OR ADVERB?

Many adverbs are formed by adding -*ly* to adjectives.

EXAMPLES: *sweet, sweetly; gentle, gently*

However, -*ly* added to a noun will usually yield an adjective.

EXAMPLES: *friend, friendly; woman, womanly*

### 4.5 COMPARISON OF MODIFIERS

Modifiers can be used to compare two or more things. The form of a modifier shows the degree of comparison. Both adjectives and adverbs have **comparative** and **superlative** forms.

The **comparative form** is used to compare two things, groups, or actions.

EXAMPLES: *His father's hands were stronger than his own.*

*My father was more courageous than I am.*

The **superlative form** is used to compare more than two things, groups, or actions.

EXAMPLES: *His father's hands were the strongest in the family.*

*My father was the most courageous of us all.*

### 4.6 REGULAR COMPARISONS

Most one-syllable and some two-syllable adjectives and adverbs have comparatives and superlatives formed by adding -*er* and -*est*. All three-syllable and most two-syllable modifiers have comparatives and superlatives formed with *more* or *most*.

| Modifier | Comparative | Superlative |
|---|---|---|
| small | smaller | smallest |
| thin | thinner | thinnest |
| sleepy | sleepier | sleepiest |
| useless | more useless | most useless |
| precisely | more precisely | most precisely |

**WATCH OUT!** Note that spelling changes must sometimes be made to form the comparatives and superlatives of modifiers.

EXAMPLES: *friendly, friendlier* (Change *y* to *i* and add the ending.)

*sad, sadder* (Double the final consonant and add the ending.)

### 4.7 IRREGULAR COMPARISONS

Some commonly used modifiers have irregular comparative and superlative forms. They are listed in the chart. You may wish to memorize them.

| Modifier | Comparative | Superlative |
|---|---|---|
| good | better | best |
| bad | worse | worst |
| far | farther *or* further | farthest *or* furthest |
| little | less *or* lesser | least |
| many | more | most |
| well | better | best |
| much | more | most |

### 4.8 PROBLEMS WITH MODIFIERS

Study the tips that follow to avoid common mistakes:

**Farther and Further** Use *farther* for distances; use *further* for everything else.

**Double Comparisons** Make a comparison by using -*er*/-*est* or by using *more*/*most*. Using -*er* with *more* or using -*est* with *most* is incorrect.

INCORRECT: *I like her more better than she likes me.*

CORRECT: *I like her better than she likes me.*

**Illogical Comparisons** An illogical or confusing comparison results when two unrelated things are compared or when something is compared with itself. The word *other* or the word *else* should be used when comparing an individual member to the rest of a group.

ILLOGICAL: *The cockroach is smarter than any insect.* (implies that the cockroach isn't an insect)

LOGICAL: *The cockroach is smarter than any other insect.* (identifies that the cockroach is an insect)

**Bad vs. Badly** *Bad,* always an adjective, is used before a noun or after a linking verb. *Badly,* always an adverb, never modifies a noun. Be sure to use the right form after a linking verb.

INCORRECT: *Ed felt badly after his team lost.*

CORRECT: *Ed felt bad after his team lost.*

**Good vs. Well** *Good* is always an adjective. It is used before a noun or after a linking verb. *Well* is often an adverb meaning "expertly" or "properly." *Well* can also be used as an adjective after a linking verb when it means "in good health."

INCORRECT: *Helen writes very good.*

CORRECT: *Helen writes very well.*

CORRECT: *Yesterday I felt bad; today I feel well.*

**Double Negatives** If you add a negative word to a sentence that is already negative, the result will be an error known as a double negative. When using *not* or *-n't* with a verb, use *any-* words, such as *anybody* or *anything,* rather than *no-* words, such as *nobody* or *nothing,* later in the sentence.

INCORRECT: *We haven't seen nobody.*

CORRECT: *We haven't seen anybody.*

Using *hardly, barely,* or *scarcely* after a negative word is also incorrect.

INCORRECT: *They couldn't barely see two feet ahead.*

CORRECT: *They could barely see two feet ahead.*

**Misplaced Modifiers** Sometimes a modifier is placed so far away from the word it modifies that the intended meaning of the sentence is unclear. Prepositional phrases and participial phrases

are often misplaced. Place modifiers as close as possible to the words they modify.

MISPLACED: *We found the child in the park who was missing.*

CLEARER: *We found the child who was missing in the park.* (The child was missing, not the park.)

**Dangling Modifiers** Sometimes a modifier doesn't appear to modify any word in a sentence. Most dangling modifiers are participial phrases or infinitive phrases.

DANGLING: *Looking out the window, his brother was seen driving by.*

CLEARER: *Looking out the window, Josh saw his brother driving by.*

### GRAMMAR PRACTICE

Choose the correct word or words from each pair in parentheses.

1. Mark Twain's attempt at studying the law did not go (good, well).

2. That wasn't the (worse, worst) of his many occupations, however.

3. He actually wasn't a (bad, badly) riverboat pilot.

4. He didn't have (no, any) confidence as a newspaper editor.

5. Still, that turned out to be the (more, most) satisfying job he ever had.

### GRAMMAR PRACTICE

Rewrite each sentence that contains a misplaced or dangling modifier. Write "correct" if the sentence is written correctly.

1. Mark Twain discovered that he was a good storyteller working as an editor.

2. Twain often added exciting details to his stories.

3. It didn't matter to Twain whether all of the details were true in his articles.

4. He wrote sixteen different articles about a single hay wagon in the paper.

5. When all else failed, he made up events.

## 5 The Sentence and Its Parts

A **sentence** is a group of words used to express a complete thought. A complete sentence has a subject and a predicate.

*For more information, see* **Quick Reference: The Sentence and Its Parts,** *page R48.*

### 5.1 KINDS OF SENTENCES

There are four basic types of sentences.

| Type | Definition | Example |
|------|-----------|---------|
| Declarative | states a fact, a wish, an intent, or a feeling | This poem is about Abraham Lincoln. |
| Interrogative | asks a question | Did you understand the metaphor? |
| Imperative | gives a command or direction | Read it more closely. |
| Exclamatory | expresses strong feeling or excitement | Whitman really admired Lincoln! |

### 5.2 COMPOUND SUBJECTS AND PREDICATES

A compound subject consists of two or more subjects that share the same verb. They are typically joined by the coordinating conjunction *and* or *or.*

> **EXAMPLE:** *A short story or novel will keep you engaged.*

A compound predicate consists of two or more predicates that share the same subject. They too are usually joined by a coordinating conjunction: *and, but,* or *or.*

> **EXAMPLE:** *The class finished all the poetry but did not read the short stories.*

### 5.3 COMPLEMENTS

A **complement** is a word or group of words that completes the meaning of the sentence. Some sentences contain only a subject and a verb. Most sentences, however, require additional words placed after the verb to complete the meaning of the sentence. There are three kinds of complements: direct objects, indirect objects, and subject complements.

**Direct objects** are words or word groups that receive the action of action verbs. A direct object answers the question *what* or *whom.*

> **EXAMPLES:** *Ellis recited the poem.* (Recited what?)
> *His performance entertained the class.* (Entertained whom?)

**Indirect objects** tell to whom or what or for whom or what the actions of verbs are performed. Indirect objects come before direct objects. In the following examples, the indirect objects are highlighted.

> **EXAMPLES:** *The teacher gave the speech a good grade.* (Gave to what?)
> *He showed his father the teacher's comments.* (Showed to whom?)

**Subject complements** come after linking verbs and identify or describe the subjects. A subject complement that names or identifies a subject is called a **predicate nominative.** Predicate nominatives include **predicate nouns** and **predicate pronouns.**

> **EXAMPLES:** *My friends are very hard workers.*
> *The best writer in the class is she.*

A subject complement that describes a subject is called a **predicate adjective.**

> **EXAMPLE:** *The pianist appeared very energetic.*

## 6 Phrases

A **phrase** is a group of related words that does not contain a subject and a predicate but functions in a sentence as a single part of speech.

### 6.1 PREPOSITIONAL PHRASES

A **prepositional phrase** is a phrase that consists of a preposition, its object, and any modifiers of the object. Prepositional phrases that modify nouns or pronouns are called **adjective phrases.** Prepositional phrases that modify verbs, adjectives, or adverbs are **adverb phrases.**

> **ADJECTIVE PHRASE:** *The central character of the story is a villain.*
> **ADVERB PHRASE:** *He reveals his nature in the first scene.*

## 6.2 APPOSITIVES AND APPOSITIVE PHRASES

An **appositive** is a noun or pronoun that identifies or renames another noun or pronoun. An **appositive phrase** includes an appositive and modifiers of it. An appositive usually follows the noun or pronoun it identifies.

An appositive can be either **essential** or **nonessential**. An **essential appositive** provides information that is needed to identify what is referred to by the preceding noun or pronoun.

> **EXAMPLE:** *This Greek myth is about the gifted woman Pandora.*

A **nonessential appositive** adds extra information about a noun or pronoun whose meaning is already clear. Nonessential appositives and appositive phrases are set off with commas.

> **EXAMPLE:** *The story, a myth, describes how evil came into the world.*

## 7 Verbals and Verbal Phrases

A **verbal** is a verb form that is used as a noun, an adjective, or an adverb. A **verbal phrase** consists of a verbal along with its modifiers and complements. There are three kinds of verbals: **infinitives, participles,** and **gerunds.**

### 7.1 INFINITIVES AND INFINITIVE PHRASES

An **infinitive** is a verb form that usually begins with *to* and functions as a noun, an adjective, or an adverb. An **infinitive phrase** consists of an infinitive plus its modifiers and complements.

> **NOUN:** *To keep a promise is difficult.* (subject)
> *Pandora tried to obey the gods.* (direct object)
> *Her chief mistake was to become too curious.* (predicate nominative)
> **ADJECTIVE:** *That was an error to regret.* (adjective modifying *error*)
> **ADVERB:** *She opened the box to satisfy her curiosity.* (adverb modifying *opened*)

Because *to* often precedes infinitives, it is usually easy to recognize them. However, sometimes *to* may be omitted.

> **EXAMPLE:** *Her husband helped her [to] forgive herself.*

## 7.2 PARTICIPLES AND PARTICIPIAL PHRASES

A **participle** is a verb form that functions as an adjective. Like adjectives, participles modify nouns and pronouns. Most participles are present-participle forms, ending in *-ing,* or past-participle forms ending in *-ed* or *-en.* In the examples below, the participles are highlighted.

> **MODIFYING A NOUN:** *The dying man had a smile on his face.*
> **MODIFYING A PRONOUN:** *Frustrated, everyone abandoned the cause.*

**Participial phrases** are participles with all their modifiers and complements.

> **MODIFYING A NOUN:** *The dogs searching for survivors are well trained.*
> **MODIFYING A PRONOUN:** *Having approved your proposal, we are ready to act.*

## 7.3 DANGLING AND MISPLACED PARTICIPLES

A participle or participial phrase should be placed as close as possible to the word that it modifies. Otherwise the meaning of the sentence may not be clear.

> **MISPLACED:** *The boys were looking for squirrels searching the trees.*
> **CLEARER:** *The boys searching the trees were looking for squirrels.*

A participle or participial phrase that does not clearly modify anything in a sentence is called a **dangling participle.** A dangling participle causes confusion because it appears to modify a word that it cannot sensibly modify. Correct a dangling participle by providing a word for the participle to modify.

> **DANGLING:** *Running like the wind, my hat fell off.* (The hat wasn't running.)
> **CLEARER:** *Running like the wind, I lost my hat.*

## 7.4 GERUNDS AND GERUND PHRASES

A **gerund** is a verb form ending in *-ing* that functions as a noun. Gerunds may perform any function nouns perform.

> **SUBJECT:** *Jogging is my favorite exercise.*
> **DIRECT OBJECT:** *My sister loves jogging.*

INDIRECT OBJECT: *She gave jogging a try last year.*

SUBJECT COMPLEMENT: *Their real passion is jogging .*

OBJECT OF PREPOSITION: *The effects of jogging .*

**Gerund phrases** are gerunds with all their modifiers and complements.

SUBJECT: *Creating Pandora was Zeus' idea.*

OBJECT OF PREPOSITION: *She suffered greatly after defying the gods.*

APPOSITIVE: *Her husband, remembering his brother Prometheus' fate, forgave her.*

---

**GRAMMAR PRACTICE**

Rewrite each sentence, adding the type of phrase shown in parentheses.

1. I read an excerpt from Anne Frank's diary. (infinitive phrase)

2. Anne was able to maintain her faith in other people. (gerund phrase)

3. Peter Van Daan eventually became Anne's good friend. (appositive phrase)

4. The Nazis found the Franks' hiding place. (prepositional phrase)

5. I know more about World War II. (participial phrase)

---

# 8 Clauses

A **clause** is a group of words that contains a subject and a predicate. There are two kinds of clauses: independent and subordinate.

## 8.1 INDEPENDENT AND SUBORDINATE CLAUSES

An **independent clause** can stand alone as a sentence, as the word *independent* suggests.

INDEPENDENT CLAUSE: *I enjoyed "Pecos Bill."*

A sentence may contain more than one independent clause.

EXAMPLE: *I read it twice, and I gave it to a friend.*

In the preceding example, the coordinating conjunction *and* joins two independent clauses.

*For more coordinating conjunctions, see **Quick Reference: Parts of Speech**, page R47.*

A **subordinate (dependent) clause** cannot stand alone as a sentence. It is subordinate to, or dependent on, an independent clause.

EXAMPLE: *After I read it, I recommended it to my friends.*

The highlighted clause cannot stand by itself.

## 8.2 ADJECTIVE CLAUSES

An **adjective clause** is a subordinate clause used as an adjective. It usually follows the noun or pronoun it modifies.

EXAMPLE: *The legend that the story retells is about a cowboy.*

Adjective clauses are typically introduced by the relative pronouns *who, whom, whose, which,* and *that.*

*For more information, see **Relative Pronouns**, page R54.*

EXAMPLE: *Pecos Bill, who was raised by coyotes, lived with them for seventeen years.*

An adjective clause can be either essential or nonessential. An **essential adjective clause** provides information that is necessary to identify the preceding noun or pronoun.

EXAMPLE: *He needed to find people who could appreciate him.*

A **nonessential adjective clause** adds additional information about a noun or pronoun whose meaning is already clear. Nonessential clauses are set off with commas.

EXAMPLE: *He carried his horse, which had broken its ankle, around his neck.*

## 8.3 ADVERB CLAUSES

An **adverb clause** is a subordinate clause that is used to modify a verb, an adjective, or an adverb. It is introduced by a subordinating conjunction.

*For examples of subordinating conjunctions, see **Noun Clauses**, page R63.*

Adverb clauses typically occur at the beginning or end of sentences.

**MODIFYING A VERB:** *When he got bored, Nick told stories.*

**MODIFYING AN ADVERB:** *Most people study more than Bob does.*

**MODIFYING AN ADJECTIVE:** *He was excited because a cyclone was forming.*

**TIP** An adverb clause should be followed by a comma when it comes before an independent clause. When an adverb clause comes after an independent clause, a comma may not be needed.

### 8.4 NOUN CLAUSES

A **noun clause** is a subordinate clause that is used as a noun. A noun clause may be used as a subject, a direct object, an indirect object, a predicate nominative, or the object of a preposition. Noun clauses are introduced either by pronouns, such as *that, what, who, whoever, which,* and *whose,* or by subordinating conjunctions, such as *how, when, where, why,* and *whether.*

*For more subordinating conjunctions, see* **Quick Reference: Parts of Speech,** *page R47.*

**TIP** Because the same words may introduce adjective and noun clauses, you need to consider how a clause functions within its sentence. To determine if a clause is a noun clause, try substituting *something* or *someone* for the clause. If you can do it, it is probably a noun clause.

**EXAMPLES:** *I know whose woods these are.*

("I know *something.*" The clause is a noun clause, direct object of the verb *know.*)

*Give a copy to whoever wants one.* ("Give a copy to *someone.*" The clause is a noun clause, object of the preposition *to.*)

**GRAMMAR PRACTICE**

Add descriptive details to each sentence by writing the type of clause indicated in parentheses.

1. Legends delight our imaginations. (adverb clause)

2. Superheroes are exciting characters. (adjective clause)

3. Don't try to copy, though. (noun clause)

4. What would your hero be able to do? (adverb clause)

5. Superheroes can inspire us to do the best work. (adjective clause)

## 9 The Structure of Sentences

When classified by their structure, there are four kinds of sentences: simple, compound, complex, and compound-complex.

### 9.1 SIMPLE SENTENCES

A **simple sentence** is a sentence that has one independent clause and no subordinate clauses.

**EXAMPLES:** *Sam ran to the theater.*

*Max waited in front of the theater.*

A simple sentence may contain a compound subject or a compound verb.

**EXAMPLES:** *Sam and Max went to the movie.* (compound subject)

*They clapped and cheered at their favorite parts.* (compound verb)

### 9.2 COMPOUND SENTENCES

A **compound sentence** consists of two or more independent clauses. The clauses in compound sentences are joined with commas and coordinating conjunctions (*and, but, or, nor, yet, for, so*) or with semicolons. Like simple sentences, compound sentences do not contain any subordinate clauses.

**EXAMPLES:** *Sam likes action movies, but Max prefers comedies.*

*The actor jumped from one building to another; he barely made the final leap.*

**WATCH OUT!** Do not confuse compound sentences with simple sentences that have compound parts.

> **EXAMPLE:** *The actor knew all the lines but didn't play the part well.*

(Here *but* joins parts of a compound predicate, not a compound sentence.)

## 9.3 COMPLEX SENTENCES

A **complex sentence** consists of one independent clause and one or more subordinate clauses.

> **EXAMPLES:** *One should not complain unless one has a better solution.*
>
> *Mr. Neiman, who is an artist, sketched pictures until the sun went down.*

## 9.4 COMPOUND-COMPLEX SENTENCES

A **compound-complex sentence** contains two or more independent clauses and one or more subordinate clauses. Compound-complex sentences are, simply, both compound and complex. If you start with a compound sentence, all you need to do to form a compound-complex sentence is add a subordinate clause.

> **COMPOUND:** *All the students knew the answer, yet they were too shy to volunteer.*
>
> **COMPOUND-COMPLEX:** *All the students knew the answer that their teacher expected, yet they were too shy to volunteer.*

## 9.5 PARALLEL STRUCTURE

When you write sentences, make sure that coordinate parts are equivalent, or **parallel,** in structure.

> **NOT PARALLEL:** *On Saturday I practiced chess and to play the flute.* (*Practice* is a verb; *to play the flute* is a phrase.)
>
> **PARALLEL:** *On Saturday I practiced chess and played the flute.* (*Practiced* and *played* are both verbs.)
>
> **NOT PARALLEL:** *I want to lose weight, becoming a musician, and good grades.* (*To lose weight* is an infinitive phrase, *becoming a musician* is a gerund phrase, and *grades* is a noun.)
>
> **PARALLEL:** *I want to lose weight, to become a musician, and to get good grades.* (*To lose, to become,* and *to get* are all infinitives.)

# 10 Writing Complete Sentences

Remember, a sentence is a group of words that expresses a complete thought. In writing that you wish to share with a reader, try to avoid both sentence fragments and run-on sentences.

## 10.1 CORRECTING FRAGMENTS

A **sentence fragment** is a group of words that is only part of a sentence. It does not express a complete thought and may be confusing to a reader or listener. A sentence fragment may be lacking a subject, a predicate, or both.

> **FRAGMENT:** *Worried about not doing well.* (no subject)
>
> **CORRECTED:** *Laura worried about not doing well.*
>
> **FRAGMENT:** *Her mother and father.* (no predicate)
>
> **CORRECTED:** *Her mother and father were both highly successful.*
>
> **FRAGMENT:** *In a gentle way.* (neither subject nor predicate)
>
> **CORRECTED:** *They tried to encourage her in a gentle way.*

In your writing, fragments may be a result of haste or incorrect punctuation. Sometimes fixing a fragment will be a matter of attaching it to a preceding or following sentence.

> **FRAGMENT:** *Laura did her best. But never felt satisfied.*
>
> **CORRECTED:** *Laura did her best but never felt satisfied.*

## 10.2 CORRECTING RUN-ON SENTENCES

A **run-on sentence** is made up of two or more sentences written as though they were one. Some run-ons have no punctuation within them. Others may have only commas where conjunctions or stronger punctuation marks are necessary.

Use your judgment in correcting run-on sentences, as you have choices. You can change a run-on to two sentences if the thoughts are not closely connected. If the thoughts are closely related, you can keep the run-on as one sentence by adding a semicolon or a conjunction.

> RUN-ON: *She joined more clubs her friendships suffered.*
>
> MAKE TWO SENTENCES: *She joined more clubs. Her friendships suffered.*
>
> RUN-ON: *She joined more clubs they took up all her time.*
>
> USE A SEMICOLON: *She joined more clubs; they took up all her time.*
>
> ADD A CONJUNCTION: *She joined more clubs, but they took up all her time.*

**WATCH OUT!** When you form compound sentences, make sure you use appropriate punctuation: a comma before a coordinating conjunction, a semicolon when there is no coordinating conjunction. A very common mistake is to use a comma alone instead of a comma and a conjunction. This error is called a **comma splice.**

> INCORRECT: *He finished the job, he left the village.*
>
> CORRECT: *He finished the job, and he left the village.*

# 11 Subject-Verb Agreement

The subject and verb in a clause must agree in number. Agreement means that if the subject is singular, the verb is also singular, and if the subject is plural, the verb is also plural.

## 11.1 BASIC AGREEMENT

Fortunately, agreement between subjects and verbs in English is simple. Most verbs show the difference between singular and plural only in the third person of the present tense. In the present tense, the third-person singular form ends in *-s*.

| Present-Tense Verb Forms | |
|---|---|
| **Singular** | **Plural** |
| I sleep | we sleep |
| you sleep | you sleep |
| she he it sleeps | they sleep |

## 11.2 AGREEMENT WITH *BE*

The verb *be* presents special problems in agreement, because this verb does not follow the usual verb patterns.

| Forms of *Be* | | | |
|---|---|---|---|
| **Present Tense** | | **Past Tense** | |
| **Singular** | **Plural** | **Singular** | **Plural** |
| I am | we are | I was | we were |
| you are | you are | you were | you were |
| she he it is | they are | she he it was | they were |

## 11.3 WORDS BETWEEN SUBJECT AND VERB

A verb agrees only with its subject. When words come between a subject and a verb, ignore them when considering proper agreement. Identify the subject and make sure the verb agrees with it.

> EXAMPLES: *Whipped cream served with berries is my favorite sweet.*
>
> *A study by scientists recommends eating berries.*

## 11.4 AGREEMENT WITH COMPOUND SUBJECTS

Use plural verbs with most compound subjects joined by the word *and*.

> EXAMPLE: *My father and his friends play chess every day.*

To confirm that you need a plural verb, you could substitute the plural pronoun *they* for *my father and his friends*.

If a compound subject is thought of as a unit, use a singular verb. Test this by substituting the singular pronoun *it*.

> EXAMPLE: *Peanut butter and jelly [it] is my brother's favorite sandwich.*

Use a singular verb with a compound subject that is preceded by *each, every,* or *many a*.

> EXAMPLE: *Each novel and short story seems grounded in personal experience.*

When the parts of a compound subject are joined by *or, nor,* or the correlative conjunctions *either . . . or* or *neither . . . nor,* make the verb agree with the noun or pronoun nearest the verb.

> **EXAMPLES:** *Cookies or ice cream is my favorite dessert.*
>
> *Either Cheryl or her friends are being invited.*
>
> *Neither ice storms nor snow is predicted today.*

## 11.5 PERSONAL PRONOUNS AS SUBJECTS

When using a personal pronoun as a subject, make sure to match it with the correct form of the verb *be.* (See the chart in Section 11.2.) Note especially that the pronoun *you* takes the forms *are* and *were,* regardless of whether it is singular or plural.

**WATCH OUT!** *You is* and *you was* are nonstandard forms and should be avoided in writing and speaking. *We was* and *they was* are also forms to be avoided.

> **INCORRECT:** *You was a good student.*
>
> **CORRECT:** *You were a good student.*
>
> **INCORRECT:** *They was starting a new school.*
>
> **CORRECT:** *They were starting a new school.*

## 11.6 INDEFINITE PRONOUNS AS SUBJECTS

Some indefinite pronouns are always singular; some are always plural.

| Singular Indefinite Pronouns | | | |
|---|---|---|---|
| another | either | neither | one |
| anybody | everybody | nobody | somebody |
| anyone | everyone | no one | someone |
| anything | everything | nothing | something |
| each | much | | |

> **EXAMPLES:** *Each of the writers was given an award.*
>
> *Somebody in the room upstairs is sleeping.*

| Plural Indefinite Pronouns | | | |
|---|---|---|---|
| both | few | many | several |

> **EXAMPLES:** *Many of the books in our library are not in circulation.*
>
> *Few have been returned recently.*

Still other indefinite pronouns may be either singular or plural.

| Singular or Plural Indefinite Pronouns | | |
|---|---|---|
| all | more | none |
| any | most | some |

The number of the indefinite pronoun *any* or *none* often depends on the intended meaning.

> **EXAMPLES:** *Any of these topics has potential for a good article.* (any one topic)
>
> *Any of these topics have potential for good articles.* (all of the many topics)

The indefinite pronouns *all, some, more, most,* and *none* are singular when they refer to quantities or parts of things. They are plural when they refer to numbers of individual things. Context will usually provide a clue.

> **EXAMPLES:** *All of the flour is gone.* (referring to a quantity)
>
> *All of the flowers are gone.* (referring to individual items)

## 11.7 INVERTED SENTENCES

A sentence in which the subject follows the verb is called an **inverted sentence.** A subject can follow a verb or part of a verb phrase in a question, a sentence beginning with *here* or *there,* or a sentence in which an adjective, an adverb, or a phrase is placed first.

> **EXAMPLES:** *There clearly are far too many cooks in this kitchen.*
>
> *What is the correct ingredient for this stew?*
>
> *Far from the frazzled cooks stands the master chef.*

**TIP** To check subject-verb agreement in some inverted sentences, place the subject before the verb. For example, change *There are many people* to *Many people are there.*

## 11.8 SENTENCES WITH PREDICATE NOMINATIVES

In a sentence containing a predicate noun (nominative), the verb should agree with the subject, not the predicate noun.

**EXAMPLES:** *The poems of Henry Wadsworth Longfellow are a unique record of U.S. history.* (*Poems* is the subject—not *record*—and it takes the plural verb *are.*)

*One unique record of U.S. history is the poems of Henry Wadsworth Longfellow.* (The subject is *record*—not *poems*—and it takes the singular verb *is.*)

## 11.9 *DON'T* AND *DOESN'T* AS AUXILIARY VERBS

The auxiliary verb *doesn't* is used with singular subjects and with the personal pronouns *she, he,* and *it.* The auxiliary verb *don't* is used with plural subjects and with the personal pronouns *I, we, you,* and *they.*

**SINGULAR:** *Doesn't the poem "Paul Revere's Ride" sound almost like a news report?*

*It doesn't sound like a poem, even though it rhymes.*

**PLURAL:** *People don't know enough about history.*

*Don't they think history is important?*

## 11.10 COLLECTIVE NOUNS AS SUBJECTS

**Collective nouns** are singular nouns that name groups of persons or things. *Team,* for example, is the collective name of a group of individuals. A collective noun takes a singular verb when the group acts as a single unit. It takes a plural verb when the members of the group act separately.

**EXAMPLES:** *Our team usually wins.* (The team as a whole wins.)

*The faculty vote differently on most issues.* (The individual members of the faculty vote.)

## 11.11 RELATIVE PRONOUNS AS SUBJECTS

When the relative pronoun *who, which,* or *that* is used as a subject in an adjective clause, the verb in the clause must agree in number with the antecedent of the pronoun.

**SINGULAR:** *The **poem** that affects me most is "Mother to Son."*

The antecedent of the relative pronoun *that* is the singular *poem;* therefore, *that* is singular and must take the singular verb *affects.*

**PLURAL:** *Langston Hughes and Gwendolyn Brooks are African-American poets who write about overcoming life's problems.*

The antecedent of the relative pronoun *who* is the plural compound subject *Langston Hughes and Gwendolyn Brooks.* Therefore *who* is plural, and it takes the plural verb *write.*

### GRAMMAR PRACTICE

Locate the subject in each sentence below. Then choose the correct verb form.

1. Daniel Keyes's story "Flowers for Algernon" (describes, describe) a mentally challenged man who takes part in a scientific experiment.
2. (Doesn't, Don't) the doctors treat him like a laboratory mouse?
3. Nobody (realizes, realize) the danger in this experiment.
4. The development of his mental abilities (become, becomes) clear in his growing language skills.
5. His perceptions, as well as his intelligence, (becomes, become) extremely sharp.
6. There (is, are) moments of joy when he falls in love with Miss Kinnian.
7. Everything (progresses, progress) well until he is fired from his job.
8. All of his insights just (makes, make) people withdraw from him.
9. Even the doctors who work with him (treat, treats) him poorly.
10. Neither Algernon's death nor Charlie's own mental failings (seems, seem) sadder than his awareness of what's happening to him.

The key to becoming an independent reader is to develop a tool kit of vocabulary strategies. By learning and practicing the strategies, you'll know what to do when you encounter unfamiliar words while reading. You'll also know how to refine the words you use for different situations—personal, school, and work.

Being a good speller is important when communicating your ideas in writing. Learning basic spelling rules and checking your spelling in a dictionary will help you spell words that you may not use frequently.

**VOCABULARY PRACTICE**
For more practice, go to the **Vocabulary Center** at **ClassZone.com.**

# 1 Using Context Clues

The context of a word is made up of the punctuation marks, words, sentences, and paragraphs that surround the word. A word's context can give you important clues about its meaning.

## 1.1 GENERAL CONTEXT

Sometimes you need to determine the meaning of an unfamiliar word by reading all the information in a passage.

> Stop teasing me! Just because you are a better tennis player than I am doesn't mean you should belittle my abilities.

You can figure out from the context that *belittle* means "make something less than it is."

## 1.2 IDIOMS, SLANG, AND FIGURATIVE LANGUAGE

An **idiom** is an expression whose overall meaning differs from the meaning of the individual words.

> A nasty case of the flu kept me under the weather. (Under the weather means "tired and sickly.")

**Slang** is informal language in which made-up words and ordinary words are used to mean something different from their meanings in formal English.

> I'm going to jazz up this salad with some walnuts. (Jazz up means "make more interesting.")

**Figurative language** is language that communicates meaning beyond the literal meaning of the words.

> The lone desert monument was like a sentinel standing guard. (Lone and standing guard help describe a sentinel.)

## 1.3 SPECIFIC CONTEXT CLUES

Sometimes writers help you understand the meanings of words by providing specific clues such as those shown in the chart.

| Specific Context Clues | | |
|---|---|---|
| **Type of Clue** | **Key Words/ Phrases** | **Example** |
| **Definition or restatement** of the meaning of the word | or, which is, that is, in other words, also known as, also called | Olympic gymnasts are very *limber,* or **flexible.** |
| **Example** following an unfamiliar word | such as, like, as if, for example, especially, including | We collected *kindling,* such as **dry twigs and branches,** to start the fire. |
| **Comparison** with a more familiar word or concept | as, like, also, similar to, in the same way, likewise | Kari's face was *luminous,* **like the rays of the sun.** |
| **Contrast** with a familiar word or experience | unlike, but, however, although, on the other hand, on the contrary | The summer was *sultry,* but the fall was **dry and cool.** |
| **Cause-and-effect** relationship in which one term is familiar | because, since, when, consequently, as a result, therefore | When the *tree fell across the road,* it **obstructed** traffic. |

For more information, see ***Vocabulary Strategy: Synonyms as Context Clues,*** *page 272,* ***Vocabulary Strategy: Idioms,*** *pages 325 and 726, and* ***Vocabulary Strategy: Antonyms and Context Clues,*** *page 1009.*

# 2 Analyzing Word Structure

Many words can be broken into smaller parts. These word parts include base words, roots, prefixes, and suffixes.

## 2.1 BASE WORDS

A **base word** is a word part that by itself is also a word. Other words or word parts can be added to base words to form new words.

*For more information, see **Vocabulary Strategy: Recognizing Base Words,** page 892.*

## 2.2 ROOTS

A **root** is a word part that contains the core meaning of the word. Many English words contain roots that come from older languages such as Greek, Latin, Old English (Anglo-Saxon), and Norse. Knowing the meaning of the word's root can help you determine the word's meaning.

| Root | Meaning | Example |
|------|---------|---------|
| *aud* (Latin) | hear | **aud**io, **aud**ition |
| *voc* (Latin) | voice | **voc**al, in**vok**e |
| *mem, ment* (Latin) | mind | **mem**ory, **ment**al, **ment**ion |
| *chron* (Greek) | time | **chron**ic, syn**chron**ize |
| *gram* (Greek) | something written | tele**gram**, **gram**mar |
| *gen* (Greek) | race, family | **gen**esis, **gen**re, **gen**ius |

*For more information, see **Vocabulary Strategy: Word Roots,** pages 117, 372, 631, 713, 937, 978, and 992.*

## 2.3 PREFIXES

A **prefix** is a word part attached to the beginning of a word or word root. Most prefixes come from Greek, Latin, or Old English.

| Prefix | Meaning | Example |
|--------|---------|---------|
| mid- | middle, center | **mid**night |
| pro- | forward | **pro**ceed, **pro**cession |
| uni- | one | **uni**form, **uni**cycle |
| tele- | view | **tele**scope |
| multi- | many, much | **multi**media, **multi**vitamins |

*For more information, see **Vocabulary Strategy: Prefixes,** pages 60, 236, and 414.*

## 2.4 SUFFIXES

A **suffix** is a word part that appears at the end of a root or base word to form a new word. Some suffixes do not change word meaning. These suffixes are

- added to nouns to change the number of persons or objects
- added to verbs to change the tense
- added to modifiers to change the degree of comparison

| Suffix | Meaning | Examples |
|--------|---------|----------|
| -s, -es | to change the number of a noun | lock + s = locks |
| -d, -ed, -ing | to change verb tense | stew + ed = stewed |
| -er, -est | to indicate comparison in modifiers | mild + er = milder<br>soft + est = softest |

Other suffixes can be added to the root or base to change the word's meaning. These suffixes can also determine a word's part of speech.

| Suffix | Meaning | Example |
|--------|---------|---------|
| -age | amount | foot**age** |
| -able, -ible | able, inclined to | read**able**, tang**ible** |
| -ant, -ent | a specific state or condition | pleas**ant**, differ**ent** |

*For more information, see **Vocabulary Strategy: Suffixes that Form Nouns,** page 74, **Vocabulary Strategy: Suffixes that Form Adjectives,** page 926.*

### Strategies for Understanding Unfamiliar Words

- Look for any prefixes or suffixes. Remove them so that you can concentrate on the base word or the root.

- See if you recognize any elements—prefix, suffix, root, or base—of the word. You may be able to guess its meaning by analyzing one or two elements.

- Think about the way the word is used in the sentence. Use the context and the word parts to make a logical guess about the word's meaning.

- Look in a dictionary to see whether you are correct.

## 3 Understanding Word Origins

### 3.1 DEVELOPMENT OF THE ENGLISH LANGUAGE

During the past 2,000 years or so, English has developed from a language spoken by a few Germanic tribes into a language that is more widely spoken and written than any other in the world. Some experts, in fact, call today's English the first truly global language. Its most valuable characteristic is its ability to change and grow, adopting new words as the need arises. The history of the English language can be divided into three main periods.

**Old English** About the year A.D. 449, Germanic people who lived on the European continent along the North Sea began a series of invasions into Britain. At that time, Britain was inhabited by the Celts, whose native language was Gaelic. Over a period of years, the raiders conquered and settled in Britain. The conquerors, known today as the Anglo-Saxons, prospered in Britain. In time, Britain became "Engla land," and the Anglo-Saxon languages evolved into "Englisc," or what modern scholars call Old English.

Old English was very different from the English we speak today. It was harsher in sound, had no silent letters, and was written phonetically. Few examples of Old English remain in our current English vocabulary. Those that do exist, however, are common words for people, places, things, and actions.

| | | |
|---|---|---|
| man (*mann*) | wife (*wif*) | child (*cild*) |
| house (*hus*) | meat (*mete*) | drink (*drincan*) |
| sleep (*slæpan*) | live (*libban*) | fight (*feohtan*) |

In the sixth and seventh centuries, missionaries from Rome and other Christian cities arrived in England, bringing with them their knowledge of religion and ancient languages. Among the most influential figures was St. Augustine, who converted thousands of Anglo-Saxons, including a king, to Christianity. As the Anglo-Saxons accepted this faith, they also accepted words from Latin and Greek.

| Latin | Greek |
|---|---|
| candle | alphabet |
| cup | angel |
| priest | box |
| noon | demon |
| scripture | school |

During the late 8th century, Viking invaders from Denmark and Norway settled in northeast England. As a result, Scandinavian words became part of Old English.

| | | |
|---|---|---|
| sky | knife | are |
| steak | leg | birth |
| they | skin | seat |
| window | them | their |

**Middle English** The Norman Conquest brought great changes to England and its language. In 1066, England was defeated by the Normans, a people from an area in France. Their leader, William the Conqueror, staged a successful invasion of England and became the nation's new monarch. With William on the throne of England, Norman French became the language of the English court, government business, nobility, and scholars. Eventually, French words were adopted in everyday vocabulary as well.

The language that evolved is called Middle English. Middle English was not as harsh-sounding as Old English and borrowed many words from Norman French.

| | | |
|---|---|---|
| attorney | joint | mallet |
| baron | jolly | marriage |
| chivalry | laundry | merchandise |
| gown | lodge | petty |

Norman French itself borrowed thousands of words from Latin and Greek, as well as from ancient Indian and Semitic languages. Consequently, Middle English also contained many of these foreign terms.

| Latin | Greek | Indian | Semitic |
|---|---|---|---|
| language | circle | ginger | camel |
| library | hour | jungle | cinnamon |
| money | lantern | orange | coffee |
| serpent | leopard | sugar | lion |
| square | magnet | pepper | syrup |

**Modern English** By the late 1400s, Middle English began to develop into Modern English. The various pronunciations, word forms, and spellings common to Middle English were becoming more uniform. One invention that aided this process was the printing press. Introduced to London around 1476, the printing press allowed printers to standardize the spellings of common English words. As a result, readers and writers of English became accustomed to following "rules" of spelling and grammar.

During this period, the English vocabulary also continued to grow as new ideas and discoveries demanded new words. As the English began to colonize and trade with other areas of the world, they borrowed foreign words. In time, the English vocabulary grew to include words from diverse languages, such as French, Dutch, Spanish, Italian, Portuguese, and Chinese. Many of these words stayed the way they were in their original languages.

| French | Dutch | Spanish | Italian |
|---|---|---|---|
| ballet | boss | canyon | diva |
| beret | caboose | rodeo | carnival |
| mirage | dock | taco | spaghetti |
| vague | skate | tornado | studio |

| Portuguese | Chinese | Japanese | Native American |
|---|---|---|---|
| cashew | chow | kamikaze | caribou |
| mango | ginseng | karaoke | moccasin |
| jaguar | kung fu | sushi | papoose |
| yam | kow tow | tsunami | tomahawk |

Today, the English language is still changing and absorbing new words. It is considered the international language of science and technology. It is also widely used in business and politics.

## 3.2 DICTIONARY AS A SOURCE OF WORD ORIGINS

Many dictionary entries provide information about a word's origin. This information often comes at the end of an entry, as in this example.

**ge•om•e•try** (jē-ŏm′ĭ-trē) *n., pl.* **-tries 1.** The mathematics of the properties, measurement, and relationships of points, lines, angles, surfaces, and solids. **2.** Arrangement. **3.** A physical arrangement suggesting geometric forms or lines. [from Greek *geōmetriā,* from *geōmetrein,* to measure land].

## 3.3 WORD FAMILIES

Words that have the same root make up a word family and have related meanings. The charts below show some common Greek and Latin roots. Notice how the meanings of the example words are related to the meanings of their roots.

| Latin Root | *circum,* around or about |
|---|---|
| English | **circumference** the boundary line of a circle |
| | **circumnavigation** the act of moving completely around |
| | **circumstance** a condition or fact surrounding an event |
| **Greek Root** | *monos,* single or alone |
| English | **monopoly** exclusive control by one group |
| | **monologue** a speech delivered by one person |
| | **monotonous** sounded or spoken in a single unvarying tone |

**TIP** Once you recognize a root in one English word, you will notice the same root in other words. Because these words develop from the same root, all words in the word family are similar in meaning.

*For more information, see **Vocabulary Strategy: Researching Word Origins,** pages 595 and 903.*

## 4 Synonyms and Antonyms

### 4.1 SYNONYMS

| Positive | Negative |
|---|---|
| slender | scrawny |
| thrifty | cheap |
| young | immature |

A **synonym** is a word with a meaning similar to that of another word. You can find synonyms in a thesaurus or a dictionary. In a dictionary, synonyms are often given as part of the definition of the word. The following word pairs are synonyms:

satisfy/please     occasionally/sometimes

rob/steal     schedule/agenda

*For more information, see **Vocabulary Strategy: Synonyms as Context Clues,** page 272.*

### 4.2 ANTONYMS

An **antonym** is a word with a meaning opposite that of another word. The following word pairs are antonyms:

accurate/incorrect     similar/different

fresh/stale     unusual/ordinary

*For more information, see **Vocabulary Strategy: Antonyms and Context Clues,** page 1009.*

## 5 Denotation and Connotation

### 5.1 DENOTATION

A word's dictionary meaning is called its **denotation.** For example, the denotation of the word *thin* is "having little flesh; spare; lean."

## 5.2 CONNOTATION

The images or feelings you connect to a word add a finer shade of meaning, called **connotation.** The connation of a word goes beyond its basic dictionary definition. Writers use connotations of words to communicate positive or negative feelings.

Make sure you understand the denotation and connotation of a word when you read it or use it in your writing.

*For more information, see* **Vocabulary Strategy: Denotations and Connotations,** *pages 693, 845, and 917.*

## 6 Analogies

An **analogy** is a comparison between two things that are similar in some way but are otherwise not alike. Analogies are sometimes used in writing when unfamiliar subjects or ideas are explained in terms of familiar ones. Analogies often appear on tests as well. In an analogy problem, the analogy is expressed using two groups of words. The relationship between the first pair of words is the same as the relationship between the second pair of words. Some analogy problems are expressed like this:

love : hate :: war: _____
**a.** soldier **b.** peace **c.** battle **d.** argument

Follow these steps to determine the correct answer:

- Read the problem as "*love* is to *hate* as **war** is to...."

- Ask yourself how the words *love* and *hate* are related. (*Love* and *hate* are antonyms.)

- Ask yourself which answer choice is an antonym of *war*. (*Peace* is an antonym of *war*, therefore *peace* is the best answer.)

*For more information, see* **Vocabulary Strategy: Analogies,** *pages 252 and 780.*

## 7 Homonyms, Homographs, and Homophones

### 7.1 HOMONYMS

**Homonyms** are words that have the same spelling and sound but have different meanings.

*The snake shed its skin in the shed behind the house.*

*Shed* can mean "to lose by natural process," but an identically spelled word means "a small structure."

Sometimes only one of the meanings of a homonym may be familiar to you. Use context clues to help you figure out the meaning of an unfamiliar word.

### 7.2 HOMOGRAPHS

**Homographs** are words that are spelled the same but have different meanings and origins. Some are also pronounced differently, as in these examples.

*Please close the door. (clōz)*
*That was a close call. (clōs)*

If you see a word used in a way that is unfamiliar to you, check a dictionary to see if it is a homograph.

*For more information, see* **Vocabulary Strategy: Homographs,** *pages 356 and 798.*

### 7.3 HOMOPHONES

**Homophones** are words that sound alike but have different meanings and spellings. The following homophones are frequently misused:

| | |
|---|---|
| it's/its | they're/their/there |
| to/too/two | stationary/stationery |

Many misused homophones are pronouns and contractions. Whenever you are unsure whether to write *your* or *you're* and *who's* or *whose*, ask yourself if you mean *you are* and *who is/has*. If you do, write the contraction. For other homophones, such as *fair* and *fare*, use the meaning of the word to help you decide which one to use.

## 8 Words with Multiple Meanings

Some words have acquired additional meanings over time that are based on the original meaning.

*I had to be replaced in the cast of the play because of the cast on my arm.*

These two uses of *cast* have different meanings, but both of them have the same origin. You will find all the meanings of *cast* listed in one entry in the dictionary.

*For more information, see* **Vocabulary Strategy: Multiple-Meaning Words,** *page 281.*

## 9 Specialized Vocabulary

**Specialized vocabulary** is special terms suited to a particular field of study or work. For example, science, mathematics, and history all have their own technical or specialized vocabularies. To figure out specialized terms, you can use context clues and reference sources, such as dictionaries on specific subjects, atlases, or manuals.

*For more information, see* **Vocabulary Strategy: Specialized Vocabulary,** *page 220.*

## 10 Using Reference Sources

### 10.1 DICTIONARIES

A **general dictionary** will tell you not only a word's definitions but also its pronunciation, parts of speech, and history and origin, or etymology.

**❶ tangible** (tăn′jə-bəl) **❷** *adj.* **❸**
**1a.** Discernible by the touch; palpable. **b.** Possible to touch. **c.** Possible to be treated as fact; real or concrete. **2.** Possible to understand or realize. **3.** Law that can be valued monetarily [Late Latin *tangibilis,* from Latin *tangere,* to touch] **❺**

**❶** Entry word
**❷** Pronunciation
**❸** Part of speech
**❹** Definitions
**❺** Etymology

A **specialized dictionary** focuses on terms related to a particular field of study or work. Use a dictionary to check the spelling of any word you are unsure of in your English class and other classes as well.

*For more information, see* **Vocabulary Strategy: Using Reference Aids,** *pages 85 and 461.*

### 10.2 THESAURI

A **thesaurus** (plural, *thesauri*) is a dictionary of synonyms. A thesaurus can be especially helpful when you find yourself using the same modifiers over and over again.

### 10.3 SYNONYM FINDERS

A **synonym finder** is often included in word-processing software. It enables you to highlight a word and be shown a display of its synonyms.

### 10.4 GLOSSARIES

A **glossary** is a list of specialized terms and their definitions. It is often found in the back of a book and sometimes includes pronunciations. Many textbooks contain glossaries. In fact, this textbook has three glossaries: the **Glossary of Literary Terms,** the **Glossary of Reading & Informational Terms,** and the **Glossary of Vocabulary in English & Spanish.** Use these glossaries to help you understand how terms are used in this textbook.

## 11 Spelling Rules

### 11.1 WORDS ENDING IN A SILENT E

Before adding a suffix beginning with a vowel or *y* to a word ending in a silent *e,* drop the *e* (with some exceptions).

**amaze + -ing = amazing**
**love + -able = lovable**
**create + -ed = created**
**nerve + -ous = nervous**

**Exceptions:** *change + -able = changeable; courage + -ous = courageous*

When adding a suffix beginning with a consonant to a word ending in a silent *e,* keep the *e* (with some exceptions).

**late + -ly = lately**
**spite + -ful = spiteful**
**noise + -less = noiseless**
**state + -ment = statement**

**Exceptions:** *truly, argument, ninth, wholly, awful,* and others

When a suffix beginning with *a* or *o* is added to a word with a final silent *e*, the final *e* is usually retained if it is preceded by a soft *c* or a soft *g*.

**bridge + -able = bridgeable**
**peace + -able = peaceable**
**outrage + -ous = outrageous**
**advantage + -ous = advantageous**

When a suffix beginning with a vowel is added to words ending in *ee* or *oe*, the final silent *e* is retained.

**agree + -ing = agreeing**     **free + -ing = freeing**
**hoe + -ing = hoeing**         **see + -ing = seeing**

## 11.2 WORDS ENDING IN Y

Before adding most suffixes to a word that ends in *y* preceded by a consonant, change the *y* to *i*.

**easy + -est = easiest**
**crazy + -est = craziest**
**silly + -ness = silliness**
**marry + -age = marriage**

**Exceptions:** *dryness, shyness,* and *slyness*

However, when you add *-ing,* the *y* does not change.

**empty + -ed = emptied**   but
**empty + -ing = emptying**

When adding a suffix to a word that ends in *y* preceded by a vowel, the *y* usually does not change.

**play + -er = player**
**employ + -ed = employed**
**coy + -ness = coyness**
**pay + -able = payable**

## 11.3 WORDS ENDING IN A CONSONANT

In one-syllable words that end in one consonant preceded by one short vowel, double the final consonant before adding a suffix beginning with a vowel, such as *-ed* or *-ing.* These are sometimes called 1+1+1 words.

**dip + -ed = dipped**        **set + -ing = setting**
**slim + -est = slimmest**    **fit + -er = fitter**

The rule does not apply to words of one syllable that end in a consonant preceded by two vowels.

**feel + -ing = feeling**     **peel + -ed = peeled**
**reap + -ed = reaped**       **loot + -ed = looted**

In words of more than one syllable, double the final consonant when (1) the word ends with one consonant preceded by one vowel and (2) when the word is accented on the last syllable.

**be•gin′   per•mit′   re•fer′**

In the following examples, note that in the new words formed with suffixes, the accent remains on the same syllable:

**be•gin′ + -ing  =  be•gin′ning  =  beginning**
**per•mit′ + -ed  =  per•mit′ted  =  permitted**

**Exceptions:** In some words with more than one syllable, though the accent remains on the same syllable when a suffix is added, the final consonant is nevertheless not doubled, as in the following examples:

**tra′vel + er  =  tra′vel•er  =  traveler**
**mar′ket + er  =  mar′ket•er  =  marketer**

In the following examples, the accent does not remain on the same syllable; thus, the final consonant is not doubled:

**re•fer′ + -ence  =  ref′er•ence  =  reference**
**con•fer′ + -ence  =  con′fer•ence  = conference**

## 11.4 PREFIXES AND SUFFIXES

When adding a prefix to a word, do not change the spelling of the base word. When a prefix creates a double letter, keep both letters.

**dis- + approve  =  disapprove**
**re- + build  =  rebuild**
**ir- + regular  =  irregular**
**mis- + spell  =  misspell**
**anti- + trust  =  antitrust**
**il- + logical  =  illogical**

When adding *-ly* to a word ending in *l,* keep both *l*'s. When adding *-ness* to a word ending in *n,* keep both *n*'s.

**careful + -ly  =  carefully**
**sudden + -ness  =  suddenness**
**final + -ly  =  finally**
**thin + -ness = thinness**

## 11.5 FORMING PLURAL NOUNS

To form the plural of most nouns, just add **-s.**

**prizes    dreams    circles    stations**

For most singular nouns ending in **o,** add **-s.**

**solos    halos    studios    photos    pianos**

For a few nouns ending in **o,** add **-es.**

**heroes    tomatoes    potatoes    echoes**

When the singular noun ends in **s, sh, ch, x,** or **z,** add **-es.**

**waitresses    brushes    ditches**

**axes    buzzes**

When a singular noun ends in **y** with a consonant before it, change the **y** to **i** and add **-es.**

**army—armies        candy—candies**
**baby—babies        diary—diaries**
**ferry—ferries        conspiracy—conspiracies**

When a vowel (**a, e, i, o, u**) comes before the **y,** just add **-s.**

**boy—boys            way—ways**
**array—arrays        alloy—alloys**
**weekday—weekdays    jockey—jockeys**

For most nouns ending in **f** or **fe,** change the **f** to **v** and add **-es** or **-s.**

**life—lives        calf—calves    knife—knives**
**thief—thieves    shelf—shelves  loaf—loaves**

For some nouns ending in **f,** add **-s** to make the plural.

**roofs    chiefs    reefs    beliefs**

Some nouns have the same form for both singular and plural.

**deer    sheep    moose    salmon    trout**

For some nouns, the plural is formed in a special way.

**man—men        goose—geese**
**ox—oxen        woman—women**
**mouse—mice     child—children**

For a compound noun written as one word, form the plural by changing the last word in the compound to its plural form.

**stepchild—stepchildren        firefly—fireflies**

If a compound noun is written as a hyphenated word or as two separate words, change the most important word to the plural form.

**brother-in-law—brothers-in-law**
**life jacket—life jackets**

## 11.6 FORMING POSSESSIVES

If a noun is singular, add **'s.**

**mother—my mother's car    Ross—Ross's desk**

**Exceptions:** The **s** after the apostrophe is dropped after *Jesus', Moses',* and certain names in classical mythology *(Zeus').* These possessive forms can thus be pronounced easily.

If a noun is plural and ends with **s,** just add an apostrophe.

**parents—my parents' car**
**the Santinis—the Santinis' house**

If a noun is plural but does not end in **s,** add **'s.**

**people—the people's choice**
**women—the women's coats**

## 11.7 SPECIAL SPELLING PROBLEMS

Only one English word ends in **-sede:** *supersede.* Three words end in **-ceed:** *exceed, proceed,* and *succeed.* All other verbs ending in the sound "seed" are spelled with **-cede.**

**concede    precede    recede    secede**

In words with **ie** or **ei,** when the sound is long **e** (as in *she*), the word is spelled *ie* except after *c* (with some exceptions).

| *i* before *e* | thief | relieve | field |
|---|---|---|---|
| | piece | grieve | pier |
| except after *c* | conceit | perceive | ceiling |
| | receive | receipt | |
| Exceptions: | either | neither | weird |
| | leisure | seize | |

# 12 Commonly Confused Words

| WORDS | DEFINITIONS | EXAMPLES |
|---|---|---|
| accept/except | The verb *accept* means "to receive or believe." *Except* is usually a preposition meaning "excluding." | Did the teacher **accept** your report? <br> Everyone smiled for the photographer **except** Jody. |
| advice/advise | *Advise* is a verb. *Advice* is a noun naming that which an *adviser* gives. | I **advise** you to take that job. <br> Whom should I ask for **advice**? |
| affect/effect | As a verb, *affect* means "to influence." *Effect* as a verb means "to cause." If you want a noun, you will almost always want *effect*. | How deeply did the news **affect** him? <br> The students tried to **effect** a change in school policy. <br> What **effect** did the acidic soil produce in the plants? |
| all ready/already | *All ready* is an adjective meaning "fully ready." *Already* is an adverb meaning "before or by this time." | He was **all ready** to go at noon. <br> I have **already** seen that movie. |
| desert/dessert | *Desert* (dĕz´ərt) means "a dry, sandy, barren region." *Desert* (dĭ-zûrt´) means "to abandon." *Dessert* (dĭ-zûrt´) is a sweet, such as cake. | The Sahara, in North Africa, is the world's largest **desert**. <br> The night guard did not **desert** his post. <br> Alison's favorite **dessert** is chocolate cake. |
| among/between | *Between* is used when you are speaking of only two things. *Among* is used for three or more. | **Between** ice cream and sherbet, I prefer the latter. <br> Gary Soto is **among** my favorite authors. |
| bring/take | *Bring* is used to denote motion toward a speaker or place. *Take* is used to denote motion away from such a person or place. | **Bring** the books over here, and I will **take** them to the library. |
| fewer/less | *Fewer* refers to the number of separate, countable units. *Less* refers to bulk quantity. | We have **less** literature and **fewer** selections in this year's curriculum. |
| leave/let | *Leave* means "to allow something to remain behind." *Let* means "to permit." | The librarian will **leave** some books on display but will not **let** us borrow any. |
| lie/lay | To *lie* is "to rest or recline." It does not take an object. *Lay* always takes an object. | Rover loves to **lie** in the sun. <br> We always **lay** some bones next to him. |
| loose/lose | *Loose* (lo͞os) means "free, not restrained"; *lose* (lo͞oz) means "to misplace or fail to find." | Who turned the horses **loose**? <br> I hope we won't **lose** any of them. |
| passed/past | *Passed* is the past tense of pass and means "went by." <br> *Past* is an adjective that means "of a former time." *Past* is also a noun that means "time gone by." | We **passed** through the Florida Keys during our vacation. <br> My **past** experiences have taught me to set my alarm. <br> Ebenezer Scrooge is a character who relives his **past**. |
| than/then | Use *than* in making comparisons. Use *then* on all other occasions. | Ramon is stronger **than** Mark. <br> Cut the grass and **then** trim the hedges. |
| two/too/to | *Two* is a number. *Too* is an adverb meaning "also" or "very." Use *to* before a verb or as a preposition. | Meg had **to** go **to** town, **too**. We had **too** much reading **to** do. **Two** chapters is **too** many. |
| their/there/they're | *Their* means "belonging to them." *There* means "in that place." *They're* is the contraction for "they are." | **There** is a movie playing at 9 P.M. **They're** going to see it with me. Sakara and Jessica drove away in **their** car after the movie. |

*Effective oral communication occurs when the audience understands a speaker's message the way the speaker intends it. Good speakers and listeners do more than simply talk and hear. They use specific techniques to present their ideas effectively, and they are attentive and critical listeners.*

# 1 Speech

In school, in business, and in community life, giving a speech can be an effective means of communicating ideas or information.

## 1.1 AUDIENCE, PURPOSE, AND OCCASION

Delivering a speech is an opportunity to share your ideas. Before you begin to prepare a speech, you will need to know *why* you are making the presentation and to *whom* you are presenting it. Understanding your purpose, the background and interests of your audience, and the occasion will help you select an appropriate focus and organizational structure for your speech.

- **Know Your Audience** What kind of group are you presenting to? Fellow classmates? A group of teachers? What are their interests and backgrounds? Understanding their different points of view can help you organize the information so that they understand and are interested in it.

- **Understand Your Purpose** Keep in mind your purpose for speaking. Are you trying to persuade the audience to do something? Perhaps you simply want to entertain them by sharing a story or experience. Being aware of your purpose will help you choose an appropriate tone for your speech. Decide whether you'll best accomplish your purpose by being serious or humorous.

- **Know the Occasion** Are you speaking at a special event? Is it formal? Will others besides you be giving speeches? Knowing what the occasion is will help you choose the proper language and the right length for your speech.

## 1.2 WRITING YOUR SPEECH

Once you understand your purpose and audience, you are ready to write your speech. Use the following guidelines to help you:

- **Create a Unified Speech** Organize your speech into paragraphs, each of which develops a single main idea. Then make sure that just as all the sentences in a paragraph support the main idea of the paragraph, all the paragraphs in your speech support the main idea of the speech.

- **Clarify Your Ideas** Make sure that you show clear relationships between ideas. Transition words can help listeners follow your ideas.
  *For more information on transitions, see the* **Writing Handbook,** *page R32.*

- **Use Appropriate Language** The subject of your speech—and the way you choose to present it—should match your audience, your purpose, and the occasion. To share a story with your classmates, you can use informal language, such as slang. For a persuasive speech in front of a school assembly, use appropriate grammar and formal, standard American English. If you are giving an informative presentation, be sure to explain any terms that the audience may not be familiar with.

- **Provide Evidence** Include relevant facts, statistics, and incidents; quote experts to support your ideas and opinions. Include specific details and visual or media displays to clarify what you are saying.

- **Arrange Details and Evidence Effectively** In a good presentation, the main thesis statement should be supported by clearly stated evidence. The evidence can be presented as details, reasons, descriptions, or examples. Use the following chart to help you arrange your ideas.

| Introduction | • Focus on one strong example or statistic. |
| | • Make sure your introduction is intense or even surprising, so that it grabs the audience's attention. |
| **Main Body** | • Try to provide at least one piece of evidence for every new idea you introduce. |
| | • Define unfamiliar terms clearly. |
| | • When possible, include well-labeled diagrams or illustrations. |
| **Conclusion** | • Leave your audience with one strong piece of evidence or a powerful detail. |

- **Use Figurative Language** To help your audience follow the main ideas of your speech, be sure to draw attention to important points with similes, metaphors, and sensory images.

- **Use Precise Language** Use precise language to convey your ideas, and vary the structure and length of your sentences. You can keep the audience's attention with a word that brings out strong emotion. You can use a question or side comment to make a personal connection with the audience.

- **Start Strong, Finish Strong** As you begin your speech, consider using a "hook"—an interesting question or statement to capture the audience's attention. At the end of the speech, restate your main ideas simply and clearly. Perhaps conclude with a powerful example or anecdote to reinforce your message.

- **Revise Your Speech** After you write your speech, revise, edit, and proofread it as you would a written report. Use a variety of sentence structures to achieve a natural rhythm. Check for correct subject-verb agreement and consistent verb tense. Correct run-on sentences and sentence fragments. Use parallel structure to emphasize ideas. Make sure you use complete sentences and correct punctuation and capitalization, even if no one else will see it. Your written speech should be clear and error free. If you notice an error in your notes while you are delivering the speech, you may not remember what you actually wanted to say.

## 1.3 DELIVERING YOUR SPEECH

Confidence is the key to a successful presentation. Use these techniques to help you prepare and present your speech:

### Prepare

- **Review Your Information** Reread your notes and review any background research. This will help you feel more confident during your speech.

- **Organize Your Notes** Some people prefer to write down only key points. Others prefer the entire script. Write each main point, or each paragraph, of your speech on a separate numbered index card. Be sure to include your most important evidence and examples.

- **Plan Your Visual Aids** If you are planning to use visual aids, such as slides, posters, charts, graphs, video clips, overhead transparencies, or computer projections, now is the time to design them and decide how to work them into your speech.

### Practice

- **Rehearse** Rehearse your speech several times, possibly in front of a practice audience. Maintain good posture by standing with your shoulders back and your head up. If you are using visual aids, arrange them in the order in which you will use them. Adapt your rate of speaking, pitch, and tone of voice to your audience and setting. Glance at your notes to refresh your memory, but avoid reading them word for word. Your delivery style should express the purpose of your speech. Use the following chart to help you.

| Purpose | Pace | Pitch | Tone |
|---|---|---|---|
| To persuade | fast but clear | same throughout | urgent |
| To inform | using plenty of pauses | same throughout | authoritative |
| To entertain | usually building to a "punch" | varied to create characters or drama | funny or dramatic |

- **Use Audience Feedback** If you had a practice audience, ask them specific questions about your delivery and the content: Did I use enough eye contact? Was my voice at the right volume? Did I stand straight, or did I slouch? Did my tone and inflection fit my purpose? Use the audience's comments to evaluate the effectiveness of your delivery.

- **Evaluate Your Performance** When you have finished each rehearsal, evaluate your performance. Did you pause to let an important point sink in or use gestures for emphasis? Make a list of the aspects of your presentation that you will try to improve for your next rehearsal.

## Present

- **Begin Your Speech** Smile, and try to look relaxed.

- **Make Eye Contact** Try to make eye contact with as many audience members as possible. This will establish personal contact and help you determine whether the audience understands your speech.

- **Remember to Pause** Pausing after important points provides emphasis and gives the audience time to think about what you're saying.

- **Speak Clearly** Speak loud enough to be heard clearly, but not so loud that your voice is overwhelming. Use a conversational tone.

- **Maintain Good Posture** Stand up straight and avoid nervous movements that may distract the audience's attention from what you are saying.

- **Use Expressive Body Language** Use facial expressions to show your feelings toward your topic. Lean forward when you make an important point; move your hands and arms for emphasis. Use your body language to show your own style and reflect your personality.

- **Watch the Audience for Responses** If the audience starts fidgeting or yawning, speak a little louder or get to your conclusion a little sooner. Use what you learn to evaluate your speech and to decide what areas need improvement. Should you make changes to the organization? Do you need to rearrange any words or sentences to clarify your meaning?

### Respond to Questions

Depending on the content of your speech, your audience may have questions. Follow these steps to make sure that you answer questions in an appropriate manner:

- Think about what your audience may ask and prepare answers before your speech.

- Tell your audience at the beginning of your speech that you will take questions at the end. This helps avoid audience interruptions during your speech.

- Call on audience members in the order in which they raise their hands.

- Repeat each question before you answer it to ensure that everyone has heard it. This step also gives you time to prepare your answer.

## 2 Different Types of Oral Presentations

### 2.1 INFORMATIVE SPEECH

When you deliver an informative speech, you give the audience new information, provide a better understanding of information, or enable the audience to use the information in a new way. An informative speech is presented in an objective way.

Use the following questions to evaluate the presentation of a peer or a public figure, or your own presentation.

**Evaluate an Informative Speech**

- Did the speaker explain the purpose of the presentation?
- Did the speaker take the audience's previous knowledge into consideration?
- Did the speaker cite a variety of sources for the information?
- Did the speaker communicate the information objectively?
- Did the speaker explain technical terms?
- Did the speaker use visual aids effectively?

## 2.2 RESEARCH PRESENTATION

An oral research presentation conveys information on a single researched topic. An effective research report will be organized around a clear thesis. It will support that thesis with details and evidence from a number of reliable sources.

- **Plan Your Report** Decide on a topic, and then narrow down that topic to find a focus.

- **Consider Your Purpose** Writing down your purpose in sentence or question form will help you develop your thesis.

- **Organize Your Material** Choose an order in which to present your information. Be sure that any main points are supported with details and evidence from sources you can cite.

Use the following guidelines to evaluate a research presentation.

### Evaluate a Research Presentation

- Did the speaker define a clear thesis?

- Did the speaker support the thesis using specific details—such as direct quotations, general concepts, or ideas—from reliable sources?

- Did the speaker summarize or paraphrase important information on the topic, when necessary?

- Did the speaker include a variety of primary and secondary sources, and explain the value of each?

- Did the speaker use charts, maps, and graphs to organize information when appropriate?

## 2.3 PERSUASIVE SPEECH

When you deliver a persuasive speech, you offer a thesis or clear statement on a subject, you provide relevant evidence to support your position, and you attempt to convince the audience to accept your point of view.

*For more information, see **Speaking and Listening: Delivering a Persuasive Speech,** page 1023.*

Use the following questions to evaluate the presentation of a peer or a public figure, or your own presentation.

### Evaluate a Persuasive Speech

- Did the speaker present a clear thesis or argument?

- Did the speaker anticipate and address audience concerns, biases, and counterarguments?

- Did the speaker use sound logic and reasoning in developing the argument?

- Did the speaker support the argument with convincing evidence, examples, facts, expert opinions, and quotations?

- Did the speaker balance emotional arguments with logical ones?

- Did the speaker use his or her tone, facial expressions, and gestures to hold the audience's interest?

- Is your reaction to the speech similar to other audience members'?

## 2.4 NARRATIVE SPEECH

When you deliver a narrative speech, you tell a story or present a subject using a story-type format. A good narrative keeps an audience informed and entertained. It also allows you to deliver a message in a creative way.

Use the following questions to evaluate a speaker or your own presentation.

### Evaluate a Narrative Speech

- Did the speaker choose a setting that makes sense and contributes to a believable narrative?

- Did the speaker locate incidents in specific places?

- Does the plot flow well?

- Did the speaker make the significance of each main event clear to the audience?

- Did the speaker use words that convey the appropriate mood and tone?

- Did the speaker use sensory details that allow the audience to experience the sights, sounds, and smells of a scene and the specific actions, gestures, and thoughts of the characters?

- Did the speaker use a range of narrative devices to keep the audience interested?

- Is your reaction to the presentation similar to other audience members'?

## 2.5 ORAL INTERPRETATION

When you read a poem, play, or story aloud, your voice can bring the literature to life.

### Oral Reading

An oral reading can be a monologue, during which you assume the voice of a single character, the narrator, or the speaker in a poem. Or it may be a dialogue, during which you take the roles of two or more characters. Use the following techniques when giving an oral reading:

- **Speak Clearly** As you speak, pronounce your words carefully and clearly.

- **Control Your Volume** Make sure that you are loud enough to be heard but not shouting.

- **Pace Yourself** Read at a moderate rate, but vary your pace if it seems appropriate to the emotions of the character or to the action.

- **Vary Your Voice** Use a different voice for each character. Stress important words and phrases. Use your voice to express different emotions.

*For more information, see **Speaking and Listening: Oral Interpretation of a Poem**, page 655.*

### Dramatic Reading

In a dramatic reading, several speakers participate in the reading of a play or your own original work. Use the following techniques in your dramatic reading:

- **Prepare** Rehearse your material several times. Become familiar with the humorous and serious parts of the script. Develop a special voice that fits the personality of the character you portray.

- **Project** As you read your lines, aim your voice toward the back of the room to allow everyone to hear you.

- **Perform** React to the other characters as if you were hearing their lines for the first time. Deliver your own lines with the appropriate emotion.

Use facial expressions, hand gestures, and other body movements to express your emotions.

### Evaluate an Oral Interpretation

- Did the speaker speak clearly?
- Did the speaker maintain eye contact with the audience?
- Did the speaker project his or her voice at the proper volume?
- Did the speaker vary the rate of speech appropriately to express emotion, mood, and action?
- Did the speaker use a different voice for each character?
- Did the speaker stress important words or phrases?
- Did the speaker use the appropriate tone, inflections, and gestures to enhance meaning?
- Did the speaker seem aware of the interpretation's effect on listeners?

### PRACTICE AND APPLY

Listen to an oral reading by a classmate or view a dramatic performance in a theater or on television. Use the preceding guidelines to evaluate it.

## 2.6 ORAL RESPONSE TO LITERATURE

An oral response to literature is your own personal interpretation of a piece written by someone else. It is a way to show an audience what a story, a poem, or an essay means to you. Use the following techniques to help you craft a response:

- **Select Carefully** In choosing a piece for your response, think about the assignment, your interest, and the audience.

- **Exhibit Understanding** Direct your audience to specific words, sentences, or paragraphs that are rich with meaning. Discuss why they are important to the piece. Explain the writer's techniques in developing plot, characterization, setting, or theme.

- **Organize Clearly** Construct your response around clear ideas, premises, or images. What elements of the literature are most important? How do they relate to the piece as a whole? Use examples and evidence to show how they provide insight and meaning.

### Evaluate an Oral Response to Literature

- Did the speaker provide an in-depth analysis of a piece of literature?
- Did the speaker call attention to specific writing techniques and passages that helped to give the piece meaning?
- Did the speaker make inferences about the piece of literature and discuss its effect on himself or herself as a reader?
- Did the speaker support inferences and judgments with references to the piece, other pieces, or personal knowledge?
- Did the speaker present his or her ideas in a clear, well-organized manner?

#### PRACTICE AND APPLY

Listen as a classmate delivers an oral response to a book or an article. Use the preceding guidelines to evaluate the presentation.

## 3 Other Types of Communication

### 3.1 CONVERSATION

Conversations are informal, but they are a very important means of communicating. When two or more people exchange messages, it is important for each person to contribute and actively listen.

### 3.2 GROUP DISCUSSION

Successful groups assign a role to each member. These roles distribute responsibility among the members and help keep discussions focused.

#### Guidelines for Discussion

- Be informed about the topic.
- Participate in the discussion.
- Ask questions and give appropriate responses.
- Don't talk while someone else is talking.
- Support statements with facts and examples.
- Listen attentively; be respectful of others.
- Work toward the goal; avoid getting sidetracked by unrelated topics.

| Role | Responsibilities |
|---|---|
| Chairperson | • Introduces topic<br>• Explains goal or purpose<br>• Participates in discussion and keeps it on track<br>• Helps resolve conflicts<br>• Helps group reach goal |
| Recorder | • Takes notes on discussion<br>• Reports on suggestions and decisions<br>• Organizes and writes up notes<br>• Participates in discussion |
| Participants | • Contribute relevant facts or ideas to discussion<br>• Respond constructively to one another's ideas<br>• Reach agreement or vote on final decision |

### 3.3 INTERVIEW

An **interview** is a formal type of conversation with a definite purpose and goal. To conduct a successful interview, use the following guidelines:

#### Prepare for the Interview

- Carefully select whom you will interview. Identify who has the kind of knowledge and experience you are looking for.
- Set a time, a date, and a place. Ask permission to record the interview.
- Learn all you can about the person you will interview or the topic you want information on.
- Prepare a list of questions. Create questions that encourage detailed responses instead of yes-or-no answers. Arrange your questions in order from most important to least important.
- Arrive on time with everything you need.

#### Conduct the Interview

- Ask your questions clearly and listen to the responses carefully. Give the person whom you are interviewing plenty of time to answer.
- Be flexible; follow up on any responses you find interesting.

- Avoid arguments; be tactful and polite.
- Even if you record an interview, take notes on important points.
- Thank the person for the interview, and ask if you can call with any follow-up questions.

### Follow Up on the Interview

- Summarize your notes or make a written copy of the recording as soon as possible.
- If any points are unclear or if information is missing, call and ask more questions while the person is still available.
- Select the most appropriate quotations to support your ideas.
- If possible, have the person you interviewed review your work to make sure you haven't misrepresented what he or she said.
- Send a thank-you note to the person in appreciation of his or her time and effort.

*For more information, see* **Speaking and Listening: Conducting an Interview:** *page 299.*

#### Evaluate an Interview

You can determine how effective your interview was by asking yourself these questions:

- Did you get the type of information you were looking for?
- Were your most important questions answered to your satisfaction?
- Were you able to keep the person being interviewed focused on the subject?

## 4 Active Listening

**Active listening** is the process of receiving, interpreting, evaluating, and responding to a message. When you listen to a class discussion or a formal speech, use the following strategies to get as much as you can from the message.

#### Listening with a Purpose

| Situation | Reason for Listening | How to Listen |
|---|---|---|
| A guest speaker talks to your class about her career. | for information, to learn something new | Listen for ideas that interest you or add to your knowledge. |
| Your friend tells you about his vacation. | for enjoyment | Maintain eye contact; make comments when appropriate. |

### Before Listening

- Learn what the topic is beforehand. You may need to read background information about the topic or learn new terms in order to understand the speaker's message.
- Think about what you know or want to know about the topic.
- Have a pen and paper to take notes.
- Establish a purpose for listening.

### While Listening

- Focus your attention on the speaker. Your facial expressions and body language should demonstrate your interest in hearing the topic. Try to ignore uncomfortable room temperature and noise.
- Listen for the speaker's purpose (usually stated at the beginning), which alerts you to main ideas.
- To help you understand the speaker's message, listen for words or phrases that signal important points, such as *to begin with, in addition, most important, finally,* and *in conclusion.*
- Listen carefully for explanations of unfamiliar terms. Use these terms to help you understand the speaker's message.
- Listen for ideas that are repeated for emphasis.
- Take notes. Write down only the most important points.
- If possible, use an outline or list format to organize main ideas and supporting points.
- Note comparisons and contrasts, causes and effects, or problems and solutions.

- As you take notes, use phrases, abbreviations, and symbols to keep up with the speaker.

- To aid your understanding, note how the speaker uses word choice, voice pitch, posture, and gestures to convey meaning.

### After Listening

- Ask questions to clarify anything that was unclear or confusing.

- Review your notes right away to make sure you understand what was said.

- Summarize and paraphrase the speaker's ideas.

- You may also wish to compare your interpretation of the speech with the interpretations of others who listened to it.

## 4.1 CRITICAL LISTENING

**Critical listening** involves evaluating a spoken message to judge its accuracy and reliability. You can use the following strategies as you listen to messages from public speakers:

- **Determine the Speaker's Purpose** Think about the background, viewpoint, and possible motives of the speaker. Separate facts from opinions. Listen carefully to details and evidence used to support the message. You may want to paraphrase the speaker's purpose and point of view to help you evaluate the speech.

- **Listen for the Main Idea** Figure out the speaker's main message before allowing yourself to be distracted by seemingly convincing facts and details. To evaluate a speaker's credibility, look for anything that may indicate bias, such as material that is unfairly slanted or contains a hidden agenda.

- **Recognize the Use of Persuasive Techniques** Speakers may present information in a particular way to persuade you to buy a product or accept an idea. Persuasive devices such as glittering generalities, either/or reasoning, and bandwagon or snob appeal may represent faulty reasoning and provide misleading information.

*For more information, see **Recognizing Persuasive Techniques**, page R21.*

- **Observe Nonverbal Messages** A speaker's gestures, facial expressions, and tone of voice should reinforce the message. If they don't, you should doubt the speaker's sincerity and his or her message's reliability.

- **Give Appropriate Feedback** An effective speaker looks for verbal and nonverbal cues from you, the listener, to see how the message is being received. For example, if you understand or agree with the message, you might nod your head. If possible, during or after a presentation, ask questions to check your understanding.

## 4.2 VERBAL FEEDBACK

At times you will be asked to give direct feedback to a speaker. You may be asked to evaluate the way the speaker delivers the presentation as well as the content of the presentation.

### Evaluate Delivery

- Did the speaker speak clearly and distinctly?
- Did the speaker pronounce words correctly?
- Did the speaker vary his or her rate of speaking?
- Did the speaker's voice sound natural and not strained?
- Was the speaker's voice loud enough?

### Evaluate Content

**Here's how to give constructive suggestions for improvement:**

**Be Specific** Instead of vague statements like "Your charts need work," offer concrete suggestions, such as "Please make the type bigger so we can read the chart from the back of the room."

**Discuss Only the Most Important Points** Don't overload the speaker with too much feedback about too many details. Focus on important points, such as

- Is the topic too advanced for the audience?
- Are the supporting details well organized?
- Is the conclusion strong or weak?

**Give Balanced Feedback** Tell the speaker not only what didn't work but also what did work: "Consider dropping the last two slides, since you covered those points earlier. The first two slides really got my attention."

*Every day, you come into contact with some form of media. Media images and messages—from television, radio, and movies to newspapers and the Internet—are all around us. With so many options, it's more important than ever to be a smart media consumer. People who are media literate know what media products are, what they mean, and who created them. They are able to analyze and evaluate the way media messages influence the world. This section introduces some of the tools you'll need to study different forms of media.*

**MEDIA TOOLS**

For more information, visit the **Media Center** at ClassZone.com.

# 1 Five Core Concepts in Media Literacy

*from* The Center for Media Literacy

The five core concepts of media literacy provide you with the basic ideas you can consider when examining media messages.

**All media messages are "constructed."** All media messages are made by someone. In fact, they are carefully thought out and researched and have attitudes and values built into them. Much of the information that you use to make sense of the world comes from the media. Therefore, it is important to know how a medium is put together so you can better understand the message it conveys.

**Media messages are constructed using a creative language with its own rules.** Each means of communication—whether it is film, television, newspapers, magazines, radio, or the Internet—has its own language and design. Therefore, the message must use the language and design of the medium that delivers the message. Thus, the medium actually shapes the message. For example, a horror film may use music to heighten suspense, or a newspaper may use a big headline to signal the importance of a story. Understanding the language of each medium can increase your enjoyment of it, as well as help you recognize any subtle attempt to persuade you.

**Different people experience the same media messages differently.** Personal factors such as age, education, and experience will affect the way a person responds to a media message. How many times has your interpretation of a film or book differed from that of a friend? Everyone interprets media messages differently.

**Media messages have embedded values and points of view.** Media messages carry underlying values, which are purposely built into them by the creators of the message. For example, a commercial's main purpose may be to persuade you to buy something, but the commercial may also aim to convince you that the product is important to a particular way of life. Understanding not only the main message but also any other points of view will help you decide whether to accept or reject the message.

**Most media messages are constructed to gain profit and/or power.** The creators of media messages often provide a commodity, such as information or entertainment, in order to make money. The bigger the audience, the more the media outlet can charge for advertising. Consequently, media outlets want to build large audiences in order to bring in more revenue from advertising. For example, a television network will create programming to appeal to the largest audience possible, in the hope that the viewer ratings will attract more advertising dollars.

# 2 Media Basics

## 2.1 MESSAGE

When a film or TV show is created, it becomes a media product. Each media product is created to send a **message,** or an expression of a belief or opinion, that serves a specific purpose. In order to understand the message, you will need to deconstruct it.

**Deconstruction** is the process of analyzing a media presentation. To analyze a media presentation you will need to ask why and how it was created, who created it, and whom it is trying to influence.

## 2.2 AUDIENCE

A **target audience** is the specific group of people that a product or presentation is aimed at. The members of a target audience usually share certain characteristics, such as age, gender, ethnic background, values, or lifestyle. For example, a target audience may be 11-to-14-year-olds who carry backpacks to school.

**Sturdy-Paks hold EVERYTHING.**

Tough and stylish, they're the perfect backpack for busy, busy students

**Demographics** are the characteristics of a population, including age, gender, profession, income, education, ethnicity, and geographical location. Media decision makers use demographics to shape their content to suit the needs and tastes of a target audience.

## 2.3 PURPOSE

The **purpose,** or intent, of a media presentation is the reason it was made. All media products—from news programs to video games—are created for a specific purpose. Identifying why a media product was invented is the first step in understanding how it can influence you. The following chart shows purposes of different media products.

| Purposes of Media Products | |
|---|---|
| **Purpose** | **Example** |
| Inform | news reports and articles, public service announcements, some Web sites |
| Persuade | advertisements, editorials, reviews, political cartoons |
| Entertain | most TV shows, films, recorded music; video games; most talk shows |

Most media products have more than one purpose. For example, TV commercials are often entertaining, but their main purpose is to persuade you to buy something. If you aren't aware of all of a media products' purposes, you may become influenced without knowing it. This chart shows some examples.

| Main and Other Purposes in Media | | |
|---|---|---|
| **Media Product** | **Main Purpose** | **Other Purposes** |
| News broadcast | to inform | to persuade you that an issue or idea is important |
| Advertisement | to persuade | to entertain you; to inform you about a product |
| Sports coverage | to entertain | to inform you about sports or athletes |

## 2.4 TYPES AND GENRES OF MEDIA

The term *media* refers to television, newspapers, magazines, radio, movies, and the Internet. Each is a **medium,** or means for carrying information, entertainment, and advertisements to a large audience.

Each type of media has different characteristics, strengths, and weaknesses. The following chart shows how several types of media deliver their messages.

| Type of Media | Characteristics |
|---|---|
| **Newspaper article** | • Provides detailed information and dramatic photographs<br>• Uses **headlines** and **subheads** to give main ideas<br>• Can't be updated until next edition or next day |
| **Television news report** | • Uses an **announcer,** or "anchor," to guide viewers through the news report<br>• Uses **video footage** to bring news to life or clarify what happened<br>• Uses **graphics** to give information at a glance<br>• Can be updated quickly |
| **Documentary** | • Tells about historic people and places, major events, and important social, political, or environmental issues<br>• Uses **footage,** or shots of photographs, interviews, news reports, and film clips, to help viewers understand the subject<br>• Features **interviews** of experts or people directly involved with the subject<br>• Uses a **voice-over narrator,** the voice of an unseen speaker, who tells viewers why the subject is important and how the information about the subject is organized |
| **Web site** | • Gives in-depth information on specialized subjects<br>• Uses **text, still images,** and **video**<br>• Allows users to select the information they want to receive by clicking on links<br>• Allows users to see when the site was last updated<br>• Can be updated quickly |

*For more information, see **Types of Media**, page 10.*

## 2.5 PRODUCERS AND CREATORS

People who control the media are known as **gatekeepers.** Gatekeepers decide what information to share with the public and the ways it will be presented. This diagram gives some examples.

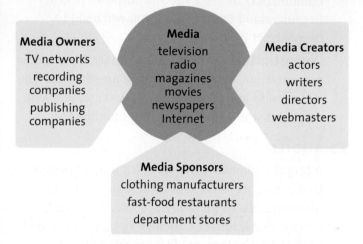

**Media Owners**
TV networks
recording companies
publishing companies

**Media**
television
radio
magazines
movies
newspapers
Internet

**Media Creators**
actors
writers
directors
webmasters

**Media Sponsors**
clothing manufacturers
fast-food restaurants
department stores

Media sponsors are companies that pay for their products to be advertised. It's important to be aware of sponsors and other gatekeepers, because they control much of what you see and hear. For example, suppose a television network executive disagrees with a particular computer company's business philosophy. As a result, she might decide not to let that company advertise on her network.

## 2.6 INFLUENCE OF MEDIA

Everywhere you go, you're bombarded by the media—advertisements, newspapers, magazines, radio, and television. Different kinds of media are all competing for your attention, telling you, "Buy this product. Listen to this music. Read this story. Look at this image. Think about this opinion." These media products are usually designed to sell you something. But they may also be sending subtle messages about values that they want you to believe in. Soda ads, for example, are intended to sell soda, but if you examine them closely, you will see that they often try to appeal to a set of values or a certain lifestyle. One message of the ad is that if you drink this soda, you will have as much fun as the people in the ad. The other message is that this lifestyle is good and desirable. TV shows, movies, and news programs also convey values and beliefs.

Media can also shape your opinions about the world. For example, news about crime shapes our understanding about how much and what type of crime is prevalent in the world around us. TV news items, talk show interviews, and commercials may shape what we think of a political candidate, a celebrity, an ethnic group, a country, or a region. As a result, our knowledge of someone or someplace could be completely based on the information we receive from television.

# 3 Film and TV

Films and television programs come in a variety of types. Films include comedies, dramas, documentaries, and animated features. Televison programs cover dramas, sitcoms, talk shows, reality shows, newscasts, and so on. Producers of films and producers of television programs rely on many of the same elements to make the action and settings seem real and to also affect the emotions of their audiences. Among these elements are scripts, visual and sound elements, special effects, and editing.

## 3.1 SCRIPT AND WRITTEN ELEMENTS

The writer and editor develop a story for television or film using a script and storyboard. A **script** is the text or words of a film or television show. A **storyboard** is a device used to plan the shooting of a movie or TV show. A storyboard is made up of drawings and brief descriptions of what is happening in each shot of a scene. The drawings of a storyboard help a director visualize how a finished scene might look before the scene is filmed. This storyboard shows some scenes that a student created.

"Runners, take your places at the starting line!"

Medium shot of Squeaky getting ready

*For more information, see **Media Study: Produce Your Own Media**, page 257.*

## 3.2 VISUAL ELEMENTS

Visual elements in film and television include camera shots and angles. A **camera shot** is a single, continuous view taken by a camera. A **camera angle** is the angle at which the camera is positioned during the recording of a shot or image. Each is carefully planned to create an effect. This chart shows what different shots are used for.

| Camera Shot/Angle | Effect |
|---|---|
| **Establishing shot** introduces viewers to the location of a scene, usually by presenting a wide view of an area | establishes the setting of a film |
| **Close-up shot** shows a close view of a person or object | helps to create emotion and make viewers feel as if they know the character |
| **Medium shot** shows a view wider than a close-up but narrower than an establishing or long shot | shows part of an object, or a character from the knees or waist up |
| **Long shot** gives a wide view of a scene, showing the full figure(s) of a person or group and the surroundings | allows the viewer to see the "big picture" and shows the relationship between characters and the environment |
| **Reaction shot** shows in some way what the subject sees | allows the viewer to see how the subject feels in order to create empathy in the viewer |
| **Low-angle shot** looks up at an object or person | makes a character, object, or scene appear more important or threatening |
| **High-angle shot** looks down on an object or person | makes a character, object, or scene seem weak or unimportant |
| **Point-of-view (POV) shot** shows a part of the story through a character's eyes | helps viewers identify with that character |

## 3.3 SOUND ELEMENTS

**Sound elements** in film and television include music, voice-over, and sound effects.

**Music** may be used to set the mood and atmosphere in a scene. Music can have a powerful effect on the way viewers feel about a story. For example, fast-paced music helps viewers feel excited during an action scene.

**Voice-over** is the voice of the unseen commentator or narrator of a film, TV program, or commercial.

**Sound effects** are the sounds added to films, TV programs, and commercials during the editing process. Sound effects, such as laugh tracks or the sounds of punches in a fight scene, can create humor, emphasize a point, or contribute to the mood.

### 3.4 SPECIAL EFFECTS

**Special effects** include computer-generated animation, manipulated video images, and fast- or slow-motion sequences in films, TV programs, and commercials.

**Animation** on film involves the frame-by-frame photography of a series of drawings or objects. When these frames are projected—at a rate of 24 per second—the illusion of movement is achieved.

A **split screen** is a special-effects shot in which two or more separate images are shown in the same frame. One example is when two people, actually a distance apart, are shown talking to each other.

### 3.5 EDITING

**Editing** is the process of selecting and arranging shots in a sequence. Moviemakers put shots together in ways that help you follow the action of a story. The editor decides which scenes or shots to use, as well as the length of each shot, the number of shots, and their sequence.

**Cut** is the transition from one shot to another. To create excitement, editors often use quick cuts, which are a series of short shots strung together.

**Dissolve** is a device in which one scene fades into another.

**Fade-in** is a device in which a white or black shot fades in to reveal the beginning of a new scene.

**Fade-out** is a device in which a shot fades to darkness to end a scene.

**Jump cut** is an abrupt and jarring change from one shot to another. A jump cut shows a break in time.

**Pace** is the length of time each shot stays on the screen and the rhythm that is created by the transitions between shots. Short, quick cuts create a fast pace in a story. Long cuts slow down a story.

## 4 News

The **news** is information on events, people, and places in your community, the region, the nation, and the world. It can be found in local newspapers, newscasts, online wire services, magazines, and documentaries. Because it's impossible to publish all the news that happens in one day in any one source, journalists have to make decisions about which stories will appear in newspapers and on newscasts. They use several factors to help them choose stories.

### 4.1 CHOOSING THE NEWS

**Newsworthiness** is the importance of an event or action that makes it worthy of media reporting. Journalists and their editors often use the following criteria in determining which stories should make the news:

**Timeliness** is the quality of being very current. Timely events usually take priority over previously reported events. For example, a tornado that strikes a residential area will be timely on the day it occurs. It may be on the front page of a newspaper or may be the lead story on a newscast.

**Widespread impact** is a characteristic of an event that could affect a large number of people. The more widespread the impact of an event, the more likely it is to be newsworthy.

**Proximity** measures the nearness of an event to a particular city, region, or country. People tend to be more interested in stories that take place close to where they live and that thus may affect them directly.

**Human interest** is a quality of stories that causes readers or listeners to feel emotions such as happiness, anger, or sadness. People are interested in reading stories about other people.

**Uniqueness** is the condition of being the only one of a kind. Unique or uncommon events or circumstances are likely to be interesting to an audience.

**Compelling video** and **photographs** grab people's attention and stay in their minds.

## 4.2 REPORTING THE NEWS

While developing a news story, a journalist makes a variety of decisions about how to construct the story, such as what information to include and how to organize it. The following elements are commonly used in news stories:

**5 *W*'s and *H*** are the six questions reporters answer when writing news stories—*who, what, when, where, why,* and *how.* It is a journalist's job to answer these questions in any type of news report. These questions also provide a structure for writing and editing a story.

**Inverted pyramid** is the means of organizing information according to importance. In the inverted-pyramid diagram below, the most important information (the answers to the 5 *W*'s and *H*) appears at the top of the pyramid. The less important details appear at the bottom. Not all stories are reported using the inverted-pyramid form. The form remains popular, however, because it helps a reader to get the important information without reading the entire story. Notice the following example.

> A new study suggests that regular exercise is key to keeping cholesterol levels low.
>
> Patients who exercised 30 minutes per day for one year decreased their cholesterol levels significantly.
>
> Researchers also suggested easy ways for people to get 30 minutes of activity daily.

**Angle or slant** is the point of view from which a story is written. Even an objective report must have an angle.

Consider these two headlines that describe the same crime story.

Painting Stolen from City Museum

Police Fail to Prevent Museum Theft

The first headline focuses on a fact. The second headline focuses on an opinion and has a negative slant.

### Standards for News Reporting

The ideal of journalism is to present news in a way that is objective, accurate, and thorough. The best news stories contain the following elements:

- **Objectivity** The story takes a balanced point of view on the issues. It is not biased, nor does it reflect a specific attitude or opinion.

- **Accuracy** The story presents factual information that can be verified.

- **Thoroughness** The story presents all sides of an issue. It includes background information, telling *who, what, when, where, why,* and *how.*

### Balanced Versus Biased Reporting

Objectivity in news reporting can be measured by how balanced or biased the story is.

**Balanced reporting** represents all sides of an issue equally and fairly. A balanced news story

- represents people and subjects in a neutral light

- treats all sides of an issue equally

- does not include inappropriate questions, such as "Why should we take pity on this thief?"

- does not show stereotypes or prejudice toward any particular race, gender, age, or religion.

- does not leave out important background information that is needed to establish a context or perspective.

**Biased reporting** is reporting in which one side is favored over another or in which the subject is unfairly represented. Biased reporting may show an overly negative view of a subject, or it may encourage racial, gender, or other stereotypes and prejudices. Sometimes biased reporting is apparent in the journalist's choice of sources.

**Sources** are the people interviewed for the news report and also any written materials and documents the journalist used for background information. From each source, the journalist gets a different point of view. To decide whether news reporting is balanced or biased, you will need to pay attention to the sources. Consider a news story on a new type of diet book. If the only source given in the story is the person who wrote the book, then the report may be biased. But if the journalist also includes the perspective of someone neutral and informed, such as a nutritionist, then the report may be more balanced. This chart shows which sources are generally considered reliable, and which tend to be considered weak.

| Sources for News Stories | |
|---|---|
| Reliable sources | Weak sources |
| • experts in a field<br>• people directly affected by the reported event (eyewitnesses)<br>• published reports that are specifically mentioned or shown | • unnamed or anonymous sources<br>• people who are not involved in the reported event (for example, people who heard about a story from a friend)<br>• research, data, or reports that are not specifically named or are referred to only in vague terms (for example, "Research shows that …") |

## 5 Advertising

**Advertising** is a sponsor's paid use of various media to promote products, services, or ideas. Some common forms of advertising are shown in the chart.

| Type of Ad | Description |
|---|---|
| Billboard | a large outdoor advertising sign |
| Print ad | typically appears in magazines and newspapers; uses eye-catching graphics and persuasive copy |
| Flyer | a print ad that is circulated by hand or mail |
| Infomercial | an extended ad on TV that usually includes detailed product information, demonstrations, and testimonials |
| Public service announcement | a message aired on radio or TV to promote ideas that are considered to be in the public interest |
| Political ad | a broadcast on radio or TV to promote political candidates |
| Trailer | a short film promoting an upcoming movie, TV show, or video game |

**Marketing** is the process of transferring products and services from producer to consumer. It involves determining the packaging and pricing of a product, how it will be promoted and advertised, and where it will be sold. One way companies market their products is by becoming media sponsors.

**Sponsors** pay for their products to be advertised. These companies hire advertising agencies to create and produce specific campaigns for their products. They then buy television or radio airtime or magazine, newspaper, or billboard space to feature ads where the target audience is sure to see them. Because selling time and space to advertisers produces much of the income the media need to function, the media need advertisers just as much as advertisers need the media.

**Product placement** is the intentional and identifiable featuring of brand-name products in movies, television shows, video games, and other media. The intention is to have viewers feel positive about a product because they see a favorite character using it. Another purpose may be to promote product recognition.

### 5.1 PERSUASIVE TECHNIQUES

**Persuasive techniques** are the methods used to convince an audience to buy a product or adopt an idea. Advertisers use a combination of visuals, sound, special effects, and words to persuade their target audience. Recognizing the following techniques can help you evaluate persuasive media messages and identify misleading information:

**Emotional appeals** use strong feelings, such as fear and pity, rather than facts to persuade consumers. An example of an appeal to fear might be, "Is your water safe to drink? Our filter system will help you be sure."

**Bandwagon appeals** use the argument that a person should believe or do something because "everyone else" does. These appeals take advantage of people's desire to be socially accepted by other people. An example of a bandwagon appeal is "Find out why everyone's talking about the hit film *A Two-Hour Story About Some Funny Characters.*"

**Slogans** are memorable phrases used in advertising campaigns. Slogans substitute catchy phrases for facts.

**Logical appeals** rely on logic and facts, appealing to a consumer's reason and his or her respect for authority. Two examples of logical appeals are expert opinions and product comparison.

**Celebrity ads** use one of the following two categories of spokesperson:

- **Celebrity authorities** are experts in a particular field. Advertisers hope that audiences will transfer the admiration they have for the person to the product. For example, a famous athlete might endorse a particular energy drink. The company selling the drink wants people to think it must work, since an athlete wouldn't want an energy drink that didn't help her perform well.

- **Celebrity spokespeople** are famous people who endorse a product. Advertisers hope that audiences will associate the product with the celebrity.

**Product comparison** is comparing between a product and its competition. Often mentioned by name, the competing product is portrayed as inferior. The intended effect is for people to question the quality of the competing product and to believe the featured product is better.

## 6 Elements of Design

The design of a media message is just as important as the words are in conveying the message. Like words, visuals are used to persuade, inform, and entertain.

Graphics and images, such as charts, diagrams, maps, timelines, photographs, illustrations, and symbols, present information that can be quickly and easily understood. The following basic elements are used to give meaning to visuals:

**Color** can be used to highlight important elements such as headlines and subheads. It can also create mood, because many colors have strong emotional or psychological impacts on the reader or viewer. For example, warm colors are often associated with happiness and comfort. Cool colors are often associated with feelings of peace and contentment or sometimes with sadness.

**Lines**—strokes or marks—can be thick or thin, long or short, and smooth or jagged. They can focus attention and create a feeling of depth. They can frame an object. They can also direct a viewer's eye or create a sense of motion.

**Texture** is the surface quality or appearance of an object. For example, an object's texture can be rough, wet, or shiny. Texture can be used to create contrast. It can also be used to make an object look "real." For example, wallpaper patterns can create a sense of depth, smoothness, or roughness, even though the texture is only visual and cannot be felt.

**Shape** is the external outline of an object. Shapes can be used to symbolize living things or geometric objects. They can emphasize visual elements and add interest. Shapes can symbolize ideas.

Notice how this movie poster uses design elements.

**Lines** Vertical lines guide the reader's eye upward to the lighted windows. This also helps create the visual perspective of a small person looking up at the large building.

**Color** Dark blues and grays suggest that the film may tell a scary story.

**Shape** The angular shapes and the placement of the two bright yellow windows combine to make the house look like a face with an evil grin.

## 7 Evaluating Media Messages

By looking closely at media products, you can see how their messages influence your opinions and your buying habits. Here are six questions to ask about any media message:

**Who made—and who sponsored—this message, and for what purpose?** The source of the message is a clue to its purpose. If the source of the message is a private company, that company may be trying to sell you a product. If the source is a government agency, that agency may be trying to promote a program or particular point of view. To discover the purpose, think about why its creator paid for and produced the message.

**Who is the target audience and how is the message specifically tailored to it?** Think about the age group, ethnic group, gender, and/or profession the message is targeting. Decide how it relates to you.

**What are the different techniques used to inform, persuade, entertain, and attract attention?** Analyze the elements, such as humor, music, special effects, and graphics, that have been used to create the message. Think about how visual and sound effects, such as symbols, color, photographs, words, and music, support the purpose behind the message.

**What messages are communicated (and/or implied) about certain people, places, events, behaviors, lifestyles, and so forth?** The media try to influence who we are, what we believe in, how we view things, and what values we hold. Look or listen closely to determine whether certain types of behavior are being depicted and if judgments or values are communicated through those behaviors. What are the biases in the message?

**How current, accurate, and believable is the information in this message?** Think about the reputation of the source. Note the broadcast or publication date of the message and whether the message might change quickly. If a report or account is not supported by facts, authoritative sources, or eyewitness accounts, you should question the message.

**What is left out of this message that might be important to know?** Think about what the message is asking you to believe. Also think about what questions come to mind as you watch, read, or listen to the message.

# Strategies and Practice for State and Standardized Tests

*The test items in this section are modeled after test formats that are used on many state and standardized tests. The strategies presented here will help you prepare for these tests. This section offers general test-taking strategies and tips for answering multiple-choice items, as well as short-response and extended-response questions in critical reading and writing. It also includes guidelines and samples for essay writing. For each test, read the tips in the margin. Then apply the tips to the practice items. You can also apply the tips to Assessment Practice Tests in this book.*

## 1 General Test-Taking Strategies

- Arrive on time and be prepared. Be sure to bring either sharpened pencils with erasers or pens—whichever you are told to bring.

- If you have any questions, ask them before the test begins. Make sure you understand the test procedures, the timing, and the rules.

- Read the test directions carefully. Look at the passages and questions to get an overview of what is expected.

- Tackle the questions one at a time rather than thinking about the whole test.

- Look for main ideas as you read passages. They are often stated at the beginning or the end of a paragraph. Sometimes the main idea is implied.

- Refer back to the reading selections as needed. For example, if a question asks about an author's attitude, you might have to reread a passage for clues.

- If you are not sure of your answer, make a logical guess. You can often arrive at the correct answer by reasoning and eliminating wrong answers.

- As you fill in answers on your answer sheet, make sure you match each test item to its numbered space on the answer sheet.

- Don't look for patterns in the positions of correct choices.

- Only change an answer if you are sure your original choice is incorrect. If you do change an answer, erase your original choice neatly and thoroughly.

- Check your answers and reread your essay.

## ❷ Critical Reading

As you advance into high school, you will be exposed to different types of writing, both fiction and nonfiction. You will read novels, persuasive essays, poems, historical documents, and scientific or technical information. Tests will measure your ability to read and analyze these kinds of writings. Test selections can range in length from 100 words to 500 or 600 words.

**Directions:** Read the selection and then answer the questions on the following page.

**SELECTION**

Walt has walked all the fourteen years of his life in suntanned, moose-hide moccasins, and he can go to the Indian camps and "talk big" with the men, and trade calico and beads with them for their precious furs. He can make bread without baking powder, yeast, or hops, shoot a moose at three hundred yards, and drive the wild wolf dogs fifty miles a day on the packed trail.

Last of all, he has a good heart, and is not afraid of the darkness and loneliness, of man or beast or thing. His father is a good man, strong and brave, and Walt is growing up like him.

Walt was born a thousand miles or so down the Yukon, in a trading post
10  below the Ramparts. After his mother died, his father and he came up on the river, step by step, from camp to camp, till now they are settled down on the Mazy May Creek in the Klondike country. Last year they and several others had spent much toil and time on the Mazy May, and endured great hardships; the creek, in turn, was just beginning to show up its richness and to reward them for their heavy labor. But with the news of their ❷ discoveries, strange men began to come and go through the short days and long nights, and many unjust things they did to the men who had worked so long upon the creek.

Si Hartman had gone away on a moose hunt, to return and find new
20  stakes driven and his claim jumped. George Lukens and his brother had lost their claims in a like manner, having delayed too long on the way to Dawson to record them. In short, it was the old story, and quite a number of the earnest, industrious prospectors had suffered similar losses.

But Walt Masters's father had recorded his claim at the start, so Walt had nothing to fear now that his father had gone on a short trip up the White River prospecting for quartz. Walt was well able to stay by himself in the cabin, cook his three meals a day, and look after things. Not only ❸ did he look after his father's claim, but he had agreed to keep an eye on the adjoining one of Loren Hall, who had started for Dawson to record it.

30  Loren Hall was an old man, and he had no dogs, so he had to travel very slowly. After he had been gone some time, word came up the river that he had broken through the ice at Rosebud Creek and frozen his feet so badly that he would not be able to travel for a couple of weeks. Then Walt Masters received the news that old Loren was nearly all right again, and about to move on afoot for Dawson as fast as a weakened man could.

## Tips: Reading Text

❶ Before reading a passage, skim the questions that follow it to help you focus your reading.

❷ Look for key ideas as you read. Competition and fairness are key ideas in this passage.

❸ Make predictions. The passage tells you that Walt is brave, strong, and resourceful. You can predict that he will be all right while his father and Loren Hall are gone.

❹ Pay attention to the connotation of words. For example, the word *stampede* in line 37 suggests something frenzied and out of control. The word is usually applied to a herd of wild animals. Here, its connotation helps describe the ruthless newcomers to the Klondike country.

Walt was worried, however; the claim was liable to be jumped at any moment because of the delay, and a fresh stampede had started in on Mazy May. He did not like the looks of the newcomers, and one day, when five of them came by with crack dog teams and the lightest of camping outfits, he could see they were prepared to make speed, and resolved to keep an eye on them. So he locked up the cabin and followed them, being at the same time careful to remain hidden.

40

—from "The King of Mazy May"
by Jack London

**Directions:** Answer these questions about the selection from "The King of Mazy May."

**1.** What can you infer about life in the Klondike from the description in lines 1–18?

   **A**   People need to use many skills to survive.

   **B**   The Klondike is a lonely place for most people.

   **C**   The competition for land makes people dishonest.

   **D**   Families purchase all of their supplies at trading posts.

**2.** The author characterizes Walt by presenting ❷

   **A**   a description of his physical appearance

   **B**   the narrator's direct comments about him

   **C**   Walt's thoughts and actions

   **D**   other characters' opinions of him.

**3.** The main conflict in this passage involves

   **A**   finding a place to trade rare furs

   **B**   traveling to town in dangerous weather

   **C**   protecting land from prospecting thieves

   **D**   hunting for moose along Mazy May Creek

**4.** Which is an effect of Loren Hall's accident? ❹

   **A**   Walt must stay alone in the cabin.

   **B**   Loren is delayed on his way to Dawson.

   **C**   Loren returns home instead of going to Dawson. ❺

   **D**   The Masters's claim is jumped.

## Tips: Multiple Choice

A multiple-choice question consists of a stem and a set of choices. The stem is in the form of a question or an incomplete sentence. One of the choices correctly answers the question or completes the sentence. Many tests offer four answer choices, but no matter how many choices are given, you can use the same strategies to guide you to the best answer.

❶ Read the stem carefully and try to answer the question before you look at the choices.

❷ Pay attention to key words in the stem. They may direct you to the correct answer. In question 2, the word *characterizes* tells you to think about how the author develops Walt's character.

❸ Read all of the choices before deciding on an answer. In question 3, you might decide to stop at choice B, because Loren Hall falls through the ice on the way to town. The main conflict, however, is about protecting land, not about Hall's difficult trip.

❹ Some questions ask you to identify cause-and-effect relationships.

❺ After reading all of the choices, eliminate any that you know are incorrect. In question 4, you can safely reject choice C, because the passage states that Loren was going to continue on to Dawson.

**Answers: 1.** C, **2.** B, **3.** C, **4.** B

# 3 Vocabulary

Most standardized tests include items that ask about the meanings of words. Some questions might refer to a passage you just read, while others might provide a sentence or paragraph followed by the answer choices.

1. Which of the following words from the passage on pages R96–R97 has a negative connotation? ❶
   A  calico (line 3)
   B  toil (line 13)
   C  industrious (line 23)
   D  careful (line 42)

2. Which word from the passage might include the Latin root meaning "hard"?
   A  endured (line 13) ❷
   B  earnest (line 23)
   C  adjoining (line 29)
   D  liable (line 36)

3. In line 28 of the passage, the idiom *keep an eye on* means ❸
   A  report to
   B  think about
   C  watch over
   D  measure

4. Read this dictionary entry for the word *claim*. Which definition represents the meaning of *claim* as used in the passage?

   > **DEFINITION**
   >
   > *v.* **1.** To demand or ask for. **2.** To state to be true; assert. *n.* **1.** A demand for something as due. **2.** Something claimed in a legal manner, especially a tract of public land. **3.** A statement of something as true.

   A  *v.* meaning 1 ❹
   B  *n.* meaning 1
   C  *n.* meaning 2
   D  *n.* meaning 3

## Tips: Word Meaning

❶ Connotation is the suggestion or feeling a word carries beyond its literal meaning. *Work* is a neutral word. *Effort* is a more positive word for work, but the word *toil* has a negative connotation.

❷ If you don't know the exact meaning of a word, look for clues in nearby sentences. For the word *endured* in line 13, read the description in the surrounding paragraph. Choice A is the best answer, because the passage is describing hard work and the difficult times the characters lived through.

❸ An idiom is an expression that has a meaning different from the meanings of its individual words. Since Walt is not literally keeping one of his eyes at Loren's claim, you can use context clues to help you figure out the meaning of the idiom *keep an eye on*. Some idioms can be found in the dictionary.

❹ Eliminate any answers that are not the same part of speech as the meaning of the word in the passage. *Claim* is used as a noun in the passsage, so you can rule out answer choice A.

**Answers:  1.** B, **2.** A, **3.** C, **4.** C

# ❹ Writing and Grammar

You will be asked to write many essays and research papers in middle school and high school. When it comes to writing, good ideas aren't enough. You need to know how to express them. That requires knowledge of English grammar, sentence structure, and usage. To measure that skill, many standardized tests ask you to identify errors or to improve sentences and paragraphs.

---

**Directions:** Read this passage and then answer the questions.

---

**PASSAGE**

❶ (1) Jack London wrote many stories about life in the Yukon. (2) He's not the only person who loves rough terrain and cold weather. (3) Each year adventurous dog-sled racers gather in Anchorage, Alaska, for the Iditarod. (4) This race covers 1,150 miles through forests, mountains, and coastlines. (5) The racers, called mushers, steer they're teams of 12 to 16 dogs from start to finish, taking only a few breaks. (6) The dogs wear special boots <u>for paw protection from cuts and frostbite</u>. (7) The first musher to reach the Yukon River checkpoint is served a seven-course dinner. (8) I hope they feed the dogs, too!

---

**1.** The correct coordinating conjunction to join sentences 1 and 2 is

❷ **A** but

**B** for

**C** or

**D** so

**2.** What change, if any, should be made to sentence 5?

**A** Change *steer* to *steers*.

**B** Change *they're* to *their*.

❸ **C** Change *teams* to *team*.

**D** Make no change.

❹ **3.** What is the best way to rewrite the underlined part of sentence 6?

**A** for cuts and frostbite protection on paws

**B** to protect their paws from cuts and frostbite

**C** for the protection of paws from cuts and frostbite

**D** in order to protect from cuts and frostbite on paws

❺ **4.** What change, if any, should be made to sentence 7?

**A** Change *reach* to *reaches*.

**B** Change *is* to *are*.

**C** Change *served* to *serving*.

**D** Make no change. ❻

## Tips: Grammar

❶ Read the entire passage to grasp its overall meaning. Pay particular attention to any underlined parts.

❷ If you are asked to combine sentences, think about how the ideas relate to each other. Use the coordinating conjunction *or* to introduce a choice. The words *for* or *so* indicate cause and effect. The word *but* expresses contrasting ideas. When you understand the connection between the two sentences, you will know which word best joins them.

❸ Some items will test your knowledge of commonly confused words. Read sentences carefully to determine how each word is used before deciding which choice is best.

❹ Before choosing a revision, read through all of the choices to decide which one is best. Your selection should produce a sentence that is grammatically correct.

❺ Some items will test your knowledge of language conventions. Make sure that pronouns agree with antecedents and that verbs agree with subjects.

❻ In test item 4, choice D says, "Make no change." Choose this answer only if the sentence is correct as it is originally written.

**Answers: 1.** A, **2.** B, **3.** B, **4.** D

# 5 Responding to Writing Prompts

Not all tests are multiple choice. Sometimes you have to develop your ideas into a paragraph or a short essay. You might be asked to interpret, summarize, or react to a reading selection.

> **Directions:** Reread the selection from "The King of Mazy May" on pages R96–R97 and follow the directions for the short and extended responses.

## SHORT RESPONSE

Write a well-organized paragraph comparing and contrasting the prospectors and the men of the "stampede."

> **SAMPLE SHORT RESPONSE**
>
> The prospectors of Mazy May, such as Walt's father and Loren Hall, **❶** couldn't be more different from the claim-jumping stampeders. The prospectors "spent much toil and time" looking for gold, willing to keep working for as long as it took. The stampeders, on the other hand, seemed not to arrive until after the prospectors had worked for a year to set up their claims. The stampeders plan to steal the claims and profit from the prospectors' hard work. Walt, who risks danger to protect his neighbor's claim, is the exact opposite of the "unjust" stampeders. **❷**

## EXTENDED RESPONSE

Discuss in two or three paragraphs the effects of the setting in the selection from "The King of Mazy May."

> **SAMPLE EXTENDED RESPONSE**
>
> The setting in "The King of Mazy May"—Klondike country—affects not only the story's plot, but also its characters and conflict.
>
> **❸** Walt is a product of his setting. His whole life, he has lived and worked in the cold weather and lonely conditions of the region. As a result, he's learned to be a good hunter and dog driver. He's become self-reliant because his father must leave on prospecting trips. The skills Walt develops in the Klondike are what make him able to protect his neighbor's claim. **❹**
>
> The setting also presents specific challenges that affect the story's plot **❸** and conflict. For example, the cold water of Rosebud Creek is what delays Loren Hall on his way to Dawson, and the "short days and long nights" seem to encourage the claim jumpers. Finally, the land along the creek is what brings both the prospectors and the thieves to the area in the first place.

## Tips: Responding to Writing Prompts

**❶** Short-response prompts are often fact-based rather than interpretive. Get right to the point in your answer, and stick to the facts.

**❷** Make sure that you write about the assigned topic. Support your answer with details from the passage, such as a quotation, a paraphrase, or an example.

**❸** When you are writing an extended response, build your paragraphs around clear topic sentences that will pull your ideas together.

**❹** If you are asked to interpret a passage, don't just copy the author's words. Try to express the ideas in your own words. Express your ideas clearly so that the reader understands your viewpoint.

**❺** Proofread your response for errors in capitalization, punctuation, spelling, or grammar.

# 6 Writing an Essay

Many tests will ask you to read a prompt and write an essay in response to it. You might be asked to write a narrative, persuasive, or expository essay. You might be asked to write a story, summarize an article, or respond to a piece of writing. It is important to read the prompt carefully and look for direction words that tell you what to write about. Because of the time constraints, an impromptu essay will not be polished. It will represent a first draft. Even so, it should be complete. Essays are scored on the following criteria:

- **Focus** Establish a point of view on your topic in the opening paragraph. Stay with that topic throughout the essay.

- **Organization** Maintain a logical progression of ideas.

- **Support for ideas** Use details and examples to develop an argument or line of thinking.

- **Style/word choice** Use words accurately and vary sentence structure.

- **Grammar** Use standard English and proofread for errors.

## Writing Prompt

In 1961, the chairman of the Federal Communications Commission called television programming "a vast wasteland." Many people still feel we would be better off without television. Write a persuasive essay of four or five paragraphs supporting or rejecting this idea.

---

**SAMPLE PERSUASIVE ESSAY**

**①** I don't agree that television is "a vast wasteland." A wasteland is an ugly place where nothing grows. So, if television were only a wasteland, that would mean that it never offered people anything beautiful or exciting. It would mean that there was no information or entertainment of value that people could get from watching television programs, and that just isn't the case.

It's true that there are many low-quality programs on TV. These programs don't teach us anything. Some shows, such as soap operas, don't show people or their lives the way they actually are. They exaggerate situations and rarely offer a positive or important message.

Other programs, however, offer interesting and important information about nature, science, history, the arts, sports, or current events. These educational and exciting programs can help us grow and improve ourselves. **②**

People who don't agree with me might say that TV turns us into couch **③** potatoes. Many people do just sit in front of the television for hours, watching whatever is on, whether it's good or bad. My answer to that point of view is that we have to be responsible in choosing the programs we watch. If viewers stopped watching bad shows, those shows would eventually be canceled.

In conclusion, TV can be worthwhile if we make good decisions about **④** its use. We just have to use our heads and take charge of the remote control.

---

## Tips: Writing an Essay

Before you begin writing, take a minute or two to gather your thoughts. You don't need to prepare a complete outline, but write the main points you want to make. In the essay here on television, program quality and personal responsibility are key issues.

**①** When writing a persuasive essay, state your point of view in the introduction.

**②** Facts and examples make your writing come to life. Use them in the body of your essay to clarify your points and to strengthen your arguments. The writer of this essay uses examples to illustrate some possible benefits of television.

**③** Try to consider the opposing viewpoint and respond to it. In the sample essay, the student notes that some people think TV "turns us into couch potatoes." Her response is that people should be responsible about what they watch.

**④** Make sure your essay has a conclusion, even if it's just a single sentence. A conclusion pulls your ideas together and lets the reader know you have finished.

**⑤** Allow time to reread what you have written. If you have to make a correction, do so neatly and legibly.

# Glossary of Literary Terms

**Act** An act is a major division within a play, similar to a chapter in a book. Each act may be further divided into smaller sections, called scenes. Plays can have as many as five acts. *The Diary of Anne Frank* has two acts. *See page 486.*

**Adventure Story** An adventure story is a literary work in which action is the main element. An adventure novel usually focuses on a main character who is on a mission and is facing many challenges and choices.

**Alliteration** Alliteration is the repetition of consonant sounds at the beginning of words. Note the repetition of the *s* sound in these lines.

> Say to them,
> say to the down-keepers,
> the sun-slappers,
> the self-soilers,
> —Gwendolyn Brooks, "Speech to the Young:
> Speech to the Progress-Toward"

*See page 613.*
*See also* **Consonance.**

**Allusion** An allusion is a reference to a famous person, place, event, or work of literature. In "The Drummer Boy of Shiloh" by Ray Bradbury, the general makes an allusion to the poet Henry Wadsworth Longfellow.
*See page 323.*

**Analogy** An analogy is a point-by-point comparison between two things that are alike in some respect. Often, writers use analogies in nonfiction to explain unfamiliar subjects or ideas in terms of familiar ones.
*See also* **Extended Metaphor; Metaphor; Simile.**

**Anecdote** An anecdote is a brief account of an interesting incident or event that is usually intended to entertain or make a point. "Manuscript Found in an Attic" is an example of an anecdote.
*See page 58.*

**Antagonist** The antagonist is a force working against the protagonist, or main character, in a story, play, or novel. The antagonist is usually another character but can be a force of nature, society itself, or an internal force within the main character. In Yoshiko Uchida's retelling of "The Wise Old Woman," the cruel young lord is the antagonist.
*See page 466.*
*See also* **Protagonist.**

**Assonance** Assonance is the repetition of vowel sounds within nonrhyming words. An example of assonance is the repetition of the short *a* sound in the following line.

> It's had tacks in it,
> —Langston Hughes, "Mother to Son"

**Author's Perspective** An author's perspective is the unique combination of ideas, values, feelings, and beliefs that influences the way the writer looks at a topic. Tone, or attitude, often reveals an author's perspective. Gary Soto writes "One Last Time" from a perspective that reflects his family's history of working in the fields and his teenage desire for status and acceptance.
*See page 817.*
*See also* **Author's Purpose; Tone.**

**Author's Purpose** A writer usually writes for one or more of these purposes: to express thoughts or feelings, to inform or explain, to persuade, and to entertain. For example, in "The Sanctuary of School," Lynda Barry's purpose is to persuade Americans to support public schools.
*See also* **Author's Perspective.**

**Autobiography** An autobiography is a writer's account of his or her own life. In almost every case, it is told from the first-person point of view. Generally, an autobiography focuses on the most significant events and people in the writer's life over a period of time. Barack Obama's *Dreams from My Father* is an autobiography.
*See page 831.*
*See also* **Memoir.**

**Ballad** A ballad is a type of narrative poem that tells a story and was originally meant to be sung or recited. Because it tells a story, a ballad has a setting, a plot, and characters. Traditional ballads are written in four-line stanzas with regular rhythm and rhyme. Folk ballads were composed orally and handed down by word of mouth. These ballads usually tell about ordinary people who have unusual adventures or perform daring deeds. A literary ballad is a poem written by a poet in imitation of the form and content of a folk ballad. "Boots of Spanish Leather" is an example of a literary ballad.

**Blank Verse** Blank verse is unrhymed poetry written in iambic pentameter. That is, each line of blank verse has five pairs of syllables. In most pairs, an unstressed syllable is followed by a stressed syllable. The most versatile of poetic forms, blank verse imitates the natural rhythms of English speech. Much of Shakespeare's drama is in blank verse.

> This day is call'd the feast of Crispian:
> He that outlives this day, and comes safe home,
> Will stand a' tiptoe when this day is named,
> —William Shakespeare, "St. Crispian's Day Speech"

**Biography** A biography is the true account of a person's life, written by another person. As such, biographies are usually told from a third-person point of view. The writer of a biography usually researches his or her subject in order to present accurate information. The best biographers strive for honesty and balance in their accounts of their subjects' lives. Ann Petry's *Harriet Tubman: Conductor on the Underground Railroad* is an example of a biography.
*See page 258.*

**Cast of Characters** In the script of a play, a cast of characters is a list of all the characters in the play, usually in order of appearance. It may include a brief description of each character.

**Character** Characters are the people, animals, or imaginary creatures who take part in the action of a work of literature. Like real people, characters display certain qualities, or character traits, that develop and change over time, and they usually have motivations, or reasons, for their behaviors.

> **Main character:** Main characters are the most important characters in literary works. Generally, the plot of a short story focuses on one main character, but a novel may have several main characters.

> **Minor characters:** The less important characters in a literary work are known as minor characters. The story is not centered on them, but they help carry out the action of the story and help the reader learn more about the main character.

> **Dynamic character:** A dynamic character is one who undergoes important changes as a plot unfolds. The changes occur because of the character's actions and experiences in the story. The changes are usually internal and may be good or bad. Main characters are usually, though not always, dynamic.

> **Static character:** A static character is one who remains the same throughout a story. The character may experience events and have interactions with other characters, but he or she is not changed because of them.

*See pages 162, 179, 189, 239.*

*See also* **Characterization; Character Traits.**

**Characterization** The way a writer creates and develops characters is known as characterization. There are four basic methods of characterization:

- The writer may make direct comments about a character through the voice of the narrator.
- The writer may describe the character's physical appearance.
- The writer may present the character's own thoughts, speech, and actions.
- The writer may present thoughts, speech, and actions of other characters.

*See pages 259, 283.*

*See also* **Character; Character Traits.**

**Character Traits** Character traits are the qualities shown by a character. Traits may be physical (brown eyes) or expressions of personality (shyness). Writers reveal the traits of their characters through methods of characterization. Sometimes writers directly state a character's traits, but more often readers need to infer traits from a character's words, actions, thoughts, appearance, and relationships. Examples of words that describe traits include *courageous, humble, generous,* and *wild.*

**Climax** The climax stage is the point of greatest interest in a story or play. The climax usually occurs toward the end of a story, after the reader has understood the conflict and become emotionally involved with the characters. At the climax, the conflict is resolved and the outcome of the plot usually becomes clear. For example, in Toni Cade Bambara's story "Raymond's Run," the climax occurs when Squeaky realizes that she doesn't have to win the race to prove her running skills; she can help her brother Raymond become a great runner.
*See pages 24, 32.*
*See also* **Plot.**

**Comedy** A comedy is a dramatic work that is light and often humorous in tone, usually ending happily with a peaceful resolution of the main conflict.

**Conflict** A conflict is a struggle between opposing forces. Almost every story has a main conflict—a conflict that is the story's focus. An external conflict involves a character who struggles against a force outside him- or herself, such as nature, a physical obstacle, or another character. An internal conflict is one that occurs within a character. A cultural conflict is a struggle that arises because of differing values, customs, or circumstances between groups of people.

**Examples:** In O. Henry's "The Ransom of Red Chief," the kidnappers are in conflict with the boy they take captive. In Laurence Yep's memoir "The Great Rat Hunt," the young Yep is torn between wanting to prove his bravery by helping his father and wanting to avoid the rat by staying with his mother. In "Out of Bounds," Rohan's family and neighbors blame the new squatters for robberies, and Rohan's parents tell him not to make contact with the squatters.

*See pages 47, 63, 119.*

*See also* **Plot.**

**Connotation** A word's connotations are the ideas and feelings associated with the word, as opposed to its dictionary definition. For example, the word *mother*, in addition to its basic meaning ("a female parent"), has connotations of love, warmth, and security.

**Consonance** Consonance is the repetition of consonant sounds within and at the end of words, as in "lonely afternoon." Consonance is unlike rhyme in that the vowel sounds preceding or following the repeated consonant sounds differ. Consonance is often used together with alliteration, assonance, and rhyme to create a musical quality, to emphasize certain words, or to unify a poem.

*See also* **Alliteration.**

**Couplet** A couplet is a rhymed pair of lines. A couplet may be written in any rhythmic pattern.

> Macavity, Macavity, there's no one like Macavity,
> He's broken every human law, he breaks the law
>   of gravity.
>             —T. S. Eliot, "Macavity: The Mystery Cat"

*See also* **Stanza.**

**Critical Essay** *See* **Essay.**

**Denotation** A word's denotation is its dictionary definition. *See also* **Connotation.**

**Description** Description is writing that helps a reader to picture events, objects, and characters. To create descriptions, writers often use imagery—words and phrases that appeal to the reader's senses.

**Dialect** A dialect is a form of a language that is spoken in a particular place or by a particular group of people. Dialects may feature unique pronunciations, vocabulary, and grammar. For example, in "The Treasure of Lemon Brown" by Walter Dean Myers, Lemon Brown speaks in a dialect that reflects his background as an African-American blues musician. His dialect includes informal grammar and nonstandard word forms.

**Dialogue** Dialogue is written conversation between two or more characters. Writers use dialogue to bring characters to life and to give readers insights into the characters' qualities, traits, and reactions to other characters. In fiction, dialogue is usually set off with quotation marks. In drama, stories are told primarily through dialogue.

**Diary** A diary is a daily record of a writer's thoughts, experiences, and feelings. As such, it is a type of autobiographical writing. The terms *diary* and *journal* are often used to mean the same thing.

*See page 520.*

**Drama** A drama, or play, is a form of literature meant to be performed by actors in front of an audience. In a drama, the characters' dialogue and actions tell the story. The written form of a play is known as a script. A script usually includes dialogue, a cast of characters, and stage directions that give instructions about performing the drama. The person who writes the drama is known as the playwright or dramatist.

**Dramatic Irony** *See* **Irony.**

**Dynamic Character** *See* **Character.**

**Elegy** An elegy is an extended meditative poem in which the speaker reflects on death—often in tribute to a person who has died recently—or on an equally serious subject. Most elegies are written in formal, dignified language and are serious in tone.

**Epic** An epic is a long narrative poem on a serious subject, presented in an elevated or formal style. It traces the adventures of a great hero whose actions reflect the ideals and values of a nation or race. Epics address universal concerns, such as good and evil, life and death, and sin and redemption. Henry Wadsworth Longfellow's *The Song of Hiawatha* is an example of an epic. The poet Homer was responsible for handing down two famous epics from ancient Greece, the *Iliad* and the *Odyssey*.

**Essay** An essay is a short work of nonfiction that deals with a single subject. There are many types of essays. An expository essay presents or explains information and ideas. A personal essay usually reflects the writer's experiences, feelings, and personality. A persuasive essay attempts to convince the reader to adopt a certain viewpoint. A critical essay evaluates a situation or a work of art.

*See pages 716, 994.*

**Exaggeration** An extreme overstatement of an idea is called an exaggeration. It is often used for purposes of emphasis or humor. In "Pecos Bill," Mary Pope Osborne exaggerates Bill's toughness and wild behavior in order to create a humorous, memorable impression of the character.

**Exposition** Exposition is the first stage of a typical story plot. The exposition provides important background information and introduces the setting and the important characters. The conflict the characters face may also be introduced in the exposition, or it may be introduced later, in the rising action.

*See pages 24, 33.*
*See also* **Plot.**

**Expository Essay** *See* **Essay.**

**Extended Metaphor** An extended metaphor is a figure of speech that compares two essentially unlike things at some length and in several ways. It does not contain the word *like* or *as*. For example, in "O Captain! My Captain!" Walt Whitman compares Abraham Lincoln to a ship's captain and the Civil War to a ship's journey. The comparison begins in the following lines and continues throughout the poem.

> O Captain! my Captain! our fearful trip is done,
> The ship has weather'd every rack, the prize we sought
>     is won,
> The port is near, the bells I hear, the people all
>     exulting,
> While follow eyes the steady keel, the vessel grim and
>     daring;
>             —Walt Whitman, "O Captain! My Captain!"

*See also* **Metaphor.**

**External Conflict** *See* **Conflict.**

**Fable** A fable is a brief tale told to illustrate a moral or teach a lesson. Often the moral of a fable appears in a distinct and memorable statement near the tale's beginning or end.

*See also* **Moral.**

**Falling Action** The falling action is the stage of the plot in which the story begins to draw to a close. The falling action comes after the climax and before the resolution. Events in the falling action show the results of the important decision or action that happened at the climax. Tension eases as the falling action begins; however, the final outcome of the story is not yet fully worked out at this stage.

*See page 24, 33.*
*See also* **Climax; Plot.**

**Fantasy** Fantasy is a type of fiction that is highly imaginative and portrays events, settings, or characters that are unrealistic. The setting might be a nonexistent world, the plot might involve magic or the supernatural, and the characters might have superhuman powers.

**Farce** Farce is a type of exaggerated comedy that features an absurd plot, ridiculous situations, and humorous dialogue. The main purpose of a farce is to keep an audience laughing. Comic devices typically used in farces include mistaken identity, wordplay (such as puns and double meanings), and exaggeration.

**Fiction** Fiction is prose writing that tells an imaginary story. The writer of a fictional work might invent all the events and characters or might base parts of the story on real people and events. The basic elements of fiction are plot, character, setting, and theme. Fiction includes both short stories and novels.

*See also* **Novel; Short Story.**

**Figurative Language** Figurative language is language that communicates meanings beyond the literal meanings of words. In figurative language, words are often used to symbolize ideas and concepts they would not otherwise be associated with. Writers use figurative language to create effects, to emphasize ideas, and to evoke emotions. Simile, metaphor, extended metaphor, hyperbole, and personification are examples of figurative language.

*See pages 576, 583, 589.*
*See also* **Hyperbole; Metaphor; Onomatopoeia; Personification; Simile.**

**First-Person Point of View** *See* **Point of View.**

**Flashback** In a literary work, a flashback is an interruption of the action to present events that took place at an earlier time. A flashback provides information that can help a reader better understand a character's current situation.
**Example:** In "Clean Sweep," Joan Bauer uses flashback to reveal what happened on the day the narrator's father died.

**Foil** A foil is a character who provides a striking contrast to another character. By using a foil, a writer can call attention to certain traits possessed by a main character or simply enhance a character by contrast. In Joseph Bruchac's "The Snapping Turtle" the boys at the rez provide a foil to the narrator.

**Folklore** The traditions, customs, and stories that are passed down within a culture are known as its folklore. Folklore includes various types of literature, such as legends, folk tales, myths, trickster tales, and fables.

*See also* **Fable; Folk Tale; Myth.**

**Folk Tale** A folk tale is a story that has been passed from generation to generation by word of mouth. Folk tales may be set in the distant past and involve supernatural events. The characters in them may be animals, people, or superhuman beings. "The Wise Old Woman" is an example of a folk tale.

**Foreshadowing** Foreshadowing occurs when a writer provides hints that suggest future events in a story. Foreshadowing creates suspense and makes readers eager to find out what will happen. For example, in W. W. Jacob's story "The Monkey's Paw," the sergeant-major's warnings about the paw foreshadow the tragedy that wishing upon it brings about.

**Form** The structure or organization of a work of writing is often called its form. The form of a poem includes the arrangement of its words and lines on the page.

**Free Verse** Free verse is poetry that does not contain regular patterns of rhythm or rhyme. The lines in free verse often flow more naturally than do rhymed, metrical lines and therefore achieve a rhythm more like that of everyday speech. Although free verse lacks conventional meter, it may contain various rhythmic and sound effects, such as repetitions of syllables or words. Free verse can be used for a variety of subjects. Billy Collins's poem "Introduction to Poetry" is an example of free verse.

*See page 586.*

*See also* **Meter; Rhyme.**

**Genre** The term *genre* refers to a category in which a work of literature is classified. The major genres in literature are fiction, nonfiction, poetry, and drama.

**Hero** A hero is a main character or protagonist in a story. In older literary works, heroes tend to be better than ordinary humans. They are typically courageous, strong, honorable, and intelligent. They are protectors of society who hold back the forces of evil and fight to make the world a better place. In modern literature, a hero may simply be the most important character in a story. Such a hero is often an ordinary person with ordinary problems.

**Historical Context** The historical context of a literary work refers to the social conditions that inspired or influenced its creation. To understand and appreciate certain works, the reader must relate them to particular events in history.

**Example:** Walt Whitman wrote his poem "O Captain! My Captain!" in 1865 in response to the assassination of Abraham Lincoln.

*See pages 729, 760, 855.*

**Historical Dramas** Historical dramas are plays that take place in the past and are based on real events. In many of these plays, the characters are also based on real historical figures. The dialogue and the action, however, are mostly created by the playwright.

**Historical Fiction** A short story or a novel can be called historical fiction when it is set in the past and includes real places and real events of historical importance. "The Drummer Boy of Shiloh" by Ray Bradbury is an example of historical fiction.

*See pages 317, 374.*

**Humor** Humor is a quality that provokes laughter or amusement. Writers create humor through exaggeration, amusing descriptions, irony, and witty and insightful dialogue. In "Roughing It," Mark Twain uses humor to tell about his poor work habits and the job he did as a reporter.

*See page 705.*

**Hyperbole** Hyperbole is a figure of speech in which the truth is exaggerated for emphasis or humorous effect.

**Idiom** An idiom is an expression that has a meaning different from the meaning of its individual words. For example, "to go to the dogs" is an idiom meaning "to go to ruin."

**Imagery** Imagery consists of descriptive words and phrases that re-create sensory experiences for the reader. Imagery usually appeals to one or more of the five senses— sight, hearing, smell, taste, and touch—to help the reader imagine exactly what is being described. Note the appeals to sight, taste, and touch in the following lines.

> I say feed me.
> She serves me red prickly pear on a spiked cactus.
>
> I say tease me.
> She sprinkles raindrops in my face on a sunny day.
> —Pat Mora, "Mi Madre"

*See pages 417, 580, 729.*

**Internal Conflict** *See* **Conflict.**

**Interview** An interview is a conversation conducted by a writer or reporter, in which facts or statements are elicited from another person, recorded, and then broadcast or published. "Interview with a Song Catcher" is based on a conversation between Brian Handwerk and Henrietta Yurchenco.

*See page 909.*

**Irony** Irony is a special kind of contrast between appearance and reality—usually one in which reality is the opposite of what it seems. One type of irony is **situational irony,** a contrast between what a reader or character expects and what actually exists or happens. For example, in O. Henry's "The Ransom of Red Chief," the kidnappers pay to get rid of the boy instead of collecting a ransom for him, as they had planned. Another type of irony is **dramatic irony,** where the reader or viewer knows something that a character does not know. In the myth "Pandora's Box," the readers know that Zeus created Pandora and her box in order to punish Prometheus, but Epimetheus isn't sure. **Verbal irony** exists when someone knowingly exaggerates or says one thing and means another. David Sedaris uses verbal irony in "Us and Them" when he says, "I could make friends if I wanted to. It just wasn't the right time." He actually means that he was unpopular.

*See pages 59, 717, 729.*

**Journal** *See* **Diary.**

**Legend** A legend is a story handed down from the past about a specific person, usually someone of heroic accomplishments. Legends usually have some basis in historical fact.

**Limerick** A limerick is a short, humorous poem composed of five lines. It usually has the rhyme scheme *aabba*, created by two rhyming couplets followed by a fifth line that rhymes with the first couplet. A limerick typically has a sing-song rhythm.

**Limited Point of View** *See* **Point of View.**

**Line** The line is the core unit of a poem. In poetry, line length is an essential element of the poem's meaning and rhythm. Line breaks, where a line of poetry ends, may coincide with grammatical units. However, a line break may also occur in the middle of a grammatical unit, therefore creating a meaningful pause or emphasis. Poets use a variety of line breaks to play with sense, grammar, and syntax and thereby create a wide range of effects.

**Lyric Poetry** A lyric poem is a short poem in which a single speaker expresses personal thoughts and feelings. Most poems other than dramatic and narrative poems are lyric poems. In ancient Greece, lyric poetry was meant to be sung. Modern lyrics are usually not intended for singing, but they are characterized by strong melodic rhythms. Lyric poetry has a variety of forms and covers many subjects, from love and death to everyday experiences. Langston Hughes's "Mother to Son" is an example of a lyric poem.

**Memoir** A memoir is a form of autobiographical writing in which a writer shares his or her personal experiences and observations of significant events or people. Often informal or even intimate in tone, memoirs usually give readers insight into the impact of historical events on people's lives. "My First Free Summer" by Julia Alvarez is a memoir.

*See page 111.*

*See also* **Autobiography.**

**Metaphor** A metaphor is a comparison of two things that are basically unlike but have some qualities in common. Unlike a simile, a metaphor does not contain the word *like* or *as*. In "Identity," the speaker of the poem compares himself to a "tall, ugly weed."

*See pages 580, 583.*

*See also* **Extended Metaphor; Figurative Language; Simile.**

**Meter** Meter is a regular pattern of stressed and unstressed syllables in a poem. The meter of a poem emphasizes the musical quality of the language. Each unit of meter, known as a foot, consists of one stressed syllable and one or two unstressed syllables. In representations of meter, a stressed syllable is indicated by the symbol (´); an unstressed syllable by the symbol (˘). The four basic types of metrical feet are the iamb, an unstressed syllable followed by a stressed syllable (˘´); the trochee, a stressed syllable followed by an unstressed syllable (´˘); the anapest, two unstressed syllables followed by a stressed syllable (˘˘´); and the dactyl, a stressed syllable followed by two unstressed syllables (´˘˘). Note the following example of stressed and unstressed syllables.

> By the shores of Gitche Gumee,
> By the shining Big-Sea-Water,
> Stood the wigwam of Nokomis,
> Daughter of the Moon, Nokomis.
> —Henry Wadsworth Longfellow, *Song of Hiawatha*

*See pages 637.*

*See also* **Rhythm.**

**Minor Character** *See* **Character.**

**Mood** Mood is the feeling or atmosphere that a writer creates for the reader. Descriptive words, imagery, and figurative language all influence the mood of a work. In "The Monkey's Paw," W. W. Jacobs creates a mood of gloom, dread, and desperation.

*See pages 312, 359.*

*See also* **Tone.**

**Moral**  A moral is a lesson that a story teaches. A moral is often stated at the end of a fable. Other times, the moral is implied.

*See also* **Fable.**

**Motivation**  *See* **Character.**

**Myth**  A myth is a traditional story, usually concerning some superhuman being or unlikely event, that was once widely believed to be true. Frequently, myths were attempts to explain natural phenomena, such as solar and lunar eclipses or the cycle of the seasons. For some peoples, myths were both a kind of science and a religion. In addition, myths served as literature and entertainment, just as they do for modern-day audiences. "Pandora's Box" is an example of a myth from ancient Greece.

*See page 455.*

**Narrative Nonfiction**  Narrative nonfiction is writing that reads much like fiction, except that the characters, setting, and events are based on real life. *An American Plague: The True and Terrifying Story of the Yellow Fever Epidemic of 1793* by Jim Murphy is an example of narrative nonfiction.

*See page 938.*

**Narrative Poetry**  Poetry that tells a story is called narrative poetry. Like fiction, a narrative poem contains characters, a setting, and a plot. It might also contain such elements of poetry as rhyme, rhythm, imagery, and figurative language. "Paul Revere's Ride" by Henry Wadsworth Longfellow is an example of a narrative poem.

**Narrator**  The narrator is the voice that tells a story. Sometimes the narrator is a character in the story. At other times, the narrator is an outside voice created by the writer. The narrator is not the same as the writer. An unreliable narrator is one who tells a story or interprets events in a way that makes readers doubt what he or she is saying. An unreliable narrator is usually a character in the story. The narrator may be unreliable for a number of different reasons. For example, the narrator may not have all the facts or may be too young to understand the situation.

*See also* **Point of View.**

**Nonfiction**  Nonfiction is writing that tells about real people, places, and events. Unlike fiction, nonfiction is mainly written to convey factual information. Nonfiction includes a wide range of writing—newspaper articles, letters, essays, biographies, movie reviews, speeches, true-life adventure stories, advertising, and more.

**Novel**  A novel is a long work of fiction. Like a short story, a novel is the product of a writer's imagination. Because a novel is considerably longer than a short story, a novelist can develop the characters and story line more thoroughly.

*See also* **Fiction.**

**Ode**  An ode is a type of lyric poem that deals with serious themes, such as justice, truth, or beauty. Odes appeal to both the imagination and the intellect, and many commemorate events or praise people or elements of nature. Alexander Pope's example of this poetic form is "Ode on Solitude."

**Omniscient Point of View**  *See* **Point of View.**

**Onomatopoeia**  Onomatopoeia is the use of words whose sounds echo their meanings, such as *buzz, whisper, gargle,* and *murmur.* As a literary technique, onomatopoeia goes beyond the use of simple echoing words. Skilled writers, especially poets, choose words whose sounds intensify images and suggest meaning. In the following lines, onomatopoeia helps the reader imagine the crying infant and the soothing mother.

> Stilled his fretful wail by saying,
> "Hush! the Naked Bear will hear thee!"
> Lulled him into slumber, singing,
> "Ewa-yea! my little owlet!"
> —Henry Wadsworth Longfellow, *Song of Hiawatha*

**Oral Literature**  Oral literature consists of stories that have been passed down by word of mouth from generation to generation. Oral literature includes folk tales, legends, and myths. In more recent times, some examples of oral literature have been written down or recorded so that the stories can be preserved.

**Parallel Episodes**  Parallel episodes occur when elements of a plot are repeated several times in the course of a story. Fairy tales often employ parallel episodes, as in the examples of "Goldilocks and the Three Bears" and "The Three Little Pigs." The short story "Flowers for Algernon" also contains several parallel episodes.

**Personal Essay**  *See* **Essay.**

**Personification**  The giving of human qualities to an animal, object, or idea is known as personification. In "the lesson of the moth," for example, the speaker, a cockroach, and the moth are personified. They have conversations with each other as if they were human.

*See page 589.*

*See also* **Figurative Language.**

**Persuasive Essay** *See* **Essay.**

**Play** *See* **Drama.**

**Playwright** *See* **Drama.**

**Plot** The series of events in a story is called the plot. The plot usually centers on a conflict, or struggle, faced by the main character. The action that the characters take to solve the problem builds toward a climax in the story. At this point, or shortly afterward, the problem is solved and the story ends. Most story plots have five stages: exposition, rising action, climax, falling action, and resolution.

*See pages 26, 33, 47.*
*See also* **Climax; Exposition; Falling Action; Rising Action.**

**Poetry** Poetry is a type of literature in which words are carefully chosen and arranged to create certain effects. Poets use a variety of sound devices, imagery, and figurative language to express emotions and ideas.

*See also* **Alliteration; Assonance; Ballad; Free Verse; Imagery; Meter; Narrative Poetry; Rhyme; Rhythm; Stanza.**

**Point of View** *Point of view* refers to the method of narration used in a short story, novel, narrative poem, or work of nonfiction. In a work told from a **first-person point of view,** the narrator is a character in the story, as in "The Tell-Tale Heart" by Edgar Allan Poe. In a work told from a **third-person point of view,** the narrative voice is outside the action, not one of the characters. If a story is told from a **third-person omniscient,** or all-knowing, point of view, as in "The Lady, or the Tiger" by Frank R. Stockton, the narrator sees into the minds of all the characters. If events are related from a **third-person limited point of view,** as in Beverly Naidoo's "Out of Bounds," the narrator tells what only one character thinks, feels, and observes.

*See pages 162, 169, 223.*
*See also* **Narrator.**

**Prop** The word *prop,* originally an abbreviation of the word *property,* refers to any physical object that is used in a drama. In the play *The Diary of Anne Frank,* the props include Anne's diary and Mrs. Van Daan's fur coat.

**Prose** The word *prose* refers to all forms of writing that are not in verse form. The term may be used to describe very different forms of writing—short stories as well as essays, for example.

**Protagonist** A protagonist is the main character in a story, play, or novel. The protagonist is involved in the main conflict of the story. Usually, the protagonist undergoes changes as the plot runs its course. In "Flowers for Algernon" by Daniel Keyes, Charlie is the protagonist.

**Radio Play** A radio play is a drama that is written specifically to be broadcast over the radio. Because the audience is not meant to see a radio play, sound effects are often used to help listeners imagine the setting and the action. The stage directions in the play's script indicate the sound effects. *The Hitchhiker* by Lucille Fletcher is an example of a radio play.

**Recurring Theme** *See* **Theme.**

**Repetition** Repetition is a technique in which a sound, word, phrase, or line is repeated for emphasis or unity. Repetition often helps to reinforce meaning and create an appealing rhythm. Note how the use of repetition in the following lines emphasizes the speaker's message about body and soul.

> You are not your body,
> you are not your bones.
> What's essential about you
> Is what can't be owned.
> —Marilyn Nelson, "Not My Bones"

*See page 625.*
*See also* **Alliteration; Sound Devices.**

**Resolution** *See* **Falling Action.**

**Rhyme** Rhyme is the occurrence of similar or identical sounds at the end of two or more words, such as *suite, heat,* and *complete.* Rhyme that occurs within a single line of poetry is internal rhyme. Rhyme that occurs at the ends of lines of poetry is called end rhyme. End rhyme that is not exact but approximate is called slant rhyme, or off rhyme. Notice the following example of slant rhyme involving the words *sky* and *signed.*

> The willow is like an etching,
> Fine-lined against the <u>sky</u>.
> The ginkgo is like a crude sketch,
> Hardly worthy to be <u>signed</u>.
> —Eve Merriam, "Simile: Willow and Ginkgo"

*See pages 578, 589, 619.*

**Rhyme Scheme** A rhyme scheme is a pattern of end rhymes in a poem. A rhyme scheme is noted by assigning a letter of the alphabet, beginning with *a*, to each line. Lines that rhyme are given the same letter. Notice the rhyme scheme of the first stanza of this poem.

> There ain't no pay beneath the sun         *a*
> As sweet as rest when a job's well done.    *a*
> I was born to work up to my grave           *b*
> But I was not born                          *c*
> To be a slave.                              *b*
> —Maya Angelou, "One More Round"

See page 619.

**Rhythm** Rhythm is a pattern of stressed and unstressed syllables in a line of poetry. Poets use rhythm to bring out the musical quality of language, to emphasize ideas, and to create moods. Devices such as alliteration, rhyme, assonance, and consonance often contribute to creating rhythm.

See pages 578, 637.
See also **Meter**.

**Rising Action** The rising action is the stage of the plot that develops the conflict, or struggle. During this stage, events occur that make the conflict more complicated. The events in the rising action build toward a climax, or turning point.

See page 33.
See also **Plot**.

**Scene** In a drama, the action is often divided into acts and scenes. Each scene presents an episode of the play's plot and typically occurs at a single place and time.

See also **Act**.

**Scenery** Scenery is a painted backdrop or other structures used to create the setting for a play.

**Science Fiction** Science fiction is fiction in which a writer explores unexpected possibilities of the past or the future, using known scientific data and theories as well as his or her creative imagination. Most science fiction writers create believable worlds, although some create fantasy worlds that have familiar elements. Isaac Asimov, the author of "Hallucination," is a famous writer of science fiction.

See also **Fantasy**.

**Screenplay** A screenplay is a play written for film.

**Script** The text of a play, film, or broadcast is called a script.

**Sensory Details** Sensory details are words and phrases that appeal to the reader's senses of sight, hearing, touch, smell, and taste. Note the use of sensory details that appeal to sight and taste in the following example.

> juniper, piñon, or something
> with hard, red berries in spring.
> You taste them, and they are sweet
> and bitter, the berries a delicacy
> —Simon Ortiz, "Canyon de Chelly"

See also **Imagery**.

**Setting** The setting of a story, poem, or play is the time and place of the action. Sometimes the setting is clear and well-defined. At other times, it is left to the reader's imagination. Elements of setting include geographic location, historical period (past, present, or future), season, time of day, and culture.

See pages 310, 317, 333, 381.

**Short Story** A short story is a work of fiction that centers on a single idea and can be read in one sitting. Generally, a short story has one main conflict that involves the characters and keeps the story moving.

See also **Fiction**.

**Simile** A simile is a figure of speech that makes a comparison between two unlike things using the word *like* or *as*.

> The willow is like a nymph with streaming hair;
> —Eve Merriam, "Simile: Willow and Ginkgo"

See pages 580, 583.
See also **Figurative Language; Metaphor**.

**Situational Irony** See **Irony**.

**Sonnet** A sonnet is a poem that has a formal structure, containing 14 lines and a specific rhyme scheme and meter. A sonnet often consists of three quatrains, or four-line units, and a final couplet. The sonnet, which means "little song," can be used for a variety of subjects. John Keats's "On the Grasshopper and Cricket" is an example of a sonnet.

See also **Couplet; Rhyme Scheme**.

**Sound Devices** Sound devices, or uses of words for their connection to the sense of hearing, can convey meaning and mood or unify a work. Some common sound devices are **alliteration, assonance, consonance, meter, onomatopoeia, repetition, rhyme,** and **rhythm.** The following poem contains alliteration, repetition, assonance, consonance, rhyme, and rhythm, all of which combine to help convey both meaning and mood.

> It's all I have to bring today—
> This, and my heart beside—
> This, and my heart, and all the fields—
> And all the meadows wide—
> Be sure you count—should I forget
> Some one the sum could tell—
> This, and my heart, and all the Bees
> Which in the Clover dwell.
> —Emily Dickinson, "It's all I have to bring today"

*See pages 283, 578, 613, 637.*
*See also* **Alliteration; Assonance; Consonance; Meter; Onomatopoeia; Repetition; Rhyme; Rhythm.**

**Speaker** In poetry, the speaker is the voice that "talks" to the reader, similar to the narrator in fiction. The speaker is not necessarily the poet. For example, in Langston Hughes's poem "Mother to Son," the speaker is an older woman, not the male poet.
*See pages 417, 597.*

**Speech** A speech is a talk or public address. The purpose of a speech may be to entertain, to explain, to persuade, to inspire, or any combination of these purposes. Chief Canasatego's speech "Educating Sons" was delivered in order to explain to the European settlers why the Iroquois were rejecting the offer of a free education.
*See pages 846, 1004.*

**Stage Directions** In the script of a play, the instructions to the actors, director, and stage crew are called the stage directions. Stage directions might suggest scenery, lighting, sound effects, and ways for actors to move and speak. Stage directions often appear in parentheses and in italic type.
*See page 87.*

**Stanza** A stanza is a group of two or more lines that form a unit in a poem. Each stanza may have the same number of lines, or the number of lines may vary. Eve Merriam's poem "Simile: Willow and Ginkgo" is divided into six stanzas.
*See also* **Couplet; Form; Poetry.**

**Static Character** *See* **Character.**

**Stereotype** In literature, characters who are defined by a single trait are known as stereotypes. Such characters do not usually demonstrate the complexities of real people. Familiar stereotypes in popular literature include the absent-minded professor and the busybody.

**Structure** The structure of a work of literature is the way in which it is put together. In poetry, structure involves the arrangement of words and lines to produce a desired effect. One structural unit in poetry is the stanza. In prose, structure involves the arrangement of such elements as sentences, paragraphs, and events. "The Wise Old Woman," for example, is structured around the three challenges set forth by Lord Higa.

**Style** A style is a manner of writing. It involves how something is said rather than what is said. For example, "New York Day Women" by Edwidge Danticat is written in a style that makes use of sentence fragments, repetition, and unusual presentation.

**Subplot** A subplot is an additional, or secondary, plot in a story. The subplot contains its own conflict, which is often separate from the main conflicts of the story.
*See page 521.*

**Surprise Ending** A surprise ending is an unexpected plot twist at the end of a story. The surprise may be a sudden turn in the action or a piece of information that gives a different perspective to the entire story. The short story writer O. Henry is famous for using this device.

**Suspense** Suspense is a feeling of growing tension and excitement felt by a reader. Suspense makes a reader curious about the outcome of a story or an event within a story. A writer creates suspense by raising questions in the reader's mind. The use of foreshadowing is one way that writers create suspense.
*See page 77.*
*See also* **Foreshadowing.**

**Symbol** A symbol is a person, a place, an object, or an activity that stands for something beyond itself. For example, a flag is a colored piece of cloth that stands for a country. A white dove is a bird that represents peace.
**Example:** In "Gil's Furniture Bought and Sold" by Sandra Cisneros, the music box represents beauty.
*See pages 442, 449, 477.*

**Tall Tale** A tall tale is a humorously exaggerated story about impossible events, often involving the supernatural abilities of the main character. Stories about folk heroes such as Pecos Bill and Paul Bunyan are typical tall tales.

**Theme** A theme is a message about life or human nature that the writer shares with the reader. In many cases, readers must infer what the writer's message is. One way of figuring out a theme is to apply the lessons learned by the main characters to people in real life. For example, a theme of *The Diary of Anne Frank* is that people are good at heart.

   **Recurring themes** are themes found in a variety of works. For example, authors from different backgrounds might express similar themes having to do with the importance of family values. Universal themes are themes that are found throughout the literature of all time periods. For example, the folk tales "The Old Grandfather and His Little Grandson" and "The Wise Old Woman" both express the theme that we should treat older people with respect.

*See pages 442, 455, 463, 485.*
*See also* **Moral.**

**Third-Person Point of View** *See* **Point of View.**

**Title** The title of a piece of writing is the name that is attached to it. A title often refers to an important aspect of the work. For example, the title "Raymond's Run" refers to the climax of the story, when Squeaky realizes she can find fulfillment in helping her brother Raymond improve his skills.

**Tone** The tone of a literary work expresses the writer's attitude toward his or her subject. Words such as *angry, sad,* and *humorous* can be used to describe different tones. For example, the tone of Mark Twain's essay "Roughing It" is humorous.

*See pages 668, 683, 735.*
*See also* **Author's Perspective; Mood.**

**Tragedy** A tragedy is a dramatic work that presents the downfall of a dignified character or characters involved in historically or socially significant events. The events in a tragic plot are set in motion by a decision that is often an error in judgment on the part of the hero. Succeeding events are linked in a cause-and-effect relationship and lead inevitably to a disastrous conclusion, usually death. William Shakespeare's *Romeo and Juliet* is a famous tragedy.

**Traits** *See* **Character Traits.**

**Turning Point** *See* **Climax.**

**Understatement** Understatement is a technique of creating emphasis by saying less than is actually or literally true. It is the opposite of hyperbole, or exaggeration. Understatement is often used to create a humorous effect.

**Universal Theme** *See* **Theme.**

**Unreliable Narrator** *See* **Narrator.**

**Verbal Irony** *See* **Irony.**

**Voice** The term *voice* refers to a writer's unique use of language that allows a reader to "hear" a human personality in the writer's work. Elements of style that contribute to a writer's voice can reveal much about the author's personality, beliefs, and attitudes.

*See page 705.*

**Word Choice** The success of any writing depends on the writer's choice of words. Words not only communicate ideas but also help describe events, characters, settings, and so on. Word choice can make a writer's work sound formal or informal, serious or humorous. A writer must choose words carefully depending on the goal of the piece of writing. For example, a writer working on a science article would probably use technical, formal words; a writer trying to establish the setting in a short story would probably use more descriptive words.

*See also* **Style.**

# Glossary of Reading and Informational Terms

**Almanac** *See* **Reference Works.**

**Analogy** An analogy is a comparison between two things that are alike in some way. Often, writers use analogies in nonfiction to explain an unfamiliar subject or idea by showing how it is like a familiar one.

**Appeal to Authority** An appeal to authority is an attempt to persuade an audience by making reference to people who are experts on a subject.

**Argument** An argument is speaking or writing that expresses a position on a problem and supports it with reasons and evidence. An argument often takes into account other points of view, anticipating and answering objections that opponents might raise.
*See also* **Claim; Counterargument; Evidence.**

**Assumption** An assumption is an opinion or belief that is taken for granted. It can be about a specific situation, a person, or the world in general. Assumptions are often unstated.

**Author's Message** An author's message is the main idea or theme of a particular work.
*See also* **Main Idea; Theme,** *Glossary of Literary Terms, page R112.*

**Author's Perspective** *See Glossary of Literary Terms, page R102.*

**Author's Position** An author's position is his or her opinion on an issue or topic.
*See also* **Claim.**

**Author's Purpose** *See Glossary of Literary Terms, page R102.*

**Autobiography** *See Glossary of Literary Terms, page R102.*

**Bias** In a piece of writing, the author's bias is the side of an issue that he or she favors. Words with extremely positive or negative connotations are often a signal of an author's bias.

**Bibliography** A bibliography is a list of related books and other materials used to write a text. Bibliographies can be good sources for further study on a subject.
*See also* **Works Consulted.**

**Biography** *See Glossary of Literary Terms, page R103.*

**Business Correspondence** Business correspondence is written business communications such as business letters, e-mails, and memos. In general, business correspondence is brief, to the point, clear, courteous, and professional.

**Cause and Effect** Two events are related by cause and effect when one event brings about, or causes, the other. The event that happens first is the **cause;** the one that follows is the **effect.** Cause and effect is also a way of organizing an entire piece of writing. It helps writers show the relationships between events or ideas.
*See also* **False Cause,** *Reading Handbook, page R24.*

**Chronological Order** Chronological order is the arrangement of events by their order of occurrence. This type of organization is used in fictional narratives and in historical writing, biography, and autobiography.

**Claim** In an argument, a claim is the writer's position on an issue or problem. Although an argument focuses on supporting one claim, a writer may make more than one claim in a text.

**Clarify** Clarifying is a strategy that helps readers understand or make clear what they are reading. Readers usually clarify by rereading, reading aloud, or discussing.

**Classification** Classification is a pattern of organization in which objects, ideas, and/or information are presented in groups, or classes, based on common characteristics.

**Cliché** A cliché is an overused expression. "Better late than never" and "hard as nails" are common examples. Good writers generally avoid clichés unless they are using them in dialogue to indicate something about a character's personality.

**Compare and Contrast** To compare and contrast is to identify the similarities and differences of two or more subjects. Compare and contrast is also a pattern of organizing an entire piece of writing.

**Conclusion** A conclusion is a statement of belief based on evidence, experience, and reasoning. A valid conclusion is one that logically follows from the facts or statements upon which it is based.

**Connect** Connecting is a reader's process of relating the content of a text to his or her own knowledge and experience.

**Consumer Documents** Consumer documents are printed materials that accompany products and services. They usually provide information about the use, care, operation, or assembly of the product or service they accompany. Some common consumer documents are applications, contracts, warranties, manuals, instructions, labels, brochures, and schedules.

**Context Clues** When you encounter an unfamiliar word, you can often use context clues to understand it. Context clues are the words or phrases surrounding the word that provide hints about the word's meaning.

**Counterargument** A counterargument is an argument made to oppose another argument. A good argument anticipates opposing viewpoints and provides counterarguments to disprove them.

**Credibility** Credibility is the believability or trustworthiness of a source and the information it provides.

**Critical Review** A critical review is an evaluation or critique by a reviewer, or critic. Types of reviews include film reviews, book reviews, music reviews, and art show reviews.

**Database** A database is a collection of information that can be quickly and easily accessed and searched and from which information can be easily retrieved. It is frequently presented in an electronic format.

**Debate** A debate is an organized exchange of opinions on an issue. In school settings, debate is usually a formal contest in which two opposing teams defend and attack a proposition.
*See also* **Argument.**

**Deductive Reasoning** Deductive reasoning is a way of thinking that begins with a generalization, presents a specific situation, and then moves forward with facts and evidence toward a logical conclusion. The following passage has a deductive argument embedded in it: "All students in the math class must take the quiz on Friday. Since Lana is in the class, she had better show up." This deductive argument can be broken down as follows: generalization—All students in the math class must take the quiz on Friday; specific situation—Lana is a student in the math class; conclusion—Therefore, Lana must take the math quiz.
*See also* **Analyzing Logic and Reasoning,** *Reading Handbook, page R22.*

**Diary** *See Glossary of Literary Terms, page R104.*

**Dictionary** *See* **Reference Works.**

**Draw Conclusions** To draw a conclusion is to make a judgment or arrive at a belief based on evidence, experience, and reasoning.

**Editorial** An editorial is an opinion piece that usually appears on the editorial page of a newspaper or as part of a news broadcast. The editorial section of the newspaper presents opinions rather than objective news reports.
*See also* **Op/Ed Piece.**

**Either/Or Fallacy** An either/or fallacy is a statement that suggests that there are only two choices available in a situation when in fact there are more than two.
*See also* **Identifying Faulty Reasoning,** *Reading Handbook, page R24.*

**Emotional Appeal** An emotional appeal is a message that creates strong feelings in order to make a point. An appeal to fear is a message that taps into people's fear of losing their safety or security. An appeal to pity is a message that taps into people's sympathy and compassion for others to build support for an idea, a cause, or a proposed action. An appeal to vanity is a message that attempts to persuade by tapping into people's desire to feel good about themselves.
*See also* **Recognizing Persuasive Techniques,** *Reading Handbook, page R21.*

**Encyclopedia** *See* **Reference Works.**

**Essay** *See Glossary of Literary Terms, page R104.*

**Ethical Appeal** In an ethical appeal, a writer links a claim to a widely accepted value in order to gain moral support for the claim. The appeal also creates an image of the writer as a trustworthy, moral person.
*See also* **Recognizing Persuasive Techniques,** *Reading Handbook, page R21.*

**Evaluate** To evaluate is to examine something carefully and to judge its value or worth. Evaluating is an important skill. A reader can evaluate the actions of a particular character, for example. A reader can also form opinions about the value of an entire work.

**Evidence** Evidence is a specific piece of information that supports a claim. Evidence can take the form of a fact, a quotation, an example, a statistic, or a personal experience, among other things.

**Expository Essay** *See* **Essay,** *Glossary of Literary Terms, page R104.*

**Fact Versus Opinion** A **fact** is a statement that can be proved, or verified. An opinion, on the other hand, is a statement that cannot be proved because it expresses a person's beliefs, feelings, or thoughts.
*See also* **Generalization; Inference.**

**Fallacy** A fallacy is an error of reasoning. Typically, a fallacy is based on an incorrect inference or a misuse of evidence.
*See also* **Either/Or Fallacy; Logical Appeal; Overgeneralization.**
*See also* **Identifying Faulty Reasoning,** *Reading Handbook, page R24.*

**Faulty Reasoning** *See* **Fallacy.**

**Feature Article** A feature article is an article in a newspaper or magazine about a topic of human interest or lifestyles.

**Generalization** A generalization is a broad statement about a class or category of people, ideas, or things based on a study of, or a belief about, only some of its members.
*See also* **Overgeneralization; Stereotyping.**

**Government Publications** Government publications are documents produced by government organizations. Pamphlets, brochures, and reports are just some of the many forms these publications take. Government publications can be good resources for a wide variety of topics.

**Graphic Aid** A graphic aid is a visual tool that is printed, handwritten, or drawn. Charts, diagrams, graphs, photographs, and maps are examples of graphic aids.
*See also* **Graphic Aids,** *Reading Handbook, page R4.*

**Graphic Organizer** A graphic organizer is a "word picture"—a visual illustration of a verbal statement—that helps a reader understand a text. Charts, tables, webs, and diagrams can all be graphic organizers. Graphic organizers and graphic aids can look the same. However, graphic organizers and graphic aids do differ in how they are used. Graphic aids help deliver important information to students using a text. Graphic organizers are actually created by students themselves. They help students understand the text or organize information.

**Historical Document** Historical documents are writings that have played a significant role in human events. The Declaration of Independence, for example, is a historical document.

**How-To Book** A how-to book explains how to do something—usually an activity, a sport, or a household project.

**Implied Main Idea** *See* **Main Idea.**

**Index** The index of a book is an alphabetized list of important topics covered in the book and the page numbers on which they can be found. An index can be used to quickly find specific information about a topic.

**Inductive Reasoning** Inductive reasoning is the process of logical reasoning that starts with observations, examples, and facts and moves on to a general conclusion or principle.
*See also* **Analyzing Logic and Reasoning,** *Reading Handbook, page R22.*

**Inference** An inference is a logical guess that is made based on facts and one's own knowledge and experience.

**Informational Text** Informational text is writing that provides factual information. It often explains an idea or teaches a process. Examples include news reports, science textbooks, software instructions, and lab reports.

**Internet** The Internet is a global, interconnected system of computer networks that allows for communication through e-mail, listservs, and the World Wide Web. The Internet connects computers and computer users throughout the world.

**Journal** A journal is a periodical publication issued by a legal, medical, or other professional organization. The term may also be used to refer to a diary or daily record.

**Loaded Language** Loaded language consists of words with strongly positive or negative connotations, intended to influence a reader's or listener's attitude.

**Logical Appeal** A logical appeal is a way of writing or speaking that relies on logic and facts. It appeals to people's reasoning or intellect rather than to their values or emotions. Flawed logical appeals—that is, errors in reasoning—are called logical fallacies.
*See also* **Fallacy.**

**Logical Argument** A logical argument is an argument in which the logical relationship between the support and claim is sound.

**Main Idea** The main idea is the central or most important idea about a topic that a writer or speaker conveys. It can be the central idea of an entire work or of just a paragraph. Often, the main idea of a paragraph is expressed in a topic sentence. However, a main idea may just be implied, or suggested, by details. A main idea is typically supported by details.

**Make Inferences** *See* **Inference.**

**Monitor** Monitoring is the strategy of checking your comprehension as you read and modifying the strategies you are using to suit your needs. Monitoring often includes the following strategies: questioning, clarifying, visualizing, predicting, connecting, and rereading.

**Narrative Nonfiction** *See Glossary of Literary Terms, page R108.*

**News Article** A news article is writing that reports on a recent event. In newspapers, news articles are usually brief and to the point, presenting the most important facts first, followed by more detailed information.

**Nonfiction** *See Glossary of Literary Terms, page R108.*

**Op/Ed Piece** An op/ed piece is an opinion piece that typically appears opposite ("op") the editorial page of a newspaper. Unlike editorials, op/ed pieces are written and submitted by readers.

**Organization** *See* **Pattern of Organization.**

**Overgeneralization** An overgeneralization is a generalization that is too broad. You can often recognize overgeneralizations by the appearance of words and phrases such as *all, everyone, every time, any, anything, no one,* or *none.* An example is "None of the city's workers really cares about keeping the environment clean." In all probability, there are many exceptions. The writer can't possibly know the feelings of every city worker.
*See also* **Identifying Faulty Reasoning,** *Reading Handbook, page R24.*

**Overview** An overview is a short summary of a story, a speech, or an essay.

**Paraphrase** Paraphrasing is the restating of information in one's own words.
*See also* **Summarize.**

**Pattern of Organization** The term *pattern of organization* refers to the way ideas and information are arranged and organized. Patterns of organization include cause and effect, chronological, compare and contrast, classification, and problem-solution, among others.
*See also* **Cause and Effect; Chronological Order; Classification; Compare and Contrast; Problem-Solution Order; Sequential Order.**
*See also* **Reading Informational Texts: Patterns of Organization,** *Reading Handbook, page R8.*

**Periodical** A periodical is a magazine or other publication that is issued on a regular basis.

**Personal Essay** *See* **Essay,** *Glossary of Literary Terms, page R104.*

**Persuasion** Persuasion is the art of swaying others' feelings, beliefs, or actions. Persuasion normally appeals to both the mind and the emotions of the reader.
*See also* **Appeal to Authority; Emotional Appeal; Ethical Appeal; Loaded Language; Logical Appeal.**
*See also* **Recognizing Persuasive Techniques,** *Reading Handbook, page R21.*

**Predict** Predicting is a reading strategy that involves using text clues to make a reasonable guess about what will happen next in a story.

**Primary Source** *See* **Source.**

**Prior Knowledge** Prior knowledge is the knowledge a reader already possesses about a topic. This information might come from personal experiences, expert accounts, books, films, or other sources.

**Problem-Solution Order** Problem-solution order is a pattern of organization in which a problem is stated and analyzed and then one or more solutions are proposed and examined.

**Propaganda** Propaganda is any form of communication that is so distorted that it conveys false or misleading information to advance a specific belief or cause.

**Public Document** Public documents are documents that were written for the public to provide information that is of public interest or concern. They include government documents, speeches, signs, and rules and regulations.
*See also* **Government Publications.**

**Reference Works** Reference works are sources that contain facts and background information on a wide range of subjects. Most reference works are good sources of reliable information because they have been reviewed by experts. The following are some common reference works: encyclopedias, dictionaries, thesauri, almanacs, atlases, and directories.

**Review** *See* **Critical Review.**

**Rhetorical Question** Rhetorical questions are those that have such obvious answers that they do not require a reply. Writers often use them to suggest that their claim is so obvious that everyone should agree with it.

**Scanning** Scanning is the process used to search through a text for a particular fact or piece of information. When you scan, you sweep your eyes across a page, looking for key words that may lead you to the information you want.

**Scope** Scope refers to a work's focus. For example, an article about Austin, Texas, that focuses on the city's history, economy, and residents has a broad scope. An article that focuses only on the restaurants in Austin has a narrower scope.

**Secondary Source** *See* **Source.**

**Sequential Order** Sequential order is a pattern of organization that shows the order of steps or stages in a process.

**Setting a Purpose** The process of establishing specific reasons for reading a text is called setting a purpose. Readers can look at a text's title, headings, and illustrations to guess what it might be about. They can then use these guesses to figure out what they want to learn from reading the text.

**Sidebar** A sidebar is additional information set in a box alongside or within a news or feature article. Popular magazines often make use of sidebars.

**Signal Words** In a text, signal words are words and phrases that help show how events or ideas are related. Some common examples of signal words are *and, but, however, nevertheless, therefore,* and *in addition.*

**Source** A source is anything that supplies information. **Primary sources** are materials created by people who witnessed or took part in the event they supply information about. Letters, diaries, autobiographies, and eyewitness accounts are primary sources. **Secondary sources** are those made by people who were not directly involved in the event or even present when it occurred. Encyclopedias, textbooks, biographies, and most news articles are examples of secondary sources.

**Speech** *See Glossary of Literary Terms, page R111.*

**Stereotyping** Stereotyping is a dangerous type of overgeneralization. It can lead to unfair judgments of people based on their ethnic background, beliefs, practices, or physical appearance.

**Summarize** To summarize is to briefly retell the main ideas of a piece of writing in one's own words.
*See also* **Paraphrase.**

**Support** Support is any information that helps to prove a claim.

**Supporting Detail** *See* **Main Idea.**

**Synthesize** To synthesize information means to take individual pieces of information and combine them in order to gain a better understanding of a subject.

**Text Feature** Text features are elements of a text, such as boldface type, headings, and subheadings, that help organize and call attention to important information. Italic type, bulleted or numbered lists, sidebars, and graphic aids such as charts, tables, timelines, illustrations, and photographs are also considered text features.
*See also* **Understanding Text Features,** *Reading Handbook, page R3.*

**Thesaurus** *See* **Reference Works.**

**Thesis Statement** A thesis statement is the main proposition that a writer attempts to support in a piece of writing.

**Topic Sentence** The topic sentence of a paragraph states the paragraph's main idea. All other sentences in the paragraph provide supporting details.

**Treatment** The way a topic is handled in a work is referred to as its treatment. Treatment includes the form the writing takes as well as the writer's purpose and tone.

**Visualize** Visualizing is the process of forming a mental picture based on written or spoken information.

**Web Site** A Web site is a collection of "pages" on the World Wide Web that is usually devoted to one specific subject. Pages are linked together and accessed by clicking hyperlinks or menus, which send the user from page to page within a Web site. Web sites are created by companies, organizations, educational institutions, branches of the government, the military, and individuals.

**Workplace Document** Workplace documents are materials that are produced or used within a work setting, usually to aid in the functioning of the workplace. They include job applications, office memos, training manuals, job descriptions, and sales reports.

**Works Cited** The term *works cited* refers to a list of all the works a writer has referred to in his or her text. This list often includes not only books and articles but also Internet sources.

**Works Consulted** The term *works consulted* refers to a list of all the works a writer consulted in order to create his or her text. It is not limited just to those works cited in the text.
*See also* **Bibliography.**

# Glossary of Vocabulary in English & Spanish

**aberration** (ăb′ə-rā′shən) *n.* an abnormal alteration
**aberración** *s.* alteración anormal

**absurd** (əb-sûrd′) *adj.* ridiculously unreasonable
**absurdo** *adj.* que va en contra de lo razonable

**accommodate** (ə-kŏm′ə-dāt) *v.* to make room for
**acomodar** *v.* albergar; contener

**acute** (ə-kyo͞ot′) *adj.* sharp; keen
**agudo** *adj.* fuerte; perspicaz

**adequately** (ăd′ĭ-kwĭt-lē) *adv.* enough to satisfy a requirement or meet a need
**adecuadamente** *adv.* de modo suficiente para cumplir un requisito o necesidad

**adorn** (ə-dôrn′) *v.* to enhance or decorate
**adornar** *v.* embellecer o decorar

**adversary** (ăd′vər-sĕr′ē) *n.* an opponent
**adversario** *s.* oponente

**aggression** (ə-grĕsh′ən) *n.* hostile or destructive behavior or action
**agresión** *s.* conducta o acción hostil o destructiva

**ajar** (ə-jär′) *adj.* partially open
**entreabierto** *adj.* parcialmente abierto

**anguished** (ăng′gwĭsht) *adj.* tormented; distressed
**angustiado** *adj.* atormentado; afligido

**annihilate** (ə-nī′ə-lāt′) *v.* to completely destroy or defeat
**aniquilar** *v.* destruir o derrotar completamente

**appendage** (ə-pĕn′dĭj) *n.* a body part, such as an arm or leg, that is attached to the main part of the body
**apéndice** *s.* parte del cuerpo pegada al tronco, como un brazo o una pierna

**apprehension** (ăp′rĭ-hĕn′shən) *n.* nervousness
**aprensión** *s.* nerviosismo

**array** (ə-rā′) *n.* a large number of items
**conjunto** *s.* gran cantidad de objetos

**arrogant** (ăr′ə-gənt) *adj.* displaying a sense of self-importance
**arrogante** *adj.* que se las da de importante

**askew** (ə-skyo͞o′) *adj.* to one side; awry
**torcido** *adj.* que no es recto ni derecho

**aspire** (ə-spīr′) *v.* to have a great ambition or an ultimate goal; to desire strongly
**aspirar** *v.* tener una gran ambición o una meta final; desear con fuerza

**assert** (ə-sûrt′) *v.* to act forcefully; to take charge
**afirmar** *v.* dejar sentado; imponer autoridad

**assurance** (ə-sho͞or′əns) *n.* a guarantee or pledge
**garantía** *s.* compromiso

**attribute** (ə-trĭb′yo͞ot) *v.* to relate to a certain cause
**atribuir** *v.* relacionar con cierta causa

**audacity** (ô-dăs′ĭ-tē) *n.* shameless daring or boldness
**audacia** *s.* atrevimiento o descaro

**authentic** (ô-thĕn′tĭk) *adj.* having a verifiable origin; not counterfeit
**auténtico** *adj.* de origen comprobado; original

**bafflement** (băf′əl-mənt) *n.* confusion; puzzlement
**desconcierto** *s.* confusión; perplejidad

**ban** (băn) *v.* to prohibit
**prohibir** *v.* negar

**barricade** (băr′ĭ-kād′) *n.* a structure that blocks passage
**barricada** *s.* estructura que bloquea el paso

**basking** (băsk′ĭng) *adj.* warming oneself pleasantly, as in sunlight
**asoleado** *adj.* expuesto al sol

**beckon** (bĕk′ən) *v.* to signal to come
**llamar** *v.* hacer señas a alguien para que se acerque

**benefactor** (bĕn′ə-făk′tər) *n.* a person who gives monetary or other aid
**benefactor** *s.* persona que da dinero o ayuda

**bewilderment** (bĭ-wĭl′dər-mənt) *n.* the state of being confused or astonished
**perplejidad** *s.* confusión o desconcierto

**bound** (bound) *v.* to leap forward
**saltar** *v.* brincar hacia adelante

**brusquely** (brŭsk′lē) *adv.* in an abrupt, sudden manner
**bruscamente** *adv.* de modo abrupto y repentino

**cache** (kăsh) *v.* to store in a hiding place
**ocultar** *v.* guardar en un escondite

**cajole** (kə-jōl') *v.* to urge gently; to coax
  **persuadir** *v.* convencer; engatusar

**cavernous** (kăv'ər-nəs) *adj.* as deep or vast as a cavern, or a large cave
  **cavernoso** *adj.* profundo y oscuro como una caverna o cueva grande

**circumstance** (sûr'kəm-stăns') *n.* a condition that affects or relates to an event or series of events
  **circunstancia** *s.* situación que rodea a un suceso o serie de sucesos

**clutch** (klŭch) *v.* to grasp and hold tightly
  **agarrar** *v.* estrechar y apretar firmemente

**collaborate** (kə-lăb'ə-rāt') *v.* to work together on a project
  **colaborar** *v.* trabajar en equipo en un proyecto

**commence** (kə-měns') *v.* to begin
  **comenzar** *v.* empezar

**commend** (kə-měnd') *v.* to speak highly of; to praise; to recommend
  **elogiar** *v.* ensalzar; recomendar

**commotion** (kə-mō'shən) *n.* a disturbance
  **conmoción** *s.* disturbio

**compel** (kəm-pěl') *v.* to pressure by force
  **compeler** *v.* obligar a la fuerza

**compensation** (kŏm'pən-sā'shən) *n.* something, such as money, received as payment
  **compensación** *s.* dinero o cosa recibida en pago

**comply** (kəm-plī') *v.* to act according to a command or request
  **cumplir** *v.* seguir una orden o una solicitud

**composer** (kəm-pō'zər) *n.* one who creates musical pieces
  **compositor** *s.* persona que crea piezas musicales

**conceive** (kən-sēv) *v.* to think of
  **concebir** *v.* idear

**concession** (kən-sěsh'ən) *n.* the act of yielding or conceding
  **concesión** *s.* acción de ceder

**conspicuous** (kən-spĭk'yōō-əs) *adj.* easy to notice; obvious
  **conspicuo** *adj.* que salta a la vista; obvio

**conspiracy** (kən-spîr'ə-sē) *n.* an agreement to perform together an illegal or wrongful act
  **conspiración** *s.* alianza para preparar una acción ilegal o indebida

**contaminate** (kən-tăm'ə-nāt') *v.* to make impure or unclean through contact
  **contaminar** *v.* dañar o alterar la pureza

**contemplate** (kŏn'təm-plāt') *v.* to consider carefully and at length
  **contemplar** *v.* considerar cuidadosamente

**contractor** (kŏn'trăk'tər) *n.* one who agrees to provide services for a specific price
  **contratista** *s.* persona que se compromete a realizar un servicio por determinado precio

**contradiction** (kŏn'trə-dĭk'shən) *n.* a denial; an expression that is opposite to
  **contradicción** *s.* negación de algo que se da por cierto; afirmación de algo contrario a lo ya dicho

**contrive** (kən-trīv') *v.* to invent or fabricate, especially by improvisation
  **ingeniarse** *v.* inventar o idear, especialmente de modo improvisado

**conventional** (kən-věn'shə-nəl) *adj.* conforming to established practice or accepted standards; traditional
  **convencional** *adj.* conforme a la práctica establecida o a estándares aceptados; tradicional

**converge** (kən-vûrj') *v.* to come together in one place; meet
  **converger** *v.* unirse en un punto; encontrarse

**conviction** (kən-vĭk'shən) *n.* a strong belief
  **convicción** *s.* creencia fuerte

**cosmic** (kŏz'mik) *adj.* universal; infinitely large
  **cósmico** *adj.* universal; infinitamente grande

**counterpart** (koun'tər-pärt') *n.* one that has the same functions and traits as another
  **contraparte** *s.* el que tiene las mismas funciones y características que otro

**craftiness** (krăf'tē-něs) *n.* deviousness or deception
  **picardía** *s.* astucia o engaño

**credulity** (krĭ-dōō'lĭ-tē) *n.* a disposition to believe too readily
  **credulidad** *s.* tendencia a creerlo todo

**crevice** (krĕv′ĭs) *n.* crack
grieta *s.* abertura larga y estrecha

**crouch** (krouch) *v.* to stoop with bent knees
acuclillarse *v.* agacharse con las rodillas dobladas

**deceive** (dĭ-sēv′) *v.* to cause to believe what is not true; to mislead
engañar *v.* hacer creer lo que no es cierto; descaminar

**decline** (dĭ-klīn′) *v.* to politely refuse
declinar *v.* rehusar cortésmente

**defy** (dĭ-fī′) *v.* to boldly oppose or resist
desafiar *v.* oponerse o resistirse

**denounce** (dĭ-nouns′) *v.* to condemn; to criticize
denunciar *v.* condenar; criticar

**depravity** (dĭ-prăv′ĭ-tē) *n.* moral corruption
depravación *s.* corrupción moral

**deprivation** (dĕp′rə-vā′shən) *n.* the condition of not having one's needs met; a lack of
privación *s.* ausencia o escasez de lo necesario para vivir

**derision** (dĭ-rĭzh′ən) *n.* ridicule
escarnio *s.* ridículo

**descendant** (dĭ-sĕn′dənt) *n.* a person whose descent can be traced to an individual or group
descendiente *s.* persona que desciende por línea directa de un individuo o grupo

**devious** (dē′vē-əs) *adj.* departing from the straight or direct course
tortuoso *adj.* desviado; sinuoso

**diatribe** (dī′ə-trīb′) *n.* bitter, abusive criticism
diatriba *s.* crítica fuerte y grosera

**diminish** (dĭ-mĭn′ĭsh′) *v.* to become smaller or less
disminuir *v.* hacerse más pequeño; mermar

**dingy** (dĭn′jē) *adj.* dirty or discolored
deslucido *adj.* sucio o manchado

**disconcert** (dĭs′kən-sûrt′) *v.* to ruffle; to frustrate by throwing into disorder
desconcertar *v.* alterar; contrariar

**disgruntle** (dĭs-grŭn′tl) *v.* to make unhappy
contrariar *v.* enfadar

**disheveled** (dĭ-shĕv′əld) *adj.* messy; untidy
desarreglado *adj.* desordenado; desaliñado

**dispel** (dĭ-spĕl′) *v.* to drive away
disipar *v.* alejar

**dowdy** (dou′dē) *adj.* out of style; shabby
fuera de moda *adj.* sin estilo o gracia

**edict** (ē′dĭkt′) *n.* a command from those in power
edicto *s.* orden de una persona de autoridad

**eliminate** (ĭ-lĭm′ə-nāt′) *v.* to remove from consideration by defeating
eliminar *v.* quitar, separar o hacer desaparecer

**eloquence** (ĕl′ə-kwəns) *n.* an ability to speak powerfully and persuasively
elocuencia *s.* eficacia para persuadir o conmover con la palabra

**emigrate** (ĕm′ĭ-grāt′) *v.* to leave one country and settle in another
emigrar *v.* dejar el país propio y establecerse en otro

**engaging** (ĕn-gāj′ĭng) *adj.* charming; likeable
agradable *adj.* simpático; encantador

**engross** (ĕn-grōs′) *v.* to completely occupy
absorber *v.* ocupar por completo

**ensnare** (ĕn-snâr′) *v.* to take or catch in something
atrapar *v.* alcanzar; coger en una trampa

**essential** (ĭ-sĕn′shəl) *adj.* having the qualities that give something its true identity
esencial *adj.* que forma parte de la naturaleza de algo

**esteem** (ĭ-stēm′) *v.* to regard with respect
estimar *v.* apreciar

**evoke** (ĭ-vōk′) *v.* to call forth; to summon
evocar *v.* traer a la memoria

**exile** (ĕk′sīl′) *n.* enforced removal from one's native country
exilio *s.* abandono obligatorio de la patria

**exotic** (ĭg-zŏt′ĭk) *adj.* foreign; unusual; exciting
exótico *adj.* extranjero; inusual; emocionante

**exploit** (ĕk′sploit′) *v.* to use for selfish purposes
explotar *v.* usar con fines egoístas

**fate** (fāt) *n.* a power that is thought to determine the course of events
   **destino** *s.* fuerza que se cree que determina el curso de los acontecimientos

**feeble** (fē'bəl) *adj.* weak or faint
   **débil** *adj.* que tiene poca fuerza o poco vigor

**fiend** (fēnd) *n.* a demon; an evil spirit
   **demonio** *s.* espíritu maligno

**foreboding** (fôr-bō'dǐng) *n.* a sense of impending misfortune
   **presentimiento** *s.* sentimiento de desgracia inminente

**foreman** (fôr'mən) *n.* the leader of a work crew
   **capataz** *s.* jefe de una cuadrilla de trabajo

**foresight** (fôr'sīt) *n.* perception of the significance of events before they have occurred
   **previsión** *s.* percepción de la importancia de algo antes de que ocurra

**fortify** (fôr'tə-fī') *v.* to make strong
   **fortificar** *v.* fortalecer

**futility** (fyōō-tǐl'ǐ-tē) *n.* uselessness
   **futilidad** *s.* lo que no tiene ninguna importancia

**glimmer** (glǐm'ər) *n.* a faint sign
   **vislumbre** *s.* señal vaga

**gnarled** (närld) *adj.* roughened, as from age or work
   **nudoso** *adj.* rugoso por la edad o el trabajo

**grimace** (grǐm'ǐs) *n.* a facial expression of pain or disgust
   **mueca** *s.* expresión facial de dolor o de asco

**grope** (grōp) *v.* to reach about with uncertainty
   **tantear** *v.* andar a tientas

**hamper** (hăm'pər) *v.* to prevent the free movement of
   **dificultar** *v.* impedir el libre movimiento

**haughtily** (hô'tə-lē) *adv.* proudly; scornfully
   **altivamente** *adv.* orgullosamente; con altanería

**hypocritical** (hǐp'ə-krǐt'ǐ-kəl) *adj.* false or deceptive
   **hipócrita** *adj.* falso o engañoso

**immaculate** (ǐ-măk'yə-lǐt) *adj.* spotless; very clean
   **inmaculado** *adj.* sin mancha; muy limpio

**immortality** (ǐm'ôr-tăl'ǐ-tē) *n.* the condition of having an endless life
   **inmortalidad** *s.* vida eterna

**impair** (ǐm-pâr') *v.* to weaken; damage
   **perjudicar** *v.* debilitar; dañar

**impart** (ǐm-pärt') *v.* to make known; reveal
   **impartir** *v.* dar a conocer; revelar

**impartial** (ǐm-pär'shəl) *adj.* not partial or biased; unprejudiced
   **imparcial** *adj.* neutral; sin prejuicio

**imply** (ǐm-plī') *v.* to express indirectly
   **implicar** *v.* expresar indirectamente

**impregnable** (ǐm-prěg'nə-bəl) *adj.* impossible to enter by force
   **impenetrable** *adj.* imposible de penetrar a la fuerza

**impromptu** (ǐm-prŏmp'tōō) *adj.* unplanned
   **improvisado** *adj.* espontáneo

**impropriety** (ǐm'prə-prī'ǐ-tē) *n.* an unsuitable or inappropriate act or quality
   **incorrección** *s.* falta de decoro; falta

**improvised** (ǐm'prə-vīzd') *adj.* to put together with little preparation or planning   **improvise** *v.*
   **improvisado** *adj.* realizado sin plan previo   **improvisar** *v.*

**impudent** (ǐm'pyə-dənt) *adj.* bold and disrespectful
   **insolente** *adj.* descarado e irrespetuoso

**incarnation** (ǐn'-kär-nā'-shən) *n.* a bodily form
   **encarnación** *s.* adopción de forma física

**inclination** (ǐn-klə-nā'shən) *n.* a tendency to prefer one thing over another
   **inclinación** *s.* tendencia a preferir una de dos cosas

**indignantly** (ǐn-dǐg'nənt-lē) *adv.* angrily
   **con indignación** *adv.* furiosamente

**indiscriminately** (ǐn'dǐ-skrǐm'ə-nǐt-lē) *adv.* without making careful distinctions or choices
   **sin discriminación** *adv.* sin criterio o discernimiento

**ineptitude** (ǐn-ěp'tǐ-tōōd') *n.* clumsiness; lack of competence
   **ineptitud** *s.* torpeza; incompetencia

**inertia** (ĭ-nûr′shə) *n.* resistance to motion, action, or change
   **inercia** *s.* resistencia al movimiento, la acción o el cambio

**inevitable** (ĭn-ĕv′ĭ-tə-bəl) *n.* that which cannot be avoided or prevented
   **inevitable** *s.* lo que no se puede evitar o prevenir

**infectious** (ĭn-fĕk′shəs) *adj.* capable of being transmitted by infection
   **infeccioso** *adj.* que se puede contagiar

**inflict** (ĭn-flĭkt′) *v.* to deal out something unpleasant or burdensome; to impose
   **infligir** *v.* someter a malos tratos o sufrimiento; imponer

**informant** (ĭn-fôr′mənt) *n.* one who gives information
   **informante** *s.* el que da información

**insolent** (ĭn′sə-lənt) *adj.* insulting; arrogant
   **insolente** *adj.* insultante; arrogante

**instill** (ĭn-stĭl′) *v.* to supply gradually
   **inculcar** *v.* infundir gradualmente

**interfere** (ĭn′tər-fîr′) *v.* to create an obstacle
   **interferir** *v.* crear un obstáculo

**intermittently** (ĭn′tər-mĭt′nt-lē) *adv.* stopping and starting at intervals
   **intermitentemente** *adv.* que se interrumpe y prosigue a intervalos

**interrogation** (ĭn-tĕr′ə-gā′shən) *n.* an official or formal questioning
   **interrogatorio** *s.* formulación oficial de preguntas

**intimate** (ĭn′tə-mĭt) *adj.* relating to one's deepest nature
   **íntimo** *adj.* relacionado con lo más profundo de una persona

**intricate** (ĭn′trĭ-kĭt) *adj.* elaborate
   **intrincado** *adj.* elaborado

**irate** (ī-rāt′) *adj.* very angry
   **airado** *adj.* furioso

**irretrievably** (ĭr′ĭ-trē′və-blē) *adv.* permanently; in a manner that cannot be reversed
   **irremediablemente** *adv.* permanentemente; de modo que no se puede cambiar

**junction** (jŭnk′shən) *n.* a place where two roads meet
   **cruce** *s.* punto de encuentro de dos caminos

**keener** (kēn′ər) *adj.* acutely sensitive
   **agudo** *adj.* muy sensible

**labyrinth** (lăb′ə-rĭnth′) *n.* a maze; an intricate structure of interconnected passages
   **laberinto** *s.* estructura formada por caminos cruzados entre sí

**languish** (lăng′gwĭsh) *v.* to lose strength and vitality
   **languidecer** *v.* perder fuerza y vitalidad

**lark** (lärk) *n.* a carefree or spirited adventure
   **travesura** *s.* aventura juguetona

**lavishly** (lăv′ĭsh-lē) *adv.* extravagantly
   **magníficamente** *adv.* con entravagancia

**legitimate** (lə-jĭt′ə-mĭt) *adj.* genuine; authentic
   **legítimo** *adj.* genuino; auténtico

**legitimately** (lə-jĭt′ə-mĭt-lē) *adv.* lawfully
   **legítimamente** *adv.* legalmente

**levitation** (lĕv′ĭ-tā′shŭn) *n.* the act of rising into the air and floating
   **levitación** *s.* elevación y suspensión en el aire

**liable** (lī′ə-bəl) *adj.* likely to
   **propenso** *adj.* que tiene inclinación a algo

**linger** (lĭng′gər) *v.* to remain or stay longer
   **quedarse** *v.* permanecer o entretenerse un rato

**listless** (lĭst′lĭs) *adj.* lacking energy
   **lánguido** *adj.* sin energía

**livelihood** (līv′lē-hŏŏd′) *n.* a means of support; a way of making a living
   **sustento** *s.* medio de ganarse la vida

**malodorous** (măl-ō′dər-əs) *adj.* having a bad odor
   **maloliente** *adj.* que huele mal

**maroon** (mə-rōōn′) *v.* to leave behind in a place from which there is little hope of escape
   **abandonar** *v.* dejar a una persona en un lugar de donde no puede salir

**meddle** (mĕd′l) *v.* to intrude or interfere
   **entrometerse** *v.* inmiscuirse o interferir

**melancholy** (mĕl′ən-kŏl′ē) *adj.* sad; depressed
   **melancólico** *adj.* triste; deprimido

**menace** (mĕn'ĭs) *n.* a possible danger; threat
  amenaza *s.* posible peligro

**merit** (mĕr'ĭt) *v.* to deserve
  merecer *v.* ser digno de

**mesmerize** (mĕz'mə-rīz') *v.* to spellbind; to enthrall
  cautivar *v.* fascinar; embelesar

**migration** (mī-grā'shən) *n.* the act of changing location seasonally
  migración *s.* cambio de lugar por temporada

**minuscule** (mĭn'ə-skyōōl') *adj.* very small; tiny
  minúsculo *adj.* muy pequeño

**mobility** (mō-bĭl'ĭ-tē) *n.* the capability of moving from place to place
  movilidad *s.* capacidad de moverse de un lugar a otro

**monotony** (mə-nŏt'n-ē) *n.* tedious sameness
  monotonía *s.* uniformidad o igualdad tediosa

**muted** (myōō'tĭd) *adj.* muffled; softened
  apagado *adj.* amortiguado; suave

**neglectful** (nĭ-glĕkt'fəl) *adj.* characterized by a failure to properly care for someone or something
  negligente *adj.* que no pone cuidado, atención o interés en lo que debe

**nondescript** (nŏn'dĭ-skrĭpt') *adj.* lacking unique qualities
  soso *adj.* sin ninguna característica distintiva

**novelty** (nŏv'əl-tē) *n.* the quality of being new
  novedad *s.* lo que es nuevo o reciente

**offense** (ə-fĕns') *n.* a violation of a moral or social code; a sin
  ofensa *s.* violación de un código moral o social; pecado

**ominous** (ŏm'ə-nəs) *adj.* threatening
  ominoso *adj.* amenazador

**opaque** (ō-pāk') *adj.* hidden; difficult or impossible to understand
  impenetrable *adj.* difícil o imposible de entender

**opportunist** (ŏp'ər-tōō'nĭst) *n.* a person who takes advantage of any opportunity, without moral regard, to achieve a goal
  oportunista *s.* persona que aprovecha toda oportunidad para alcanzar una meta, sin consideraciones morales

**opposition** (ŏp'ə-zĭsh'ən) *n.* the act of opposing or resisting
  oposición *s.* acción de oponer u oponerse

**oratory** (ôr'ə-tôr'ē) *n.* the art of making speeches
  oratoria *s.* arte de dar discursos

**pandemonium** (păn'də-mō'nē-əm) *n.* wild uproar or noise
  pandemónium *s.* gran ruido y confusión

**patronize** (pā'trə-nīz') *v.* to go to as a customer
  frecuentar *v.* ser cliente de

**peril** (pĕr'əl) *n.* danger
  peligro *s.* riesgo

**perpetual** (pər-pĕch'ōō-əl) *adj.* continuing without interruption
  perpetuo *adj.* sin interrupción

**perseverance** (pûr'sə-vîr'əns) *n.* steady persistence in sticking to a course of action
  perseverancia *s.* firmeza y constancia en un curso de acción

**pervasive** (pər-vā'sĭv) *adj.* present throughout
  omnipresente *adj.* que está en todas partes

**philosophy** (fĭ-lŏs'ə-fē) *n.* a system of values or beliefs
  filosofía *s.* sistema de valores o creencias

**pinnacle** (pĭn'ə-kəl) *n.* a peak; a pointed top
  pináculo *s.* cumbre; cima

**ponder** (pŏn'dər) *v.* to think or consider carefully
  considerar *v.* pensar o reflexionar con atención

**potential** (pə-tĕn'shəl) *n.* the ability to grow or develop
  potenial *s.* capacidad de crecimiento o desarrollo

**predicament** (prĭ-dĭk'ə-mənt) *n.* an unpleasant situation from which it is difficult to free oneself
  aprieto *s.* situación incómoda de la que es difícil zafarse

**primitive** (prĭm'ĭ-tĭv) *adj.* of or relating to a nonindustrial, often tribal, culture
  primitivo *adj.* relacionado con una cultura no industrial o tribal

**prodigy** (prŏd'ə-jē) *n.* a person with an exceptional talent
  prodigio *s.* persona con un talento excepcional

**progressiveness** (prə-grĕs′ĭv-nĭs) *n.* the state of advancing toward better conditions or new policies, ideas, or methods
　　**progresismo** *s.* avance hacia mejores condiciones, o nuevas medidas, ideas o métodos

**propaganda** (prŏp′ə-găn′də) *n.* information that supports a certain cause
　　**propaganda** *s.* información que apoya una causa

**proportional** (prə-pôr′shə-nəl) *adj.* having a constant relation in degree or number
　　**proporcional** *adj.* que tiene una relación constante de grado o cantidad

**proposition** (prŏp′ə-zĭsh′ən) *n.* a suggested plan
　　**propuesta** *s.* plan sugerido

**propriety** (prə-prī′ĭ-tē) *n.* the quality of being proper; appropriateness
　　**corrección** *s.* decoro; conveniencia

**provisions** (prə-vĭzh′ənz) *n.* necessary supplies; food
　　**provisiones** *s.* suministros necesarios; alimentos

**provoke** (prə-vōk′) *v.* to cause; to bring up
　　**provocar** *v.* causar; suscitar

**pungent** (pŭn′jənt) *adj.* sharp or intense
　　**acre** *adj.* agudo o intenso

**puritanical** (pyŏŏr-ĭ-tăn′ĭ-kəl) *adj.* strictly observant of religious practices; sternly moral
　　**puritano** *adj.* que cumple con rigor las prácticas religiosas; severamente moral

**pursuit** (pər-sōōt′) *n.* the act of chasing
　　**persecución** *v.* seguimiento

**ramble** (răm′bəl) *v.* to talk at length and aimlessly
　　**divagar** *v.* hablar sin parar y sin ton ni son

**ransom** (răn′səm) *n.* payment demanded for the release of a person or property
　　**rescate** *s.* dinero que se pide o se paga por la liberación de una persona o propiedad

**rationalize** (răsh′ə-nə-līz′) *v.* to make explanations for one's behavior
　　**justificar** *v.* dar explicaciones racionales de la conducta propia

**ravage** (răv′ĭj) *n.* serious damage or destruction
　　**devastación** *s.* daño o destrucción grave

**recuperation** (rĭ-kōō′pə-rā′shən) *n.* a return to health or strength; recovery
　　**recuperación** *s.* regreso a la salud; mejoría

**refrain** (rĭ-frān′) *v.* to hold oneself back; to stop
　　**refrenar** *v.* contener, dominar o hacer menos violento; parar

**refuge** (rĕf′yōōj) *n.* a source of comfort in times of trouble
　　**refugio** *v.* fuente de consuelo en momentos de dificultad

**refute** (rĭ-fyōōt′) *v.* to prove as false
　　**refutar** *v.* demostrar que es falso

**rehabilitation** (rē′hə-bĭl′ĭ-tā′shən) *n.* the process of restoring someone to physical capability, usually through exercise and physical therapy
　　**rehabilitación** *s.* proceso de restaurar capacidades físicas con ejercicio y fisioterapia

**relay** (rē′lā) *n.* a race in which several team members take turns running to complete the race
　　**carrera de relevos** *s.* carrera en que los corredores de cada equipo se van relevando

**remorse** (rĭ-môrs′) *n.* sorrow; regret
　　**remordimiento** *s.* pesar; arrepentimiento

**remote** (rĭ-mōt′) *adj.* located far away
　　**remoto** *adj.* lejano

**rendition** (rĕn-dĭsh′ən) *n.* a pictorial representation; an interpretation
　　**interpretación** *s.* representación pictórica

**replete** (rĭ-plēt′) *adj.* abundantly supplied
　　**repleto** *adj.* lleno; atiborrado

**reserve** (rĭ-zûrv′) *n.* self-restraint in the way one looks or acts
　　**reserva** *s.* discreción o comedimiento en la forma de presentarse y de actuar

**resignation** (rĕz′ĭg-nā′shən) *n.* acceptance of something that is inescapable
　　**resignación** *s.* conformidad para aceptar lo que no tiene remedio

**resolute** (rĕz′ə-lōōt′) *adj.* firm or determined
　　**resuelto** *adj.* firme o decidido

**restrain** (rĭ-strān′) *v.* to hold back; to control
   **refrenar** *v.* contener; controlar

**retort** (rĭ-tôrt′) *n.* a quick, sharp, witty reply
   **réplica** *s.* respuesta rápida e ingeniosa

**rigid** (rĭj′ĭd) *adj.* inflexible; strict
   **rígido** *adj.* inflexible; estricto

**sacred** (sā′krĭd) *adj.* holy; worthy of religious veneration or respect
   **sagrado** *adj.* santo; digno de veneración o respeto religioso

**sanctuary** (săngk′chōō-ĕr′ē) *n.* a place of refuge
   **santuario** *s.* lugar de refugio

**savage** (săv′ĭj) *n.* a person regarded as primitive or uncivilized
   **salvaje** *s.* persona a quien se considera primitiva o incivilizada

**scale** (skāl) *v.* to climb up or over; ascend
   **escalar** *v.* subir; ascender

**searing** (sîr′ĭng) *adj.* hot enough to burn, char, or scorch
   **abrasador** *adj.* que quema o chamusca

**sect** (sĕkt) *n.* a religious group
   **secta** *s.* grupo religioso

**secure** (sĭ-kyŏŏr′) *adj.* safe; protected; free from fear or anxiety
   **seguro** *adj.* a salvo; protegido; libre de temores

**sensation** (sĕn-sā′shən) *n.* a state of great interest and excitement
   **sensación** *s.* estado de gran interés y emoción; furor

**sensational** (sĕn-sā′shə-nəl) *adj.* intended to arouse strong curiosity or interest, especially through exaggerated details
   **sensacional** *adj.* que llama fuertemente la atención, la curiosidad o el interés, especialmente con detalles exagerados

**serendipitous** (sĕr′ən-dĭp′ĭ-təs) *adj.* found by fortunate accident
   **fortuito** *adj.* hallado por buena suerte

**sheepishly** (shē′pĭsh-lē) *adv.* meekly; with embarrassment
   **tímidamente** *adv.* mansamente; con vergüenza

**sidekick** (sīd′kĭk′) *n.* a close friend
   **compañero** *s.* buen amigo

**sinister** (sĭn′ĭ-stər) *adj.* suggesting or threatening evil
   **siniestro** *adj.* malo o con mala intención

**solemn** (sŏl′əm) *adj.* deeply serious
   **solemne** *adj.* profundamente serio

**specialization** (spĕsh′ə-lĭ-za′shən) *n.* a focus on a particular area of study
   **especialización** *s.* preparación en determinada área de estudio

**stealthily** (stĕl′thə-lē) *adv.* cautiously; secretly
   **furtivamente** *adv.* secretamente; a hurtadillas

**sterile** (stĕr′əl) *adj.* barren; lacking vitality
   **estéril** *adj.* árido; sin vitalidad

**stifled** (stī′fəld) *adj.* smothered  **stifle** *v.*
   **sofocado** *adj.* ahogado  **sofocar** *v.*

**stipulation** (stĭp′yə-lā′shən) *n.* the act of laying down a condition or agreement
   **estipulación** *s.* acción de definir condiciones o acuerdos

**stoop** (stōōp) *v.* to bend forward and down from the waist or the middle of the back
   **encorvarse** *v.* doblarse por la cintura o la espalda hacia delante

**straddle** (străd′l) *v.* to be on both sides of
   **estar entre dos aguas** *v.* estar por ambas partes

**straggle** (străg′əl) *v.* to spread out in a scattered group
   **dispersar** *v.* separarse en un grupo extendido en distintas direcciones

**strew** (strōō) *v.* to spread here and there; scatter
   **esparcir** *v.* derramar; dispersar

**suavity** (swä′vĭ-tē) *n.* graceful politeness
   **urbanidad** *s.* cortesía y afabilidad

**subordinate** (sə-bôr′dn-ĭt) *adj.* secondary; belonging to a lower rank
   **subordinado** *adj.* secundario; de un rango inferior

**subtle** (sŭt′l) *adj.* slight; difficult to detect
   **sutil** *adj.* leve; imperceptible

**sullen** (sŭl'ən) *adj.* showing silent resentment; sulky
**hosco** *adj.* resentido; huraño

**summon** (sŭm'ən) *v.* to send for; call
**llamar** *v.* mandar a traer

**surrender** (sə-rĕn'dər) *v.* to give up possession or control to another
**rendir** *v.* entregar posesiones o control

**tactic** (tăk'tĭk) *n.* a maneuver to achieve a goal
**táctica** *s.* maniobra para alcanzar una meta

**tangible** (tăn'jə-bəl) *adj.* able to be seen, touched, or understood
**tangible** *adj.* que se puede ver, tocar o entender

**tentatively** (tĕn'tə-tĭv-lē) *adv.* uncertainly or hesitantly
**tentativamente** *adv.* provisionalmente; con vacilación

**tolerable** (tŏl'ər-ə-bəl) *adj.* fairly good; passable
**tolerable** *adj.* regular; pasable

**traipse** (trāps) *v.* to walk or tramp around
**recorrer** *v.* andar de un lado para otro

**transcendent** (trăn-sĕn'dənt) *adj.* being above the material world
**trascendente** *adj.* por encima del mundo material

**treacherous** (trĕch'ər-əs) *adj.* not to be relied on; untrustworthy
**traicionero** *adj.* traidor; desleal

**tremor** (trĕm'ər) *n.* nervous trembling
**temblor** *s.* estremecimiento nervioso

**turmoil** (tûr'moil') *n.* a state of extreme confusion or agitation
**agitación** *s.* estado de extrema confusión o caos

**unabashed** (ŭn'ə-băsht') *adj.* obvious; bold
**descarado** *adj.* desenfadado; sin inmutarse

**undaunted** (ŭn-dôn'tĭd) *adj.* not discouraged; courageous
**intrépido** *adj.* impertérrito; sin desanimarse

**unravel** (ŭn-răv'əl) *v.* to undo; come apart
**deshilachar** *v.* deshacer; desenredar

**unseemly** (ŭn-sēm'lē) *adj.* inappropriate
**indecoroso** *adj.* impropio

**valiant** (văl'yənt) *adj.* brave
**valiente** *adj.* valeroso

**vehemently** (vē'ə-mənt-lē) *adv.* with intense emotion
**vehementemente** *adv.* con intensa emoción

**vermin** (vûr'mĭn) *n.*, *pl.* destructive and annoying insects and small animals, such as cockroaches and rats
**alimañas** *s.* insectos y animalitos destructivos e indeseables, como cucarachas y ratas

**vex** (vĕks) *v.* to disturb; to annoy
**irritar** *v.* molestar; sacar de quicio

**vigilant** (vĭj'ə-lənt) *adj.* watchful; alert
**vigilante** *adj.* atento; alerta

**vigilantly** (vĭj'ə-lənt-lē) *adv.* watchfully
**vigilantemente** *adv.* con atención

**vigorously** (vĭg'ər-əs-lē) *adv.* energetically
**vigorosamente** *adv.* enérgicamente

**vileness** (vīl'nəs) *n.* unpleasantness; disgusting quality
**vileza** *s.* inmundicia; asquerosidad

**virtuoso** (vûr'chōō-ō'sō) *n.* a musician with excellent abilities, techniques, and/or an attractive personal style
**virtuoso** *s.* músico de excelentes aptitudes, técnicas y/o estilo personal atractivo

**volatile** (vŏl'ə-tl) *adj.* difficult to define or pin down; unpredictable
**volátil** *adj.* inconstante o mudable; imprevisible

**waver** (wā'vər) *v.* to exhibit indecision; to hesitate
**flaquear** *v.* mostrar indecisión; vacilar

**wince** (wĭns) *v.* to flinch or shrink in pain or distress
**estremecerse** *v.* encogerse o contraerse por dolor o malestar

**yield** (yēld) *v.* to give in to another
**ceder** *v.* rendir

# Pronunciation Key

| Symbol | Examples | Symbol | Examples | Symbol | Examples |
|--------|----------|--------|----------|--------|----------|
| ă | **at**, g**as** | m | **m**an, see**m** | v | **v**an, sa**ve** |
| ā | **a**pe, d**ay** | n | **n**ight, mitt**en** | w | **w**eb, t**w**ice |
| ä | f**a**ther, b**ar**n | ng | si**ng**, ha**ng**er | y | **y**ard, law**y**er |
| âr | **f**air, **d**are | ŏ | **o**dd, n**o**t | z | **z**oo, rea**s**on |
| b | **b**ell, ta**b**le | ō | **o**pen, r**oa**d, gr**ow** | zh | trea**s**ure, gara**ge** |
| ch | **ch**in, lun**ch** | ô | **aw**ful, b**ough**t, h**o**rse | ə | **a**wake, ev**e**n, penc**i**l, |
| d | **d**ig, bor**ed** | oi | c**oi**n, b**oy** | | pil**o**t, foc**u**s |
| ĕ | **e**gg, t**e**n | ŏŏ | l**oo**k, f**u**ll | ər | p**er**form, lett**er** |
| ē | **e**vil, s**ee**, m**ea**l | ōō | r**oo**t, gl**ue**, thr**ough** | | |
| f | **f**all, lau**gh**, **ph**rase | ou | **ou**t, c**ow** | | |
| g | **g**old, bi**g** | p | **p**ig, ca**p** | **Sounds in Foreign Words** | |
| h | **h**it, in**h**ale | r | **r**ose, sta**r** | KH | *German* i**ch**, au**ch**; |
| hw | **wh**ite, every**wh**ere | s | **s**it, fa**c**e | | *Scottish* lo**ch** |
| ĭ | **i**nch, f**i**t | sh | **sh**e, ma**sh** | N | *French* e**n**tre, bo**n**, fi**n** |
| ī | **i**dle, m**y**, tr**ie**d | t | **t**ap, hopp**ed** | œ | *French* f**eu**, c**œu**r; |
| îr | **d**ear, **h**ere | th | **th**ing, wi**th** | | *German* sch**ö**n |
| j | **j**ar, **g**em, ba**dge** | *th* | **th**en, o**th**er | ü | *French* **u**tile, r**ue**; |
| k | **k**eep, **c**at, lu**ck** | ŭ | **u**p, n**u**t | | *German* gr**ü**n |
| l | **l**oad, ratt**le** | ûr | **f**ur, **ear**n, **b**ird, **w**orm | | |

**Stress Marks**

′    This mark indicates that the preceding syllable receives the primary stress. For example, in the word *language,* the first syllable is stressed: lăng′gwĭj.

′    This mark is used only in words in which more than one syllable is stressed. It indicates that the preceding syllable is stressed, but somewhat more weakly than the syllable receiving the primary stress. In the word *literature,* for example, the first syllable receives the primary stress, and the last syllable receives a weaker stress: lĭt′ər-ə-chŏŏr′.

Adapted from *The American Heritage Dictionary of the English Language,* fourth edition. Copyright © 2000 by Houghton Mifflin Company. Used with the permission of Houghton Mifflin Company.

# INDEX OF FINE ART

# Index of Skills

## A

Academic vocabulary, 33, 44, 47, 60, 63, 74, 77, 85, 87, 111, 117, 119, 130, 169, 189, 220, 223, 236, 239, 252, 259, 272, 275, 281, 317, 325, 333, 356, 359, 372, 381, 394, 396, 414, 455, 461, 463, 474, 485, 589, 595, 625, 631, 673, 680, 683, 693, 705, 713, 717, 726, 767, 780, 783, 798, 817, 828, 831, 845, 885, 892, 895, 903, 909, 917, 919, 926, 929, 937, 969, 979, 985, 992, 995, 1001, 1003, 1009. *See also* Specialized vocabulary.
Act (in a play), 7, 488, 522, R103
Active listening, R84–R85
Active reading, 12–15
Active voice, of verbs, 483, 566, 1022, R57
Ad campaigns, 980–983
    creating, 983
    strategies for viewing, 982
Adjective clauses, R62
    essential, R62
    nonessential, R62
Adjective phrases, R60
Adjectives, R47, R57–R59
    versus adverbs, R58
    comparative forms, 221, R58
    predicate, R57, R60
    proper, R51
    punctuation between, 603, R49
    superlative forms, 221, R58
Adverb clauses, R62–R63
Adverb phrases, R60
Adverbs, R48, R58–R59. *See also* Modifiers.
    versus adjectives, R58
    comparative forms, 221, R58
    superlative forms, 221, R58
Advertising, 980–983, R92–R93
    billboards, R92
    celebrities in, R93
    demographics, R87
    flyer, R92
    infomercial, R92
    marketing, R92
    political ads, R92
    print ads, 981, R92
    product comparison, R93
    product placement, R92
    promotional web sites, 981
    public service announcement, R92
    sponsors, R92

target audience, 981–982, R87
teaser trailers, 981
trailers, 981, R92
Affixes. *See* Prefixes; Suffixes.
Agreement
    pronoun-antecedent, 99, 152, R52–R53
    subject-verb, 373, 432, R65
Alliteration, 578, 579, 581, 602, 613, R102. *See also* Sound devices.
Almanacs, 1040, 1042. *See also* References.
Analogies, 252, 780, R71, R102, R113. *See also* Rhetorical devices.
Analysis, writing, 61, 109, 271, 358, 395, 453, 647, 727, 1015, R39–R40
    options for organization, R39–R40
    rubric for, R39
Anecdote, 58, R102
    identifying, 271
    in student writing, R30, R41
Antecedent-pronoun agreement, 99, 152, R52–R53
Antonyms, 1009, R72
Apostrophes, 75, 152, R50
Appeals, R21. *See also* Arguments; Persuasive techniques.
    by association, 964, R21
    to authority, R110
    bandwagon, 964, R21, R91
    emotional, 964, 985, 1022, R21, R93, R114
    ethical, 964, 985, R21, R114
    logical, R21, R91, R115
    to loyalty, R21
    to pity, fear, or vanity, 964, R21
    snob appeal, R21
Appositives and appositive phrases, 681, 750, R61
Arguments, 962–963, 969–977, 1024, 1025, R20, R113. *See also* Appeals; Persuasive techniques; Persuasive writing.
    claims, 962–963, 969–977, R20, R113
    counterarguments, 962, 969–977, 1020, 1024, R20, R26, R40, R114
    deductive, R23, R114
    elements of, 962–963, 969–977, R20
    evidence, 331, 553, 635, 962–963, 966, 969–977, 1000, R20, R22, R25–R26, R41, R78, R81, R83, R114
    faulty, R24, R115. *See also* Fallacies.
    inductive, R22, R115
    opposing. *See* counterarguments, *above*.

reasons, 962–963, 969, R20
strategies for determining strong, R26
strategies for reading, R20
support, 962, 969, 973, R20, R117
writing, R40–R41
Art. *See* Visuals.
Articles (written). *See* Feature articles; Magazine articles; News articles; Newspapers, articles in.
Articulation. *See* Speaking strategies.
Artistic effects. *See* Media presentations.
Assessment practice, 152–157, 300–305, 432–437, 566–571, 750–755, 868–873, 952–957, 1024–1029, R95–R101
    reading comprehension, 152–155, 300–303, 432–435, 566–569, 750–753, 868–871, 952–955, 1024–1027, R96–R97
    vocabulary, 156, 304, 436, 754, 872, 956, 1028, R98
    writing and grammar, 157, 305, 437, 571, 755, 873, 957, 1029, R99
    written response, 155, 303, 435, 569, 753, 871, 955, 1027, R100–R101
Assonance, 578, 613, R102
Atlases, 1040, 1042. *See also* References.
Attitudes, evaluating, 797
Audience
    media, 107, 255, 981–982, R87
    speaking and listening, R86
    target, 981–982, R87
Authority. *See* Arguments; Sources.
Author's background, 33, 169, 189, 223, 239, 259, 275, 283, 317, 333, 359, 381, 397, 417, 449, 455, 463, 477, 485, 583, 589, 597, 605, 613, 619, 625, 637, 673, 683, 698, 705, 717, 729, 735, 767, 783, 801, 810, 817, 831, 855, 868, 885, 895, 909, 919, 929, 938, 969, 985, 995, 1003, 1011
    influence of, 33, 705, 760–765, 767–779, 868
Author's intent. *See* Author's purpose.
Author's message, 442, 444, 455, R113. *See also* Main ideas; Theme.
Author's perspective, R102
    analysis of, 116, 817–827, 868
Author's point of view. *See* Author's perspective.
Author's position, R113. *See also* Claims.

Author's purpose, 929–936, 995–1000, 1024, R102
  analysis of, 740, 936, 1000
Author's style. *See* Style.
Author's viewpoint. *See* Author's perspective.
Autobiography, 8, 830, 868, R102.
    *See also* Memoirs.
  analysis of, 831–844

## B

Ballads, 636, R102
  analysis of, 291, 637–646
Bandwagon appeal, 964, R21, R85, R93
Bar graphs, R5
Base words, 394, 892, 952, R69, R73. *See also* Words parts; Word roots.
Bias, R113
  identifying, in sources, 1038, 1042, R25, R85
  in reporting, R92
Bibliography, 1043, R113. *See also* Works cited.
  MLA citation guidelines, 1066
Biography, 8–9, 258, 274, R103
  analysis of, 275–280
Boldface type, as text feature, R3, R15
Book excerpts, 632–635, 859, 938
Books, as a resource, 1040
  parts of, 1043
Brainstorming, 358, 416, 612, 827, 907
Bulleted list, as text feature, 878, 885, R3
Business correspondence, R43–R45, R113.
    *See also* Workplace and technical writing.
  formats for, R43–R45
  key techniques, R42–R43

## C

Camera shots in film and video, R89.
    *See also* Media elements and techniques.
  close-up, 107, 255, 257, R89
  establishing, R89
  high-angle, R89
  long, 255, 257, R89
  low-angle, R89
  medium, 107, R89
  point-of-view, R89
  reaction, 255, 256, 257, R89
Capitalization, R51
  of countries, 543, 566, R51
  of ethnicities, 543, 566, R51
  of languages, 543, 566, R51
  of names of organizations, 543, 979, 1024, R51
  of nationalities, 543, R51
  of proper nouns, 543, 979, R51

of religions, 543, R51
of titles of works, 893, 952, R51
Captions, R3, R14
Career-related writing. *See* Business correspondence; Workplace and technical writing.
Case, pronoun, 131, R52–R53
  nominative, R52–R53
  objective, 131, R52–R53
  possessive, R52–R53
Catalogs, online, 1041
Cause-and-effect essay, 860–866
  analysis of, 861–862
  key traits, 860
  options for organization, 864
  rubric for, 866
Cause-and-effect organization, R10–R11, R38, R112. *See also* Patterns of organization.
  signal words for, R10, R32, R68
Cause-and-effect relationships, reading, 111–116, 152, 868, 1000, R10–R11
  in nonfiction, 831–844, 995–1000
Cause-effect diagrams, 111, R10, R38
CD-ROMs, of reference works, 1040
Character sketch, writing, 273, 681
Characterization, R103
  analysis of, 259–271, 280, 300, 679, 809
  in drama, 521, 1014
  in poetry, 283–291
Characters, 5, R103. *See also* Character types; Characterization.
  analysis of, 43, 116, 129, 179, 300, 310–311, 521, 542, 1014
  comparing and contrasting, 43, 235, 251, 256, 291, 355, 452, 473
  in drama, 485, 521, 542, 1014
  in film, 107–109
  motivation of, 73, 166, 167
  in narrative poetry, 133
  settings and, 310–311
Chain of events, R38. *See also* Cause-and-effect organization.
Character traits, 164–165, R103
  analysis of, 116, 167, 189–215, 216–219
Character types
  dynamic, R103
  main, 239–247, 248–251, R103
  minor, R103
  static, R103
Charts. *See* Graphic aids; Graphic organizers.
Choice of words. *See* Word choice.
Chronological order, 119–129, 148, 327, 938, R9, R36, R113. *See also* Patterns of organization.
  signal words for, 119, R9

Circle graphs, R5
Circular reasoning, 950, R24. *See also* Fallacies; Reasoning.
Citation of sources. *See* MLA citation guidelines; Works cited.
Claims, in argument, 962, 969, R20, R113
Clarifying, 43, 59, 73, 84, 98, 108, 116, 129, 143, 179, 187, 219, 235, 256, 271, 280, 291, 324, 355, 371, 393, 413, 452, 460, 473, 521, 542, 556, 635, 646, 679, 697, 712, 725, 733, 740, 809, 844, 849, 852, 891, 906, 916, 936, 977, 991, 1000, 1014, R113. *See also* Monitoring.
  as reading strategy, 597–602
Clauses, R62–R63
  adjective, R62
  adverb, R62–R63
  dependent (subordinate), 273, 727, 750, R62
  essential, R61
  as fragments, 273, R64
  independent (main), 273, 714, 727, 750, R62
  nonessential, R61
  noun, R63
  punctuation of, R49
Cliché, 298, R113
Climax, 26, 33, R103. *See also* Plot.
  conflict at, 26
Cluster diagram, 147, 295, 1034
Coherence in compositions and paragraphs, R31
Collage, creating, 758
Colons, 799, 868, R50
Combining sentences, 237, 681
Comic strip, 290
Commas, R49
  in addresses, R49
  adjectives and, 603, R49
  in compound sentences, 61, R49
  with coordinating conjunction, 61, R49
  in dates, R49
  after introductory words or phrases, 866, 927, 952, R49
  in letters, R49
  with parenthetical expression, R49
  with quotation marks, 150
  in run-on sentences, 61, R65
  versus semicolon, 61
  in series, 603, 656, 829, R49
Comma splices, R65
Commercials. *See* Advertising.
Commonly confused words, R77
Comparative form of modifiers, 221, 300, R58

520, 545, 632, 694, 715, 846, 859, 883, 884, 894, 918, 928, 934, 952, 966, 968, 974, 984, 988, 1024, 1025, R115. *See also* Consumer documents; Nonfiction; Public documents; Reading for information; Workplace documents.
   strategies for reading, 8–9, 878–883, R3–R19
Informative articles, 141, 184, 883, 934, 952, 968. *See also* Magazine articles; News articles.
Informative writing. *See* Expository writing.
Inquiry and research, 43, 84, 179, 452, 779, 977, 1000
Instruction manuals, R16
Interjections, R47
Internal conflict, 24
   analysis of, 63–73
Internet, 1037–1039, 1050, R3–R19, R115. *See also* Electronic media; References; Web sites.
Interviews, 547, 909–916, R83, R107
   analysis of, 553, R83
   conducting, 299, R83
   following up on, R83
   mock, 712
   preparing for, 299, R83
   as a research source, 1049
Introductions, R30–R31
   thought-provoking, 429
Irony, analysis of, 717–725, 750, 1008, R107
Issues
   debating, R79
   evading, as logical fallacy, R24
Italic type. *See also* Formatting.
   for titles, 647, R50

## J

Job advertisement, 893
Journal articles, 326–331
Journal entries, 72, 799
Journalism, R90–R92
Journals (published), 327, R115. *See also* References.
Judgments, making, 73, 271, 280, 413, 679, 712, 725, 797, 916, 991

## K

Key, on map, R7
Key traits of effective writing, 18, 144, 292, 424, 558, 648, 742, 860, 994, 1016, 1052
Keyword search, 1037–1038

## L

Language. *See also* Word choice.
   descriptive, R34–R35
   figurative. *See* Figurative language.
   humorous, R106
   informal, R68, R78
   loaded, 964, R25, R115
   persuasive. See Persuasive techniques.
   precise, R29
   slang, R68
Latin word parts. *See also* Word roots.
   affixes, 60, 236, R69
   word roots, 117, 152, 372, 631, 656, 713, 750, 937, 992, 1024, R69
Layout. *See* Formatting.
Legend (on map), R7
Letters
   business, R43, R113
   to the editor, 829, 979
   published, 270, 1006
   writing, 357, 395, 781, 927
Library
   catalog in, 1041
   classification systems for books in, 1051
   research in, 1040–1041
Library of Congress classification system, 1051
Line graphs, R5
Lines, in poetry, 6, 482, R2, R107
   analysis of, 460, 587, 594
Listening skills, R84–R86. *See also* Speaking.
Lists, as graphic organizers, 22, 46, 76, 84, 132, 168, 308, 454, 462, 574, 588, 618, 734, 766, 854, 858, 876, 968, 984
Literary analysis, 33, 43, 47, 59, 63, 73, 77, 84, 87, 98, 111, 116, 119, 129, 133, 139, 169, 179, 189, 219, 223, 235, 239, 251, 259, 271, 275, 280, 283, 291, 317, 324, 333, 355, 359, 371, 381, 417, 423, 449, 452, 455, 460, 463, 473, 477, 482, 485, 521, 542, 583, 587, 589, 594, 597, 602, 605, 610, 613, 617, 619, 623, 630, 637, 646, 673, 679, 683, 692, 705, 712, 717, 725, 729, 733, 735, 740, 767, 779, 783, 797, 801, 809, 817, 827, 831, 844, 855, 858, 1011, 1014
Literary analysis, writing, 742–748
   key traits, 742
   options for organization, 746
   rubric for, 748
Literary criticism, 59, 235, 355, 587, 646, 692, 844, 1014
   author's background, 797

Literary elements and devices. *See also* Characters; Conflict; Plot; Poetic elements and devices; Point of view; Settings; Theme.
   alliteration, 613, R102
   assonance, 613
   author's background, influence of, 33, 705, 760–765, 767–779
   author's perspective, 116, 817–827, R102
   characterization, 259–271, 280, 300, 679, 809
   characters, 43, 235, 251, 256, 291, 300, 452, 473, 1014, R103
   characters, main, 239–247, 248–251
   character traits, 116, 164–165, 167, 189–215, 216–219
   conflict, 24–25, 27–31, 33, 47–59, 152, 235, 783–797, R103
   couplet, 589–594, R104
   dialogue, 7, R104
   extended metaphors, 589, R105
   figurative language, 589–594, 617, R105
   flashbacks, 63, 542, R105
   foreshadowing, 87–98, 219
   historical context, 111, 133, 259, 359, 397, 673, 683, 729–733, 855–858, 919, 1003–1008, 1011
   hyperbole, 705, R106
   imagery, 417–423, 432, 623, 750, 868, 982, 1000, R106
   irony, 717–725, 750, 1008, R107
   memoirs, 110, 118, 380, 704, 750, 816, R107
   metaphors, 583–587, 602, 654, R107
   meter, 637–646, R107
   mood, 312–313, 314–315, 359–371, 432, R108
   personification, 589, R109
   persuasion, 1011–1014
   plot, 5, 27–31, 33–43, 333–355, R2, R109
   point of view, 162–167, 223–235, 300
   repetition, 283, 625–630, R109
   rhyme, 6, 283, R109
   rhyme scheme, 619–623, R110
   rhythm, 6, 283, 654, R2, R110
   setting, 5, 311, 314–315, 317–324, 333–355, 433, R111
   similes, 583–587, 654, R110
   sound devices, 283–291, 613–617, R111
   speakers, 417–423, 597–602, 654, 740, R111
   stanzas, 6, 583–587, 602, 654, R111
   style 673–679, 712, 729–733
   suspense, 77–84, 139, 152

## N

Name-calling, as logical fallacy, 991, R24, R25

Narrative and expressive writing, R36–R37
  alternative ending, 373
  character sketch, 681
  description, 45, 131
  dialogue, 75
  journal, 72, 799
  options for organization, R36–R37
  personal narrative, 144–150
  poem, 594
  postcard, 61
  retelling, 237
  rubric for, R36
  scene, 99, 681
  short stories, 558–564, 647

Narrative elements. *See* Character; Conflict; Plot; Point of view; Setting; Theme.

Narrative essays, 354, 718, 994

Narrative nonfiction, 8, 110, 118, 258, 275–280, 380, 704, 750, 816, 830–844, 868, R108. *See also* Literary nonfiction.

Narrative poetry, 132, 133–139, 282, 476, 608, 636–646, 732, 734, 738, 826, 854, 856, R107
  analysis of, 133–139

Narrators, 77–84, R107. *See also* Point of view.
  first-person, 162–163, 223–235
  third-person limited, 162, 169–179
  third-person omniscient, 162–163

Negatives, double, R59

News, R90–R92. *See also* Media genres and types.
  angle, R91
  balance in reporting, R91
  bias in reporting, R92
  features, R115
  five W's and H questions, R91
  human interest, R88
  inverted pyramid organization, R89
  objectivity, R91
  reporting, R91–R92
  slant, R91
  sources for, R92
  thoroughness, R91
  timeliness, R90
  uniqueness, R90
  widespread impact, R90

News articles, 8, 186, 545, 694, 715, R14, R116. *See also* News; Newspapers, articles in.

News reports, 904–907. *See also* News.
  viewing guide for, 906

Newspapers, R90, R92

articles in, 8, 186, 545, 694, 715, R14
  evaluating, 1048
  as a reference, 1040, 1044
  strategies for reading, R14

Nonfiction, R108. *See also* Nonfiction, types of; Patterns of organization.
  author's purpose in, 929–936, 995–1000
  books as reference, 1043
  conflict in, 119–129
  evaluation of, 1047
  graphic aids in, 895–902
  historical context, 1003–1008
  persuasion in, 985–991
  scope, 397–404, 405–413
  setting in, 381–393
  strategies for reading, R2
  text features in, 891, 878–883, 885–891, R3–R7

Nonfiction, types of, 4, 8–9. *See also* Informational texts.
  anecdotes, 58, R102
  arguments, 969–977, 1024, 1025
  autobiographies, 8, 830, 868, R102
  biographies, 8–9, 258, 274, R103
  book excerpts, 632–635, 859, 938
  diaries, 520
  editorials, 966, R114
  electronic texts, R19
  essays, 8, 354, 718, 994
  feature articles, 8–9, 884, 919–925, R14, R115
  interviews, 547, 908–916
  journals, 327
  letters, 270, 1006
  magazine articles, 396, 405, 894, 918, 928
  memoirs, 110, 118, 380, 704, 750, 816, R107
  narrative nonfiction, 8, 110, 118, 258, 275–280, 380, 704, 750, 816, 830–844, 868, R108
  news articles, 8, 186, 545, 694–697, 715, R14, R116
  online articles, 141, 184, 883, 934, 968
  opinion pieces, 974, 988
  position statement, 984
  speeches, 8, 846, 1002

Note cards, 1036, 1058

Note taking, 140–143, 632–635, 882, 1036, 1059, 1061, R4, R84, R85. *See also* Graphic organizers.

Noun clauses, R63

Nouns
  abstract, R46
  as antecedent, R67

capitalization of, 979, R51
collective, R46, R67
common, R46, R52
compound, R46, R76
concrete, R46
formed from suffixes, 74
plural, 75, R46, R52, R73
possessive, 75, 152, R46, R52, R74
precise, R29
predicate, R60, R67
proper, R46, R52
singular, 75, R46, R52

Novellas, 5, 810

Novels and novel excerpts, 5, 300, 301, 433, 698, 869R108
  historical, 374
  mystery, 100

## O

Objections, anticipating, R20, R41

Object pronoun, R52

Objects
  direct, R48, R60
  indirect, R48, R60
  use of whom as, R54

Observation, as a research source, 1049

Ode, 622, 728, R108

Online article, 141, 184, 883, 934, 968

Online catalog, 1041

Online information. *See* Internet; Web sites.

Onomatopoeia, 130, 646, R108

Opinion pieces, 974, 988

Opinions
  in conclusions, R33
  editorial, 966, R114
  evaluating, R25–R26
  expert, 905, R25, R81, R83, R85, R93
  explaining, 373, 977
  versus facts, 909–916, 969–977, 1024, R41, R81, R83, R85, R114
  supporting, 635, R20, R41, R83

Opinion statement. *See* Persuasion.

Opposing argument. *See* Counterarguments.

Opposing viewpoint. *See* Counterarguments.

Oral interpretation, 655, R82

Oral presentations R78–R84. *See also* Speaking strategies.
  debate, 977
  descriptive speech, R79
  informative speech, R78
  oral interpretation of a poem, 655, R82
  oral reading, 725
  oral report, 951
  persuasive speech, 1023, R81
  problem-solution presentation, R81
  response to literature, R82

meter, 578, 637–646, R107

onomatopoeia, 130, 646, R108

personification, 580, 589, R109

repetition, 283, 578–579, 625–630, 730–740, 855–858, R109

rhyme, 6, 283, 578–579, R109–R110

rhyme scheme, 578, 619–623, R110

rhythm, 6, 283, 578–579, 625, 637–646, 654, R110

sound devices, 283, 578–579, 613–617, 855, R111

speaker, 417–423, 576, 597–602, 613, 654, 740, R111

stanzas, 6, 576, 577, 579, 583–587, 602, 654, R111

style, 729–733, R111

symbols, 477–482, 610, R112

Poetic forms

ballad, 288, 636, R102

couplet, 588–594, R104

epic, 640, R104

free verse, 391, 420, 582, 586, 596, 254, 654, 628, R106

lyric, 481, 593, 604, 612, 618, 657, R107

narrative, 132, 282, 476, 608, 636, 732, 734, 738, 826, 854, 856, R107

ode, 622, 728, R108

sonnet, 618, R111

Poetry, 4, 6, R109. *See also* Poetic devices and elements; Poetic forms.

characterization in, 283–291

comparing and contrasting, 740

interpreting, 423, 610, 630, 740

oral interpretation of, 655

strategies for reading, 625–630, R2

Point of view, 162–163, 300, R109. *See also* Narrators.

first-person, 162–163, 223–235

third-person limited, 162, 169–179

third-person omniscient, 162–163

Political cartoons, 850–853, R87

Positions. *See* Author's position; Claims; Thesis statements.

Position statement, 984

Possessive forms, R46, R50, R52, R53

punctuation of, 75, 152, R50

Posture, in oral presentation, R79, R80, R85

Power presentations, 431. *See also* Oral presentations.

Predicate adjectives, R57

Predicate nominatives, R60, R61, R63, R67

Predicates, 41, 45, R60

complete, R48

compound, R60, R64

simple, R48

Predicting, 47–59, 359–371, 797, R116

Prefixes, 60, 236, 300, 414, R69. *See also* Word parts.

Greek, R69

Latin, 60, 236, R69

punctuation with, R50

spelling with, R73

Prejudice. *See* Bias.

Prepositional phrases, 357, R48, R60

between subject and verb, 453

correct placement of, 357, 748

Prepositions, 357, R47, R48, R53, R60, R77

Presentations. *See* Oral presentations.

Previewing, R4

Prewriting, 17, 147, 295, 427, 561, 651, 745, 863, 947, 1019, 1056, R28. *See also* Graphic organizers; Writing process.

Primary sources, 326–331, R28

versus secondary sources, 1042–1043

Print ads, 981

Prior knowledge, R116

Problem-solution essay, 944–950

analysis of, 945–946

key traits, 944

options for organization, 948, R39

rubric for, 950, R39

Problem-solution order, R13, R116

Procedures. *See* Business and technical writing.

Process analysis, R39

Promotional web site, 981

Prompts, responding to, 45, 61, 75, 99, 131, 143, 144, 181, 187, 221, 237, 253, 273, 331, 357, 373, 395, 415, 424, 453, 475, 483, 543, 553, 558, 603, 611, 635, 647, 681, 697, 714, 727, 741, 742, 893, 927, 944, 979, 993, 1015, 1016, 1052, R100–R101. *See also* Reading-writing connection; Writing for assessment.

Pronouns, R52–R55

agreement with antecedent, 99, 152, R52–R53

capitalization of, R51

case of, 131, R52–R53

demonstrative, R46, R54

first-person, R52

gender of, R52

indefinite, 395, R46, R54, R66

intensive, R46, R53

interrogative, R46, R54

nominative, R52–R53, R60

number of, 99, 395, R52, R65

object, 131, R52–R53

personal, R46, R52, R53, R54

person of, R52

possessive, R52, R53, R54

predicate, R60

reference problems, R55

reflexive, R46, R53

relative, R46, R54, R62, R67

second-person, R52

subject, 131, 395, R52, R53

third-person, R52

verb agreement with, 395, 432, R66

Proofreading, 150, 298, 430, 564, 654, 748, 950, 1022, R29. *See also* Revising and editing.

of test responses, R100–R101

Propaganda, R25, R116

Public documents, R17, R116. *See also* Nonfiction, types of; Speech.

Public service announcements, R87, R92

Publishing, 17, 150, 298, 430, 564, 654, 748, 950, 1022, 1066, R29

Punctuation, R49–R50

apostrophes, 75, 152, R50

colons, 799, 868, R50

commas, 61, 150, 603, 866, 927, 952, R49

dashes, R50

of dialogue, 150

ellipses, R50

end marks, 61, R49

exclamation points, R49, R60

hyphens, R50

after introductory words or phrases, 866, 927, 952, R49

italic type, 647, R50

parentheses, R50

periods, R49

of possessive forms, 75, 152, R50

question marks, R49

quick reference chart, R49

quotation marks, 150, 647, R50

semicolons, 61, 829, 868, R49

of series of items, 603, 656, 829, R65

of titles, 656

Purpose for reading, setting, 239–247, 248–251, 397–404, 405–413, 463–473, 605–610, 735–740, 985–991, R117

## Q

Questioning, R2. *See also* Monitoring.

Question marks, R49

Questions, R30, R33. *See also* Interviews; Research; Sentences.

Questions, in research report, 1036

interpreting, 482

research, 1036

rhetorical, R116

as text feature, R3

Quick reference charts
  capitalization, R51
  parts of speech, R46
  punctuation, R49–R50
  sentence and its parts, R48
Quickwriting, 32, 43, 110, 222, 258, 282,
    332, 380, 448, 582, 604, 624, 672,
    728, 816, 928, 1010, 1054. *See also*
    Freewriting.
Quotation marks, R50
  commas with, 150
  to enclose Internet search terms, 1037
  to set off speaker's exact words, 150
  with titles, 647
Quotations, R14, R28. *See also* Plagiarism;
    Works cited.
  analysis of, 925, 936
  capitalization in, R51
  in elaboration, R34
  ellipses in, R50
  of poems and songs, 654
  punctuation with, 150, 654, R50

## R

Radio plays, reading, 87–98, R109
Reading comprehension, assessment practice,
    152–155, 300–303, 432–435, 566–
    569, 750–753, 868–871, 952–955,
    1024–1029, R96–R97
Reading for information. *See also*
    Informational texts; Reading skills and
    strategies.
  anecdote, 58
  book excerpts, 632–635, 859
  citing evidence, R20, R114
  comic strip, 290
  compare and contrast, 143
  diary entry, 520
  electronic texts, R19. *See also* online
    articles, *below.*
  feature articles, 182–187, R115
  generalizations, making, 553
  history article, 140–143, 182–187
  information, evaluating, R25–R26
  informational texts, 588, R14–R19
  interview, 547
  journal, 326–331
  letter, 270
  maps, R7
  math article, 694
  newspaper articles, 545, 715, R14
  notes, 632–635
  online articles, 141, 184, 883, 934, 968
  opinion, supporting, 635
  personal essay, 354
  political cartoons, R87

primary sources, 326–331
  scope, identifying, 182–187
  sources, evaluating for usefulness, 187
  speech, 846–849
  synthesizing, 544–553, R117
  text features, using, R3–R7
  timeline, 183
  treatment, identifying, 846–849
Reading rate, 902
  adjusting to purpose, 895–902
Reading skills and strategies
  author's opinions, actions, or statements,
    evaluating, 717–725
  cause and effect, 111–116, 152, 831–844,
    995–1000
  chronological order, tracing, 119–129
  clarifying, 43, 59, 73, 84, 98, 108, 116,
    129, 143, 179, 187, 219, 235, 256, 271,
    280, 291, 324, 355, 371, 393, 413,
    452, 460, 473, 521, 542, 556, 597–
    602, 635, 646, 679, 697, 712, 725,
    733, 740, 809, 844, 849, 852, 891,
    906, 916, 936, 977, 991, 1000, 1014
  comparing and contrasting, 43, 129,
    143, 251, 256, 291, 355, 381–393, 452,
    473, 556, 602, 623, 740, 767–779,
    827, 853, 858, 902, 936, 977, 982,
    1003–1008, 1014, R11–R13
  conclusions, drawing, 43, 59, 84, 98,
    116, 139, 223–235, 251, 291, 331, 371,
    452, 477–482, 542, 566, 610, 630,
    679, 692, 725, 740, 809, 844, 891,
    902, 1000, R23
  connecting, 58, 140–143, 182–187,
    270, 290, 326–331, 354, 391–92,
    520, 544–553, 692–697, 715, 826,
    846–849, 859, 974, R2
  fact and opinion, distinguishing, 909–
    916, 969–977, R114
  figurative language, analysis of, 589–
    594, 817–827, 855–858
  graphic aids, using, 183, 694–697, R4–
    R7, R14, R16
  historical context, understanding,
    729–733
  inferences, making, 84, 98, 251, 291,
    300, 423, 449–452, 602, 610, 613–
    617, 630, 646, 733, 740, 779, 827,
    1000, R115
  long stories, reading, 189–215, 216–219
  main idea, 275–280, 880–881, 919–925,
    R8–R9
  monitoring, 259–271, 705–712, 929–
    936, R115
  myths, reading, 455–460
  narrator, evaluating, 77–84

note taking, 140–143, R4
  outlines, 632–635, R4
  paraphrasing, 133–139, 619–623, 683–
    692, 1011–1014, R116
  poetry, reading, 625–630
  predicting, 47–59, 359–371, 797
  primary sources, reading, 326–331
  purpose for reading, setting, 239–247,
    248–251, 397–404, 405–413, 463–
    473, 605–610, 735–740, 985–991
  radio plays, reading 87–98
  reading rate, adjusting, 895–902, R27
  recalling, 43, 59 73, 84, 98, 108, 116,
    129, 139, 143, 179. 187, 219, 235, 251,
    256, 271, 280, 291, 324, 331, 355,
    371, 393, 413, 423, 452, 460, 473,
    482, 521, 542, 553, 556, 587, 594,
    602, 610, 617, 635, 646, 679, 692,
    697, 712, 725, 733, 740, 779, 797,
    809, 827, 844, 849, 858, 891, 902,
    906, 925, 936, 977, 991, 1000, 1008,
    1014
  representing, 59, 139, 251, 423, 460,
    594, 602, 617, 692, 779, 797, 902
  scope, identifying, 182–187
  sequence, identifying, 63–73, 673–679
  sound devices, recognizing, 283–291
  story mapping, 485–521, 522–542
  summarizing, 73, 84, 139, 187, 271, 331,
    452, 482, 542, 553, 637–646, 809,
    827, 844, 885–891, 916, 936, 1008
  synthesizing, 544–553, 697, R117
  visualizing, 235, 333–355, 482,
    583–587, 610, 779, 801–809, R117
Reading-writing connection, 45, 61, 75, 99,
    131, 181, 221, 237, 273, 357, 373,
    395, 453, 483, 543, 603, 647, 681,
    714, 727, 781, 799, 829, 893, 927,
    979, 1015
Reasoning, R22–R24
  circular, R24
  deductive, R23, R111
  errors in. *See* Fallacies.
  evaluating, R25–R26
  inductive, R22, R115
Reasons, for claim, 962, 969, R20
Recalling, 43, 59 73, 84, 98, 108, 116, 129,
    139, 143, 179. 187, 219, 235, 251,
    256, 271, 280, 291, 324, 331, 355,
    371, 393, 413, 423, 452, 460, 473,
    482, 521, 542, 553, 556, 587, 594,
    602, 610, 617, 635, 646, 679, 692,
    697, 712, 725, 733, 740, 779, 797,
    809, 827, 844, 849, 858, 891, 902,
    906, 925, 936, 977, 991, 1000, 1008,
    1014

Word origins, 595, 656, 903, R70–R72. *See also* Word roots.

Word parts
  base words, 394, 892, 952, R69, R75
  prefixes, 60, 236, 300, 414, R69–R70, R75
  roots, 117, 152, 372, 631, 713, 750, 937, 978, 992, R69–R70
  suffixes, 74, 474, 926, 952, R69–R70, R74–R75

Word roots, R69–R70
  Greek, 978, 1024, R70
  Latin, 117, 152, 372, 631, 656, 713, 750, 937, 992, 1024, R70

Word structure. See Word parts.

Workplace and technical writing, R42–R45, R117. *See also* Business writing.
  audience for, R43
  business correspondence, 779, 863, R43, R113
  e-mail, R44
  formats for, R43–R45
  instructions, 493, R44
  key techniques, R42, R43
  memo, R44
  matching organization to content of, R42
  rubric for, R42

Workplace documents, 8, R14, R18, R43–R45. *See also* Business writing; Workplace and technical writing.
  strategies for reading, R18

Works cited, 1066, R117
  MLA citation guidelines, 1066
  preparing list, 1063

World Wide Web. *See* Internet.

Writer's message. *See* Author's message.

Writing, 16–19, R28–R45
  about literature, 144, 292, 424, 558, 648, 742, 860, 994, 1016
  audience, 16, R28, R34
  format of, 16, R34–R45
  goals in, R34
  peer response. *See* Peer response.
  prompts, 45, 61, 75, 99, 131, 143, 144, 181, 187, 221, 237, 253, 273, 331, 357, 373, 395, 415, 424, 453, 475, 483, 543, 553, 558, 603, 611, 635, 647, 681, 697, 714, 727, 741, 742, 893, 927, 944, 979, 993, 1015, 1016, 1052, R100–R101. *See also* Reading-writing connection; Writing for assessment.
  purpose for, 16, R28

Writing and grammar, assessment practice, 157, 305, 437, 571, 755, 873, 957, 1029, R99

Writing for assessment, 253, 415, 475, 611, 741, 993

Writing modes. *See* Descriptive writing; Expository writing; Narrative writing; Persuasive writing; Writing about literature.

Writing process, R28–R45
  drafting, 17, 148, 296, 428, 561, 652, 746, 864, 948, 1020, 1062–1063, R28
  peer response in, 150, 298, 430, 564, 654, 748, 866, 950, 1022, 1066, R29
  prewriting, 17, 147, 295, 427, 561, 651, 745, 863, 947, 1019, 1056, R28
  proofreading, 150, 298, 430, 564, 654, 748, 950, 1022, R29
  publishing, 17, 150, 298, 430, 564, 654, 748, 950, 1022, 1066
  reflecting, R29
  researching, 1057–1061
  revising and editing, 17, 149, 297, 429, 561, 653, 747, 865, 949, 1021, 1064–1065, R29

Writing skills and strategies. *See also* Reading-writing connection.
  analogies, R73, R102, R113
  anecdotes, R30, R79, R102
  cause and effect, R32
  coherence, R29, R31–R32
  compare and contrast, R32
  description, R102
  details, R34–R35
  dialogue, 148, R36
  elaboration, R33–R34
  examples, R34
  humor, R104
  introduction, 429
  organization. *See* Patterns of organization.
  precise language, 429, R29
  quotations, R28, R34
  sensory language, 149
  tone, R29, R30, R31, R36, R39, R40, R41, R42, R43
  transitions, 866, R32
  word choice, R101

Written response, assessment practice, 155, 303, 435, 569, 753, 871, 955, 1027, R100–R101

# INDEX OF TITLES & AUTHORS

Page numbers that appear in italics refer to biographical information.

# ACKNOWLEDGMENTS

## UNIT 1

**Houghton Mifflin:** Excerpt from *Johnny Tremain* by Esther Forbes. Copyright © 1943 by Esther Forbes Hoskins. Copyright © renewed 1971 by Linwood M. Erskine, Jr., Executor of the Estate of Esther Forbes Hoskins. Reprinted by permission of Houghton Mifflin Company. All rights reserved.

**Random House:** "Raymond's Run," from *Gorilla, My Love* by Toni Cade Bambara. Copyright © 1971 by Toni Cade Bambara. Used by permission of Random House, Inc.

**The Carol Mann Agency:** "Manuscript Found in the Attic" by Marcus Rosenbaum, from *I Thought My Father Was a God: And Other True Tales from NPR's National Story Project* edited by Paul Auster. Copyright © 2001 by Paul Auster. Reprinted by permission of The Carol Mann Agency.

**Sterling Lord Literistic:** "Clean Sweep" by Joan Bauer, from *Shelf Life, Stories by the Book* edited by Gary Paulsen. Copyright © 2003 by Joan Bauer. Reprinted by permission of SLL/Sterling Lord Literistic, Inc.

**William Morris Agency:** "The Hitchhiker" by Lucille Fletcher, from *Radio's Best Plays*. Copyright © 1947, 1952, renewed 1980 by Lucille Fletcher. Reprinted by permission of William Morris Agency, LLC, on behalf of the author.

**Random House:** Excerpt from *Hoot* by Carl Hiassen. Copyright © 2002 by Carl Hiassen. Used by permission of Alfred A. Knopf, an imprint of Random House Children's Books, a division of Random House, Inc.

**Susan Bergholz Literary Services:** "My First Free Summer" by Julia Alvarez, first published in *Better Homes and Gardens*, August 2003. Copyright © 2003 by Julia Alvarez. Reprinted by permission of Susan Bergholz Literary Services, New York. All rights reserved.

**Laurence Yep:** "The Great Rat Hunt" by Laurence Yep, from *When I Was Your Age: Original Stories about Growing Up*, edited by Amy Ehrlich. Copyright © 1996 by Laurence Yep. Reprinted by permission of the author.

## UNIT 2

**Harcourt:** Excerpt from "Broken Chain," from *Baseball in April and Other Stories* by Gary Soto. Copyright © 1990 by Gary Soto. Reprinted by permission of Harcourt, Inc.

**Miriam Altshuler Literary Agency:** "The Treasure of Lemon Brown" by Walter Dean Myers, *Boys' Life,* March 1983. Copyright © 1983 by Walter Dean Myers. Reprinted by permission of Miriam Altshuler Literary Agency, on behalf of Walter Dean Myers.

**The New York Times:** Excerpts from "Blues Musicians Get Help Overcoming Hard Times" by Andrew Jacobs, from the *New York Times*, March 21, 2004. Copyright © 2004 by the New York Times Co. Reprinted with permission.

**Daniel Keyes:** "Flowers for Algernon" by Daniel Keyes, from *The Magazine of Fantasy and Science Fiction*. Copyright © 1959, 1987 by Daniel Keyes. Reprinted by permission of the author. All rights reserved.

**G.P. Putnam's Sons:** "Rules of the Game," from *The Joy Luck Club* by Amy Tan. Copyright © 1989 by Amy Tan. Used by permission of G.P. Putnam's Sons, a division of Penguin Group (USA) Inc.

**Virginia Driving Hawk Sneve:** "The Medicine Bag" by Driving Hawk, from *Boy's Life*, March 1975. Copyright © 1975 by Virginia Driving Hawk Sneve. Used by permission of the author.

**Scholastic:** "Who Are You Today, Maria?" from *Call Me Maria* by Judith Ortiz Cofer. Copyright © 2004 by Judith Ortiz Cofer. Published by Scholastic Inc./Orchard Books. Reprinted by permission.

**Russell & Volkening:** "The Railroad Runs to Canada" and "Go On or Die," from *Harriet Tubman: Conductor of the Underground Railroad* by Ann Petry. Copyright © 1955 by Ann Petry, renewed 1983 by Ann Petry. Reprinted by permission of Russell & Volkening as agents for the author.

**Houghton Mifflin:** "The Mysterious Mr. Lincoln," from *Lincoln: A Photobiography* by Russell Freedman. Copyright © 1987 by Russell Freedman. Reprinted by permission of Houghton Mifflin Company. All rights reserved.

**John Steventon:** Excerpt from "Tribute to John Henry" by John Steventon. Used by permission of the author.

## UNIT 3

**Bancroft Library:** Excerpt from *Journey to Topaz: A Story of the Japanese-American Evacuation* by Yoshiko Uchida. Copyright © 1971 by Yoshiko Uchida. Courtesy of the Bancroft Library, University of California, Berkeley.

**Don Congdon:** "The Drummer Boy of Shiloh" by Ray Bradbury. Copyright © 1960 by the Curtis Publishing Company, renewed 1988 by Ray Bradbury. Reprinted by permission of Don Congdon Associates, Inc.

**Ralph M. Vicinanza:** "Hallucination" by Isaac Asimov, from *Gold, The Final Science Fiction Collection*. Copyright © 1995 by Nightfall Inc./The Estate of Isaac Asimov. All rights reserved. Reprinted by permission of Ralph M. Vicinanza, Ltd.

**Prometheus Books:** Excerpt from "Ellis Island and I," from *The Tyrannosaurus Prescription and 100 Other Essays* by Isaac Asimov (Amherst, NY: Prometheus Books). Copyright © 1989 by Isaac Asimov. Reprinted by permission of the publisher.

**Dial Books for Young Readers:** Excerpt from *Roll of Thunder, Hear My Cry* by Mildred Taylor. Copyright © 1976 by Mildred D. Taylor. Used by permission of Dial Books for Young Readers, A Division of Penguin Young Readers Group, A Member of Penguin Group (USA) Inc., 345 Hudson Street, New York, NY 10014. All rights reserved.

**Naomi Shihab Nye:** Excerpt from "Thank You in Arabic" by Naomi Shihab Nye. Copyright © 1995 by Naomi Shihab Nye. First published in *Going Where I'm Coming From* by arrangement with the author. Used by permission of the author, Naomi Shihab Nye, 2006.

**Naomi Shihab Nye:** "My Father and the Figtree," from *19 Varieties of Gazelle: Poems of the Middle East* by Naomi Shihab Nye. Copyright © 1994, 1995, 1998, 2002 by Naomi Shihab Nye. Reprinted with permission.

**The Wylie Agency:** Excerpts from "Leaving Desire, The Ninth Ward after the Hurricane" by Jon Lee Anderson, from the *New Yorker,* September 19, 2005. Copyright © 2005 by Jon Lee Anderson. Used by permission of the Wylie Agency, as agents for the author.

**Arte Público Press:** "Mi Madre," from *Chants* by Pat Mora. Copyright © 1986 by Arte Público Press—University of Houston. Reprinted with permission from Arte Público Press.

**Simon J. Ortiz:** "Canyon de Chelly" by Simon J. Ortiz, originally published in *Woven Stone,* University of Arizona Press, Tucson, AZ. Copyright © 1992 by Simon J. Ortiz. Permission granted by the author.

## UNIT 4

**Scholastic:** "Abuela Invents the Zero," from *An Island Like You: Stories of the Barrio* by Judith Ortiz Cofer. Copyright © 2005 by Judith Ortiz Cofer. Reprinted by permission of Orchard Books/Scholastic Inc.

**Susan Bergholz Literary Services:** "Gil's Furniture Bought & Sold," from *The House on Mango Street* by Sandra Cisneros. Copyright © 1984 by Sandra Cisneros. Published by Vintage Books, a division of Random House, Inc., and in hardcover by Alfred A. Knopf in 1994. Reprinted by permission of Susan Bergholz Literary Services, New York. All rights reserved.

**M. Evans:** "Pandora . . . The Fateful Casket," from *The Firebringer and Other Great Stories, Fifty-Five Legends That Will Live Forever* by Louis Untermeyer. Copyright © 1968 by Louis Untermeyer. Reprinted by permission of M. Evans, an imprint of Taylor Trade Publishing, Lanham, MD.

**Little Simon:** "The Old Grandfather and His Little Grandson," from *Twenty-Two Russian Tales for Young Children* by Leo Tolstoy, translated by Miriam Morton. Translation copyright © 1969 by Miriam Morton. Reprinted by permission of Little Simon, an imprint of Simon & Schuster Children's Publishing Division.

**Bancroft Library:** "The Wise Old Woman," from *The Sea of Gold and Other Tales from Japan* adapted by Yoshiko Uchida. Copyright © 1965 by Yoshiko Uchida. Courtesy of the Bancroft Library, University of California, Berkeley.

**Teresa Palomo Acosta:** "My Mother Pieced Quilts" by Teresa Palomo Acosta, from *Festival de Flor y Canto: An Anthology of Chicano Literature.* Copyright © by Teresa Palomo Acosta. Used by permission of the author.

**BOA Editions:** "quilting," from *Quilting: Poems 1987–1990* by Lucille Clifton. Copyright © 1991 by Lucille Clifton. Reprinted by permission of BOA Editions, Ltd.

**Random House:** *The Diary of Anne Frank* by Frances Goodrich and Albert Hackett. Copyright © 1956 by Albert Hackett, Frances Goodrich Hackett, and Otto Frank. Used by permission of Random House, Inc.

**Doubleday:** Excerpt from *The Diary of a Young Girl: the Definitive Edition* by Anne Frank. Edited by Otto H. Frank and Mirjam Pressler. Translated by Susan Massotty. Copyright © 1995 by Doubleday. Used by permission of Doubleday, a division of Random House, Inc.

**Gerda Klein:** Excerpts from "A Diary from Another World" by Gerda Weissman Klein, from *Buffalo News.* Used by permission of the author.

## UNIT 5

**Rosina M. Albi:** Excerpt from "Street Corner Flight" by Norma Landa Flores, from *Sighs and Songs of Aztlan* edited by F. E. Albi and J. G. Nieto. Copyright © 1975 by F. E. Albi and J. G. Nieto. Reprinted by permission of Rosina M. Albi.

**The Overlook Press:** Excerpt from "That Day," from *I Remember Root River* by David Kherdian. Copyright © 1978 by David Kherdian. Used by permission of the Overlook Press.

**Henry Holt and Company:** "Stopping by Woods on a Snowy Evening," from *The Poetry of Robert Frost* edited by Edward Connery Lathem. Copyright 1923, 1969 by Henry Holt and Company. Copyright © 1951 by Robert Frost. Reprinted by permission of Henry Holt and Company, LLC.

**HarperCollins:** Excerpt from "Chrysalis Diary" from *Joyful Noise: Poems for Two Voices* by Paul Fleischman. Copyright © 1988 by Paul Fleischman. Used by permission of HarperCollins Publishers.

**Okpaku Communications:** "Sunset," from *Sounds of a Cowhide Drum* by Oswald Mbuyiseni Mtshali. Copyright © 1972 by the Third Press, Joseph Okpaku Publishing Company. Used by permission of Okpaku Communication Corporation.

**Houghton Mifflin:** Excerpt from "Water Picture," from *Nature: Poems Old and New* by May Swenson. Copyright © 1994 by the Literary Estate of May Swenson. Reprinted by permission of Houghton Mifflin Company. All rights reserved.

**New Directions:** "Aware," from *This Great Unknowing: Last Poems* by Denise Levertov. Copyright © 1999 by the Denise Levertov Literary Trust, Paul A. Lacey and Valerie Trueblood Rapport, Co-Trustees. Reprinted by permission of New Directions Publishing Corp.

**The University of Georgia Press:** "Lineage," from *For My People* by Margaret Walker. Copyright © 1942 by Yale University Press. Reprinted by permission of the University of Georgia Press.

**Marian Reiner:** "Simile: Willow and Ginkgo," from *It Doesn't Always Have to Rhyme* by Eve Merriam. Copyright © 1964 by Eve Merriam. Used by permission of Marian Reiner.

**University of Arkansas Press:** "Introduction to Poetry," from *The Apple That Astonished Paris* by Billy Collins. Copyright © 1988 by Billy Collins. Reprinted by permission of the University of Arkansas Press.

**Harcourt:** "Macavity: The Mystery Cat," from *Old Possum's Book of Practical Cats* by T. S. Eliot. Copyright © 1939 by T. S. Eliot and renewed 1967 by Esme Valerie Eliot. Reprinted by permission of Harcourt, Inc.

**Doubleday:** "The Lesson of the Moth," from *Archy and Mehitabel* by Don Marquis. Copyright © 1927 by Doubleday. Used by permission of Doubleday, a division of Random House, Inc.

**Harvard University Press and the Trustees of Amherst College:** "It's all I have to bring today" by Emily Dickinson, from *The Poems of Emily Dickinson*, Thomas J. Johnson, ed., Cambridge, Mass.: The Belknap Press of Harvard University Press. Copyright © 1951, 1955, 1979, 1983 by the President and Fellows of Harvard College. Reprinted by permission of the publishers and the Trustees of Amherst College.

**Harcourt:** "We Alone," from *Horses Make a Landscape Look More Beautiful: Poems by Alice Walker.* Copyright © 1984 by Alice Walker. Reprinted by permission of Harcourt, Inc.

**Brooks Permissions:** "Speech to the Young: Speech to the Progress-Toward," from *Blacks* by Gwendolyn Brooks. Copyright © by Gwendolyn Brooks. Reprinted by consent of Brooks Permissions.

**Alfred A. Knopf:** "Mother to Son," from *The Collected Poems of Langston Hughes* by Langston Hughes. Copyright © 1994 by the Estate of Langston Hughes. Used by permission of Alfred A. Knopf, a division of Random House, Inc.

**Random House:** "One More Round," from *And Still I Rise* by Maya Angelou. Copyright © 1978 by Maya Angelou. Used by permission of Random House, Inc.

**Boyds Mills Press:** "Not My Bones," from *Fortune's Bones, The Manumission Requiem* by Marilyn Nelson (Front Street, an imprint of Boyds Mills Press, 2003.) Poem copyright © 2003 by Marilyn Nelson. Reprinted with the permission of Boyds Mills Press, Inc.

**Special Rider Music:** "Boots of Spanish Leather" by Bob Dylan. Copyright © 1963 by Warner Bros. Inc. Copyright renewed 1991 by Special Rider Music. All rights reserved. International copyright secured. Reprinted by permission.

## UNIT 6

**The C. S. Lewis Company:** Excerpt from *The Voyage of the Dawn Treader* by C. S. Lewis. Copyright © 1952 by C. S. Lewis Pte. Ltd. Extract reprinted by permission.

**Brandt & Hochman:** Excerpt from "The Truth About the World" by Lloyd Alexander. Copyright © 2005 by Lloyd Alexander. First published in *Guys Write for Guys Read* (Viking, 2005.) Reprinted by permission of Brandt & Hochman Literary Agents, Inc. All rights reserved.

**Soho Press:** Excerpt from *Krik? Krak!* by Edwidge Danticat. Copyright © 1991, 1992, 1993, 1994, and 1995 by Edwidge Danticat. Reprinted by permission of Soho Press, Inc.

**The New York Times:** Adaptation of "Behind Monty Hall's Doors: Puzzle, Debate and Answer?" by John Tierney, from the *New York Times*. Copyright © 1991 by the New York Times Company. Reprinted with permission.

**Atheneum Books for Young Readers:** Excerpt from *Kira-Kira* by Cynthia Kadohata. Copyright © 2004 by Cynthia Kadohata. Reprinted with the permission of Atheneum Books for Young Readers, an imprint of Simon & Schuster Children's Publishing Division.

**Little, Brown and Co:** Excerpt from *Dress Your Family in Corduroy and Denim* by David Sedaris. Copyright © 2004 by David Sedaris. By permission of Little, Brown and Co., Inc.

## UNIT 7

**BOA Editions:** "Eating Together," from *Rose*, by Li-Young Lee. Copyright © 1986 by Li-Young Lee. Reprinted by permission of BOA Editions, Ltd.

**Susan Bergholz:** "Dusting," from *Homecoming: New and Collected Poems* by Julia Alvarez. Copyright © 1984, 1996 by Julia Alvarez. Used by permission of Susan Bergholz.

**Barbara S. Kouts:** "The Snapping Turtle" by Joseph Bruchac, from *When I Was Your Age*, Vol. Two, Candlewick Press, 1999. Copyright © 1999 by Joseph Bruchac. Reprinted by permission of Barbara S. Kouts Literary Agency.

**Viking Penguin:** Excerpt from *The Pearl* by John Steinbeck. Copyright © 1945 by John Steinbeck. Copyright © renewed 1973 by Elaine Steinbeck, Thom Steinbeck, and John Steinbeck IV. Used by permission of Viking Penguin, a division of Penguin Group (USA) Inc.

**Gary Soto:** "One Last Time," from *Living Up the Street* by Gary Soto. Copyright © 1985 by Gary Soto. Used by permission of the author.

**Harcourt:** "How Things Work," from *A Fire in My Hands* by Gary Soto. Copyright © 2006, 1999 by Gary Soto. Reprinted by permission of Harcourt, Inc. This material may not be reproduced in any form or by any means without the prior written permission of the publisher.

**The University of Georgia Press:** "Sit-ins" and "I Want to Write," from *This Is My Century, New and Collected Poems* by Margaret Walker. Copyright © 1989 by Margaret Walker Alexander. Reprinted by permission of the University of Georgia Press.

**Scholastic:** Excerpt from *A Dream of Freedom: The Civil Rights Movement from 1954 to 1968* by Diane McWhorter. Copyright © 2004 by Diane McWhorter. Reprinted by permission of Scholastic Inc./Nonfiction.

## UNIT 8

**National Geographic Society:** "Female Android Debuts in S. Korea" by Victoria Gilman, from *National Geographic News*, May 15, 2006. Copyright © 2006 by National Geographic Society. Reprinted by permission of the National Geographic Society.

**National Geographic Society:** Excerpt from "Escape from the Blaze" by Michael Burgan, from *National Geographic World*, September 1988. Copyright © 1988 by National Geographic Society. Reprinted by permission of the National Geographic Society.

**National Geographic Society:** "The Spider Man Behind Spider-Man" by Bijal P. Trivedi, from *National Geographic Today*, May 2, 2002. Copyright © 2002 by National Geographic Society. Reprinted by permission of the National Geographic Society.

**National Geographic Society:** Excerpts from "Over the Top: The True Adventures of a Volcano Chaser" by Renee Skelton, from *National Geographic World*, June 2001. Copyright © 2001 by National Geographic Society. Reprinted by permission of the National Geographic Society.

**National Geographic Society:** Excerpt from "Q&A: 'Songcatcher' Pioneer on Musical Heritage" by Brian Handwerk, from *National Geographic News*, June 16, 2003. Copyright © 2003 by National Geographic Society. Reprinted by permission of the National Geographic Society.

**The New York Times:** Excerpt from "Robo-Legs" by Michael Marriott, from the *New York Times*, June 20, 2005. Copyright © 2005 by the New York Times. Reprinted with permission.

**Houghton Mifflin:** Excerpt from *An American Plague: The True and Terrifying Story of the Yellow Fever Epidemic of 1793* by Jim Murphy. Copyright © 2003 by Jim Murphy. Reprinted by permission of Clarion Books, an imprint of Houghton Mifflin Company. All rights reserved.

## UNIT 9

**NASPE:** "Position on Dodgeball in Physical Education" by NASPE. Reprinted with permission from the National Association for Sport and Physical Education (NASPE), 1900 Association Drive, Reston, VA 20191-1599.

**Sports Illustrated:** Excerpts from "The Weak Shall Inherit the Gym" by Rick Reilly, from *Sports Illustrated*, May 14, 2001. Copyright © 2001 by Time Inc. Reprinted courtesy of *Sports Illustrated*. All rights reserved.

**The New York Times:** "The Sanctuary of School" by Lynda Barry, from the *New York Times*, January 5, 1992. Copyright © 1992 by the New York Times. Reprinted with permission.

The editors have made every effort to trace the ownership of all copyrighted material found in this book and to make full acknowledgment for its use. Omissions brought to our attention will be corrected in a subsequent edition.

## CONSULTANTS

**Title page** © Image 100/PunchStock; Photo © Duane McCubrey; Photo © Mark Schmidt; Photo © Bruce Forrester; Photo © McDougal Littell; Photo © Howard Gollub; Photo © Tamra Stallings; Photo © Mark Schmidt; Photo © Robert J. Marzano; Photo © McDougal Littell; Photo © Dawson & Associates Photography; Photo © Gitchell's Studio Photo © Michael Romeo; Photo © Monica Ani; Photo © William McBride; Photo © Bill Caldwell; Photo © Gabriel Pauluzzi; Photo © Steven Scheffler.

## TABLE OF CONTENTS

**Contents in Brief verso** *top* © Edwin Wallace/Mary Evans Picture Library; *bottom, Deer Spirit Helper*, Joe Geshick. Oil. © Joe Geshick; *top* © Steve Bloom/Getty Images; *bottom* © Getty Images; **Unit 1 verso** *top left* Illustration by Howard Simpson; *top right* © er Productions/Getty Images; *bottom* Courtesy American Library Association; **recto** © PunchStock; **Unit 2 verso** *left* From *Harlem* by Walter Dean Myers, illustrated by Christopher Myers. © 1997 by Christopher Myers. Reprinted by permission of Scholastic, Inc.; *right, Frida* (2004), Maria Sanchez. Acrylic on canvas. C. Perez Collection. © Maria Sanchez; **recto** © PunchStock; **Unit 3 verso** *top left, Jerusalem* (1984), Tamam Al-akhal. Palestine. Oil on canvas, 50 cm × 70 cm. Private collection; *top right* © Jupiter Images; *bottom* Courtesy American Library Association; **recto** © PunchStock; **Unit 4 verso** *left, Crossing Borders* (1995), Diedre Scherer. Fabric and thread. © Diedre Scherer; *right* © Joan Marcus; **recto** © PunchStock; **Unit 5 verso** *left, Aspiration* (1936), Aaron Douglas. Oil on canvas, 60″ × 60″. © Fine Arts Museums of San Francisco purchase, the estate of Thurlow E. Tibbs, Jr., the Museum Society Auxiliary, American Art Trust Fund, Unrestricted Art Trust Fund, partial gift of Dr. Ernest A. Bates, Sharon Bell, Jo-Ann Beverly, Barbara Carleton, Dr. and Mrs. Arthur H. Coleman, Dr. and Mrs. Coyness Ennix, Jr., Nicole Y. Ennix, Mr. and Mrs. Gary Francois, Dennis L. Franklin, Mr. and Mrs. Maxwell C. Gillette, Mr. and Mrs. Richard Goodyear, Zuretti L. Goosby, Marion E. Greene, Mrs. Vivian S. W. Hambrick, Laurie Gibbs Harris, Arlene Hollis, Louis A. and Letha Jeanpierre, Daniel and Jackie Johnson, Jr., Stephen L. Johnson, Mr. and Mrs. Arthur Lathan, Lewis and Ribbs Mortuary Garden Chapel, Mr. and Mrs. Gary Love, Glenn R. Nance, Mr. and Mrs. Harry S. Parker III, Mr. and Mrs. Carr T. Preston, Fannie Preston, Pamela R. Ransom, Dr. and Mrs. Benjamin F. Reed, San Francisco Black Chamber of Commerce, San Francisco Chapter of Links, Inc., San Francisco Chapter of the N.A.A.C.P., Sigma Pi Phi Fraternity, Dr. Ella Mae Simmons, Mr. Calvin R. Swinson, Joseph B. Williams, Mr. and Mrs. Alfred S. Wilsey, and the people of the Bay Area, 1997.84; *right* © Corbis; **recto** © PunchStock; **Unit 6 verso** *top left, Lincoln 2*, Wendy Allen. Oil on canvas. © Wendy Allen; *top, right Californians Catching Wild Horses with Riata* (about 1851), Hugo Wilhelm Arthur Nahl. Oil on canvas mounted on masonite. Courtesy of the Oakland Museum of California Kahn Collection (A65.57) © Laurie Platt Winfrey/Oakland Museum/The Art Archive; *bottom* Courtesy

American Library Association; **recto** © PunchStock; **Unit 7 verso** *top left* © Steve McCurry/Magnum Photos; *top right* Illustration by Michael McCurdy. © 1991 by Michael McCurdy, from *American Tall Tales* by Mary Pope Osborne. Used by permission of Alfred A. Knopf, an imprint of Random House Children's Books, a division of Random House, Inc.; *bottom* AP/Wide World Photos; **recto** © PunchStock; **Unit 8 verso** *left* © Science Source/Photo Researchers, Inc.; *right* © Carsten Peter/National Geographic Image Collection; **recto** *top* Courtesy American Library Association; *bottom* © PunchStock; **Unit 9 verso** *left* © Getty Images; *right* © Steve Bly/ Alamy Images; **recto** © PunchStock; **Unit 10** *left, collage, top* © Gary Walts/Syracuse Newspapers/The Image Works, Inc.; *center* © Gregor Schuster/Iconica/Getty Images; *bottom left* © Syracuse Newspapers/The Image Works, Inc.; *bottom right* Marcio Jose Sanchez/AP/Wide World Photos; *right photo* © Getty Images.

## INTRODUCTORY UNIT

**1** *left, The Promenade, Fifth Avenue* (1986), Bill Jacklin. Oil on canvas, 243.6 cm × 182.7 cm. Private collection. © Bill Jacklin/ Bridgeman Art Library; *top right* © Bill Brooks/Masterfile; *bottom right* Detail of *Harriet Tubman* (1945), William H. Johnson. Oil on paperboard, sheet, 29⅜″ × 23⅜″. Smithsonian American Art Museum, Washington, D.C. © Smithsonian American Art Museum, Washington, D.C./Art Resource, New York; **2** *left, The Olive Tree* (2005), Ismail Shammout. Palestine. Oil on canvas, 60 cm × 80 cm. Private collection; *right* Fort Sumter National Monument/National Park Service; **3** *left* © Getty Images; *right, Communion*, Joe Geshick. © Joe Geshick; **6** © Stephen Stickler/Getty Images; **8** *top to bottom* Library of Congress; © Getty Images; © Rick Wilking/Reuters/Corbis; © Carsten Peter/National Geographic Image Collection; Commuter Rail Division of the Regional Transportation Authority, d/b/a/ Metra; **9** © Jerry Cooke/Corbis; **10** *top to bottom Whale Rider* footage provided courtesy of South Pacific Pictures Limited. © South Pacific Pictures Limited and ApolloMedia GmbH & Co 5 Filmproduktion KG 2002/© Newmarket/Courtesy The Everett Collection; © Gary Hershorn/Reuters/Corbis; Photo by Will Hart/© NBC/Courtesy of the Everett Collection/The Everett Collection; Footage courtesy of Lucasfilm Ltd. *Star Wars: Episode III-Revenge of the Sith* © 2005 Lucasfilm Ltd. & TM. All rights reserved. Used under authorization. Unauthorized duplication is a violation of applicable law; © James Leynse/Corbis; **13** © Gusto Images/Getty Images; **16** *left* © Comstock Images/Age Fotostock; *center* © SW Productions/Getty Images; *right-top background* © 2007 *The Daily Northwestern*; *right-top right* © Carsten Peter/ National Geographic Image Collection; *right: center cover background* © Bob Gelberg/Sharpshooters; *frontispiece background* The Granger Collection, New York; Amelia Earhart: © Albert L. Bresnik; Maya Lin: © 1999 Richard Howard/Black Star; Juan Seguín: Detail of *Juan Seguín* (1838), Jefferson Wright. Texas State Library and Archives Commission; Harry S. Truman: White House Collection. © White House Historical Association. Courtesy of the Harry S. Truman Library; Ida Bell Wells: The Granger Collection, New York; Abigail Adams: *Portrait traditionally said to be Abigail Adams* (about 1795), artist unknown. Oil on canvas, 30¼″ × 26½″, N-150.55. Photograph by Richard Walker. Copyright © New York State Historical Association, Cooperstown, New York; Zitkala-Sa: Negative no. Mss 299, Tom Perry Special Collections, William F. Hansen Collection, Photographic Archives, Harold B. Lee Library, Brigham Young University, Provo, Utah; Benjamin Franklin: © Joseph-Siffrede Duplessis/Wood River Gallery/PNI; Abraham Lincoln: Library of Congress; Martin Luther King, Jr: Photograph by Howard Sochrer/*Life* magazine © Time Inc; *right: left bottom* © Time & Life Pictures/Getty Images; *right: bottom center* © Regin Igloria; *right* Photograph by Sharon Hoogstraten; **17** *left* © Google; *right* © Ragnar Schmuck/Getty Images; **18** © Jupiter Images; **19** *left* © ImageSource/Age Fotostock; *center* © Susan Wides/PunchStock; *right* © Corbis/Age Fotostock America, Inc.

## UNIT 1

**21** *left* Illustrations © 2004 by Jan Peng-Wang. From *A Song for Ba*, text © 2004 by Paul Yee. First published in Canada by Groundwood Books, Ltd. Reprinted by permission of the publisher; *right background* © StockAB/Alamy Images; *right foreground* © Michael Kelley/Getty Images; **22** Cover of *Dragon of the Lost Sea* by Laurence Yep. © 1982 by Laurence Yep. Reprinted by permission of HarperCollins Children's Books, a division of HarperCollins Publishers, New York. Photo by Sharon Hoogstraten; **22–23** © Adam Woolfitt/Corbis; **24** *left* © Corbis; *center left* © Terje Rakke/Getty Images; *center right* © Dean Conger/Corbis; *right* © Medioimages/Getty Images; **27** © Vance Lessard/Getty Images; **31** © Photodisc/Getty Images; **32** © 2005 Getty Images; **33** © Schomburg Center for Research in Black Culture, New York Public Library/Art Resource, New York; **35** *foreground* © Michael Kelley/Getty Images; *background* © StockAB/Alamy Images; **37** © Lise Gagne/istockphoto.com; **39** © Ingram Publishing Royalty Free Photography/Fotosearch Stock Photography; **42** © er Productions/Getty Images; **46** © Warner Bros./Photofest; **47** © Bettmann/Corbis; **50** The Granger Collection, New York; **58** © Brown Brothers, Sterling, PA; **62** Photograph by Sharon Hoogstraten; **63** Photo by Jim Lundquist; **65** © Didier Robcis/Getty Images; **66** © Andrew Syred/Photo Researchers, Inc.; **68** © Dennis Novak/Getty Images; **72** © Peter Marlow/Magnum Photos; **76** © Nick Koudis/Getty Images; **77** © Bettmann/Corbis; **86** © Louie Psihoyos/Science Faction; **87** © CBS/Landov; **89** © Gene Laughter, 2006; **90** © Ferdinando Scianna/Magnum Photos; **93** © Raymond Depardon/Magnum Photos; **96** © Andreas Feininger/Time & Life Pictures/Getty Images; **100** *top* © Les Cunliffe/Age Fotostock America, Inc.; *bottom* © Jerry Bauer; **100–101** © David R. Frazier Photolibrary, Inc./Alamy Images; **101** *top* Courtesy American Library Association; *bottom* Cover of *Hoot* by Carl Hiaasen. © 2002 by Carl Hiaasen. Cover design and illustration © 2004 by Alfred A. Knopf. Reprinted by permission of Alfred A. Knopf, an imprint of Random House Children's Books, a division of Random House, Inc.; **102–103** © Paul Harris/Getty Images; **104–105** © Junichi Kusaka/MIXA Co., Ltd./Alamy; **106, 107** © Warner Bother/Courtesy The Everett Collection; **108** *top, center* © Warner Brothers Entertainment Inc. All rights reserved; *bottom* © PunchStock; **110** © Reg Charity/Corbis; **111** © Bill Eichner. Reprinted by permission of Susan Bergholz Literary Services, New York. All rights reserved; **113** *The Stillness of an Afternoon* (2003), Bo Bartlett. Oil on panel, 18½" × 21". Courtesy of the artist and P.P.O.W. Gallery, New York; **114** © GeoNova LLC; **118** © Getty Images; **119** Courtesy of Laurence Yep; **121, 125, 128** Illustrations © 2004 by Jan Peng-

Wang. From *A Song for Ba*, text © 2004 by Paul Yee. First published in Canada by Groundwood Books, Ltd. Reprinted by permission of the publisher; **132** © AFP/Getty Images; **133** © Stock Montage; **135** Illustration © 2001 by Christopher Bing. From *The Midnight Ride of Paul Revere* by Henry Wadsworth Longfellow, graved and painted by Christopher Bing. Reprinted by permission of Handprint Books, New York; **136** © Raymond Gehman/Getty Images; **138** © Bill Brooks/Alamy Images; **140** Illustration © 2001 by Christopher Bing. From *The Midnight Ride of Paul Revere* by Henry Wadsworth Longfellow, graved and painted by Christopher Bing. Reprinted by permission of Handprint Books, New York; **141** *top* PBS ® and the PBS logo are registered trademarks of the Public Broadcasting Service and are used with permission. All rights reserved; *bottom William Dawes* (unknown), attributed to John Johnston. Oil on canvas, 35" × 29". © Collection of the Evanston Historical Society, Evanston, Illinois; **142** © GeoNova LLC; **144, 150** © Craig Aurness/Corbis; **151** © Thinkstock/PunchStock; **158** © Siede Preis/Photodisc/Getty Images.

## UNIT 2

**159** *left* © Mary Grace Long/Getty Images; *right* Detail of *They Moved Them* (1991), David Behrens. Oil glazing, 9¼" × 14½". © David Behrens, www.davidbehrens.com; **160** © BBC Films/Photofest; **160–161** *center* © DreamWorks Animation/Zuma/Corbis; **163** © Jamie Thorpe/ShutterStock; **164** © Digital Vision/PunchStock; **168** © Clarissa Leahy/Getty Images; **169** © Jerry Bauer; **171, 174, 18** From *Harlem* by Walter Dean Myers, illustrated by Christopher Myers. © 1997 by Christopher Myers. Reprinted by permission of Scholastic, Inc.; **183** *top left* The Granger Collection, New York; *top right* © Bettmann/Corbis; *bottom left* © Getty Images; *bottom right* © Bob Adelman/Magnum Photos; **184** *left, right* AP/Wide World Photos; *center left* The Granger Collection, New York; *center right* © Bettmann/Corbis; **186** The New York Times Company; **188** © Paul Eekhoff/Masterfile; **189** *top* © Beth Gwinn, Photographer; **189** *bottom* CBS/Landov; **191** Detail of *Mean Dog* (1998), Sylvia Chesley Smith. © Sylvia Chesley Smith/Corbis; **192** The Granger Collection, New York; **195** Corbis; **198** Todd Davidson/Illustration Works; **203** Images.com/Corbis; **205** Todd Davidson/Stock Illustration RF/Getty Images; **209** © Todd Davidson PTY Ltd/The Image Bank/Getty Images; **213** © Images.com/Corbis; **217** © Selmur/Cinema Rel. Corp./The Kobal Collection; **222** © Ariel Skelley/Corbis; **223** © Jennifer Graylock/AP/Wide World Photos; **225** © Mary Grace Long/Getty Images; **227** © Morton Beebe/Corbis; **230** © Martin Barraud/Getty Images; **234** © Corbis; **238** © Lindsay Hebberd/Corbis; **239** *top* Courtesy of Virginia Driving Hawk Sneve; *bottom* Photo of Judith Ortiz Cofer is reprinted with permission from the publisher Arte Publico Press. © 2005, University of Houston, Houston, Texas; **242** © GeoNova LLC; **245** Photo by Sharon Hoogstraten; **254** *Whale Rider* footage provided courtesy of South Pacific Pictures Limited, © South Pacific Pictures Limited and ApolloMedia GmbH & Co 5 Filmproduktion KG 2002/© Newmarket/Courtesy The Everett Collection; **255, 256** *top Whale Rider* footage provided courtesy of South Pacific Pictures Limited. © South Pacific Pictures Limited and ApolloMedia GmbH & Co 5 Filmproduktion KG 2002; **256** *bottom* © Digitalvision/PunchStock; **258** AP/Wide World Photos; **259** Courtesy of The Connecticut Women's Hall of Fame; **261** *Harriet Tubman* (1945), William H. Johnson. Oil on paperboard, sheet,

29⅜″ × 23⅜″. Smithsonian American Art Museum, Washington, D.C. © Smithsonian American Art Museum, Washington, D.C./ Art Resource, New York; **262** *Through Forest, Through Rivers, Up Mountains* (1967), Jacob Lawrence. Tempera, gouache and pencil on paper, 15¹¹⁄₁₆″ × 26⅞″. The Joseph H. Hirshhorn Bequest, 1981. Smithsonian Institution, Hirshhorn Museum and Sculpture Garden. Photo by Lee Stalsworth. © 2007 The Jacob and Gwendolyn Lawrence Foundation, Seattle/Artists Rights Society (ARS), New York. Reproduction, including downloading of Lawrence works is prohibited by copyright laws and international conventions without the express written permission of Artists Rights Society (ARS), New York; **264** © GeoNova LLC; **267** *An Underground Railroad* (1967), Jacob Lawrence. Gouache and tempera on paper, 14¼″ × 13″. Collection of Marylin Bender Altschul, New York. © 2007 The Jacob and Gwendolyn Lawrence Foundation, Seattle/Artists Rights Society (ARS), New York. Reproduction, including downloading of Lawrence works is prohibited by copyright laws and international conventions without the express written permission of Artists Rights Society (ARS), New York; **269** *Harriet and the Promised Land No. 15: Canada Bound* (1967), Jacob Lawrence. Gouache and tempera over black colored pencil on very rough cream, 16½″ × 28¼″. The University of Michigan Museum of Art. Gift of Dr. James and Vivian Curtis. (1997/1.531). © 2007 The Jacob and Gwendolyn Lawrence Foundation, Seattle/ Artists Rights Society (ARS), New York. Reproduction, including downloading of Lawrence works is prohibited by copyright laws and international conventions without the express written permission of Artists Rights Society (ARS), New York; **270** *top* © National Archives, Washington, D.C./The Art Archive; *frame* Library of Congress; *signature* © North Wind/North Wind Picture Archives. All rights reserved; **271** © GeoNova LLC; **274** © Grant Faint/Getty Images; **275** © Evans Chan; **277, 279** Library of Congress; **280** © William Manning/Corbis; **282** © Sean Justice/Getty Images; **283** The Granger Collection, New York; **285** Fort Sumter National Monument/National Park Service; **288** © Corbis; **290** © 2003 John Steventon/www. HappyGlyphs.com; **292, 298** © Joseph Sohm; ChromoSohm Inc./Corbis; **299** © Spencer Grant/PhotoEdit; **306** © Siede Preis/ Photodisc/Getty Images.

## UNIT 3

**307** *left, Letter From Home.* Mort Künstler. © 2000 Mort Künstler, Inc.; *right* © David De Lossy/Getty Images; **308** Cover of *Journey to the Center of the Earth* by Jules Verne. Cover illustration by Robin Koni. © 1965, Penguin Books. Reprinted by permission of Puffin Books, a member of Penguin Group (USA) Inc., 345 Hudson Street, New York, NY 10014. All rights reserved; **308–309** © Corbis; **310** *top* © Image Source/Alamy Images; *bottom* © Patrick Pleul/ epa/Corbis; **312** *left* © AL/ShutterStock; *center* © William Gottlieb/ Corbis; *right* © Piotr Przeszlo/ShutterStock; **313** © Elisabeth Perotin/ ShutterStock; **316** © Aflo Foto Agency/Alamy Images; **317** © Bassouls Sophie/Corbis Sygma; **319** *The Musician,* Dale Gallon. Courtesy of Gallon Historical Art, Gettysburg, Pennsylvania; **320** *Letter From Home.* Mort Künstler. © 2000 Mort Künstler, Inc.; **322** © GeoNova LLC; **326** *The Musician,* Dale Gallon. Courtesy of Gallon Historical Art, Gettysburg, Pennsylvania; **327, 328** The Granger Collection, New York; **332** © Neil Beckerman/Getty Images; **333** © Alex Gotfryd/ Corbis; **335** © Bill Brooks/Masterfile; **336** © Ryan McVay/Getty Images; **338** © Photononstop/photolibrary; **343** © Awilli/zefa/

Corbis; **347** © John Stuart/Mira; **350–351** © Jupiter Images; **354** *left* © Douglas Kirkland/Corbis; *top right* The Granger Collection, New York; *bottom right* Mary Evans Picture Library; **358** *bottom* © Sagel & Kranefeld/zefa/Corbis; **359** The Granger Collection, New York; **361** © Adrian Bailey/Getty Images; **362** © John Beatty/ Getty Images; **365** *background* © Skye Chalmers/Getty Images; *center* © Theo Allofs/Getty Images; **369** © Barnaby Hall/Getty Images; **374** *top* © Les Cunliffe/Age Fotostock America, Inc.; *bottom* © Nancy N. Jacobs; **374–375** © Alan R. Moller/Getty Images; **375** *top* Courtesy American Library Association; *bottom* Cover illustration by Michael Steirnagle/Book © McDougal Littell; **376–377** © Joe Baraban/Alamy Images; **378–379** © Joe Sohm/Visions of America, LLC/Alamy Images; **380** © Ralph Lee Hopkins/Getty Images; **381** Photo by Madison Nye; **384** © GeoNova LLC; **391** © Darryl T. Branch/Photo Researchers, Inc.; **392** © Photocuisine Photography/ Veer; **396** © Enigma/Alamy Images; **397** *top* © Underwood & Underwood/Corbis; *bottom* © San Francisco Chronicle; **398** © Bettmann/Corbis; **400** © Corbis; **403** © Bettmann/Corbis; **406** © Photo by Shawn Alladio; **408, 409** © Rick Wilking/ Reuters/Corbis; **416** © Richard H. Johnston/Getty Images; **417** *top* Courtesy Pat Mora; *bottom* Photo by David Burkhalter. Reprinted by permission of the University of Arizona Press; **424, 430** © Daryl Benson/Masterfile; **431** *left foreground* © Michael J. Doolittle/The Image Works, Inc.; *left background* © Bill Brooks/ Masterfile; *top right* © Ecliptic Blue/ShutterStock; *bottom right* © Bill Brooks/Masterfile; **438** © Siede Preis/Photodisc/Getty Images.

## UNIT 4

**439** *left, The Moon and the Abandoned Old Woman* (1891), Yoshitoshi. © Asian Art & Archaeology, Inc./Corbis; *right* © JIStock/Masterfile; **440–441** © Matthias Kulka/zefa/Corbis; **442** *left* © BananaStock/ PunchStock; *center left* © Jennifer Hulshizer/Star Ledger/Corbis; *center right* © Abode/Beateworks/Corbis; *right* © Digital Vision/ PunchStock; **443** © Nikolajs Strigins/ShutterStock; **448** © Atlantide Phototravel/Corbis; **449** © Gene Blevins/Corbis; **450** *top* © Image Source/PunchStock; *bottom* © Photodisc/Getty Images; **451** © ICP/ Alamy Images; **454** © Pat Doyle/Corbis; **455** © Getty Images; **460** © Corbis; **462** © Hermes/Age Fotostock; **463** *top* © Time Life Pictures/Getty Images; *bottom* © June Finfer; **465** *Beggar and a Boy* (1903), Pablo Picasso. Oil on canvas, 125 cm × 92 cm. Pushkin Museum, Moscow. © Bridgeman Art Library. © 2007 Estate of Pablo Picasso/Artists Rights Society (ARS), New York. Reproduction, including downloading of Picasso works is prohibited by copyright laws and international conventions without the express written permission of Artists Rights Society (ARS), New York; **468** © GeoNova LLC; **476** Photograph by Sharon Hoogstraten; **477** *top* © Courtesy of the author; *bottom* © Michael Glaser; **479** *American Childhood* (1995), Jan Burch Cochran. Fabric, beads, buttons, paint, baby dress, gloves. Machine pieced, hand appliquéd using beads, hand embellished. 53″ × 42″. Collection of Pam Monfort; **482** Photo by Sharon Hoogstraten; *top left* © Getty Images; *bottom left* © Regin Igloria; *bottom right* © Getty Images; **484** © Getty Images; **485** AP/Wide World Photos; **487, 489, 494, 501, 505, 511, 514** © Joan Marcus; **520** © Getty Images; **523, 527, 533** © Joan Marcus; **541** *The Diary of Anne Frank* (2006), Oregon Shakespeare Festival. Tony De Bruno as Otto Frank. Photo © David Cooper Photography; **544** © Joan Marcus; **545, 546, 547** © Getty Images; **548** *left* Courtesy of Harry Goldsmith (Estate). © United States Holocaust Memorial Museum. The views and opinions expressed in the book and the context in which the images are used do not necessarily reflect the views or policy of, nor imply approval or endorsement by, the United States Holocaust Memorial Museum; *right* Courtesy of Hannah Kastan Weiss. © United States Holocaust Memorial Museum. The views and opinions expressed in the book and the context in which the images are used do not necessarily reflect the views or policy of, nor imply approval or endorsement by, the United States Holocaust Memorial Museum; **549** The Granger Collection, New York; **551** Courtesy of Madalae Fraser. © United States Holocaust Memorial Museum. The views and opinions expressed in the book and the context in which the images are used do not necessarily reflect the views or policy of, nor imply approval or endorsement by, the United States Holocaust Memorial Museum; **554** © Getty Images; **555** *top* Scene from *Anne Frank Remembered* appears courtesy of Sony Pictures Classics, Inc.; *center right, center left* © The Everett Collection; *bottom* © Anne Frank Stichting/Allard Bovenberg/2003 Getty Images; **556** © Getty Images; **557** *top left* © Kayte M. Deioma/PhotoEdit; *top center* © Myrleen Ferguson Cate/PhotoEdit; *top right* AP/Wide World Photos; **557** *bottom left* © Michael Newman/PhotoEdit; *bottom center* © Frank Siteman/ PhotoEdit; *bottom right* © Michael Newman/PhotoEdit; **558, 564** © Richard Sisk/Jupiter Images; **565** © James Woodson/Getty Images; **572** © Siede Preis/Photodisc/Getty Images.

## UNIT 5

**573** *left, La Promenade en Mer* (1988), Jean Plichart. Copper engraving. © SuperStock; *right* © Ted Mead/Getty Images; **574–575** © Photograph by Bac To Trong; **576** *foreground* © Corbis; *background* © Getty Images; **577** © Image Club Graphics; **578** © Getty Images; **579** © Laurie Barr/ShutterStock; **580** *top left* © Corbis; *bottom left* © Merryl McNaughton/ShutterStock; *right* © Robert Blomkvist/ ShutterStock; **581** *top* © Piotr Przeszlo/ShutterStock; *bottom* © Karin Lau/ShutterStock; **582** Designed by Lisa Brennan; **583** *top* © The Schlesinger Library, Radcliffe Institute, Harvard University; *bottom* © Christopher Felver/Corbis; **588** © Masterfile; **589** *top* © Bettmann/ Corbis; *bottom* © Bettmann/Corbis; **591** © G. K. Hart/Vikki Hart/ Getty Images; **593** © SuperStock; **596** © Big Cheese Photo LLC/ Alamy Images; **597** *top* © Getty Images; *bottom* Photograph by Norberto E. Martinez/University of Texas at Brownsville and Texas Southmost College; **599** © PIER/Getty Images; **602** © David Scharf/Science Photo Library/Photo Researchers, Inc.; **604** © Lori Adamski Peek/Getty Images; **605** *top* The Granger Collection, New York; *bottom* © Getty Images; **607** © Paul Edmondson/Getty Images; **609** © Ted Mead/Getty Images; **612** Designed by Lisa Brennan; **613** *top* © Nancy E. Crampton; *bottom* © Corbis; **618** © Just One Productions/Photofest; **619** *top* The Granger Collection, New York; *bottom, Alexander Pope* (1740), William Hoare. The Granger Collection, New York; **621** © Corbis; **624** © Mango Productions/Corbis; **625** *top* © Getty Images; *bottom* © Peter Morenus; **627** *Aspiration* (1936), Aaron Douglas. Oil on canvas, 60″ × 60″. © Fine Arts Museums of San Francisco purchase, the estate of Thurlow E. Tibbs, Jr., the Museum Society Auxiliary, American Art Trust Fund, Unrestricted Art Trust Fund, partial gift of Dr. Ernest A. Bates, Sharon Bell, Jo-Ann Beverly, Barbara Carleton, Dr. and Mrs. Arthur H. Coleman, Dr. and Mrs. Coyness Ennix, Jr., Nicole Y. Ennix, Mr. and Mrs. Gary Francois, Dennis L. Franklin, Mr. and Mrs. Maxwell C.

Gillette, Mr. and Mrs. Richard Goodyear, Zuretti L. Goosby, Marion E. Greene, Mrs. Vivian S. W. Hambrick, Laurie Gibbs Harris, Arlene Hollis, Louis A. and Letha Jeanpierre, Daniel and Jackie Johnson, Jr., Stephen L. Johnson, Mr. and Mrs. Arthur Lathan, Lewis and Ribbs Mortuary Garden Chapel, Mr. and Mrs. Gary Love, Glenn R. Nance, Mr. and Mrs. Harry S. Parker III, Mr. and Mrs. Carr T. Preston, Fannie Preston, Pamela R. Ransom, Dr. and Mrs. Benjamin F. Reed, San Francisco Black Chamber of Commerce, San Francisco Chapter of Links, Inc., San Francisco Chapter of the N.A.A.C.P., Sigma Pi Phi Fraternity, Dr. Ella Mae Simmons, Mr. Calvin R. Swinson, Joseph B. Williams, Mr. and Mrs. Alfred S. Wilsey, and the people of the Bay Area, 1997.84; **629** Facial Reconstruction of Fortune by Frank Bender. © Mattatuck Museum Arts and History Center, Waterbury, Connecticut; **632** *Fortune* (2001), William B. Westwood. © William B. Westwood; **633** Facial Reconstruction of Fortune by Frank Bender. © Mattatuck Museum Arts and History Center, Waterbury, Connecticutt.; **636** © Paul Panayiotou/Alamy Images; **637** *top* © Getty Images; *bottom* © Stock Montage; **648, 654** © Daryl Benson/Masterfile; **655** © Larry Williams/Corbis; **662** © Siede Preis/ Photodisc/Getty Images.

## UNIT 6

**663** *right, The Promenade, Fifth Avenue* (1986), Bill Jacklin. Oil on canvas, 243.6 cm × 182.7 cm. Private collection. © Bill Jacklin/ Bridgeman Art Library; *left* © Sherman Hines/Masterfile; **664** *top left* © Pierre Vauthey/Corbis Sygma; *top center left* © The Everett Collection; *top center* © Universal TV/The Kobal Collection; *top right* © Charles Sykes/Rex Features/Courtesy The Everett Collection; *bottom far left* © The Everett Collection; *2nd bottom left* © John Rogers/Getty Images; *bottom center* © John Springer Collection/ Corbis; *bottom center right* © The Everett Collection; *bottom right* © Roger Ressmeyer/Corbis; **665** © Bettmann/Corbis; **666** *top* © Robert Kyllo/ShutterStock; *center* © Zina Seletskaya/ShutterStock; *bottom* © ANP/ShutterStock; **668** *top left* © Jerry Bauer; *bottom left* Photo Siang Chitsa-Ard/Courtesy William Sleator; *background* © Albo/ShutterStock; **669** © Paul Maguire/ShutterStock; **670** © Aga & Miko Materne (arsat)/ShutterStock; **672** © Chad Baker/Ryan McVay/Getty Images; **673** © Getty Images; **676** © GeoNova LLC; **682** © Eyebyte/Alamy Images; **683** © The New York Public Library; **686** © T. Papageorgiou/Age Fotostock America, Inc.; **694** *Spring* (1894), Lawrence Alma-Tadema. Oil on canvas, 70 1/4″ x 31 1/2″. The J. Paul Getty Museum, Los Angeles. (72.PA.3). © J. Paul Getty Trust; **695** *top* The New York Times Company; *bottom, Let's Make a Deal,* Host Monty Hall, 1963–1976. © The Everett Collection; **696** The New York Times Company; **698** *top* © Les Cunliffe/Age Fotostock America, Inc.; *bottom* Reed Saxon/AP/Wide World Photos; **698–699** © Reuters/Corbis; **699** *top* Courtesy American Library Association; *bottom* Cover of *Kira-Kira* by Cynthia Kadohata. © 2004 by Cynthia Kadohata. Cover photo © Julia Kuskin. Reprinted by permission of Atheneum Books for Young Readers, an imprint of Simon and Schuster Children's Publishing Division, New York; **700–701** © Bryan Mullennix/Getty Images; **702–703** © Ken Ross/Getty Images; **705** Library of Congress; **707** The Granger Collection, New York; **709** Library of Congress; **711** The Granger Collection, New York; **715** © Michael Newman/PhotoEdit; **716** © Chuck Pefley/Alamy Images; **717** © Hugh Hamrick; **720** © Christopher Stevenson/Getty Images; **723** Photograph by Sharon

Hoogstraten; **728** © Kevin Fleming/Corbis; **729** National Archives; **734** © American Solar Challenge/Getty Images; **735** *top* The Granger Collection, New York; *bottom* Courtesy of Fernando R. Montemayor; **739** *Californians Catching Wild Horses with Riata* (about 1851), Hugo Wilhelm Arthur Nahl. Oil on canvas mounted on masonite. Courtesy of the Oakland Museum of California Kahn Collection (A65.57) © Laurie Platt Winfrey/OaklandMuseum/The Art Archive; **742**, **748** © J. David Andrews/Masterfile; **749** © Taxi/Getty Images; **756** © Siede Preis/Photodisc/Getty Images.

## UNIT 7

**757** *left, Los Comaradas del Barrio* (1976), Jesse Treviño. Acrylic on canvas, 36″ × 48″. Collection of the artist; *right* © Ric Ergenbright/Corbis; **758** © PunchStock; **760** *left* © Getty Images; *right* © Margaretta Mitchell; *bottom* © Photodisc; **761** *top foreground* © Getty Images; *top background* © Artbeats; *bottom* Photo by Bill Eichner; **762** © Bettmann/Corbis; **763** © Hulton-Deutsch Collection/Corbis; **764** *top* Photo by Christine Lee Zilka; *center* © Ryan McVay/Getty Images; *bottom* © Corbis; **765** © Ryan McVay/Getty Images; **766** © Ariel Skelley/Corbis; **767** Courtesy Joseph Bruchac/Michael Greenlar; **771** © Betsy Cullen/Getty Images; **776** *backgound* © Skye Chalmers/Getty Images; *foreground* © Georgette Douwma/Photo Researchers, Inc.; **782** © Richard Wahlstrom/Getty Images; **783** © Colin Izod; **785** © Richard I'Anson/Lonely Planet Images; **786** Marriage necklace or Thali (1800). India (Madras). Golden pendants on black thread. (CT17149). Victoria & Albert Museum, London. © Victoria & Albert Museum, London/Art Resource, New York; **787** © Per-Anders Pettersson/Getty Images; **788** © GeoNova LLC; **793** © Robert Harding Picture Library Ltd/Alamy Images; **795** © Steve McCurry/Magnum Photos; **797** © Gideon Mendel/Corbis; **800** © Will & Deni McIntyre/Corbis; **801** © Paul Coughlin; **803**, **807** Illustration by Michael McCurdy. © 1991 by Michael McCurdy, from *American Tall Tales* by Mary Pope Osborne. Used by permission of Alfred A. Knopf, an imprint of Random House Children's Books, a division of Random House, Inc.; **810** *top* © Les Cunliffe/Age Fotostock America, Inc.; *bottom* © Bettmann/Corbis; **810–811** © Adalberto Rios Lanz/Sexto Sol/Getty Images; **811** *top* AP/Wide World Photos; *bottom* From *The Pearl* by John Steinbeck. © 2003. Reprinted with permission of Gale, a division of Thomson Learning. www.thomsonrights.com; **812–813** © Dania Delimont/Alamy Images; **814–815** © Kenny Johnson/Getty Images; **816** © Mike Powell/Getty Images; **817** Photo © Gary Soto. Courtesy of Gary Soto; **826** © Creatas/Superstock; **830** © Getty Images; **831** © Paul Mounce/Corbis; **833** © Punahou School, Hawaii; **834** © GeoNova LLC; **837** © Ric Ergenbright/Corbis; **840** © Veer; *inset right* © CBS/Photofest; **843** © Corbis; **846** © Punahou School, Hawaii; **847** © Rick Wilking/Reuters/Corbis; **850** © 2006 Larry Wright. *The Detroit News*. All rights reserved. Courtesy of Cagle Cartoons, Inc.; **852** *left* The Granger Collection, New York; *bottom* © Corbis; **853** © Jupiter Images Corporation; **854** © Paul Carstairs/Alamy Images; **855** © Tom Roster Photographer; **856** Illustration by Jerome Lagarrrigue, from *Going North* by Janice N. Harrington. Pictures © 2005 by Jerome Lagarigue. Reprinted by permission of Farrar, Straus and Giroux; **857** From *Freedom on the Menu: The Greensboro Sit-ins* by Carole Boston Weatherford. Illustrated by Jerome La Garrigue. Painting © 2005 by Jerome La Garrigue. Used by permission of Dial Books for Young Readers, a division of Penguin Young Readers Group, a member of Penguin Group (USA) Inc., 345 Hudson Street, New York, NY 10014. All rights reserved; **859** © Jack Moebes/Corbis; **860**, **866** © Jason Ernst/Age Fotostock America, Inc.; **867** © Jeff Greenberg/Age Fotostock; **874**© Siede Preis/Photodisc/Getty Images.

## UNIT 8

**875** *left* © Carsten Peter/National Geographic Image Collection; *right* © Columbia/Marvel/The Kobal Collection; **876** *left* Jacket of *1000 Great Rail-Trails, A Comprehensive Directory*. Cover photos: background @ Mark Windom/Index Stock Imagery and PhotoDisc, Inc.; inset photos © PhotoDisc, Inc. Reprinted by permission of The Globe Pequot Press, Guilford, Connecticut; *center* © Tom Schierlitz/Getty Images; *bottom center left* © Jules Frazier/Getty Images; *right* © Corbis; **878** *top left* © Artville; *top right* © Stockfood Creative/Getty Images; *bottom* © Foodpix/Jupiter Images; **879** © Denis Scott/Corbis; **880** © Sanford/Agliolo/Corbis; **881** *top* © Yonhap; *bottom* © Steve Kaufman/Corbis; **883** *top* © Bettmann/Corbis; *bottom* © Blake Little/Getty Images; **884** © LWA-Dann Tardif/Corbis; **885** Courtesy of the author; **887** AP/Wide World Photos; *inset right* © Columbia/Marvel/The Kobal Collection; **890** © Peter J. Bryant/Biological Photo Service. All rights reserved; **894** © Corbis; **895**, **896–897** © Carsten Peter/National Geographic Image Collection; **898** *top* © GeoNova LLC; *bottom left* Seated man. Victim of the eruption of Mount Vesuvius. Palestra Grande, Pompeii, Italy. © Scala/Art Resource, New York; *bottom center* © Corbis; *bottom right* © Layne Kennedy/Corbis; **899** © Carsten Peter/National Geographic Image Collection; **900** *top* Illustration by Richard Bonson/Wildlife Art Ltd.; **900–901**, **901** © Carsten Peter/National Geographic Image Collection; **904** NASA Kennedy Space Center (NASA-KSC); **905** *left* © Jim Ruymen/Reuters/Corbis, *CBS Evening News* : NASA Scientists succeed in colliding with a comet with Deep Impact spacecraft-Courtesy CBS News Archives; *right: top left* NASA/JPL/University of Maryland/AP/Wide World Photos; *top center left, top center right; top right* NASA Jet Propulsion Laboratory; *bottom left* NASA/AP/Wide World Photos; *bottom center, bottom right* NASA Jet Propulsion Laboratory; **906** *top left* AP/Wide World Photos; *bottom left, background* © NASA/JPL/epa/Corbis; **908** © Hugh Sitton/zefa/Corbis; **909** © Alice Handwerk; **911** © Mark Christmas/National Geographic Image Collection; **912** Courtesy Henrietta Yurchenco; **915** Photo by Joaquin A. Huerta A./Courtesy Henrietta Yurchenco; **918** © Taili Song Roth/Corbis; **919** Courtesy Jan McGirk; **920** © Robert Nickelsberg/Getty Images; **922** © GeoNova LLC; **924** © Robert Nickelsberg/Getty Images; **925** © Mark Richards/ZUMA/Corbis; **928** © Adam Gault/Getty Images; **929** © Tony Cenicola/*The New York Times*; **930**, **932** Courtesy of Hanger Prosthetics & Orthotics, Inc. www.hanger.com; **933** © Dith Pran/*New York Times*/Redux; **934** *left* © Science VU/Visuals Unlimited; *right* PBS ® and the PBS logo are registered trademarks of the Public Broadcasting Service and are used with permission. All rights reserved; **935** © Science Source/Photo Researchers, Inc.; **938** *top* © Les Cunliffe/Age Fotostock America, Inc.; *bottom* © Arthur Cohen; **938–939** The Granger Collection, New York; **939** *top* Courtesy American Library Association; *bottom* Cover of *An American Plague: The True and Terrifying Story of the Yellow Fever Epidemic of 1793* by Jim Murphy. Copyright © 2003 by Jim Murphy. Reprinted by permission of Clarion Books, an imprint of Houghton Mifflin Company; **940–941, 942–943** The Granger Collection, New York; **944, 950** © Alain Choisnet/Getty Images; **951** © Michael Newman/PhotoEdit; **953** *top* © Harpe/Peter Arnold, Inc.; *bottom* © Jeffrey L. Rotman/Corbis; **958** © Siede Preis/Photodisc/Getty Images.

## UNIT 9

**959** *left* © Peter Finger/Corbis; *right* © Getty Images; **960–961** © Louie Psihoyos/Corbis; **962** © Ronnie Kaufman/Corbis; **963** *top* © C. Fleurent/photocuisine/Corbis; *bottom* © Artville; **965** © Ken Kaminesky/Take 2 Productions/Corbis; **967** © David Woods/Corbis; **968** © Steve Bloom/Getty Images; **969** *top* Courtesy Rob Laidlaw; *bottom* © The Wildlife Society, Bethesda, Maryland; **970** © Getty Images; **974** Reprinted courtesy of the *Boston Globe* via Copyright Clearance Center; **975** © ALI BURAFI/AFP/Getty Images; **980** *top* © Getty Images; *bottom* Francois Mori/AP/Wide World Photos; **981** *top, bottom,* **982** *left* Footage courtesy of Lucasfilm Ltd. *Star Wars: Episode III-Revenge of the Sith* © 2005 Lucasfilm Ltd. & TM. All rights reserved. Used under authorization. Unauthorized duplication is a violation of applicable law; *background* © Getty Images; **983** *center* © Stockbyte; *right* © Getty Images; **984** © Todd Gipstein/Corbis; **985** © Sports Illustrated; **986** Courtesy of the National Association for Sport and Physical Eduction; **987** © Chris Clinton/Getty Images; **988** © Sports Illustrated; **989** © Peter Finger/Corbis; **994** © 2004 Twentieth Century Fox/Photofest; **995** Courtesy of Darhansoff, Verrill, and Feldman Agency; **996** The New York Times Company; **997** © Lynda Barry; **1002** © Corbis; **1003** © GeoNova LLC; **1005** © Steve Bly/Alamy Images; **1007** © Saulius T. Kondrotas/Alamy Images; **1008** The Granger Collection, New York; **1010** *top* Courtesy of the American Red Cross; *bottom* AP/Wide World Photos; **1011** © National Portrait Gallery, London; **1013** © Renaissance Films/BBC/Curzon Films/The Kobal Collection; **1014** © Royal Armouries Museum, Leeds, United Kingdom; **1016, 1022** © Sam Barricklow/Jupiterimages Corporation; **1023** © Dirk Anschutz/Getty Images; **1030** © Siede Preis/Photodisc/Getty Images.

## UNIT 10 RESEARCH

**1031** *left* © Getty Images; *right collage, top* © Gary Walts/Syracuse Newspapers/The Image Works, Inc.; *center* © Gregor Schuster/Iconica/Getty Images; *bottom left* © Syracuse Newspapers/The Image Works, Inc.; *bottom right* Marcio Jose Sanchez/AP/Wide World Photos; **1032–1033** © Robin Sachs/PhotoEdit; **1034** *foreground* © CSAImages.com; *background* © Laurent Hamels/Age Fotostock America, Inc.; **1038** © Google; **1039** Courtesy of the Smithsonian National Museum of American History, Lemuelson Center; *inset* Lemulson Center/Smithsonian Website; Smithsonian Institution, www. SmithsonianInstitution.org; **1043** © Garry Gay/Getty Images; **1046** *inset-spurs* © Bob Brown/*Richmond Times-Dispatch*/AP/Wide World Photos; **1047** *left* Marcio Jose Sanchez/AP/Wide World Photos; *right* © Rubberball Productions; **1048, 1051** © Punchstock/Royalty Free; **1052, 1066** © Walter Bibikow/Jupiter Images; **1067** © David Kennedy/AgeFotostock.

## STUDENT RESOURCE BANK

**R03** © Ben Mangor/SuperStock Inc.; **R05** *Bar graph* © Sense Interactive Multimedia/Royalty Free; **R06** *top* © Illustration by Gary Hincks; *bottom* Cross-section of a Roman road. Illustration by Peter Bull; **R07** © GeoNova LLC; **R14** *top* © 1998 The Washington Times LLC; *bottom* © Bill Ballenberg; **R15** *top* © 2004 Doak Heyser; *bottom* © Pam Gardner; Frank Lane Picture Agency/Corbis; **R19** © Carsten Peter/National Geographic Image Collection; **R87** *left* © Corbis; *right* © Comstock; **R94** © Sony Pictures/Courtesy Everett Collection.

## BACK COVER © Image 100/PunchStock.

# GRADE EIGHT

*During the eighth-grade year, students begin to look forward to high school. Grade 8 standards get students ready for the challenges and transition to come. Students begin to study the history and the development of English vocabulary. They continue to read a variety of grade-level-appropriate classic and contemporary literature, nonfiction, poetry, and plays, and they begin to compare and contrast the different types of writing as well as different perspectives on similar topics or themes. They evaluate the logic of informational texts and analyze how literature reflects the backgrounds, attitudes, and beliefs of the authors. They not only write or deliver research reports but also conduct their own research. They use the conventions of Standard English correctly. They deliver a variety of types of presentations and effectively respond to questions and concerns from the audience.*

## Standard 1
## READING: Word Recognition, Fluency, and Vocabulary Development

*Students use their knowledge of word parts and word relationships, as well as context (the meaning of the text around a word), to determine the meaning of specialized vocabulary and to understand the precise meaning of grade-level-appropriate words.*

*Vocabulary and Concept Development*

8.1.1    Analyze idioms and comparisons — such as analogies, metaphors, and similes — to infer the literal and figurative meanings of phrases.
- Idioms: expressions that cannot be understood just by knowing the meanings of the words in the expression, such as *to be an old hand at something* or *to get one's feet wet*
- Analogies: comparisons of the similar aspects of two different things
- Metaphors: implied comparisons, such as *The stars were brilliant diamonds in the night sky.*
- Similes: comparisons that use *like* or *as*, such as *The stars were like a million diamonds in the sky.*

8.1.2    Understand the influence of historical events on English word meaning and vocabulary expansion.
Example: Recognize how the early influences of Spanish explorers in North America expanded American English vocabulary, adding words such as *tornado, tomato,* and *patio.*

8.1.3    Verify the meaning of a word in its context, even when its meaning is not directly stated, through the use of definition, restatement, example, comparison, or contrast.
Example: Understand the meaning of *pickle* in a sentence, such as *The pickle was an important part of metal working.* Use a dictionary to help clarify the use of the word *pickle* in this context.

## Standard 2
## READING: Comprehension and Analysis of Nonfiction and Informational Text

*Students read and understand grade-level-appropriate material. The selections in the* **Indiana Reading List** *(www.doe.state.in.us/standards/readinglist.html) illustrate the quality and complexity of the materials to be read by students. At Grade 8, in addition to regular classroom reading, students read a variety of nonfiction, such as biographies, autobiographies, books in many different subject areas, magazines, newspapers, reference and technical materials, and online information.*

*Structural Features of Informational and Technical Materials*

8.2.1    Compare and contrast the features and elements of consumer materials to gain meaning from documents.
Example: Compare examples of a variety of instructional or technical manuals, such as those for a computer, hair appliance, camera, or electronic game, brought to class by different students. Describe what features make certain instructions easier than others to understand and follow.

8.2.2    Analyze text that uses proposition (statement of argument) and support patterns.
Example: Read and analyze the organization of the "pro" and the "con" editorials on a topic of interest in *USA Today*. In each, decide if the argument is simply and clearly stated. Decide if there are at least three major points in support of the argument, with the strongest argument given first.

8.2.7    Analyze the structure, format, and purpose of informational materials (such as textbooks, newspapers, instructional or technical manuals, and public documents).

*Analysis of Grade-Level-Appropriate Nonfiction and Informational Text*

8.2.3    Find similarities and differences between texts in the treatment, amount of coverage, or organization of ideas.
         Example: Read articles or biographies about cultural or historical figures with Indiana connections such as Supreme Court
         Justice Sherman Minton or leaders in the Underground Railroad movement Levi and Catharine Coffin. Compare the amount
         of or types of coverage such figures received.

8.2.4    Compare the original text to a summary to determine whether the summary accurately describes the main ideas, includes
         important details, and conveys the underlying meaning.
         Example: After writing summaries or creating graphic organizers on an informational text read for class, exchange the
         summary or organizer with another student. Evaluate this classmate's summary, based on how well the student describes the
         most important elements of the text.

8.2.5    Use information from a variety of consumer and public documents to explain a situation or decision and to solve a problem.
         Example: Decide which is the most practical and economical wireless telephone to purchase by reading articles, brochures,
         Web pages, and other consumer sources, such as *Consumer Reports*.

8.2.8    Understand and explain the use of simple equipment by following directions in a technical manual.

8.2.9    Make reasonable statements and draw conclusions about a text, supporting them with accurate examples.

*Expository (Informational) Critique*

8.2.6    Evaluate the logic (inductive or deductive argument), internal consistency, and structural patterns of text.
         Example: Read *The Brooklyn Bridge: They Said It Couldn't Be Built* by Judith St. George and evaluate the techniques and the
         effectiveness of the development of the main idea of the book.

# Standard 3
# READING: Comprehension and Analysis of Literary Text

*Students read and respond to grade-level-appropriate historically or culturally significant works of literature, such as the
selections in the* **Indiana Reading List** *(www.doe.state.in.us/standards/readinglist.html), which illustrate the quality and
complexity of the materials to be read by students. At Grade 8, students read a wide variety of fiction, such as classic
and contemporary literature, historical fiction, fantasy, science fiction, mysteries, adventures, folklore, mythology,
poetry, short stories, dramas, and other genres.*

*Structural Features of Literature*

8.3.1    Determine and articulate the relationship between the purposes and characteristics of different forms of poetry (including
         ballads, lyrics, couplets, epics, elegies, odes, and sonnets).
         • Ballad: a poem that tells a story
         • Lyric: words set to music
         • Couplet: two successive lines of verse that rhyme
         • Epic: a long poem that describes heroic deeds or adventures
         • Elegy: a mournful poem for the dead
         • Ode: a poem of praise
         • Sonnet: a rhymed poem of 14 lines
         Example: Describe the different forms of poetry. Compare poems such as John Ciardi's "Elegy for Jog," Pablo Neruda's "Odes
         to Common Things," and Edgar Allan Poe's sonnet "To Science."

*Analysis of Grade-Level-Appropriate Literary Text*

8.3.2    Evaluate the structural elements of the plot, such as subplots, parallel episodes, and climax; the plot's development; and the
         way in which conflicts are (or are not) addressed and resolved.
         Example: Read a book, such as *Holes* by Louis Sachar, and discuss how the plot is developed, including the climax and its
         resolution and how different subplots are incorporated into the story.

8.3.3    Compare and contrast the motivations and reactions of literary characters from different historical eras confronting either
         similar situations and conflicts or similar hypothetical situations.
         Example: Compare literary works that deal with the theme of the impact of war, both on those who fight in the battles and
         those who remain at home. Works could include Walt Whitman's poem "Drum-Taps" from the Civil War period, John Hersey's
         novel *A Bell for Adano* from World War II, or Graham Greene's novel *The Quiet American*, set in Vietnam at the beginning of
         the Vietnam conflict.

8.3.4    Analyze the importance of the setting to the mood, tone, and meaning of the text.

Example: Discuss the importance of the setting, including the place, the time period, and the customs, to books, such as *Friendly Persuasion* by Jessamyn West or *Stranded* by Ben Mikaelsen.

8.3.5 Identify and analyze recurring themes (such as good versus evil) that appear frequently across traditional and contemporary works.

Example: Explore the theme that heroism demands unusual courage and risk-taking. Read classic myths found in Alice Low's *The MacMillan Book of Greek Gods and Myths* or dramatic literature such as Rod Serling's television play *Requiem for a Heavyweight* to identify what both real and imaginary heroes have done.

8.3.6 Identify significant literary devices, such as metaphor, symbolism, dialect or quotations, and irony, which define a writer's style and use those elements to interpret the work.

- Metaphor: an implied comparison in which a word or phrase is used in place of another, such as *He was drowning in money*.
- Symbolism: the use of an object to represent something else; for example, a dove might symbolize peace.
- Dialect: the vocabulary, grammar, and pronunciation used by people in different regions.
- Irony: the use of words to express the opposite of the literal meaning of the words, often to be humorous.

Example: Read several short stories by Mark Twain and discuss his use of dialect in his stories. Watch Alan Jay Lerner and Frederick Loewe's musical *My Fair Lady*, an adaptation of Bernard Shaw's *Pygmalion*, and discuss how the musical presents dialect and how this dialect is important to the conflict in the story.

8.3.8 Contrast points of view — such as first person, third person, third person limited and third person omniscient, and subjective and objective — in narrative text and explain how they affect the overall theme of the work.

- First person: the narrator tells the story from the "I" perspective.
- Third person: the narrator tells the story from an outside perspective.
- Limited narration: the narrator does not know all thoughts of all characters.
- Omniscient narration: the narrator knows all thoughts of all characters.
- Subjective: the point of view involves a personal perspective.
- Objective: the point of view is from a distanced, informational perspective, as in a news report.

8.3.9 Analyze the relevance of setting (places, times, customs) to mood, tone, and meaning of text.

*Literary Criticism*

8.3.7 Analyze a work of literature, showing how it reflects the heritage, traditions, attitudes, and beliefs of its author.

Example: Read books by Charles Major such as *The Bears of Blue River or Uncle Tom Andy Bill* to analyze how he incorporates his understanding of frontier Indiana attitudes.

## Standard 4
## WRITING: Processes and Features

*Students discuss, list, and graphically organize writing ideas. They write clear, coherent, and focused essays. Students progress through the stages of the writing process and proofread, edit, and revise writing.*

*Organization and Focus*

8.4.1 Discuss ideas for writing, keep a list or notebook of ideas, and use graphic organizers to plan writing.

8.4.2 Create compositions that have a clear message, a coherent thesis (a statement of position on the topic), and end with a clear and well-supported conclusion.

8.4.3 Support theses or conclusions with analogies (comparisons), paraphrases, quotations, opinions from experts, and similar devices.

8.4.10 Create an organizational structure that balances all aspects of the composition and uses effective transitions between sentences to unify important ideas.

*Research Process and Technology*

8.4.4 Plan and conduct multiple-step information searches using computer networks.

8.4.5 Achieve an effective balance between researched information and original ideas.

8.4.6 Use a computer to create documents by using word-processing skills and publishing programs; develop simple databases and spreadsheets to manage information and prepare reports.

*Evaluation and Revision*

8.4.7 Review, evaluate, and revise writing for meaning and clarity.

8.4.11 Identify topics; ask and evaluate questions; and develop ideas leading to inquiry, investigation, and research.

8.4.8    Edit and proofread one's own writing, as well as that of others, using an editing checklist or set of rules, with specific examples of corrections of frequent errors.

8.4.9    Revise writing for word choice; appropriate organization; consistent point of view; and transitions among paragraphs, passages, and ideas.

## Standard 5
## WRITING: Applications
## (Different Types of Writing and Their Characteristics)

*At Grade 8, students continue to write narrative, expository (informational), persuasive, and descriptive essays (research reports of 700 to 1,000 words or more). Students are introduced to writing technical documents. Student writing demonstrates a command of Standard English and the research, organizational, and drafting strategies outlined in Standard 4 — Writing Processes and Features. Writing demonstrates an awareness of the audience (intended reader) and purpose for writing.*

*In addition to producing the different writing forms introduced in earlier grades, such as letters, Grade 8 students use the writing strategies outlined in Standard 4 — Writing Processes and Features to:*

8.5.1    Write biographies, autobiographies, and short stories that:
• tell about an incident, event, or situation, using well-chosen details.
• reveal the significance of, or the writer's attitude about, the subject.
• use narrative and descriptive strategies, including relevant dialogue, specific action, physical description, background description, and comparison or contrast of characters.
Example: Write an autobiographical account of one of your most memorable first days of school. Describe the day and its importance clearly enough so the reader can see and feel the day from your perspective.

8.5.2    Write responses to literature that:
• demonstrate careful reading and insight into interpretations.
• connect response to the writer's techniques and to specific textual references.
• make supported inferences about the effects of a literary work on its audience.
• support statements with evidence from the text.
Example: After reading *The Giver* by Lois Lowry, write a final chapter to the book, describing what happens to the main character after the point where Lowry ends the book. Then, plan a class presentation explaining the new ending and how it is supported by the rest of the book.

8.5.4    Write persuasive compositions that:
• include a well-defined thesis that makes a clear and knowledgeable appeal.
• present detailed evidence, examples, and reasoning to support effective arguments and emotional appeals.
• provide details, reasons, and examples, arranging them effectively by anticipating and answering reader concerns and counterarguments.
Example: Using the research completed on public transportation, write a persuasive letter to the mayor on why the community should or should not invest more resources into public transportation.

8.5.5    Write technical documents that:
• identify the sequence of activities needed to design a system, operate a tool, or explain the bylaws of an organization's constitution or guidelines.
• include all the factors and variables that need to be considered.
• use formatting techniques, including headings and changing the fonts (typeface) to aid comprehension.
Example: Write a report of a science experiment that was conducted in class, describing both the process and the scientific conclusions. Describe the steps clearly, using precise scientific vocabulary, so that another reader could follow exactly what the experiment involved and could understand the reasoning behind the conclusion. Add graphics and text design to make the content clearer and easier to follow.

8.5.6    Write using precise word choices to make writing interesting and exact.
Example: Write stories, reports, articles, and letters using a variety of word choices. (Use *adequately* instead of *enough*. Use *encyclopedia* or *mystery novel* instead of *book*.)

8.5.7    Write for different purposes and to a specific audience or person, adjusting tone and style as necessary.
Example: Write a letter to the editor in response to an opinion column in your school or community newspaper.

*Research Application*

8.5.3    Write or deliver a research report that has been developed using a systematic research process (defines the topic, gathers information, determines credibility, reports findings) and that:
   •uses information from a variety of sources (books, technology, multimedia) and documents sources independently by using a consistent format for citations.
   • demonstrates that information that has been gathered has been summarized and that the topic has been refined through this process.
   • demonstrates that sources have been evaluated for accuracy, bias, and credibility.
   • organizes information by categorizing and sequencing, and demonstrates the distinction between one's own ideas from the ideas of others, and includes a bibliography (Works Cited).
   Example: Research the topic of the benefits and drawbacks of public transportation. Conduct research to learn why some experts argue that we should use more public transportation. Survey parents and friends to find out how often they use public transportation for school, business, or pleasure travel. Summarize the findings and write a report on the pros and cons of public transportation.

# Standard 6
# WRITING: English Language Conventions
*Students write using Standard English conventions appropriate to this grade level.*

*Sentence Structure*

8.6.1    Use correct and varied sentence types (simple, compound, complex, and compound-complex) and sentence openings to present a lively and effective personal style.
8.6.2    Identify and use parallelism (use consistent elements of grammar when compiling a list) in all writing to present items in a series and items juxtaposed for emphasis.
   • Correct: *Students having difficulty and needing help should stay after class.*
   • Incorrect: *Students having difficulty and who need help should stay after class.*
8.6.3    Use subordination, coordination, noun phrases that function as adjectives (*These gestures — acts of friendship — were noticed but not appreciated.*), and other devices to indicate clearly the relationship between ideas.

*Grammar*

8.6.4    Edit written manuscripts to ensure that correct grammar is used.
8.6.8    Identify and use infinitives (the word *to* followed by the base form of a verb, such as *to understand* or *to learn*) and participles (made by adding *-ing, -d, -ed, -n, -en,* or *-t* to the base form of the verb, such as *dreaming, chosen, built,* and *grown*).

*Punctuation*

8.6.5    Use correct punctuation.

*Capitalization*

8.6.6    Use correct capitalization.

*Spelling*

8.6.7    Use correct spelling conventions.

# Standard 7
# LISTENING AND SPEAKING:
# Skills, Strategies, and Applications
*Students deliver focused, coherent presentations that convey ideas clearly and relate to the background and interests of the audience. They evaluate the content of oral communication. Students deliver well-organized formal presentations using traditional speech strategies, including narration, exposition, persuasion, and description. Students use the same Standard English conventions for oral speech that they use in their writing.*

*Comprehension*

8.7.1    Paraphrase (restate) a speaker's purpose and point of view and ask questions concerning the speaker's content, delivery, and attitude toward the subject.

*Organization and Delivery of Oral Communication*

8.7.2    Match the message, vocabulary, voice modulation (changes in tone), expression, and tone to the audience and purpose.

8.7.3    Outline the organization of a speech, including an introduction; transitions, previews, and summaries; a logically developed body; and an effective conclusion.

8.7.4    Use precise language, action verbs, sensory details, appropriate and colorful modifiers (describing words, such as adverbs and adjectives), and the active (*I recommend that you write drafts.*) rather than the passive voice (*The writing of drafts is recommended.*) in ways that enliven oral presentations.

8.7.5    Use appropriate grammar, word choice, enunciation (clear speech), and pace (timing) during formal presentations.

8.7.6    Use audience feedback, including both verbal and nonverbal cues, to reconsider and modify the organizational structure and/or to rearrange words and sentences for clarification of meaning.

*Analysis and Evaluation of Oral and Media Communications*

8.7.7    Analyze oral interpretations of literature, including language choice and delivery, and the effect of the interpretations on the listener.

8.7.8    Evaluate the credibility of a speaker, including whether the speaker has hidden agendas or presents slanted or biased material.

8.7.9    Interpret and evaluate the various ways in which visual image makers (such as graphic artists, illustrators, and news photographers) communicate information and affect impressions and opinions.

*Speaking Applications*

8.7.10    Deliver narrative presentations, such as biographical or autobiographical information that:
- relate a clear incident, event, or situation, using well-chosen details.
- reveal the significance of the incident, event, or situation.
- use narrative and descriptive strategies to support the presentation, including relevant dialogue, specific action, physical description, background description, and comparison or contrast of characters.

8.7.15    Deliver descriptive presentations that:
- establish a clear point of view on the subject of the presentation.
- establish the presenter's relationship with the subject of the presentation (whether the presentation is made as an uninvolved observer or by someone who is personally involved).
- contain effective, factual descriptions of appearance, concrete images, shifting perspectives, and sensory details.

8.7.11    Deliver oral responses to literature that:
- interpret a reading and provide insight.
- connect personal responses to the writer's techniques and to specific textual references.
- make supported inferences about the effects of a literary work on its audience.
- support judgments through references to the text, other works, other authors, or personal knowledge.

8.7.12    Deliver research presentations that:
- define a thesis (a position on the topic).
- research important ideas, concepts, and direct quotations from significant information sources and paraphrase and summarize important perspectives on the topic.
- use a variety of research sources and distinguish the nature and value of each.
- present information on charts, maps, and graphs.

8.7.13    Deliver persuasive presentations that:
- include a well-defined thesis (position on the topic).
- differentiate fact from opinion and support arguments with detailed evidence, examples, reasoning, and persuasive language.
- anticipate and effectively answer listener concerns and counterarguments through the inclusion and arrangement of details, reasons, examples, and other elements.
- maintain a reasonable tone.

8.7.14    Recite poems (of four to six stanzas), sections of speeches, or dramatic soliloquies (sections of plays in which characters speak out loud to themselves) using voice modulation, tone, and gestures expressively to enhance the meaning.

# EXTENDED RESPONSE WRITING APPLICATIONS OVERVIEW
## GRADES 6–12

| Score | Does the writing sample |
|---|---|
| **4** | • fully accomplish the task?<br>• include many relevant ideas?<br>• organize ideas logically?<br>• exhibit very good word usage?<br>• demonstrate very good writing technique?<br>• demonstrate effective adjustment of language and tone to task and reader? |
| **Score** | **Does the writing sample** |
| **3** | • accomplish the task?<br>• include relevant ideas?<br>• organize ideas logically?<br>• exhibit good word usage?<br>• demonstrate good writing technique?<br>• demonstrate an attempt to adjust language and tone to task and reader? |
| **Score** | **Does the writing sample** |
| **2** | • minimally accomplish the task?<br>• include some relevant ideas?<br>• exhibit an attempt to organize ideas logically?<br>• exhibit ordinary word usage?<br>• demonstrate adequate writing technique?<br>• demonstrate an attempt to adjust language and tone to task and reader? |
| **Score** | **Does the writing sample** |
| **1** | • only partially accomplish or fail to accomplish the task?<br>• include few relevant ideas?<br>• exhibit a minimal attempt to organize ideas logically?<br>• exhibit minimal word usage?<br>• demonstrate minimal or less than minimal writing technique?<br>• demonstrate language and tone that may be inappropriate to task and reader? |

**NOTE:** This chart is only a brief summary of the score points. It is not appropriate to use this summary as the sole tool in scoring student papers. The more in-depth Extended Response Writing Applications Rubric is used for the actual scoring of *ISTEP+* student papers.

These scoring rubrics are used for students tested on the fall *ISTEP+* assessment in Grades 6–12.

# EXTENDED RESPONSE WRITING APPLICATIONS RUBRIC

## GRADES 6–12

## SCORE POINT 4

**A Score Point 4 paper represents a solid performance. It fully accomplishes the task.**

### Ideas and Content

**Does the writing sample fully accomplish the task (e.g., support an opinion, summarize, tell a story, or write an article)? Does it**
- present a unifying theme or main idea without going off on tangents?
- stay focused on topic and task?

**Does the writing sample include many relevant ideas? Does it**
- provide ample information and more than adequate supporting details that are developed?
- explore many facets of the topic?

### Organization

**Are the ideas in the writing sample organized logically? Does the writing**
- present a meaningful, cohesive whole with a beginning, a middle, and an end (i.e., include a solid introduction and conclusion)?
- progress in an order that enhances meaning of text?
- include smooth transitions (e.g., use topic sentences) between sentences and paragraphs to enhance meaning of text? (Writing may have an occasional lapse.)

### Style

**Does the writing sample exhibit very good word usage? Does it**
- include vocabulary to make explanations detailed and precise, descriptions rich, and actions clear and vivid?
- demonstrate control of vocabulary?

**Does the writing sample demonstrate very good writing technique?**
- Is the writing very fluent?
- Does it include varied sentence patterns, including complex sentences?
- Does it demonstrate use of writer's techniques (e.g., literary conventions such as imagery and dialogue and/or literary genres such as humor and suspense)?

### Voice

**Does the writing sample demonstrate effective adjustment of language and tone to task and reader? Does it**
- exhibit appropriate register (e.g., formal, personal, or dialect) to suit task?
- demonstrate a sense of audience?
- exhibit an original perspective (e.g., authoritative, lively, and/or exciting)?

**NOTE:** These scoring rubrics are used for students tested on the fall *ISTEP+* assessment in Grades 6–12.

# EXTENDED RESPONSE WRITING APPLICATIONS RUBRIC

## GRADES 6–12

## SCORE POINT 3

A Score Point 3 paper represents a good performance. It accomplishes the task, but generally needs to exhibit more development, better organization, or a more sophisticated writing style to receive a higher score.

### Ideas and Content

**Does the writing sample accomplish the task (e.g., support an opinion, summarize, tell a story, or write an article)? Does it**
- present a unifying theme or main idea? (Writing may include minor tangents.)
- stay mostly focused on topic and task?

**Does the writing sample include relevant ideas? Does it**
- include sufficient information and supporting details? (Details may not be fully developed; ideas may be listed.)
- explore some facets of the topic?

### Organization

**Are the ideas in the writing sample organized logically? Does the writing**
- present a meaningful whole with a beginning, a middle, and an end despite an occasional lapse (e.g., a weak introduction or conclusion)?
- generally progress in an order that enhances meaning of text?
- include transitions between sentences and paragraphs to enhance meaning of text? (Transitions may be rough, although some topic sentences are included.)

### Style

**Does the writing sample exhibit good word usage? Does it**
- include vocabulary that is appropriately chosen, with words that clearly convey the writer's meaning?
- demonstrate control of basic vocabulary?

**Does the writing sample demonstrate good writing technique?**
- Is the writing fluent?
- Does it exhibit some varied sentence patterns, including some complex sentences?
- Does it demonstrate an attempt to use writer's techniques (e.g., literary conventions such as imagery and dialogue and/or literary genres such as humor and suspense)?

### Voice

**Does the writing sample demonstrate an attempt to adjust language and tone to task and reader? Does it**
- generally exhibit appropriate register (e.g., formal, personal, or dialect) to suit task? (The writing may occasionally slip out of register.)
- demonstrate some sense of audience?
- attempt an original perspective?

**NOTE:** These scoring rubrics are used for students tested on the fall *ISTEP+* assessment in Grades 6–12.

# EXTENDED RESPONSE WRITING APPLICATIONS RUBRIC

## GRADES 6–12

## SCORE POINT 2

**A Score Point 2 paper represents a performance that minimally accomplishes the task. Some elements of development, organization, and writing style are weak.**

### Ideas and Content

**Does the writing sample minimally accomplish the task (e.g., support an opinion, summarize, tell a story, or write an article)? Does it**
- attempt a unifying theme or main idea?
- stay somewhat focused on topic and task?

**Does the writing sample include some relevant ideas? Does it**
- include some information with only a few details, or list ideas without supporting details?
- explore some facets of the topic?

### Organization

**Is there an attempt to logically organize ideas in the writing sample? Does the writing**
- have a beginning, a middle, or an end that may be weak or absent?
- demonstrate an attempt to progress in an order that enhances meaning? (Progression of text may sometimes be unclear or out of order.)
- demonstrate an attempt to include transitions? (Are some topic sentences used? Are transitions between sentences and paragraphs weak or absent?)

### Style

**Does the writing sample exhibit ordinary word usage? Does it**
- contain basic vocabulary, with words that are predictable and common?
- demonstrate some control of vocabulary?

**Does the writing sample demonstrate adequate writing technique?**
- Is the writing generally fluent?
- Does it contain mostly simple sentences (although there may be an attempt at more varied sentence patterns)?
- Is it generally ordinary and predictable?

### Voice

**Does the writing sample demonstrate an attempt to adjust language and tone to task and reader? Does it**
- demonstrate a difficulty in establishing a register (e.g., formal, personal, or dialect)?
- demonstrate little sense of audience?
- generally lack an original perspective?

**NOTE:** These scoring rubrics are used for students tested on the fall *ISTEP+* assessment in Grades 6–12.

# EXTENDED RESPONSE WRITING APPLICATIONS RUBRIC

## GRADES 6–12

## SCORE POINT 1

A Score Point 1 paper represents a performance that only partially accomplishes or fails to accomplish the task. Some responses may exhibit difficulty maintaining a focus. Others may be too brief to provide sufficient development of the topic or evidence of adequate organizational or writing style.

### Ideas and Content

**Does the writing sample only partially accomplish or fail to accomplish the task (e.g., support an opinion, summarize, tell a story, or write an article)?**
- Writing may attempt a main idea, or the main idea may be difficult to discern.
- Does the writing sometimes lose focus or ineffectively establish focus?

**Does the writing sample include few relevant ideas?**
- Does the writing sample include little information and few or no details?
- Writing may explore only one or two facets of the topic.

### Organization

**Is there a minimal attempt to logically organize ideas in the writing sample?**
- Does the writing have only one or two of the three elements: beginning, middle, and end?
- Is the writing sometimes difficult to follow? (Progression of text may be confusing, unclear, or difficult to discern.)
- Are transitions weak or absent (e.g., few or no topic sentences)?

### Style

**Does the writing sample exhibit minimal word usage? Does it**
- contain limited vocabulary? (Words may be used incorrectly.)
- demonstrate minimal or less than minimal control of vocabulary?

**Does the writing sample demonstrate minimal or less than minimal writing technique?**
- Does the writing exhibit some or little fluency?
- Does it rely mostly on simple sentences or demonstrate problems with sentence patterns?
- Is it often repetitive, predictable, or dull?

### Voice

**Does the writing sample demonstrate language and tone that may be inappropriate to task and reader? Does it**
- demonstrate use of a register inappropriate to the task (e.g., slang or dialect in a formal setting)?
- demonstrate little or no sense of audience?
- lack an original perspective?

**NOTE**: These scoring rubrics are used for students tested on the fall *ISTEP+* assessment in Grades 6–12.

# LANGUAGE CONVENTIONS RUBRIC
## GRADES 6–8

| Score | Does the writing sample exhibit a good command of language skills? |
|---|---|
| **4** | In a Score Point 4 paper, there are no errors that impair the flow of communication. Errors are infrequent and will generally be of the first-draft variety; they have a minor impact on the overall communication.<br>• Do words have very few or no capitalization errors?<br>• Do sentences have very few or no punctuation errors?<br>• Do words have very few or no spelling errors?<br>• Do sentences have very few or no grammar or word usage errors?<br>• Writing has very few or no paragraphing errors.<br>• Writing has very few or no run-on sentences or sentence fragments. |

| Score | Does the writing sample exhibit an adequate command of language skills? |
|---|---|
| **3** | In a Score Point 3 paper, errors are occasional but do not impede the flow of communication; the writer's meaning is not seriously obscured by errors in language conventions.<br>• Do words have occasional capitalization errors?<br>• Do sentences have occasional punctuation errors?<br>• Do words have occasional spelling errors?<br>• Do sentences have occasional grammar or word usage errors?<br>• Writing may have occasional paragraphing errors.<br>• Writing may have run-on sentences or sentence fragments. |

| Score | Does the writing sample exhibit a minimal command of language skills? |
|---|---|
| **2** | In a Score Point 2 paper, errors are typically frequent and may cause the reader to stop and reread part of the writing. While some aspects of the writing may be more consistently correct than others, the existing errors do impair communication. With a little extra effort on the reader's part, it is still possible to discern most, if not all, of what the writer is trying to communicate.<br>• Do words have frequent capitalization errors?<br>• Do sentences have frequent punctuation errors?<br>• Do words have frequent spelling errors?<br>• Do sentences have frequent grammar or word usage errors?<br>• Writing may have errors in paragraphing, or paragraphing may be missing.<br>• Writing is likely to have run-on sentences or sentence fragments. |

| Score | Does the writing sample exhibit a less than minimal command of language skills? |
|---|---|
| **1** | In a Score Point 1 paper, errors are serious and numerous; they often cause the reader to struggle to discern the writer's meaning. Errors are frequently of a wide variety. There may be sections where it is impossible to ascertain what the writer is attempting to communicate.<br>• Do words have many capitalization errors?<br>• Do sentences have many punctuation errors?<br>• Do words have many spelling errors?<br>• Do sentences have many grammar and word usage errors?<br>• Writing may have errors in paragraphing, or paragraphing may be missing.<br>• Writing is likely to have run-on sentences or sentence fragments. |

**NOTE**: These rubrics are applied holistically, with no element of the rubric intended to supersede any other element. The variety and proportion of errors in relation to the length of the writing sample are considered. A very brief paper consisting of two or three sentences may receive no more than 2 score points.

These scoring rubrics are used for students tested on the fall *ISTEP+* assessment in Grades 6–8.

# WRITING APPLICATIONS OVERVIEW
## GRADES 6–12

| Score Level | Ideas and Content | Organization |
|---|---|---|
| | **Does the writing sample** | **Does the writing sample** |
| 6 | • fully accomplish the task?<br>• include thorough, relevant, and complete ideas? | • organize ideas logically? |
| 5 | • fully accomplish the task?<br>• include many relevant ideas? | • organize ideas logically? |
| 4 | • accomplish the task?<br>• include relevant ideas? | • organize ideas logically? |
| 3 | • minimally accomplish the task?<br>• include some relevant ideas? | • exhibit an attempt to organize ideas logically? |
| 2 | • only partially accomplish the task?<br>• include few relevant ideas? | • exhibit a minimal attempt to exhibit ideas logically? |
| 1 | • fail to accomplish the task?<br>• include very few relevant ideas? | • organize ideas illogically? |

| Score Level | Style | Voice |
|---|---|---|
| | **Does the writing sample** | **Does the writing sample** |
| 6 | • exhibit exceptional word usage?<br>• demonstrate exceptional writing technique? | • demonstrate effective adjustment of language and tone to task and reader? |
| 5 | • exhibit very good word usage?<br>• demonstrate very good writing technique? | • demonstrate effective adjustment of language and tone to task and reader? |
| 4 | • exhibit good word usage?<br>• demonstrate good writing technique? | • demonstrate an attempt to adjust language and tone to task and reader? |
| 3 | • exhibit ordinary word usage?<br>• demonstrate average writing technique? | • demonstrate an attempt to adjust language and tone to task and reader? |
| 2 | • exhibit minimal word usage?<br>• demonstrate minimal writing technique? | • demonstrate language and tone that may be inappropriate to task and reader? |
| 1 | • exhibit less than minimal word usage?<br>• demonstrate less than minimal writing technique? | • demonstrate language and tone that may be inappropriate to task and reader? |

**NOTE:** This chart is only a brief summary of the score points. It is not appropriate to use this summary as the sole tool in scoring student papers. The more in-depth Writing Applications Rubric is used for the actual scoring of *ISTEP+* student papers.
These scoring rubrics are used for students tested on the fall *ISTEP+* assessment in Grades 6–12.

# WRITING APPLICATIONS RUBRIC
## GRADES 6–12

## SCORE POINT 6

**A Score Point 6 paper is rare. It fully accomplishes the task in a thorough and insightful manner and has a distinctive quality that sets it apart as an outstanding performance.**

### Ideas and Content

**Does the writing sample fully accomplish the task (e.g., support an opinion, summarize, tell a story, or write an article)? Does it**
- present a unifying theme or main idea without going off on tangents?
- stay completely focused on topic and task?

**Does the writing sample include thorough, relevant, and complete ideas? Does it**
- include in-depth information and exceptional supporting details that are fully developed?
- fully explore many facets of the topic?

### Organization

**Are the ideas in the writing sample organized logically? Does the writing**
- present a meaningful, cohesive whole with a beginning, a middle, and an end (i.e., include an inviting introduction and a strong conclusion)?
- progress in an order that enhances meaning?
- include smooth transitions between ideas, sentences, and paragraphs to enhance meaning of text (i.e., have a clear connection of ideas and use topic sentences)?

### Style

**Does the writing sample exhibit exceptional word usage? Does it**
- include vocabulary to make explanations detailed and precise, descriptions rich, and actions clear and vivid (e.g., varied word choices, action words, appropriate modifiers, sensory details)?
- demonstrate control of a challenging vocabulary?

**Does the writing sample demonstrate exceptional writing technique?**
- Is the writing exceptionally fluent?
- Does it include varied sentence patterns, including complex sentences?
- Does it demonstrate use of writer's techniques (e.g., literary conventions such as imagery and dialogue and/or literary genres such as humor and suspense)?

### Voice

**Does the writing sample demonstrate effective adjustment of language and tone to task and reader? Does it**
- exhibit appropriate register (e.g., formal, personal, or dialect) to suit task?
- demonstrate a strong sense of audience?
- exhibit an original perspective (e.g., authoritative, lively, and/or exciting)?

**NOTE:** These scoring rubrics are used for students tested on the fall *ISTEP+* assessment in Grades 6–12.

# WRITING APPLICATIONS RUBRIC
## GRADES 6–12

## SCORE POINT 5

A Score Point 5 paper represents a solid performance. It fully accomplishes the task, but lacks the overall level of sophistication and consistency of a Score Point 6 paper.

### Ideas and Content

Does the writing sample fully accomplish the task (e.g., support an opinion, summarize, tell a story, or write an article)? Does it
- present a unifying theme or main idea without going off on tangents?
- stay focused on topic and task?

Does the writing sample include many relevant ideas? Does it
- provide in-depth information and more than adequate supporting details that are developed?
- explore many facets of the topic?

### Organization

Are the ideas in the writing sample organized logically? Does the writing
- present a meaningful, cohesive whole with a beginning, a middle, and an end (i.e., include a solid introduction and conclusion)?
- progress in an order that enhances meaning of text?
- include smooth transitions (e.g., use topic sentences) between sentences and paragraphs to enhance meaning of text? (Writing may have an occasional lapse.)

### Style

Does the writing sample exhibit very good word usage? Does it
- include vocabulary to make explanations detailed and precise, descriptions rich, and actions clear and vivid?
- demonstrate control of vocabulary?

Does the writing sample demonstrate very good writing technique?
- Is the writing very fluent?
- Does it include varied sentence patterns, including complex sentences?
- Does it demonstrate use of writer's techniques (e.g., literary conventions such as imagery and dialogue and/or literary genres such as humor and suspense)?

### Voice

Does the writing sample demonstrate effective adjustment of language and tone to task and reader? Does it
- exhibit appropriate register (e.g., formal, personal, or dialect) to suit task?
- demonstrate a sense of audience?
- exhibit an original perspective (e.g., authoritative, lively, and/or exciting)?

NOTE: These scoring rubrics are used for students tested on the fall *ISTEP+* assessment in Grades 6–12.

# WRITING APPLICATIONS RUBRIC
## GRADES 6–12

## SCORE POINT 4

**A Score Point 4 paper represents a good performance. It accomplishes the task, but generally needs to exhibit more development, better organization, or a more sophisticated writing style to receive a higher score.**

### Ideas and Content

**Does the writing sample accomplish the task (e.g., support an opinion, summarize, tell a story, or write an article)? Does it**
- present a unifying theme or main idea? (Writing may include minor tangents.)
- stay mostly focused on topic and task?

**Does the writing sample include relevant ideas? Does it**
- include sufficient information and supporting details? (Details may not be fully developed; ideas may be listed.)
- explore some facets of the topic?

### Organization

**Are the ideas in the writing sample organized logically? Does the writing**
- present a meaningful whole with a beginning, a middle, and an end despite an occasional lapse (e.g., a weak introduction or conclusion)?
- generally progress in an order that enhances meaning of text?
- include transitions between sentences and paragraphs to enhance meaning of text? (Transitions may be rough, although some topic sentences are included.)

### Style

**Does the writing sample exhibit good word usage? Does it**
- include vocabulary that is appropriately chosen, with words that clearly convey the writer's meaning?
- demonstrate control of basic vocabulary?

**Does the writing sample demonstrate good writing technique?**
- Is the writing fluent?
- Does it exhibit some varied sentence patterns, including some complex sentences?
- Does it demonstrate an attempt to use writer's techniques (e.g., literary conventions such as imagery and dialogue and/or literary genres such as humor and suspense)?

### Voice

**Does the writing sample demonstrate an attempt to adjust language and tone to task and reader? Does it**
- generally exhibit appropriate register (e.g., formal, personal, or dialect) to suit task? (The writing may occasionally slip out of register.)
- demonstrate some sense of audience?
- attempt an original perspective?

**NOTE:** These scoring rubrics are used for students tested on the fall *ISTEP+* assessment in Grades 6–12.

# WRITING APPLICATIONS RUBRIC
## GRADES 6–12

## SCORE POINT 3

**A Score Point 3 paper represents a performance that minimally accomplishes the task. Some elements of development, organization, and writing style are weak.**

### Ideas and Content

**Does the writing sample minimally accomplish the task (e.g., support an opinion, summarize, tell a story, or write an article)? Does it**
- attempt a unifying theme or main idea?
- stay somewhat focused on topic and task?

**Does the writing sample include some relevant ideas? Does it**
- include some information with only a few details, or list ideas without supporting details?
- explore some facets of the topic?

### Organization

**Is there an attempt to logically organize ideas in the writing sample? Does the writing**
- have a beginning, a middle, or an end that may be weak or absent?
- demonstrate an attempt to progress in an order that enhances meaning? (Progression of text may sometimes be unclear or out of order.)
- demonstrate an attempt to include transitions? (Are some topic sentences used? Are transitions between sentences and paragraphs weak or absent?)

### Style

**Does the writing sample exhibit ordinary word usage? Does it**
- contain basic vocabulary, with words that are predictable and common?
- demonstrate some control of vocabulary?

**Does the writing sample demonstrate average writing technique?**
- Is the writing generally fluent?
- Does it contain mostly simple sentences (although there may be an attempt at more varied sentence patterns)?
- Is it generally ordinary and predictable?

### Voice

**Does the writing sample demonstrate an attempt to adjust language and tone to task and reader? Does it**
- demonstrate a difficulty in establishing a register (e.g., formal, personal, or dialect)?
- demonstrate little sense of audience?
- generally lack an original perspective?

**NOTE:** These scoring rubrics are used for students tested on the fall *ISTEP+* assessment in Grades 6–12.

# WRITING APPLICATIONS RUBRIC
## GRADES 6–12

## SCORE POINT 2

A Score Point 2 paper represents a performance that only partially accomplishes the task. Some responses may exhibit difficulty maintaining a focus. Others may be too brief to provide sufficient development of the topic or evidence of adequate organizational or writing style.

### Ideas and Content

**Does the writing sample only partially accomplish the task (e.g., support an opinion, summarize, tell a story, or write an article)? Does it**
- attempt a main idea?
- sometimes lose focus or ineffectively display focus?

**Does the writing sample include few relevant ideas? Does it**
- include little information and few or no details?
- explore only one or two facets of the topic?

### Organization

**Is there a minimal attempt to logically organize ideas in the writing sample?**
- Does the writing have only one or two of the three elements: beginning, middle, and end?
- Is the writing sometimes difficult to follow? (Progression of text may be confusing or unclear.)
- Are transitions weak or absent (e.g., few or no topic sentences)?

### Style

**Does the writing sample exhibit minimal word usage? Does it**
- contain limited vocabulary? (Some words may be used incorrectly.)
- demonstrate minimal control of vocabulary?

**Does the writing sample demonstrate minimal writing technique?**
- Does the writing exhibit some fluency?
- Does it rely mostly on simple sentences?
- Is it often repetitive, predictable, or dull?

### Voice

**Does the writing sample demonstrate language and tone that may be inappropriate to task and reader? Does it**
- demonstrate use of a register inappropriate to the task (e.g., slang or dialect in a formal setting)?
- demonstrate little or no sense of audience?
- lack an original perspective?

**NOTE:** These scoring rubrics are used for students tested on the fall *ISTEP+* assessment in Grades 6-12.

# WRITING APPLICATIONS RUBRIC
## GRADES 6–12

## SCORE POINT 1

A Score Point 1 paper represents a performance that fails to accomplish the task. It exhibits considerable difficulty in areas of development, organization, and writing style. The writing is generally either very brief or rambling and repetitive, sometimes resulting in a response that may be difficult to read or comprehend.

### Ideas and Content

**Does the writing sample fail to accomplish the task (e.g., support an opinion, summarize, tell a story, or write an article)? Is it**
- difficult for the reader to discern the main idea?
- too brief or too repetitive to establish or maintain a focus?

**Does the writing sample include very few relevant ideas?**
- Does it include little information with few or no details or unrelated details?
- Is it unsuccessful in attempts to explore any facets of the prompt?

### Organization

**Are the ideas in the writing sample organized illogically?**
- Does it have only one or two of the three elements: beginning, middle, or end?
- Is it difficult to follow, with the order possibly difficult to discern?
- Are transitions weak or absent (e.g., without topic sentences)?

### Style

**Does the writing sample exhibit less than minimal word usage? Does it**
- contain limited vocabulary, with many words used incorrectly?
- demonstrate minimal or less than minimal control of vocabulary?

**Does the writing sample demonstrate less than minimal writing technique? Does it**
- lack fluency?
- demonstrate problems with sentence patterns?
- consist of writing that is flat and lifeless?

### Voice

**Does the writing sample demonstrate language and tone that may be inappropriate to task and reader? Does it**
- demonstrate difficulty in choosing an appropriate register?
- demonstrate a lack of a sense of audience?
- lack an original perspective?

**NOTE:** These scoring rubrics are used for students tested on the fall *ISTEP+* assessment in Grades 6–12.